# Algorithm Design

# Algorithm Design

## JON KLEINBERG · ÉVA TARDOS

### Cornell University

PEARSON

Addison
Wesley

Boston  San Francisco  New York
London  Toronto  Sydney  Tokyo  Singapore  Madrid
Mexico City  Munich  Paris  Cape Town  Hong Kong  Montreal

Acquisitions Editor:  *Matt Goldstein*
Project Editor:  *Maite Suarez-Rivas*
Production Supervisor:  *Marilyn Lloyd*
Marketing Manager:  *Michelle Brown*
Marketing Coordinator:  *Jake Zavracky*
Project Management:  *Windfall Software*
Composition:  *Windfall Software, using ZzTEX*
Copyeditor:  *Carol Leyba*
Technical Illustration:  *Dartmouth Publishing*
Proofreader:  *Jennifer McClain*
Indexer:  *Ted Laux*
Cover Design:  *Joyce Cosentino Wells*
Cover Photo:  *© 2005 Tim Laman / National Geographic. A pair of weaverbirds work together on their nest in Africa.*
Prepress and Manufacturing:  *Caroline Fell*
Printer:  *Courier Westford*

Access the latest information about Addison-Wesley titles from our World Wide Web site: http://www.aw-bc.com/computing

Many of the designations used by manufacturers and sellers to distinguish their products are claimed as trademarks. Where those designations appear in this book, and Addison-Wesley was aware of a trademark claim, the designations have been printed in initial caps or all caps.

The programs and applications presented in this book have been included for their instructional value. They have been tested with care, but are not guaranteed for any particular purpose. The publisher does not offer any warranties or representations, nor does it accept any liabilities with respect to the programs or applications.

ISBN 0-321-37291-3
1 2 3 4 5 6 7 8 9 10-CRW-08 07 06 05

# *About the Authors*

Jon Kleinberg is a professor of Computer Science at Cornell University. He received his Ph.D. from M.I.T. in 1996. He is the recipient of an NSF Career Award, an ONR Young Investigator Award, an IBM Outstanding Innovation Award, the National Academy of Sciences Award for Initiatives in Research, research fellowships from the Packard and Sloan Foundations, and teaching awards from the Cornell Engineering College and Computer Science Department.

Kleinberg's research is centered around algorithms, particularly those concerned with the structure of networks and information, and with applications to information science, optimization, data mining, and computational biology. His work on network analysis using hubs and authorities helped form the foundation for the current generation of Internet search engines.

Éva Tardos is a professor of Computer Science at Cornell University. She received her Ph.D. from Eötvös University in Budapest, Hungary in 1984. She is a member of the American Academy of Arts and Sciences, and an ACM Fellow; she is the recipient of an NSF Presidential Young Investigator Award, the Fulkerson Prize, research fellowships from the Guggenheim, Packard, and Sloan Foundations, and teaching awards from the Cornell Engineering College and Computer Science Department.

Tardos's research interests are focused on the design and analysis of algorithms for problems on graphs or networks. She is most known for her work on network-flow algorithms and approximation algorithms for network problems. Her recent work focuses on algorithmic game theory, an emerging area concerned with designing systems and algorithms for selfish users.

# Contents

---

* The star indicates an optional section. (See the Preface for more information about the relationships among the chapters and sections.)

# *Preface*

Algorithmic ideas are pervasive, and their reach is apparent in examples both within computer science and beyond. Some of the major shifts in Internet routing standards can be viewed as debates over the deficiencies of one shortest-path algorithm and the relative advantages of another. The basic notions used by biologists to express similarities among genes and genomes have algorithmic definitions. The concerns voiced by economists over the feasibility of combinatorial auctions in practice are rooted partly in the fact that these auctions contain computationally intractable search problems as special cases. And algorithmic notions aren't just restricted to well-known and long-standing problems; one sees the reflections of these ideas on a regular basis, in novel issues arising across a wide range of areas. The scientist from Yahoo! who told us over lunch one day about their system for serving ads to users was describing a set of issues that, deep down, could be modeled as a network flow problem. So was the former student, now a management consultant working on staffing protocols for large hospitals, whom we happened to meet on a trip to New York City.

The point is not simply that algorithms have many applications. The deeper issue is that the subject of algorithms is a powerful lens through which to view the field of computer science in general. Algorithmic problems form the heart of computer science, but they rarely arrive as cleanly packaged, mathematically precise questions. Rather, they tend to come bundled together with lots of messy, application-specific detail, some of it essential, some of it extraneous. As a result, the algorithmic enterprise consists of two fundamental components: the task of getting to the mathematically clean core of a problem, and then the task of identifying the appropriate algorithm design techniques, based on the structure of the problem. These two components interact: the more comfortable one is with the full array of possible design techniques, the more one starts to recognize the clean formulations that lie within messy problems out in the world. At their most effective, then, algorithmic ideas do not just provide solutions to well-posed problems; they form the language that lets you cleanly express the underlying questions.

The goal of our book is to convey this approach to algorithms, as a design process that begins with problems arising across the full range of computing applications, builds on an understanding of algorithm design techniques, and results in the development of efficient solutions to these problems. We seek to explore the role of algorithmic ideas in computer science generally, and relate these ideas to the range of precisely formulated problems for which we can design and analyze algorithms. In other words, what are the underlying issues that motivate these problems, and how did we choose these particular ways of formulating them? How did we recognize which design principles were appropriate in different situations?

In keeping with this, our goal is to offer advice on how to identify clean algorithmic problem formulations in complex issues from different areas of computing and, from this, how to design efficient algorithms for the resulting problems. Sophisticated algorithms are often best understood by reconstructing the sequence of ideas—including false starts and dead ends—that led from simpler initial approaches to the eventual solution. The result is a style of exposition that does not take the most direct route from problem statement to algorithm, but we feel it better reflects the way that we and our colleagues genuinely think about these questions.

## Overview

The book is intended for students who have completed a programming-based two-semester introductory computer science sequence (the standard "CS1/CS2" courses) in which they have written programs that implement basic algorithms, manipulate discrete structures such as trees and graphs, and apply basic data structures such as arrays, lists, queues, and stacks. Since the interface between CS1/CS2 and a first algorithms course is not entirely standard, we begin the book with self-contained coverage of topics that at some institutions are familiar to students from CS1/CS2, but which at other institutions are included in the syllabi of the first algorithms course. This material can thus be treated either as a review or as new material; by including it, we hope the book can be used in a broader array of courses, and with more flexibility in the prerequisite knowledge that is assumed.

In keeping with the approach outlined above, we develop the basic algorithm design techniques by drawing on problems from across many areas of computer science and related fields. To mention a few representative examples here, we include fairly detailed discussions of applications from systems and networks (caching, switching, interdomain routing on the Internet), artificial intelligence (planning, game playing, Hopfield networks), computer vision (image segmentation), data mining (change-point detection, clustering), operations research (airline scheduling), and computational biology (sequence alignment, RNA secondary structure).

The notion of computational intractability, and NP-completeness in particular, plays a large role in the book. This is consistent with how we think about the overall process of algorithm design. Some of the time, an interesting problem arising in an application area will be amenable to an efficient solution, and some of the time it will be provably NP-complete; in order to fully address a new algorithmic problem, one should be able to explore both of these options with equal familiarity. Since so many natural problems in computer science are NP-complete, the development of methods to deal with intractable problems has become a crucial issue in the study of algorithms, and our book heavily reflects this theme. The discovery that a problem is NP-complete should not be taken as the end of the story, but as an invitation to begin looking for approximation algorithms, heuristic local search techniques, or tractable special cases. We include extensive coverage of each of these three approaches.

## Problems and Solved Exercises

An important feature of the book is the collection of problems. Across all chapters, the book includes over 200 problems, almost all of them developed and class-tested in homework or exams as part of our teaching of the course at Cornell. We view the problems as a crucial component of the book, and they are structured in keeping with our overall approach to the material. Most of them consist of extended verbal descriptions of a problem arising in an application area in computer science or elsewhere out in the world, and part of the problem is to practice what we discuss in the text: setting up the necessary notation and formalization, designing an algorithm, and then analyzing it and proving it correct. (We view a complete answer to one of these problems as consisting of all these components: a fully explained algorithm, an analysis of the running time, and a proof of correctness.) The ideas for these problems come in large part from discussions we have had over the years with people working in different areas, and in some cases they serve the dual purpose of recording an interesting (though manageable) application of algorithms that we haven't seen written down anywhere else.

To help with the process of working on these problems, we include in each chapter a section entitled "Solved Exercises," where we take one or more problems and describe how to go about formulating a solution. The discussion devoted to each solved exercise is therefore significantly longer than what would be needed simply to write a complete, correct solution (in other words, significantly longer than what it would take to receive full credit if these were being assigned as homework problems). Rather, as with the rest of the text, the discussions in these sections should be viewed as trying to give a sense of the larger process by which one might think about problems of this type, culminating in the specification of a precise solution.

It is worth mentioning two points concerning the use of these problems as homework in a course. First, the problems are sequenced roughly in order of increasing difficulty, but this is only an approximate guide and we advise against placing too much weight on it: since the bulk of the problems were designed as homework for our undergraduate class, large subsets of the problems in each chapter are really closely comparable in terms of difficulty. Second, aside from the lowest-numbered ones, the problems are designed to involve some investment of time, both to relate the problem description to the algorithmic techniques in the chapter, and then to actually design the necessary algorithm. In our undergraduate class, we have tended to assign roughly three of these problems per week.

## Pedagogical Features and Supplements

In addition to the problems and solved exercises, the book has a number of further pedagogical features, as well as additional supplements to facilitate its use for teaching.

As noted earlier, a large number of the sections in the book are devoted to the formulation of an algorithmic problem—including its background and underlying motivation—and the design and analysis of an algorithm for this problem. To reflect this style, these sections are consistently structured around a sequence of subsections: "The Problem," where the problem is described and a precise formulation is worked out; "Designing the Algorithm," where the appropriate design technique is employed to develop an algorithm; and "Analyzing the Algorithm," which proves properties of the algorithm and analyzes its efficiency. These subsections are highlighted in the text with an icon depicting a feather. In cases where extensions to the problem or further analysis of the algorithm is pursued, there are additional subsections devoted to these issues. The goal of this structure is to offer a relatively uniform style of presentation that moves from the initial discussion of a problem arising in a computing application through to the detailed analysis of a method to solve it.

A number of supplements are available in support of the book itself. An instructor's manual works through all the problems, providing full solutions to each. A set of lecture slides, developed by Kevin Wayne of Princeton University, is also available; these slides follow the order of the book's sections and can thus be used as the foundation for lectures in a course based on the book. These files are available at *www.aw.com*. For instructions on obtaining a professor login and password, search the site for either "Kleinberg" or "Tardos" or contact your local Addison-Wesley representative.

Finally, we would appreciate receiving feedback on the book. In particular, as in any book of this length, there are undoubtedly errors that have remained in the final version. Comments and reports of errors can be sent to us by e-mail, at the address algbook@cs.cornell.edu; please include the word "feedback" in the subject line of the message.

## Chapter-by-Chapter Synopsis

Chapter 1 starts by introducing some representative algorithmic problems. We begin immediately with the Stable Matching Problem, since we feel it sets up the basic issues in algorithm design more concretely and more elegantly than any abstract discussion could: stable matching is motivated by a natural though complex real-world issue, from which one can abstract an interesting problem statement and a surprisingly effective algorithm to solve this problem. The remainder of Chapter 1 discusses a list of five "representative problems" that foreshadow topics from the remainder of the course. These five problems are interrelated in the sense that they are all variations and/or special cases of the Independent Set Problem; but one is solvable by a greedy algorithm, one by dynamic programming, one by network flow, one (the Independent Set Problem itself) is NP-complete, and one is PSPACE-complete. The fact that closely related problems can vary greatly in complexity is an important theme of the book, and these five problems serve as milestones that reappear as the book progresses.

Chapters 2 and 3 cover the interface to the CS1/CS2 course sequence mentioned earlier. Chapter 2 introduces the key mathematical definitions and notations used for analyzing algorithms, as well as the motivating principles behind them. It begins with an informal overview of what it means for a problem to be computationally tractable, together with the concept of polynomial time as a formal notion of efficiency. It then discusses growth rates of functions and asymptotic analysis more formally, and offers a guide to commonly occurring functions in algorithm analysis, together with standard applications in which they arise. Chapter 3 covers the basic definitions and algorithmic primitives needed for working with graphs, which are central to so many of the problems in the book. A number of basic graph algorithms are often implemented by students late in the CS1/CS2 course sequence, but it is valuable to present the material here in a broader algorithm design context. In particular, we discuss basic graph definitions, graph traversal techniques such as breadth-first search and depth-first search, and directed graph concepts including strong connectivity and topological ordering.

Chapters 2 and 3 also present many of the basic data structures that will be used for implementing algorithms throughout the book; more advanced data structures are presented in subsequent chapters. Our approach to data structures is to introduce them as they are needed for the implementation of the algorithms being developed in the book. Thus, although many of the data structures covered here will be familiar to students from the CS1/CS2 sequence, our focus is on these data structures in the broader context of algorithm design and analysis.

Chapters 4 through 7 cover four major algorithm design techniques: greedy algorithms, divide and conquer, dynamic programming, and network flow. With greedy algorithms, the challenge is to recognize when they work and when they don't; our coverage of this topic is centered around a way of classifying the kinds of arguments used to prove greedy algorithms correct. This chapter concludes with some of the main applications of greedy algorithms, for shortest paths, undirected and directed spanning trees, clustering, and compression. For divide and conquer, we begin with a discussion of strategies for solving recurrence relations as bounds on running times; we then show how familiarity with these recurrences can guide the design of algorithms that improve over straightforward approaches to a number of basic problems, including the comparison of rankings, the computation of closest pairs of points in the plane, and the Fast Fourier Transform. Next we develop dynamic programming by starting with the recursive intuition behind it, and subsequently building up more and more expressive recurrence formulations through applications in which they naturally arise. This chapter concludes with extended discussions of the dynamic programming approach to two fundamental problems: sequence alignment, with applications in computational biology; and shortest paths in graphs, with connections to Internet routing protocols. Finally, we cover algorithms for network flow problems, devoting much of our focus in this chapter to discussing a large array of different flow applications. To the extent that network flow is covered in algorithms courses, students are often left without an appreciation for the wide range of problems to which it can be applied; we try to do justice to its versatility by presenting applications to load balancing, scheduling, image segmentation, and a number of other problems.

Chapters 8 and 9 cover computational intractability. We devote most of our attention to NP-completeness, organizing the basic NP-complete problems thematically to help students recognize candidates for reductions when they encounter new problems. We build up to some fairly complex proofs of NP-completeness, with guidance on how one goes about constructing a difficult reduction. We also consider types of computational hardness beyond NP-completeness, particularly through the topic of PSPACE-completeness. We find this is a valuable way to emphasize that intractability doesn't end at NP-completeness, and PSPACE-completeness also forms the underpinning for some central notions from artificial intelligence—planning and game playing—that would otherwise not find a place in the algorithmic landscape we are surveying.

Chapters 10 through 12 cover three major techniques for dealing with computationally intractable problems: identification of structured special cases, approximation algorithms, and local search heuristics. Our chapter on tractable special cases emphasizes that instances of NP-complete problems arising in practice may not be nearly as hard as worst-case instances, because they often contain some structure that can be exploited in the design of an efficient algorithm. We illustrate how NP-complete problems are often efficiently solvable when restricted to tree-structured inputs, and we conclude with an extended discussion of tree decompositions of graphs. While this topic is more suitable for a graduate course than for an undergraduate one, it is a technique with considerable practical utility for which it is hard to find an existing accessible reference for students. Our chapter on approximation algorithms discusses both the process of designing effective algorithms and the task of understanding the optimal solution well enough to obtain good bounds on it. As design techniques for approximation algorithms, we focus on greedy algorithms, linear programming, and a third method we refer to as "pricing," which incorporates ideas from each of the first two. Finally, we discuss local search heuristics, including the Metropolis algorithm and simulated annealing. This topic is often missing from undergraduate algorithms courses, because very little is known in the way of provable guarantees for these algorithms; however, given their widespread use in practice, we feel it is valuable for students to know something about them, and we also include some cases in which guarantees can be proved.

Chapter 13 covers the use of randomization in the design of algorithms. This is a topic on which several nice graduate-level books have been written. Our goal here is to provide a more compact introduction to some of the ways in which students can apply randomized techniques using the kind of background in probability one typically gains from an undergraduate discrete math course.

## Use of the Book

The book is primarily designed for use in a first undergraduate course on algorithms, but it can also be used as the basis for an introductory graduate course.

When we use the book at the undergraduate level, we spend roughly one lecture per numbered section; in cases where there is more than one lecture's worth of material in a section (for example, when a section provides further applications as additional examples), we treat this extra material as a supplement that students can read about outside of lecture. We skip the starred sections; while these sections contain important topics, they are less central to the development of the subject, and in some cases they are harder as well. We also tend to skip one or two other sections per chapter in the first half of the book (for example, we tend to skip Sections 4.3, 4.7–4.8, 5.5–5.6, 6.5, 7.6, and 7.11). We cover roughly half of each of Chapters 11–13.

This last point is worth emphasizing: rather than viewing the later chapters as "advanced," and hence off-limits to undergraduate algorithms courses, we have designed them with the goal that the first few sections of each should be accessible to an undergraduate audience. Our own undergraduate course involves material from all these chapters, as we feel that all of these topics have an important place at the undergraduate level.

Finally, we treat Chapters 2 and 3 primarily as a review of material from earlier courses; but, as discussed above, the use of these two chapters depends heavily on the relationship of each specific course to its prerequisites.

The resulting syllabus looks roughly as follows: Chapter 1; Chapters 4–8 (excluding 4.3, 4.7–4.9, 5.5–5.6, 6.5, 6.10, 7.4, 7.6, 7.11, and 7.13); Chapter 9 (briefly); Chapter 10, Sections.10.1 and 10.2; Chapter 11, Sections 11.1, 11.2, 11.6, and 11.8; Chapter 12, Sections 12.1–12.3; and Chapter 13, Sections 13.1–13.5.

The book also naturally supports an introductory graduate course on algorithms. Our view of such a course is that it should introduce students destined for research in all different areas to the important current themes in algorithm design. Here we find the emphasis on formulating problems to be useful as well, since students will soon be trying to define their own research problems in many different subfields. For this type of course, we cover the later topics in Chapters 4 and 6 (Sections 4.5–4.9 and 6.5–6.10), cover all of Chapter 7 (moving more rapidly through the early sections), quickly cover NP-completeness in Chapter 8 (since many beginning graduate students will have seen this topic as undergraduates), and then spend the remainder of the time on Chapters 10–13. Although our focus in an introductory graduate course is on the more advanced sections, we find it useful for the students to have the full book to consult for reviewing or filling in background knowledge, given the range of different undergraduate backgrounds among the students in such a course.

Finally, the book can be used to support self-study by graduate students, researchers, or computer professionals who want to get a sense for how they might be able to use particular algorithm design techniques in the context of their own work. A number of graduate students and colleagues have used portions of the book in this way.

## Acknowledgments

This book grew out of the sequence of algorithms courses that we have taught at Cornell. These courses have grown, as the field has grown, over a number of years, and they reflect the influence of the Cornell faculty who helped to shape them during this time, including Juris Hartmanis, Monika Henzinger, John Hopcroft, Dexter Kozen, Ronitt Rubinfeld, and Sam Toueg. More generally, we would like to thank all our colleagues at Cornell for countless discussions both on the material here and on broader issues about the nature of the field.

The course staffs we've had in teaching the subject have been tremendously helpful in the formulation of this material. We thank our undergraduate and graduate teaching assistants, Siddharth Alexander, Rie Ando, Elliot Anshelevich, Lars Backstrom, Steve Baker, Ralph Benzinger, John Bicket, Doug Burdick, Mike Connor, Vladimir Dizhoor, Shaddin Doghmi, Alexander Druyan, Bowei Du, Sasha Evfimievski, Ariful Gani, Vadim Grinshpun, Ara Hayrapetyan, Chris Jeuell, Igor Kats, Omar Khan, Mikhail Kobyakov, Alexei Kopylov, Brian Kulis, Amit Kumar, Yeongwee Lee, Henry Lin, Ashwin Machanavajjhala, Ayan Mandal, Bill McCloskey, Leonid Meyerguz, Evan Moran, Niranjan Nagarajan, Tina Nolte, Travis Ortogero, Martin Pál, Jon Peress, Matt Piotrowski, Joe Polastre, Mike Priscott, Xin Qi, Venu Ramasubramanian, Aditya Rao, David Richardson, Brian Sabino, Rachit Siamwalla, Sebastian Silgardo, Alex Slivkins, Chaitanya Swamy, Perry Tam, Nadya Travinin, Sergei Vassilvitskii, Matthew Wachs, Tom Wexler, Shan-Leung Maverick Woo, Justin Yang, and Misha Zatsman. Many of them have provided valuable insights, suggestions, and comments on the text. We also thank all the students in these classes who have provided comments and feedback on early drafts of the book over the years.

For the past several years, the development of the book has benefited greatly from the feedback and advice of colleagues who have used prepublication drafts for teaching. Anna Karlin fearlessly adopted a draft as her course textbook at the University of Washington when it was still in an early stage of development; she was followed by a number of people who have used it either as a course textbook or as a resource for teaching: Paul Beame, Allan Borodin, Devdatt Dubhashi, David Kempe, Gene Kleinberg, Dexter Kozen, Amit Kumar, Mike Molloy, Yuval Rabani, Tim Roughgarden, Alexa Sharp, Shanghua Teng, Aravind Srinivasan, Dieter van Melkebeek, Kevin Wayne, Tom Wexler, and

Sue Whitesides. We deeply appreciate their input and advice, which has informed many of our revisions to the content. We would like to additionally thank Kevin Wayne for producing supplementary material associated with the book, which promises to greatly extend its utility to future instructors.

In a number of other cases, our approach to particular topics in the book reflects the infuence of specific colleagues. Many of these contributions have undoubtedly escaped our notice, but we especially thank Yuri Boykov, Ron Elber, Dan Huttenlocher, Bobby Kleinberg, Evie Kleinberg, Lillian Lee, David McAllester, Mark Newman, Prabhakar Raghavan, Bart Selman, David Shmoys, Steve Strogatz, Olga Veksler, Duncan Watts, and Ramin Zabih.

It has been a pleasure working with Addison Wesley over the past year. First and foremost, we thank Matt Goldstein for all his advice and guidance in this process, and for helping us to synthesize a vast amount of review material into a concrete plan that improved the book. Our early conversations about the book with Susan Hartman were extremely valuable as well. We thank Matt and Susan, together with Michelle Brown, Marilyn Lloyd, Patty Mahtani, and Maite Suarez-Rivas at Addison Wesley, and Paul Anagnostopoulos and Jacqui Scarlott at Windfall Software, for all their work on the editing, production, and management of the project. We further thank Paul and Jacqui for their expert composition of the book. We thank Joyce Wells for the cover design, Nancy Murphy of Dartmouth Publishing for her work on the figures, Ted Laux for the indexing, and Carol Leyba and Jennifer McClain for the copyediting and proofreading.

We thank Anselm Blumer (Tufts University), Richard Chang (University of Maryland, Baltimore County), Kevin Compton (University of Michigan), Diane Cook (University of Texas, Arlington), Sariel Har-Peled (University of Illinois, Urbana-Champaign), Sanjeev Khanna (University of Pennsylvania), Philip Klein (Brown University), David Matthias (Ohio State University), Adam Meyerson (UCLA), Michael Mitzenmacher (Harvard University), Stephan Olariu (Old Dominion University), Mohan Paturi (UC San Diego), Edgar Ramos (University of Illinois, Urbana-Champaign), Sanjay Ranka (University of Florida, Gainesville), Leon Reznik (Rochester Institute of Technology), Subhash Suri (UC Santa Barbara), Dieter van Melkebeek (University of Wisconsin, Madison), and Bulent Yener (Rensselaer Polytechnic Institute) who generously contributed their time to provide detailed and thoughtful reviews of the manuscript; their comments led to numerous improvements, both large and small, in the final version of the text.

Finally, we thank our families—Lillian and Alice, and David, Rebecca, and Amy. We appreciate their support, patience, and many other contributions more than we can express in any acknowledgments here.

This book was begun amid the irrational exuberance of the late nineties, when the arc of computing technology seemed, to many of us, briefly to pass through a place traditionally occupied by celebrities and other inhabitants of the pop-cultural firmament. (It was probably just in our imaginations.) Now, several years after the hype and stock prices have come back to earth, one can appreciate that in some ways computer science was forever changed by this period, and in other ways it has remained the same: the driving excitement that has characterized the field since its early days is as strong and enticing as ever, the public's fascination with information technology is still vibrant, and the reach of computing continues to extend into new disciplines. And so to all students of the subject, drawn to it for so many different reasons, we hope you find this book an enjoyable and useful guide wherever your computational pursuits may take you.

Jon Kleinberg
Éva Tardos
Ithaca, 2005

# Chapter 1

## Introduction: Some Representative Problems

### 1.1 A First Problem: Stable Matching

As an opening topic, we look at an algorithmic problem that nicely illustrates many of the themes we will be emphasizing. It is motivated by some very natural and practical concerns, and from these we formulate a clean and simple statement of a problem. The algorithm to solve the problem is very clean as well, and most of our work will be spent in proving that it is correct and giving an acceptable bound on the amount of time it takes to terminate with an answer. The problem itself—the *Stable Matching Problem*—has several origins.

### The Problem

The Stable Matching Problem originated, in part, in 1962, when David Gale and Lloyd Shapley, two mathematical economists, asked the question: Could one design a college admissions process, or a job recruiting process, that was *self-enforcing*? What did they mean by this?

To set up the question, let's first think informally about the kind of situation that might arise as a group of friends, all juniors in college majoring in computer science, begin applying to companies for summer internships. The crux of the application process is the interplay between two different types of parties: companies (the employers) and students (the applicants). Each applicant has a preference ordering on companies, and each company—once the applications come in—forms a preference ordering on its applicants. Based on these preferences, companies extend offers to some of their applicants, applicants choose which of their offers to accept, and people begin heading off to their summer internships.

Gale and Shapley considered the sorts of things that could start going wrong with this process, in the absence of any mechanism to enforce the status quo. Suppose, for example, that your friend Raj has just accepted a summer job at the large telecommunications company CluNet. A few days later, the small start-up company WebExodus, which had been dragging its feet on making a few final decisions, calls up Raj and offers him a summer job as well. Now, Raj actually prefers WebExodus to CluNet—won over perhaps by the laid-back, anything-can-happen atmosphere—and so this new development may well cause him to retract his acceptance of the CluNet offer and go to WebExodus instead. Suddenly down one summer intern, CluNet offers a job to one of its wait-listed applicants, who promptly retracts his previous acceptance of an offer from the software giant Babelsoft, and the situation begins to spiral out of control.

Things look just as bad, if not worse, from the other direction. Suppose that Raj's friend Chelsea, destined to go to Babelsoft but having just heard Raj's story, calls up the people at WebExodus and says, "You know, I'd really rather spend the summer with you guys than at Babelsoft." They find this very easy to believe; and furthermore, on looking at Chelsea's application, they realize that they would have rather hired her than some other student who actually *is* scheduled to spend the summer at WebExodus. In this case, if WebExodus were a slightly less scrupulous company, it might well find some way to retract its offer to this other student and hire Chelsea instead.

Situations like this can rapidly generate a lot of chaos, and many people—both applicants and employers—can end up unhappy with the process as well as the outcome. What has gone wrong? One basic problem is that the process is not self-enforcing—if people are allowed to act in their self-interest, then it risks breaking down.

We might well prefer the following, more stable situation, in which self-interest itself prevents offers from being retracted and redirected. Consider another student, who has arranged to spend the summer at CluNet but calls up WebExodus and reveals that he, too, would rather work for them. But in this case, based on the offers already accepted, they are able to reply, "No, it turns out that we prefer each of the students we've accepted to you, so we're afraid there's nothing we can do." Or consider an employer, earnestly following up with its top applicants who went elsewhere, being told by each of them, "No, I'm happy where I am." In such a case, all the outcomes are stable—there are no further outside deals that can be made.

So this is the question Gale and Shapley asked: Given a set of preferences among employers and applicants, can we assign applicants to employers so that for every employer $E$, and every applicant $A$ who is not scheduled to work for $E$, at least one of the following two things is the case?

(i) *E* prefers every one of its accepted applicants to *A*; or

(ii) *A* prefers her current situation over working for employer *E*.

If this holds, the outcome is stable: individual self-interest will prevent any applicant/employer deal from being made behind the scenes.

Gale and Shapley proceeded to develop a striking algorithmic solution to this problem, which we will discuss presently. Before doing this, let's note that this is not the only origin of the Stable Matching Problem. It turns out that for a decade before the work of Gale and Shapley, unbeknownst to them, the National Resident Matching Program had been using a very similar procedure, with the same underlying motivation, to match residents to hospitals. Indeed, this system, with relatively little change, is still in use today.

This is one testament to the problem's fundamental appeal. And from the point of view of this book, it provides us with a nice first domain in which to reason about some basic combinatorial definitions and the algorithms that build on them.

***Formulating the Problem*** To get at the essence of this concept, it helps to make the problem as clean as possible. The world of companies and applicants contains some distracting asymmetries. Each applicant is looking for a single company, but each company is looking for many applicants; moreover, there may be more (or, as is sometimes the case, fewer) applicants than there are available slots for summer jobs. Finally, each applicant does not typically apply to every company.

It is useful, at least initially, to eliminate these complications and arrive at a more "bare-bones" version of the problem: each of $n$ applicants applies to each of $n$ companies, and each company wants to accept a *single* applicant. We will see that doing this preserves the fundamental issues inherent in the problem; in particular, our solution to this simplified version will extend directly to the more general case as well.

Following Gale and Shapley, we observe that this special case can be viewed as the problem of devising a system by which each of $n$ men and $n$ women can end up getting married: our problem naturally has the analogue of two "genders"—the applicants and the companies—and in the case we are considering, everyone is seeking to be paired with exactly one individual of the opposite gender.[1]

---

[1] Gale and Shapley considered the same-sex Stable Matching Problem as well, where there is only a single gender. This is motivated by related applications, but it turns out to be fairly different at a technical level. Given the applicant-employer application we're considering here, we'll be focusing on the version with two genders.

So consider a set $M = \{m_1, \ldots, m_n\}$ of $n$ men, and a set $W = \{w_1, \ldots, w_n\}$ of $n$ women. Let $M \times W$ denote the set of all possible ordered pairs of the form $(m, w)$, where $m \in M$ and $w \in W$. A *matching* $S$ is a *set* of ordered pairs, each from $M \times W$, with the property that each member of $M$ and each member of $W$ appears in at most one pair in $S$. A *perfect matching* $S'$ is a matching with the property that each member of $M$ and each member of $W$ appears in *exactly* one pair in $S'$.

Matchings and perfect matchings are objects that will recur frequently throughout the book; they arise naturally in modeling a wide range of algorithmic problems. In the present situation, a perfect matching corresponds simply to a way of pairing off the men with the women, in such a way that everyone ends up married to somebody, and nobody is married to more than one person—there is neither singlehood nor polygamy.

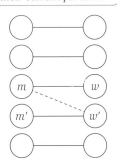

An instability: $m$ and $w'$ each prefer the other to their current partners.

**Figure 1.1** Perfect matching $S$ with instability $(m, w')$.

Now we can add the notion of *preferences* to this setting. Each man $m \in M$ *ranks* all the women; we will say that $m$ *prefers $w$ to $w'$* if $m$ ranks $w$ higher than $w'$. We will refer to the ordered ranking of $m$ as his *preference list*. We will not allow ties in the ranking. Each woman, analogously, ranks all the men.

Given a perfect matching $S$, what can go wrong? Guided by our initial motivation in terms of employers and applicants, we should be worried about the following situation: There are two pairs $(m, w)$ and $(m', w')$ in $S$ (as depicted in Figure 1.1) with the property that $m$ prefers $w'$ to $w$, and $w'$ prefers $m$ to $m'$. In this case, there's nothing to stop $m$ and $w'$ from abandoning their current partners and heading off together; the set of marriages is not self-enforcing. We'll say that such a pair $(m, w')$ is an *instability* with respect to $S$: $(m, w')$ does not belong to $S$, but each of $m$ and $w'$ prefers the other to their partner in $S$.

Our goal, then, is a set of marriages with no instabilities. We'll say that a matching $S$ is *stable* if (i) it is perfect, and (ii) there is no instability with respect to $S$. Two questions spring immediately to mind:

- Does there exist a stable matching for every set of preference lists?
- Given a set of preference lists, can we efficiently construct a stable matching if there is one?

***Some Examples*** To illustrate these definitions, consider the following two very simple instances of the Stable Matching Problem.

First, suppose we have a set of two men, $\{m, m'\}$, and a set of two women, $\{w, w'\}$. The preference lists are as follows:

$m$ prefers $w$ to $w'$.

$m'$ prefers $w$ to $w'$.

$w$ prefers $m$ to $m'$.

$w'$ prefers $m$ to $m'$.

If we think about this set of preference lists intuitively, it represents complete agreement: the men agree on the order of the women, and the women agree on the order of the men. There is a unique stable matching here, consisting of the pairs $(m, w)$ and $(m', w')$. The other perfect matching, consisting of the pairs $(m', w)$ and $(m, w')$, would not be a stable matching, because the pair $(m, w)$ would form an instability with respect to this matching. (Both $m$ and $w$ would want to leave their respective partners and pair up.)

Next, here's an example where things are a bit more intricate. Suppose the preferences are

$m$ prefers $w$ to $w'$.

$m'$ prefers $w'$ to $w$.

$w$ prefers $m'$ to $m$.

$w'$ prefers $m$ to $m'$.

What's going on in this case? The two men's preferences mesh perfectly with each other (they rank different women first), and the two women's preferences likewise mesh perfectly with each other. But the men's preferences clash completely with the women's preferences.

In this second example, there are two different stable matchings. The matching consisting of the pairs $(m, w)$ and $(m', w')$ is stable, because both men are as happy as possible, so neither would leave their matched partner. But the matching consisting of the pairs $(m', w)$ and $(m, w')$ is also stable, for the complementary reason that both women are as happy as possible. This is an important point to remember as we go forward—it's possible for an instance to have more than one stable matching.

## Designing the Algorithm

We now show that there exists a stable matching for every set of preference lists among the men and women. Moreover, our means of showing this will also answer the second question that we asked above: we will give an efficient algorithm that takes the preference lists and constructs a stable matching.

Let us consider some of the basic ideas that motivate the algorithm.

- Initially, everyone is unmarried. Suppose an unmarried man $m$ chooses the woman $w$ who ranks highest on his preference list and *proposes* to her. Can we declare immediately that $(m, w)$ will be one of the pairs in our final stable matching? Not necessarily: at some point in the future, a man $m'$ whom $w$ prefers may propose to her. On the other hand, it would be

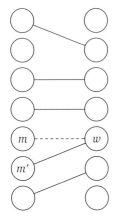

Woman $w$ will become engaged to $m$ if she prefers him to $m'$.

$m$

$m'$

**Figure 1.2** An intermediate state of the G-S algorithm when a free man $m$ is proposing to a woman $w$.

dangerous for $w$ to reject $m$ right away; she may never receive a proposal from someone she ranks as highly as $m$. So a natural idea would be to have the pair $(m, w)$ enter an intermediate state—*engagement*.

- Suppose we are now at a state in which some men and women are *free*—not engaged—and some are engaged. The next step could look like this. An arbitrary free man $m$ chooses the highest-ranked woman $w$ to whom he has not yet proposed, and he proposes to her. If $w$ is also free, then $m$ and $w$ become engaged. Otherwise, $w$ is already engaged to some other man $m'$. In this case, she determines which of $m$ or $m'$ ranks higher on her preference list; this man becomes engaged to $w$ and the other becomes free.

- Finally, the algorithm will terminate when no one is free; at this moment, all engagements are declared final, and the resulting perfect matching is returned.

Here is a concrete description of the *Gale-Shapley algorithm*, with Figure 1.2 depicting a state of the algorithm.

```
Initially all m ∈ M and w ∈ W are free
While there is a man m who is free and hasn't proposed to
every woman
    Choose such a man m
    Let w be the highest-ranked woman in m's preference list
        to whom m has not yet proposed
    If w is free then
        (m, w) become engaged
    Else w is currently engaged to m'
        If w prefers m' to m then
            m remains free
        Else w prefers m to m'
            (m, w) become engaged
            m' becomes free
        Endif
    Endif
Endwhile
Return the set S of engaged pairs
```

An intriguing thing is that, although the G-S algorithm is quite simple to state, it is not immediately obvious that it returns a stable matching, or even a perfect matching. We proceed to prove this now, through a sequence of intermediate facts.

## Analyzing the Algorithm

First consider the view of a woman $w$ during the execution of the algorithm. For a while, no one has proposed to her, and she is free. Then a man $m$ may propose to her, and she becomes engaged. As time goes on, she may receive additional proposals, accepting those that increase the rank of her partner. So we discover the following.

**(1.1)** *w remains engaged from the point at which she receives her first proposal; and the sequence of partners to which she is engaged gets better and better (in terms of her preference list).*

The view of a man $m$ during the execution of the algorithm is rather different. He is free until he proposes to the highest-ranked woman on his list; at this point he may or may not become engaged. As time goes on, he may alternate between being free and being engaged; however, the following property does hold.

**(1.2)** *The sequence of women to whom m proposes gets worse and worse (in terms of his preference list).*

Now we show that the algorithm terminates, and give a bound on the maximum number of iterations needed for termination.

**(1.3)** *The G-S algorithm terminates after at most $n^2$ iterations of the* `While` *loop.*

**Proof.** A useful strategy for upper-bounding the running time of an algorithm, as we are trying to do here, is to find a measure of *progress*. Namely, we seek some precise way of saying that each step taken by the algorithm brings it closer to termination.

In the case of the present algorithm, each iteration consists of some man proposing (for the only time) to a woman he has never proposed to before. So if we let $\mathcal{P}(t)$ denote the set of pairs $(m, w)$ such that $m$ has proposed to $w$ by the end of iteration $t$, we see that for all $t$, the size of $\mathcal{P}(t + 1)$ is strictly greater than the size of $\mathcal{P}(t)$. But there are only $n^2$ possible pairs of men and women in total, so the value of $\mathcal{P}(\cdot)$ can increase at most $n^2$ times over the course of the algorithm. It follows that there can be at most $n^2$ iterations. ■

Two points are worth noting about the previous fact and its proof. First, there are executions of the algorithm (with certain preference lists) that can involve close to $n^2$ iterations, so this analysis is not far from the best possible. Second, there are many quantities that would not have worked well as a *progress measure* for the algorithm, since they need not strictly increase in each iteration. For example, the number of free individuals could remain constant from one iteration to the next, as could the number of engaged pairs. Thus, these quantities could not be used directly in giving an upper bound on the maximum possible number of iterations, in the style of the previous paragraph.

Let us now establish that the set $S$ returned at the termination of the algorithm is in fact a perfect matching. Why is this not immediately obvious? Essentially, we have to show that no man can "fall off" the end of his preference list; the only way for the `While` loop to exit is for there to be no free man. In this case, the set of engaged couples would indeed be a perfect matching.

So the main thing we need to show is the following.

**(1.4)**    *If $m$ is free at some point in the execution of the algorithm, then there is a woman to whom he has not yet proposed.*

**Proof.** Suppose there comes a point when $m$ is free but has already proposed to every woman. Then by (1.1), each of the $n$ women is engaged at this point in time. Since the set of engaged pairs forms a matching, there must also be $n$ engaged men at this point in time. But there are only $n$ men total, and $m$ is not engaged, so this is a contradiction.  ■

**(1.5)**    *The set $S$ returned at termination is a perfect matching.*

**Proof.** The set of engaged pairs always forms a matching. Let us suppose that the algorithm terminates with a free man $m$. At termination, it must be the case that $m$ had already proposed to every woman, for otherwise the `While` loop would not have exited. But this contradicts (1.4), which says that there cannot be a free man who has proposed to every woman.  ■

Finally, we prove the main property of the algorithm—namely, that it results in a stable matching.

**(1.6)**    *Consider an execution of the G-S algorithm that returns a set of pairs S. The set S is a stable matching.*

**Proof.** We have already seen, in (1.5), that $S$ is a perfect matching. Thus, to prove $S$ is a stable matching, we will assume that there is an instability with respect to $S$ and obtain a contradiction. As defined earlier, such an instability would involve two pairs, $(m, w)$ and $(m', w')$, in $S$ with the properties that

- $m$ prefers $w'$ to $w$, and
- $w'$ prefers $m$ to $m'$.

In the execution of the algorithm that produced $S$, $m$'s last proposal was, by definition, to $w$. Now we ask: Did $m$ propose to $w'$ at some earlier point in this execution? If he didn't, then $w$ must occur higher on $m$'s preference list than $w'$, contradicting our assumption that $m$ prefers $w'$ to $w$. If he did, then he was rejected by $w'$ in favor of some other man $m''$, whom $w'$ prefers to $m$. $m'$ is the final partner of $w'$, so either $m'' = m'$ or, by (1.1), $w'$ prefers her final partner $m'$ to $m''$; either way this contradicts our assumption that $w'$ prefers $m$ to $m'$.

It follows that $S$ is a stable matching.    ■

## Extensions

We began by defining the notion of a stable matching; we have just proven that the G-S algorithm actually constructs one. We now consider some further questions about the behavior of the G-S algorithm and its relation to the properties of different stable matchings.

To begin with, recall that we saw an example earlier in which there could be multiple stable matchings. To recap, the preference lists in this example were as follows:

> $m$ prefers $w$ to $w'$.
> $m'$ prefers $w'$ to $w$.
> $w$ prefers $m'$ to $m$.
> $w'$ prefers $m$ to $m'$.

Now, in any execution of the Gale-Shapley algorithm, $m$ will become engaged to $w$, $m'$ will become engaged to $w'$ (perhaps in the other order), and things will stop there. Thus, the *other* stable matching, consisting of the pairs $(m', w)$ and $(m, w')$, is not attainable from an execution of the G-S algorithm in which the men propose. On the other hand, it would be reached if we ran a version of the algorithm in which the women propose. And in larger examples, with more than two people on each side, we can have an even larger collection of possible stable matchings, many of them not achievable by any natural algorithm.

This example shows a certain "unfairness" in the G-S algorithm, favoring men. If the men's preferences mesh perfectly (they all list different women as their first choice), then in all runs of the G-S algorithm all men end up matched with their first choice, independent of the preferences of the women. If the women's preferences clash completely with the men's preferences (as was the case in this example), then the resulting stable matching is as bad as possible for the women. So this simple set of preference lists compactly summarizes a world in which *someone* is destined to end up unhappy: women are unhappy if men propose, and men are unhappy if women propose.

Let's now analyze the G-S algorithm in more detail and try to understand how general this "unfairness" phenomenon is.

To begin with, our example reinforces the point that the G-S algorithm is actually underspecified: as long as there is a free man, we are allowed to choose *any* free man to make the next proposal. Different choices specify different executions of the algorithm; this is why, to be careful, we stated (1.6) as "Consider an execution of the G-S algorithm that returns a set of pairs *S*," instead of "Consider the set *S* returned by the G-S algorithm."

Thus, we encounter another very natural question: Do all executions of the G-S algorithm yield the same matching? This is a genre of question that arises in many settings in computer science: we have an algorithm that runs *asynchronously*, with different independent components performing actions that can be interleaved in complex ways, and we want to know how much variability this asynchrony causes in the final outcome. To consider a very different kind of example, the independent components may not be men and women but electronic components activating parts of an airplane wing; the effect of asynchrony in their behavior can be a big deal.

In the present context, we will see that the answer to our question is surprisingly clean: all executions of the G-S algorithm yield the same matching. We proceed to prove this now.

***All Executions Yield the Same Matching***   There are a number of possible ways to prove a statement such as this, many of which would result in quite complicated arguments. It turns out that the easiest and most informative approach for us will be to uniquely *characterize* the matching that is obtained and then show that all executions result in the matching with this characterization.

What is the characterization? We'll show that each man ends up with the "best possible partner" in a concrete sense. (Recall that this is true if all men prefer different women.) First, we will say that a woman *w* is a *valid partner* of a man *m* if there is a stable matching that contains the pair $(m, w)$. We will say that *w* is the *best valid partner* of *m* if *w* is a valid partner of *m*, and no woman whom *m* ranks higher than *w* is a valid partner of his. We will use *best*(*m*) to denote the best valid partner of *m*.

Now, let $S^*$ denote the set of pairs $\{(m, best(m)) : m \in M\}$. We will prove the following fact.

**(1.7)**   *Every execution of the G-S algorithm results in the set $S^*$.*

This statement is surprising at a number of levels. First of all, as defined, there is no reason to believe that $S^*$ is a matching at all, let alone a stable matching. After all, why couldn't it happen that two men have the same best valid partner? Second, the result shows that the G-S algorithm gives the best possible outcome for every man simultaneously; there is no stable matching in which any of the men could have hoped to do better. And finally, it answers our question above by showing that the order of proposals in the G-S algorithm has absolutely no effect on the final outcome.

Despite all this, the proof is not so difficult.

**Proof.** Let us suppose, by way of contradiction, that some execution $\mathcal{E}$ of the G-S algorithm results in a matching $S$ in which some man is paired with a woman who is not his best valid partner. Since men propose in decreasing order of preference, this means that some man is rejected by a valid partner during the execution $\mathcal{E}$ of the algorithm. So consider the first moment during the execution $\mathcal{E}$ in which some man, say $m$, is rejected by a valid partner $w$. Again, since men propose in decreasing order of preference, and since this is the first time such a rejection has occurred, it must be that $w$ is $m$'s best valid partner $best(m)$.

The rejection of $m$ by $w$ may have happened either because $m$ proposed and was turned down in favor of $w$'s existing engagement, or because $w$ broke her engagement to $m$ in favor of a better proposal. But either way, at this moment $w$ forms or continues an engagement with a man $m'$ whom she prefers to $m$.

Since $w$ is a valid partner of $m$, there exists a stable matching $S'$ containing the pair $(m, w)$. Now we ask: Who is $m'$ paired with in this matching? Suppose it is a woman $w' \neq w$.

Since the rejection of $m$ by $w$ was the first rejection of a man by a valid partner in the execution $\mathcal{E}$, it must be that $m'$ had not been rejected by any valid partner at the point in $\mathcal{E}$ when he became engaged to $w$. Since he proposed in decreasing order of preference, and since $w'$ is clearly a valid partner of $m'$, it must be that $m'$ prefers $w$ to $w'$. But we have already seen that $w$ prefers $m'$ to $m$, for in execution $\mathcal{E}$ she rejected $m$ in favor of $m'$. Since $(m', w) \notin S'$, it follows that $(m', w)$ is an instability in $S'$.

This contradicts our claim that $S'$ is stable and hence contradicts our initial assumption. ∎

So for the men, the G-S algorithm is ideal. Unfortunately, the same cannot be said for the women. For a woman $w$, we say that $m$ is a valid partner if there is a stable matching that contains the pair $(m, w)$. We say that $m$ is the *worst valid partner* of $w$ if $m$ is a valid partner of $w$, and no man whom $w$ ranks lower than $m$ is a valid partner of hers.

**(1.8)** *In the stable matching $S^*$, each woman is paired with her worst valid partner.*

**Proof.** Suppose there were a pair $(m, w)$ in $S^*$ such that $m$ is not the worst valid partner of $w$. Then there is a stable matching $S'$ in which $w$ is paired with a man $m'$ whom she likes less than $m$. In $S'$, $m$ is paired with a woman $w' \neq w$; since $w$ is the best valid partner of $m$, and $w'$ is a valid partner of $m$, we see that $m$ prefers $w$ to $w'$.

But from this it follows that $(m, w)$ is an instability in $S'$, contradicting the claim that $S'$ is stable and hence contradicting our initial assumption. ∎

Thus, we find that our simple example above, in which the men's preferences clashed with the women's, hinted at a very general phenomenon: for any input, the side that does the proposing in the G-S algorithm ends up with the best possible stable matching (from their perspective), while the side that does not do the proposing correspondingly ends up with the worst possible stable matching.

## 1.2 Five Representative Problems

The Stable Matching Problem provides us with a rich example of the process of algorithm design. For many problems, this process involves a few significant steps: formulating the problem with enough mathematical precision that we can ask a concrete question and start thinking about algorithms to solve it; designing an algorithm for the problem; and analyzing the algorithm by proving it is correct and giving a bound on the running time so as to establish the algorithm's efficiency.

This high-level strategy is carried out in practice with the help of a few fundamental design techniques, which are very useful in assessing the inherent complexity of a problem and in formulating an algorithm to solve it. As in any area, becoming familiar with these design techniques is a gradual process; but with experience one can start recognizing problems as belonging to identifiable genres and appreciating how subtle changes in the statement of a problem can have an enormous effect on its computational difficulty.

To get this discussion started, then, it helps to pick out a few representative milestones that we'll be encountering in our study of algorithms: cleanly formulated problems, all resembling one another at a general level, but differing greatly in their difficulty and in the kinds of approaches that one brings to bear on them. The first three will be solvable efficiently by a sequence of increasingly subtle algorithmic techniques; the fourth marks a major turning point in our discussion, serving as an example of a problem believed to be unsolvable by any efficient algorithm; and the fifth hints at a class of problems believed to be harder still.

The problems are self-contained and are all motivated by computing applications. To talk about some of them, though, it will help to use the terminology of *graphs*. While graphs are a common topic in earlier computer science courses, we'll be introducing them in a fair amount of depth in Chapter 3; due to their enormous expressive power, we'll also be using them extensively throughout the book. For the discussion here, it's enough to think of a graph $G$ as simply a way of encoding pairwise relationships among a set of objects. Thus, $G$ consists of a pair of sets $(V, E)$—a collection $V$ of *nodes* and a collection $E$ of *edges*, each of which "joins" two of the nodes. We thus represent an edge $e \in E$ as a two-element subset of $V$: $e = \{u, v\}$ for some $u, v \in V$, where we call $u$ and $v$ the *ends* of $e$. We typically draw graphs as in Figure 1.3, with each node as a small circle and each edge as a line segment joining its two ends.

Let's now turn to a discussion of the five representative problems.

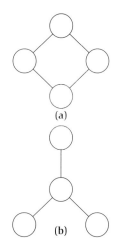

**Figure 1.3** Each of (a) and (b) depicts a graph on four nodes.

## Interval Scheduling

Consider the following very simple scheduling problem. You have a resource—it may be a lecture room, a supercomputer, or an electron microscope—and many people request to use the resource for periods of time. A *request* takes the form: Can I reserve the resource starting at time $s$, until time $f$? We will assume that the resource can be used by at most one person at a time. A scheduler wants to accept a subset of these requests, rejecting all others, so that the accepted requests do not overlap in time. The goal is to maximize the number of requests accepted.

More formally, there will be $n$ requests labeled $1, \ldots, n$, with each request $i$ specifying a start time $s_i$ and a finish time $f_i$. Naturally, we have $s_i < f_i$ for all $i$. Two requests $i$ and $j$ are *compatible* if the requested intervals do not overlap: that is, either request $i$ is for an earlier time interval than request $j$ ($f_i \leq s_j$), or request $i$ is for a later time than request $j$ ($f_j \leq s_i$). We'll say more generally that a subset $A$ of requests is compatible if all pairs of requests $i, j \in A$, $i \neq j$ are compatible. The goal is to select a compatible subset of requests of maximum possible size.

We illustrate an instance of this *Interval Scheduling Problem* in Figure 1.4. Note that there is a single compatible set of size 4, and this is the largest compatible set.

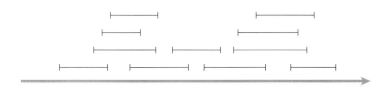

**Figure 1.4** An instance of the Interval Scheduling Problem.

We will see shortly that this problem can be solved by a very natural algorithm that orders the set of requests according to a certain heuristic and then "greedily" processes them in one pass, selecting as large a compatible subset as it can. This will be typical of a class of *greedy algorithms* that we will consider for various problems—myopic rules that process the input one piece at a time with no apparent look-ahead. When a greedy algorithm can be shown to find an optimal solution for all instances of a problem, it's often fairly surprising. We typically learn something about the structure of the underlying problem from the fact that such a simple approach can be optimal.

## Weighted Interval Scheduling

In the Interval Scheduling Problem, we sought to maximize the *number* of requests that could be accommodated simultaneously. Now, suppose more generally that each request interval $i$ has an associated *value*, or *weight*, $v_i > 0$; we could picture this as the amount of money we will make from the $i^{\text{th}}$ individual if we schedule his or her request. Our goal will be to find a compatible subset of intervals of maximum total value.

The case in which $v_i = 1$ for each $i$ is simply the basic Interval Scheduling Problem; but the appearance of arbitrary values changes the nature of the maximization problem quite a bit. Consider, for example, that if $v_1$ exceeds the sum of all other $v_i$, then the optimal solution must include interval 1 regardless of the configuration of the full set of intervals. So any algorithm for this problem must be very sensitive to the values, and yet degenerate to a method for solving (unweighted) interval scheduling when all the values are equal to 1.

There appears to be no simple greedy rule that walks through the intervals one at a time, making the correct decision in the presence of arbitrary values. Instead, we employ a technique, *dynamic programming*, that builds up the optimal value over all possible solutions in a compact, tabular way that leads to a very efficient algorithm.

## Bipartite Matching

When we considered the Stable Matching Problem, we defined a *matching* to be a set of ordered pairs of men and women with the property that each man and each woman belong to at most one of the ordered pairs. We then defined a *perfect matching* to be a matching in which every man and every woman belong to some pair.

We can express these concepts more generally in terms of graphs, and in order to do this it is useful to define the notion of a *bipartite graph*. We say that a graph $G = (V, E)$ is *bipartite* if its node set $V$ can be partitioned into sets $X$

and $Y$ in such a way that every edge has one end in $X$ and the other end in $Y$. A bipartite graph is pictured in Figure 1.5; often, when we want to emphasize a graph's "bipartiteness," we will draw it this way, with the nodes in $X$ and $Y$ in two parallel columns. But notice, for example, that the two graphs in Figure 1.3 are also bipartite.

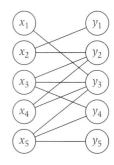

**Figure 1.5** A bipartite graph.

Now, in the problem of finding a stable matching, matchings were built from pairs of men and women. In the case of bipartite graphs, the edges are pairs of nodes, so we say that a matching in a graph $G = (V, E)$ is a set of edges $M \subseteq E$ with the property that each node appears in at most one edge of $M$. $M$ is a perfect matching if every node appears in exactly one edge of $M$.

To see that this does capture the same notion we encountered in the Stable Matching Problem, consider a bipartite graph $G'$ with a set $X$ of $n$ men, a set $Y$ of $n$ women, and an edge from every node in $X$ to every node in $Y$. Then the matchings and perfect matchings in $G'$ are precisely the matchings and perfect matchings among the set of men and women.

In the Stable Matching Problem, we added preferences to this picture. Here, we do not consider preferences; but the nature of the problem in arbitrary bipartite graphs adds a different source of complexity: there is not necessarily an edge from every $x \in X$ to every $y \in Y$, so the set of possible matchings has quite a complicated structure. In other words, it is as though only certain pairs of men and women are willing to be paired off, and we want to figure out how to pair off many people in a way that is consistent with this. Consider, for example, the bipartite graph $G$ in Figure 1.5: there are many matchings in $G$, but there is only one perfect matching. (Do you see it?)

Matchings in bipartite graphs can model situations in which objects are being *assigned* to other objects. Thus, the nodes in $X$ can represent jobs, the nodes in $Y$ can represent machines, and an edge $(x_i, y_j)$ can indicate that machine $y_j$ is capable of processing job $x_i$. A perfect matching is then a way of assigning each job to a machine that can process it, with the property that each machine is assigned exactly one job. In the spring, computer science departments across the country are often seen pondering a bipartite graph in which $X$ is the set of professors in the department, $Y$ is the set of offered courses, and an edge $(x_i, y_j)$ indicates that professor $x_i$ is capable of teaching course $y_j$. A perfect matching in this graph consists of an assignment of each professor to a course that he or she can teach, in such a way that every course is covered.

Thus the *Bipartite Matching Problem* is the following: Given an arbitrary bipartite graph $G$, find a matching of maximum size. If $|X| = |Y| = n$, then there is a perfect matching if and only if the maximum matching has size $n$. We will find that the algorithmic techniques discussed earlier do not seem adequate for providing an efficient algorithm for this problem. There is, however, a very elegant and efficient algorithm to find a maximum matching; it inductively builds up larger and larger matchings, selectively backtracking along the way. This process is called *augmentation*, and it forms the central component in a large class of efficiently solvable problems called *network flow problems*.

## Independent Set

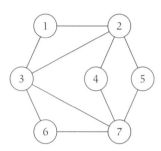

**Figure 1.6** A graph whose largest independent set has size 4.

Now let's talk about an extremely general problem, which includes most of these earlier problems as special cases. Given a graph $G = (V, E)$, we say a set of nodes $S \subseteq V$ is *independent* if no two nodes in $S$ are joined by an edge. The *Independent Set Problem* is, then, the following: Given $G$, find an independent set that is as large as possible. For example, the maximum size of an independent set in the graph in Figure 1.6 is four, achieved by the four-node independent set $\{1, 4, 5, 6\}$.

The Independent Set Problem encodes any situation in which you are trying to choose from among a collection of objects and there are pairwise *conflicts* among some of the objects. Say you have $n$ friends, and some pairs of them don't get along. How large a group of your friends can you invite to dinner if you don't want any interpersonal tensions? This is simply the largest independent set in the graph whose nodes are your friends, with an edge between each conflicting pair.

Interval Scheduling and Bipartite Matching can both be encoded as special cases of the Independent Set Problem. For Interval Scheduling, define a graph $G = (V, E)$ in which the nodes are the intervals and there is an edge between each pair of them that overlap; the independent sets in $G$ are then just the compatible subsets of intervals. Encoding Bipartite Matching as a special case of Independent Set is a little trickier to see. Given a bipartite graph $G' = (V', E')$, the objects being chosen are edges, and the conflicts arise between two edges that share an end. (These, indeed, are the pairs of edges that cannot belong to a common matching.) So we define a graph $G = (V, E)$ in which the node set $V$ is equal to the edge set $E'$ of $G'$. We define an edge between each pair of elements in $V$ that correspond to edges of $G'$ with a common end. We can now check that the independent sets of $G$ are precisely the matchings of $G'$. While it is not complicated to check this, it takes a little concentration to deal with this type of "edges-to-nodes, nodes-to-edges" transformation.[2]

---

[2] For those who are curious, we note that not every instance of the Independent Set Problem can arise in this way from Interval Scheduling or from Bipartite Matching; the full Independent Set Problem really is more general. The graph in Figure 1.3(a) cannot arise as the "conflict graph" in an instance of

Given the generality of the Independent Set Problem, an efficient algorithm to solve it would be quite impressive. It would have to implicitly contain algorithms for Interval Scheduling, Bipartite Matching, and a host of other natural optimization problems.

The current status of Independent Set is this: no efficient algorithm is known for the problem, and it is conjectured that no such algorithm exists. The obvious brute-force algorithm would try all subsets of the nodes, checking each to see if it is independent, and then recording the largest one encountered. It is possible that this is close to the best we can do on this problem. We will see later in the book that Independent Set is one of a large class of problems that are termed *NP-complete*. No efficient algorithm is known for any of them; but they are all *equivalent* in the sense that a solution to any one of them would imply, in a precise sense, a solution to all of them.

Here's a natural question: Is there anything good we can say about the complexity of the Independent Set Problem? One positive thing is the following: If we have a graph $G$ on 1,000 nodes, and we want to convince you that it contains an independent set $S$ of size 100, then it's quite easy. We simply show you the graph $G$, circle the nodes of $S$ in red, and let you check that no two of them are joined by an edge. So there really seems to be a great difference in difficulty between *checking* that something is a large independent set and actually *finding* a large independent set. This may look like a very basic observation—and it is—but it turns out to be crucial in understanding this class of problems. Furthermore, as we'll see next, it's possible for a problem to be so hard that there isn't even an easy way to "check" solutions in this sense.

## Competitive Facility Location

Finally, we come to our fifth problem, which is based on the following two-player game. Consider two large companies that operate café franchises across the country—let's call them JavaPlanet and Queequeg's Coffee—and they are currently competing for market share in a geographic area. First JavaPlanet opens a franchise; then Queequeg's Coffee opens a franchise; then JavaPlanet; then Queequeg's; and so on. Suppose they must deal with zoning regulations that require no two franchises be located too close together, and each is trying to make its locations as convenient as possible. Who will win?

Let's make the rules of this "game" more concrete. The geographic region in question is divided into $n$ zones, labeled $1, 2, \ldots, n$. Each zone $i$ has a

---

Interval Scheduling, and the graph in Figure 1.3(b) cannot arise as the "conflict graph" in an instance of Bipartite Matching.

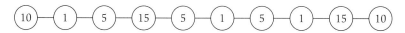

**Figure 1.7** An instance of the Competitive Facility Location Problem.

value $b_i$, which is the revenue obtained by either of the companies if it opens a franchise there. Finally, certain pairs of zones $(i, j)$ are *adjacent*, and local zoning laws prevent two adjacent zones from each containing a franchise, regardless of which company owns them. (They also prevent two franchises from being opened in the same zone.) We model these conflicts via a graph $G = (V, E)$, where $V$ is the set of zones, and $(i, j)$ is an edge in $E$ if the zones $i$ and $j$ are adjacent. The zoning requirement then says that the full set of franchises opened must form an independent set in $G$.

Thus our game consists of two players, $P_1$ and $P_2$, alternately selecting nodes in $G$, with $P_1$ moving first. At all times, the set of all selected nodes must form an independent set in $G$. Suppose that player $P_2$ has a target bound $B$, and we want to know: is there a strategy for $P_2$ so that no matter how $P_1$ plays, $P_2$ will be able to select a set of nodes with a total value of at least $B$? We will call this an instance of the *Competitive Facility Location Problem*.

Consider, for example, the instance pictured in Figure 1.7, and suppose that $P_2$'s target bound is $B = 20$. Then $P_2$ does have a winning strategy. On the other hand, if $B = 25$, then $P_2$ does not.

One can work this out by looking at the figure for a while; but it requires some amount of case-checking of the form, "If $P_1$ goes here, then $P_2$ will go there; but if $P_1$ goes over there, then $P_2$ will go here. . . . " And this appears to be intrinsic to the problem: not only is it computationally difficult to determine whether $P_2$ has a winning strategy; on a reasonably sized graph, it would even be hard for us to *convince* you that $P_2$ has a winning strategy. There does not seem to be a short proof we could present; rather, we'd have to lead you on a lengthy case-by-case analysis of the set of possible moves.

This is in contrast to the Independent Set Problem, where we believe that finding a large solution is hard but checking a proposed large solution is easy. This contrast can be formalized in the class of *PSPACE-complete problems*, of which Competitive Facility Location is an example. PSPACE-complete problems are believed to be strictly harder than NP-complete problems, and this conjectured lack of short "proofs" for their solutions is one indication of this greater hardness. The notion of PSPACE-completeness turns out to capture a large collection of problems involving game-playing and planning; many of these are fundamental issues in the area of artificial intelligence.

# Solved Exercises

### Solved Exercise 1

Consider a town with $n$ men and $n$ women seeking to get married to one another. Each man has a preference list that ranks all the women, and each woman has a preference list that ranks all the men.

The set of all $2n$ people is divided into two categories: *good* people and *bad* people. Suppose that for some number $k$, $1 \leq k \leq n - 1$, there are $k$ good men and $k$ good women; thus there are $n - k$ bad men and $n - k$ bad women.

Everyone would rather marry any good person than any bad person. Formally, each preference list has the property that it ranks each good person of the opposite gender higher than each bad person of the opposite gender: its first $k$ entries are the good people (of the opposite gender) in some order, and its next $n - k$ are the bad people (of the opposite gender) in some order.

Show that in every stable matching, every good man is married to a good woman.

**Solution**    A natural way to get started thinking about this problem is to assume the claim is false and try to work toward obtaining a contradiction. What would it mean for the claim to be false? There would exist some stable matching $M$ in which a good man $m$ was married to a bad woman $w$.

Now, let's consider what the other pairs in $M$ look like. There are $k$ good men and $k$ good women. Could it be the case that every good woman is married to a good man in this matching $M$? No: one of the good men (namely, $m$) is already married to a bad woman, and that leaves only $k - 1$ other good men. So even if all of them were married to good women, that would still leave some good woman who is married to a bad man.

Let $w'$ be such a good woman, who is married to a bad man. It is now easy to identify an instability in $M$: consider the pair $(m, w')$. Each is good, but is married to a bad partner. Thus, each of $m$ and $w'$ prefers the other to their current partner, and hence $(m, w')$ is an instability. This contradicts our assumption that $M$ is stable, and hence concludes the proof.

## Solved Exercise 2

We can think about a generalization of the Stable Matching Problem in which certain man-woman pairs are explicitly *forbidden*. In the case of employers and applicants, we could imagine that certain applicants simply lack the necessary qualifications or certifications, and so they cannot be employed at certain companies, however desirable they may seem. Using the analogy to marriage between men and women, we have a set $M$ of $n$ men, a set $W$ of $n$ women, and a set $F \subseteq M \times W$ of pairs who are simply *not allowed* to get married. Each man $m$ ranks all the women $w$ for which $(m, w) \notin F$, and each woman $w'$ ranks all the men $m'$ for which $(m', w') \notin F$.

In this more general setting, we say that a matching $S$ is *stable* if it does not exhibit any of the following types of instability.

(i) There are two pairs $(m, w)$ and $(m', w')$ in $S$ with the property that $(m, w') \notin F$, $m$ prefers $w'$ to $w$, and $w'$ prefers $m$ to $m'$. *(The usual kind of instability.)*

(ii) There is a pair $(m, w) \in S$, and a man $m'$, so that $m'$ is not part of any pair in the matching, $(m', w) \notin F$, and $w$ prefers $m'$ to $m$. *(A single man is more desirable and not forbidden.)*

(iii) There is a pair $(m, w) \in S$, and a woman $w'$, so that $w'$ is not part of any pair in the matching, $(m, w') \notin F$, and $m$ prefers $w'$ to $w$. *(A single woman is more desirable and not forbidden.)*

(iv) There is a man $m$ and a woman $w$, neither of whom is part of any pair in the matching, so that $(m, w) \notin F$. *(There are two single people with nothing preventing them from getting married to each other.)*

Note that under these more general definitions, a stable matching need not be a perfect matching.

Now we can ask: For every set of preference lists and every set of forbidden pairs, is there always a stable matching? Resolve this question by doing one of the following two things: (a) give an algorithm that, for any set of preference lists and forbidden pairs, produces a stable matching; or (b) give an example of a set of preference lists and forbidden pairs for which there is no stable matching.

***Solution***   The Gale-Shapley algorithm is remarkably robust to variations on the Stable Matching Problem. So, if you're faced with a new variation of the problem and can't find a counterexample to stability, it's often a good idea to check whether a direct adaptation of the G-S algorithm will in fact produce stable matchings.

That turns out to be the case here. We will show that there is always a stable matching, even in this more general model with forbidden pairs, and we will do this by adapting the G-S algorithm. To do this, let's consider why the original G-S algorithm can't be used directly. The difficulty, of course, is that the G-S algorithm doesn't know anything about forbidden pairs, and so the condition in the While loop,

```
While there is a man m who is free and hasn't proposed to
every woman,
```

won't work: we don't want $m$ to propose to a woman $w$ for which the pair $(m, w)$ is forbidden.

Thus, let's consider a variation of the G-S algorithm in which we make only one change: we modify the `While` loop to say,

While there is a man $m$ who is free and hasn't proposed to every woman $w$ for which $(m, w) \notin F$.

Here is the algorithm in full.

```
Initially all m ∈ M and w ∈ W are free
While there is a man m who is free and hasn't proposed to
every woman w for which (m, w) ∉ F
   Choose such a man m
   Let w be the highest-ranked woman in m's preference list
       to which m has not yet proposed
   If w is free then
     (m, w) become engaged
   Else w is currently engaged to m'
       If w prefers m' to m then
           m remains free
       Else w prefers m to m'
           (m, w) become engaged
           m' becomes free
       Endif
   Endif
Endwhile
Return the set S of engaged pairs
```

We now prove that this yields a stable matching, under our new definition of stability.

To begin with, facts (1.1), (1.2), and (1.3) from the text remain true (in particular, the algorithm will terminate in at most $n^2$ iterations). Also, we don't have to worry about establishing that the resulting matching $S$ is perfect (indeed, it may not be). We also notice an additional pairs of facts. If $m$ is a man who is not part of a pair in $S$, then $m$ must have proposed to every nonforbidden woman; and if $w$ is a woman who is not part of a pair in $S$, then it must be that no man ever proposed to $w$.

Finally, we need only show

**(1.9)** *There is no instability with respect to the returned matching S.*

**Proof.** Our general definition of instability has four parts: This means that we have to make sure that none of the four bad things happens.

First, suppose there is an instability of type (i), consisting of pairs $(m, w)$ and $(m', w')$ in $S$ with the property that $(m, w') \notin F$, $m$ prefers $w'$ to $w$, and $w'$ prefers $m$ to $m'$. It follows that $m$ must have proposed to $w'$; so $w'$ rejected $m$, and thus she prefers her final partner to $m$—a contradiction.

Next, suppose there is an instability of type (ii), consisting of a pair $(m, w) \in S$, and a man $m'$, so that $m'$ is not part of any pair in the matching, $(m', w) \notin F$, and $w$ prefers $m'$ to $m$. Then $m'$ must have proposed to $w$ and been rejected; again, it follows that $w$ prefers her final partner to $m'$—a contradiction.

Third, suppose there is an instability of type (iii), consisting of a pair $(m, w) \in S$, and a woman $w'$, so that $w'$ is not part of any pair in the matching, $(m, w') \notin F$, and $m$ prefers $w'$ to $w$. Then no man proposed to $w'$ at all; in particular, $m$ never proposed to $w'$, and so he must prefer $w$ to $w'$—a contradiction.

Finally, suppose there is an instability of type (iv), consisting of a man $m$ and a woman $w$, neither of which is part of any pair in the matching, so that $(m, w) \notin F$. But for $m$ to be single, he must have proposed to every nonforbidden woman; in particular, he must have proposed to $w$, which means she would no longer be single—a contradiction.  ■

# Exercises

1. Decide whether you think the following statement is true or false. If it is true, give a short explanation. If it is false, give a counterexample.

   *True or false?   In every instance of the Stable Matching Problem, there is a stable matching containing a pair $(m, w)$ such that $m$ is ranked first on the preference list of $w$ and $w$ is ranked first on the preference list of $m$.*

2. Decide whether you think the following statement is true or false. If it is true, give a short explanation. If it is false, give a counterexample.

   *True or false?   Consider an instance of the Stable Matching Problem in which there exists a man $m$ and a woman $w$ such that $m$ is ranked first on the preference list of $w$ and $w$ is ranked first on the preference list of $m$. Then in every stable matching $S$ for this instance, the pair $(m, w)$ belongs to $S$.*

3. There are many other settings in which we can ask questions related to some type of "stability" principle. Here's one, involving competition between two enterprises.

Suppose we have two television networks, whom we'll call $A$ and $B$. There are $n$ prime-time programming slots, and each network has $n$ TV shows. Each network wants to devise a *schedule*—an assignment of each show to a distinct slot—so as to attract as much market share as possible.

Here is the way we determine how well the two networks perform relative to each other, given their schedules. Each show has a fixed *rating*, which is based on the number of people who watched it last year; we'll assume that no two shows have exactly the same rating. A network *wins* a given time slot if the show that it schedules for the time slot has a larger rating than the show the other network schedules for that time slot. The goal of each network is to win as many time slots as possible.

Suppose in the opening week of the fall season, Network $A$ reveals a schedule $S$ and Network $B$ reveals a schedule $T$. On the basis of this pair of schedules, each network wins certain time slots, according to the rule above. We'll say that the pair of schedules $(S, T)$ is *stable* if neither network can unilaterally change its own schedule and win more time slots. That is, there is no schedule $S'$ such that Network $A$ wins more slots with the pair $(S', T)$ than it did with the pair $(S, T)$; and symmetrically, there is no schedule $T'$ such that Network $B$ wins more slots with the pair $(S, T')$ than it did with the pair $(S, T)$.

The analogue of Gale and Shapley's question for this kind of stability is the following: For every set of TV shows and ratings, is there always a stable pair of schedules? Resolve this question by doing one of the following two things:

(a) give an algorithm that, for any set of TV shows and associated ratings, produces a stable pair of schedules; or

(b) give an example of a set of TV shows and associated ratings for which there is no stable pair of schedules.

4. Gale and Shapley published their paper on the Stable Matching Problem in 1962; but a version of their algorithm had already been in use for ten years by the National Resident Matching Program, for the problem of assigning medical residents to hospitals.

Basically, the situation was the following. There were $m$ hospitals, each with a certain number of available positions for hiring residents. There were $n$ medical students graduating in a given year, each interested in joining one of the hospitals. Each hospital had a ranking of the students in order of preference, and each student had a ranking of the hospitals in order of preference. We will assume that there were more students graduating than there were slots available in the $m$ hospitals.

The interest, naturally, was in finding a way of assigning each student to at most one hospital, in such a way that all available positions in all hospitals were filled. (Since we are assuming a surplus of students, there would be some students who do not get assigned to any hospital.)

We say that an assignment of students to hospitals is *stable* if neither of the following situations arises.

- First type of instability: There are students $s$ and $s'$, and a hospital $h$, so that
  - $s$ is assigned to $h$, and
  - $s'$ is assigned to no hospital, and
  - $h$ prefers $s'$ to $s$.
- Second type of instability: There are students $s$ and $s'$, and hospitals $h$ and $h'$, so that
  - $s$ is assigned to $h$, and
  - $s'$ is assigned to $h'$, and
  - $h$ prefers $s'$ to $s$, and
  - $s'$ prefers $h$ to $h'$.

So we basically have the Stable Matching Problem, except that (i) hospitals generally want more than one resident, and (ii) there is a surplus of medical students.

Show that there is always a stable assignment of students to hospitals, and give an algorithm to find one.

5. The Stable Matching Problem, as discussed in the text, assumes that all men and women have a fully ordered list of preferences. In this problem we will consider a version of the problem in which men and women can be *indifferent* between certain options. As before we have a set $M$ of $n$ men and a set $W$ of $n$ women. Assume each man and each woman ranks the members of the opposite gender, but now we allow ties in the ranking. For example (with $n = 4$), a woman could say that $m_1$ is ranked in first place; second place is a tie between $m_2$ and $m_3$ (she has no preference between them); and $m_4$ is in last place. We will say that $w$ *prefers* $m$ to $m'$ if $m$ is ranked higher than $m'$ on her preference list (they are not tied).

With indifferences in the rankings, there could be two natural notions for stability. And for each, we can ask about the existence of stable matchings, as follows.

(a) A *strong instability* in a perfect matching $S$ consists of a man $m$ and a woman $w$, such that each of $m$ and $w$ prefers the other to their partner in $S$. Does there always exist a perfect matching with no strong instability? Either give an example of a set of men and women with preference lists for which every perfect matching has a strong instability; or give an algorithm that is guaranteed to find a perfect matching with no strong instability.

**(b)** A *weak instability* in a perfect matching $S$ consists of a man $m$ and a woman $w$, such that their partners in $S$ are $w'$ and $m'$, respectively, and one of the following holds:

- $m$ prefers $w$ to $w'$, and $w$ either prefers $m$ to $m'$ or is indifferent between these two choices; or
- $w$ prefers $m$ to $m'$, and $m$ either prefers $w$ to $w'$ or is indifferent between these two choices.

In other words, the pairing between $m$ and $w$ is either preferred by both, or preferred by one while the other is indifferent. Does there always exist a perfect matching with no weak instability? Either give an example of a set of men and women with preference lists for which every perfect matching has a weak instability; or give an algorithm that is guaranteed to find a perfect matching with no weak instability.

6. Peripatetic Shipping Lines, Inc., is a shipping company that owns $n$ ships and provides service to $n$ ports. Each of its ships has a *schedule* that says, for each day of the month, which of the ports it's currently visiting, or whether it's out at sea. (You can assume the "month" here has $m$ days, for some $m > n$.) Each ship visits each port for exactly one day during the month. For safety reasons, PSL Inc. has the following strict requirement:

(†)   *No two ships can be in the same port on the same day.*

The company wants to perform maintenance on all the ships this month, via the following scheme. They want to *truncate* each ship's schedule: for each ship $S_i$, there will be some day when it arrives in its scheduled port and simply remains there for the rest of the month (for maintenance). This means that $S_i$ will not visit the remaining ports on its schedule (if any) that month, but this is okay. So the *truncation* of $S_i$'s schedule will simply consist of its original schedule up to a certain specified day on which it is in a port $P$; the remainder of the truncated schedule simply has it remain in port $P$.

Now the company's question to you is the following: Given the schedule for each ship, find a truncation of each so that condition (†) continues to hold: no two ships are ever in the same port on the same day.

Show that such a set of truncations can always be found, and give an algorithm to find them.

**Example.** Suppose we have two ships and two ports, and the "month" has four days. Suppose the first ship's schedule is

>   *port $P_1$; at sea; port $P_2$; at sea*

and the second ship's schedule is

>   *at sea; port $P_1$; at sea; port $P_2$*

Then the (only) way to choose truncations would be to have the first ship remain in port $P_2$ starting on day 3, and have the second ship remain in port $P_1$ starting on day 2.

7. Some of your friends are working for CluNet, a builder of large communication networks, and they are looking at algorithms for switching in a particular type of input/output crossbar.

    Here is the setup. There are $n$ *input wires* and $n$ *output wires*, each directed from a *source* to a *terminus*. Each input wire meets each output wire in exactly one distinct point, at a special piece of hardware called a *junction box*. Points on the wire are naturally ordered in the direction from source to terminus; for two distinct points $x$ and $y$ on the same wire, we say that $x$ is *upstream* from $y$ if $x$ is closer to the source than $y$, and otherwise we say $x$ is *downstream* from $y$. The order in which one input wire meets the output wires is not necessarily the same as the order in which another input wire meets the output wires. (And similarly for the orders in which output wires meet input wires.) Figure 1.8 gives an example of such a collection of input and output wires.

    Now, here's the switching component of this situation. Each input wire is carrying a distinct data stream, and this data stream must be *switched* onto one of the output wires. If the stream of Input $i$ is switched onto Output $j$, at junction box $B$, then this stream passes through all junction boxes upstream from $B$ on Input $i$, then through $B$, then through all junction boxes downstream from $B$ on Output $j$. It does not matter which input data stream gets switched onto which output wire, but each input data stream must be switched onto a *different* output wire. Furthermore—and this is the tricky constraint—no two data streams can pass through the same junction box following the switching operation.

    Finally, here's the problem. Show that for any specified pattern in which the input wires and output wires meet each other (each pair meeting exactly once), a valid switching of the data streams can always be found—one in which each input data stream is switched onto a different output, and no two of the resulting streams pass through the same junction box. Additionally, give an algorithm to find such a valid switching.

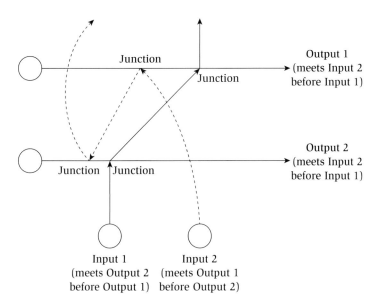

**Figure 1.8** An example with two input wires and two output wires. Input 1 has its junction with Output 2 upstream from its junction with Output 1; Input 2 has its junction with Output 1 upstream from its junction with Output 2. A valid solution is to switch the data stream of Input 1 onto Output 2, and the data stream of Input 2 onto Output 1. On the other hand, if the stream of Input 1 were switched onto Output 1, and the stream of Input 2 were switched onto Output 2, then both streams would pass through the junction box at the meeting of Input 1 and Output 2—and this is not allowed.

8. For this problem, we will explore the issue of *truthfulness* in the Stable Matching Problem and specifically in the Gale-Shapley algorithm. The basic question is: Can a man or a woman end up better off by lying about his or her preferences? More concretely, we suppose each participant has a true preference order. Now consider a woman $w$. Suppose $w$ prefers man $m$ to $m'$, but both $m$ and $m'$ are low on her list of preferences. Can it be the case that by switching the order of $m$ and $m'$ on her list of preferences (i.e., by falsely claiming that she prefers $m'$ to $m$) and running the algorithm with this false preference list, $w$ will end up with a man $m''$ that she truly prefers to both $m$ and $m'$? (We can ask the same question for men, but will focus on the case of women for purposes of this question.)

   Resolve this question by doing one of the following two things:

   (a) Give a proof that, for any set of preference lists, switching the order of a pair on the list cannot improve a woman's partner in the Gale-Shapley algorithm; or

(b) Give an example of a set of preference lists for which there is a switch that would improve the partner of a woman who switched preferences.

## Notes and Further Reading

The Stable Matching Problem was first defined and analyzed by Gale and Shapley (1962); according to David Gale, their motivation for the problem came from a story they had recently read in the *New Yorker* about the intricacies of the college admissions process (Gale, 2001). Stable matching has grown into an area of study in its own right, covered in books by Gusfield and Irving (1989) and Knuth (1997c). Gusfield and Irving also provide a nice survey of the "parallel" history of the Stable Matching Problem as a technique invented for matching applicants with employers in medicine and other professions.

As discussed in the chapter, our five representative problems will be central to the book's discussions, respectively, of greedy algorithms, dynamic programming, network flow, NP-completeness, and PSPACE-completeness. We will discuss the problems in these contexts later in the book.

# Chapter 2

## Basics of Algorithm Analysis

Analyzing algorithms involves thinking about how their resource requirements—the amount of time and space they use—will scale with increasing input size. We begin this chapter by talking about how to put this notion on a concrete footing, as making it concrete opens the door to a rich understanding of computational tractability. Having done this, we develop the mathematical machinery needed to talk about the way in which different functions scale with increasing input size, making precise what it means for one function to grow faster than another.

We then develop running-time bounds for some basic algorithms, beginning with an implementation of the Gale-Shapley algorithm from Chapter 1 and continuing to a survey of many different running times and certain characteristic types of algorithms that achieve these running times. In some cases, obtaining a good running-time bound relies on the use of more sophisticated data structures, and we conclude this chapter with a very useful example of such a data structure: priority queues and their implementation using heaps.

## 2.1 Computational Tractability

A major focus of this book is to find efficient algorithms for computational problems. At this level of generality, our topic seems to encompass the whole of computer science; so what is specific to our approach here?

First, we will try to identify broad themes and design principles in the development of algorithms. We will look for paradigmatic problems and approaches that illustrate, with a minimum of irrelevant detail, the basic approaches to designing efficient algorithms. At the same time, it would be pointless to pursue these design principles in a vacuum, so the problems and approaches we consider are drawn from fundamental issues that arise throughout computer science, and a general study of algorithms turns out to serve as a nice survey of computational ideas that arise in many areas.

Another property shared by many of the problems we study is their fundamentally *discrete* nature. That is, like the Stable Matching Problem, they will involve an implicit search over a large set of combinatorial possibilities; and the goal will be to efficiently find a solution that satisfies certain clearly delineated conditions.

As we seek to understand the general notion of computational efficiency, we will focus primarily on efficiency in running time: we want algorithms that run quickly. But it is important that algorithms be efficient in their use of other resources as well. In particular, the amount of *space* (or memory) used by an algorithm is an issue that will also arise at a number of points in the book, and we will see techniques for reducing the amount of space needed to perform a computation.

## Some Initial Attempts at Defining Efficiency

The first major question we need to answer is the following: How should we turn the fuzzy notion of an "efficient" algorithm into something more concrete?

A first attempt at a working definition of *efficiency* is the following.

Proposed Definition of Efficiency (1): *An algorithm is efficient if, when implemented, it runs quickly on real input instances.*

Let's spend a little time considering this definition. At a certain level, it's hard to argue with: one of the goals at the bedrock of our study of algorithms is solving real problems quickly. And indeed, there is a significant area of research devoted to the careful implementation and profiling of different algorithms for discrete computational problems.

But there are some crucial things missing from this definition, even if our main goal is to solve real problem instances quickly on real computers. The first is the omission of *where*, and *how well*, we implement an algorithm. Even bad algorithms can run quickly when applied to small test cases on extremely fast processors; even good algorithms can run slowly when they are coded sloppily. Also, what is a "real" input instance? We don't know the full range of input instances that will be encountered in practice, and some input instances can be much harder than others. Finally, this proposed definition above does not consider how well, or badly, an algorithm may *scale* as problem sizes grow to unexpected levels. A common situation is that two very different algorithms will perform comparably on inputs of size 100; multiply the input size tenfold, and one will still run quickly while the other consumes a huge amount of time.

So what we could ask for is a concrete definition of efficiency that is platform-independent, instance-independent, and of predictive value with respect to increasing input sizes. Before focusing on any specific consequences of this claim, we can at least explore its implicit, high-level suggestion: that we need to take a more mathematical view of the situation.

We can use the Stable Matching Problem as an example to guide us. The input has a natural "size" parameter $N$; we could take this to be the total size of the representation of all preference lists, since this is what any algorithm for the problem will receive as input. $N$ is closely related to the other natural parameter in this problem: $n$, the number of men and the number of women. Since there are $2n$ preference lists, each of length $n$, we can view $N = 2n^2$, suppressing more fine-grained details of how the data is represented. In considering the problem, we will seek to describe an algorithm at a high level, and then analyze its running time mathematically as a function of this input size $N$.

## Worst-Case Running Times and Brute-Force Search

To begin with, we will focus on analyzing the *worst-case* running time: we will look for a bound on the largest possible running time the algorithm could have over all inputs of a given size $N$, and see how this scales with $N$. The focus on worst-case performance initially seems quite draconian: what if an algorithm performs well on most instances and just has a few pathological inputs on which it is very slow? This certainly is an issue in some cases, but in general the worst-case analysis of an algorithm has been found to do a reasonable job of capturing its efficiency in practice. Moreover, once we have decided to go the route of mathematical analysis, it is hard to find an effective alternative to worst-case analysis. Average-case analysis—the obvious appealing alternative, in which one studies the performance of an algorithm averaged over "random" instances—can sometimes provide considerable insight, but very often it can also become a quagmire. As we observed earlier, it's very hard to express the full range of input instances that arise in practice, and so attempts to study an algorithm's performance on "random" input instances can quickly devolve into debates over how a random input should be generated: the same algorithm can perform very well on one class of random inputs and very poorly on another. After all, real inputs to an algorithm are generally not being produced from a random distribution, and so average-case analysis risks telling us more about the means by which the random inputs were generated than about the algorithm itself.

So in general we will think about the worst-case analysis of an algorithm's running time. But what is a reasonable analytical benchmark that can tell us whether a running-time bound is impressive or weak? A first simple guide is by comparison with brute-force search over the search space of possible solutions.

Let's return to the example of the Stable Matching Problem. Even when the size of a Stable Matching input instance is relatively small, the *search space* it defines is enormous (there are $n!$ possible perfect matchings between $n$ men and $n$ women), and we need to find a matching that is stable. The natural "brute-force" algorithm for this problem would plow through all perfect matchings by enumeration, checking each to see if it is stable. The surprising punchline, in a sense, to our solution of the Stable Matching Problem is that we needed to spend time proportional only to $N$ in finding a stable matching from among this stupendously large space of possibilities. This was a conclusion we reached at an *analytical level*. We did not implement the algorithm and try it out on sample preference lists; we reasoned about it mathematically. Yet, at the same time, our analysis indicated how the algorithm could be implemented in practice and gave fairly conclusive evidence that it would be a big improvement over exhaustive enumeration.

This will be a common theme in most of the problems we study: a compact representation, implicitly specifying a giant search space. For most of these problems, there will be an obvious brute-force solution: try all possibilities and see if any one of them works. Not only is this approach almost always too slow to be useful, it is an intellectual cop-out; it provides us with absolutely no insight into the structure of the problem we are studying. And so if there is a common thread in the algorithms we emphasize in this book, it would be the following alternative definition of efficiency.

> Proposed Definition of Efficiency (2): *An algorithm is efficient if it achieves qualitatively better worst-case performance, at an analytical level, than brute-force search.*

This will turn out to be a very useful working definition for us. Algorithms that improve substantially on brute-force search nearly always contain a valuable heuristic idea that makes them work; and they tell us something about the intrinsic structure, and computational tractability, of the underlying problem itself.

But if there is a problem with our second working definition, it is vagueness. What do we mean by "qualitatively better performance?" This suggests that we consider the actual running time of algorithms more carefully, and try to quantify what a reasonable running time would be.

## Polynomial Time as a Definition of Efficiency

When people first began analyzing discrete algorithms mathematically—a thread of research that began gathering momentum through the 1960s—

a consensus began to emerge on how to quantify the notion of a "reasonable" running time. Search spaces for natural combinatorial problems tend to grow exponentially in the size $N$ of the input; if the input size increases by one, the number of possibilities increases multiplicatively. We'd like a good algorithm for such a problem to have a better scaling property: when the input size increases by a constant factor—say, a factor of 2—the algorithm should only slow down by some constant factor $C$.

Arithmetically, we can formulate this scaling behavior as follows. Suppose an algorithm has the following property: There are absolute constants $c > 0$ and $d > 0$ so that on every input instance of size $N$, its running time is bounded by $cN^d$ primitive computational steps. (In other words, its running time is at most proportional to $N^d$.) For now, we will remain deliberately vague on what we mean by the notion of a "primitive computational step"— but it can be easily formalized in a model where each step corresponds to a single assembly-language instruction on a standard processor, or one line of a standard programming language such as C or Java. In any case, if this running-time bound holds, for some $c$ and $d$, then we say that the algorithm has a *polynomial running time*, or that it is a *polynomial-time algorithm*. Note that any polynomial-time bound has the scaling property we're looking for. If the input size increases from $N$ to $2N$, the bound on the running time increases from $cN^d$ to $c(2N)^d = c \cdot 2^d N^d$, which is a slow-down by a factor of $2^d$. Since $d$ is a constant, so is $2^d$; of course, as one might expect, lower-degree polynomials exhibit better scaling behavior than higher-degree polynomials.

From this notion, and the intuition expressed above, emerges our third attempt at a working definition of efficiency.

Proposed Definition of Efficiency (3): *An algorithm is efficient if it has a polynomial running time.*

Where our previous definition seemed overly vague, this one seems much too prescriptive. Wouldn't an algorithm with running time proportional to $n^{100}$—and hence polynomial—be hopelessly inefficient? Wouldn't we be relatively pleased with a nonpolynomial running time of $n^{1+.02(\log n)}$? The answers are, of course, "yes" and "yes." And indeed, however much one may try to abstractly motivate the definition of efficiency in terms of polynomial time, a primary justification for it is this: *It really works.* Problems for which polynomial-time algorithms exist almost invariably turn out to have algorithms with running times proportional to very moderately growing polynomials like $n$, $n \log n$, $n^2$, or $n^3$. Conversely, problems for which no polynomial-time algorithm is known tend to be very difficult in practice. There are certainly exceptions to this principle in both directions: there are cases, for example, in

**Table 2.1** The running times (rounded up) of different algorithms on inputs of increasing size, for a processor performing a million high-level instructions per second. In cases where the running time exceeds $10^{25}$ years, we simply record the algorithm as taking a very long time.

|  | $n$ | $n \log_2 n$ | $n^2$ | $n^3$ | $1.5^n$ | $2^n$ | $n!$ |
|---|---|---|---|---|---|---|---|
| $n = 10$ | < 1 sec | < 1 sec | < 1 sec | < 1 sec | < 1 sec | < 1 sec | 4 sec |
| $n = 30$ | < 1 sec | < 1 sec | < 1 sec | < 1 sec | < 1 sec | 18 min | $10^{25}$ years |
| $n = 50$ | < 1 sec | < 1 sec | < 1 sec | < 1 sec | 11 min | 36 years | very long |
| $n = 100$ | < 1 sec | < 1 sec | < 1 sec | 1 sec | 12,892 years | $10^{17}$ years | very long |
| $n = 1,000$ | < 1 sec | < 1 sec | 1 sec | 18 min | very long | very long | very long |
| $n = 10,000$ | < 1 sec | < 1 sec | 2 min | 12 days | very long | very long | very long |
| $n = 100,000$ | < 1 sec | 2 sec | 3 hours | 32 years | very long | very long | very long |
| $n = 1,000,000$ | 1 sec | 20 sec | 12 days | 31,710 years | very long | very long | very long |

which an algorithm with exponential worst-case behavior generally runs well on the kinds of instances that arise in practice; and there are also cases where the best polynomial-time algorithm for a problem is completely impractical due to large constants or a high exponent on the polynomial bound. All this serves to reinforce the point that our emphasis on worst-case, polynomial-time bounds is only an abstraction of practical situations. But overwhelmingly, the concrete mathematical definition of polynomial time has turned out to correspond surprisingly well in practice to what we observe about the efficiency of algorithms, and the tractability of problems, in real life.

One further reason why the mathematical formalism and the empirical evidence seem to line up well in the case of polynomial-time solvability is that the gulf between the growth rates of polynomial and exponential functions is enormous. Suppose, for example, that we have a processor that executes a million high-level instructions per second, and we have algorithms with running-time bounds of $n$, $n \log_2 n$, $n^2$, $n^3$, $1.5^n$, $2^n$, and $n!$. In Table 2.1, we show the running times of these algorithms (in seconds, minutes, days, or years) for inputs of size $n = 10, 30, 50, 100, 1,000, 10,000, 100,000$, and $1,000,000$.

There is a final, fundamental benefit to making our definition of efficiency so specific: it becomes negatable. It becomes possible to express the notion that *there is no efficient algorithm for a particular problem*. In a sense, being able to do this is a prerequisite for turning our study of algorithms into good science, for it allows us to ask about the existence or nonexistence of efficient algorithms as a well-defined question. In contrast, both of our previous definitions were completely subjective, and hence limited the extent to which we could discuss certain issues in concrete terms.

In particular, the first of our definitions, which was tied to the specific implementation of an algorithm, turned efficiency into a moving target: as processor speeds increase, more and more algorithms fall under this notion of efficiency. Our definition in terms of polynomial time is much more an absolute notion; it is closely connected with the idea that each problem has an intrinsic level of computational tractability: some admit efficient solutions, and others do not.

## 2.2 Asymptotic Order of Growth

Our discussion of computational tractability has turned out to be intrinsically based on our ability to express the notion that an algorithm's worst-case running time on inputs of size $n$ grows at a rate that is at most proportional to some function $f(n)$. The function $f(n)$ then becomes a bound on the running time of the algorithm. We now discuss a framework for talking about this concept.

We will mainly express algorithms in the pseudo-code style that we used for the Gale-Shapley algorithm. At times we will need to become more formal, but this style of specifying algorithms will be completely adequate for most purposes. When we provide a bound on the running time of an algorithm, we will generally be counting the number of such pseudo-code steps that are executed; in this context, one *step* will consist of assigning a value to a variable, looking up an entry in an array, following a pointer, or performing an arithmetic operation on a fixed-size integer.

When we seek to say something about the running time of an algorithm on inputs of size $n$, one thing we could aim for would be a very concrete statement such as, "On any input of size $n$, the algorithm runs for at most $1.62n^2 + 3.5n + 8$ steps." This may be an interesting statement in some contexts, but as a general goal there are several things wrong with it. First, getting such a precise bound may be an exhausting activity, and more detail than we wanted anyway. Second, because our ultimate goal is to identify broad classes of algorithms that have similar behavior, we'd actually like to classify running times at a coarser level of granularity so that similarities among different algorithms, and among different problems, show up more clearly. And finally, extremely detailed statements about the number of steps an algorithm executes are often—in a strong sense—meaningless. As just discussed, we will generally be counting steps in a pseudo-code specification of an algorithm that resembles a high-level programming language. Each one of these steps will typically unfold into some fixed number of primitive steps when the program is compiled into an intermediate representation, and then into some further number of steps depending on the particular architecture being used to do the computing. So the most we can safely say is that as we look at different levels of computational abstraction, the notion of a "step" may grow or shrink by a constant factor—for example, if it takes 25 low-level machine instructions to perform one operation in our high-level language, then our algorithm that took at most $1.62n^2 + 3.5n + 8$ steps can also be viewed as taking $40.5n^2 + 87.5n + 200$ steps when we analyze it at a level that is closer to the actual hardware.

## $O$, $\Omega$, and $\Theta$

For all these reasons, we want to express the growth rate of running times and other functions in a way that is insensitive to constant factors and low-order terms. In other words, we'd like to be able to take a running time like the one we discussed above, $1.62n^2 + 3.5n + 8$, and say that it grows like $n^2$, up to constant factors. We now discuss a precise way to do this.

*Asymptotic Upper Bounds*   Let $T(n)$ be a function—say, the worst-case running time of a certain algorithm on an input of size $n$. (We will assume that all the functions we talk about here take nonnegative values.) Given another function $f(n)$, we say that $T(n)$ *is* $O(f(n))$ (read as "$T(n)$ is order $f(n)$") if, for sufficiently large $n$, the function $T(n)$ is bounded above by a constant multiple of $f(n)$. We will also sometimes write this as $T(n) = O(f(n))$. More precisely, $T(n)$ is $O(f(n))$ if there exist constants $c > 0$ and $n_0 \geq 0$ so that for all $n \geq n_0$, we have $T(n) \leq c \cdot f(n)$. In this case, we will say that $T$ is *asymptotically upper-bounded by* $f$. It is important to note that this definition requires a constant $c$ to exist that works for *all* $n$; in particular, $c$ cannot depend on $n$.

As an example of how this definition lets us express upper bounds on running times, consider an algorithm whose running time (as in the earlier discussion) has the form $T(n) = pn^2 + qn + r$ for positive constants $p$, $q$, and $r$. We'd like to claim that any such function is $O(n^2)$. To see why, we notice that for all $n \geq 1$, we have $qn \leq qn^2$, and $r \leq rn^2$. So we can write

$$T(n) = pn^2 + qn + r \leq pn^2 + qn^2 + rn^2 = (p + q + r)n^2$$

for all $n \geq 1$. This inequality is exactly what the definition of $O(\cdot)$ requires: $T(n) \leq cn^2$, where $c = p + q + r$.

Note that $O(\cdot)$ expresses only an upper bound, not the exact growth rate of the function. For example, just as we claimed that the function $T(n) = pn^2 + qn + r$ is $O(n^2)$, it's also correct to say that it's $O(n^3)$. Indeed, we just argued that $T(n) \leq (p + q + r)n^2$, and since we also have $n^2 \leq n^3$, we can conclude that $T(n) \leq (p + q + r)n^3$ as the definition of $O(n^3)$ requires. The fact that a function can have many upper bounds is not just a trick of the notation; it shows up in the analysis of running times as well. There are cases where an algorithm has been proved to have running time $O(n^3)$; some years pass, people analyze the same algorithm more carefully, and they show that in fact its running time is $O(n^2)$. There was nothing wrong with the first result; it was a correct upper bound. It's simply that it wasn't the "tightest" possible running time.

*Asymptotic Lower Bounds*   There is a complementary notation for lower bounds. Often when we analyze an algorithm—say we have just proven that its worst-case running time $T(n)$ is $O(n^2)$—we want to show that this upper bound is the best one possible. To do this, we want to express the notion that for arbitrarily large input sizes $n$, the function $T(n)$ is *at least* a constant multiple of some specific function $f(n)$. (In this example, $f(n)$ happens to be $n^2$.) Thus, we say that $T(n)$ is $\Omega(f(n))$ (also written $T(n) = \Omega(f(n))$) if there exist constants $\epsilon > 0$ and $n_0 \geq 0$ so that for all $n \geq n_0$, we have $T(n) \geq \epsilon \cdot f(n)$. By analogy with $O(\cdot)$ notation, we will refer to $T$ in this case as being *asymptotically lower-bounded by $f$*. Again, note that the constant $\epsilon$ must be fixed, independent of $n$.

This definition works just like $O(\cdot)$, except that we are bounding the function $T(n)$ from below, rather than from above. For example, returning to the function $T(n) = pn^2 + qn + r$, where $p$, $q$, and $r$ are positive constants, let's claim that $T(n) = \Omega(n^2)$. Whereas establishing the upper bound involved "inflating" the terms in $T(n)$ until it looked like a constant times $n^2$, now we need to do the opposite: we need to reduce the size of $T(n)$ until it looks like a constant times $n^2$. It is not hard to do this; for all $n \geq 0$, we have

$$T(n) = pn^2 + qn + r \geq pn^2,$$

which meets what is required by the definition of $\Omega(\cdot)$ with $\epsilon = p > 0$.

Just as we discussed the notion of "tighter" and "weaker" upper bounds, the same issue arises for lower bounds. For example, it is correct to say that our function $T(n) = pn^2 + qn + r$ is $\Omega(n)$, since $T(n) \geq pn^2 \geq pn$.

*Asymptotically Tight Bounds*   If we can show that a running time $T(n)$ is both $O(f(n))$ and also $\Omega(f(n))$, then in a natural sense we've found the "right" bound: $T(n)$ grows exactly like $f(n)$ to within a constant factor. This, for example, is the conclusion we can draw from the fact that $T(n) = pn^2 + qn + r$ is both $O(n^2)$ and $\Omega(n^2)$.

There is a notation to express this: if a function $T(n)$ is both $O(f(n))$ and $\Omega(f(n))$, we say that $T(n)$ is $\Theta(f(n))$. In this case, we say that $f(n)$ is an *asymptotically tight bound* for $T(n)$. So, for example, our analysis above shows that $T(n) = pn^2 + qn + r$ is $\Theta(n^2)$.

Asymptotically tight bounds on worst-case running times are nice things to find, since they characterize the worst-case performance of an algorithm precisely up to constant factors. And as the definition of $\Theta(\cdot)$ shows, one can obtain such bounds by closing the gap between an upper bound and a lower bound. For example, sometimes you will read a (slightly informally phrased) sentence such as "An upper bound of $O(n^3)$ has been shown on the worst-case running time of the algorithm, but there is no example known on which the algorithm runs for more than $\Omega(n^2)$ steps." This is implicitly an invitation to search for an asymptotically tight bound on the algorithm's worst-case running time.

Sometimes one can also obtain an asymptotically tight bound directly by computing a limit as $n$ goes to infinity. Essentially, if the ratio of functions $f(n)$ and $g(n)$ converges to a positive constant as $n$ goes to infinity, then $f(n) = \Theta(g(n))$.

**(2.1)**    *Let f and g be two functions that*

$$\lim_{n \to \infty} \frac{f(n)}{g(n)}$$

*exists and is equal to some number $c > 0$. Then $f(n) = \Theta(g(n))$.*

**Proof.** We will use the fact that the limit exists and is positive to show that $f(n) = O(g(n))$ and $f(n) = \Omega(g(n))$, as required by the definition of $\Theta(\cdot)$.

Since

$$\lim_{n \to \infty} \frac{f(n)}{g(n)} = c > 0,$$

it follows from the definition of a limit that there is some $n_0$ beyond which the ratio is always between $\frac{1}{2}c$ and $2c$. Thus, $f(n) \le 2cg(n)$ for all $n \ge n_0$, which implies that $f(n) = O(g(n))$; and $f(n) \ge \frac{1}{2}cg(n)$ for all $n \ge n_0$, which implies that $f(n) = \Omega(g(n))$. ■

## Properties of Asymptotic Growth Rates

Having seen the definitions of $O$, $\Omega$, and $\Theta$, it is useful to explore some of their basic properties.

*Transitivity*    A first property is *transitivity*: if a function $f$ is asymptotically upper-bounded by a function $g$, and if $g$ in turn is asymptotically upper-bounded by a function $h$, then $f$ is asymptotically upper-bounded by $h$. A similar property holds for lower bounds. We write this more precisely as follows.

**(2.2)**

(a)  *If $f = O(g)$ and $g = O(h)$, then $f = O(h)$.*

(b)  *If $f = \Omega(g)$ and $g = \Omega(h)$, then $f = \Omega(h)$.*

**Proof.** We'll prove part (a) of this claim; the proof of part (b) is very similar.

For (a), we're given that for some constants $c$ and $n_0$, we have $f(n) \le cg(n)$ for all $n \ge n_0$. Also, for some (potentially different) constants $c'$ and $n'_0$, we have $g(n) \le c'h(n)$ for all $n \ge n'_0$. So consider any number $n$ that is at least as large as both $n_0$ and $n'_0$. We have $f(n) \le cg(n) \le cc'h(n)$, and so $f(n) \le cc'h(n)$ for all $n \ge \max(n_0, n'_0)$. This latter inequality is exactly what is required for showing that $f = O(h)$. ∎

Combining parts (a) and (b) of (2.2), we can obtain a similar result for asymptotically tight bounds. Suppose we know that $f = \Theta(g)$ and that $g = \Theta(h)$. Then since $f = O(g)$ and $g = O(h)$, we know from part (a) that $f = O(h)$; since $f = \Omega(g)$ and $g = \Omega(h)$, we know from part (b) that $f = \Omega(h)$. It follows that $f = \Theta(h)$. Thus we have shown

**(2.3)** If $f = \Theta(g)$ and $g = \Theta(h)$, then $f = \Theta(h)$.

**Sums of Functions** It is also useful to have results that quantify the effect of adding two functions. First, if we have an asymptotic upper bound that applies to each of two functions $f$ and $g$, then it applies to their sum.

**(2.4)** Suppose that $f$ and $g$ are two functions such that for some other function $h$, we have $f = O(h)$ and $g = O(h)$. Then $f + g = O(h)$.

**Proof.** We're given that for some constants $c$ and $n_0$, we have $f(n) \le ch(n)$ for all $n \ge n_0$. Also, for some (potentially different) constants $c'$ and $n'_0$, we have $g(n) \le c'h(n)$ for all $n \ge n'_0$. So consider any number $n$ that is at least as large as both $n_0$ and $n'_0$. We have $f(n) + g(n) \le ch(n) + c'h(n)$. Thus $f(n) + g(n) \le (c + c')h(n)$ for all $n \ge \max(n_0, n'_0)$, which is exactly what is required for showing that $f + g = O(h)$. ∎

There is a generalization of this to sums of a fixed constant number of functions $k$, where $k$ may be larger than two. The result can be stated precisely as follows; we omit the proof, since it is essentially the same as the proof of (2.4), adapted to sums consisting of $k$ terms rather than just two.

**(2.5)** Let $k$ be a fixed constant, and let $f_1, f_2, \ldots, f_k$ and $h$ be functions such that $f_i = O(h)$ for all $i$. Then $f_1 + f_2 + \cdots + f_k = O(h)$.

There is also a consequence of (2.4) that covers the following kind of situation. It frequently happens that we're analyzing an algorithm with two high-level parts, and it is easy to show that one of the two parts is slower than the other. We'd like to be able to say that the running time of the whole algorithm is asymptotically comparable to the running time of the slow part. Since the overall running time is a sum of two functions (the running times of the two parts), results on asymptotic bounds for sums of functions are directly relevant.

**(2.6)** *Suppose that f and g are two functions (taking nonnegative values) such that $g = O(f)$. Then $f + g = \Theta(f)$. In other words, f is an asymptotically tight bound for the combined function $f + g$.*

**Proof.** Clearly $f + g = \Omega(f)$, since for all $n \geq 0$, we have $f(n) + g(n) \geq f(n)$. So to complete the proof, we need to show that $f + g = O(f)$.

But this is a direct consequence of (2.4): we're given the fact that $g = O(f)$, and also $f = O(f)$ holds for any function, so by (2.4) we have $f + g = O(f)$. ■

This result also extends to the sum of any fixed, constant number of functions: the most rapidly growing among the functions is an asymptotically tight bound for the sum.

## Asymptotic Bounds for Some Common Functions

There are a number of functions that come up repeatedly in the analysis of algorithms, and it is useful to consider the asymptotic properties of some of the most basic of these: polynomials, logarithms, and exponentials.

*Polynomials*   Recall that a polynomial is a function that can be written in the form $f(n) = a_0 + a_1 n + a_2 n^2 + \cdots + a_d n^d$ for some integer constant $d > 0$, where the final coefficient $a_d$ is nonzero. This value $d$ is called the *degree* of the polynomial. For example, the functions of the form $pn^2 + qn + r$ (with $p \neq 0$) that we considered earlier are polynomials of degree 2.

A basic fact about polynomials is that their asymptotic rate of growth is determined by their "high-order term"—the one that determines the degree. We state this more formally in the following claim. Since we are concerned here only with functions that take nonnegative values, we will restrict our attention to polynomials for which the high-order term has a positive coefficient $a_d > 0$.

**(2.7)** *Let f be a polynomial of degree d, in which the coefficient $a_d$ is positive. Then $f = O(n^d)$.*

**Proof.** We write $f = a_0 + a_1 n + a_2 n^2 + \cdots + a_d n^d$, where $a_d > 0$. The upper bound is a direct application of (2.5). First, notice that coefficients $a_j$ for $j < d$ may be negative, but in any case we have $a_j n^j \leq |a_j| n^d$ for all $n \geq 1$. Thus each term in the polynomial is $O(n^d)$. Since $f$ is a sum of a constant number of functions, each of which is $O(n^d)$, it follows from (2.5) that $f$ is $O(n^d)$. ■

One can also show that under the conditions of (2.7), we have $f = \Omega(n^d)$, and hence it follows that in fact $f = \Theta(n^d)$.

This is a good point at which to discuss the relationship between these types of asymptotic bounds and the notion of *polynomial time*, which we arrived at in the previous section as a way to formalize the more elusive concept of efficiency. Using $O(\cdot)$ notation, it's easy to formally define polynomial time: a *polynomial-time algorithm* is one whose running time $T(n)$ is $O(n^d)$ for some constant $d$, where $d$ is independent of the input size.

So algorithms with running-time bounds like $O(n^2)$ and $O(n^3)$ are polynomial-time algorithms. But it's important to realize that an algorithm can be polynomial time even if its running time is not written as $n$ raised to some integer power. To begin with, a number of algorithms have running times of the form $O(n^x)$ for some number $x$ that is not an integer. For example, in Chapter 5 we will see an algorithm whose running time is $O(n^{1.59})$; we will also see exponents less than 1, as in bounds like $O(\sqrt{n}) = O(n^{1/2})$.

To take another common kind of example, we will see many algorithms whose running times have the form $O(n \log n)$. Such algorithms are also polynomial time: as we will see next, $\log n \le n$ for all $n \ge 1$, and hence $n \log n \le n^2$ for all $n \ge 1$. In other words, if an algorithm has running time $O(n \log n)$, then it also has running time $O(n^2)$, and so it is a polynomial-time algorithm.

***Logarithms*** Recall that $\log_b n$ is the number $x$ such that $b^x = n$. One way to get an approximate sense of how fast $\log_b n$ grows is to note that, if we round it down to the nearest integer, it is one less than the number of digits in the base-$b$ representation of the number $n$. (Thus, for example, $1 + \log_2 n$, rounded down, is the number of bits needed to represent $n$.)

So logarithms are very slowly growing functions. In particular, for every base $b$, the function $\log_b n$ is asymptotically bounded by every function of the form $n^x$, even for (noninteger) values of $x$ arbitrary close to 0.

**(2.8)** *For every $b > 1$ and every $x > 0$, we have $\log_b n = O(n^x)$.*

One can directly translate between logarithms of different bases using the following fundamental identity:

$$\log_a n = \frac{\log_b n}{\log_b a}.$$

This equation explains why you'll often notice people writing bounds like $O(\log n)$ without indicating the base of the logarithm. This is not sloppy usage: the identity above says that $\log_a n = \frac{1}{\log_b a} \cdot \log_b n$, so the point is that $\log_a n = \Theta(\log_b n)$, and the base of the logarithm is not important when writing bounds using asymptotic notation.

***Exponentials***   Exponential functions are functions of the form $f(n) = r^n$ for some constant base $r$. Here we will be concerned with the case in which $r > 1$, which results in a very fast-growing function.

In particular, where polynomials raise $n$ to a fixed exponent, exponentials raise a fixed number to $n$ as a power; this leads to much faster rates of growth. One way to summarize the relationship between polynomials and exponentials is as follows.

**(2.9)**   *For every $r > 1$ and every $d > 0$, we have $n^d = O(r^n)$.*

In particular, every exponential grows faster than every polynomial. And as we saw in Table 2.1, when you plug in actual values of $n$, the differences in growth rates are really quite impressive.

Just as people write $O(\log n)$ without specifying the base, you'll also see people write "The running time of this algorithm is exponential," without specifying which exponential function they have in mind. Unlike the liberal use of $\log n$, which is justified by ignoring constant factors, this generic use of the term "exponential" is somewhat sloppy. In particular, for different bases $r > s > 1$, it is never the case that $r^n = \Theta(s^n)$. Indeed, this would require that for some constant $c > 0$, we would have $r^n \leq cs^n$ for all sufficiently large $n$. But rearranging this inequality would give $(r/s)^n \leq c$ for all sufficiently large $n$. Since $r > s$, the expression $(r/s)^n$ is tending to infinity with $n$, and so it cannot possibly remain bounded by a fixed constant $c$.

So asymptotically speaking, exponential functions are all different. Still, it's usually clear what people intend when they inexactly write "The running time of this algorithm is exponential"—they typically mean that the running time grows at least as fast as *some* exponential function, and all exponentials grow so fast that we can effectively dismiss this algorithm without working out further details of the exact running time. This is not entirely fair. Occasionally there's more going on with an exponential algorithm than first appears, as we'll see, for example, in Chapter 10; but as we argued in the first section of this chapter, it's a reasonable rule of thumb.

Taken together, then, logarithms, polynomials, and exponentials serve as useful landmarks in the range of possible functions that you encounter when analyzing running times. Logarithms grow more slowly than polynomials, and polynomials grow more slowly than exponentials.

## 2.3 Implementing the Stable Matching Algorithm Using Lists and Arrays

We've now seen a general approach for expressing bounds on the running time of an algorithm. In order to asymptotically analyze the running time of an algorithm expressed in a high-level fashion—as we expressed the Gale-Shapley Stable Matching algorithm in Chapter 1, for example—one doesn't have to actually program, compile, and execute it, but one does have to think about how the data will be represented and manipulated in an implementation of the algorithm, so as to bound the number of computational steps it takes.

The implementation of basic algorithms using data structures is something that you probably have had some experience with. In this book, data structures will be covered in the context of implementing specific algorithms, and so we will encounter different data structures based on the needs of the algorithms we are developing. To get this process started, we consider an implementation of the Gale-Shapley Stable Matching algorithm; we showed earlier that the algorithm terminates in at most $n^2$ iterations, and our implementation here provides a corresponding worst-case running time of $O(n^2)$, counting actual computational steps rather than simply the total number of iterations. To get such a bound for the Stable Matching algorithm, we will only need to use two of the simplest data structures: *lists* and *arrays*. Thus, our implementation also provides a good chance to review the use of these basic data structures as well.

In the Stable Matching Problem, each man and each woman has a ranking of all members of the opposite gender. The very first question we need to discuss is how such a ranking will be represented. Further, the algorithm maintains a matching and will need to know at each step which men and women are free, and who is matched with whom. In order to implement the algorithm, we need to decide which data structures we will use for all these things.

An important issue to note here is that the choice of data structure is up to the algorithm designer; for each algorithm we will choose data structures that make it efficient and easy to implement. In some cases, this may involve *preprocessing* the input to convert it from its given input representation into a data structure that is more appropriate for the problem being solved.

## Arrays and Lists

To start our discussion we will focus on a single list, such as the list of women in order of preference by a single man. Maybe the simplest way to keep a list of $n$ elements is to use an array $A$ of length $n$, and have $A[i]$ be the $i^{th}$ element of the list. Such an array is simple to implement in essentially all standard programming languages, and it has the following properties.

- We can answer a query of the form "What is the $i^{th}$ element on the list?" in $O(1)$ time, by a direct access to the value $A[i]$.

- If we want to determine whether a particular element $e$ belongs to the list (i.e., whether it is equal to $A[i]$ for some $i$), we need to check the elements one by one in $O(n)$ time, assuming we don't know anything about the order in which the elements appear in $A$.

- If the array elements are sorted in some clear way (either numerically or alphabetically), then we can determine whether an element $e$ belongs to the list in $O(\log n)$ time using *binary search*; we will not need to use binary search for any part of our stable matching implementation, but we will have more to say about it in the next section.

An array is less good for dynamically maintaining a list of elements that changes over time, such as the list of free men in the Stable Matching algorithm; since men go from being free to engaged, and potentially back again, a list of free men needs to grow and shrink during the execution of the algorithm. It is generally cumbersome to frequently add or delete elements to a list that is maintained as an array.

An alternate, and often preferable, way to maintain such a dynamic set of elements is via a linked list. In a linked list, the elements are sequenced together by having each element point to the next in the list. Thus, for each element $v$ on the list, we need to maintain a pointer to the next element; we set this pointer to *null* if $i$ is the last element. We also have a pointer `First` that points to the first element. By starting at `First` and repeatedly following pointers to the next element until we reach *null*, we can thus traverse the entire contents of the list in time proportional to its length.

A generic way to implement such a linked list, when the set of possible elements may not be fixed in advance, is to allocate a record $e$ for each element that we want to include in the list. Such a record would contain a field $e$.`val` that contains the value of the element, and a field $e$.`Next` that contains a pointer to the next element in the list. We can create a *doubly linked list*, which is traversable in both directions, by also having a field $e$.`Prev` that contains a pointer to the previous element in the list. ($e$.`Prev` = *null* if $e$ is the first element.) We also include a pointer `Last`, analogous to `First`, that points to the last element in the list. A schematic illustration of part of such a list is shown in the first line of Figure 2.1.

A doubly linked list can be modified as follows.

- *Deletion.* To delete the element $e$ from a doubly linked list, we can just "splice it out" by having the previous element, referenced by $e$.`Prev`, and the next element, referenced by $e$.`Next`, point directly to each other. The deletion operation is illustrated in Figure 2.1.
- *Insertion.* To insert element $e$ between elements $d$ and $f$ in a list, we "splice it in" by updating $d$.`Next` and $f$.`Prev` to point to $e$, and the `Next` and `Prev` pointers of $e$ to point to $d$ and $f$, respectively. This operation is

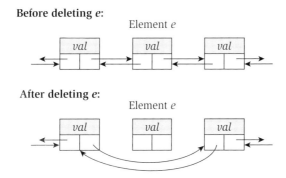

**Figure 2.1** A schematic representation of a doubly linked list, showing the deletion of an element $e$.

essentially the reverse of deletion, and indeed one can see this operation at work by reading Figure 2.1 from bottom to top.

Inserting or deleting $e$ at the beginning of the list involves updating the `First` pointer, rather than updating the record of the element before $e$.

While lists are good for maintaining a dynamically changing set, they also have disadvantages. Unlike arrays, we cannot find the $i^{\text{th}}$ element of the list in $O(1)$ time: to find the $i^{\text{th}}$ element, we have to follow the `Next` pointers starting from the beginning of the list, which takes a total of $O(i)$ time.

Given the relative advantages and disadvantages of arrays and lists, it may happen that we receive the input to a problem in one of the two formats and want to convert it into the other. As discussed earlier, such preprocessing is often useful; and in this case, it is easy to convert between the array and list representations in $O(n)$ time. This allows us to freely choose the data structure that suits the algorithm better and not be constrained by the way the information is given as input.

## Implementing the Stable Matching Algorithm

Next we will use arrays and linked lists to implement the Stable Matching algorithm from Chapter 1. We have already shown that the algorithm terminates in at most $n^2$ iterations, and this provides a type of upper bound on the running time. However, if we actually want to implement the G-S algorithm so that it runs in time proportional to $n^2$, we need to be able to implement each iteration in constant time. We discuss how to do this now.

For simplicity, assume that the set of men and women are both $\{1, \ldots, n\}$. To ensure this, we can order the men and women (say, alphabetically), and associate number $i$ with the $i^{\text{th}}$ man $m_i$ or $i^{\text{th}}$ women $w_i$ in this order. This assumption (or notation) allows us to define an array indexed by all men or all women. We need to have a preference list for each man and for each woman. To do this we will have two arrays, one for women's preference lists and one for the men's preference lists; we will use $\mathtt{ManPref}[m, i]$ to denote the $i^{\text{th}}$ woman on man $m$'s preference list, and similarly $\mathtt{WomanPref}[w, i]$ to be the $i^{\text{th}}$ man on the preference list of woman $w$. Note that the amount of space needed to give the preferences for all $2n$ individuals is $O(n^2)$, as each person has a list of length $n$.

We need to consider each step of the algorithm and understand what data structure allows us to implement it efficiently. Essentially, we need to be able to do each of four things in constant time.

1. We need to be able to identify a free man.
2. We need, for a man $m$, to be able to identify the highest-ranked woman to whom he has not yet proposed.
3. For a woman $w$, we need to decide if $w$ is currently engaged, and if she is, we need to identify her current partner.
4. For a woman $w$ and two men $m$ and $m'$, we need to be able to decide, again in constant time, which of $m$ or $m'$ is preferred by $w$.

First, consider selecting a free man. We will do this by maintaining the set of free men as a linked list. When we need to select a free man, we take the first man $m$ on this list. We delete $m$ from the list if he becomes engaged, and possibly insert a different man $m'$, if some other man $m'$ becomes free. In this case, $m'$ can be inserted at the front of the list, again in constant time.

Next, consider a man $m$. We need to identify the highest-ranked woman to whom he has not yet proposed. To do this we will need to maintain an extra array $\mathtt{Next}$ that indicates for each man $m$ the position of the next woman he will propose to on his list. We initialize $\mathtt{Next}[m] = 1$ for all men $m$. If a man $m$ needs to propose to a woman, he'll propose to $w = \mathtt{ManPref}[m, \mathtt{Next}[m]]$, and once he proposes to $w$, we increment the value of $\mathtt{Next}[m]$ by one, regardless of whether or not $w$ accepts the proposal.

Now assume man $m$ proposes to woman $w$; we need to be able to identify the man $m'$ that $w$ is engaged to (if there is such a man). We can do this by maintaining an array $\mathtt{Current}$ of length $n$, where $\mathtt{Current}[w]$ is the woman $w$'s current partner $m'$. We set $\mathtt{Current}[w]$ to a special null symbol when we need to indicate that woman $w$ is not currently engaged; at the start of the algorithm, $\mathtt{Current}[w]$ is initialized to this null symbol for all women $w$.

To sum up, the data structures we have set up thus far can implement the operations (1)–(3) in $O(1)$ time each.

Maybe the trickiest question is how to maintain women's preferences to keep step (4) efficient. Consider a step of the algorithm, when man $m$ proposes to a woman $w$. Assume $w$ is already engaged, and her current partner is $m' = $Current$[w]$. We would like to decide in $O(1)$ time if woman $w$ prefers $m$ or $m'$. Keeping the women's preferences in an array WomanPref, analogous to the one we used for men, does not work, as we would need to walk through $w$'s list one by one, taking $O(n)$ time to find $m$ and $m'$ on the list. While $O(n)$ is still polynomial, we can do a lot better if we build an auxiliary data structure at the beginning.

At the start of the algorithm, we create an $n \times n$ array Ranking, where Ranking$[w, m]$ contains the rank of man $m$ in the sorted order of $w$'s preferences. By a single pass through $w$'s preference list, we can create this array in linear time for each woman, for a total initial time investment proportional to $n^2$. Then, to decide which of $m$ or $m'$ is preferred by $w$, we simply compare the values Ranking$[w, m]$ and Ranking$[w, m']$.

This allows us to execute step (4) in constant time, and hence we have everything we need to obtain the desired running time.

**(2.10)**    *The data structures described above allow us to implement the G-S algorithm in $O(n^2)$ time.*

## 2.4 A Survey of Common Running Times

When trying to analyze a new algorithm, it helps to have a rough sense of the "landscape" of different running times. Indeed, there are styles of analysis that recur frequently, and so when one sees running-time bounds like $O(n)$, $O(n \log n)$, and $O(n^2)$ appearing over and over, it's often for one of a very small number of distinct reasons. Learning to recognize these common styles of analysis is a long-term goal. To get things under way, we offer the following survey of common running-time bounds and some of the typical approaches that lead to them.

Earlier we discussed the notion that most problems have a natural "search space"—the set of all possible solutions—and we noted that a unifying theme in algorithm design is the search for algorithms whose performance is more efficient than a brute-force enumeration of this search space. In approaching a new problem, then, it often helps to think about two kinds of bounds: one on the running time you hope to achieve, and the other on the size of the problem's natural search space (and hence on the running time of a brute-force algorithm for the problem). The discussion of running times in this section will begin in many cases with an analysis of the brute-force algorithm, since it is a useful way to get one's bearings with respect to a problem; the task of improving on such algorithms will be our goal in most of the book.

## Linear Time

An algorithm that runs in $O(n)$, or linear, time has a very natural property: its running time is at most a constant factor times the size of the input. One basic way to get an algorithm with this running time is to process the input in a single pass, spending a constant amount of time on each item of input encountered. Other algorithms achieve a linear time bound for more subtle reasons. To illustrate some of the ideas here, we consider two simple linear-time algorithms as examples.

***Computing the Maximum***   Computing the maximum of $n$ numbers, for example, can be performed in the basic "one-pass" style. Suppose the numbers are provided as input in either a list or an array. We process the numbers $a_1, a_2, \ldots, a_n$ in order, keeping a running estimate of the maximum as we go. Each time we encounter a number $a_i$, we check whether $a_i$ is larger than our current estimate, and if so we update the estimate to $a_i$.

```
max = a₁
For i = 2 to n
  If aᵢ > max then
    set max = aᵢ
  Endif
Endfor
```

In this way, we do constant work per element, for a total running time of $O(n)$.

Sometimes the constraints of an application force this kind of one-pass algorithm on you—for example, an algorithm running on a high-speed switch on the Internet may see a stream of packets flying past it, and it can try computing anything it wants to as this stream passes by, but it can only perform a constant amount of computational work on each packet, and it can't save the stream so as to make subsequent scans through it. Two different subareas of algorithms, *online algorithms* and *data stream algorithms*, have developed to study this model of computation.

***Merging Two Sorted Lists***   Often, an algorithm has a running time of $O(n)$, but the reason is more complex. We now describe an algorithm for merging two sorted lists that stretches the one-pass style of design just a little, but still has a linear running time.

Suppose we are given two lists of $n$ numbers each, $a_1, a_2, \ldots, a_n$ and $b_1, b_2, \ldots, b_n$, and each is already arranged in ascending order. We'd like to merge these into a single list $c_1, c_2, \ldots, c_{2n}$ that is also arranged in ascending order. For example, merging the lists $2, 3, 11, 19$ and $4, 9, 16, 25$ results in the output $2, 3, 4, 9, 11, 16, 19, 25$.

To do this, we could just throw the two lists together, ignore the fact that they're separately arranged in ascending order, and run a sorting algorithm. But this clearly seems wasteful; we'd like to make use of the existing order in the input. One way to think about designing a better algorithm is to imagine performing the merging of the two lists by hand: suppose you're given two piles of numbered cards, each arranged in ascending order, and you'd like to produce a single ordered pile containing all the cards. If you look at the top card on each stack, you know that the smaller of these two should go first on the output pile; so you could remove this card, place it on the output, and now iterate on what's left.

In other words, we have the following algorithm.

---

To merge sorted lists $A = a_1, \ldots, a_n$ and $B = b_1, \ldots, b_n$:
  Maintain a *Current* pointer into each list, initialized to
    point to the front elements
  While both lists are nonempty:
    Let $a_i$ and $b_j$ be the elements pointed to by the *Current* pointer
    Append the smaller of these two to the output list
    Advance the *Current* pointer in the list from which the
      smaller element was selected
  EndWhile
  Once one list is empty, append the remainder of the other list
    to the output

---

See Figure 2.2 for a picture of this process.

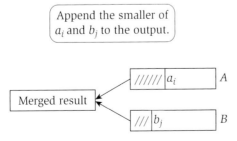

**Figure 2.2** To merge sorted lists $A$ and $B$, we repeatedly extract the smaller item from the front of the two lists and append it to the output.

Now, to show a linear-time bound, one is tempted to describe an argument like what worked for the maximum-finding algorithm: "We do constant work per element, for a total running time of $O(n)$." But it is actually not true that we do only constant work per element. Suppose that $n$ is an even number, and consider the lists $A = 1, 3, 5, \ldots, 2n - 1$ and $B = n, n + 2, n + 4, \ldots, 3n - 2$. The number $b_1$ at the front of list $B$ will sit at the front of the list for $n/2$ iterations while elements from $A$ are repeatedly being selected, and hence it will be involved in $\Omega(n)$ comparisons. Now, it is true that each element can be involved in at most $O(n)$ comparisons (at worst, it is compared with each element in the other list), and if we sum this over all elements we get a running-time bound of $O(n^2)$. This is a correct bound, but we can show something much stronger.

The better way to argue is to bound the number of iterations of the While loop by an "accounting" scheme. Suppose we *charge* the cost of each iteration to the element that is selected and added to the output list. An element can be charged only once, since at the moment it is first charged, it is added to the output and never seen again by the algorithm. But there are only $2n$ elements total, and the cost of each iteration is accounted for by a charge to some element, so there can be at most $2n$ iterations. Each iteration involves a constant amount of work, so the total running time is $O(n)$, as desired.

While this merging algorithm iterated through its input lists in order, the "interleaved" way in which it processed the lists necessitated a slightly subtle running-time analysis. In Chapter 3 we will see linear-time algorithms for graphs that have an even more complex flow of control: they spend a constant amount of time on each node and edge in the underlying graph, but the order in which they process the nodes and edges depends on the structure of the graph.

## $O(n \log n)$ **Time**

$O(n \log n)$ is also a very common running time, and in Chapter 5 we will see one of the main reasons for its prevalence: it is the running time of any algorithm that splits its input into two equal-sized pieces, solves each piece recursively, and then combines the two solutions in linear time.

Sorting is perhaps the most well-known example of a problem that can be solved this way. Specifically, the *Mergesort* algorithm divides the set of input numbers into two equal-sized pieces, sorts each half recursively, and then merges the two sorted halves into a single sorted output list. We have just seen that the merging can be done in linear time; and Chapter 5 will discuss how to analyze the recursion so as to get a bound of $O(n \log n)$ on the overall running time.

One also frequently encounters $O(n \log n)$ as a running time simply because there are many algorithms whose most expensive step is to sort the input. For example, suppose we are given a set of $n$ time-stamps $x_1, x_2, \ldots, x_n$ on which copies of a file arrived at a server, and we'd like to find the largest interval of time between the first and last of these time-stamps during which no copy of the file arrived. A simple solution to this problem is to first sort the time-stamps $x_1, x_2, \ldots, x_n$ and then process them in sorted order, determining the sizes of the gaps between each number and its successor in ascending order. The largest of these gaps is the desired subinterval. Note that this algorithm requires $O(n \log n)$ time to sort the numbers, and then it spends constant work on each number in ascending order. In other words, the remainder of the algorithm after sorting follows the basic recipe for linear time that we discussed earlier.

## Quadratic Time

Here's a basic problem: suppose you are given $n$ points in the plane, each specified by $(x, y)$ coordinates, and you'd like to find the pair of points that are closest together. The natural brute-force algorithm for this problem would enumerate all pairs of points, compute the distance between each pair, and then choose the pair for which this distance is smallest.

What is the running time of this algorithm? The number of pairs of points is $\binom{n}{2} = \frac{n(n-1)}{2}$, and since this quantity is bounded by $\frac{1}{2}n^2$, it is $O(n^2)$. More crudely, the number of pairs is $O(n^2)$ because we multiply the number of ways of choosing the first member of the pair (at most $n$) by the number of ways of choosing the second member of the pair (also at most $n$). The distance between points $(x_i, y_i)$ and $(x_j, y_j)$ can be computed by the formula $\sqrt{(x_i - x_j)^2 + (y_i - y_j)^2}$ in constant time, so the overall running time is $O(n^2)$. This example illustrates a very common way in which a running time of $O(n^2)$ arises: performing a search over all pairs of input items and spending constant time per pair.

Quadratic time also arises naturally from a pair of *nested loops*: An algorithm consists of a loop with $O(n)$ iterations, and each iteration of the loop launches an internal loop that takes $O(n)$ time. Multiplying these two factors of $n$ together gives the running time.

The brute-force algorithm for finding the closest pair of points can be written in an equivalent way with two nested loops:

```
For each input point (xᵢ, yᵢ)
   For each other input point (xⱼ, yⱼ)
      Compute distance d = √(xᵢ − xⱼ)² + (yᵢ − yⱼ)²
```

```
       If d is less than the current minimum, update minimum to d
    Endfor
  Endfor
```

Note how the "inner" loop, over $(x_j, y_j)$, has $O(n)$ iterations, each taking constant time; and the "outer" loop, over $(x_i, y_i)$, has $O(n)$ iterations, each invoking the inner loop once.

It's important to notice that the algorithm we've been discussing for the Closest-Pair Problem really is just the brute-force approach: the natural search space for this problem has size $O(n^2)$, and we're simply enumerating it. At first, one feels there is a certain inevitability about this quadratic algorithm—we have to measure all the distances, don't we?—but in fact this is an illusion. In Chapter 5 we describe a very clever algorithm that finds the closest pair of points in the plane in only $O(n \log n)$ time, and in Chapter 13 we show how randomization can be used to reduce the running time to $O(n)$.

## Cubic Time

More elaborate sets of nested loops often lead to algorithms that run in $O(n^3)$ time. Consider, for example, the following problem. We are given sets $S_1, S_2, \ldots, S_n$, each of which is a subset of $\{1, 2, \ldots, n\}$, and we would like to know whether some pair of these sets is disjoint—in other words, has no elements in common.

What is the running time needed to solve this problem? Let's suppose that each set $S_i$ is represented in such a way that the elements of $S_i$ can be listed in constant time per element, and we can also check in constant time whether a given number $p$ belongs to $S_i$. The following is a direct way to approach the problem.

```
For pair of sets S_i and S_j
   Determine whether S_i and S_j have an element in common
Endfor
```

This is a concrete algorithm, but to reason about its running time it helps to open it up (at least conceptually) into three nested loops.

```
For each set S_i
   For each other set S_j
      For each element p of S_i
         Determine whether p also belongs to S_j
      Endfor
      If no element of S_i belongs to S_j then
```

```
        Report that S_i and S_j are disjoint
      Endif
   Endfor
Endfor
```

Each of the sets has maximum size $O(n)$, so the innermost loop takes time $O(n)$. Looping over the sets $S_j$ involves $O(n)$ iterations around this innermost loop; and looping over the sets $S_i$ involves $O(n)$ iterations around this. Multiplying these three factors of $n$ together, we get the running time of $O(n^3)$.

For this problem, there are algorithms that improve on $O(n^3)$ running time, but they are quite complicated. Furthermore, it is not clear whether the improved algorithms for this problem are practical on inputs of reasonable size.

## $O(n^k)$ Time

In the same way that we obtained a running time of $O(n^2)$ by performing brute-force search over all pairs formed from a set of $n$ items, we obtain a running time of $O(n^k)$ for any constant $k$ when we search over all subsets of size $k$.

Consider, for example, the problem of finding independent sets in a graph, which we discussed in Chapter 1. Recall that a set of nodes is independent if no two are joined by an edge. Suppose, in particular, that for some fixed constant $k$, we would like to know if a given $n$-node input graph $G$ has an independent set of size $k$. The natural brute-force algorithm for this problem would enumerate all subsets of $k$ nodes, and for each subset $S$ it would check whether there is an edge joining any two members of $S$. That is,

```
For each subset S of k nodes
   Check whether S constitutes an independent set
   If S is an independent set then
      Stop and declare success
   Endif
Endfor
If no k-node independent set was found then
   Declare failure
Endif
```

To understand the running time of this algorithm, we need to consider two quantities. First, the total number of $k$-element subsets in an $n$-element set is

$$\binom{n}{k} = \frac{n(n-1)(n-2)\cdots(n-k+1)}{k(k-1)(k-2)\cdots(2)(1)} \leq \frac{n^k}{k!}.$$

Since we are treating $k$ as a constant, this quantity is $O(n^k)$. Thus, the outer loop in the algorithm above will run for $O(n^k)$ iterations as it tries all $k$-node subsets of the $n$ nodes of the graph.

Inside this loop, we need to test whether a given set $S$ of $k$ nodes constitutes an independent set. The definition of an independent set tells us that we need to check, for each pair of nodes, whether there is an edge joining them. Hence this is a search over pairs, like we saw earlier in the discussion of quadratic time; it requires looking at $\binom{k}{2}$, that is, $O(k^2)$, pairs and spending constant time on each.

Thus the total running time is $O(k^2 n^k)$. Since we are treating $k$ as a constant here, and since constants can be dropped in $O(\cdot)$ notation, we can write this running time as $O(n^k)$.

Independent Set is a principal example of a problem believed to be computationally hard, and in particular it is believed that no algorithm to find $k$-node independent sets in arbitrary graphs can avoid having some dependence on $k$ in the exponent. However, as we will discuss in Chapter 10 in the context of a related problem, even once we've conceded that brute-force search over $k$-element subsets is necessary, there can be different ways of going about this that lead to significant differences in the efficiency of the computation.

## Beyond Polynomial Time

The previous example of the Independent Set Problem starts us rapidly down the path toward running times that grow faster than any polynomial. In particular, two kinds of bounds that come up very frequently are $2^n$ and $n!$, and we now discuss why this is so.

Suppose, for example, that we are given a graph and want to find an independent set of *maximum* size (rather than testing for the existence of one with a given number of nodes). Again, people don't know of algorithms that improve significantly on brute-force search, which in this case would look as follows.

```
For each subset S of nodes
   Check whether S constitutes an independent set
   If S is a larger independent set than the largest seen so far then
      Record the size of S as the current maximum
   Endif
Endfor
```

This is very much like the brute-force algorithm for $k$-node independent sets, except that now we are iterating over *all* subsets of the graph. The total number of subsets of an $n$-element set is $2^n$, and so the outer loop in this algorithm will run for $2^n$ iterations as it tries all these subsets. Inside the loop, we are checking all pairs from a set $S$ that can be as large as $n$ nodes, so each iteration of the loop takes at most $O(n^2)$ time. Multiplying these two together, we get a running time of $O(n^2 2^n)$.

Thus see that $2^n$ arises naturally as a running time for a search algorithm that must consider all subsets. In the case of Independent Set, something at least nearly this inefficient appears to be necessary; but it's important to keep in mind that $2^n$ is the size of the search space for many problems, and for many of them we will be able to find highly efficient polynomial-time algorithms. For example, a brute-force search algorithm for the Interval Scheduling Problem that we saw in Chapter 1 would look very similar to the algorithm above: try all subsets of intervals, and find the largest subset that has no overlaps. But in the case of the Interval Scheduling Problem, as opposed to the Independent Set Problem, we will see (in Chapter 4) how to find an optimal solution in $O(n \log n)$ time. This is a recurring kind of dichotomy in the study of algorithms: two algorithms can have very similar-looking search spaces, but in one case you're able to bypass the brute-force search algorithm, and in the other you aren't.

The function $n!$ grows even more rapidly than $2^n$, so it's even more menacing as a bound on the performance of an algorithm. Search spaces of size $n!$ tend to arise for one of two reasons. First, $n!$ is the number of ways to match up $n$ items with $n$ other items—for example, it is the number of possible perfect matchings of $n$ men with $n$ women in an instance of the Stable Matching Problem. To see this, note that there are $n$ choices for how we can match up the first man; having eliminated this option, there are $n - 1$ choices for how we can match up the second man; having eliminated these two options, there are $n - 2$ choices for how we can match up the third man; and so forth. Multiplying all these choices out, we get $n(n - 1)(n - 2) \cdots (2)(1) = n!$

Despite this enormous set of possible solutions, we were able to solve the Stable Matching Problem in $O(n^2)$ iterations of the proposal algorithm. In Chapter 7, we will see a similar phenomenon for the Bipartite Matching Problem we discussed earlier; if there are $n$ nodes on each side of the given bipartite graph, there can be up to $n!$ ways of pairing them up. However, by a fairly subtle search algorithm, we will be able to find the largest bipartite matching in $O(n^3)$ time.

The function $n!$ also arises in problems where the search space consists of all ways to arrange $n$ items in order. A basic problem in this genre is the Traveling Salesman Problem: given a set of $n$ cities, with distances between all pairs, what is the shortest tour that visits all cities? We assume that the salesman starts and ends at the first city, so the crux of the problem is the implicit search over all orders of the remaining $n - 1$ cities, leading to a search space of size $(n - 1)!$. In Chapter 8, we will see that Traveling Salesman is another problem that, like Independent Set, belongs to the class of NP-complete problems and is believed to have no efficient solution.

## Sublinear Time

Finally, there are cases where one encounters running times that are asymptotically smaller than linear. Since it takes linear time just to read the input, these situations tend to arise in a model of computation where the input can be "queried" indirectly rather than read completely, and the goal is to minimize the amount of querying that must be done.

Perhaps the best-known example of this is the binary search algorithm. Given a sorted array $A$ of $n$ numbers, we'd like to determine whether a given number $p$ belongs to the array. We could do this by reading the entire array, but we'd like to do it much more efficiently, taking advantage of the fact that the array is sorted, by carefully *probing* particular entries. In particular, we probe the middle entry of $A$ and get its value—say it is $q$—and we compare $q$ to $p$. If $q = p$, we're done. If $q > p$, then in order for $p$ to belong to the array $A$, it must lie in the lower half of $A$; so we ignore the upper half of $A$ from now on and recursively apply this search in the lower half. Finally, if $q < p$, then we apply the analogous reasoning and recursively search in the upper half of $A$.

The point is that in each step, there's a region of $A$ where $p$ might possibly be; and we're shrinking the size of this region by a factor of two with every probe. So how large is the "active" region of $A$ after $k$ probes? It starts at size $n$, so after $k$ probes it has size at most $(\frac{1}{2})^k n$.

Given this, how long will it take for the size of the active region to be reduced to a constant? We need $k$ to be large enough so that $(\frac{1}{2})^k = O(1/n)$, and to do this we can choose $k = \log_2 n$. Thus, when $k = \log_2 n$, the size of the active region has been reduced to a constant, at which point the recursion bottoms out and we can search the remainder of the array directly in constant time.

So the running time of binary search is $O(\log n)$, because of this successive shrinking of the search region. In general, $O(\log n)$ arises as a time bound whenever we're dealing with an algorithm that does a constant amount of work in order to throw away a constant *fraction* of the input. The crucial fact is that $O(\log n)$ such iterations suffice to shrink the input down to constant size, at which point the problem can generally be solved directly.

# 2.5 A More Complex Data Structure: Priority Queues

Our primary goal in this book was expressed at the outset of the chapter: we seek algorithms that improve qualitatively on brute-force search, and in general we use polynomial-time solvability as the concrete formulation of this. Typically, achieving a polynomial-time solution to a nontrivial problem is not something that depends on fine-grained implementation details; rather, the difference between exponential and polynomial is based on overcoming higher-level obstacles. Once one has an efficient algorithm to solve a problem, however, it is often possible to achieve further improvements in running time by being careful with the implementation details, and sometimes by using more complex data structures.

Some complex data structures are essentially tailored for use in a single kind of algorithm, while others are more generally applicable. In this section, we describe one of the most broadly useful sophisticated data structures, the *priority queue.* Priority queues will be useful when we describe how to implement some of the graph algorithms developed later in the book. For our purposes here, it is a useful illustration of the analysis of a data structure that, unlike lists and arrays, must perform some nontrivial processing each time it is invoked.

## The Problem

In the implementation of the Stable Matching algorithm in Section 2.3, we discussed the need to maintain a dynamically changing set $S$ (such as the set of all free men in that case). In such situations, we want to be able to add elements to and delete elements from the set $S$, and we want to be able to select an element from $S$ when the algorithm calls for it. A priority queue is designed for applications in which elements have a *priority value,* or *key,* and each time we need to select an element from $S$, we want to take the one with highest priority.

A priority queue is a data structure that maintains a set of elements $S$, where each element $v \in S$ has an associated value $\text{key}(v)$ that denotes the priority of element $v$; smaller keys represent higher priorities. Priority queues support the addition and deletion of elements from the set, and also the selection of the element with smallest key. Our implementation of priority queues will also support some additional operations that we summarize at the end of the section.

A motivating application for priority queues, and one that is useful to keep in mind when considering their general function, is the problem of managing real-time events such as the scheduling of processes on a computer. Each process has a priority, or urgency, but processes do not arrive in order of their priorities. Rather, we have a current set of active processes, and we want to be able to extract the one with the currently highest priority and run it. We can maintain the set of processes in a priority queue, with the key of a process representing its priority value. Scheduling the highest-priority process corresponds to selecting the element with minimum key from the priority queue; concurrent with this, we will also be inserting new processes as they arrive, according to their priority values.

How efficiently do we hope to be able to execute the operations in a priority queue? We will show how to implement a priority queue containing at most $n$ elements at any time so that elements can be added and deleted, and the element with minimum key selected, in $O(\log n)$ time per operation.

Before discussing the implementation, let us point out a very basic application of priority queues that highlights why $O(\log n)$ time per operation is essentially the "right" bound to aim for.

**(2.11)**  *A sequence of $O(n)$ priority queue operations can be used to sort a set of n numbers.*

**Proof.** Set up a priority queue $H$, and insert each number into $H$ with its value as a key. Then extract the smallest number one by one until all numbers have been extracted; this way, the numbers will come out of the priority queue in sorted order.  ∎

Thus, with a priority queue that can perform insertion and the extraction of minima in $O(\log n)$ per operation, we can sort $n$ numbers in $O(n \log n)$ time. It is known that, in a comparison-based model of computation (when each operation accesses the input only by comparing a pair of numbers), the time needed to sort must be at least proportional to $n \log n$, so (2.11) highlights a sense in which $O(\log n)$ time per operation is the best we can hope for. We should note that the situation is a bit more complicated than this: implementations of priority queues more sophisticated than the one we present here can improve the running time needed for certain operations, and add extra functionality. But (2.11) shows that any sequence of priority queue operations that results in the sorting of $n$ numbers must take time at least proportional to $n \log n$ in total.

## A Data Structure for Implementing a Priority Queue

We will use a data structure called a *heap* to implement a priority queue. Before we discuss the structure of heaps, we should consider what happens with some simpler, more natural approaches to implementing the functions of a priority queue. We could just have the elements in a list, and separately have a pointer labeled Min to the one with minimum key. This makes adding new elements easy, but extraction of the minimum hard. Specifically, finding the minimum is quick—we just consult the Min pointer—but after removing this minimum element, we need to update the Min pointer to be ready for the next operation, and this would require a scan of all elements in $O(n)$ time to find the new minimum.

This complication suggests that we should perhaps maintain the elements in the sorted order of the keys. This makes it easy to extract the element with smallest key, but now how do we add a new element to our set? Should we have the elements in an array, or a linked list? Suppose we want to add $s$ with key value key($s$). If the set $S$ is maintained as a sorted array, we can use binary search to find the array position where $s$ should be inserted in $O(\log n)$ time, but to insert $s$ in the array, we would have to move all later elements one position to the right. This would take $O(n)$ time. On the other hand, if we maintain the set as a sorted doubly linked list, we could insert it in $O(1)$ time into any position, but the doubly linked list would not support binary search, and hence we may need up to $O(n)$ time to find the position where $s$ should be inserted.

***The Definition of a Heap***   So in all these simple approaches, at least one of the operations can take up to $O(n)$ time—much more than the $O(\log n)$ per operation that we're hoping for. This is where heaps come in. The *heap* data structure combines the benefits of a sorted array and list for purposes of this application. Conceptually, we think of a heap as a balanced binary tree as shown on the left of Figure 2.3. The tree will have a root, and each node can have up to two children, a left and a right child. The keys in such a binary tree are said to be in *heap order* if the key of any element is at least as large as the key of the element at its parent node in the tree. In other words,

> Heap order: For every element $v$, at a node $i$, the element $w$ at $i$'s parent satisfies key($w$) $\leq$ key($v$).

In Figure 2.3 the numbers in the nodes are the keys of the corresponding elements.

Before we discuss how to work with a heap, we need to consider what data structure should be used to represent it. We can use pointers: each node at the heap could keep the element it stores, its key, and three pointers pointing to the two children and the parent of the heap node. We can avoid using pointers, however, if a bound $N$ is known in advance on the total number of elements that will ever be in the heap at any one time. Such heaps can be maintained in an array $H$ indexed by $i = 1, \ldots, N$. We will think of the heap nodes as corresponding to the positions in this array. $H[1]$ is the root, and for any node

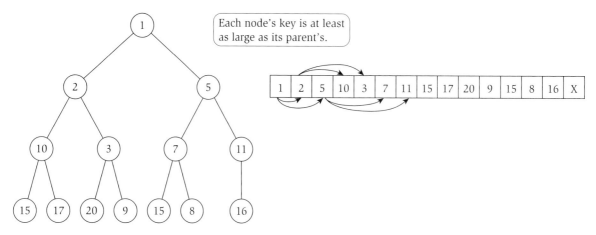

**Figure 2.3** Values in a heap shown as a binary tree on the left, and represented as an array on the right. The arrows show the children for the top three nodes in the tree.

at position $i$, the children are the nodes at positions $\texttt{leftChild}(i) = 2i$ and $\texttt{rightChild}(i) = 2i + 1$. So the two children of the root are at positions 2 and 3, and the parent of a node at position $i$ is at position $\texttt{parent}(i) = \lfloor i/2 \rfloor$. If the heap has $n < N$ elements at some time, we will use the first $n$ positions of the array to store the $n$ heap elements, and use $\texttt{length}(H)$ to denote the number of elements in $H$. This representation keeps the heap balanced at all times. See the right-hand side of Figure 2.3 for the array representation of the heap on the left-hand side.

### Implementing the Heap Operations

The heap element with smallest key is at the root, so it takes $O(1)$ time to identify the minimal element. How do we add or delete heap elements? First consider adding a new heap element $v$, and assume that our heap $H$ has $n < N$ elements so far. Now it will have $n + 1$ elements. To start with, we can add the new element $v$ to the final position $i = n + 1$, by setting $\texttt{H}[i] = v$. Unfortunately, this does not maintain the heap property, as the key of element $v$ may be smaller than the key of its parent. So we now have something that is almost a heap, except for a small "damaged" part where $v$ was pasted on at the end.

We will use the procedure $\texttt{Heapify-up}$ to fix our heap. Let $j = \texttt{parent}(i) = \lfloor i/2 \rfloor$ be the parent of the node $i$, and assume $\texttt{H}[j] = w$. If $\texttt{key}[v] < \texttt{key}[w]$, then we will simply swap the positions of $v$ and $w$. This will fix the heap property at position $i$, but the resulting structure will possibly fail to satisfy the heap property at position $j$—in other words, the site of the "damage" has moved upward from $i$ to $j$. We thus call the process recursively from position

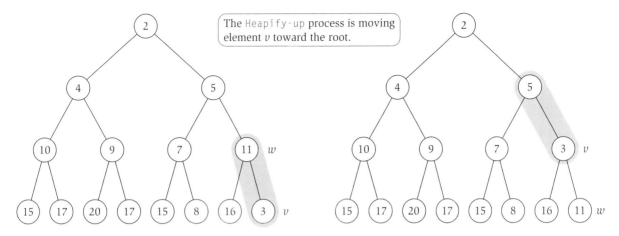

**Figure 2.4** The Heapify-up process. Key 3 (at position 16) is too small (on the left). After swapping keys 3 and 11, the heap violation moves one step closer to the root of the tree (on the right).

$j = \texttt{parent}(i)$ to continue fixing the heap by pushing the damaged part upward. Figure 2.4 shows the first two steps of the process after an insertion.

```
Heapify-up(H,i):
  If i > 1 then
    let j = parent(i) = ⌊i/2⌋
    If key[H[i]]<key[H[j]] then
      swap the array entries H[i] and H[j]
      Heapify-up(H,j)
    Endif
  Endif
```

To see why Heapify-up works, eventually restoring the heap order, it helps to understand more fully the structure of our slightly damaged heap in the middle of this process. Assume that $H$ is an array, and $v$ is the element in position $i$. We say that $H$ is almost a heap with the key of $H[i]$ too small, if there is a value $\alpha \geq \texttt{key}(v)$ such that raising the value of $\texttt{key}(v)$ to $\alpha$ would make the resulting array satisfy the heap property. (In other words, element $v$ in $H[i]$ is too small, but raising it to $\alpha$ would fix the problem.) One important point to note is that if $H$ is almost a heap with the key of the root (i.e., $H[1]$) too small, then in fact it is a heap. To see why this is true, consider that if raising the value of $H[1]$ to $\alpha$ would make $H$ a heap, then the value of $H[1]$ must also be smaller than both its children, and hence it already has the heap-order property.

**(2.12)**    *The procedure* Heapify-up(*H*, *i*) *fixes the heap property in* $O(\log i)$ *time, assuming that the array H is almost a heap with the key of H*[*i*] *too small. Using* Heapify-up *we can insert a new element in a heap of n elements in* $O(\log n)$ *time.*

**Proof.** We prove the statement by induction on $i$. If $i = 1$ there is nothing to prove, since we have already argued that in this case $H$ is actually a heap. Now consider the case in which $i > 1$: Let $v = H[i]$, $j = \texttt{parent}(i)$, $w = H[j]$, and $\beta = \texttt{key}(w)$. Swapping elements $v$ and $w$ takes $O(1)$ time. We claim that after the swap, the array $H$ is either a heap or almost a heap with the key of $H[j]$ (which now holds $v$) too small. This is true, as setting the key value at node $j$ to $\beta$ would make $H$ a heap.

So by the induction hypothesis, applying Heapify-up($j$) recursively will produce a heap as required. The process follows the tree-path from position $i$ to the root, so it takes $O(\log i)$ time.

To insert a new element in a heap, we first add it as the last element. If the new element has a very large key value, then the array is a heap. Otherwise, it is almost a heap with the key value of the new element too small. We use Heapify-up to fix the heap property.  ∎

Now consider deleting an element. Many applications of priority queues don't require the deletion of arbitrary elements, but only the extraction of the minimum. In a heap, this corresponds to identifying the key at the root (which will be the minimum) and then deleting it; we will refer to this operation as ExtractMin(*H*). Here we will implement a more general operation Delete(*H*, *i*), which will delete the element in position $i$. Assume the heap currently has $n$ elements. After deleting the element $H[i]$, the heap will have only $n - 1$ elements; and not only is the heap-order property violated, there is actually a "hole" at position $i$, since $H[i]$ is now empty. So as a first step, to patch the hole in $H$, we move the element $w$ in position $n$ to position $i$. After doing this, $H$ at least has the property that its $n - 1$ elements are in the first $n - 1$ positions, as required, but we may well still not have the heap-order property.

However, the only place in the heap where the order might be violated is position $i$, as the key of element $w$ may be either too small or too big for the position $i$. If the key is too small (that is, the violation of the heap property is between node $i$ and its parent), then we can use Heapify-up($i$) to reestablish the heap order. On the other hand, if key[$w$] is too big, the heap property may be violated between $i$ and one or both of its children. In this case, we will use a procedure called Heapify-down, closely analogous to Heapify-up, that

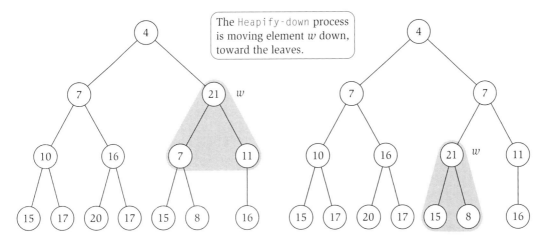

**Figure 2.5** The Heapify−down process:. Key 21 (at position 3) is too big (on the left). After swapping keys 21 and 7, the heap violation moves one step closer to the bottom of the tree (on the right).

swaps the element at position $i$ with one of its children and proceeds down the tree recursively. Figure 2.5 shows the first steps of this process.

```
Heapify-down(H,i):
  Let n = length(H)
  If 2i > n then
    Terminate with H unchanged
  Else if 2i < n then
    Let left = 2i, and right = 2i + 1
    Let j be the index that minimizes key[H[left]] and key[H[right]]
  Else if 2i = n then
    Let j = 2i
  Endif
  If key[H[j]] < key[H[i]] then
    swap the array entries H[i] and H[j]
    Heapify-down(H, j)
  Endif
```

Assume that $H$ is an array and $w$ is the element in position $i$. We say that *H is almost a heap with the key of H[i] too big*, if there is a value $\alpha \leq \mathrm{key}(w)$ such that lowering the value of $\mathrm{key}(w)$ to $\alpha$ would make the resulting array satisfy the heap property. Note that if $H[i]$ corresponds to a leaf in the heap (i.e., it has no children), and $H$ is almost a heap with $H[i]$ too big, then in fact $H$ is a heap. Indeed, if lowering the value in $H[i]$ would make $H$ a heap, then

$H[i]$ is already larger than its parent and hence it already has the heap-order property.

**(2.13)** *The procedure* Heapify-down$(H, i)$ *fixes the heap property in* $O(\log n)$ *time, assuming that $H$ is almost a heap with the key value of $H[i]$ too big. Using* Heapify-up *or* Heapify-down *we can delete a new element in a heap of $n$ elements in* $O(\log n)$ *time.*

**Proof.** We prove that the process fixes the heap by reverse induction on the value $i$. Let $n$ be the number of elements in the heap. If $2i > n$, then, as we just argued above, $H$ is a heap and hence there is nothing to prove. Otherwise, let $j$ be the child of $i$ with smaller key value, and let $w = H[j]$. Swapping the array elements $w$ and $v$ takes $O(1)$ time. We claim that the resulting array is either a heap or almost a heap with $H[j] = v$ too big. This is true as setting $\text{key}(v) = \text{key}(w)$ would make $H$ a heap. Now $j \geq 2i$, so by the induction hypothesis, the recursive call to Heapify-down fixes the heap property.

The algorithm repeatedly swaps the element originally at position $i$ down, following a tree-path, so in $O(\log n)$ iterations the process results in a heap.

To use the process to remove an element $v = H[i]$ from the heap, we replace $H[i]$ with the last element in the array, $H[n] = w$. If the resulting array is not a heap, it is almost a heap with the key value of $H[i]$ either too small or too big. We use Heapify-down or Heapify-down to fix the heap property in $O(\log n)$ time. ■

## Implementing Priority Queues with Heaps

The heap data structure with the Heapify-down and Heapify-up operations can efficiently implement a priority queue that is constrained to hold at most $N$ elements at any point in time. Here we summarize the operations we will use.

- StartHeap$(N)$ returns an empty heap $H$ that is set up to store at most $N$ elements. This operation takes $O(N)$ time, as it involves initializing the array that will hold the heap.
- Insert$(H, v)$ inserts the item $v$ into heap $H$. If the heap currently has $n$ elements, this takes $O(\log n)$ time.
- FindMin$(H)$ identifies the minimum element in the heap $H$ but does not remove it. This takes $O(1)$ time.
- Delete$(H, i)$ deletes the element in heap position $i$. This is implemented in $O(\log n)$ time for heaps that have $n$ elements.
- ExtractMin$(H)$ identifies and deletes an element with minimum key value from a heap. This is a combination of the preceding two operations, and so it takes $O(\log n)$ time.

There is a second class of operations in which we want to operate on elements by name, rather than by their position in the heap. For example, in a number of graph algorithms that use heaps, the heap elements are nodes of the graph with key values that are computed during the algorithm. At various points in these algorithms, we want to operate on a particular node, regardless of where it happens to be in the heap.

To be able to access given elements of the priority queue efficiently, we simply maintain an additional array Position that stores the current position of each element (each node) in the heap. We can now implement the following further operations.

- To delete the element $v$, we apply Delete($H$,Position[$v$]). Maintaining this array does not increase the overall running time, and so we can delete an element $v$ from a heap with $n$ nodes in $O(\log n)$ time.

- An additional operation that is used by some algorithms is ChangeKey $(H, v, \alpha)$, which changes the key value of element $v$ to key$(v) = \alpha$. To implement this operation in $O(\log n)$ time, we first need to be able to identify the position of element $v$ in the array, which we do by using the array Position. Once we have identified the position of element $v$, we change the key and then apply Heapify-up or Heapify-down as appropriate.

## Solved Exercises

### Solved Exercise 1

Take the following list of functions and arrange them in ascending order of growth rate. That is, if function $g(n)$ immediately follows function $f(n)$ in your list, then it should be the case that $f(n)$ is $O(g(n))$.

$$f_1(n) = 10^n$$
$$f_2(n) = n^{1/3}$$
$$f_3(n) = n^n$$
$$f_4(n) = \log_2 n$$
$$f_5(n) = 2^{\sqrt{\log_2 n}}$$

**Solution**   We can deal with functions $f_1$, $f_2$, and $f_4$ very easily, since they belong to the basic families of exponentials, polynomials, and logarithms. In particular, by (2.8), we have $f_4(n) = O(f_2(n))$; and by (2.9), we have $f_2(n) = O(f_1(n))$.

Now, the function $f_3$ isn't so hard to deal with. It starts out smaller than $10^n$, but once $n \geq 10$, then clearly $10^n \leq n^n$. This is exactly what we need for the definition of $O(\cdot)$ notation: for all $n \geq 10$, we have $10^n \leq cn^n$, where in this case $c = 1$, and so $10^n = O(n^n)$.

Finally, we come to function $f_5$, which is admittedly kind of strange-looking. A useful rule of thumb in such situations is to try taking logarithms to see whether this makes things clearer. In this case, $\log_2 f_5(n) = \sqrt{\log_2 n} = (\log_2 n)^{1/2}$. What do the logarithms of the other functions look like? $\log f_4(n) = \log_2 \log_2 n$, while $\log f_2(n) = \frac{1}{3} \log_2 n$. All of these can be viewed as functions of $\log_2 n$, and so using the notation $z = \log_2 n$, we can write

$$\log f_2(n) = \frac{1}{3}z$$

$$\log f_4(n) = \log_2 z$$

$$\log f_5(n) = z^{1/2}$$

Now it's easier to see what's going on. First, for $z \geq 16$, we have $\log_2 z \leq z^{1/2}$. But the condition $z \geq 16$ is the same as $n \geq 2^{16} = 65,536$; thus once $n \geq 2^{16}$ we have $\log f_4(n) \leq \log f_5(n)$, and so $f_4(n) \leq f_5(n)$. Thus we can write $f_4(n) = O(f_5(n))$. Similarly we have $z^{1/2} \leq \frac{1}{3}z$ once $z \geq 9$—in other words, once $n \geq 2^9 = 512$. For $n$ above this bound we have $\log f_5(n) \leq \log f_2(n)$ and hence $f_5(n) \leq f_2(n)$, and so we can write $f_5(n) = O(f_2(n))$. Essentially, we have discovered that $2^{\sqrt{\log_2 n}}$ is a function whose growth rate lies somewhere between that of logarithms and polynomials.

Since we have sandwiched $f_5$ between $f_4$ and $f_2$, this finishes the task of putting the functions in order.

## Solved Exercise 2

Let $f$ and $g$ be two functions that take nonnegative values, and suppose that $f = O(g)$. Show that $g = \Omega(f)$.

**Solution**    This exercise is a way to formalize the intuition that $O(\cdot)$ and $\Omega(\cdot)$ are in a sense opposites. It is, in fact, not difficult to prove; it is just a matter of unwinding the definitions.

We're given that, for some constants $c$ and $n_0$, we have $f(n) \leq cg(n)$ for all $n \geq n_0$. Dividing both sides by $c$, we can conclude that $g(n) \geq \frac{1}{c}f(n)$ for all $n \geq n_0$. But this is exactly what is required to show that $g = \Omega(f)$: we have established that $g(n)$ is at least a constant multiple of $f(n)$ (where the constant is $\frac{1}{c}$), for all sufficiently large $n$ (at least $n_0$).

## Exercises

1. Suppose you have algorithms with the five running times listed below. (Assume these are the exact running times.) How much slower do each of these algorithms get when you (a) double the input size, or (b) increase the input size by one?

   **(a)** $n^2$

   **(b)** $n^3$

   **(c)** $100n^2$

   **(d)** $n \log n$

   **(e)** $2^n$

2. Suppose you have algorithms with the six running times listed below. (Assume these are the exact number of operations performed as a function of the input size $n$.) Suppose you have a computer that can perform $10^{10}$ operations per second, and you need to compute a result in at most an hour of computation. For each of the algorithms, what is the largest input size $n$ for which you would be able to get the result within an hour?

   **(a)** $n^2$

   **(b)** $n^3$

   **(c)** $100n^2$

   **(d)** $n \log n$

   **(e)** $2^n$

   **(f)** $2^{2^n}$

3. Take the following list of functions and arrange them in ascending order of growth rate. That is, if function $g(n)$ immediately follows function $f(n)$ in your list, then it should be the case that $f(n)$ is $O(g(n))$.

$$f_1(n) = n^{2.5}$$
$$f_2(n) = \sqrt{2n}$$
$$f_3(n) = n + 10$$
$$f_4(n) = 10^n$$
$$f_5(n) = 100^n$$
$$f_6(n) = n^2 \log n$$

4. Take the following list of functions and arrange them in ascending order of growth rate. That is, if function $g(n)$ immediately follows function $f(n)$ in your list, then it should be the case that $f(n)$ is $O(g(n))$.

$$g_1(n) = 2^{\sqrt{\log n}}$$
$$g_2(n) = 2^n$$
$$g_4(n) = n^{4/3}$$
$$g_3(n) = n(\log n)^3$$
$$g_5(n) = n^{\log n}$$
$$g_6(n) = 2^{2^n}$$
$$g_7(n) = 2^{n^2}$$

5. Assume you have functions $f$ and $g$ such that $f(n)$ is $O(g(n))$. For each of the following statements, decide whether you think it is true or false and give a proof or counterexample.

   **(a)** $\log_2 f(n)$ is $O(\log_2 g(n))$.

   **(b)** $2^{f(n)}$ is $O(2^{g(n)})$.

   **(c)** $f(n)^2$ is $O(g(n)^2)$.

6. Consider the following basic problem. You're given an array $A$ consisting of $n$ integers $A[1], A[2], \ldots, A[n]$. You'd like to output a two-dimensional $n$-by-$n$ array $B$ in which $B[i,j]$ (for $i < j$) contains the sum of array entries $A[i]$ through $A[j]$—that is, the sum $A[i] + A[i+1] + \cdots + A[j]$. (The value of array entry $B[i,j]$ is left unspecified whenever $i \geq j$, so it doesn't matter what is output for these values.)

   Here's a simple algorithm to solve this problem.

```
For i = 1, 2, . . . , n
  For j = i + 1, i + 2, . . . , n
      Add up array entries A[i] through A[j]
      Store the result in B[i, j]
  Endfor
Endfor
```

   **(a)** For some function $f$ that you should choose, give a bound of the form $O(f(n))$ on the running time of this algorithm on an input of size $n$ (i.e., a bound on the number of operations performed by the algorithm).

   **(b)** For this same function $f$, show that the running time of the algorithm on an input of size $n$ is also $\Omega(f(n))$. (This shows an asymptotically tight bound of $\Theta(f(n))$ on the running time.)

   **(c)** Although the algorithm you analyzed in parts (a) and (b) is the most natural way to solve the problem—after all, it just iterates through the relevant entries of the array $B$, filling in a value for each—it contains some highly unnecessary sources of inefficiency. Give a different algorithm to solve this problem, with an asymptotically better running time. In other words, you should design an algorithm with running time $O(g(n))$, where $\lim_{n\to\infty} g(n)/f(n) = 0$.

7. There's a class of folk songs and holiday songs in which each verse consists of the previous verse, with one extra line added on. "The Twelve Days of Christmas" has this property; for example, when you get to the fifth verse, you sing about the five golden rings and then, reprising the lines from the fourth verse, also cover the four calling birds, the three French hens, the two turtle doves, and of course the partridge in the pear tree. The Aramaic song "Had gadya" from the Passover Haggadah works like this as well, as do many other songs.

   These songs tend to last a long time, despite having relatively short scripts. In particular, you can convey the words plus instructions for one of these songs by specifying just the new line that is added in each verse, without having to write out all the previous lines each time. (So the phrase "five golden rings" only has to be written once, even though it will appear in verses five and onward.)

   There's something asymptotic that can be analyzed here. Suppose, for concreteness, that each line has a length that is bounded by a constant $c$, and suppose that the song, when sung out loud, runs for $n$ words total. Show how to encode such a song using a script that has length $f(n)$, for a function $f(n)$ that grows as slowly as possible.

8. You're doing some stress-testing on various models of glass jars to determine the height from which they can be dropped and still not break. The setup for this experiment, on a particular type of jar, is as follows. You have a ladder with $n$ rungs, and you want to find the highest rung from which you can drop a copy of the jar and not have it break. We call this the *highest safe rung*.

   It might be natural to try binary search: drop a jar from the middle rung, see if it breaks, and then recursively try from rung $n/4$ or $3n/4$ depending on the outcome. But this has the drawback that you could break a lot of jars in finding the answer.

   If your primary goal were to conserve jars, on the other hand, you could try the following strategy. Start by dropping a jar from the first rung, then the second rung, and so forth, climbing one higher each time until the jar breaks. In this way, you only need a single jar—at the moment it breaks, you have the correct answer—but you may have to drop it $n$ times (rather than $\log n$ as in the binary search solution).

So here is the trade-off: it seems you can perform fewer drops if you're willing to break more jars. To understand better how this trade-off works at a quantitative level, let's consider how to run this experiment given a fixed "budget" of $k \geq 1$ jars. In other words, you have to determine the correct answer—the highest safe rung—and can use at most $k$ jars in doing so.

   **(a)** Suppose you are given a budget of $k = 2$ jars. Describe a strategy for finding the highest safe rung that requires you to drop a jar at most $f(n)$ times, for some function $f(n)$ that grows slower than linearly. (In other words, it should be the case that $\lim_{n \to \infty} f(n)/n = 0$.)

   **(b)** Now suppose you have a budget of $k > 2$ jars, for some given $k$. Describe a strategy for finding the highest safe rung using at most $k$ jars. If $f_k(n)$ denotes the number of times you need to drop a jar according to your strategy, then the functions $f_1, f_2, f_3, \ldots$ should have the property that each grows asymptotically slower than the previous one: $\lim_{n \to \infty} f_k(n)/f_{k-1}(n) = 0$ for each $k$.

## Notes and Further Reading

Polynomial-time solvability emerged as a formal notion of efficiency by a gradual process, motivated by the work of a number of researchers including Cobham, Rabin, Edmonds, Hartmanis, and Stearns. The survey by Sipser (1992) provides both a historical and technical perspective on these developments. Similarly, the use of asymptotic order of growth notation to bound the running time of algorithms—as opposed to working out exact formulas with leading coefficients and lower-order terms—is a modeling decision that was quite non-obvious at the time it was introduced; Tarjan's Turing Award lecture (1987) offers an interesting perspective on the early thinking of researchers including Hopcroft, Tarjan, and others on this issue. Further discussion of asymptotic notation and the growth of basic functions can be found in Knuth (1997a).

The implementation of priority queues using heaps, and the application to sorting, is generally credited to Williams (1964) and Floyd (1964). The priority queue is an example of a nontrivial data structure with many applications; in later chapters we will discuss other data structures as they become useful for the implementation of particular algorithms. We will consider the Union-Find data structure in Chapter 4 for implementing an algorithm to find minimum-cost spanning trees, and we will discuss randomized hashing in Chapter 13. A number of other data structures are discussed in the book by Tarjan (1983). The LEDA library (Library of Efficient Datatypes and Algorithms) of Mehlhorn and Näher (1999) offers an extensive library of data structures useful in combinatorial and geometric applications.

***Notes on the Exercises*** Exercise 8 is based on a problem we learned from Sam Toueg.

# Chapter 3

## Graphs

Our focus in this book is on problems with a discrete flavor. Just as continuous mathematics is concerned with certain basic structures such as real numbers, vectors, and matrices, discrete mathematics has developed basic combinatorial structures that lie at the heart of the subject. One of the most fundamental and expressive of these is the *graph*.

The more one works with graphs, the more one tends to see them everywhere. Thus, we begin by introducing the basic definitions surrounding graphs, and list a spectrum of different algorithmic settings where graphs arise naturally. We then discuss some basic algorithmic primitives for graphs, beginning with the problem of *connectivity* and developing some fundamental graph search techniques.

## 3.1 Basic Definitions and Applications

Recall from Chapter 1 that a graph $G$ is simply a way of encoding pairwise relationships among a set of objects: it consists of a collection $V$ of *nodes* and a collection $E$ of *edges*, each of which "joins" two of the nodes. We thus represent an edge $e \in E$ as a two-element subset of $V$: $e = \{u, v\}$ for some $u, v \in V$, where we call $u$ and $v$ the *ends* of $e$.

Edges in a graph indicate a symmetric relationship between their ends. Often we want to encode asymmetric relationships, and for this we use the closely related notion of a *directed graph*. A directed graph $G'$ consists of a set of nodes $V$ and a set of *directed edges* $E'$. Each $e' \in E'$ is an *ordered pair* $(u, v)$; in other words, the roles of $u$ and $v$ are not interchangeable, and we call $u$ the *tail* of the edge and $v$ the *head*. We will also say that edge $e'$ *leaves node* $u$ and *enters node* $v$.

When we want to emphasize that the graph we are considering is not directed, we will call it an *undirected graph*; by default, however, the term "graph" will mean an undirected graph. It is also worth mentioning two warnings in our use of graph terminology. First, although an edge $e$ in an undirected graph should properly be written as a *set* of nodes $\{u, v\}$, one will more often see it written (even in this book) in the notation used for ordered pairs: $e = (u, v)$. Second, a *node* in a graph is also frequently called a *vertex*; in this context, the two words have exactly the same meaning.

***Examples of Graphs***    Graphs are very simple to define: we just take a collection of things and join some of them by edges. But at this level of abstraction, it's hard to appreciate the typical kinds of situations in which they arise. Thus, we propose the following list of specific contexts in which graphs serve as important models. The list covers a lot of ground, and it's not important to remember everything on it; rather, it will provide us with a lot of useful examples against which to check the basic definitions and algorithmic problems that we'll be encountering later in the chapter. Also, in going through the list, it's useful to digest the meaning of the nodes and the meaning of the edges in the context of the application. In some cases the nodes and edges both correspond to physical objects in the real world, in others the nodes are real objects while the edges are virtual, and in still others both nodes and edges are pure abstractions.

1. *Transportation networks.* The map of routes served by an airline carrier naturally forms a graph: the nodes are airports, and there is an edge from $u$ to $v$ if there is a nonstop flight that departs from $u$ and arrives at $v$. Described this way, the graph is directed; but in practice when there is an edge $(u, v)$, there is almost always an edge $(v, u)$, so we would not lose much by treating the airline route map as an undirected graph with edges joining pairs of airports that have nonstop flights each way. Looking at such a graph (you can generally find them depicted in the backs of in-flight airline magazines), we'd quickly notice a few things: there are often a small number of hubs with a very large number of incident edges; and it's possible to get between any two nodes in the graph via a very small number of intermediate stops.

   Other transportation networks can be modeled in a similar way. For example, we could take a rail network and have a node for each terminal, and an edge joining $u$ and $v$ if there's a section of railway track that goes between them without stopping at any intermediate terminal. The standard depiction of the subway map in a major city is a drawing of such a graph.

2. *Communication networks.* A collection of computers connected via a communication network can be naturally modeled as a graph in a few

different ways. First, we could have a node for each computer and an edge joining $u$ and $v$ if there is a direct physical link connecting them. Alternatively, for studying the large-scale structure of the Internet, people often define a node to be the set of all machines controlled by a single Internet service provider, with an edge joining $u$ and $v$ if there is a direct *peering relationship* between them—roughly, an agreement to exchange data under the standard BGP protocol that governs global Internet routing. Note that this latter network is more "virtual" than the former, since the links indicate a formal agreement in addition to a physical connection.

In studying wireless networks, one typically defines a graph where the nodes are computing devices situated at locations in physical space, and there is an edge from $u$ to $v$ if $v$ is close enough to $u$ to receive a signal from it. Note that it's often useful to view such a graph as directed, since it may be the case that $v$ can hear $u$'s signal but $u$ cannot hear $v$'s signal (if, for example, $u$ has a stronger transmitter). These graphs are also interesting from a geometric perspective, since they roughly correspond to putting down points in the plane and then joining pairs that are close together.

3. *Information networks.* The World Wide Web can be naturally viewed as a directed graph, in which nodes correspond to Web pages and there is an edge from $u$ to $v$ if $u$ has a hyperlink to $v$. The directedness of the graph is crucial here; many pages, for example, link to popular news sites, but these sites clearly do not reciprocate all these links. The structure of all these hyperlinks can be used by algorithms to try inferring the most important pages on the Web, a technique employed by most current search engines.

The hypertextual structure of the Web is anticipated by a number of information networks that predate the Internet by many decades. These include the network of cross-references among articles in an encyclopedia or other reference work, and the network of bibliographic citations among scientific papers.

4. *Social networks.* Given any collection of people who interact (the employees of a company, the students in a high school, or the residents of a small town), we can define a network whose nodes are people, with an edge joining $u$ and $v$ if they are friends with one another. We could have the edges mean a number of different things instead of friendship: the undirected edge $(u, v)$ could mean that $u$ and $v$ have had a romantic relationship or a financial relationship; the directed edge $(u, v)$ could mean that $u$ seeks advice from $v$, or that $u$ lists $v$ in his or her e-mail address book. One can also imagine bipartite social networks based on a

notion of *affiliation*: given a set $X$ of people and a set $Y$ of organizations, we could define an edge between $u \in X$ and $v \in Y$ if person $u$ belongs to organization $v$.

Networks such as this are used extensively by sociologists to study the dynamics of interaction among people. They can be used to identify the most "influential" people in a company or organization, to model trust relationships in a financial or political setting, and to track the spread of fads, rumors, jokes, diseases, and e-mail viruses.

5. *Dependency networks.* It is natural to define directed graphs that capture the interdependencies among a collection of objects. For example, given the list of courses offered by a college or university, we could have a node for each course and an edge from $u$ to $v$ if $u$ is a prerequisite for $v$. Given a list of functions or modules in a large software system, we could have a node for each function and an edge from $u$ to $v$ if $u$ invokes $v$ by a function call. Or given a set of species in an ecosystem, we could define a graph—a *food web*—in which the nodes are the different species and there is an edge from $u$ to $v$ if $u$ consumes $v$.

This is far from a complete list, too far to even begin tabulating its omissions. It is meant simply to suggest some examples that are useful to keep in mind when we start thinking about graphs in an algorithmic context.

**Paths and Connectivity**    One of the fundamental operations in a graph is that of traversing a sequence of nodes connected by edges. In the examples just listed, such a traversal could correspond to a user browsing Web pages by following hyperlinks; a rumor passing by word of mouth from you to someone halfway around the world; or an airline passenger traveling from San Francisco to Rome on a sequence of flights.

With this notion in mind, we define a *path* in an undirected graph $G = (V, E)$ to be a sequence $P$ of nodes $v_1, v_2, \ldots, v_{k-1}, v_k$ with the property that each consecutive pair $v_i, v_{i+1}$ is joined by an edge in $G$. $P$ is often called a path *from $v_1$ to $v_k$*, or a $v_1$-$v_k$ path. For example, the nodes $4, 2, 1, 7, 8$ form a path in Figure 3.1. A path is called *simple* if all its vertices are distinct from one another. A *cycle* is a path $v_1, v_2, \ldots, v_{k-1}, v_k$ in which $k > 2$, the first $k - 1$ nodes are all distinct, and $v_1 = v_k$—in other words, the sequence of nodes "cycles back" to where it began. All of these definitions carry over naturally to directed graphs, with the following change: in a directed path or cycle, each pair of consecutive nodes has the property that $(v_i, v_{i+1})$ is an edge. In other words, the sequence of nodes in the path or cycle must respect the directionality of edges.

We say that an undirected graph is *connected* if, for every pair of nodes $u$ and $v$, there is a path from $u$ to $v$. Choosing how to define connectivity of a

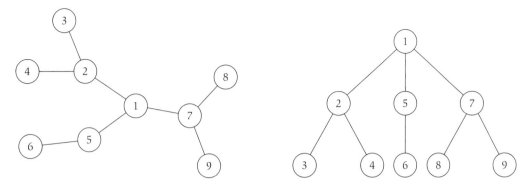

**Figure 3.1** Two drawings of the same tree. On the right, the tree is rooted at node 1.

directed graph is a bit more subtle, since it's possible for $u$ to have a path to $v$ while $v$ has no path to $u$. We say that a directed graph is *strongly connected* if, for every two nodes $u$ and $v$, there is a path from $u$ to $v$ and a path from $v$ to $u$.

In addition to simply knowing about the existence of a path between some pair of nodes $u$ and $v$, we may also want to know whether there is a *short* path. Thus we define the *distance* between two nodes $u$ and $v$ to be the minimum number of edges in a $u$-$v$ path. (We can designate some symbol like $\infty$ to denote the distance between nodes that are not connected by a path.) The term *distance* here comes from imagining $G$ as representing a communication or transportation network; if we want to get from $u$ to $v$, we may well want a route with as few "hops" as possible.

***Trees*** We say that an undirected graph is a *tree* if it is connected and does not contain a cycle. For example, the two graphs pictured in Figure 3.1 are trees. In a strong sense, trees are the simplest kind of connected graph: deleting any edge from a tree will disconnect it.

For thinking about the structure of a tree $T$, it is useful to *root* it at a particular node $r$. Physically, this is the operation of grabbing $T$ at the node $r$ and letting the rest of it hang downward under the force of gravity, like a mobile. More precisely, we "orient" each edge of $T$ away from $r$; for each other node $v$, we declare the *parent* of $v$ to be the node $u$ that directly precedes $v$ on its path from $r$; we declare $w$ to be a *child* of $v$ if $v$ is the parent of $w$. More generally, we say that $w$ is a *descendant* of $v$ (or $v$ is an *ancestor* of $w$) if $v$ lies on the path from the root to $w$; and we say that a node $x$ is a *leaf* if it has no descendants. Thus, for example, the two pictures in Figure 3.1 correspond to the same tree $T$—the same pairs of nodes are joined by edges—but the drawing on the right represents the result of rooting $T$ at node 1.

Rooted trees are fundamental objects in computer science, because they encode the notion of a *hierarchy*. For example, we can imagine the rooted tree in Figure 3.1 as corresponding to the organizational structure of a tiny nine-person company; employees 3 and 4 report to employee 2; employees 2, 5, and 7 report to employee 1; and so on. Many Web sites are organized according to a tree-like structure, to facilitate navigation. A typical computer science department's Web site will have an entry page as the root; the *People* page is a child of this entry page (as is the *Courses* page); pages entitled *Faculty* and *Students* are children of the *People* page; individual professors' home pages are children of the *Faculty* page; and so on.

For our purposes here, rooting a tree $T$ can make certain questions about $T$ conceptually easy to answer. For example, given a tree $T$ on $n$ nodes, how many edges does it have? Each node other than the root has a single edge leading "upward" to its parent; and conversely, each edge leads upward from precisely one non-root node. Thus we have very easily proved the following fact.

**(3.1)**   *Every n-node tree has exactly n − 1 edges.*

In fact, the following stronger statement is true, although we do not prove it here.

**(3.2)**   *Let G be an undirected graph on n nodes. Any two of the following statements implies the third.*

 *(i)  G is connected.*

 *(ii)  G does not contain a cycle.*

*(iii)  G has n − 1 edges.*

We now turn to the role of trees in the fundamental algorithmic idea of *graph traversal*.

## 3.2  Graph Connectivity and Graph Traversal

Having built up some fundamental notions regarding graphs, we turn to a very basic algorithmic question: node-to-node connectivity. Suppose we are given a graph $G = (V, E)$ and two particular nodes $s$ and $t$. We'd like to find an efficient algorithm that answers the question: Is there a path from $s$ to $t$ in $G$? We will call this the problem of determining *s-t connectivity*.

For very small graphs, this question can often be answered easily by visual inspection. But for large graphs, it can take some work to search for a path. Indeed, the *s-t* Connectivity Problem could also be called the *Maze-Solving* Problem. If we imagine $G$ as a maze with a room corresponding to each node, and a hallway corresponding to each edge that joins nodes (rooms) together,

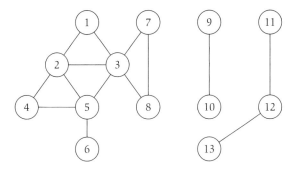

**Figure 3.2** In this graph, node 1 has paths to nodes 2 through 8, but not to nodes 9 through 13.

then the problem is to start in a room $s$ and find your way to another designated room $t$. How efficient an algorithm can we design for this task?

In this section, we describe two natural algorithms for this problem at a high level: breadth-first search (BFS) and depth-first search (DFS). In the next section we discuss how to implement each of these efficiently, building on a data structure for representing a graph as the input to an algorithm.

## Breadth-First Search

Perhaps the simplest algorithm for determining $s$-$t$ connectivity is *breadth-first search* (BFS), in which we explore outward from $s$ in all possible directions, adding nodes one "layer" at a time. Thus we start with $s$ and include all nodes that are joined by an edge to $s$—this is the first layer of the search. We then include all additional nodes that are joined by an edge to any node in the first layer—this is the second layer. We continue in this way until no new nodes are encountered.

In the example of Figure 3.2, starting with node 1 as $s$, the first layer of the search would consist of nodes 2 and 3, the second layer would consist of nodes 4, 5, 7, and 8, and the third layer would consist just of node 6. At this point the search would stop, since there are no further nodes that could be added (and in particular, note that nodes 9 through 13 are never reached by the search).

As this example reinforces, there is a natural physical interpretation to the algorithm. Essentially, we start at $s$ and "flood" the graph with an expanding wave that grows to visit all nodes that it can reach. The layer containing a node represents the point in time at which the node is reached.

We can define the layers $L_1, L_2, L_3, \ldots$ constructed by the BFS algorithm more precisely as follows.

- Layer $L_1$ consists of all nodes that are neighbors of $s$. (For notational reasons, we will sometimes use layer $L_0$ to denote the set consisting just of $s$.)

- Assuming that we have defined layers $L_1, \ldots, L_j$, then layer $L_{j+1}$ consists of all nodes that do not belong to an earlier layer and that have an edge to a node in layer $L_j$.

Recalling our definition of the distance between two nodes as the minimum number of edges on a path joining them, we see that layer $L_1$ is the set of all nodes at distance 1 from $s$, and more generally layer $L_j$ is the set of all nodes at distance exactly $j$ from $s$. A node fails to appear in any of the layers if and only if there is no path to it. Thus, BFS is not only determining the nodes that $s$ can reach, it is also computing shortest paths to them. We sum this up in the following fact.

**(3.3)**    *For each j $\geq$ 1, layer $L_j$ produced by BFS consists of all nodes at distance exactly j from s. There is a path from s to t if and only if t appears in some layer.*

A further property of breadth-first search is that it produces, in a very natural way, a tree $T$ rooted at $s$ on the set of nodes reachable from $s$. Specifically, for each such node $v$ (other than $s$), consider the moment when $v$ is first "discovered" by the BFS algorithm; this happens when some node $u$ in layer $L_j$ is being examined, and we find that it has an edge to the previously unseen node $v$. At this moment, we add the edge $(u, v)$ to the tree $T$—$u$ becomes the parent of $v$, representing the fact that $u$ is "responsible" for completing the path to $v$. We call the tree $T$ that is produced in this way a *breadth-first search tree*.

Figure 3.3 depicts the construction of a BFS tree rooted at node 1 for the graph in Figure 3.2. The solid edges are the edges of $T$; the dotted edges are edges of $G$ that do not belong to $T$. The execution of BFS that produces this tree can be described as follows.

(a) Starting from node 1, layer $L_1$ consists of the nodes $\{2, 3\}$.

(b) Layer $L_2$ is then grown by considering the nodes in layer $L_1$ in order (say, first 2, then 3). Thus we discover nodes 4 and 5 as soon as we look at 2, so 2 becomes their parent. When we consider node 2, we also discover an edge to 3, but this isn't added to the BFS tree, since we already know about node 3.

We first discover nodes 7 and 8 when we look at node 3. On the other hand, the edge from 3 to 5 is another edge of $G$ that does not end up in

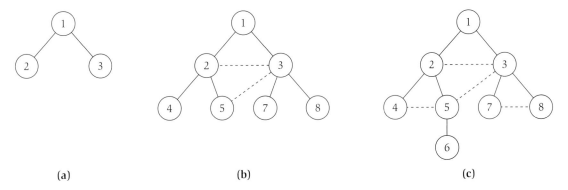

(a)     (b)     (c)

**Figure 3.3** The construction of a breadth-first search tree $T$ for the graph in Figure 3.2, with (a), (b), and (c) depicting the successive layers that are added. The solid edges are the edges of $T$; the dotted edges are in the connected component of $G$ containing node 1, but do not belong to $T$.

the BFS tree, because by the time we look at this edge out of node 3, we already know about node 5.

(c) We then consider the nodes in layer $L_2$ in order, but the only new node discovered when we look through $L_2$ is node 6, which is added to layer $L_3$. Note that the edges $(4, 5)$ and $(7, 8)$ don't get added to the BFS tree, because they don't result in the discovery of new nodes.

(d) No new nodes are discovered when node 6 is examined, so nothing is put in layer $L_4$, and the algorithm terminates. The full BFS tree is depicted in Figure 3.3(c).

We notice that as we ran BFS on this graph, the nontree edges all either connected nodes in the same layer, or connected nodes in adjacent layers. We now prove that this is a property of BFS trees in general.

**(3.4)** *Let $T$ be a breadth-first search tree, let $x$ and $y$ be nodes in $T$ belonging to layers $L_i$ and $L_j$ respectively, and let $(x, y)$ be an edge of $G$. Then $i$ and $j$ differ by at most 1.*

**Proof.** Suppose by way of contradiction that $i$ and $j$ differed by more than 1; in particular, suppose $i < j - 1$. Now consider the point in the BFS algorithm when the edges incident to $x$ were being examined. Since $x$ belongs to layer $L_i$, the only nodes discovered from $x$ belong to layers $L_{i+1}$ and earlier; hence, if $y$ is a neighbor of $x$, then it should have been discovered by this point at the latest and hence should belong to layer $L_{i+1}$ or earlier. ∎

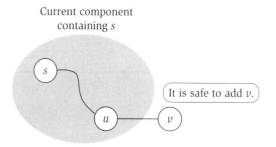

Figure 3.4 When growing the connected component containing $s$, we look for nodes like $v$ that have not yet been visited.

## Exploring a Connected Component

The set of nodes discovered by the BFS algorithm is precisely those reachable from the starting node $s$. We will refer to this set $R$ as the *connected component* of $G$ containing $s$; and once we know the connected component containing $s$, we can simply check whether $t$ belongs to it so as to answer the question of *s-t* connectivity.

Now, if one thinks about it, it's clear that BFS is just one possible way to produce this component. At a more general level, we can build the component $R$ by "exploring" $G$ in any order, starting from $s$. To start off, we define $R = \{s\}$. Then at any point in time, if we find an edge $(u, v)$ where $u \in R$ and $v \notin R$, we can add $v$ to $R$. Indeed, if there is a path $P$ from $s$ to $u$, then there is a path from $s$ to $v$ obtained by first following $P$ and then following the edge $(u, v)$. Figure 3.4 illustrates this basic step in growing the component $R$.

Suppose we continue growing the set $R$ until there are no more edges leading out of $R$; in other words, we run the following algorithm.

```
R will consist of nodes to which s has a path
Initially R = {s}
While there is an edge (u, v) where u ∈ R and v ∉ R
  Add v to R
Endwhile
```

Here is the key property of this algorithm.

**(3.5)** *The set R produced at the end of the algorithm is precisely the connected component of G containing s.*

**Proof.** We have already argued that for any node $v \in R$, there is a path from $s$ to $v$.

Now, consider a node $w \notin R$, and suppose by way of contradiction, that there is an $s$-$w$ path $P$ in $G$. Since $s \in R$ but $w \notin R$, there must be a first node $v$ on $P$ that does not belong to $R$; and this node $v$ is not equal to $s$. Thus there is a node $u$ immediately preceding $v$ on $P$, so $(u, v)$ is an edge. Moreover, since $v$ is the first node on $P$ that does not belong to $R$, we must have $u \in R$. It follows that $(u, v)$ is an edge where $u \in R$ and $v \notin R$; this contradicts the stopping rule for the algorithm. ■

For any node $t$ in the component $R$, observe that it is easy to recover the actual path from $s$ to $t$ along the lines of the argument above: we simply record, for each node $v$, the edge $(u, v)$ that was considered in the iteration in which $v$ was added to $R$. Then, by tracing these edges backward from $t$, we proceed through a sequence of nodes that were added in earlier and earlier iterations, eventually reaching $s$; this defines an $s$-$t$ path.

To conclude, we notice that the general algorithm we have defined to grow $R$ is underspecified, so how do we decide which edge to consider next? The BFS algorithm arises, in particular, as a particular way of ordering the nodes we visit—in successive layers, based on their distance from $s$. But there are other natural ways to grow the component, several of which lead to efficient algorithms for the connectivity problem while producing search patterns with different structures. We now go on to discuss a different one of these algorithms, *depth-first search*, and develop some of its basic properties.

## Depth-First Search

Another natural method to find the nodes reachable from $s$ is the approach you might take if the graph $G$ were truly a maze of interconnected rooms and you were walking around in it. You'd start from $s$ and try the first edge leading out of it, to a node $v$. You'd then follow the first edge leading out of $v$, and continue in this way until you reached a "dead end"—a node for which you had already explored all its neighbors. You'd then backtrack until you got to a node with an unexplored neighbor, and resume from there. We call this algorithm *depth-first search* (DFS), since it explores $G$ by going as deeply as possible and only retreating when necessary.

DFS is also a particular implementation of the generic component-growing algorithm that we introduced earlier. It is most easily described in recursive form: we can invoke DFS from any starting point but maintain global knowledge of which nodes have already been explored.

```
DFS(u):
  Mark u as "Explored" and add u to R
  For each edge (u,v) incident to u
    If v is not marked "Explored" then
      Recursively invoke DFS(v)
    Endif
  Endfor
```

To apply this to *s-t* connectivity, we simply declare all nodes initially to be not explored, and invoke *DFS(s)*.

There are some fundamental similarities and some fundamental differences between DFS and BFS. The similarities are based on the fact that they both build the connected component containing *s*, and we will see in the next section that they achieve qualitatively similar levels of efficiency.

While DFS ultimately visits exactly the same set of nodes as BFS, it typically does so in a very different order; it probes its way down long paths, potentially getting very far from *s*, before backing up to try nearer unexplored nodes. We can see a reflection of this difference in the fact that, like BFS, the DFS algorithm yields a natural rooted tree *T* on the component containing *s*, but the tree will generally have a very different structure. We make *s* the root of the tree *T*, and make *u* the parent of *v* when *u* is responsible for the discovery of *v*. That is, whenever *DFS(v)* is invoked directly during the call to *DFS(u)*, we add the edge $(u, v)$ to *T*. The resulting tree is called a *depth-first search tree* of the component *R*.

Figure 3.5 depicts the construction of a DFS tree rooted at node 1 for the graph in Figure 3.2. The solid edges are the edges of *T*; the dotted edges are edges of *G* that do not belong to *T*. The execution of DFS begins by building a path on nodes $1, 2, 3, 5, 4$. The execution reaches a dead end at 4, since there are no new nodes to find, and so it "backs up" to 5, finds node 6, backs up again to 3, and finds nodes 7 and 8. At this point there are no new nodes to find in the connected component, so all the pending recursive DFS calls terminate, one by one, and the execution comes to an end. The full DFS tree is depicted in Figure 3.5(g).

This example suggests the characteristic way in which DFS trees look different from BFS trees. Rather than having root-to-leaf paths that are as short as possible, they tend to be quite narrow and deep. However, as in the case of BFS, we can say something quite strong about the way in which nontree edges of *G* must be arranged relative to the edges of a DFS tree *T*: as in the figure, nontree edges can only connect ancestors of *T* to descendants.

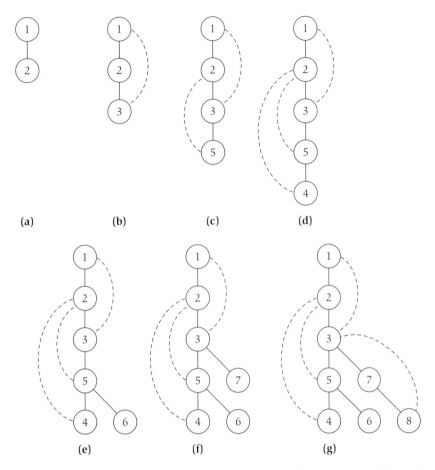

**Figure 3.5** The construction of a depth-first search tree $T$ for the graph in Figure 3.2, with (a) through (g) depicting the nodes as they are discovered in sequence. The solid edges are the edges of $T$; the dotted edges are edges of $G$ that do not belong to $T$.

To establish this, we first observe the following property of the DFS algorithm and the tree that it produces.

**(3.6)** *For a given recursive call DFS(u), all nodes that are marked "Explored" between the invocation and end of this recursive call are descendants of u in T.*

Using (3.6), we prove

**(3.7)** *Let T be a depth-first search tree, let x and y be nodes in T, and let (x, y) be an edge of G that is not an edge of T. Then one of x or y is an ancestor of the other.*

**Proof.** Suppose that $(x, y)$ is an edge of $G$ that is not an edge of $T$, and suppose without loss of generality that $x$ is reached first by the DFS algorithm. When the edge $(x, y)$ is examined during the execution of $DFS(x)$, it is not added to $T$ because $y$ is marked "Explored." Since $y$ was not marked "Explored" when $DFS(x)$ was first invoked, it is a node that was discovered between the invocation and end of the recursive call $DFS(x)$. It follows from (3.6) that $y$ is a descendant of $x$.  ∎

## The Set of All Connected Components

So far we have been talking about the connected component containing a particular node $s$. But there is a connected component associated with each node in the graph. What is the relationship between these components?

In fact, this relationship is highly structured and is expressed in the following claim.

**(3.8)** *For any two nodes $s$ and $t$ in a graph, their connected components are either identical or disjoint.*

This is a statement that is very clear intuitively, if one looks at a graph like the example in Figure 3.2. The graph is divided into multiple pieces with no edges between them; the largest piece is the connected component of nodes 1 through 8, the medium piece is the connected component of nodes 11, 12, and 13, and the smallest piece is the connected component of nodes 9 and 10. To prove the statement in general, we just need to show how to define these "pieces" precisely for an arbitrary graph.

**Proof.** Consider any two nodes $s$ and $t$ in a graph $G$ with the property that there is a path between $s$ and $t$. We claim that the connected components containing $s$ and $t$ are the same set. Indeed, for any node $v$ in the component of $s$, the node $v$ must also be reachable from $t$ by a path: we can just walk from $t$ to $s$, and then on from $s$ to $v$. The same reasoning works with the roles of $s$ and $t$ reversed, and so a node is in the component of one if and only if it is in the component of the other.

On the other hand, if there is no path between $s$ and $t$, then there cannot be a node $v$ that is in the connected component of each. For if there were such a node $v$, then we could walk from $s$ to $v$ and then on to $t$, constructing a path between $s$ and $t$. Thus, if there is no path between $s$ and $t$, then their connected components are disjoint.  ∎

This proof suggests a natural algorithm for producing all the connected components of a graph, by growing them one component at a time. We start with an arbitrary node $s$, and we use BFS (or DFS) to generate its connected component. We then find a node $v$ (if any) that was not visited by the search from $s$, and iterate, using BFS starting from $v$, to generate its connected component—which, by (3.8), will be disjoint from the component of $s$. We continue in this way until all nodes have been visited.

# 3.3 Implementing Graph Traversal Using Queues and Stacks

So far we have been discussing basic algorithmic primitives for working with graphs without mentioning any implementation details. Here we discuss how to use lists and arrays to represent graphs, and we discuss the trade-offs between the different representations. Then we use these data structures to implement the graph traversal algorithms breadth-first search (BFS) and depth-first search (DFS) efficiently. We will see that BFS and DFS differ essentially only in that one uses a *queue* and the other uses a *stack*, two simple data structures that we will describe later in this section.

## Representing Graphs

There are two basic ways to represent graphs: by an *adjacency matrix* and by an *adjacency list* representation. Throughout the book we will use the adjacency list representation. We start, however, by reviewing both of these representations and discussing the trade-offs between them.

A graph $G = (V, E)$ has two natural input parameters, the number of nodes $|V|$, and the number of edges $|E|$. We will use $n = |V|$ and $m = |E|$ to denote these, respectively. Running times will be given in terms of both of these two parameters. As usual, we will aim for polynomial running times, and lower-degree polynomials are better. However, with two parameters in the running time, the comparison is not always so clear. Is $O(m^2)$ or $O(n^3)$ a better running time? This depends on what the relation is between $n$ and $m$. With at most one edge between any pair of nodes, the number of edges $m$ can be at most $\binom{n}{2} \leq n^2$. On the other hand, in many applications the graphs of interest are connected, and by (3.1), connected graphs must have at least $m \geq n - 1$ edges. But these comparisons do not always tell us which of two running times (such as $m^2$ and $n^3$) are better, so we will tend to keep the running times in terms of both of these parameters. In this section we aim to implement the basic graph search algorithms in time $O(m + n)$. We will refer to this as *linear time*, since it takes $O(m + n)$ time simply to read the input. Note that when we work with connected graphs, a running time of $O(m + n)$ is the same as $O(m)$, since $m \geq n - 1$.

Consider a graph $G = (V, E)$ with $n$ nodes, and assume the set of nodes is $V = \{1, \ldots, n\}$. The simplest way to represent a graph is by an *adjacency matrix*, which is an $n \times n$ matrix $A$ where $A[u, v]$ is equal to 1 if the graph contains the edge $(u, v)$ and 0 otherwise. If the graph is undirected, the matrix $A$ is symmetric, with $A[u, v] = A[v, u]$ for all nodes $u, v \in V$. The adjacency matrix representation allows us to check in $O(1)$ time if a given edge $(u, v)$ is present in the graph. However, the representation has two basic disadvantages.

- The representation takes $\Theta(n^2)$ space. When the graph has many fewer edges than $n^2$, more compact representations are possible.
- Many graph algorithms need to examine all edges incident to a given node $v$. In the adjacency matrix representation, doing this involves considering all other nodes $w$, and checking the matrix entry $A[v, w]$ to see whether the edge $(v, w)$ is present—and this takes $\Theta(n)$ time. In the worst case, $v$ may have $\Theta(n)$ incident edges, in which case checking all these edges will take $\Theta(n)$ time regardless of the representation. But many graphs in practice have significantly fewer edges incident to most nodes, and so it would be good to be able to find all these incident edges more efficiently.

The representation of graphs used throughout the book is the adjacency list, which works better for sparse graphs—that is, those with many fewer than $n^2$ edges. In the *adjacency list* representation there is a record for each node $v$, containing a list of the nodes to which $v$ has edges. To be precise, we have an array Adj, where Adj[$v$] is a record containing a list of all nodes adjacent to node $v$. For an undirected graph $G = (V, E)$, each edge $e = (v, w) \in E$ occurs on two adjacency lists: node $w$ appears on the list for node $v$, and node $v$ appears on the list for node $w$.

Let's compare the adjacency matrix and adjacency list representations. First consider the space required by the representation. An adjacency matrix requires $O(n^2)$ space, since it uses an $n \times n$ matrix. In contrast, we claim that the adjacency list representation requires only $O(m + n)$ space. Here is why. First, we need an array of pointers of length $n$ to set up the lists in Adj, and then we need space for all the lists. Now, the lengths of these lists may differ from node to node, but we argued in the previous paragraph that overall, each edge $e = (v, w)$ appears in exactly two of the lists: the one for $v$ and the one for $w$. Thus the total length of all lists is $2m = O(m)$.

Another (essentially equivalent) way to justify this bound is as follows. We define the *degree* $n_v$ of a node $v$ to be the number of incident edges it has. The length of the list at Adj[$v$] is list is $n_v$, so the total length over all nodes is $O\left(\sum_{v \in V} n_v\right)$. Now, the sum of the degrees in a graph is a quantity that often comes up in the analysis of graph algorithms, so it is useful to work out what this sum is.

**(3.9)**   $\sum_{v \in V} n_v = 2m.$

**Proof.** Each edge $e = (v, w)$ contributes exactly twice to this sum: once in the quantity $n_v$ and once in the quantity $n_w$. Since the sum is the total of the contributions of each edge, it is $2m$.  ∎

We sum up the comparison between adjacency matrices and adjacency lists as follows.

**(3.10)** *The adjacency matrix representation of a graph requires $O(n^2)$ space, while the adjacency list representation requires only $O(m + n)$ space.*

Since we have already argued that $m \leq n^2$, the bound $O(m + n)$ is never worse than $O(n^2)$; and it is much better when the underlying graph is *sparse*, with $m$ much smaller than $n^2$.

Now we consider the ease of accessing the information stored in these two different representations. Recall that in an adjacency matrix we can check in $O(1)$ time if a particular edge $(u, v)$ is present in the graph. In the adjacency list representation, this can take time proportional to the degree $O(n_v)$: we have to follow the pointers on $u$'s adjacency list to see if edge $v$ occurs on the list. On the other hand, if the algorithm is currently looking at a node $u$, it can read the list of neighbors in constant time per neighbor.

In view of this, the adjacency list is a natural representation for exploring graphs. If the algorithm is currently looking at a node $u$, it can read this list of neighbors in constant time per neighbor; move to a neighbor $v$ once it encounters it on this list in constant time; and then be ready to read the list associated with node $v$. The list representation thus corresponds to a physical notion of "exploring" the graph, in which you learn the neighbors of a node $u$ once you arrive at $u$, and can read them off in constant time per neighbor.

## Queues and Stacks

Many algorithms have an inner step in which they need to process a set of elements, such the set of all edges adjacent to a node in a graph, the set of visited nodes in BFS and DFS, or the set of all free men in the Stable Matching algorithm. For this purpose, it is natural to maintain the set of elements to be considered in a linked list, as we have done for maintaining the set of free men in the Stable Matching algorithm.

One important issue that arises is the order in which to consider the elements in such a list. In the Stable Matching algorithm, the order in which we considered the free men did not affect the outcome, although this required a fairly subtle proof to verify. In many other algorithms, such as DFS and BFS, the order in which elements are considered is crucial.

Two of the simplest and most natural options are to maintain a set of elements as either a queue or a stack. A *queue* is a set from which we extract elements in *first-in, first-out* (FIFO) order: we select elements in the same order in which they were added. A *stack* is a set from which we extract elements in *last-in, first-out* (LIFO) order: each time we select an element, we choose the one that was added most recently. Both queues and stacks can be easily implemented via a doubly linked list. In both cases, we always select the first element on our list; the difference is in where we insert a new element. In a queue a new element is added to the end of the list as the last element, while in a stack a new element is placed in the first position on the list. Recall that a doubly linked list has explicit `First` and `Last` pointers to the beginning and end, respectively, so each of these insertions can be done in constant time.

Next we will discuss how to implement the search algorithms of the previous section in linear time. We will see that BFS can be thought of as using a queue to select which node to consider next, while DFS is effectively using a stack.

## Implementing Breadth-First Search

The adjacency list data structure is ideal for implementing breadth-first search. The algorithm examines the edges leaving a given node one by one. When we are scanning the edges leaving $u$ and come to an edge $(u, v)$, we need to know whether or not node $v$ has been previously discovered by the search. To make this simple, we maintain an array `Discovered` of length $n$ and set `Discovered`$[v] = true$ as soon as our search first sees $v$. The algorithm, as described in the previous section, constructs layers of nodes $L_1, L_2, \ldots$, where $L_i$ is the set of nodes at distance $i$ from the source $s$. To maintain the nodes in a layer $L_i$, we have a list $L[i]$ for each $i = 0, 1, 2, \ldots$.

```
BFS(s):
  Set Discovered[s] = true and Discovered[v] = false for all other v
  Initialize L[0] to consist of the single element s
  Set the layer counter i = 0
  Set the current BFS tree T = ∅
  While L[i] is not empty
    Initialize an empty list L[i + 1]
    For each node u ∈ L[i]
      Consider each edge (u, v) incident to u
      If Discovered[v] = false then
        Set Discovered[v] = true
        Add edge (u, v) to the tree T
```

```
        Add v to the list L[i + 1]
     Endif
  Endfor
  Increment the layer counter i by one
Endwhile
```

In this implementation it does not matter whether we manage each list $L[i]$ as a queue or a stack, since the algorithm is allowed to consider the nodes in a layer $L_i$ in any order.

**(3.11)** *The above implementation of the BFS algorithm runs in time $O(m + n)$ (i.e., linear in the input size), if the graph is given by the adjacency list representation.*

**Proof.** As a first step, it is easy to bound the running time of the algorithm by $O(n^2)$ (a weaker bound than our claimed $O(m + n)$). To see this, note that there are at most $n$ lists $L[i]$ that we need to set up, so this takes $O(n)$ time. Now we need to consider the nodes $u$ on these lists. Each node occurs on at most one list, so the For loop runs at most $n$ times over all iterations of the While loop. When we consider a node $u$, we need to look through all edges $(u, v)$ incident to $u$. There can be at most $n$ such edges, and we spend $O(1)$ time considering each edge. So the total time spent on one iteration of the For loop is at most $O(n)$. We've thus concluded that there are at most $n$ iterations of the For loop, and that each iteration takes at most $O(n)$ time, so the total time is at most $O(n^2)$.

To get the improved $O(m + n)$ time bound, we need to observe that the For loop processing a node $u$ can take less than $O(n)$ time if $u$ has only a few neighbors. As before, let $n_u$ denote the degree of node $u$, the number of edges incident to $u$. Now, the time spent in the For loop considering edges incident to node $u$ is $O(n_u)$, so the total over all nodes is $O(\sum_{u \in V} n_u)$. Recall from (3.9) that $\sum_{u \in V} n_u = 2m$, and so the total time spent considering edges over the whole algorithm is $O(m)$. We need $O(n)$ additional time to set up lists and manage the array Discovered. So the total time spent is $O(m + n)$ as claimed. ∎

We described the algorithm using up to $n$ separate lists $L[i]$ for each layer $L_i$. Instead of all these distinct lists, we can implement the algorithm using a single list $L$ that we maintain as a queue. In this way, the algorithm processes nodes in the order they are first discovered: each time a node is discovered, it is added to the end of the queue, and the algorithm always processes the edges out of the node that is currently first in the queue.

If we maintain the discovered nodes in this order, then all nodes in layer $L_i$ will appear in the queue ahead of all nodes in layer $L_{i+1}$, for $i = 0, 1, 2 \ldots$. Thus, all nodes in layer $L_i$ will be considered in a contiguous sequence, followed by all nodes in layer $L_{i+1}$, and so forth. Hence this implementation in terms of a single queue will produce the same result as the BFS implementation above.

## Implementing Depth-First Search

We now consider the depth-first search algorithm. In the previous section we presented DFS as a recursive procedure, which is a natural way to specify it. However, it can also be viewed as almost identical to BFS, with the difference that it maintains the nodes to be processed in a stack, rather than in a queue. Essentially, the recursive structure of DFS can be viewed as pushing nodes onto a stack for later processing, while moving on to more freshly discovered nodes. We now show how to implement DFS by maintaining this stack of nodes to be processed explicitly.

In both BFS and DFS, there is a distinction between the act of *discovering* a node $v$—the first time it is seen, when the algorithm finds an edge leading to $v$—and the act of *exploring* a node $v$, when all the incident edges to $v$ are scanned, resulting in the potential discovery of further nodes. The difference between BFS and DFS lies in the way in which discovery and exploration are interleaved.

In BFS, once we started to explore a node $u$ in layer $L_i$, we added all its newly discovered neighbors to the next layer $L_{i+1}$, and we deferred actually exploring these neighbors until we got to the processing of layer $L_{i+1}$. In contrast, DFS is more impulsive: when it explores a node $u$, it scans the neighbors of $u$ until it finds the first not-yet-explored node $v$ (if any), and then it immediately shifts attention to exploring $v$.

To implement the exploration strategy of DFS, we first add *all* of the nodes adjacent to $u$ to our list of nodes to be considered, but after doing this we proceed to explore a new neighbor $v$ of $u$. As we explore $v$, in turn, we add the neighbors of $v$ to the list we're maintaining, but we do so in stack order, so that these neighbors will be explored before we return to explore the other neighbors of $u$. We only come back to other nodes adjacent to $u$ when there are no other nodes left.

In addition, we use an array Explored analogous to the Discovered array we used for BFS. The difference is that we only set Explored[$v$] to be true when we scan $v$'s incident edges (when the DFS search is at $v$), while BFS sets Discovered[$v$] to true as soon as $v$ is first discovered. The implementation in full looks as follows.

```
DFS(s):
  Initialize S to be a stack with one element s
  While S is not empty
    Take a node u from S
    If Explored[u] = false then
        Set Explored[u] = true
        For each edge (u, v) incident to u
            Add v to the stack S
        Endfor
    Endif
  Endwhile
```

There is one final wrinkle to mention. Depth-first search is underspecified, since the adjacency list of a node being explored can be processed in any order. Note that the above algorithm, because it pushes all adjacent nodes onto the stack before considering any of them, in fact processes each adjacency list in the reverse order relative to the recursive version of DFS in the previous section.

**(3.12)** *The above algorithm implements DFS, in the sense that it visits the nodes in exactly the same order as the recursive DFS procedure in the previous section (except that each adjacency list is processed in reverse order).*

If we want the algorithm to also find the DFS tree, we need to have each node $u$ on the stack $S$ maintain the node that "caused" $u$ to get added to the stack. This can be easily done by using an array parent and setting parent$[v] = u$ when we add node $v$ to the stack due to edge $(u, v)$. When we mark a node $u \neq s$ as Explored, we also can add the edge $(u, \text{parent}[u])$ to the tree $T$. Note that a node $v$ may be in the stack $S$ multiple times, as it can be adjacent to multiple nodes $u$ that we explore, and each such node adds a copy of $v$ to the stack $S$. However, we will only use one of these copies to explore node $v$, the copy that we add last. As a result, it suffices to maintain one value parent$[v]$ for each node $v$ by simply overwriting the value parent$[v]$ every time we add a new copy of $v$ to the stack $S$.

The main step in the algorithm is to add and delete nodes to and from the stack $S$, which takes $O(1)$ time. Thus, to bound the running time, we need to bound the number of these operations. To count the number of stack operations, it suffices to count the number of nodes added to $S$, as each node needs to be added once for every time it can be deleted from $S$.

How many elements ever get added to $S$? As before, let $n_v$ denote the degree of node $v$. Node $v$ will be added to the stack $S$ every time one of its $n_v$ adjacent nodes is explored, so the total number of nodes added to $S$ is at most $\sum_u n_v = 2m$. This proves the desired $O(m + n)$ bound on the running time of DFS.

> **(3.13)**    *The above implementation of the DFS algorithm runs in time $O(m + n)$ (i.e., linear in the input size), if the graph is given by the adjacency list representation.*

### Finding the Set of All Connected Components

In the previous section we talked about how one can use BFS (or DFS) to find all connected components of a graph. We start with an arbitrary node $s$, and we use BFS (or DFS) to generate its connected component. We then find a node $v$ (if any) that was not visited by the search from $s$ and iterate, using BFS (or DFS) starting from $v$ to generate its connected component—which, by (3.8), will be disjoint from the component of $s$. We continue in this way until all nodes have been visited.

Although we earlier expressed the running time of BFS and DFS as $O(m + n)$, where $m$ and $n$ are the total number of edges and nodes in the graph, both BFS and DFS in fact spend work only on edges and nodes in the connected component containing the starting node. (They never see any of the other nodes or edges.) Thus the above algorithm, although it may run BFS or DFS a number of times, only spends a constant amount of work on a given edge or node in the iteration when the connected component it belongs to is under consideration. Hence the overall running time of this algorithm is still $O(m + n)$.

## 3.4  Testing Bipartiteness: An Application of Breadth-First Search

Recall the definition of a bipartite graph: it is one where the node set $V$ can be partitioned into sets $X$ and $Y$ in such a way that every edge has one end in $X$ and the other end in $Y$. To make the discussion a little smoother, we can imagine that the nodes in the set $X$ are colored red, and the nodes in the set $Y$ are colored blue. With this imagery, we can say a graph is bipartite if it is possible to color its nodes red and blue so that every edge has one red end and one blue end.

### The Problem

In the earlier chapters, we saw examples of bipartite graphs. Here we start by asking: What are some natural examples of a nonbipartite graph, one where no such partition of $V$ is possible?

Clearly a triangle is not bipartite, since we can color one node red, another one blue, and then we can't do anything with the third node. More generally, consider a cycle $C$ of odd length, with nodes numbered $1, 2, 3, \ldots, 2k, 2k+1$. If we color node 1 red, then we must color node 2 blue, and then we must color node 3 red, and so on—coloring odd-numbered nodes red and even-numbered nodes blue. But then we must color node $2k+1$ red, and it has an edge to node 1, which is also red. This demonstrates that there's no way to partition $C$ into red and blue nodes as required. More generally, if a graph $G$ simply *contains* an odd cycle, then we can apply the same argument; thus we have established the following.

**(3.14)**   *If a graph G is bipartite, then it cannot contain an odd cycle.*

It is easy to recognize that a graph is bipartite when appropriate sets $X$ and $Y$ (i.e., red and blue nodes) have actually been identified for us; and in many settings where bipartite graphs arise, this is natural. But suppose we encounter a graph $G$ with no annotation provided for us, and we'd like to determine for ourselves whether it is bipartite—that is, whether there exists a partition into red and blue nodes, as required. How difficult is this? We see from (3.14) that an odd cycle is one simple "obstacle" to a graph's being bipartite. Are there other, more complex obstacles to bipartitness?

### Designing the Algorithm

In fact, there is a very simple procedure to test for bipartiteness, and its analysis can be used to show that odd cycles are the *only* obstacle. First we assume the graph $G$ is connected, since otherwise we can first compute its connected components and analyze each of them separately. Next we pick any node $s \in V$ and color it red; there is no loss in doing this, since $s$ must receive some color. It follows that all the neighbors of $s$ must be colored blue, so we do this. It then follows that all the neighbors of *these* nodes must be colored red, their neighbors must be colored blue, and so on, until the whole graph is colored. At this point, either we have a valid red/blue coloring of $G$, in which every edge has ends of opposite colors, or there is some edge with ends of the same color. In this latter case, it seems clear that there's nothing we could have done: $G$ simply is not bipartite. We now want to argue this point precisely and also work out an efficient way to perform the coloring.

The first thing to notice is that the coloring procedure we have just described is essentially identical to the description of BFS: we move outward from $s$, coloring nodes as soon as we first encounter them. Indeed, another way to describe the coloring algorithm is as follows: we perform BFS, coloring

$s$ red, all of layer $L_1$ blue, all of layer $L_2$ red, and so on, coloring odd-numbered layers blue and even-numbered layers red.

We can implement this on top of BFS, by simply taking the implementation of BFS and adding an extra array Color over the nodes. Whenever we get to a step in BFS where we are adding a node $v$ to a list $L[i+1]$, we assign Color$[v]$ = red if $i+1$ is an even number, and Color$[v]$ = blue if $i+1$ is an odd number. At the end of this procedure, we simply scan all the edges and determine whether there is any edge for which both ends received the same color. Thus, the total running time for the coloring algorithm is $O(m+n)$, just as it is for BFS.

## Analyzing the Algorithm

We now prove a claim that shows this algorithm correctly determines whether $G$ is bipartite, and it also shows that we can find an odd cycle in $G$ whenever it is not bipartite.

**(3.15)**    *Let $G$ be a connected graph, and let $L_1, L_2, \ldots$ be the layers produced by BFS starting at node $s$. Then exactly one of the following two things must hold.*

(i)    *There is no edge of $G$ joining two nodes of the same layer. In this case $G$ is a bipartite graph in which the nodes in even-numbered layers can be colored red, and the nodes in odd-numbered layers can be colored blue.*

(ii)    *There is an edge of $G$ joining two nodes of the same layer. In this case, $G$ contains an odd-length cycle, and so it cannot be bipartite.*

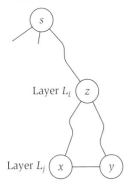

The cycle through $x, y$, and $z$ has odd length.

Layer $L_i$   $z$

Layer $L_j$   $x$ —— $y$

**Figure 3.6** If two nodes $x$ and $y$ in the same layer are joined by an edge, then the cycle through $x, y$, and their lowest common ancestor $z$ has odd length, demonstrating that the graph cannot be bipartite.

**Proof.**  First consider case (i), where we suppose that there is no edge joining two nodes of the same layer. By (3.4), we know that every edge of $G$ joins nodes either in the same layer or in adjacent layers. Our assumption for case (i) is precisely that the first of these two alternatives never happens, so this means that *every* edge joins two nodes in adjacent layers. But our coloring procedure gives nodes in adjacent layers the opposite colors, and so every edge has ends with opposite colors. Thus this coloring establishes that $G$ is bipartite.

Now suppose we are in case (ii); why must $G$ contain an odd cycle? We are told that $G$ contains an edge joining two nodes of the same layer. Suppose this is the edge $e = (x, y)$, with $x, y \in L_j$. Also, for notational reasons, recall that $L_0$ ("layer 0") is the set consisting of just $s$. Now consider the BFS tree $T$ produced by our algorithm, and let $z$ be the node whose layer number is as large as possible, subject to the condition that $z$ is an ancestor of both $x$ and $y$ in $T$; for obvious reasons, we can call $z$ the *lowest common ancestor* of $x$ and $y$. Suppose $z \in L_i$, where $i < j$. We now have the situation pictured in Figure 3.6. We consider the cycle $C$ defined by following the $z$-$x$ path in $T$, then the edge $e$, and then the $y$-$z$ path in $T$. The length of this cycle is $(j - i) + 1 + (j - i)$, adding the length of its three parts separately; this is equal to $2(j - i) + 1$, which is an odd number. ∎

## 3.5 Connectivity in Directed Graphs

Thus far, we have been looking at problems on undirected graphs; we now consider the extent to which these ideas carry over to the case of directed graphs.

Recall that in a directed graph, the edge $(u, v)$ has a direction: it goes from $u$ to $v$. In this way, the relationship between $u$ and $v$ is asymmetric, and this has qualitative effects on the structure of the resulting graph. In Section 3.1, for example, we discussed the World Wide Web as an instance of a large, complex directed graph whose nodes are pages and whose edges are hyperlinks. The act of browsing the Web is based on following a sequence of edges in this directed graph; and the directionality is crucial, since it's not generally possible to browse "backwards" by following hyperlinks in the reverse direction.

At the same time, a number of basic definitions and algorithms have natural analogues in the directed case. This includes the adjacency list representation and graph search algorithms such as BFS and DFS. We now discuss these in turn.

### Representing Directed Graphs

In order to represent a directed graph for purposes of designing algorithms, we use a version of the adjacency list representation that we employed for undirected graphs. Now, instead of each node having a single list of neighbors, each node has two lists associated with it: one list consists of nodes *to which* it has edges, and a second list consists of nodes *from which* it has edges. Thus an algorithm that is currently looking at a node $u$ can read off the nodes reachable by going one step forward on a directed edge, as well as the nodes that would be reachable if one went one step in the reverse direction on an edge from $u$.

### The Graph Search Algorithms

Breadth-first search and depth-first search are almost the same in directed graphs as they are in undirected graphs. We will focus here on BFS. We start at a node $s$, define a first layer of nodes to consist of all those to which $s$ has an edge, define a second layer to consist of all additional nodes to which these first-layer nodes have an edge, and so forth. In this way, we discover nodes layer by layer as they are reached in this outward search from $s$, and the nodes in layer $j$ are precisely those for which the shortest path *from* $s$ has exactly $j$ edges. As in the undirected case, this algorithm performs at most constant work for each node and edge, resulting in a running time of $O(m + n)$.

It is important to understand what this directed version of BFS is computing. In directed graphs, it is possible for a node $s$ to have a path to a node $t$ even though $t$ has no path to $s$; and what directed BFS is computing is the set of all nodes $t$ with the property that $s$ has a path to $t$. Such nodes may or may not have paths back to $s$.

There is a natural analogue of depth-first search as well, which also runs in linear time and computes the same set of nodes. It is again a recursive procedure that tries to explore as deeply as possible, in this case only following edges according to their inherent direction. Thus, when DFS is at a node $u$, it recursively launches a depth-first search, in order, for each node to which $u$ has an edge.

Suppose that, for a given node $s$, we wanted the set of nodes with paths to $s$, rather than the set of nodes to which $s$ has paths. An easy way to do this would be to define a new directed graph, $G^{rev}$, that we obtain from $G$ simply by reversing the direction of every edge. We could then run BFS or DFS in $G^{rev}$; a node has a path *from* $s$ in $G^{rev}$ if and only if it has a path *to* $s$ in $G$.

## Strong Connectivity

Recall that a directed graph is *strongly connected* if, for every two nodes $u$ and $v$, there is a path from $u$ to $v$ and a path from $v$ to $u$. It's worth also formulating some terminology for the property at the heart of this definition; let's say that two nodes $u$ and $v$ in a directed graph are *mutually reachable* if there is a path from $u$ to $v$ and also a path from $v$ to $u$. (So a graph is strongly connected if every pair of nodes is mutually reachable.)

Mutual reachability has a number of nice properties, many of them stemming from the following simple fact.

**(3.16)**   *If $u$ and $v$ are mutually reachable, and $v$ and $w$ are mutually reachable, then $u$ and $w$ are mutually reachable.*

**Proof.** To construct a path from $u$ to $w$, we first go from $u$ to $v$ (along the path guaranteed by the mutual reachability of $u$ and $v$), and then on from $v$ to $w$ (along the path guaranteed by the mutual reachability of $v$ and $w$). To construct a path from $w$ to $u$, we just reverse this reasoning: we first go from $w$ to $v$ (along the path guaranteed by the mutual reachability of $v$ and $w$), and then on from $v$ to $u$ (along the path guaranteed by the mutual reachability of $u$ and $v$).   ■

There is a simple linear-time algorithm to test if a directed graph is strongly connected, implicitly based on (3.16). We pick any node $s$ and run BFS in $G$ starting from $s$. We then also run BFS starting from $s$ in $G^{rev}$. Now, if one of these two searches fails to reach every node, then clearly $G$ is not strongly connected. But suppose we find that $s$ has a path to every node, and that every node has a path to $s$. Then $s$ and $v$ are mutually reachable for every $v$, and so it follows that *every* two nodes $u$ and $v$ are mutually reachable: $s$ and $u$ are mutually reachable, and $s$ and $v$ are mutually reachable, so by (3.16) we also have that $u$ and $v$ are mutually reachable.

By analogy with connected components in an undirected graph, we can define the *strong component* containing a node $s$ in a directed graph to be the set of all $v$ such that $s$ and $v$ are mutually reachable. If one thinks about it, the algorithm in the previous paragraph is really computing the strong component containing $s$: we run BFS starting from $s$ both in $G$ and in $G^{rev}$; the set of nodes reached by *both* searches is the set of nodes with paths to *and* from $s$, and hence this set is the strong component containing $s$.

There are further similarities between the notion of connected components in undirected graphs and strong components in directed graphs. Recall that connected components naturally partitioned the graph, since any two were either identical or disjoint. Strong components have this property as well, and for essentially the same reason, based on (3.16).

**(3.17)** *For any two nodes s and t in a directed graph, their strong components are either identical or disjoint.*

**Proof.** Consider any two nodes $s$ and $t$ that are mutually reachable; we claim that the strong components containing $s$ and $t$ are identical. Indeed, for any node $v$, if $s$ and $v$ are mutually reachable, then by (3.16), $t$ and $v$ are mutually reachable as well. Similarly, if $t$ and $v$ are mutually reachable, then again by (3.16), $s$ and $v$ are mutually reachable.

On the other hand, if $s$ and $t$ are not mutually reachable, then there cannot be a node $v$ that is in the strong component of each. For if there were such a node $v$, then $s$ and $v$ would be mutually reachable, and $v$ and $t$ would be mutually reachable, so from (3.16) it would follow that $s$ and $t$ were mutually reachable. ∎

In fact, although we will not discuss the details of this here, with more work it is possible to compute the strong components for all nodes in a total time of $O(m + n)$.

# 3.6 Directed Acyclic Graphs and Topological Ordering

If an undirected graph has no cycles, then it has an extremely simple structure: each of its connected components is a tree. But it is possible for a directed graph to have no (directed) cycles and still have a very rich structure. For example, such graphs can have a large number of edges: if we start with the node

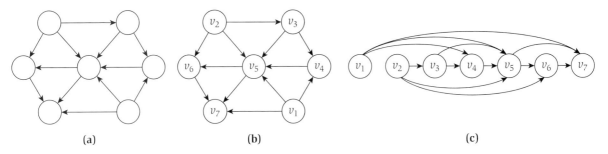

In a topological ordering, all edges point from left to right.

(a)                    (b)                    (c)

**Figure 3.7** (a) A directed acyclic graph. (b) The same DAG with a topological ordering, specified by the labels on each node. (c) A different drawing of the same DAG, arranged so as to emphasize the topological ordering.

set $\{1, 2, \ldots, n\}$ and include an edge $(i, j)$ whenever $i < j$, then the resulting directed graph has $\binom{n}{2}$ edges but no cycles.

If a directed graph has no cycles, we call it—naturally enough—a *directed acyclic graph*, or a *DAG* for short. (The term *DAG* is typically pronounced as a word, not spelled out as an acronym.) In Figure 3.7(a) we see an example of a DAG, although it may take some checking to convince oneself that it really has no directed cycles.

### The Problem

DAGs are a very common structure in computer science, because many kinds of dependency networks of the type we discussed in Section 3.1 are acyclic. Thus DAGs can be used to encode *precedence relations* or *dependencies* in a natural way. Suppose we have a set of tasks labeled $\{1, 2, \ldots, n\}$ that need to be performed, and there are dependencies among them stipulating, for certain pairs $i$ and $j$, that $i$ must be performed before $j$. For example, the tasks may be courses, with prerequisite requirements stating that certain courses must be taken before others. Or the tasks may correspond to a pipeline of computing jobs, with assertions that the output of job $i$ is used in determining the input to job $j$, and hence job $i$ must be done before job $j$.

We can represent such an interdependent set of tasks by introducing a node for each task, and a directed edge $(i, j)$ whenever $i$ must be done before $j$. If the precedence relation is to be at all meaningful, the resulting graph $G$ must be a DAG. Indeed, if it contained a cycle $C$, there would be no way to do any of the tasks in $C$: since each task in $C$ cannot begin until some other one completes, no task in $C$ could ever be done, since none could be done first.

Let's continue a little further with this picture of DAGs as precedence relations. Given a set of tasks with dependencies, it would be natural to seek a valid order in which the tasks could be performed, so that all dependencies are respected. Specifically, for a directed graph $G$, we say that a *topological ordering* of $G$ is an ordering of its nodes as $v_1, v_2, \ldots, v_n$ so that for every edge $(v_i, v_j)$, we have $i < j$. In other words, all edges point "forward" in the ordering. A topological ordering on tasks provides an order in which they can be safely performed; when we come to the task $v_j$, all the tasks that are required to precede it have already been done. In Figure 3.7(b) we've labeled the nodes of the DAG from part (a) with a topological ordering; note that each edge indeed goes from a lower-indexed node to a higher-indexed node.

In fact, we can view a topological ordering of $G$ as providing an immediate "proof" that $G$ has no cycles, via the following.

**(3.18)**  *If $G$ has a topological ordering, then $G$ is a DAG.*

**Proof.** Suppose, by way of contradiction, that $G$ has a topological ordering $v_1, v_2, \ldots, v_n$, and also has a cycle $C$. Let $v_i$ be the lowest-indexed node on $C$, and let $v_j$ be the node on $C$ just before $v_i$—thus $(v_j, v_i)$ is an edge. But by our choice of $i$, we have $j > i$, which contradicts the assumption that $v_1, v_2, \ldots, v_n$ was a topological ordering.  ■

The proof of acyclicity that a topological ordering provides can be very useful, even visually. In Figure 3.7(c), we have drawn the same graph as in (a) and (b), but with the nodes laid out in the topological ordering. It is immediately clear that the graph in (c) is a DAG since each edge goes from left to right.

*Computing a Topological Ordering*   The main question we consider here is the converse of (3.18): Does every DAG have a topological ordering, and if so, how do we find one efficiently? A method to do this for every DAG would be very useful: it would show that for any precedence relation on a set of tasks without cycles, there is an efficiently computable order in which to perform the tasks.

## Designing and Analyzing the Algorithm

In fact, the converse of (3.18) does hold, and we establish this via an efficient algorithm to compute a topological ordering. The key to this lies in finding a way to get started: which node do we put at the beginning of the topological ordering? Such a node $v_1$ would need to have no incoming edges, since any such incoming edge would violate the defining property of the topological ordering, that all edges point forward. Thus, we need to prove the following fact.

**(3.19)**    *In every DAG G, there is a node v with no incoming edges.*

**Proof.** Let $G$ be a directed graph in which every node has at least one incoming edge. We show how to find a cycle in $G$; this will prove the claim. We pick any node $v$, and begin following edges backward from $v$: since $v$ has at least one incoming edge $(u, v)$, we can walk backward to $u$; then, since $u$ has at least one incoming edge $(x, u)$, we can walk backward to $x$; and so on. We can continue this process indefinitely, since every node we encounter has an incoming edge. But after $n + 1$ steps, we will have visited some node $w$ twice. If we let $C$ denote the sequence of nodes encountered between successive visits to $w$, then clearly $C$ forms a cycle.  ∎

In fact, the existence of such a node $v$ is all we need to produce a topological ordering of $G$ by induction. Specifically, let us claim by induction that every DAG has a topological ordering. This is clearly true for DAGs on one or two nodes. Now suppose it is true for DAGs with up to some number of nodes $n$. Then, given a DAG $G$ on $n + 1$ nodes, we find a node $v$ with no incoming edges, as guaranteed by (3.19). We place $v$ first in the topological ordering; this is safe, since all edges out of $v$ will point forward. Now $G - \{v\}$ is a DAG, since deleting $v$ cannot create any cycles that weren't there previously. Also, $G - \{v\}$ has $n$ nodes, so we can apply the induction hypothesis to obtain a topological ordering of $G - \{v\}$. We append the nodes of $G - \{v\}$ in this order after $v$; this is an ordering of $G$ in which all edges point forward, and hence it is a topological ordering.

Thus we have proved the desired converse of (3.18).

**(3.20)**    *If G is a DAG, then G has a topological ordering.*

The inductive proof contains the following algorithm to compute a topological ordering of $G$.

```
To compute a topological ordering of G:
Find a node v with no incoming edges and order it first
Delete v from G
Recursively compute a topological ordering of G-{v}
  and append this order after v
```

In Figure 3.8 we show the sequence of node deletions that occurs when this algorithm is applied to the graph in Figure 3.7. The shaded nodes in each iteration are those with no incoming edges; the crucial point, which is what

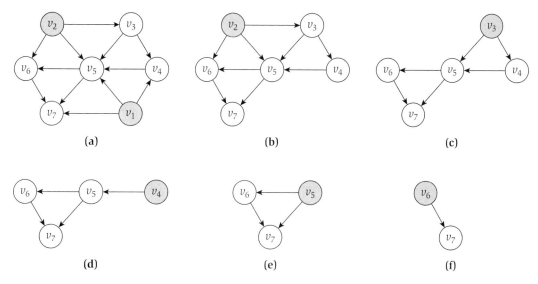

**Figure 3.8** Starting from the graph in Figure 3.7, nodes are deleted one by one so as to be added to a topological ordering. The shaded nodes are those with no incoming edges; note that there is always at least one such edge at every stage of the algorithm's execution.

(3.19) guarantees, is that when we apply this algorithm to a DAG, there will always be at least one such node available to delete.

To bound the running time of this algorithm, we note that identifying a node $v$ with no incoming edges, and deleting it from $G$, can be done in $O(n)$ time. Since the algorithm runs for $n$ iterations, the total running time is $O(n^2)$.

This is not a bad running time; and if $G$ is very dense, containing $\Theta(n^2)$ edges, then it is linear in the size of the input. But we may well want something better when the number of edges $m$ is much less than $n^2$. In such a case, a running time of $O(m + n)$ could be a significant improvement over $\Theta(n^2)$.

In fact, we can achieve a running time of $O(m + n)$ using the same high-level algorithm—iteratively deleting nodes with no incoming edges. We simply have to be more efficient in finding these nodes, and we do this as follows.

We declare a node to be "active" if it has not yet been deleted by the algorithm, and we explicitly maintain two things:

(a) for each node $w$, the number of incoming edges that $w$ has from active nodes; and

(b) the set $S$ of all active nodes in $G$ that have no incoming edges from other active nodes.

At the start, all nodes are active, so we can initialize (a) and (b) with a single pass through the nodes and edges. Then, each iteration consists of selecting a node $v$ from the set $S$ and deleting it. After deleting $v$, we go through all nodes $w$ to which $v$ had an edge, and subtract one from the number of active incoming edges that we are maintaining for $w$. If this causes the number of active incoming edges to $w$ to drop to zero, then we add $w$ to the set $S$. Proceeding in this way, we keep track of nodes that are eligible for deletion at all times, while spending constant work per edge over the course of the whole algorithm.

## Solved Exercises

### Solved Exercise 1

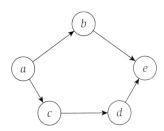

Figure 3.9 How many topological orderings does this graph have?

Consider the directed acyclic graph $G$ in Figure 3.9. How many topological orderings does it have?

**Solution**    Recall that a topological ordering of $G$ is an ordering of the nodes as $v_1, v_2, \ldots, v_n$ so that all edges point "forward": for every edge $(v_i, v_j)$, we have $i < j$.

So one way to answer this question would be to write down all $5 \cdot 4 \cdot 3 \cdot 2 \cdot 1 = 120$ possible orderings and check whether each is a topological ordering. But this would take a while.

Instead, we think about this as follows. As we saw in the text (or reasoning directly from the definition), the first node in a topological ordering must be one that has no edge coming into it. Analogously, the last node must be one that has no edge leaving it. Thus, in every topological ordering of $G$, the node $a$ must come first and the node $e$ must come last.

Now we have to figure how the nodes $b$, $c$, and $d$ can be arranged in the middle of the ordering. The edge $(c, d)$ enforces the requirement that $c$ must come before $d$; but $b$ can be placed anywhere relative to these two: before both, between $c$ and $d$, or after both. This exhausts all the possibilities, and so we conclude that there are three possible topological orderings:

$$a, b, c, d, e$$

$$a, c, b, d, e$$

$$a, c, d, b, e$$

### Solved Exercise 2

Some friends of yours are working on techniques for coordinating groups of mobile robots. Each robot has a radio transmitter that it uses to communicate with a base station, and your friends find that if the robots get too close to one another, then there are problems with interference among the transmitters. So a natural problem arises: how to plan the motion of the robots in such a way that each robot gets to its intended destination, but in the process the robots don't come close enough together to cause interference problems.

We can model this problem abstractly as follows. Suppose that we have an undirected graph $G = (V, E)$, representing the floor plan of a building, and there are two robots initially located at nodes $a$ and $b$ in the graph. The robot at node $a$ wants to travel to node $c$ along a path in $G$, and the robot at node $b$ wants to travel to node $d$. This is accomplished by means of a *schedule*: at each time step, the schedule specifies that one of the robots moves across a single edge, from one node to a neighboring node; at the end of the schedule, the robot from node $a$ should be sitting on $c$, and the robot from $b$ should be sitting on $d$.

A schedule is *interference-free* if there is no point at which the two robots occupy nodes that are at a distance $\leq r$ from one another in the graph, for a given parameter $r$. We'll assume that the two starting nodes $a$ and $b$ are at a distance greater than $r$, and so are the two ending nodes $c$ and $d$.

Give a polynomial-time algorithm that decides whether there exists an interference-free schedule by which each robot can get to its destination.

***Solution*** This is a problem of the following general flavor. We have a set of possible *configurations* for the robots, where we define a configuration to be a choice of location for each one. We are trying to get from a given starting configuration $(a, b)$ to a given ending configuration $(c, d)$, subject to constraints on how we can move between configurations (we can only change one robot's location to a neighboring node), and also subject to constraints on which configurations are "legal."

This problem can be tricky to think about if we view things at the level of the underlying graph $G$: for a given configuration of the robots—that is, the current location of each one—it's not clear what rule we should be using to decide how to move one of the robots next. So instead we apply an idea that can be very useful for situations in which we're trying to perform this type of search. We observe that our problem looks a lot like a path-finding problem, not in the original graph $G$ but in the space of all possible configurations.

Let us define the following (larger) graph $H$. The node set of $H$ is the set of all possible configurations of the robots; that is, $H$ consists of all possible pairs of nodes in $G$. We join two nodes of $H$ by an edge if they represent configurations that could be consecutive in a schedule; that is, $(u, v)$ and $(u', v')$ will be joined by an edge in $H$ if one of the pairs $u, u'$ or $v, v'$ are equal, and the other pair corresponds to an edge in $G$.

We can already observe that paths in $H$ from $(a, b)$ to $(c, d)$ correspond to schedules for the robots: such a path consists precisely of a sequence of configurations in which, at each step, one robot crosses a single edge in $G$. However, we have not yet encoded the notion that the schedule should be interference-free.

To do this, we simply delete from $H$ all nodes that correspond to configurations in which there would be interference. Thus we define $H'$ to be the graph obtained from $H$ by deleting all nodes $(u, v)$ for which the distance between $u$ and $v$ in $G$ is at most $r$.

The full algorithm is then as follows. We construct the graph $H'$, and then run the connectivity algorithm from the text to determine whether there is a path from $(a, b)$ to $(c, d)$. The correctness of the algorithm follows from the fact that paths in $H'$ correspond to schedules, and the nodes in $H'$ correspond precisely to the configurations in which there is no interference.

Finally, we need to consider the running time. Let $n$ denote the number of nodes in $G$, and $m$ denote the number of edges in $G$. We'll analyze the running time by doing three things: (1) bounding the size of $H'$ (which will in general be larger than $G$), (2) bounding the time it takes to construct $H'$, and (3) bounding the time it takes to search for a path from $(a, b)$ to $(c, d)$ in $H$.

1. First, then, let's consider the size of $H'$. $H'$ has at most $n^2$ nodes, since its nodes correspond to pairs of nodes in $G$. Now, how many edges does $H'$ have? A node $(u, v)$ will have edges to $(u', v)$ for each neighbor $u'$ of $u$ in $G$, and to $(u, v')$ for each neighbor $v'$ of $v$ in $G$. A simple upper bound says that there can be at most $n$ choices for $(u', v)$, and at most $n$ choices for $(u, v')$, so there are at most $2n$ edges incident to each node of $H'$. Summing over the (at most) $n^2$ nodes of $H'$, we have $O(n^3)$ edges.

   (We can actually give a better bound of $O(mn)$ on the number of edges in $H'$, by using the bound (3.9) we proved in Section 3.3 on the sum of the degrees in a graph. We'll leave this as a further exercise.)

2. Now we bound the time needed to construct $H'$. We first build $H$ by enumerating all pairs of nodes in $G$ in time $O(n^2)$, and constructing edges using the definition above in time $O(n)$ per node, for a total of $O(n^3)$. Now we need to figure out which nodes to delete from $H$ so as to produce $H'$. We can do this as follows. For each node $u$ in $G$, we run a breadth-first search from $u$ and identify all nodes $v$ within distance $r$ of $u$. We list all these pairs $(u, v)$ and delete them from $H$. Each breadth-first search in $G$ takes time $O(m + n)$, and we're doing one from each node, so the total time for this part is $O(mn + n^2)$.

3. Now we have $H'$, and so we just need to decide whether there is a path from $(a, b)$ to $(c, d)$. This can be done using the connectivity algorithm from the text in time that is linear in the number of nodes and edges of $H'$. Since $H'$ has $O(n^2)$ nodes and $O(n^3)$ edges, this final step takes polynomial time as well.

## Exercises

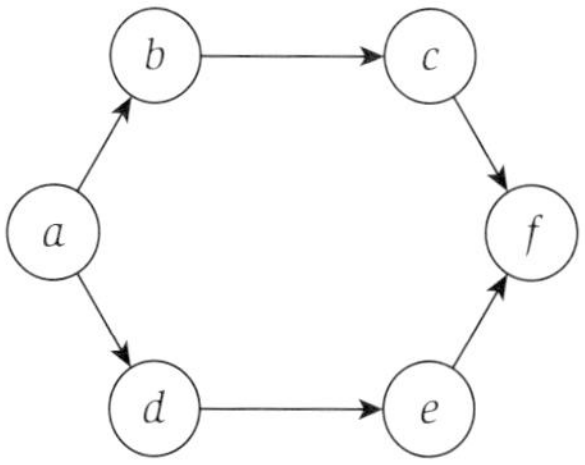

1. Consider the directed acyclic graph $G$ in Figure 3.10. How many topological orderings does it have?

**Figure 3.10** How many topological orderings does this graph have?

2. Give an algorithm to detect whether a given undirected graph contains a cycle. If the graph contains a cycle, then your algorithm should output one. (It should not output all cycles in the graph, just one of them.) The running time of your algorithm should be $O(m + n)$ for a graph with $n$ nodes and $m$ edges.

3. The algorithm described in Section 3.6 for computing a topological ordering of a DAG repeatedly finds a node with no incoming edges and deletes it. This will eventually produce a topological ordering, provided that the input graph really is a DAG.

   But suppose that we're given an arbitrary graph that may or may not be a DAG. Extend the topological ordering algorithm so that, given an input directed graph $G$, it outputs one of two things: (a) a topological ordering, thus establishing that $G$ is a DAG; or (b) a cycle in $G$, thus establishing that $G$ is not a DAG. The running time of your algorithm should be $O(m + n)$ for a directed graph with $n$ nodes and $m$ edges.

4. Inspired by the example of that great Cornellian, Vladimir Nabokov, some of your friends have become amateur lepidopterists (they study butterflies). Often when they return from a trip with specimens of butterflies, it is very difficult for them to tell how many distinct species they've caught—thanks to the fact that many species look very similar to one another.

   One day they return with $n$ butterflies, and they believe that each belongs to one of two different species, which we'll call $A$ and $B$ for purposes of this discussion. They'd like to divide the $n$ specimens into two groups—those that belong to $A$ and those that belong to $B$—but it's very hard for them to directly label any one specimen. So they decide to adopt the following approach.

For each pair of specimens $i$ and $j$, they study them carefully side by side. If they're confident enough in their judgment, then they label the pair $(i, j)$ either "same" (meaning they believe them both to come from the same species) or "different" (meaning they believe them to come from different species). They also have the option of rendering no judgment on a given pair, in which case we'll call the pair *ambiguous*.

So now they have the collection of $n$ specimens, as well as a collection of $m$ judgments (either "same" or "different") for the pairs that were not declared to be ambiguous. They'd like to know if this data is consistent with the idea that each butterfly is from one of species $A$ or $B$. So more concretely, we'll declare the $m$ judgments to be *consistent* if it is possible to label each specimen either $A$ or $B$ in such a way that for each pair $(i, j)$ labeled "same," it is the case that $i$ and $j$ have the same label; and for each pair $(i, j)$ labeled "different," it is the case that $i$ and $j$ have different labels. They're in the middle of tediously working out whether their judgments are consistent, when one of them realizes that you probably have an algorithm that would answer this question right away.

Give an algorithm with running time $O(m + n)$ that determines whether the $m$ judgments are consistent.

5. A binary tree is a rooted tree in which each node has at most two children. Show by induction that in any binary tree the number of nodes with two children is exactly one less than the number of leaves.

6. We have a connected graph $G = (V, E)$, and a specific vertex $u \in V$. Suppose we compute a depth-first search tree rooted at $u$, and obtain a tree $T$ that includes all nodes of $G$. Suppose we then compute a breadth-first search tree rooted at $u$, and obtain the same tree $T$. Prove that $G = T$. (In other words, if $T$ is both a depth-first search tree and a breadth-first search tree rooted at $u$, then $G$ cannot contain any edges that do not belong to $T$.)

7. Some friends of yours work on wireless networks, and they're currently studying the properties of a network of $n$ mobile devices. As the devices move around (actually, as their human owners move around), they define a graph at any point in time as follows: there is a node representing each of the $n$ devices, and there is an edge between device $i$ and device $j$ if the physical locations of $i$ and $j$ are no more than 500 meters apart. (If so, we say that $i$ and $j$ are "in range" of each other.)

They'd like it to be the case that the network of devices is connected at all times, and so they've constrained the motion of the devices to satisfy the following property: at all times, each device $i$ is within 500 meters of at least $n/2$ of the other devices. (We'll assume $n$ is an even number.) What they'd like to know is: Does this property by itself guarantee that the network will remain connected?

Here's a concrete way to formulate the question as a claim about graphs.

> *Claim: Let G be a graph on n nodes, where n is an even number. If every node of G has degree at least n/2, then G is connected.*

Decide whether you think the claim is true or false, and give a proof of either the claim or its negation.

8. A number of stories in the press about the structure of the Internet and the Web have focused on some version of the following question: How far apart are typical nodes in these networks? If you read these stories carefully, you find that many of them are confused about the difference between the *diameter* of a network and the *average distance* in a network; they often jump back and forth between these concepts as though they're the same thing.

As in the text, we say that the *distance* between two nodes $u$ and $v$ in a graph $G = (V, E)$ is the minimum number of edges in a path joining them; we'll denote this by $dist(u, v)$. We say that the *diameter* of $G$ is the maximum distance between any pair of nodes; and we'll denote this quantity by $diam(G)$.

Let's define a related quantity, which we'll call the *average pairwise distance* in $G$ (denoted $apd(G)$). We define $apd(G)$ to be the average, over all $\binom{n}{2}$ sets of two distinct nodes $u$ and $v$, of the distance between $u$ and $v$. That is,

$$apd(G) = \left[ \sum_{\{u,v\} \subseteq V} dist(u, v) \right] / \binom{n}{2}.$$

Here's a simple example to convince yourself that there are graphs $G$ for which $diam(G) \neq apd(G)$. Let $G$ be a graph with three nodes $u, v, w$, and with the two edges $\{u, v\}$ and $\{v, w\}$. Then

$$diam(G) = dist(u, w) = 2,$$

while

$$apd(G) = [dist(u, v) + dist(u, w) + dist(v, w)]/3 = 4/3.$$

Of course, these two numbers aren't all *that* far apart in the case of this three-node graph, and so it's natural to ask whether there's always a close relation between them. Here's a claim that tries to make this precise.

*Claim: There exists a positive natural number c so that for all connected graphs G, it is the case that*

$$\frac{diam(G)}{apd(G)} \leq c.$$

Decide whether you think the claim is true or false, and give a proof of either the claim or its negation.

9. There's a natural intuition that two nodes that are far apart in a communication network—separated by many hops—have a more tenuous connection than two nodes that are close together. There are a number of algorithmic results that are based to some extent on different ways of making this notion precise. Here's one that involves the susceptibility of paths to the deletion of nodes.

Suppose that an $n$-node undirected graph $G = (V, E)$ contains two nodes $s$ and $t$ such that the distance between $s$ and $t$ is strictly greater than $n/2$. Show that there must exist some node $v$, not equal to either $s$ or $t$, such that deleting $v$ from $G$ destroys all $s$-$t$ paths. (In other words, the graph obtained from $G$ by deleting $v$ contains no path from $s$ to $t$.) Give an algorithm with running time $O(m + n)$ to find such a node $v$.

10. A number of art museums around the country have been featuring work by an artist named Mark Lombardi (1951–2000), consisting of a set of intricately rendered graphs. Building on a great deal of research, these graphs encode the relationships among people involved in major political scandals over the past several decades: the nodes correspond to participants, and each edge indicates some type of relationship between a pair of participants. And so, if you peer closely enough at the drawings, you can trace out ominous-looking paths from a high-ranking U.S. government official, to a former business partner, to a bank in Switzerland, to a shadowy arms dealer.

Such pictures form striking examples of *social networks*, which, as we discussed in Section 3.1, have nodes representing people and organizations, and edges representing relationships of various kinds. And the short paths that abound in these networks have attracted considerable attention recently, as people ponder what they mean. In the case of Mark Lombardi's graphs, they hint at the short set of steps that can carry you from the reputable to the disreputable.

Of course, a single, spurious short path between nodes $v$ and $w$ in such a network may be more coincidental than anything else; a large number of short paths between $v$ and $w$ can be much more convincing. So in addition to the problem of computing a single shortest $v$-$w$ path in a graph $G$, social networks researchers have looked at the problem of determining the *number* of shortest $v$-$w$ paths.

This turns out to be a problem that can be solved efficiently. Suppose we are given an undirected graph $G = (V, E)$, and we identify two nodes $v$ and $w$ in $G$. Give an algorithm that computes the number of shortest $v$-$w$ paths in $G$. (The algorithm should not list all the paths; just the number suffices.) The running time of your algorithm should be $O(m + n)$ for a graph with $n$ nodes and $m$ edges.

11. You're helping some security analysts monitor a collection of networked computers, tracking the spread of an online virus. There are $n$ computers in the system, labeled $C_1, C_2, \ldots, C_n$, and as input you're given a collection of *trace data* indicating the times at which pairs of computers communicated. Thus the data is a sequence of ordered triples $(C_i, C_j, t_k)$; such a triple indicates that $C_i$ and $C_j$ exchanged bits at time $t_k$. There are $m$ triples total.

We'll assume that the triples are presented to you in sorted order of time. For purposes of simplicity, we'll assume that each pair of computers communicates at most once during the interval you're observing.

The security analysts you're working with would like to be able to answer questions of the following form: If the virus was inserted into computer $C_a$ at time $x$, could it possibly have infected computer $C_b$ by time $y$? The mechanics of infection are simple: if an infected computer $C_i$ communicates with an uninfected computer $C_j$ at time $t_k$ (in other words, if one of the triples $(C_i, C_j, t_k)$ or $(C_j, C_i, t_k)$ appears in the trace data), then computer $C_j$ becomes infected as well, starting at time $t_k$. Infection can thus spread from one machine to another across a *sequence* of communications, provided that no step in this sequence involves a move backward in time. Thus, for example, if $C_i$ is infected by time $t_k$, and the trace data contains triples $(C_i, C_j, t_k)$ and $(C_j, C_q, t_r)$, where $t_k \leq t_r$, then $C_q$ will become infected via $C_j$. (Note that it is okay for $t_k$ to be equal to $t_r$; this would mean that $C_j$ had open connections to both $C_i$ and $C_q$ at the same time, and so a virus could move from $C_i$ to $C_q$.)

For example, suppose $n = 4$, the trace data consists of the triples

$$(C_1, C_2, 4), \quad (C_2, C_4, 8), \quad (C_3, C_4, 8), \quad (C_1, C_4, 12),$$

and the virus was inserted into computer $C_1$ at time 2. Then $C_3$ would be infected at time 8 by a sequence of three steps: first $C_2$ becomes infected at time 4, then $C_4$ gets the virus from $C_2$ at time 8, and then $C_3$ gets the virus from $C_4$ at time 8. On the other hand, if the trace data were

$$(C_2, C_3, 8), \quad (C_1, C_4, 12), \quad (C_1, C_2, 14),$$

and again the virus was inserted into computer $C_1$ at time 2, then $C_3$ would not become infected during the period of observation: although $C_2$ becomes infected at time 14, we see that $C_3$ only communicates with $C_2$ *before* $C_2$ was infected. There is no sequence of communications moving forward in time by which the virus could get from $C_1$ to $C_3$ in this second example.

Design an algorithm that answers questions of this type: given a collection of trace data, the algorithm should decide whether a virus introduced at computer $C_a$ at time $x$ could have infected computer $C_b$ by time $y$. The algorithm should run in time $O(m + n)$.

12. You're helping a group of ethnographers analyze some oral history data they've collected by interviewing members of a village to learn about the lives of people who've lived there over the past two hundred years.

From these interviews, they've learned about a set of $n$ people (all of them now deceased), whom we'll denote $P_1, P_2, \ldots, P_n$. They've also collected facts about when these people lived relative to one another. Each fact has one of the following two forms:

- For some $i$ and $j$, person $P_i$ died before person $P_j$ was born; or
- for some $i$ and $j$, the life spans of $P_i$ and $P_j$ overlapped at least partially.

Naturally, they're not sure that all these facts are correct; memories are not so good, and a lot of this was passed down by word of mouth. So what they'd like you to determine is whether the data they've collected is at least internally consistent, in the sense that there could have existed a set of people for which all the facts they've learned simultaneously hold.

Give an efficient algorithm to do this: either it should produce proposed dates of birth and death for each of the $n$ people so that all the facts hold true, or it should report (correctly) that no such dates can exist—that is, the facts collected by the ethnographers are not internally consistent.

## Notes and Further Reading

The theory of graphs is a large topic, encompassing both algorithmic and non-algorithmic issues. It is generally considered to have begun with a paper by

Euler (1736), grown through interest in graph representations of maps and chemical compounds in the nineteenth century, and emerged as a systematic area of study in the twentieth century, first as a branch of mathematics and later also through its applications to computer science. The books by Berge (1976), Bollobas (1998), and Diestel (2000) provide substantial further coverage of graph theory. Recently, extensive data has become available for studying large networks that arise in the physical, biological, and social sciences, and there has been interest in understanding properties of networks that span all these different domains. The books by Barabasi (2002) and Watts (2002) discuss this emerging area of research, with presentations aimed at a general audience.

The basic graph traversal techniques covered in this chapter have numerous applications. We will see a number of these in subsequent chapters, and we refer the reader to the book by Tarjan (1983) for further results.

***Notes on the Exercises*** Exercise 12 is based on a result of Martin Golumbic and Ron Shamir.

# Chapter 4

## Greedy Algorithms

In *Wall Street*, that iconic movie of the 1980s, Michael Douglas gets up in front of a room full of stockholders and proclaims, "Greed . . . is good. Greed is right. Greed works." In this chapter, we'll be taking a much more understated perspective as we investigate the pros and cons of short-sighted greed in the design of algorithms. Indeed, our aim is to approach a number of different computational problems with a recurring set of questions: Is greed good? Does greed work?

It is hard, if not impossible, to define precisely what is meant by a *greedy algorithm*. An algorithm is greedy if it builds up a solution in small steps, choosing a decision at each step myopically to optimize some underlying criterion. One can often design many different greedy algorithms for the same problem, each one locally, incrementally optimizing some different measure on its way to a solution.

When a greedy algorithm succeeds in solving a nontrivial problem optimally, it typically implies something interesting and useful about the structure of the problem itself; there is a local decision rule that one can use to construct optimal solutions. And as we'll see later, in Chapter 11, the same is true of problems in which a greedy algorithm can produce a solution that is guaranteed to be *close* to optimal, even if it does not achieve the precise optimum. These are the kinds of issues we'll be dealing with in this chapter. It's easy to invent greedy algorithms for almost any problem; finding cases in which they work well, and proving that they work well, is the interesting challenge.

The first two sections of this chapter will develop two basic methods for proving that a greedy algorithm produces an optimal solution to a problem. One can view the first approach as establishing that *the greedy algorithm stays ahead*. By this we mean that if one measures the greedy algorithm's progress in a step-by-step fashion, one sees that it does better than any other algorithm at each step; it then follows that it produces an optimal solution. The second approach is known as an *exchange argument*, and it is more general: one considers any possible solution to the problem and gradually transforms it into the solution found by the greedy algorithm without hurting its quality. Again, it will follow that the greedy algorithm must have found a solution that is at least as good as any other solution.

Following our introduction of these two styles of analysis, we focus on several of the most well-known applications of greedy algorithms: *shortest paths in a graph*, the *Minimum Spanning Tree Problem*, and the construction of *Huffman codes* for performing data compression. They each provide nice examples of our analysis techniques. We also explore an interesting relationship between minimum spanning trees and the long-studied problem of *clustering*. Finally, we consider a more complex application, the *Minimum-Cost Arborescence Problem*, which further extends our notion of what a greedy algorithm is.

## 4.1 Interval Scheduling: The Greedy Algorithm Stays Ahead

Let's recall the Interval Scheduling Problem, which was the first of the five representative problems we considered in Chapter 1. We have a set of requests $\{1, 2, \ldots, n\}$; the $i^{\text{th}}$ request corresponds to an interval of time starting at $s(i)$ and finishing at $f(i)$. (Note that we are slightly changing the notation from Section 1.2, where we used $s_i$ rather than $s(i)$ and $f_i$ rather than $f(i)$. This change of notation will make things easier to talk about in the proofs.) We'll say that a subset of the requests is *compatible* if no two of them overlap in time, and our goal is to accept as large a compatible subset as possible. Compatible sets of maximum size will be called *optimal*.

### Designing a Greedy Algorithm

Using the Interval Scheduling Problem, we can make our discussion of greedy algorithms much more concrete. The basic idea in a greedy algorithm for interval scheduling is to use a simple rule to select a first request $i_1$. Once a request $i_1$ is accepted, we reject all requests that are not compatible with $i_1$. We then select the next request $i_2$ to be accepted, and again reject all requests that are not compatible with $i_2$. We continue in this fashion until we run out of requests. The challenge in designing a good greedy algorithm is in deciding which simple rule to use for the selection—and there are many natural rules for this problem that do not give good solutions.

Let's try to think of some of the most natural rules and see how they work.

- The most obvious rule might be to always select the available request that starts earliest—that is, the one with minimal start time $s(i)$. This way our resource starts being used as quickly as possible.

  This method does not yield an optimal solution. If the earliest request $i$ is for a very long interval, then by accepting request $i$ we may have to reject a lot of requests for shorter time intervals. Since our goal is to satisfy as many requests as possible, we will end up with a suboptimal solution. In a really bad case—say, when the finish time $f(i)$ is the maximum among all requests—the accepted request $i$ keeps our resource occupied for the whole time. In this case our greedy method would accept a single request, while the optimal solution could accept many. Such a situation is depicted in Figure 4.1(a).

- This might suggest that we should start out by accepting the request that requires the smallest interval of time—namely, the request for which $f(i) - s(i)$ is as small as possible. As it turns out, this is a somewhat better rule than the previous one, but it still can produce a suboptimal schedule. For example, in Figure 4.1(b), accepting the short interval in the middle would prevent us from accepting the other two, which form an optimal solution.

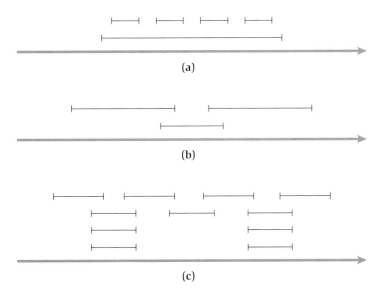

**Figure 4.1** Some instances of the Interval Scheduling Problem on which natural greedy algorithms fail to find the optimal solution. In (a), it does not work to select the interval that starts earliest; in (b), it does not work to select the shortest interval; and in (c), it does not work to select the interval with the fewest conflicts.

- In the previous greedy rule, our problem was that the second request competes with both the first and the third—that is, accepting this request made us reject two other requests. We could design a greedy algorithm that is based on this idea: for each request, we count the number of other requests that are not compatible, and accept the request that has the fewest number of noncompatible requests. (In other words, we select the interval with the fewest "conflicts.") This greedy choice would lead to the optimum solution in the previous example. In fact, it is quite a bit harder to design a bad example for this rule; but it can be done, and we've drawn an example in Figure 4.1(c). The unique optimal solution in this example is to accept the four requests in the top row. The greedy method suggested here accepts the middle request in the second row and thereby ensures a solution of size no greater than three.

A greedy rule that does lead to the optimal solution is based on a fourth idea: we should accept first the request that finishes first, that is, the request $i$ for which $f(i)$ is as small as possible. This is also quite a natural idea: we ensure that our resource becomes free as soon as possible while still satisfying one request. In this way we can maximize the time left to satisfy other requests.

Let us state the algorithm a bit more formally. We will use $R$ to denote the set of requests that we have neither accepted nor rejected yet, and use $A$ to denote the set of accepted requests. For an example of how the algorithm runs, see Figure 4.2.

```
Initially let R be the set of all requests, and let A be empty
While R is not yet empty
  Choose a request i ∈ R that has the smallest finishing time
  Add request i to A
  Delete all requests from R that are not compatible with request i
EndWhile
Return the set A as the set of accepted requests
```

## Analyzing the Algorithm

While this greedy method is quite natural, it is certainly not obvious that it returns an optimal set of intervals. Indeed, it would only be sensible to reserve judgment on its optimality: the ideas that led to the previous nonoptimal versions of the greedy method also seemed promising at first.

As a start, we can immediately declare that the intervals in the set $A$ returned by the algorithm are all compatible.

**(4.1)**    *A is a compatible set of requests.*

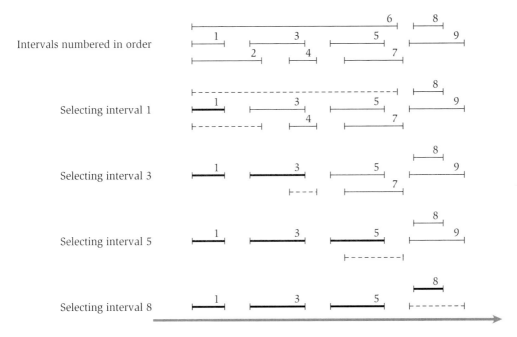

**Figure 4.2** Sample run of the Interval Scheduling Algorithm. At each step the selected intervals are darker lines, and the intervals deleted at the corresponding step are indicated with dashed lines.

What we need to show is that this solution is optimal. So, for purposes of comparison, let $\mathcal{O}$ be an optimal set of intervals. Ideally one might want to show that $A = \mathcal{O}$, but this is too much to ask: there may be many optimal solutions, and at best $A$ is equal to a single one of them. So instead we will simply show that $|A| = |\mathcal{O}|$, that is, that $A$ contains the same number of intervals as $\mathcal{O}$ and hence is also an optimal solution.

The idea underlying the proof, as we suggested initially, will be to find a sense in which our greedy algorithm "stays ahead" of this solution $\mathcal{O}$. We will compare the partial solutions that the greedy algorithm constructs to initial segments of the solution $\mathcal{O}$, and show that the greedy algorithm is doing better in a step-by-step fashion.

We introduce some notation to help with this proof. Let $i_1, \ldots, i_k$ be the set of requests in $A$ in the order they were added to $A$. Note that $|A| = k$. Similarly, let the set of requests in $\mathcal{O}$ be denoted by $j_1, \ldots, j_m$. Our goal is to prove that $k = m$. Assume that the requests in $\mathcal{O}$ are also ordered in the natural left-to-right order of the corresponding intervals, that is, in the order of the start and finish points. Note that the requests in $\mathcal{O}$ are compatible, which implies that the start points have the same order as the finish points.

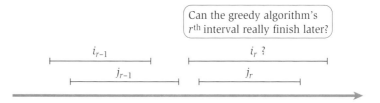

**Figure 4.3** The inductive step in the proof that the greedy algorithm stays ahead.

Our intuition for the greedy method came from wanting our resource to become free again as soon as possible after satisfying the first request. And indeed, our greedy rule guarantees that $f(i_1) \leq f(j_1)$. This is the sense in which we want to show that our greedy rule "stays ahead"—that each of its intervals finishes at least as soon as the corresponding interval in the set $\mathcal{O}$. Thus we now prove that for each $r \geq 1$, the $r^{\text{th}}$ accepted request in the algorithm's schedule finishes no later than the $r^{\text{th}}$ request in the optimal schedule.

**(4.2)**    *For all indices $r \leq k$ we have $f(i_r) \leq f(j_r)$.*

**Proof.** We will prove this statement by induction. For $r = 1$ the statement is clearly true: the algorithm starts by selecting the request $i_1$ with minimum finish time.

Now let $r > 1$. We will assume as our induction hypothesis that the statement is true for $r - 1$, and we will try to prove it for $r$. As shown in Figure 4.3, the induction hypothesis lets us assume that $f(i_{r-1}) \leq f(j_{r-1})$. In order for the algorithm's $r^{\text{th}}$ interval not to finish earlier as well, it would need to "fall behind" as shown. But there's a simple reason why this could not happen: rather than choose a later-finishing interval, the greedy algorithm always has the option (at worst) of choosing $j_r$ and thus fulfilling the induction step.

We can make this argument precise as follows. We know (since $\mathcal{O}$ consists of compatible intervals) that $f(j_{r-1}) \leq s(j_r)$. Combining this with the induction hypothesis $f(i_{r-1}) \leq f(j_{r-1})$, we get $f(i_{r-1}) \leq s(j_r)$. Thus the interval $j_r$ is in the set $R$ of available intervals at the time when the greedy algorithm selects $i_r$. The greedy algorithm selects the available interval with *smallest* finish time; since interval $j_r$ is one of these available intervals, we have $f(i_r) \leq f(j_r)$. This completes the induction step.  ∎

Thus we have formalized the sense in which the greedy algorithm is remaining ahead of $\mathcal{O}$: for each $r$, the $r^{\text{th}}$ interval it selects finishes at least as soon as the $r^{\text{th}}$ interval in $\mathcal{O}$. We now see why this implies the optimality of the greedy algorithm's set $A$.

**(4.3)**    *The greedy algorithm returns an optimal set A.*

**Proof.** We will prove the statement by contradiction. If $A$ is not optimal, then an optimal set $\mathcal{O}$ must have more requests, that is, we must have $m > k$. Applying (4.2) with $r = k$, we get that $f(i_k) \leq f(j_k)$. Since $m > k$, there is a request $j_{k+1}$ in $\mathcal{O}$. This request starts after request $j_k$ ends, and hence after $i_k$ ends. So after deleting all requests that are not compatible with requests $i_1, \ldots, i_k$, the set of possible requests $R$ still contains $j_{k+1}$. But the greedy algorithm stops with request $i_k$, and it is only supposed to stop when $R$ is empty—a contradiction. ∎

***Implementation and Running Time***    We can make our algorithm run in time $O(n \log n)$ as follows. We begin by sorting the $n$ requests in order of finishing time and labeling them in this order; that is, we will assume that $f(i) \leq f(j)$ when $i < j$. This takes time $O(n \log n)$. In an additional $O(n)$ time, we construct an array $S[1 \ldots n]$ with the property that $S[i]$ contains the value $s(i)$.

We now select requests by processing the intervals in order of increasing $f(i)$. We always select the first interval; we then iterate through the intervals in order until reaching the first interval $j$ for which $s(j) \geq f(1)$; we then select this one as well. More generally, if the most recent interval we've selected ends at time $f$, we continue iterating through subsequent intervals until we reach the first $j$ for which $s(j) \geq f$. In this way, we implement the greedy algorithm analyzed above in one pass through the intervals, spending constant time per interval. Thus this part of the algorithm takes time $O(n)$.

## Extensions

The Interval Scheduling Problem we considered here is a quite simple scheduling problem. There are many further complications that could arise in practical settings. The following point out issues that we will see later in the book in various forms.

- In defining the problem, we assumed that all requests were known to the scheduling algorithm when it was choosing the compatible subset. It would also be natural, of course, to think about the version of the problem in which the scheduler needs to make decisions about accepting or rejecting certain requests before knowing about the full set of requests. Customers (requestors) may well be impatient, and they may give up and leave if the scheduler waits too long to gather information about all other requests. An active area of research is concerned with such *on-line* algorithms, which must make decisions as time proceeds, without knowledge of future input.

- Our goal was to maximize the number of satisfied requests. But we could picture a situation in which each request has a different value to us. For example, each request $i$ could also have a value $v_i$ (the amount gained by satisfying request $i$), and the goal would be to maximize our income: the sum of the values of all satisfied requests. This leads to the *Weighted Interval Scheduling Problem*, the second of the representative problems we described in Chapter 1.

There are many other variants and combinations that can arise. We now discuss one of these further variants in more detail, since it forms another case in which a greedy algorithm can be used to produce an optimal solution.

## A Related Problem: Scheduling All Intervals

***The Problem***   In the Interval Scheduling Problem, there is a single resource and many requests in the form of time intervals, so we must choose which requests to accept and which to reject. A related problem arises if we have many identical resources available and we wish to schedule *all* the requests using as few resources as possible. Because the goal here is to partition all intervals across multiple resources, we will refer to this as the *Interval Partitioning* Problem.[1]

For example, suppose that each request corresponds to a lecture that needs to be scheduled in a classroom for a particular interval of time. We wish to satisfy all these requests, using as few classrooms as possible. The classrooms at our disposal are thus the multiple resources, and the basic constraint is that any two lectures that overlap in time must be scheduled in different classrooms. Equivalently, the interval requests could be jobs that need to be processed for a specific period of time, and the resources are machines capable of handling these jobs. Much later in the book, in Chapter 10, we will see a different application of this problem in which the intervals are routing requests that need to be allocated bandwidth on a fiber-optic cable.

As an illustration of the problem, consider the sample instance in Figure 4.4(a). The requests in this example can all be scheduled using three resources; this is indicated in Figure 4.4(b), where the requests are rearranged into three rows, each containing a set of nonoverlapping intervals. In general, one can imagine a solution using $k$ resources as a rearrangement of the requests into $k$ rows of nonoverlapping intervals: the first row contains all the intervals

---

[1] The problem is also referred to as the *Interval Coloring Problem*; the terminology arises from thinking of the different resources as having distinct colors—all the intervals assigned to a particular resource are given the corresponding color.

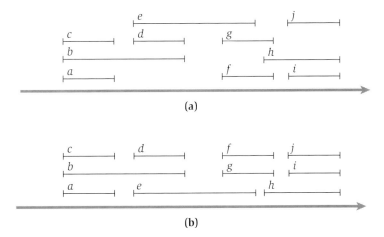

**Figure 4.4** (a) An instance of the Interval Partitioning Problem with ten intervals (*a* through *j*). (b) A solution in which all intervals are scheduled using three resources: each row represents a set of intervals that can all be scheduled on a single resource.

assigned to the first resource, the second row contains all those assigned to the second resource, and so forth.

Now, is there any hope of using just two resources in this sample instance? Clearly the answer is no. We need at least three resources since, for example, intervals *a*, *b*, and *c* all pass over a common point on the time-line, and hence they all need to be scheduled on different resources. In fact, one can make this last argument in general for any instance of Interval Partitioning. Suppose we define the *depth* of a set of intervals to be the maximum number that pass over any single point on the time-line. Then we claim

**(4.4)** *In any instance of Interval Partitioning, the number of resources needed is at least the depth of the set of intervals.*

**Proof.** Suppose a set of intervals has depth $d$, and let $I_1, \ldots, I_d$ all pass over a common point on the time-line. Then each of these intervals must be scheduled on a different resource, so the whole instance needs at least $d$ resources. ∎

We now consider two questions, which turn out to be closely related. First, can we design an efficient algorithm that schedules all intervals using the minimum possible number of resources? Second, is there always a schedule using a number of resources that is *equal* to the depth? In effect, a positive answer to this second question would say that the only obstacles to partitioning intervals are purely local—a set of intervals all piled over the same point. It's not immediately clear that there couldn't exist other, "long-range" obstacles that push the number of required resources even higher.

We now design a simple greedy algorithm that schedules all intervals using a number of resources equal to the depth. This immediately implies the optimality of the algorithm: in view of (4.4), no solution could use a number of resources that is smaller than the depth. The analysis of our algorithm will therefore illustrate another general approach to proving optimality: one finds a simple, "structural" bound asserting that every possible solution must have at least a certain value, and then one shows that the algorithm under consideration always achieves this bound.

***Designing the Algorithm***   Let $d$ be the depth of the set of intervals; we show how to assign a *label* to each interval, where the labels come from the set of numbers $\{1, 2, \ldots, d\}$, and the assignment has the property that overlapping intervals are labeled with different numbers. This gives the desired solution, since we can interpret each number as the name of a resource, and the label of each interval as the name of the resource to which it is assigned.

The algorithm we use for this is a simple one-pass greedy strategy that orders intervals by their starting times. We go through the intervals in this order, and try to assign to each interval we encounter a label that hasn't already been assigned to any previous interval that overlaps it. Specifically, we have the following description.

---

```
Sort the intervals by their start times, breaking ties arbitrarily
Let I₁, I₂, . . . , Iₙ denote the intervals in this order
For j = 1, 2, 3, . . . , n
  For each interval Iᵢ that precedes Iⱼ in sorted order and overlaps it
    Exclude the label of Iᵢ from consideration for Iⱼ
  Endfor
  If there is any label from {1, 2, . . . , d} that has not been excluded then
    Assign a nonexcluded label to Iⱼ
  Else
    Leave Iⱼ unlabeled
  Endif
Endfor
```

---

***Analyzing the Algorithm***   We claim the following.

**(4.5)**   *If we use the greedy algorithm above, every interval will be assigned a label, and no two overlapping intervals will receive the same label.*

**Proof.**   First let's argue that no interval ends up unlabeled. Consider one of the intervals $I_j$, and suppose there are $t$ intervals earlier in the sorted order that overlap it. These $t$ intervals, together with $I_j$, form a set of $t + 1$ intervals that all pass over a common point on the time-line (namely, the start time of

$I_j$), and so $t + 1 \leq d$. Thus $t \leq d - 1$. It follows that at least one of the $d$ labels is not excluded by this set of $t$ intervals, and so there is a label that can be assigned to $I_j$.

Next we claim that no two overlapping intervals are assigned the same label. Indeed, consider any two intervals $I$ and $I'$ that overlap, and suppose $I$ precedes $I'$ in the sorted order. Then when $I'$ is considered by the algorithm, $I$ is in the set of intervals whose labels are excluded from consideration; consequently, the algorithm will not assign to $I'$ the label that it used for $I$. $\quad\blacksquare$

The algorithm and its analysis are very simple. Essentially, if you have $d$ labels at your disposal, then as you sweep through the intervals from left to right, assigning an available label to each interval you encounter, you can never reach a point where all the labels are currently in use.

Since our algorithm is using $d$ labels, we can use (4.4) to conclude that it is, in fact, always using the minimum possible number of labels. We sum this up as follows.

**(4.6)** *The greedy algorithm above schedules every interval on a resource, using a number of resources equal to the depth of the set of intervals. This is the optimal number of resources needed.*

## 4.2 Scheduling to Minimize Lateness: An Exchange Argument

We now discuss a scheduling problem related to the one with which we began the chapter. Despite the similarities in the problem formulation and in the greedy algorithm to solve it, the proof that this algorithm is optimal will require a more sophisticated kind of analysis.

### The Problem

Consider again a situation in which we have a single resource and a set of $n$ requests to use the resource for an interval of time. Assume that the resource is available starting at time $s$. In contrast to the previous problem, however, each request is now more flexible. Instead of a start time and finish time, the request $i$ has a deadline $d_i$, and it requires a contiguous time interval of length $t_i$, but it is willing to be scheduled at any time before the deadline. Each accepted request must be assigned an interval of time of length $t_i$, and different requests must be assigned nonoverlapping intervals.

There are many objective functions we might seek to optimize when faced with this situation, and some are computationally much more difficult than

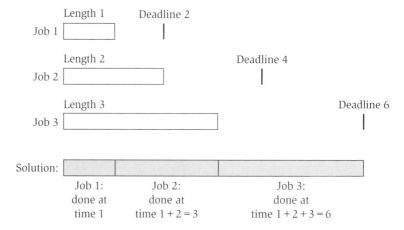

**Figure 4.5** A sample instance of scheduling to minimize lateness.

others. Here we consider a very natural goal that can be optimized by a greedy algorithm. Suppose that we plan to satisfy each request, but we are allowed to let certain requests run late. Thus, beginning at our overall start time $s$, we will assign each request $i$ an interval of time of length $t_i$; let us denote this interval by $[s(i), f(i)]$, with $f(i) = s(i) + t_i$. Unlike the previous problem, then, the algorithm must actually determine a start time (and hence a finish time) for each interval.

We say that a request $i$ is *late* if it misses the deadline, that is, if $f(i) > d_i$. The *lateness* of such a request $i$ is defined to be $l_i = f(i) - d_i$. We will say that $l_i = 0$ if request $i$ is not late. The goal in our new optimization problem will be to schedule all requests, using nonoverlapping intervals, so as to minimize the *maximum lateness*, $L = \max_i l_i$. This problem arises naturally when scheduling jobs that need to use a single machine, and so we will refer to our requests as *jobs*.

Figure 4.5 shows a sample instance of this problem, consisting of three jobs: the first has length $t_1 = 1$ and deadline $d_1 = 2$; the second has $t_2 = 2$ and $d_2 = 4$; and the third has $t_3 = 3$ and $d_3 = 6$. It is not hard to check that scheduling the jobs in the order $1, 2, 3$ incurs a maximum lateness of 0.

### Designing the Algorithm

What would a greedy algorithm for this problem look like? There are several natural greedy approaches in which we look at the data $(t_i, d_i)$ about the jobs and use this to order them according to some simple rule.

- One approach would be to schedule the jobs in order of increasing length $t_i$, so as to get the short jobs out of the way quickly. This immediately looks too simplistic, since it completely ignores the deadlines of the jobs. And indeed, consider a two-job instance where the first job has $t_1 = 1$ and $d_1 = 100$, while the second job has $t_2 = 10$ and $d_2 = 10$. Then the second job has to be started right away if we want to achieve lateness $L = 0$, and scheduling the second job first is indeed the optimal solution.

- The previous example suggests that we should be concerned about jobs whose available *slack time* $d_i - t_i$ is very small—they're the ones that need to be started with minimal delay. So a more natural greedy algorithm would be to sort jobs in order of increasing slack $d_i - t_i$.

  Unfortunately, this greedy rule fails as well. Consider a two-job instance where the first job has $t_1 = 1$ and $d_1 = 2$, while the second job has $t_2 = 10$ and $d_2 = 10$. Sorting by increasing slack would place the second job first in the schedule, and the first job would incur a lateness of 9. (It finishes at time 11, nine units beyond its deadline.) On the other hand, if we schedule the first job first, then it finishes on time and the second job incurs a lateness of only 1.

There is, however, an equally basic greedy algorithm that always produces an optimal solution. We simply sort the jobs in increasing order of their deadlines $d_i$, and schedule them in this order. (This rule is often called *Earliest Deadline First*.) There is an intuitive basis to this rule: we should make sure that jobs with earlier deadlines get completed earlier. At the same time, it's a little hard to believe that this algorithm always produces optimal solutions— specifically because it never looks at the lengths of the jobs. Earlier we were skeptical of the approach that sorted by length on the grounds that it threw away half the input data (i.e., the deadlines); but now we're considering a solution that throws away the other half of the data. Nevertheless, Earliest Deadline First does produce optimal solutions, and we will now prove this.

First we specify some notation that will be useful in talking about the algorithm. By renaming the jobs if necessary, we can assume that the jobs are labeled in the order of their deadlines, that is, we have

$$d_1 \leq \ldots \leq d_n.$$

We will simply schedule all jobs in this order. Again, let $s$ be the start time for all jobs. Job 1 will start at time $s = s(1)$ and end at time $f(1) = s(1) + t_1$; Job 2 will start at time $s(2) = f(1)$ and end at time $f(2) = s(2) + t_2$; and so forth. We will use $f$ to denote the finishing time of the last scheduled job. We write this algorithm here.

---

```
Order the jobs in order of their deadlines
Assume for simplicity of notation that d₁ ≤ ... ≤ dₙ
Initially, f = s
```

```
Consider the jobs i = 1,...,n in this order
    Assign job i to the time interval from s(i) = f to f(i) = f + tᵢ
    Let f = f + tᵢ
End
Return the set of scheduled intervals [s(i), f(i)] for i = 1,...,n
```

### ✎ Analyzing the Algorithm

To reason about the optimality of the algorithm, we first observe that the schedule it produces has no "gaps"—times when the machine is not working yet there are jobs left. The time that passes during a gap will be called *idle time:* there is work to be done, yet for some reason the machine is sitting idle. Not only does the schedule $A$ produced by our algorithm have no idle time; it is also very easy to see that there is an optimal schedule with this property. We do not write down a proof for this.

**(4.7)**    *There is an optimal schedule with no idle time.*

Now, how can we prove that our schedule $A$ is optimal, that is, its maximum lateness $L$ is as small as possible? As in previous analyses, we will start by considering an optimal schedule $\mathcal{O}$. Our plan here is to gradually modify $\mathcal{O}$, preserving its optimality at each step, but eventually transforming it into a schedule that is identical to the schedule $A$ found by the greedy algorithm. We refer to this type of analysis as an *exchange argument*, and we will see that it is a powerful way to think about greedy algorithms in general.

We first try characterizing schedules in the following way. We say that a schedule $A'$ has an *inversion* if a job $i$ with deadline $d_i$ is scheduled before another job $j$ with earlier deadline $d_j < d_i$. Notice that, by definition, the schedule $A$ produced by our algorithm has no inversions. If there are jobs with identical deadlines then there can be many different schedules with no inversions. However, we can show that all these schedules have the same maximum lateness $L$.

**(4.8)**    *All schedules with no inversions and no idle time have the same maximum lateness.*

**Proof.** If two different schedules have neither inversions nor idle time, then they might not produce exactly the same order of jobs, but they can only differ in the order in which jobs with identical deadlines are scheduled. Consider such a deadline $d$. In both schedules, the jobs with deadline $d$ are all scheduled consecutively (after all jobs with earlier deadlines and before all jobs with later deadlines). Among the jobs with deadline $d$, the last one has the greatest lateness, and this lateness does not depend on the order of the jobs. ∎

The main step in showing the optimality of our algorithm is to establish that there is an optimal schedule that has no inversions and no idle time. To do this, we will start with any optimal schedule having no idle time; we will then convert it into a schedule with no inversions without increasing its maximum lateness. Thus the resulting scheduling after this conversion will be optimal as well.

**(4.9)**   *There is an optimal schedule that has no inversions and no idle time.*

**Proof.** By (4.7), there is an optimal schedule $\mathcal{O}$ with no idle time. The proof will consist of a sequence of statements. The first of these is simple to establish.

(a)   *If $\mathcal{O}$ has an inversion, then there is a pair of jobs $i$ and $j$ such that $j$ is scheduled immediately after $i$ and has $d_j < d_i$.*

Indeed, consider an inversion in which a job $a$ is scheduled sometime before a job $b$, and $d_a > d_b$. If we advance in the scheduled order of jobs from $a$ to $b$ one at a time, there has to come a point at which the deadline we see decreases for the first time. This corresponds to a pair of consecutive jobs that form an inversion.

Now suppose $\mathcal{O}$ has at least one inversion, and by (a), let $i$ and $j$ be a pair of inverted requests that are consecutive in the scheduled order. We will decrease the number of inversions in $\mathcal{O}$ by swapping the requests $i$ and $j$ in the schedule $\mathcal{O}$. The pair $(i, j)$ formed an inversion in $\mathcal{O}$, this inversion is eliminated by the swap, and no new inversions are created. Thus we have

(b)   *After swapping $i$ and $j$ we get a schedule with one less inversion.*

The hardest part of this proof is to argue that the inverted schedule is also optimal.

(c)   *The new swapped schedule has a maximum lateness no larger than that of $\mathcal{O}$.*

It is clear that if we can prove (c), then we are done. The initial schedule $\mathcal{O}$ can have at most $\binom{n}{2}$ inversions (if all pairs are inverted), and hence after at most $\binom{n}{2}$ swaps we get an optimal schedule with no inversions.

So we now conclude by proving (c), showing that by swapping a pair of consecutive, inverted jobs, we do not increase the maximum lateness $L$ of the schedule.   ∎

**Proof of (c).** We invent some notation to describe the schedule $\mathcal{O}$: assume that each request $r$ is scheduled for the time interval $[s(r), f(r)]$ and has lateness $l'_r$. Let $L' = \max_r l'_r$ denote the maximum lateness of this schedule.

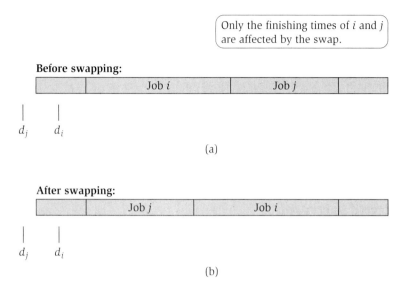

Figure 4.6 The effect of swapping two consecutive, inverted jobs.

Let $\overline{\mathcal{O}}$ denote the swapped schedule; we will use $\overline{s}(r)$, $\overline{f}(r)$, $\overline{l}_r$, and $\overline{L}$ to denote the corresponding quantities in the swapped schedule.

Now recall our two adjacent, inverted jobs $i$ and $j$. The situation is roughly as pictured in Figure 4.6. The finishing time of $j$ before the swap is exactly equal to the finishing time of $i$ after the swap. Thus all jobs other than jobs $i$ and $j$ finish at the same time in the two schedules. Moreover, job $j$ will get finished earlier in the new schedule, and hence the swap does not increase the lateness of job $j$.

Thus the only thing to worry about is job $i$: its lateness may have been increased, and what if this actually raises the maximum lateness of the whole schedule? After the swap, job $i$ finishes at time $f(j)$, when job $j$ was finished in the schedule $\mathcal{O}$. If job $i$ is late in this new schedule, its lateness is $\overline{l}_i = \overline{f}(i) - d_i = f(j) - d_i$. But the crucial point is that $i$ cannot be *more late* in the schedule $\overline{\mathcal{O}}$ than $j$ was in the schedule $\mathcal{O}$. Specifically, our assumption $d_i > d_j$ implies that

$$\overline{l}_i = f(j) - d_i < f(j) - d_j = l'_j.$$

Since the lateness of the schedule $\mathcal{O}$ was $L' \geq l'_j > \overline{l}_i$, this shows that the swap does not increase the maximum lateness of the schedule. ∎

The optimality of our greedy algorithm now follows immediately.

> **(4.10)**  *The schedule A produced by the greedy algorithm has optimal maximum lateness L.*

**Proof.** Statement (4.9) proves that an optimal schedule with no inversions exists. Now by (4.8) all schedules with no inversions have the same maximum lateness, and so the schedule obtained by the greedy algorithm is optimal. ∎

## Extensions

There are many possible generalizations of this scheduling problem. For example, we assumed that all jobs were available to start at the common start time $s$. A natural, but harder, version of this problem would contain requests $i$ that, in addition to the deadline $d_i$ and the requested time $t_i$, would also have an earliest possible starting time $r_i$. This earliest possible starting time is usually referred to as the *release time*. Problems with release times arise naturally in scheduling problems where requests can take the form: Can I reserve the room for a two-hour lecture, sometime between 1 P.M. and 5 P.M.? Our proof that the greedy algorithm finds an optimal solution relied crucially on the fact that all jobs were available at the common start time $s$. (Do you see where?) Unfortunately, as we will see later in the book, in Chapter 8, this more general version of the problem is much more difficult to solve optimally.

## 4.3 Optimal Caching: A More Complex Exchange Argument

We now consider a problem that involves processing a sequence of requests of a different form, and we develop an algorithm whose analysis requires a more subtle use of the exchange argument. The problem is that of *cache maintenance*.

### The Problem

To motivate caching, consider the following situation. You're working on a long research paper, and your draconian library will only allow you to have eight books checked out at once. You know that you'll probably need more than this over the course of working on the paper, but at any point in time, you'd like to have ready access to the eight books that are most relevant at that time. How should you decide which books to check out, and when should you return some in exchange for others, to minimize the number of times you have to exchange a book at the library?

This is precisely the problem that arises when dealing with a *memory hierarchy*: There is a small amount of data that can be accessed very quickly, and a large amount of data that requires more time to access; and you must decide which pieces of data to have close at hand.

Memory hierarchies have been a ubiquitous feature of computers since very early in their history. To begin with, data in the main memory of a processor can be accessed much more quickly than the data on its hard disk; but the disk has much more storage capacity. Thus, it is important to keep the most regularly used pieces of data in main memory, and go to disk as infrequently as possible. The same phenomenon, qualitatively, occurs with on-chip caches in modern processors. These can be accessed in a few cycles, and so data can be retrieved from cache much more quickly than it can be retrieved from main memory. This is another level of hierarchy: small caches have faster access time than main memory, which in turn is smaller and faster to access than disk. And one can see extensions of this hierarchy in many other settings. When one uses a Web browser, the disk often acts as a cache for frequently visited Web pages, since going to disk is still much faster than downloading something over the Internet.

*Caching* is a general term for the process of storing a small amount of data in a fast memory so as to reduce the amount of time spent interacting with a slow memory. In the previous examples, the on-chip cache reduces the need to fetch data from main memory, the main memory acts as a cache for the disk, and the disk acts as a cache for the Internet. (Much as your desk acts as a cache for the campus library, and the assorted facts you're able to remember without looking them up constitute a cache for the books on your desk.)

For caching to be as effective as possible, it should generally be the case that when you go to access a piece of data, it is already in the cache. To achieve this, a *cache maintenance* algorithm determines what to keep in the cache and what to evict from the cache when new data needs to be brought in.

Of course, as the caching problem arises in different settings, it involves various different considerations based on the underlying technology. For our purposes here, though, we take an abstract view of the problem that underlies most of these settings. We consider a set $U$ of $n$ pieces of data stored in *main memory*. We also have a faster memory, the *cache*, that can hold $k < n$ pieces of data at any one time. We will assume that the cache initially holds some set of $k$ items. A sequence of data items $D = d_1, d_2, \ldots, d_m$ drawn from $U$ is presented to us—this is the sequence of memory references we must process—and in processing them we must decide at all times which $k$ items to keep in the cache. When item $d_i$ is presented, we can access it very quickly if it is already in the cache; otherwise, we are required to bring it from main memory into the cache and, if the cache is full, to *evict* some other piece of data that is currently in the cache to make room for $d_i$. This is called a *cache miss*, and we want to have as few of these as possible.

Thus, on a particular sequence of memory references, a cache maintenance algorithm determines an *eviction schedule*—specifying which items should be evicted from the cache at which points in the sequence—and this determines the contents of the cache and the number of misses over time. Let's consider an example of this process.

- Suppose we have three items $\{a, b, c\}$, the cache size is $k = 2$, and we are presented with the sequence

$$a, b, c, b, c, a, b.$$

Suppose that the cache initially contains the items $a$ and $b$. Then on the third item in the sequence, we could evict $a$ so as to bring in $c$; and on the sixth item we could evict $c$ so as to bring in $a$; we thereby incur two cache misses over the whole sequence. After thinking about it, one concludes that any eviction schedule for this sequence must include at least two cache misses.

Under real operating conditions, cache maintenance algorithms must process memory references $d_1, d_2, \ldots$ without knowledge of what's coming in the future; but for purposes of evaluating the quality of these algorithms, systems researchers very early on sought to understand the nature of the optimal solution to the caching problem. Given a full sequence $S$ of memory references, what is the eviction schedule that incurs as few cache misses as possible?

## Designing and Analyzing the Algorithm

In the 1960s, Les Belady showed that the following simple rule will always incur the minimum number of misses:

When $d_i$ needs to be brought into the cache,
    evict the item that is needed the farthest into the future

We will call this the *Farthest-in-Future Algorithm*. When it is time to evict something, we look at the next time that each item in the cache will be referenced, and choose the one for which this is as late as possible.

This is a very natural algorithm. At the same time, the fact that it is optimal on all sequences is somewhat more subtle than it first appears. Why evict the item that is needed farthest in the future, as opposed, for example, to the one that will be used least frequently in the future? Moreover, consider a sequence like

$$a, b, c, d, a, d, e, a, d, b, c$$

with $k = 3$ and items $\{a, b, c\}$ initially in the cache. The Farthest-in-Future rule will produce a schedule $S$ that evicts $c$ on the fourth step and $b$ on the seventh step. But there are other eviction schedules that are just as good. Consider the schedule $S'$ that evicts $b$ on the fourth step and $c$ on the seventh step, incurring the same number of misses. So in fact it's easy to find cases where schedules produced by rules other than Farthest-in-Future are also optimal; and given this flexibility, why might a deviation from Farthest-in-Future early on not yield an actual savings farther along in the sequence? For example, on the seventh step in our example, the schedule $S'$ is actually evicting an item ($c$) that is needed *farther* into the future than the item evicted at this point by Farthest-in-Future, since Farthest-in-Future gave up $c$ earlier on.

These are some of the kinds of things one should worry about before concluding that Farthest-in-Future really is optimal. In thinking about the example above, we quickly appreciate that it doesn't really matter whether $b$ or $c$ is evicted at the fourth step, since the other one should be evicted at the seventh step; so given a schedule where $b$ is evicted first, we can swap the choices of $b$ and $c$ without changing the cost. This reasoning—swapping one decision for another—forms the first outline of an *exchange argument* that proves the optimality of Farthest-in-Future.

Before delving into this analysis, let's clear up one important issue. All the cache maintenance algorithms we've been considering so far produce schedules that only bring an item $d$ into the cache in a step $i$ if there is a request to $d$ in step $i$, and $d$ is not already in the cache. Let us call such a schedule *reduced*—it does the minimal amount of work necessary in a given step. But in general one could imagine an algorithm that produced schedules that are not reduced, by bringing in items in steps when they are not requested. We now show that for every nonreduced schedule, there is an equally good reduced schedule.

Let $S$ be a schedule that may not be reduced. We define a new schedule $\overline{S}$—the *reduction* of $S$—as follows. In any step $i$ where $S$ brings in an item $d$ that has not been requested, our construction of $\overline{S}$ "pretends" to do this but actually leaves $d$ in main memory. It only really brings $d$ into the cache in the next step $j$ after this in which $d$ is requested. In this way, the cache miss incurred by $\overline{S}$ in step $j$ can be charged to the earlier cache operation performed by $S$ in step $i$, when it brought in $d$. Hence we have the following fact.

**(4.11)**   $\overline{S}$ *is a reduced schedule that brings in at most as many items as the schedule $S$.*

Note that for any reduced schedule, the number of items that are brought in is exactly the number of misses.

*Proving the Optimalthy of Farthest-in-Future* We now proceed with the exchange argument showing that Farthest-in-Future is optimal. Consider an arbitrary sequence $D$ of memory references; let $S_{FF}$ denote the schedule produced by Farthest-in-Future, and let $S^*$ denote a schedule that incurs the minimum possible number of misses. We will now gradually "transform" the schedule $S^*$ into the schedule $S_{FF}$, one eviction decision at a time, without increasing the number of misses.

Here is the basic fact we use to perform one step in the transformation.

**(4.12)** *Let S be a reduced schedule that makes the same eviction decisions as $S_{FF}$ through the first j items in the sequence, for a number j. Then there is a reduced schedule S' that makes the same eviction decisions as $S_{FF}$ through the first $j + 1$ items, and incurs no more misses than S does.*

**Proof.** Consider the $(j + 1)^{st}$ request, to item $d = d_{j+1}$. Since $S$ and $S_{FF}$ have agreed up to this point, they have the same cache contents. If $d$ is in the cache for both, then no eviction decision is necessary (both schedules are reduced), and so $S$ in fact agrees with $S_{FF}$ through step $j + 1$, and we can set $S' = S$. Similarly, if $d$ needs to be brought into the cache, but $S$ and $S_{FF}$ both evict the same item to make room for $d$, then we can again set $S' = S$.

So the interesting case arises when $d$ needs to be brought into the cache, and to do this $S$ evicts item $f$ while $S_{FF}$ evicts item $e \neq f$. Here $S$ and $S_{FF}$ do not already agree through step $j + 1$ since $S$ has $e$ in cache while $S_{FF}$ has $f$ in cache. Hence we must actually do something nontrivial to construct $S'$.

As a first step, we should have $S'$ evict $e$ rather than $f$. Now we need to further ensure that $S'$ incurs no more misses than $S$. An easy way to do this would be to have $S'$ agree with $S$ for the remainder of the sequence; but this is no longer possible, since $S$ and $S'$ have slightly different caches from this point onward. So instead we'll have $S'$ try to get its cache back to the same state as $S$ as quickly as possible, while not incurring unnecessary misses. Once the caches are the same, we can finish the construction of $S'$ by just having it behave like $S$.

Specifically, from request $j + 2$ onward, $S'$ behaves exactly like $S$ until one of the following things happens for the first time.

(i) There is a request to an item $g \neq e, f$ that is not in the cache of $S$, and $S$ evicts $e$ to make room for it. Since $S'$ and $S$ only differ on $e$ and $f$, it must be that $g$ is not in the cache of $S'$ either; so we can have $S'$ evict $f$, and now the caches of $S$ and $S'$ are the same. We can then have $S'$ behave exactly like $S$ for the rest of the sequence.

(ii) There is a request to $f$, and $S$ evicts an item $e'$. If $e' = e$, then we're all set: $S'$ can simply access $f$ from the cache, and after this step the caches of $S$ and $S'$ will be the same. If $e' \neq e$, then we have $S'$ evict $e'$ as well, and bring in $e$ from main memory; this too results in $S$ and $S'$ having the same caches. However, we must be careful here, since $S'$ is no longer a reduced schedule: it brought in $e$ when it wasn't immediately needed. So to finish this part of the construction, we further transform $S'$ to its reduction $\overline{S'}$ using (4.11); this doesn't increase the number of items brought in by $S'$, and it still agrees with $S_{FF}$ through step $j + 1$.

Hence, in both these cases, we have a new reduced schedule $S'$ that agrees with $S_{FF}$ through the first $j + 1$ items and incurs no more misses than $S$ does. And crucially—here is where we use the defining property of the Farthest-in-Future Algorithm—one of these two cases will arise *before* there is a reference to $e$. This is because in step $j + 1$, Farthest-in-Future evicted the item ($e$) that would be needed farthest in the future; so before there could be a request to $e$, there would have to be a request to $f$, and then case (ii) above would apply. ∎

Using this result, it is easy to complete the proof of optimality. We begin with an optimal schedule $S^*$, and use (4.12) to construct a schedule $S_1$ that agrees with $S_{FF}$ through the first step. We continue applying (4.12) inductively for $j = 1, 2, 3, \ldots, m$, producing schedules $S_j$ that agree with $S_{FF}$ through the first $j$ steps. Each schedule incurs no more misses than the previous one; and by definition $S_m = S_{FF}$, since it agrees with it through the whole sequence. Thus we have

**(4.13)**   *$S_{FF}$ incurs no more misses than any other schedule $S^*$ and hence is optimal.*

## Extensions: Caching under Real Operating Conditions

As mentioned in the previous subsection, Belady's optimal algorithm provides a benchmark for caching performance; but in applications, one generally must make eviction decisions on the fly without knowledge of future requests. Experimentally, the best caching algorithms under this requirement seem to be variants of the *Least-Recently-Used* (LRU) Principle, which proposes evicting the item from the cache that was referenced *longest ago*.

If one thinks about it, this is just Belady's Algorithm with the direction of time reversed—longest in the past rather than farthest in the future. It is effective because applications generally exhibit *locality of reference*: a running program will generally keep accessing the things it has just been accessing. (It is easy to invent pathological exceptions to this principle, but these are relatively rare in practice.) Thus one wants to keep the more recently referenced items in the cache.

Long after the adoption of LRU in practice, Sleator and Tarjan showed that one could actually provide some theoretical analysis of the performance of LRU, bounding the number of misses it incurs relative to Farthest-in-Future. We will discuss this analysis, as well as the analysis of a randomized variant on LRU, when we return to the caching problem in Chapter 13.

## 4.4 Shortest Paths in a Graph

Some of the basic algorithms for graphs are based on greedy design principles. Here we apply a greedy algorithm to the problem of finding shortest paths, and in the next section we look at the construction of minimum-cost spanning trees.

### The Problem

As we've seen, graphs are often used to model networks in which one travels from one point to another—traversing a sequence of highways through interchanges, or traversing a sequence of communication links through intermediate routers. As a result, a basic algorithmic problem is to determine the shortest path between nodes in a graph. We may ask this as a point-to-point question: Given nodes $u$ and $v$, what is the shortest $u$-$v$ path? Or we may ask for more information: Given a *start node* $s$, what is the shortest path from $s$ to each other node?

The concrete setup of the shortest paths problem is as follows. We are given a directed graph $G = (V, E)$, with a designated start node $s$. We assume that $s$ has a path to every other node in $G$. Each edge $e$ has a length $\ell_e \geq 0$, indicating the time (or distance, or cost) it takes to traverse $e$. For a path $P$, the *length of P*—denoted $\ell(P)$—is the sum of the lengths of all edges in $P$. Our goal is to determine the shortest path from $s$ to every other node in the graph. We should mention that although the problem is specified for a directed graph, we can handle the case of an undirected graph by simply replacing each undirected edge $e = (u, v)$ of length $\ell_e$ by two directed edges $(u, v)$ and $(v, u)$, each of length $\ell_e$.

### Designing the Algorithm

In 1959, Edsger Dijkstra proposed a very simple greedy algorithm to solve the single-source shortest-paths problem. We begin by describing an algorithm that just determines the *length* of the shortest path from $s$ to each other node in the graph; it is then easy to produce the paths as well. The algorithm maintains a set $S$ of vertices $u$ for which we have determined a shortest-path distance $d(u)$ from $s$; this is the "explored" part of the graph. Initially $S = \{s\}$, and $d(s) = 0$. Now, for each node $v \in V - S$, we determine the shortest path that can be constructed by traveling along a path through the explored part $S$ to some $u \in S$, followed by the single edge $(u, v)$. That is, we consider the quantity

$d'(v) = \min_{e=(u,v):u\in S} d(u) + \ell_e$. We choose the node $v \in V - S$ for which this quantity is minimized, add $v$ to $S$, and define $d(v)$ to be the value $d'(v)$.

---

```
Dijkstra's Algorithm (G, ℓ)
Let S be the set of explored nodes
    For each u ∈ S, we store a distance d(u)
Initially S = {s} and d(s) = 0
While S ≠ V
    Select a node v ∉ S with at least one edge from S for which
        d'(v) = min_{e=(u,v):u∈S} d(u) + ℓ_e is as small as possible
    Add v to S and define d(v) = d'(v)
EndWhile
```

---

It is simple to produce the $s$-$u$ paths corresponding to the distances found by Dijkstra's Algorithm. As each node $v$ is added to the set $S$, we simply record the edge $(u, v)$ on which it achieved the value $\min_{e=(u,v):u\in S} d(u) + \ell_e$. The path $P_v$ is implicitly represented by these edges: if $(u, v)$ is the edge we have stored for $v$, then $P_v$ is just (recursively) the path $P_u$ followed by the single edge $(u, v)$. In other words, to construct $P_v$, we simply start at $v$; follow the edge we have stored for $v$ in the reverse direction to $u$; then follow the edge we have stored for $u$ in the reverse direction to its predecessor; and so on until we reach $s$. Note that $s$ must be reached, since our backward walk from $v$ visits nodes that were added to $S$ earlier and earlier.

To get a better sense of what the algorithm is doing, consider the snapshot of its execution depicted in Figure 4.7. At the point the picture is drawn, two iterations have been performed: the first added node $u$, and the second added node $v$. In the iteration that is about to be performed, the node $x$ will be added because it achieves the smallest value of $d'(x)$; thanks to the edge $(u, x)$, we have $d'(x) = d(u) + l_{ux} = 2$. Note that attempting to add $y$ or $z$ to the set $S$ at this point would lead to an incorrect value for their shortest-path distances; ultimately, they will be added because of their edges from $x$.

### Analyzing the Algorithm

We see in this example that Dijkstra's Algorithm is doing the right thing and avoiding recurring pitfalls: growing the set $S$ by the wrong node can lead to an overestimate of the shortest-path distance to that node. The question becomes: Is it always true that when Dijkstra's Algorithm adds a node $v$, we get the true shortest-path distance to $v$?

We now answer this by proving the correctness of the algorithm, showing that the paths $P_u$ really are shortest paths. Dijkstra's Algorithm is greedy in

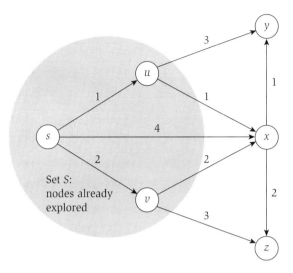

**Figure 4.7** A snapshot of the execution of Dijkstra's Algorithm. The next node that will be added to the set $S$ is $x$, due to the path through $u$.

the sense that we always form the shortest new $s$-$v$ path we can make from a path in $S$ followed by a single edge. We prove its correctness using a variant of our first style of analysis: we show that it "stays ahead" of all other solutions by establishing, inductively, that each time it selects a path to a node $v$, that path is shorter than every other possible path to $v$.

**(4.14)** *Consider the set $S$ at any point in the algorithm's execution. For each $u \in S$, the path $P_u$ is a shortest $s$-$u$ path.*

Note that this fact immediately establishes the correctness of Dijkstra's Algorithm, since we can apply it when the algorithm terminates, at which point $S$ includes all nodes.

**Proof.** We prove this by induction on the size of $S$. The case $|S| = 1$ is easy, since then we have $S = \{s\}$ and $d(s) = 0$. Suppose the claim holds when $|S| = k$ for some value of $k \geq 1$; we now grow $S$ to size $k + 1$ by adding the node $v$. Let $(u, v)$ be the final edge on our $s$-$v$ path $P_v$.

By induction hypothesis, $P_u$ is the shortest $s$-$u$ path for each $u \in S$. Now consider any other $s$-$v$ path $P$; we wish to show that it is at least as long as $P_v$. In order to reach $v$, this path $P$ must leave the set $S$ *somewhere*; let $y$ be the first node on $P$ that is not in $S$, and let $x \in S$ be the node just before $y$.

The situation is now as depicted in Figure 4.8, and the crux of the proof is very simple: $P$ cannot be shorter than $P_v$ because it is already at least as

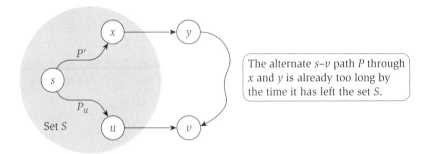

**Figure 4.8** The shortest path $P_v$ and an alternate $s$-$v$ path $P$ through the node $y$.

long as $P_v$ by the time it has left the set $S$. Indeed, in iteration $k + 1$, Dijkstra's Algorithm must have considered adding node $y$ to the set $S$ via the edge $(x, y)$ and rejected this option in favor of adding $v$. This means that there is no path from $s$ to $y$ through $x$ that is shorter than $P_v$. But the subpath of $P$ up to $y$ is such a path, and so this subpath is at least as long as $P_v$. Since edge lengths are nonnegative, the full path $P$ is at least as long as $P_v$ as well.

This is a complete proof; one can also spell out the argument in the previous paragraph using the following inequalities. Let $P'$ be the subpath of $P$ from $s$ to $x$. Since $x \in S$, we know by the induction hypothesis that $P_x$ is a shortest $s$-$x$ path (of length $d(x)$), and so $\ell(P') \geq \ell(P_x) = d(x)$. Thus the subpath of $P$ out to node $y$ has length $\ell(P') + \ell(x, y) \geq d(x) + \ell(x, y) \geq d'(y)$, and the full path $P$ is at least as long as this subpath. Finally, since Dijkstra's Algorithm selected $v$ in this iteration, we know that $d'(y) \geq d'(v) = \ell(P_v)$. Combining these inequalities shows that $\ell(P) \geq \ell(P') + \ell(x, y) \geq \ell(P_v)$. ∎

Here are two observations about Dijkstra's Algorithm and its analysis. First, the algorithm does not always find shortest paths if some of the edges can have negative lengths. (Do you see where the proof breaks?) Many shortest-path applications involve negative edge lengths, and a more complex algorithm—due to Bellman and Ford—is required for this case. We will see this algorithm when we consider the topic of dynamic programming.

The second observation is that Dijkstra's Algorithm is, in a sense, even simpler than we've described here. Dijkstra's Algorithm is really a "continuous" version of the standard breadth-first search algorithm for traversing a graph, and it can be motivated by the following physical intuition. Suppose the edges of $G$ formed a system of pipes filled with water, joined together at the nodes; each edge $e$ has length $\ell_e$ and a fixed cross-sectional area. Now suppose an extra droplet of water falls at node $s$ and starts a wave from $s$. As the wave expands out of node $s$ at a constant speed, the expanding sphere of wavefront reaches nodes in increasing order of their distance from $s$. It is easy to believe (and also true) that the path taken by the wavefront to get to any node $v$ is a shortest path. Indeed, it is easy to see that this is exactly the path to $v$ found by Dijkstra's Algorithm, and that the nodes are discovered by the expanding water in the same order that they are discovered by Dijkstra's Algorithm.

***Implementation and Running Time*** To conclude our discussion of Dijkstra's Algorithm, we consider its running time. There are $n - 1$ iterations of the While loop for a graph with $n$ nodes, as each iteration adds a new node $v$ to $S$. Selecting the correct node $v$ efficiently is a more subtle issue. One's first impression is that each iteration would have to consider each node $v \notin S$, and go through all the edges between $S$ and $v$ to determine the minimum $\min_{e=(u,v):u\in S} d(u) + \ell_e$, so that we can select the node $v$ for which this minimum is smallest. For a graph with $m$ edges, computing all these minima can take $O(m)$ time, so this would lead to an implementation that runs in $O(mn)$ time.

We can do considerably better if we use the right data structures. First, we will explicitly maintain the values of the minima $d'(v) = \min_{e=(u,v):u\in S} d(u) + \ell_e$ for each node $v \in V - S$, rather than recomputing them in each iteration. We can further improve the efficiency by keeping the nodes $V - S$ in a priority queue with $d'(v)$ as their keys. Priority queues were discussed in Chapter 2; they are data structures designed to maintain a set of $n$ elements, each with a key. A priority queue can efficiently insert elements, delete elements, change an element's key, and extract the element with the minimum key. We will need the third and fourth of the above operations: ChangeKey and ExtractMin.

How do we implement Dijkstra's Algorithm using a priority queue? We put the nodes $V$ in a priority queue with $d'(v)$ as the key for $v \in V$. To select the node $v$ that should be added to the set $S$, we need the ExtractMin operation. To see how to update the keys, consider an iteration in which node $v$ is added to $S$, and let $w \notin S$ be a node that remains in the priority queue. What do we have to do to update the value of $d'(w)$? If $(v, w)$ is not an edge, then we don't have to do anything: the set of edges considered in the minimum $\min_{e=(u,w):u\in S} d(u) + \ell_e$ is exactly the same before and after adding $v$ to $S$. If $e' = (v, w) \in E$, on the other hand, then the new value for the key is $\min(d'(w), d(v) + \ell_{e'})$. If $d'(w) > d(v) + \ell_{e'}$ then we need to use the ChangeKey operation to decrease the key of node $w$ appropriately. This ChangeKey operation can occur at most once per edge, when the tail of the edge $e'$ is added to $S$. In summary, we have the following result.

> **(4.15)**   *Using a priority queue, Dijkstra's Algorithm can be implemented on a graph with n nodes and m edges to run in $O(m)$ time, plus the time for n* `ExtractMin` *and m* `ChangeKey` *operations.*

Using the heap-based priority queue implementation discussed in Chapter 2, each priority queue operation can be made to run in $O(\log n)$ time. Thus the overall time for the implementation is $O(m \log n)$.

## 4.5 The Minimum Spanning Tree Problem

We now apply an exchange argument in the context of a second fundamental problem on graphs: the Minimum Spanning Tree Problem.

### The Problem

Suppose we have a set of locations $V = \{v_1, v_2, \ldots, v_n\}$, and we want to build a communication network on top of them. The network should be connected—there should be a path between every pair of nodes—but subject to this requirement, we wish to build it as cheaply as possible.

For certain pairs $(v_i, v_j)$, we may build a direct link between $v_i$ and $v_j$ for a certain cost $c(v_i, v_j) > 0$. Thus we can represent the set of possible links that may be built using a graph $G = (V, E)$, with a positive *cost* $c_e$ associated with each edge $e = (v_i, v_j)$. The problem is to find a subset of the edges $T \subseteq E$ so that the graph $(V, T)$ is connected, and the total cost $\sum_{e \in T} c_e$ is as small as possible. (We will assume that the full graph $G$ is connected; otherwise, no solution is possible.)

Here is a basic observation.

> **(4.16)**   *Let T be a minimum-cost solution to the network design problem defined above. Then $(V, T)$ is a tree.*

**Proof.** By definition, $(V, T)$ must be connected; we show that it also will contain no cycles. Indeed, suppose it contained a cycle $C$, and let $e$ be any edge on $C$. We claim that $(V, T - \{e\})$ is still connected, since any path that previously used the edge $e$ can now go "the long way" around the remainder of the cycle $C$ instead. It follows that $(V, T - \{e\})$ is also a valid solution to the problem, and it is cheaper—a contradiction.   ∎

If we allow some edges to have 0 cost (that is, we assume only that the costs $c_e$ are nonnegative), then a minimum-cost solution to the network design problem may have extra edges—edges that have 0 cost and could optionally be deleted. But even in this case, there is always a minimum-cost solution that is a tree. Starting from any optimal solution, we could keep deleting edges on cycles until we had a tree; with nonnegative edges, the cost would not increase during this process.

We will call a subset $T \subseteq E$ a *spanning tree* of $G$ if $(V, T)$ is a tree. Statement (4.16) says that the goal of our network design problem can be rephrased as that of finding the cheapest spanning tree of the graph; for this reason, it is generally called the *Minimum Spanning Tree Problem*. Unless $G$ is a very simple graph, it will have exponentially many different spanning trees, whose structures may look very different from one another. So it is not at all clear how to efficiently find the cheapest tree from among all these options.

## 🖋 Designing Algorithms

As with the previous problems we've seen, it is easy to come up with a number of natural greedy algorithms for the problem. But curiously, and fortunately, this is a case where *many* of the first greedy algorithms one tries turn out to be correct: they each solve the problem optimally. We will review a few of these algorithms now and then discover, via a nice pair of exchange arguments, some of the underlying reasons for this plethora of simple, optimal algorithms.

Here are three greedy algorithms, each of which correctly finds a minimum spanning tree.

- One simple algorithm starts without any edges at all and builds a spanning tree by successively inserting edges from $E$ in order of increasing cost. As we move through the edges in this order, we insert each edge $e$ as long as it does not create a cycle when added to the edges we've already inserted. If, on the other hand, inserting $e$ would result in a cycle, then we simply discard $e$ and continue. This approach is called *Kruskal's Algorithm*.

- Another simple greedy algorithm can be designed by analogy with Dijkstra's Algorithm for paths, although, in fact, it is even simpler to specify than Dijkstra's Algorithm. We start with a root node $s$ and try to greedily grow a tree from $s$ outward. At each step, we simply add the node that can be attached as cheaply as possibly to the partial tree we already have.

    More concretely, we maintain a set $S \subseteq V$ on which a spanning tree has been constructed so far. Initially, $S = \{s\}$. In each iteration, we grow $S$ by one node, adding the node $v$ that minimizes the "attachment cost" $\min_{e=(u,v):u\in S} c_e$, and including the edge $e = (u, v)$ that achieves this minimum in the spanning tree. This approach is called *Prim's Algorithm*.

- Finally, we can design a greedy algorithm by running sort of a "backward" version of Kruskal's Algorithm. Specifically, we start with the full graph $(V, E)$ and begin deleting edges in order of decreasing cost. As we get to each edge $e$ (starting from the most expensive), we delete it as

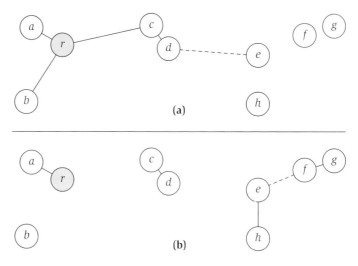

**Figure 4.9** Sample run of the Minimum Spanning Tree Algorithms of (a) Prim and (b) Kruskal, on the same input. The first 4 edges added to the spanning tree are indicated by solid lines; the next edge to be added is a dashed line.

long as doing so would not actually disconnect the graph we currently have. For want of a better name, this approach is generally called the *Reverse-Delete Algorithm* (as far as we can tell, it's never been named after a specific person).

For example, Figure 4.9 shows the first four edges added by Prim's and Kruskal's Algorithms respectively, on a geometric instance of the Minimum Spanning Tree Problem in which the cost of each edge is proportional to the geometric distance in the plane.

The fact that each of these algorithms is guaranteed to produce an optimal solution suggests a certain "robustness" to the Minimum Spanning Tree Problem—there are many ways to get to the answer. Next we explore some of the underlying reasons why so many different algorithms produce minimum-cost spanning trees.

### Analyzing the Algorithms

All these algorithms work by repeatedly inserting or deleting edges from a partial solution. So, to analyze them, it would be useful to have in hand some basic facts saying when it is "safe" to include an edge in the minimum spanning tree, and, correspondingly, when it is safe to eliminate an edge on the grounds that it couldn't possibly be in the minimum spanning tree. For purposes of the analysis, we will make the simplifying assumption that all edge costs are distinct from one another (i.e., no two are equal). This assumption makes it easier to express the arguments that follow, and we will show later in this section how this assumption can be easily eliminated.

**When Is It Safe to Include an Edge in the Minimum Spanning Tree?** The crucial fact about edge insertion is the following statement, which we will refer to as the *Cut Property*.

**(4.17)** *Assume that all edge costs are distinct. Let S be any subset of nodes that is neither empty nor equal to all of V, and let edge $e = (v, w)$ be the minimum-cost edge with one end in S and the other in $V - S$. Then every minimum spanning tree contains the edge $e$.*

**Proof.** Let $T$ be a spanning tree that does not contain $e$; we need to show that $T$ does not have the minimum possible cost. We'll do this using an exchange argument: we'll identify an edge $e'$ in $T$ that is more expensive than $e$, and with the property exchanging $e$ for $e'$ results in another spanning tree. This resulting spanning tree will then be cheaper than $T$, as desired.

The crux is therefore to find an edge that can be successfully exchanged with $e$. Recall that the ends of $e$ are $v$ and $w$. $T$ is a spanning tree, so there must be a path $P$ in $T$ from $v$ to $w$. Starting at $v$, suppose we follow the nodes of $P$ in sequence; there is a first node $w'$ on $P$ that is in $V - S$. Let $v' \in S$ be the node just before $w'$ on $P$, and let $e' = (v', w')$ be the edge joining them. Thus, $e'$ is an edge of $T$ with one end in $S$ and the other in $V - S$. See Figure 4.10 for the situation at this stage in the proof.

If we exchange $e$ for $e'$, we get a set of edges $T' = T - \{e'\} \cup \{e\}$. We claim that $T'$ is a spanning tree. Clearly $(V, T')$ is connected, since $(V, T)$ is connected, and any path in $(V, T)$ that used the edge $e' = (v', w')$ can now be "rerouted" in $(V, T')$ to follow the portion of $P$ from $v'$ to $v$, then the edge $e$, and then the portion of $P$ from $w$ to $w'$. To see that $(V, T')$ is also acyclic, note that the only cycle in $(V, T' \cup \{e'\})$ is the one composed of $e$ and the path $P$, and this cycle is not present in $(V, T')$ due to the deletion of $e'$.

We noted above that the edge $e'$ has one end in $S$ and the other in $V - S$. But $e$ is the cheapest edge with this property, and so $c_e < c_{e'}$. (The inequality is strict since no two edges have the same cost.) Thus the total cost of $T'$ is less than that of $T$, as desired. ■

The proof of (4.17) is a bit more subtle than it may first appear. To appreciate this subtlety, consider the following shorter but incorrect argument for (4.17). Let $T$ be a spanning tree that does not contain $e$. Since $T$ is a spanning tree, it must contain an edge $f$ with one end in $S$ and the other in $V - S$. Since $e$ is the cheapest edge with this property, we have $c_e < c_f$, and hence $T - \{f\} \cup \{e\}$ is a spanning tree that is cheaper than $T$.

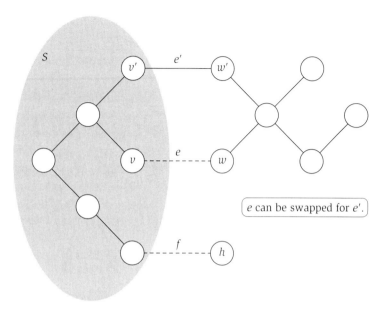

**Figure 4.10** Swapping the edge $e$ for the edge $e'$ in the spanning tree $T$, as described in the proof of (4.17).

The problem with this argument is not in the claim that $f$ exists, or that $T - \{f\} \cup \{e\}$ is cheaper than $T$. The difficulty is that $T - \{f\} \cup \{e\}$ may not be a spanning tree, as shown by the example of the edge $f$ in Figure 4.10. The point is that we can't prove (4.17) by simply picking *any* edge in $T$ that crosses from $S$ to $V - S$; some care must be taken to find the right one.

**The Optimality of Kruskal's and Prim's Algorithms**    We can now easily prove the optimality of both Kruskal's Algorithm and Prim's Algorithm. The point is that both algorithms only include an edge when it is justified by the Cut Property (4.17).

**(4.18)** *Kruskal's Algorithm produces a minimum spanning tree of G.*

**Proof.** Consider any edge $e = (v, w)$ added by Kruskal's Algorithm, and let $S$ be the set of all nodes to which $v$ has a path at the moment just before $e$ is added. Clearly $v \in S$, but $w \notin S$, since adding $e$ does not create a cycle. Moreover, no edge from $S$ to $V - S$ has been encountered yet, since any such edge could have been added without creating a cycle, and hence would have been added by Kruskal's Algorithm. Thus $e$ is the cheapest edge with one end in $S$ and the other in $V - S$, and so by (4.17) it belongs to every minimum spanning tree.

So if we can show that the output $(V, T)$ of Kruskal's Algorithm is in fact a spanning tree of $G$, then we will be done. Clearly $(V, T)$ contains no cycles, since the algorithm is explicitly designed to avoid creating cycles. Further, if $(V, T)$ were not connected, then there would exist a nonempty subset of nodes $S$ (not equal to all of $V$) such that there is no edge from $S$ to $V - S$. But this contradicts the behavior of the algorithm: we know that since $G$ is connected, there is at least one edge between $S$ and $V - S$, and the algorithm will add the first of these that it encounters. ∎

**(4.19)** *Prim's Algorithm produces a minimum spanning tree of G.*

**Proof.** For Prim's Algorithm, it is also very easy to show that it only adds edges belonging to every minimum spanning tree. Indeed, in each iteration of the algorithm, there is a set $S \subseteq V$ on which a partial spanning tree has been constructed, and a node $v$ and edge $e$ are added that minimize the quantity $\min_{e=(u,v):u\in S} c_e$. By definition, $e$ is the cheapest edge with one end in $S$ and the other end in $V - S$, and so by the Cut Property (4.17) it is in every minimum spanning tree. 

It is also straightforward to show that Prim's Algorithm produces a spanning tree of $G$, and hence it produces a minimum spanning tree. ∎

**When Can We Guarantee an Edge Is Not in the Minimum Spanning Tree?** The crucial fact about edge deletion is the following statement, which we will refer to as the *Cycle Property*.

**(4.20)** *Assume that all edge costs are distinct. Let C be any cycle in G, and let edge $e = (v, w)$ be the most expensive edge belonging to C. Then e does not belong to any minimum spanning tree of G.*

**Proof.** Let $T$ be a spanning tree that contains $e$; we need to show that $T$ does not have the minimum possible cost. By analogy with the proof of the Cut Property (4.17), we'll do this with an exchange argument, swapping $e$ for a cheaper edge in such a way that we still have a spanning tree.

So again the question is: How do we find a cheaper edge that can be exchanged in this way with $e$? Let's begin by deleting $e$ from $T$; this partitions the nodes into two components: $S$, containing node $v$; and $V - S$, containing node $w$. Now, the edge we use in place of $e$ should have one end in $S$ and the other in $V - S$, so as to stitch the tree back together.

We can find such an edge by following the cycle $C$. The edges of $C$ other than $e$ form, by definition, a path $P$ with one end at $v$ and the other at $w$. If we follow $P$ from $v$ to $w$, we begin in $S$ and end up in $V - S$, so there is some

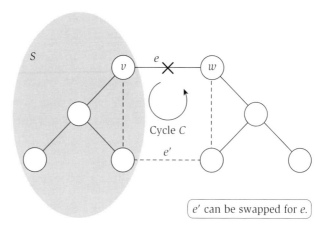

**Figure 4.11** Swapping the edge $e'$ for the edge $e$ in the spanning tree $T$, as described in the proof of (4.20).

edge $e'$ on $P$ that crosses from $S$ to $V - S$. See Figure 4.11 for an illustration of this.

Now consider the set of edges $T' = T - \{e\} \cup \{e'\}$. Arguing just as in the proof of the Cut Property (4.17), the graph $(V, T')$ is connected and has no cycles, so $T'$ is a spanning tree of $G$. Moreover, since $e$ is the most expensive edge on the cycle $C$, and $e'$ belongs to $C$, it must be that $e'$ is cheaper than $e$, and hence $T'$ is cheaper than $T$, as desired. ∎

**The Optimality of the Reverse-Delete Algorithm**   Now that we have the Cycle Property (4.20), it is easy to prove that the Reverse-Delete Algorithm produces a minimum spanning tree. The basic idea is analogous to the optimality proofs for the previous two algorithms: Reverse-Delete only adds an edge when it is justified by (4.20).

**(4.21)**    *The Reverse-Delete Algorithm produces a minimum spanning tree of G.*

**Proof.** Consider any edge $e = (v, w)$ removed by Reverse-Delete. At the time that $e$ is removed, it lies on a cycle $C$; and since it is the first edge encountered by the algorithm in decreasing order of edge costs, it must be the most expensive edge on $C$. Thus by (4.20), $e$ does not belong to any minimum spanning tree.

So if we show that the output $(V, T)$ of Reverse-Delete is a spanning tree of $G$, we will be done. Clearly $(V, T)$ is connected, since the algorithm never removes an edge when this will disconnect the graph. Now, suppose by way of contradiction that $(V, T)$ contains a cycle $C$. Consider the most expensive edge $e$ on $C$, which would be the first one encountered by the algorithm. This edge should have been removed, since its removal would not have disconnected the graph, and this contradicts the behavior of Reverse-Delete. ∎

While we will not explore this further here, the combination of the Cut Property (4.17) and the Cycle Property (4.20) implies that something even more general is going on. *Any* algorithm that builds a spanning tree by repeatedly including edges when justified by the Cut Property and deleting edges when justified by the Cycle Property—in any order at all—will end up with a minimum spanning tree. This principle allows one to design natural greedy algorithms for this problem beyond the three we have considered here, and it provides an explanation for why so many greedy algorithms produce optimal solutions for this problem.

***Eliminating the Assumption that All Edge Costs Are Distinct*** Thus far, we have assumed that all edge costs are distinct, and this assumption has made the analysis cleaner in a number of places. Now, suppose we are given an instance of the Minimum Spanning Tree Problem in which certain edges have the same cost – how can we conclude that the algorithms we have been discussing still provide optimal solutions?

There turns out to be an easy way to do this: we simply take the instance and perturb all edge costs by different, extremely small numbers, so that they all become distinct. Now, any two costs that differed originally will still have the same relative order, since the perturbations are so small; and since all of our algorithms are based on just comparing edge costs, the perturbations effectively serve simply as "tie-breakers" to resolve comparisons among costs that used to be equal.

Moreover, we claim that any minimum spanning tree $T$ for the new, perturbed instance must have also been a minimum spanning tree for the original instance. To see this, we note that if $T$ cost more than some tree $T^*$ in the original instance, then for small enough perturbations, the change in the cost of $T$ cannot be enough to make it better than $T^*$ under the new costs. Thus, if we run any of our minimum spanning tree algorithms, using the perturbed costs for comparing edges, we will produce a minimum spanning tree $T$ that is also optimal for the original instance.

## Implementing Prim's Algorithm

We next discuss how to implement the algorithms we have been considering so as to obtain good running-time bounds. We will see that both Prim's and Kruskal's Algorithms can be implemented, with the right choice of data structures, to run in $O(m \log n)$ time. We will see how to do this for Prim's Algorithm here, and defer discussing the implementation of Kruskal's Algorithm to the next section. Obtaining a running time close to this for the Reverse-Delete Algorithm is difficult, so we do not focus on Reverse-Delete in this discussion.

For Prim's Algorithm, while the proof of correctness was quite different from the proof for Dijkstra's Algorithm for the Shortest-Path Algorithm, the implementations of Prim and Dijkstra are almost identical. By analogy with Dijkstra's Algorithm, we need to be able to decide which node $v$ to add next to the growing set $S$, by maintaining the attachment costs $a(v) = \min_{e=(u,v):u \in S} c_e$ for each node $v \in V - S$. As before, we keep the nodes in a priority queue with these attachment costs $a(v)$ as the keys; we select a node with an `ExtractMin` operation, and update the attachment costs using `ChangeKey` operations. There are $n - 1$ iterations in which we perform `ExtractMin`, and we perform `ChangeKey` at most once for each edge. Thus we have

**(4.22)**    *Using a priority queue, Prim's Algorithm can be implemented on a graph with n nodes and m edges to run in $O(m)$ time, plus the time for n* `ExtractMin`, *and m* `ChangeKey` *operations.*

As with Dijkstra's Algorithm, if we use a heap-based priority queue we can implement both `ExtractMin` and `ChangeKey` in $O(\log n)$ time, and so get an overall running time of $O(m \log n)$.

## Extensions

The minimum spanning tree problem emerged as a particular formulation of a broader *network design* goal—finding a good way to connect a set of sites by installing edges between them. A minimum spanning tree optimizes a particular goal, achieving connectedness with minimum total edge cost. But there are a range of further goals one might consider as well.

We may, for example, be concerned about point-to-point distances in the spanning tree we build, and be willing to reduce these even if we pay more for the set of edges. This raises new issues, since it is not hard to construct examples where the minimum spanning tree does not minimize point-to-point distances, suggesting some tension between these goals.

Alternately, we may care more about the *congestion* on the edges. Given traffic that needs to be routed between pairs of nodes, one could seek a spanning tree in which no single edge carries more than a certain amount of this traffic. Here too, it is easy to find cases in which the minimum spanning tree ends up concentrating a lot of traffic on a single edge.

More generally, it is reasonable to ask whether a spanning tree is even the right kind of solution to our network design problem. A tree has the property that destroying any one edge disconnects it, which means that trees are not at all robust against failures. One could instead make resilience an explicit goal, for example seeking the cheapest connected network on the set of sites that remains connected after the deletion of any one edge.

All of these extensions lead to problems that are computationally much harder than the basic Minimum Spanning Tree problem, though due to their importance in practice there has been research on good heuristics for them.

# 4.6 Implementing Kruskal's Algorithm: The Union-Find Data Structure

One of the most basic graph problems is to find the set of connected components. In Chapter 3 we discussed linear-time algorithms using BFS or DFS for finding the connected components of a graph.

In this section, we consider the scenario in which a graph evolves through the addition of edges. That is, the graph has a fixed population of nodes, but it grows over time by having edges appear between certain pairs of nodes. Our goal is to maintain the set of connected components of such a graph throughout this evolution process. When an edge is added to the graph, we don't want to have to recompute the connected components from scratch. Rather, we will develop a data structure that we call the Union-Find structure, which will store a representation of the components in a way that supports rapid searching and updating.

This is exactly the data structure needed to implement Kruskal's Algorithm efficiently. As each edge $e = (v, w)$ is considered, we need to efficiently find the identities of the connected components containing $v$ and $w$. If these components are different, then there is no path from $v$ and $w$, and hence edge $e$ should be included; but if the components are the same, then there is a $v$-$w$ path on the edges already included, and so $e$ should be omitted. In the event that $e$ is included, the data structure should also support the efficient merging of the components of $v$ and $w$ into a single new component.

## The Problem

The Union-Find data structure allows us to maintain disjoint sets (such as the components of a graph) in the following sense. Given a node $u$, the operation Find($u$) will return the name of the set containing $u$. This operation can be used to test if two nodes $u$ and $v$ are in the same set, by simply checking if Find($u$) = Find($v$). The data structure will also implement an operation Union($A, B$) to take two sets $A$ and $B$ and merge them to a single set.

These operations can be used to maintain connected components of an evolving graph $G = (V, E)$ as edges are added. The sets will be the connected components of the graph. For a node $u$, the operation Find($u$) will return the name of the component containing $u$. If we add an edge $(u, v)$ to the graph, then we first test if $u$ and $v$ are already in the same connected component (by testing if $\text{Find}(u) = \text{Find}(v)$). If they are not, then $\text{Union}(\text{Find}(u),\text{Find}(v))$ can be used to merge the two components into one. It is important to note that the $\text{Union-Find}$ data structure can only be used to maintain components of a graph as we *add* edges; it is not designed to handle the effects of edge deletion, which may result in a single component being "split" into two.

To summarize, the $\text{Union-Find}$ data structure will support three operations.

- $\text{MakeUnionFind}(S)$ for a set $S$ will return a $\text{Union-Find}$ data structure on set $S$ where all elements are in separate sets. This corresponds, for example, to the connected components of a graph with no edges. Our goal will be to implement $\text{MakeUnionFind}$ in time $O(n)$ where $n = |S|$.

- For an element $u \in S$, the operation $\text{Find}(u)$ will return the name of the set containing $u$. Our goal will be to implement $\text{Find}(u)$ in $O(\log n)$ time. Some implementations that we discuss will in fact take only $O(1)$ time for this operation.

- For two sets $A$ and $B$, the operation $\text{Union}(A, B)$ will change the data structure by merging the sets $A$ and $B$ into a single set. Our goal will be to implement $\text{Union}$ in $O(\log n)$ time.

Let's briefly discuss what we mean by the *name* of a set—for example, as returned by the $\text{Find}$ operation. There is a fair amount of flexibility in defining the names of the sets; they should simply be consistent in the sense that $\text{Find}(v)$ and $\text{Find}(w)$ should return the same name if $v$ and $w$ belong to the same set, and different names otherwise. In our implementations, we will name each set using one of the elements it contains.

## A Simple Data Structure for Union-Find

Maybe the simplest possible way to implement a $\text{Union-Find}$ data structure is to maintain an array $\text{Component}$ that contains the name of the set currently containing each element. Let $S$ be a set, and assume it has $n$ elements denoted $\{1, \ldots, n\}$. We will set up an array $\text{Component}$ of size $n$, where $\text{Component}[s]$ is the name of the set containing $s$. To implement $\text{MakeUnionFind}(S)$, we set up the array and initialize it to $\text{Component}[s] = s$ for all $s \in S$. This implementation makes $\text{Find}(v)$ easy: it is a simple lookup and takes only $O(1)$ time. However, $\text{Union}(A, B)$ for two sets $A$ and $B$ can take as long as $O(n)$ time, as we have to update the values of $\text{Component}[s]$ for all elements in sets $A$ and $B$.

To improve this bound, we will do a few simple optimizations. First, it is useful to explicitly maintain the list of elements in each set, so we don't have to look through the whole array to find the elements that need updating. Further, we save some time by choosing the name for the union to be the name of one of the sets, say, set $A$: this way we only have to update the values Component$[s]$ for $s \in B$, but not for any $s \in A$. Of course, if set $B$ is large, this idea by itself doesn't help very much. Thus we add one further optimization. When set $B$ is big, we may want to keep its name and change Component$[s]$ for all $s \in A$ instead. More generally, we can maintain an additional array size of length $n$, where size$[A]$ is the size of set $A$, and when a Union$(A, B)$ operation is performed, we use the name of the larger set for the union. This way, fewer elements need to have their Component values updated.

Even with these optimizations, the worst case for a Union operation is still $O(n)$ time; this happens if we take the union of two large sets $A$ and $B$, each containing a constant fraction of all the elements. However, such bad cases for Union cannot happen very often, as the resulting set $A \cup B$ is even bigger. How can we make this statement more precise? Instead of bounding the worst-case running time of a single Union operation, we can bound the total (or average) running time of a sequence of $k$ Union operations.

**(4.23)** *Consider the array implementation of the* Union-Find *data structure for some set $S$ of size $n$, where unions keep the name of the larger set. The* Find *operation takes $O(1)$ time,* MakeUnionFind$(S)$ *takes $O(n)$ time, and any sequence of $k$* Union *operations takes at most $O(k \log k)$ time.*

**Proof.** The claims about the MakeUnionFind and Find operations are easy to verify. Now consider a sequence of $k$ Union operations. The only part of a Union operation that takes more than $O(1)$ time is updating the array Component. Instead of bounding the time spent on one Union operation, we will bound the total time spent updating Component$[v]$ for an element $v$ throughout the sequence of $k$ operations.

Recall that we start the data structure from a state when all $n$ elements are in their own separate sets. A single Union operation can consider at most two of these original one-element sets, so after any sequence of $k$ Union operations, all but at most $2k$ elements of $S$ have been completely untouched. Now consider a particular element $v$. As $v$'s set is involved in a sequence of Union operations, its size grows. It may be that in some of these Unions, the value of Component$[v]$ is updated, and in others it is not. But our convention is that the union uses the name of the larger set, so in every update to Component$[v]$ the size of the set containing $v$ at least doubles. The size of $v$'s set starts out at 1, and the maximum possible size it can reach is $2k$ (since we argued above that all but at most $2k$ elements are untouched by Union operations). Thus Component$[v]$ gets updated at most $\log_2(2k)$ times throughout the process. Moreover, at most $2k$ elements are involved in any Union operations at all, so we get a bound of $O(k \log k)$ for the time spent updating `Component` values in a sequence of $k$ `Union` operations.    ■

While this bound on the average running time for a sequence of $k$ operations is good enough in many applications, including implementing Kruskal's Algorithm, we will try to do better and reduce the *worst-case* time required. We'll do this at the expense of raising the time required for the `Find` operation to $O(\log n)$.

### A Better Data Structure for Union-Find

The data structure for this alternate implementation uses pointers. Each node $v \in S$ will be contained in a record with an associated pointer to the name of the set that contains $v$. As before, we will use the elements of the set $S$ as possible set names, naming each set after one of its elements. For the `MakeUnionFind`$(S)$ operation, we initialize a record for each element $v \in S$ with a pointer that points to itself (or is defined as a `null` pointer), to indicate that $v$ is in its own set.

Consider a `Union` operation for two sets $A$ and $B$, and assume that the name we used for set $A$ is a node $v \in A$, while set $B$ is named after node $u \in B$. The idea is to have either $u$ or $v$ be the name of the combined set; assume we select $v$ as the name. To indicate that we took the union of the two sets, and that the name of the union set is $v$, we simply update $u$'s pointer to point to $v$. We do not update the pointers at the other nodes of set $B$.

As a result, for elements $w \in B$ other than $u$, the name of the set they belong to must be computed by following a sequence of pointers, first leading them to the "old name" $u$ and then via the pointer from $u$ to the "new name" $v$. See Figure 4.12 for what such a representation looks like. For example, the two sets in Figure 4.12 could be the outcome of the following sequence of `Union` operations: `Union`$(w, u)$, `Union`$(s, u)$, `Union`$(t, v)$, `Union`$(z, v)$, `Union`$(i, x)$, `Union`$(y, j)$, `Union`$(x, j)$, and `Union`$(u, v)$.

This pointer-based data structure implements `Union` in $O(1)$ time: all we have to do is to update one pointer. But a `Find` operation is no longer constant time, as we have to follow a sequence of pointers through a history of old names the set had, in order to get to the current name. How long can a `Find`$(u)$ operation take? The number of steps needed is exactly the number of times the set containing node $u$ had to change its name, that is, the number of times the `Component`$[u]$ array position would have been updated in our previous array representation. This can be as large as $O(n)$ if we are not careful with choosing set names. To reduce the time required for a `Find` operation, we will use the same optimization we used before: keep the name of the larger set as the name of the union. The sequence of `Union`s that produced the data

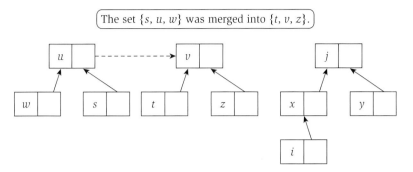

**Figure 4.12** A Union-Find data structure using pointers. The data structure has only two sets at the moment, named after nodes $v$ and $j$. The dashed arrow from $u$ to $v$ is the result of the last Union operation. To answer a Find query, we follow the arrows until we get to a node that has no outgoing arrow. For example, answering the query Find($i$) would involve following the arrows $i$ to $x$, and then $x$ to $j$.

structure in Figure 4.12 followed this convention. To implement this choice efficiently, we will maintain an additional field with the nodes: the size of the corresponding set.

**(4.24)** *Consider the above pointer-based implementation of the Union-Find data structure for some set S of size n, where unions keep the name of the larger set. A Union operation takes $O(1)$ time, MakeUnionFind(S) takes $O(n)$ time, and a Find operation takes $O(\log n)$ time.*

**Proof.** The statements about Union and MakeUnionFind are easy to verify. The time to evaluate Find($v$) for a node $v$ is the number of times the set containing node $v$ changes its name during the process. By the convention that the union keeps the name of the larger set, it follows that every time the name of the set containing node $v$ changes, the size of this set at least doubles. Since the set containing $v$ starts at size 1 and is never larger than $n$, its size can double at most $\log_2 n$ times, and so there can be at most $\log_2 n$ name changes. ∎

## Further Improvements

Next we will briefly discuss a natural optimization in the pointer-based Union-Find data structure that has the effect of speeding up the Find operations. Strictly speaking, this improvement will not be necessary for our purposes in this book: for all the applications of Union-Find data structures that we consider, the $O(\log n)$ time per operation is good enough in the sense that further improvement in the time for operations would not translate to improvements in the overall running time of the algorithms where we use them. (The Union–Find operations will not be the only computational bottleneck in the running time of these algorithms.)

To motivate the improved version of the data structure, let us first discuss a bad case for the running time of the pointer-based Union–Find data structure. First we build up a structure where one of the Find operations takes about log $n$ time. To do this, we can repeatedly take Unions of equal-sized sets. Assume $v$ is a node for which the Find($v$) operation takes about log $n$ time. Now we can issue Find($v$) repeatedly, and it takes log $n$ for each such call. Having to follow the same sequence of log $n$ pointers every time for finding the name of the set containing $v$ is quite redundant: after the first request for Find($v$), we already "know" the name $x$ of the set containing $v$, and we also know that all other nodes that we touched during our path from $v$ to the current name also are all contained in the set $x$. So in the improved implementation, we will *compress* the path we followed after every Find operation by resetting all pointers along the path to point to the current name of the set. No information is lost by doing this, and it makes subsequent Find operations run more quickly. See Figure 4.13 for a Union–Find data structure and the result of Find($v$) using path compression.

Now consider the running time of the operations in the resulting implementation. As before, a Union operation takes $O(1)$ time and MakeUnion-Find($S$) takes $O(n)$ time to set up a data structure for a set of size $n$. How did the time required for a Find($v$) operation change? Some Find operations can still take up to log $n$ time; and for some Find operations we actually increase

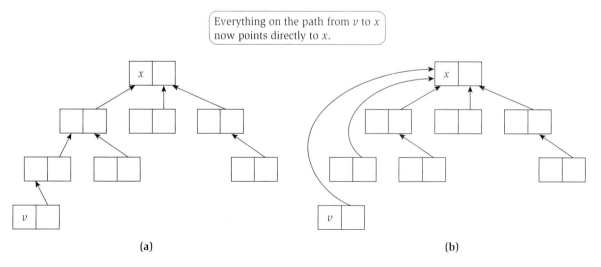

**Figure 4.13** (a) An instance of a Union–Find data structure; and (b) the result of the operation Find($v$) on this structure, using path compression.

the time, since after finding the name $x$ of the set containing $v$, we have to go back through the same path of pointers from $v$ to $x$, and reset each of these pointers to point to $x$ directly. But this additional work can at most double the time required, and so does not change the fact that a Find takes at most $O(\log n)$ time. The real gain from compression is in making subsequent calls to Find cheaper, and this can be made precise by the same type of argument we used in (4.23): bounding the total time for a sequence of $n$ Find operations, rather than the worst-case time for any one of them. Although we do not go into the details here, a sequence of $n$ Find operations employing compression requires an amount of time that is extremely close to linear in $n$; the actual upper bound is $O(n\alpha(n))$, where $\alpha(n)$ is an extremely slow-growing function of $n$ called the *inverse Ackermann function*. (In particular, $\alpha(n) \leq 4$ for any value of $n$ that could be encountered in practice.)

### Implementing Kruskal's Algorithm

Now we'll use the Union-Find data structure to implement Kruskal's Algorithm. First we need to sort the edges by cost. This takes time $O(m \log m)$. Since we have at most one edge between any pair of nodes, we have $m \leq n^2$ and hence this running time is also $O(m \log n)$.

After the sorting operation, we use the Union-Find data structure to maintain the connected components of $(V, T)$ as edges are added. As each edge $e = (v, w)$ is considered, we compute Find($u$) and Find($v$) and test if they are equal to see if $v$ and $w$ belong to different components. We use Union(Find($u$),Find($v$)) to merge the two components, if the algorithm decides to include edge $e$ in the tree $T$.

We are doing a total of at most $2m$ Find and $n - 1$ Union operations over the course of Kruskal's Algorithm. We can use either (4.23) for the array-based implementation of Union-Find, or (4.24) for the pointer-based implementation, to conclude that this is a total of $O(m \log n)$ time. (While more efficient implementations of the Union-Find data structure are possible, this would not help the running time of Kruskal's Algorithm, which has an unavoidable $O(m \log n)$ term due to the initial sorting of the edges by cost.)

To sum up, we have

**(4.25)** *Kruskal's Algorithm can be implemented on a graph with n nodes and m edges to run in $O(m \log n)$ time.*

## 4.7 Clustering

We motivated the construction of minimum spanning trees through the problem of finding a low-cost network connecting a set of sites. But minimum spanning trees arise in a range of different settings, several of which appear on the surface to be quite different from one another. An appealing example is the role that minimum spanning trees play in the area of *clustering*.

## The Problem

Clustering arises whenever one has a collection of objects—say, a set of photographs, documents, or microorganisms—that one is trying to classify or organize into coherent groups. Faced with such a situation, it is natural to look first for measures of how similar or dissimilar each pair of objects is. One common approach is to define a *distance function* on the objects, with the interpretation that objects at a larger distance from one another are less similar to each other. For points in the physical world, distance may actually be related to their physical distance; but in many applications, distance takes on a much more abstract meaning. For example, we could define the distance between two species to be the number of years since they diverged in the course of evolution; we could define the distance between two images in a video stream as the number of corresponding pixels at which their intensity values differ by at least some threshold.

Now, given a distance function on the objects, the clustering problem seeks to divide them into groups so that, intuitively, objects within the same group are "close," and objects in different groups are "far apart." Starting from this vague set of goals, the field of clustering branches into a vast number of technically different approaches, each seeking to formalize this general notion of what a good set of groups might look like.

***Clusterings of Maximum Spacing***    Minimum spanning trees play a role in one of the most basic formalizations, which we describe here. Suppose we are given a set $U$ of $n$ objects, labeled $p_1, p_2, \ldots, p_n$. For each pair, $p_i$ and $p_j$, we have a numerical distance $d(p_i, p_j)$. We require only that $d(p_i, p_i) = 0$; that $d(p_i, p_j) > 0$ for distinct $p_i$ and $p_j$; and that distances are symmetric: $d(p_i, p_j) = d(p_j, p_i)$.

Suppose we are seeking to divide the objects in $U$ into $k$ groups, for a given parameter $k$. We say that a *k-clustering* of $U$ is a partition of $U$ into $k$ nonempty sets $C_1, C_2, \ldots, C_k$. We define the *spacing* of a $k$-clustering to be the minimum distance between any pair of points lying in different clusters. Given that we want points in different clusters to be far apart from one another, a natural goal is to seek the $k$-clustering with the maximum possible spacing.

The question now becomes the following. There are exponentially many different $k$-clusterings of a set $U$; how can we efficiently find the one that has maximum spacing?

## ✐ Designing the Algorithm

To find a clustering of maximum spacing, we consider growing a graph on the vertex set $U$. The connected components will be the clusters, and we will try to bring nearby points together into the same cluster as rapidly as possible. (This way, they don't end up as points in different clusters that are very close together.) Thus we start by drawing an edge between the closest pair of points. We then draw an edge between the next closest pair of points. We continue adding edges between pairs of points, in order of increasing distance $d(p_i, p_j)$. In this way, we are growing a graph $H$ on $U$ edge by edge, with connected components corresponding to clusters. Notice that we are only interested in the connected components of the graph $H$, not the full set of edges; so if we are about to add the edge $(p_i, p_j)$ and find that $p_i$ and $p_j$ already belong to the same cluster, we will refrain from adding the edge—it's not necessary, because it won't change the set of components. In this way, our graph-growing process will never create a cycle; so $H$ will actually be a union of trees. Each time we add an edge that spans two distinct components, it is as though we have merged the two corresponding clusters. In the clustering literature, the iterative merging of clusters in this way is often termed *single-link clustering*, a special case of *hierarchical agglomerative clustering*. (*Agglomerative* here means that we combine clusters; *single-link* means that we do so as soon as a single link joins them together.) See Figure 4.14 for an example of an instance with $k = 3$ clusters where this algorithm partitions the points into an intuitively natural grouping.

What is the connection to minimum spanning trees? It's very simple: although our graph-growing procedure was motivated by this cluster-merging idea, our procedure is precisely Kruskal's Minimum Spanning Tree Algorithm. We are doing exactly what Kruskal's Algorithm would do if given a graph $G$ on $U$ in which there was an edge of cost $d(p_i, p_j)$ between each pair of nodes $(p_i, p_j)$. The only difference is that we seek a $k$-clustering, so we stop the procedure once we obtain $k$ connected components.

In other words, we are running Kruskal's Algorithm but stopping it just before it adds its last $k - 1$ edges. This is equivalent to taking the full minimum spanning tree $T$ (as Kruskal's Algorithm would have produced it), deleting the $k - 1$ most expensive edges (the ones that we never actually added), and defining the $k$-clustering to be the resulting connected components $C_1, C_2, \ldots, C_k$. Thus, iteratively merging clusters is equivalent to computing a minimum spanning tree and deleting the most expensive edges.

## ✐ Analyzing the Algorithm

Have we achieved our goal of producing clusters that are as spaced apart as possible? The following claim shows that we have.

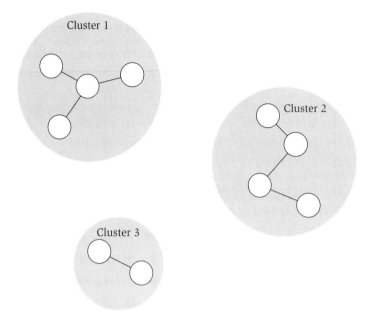

**Figure 4.14** An example of single-linkage clustering with $k = 3$ clusters. The clusters are formed by adding edges between points in order of increasing distance.

**(4.26)** *The components $C_1, C_2, \ldots, C_k$ formed by deleting the $k - 1$ most expensive edges of the minimum spanning tree $T$ constitute a $k$-clustering of maximum spacing.*

**Proof.** Let $\mathcal{C}$ denote the clustering $C_1, C_2, \ldots, C_k$. The spacing of $\mathcal{C}$ is precisely the length $d^*$ of the $(k - 1)^{\text{st}}$ most expensive edge in the minimum spanning tree; this is the length of the edge that Kruskal's Algorithm would have added next, at the moment we stopped it.

Now consider some other $k$-clustering $\mathcal{C}'$, which partitions $U$ into non-empty sets $C_1', C_2', \ldots, C_k'$. We must show that the spacing of $\mathcal{C}'$ is at most $d^*$.

Since the two clusterings $\mathcal{C}$ and $\mathcal{C}'$ are not the same, it must be that one of our clusters $C_r$ is not a subset of any of the $k$ sets $C_s'$ in $\mathcal{C}'$. Hence there are points $p_i, p_j \in C_r$ that belong to different clusters in $\mathcal{C}'$—say, $p_i \in C_s'$ and $p_j \in C_t' \neq C_s'$.

Now consider the picture in Figure 4.15. Since $p_i$ and $p_j$ belong to the same component $C_r$, it must be that Kruskal's Algorithm added all the edges of a $p_i$-$p_j$ path $P$ before we stopped it. In particular, this means that each edge on

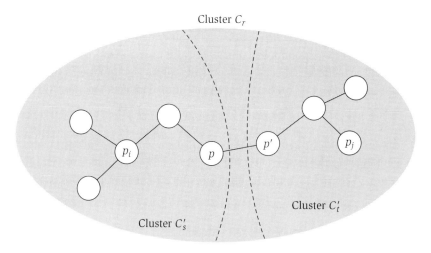

**Figure 4.15** An illustration of the proof of (4.26), showing that the spacing of any other clustering can be no larger than that of the clustering found by the single-linkage algorithm.

$P$ has length at most $d^*$. Now, we know that $p_i \in C'_s$ but $p_j \notin C'_s$; so let $p'$ be the first node on $P$ that does not belong to $C'_s$, and let $p$ be the node on $P$ that comes just before $p'$. We have just argued that $d(p, p') \le d^*$, since the edge $(p, p')$ was added by Kruskal's Algorithm. But $p$ and $p'$ belong to different sets in the clustering $\mathcal{C}'$, and hence the spacing of $\mathcal{C}'$ is at most $d(p, p') \le d^*$. This completes the proof. ∎

## 4.8 Huffman Codes and Data Compression

In the Shortest-Path and Minimum Spanning Tree Problems, we've seen how greedy algorithms can be used to commit to certain parts of a solution (edges in a graph, in these cases), based entirely on relatively short-sighted considerations. We now consider a problem in which this style of "committing" is carried out in an even looser sense: a greedy rule is used, essentially, to shrink the size of the problem instance, so that an equivalent smaller problem can then be solved by recursion. The greedy operation here is proved to be "safe," in the sense that solving the smaller instance still leads to an optimal solution for the original instance, but the global consequences of the initial greedy decision do not become fully apparent until the full recursion is complete.

The problem itself is one of the basic questions in the area of *data compression*, an area that forms part of the foundations for digital communication.

## The Problem

*Encoding Symbols Using Bits*    Since computers ultimately operate on sequences of *bits* (i.e., sequences consisting only of the symbols 0 and 1), one needs encoding schemes that take text written in richer alphabets (such as the alphabets underpinning human languages) and converts this text into long strings of bits.

The simplest way to do this would be to use a fixed number of bits for each symbol in the alphabet, and then just concatenate the bit strings for each symbol to form the text. To take a basic example, suppose we wanted to encode the 26 letters of English, plus the space (to separate words) and five punctuation characters: comma, period, question mark, exclamation point, and apostrophe. This would give us 32 symbols in total to be encoded. Now, you can form $2^b$ different sequences out of $b$ bits, and so if we use 5 bits per symbol, then we can encode $2^5 = 32$ symbols—just enough for our purposes. So, for example, we could let the bit string 00000 represent $a$, the bit string 00001 represent $b$, and so forth up to 11111, which could represent the apostrophe. Note that the mapping of bit strings to symbols is arbitrary; the point is simply that five bits per symbol is sufficient. In fact, encoding schemes like ASCII work precisely this way, except that they use a larger number of bits per symbol so as to handle larger character sets, including capital letters, parentheses, and all those other special symbols you see on a typewriter or computer keyboard.

Let's think about our bare-bones example with just 32 symbols. Is there anything more we could ask for from an encoding scheme? We couldn't ask to encode each symbol using just four bits, since $2^4$ is only 16—not enough for the number of symbols we have. Nevertheless, it's not clear that over large stretches of text, we really need to be spending an *average* of five bits per symbol. If we think about it, the letters in most human alphabets do not get used equally frequently. In English, for example, the letters $e$, $t$, $a$, $o$, $i$, and $n$ get used much more frequently than $q$, $j$, $x$, and $z$ (by more than an order of magnitude). So it's really a tremendous waste to translate them all into the same number of bits; instead we could use a small number of bits for the frequent letters, and a larger number of bits for the less frequent ones, and hope to end up using fewer than five bits per letter when we average over a long string of typical text.

This issue of reducing the average number of bits per letter is a fundamental problem in the area of *data compression*. When large files need to be shipped across communication networks, or stored on hard disks, it's important to represent them as compactly as possible, subject to the requirement that a subsequent reader of the file should be able to correctly reconstruct it. A huge amount of research is devoted to the design of *compression algorithms* that can take files as input and reduce their space through efficient encoding schemes.

We now describe one of the fundamental ways of formulating this issue, building up to the question of how we might construct the *optimal* way to take advantage of the nonuniform frequencies of the letters. In one sense, such an optimal solution is a very appealing answer to the problem of compressing data: it squeezes all the available gains out of nonuniformities in the frequencies. At the end of the section, we will discuss how one can make further progress in compression, taking advantage of features other than nonuniform frequencies.

**Variable-Length Encoding Schemes**   Before the Internet, before the digital computer, before the radio and telephone, there was the telegraph. Communicating by telegraph was a lot faster than the contemporary alternatives of hand-delivering messages by railroad or on horseback. But telegraphs were only capable of transmitting pulses down a wire, and so if you wanted to send a message, you needed a way to encode the text of your message as a sequence of pulses.

To deal with this issue, the pioneer of telegraphic communication, Samuel Morse, developed *Morse code*, translating each letter into a sequence of *dots* (short pulses) and *dashes* (long pulses). For our purposes, we can think of dots and dashes as zeros and ones, and so this is simply a mapping of symbols into bit strings, just as in ASCII. Morse understood the point that one could communicate more efficiently by encoding frequent letters with short strings, and so this is the approach he took. (He consulted local printing presses to get frequency estimates for the letters in English.) Thus, Morse code maps *e* to 0 (a single dot), *t* to 1 (a single dash), *a* to 01 (dot-dash), and in general maps more frequent letters to shorter bit strings.

In fact, Morse code uses such short strings for the letters that the encoding of words becomes ambiguous. For example, just using what we know about the encoding of *e*, *t*, and *a*, we see that the string 0101 could correspond to any of the sequences of letters *eta*, *aa*, *etet*, or *aet*. (There are other possibilities as well, involving other letters.) To deal with this ambiguity, Morse code transmissions involve short pauses between letters (so the encoding of *aa* would actually be dot-dash-pause-dot-dash-pause). This is a reasonable solution—using very short bit strings and then introducing pauses—but it means that we haven't actually encoded the letters using just 0 and 1; we've actually encoded it using a three-letter alphabet of 0, 1, and "pause." Thus, if we really needed to encode everything using only the bits 0 and 1, there would need to be some further encoding in which the pause got mapped to bits.

*Prefix Codes*    The ambiguity problem in Morse code arises because there exist pairs of letters where the bit string that encodes one letter is a *prefix* of the bit string that encodes another. To eliminate this problem, and hence to obtain an encoding scheme that has a well-defined interpretation for every sequence of bits, it is enough to map letters to bit strings in such a way that no encoding is a prefix of any other.

Concretely, we say that a *prefix code* for a set $S$ of letters is a function $\gamma$ that maps each letter $x \in S$ to some sequence of zeros and ones, in such a way that for distinct $x, y \in S$, the sequence $\gamma(x)$ is not a prefix of the sequence $\gamma(y)$.

Now suppose we have a text consisting of a sequence of letters $x_1 x_2 x_3 \cdots x_n$. We can convert this to a sequence of bits by simply encoding each letter as a bit sequence using $\gamma$ and then concatenating all these bit sequences together: $\gamma(x_1)\gamma(x_2) \cdots \gamma(x_n)$. If we then hand this message to a recipient who knows the function $\gamma$, they will be able to reconstruct the text according to the following rule.

- Scan the bit sequence from left to right.
- As soon as you've seen enough bits to match the encoding of some letter, output this as the first letter of the text. This must be the correct first letter, since no shorter or longer prefix of the bit sequence could encode any other letter.
- Now delete the corresponding set of bits from the front of the message and iterate.

In this way, the recipient can produce the correct set of letters without our having to resort to artificial devices like pauses to separate the letters.

For example, suppose we are trying to encode the set of five letters $S = \{a, b, c, d, e\}$. The encoding $\gamma_1$ specified by

$$\gamma_1(a) = 11$$
$$\gamma_1(b) = 01$$
$$\gamma_1(c) = 001$$
$$\gamma_1(d) = 10$$
$$\gamma_1(e) = 000$$

is a prefix code, since we can check that no encoding is a prefix of any other. Now, for example, the string *cecab* would be encoded as 0010000011101. A recipient of this message, knowing $\gamma_1$, would begin reading from left to right. Neither 0 nor 00 encodes a letter, but 001 does, so the recipient concludes that the first letter is $c$. This is a safe decision, since no longer sequence of bits beginning with 001 could encode a different letter. The recipient now iterates on the rest of the message, 0000011101; next they will conclude that the second letter is $e$, encoded as 000.

**Optimal Prefix Codes** We've been doing all this because some letters are more frequent than others, and we want to take advantage of the fact that more frequent letters can have shorter encodings. To make this objective precise, we now introduce some notation to express the frequencies of letters.

Suppose that for each letter $x \in S$, there is a frequency $f_x$, representing the fraction of letters in the text that are equal to $x$. In other words, assuming there are $n$ letters total, $nf_x$ of these letters are equal to $x$. We notice that the frequencies sum to 1; that is, $\sum_{x \in S} f_x = 1$.

Now, if we use a prefix code $\gamma$ to encode the given text, what is the total length of our encoding? This is simply the sum, over all letters $x \in S$, of the number of times $x$ occurs times the length of the bit string $\gamma(x)$ used to encode $x$. Using $|\gamma(x)|$ to denote the length $\gamma(x)$, we can write this as

$$\text{encoding length} = \sum_{x \in S} nf_x|\gamma(x)| = n \sum_{x \in S} f_x|\gamma(x)|.$$

Dropping the leading coefficient of $n$ from the final expression gives us $\sum_{x \in S} f_x|\gamma(x)|$, the *average* number of bits required per letter. We denote this quantity by $\text{ABL}(\gamma)$.

To continue the earlier example, suppose we have a text with the letters $S = \{a, b, c, d, e\}$, and their frequencies are as follows:

$$f_a = .32, \quad f_b = .25, \quad f_c = .20, \quad f_d = .18, \quad f_e = .05.$$

Then the average number of bits per letter using the prefix code $\gamma_1$ defined previously is

$$.32 \cdot 2 + .25 \cdot 2 + .20 \cdot 3 + .18 \cdot 2 + .05 \cdot 3 = 2.25.$$

It is interesting to compare this to the average number of bits per letter using a fixed-length encoding. (Note that a fixed-length encoding is a prefix code: if all letters have encodings of the same length, then clearly no encoding can be a prefix of any other.) With a set $S$ of five letters, we would need three bits per letter for a fixed-length encoding, since two bits could only encode four letters. Thus, using the code $\gamma_1$ reduces the bits per letter from 3 to 2.25, a savings of 25 percent.

And, in fact, $\gamma_1$ is not the best we can do in this example. Consider the prefix code $\gamma_2$ given by

$$\gamma_2(a) = 11$$
$$\gamma_2(b) = 10$$
$$\gamma_2(c) = 01$$
$$\gamma_2(d) = 001$$
$$\gamma_2(e) = 000$$

The average number of bits per letter using $\gamma_2$ is

$$.32 \cdot 2 + .25 \cdot 2 + .20 \cdot 2 + .18 \cdot 3 + .05 \cdot 3 = 2.23.$$

So now it is natural to state the underlying question. Given an alphabet and a set of frequencies for the letters, we would like to produce a prefix code that is as efficient as possible—namely, a prefix code that minimizes the average number of bits per letter $\mathrm{ABL}(\gamma) = \sum_{x \in S} f_x |\gamma(x)|$. We will call such a prefix code *optimal*.

### Designing the Algorithm

The search space for this problem is fairly complicated; it includes all possible ways of mapping letters to bit strings, subject to the defining property of prefix codes. For alphabets consisting of an extremely small number of letters, it is feasible to search this space by brute force, but this rapidly becomes infeasible.

We now describe a greedy method to construct an optimal prefix code very efficiently. As a first step, it is useful to develop a tree-based means of representing prefix codes that exposes their structure more clearly than simply the lists of function values we used in our previous examples.

***Representing Prefix Codes Using Binary Trees***    Suppose we take a rooted tree $T$ in which each node that is not a leaf has at most two children; we call such a tree a *binary tree*. Further suppose that the number of leaves is equal to the size of the alphabet $S$, and we label each leaf with a distinct letter in $S$.

Such a labeled binary tree $T$ naturally describes a prefix code, as follows. For each letter $x \in S$, we follow the path from the root to the leaf labeled $x$; each time the path goes from a node to its left child, we write down a 0, and each time the path goes from a node to its right child, we write down a 1. We take the resulting string of bits as the encoding of $x$.

Now we observe

**(4.27)**    *The encoding of S constructed from T is a prefix code.*

**Proof.** In order for the encoding of $x$ to be a prefix of the encoding of $y$, the path from the root to $x$ would have to be a prefix of the path from the root to $y$. But this is the same as saying that $x$ would lie on the path from the root to $y$, which isn't possible if $x$ is a leaf. ■

This relationship between binary trees and prefix codes works in the other direction as well. Given a prefix code $\gamma$, we can build a binary tree recursively as follows. We start with a root; all letters $x \in S$ whose encodings begin with a 0 will be leaves in the left subtree of the root, and all letters $y \in S$ whose encodings begin with a 1 will be leaves in the right subtree of the root. We now build these two subtrees recursively using this rule.

For example, the labeled tree in Figure 4.16(a) corresponds to the prefix code $\gamma_0$ specified by

$$\gamma_0(a) = 1$$
$$\gamma_0(b) = 011$$
$$\gamma_0(c) = 010$$
$$\gamma_0(d) = 001$$
$$\gamma_0(e) = 000$$

To see this, note that the leaf labeled $a$ is obtained by simply taking the right-hand edge out of the root (resulting in an encoding of 1); the leaf labeled $e$ is obtained by taking three successive left-hand edges starting from the root; and analogous explanations apply for $b$, $c$, and $d$. By similar reasoning, one can see that the labeled tree in Figure 4.16(b) corresponds to the prefix code $\gamma_1$ defined earlier, and the labeled tree in Figure 4.16(c) corresponds to the prefix code $\gamma_2$ defined earlier. Note also that the binary trees for the two prefix codes $\gamma_1$ and $\gamma_2$ are identical in structure; only the labeling of the leaves is different. The tree for $\gamma_0$, on the other hand, has a different structure.

Thus the search for an optimal prefix code can be viewed as the search for a binary tree $T$, together with a labeling of the leaves of $T$, that minimizes the average number of bits per letter. Moreover, this average quantity has a natural interpretation in the terms of the structure of $T$: the length of the encoding of a letter $x \in S$ is simply the length of the path from the root to the leaf labeled $x$. We will refer to the length of this path as the *depth* of the leaf, and we will denote the depth of a leaf $v$ in $T$ simply by $\text{depth}_T(v)$. (As two bits of notational convenience, we will drop the subscript $T$ when it is clear from context, and we will often use a letter $x \in S$ to also denote the leaf that is labeled by it.) Thus we are seeking the labeled tree that minimizes the weighted average of the depths of all leaves, where the average is weighted by the frequencies of the letters that label the leaves: $\sum_{x \in S} f_x \cdot \text{depth}_T(x)$. We will use ABL($T$) to denote this quantity.

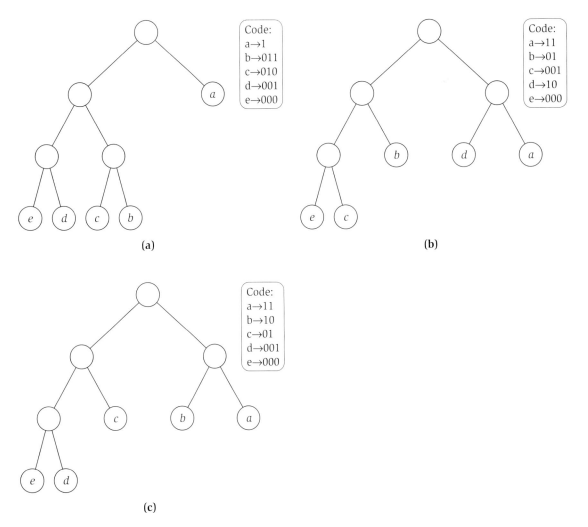

**Figure 4.16** Parts (a), (b), and (c) of the figure depict three different prefix codes for the alphabet $S = \{a, b, c, d, e\}$.

As a first step in considering algorithms for this problem, let's note a simple fact about the optimal tree. For this fact, we need a definition: we say that a binary tree is *full* if each node that is not a leaf has two children. (In other words, there are no nodes with exactly one child.) Note that all three binary trees in Figure 4.16 are full.

**(4.28)** *The binary tree corresponding to the optimal prefix code is full.*

**Proof.** This is easy to prove using an exchange argument. Let $T$ denote the binary tree corresponding to the optimal prefix code, and suppose it contains a node $u$ with exactly one child $v$. Now convert $T$ into a tree $T'$ by replacing node $u$ with $v$.

To be precise, we need to distinguish two cases. If $u$ was the root of the tree, we simply delete node $u$ and use $v$ as the root. If $u$ is not the root, let $w$ be the parent of $u$ in $T$. Now we delete node $u$ and make $v$ be a child of $w$ in place of $u$. This change decreases the number of bits needed to encode any leaf in the subtree rooted at node $u$, and it does not affect other leaves. So the prefix code corresponding to $T'$ has a smaller average number of bits per letter than the prefix code for $T$, contradicting the optimality of $T$. ■

***A First Attempt: The Top-Down Approach*** Intuitively, our goal is to produce a labeled binary tree in which the leaves are as close to the root as possible. This is what will give us a small average leaf depth.

A natural way to do this would be to try building a tree from the top down by "packing" the leaves as tightly as possible. So suppose we try to split the alphabet $S$ into two sets $S_1$ and $S_2$, such that the total frequency of the letters in each set is exactly $\frac{1}{2}$. If such a perfect split is not possible, then we can try for a split that is as nearly balanced as possible. We then recursively construct prefix codes for $S_1$ and $S_2$ independently, and make these the two subtrees of the root. (In terms of bit strings, this would mean sticking a 0 in front of the encodings we produce for $S_1$, and sticking a 1 in front of the encodings we produce for $S_2$.)

It is not entirely clear how we should concretely define this "nearly balanced" split of the alphabet, but there are ways to make this precise. The resulting encoding schemes are called *Shannon-Fano* codes, named after Claude Shannon and Robert Fano, two of the major early figures in the area of *information theory*, which deals with representing and encoding digital information. These types of prefix codes can be fairly good in practice, but for our present purposes they represent a kind of dead end: no version of this top-down splitting strategy is guaranteed to always produce an optimal prefix code. Consider again our example with the five-letter alphabet $S = \{a, b, c, d, e\}$ and frequencies

$$f_a = .32, \quad f_b = .25, \quad f_c = .20, \quad f_d = .18, \quad f_e = .05.$$

There is a unique way to split the alphabet into two sets of equal frequency: $\{a, d\}$ and $\{b, c, e\}$. For $\{a, d\}$, we can use a single bit to encode each. For $\{b, c, e\}$, we need to continue recursively, and again there is a unique way to split the set into two subsets of equal frequency. The resulting code corresponds to the code $\gamma_1$, given by the labeled tree in Figure 4.16(b); and we've already seen that $\gamma_1$ is not as efficient as the prefix code $\gamma_2$ corresponding to the labeled tree in Figure 4.16(c).

Shannon and Fano knew that their approach did not always yield the optimal prefix code, but they didn't see how to compute the optimal code without brute-force search. The problem was solved a few years later by David Huffman, at the time a graduate student who learned about the question in a class taught by Fano.

We now describe the ideas leading up to the greedy approach that Huffman discovered for producing optimal prefix codes.

***What If We Knew the Tree Structure of the Optimal Prefix Code?*** A technique that is often helpful in searching for an efficient algorithm is to assume, as a thought experiment, that one knows something partial about the optimal solution, and then to see how one would make use of this partial knowledge in finding the complete solution. (Later, in Chapter 6, we will see in fact that this technique is a main underpinning of the *dynamic programming* approach to designing algorithms.)

For the current problem, it is useful to ask: What if someone gave us the binary tree $T^*$ that corresponded to an optimal prefix code, but not the labeling of the leaves? To complete the solution, we would need to figure out which letter should label which leaf of $T^*$, and then we'd have our code. How hard is this?

In fact, this is quite easy. We begin by formulating the following basic fact.

**(4.29)** *Suppose that u and v are leaves of $T^*$, such that depth$(u) <$ depth$(v)$. Further, suppose that in a labeling of $T^*$ corresponding to an optimal prefix code, leaf u is labeled with $y \in S$ and leaf v is labeled with $z \in S$. Then $f_y \geq f_z$.*

**Proof.** This has a quick proof using an exchange argument. If $f_y < f_z$, then consider the code obtained by exchanging the labels at the nodes $u$ and $v$. In the expression for the average number of bits per letter, ABL$(T^*) = \sum_{x \in S} f_x$ depth$(x)$, the effect of this exchange is as follows: the multiplier on $f_y$ increases (from depth$(u)$ to depth$(v)$), and the multiplier on $f_z$ decreases by the same amount (from depth$(v)$ to depth$(u)$).

Thus the change to the overall sum is (depth$(v) -$ depth$(u))(f_y - f_z)$. If $f_y < f_z$, this change is a negative number, contradicting the supposed optimality of the prefix code that we had before the exchange. ∎

We can see the idea behind (4.29) in Figure 4.16(b): a quick way to see that the code here is not optimal is to notice that it can be improved by exchanging the positions of the labels $c$ and $d$. Having a lower-frequency letter at a strictly smaller depth than some other higher-frequency letter is precisely what (4.29) rules out for an optimal solution.

Statement (4.29) gives us the following intuitively natural, and optimal, way to label the tree $T^*$ if someone should give it to us. We first take all leaves of depth 1 (if there are any) and label them with the highest-frequency letters in any order. We then take all leaves of depth 2 (if there are any) and label them with the next-highest-frequency letters in any order. We continue through the leaves in order of increasing depth, assigning letters in order of decreasing frequency. The point is that this can't lead to a suboptimal labeling of $T^*$, since any supposedly better labeling would be susceptible to the exchange in (4.29). It is also crucial to note that, among the labels we assign to a block of leaves all at the same depth, it doesn't matter which label we assign to which leaf. Since the depths are all the same, the corresponding multipliers in the expression $\sum_{x \in S} f_x |\gamma(x)|$ are the same, and so the choice of assignment among leaves of the same depth doesn't affect the average number of bits per letter.

But how is all this helping us? We don't have the structure of the optimal tree $T^*$, and since there are exponentially many possible trees (in the size of the alphabet), we aren't going to be able to perform a brute-force search over all of them.

In fact, our reasoning about $T^*$ becomes very useful if we think not about the very beginning of this labeling process, with the leaves of minimum depth, but about the very end, with the leaves of maximum depth—the ones that receive the letters with lowest frequency. Specifically, consider a leaf $v$ in $T^*$ whose depth is as large as possible. Leaf $v$ has a parent $u$, and by (4.28) $T^*$ is a full binary tree, so $u$ has another child $w$. We refer to $v$ and $w$ as *siblings*, since they have a common parent. Now, we have

**(4.30)** $w$ *is a leaf of* $T^*$.

**Proof.** If $w$ were not a leaf, there would be some leaf $w'$ in the subtree below it. But then $w'$ would have a depth greater than that of $v$, contradicting our assumption that $v$ is a leaf of maximum depth in $T^*$. ∎

So $v$ and $w$ are sibling leaves that are as deep as possible in $T^*$. Thus our level-by-level process of labeling $T^*$, as justified by (4.29), will get to the level containing $v$ and $w$ last. The leaves at this level will get the lowest-frequency letters. Since we have already argued that the order in which we assign these letters to the leaves within this level doesn't matter, there is an optimal labeling in which $v$ and $w$ get the two lowest-frequency letters of all.

We sum this up in the following claim.

**(4.31)** *There is an optimal prefix code, with corresponding tree* $T^*$, *in which the two lowest-frequency letters are assigned to leaves that are siblings in* $T^*$.

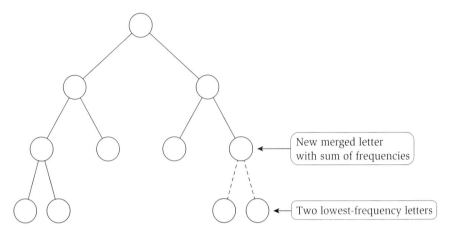

**Figure 4.17** There is an optimal solution in which the two lowest-frequency letters label sibling leaves; deleting them and labeling their parent with a new letter having the combined frequency yields an instance with a smaller alphabet.

***An Algorithm to Construct an Optimal Prefix Code***  Suppose that $y^*$ and $z^*$ are the two lowest-frequency letters in $S$. (We can break ties in the frequencies arbitrarily.) Statement (4.31) is important because it tells us something about where $y^*$ and $z^*$ go in the optimal solution; it says that it is safe to "lock them together" in thinking about the solution, because we know they end up as sibling leaves below a common parent. In effect, this common parent acts like a "meta-letter" whose frequency is the sum of the frequencies of $y^*$ and $z^*$.

This directly suggests an algorithm: we replace $y^*$ and $z^*$ with this meta-letter, obtaining an alphabet that is one letter smaller. We recursively find a prefix code for the smaller alphabet, and then "open up" the meta-letter back into $y^*$ and $z^*$ to obtain a prefix code for $S$. This recursive strategy is depicted in Figure 4.17.

A concrete description of the algorithm is as follows.

```
To construct a prefix code for an alphabet S, with given frequencies:
  If S has two letters then
    Encode one letter using 0 and the other letter using 1
  Else
    Let y* and z* be the two lowest-frequency letters
    Form a new alphabet S' by deleting y* and z* and
      replacing them with a new letter ω of frequency f_y* + f_z*
    Recursively construct a prefix code γ' for S', with tree T'
    Define a prefix code for S as follows:
      Start with T'
```

```
        Take the leaf labeled ω and add two children below it
            labeled y* and z*
    Endif
```

We refer to this as *Huffman's Algorithm*, and the prefix code that it produces for a given alphabet is accordingly referred to as a *Huffman code*. In general, it is clear that this algorithm always terminates, since it simply invokes a recursive call on an alphabet that is one letter smaller. Moreover, using (4.31), it will not be difficult to prove that the algorithm in fact produces an optimal prefix code. Before doing this, however, we pause to note some further observations about the algorithm.

First let's consider the behavior of the algorithm on our sample instance with $S = \{a, b, c, d, e\}$ and frequencies

$$f_a = .32, \quad f_b = .25, \quad f_c = .20, \quad f_d = .18, \quad f_e = .05.$$

The algorithm would first merge $d$ and $e$ into a single letter—let's denote it $(de)$—of frequency $.18 + .05 = .23$. We now have an instance of the problem on the four letters $S' = \{a, b, c, (de)\}$. The two lowest-frequency letters in $S'$ are $c$ and $(de)$, so in the next step we merge these into the single letter $(cde)$ of frequency $.20 + .23 = .43$. This gives us the three-letter alphabet $\{a, b, (cde)\}$. Next we merge $a$ and $b$, and this gives us a two-letter alphabet, at which point we invoke the base case of the recursion. If we unfold the result back through the recursive calls, we get the tree pictured in Figure 4.16(c).

It is interesting to note how the greedy rule underlying Huffman's Algorithm—the merging of the two lowest-frequency letters—fits into the structure of the algorithm as a whole. Essentially, at the time we merge these two letters, we don't know exactly how they will fit into the overall code. Rather, we simply commit to having them be children of the same parent, and this is enough to produce a new, equivalent problem with one less letter.

Moreover, the algorithm forms a natural contrast with the earlier approach that led to suboptimal Shannon-Fano codes. That approach was based on a top-down strategy that worried first and foremost about the top-level split in the binary tree—namely, the two subtrees directly below the root. Huffman's Algorithm, on the other hand, follows a bottom-up approach: it focuses on the leaves representing the two lowest-frequency letters, and then continues by recursion.

## Analyzing the Algorithm

*The Optimality of the Algorithm*   We first prove the optimality of Huffman's Algorithm. Since the algorithm operates recursively, invoking itself on smaller and smaller alphabets, it is natural to try establishing optimality by induction on the size of the alphabet. Clearly it is optimal for all two-letter alphabets (since it uses only one bit per letter). So suppose by induction that it is optimal for all alphabets of size $k - 1$, and consider an input instance consisting of an alphabet $S$ of size $k$.

Let's quickly recap the behavior of the algorithm on this instance. The algorithm merges the two lowest-frequency letters $y^*, z^* \in S$ into a single letter $\omega$, calls itself recursively on the smaller alphabet $S'$ (in which $y^*$ and $z^*$ are replaced by $\omega$), and by induction produces an optimal prefix code for $S'$, represented by a labeled binary tree $T'$. It then extends this into a tree $T$ for $S$, by attaching leaves labeled $y^*$ and $z^*$ as children of the node in $T'$ labeled $\omega$.

There is a close relationship between $\text{ABL}(T)$ and $\text{ABL}(T')$. (Note that the former quantity is the average number of bits used to encode letters in $S$, while the latter quantity is the average number of bits used to encode letters in $S'$.)

**(4.32)**    $\text{ABL}(T') = \text{ABL}(T) - f_\omega.$

**Proof.** The depth of each letter $x$ other than $y^*, z^*$ is the same in both $T$ and $T'$. Also, the depths of $y^*$ and $z^*$ in $T$ are each one greater than the depth of $\omega$ in $T'$. Using this, plus the fact that $f_\omega = f_{y^*} + f_{z^*}$, we have

$$\text{ABL}(T) = \sum_{x \in S} f_x \cdot \text{depth}_T(x)$$

$$= f_{y^*} \cdot \text{depth}_T(y^*) + f_{z^*} \cdot \text{depth}_T(z^*) + \sum_{x \neq y^*, z^*} f_x \cdot \text{depth}_T(x)$$

$$= (f_{y^*} + f_{z^*}) \cdot (1 + \text{depth}_{T'}(\omega)) + \sum_{x \neq y^*, z^*} f_x \cdot \text{depth}_{T'}(x)$$

$$= f_\omega \cdot (1 + \text{depth}_{T'}(\omega)) + \sum_{x \neq y^*, z^*} f_x \cdot \text{depth}_{T'}(x)$$

$$= f_\omega + f_\omega \cdot \text{depth}_{T'}(\omega) + \sum_{x \neq y^*, z^*} f_x \cdot \text{depth}_{T'}(x)$$

$$= f_\omega + \sum_{x \in S'} f_x \cdot \text{depth}_{T'}(x)$$

$$= f_\omega + \text{ABL}(T'). \quad \blacksquare$$

Using this, we now prove optimality as follows.

**(4.33)**    *The Huffman code for a given alphabet achieves the minimum average number of bits per letter of any prefix code.*

**Proof.** Suppose by way of contradiction that the tree $T$ produced by our greedy algorithm is not optimal. This means that there is some labeled binary tree $Z$

such that $\text{ABL}(Z) < \text{ABL}(T)$; and by (4.31), there is such a tree $Z$ in which the leaves representing $y^*$ and $z^*$ are siblings.

It is now easy to get a contradiction, as follows. If we delete the leaves labeled $y^*$ and $z^*$ from $Z$, and label their former parent with $\omega$, we get a tree $Z'$ that defines a prefix code for $S'$. In the same way that $T$ is obtained from $T'$, the tree $Z$ is obtained from $Z'$ by adding leaves for $y^*$ and $z^*$ below $\omega$; thus the identity in (4.32) applies to $Z$ and $Z'$ as well: $\text{ABL}(Z') = \text{ABL}(Z) - f_{\omega}$.

But we have assumed that $\text{ABL}(Z) < \text{ABL}(T)$; subtracting $f_{\omega}$ from both sides of this inequality we get $\text{ABL}(Z') < \text{ABL}(T')$, which contradicts the optimality of $T'$ as a prefix code for $S'$. ∎

***Implementation and Running Time***   It is clear that Huffman's Algorithm can be made to run in polynomial time in $k$, the number of letters in the alphabet. The recursive calls of the algorithm define a sequence of $k - 1$ iterations over smaller and smaller alphabets, and each iteration except the last consists simply of identifying the two lowest-frequency letters and merging them into a single letter that has the combined frequency. Even without being careful about the implementation, identifying the lowest-frequency letters can be done in a single scan of the alphabet, in time $O(k)$, and so summing this over the $k - 1$ iterations gives $O(k^2)$ time.

But in fact Huffman's Algorithm is an ideal setting in which to use a priority queue. Recall that a priority queue maintains a set of $k$ elements, each with a numerical key, and it allows for the insertion of new elements and the extraction of the element with the minimum key. Thus we can maintain the alphabet $S$ in a priority queue, using each letter's frequency as its key. In each iteration we just extract the minimum twice (this gives us the two lowest-frequency letters), and then we insert a new letter whose key is the sum of these two minimum frequencies. Our priority queue now contains a representation of the alphabet that we need for the next iteration.

Using an implementation of priority queues via heaps, as in Chapter 2, we can make each insertion and extraction of the minimum run in time $O(\log k)$; hence, each iteration—which performs just three of these operations—takes time $O(\log k)$. Summing over all $k$ iterations, we get a total running time of $O(k \log k)$.

## Extensions

The structure of optimal prefix codes, which has been our focus here, stands as a fundamental result in the area of data compression. But it is important to understand that this optimality result does not by any means imply that we have found the best way to compress data under all circumstances.

What more could we want beyond an optimal prefix code? First, consider an application in which we are transmitting black-and-white images: each image is a 1,000-by-1,000 array of pixels, and each pixel takes one of the two values *black* or *white*. Further, suppose that a typical image is almost entirely white: roughly 1,000 of the million pixels are black, and the rest are white. Now, if we wanted to compress such an image, the whole approach of prefix codes has very little to say: we have a text of length one million over the two-letter alphabet {*black*, *white*}. As a result, the text is already encoded using one bit per letter—the lowest possible in our framework.

It is clear, though, that such images should be highly compressible. Intuitively, one ought to be able to use a "fraction of a bit" for each white pixel, since they are so overwhelmingly frequent, at the cost of using multiple bits for each black pixel. (In an extreme version, sending a list of $(x, y)$ coordinates for each black pixel would be an improvement over sending the image as a text with a million bits.) The challenge here is to define an encoding scheme where the notion of using fractions of bits is well-defined. There are results in the area of data compression, however, that do just this; *arithmetic coding* and a range of other techniques have been developed to handle settings like this.

A second drawback of prefix codes, as defined here, is that they cannot *adapt* to changes in the text. Again let's consider a simple example. Suppose we are trying to encode the output of a program that produces a long sequence of letters from the set {$a, b, c, d$}. Further suppose that for the first half of this sequence, the letters $a$ and $b$ occur equally frequently, while $c$ and $d$ do not occur at all; but in the second half of this sequence, the letters $c$ and $d$ occur equally frequently, while $a$ and $b$ do not occur at all. In the framework developed in this section, we are trying to compress a text over the four-letter alphabet {$a, b, c, d$}, and all letters are equally frequent. Thus each would be encoded with two bits.

But what's really happening in this example is that the frequency remains stable for half the text, and then it changes radically. So one could get away with just one bit per letter, plus a bit of extra overhead, as follows.

- Begin with an encoding in which the bit 0 represents $a$ and the bit 1 represents $b$.
- Halfway into the sequence, insert some kind of instruction that says, "We're changing the encoding now. From now on, the bit 0 represents $c$ and the bit 1 represents $d$."
- Use this new encoding for the rest of the sequence.

The point is that investing a small amount of space to describe a new encoding can pay off many times over if it reduces the average number of bits per letter over a long run of text that follows. Such approaches, which change the encoding in midstream, are called *adaptive* compression schemes, and for many kinds of data they lead to significant improvements over the static method we've considered here.

These issues suggest some of the directions in which work on data compression has proceeded. In many of these cases, there is a trade-off between the power of the compression technique and its computational cost. In particular, many of the improvements to Huffman codes just described come with a corresponding increase in the computational effort needed both to produce the compressed version of the data and also to decompress it and restore the original text. Finding the right balance among these trade-offs is a topic of active research.

## * 4.9 Minimum-Cost Arborescences: A Multi-Phase Greedy Algorithm

As we've seen more and more examples of greedy algorithms, we've come to appreciate that there can be considerable diversity in the way they operate. Many greedy algorithms make some sort of an initial "ordering" decision on the input, and then process everything in a one-pass fashion. Others make more incremental decisions—still local and opportunistic, but without a global "plan" in advance. In this section, we consider a problem that stresses our intuitive view of greedy algorithms still further.

### The Problem

The problem is to compute a minimum-cost *arborescence* of a directed graph. This is essentially an analogue of the Minimum Spanning Tree Problem for directed, rather than undirected, graphs; we will see that the move to directed graphs introduces significant new complications. At the same time, the style of the algorithm has a strongly greedy flavor, since it still constructs a solution according to a local, myopic rule.

We begin with the basic definitions. Let $G = (V, E)$ be a directed graph in which we've distinguished one node $r \in V$ as a *root*. An *arborescence* (with respect to $r$) is essentially a directed spanning tree rooted at $r$. Specifically, it is a subgraph $T = (V, F)$ such that $T$ is a spanning tree of $G$ if we ignore the direction of edges; and there is a path in $T$ from $r$ to each other node $v \in V$ if we take the direction of edges into account. Figure 4.18 gives an example of two different arborescences in the same directed graph.

There is a useful equivalent way to characterize arborescences, and this is as follows.

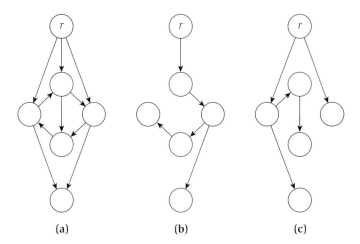

**Figure 4.18** A directed graph can have many different arborescences. Parts (b) and (c) depict two different aborescences, both rooted at node $r$, for the graph in part (a).

**(4.34)** *A subgraph $T = (V, F)$ of $G$ is an arborescence with respect to root $r$ if and only if $T$ has no cycles, and for each node $v \neq r$, there is exactly one edge in $F$ that enters $v$.*

**Proof.** If $T$ is an arborescence with root $r$, then indeed every other node $v$ has exactly one edge entering it: this is simply the last edge on the unique $r$-$v$ path.

Conversely, suppose $T$ has no cycles, and each node $v \neq r$ has exactly one entering edge. In order to establish that $T$ is an arborescence, we need only show that there is a directed path from $r$ to each other node $v$. Here is how to construct such a path. We start at $v$ and repeatedly follow edges in the backward direction. Since $T$ has no cycles, we can never return to a node we've previously visited, and thus this process must terminate. But $r$ is the only node without incoming edges, and so the process must in fact terminate by reaching $r$; the sequence of nodes thus visited yields a path (in the reverse direction) from $r$ to $v$. ■

It is easy to see that, just as every connected graph has a spanning tree, a directed graph has an arborescence rooted at $r$ provided that $r$ can reach every node. Indeed, in this case, the edges in a breadth-first search tree rooted at $r$ will form an arborescence.

**(4.35)** *A directed graph $G$ has an arborescence rooted at $r$ if and only if there is a directed path from $r$ to each other node.*

The basic problem we consider here is the following. We are given a directed graph $G = (V, E)$, with a distinguished root node $r$ and with a non-negative cost $c_e \geq 0$ on each edge, and we wish to compute an arborescence rooted at $r$ of minimum total cost. (We will refer to this as an *optimal* arborescence.) We will assume throughout that $G$ at least has an arborescence rooted at $r$; by (4.35), this can be easily checked at the outset.

### Designing the Algorithm

Given the relationship between arborescences and trees, the minimum-cost arborescence problem certainly has a strong initial resemblance to the Minimum Spanning Tree Problem for undirected graphs. Thus it's natural to start by asking whether the ideas we developed for that problem can be carried over directly to this setting. For example, must the minimum-cost arborescence contain the cheapest edge in the whole graph? Can we safely delete the most expensive edge on a cycle, confident that it cannot be in the optimal arborescence?

Clearly the cheapest edge $e$ in $G$ will not belong to the optimal arborescence if $e$ enters the root, since the arborescence we're seeking is not supposed to have any edges entering the root. But even if the cheapest edge in $G$ belongs to *some* arborescence rooted at $r$, it need not belong to the optimal one, as the example of Figure 4.19 shows. Indeed, including the edge of cost 1 in Figure 4.19 would prevent us from including the edge of cost 2 out of the root $r$ (since there can only be one entering edge per node); and this in turn would force us to incur an unacceptable cost of 10 when we included one of

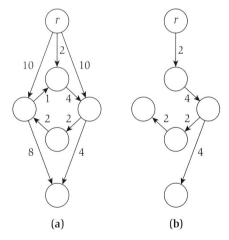

(a)           (b)

**Figure 4.19** (a) A directed graph with costs on its edges, and (b) an optimal arborescence rooted at $r$ for this graph.

the other edges out of $r$. This kind of argument never clouded our thinking in the Minimum Spanning Tree Problem, where it was always safe to plunge ahead and include the cheapest edge; it suggests that finding the optimal arborescence may be a significantly more complicated task. (It's worth noticing that the optimal arborescence in Figure 4.19 also includes the most expensive edge on a cycle; with a different construction, one can even cause the optimal arborescence to include the most expensive edge in the whole graph.)

Despite this, it is possible to design a greedy type of algorithm for this problem; it's just that our myopic rule for choosing edges has to be a little more sophisticated. First let's consider a little more carefully what goes wrong with the general strategy of including the cheapest edges. Here's a particular version of this strategy: for each node $v \neq r$, select the cheapest edge entering $v$ (breaking ties arbitrarily), and let $F^*$ be this set of $n - 1$ edges. Now consider the subgraph $(V, F^*)$. Since we know that the optimal arborescence needs to have exactly one edge entering each node $v \neq r$, and $(V, F^*)$ represents the cheapest possible way of making these choices, we have the following fact.

**(4.36)** *If $(V, F^*)$ is an arborescence, then it is a minimum-cost arborescence.*

So the difficulty is that $(V, F^*)$ may not be an arborescence. In this case, (4.34) implies that $(V, F^*)$ must contain a cycle $C$, which does not include the root. We now must decide how to proceed in this situation.

To make matters somewhat clearer, we begin with the following observation. Every arborescence contains exactly one edge entering each node $v \neq r$; so if we pick some node $v$ and subtract a uniform quantity from the cost of every edge entering $v$, then the total cost of every arborescence changes by exactly the same amount. This means, essentially, that the actual cost of the cheapest edge entering $v$ is not important; what matters is the cost of all other edges entering $v$ *relative* to this. Thus let $y_v$ denote the minimum cost of any edge entering $v$. For each edge $e = (u, v)$, with cost $c_e \geq 0$, we define its *modified cost* $c'_e$ to be $c_e - y_v$. Note that since $c_e \geq y_v$, all the modified costs are still nonnegative. More crucially, our discussion motivates the following fact.

**(4.37)** *$T$ is an optimal arborescence in $G$ subject to costs $\{c_e\}$ if and only if it is an optimal arborescence subject to the modified costs $\{c'_e\}$.*

**Proof.** Consider an arbitrary arborescence $T$. The difference between its cost with costs $\{c_e\}$ and $\{c'_e\}$ is exactly $\sum_{v \neq r} y_v$—that is,

$$\sum_{e \in T} c_e - \sum_{e \in T} c'_e = \sum_{v \neq r} y_v.$$

This is because an arborescence has exactly one edge entering each node $v$ in the sum. Since the difference between the two costs is independent of the choice of the arborescence $T$, we see that $T$ has minimum cost subject to $\{c_e\}$ if and only if it has minimum cost subject to $\{c'_e\}$. ∎

We now consider the problem in terms of the costs $\{c'_e\}$. All the edges in our set $F^*$ have cost 0 under these modified costs; and so if $(V, F^*)$ contains a cycle $C$, we know that all edges in $C$ have cost 0. This suggests that we can afford to use as many edges from $C$ as we want (consistent with producing an arborescence), since including edges from $C$ doesn't raise the cost.

Thus our algorithm continues as follows. We contract $C$ into a single *supernode*, obtaining a smaller graph $G' = (V', E')$. Here, $V'$ contains the nodes of $V - C$, plus a single node $c^*$ representing $C$. We transform each edge $e \in E$ to an edge $e' \in E'$ by replacing each end of $e$ that belongs to $C$ with the new node $c^*$. This can result in $G'$ having parallel edges (i.e., edges with the same ends), which is fine; however, we delete self-loops from $E'$—edges that have both ends equal to $c^*$. We recursively find an optimal arborescence in this smaller graph $G'$, subject to the costs $\{c'_e\}$. The arborescence returned by this recursive call can be converted into an arborescence of $G$ by including all but one edge on the cycle $C$.

In summary, here is the full algorithm.

```
For each node v ≠ r
    Let y_v be the minimum cost of an edge entering node v
    Modify the costs of all edges e entering v to c'_e = c_e − y_v
Choose one 0-cost edge entering each v ≠ r, obtaining a set F*
If F* forms an arborescence, then return it
Else there is a directed cycle C ⊆ F*
    Contract C to a single supernode, yielding a graph G' = (V', E')
    Recursively find an optimal arborescence (V', F') in G'
            with costs {c'_e}
    Extend (V', F') to an arborescence (V, F) in G
            by adding all but one edge of C
```

## Analyzing the Algorithm

It is easy to implement this algorithm so that it runs in polynomial time. But does it lead to an optimal arborescence? Before concluding that it does, we need to worry about the following point: not every arborescence in $G$ corresponds to an arborescence in the contracted graph $G'$. Could we perhaps "miss" the true optimal arborescence in $G$ by focusing on $G'$? What is true is the following.

The arborescences of $G'$ are in one-to-one correspondence with arborescences of $G$ *that have exactly one edge entering the cycle $C$*; and these corresponding arborescences have the same cost with respect to $\{c'_e\}$, since $C$ consists of 0-cost edges. (We say that an edge $e = (u, v)$ enters $C$ if $v$ belongs to $C$ but $u$ does not.) So to prove that our algorithm finds an optimal arborescence in $G$, we must prove that $G$ has an optimal arborescence with exactly one edge entering $C$. We do this now.

**(4.38)**  *Let $C$ be a cycle in $G$ consisting of edges of cost 0, such that $r \notin C$. Then there is an optimal arborescence rooted at $r$ that has exactly one edge entering $C$.*

**Proof.**  Consider an optimal arborescence $T$ in $G$. Since $r$ has a path in $T$ to every node, there is at least one edge of $T$ that enters $C$. If $T$ enters $C$ exactly once, then we are done. Otherwise, suppose that $T$ enters $C$ more than once. We show how to modify it to obtain an arborescence of no greater cost that enters $C$ exactly once.

Let $e = (a, b)$ be an edge entering $C$ that lies on as short a path as possible from $r$; this means in particular that no edges on the path from $r$ to $a$ can enter $C$. We delete all edges of $T$ that enter $C$, except for the edge $e$. We add in all edges of $C$ except for the one edge that enters $b$, the head of edge $e$. Let $T'$ denote the resulting subgraph of $G$.

We claim that $T'$ is also an arborescence. This will establish the result, since the cost of $T'$ is clearly no greater than that of $T$: the only edges of $T'$ that do not also belong to $T$ have cost 0. So why is $T'$ an arborescence? Observe that $T'$ has exactly one edge entering each node $v \neq r$, and no edge entering $r$. So $T'$ has exactly $n - 1$ edges; hence if we can show there is an $r$-$v$ path in $T'$ for each $v$, then $T'$ must be connected in an undirected sense, and hence a tree. Thus it would satisfy our initial definition of an arborescence.

So consider any node $v \neq r$; we must show there is an $r$-$v$ path in $T'$. If $v \in C$, we can use the fact that the path in $T$ from $r$ to $e$ has been preserved in the construction of $T'$; thus we can reach $v$ by first reaching $e$ and then following the edges of the cycle $C$. Now suppose that $v \notin C$, and let $P$ denote the $r$-$v$ path in $T$. If $P$ did not touch $C$, then it still exists in $T'$. Otherwise, let $w$ be the last node in $P \cap C$, and let $P'$ be the subpath of $P$ from $w$ to $v$. Observe that all the edges in $P'$ still exist in $T'$. We have already argued that $w$ is reachable from $r$ in $T'$, since it belongs to $C$. Concatenating this path to $w$ with the subpath $P'$ gives us a path to $v$ as well.  ∎

We can now put all the pieces together to argue that our algorithm is correct.

**(4.39)**   *The algorithm finds an optimal arborescence rooted at r in G.*

**Proof.** The proof is by induction on the number of nodes in $G$. If the edges of $F$ form an arborescence, then the algorithm returns an optimal arborescence by (4.36). Otherwise, we consider the problem with the modified costs $\{c'_e\}$, which is equivalent by (4.37). After contracting a 0-cost cycle $C$ to obtain a smaller graph $G'$, the algorithm produces an optimal arborescence in $G'$ by the inductive hypothesis. Finally, by (4.38), there is an optimal arborescence in $G$ that corresponds to the optimal arborescence computed for $G'$. ■

# Solved Exercises

## Solved Exercise 1

Suppose that three of your friends, inspired by repeated viewings of the horror-movie phenomenon *The Blair Witch Project*, have decided to hike the Appalachian Trail this summer. They want to hike as much as possible per day but, for obvious reasons, not after dark. On a map they've identified a large set of good *stopping points* for camping, and they're considering the following system for deciding when to stop for the day. Each time they come to a potential stopping point, they determine whether they can make it to the next one before nightfall. If they can make it, then they keep hiking; otherwise, they stop.

Despite many significant drawbacks, they claim this system does have one good feature. "Given that we're only hiking in the daylight," they claim, "it minimizes the number of camping stops we have to make."

Is this true? The proposed system is a greedy algorithm, and we wish to determine whether it minimizes the number of stops needed.

To make this question precise, let's make the following set of simplifying assumptions. We'll model the Appalachian Trail as a long line segment of length $L$, and assume that your friends can hike $d$ miles per day (independent of terrain, weather conditions, and so forth). We'll assume that the potential stopping points are located at distances $x_1, x_2, \ldots, x_n$ from the start of the trail. We'll also assume (very generously) that your friends are always correct when they estimate whether they can make it to the next stopping point before nightfall.

We'll say that a set of stopping points is *valid* if the distance between each adjacent pair is at most $d$, the first is at distance at most $d$ from the start of the trail, and the last is at distance at most $d$ from the end of the trail. Thus a set of stopping points is valid if one could camp only at these places and still make it across the whole trail. We'll assume, naturally, that the full set of $n$ stopping points is valid; otherwise, there would be no way to make it the whole way.

We can now state the question as follows. Is your friends' greedy algorithm—hiking as long as possible each day—*optimal*, in the sense that it finds a valid set whose size is as small as possible?

***Solution***    Often a greedy algorithm looks correct when you first encounter it, so before succumbing too deeply to its intuitive appeal, it's useful to ask: why might it not work? What should we be worried about?

There's a natural concern with this algorithm: Might it not help to stop early on some day, so as to get better synchronized with camping opportunities on future days? But if you think about it, you start to wonder whether this could really happen. Could there really be an alternate solution that intentionally lags behind the greedy solution, and then puts on a burst of speed and passes the greedy solution? How could it pass it, given that the greedy solution travels as far as possible each day?

This last consideration starts to look like the outline of an argument based on the "staying ahead" principle from Section 4.1. Perhaps we can show that as long as the greedy camping strategy is ahead on a given day, no other solution can catch up and overtake it the next day.

We now turn this into a proof showing the algorithm is indeed optimal, identifying a natural sense in which the stopping points it chooses "stay ahead" of any other legal set of stopping points. Although we are following the style of proof from Section 4.1, it's worth noting an interesting contrast with the Interval Scheduling Problem: there we needed to prove that a greedy algorithm maximized a quantity of interest, whereas here we seek to minimize a certain quantity.

Let $R = \{x_{p_1}, \ldots, x_{p_k}\}$ denote the set of stopping points chosen by the greedy algorithm, and suppose by way of contradiction that there is a smaller valid set of stopping points; let's call this smaller set $S = \{x_{q_1}, \ldots, x_{q_m}\}$, with $m < k$.

To obtain a contradiction, we first show that the stopping point reached by the greedy algorithm on each day $j$ is farther than the stopping point reached under the alternate solution. That is,

**(4.40)**    *For each $j = 1, 2, \ldots, m$, we have $x_{p_j} \geq x_{q_j}$.*

**Proof.** We prove this by induction on $j$. The case $j = 1$ follows directly from the definition of the greedy algorithm: your friends travel as long as possible on the first day before stopping. Now let $j > 1$ and assume that the claim is true for all $i < j$. Then

$$x_{q_j} - x_{q_{j-1}} \leq d,$$

since $S$ is a valid set of stopping points, and

$$x_{q_j} - x_{p_{j-1}} \leq x_{q_j} - x_{q_{j-1}}$$

since $x_{p_{j-1}} \geq x_{q_{j-1}}$ by the induction hypothesis. Combining these two inequalities, we have

$$x_{q_j} - x_{p_{j-1}} \leq d.$$

This means that your friends have the option of hiking all the way from $x_{p_{j-1}}$ to $x_{q_j}$ in one day; and hence the location $x_{p_j}$ at which they finally stop can only be farther along than $x_{q_j}$. (Note the similarity with the corresponding proof for the Interval Scheduling Problem: here too the greedy algorithm is staying ahead because, at each step, the choice made by the alternate solution is one of its valid options.) ∎

Statement (4.40) implies in particular that $x_{q_m} \leq x_{p_m}$. Now, if $m < k$, then we must have $x_{p_m} < L - d$, for otherwise your friends would never have needed to stop at the location $x_{p_{m+1}}$. Combining these two inequalities, we have concluded that $x_{q_m} < L - d$; but this contradicts the assumption that $S$ is a valid set of stopping points.

Consequently, we cannot have $m < k$, and so we have proved that the greedy algorithm produces a valid set of stopping points of minimum possible size.

## Solved Exercise 2

Your friends are starting a security company that needs to obtain licenses for $n$ different pieces of cryptographic software. Due to regulations, they can only obtain these licenses at the rate of at most one per month.

Each license is currently selling for a price of \$100. However, they are all becoming more expensive according to exponential growth curves: in particular, the cost of license $j$ increases by a factor of $r_j > 1$ each month, where $r_j$ is a given parameter. This means that if license $j$ is purchased $t$ months from now, it will cost $100 \cdot r_j^t$. We will assume that all the price growth rates are distinct; that is, $r_i \neq r_j$ for licenses $i \neq j$ (even though they start at the same price of \$100).

The question is: Given that the company can only buy at most one license a month, in which order should it buy the licenses so that the total amount of money it spends is as small as possible?

Give an algorithm that takes the $n$ rates of price growth $r_1, r_2, \ldots, r_n$, and computes an order in which to buy the licenses so that the total amount of money spent is minimized. The running time of your algorithm should be polynomial in $n$.

**Solution**    Two natural guesses for a good sequence would be to sort the $r_i$ in decreasing order, or to sort them in increasing order. Faced with alternatives like this, it's perfectly reasonable to work out a small example and see if the example eliminates at least one of them. Here we could try $r_1 = 2$, $r_2 = 3$, and $r_3 = 4$. Buying the licenses in increasing order results in a total cost of

$$100(2 + 3^2 + 4^3) = 7,500,$$

while buying them in decreasing order results in a total cost of

$$100(4 + 3^2 + 2^3) = 2,100.$$

This tells us that increasing order is not the way to go. (On the other hand, it doesn't tell us immediately that decreasing order is the right answer, but our goal was just to eliminate one of the two options.)

Let's try proving that sorting the $r_i$ in decreasing order in fact always gives the optimal solution. When a greedy algorithm works for problems like this, in which we put a set of things in an optimal order, we've seen in the text that it's often effective to try proving correctness using an exchange argument.

To do this here, let's suppose that there is an optimal solution $O$ that differs from our solution $S$. (In other words, $S$ consists of the licenses sorted in decreasing order.) So this optimal solution $O$ must contain an inversion—that is, there must exist two neighboring months $t$ and $t+1$ such that the price increase rate of the license bought in month $t$ (let us denote it by $r_t$) is less than that bought in month $t+1$ (similarly, we use $r_{t+1}$ to denote this). That is, we have $r_t < r_{t+1}$.

We claim that by exchanging these two purchases, we can strictly improve our optimal solution, which contradicts the assumption that $O$ was optimal. Therefore if we succeed in showing this, we will successfully show that our algorithm is indeed the correct one.

Notice that if we swap these two purchases, the rest of the purchases are identically priced. In $O$, the amount paid during the two months involved in the swap is $100(r_t^t + r_{t+1}^{t+1})$. On the other hand, if we swapped these two purchases, we would pay $100(r_{t+1}^t + r_t^{t+1})$. Since the constant 100 is common to both expressions, we want to show that the second term is less than the first one. So we want to show that

$$r_{t+1}^t + r_t^{t+1} < r_t^t + r_{t+1}^{t+1}$$

$$r_t^{t+1} - r_t^t < r_{t+1}^{t+1} - r_{t+1}^t$$

$$r_t^t(r_t - 1) < r_{t+1}^t(r_{t+1} - 1).$$

But this last inequality is true simply because $r_i > 1$ for all $i$ and since $r_t < r_{t+1}$.

This concludes the proof of correctness. The running time of the algorithm is $O(n \log n)$, since the sorting takes that much time and the rest (outputting) is linear. So the overall running time is $O(n \log n)$.

*Note:* It's interesting to note that things become much less straightforward if we vary this question even a little. Suppose that instead of buying licenses whose prices increase, you're trying to sell off equipment whose cost is depreciating. Item $i$ depreciates at a factor of $r_i < 1$ per month, starting from $100, so if you sell it $t$ months from now you will receive $100 \cdot r_i^t$. (In other words, the exponential rates are now less than 1, instead of greater than 1.) If you can only sell one item per month, what is the optimal order in which to sell them? Here, it turns out that there are cases in which the optimal solution doesn't put the rates in either increasing or decreasing order (as in the input $\frac{3}{4}, \frac{1}{2}, \frac{1}{100}$).

## Solved Exercise 3

Suppose you are given a connected graph $G$, with edge costs that you may assume are all distinct. $G$ has $n$ vertices and $m$ edges. A particular edge $e$ of $G$ is specified. Give an algorithm with running time $O(m + n)$ to decide whether $e$ is contained in a minimum spanning tree of $G$.

***Solution*** From the text, we know of two rules by which we can conclude whether an edge $e$ belongs to a minimum spanning tree: the Cut Property (4.17) says that $e$ is in every minimum spanning tree when it is the cheapest edge crossing from some set $S$ to the complement $V - S$; and the Cycle Property (4.20) says that $e$ is in no minimum spanning tree if it is the most expensive edge on some cycle $C$. Let's see if we can make use of these two rules as part of an algorithm that solves this problem in linear time.

Both the Cut and Cycle Properties are essentially talking about how $e$ relates to the set of edges that are *cheaper* than $e$. The Cut Property can be viewed as asking: Is there some set $S \subseteq V$ so that in order to get from $S$ to $V - S$ without using $e$, we need to use an edge that is more expensive than $e$? And if we think about the cycle $C$ in the statement of the Cycle Property, going the "long way" around $C$ (avoiding $e$) can be viewed as an alternate route between the endpoints of $e$ that only uses cheaper edges.

Putting these two observations together suggests that we should try proving the following statement.

**(4.41)** *Edge $e = (v, w)$ does not belong to a minimum spanning tree of $G$ if and only if $v$ and $w$ can be joined by a path consisting entirely of edges that are cheaper than $e$.*

**Proof.** First suppose that $P$ is a $v$-$w$ path consisting entirely of edges cheaper than $e$. If we add $e$ to $P$, we get a cycle on which $e$ is the most expensive edge. Thus, by the Cycle Property, $e$ does not belong to a minimum spanning tree of $G$.

On the other hand, suppose that $v$ and $w$ cannot be joined by a path consisting entirely of edges cheaper than $e$. We will now identify a set $S$ for which $e$ is the cheapest edge with one end in $S$ and the other in $V - S$; if we can do this, the Cut Property will imply that $e$ belongs to every minimum spanning tree. Our set $S$ will be the set of all nodes that are reachable from $v$ using a path consisting only of edges that are cheaper than $e$. By our assumption, we have $w \in V - S$. Also, by the definition of $S$, there cannot be an edge $f = (x, y)$ that is cheaper than $e$, and for which one end $x$ lies in $S$ and the other end $y$ lies in $V - S$. Indeed, if there were such an edge $f$, then since the node $x$ is reachable from $v$ using only edges cheaper than $e$, the node $y$ would be reachable as well. Hence $e$ is the cheapest edge with one end in $S$ and the other in $V - S$, as desired, and so we are done.  ∎

Given this fact, our algorithm is now simply the following. We form a graph $G'$ by deleting from $G$ all edges of weight greater than $c_e$ (as well as deleting $e$ itself). We then use one of the connectivity algorithms from Chapter 3 to determine whether there is a path from $v$ to $w$ in $G'$. Statement (4.41) says that $e$ belongs to a minimum spanning tree if and only if there is no such path.

The running time of this algorithm is $O(m + n)$ to build $G'$, and $O(m + n)$ to test for a path from $v$ to $w$.

# Exercises

1. Decide whether you think the following statement is true or false. If it is true, give a short explanation. If it is false, give a counterexample.

   *Let $G$ be an arbitrary connected, undirected graph with a distinct cost $c(e)$ on every edge $e$. Suppose $e^*$ is the cheapest edge in $G$; that is, $c(e^*) < c(e)$ for every* *edge e ≠ e\*. Then there is a minimum spanning tree T of G that contains the edge e\*.*

2. For each of the following two statements, decide whether it is true or false. If it is true, give a short explanation. If it is false, give a counterexample.

   **(a)** Suppose we are given an instance of the Minimum Spanning Tree Problem on a graph $G$, with edge costs that are all positive and distinct. Let $T$ be a minimum spanning tree for this instance. Now suppose we replace each edge cost $c_e$ by its square, $c_e^2$, thereby creating a new instance of the problem with the same graph but different costs.

   True or false?    $T$ must still be a minimum spanning tree for this new instance.

   **(b)** Suppose we are given an instance of the Shortest $s$-$t$ Path Problem on a directed graph $G$. We assume that all edge costs are positive and distinct. Let $P$ be a minimum-cost $s$-$t$ path for this instance. Now suppose we replace each edge cost $c_e$ by its square, $c_e^2$, thereby creating a new instance of the problem with the same graph but different costs.

   True or false?    $P$ must still be a minimum-cost $s$-$t$ path for this new instance.

3. You are consulting for a trucking company that does a large amount of business shipping packages between New York and Boston. The volume is high enough that they have to send a number of trucks each day between the two locations. Trucks have a fixed limit $W$ on the maximum amount of weight they are allowed to carry. Boxes arrive at the New York station one by one, and each package $i$ has a weight $w_i$. The trucking station is quite small, so at most one truck can be at the station at any time. Company policy requires that boxes are shipped in the order they arrive; otherwise, a customer might get upset upon seeing a box that arrived after his make it to Boston faster. At the moment, the company is using a simple greedy algorithm for packing: they pack boxes in the order they arrive, and whenever the next box does not fit, they send the truck on its way.

   But they wonder if they might be using too many trucks, and they want your opinion on whether the situation can be improved. Here is how they are thinking. Maybe one could decrease the number of trucks needed by sometimes sending off a truck that was less full, and in this way allow the next few trucks to be better packed.

Prove that, for a given set of boxes with specified weights, the greedy algorithm currently in use actually minimizes the number of trucks that are needed. Your proof should follow the type of analysis we used for the Interval Scheduling Problem: it should establish the optimality of this greedy packing algorithm by identifying a measure under which it "stays ahead" of all other solutions.

4. Some of your friends have gotten into the burgeoning field of *time-series data mining*, in which one looks for patterns in sequences of events that occur over time. Purchases at stock exchanges—what's being bought— are one source of data with a natural ordering in time. Given a long sequence $S$ of such events, your friends want an efficient way to detect certain "patterns" in them—for example, they may want to know if the four events

> buy Yahoo, buy eBay, buy Yahoo, buy Oracle

occur in this sequence $S$, in order but not necessarily consecutively.

They begin with a collection of possible *events* (e.g., the possible transactions) and a sequence $S$ of $n$ of these events. A given event may occur multiple times in $S$ (e.g., Yahoo stock may be bought many times in a single sequence $S$). We will say that a sequence $S'$ is a *subsequence* of $S$ if there is a way to delete certain of the events from $S$ so that the remaining events, in order, are equal to the sequence $S'$. So, for example, the sequence of four events above is a subsequence of the sequence

> buy Amazon, buy Yahoo, buy eBay, buy Yahoo, buy Yahoo, buy Oracle

Their goal is to be able to dream up short sequences and quickly detect whether they are subsequences of $S$. So this is the problem they pose to you: Give an algorithm that takes two sequences of events—$S'$ of length $m$ and $S$ of length $n$, each possibly containing an event more than once—and decides in time $O(m + n)$ whether $S'$ is a subsequence of $S$.

5. Let's consider a long, quiet country road with houses scattered very sparsely along it. (We can picture the road as a long line segment, with an eastern endpoint and a western endpoint.) Further, let's suppose that despite the bucolic setting, the residents of all these houses are avid cell phone users. You want to place cell phone base stations at certain points along the road, so that every house is within four miles of one of the base stations.

Give an efficient algorithm that achieves this goal, using as few base stations as possible.

**6.** Your friend is working as a camp counselor, and he is in charge of organizing activities for a set of junior-high-school-age campers. One of his plans is the following mini-triathalon exercise: each contestant must swim 20 laps of a pool, then bike 10 miles, then run 3 miles. The plan is to send the contestants out in a staggered fashion, via the following rule: the contestants must use the pool one at a time. In other words, first one contestant swims the 20 laps, gets out, and starts biking. As soon as this first person is out of the pool, a second contestant begins swimming the 20 laps; as soon as he or she is out and starts biking, a third contestant begins swimming . . . and so on.)

Each contestant has a projected *swimming time* (the expected time it will take him or her to complete the 20 laps), a projected *biking time* (the expected time it will take him or her to complete the 10 miles of bicycling), and a projected *running time* (the time it will take him or her to complete the 3 miles of running). Your friend wants to decide on a *schedule* for the triathalon: an order in which to sequence the starts of the contestants. Let's say that the *completion time* of a schedule is the earliest time at which all contestants will be finished with all three legs of the triathalon, assuming they each spend exactly their projected swimming, biking, and running times on the three parts. (Again, note that participants can bike and run simultaneously, but at most one person can be in the pool at any time.) What's the best order for sending people out, if one wants the whole competition to be over as early as possible? More precisely, give an efficient algorithm that produces a schedule whose completion time is as small as possible.

**7.** The wildly popular Spanish-language search engine El Goog needs to do a serious amount of computation every time it recompiles its index. Fortunately, the company has at its disposal a single large supercomputer, together with an essentially unlimited supply of high-end PCs.

They've broken the overall computation into $n$ distinct jobs, labeled $J_1, J_2, \ldots, J_n$, which can be performed completely independently of one another. Each job consists of two stages: first it needs to be *preprocessed* on the supercomputer, and then it needs to be *finished* on one of the PCs. Let's say that job $J_i$ needs $p_i$ seconds of time on the supercomputer, followed by $f_i$ seconds of time on a PC.

Since there are at least $n$ PCs available on the premises, the finishing of the jobs can be performed fully in parallel—all the jobs can be processed at the same time. However, the supercomputer can only work on a single job at a time, so the system managers need to work out an order in which to feed the jobs to the supercomputer. As soon as the first job in order is done on the supercomputer, it can be handed off to a PC for finishing; at that point in time a second job can be fed to the supercomputer; when the second job is done on the supercomputer, it can proceed to a PC regardless of whether or not the first job is done (since the PCs work in parallel); and so on.

Let's say that a *schedule* is an ordering of the jobs for the supercomputer, and the *completion time* of the schedule is the earliest time at which all jobs will have finished processing on the PCs. This is an important quantity to minimize, since it determines how rapidly El Goog can generate a new index.

Give a polynomial-time algorithm that finds a schedule with as small a completion time as possible.

8. Suppose you are given a connected graph $G$, with edge costs that are all distinct. Prove that $G$ has a unique minimum spanning tree.

9. One of the basic motivations behind the Minimum Spanning Tree Problem is the goal of designing a spanning network for a set of nodes with minimum *total* cost. Here we explore another type of objective: designing a spanning network for which the *most expensive* edge is as cheap as possible.

   Specifically, let $G = (V, E)$ be a connected graph with $n$ vertices, $m$ edges, and positive edge costs that you may assume are all distinct. Let $T = (V, E')$ be a spanning tree of $G$; we define the *bottleneck edge* of $T$ to be the edge of $T$ with the greatest cost.

   A spanning tree $T$ of $G$ is a *minimum-bottleneck spanning tree* if there is no spanning tree $T'$ of $G$ with a cheaper bottleneck edge.

   (a) Is every minimum-bottleneck tree of $G$ a minimum spanning tree of $G$? Prove or give a counterexample.

   (b) Is every minimum spanning tree of $G$ a minimum-bottleneck tree of $G$? Prove or give a counterexample.

10. Let $G = (V, E)$ be an (undirected) graph with costs $c_e \geq 0$ on the edges $e \in E$. Assume you are given a minimum-cost spanning tree $T$ in $G$. Now assume that a new edge is added to $G$, connecting two nodes $v, w \in V$ with cost $c$.

    (a) Give an efficient algorithm to test if $T$ remains the minimum-cost spanning tree with the new edge added to $G$ (but not to the tree $T$). Make your algorithm run in time $O(|E|)$. Can you do it in $O(|V|)$ time? Please note any assumptions you make about what data structure is used to represent the tree $T$ and the graph $G$.

(b) Suppose $T$ is no longer the minimum-cost spanning tree. Give a linear-time algorithm (time $O(|E|)$) to update the tree $T$ to the new minimum-cost spanning tree.

11. Suppose you are given a connected graph $G = (V, E)$, with a cost $c_e$ on each edge $e$. In an earlier problem, we saw that when all edge costs are distinct, $G$ has a unique minimum spanning tree. However, $G$ may have many minimum spanning trees when the edge costs are not all distinct. Here we formulate the question: Can Kruskal's Algorithm be made to find all the minimum spanning trees of $G$?

Recall that Kruskal's Algorithm sorted the edges in order of increasing cost, then greedily processed edges one by one, adding an edge $e$ as long as it did not form a cycle. When some edges have the same cost, the phrase "in order of increasing cost" has to be specified a little more carefully: we'll say that an ordering of the edges is *valid* if the corresponding sequence of edge costs is nondecreasing. We'll say that a *valid execution* of Kruskal's Algorithm is one that begins with a valid ordering of the edges of $G$.

For any graph $G$, and any minimum spanning tree $T$ of $G$, is there a valid execution of Kruskal's Algorithm on $G$ that produces $T$ as output? Give a proof or a counterexample.

12. Suppose you have $n$ video streams that need to be sent, one after another, over a communication link. Stream $i$ consists of a total of $b_i$ bits that need to be sent, at a constant rate, over a period of $t_i$ seconds. You cannot send two streams at the same time, so you need to determine a *schedule* for the streams: an order in which to send them. Whichever order you choose, there cannot be any delays between the end of one stream and the start of the next. Suppose your schedule starts at time 0 (and therefore ends at time $\sum_{i=1}^{n} t_i$, whichever order you choose). We assume that all the values $b_i$ and $t_i$ are positive integers.

Now, because you're just one user, the link does not want you taking up too much bandwidth, so it imposes the following constraint, using a fixed parameter $r$:

(∗) *For each natural number $t > 0$, the total number of bits you send over the time interval from 0 to $t$ cannot exceed $rt$.*

Note that this constraint is only imposed for time intervals that start at 0, *not* for time intervals that start at any other value.

We say that a schedule is *valid* if it satisfies the constraint (∗) imposed by the link.

**The Problem.** Given a set of $n$ streams, each specified by its number of bits $b_i$ and its time duration $t_i$, as well as the link parameter $r$, determine whether there exists a valid schedule.

**Example.** Suppose we have $n = 3$ streams, with

$$(b_1, t_1) = (2000, 1), \quad (b_2, t_2) = (6000, 2), \quad (b_3, t_3) = (2000, 1),$$

and suppose the link's parameter is $r = 5000$. Then the schedule that runs the streams in the order $1, 2, 3$, is valid, since the constraint $(*)$ is satisfied:

> $t = 1$: *the whole first stream has been sent, and* $2000 < 5000 \cdot 1$
> $t = 2$: *half of the second stream has also been sent,*
>         *and* $2000 + 3000 < 5000 \cdot 2$
> *Similar calculations hold for* $t = 3$ *and* $t = 4$.

(a)  Consider the following claim:

> Claim: There exists a valid schedule if and only if each stream $i$ satisfies $b_i \le rt_i$.

Decide whether you think the claim is true or false, and give a proof of either the claim or its negation.

(b)  Give an algorithm that takes a set of $n$ streams, each specified by its number of bits $b_i$ and its time duration $t_i$, as well as the link parameter $r$, and determines whether there exists a valid schedule. The running time of your algorithm should be polynomial in $n$.

13. A small business—say, a photocopying service with a single large machine—faces the following scheduling problem. Each morning they get a set of jobs from customers. They want to do the jobs on their single machine in an order that keeps their customers happiest. Customer $i$'s job will take $t_i$ time to complete. Given a schedule (i.e., an ordering of the jobs), let $C_i$ denote the finishing time of job $i$. For example, if job $j$ is the first to be done, we would have $C_j = t_j$; and if job $j$ is done right after job $i$, we would have $C_j = C_i + t_j$. Each customer $i$ also has a given weight $w_i$ that represents his or her importance to the business. The happiness of customer $i$ is expected to be dependent on the finishing time of $i$'s job. So the company decides that they want to order the jobs to minimize the weighted sum of the completion times, $\sum_{i=1}^{n} w_i C_i$.

   Design an efficient algorithm to solve this problem. That is, you are given a set of $n$ jobs with a processing time $t_i$ and a weight $w_i$ for each job. You want to order the jobs so as to minimize the weighted sum of the completion times, $\sum_{i=1}^{n} w_i C_i$.

   **Example.** Suppose there are two jobs: the first takes time $t_1 = 1$ and has weight $w_1 = 10$, while the second job takes time $t_2 = 3$ and has weight

$w_2 = 2$. Then doing job 1 first would yield a weighted completion time of $10 \cdot 1 + 2 \cdot 4 = 18$, while doing the second job first would yield the larger weighted completion time of $10 \cdot 4 + 2 \cdot 3 = 46$.

14. You're working with a group of security consultants who are helping to monitor a large computer system. There's particular interest in keeping track of processes that are labeled "sensitive." Each such process has a designated start time and finish time, and it runs continuously between these times; the consultants have a list of the planned start and finish times of all sensitive processes that will be run that day.

   As a simple first step, they've written a program called status_check that, when invoked, runs for a few seconds and records various pieces of logging information about all the sensitive processes running on the system at that moment. (We'll model each invocation of status_check as lasting for only this single point in time.) What they'd like to do is to run status_check as few times as possible during the day, but enough that for each sensitive process $P$, status_check is invoked at least once during the execution of process $P$.

   **(a)** Give an efficient algorithm that, given the start and finish times of all the sensitive processes, finds as small a set of times as possible at which to invoke status_check, subject to the requirement that status_check is invoked at least once during each sensitive process $P$.

   **(b)** While you were designing your algorithm, the security consultants were engaging in a little back-of-the-envelope reasoning. "Suppose we can find a set of $k$ sensitive processes with the property that no two are ever running at the same time. Then clearly your algorithm will need to invoke status_check at least $k$ times: no one invocation of status_check can handle more than one of these processes."

   This is true, of course, and after some further discussion, you all begin wondering whether something stronger is true as well, a kind of converse to the above argument. Suppose that $k^*$ is the largest value of $k$ such that one can find a set of $k$ sensitive processes with no two ever running at the same time. Is it the case that there must be a set of $k^*$ times at which you can run status_check so that some invocation occurs during the execution of each sensitive process? (In other words, the kind of argument in the previous paragraph is really the only thing forcing you to need a lot of invocations of status_check.) Decide whether you think this claim is true or false, and give a proof or a counterexample.

**15.** The manager of a large student union on campus comes to you with the following problem. She's in charge of a group of $n$ students, each of whom is scheduled to work one *shift* during the week. There are different jobs associated with these shifts (tending the main desk, helping with package delivery, rebooting cranky information kiosks, etc.), but we can view each shift as a single contiguous interval of time. There can be multiple shifts going on at once.

She's trying to choose a subset of these $n$ students to form a *supervising committee* that she can meet with once a week. She considers such a committee to be *complete* if, for every student not on the committee, that student's shift overlaps (at least partially) the shift of some student who is on the committee. In this way, each student's performance can be observed by at least one person who's serving on the committee.

Give an efficient algorithm that takes the schedule of $n$ shifts and produces a complete supervising committee containing as few students as possible.

**Example.** Suppose $n = 3$, and the shifts are

> *Monday 4 P.M.–Monday 8 P.M.,*
> *Monday 6 P.M.–Monday 10 P.M.,*
> *Monday 9 P.M.–Monday 11 P.M..*

Then the smallest complete supervising committee would consist of just the second student, since the second shift overlaps both the first and the third.

**16.** Some security consultants working in the financial domain are currently advising a client who is investigating a potential money-laundering scheme. The investigation thus far has indicated that $n$ suspicious transactions took place in recent days, each involving money transferred into a single account. Unfortunately, the sketchy nature of the evidence to date means that they don't know the identity of the account, the amounts of the transactions, or the exact times at which the transactions took place. What they do have is an *approximate time-stamp* for each transaction; the evidence indicates that transaction $i$ took place at time $t_i \pm e_i$, for some "margin of error" $e_i$. (In other words, it took place sometime between $t_i - e_i$ and $t_i + e_i$.) Note that different transactions may have different margins of error.

In the last day or so, they've come across a bank account that (for other reasons we don't need to go into here) they suspect might be the one involved in the crime. There are $n$ recent *events* involving the account, which took place at times $x_1, x_2, \ldots, x_n$. To see whether it's plausible that this really is the account they're looking for, they're wondering whether it's possible to associate each of the account's $n$ events with a distinct one of the $n$ suspicious transactions in such a way that, if the account event at time $x_i$ is associated with the suspicious transaction that occurred approximately at time $t_j$, then $|t_j - x_i| \le e_j$. (In other words, they want to know if the activity on the account lines up with the suspicious transactions to within the margin of error; the tricky part here is that they don't know which account event to associate with which suspicious transaction.)

Give an efficient algorithm that takes the given data and decides whether such an association exists. If possible, you should make the running time be at most $O(n^2)$.

17. Consider the following variation on the Interval Scheduling Problem. You have a processor that can operate 24 hours a day, every day. People submit requests to run *daily jobs* on the processor. Each such job comes with a *start time* and an *end time*; if the job is accepted to run on the processor, it must run continuously, every day, for the period between its start and end times. (Note that certain jobs can begin before midnight and end after midnight; this makes for a type of situation different from what we saw in the Interval Scheduling Problem.)

Given a list of $n$ such jobs, your goal is to accept as many jobs as possible (regardless of their length), subject to the constraint that the processor can run at most one job at any given point in time. Provide an algorithm to do this with a running time that is polynomial in $n$. You may assume for simplicity that no two jobs have the same start or end times.

**Example.** Consider the following four jobs, specified by *(start-time, end-time)* pairs.

(6 P.M., 6 A.M.), (9 P.M., 4 A.M.), (3 A.M., 2 P.M.), (1 P.M., 7 P.M.).

The optimal solution would be to pick the two jobs (9 P.M., 4 A.M.) and (1 P.M., 7 P.M.), which can be scheduled without overlapping.

18. Your friends are planning an expedition to a small town deep in the Canadian north next winter break. They've researched all the travel options and have drawn up a directed graph whose nodes represent intermediate destinations and edges represent the roads between them.

In the course of this, they've also learned that extreme weather causes roads in this part of the world to become quite slow in the winter and may cause large travel delays. They've found an excellent travel Web site that can accurately predict how fast they'll be able to travel along the roads; however, the speed of travel depends on the time of year. More precisely, the Web site answers queries of the following form: given an edge $e = (v, w)$ connecting two sites $v$ and $w$, and given a proposed starting time $t$ from location $v$, the site will return a value $f_e(t)$, the predicted arrival time at $w$. The Web site guarantees that $f_e(t) \geq t$ for all edges $e$ and all times $t$ (you can't travel backward in time), and that $f_e(t)$ is a monotone increasing function of $t$ (that is, you do not arrive earlier by starting later). Other than that, the functions $f_e(t)$ may be arbitrary. For example, in areas where the travel time does not vary with the season, we would have $f_e(t) = t + \ell_e$, where $\ell_e$ is the time needed to travel from the beginning to the end of edge $e$.

Your friends want to use the Web site to determine the fastest way to travel through the directed graph from their starting point to their intended destination. (You should assume that they start at time $0$, and that all predictions made by the Web site are completely correct.) Give a polynomial-time algorithm to do this, where we treat a single query to the Web site (based on a specific edge $e$ and a time $t$) as taking a single computational step.

19. A group of network designers at the communications company CluNet find themselves facing the following problem. They have a connected graph $G = (V, E)$, in which the nodes represent sites that want to communicate. Each edge $e$ is a communication link, with a given available bandwidth $b_e$.

For each pair of nodes $u, v \in V$, they want to select a single $u$-$v$ path $P$ on which this pair will communicate. The *bottleneck rate* $b(P)$ of this path $P$ is the minimum bandwidth of any edge it contains; that is, $b(P) = \min_{e \in P} b_e$. The *best achievable bottleneck rate* for the pair $u, v$ in $G$ is simply the maximum, over all $u$-$v$ paths $P$ in $G$, of the value $b(P)$.

It's getting to be very complicated to keep track of a path for each pair of nodes, and so one of the network designers makes a bold suggestion: Maybe one can find a spanning tree $T$ of $G$ so that for *every* pair of nodes $u, v$, the unique $u$-$v$ path in the tree actually attains the best achievable bottleneck rate for $u, v$ in $G$. (In other words, even if you could choose any $u$-$v$ path in the whole graph, you couldn't do better than the $u$-$v$ path in $T$.)

This idea is roundly heckled in the offices of CluNet for a few days, and there's a natural reason for the skepticism: each pair of nodes might want a very different-looking path to maximize its bottleneck rate; why should there be a single tree that simultaneously makes everybody happy? But after some failed attempts to rule out the idea, people begin to suspect it could be possible.

Show that such a tree exists, and give an efficient algorithm to find one. That is, give an algorithm constructing a spanning tree $T$ in which, for each $u, v \in V$, the bottleneck rate of the $u$-$v$ path in $T$ is equal to the best achievable bottleneck rate for the pair $u, v$ in $G$.

20. Every September, somewhere in a far-away mountainous part of the world, the county highway crews get together and decide which roads to keep clear through the coming winter. There are $n$ towns in this county, and the road system can be viewed as a (connected) graph $G = (V, E)$ on this set of towns, each edge representing a road joining two of them. In the winter, people are high enough up in the mountains that they stop worrying about the *length* of roads and start worrying about their *altitude*—this is really what determines how difficult the trip will be.

So each road—each edge $e$ in the graph—is annotated with a number $a_e$ that gives the altitude of the highest point on the road. We'll assume that no two edges have exactly the same altitude value $a_e$. The *height* of a path $P$ in the graph is then the maximum of $a_e$ over all edges $e$ on $P$. Finally, a path between towns $i$ and $j$ is declared to be *winter-optimal* if it achieves the minimum possible height over all paths from $i$ to $j$.

The highway crews are going to select a set $E' \subseteq E$ of the roads to keep clear through the winter; the rest will be left unmaintained and kept off limits to travelers. They all agree that whichever subset of roads $E'$ they decide to keep clear, it should have the property that $(V, E')$ is a connected subgraph; and more strongly, for every pair of towns $i$ and $j$, the height of the winter-optimal path in $(V, E')$ should be no greater than it is in the full graph $G = (V, E)$. We'll say that $(V, E')$ is a *minimum-altitude connected subgraph* if it has this property.

Given that they're going to maintain this key property, however, they otherwise want to keep as few roads clear as possible. One year, they hit upon the following conjecture:

> The minimum spanning tree of G, with respect to the edge weights $a_e$, is a minimum-altitude connected subgraph.

(In an earlier problem, we claimed that there is a unique minimum spanning tree when the edge weights are distinct. Thus, thanks to the assumption that all $a_e$ are distinct, it is okay for us to speak of *the* minimum spanning tree.)

Initially, this conjecture is somewhat counterintuitive, since the minimum spanning tree is trying to minimize the *sum* of the values $a_e$, while the goal of minimizing altitude seems to be asking for a fairly different thing. But lacking an argument to the contrary, they begin considering an even bolder second conjecture:

> *A subgraph* $(V, E')$ *is a minimum-altitude connected subgraph if and only if it contains the edges of the minimum spanning tree.*

Note that this second conjecture would immediately imply the first one, since a minimum spanning tree contains its own edges.

So here's the question.

**(a)** Is the first conjecture true, for all choices of $G$ and distinct altitudes $a_e$? Give a proof or a counterexample with explanation.

**(b)** Is the second conjecture true, for all choices of $G$ and distinct altitudes $a_e$? Give a proof or a counterexample with explanation.

21. Let us say that a graph $G = (V, E)$ is a *near-tree* if it is connected and has at most $n + 8$ edges, where $n = |V|$. Give an algorithm with running time $O(n)$ that takes a near-tree $G$ with costs on its edges, and returns a minimum spanning tree of $G$. You may assume that all the edge costs are distinct.

22. Consider the Minimum Spanning Tree Problem on an undirected graph $G = (V, E)$, with a cost $c_e \geq 0$ on each edge, where the costs may not all be different. If the costs are not all distinct, there can in general be many distinct minimum-cost solutions. Suppose we are given a spanning tree $T \subseteq E$ with the guarantee that for every $e \in T$, $e$ belongs to *some* minimum-cost spanning tree in $G$. Can we conclude that $T$ itself must be a minimum-cost spanning tree in $G$? Give a proof or a counterexample with explanation.

23. Recall the problem of computing a minimum-cost arborescence in a directed graph $G = (V, E)$, with a cost $c_e \geq 0$ on each edge. Here we will consider the case in which $G$ is a directed acyclic graph—that is, it contains no directed cycles.

As in general directed graphs, there can be many distinct minimum-cost solutions. Suppose we are given a directed acyclic graph $G = (V, E)$, and an arborescence $A \subseteq E$ with the guarantee that for every $e \in A$, $e$ belongs to *some* minimum-cost arborescence in $G$. Can we conclude that $A$ itself must be a minimum-cost arborescence in $G$? Give a proof or a counterexample with explanation.

24. Timing circuits are a crucial component of VLSI chips. Here's a simple model of such a timing circuit. Consider a complete balanced binary tree with $n$ leaves, where $n$ is a power of two. Each edge $e$ of the tree has an associated length $\ell_e$, which is a positive number. The *distance* from the root to a given leaf is the sum of the lengths of all the edges on the path from the root to the leaf.

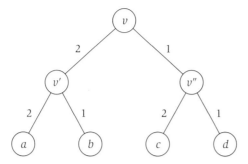

**Figure 4.20** An instance of the zero-skew problem, described in Exercise 23.

The root generates a *clock signal* which is propagated along the edges to the leaves. We'll assume that the time it takes for the signal to reach a given leaf is proportional to the distance from the root to the leaf.

Now, if all leaves do not have the same distance from the root, then the signal will not reach the leaves at the same time, and this is a big problem. We want the leaves to be completely synchronized, and all to receive the signal at the same time. To make this happen, we will have to *increase* the lengths of certain edges, so that all root-to-leaf paths have the same length (we're not able to shrink edge lengths). If we achieve this, then the tree (with its new edge lengths) will be said to have *zero skew*. Our goal is to achieve zero skew in a way that keeps the sum of all the edge lengths as small as possible.

Give an algorithm that increases the lengths of certain edges so that the resulting tree has zero skew and the total edge length is as small as possible.

**Example.** Consider the tree in Figure 4.20, in which letters name the nodes and numbers indicate the edge lengths.

The unique optimal solution for this instance would be to take the three length-1 edges and increase each of their lengths to 2. The resulting tree has zero skew, and the total edge length is 12, the smallest possible.

25. Suppose we are given a set of points $P = \{p_1, p_2, \ldots, p_n\}$, together with a distance function $d$ on the set $P$; $d$ is simply a function on pairs of points in $P$ with the properties that $d(p_i, p_j) = d(p_j, p_i) > 0$ if $i \neq j$, and that $d(p_i, p_i) = 0$ for each $i$.

We define a *hierarchical metric* on $P$ to be any distance function $\tau$ that can be constructed as follows. We build a rooted tree $T$ with $n$ leaves, and we associate with each node $v$ of $T$ (both leaves and internal nodes) a *height* $h_v$. These heights must satisfy the properties that $h(v) = 0$ for each leaf $v$, and if $u$ is the parent of $v$ in $T$, then $h(u) \geq h(v)$. We place each point in $P$ at a distinct leaf in $T$. Now, for any pair of points $p_i$ and $p_j$, their distance $\tau(p_i, p_j)$ is defined as follows. We determine the least common ancestor $v$ in $T$ of the leaves containing $p_i$ and $p_j$, and define $\tau(p_i, p_j) = h_v$.

We say that a hierarchical metric $\tau$ is *consistent* with our distance function $d$ if, for all pairs $i, j$, we have $\tau(p_i, p_j) \leq d(p_i, p_j)$.

Give a polynomial-time algorithm that takes the distance function $d$ and produces a hierarchical metric $\tau$ with the following properties.

(i)   $\tau$ is consistent with $d$, and

(ii)  if $\tau'$ is any other hierarchical metric consistent with $d$, then $\tau'(p_i, p_j) \leq \tau(p_i, p_j)$ for each pair of points $p_i$ and $p_j$.

26. One of the first things you learn in calculus is how to minimize a differentiable function such as $y = ax^2 + bx + c$, where $a > 0$. The Minimum Spanning Tree Problem, on the other hand, is a minimization problem of a very different flavor: there are now just a finite number of possibilities for how the minimum might be achieved—rather than a continuum of possibilities—and we are interested in how to perform the computation without having to exhaust this (huge) finite number of possibilities.

One can ask what happens when these two minimization issues are brought together, and the following question is an example of this. Suppose we have a connected graph $G = (V, E)$. Each edge $e$ now has a *time-varying edge cost* given by a function $f_e : \mathbf{R} \rightarrow \mathbf{R}$. Thus, at time $t$, it has cost $f_e(t)$. We'll assume that all these functions are positive over their entire range. Observe that the set of edges constituting the minimum spanning tree of $G$ may change over time. Also, of course, the cost of the minimum spanning tree of $G$ becomes a function of the time $t$; we'll denote this function $c_G(t)$. A natural problem then becomes: find a value of $t$ at which $c_G(t)$ is minimized.

Suppose each function $f_e$ is a polynomial of degree 2: $f_e(t) = a_e t^2 + b_e t + c_e$, where $a_e > 0$. Give an algorithm that takes the graph $G$ and the values $\{(a_e, b_e, c_e) : e \in E\}$ and returns a value of the time $t$ at which the minimum spanning tree has minimum cost. Your algorithm should run in time polynomial in the number of nodes and edges of the graph $G$. You may assume that arithmetic operations on the numbers $\{(a_e, b_e, c_e)\}$ can be done in constant time per operation.

27. In trying to understand the combinatorial structure of spanning trees, we can consider the space of *all* possible spanning trees of a given graph and study the properties of this space. This is a strategy that has been applied to many similar problems as well.

Here is one way to do this. Let $G$ be a connected graph, and $T$ and $T'$ two different spanning trees of $G$. We say that $T$ and $T'$ are *neighbors* if $T$ contains exactly one edge that is not in $T'$, and $T'$ contains exactly one edge that is not in $T$.

Now, from any graph $G$, we can build a (large) graph $\mathcal{H}$ as follows. The nodes of $\mathcal{H}$ are the spanning trees of $G$, and there is an edge between two nodes of $\mathcal{H}$ if the corresponding spanning trees are neighbors.

Is it true that, for any connected graph $G$, the resulting graph $\mathcal{H}$ is connected? Give a proof that $\mathcal{H}$ is always connected, or provide an example (with explanation) of a connected graph $G$ for which $\mathcal{H}$ is not connected.

28. Suppose you're a consultant for the networking company CluNet, and they have the following problem. The network that they're currently working on is modeled by a connected graph $G = (V, E)$ with $n$ nodes. Each edge $e$ is a fiber-optic cable that is owned by one of two companies— creatively named $X$ and $Y$—and leased to CluNet.

Their plan is to choose a spanning tree $T$ of $G$ and upgrade the links corresponding to the edges of $T$. Their business relations people have already concluded an agreement with companies $X$ and $Y$ stipulating a number $k$ so that in the tree $T$ that is chosen, $k$ of the edges will be owned by $X$ and $n - k - 1$ of the edges will be owned by $Y$.

CluNet management now faces the following problem. It is not at all clear to them whether there even *exists* a spanning tree $T$ meeting these conditions, or how to find one if it exists. So this is the problem they put to you: Give a polynomial-time algorithm that takes $G$, with each edge labeled $X$ or $Y$, and either (i) returns a spanning tree with exactly $k$ edges labeled $X$, or (ii) reports correctly that no such tree exists.

29. Given a list of $n$ natural numbers $d_1, d_2, \ldots, d_n$, show how to decide in polynomial time whether there exists an undirected graph $G = (V, E)$ whose node degrees are precisely the numbers $d_1, d_2, \ldots, d_n$. (That is, if $V = \{v_1, v_2, \ldots, v_n\}$, then the degree of $v_i$ should be exactly $d_i$.) $G$ should not contain multiple edges between the same pair of nodes, or "loop" edges with both endpoints equal to the same node.

30. Let $G = (V, E)$ be a graph with $n$ nodes in which each pair of nodes is joined by an edge. There is a positive weight $w_{ij}$ on each edge $(i, j)$; and we will assume these weights satisfy the *triangle inequality* $w_{ik} \leq w_{ij} + w_{jk}$. For a subset $V' \subseteq V$, we will use $G[V']$ to denote the subgraph (with edge weights) induced on the nodes in $V'$.

We are given a set $X \subseteq V$ of $k$ *terminals* that must be connected by edges. We say that a *Steiner tree* on $X$ is a set $Z$ so that $X \subseteq Z \subseteq V$, together with a spanning subtree $T$ of $G[Z]$. The *weight* of the Steiner tree is the weight of the tree $T$.

Show that the problem of finding a minimum-weight Steiner tree on $X$ can be solved in time $O(n^{O(k)})$.

31. Let's go back to the original motivation for the Minimum Spanning Tree Problem. We are given a connected, undirected graph $G = (V, E)$ with positive edge lengths $\{\ell_e\}$, and we want to find a spanning subgraph of it. Now suppose we are willing to settle for a subgraph $H = (V, F)$ that is "denser" than a tree, and we are interested in guaranteeing that, for each pair of vertices $u, v \in V$, the length of the shortest $u$-$v$ path in $H$ is not much longer than the length of the shortest $u$-$v$ path in $G$. By the *length* of a path $P$ here, we mean the sum of $\ell_e$ over all edges $e$ in $P$.

Here's a variant of Kruskal's Algorithm designed to produce such a subgraph.

- First we sort all the edges in order of increasing length. (You may assume all edge lengths are distinct.)

- We then construct a subgraph $H = (V, F)$ by considering each edge in order.

- When we come to edge $e = (u, v)$, we add $e$ to the subgraph $H$ if there is currently no $u$-$v$ path in $H$. (This is what Kruskal's Algorithm would do as well.) On the other hand, if there is a $u$-$v$ path in $H$, we let $d_{uv}$ denote the length of the shortest such path; again, length is with respect to the values $\{\ell_e\}$. We add $e$ to $H$ if $3\ell_e < d_{uv}$.

In other words, we add an edge even when $u$ and $v$ are already in the same connected component, provided that the addition of the edge reduces their shortest-path distance by a sufficient amount.

Let $H = (V, F)$ be the subgraph of $G$ returned by the algorithm.

(a) Prove that for every pair of nodes $u, v \in V$, the length of the shortest $u$-$v$ path in $H$ is at most three times the length of the shortest $u$-$v$ path in $G$.

(b) Despite its ability to approximately preserve shortest-path distances, the subgraph $H$ produced by the algorithm cannot be too dense. Let $f(n)$ denote the maximum number of edges that can possibly be produced as the output of this algorithm, over all $n$-node input graphs with edge lengths. Prove that

$$\lim_{n \to \infty} \frac{f(n)}{n^2} = 0.$$

32. Consider a directed graph $G = (V, E)$ with a root $r \in V$ and nonnegative costs on the edges. In this problem we consider variants of the minimum-cost arborescence algorithm.

   (a) The algorithm discussed in Section 4.9 works as follows. We modify the costs, consider the subgraph of zero-cost edges, look for a directed cycle in this subgraph, and contract it (if one exists). Argue briefly that instead of looking for cycles, we can instead identify and contract strong components of this subgraph.

   (b) In the course of the algorithm, we defined $y_v$ to be the minimum cost of an edge entering $v$, and we modified the costs of all edges $e$ entering node $v$ to be $c'_e = c_e - y_v$. Suppose we instead use the following modified cost: $c''_e = \max(0, c_e - 2y_v)$. This new change is likely to turn more edges to 0 cost. Suppose now we find an arborescence $T$ of 0 cost. Prove that this $T$ has cost at most twice the cost of the minimum-cost arborescence in the original graph.

   (c) Assume you do not find an arborescence of 0 cost. Contract all 0-cost strong components and recursively apply the same procedure on the resulting graph until an arborescence is found. Prove that this $T$ has cost at most twice the cost of the minimum-cost arborescence in the original graph.

33. Suppose you are given a directed graph $G = (V, E)$ in which each edge has a cost of either 0 or 1. Also suppose that $G$ has a node $r$ such that there is a path from $r$ to every other node in $G$. You are also given an integer $k$. Give a polynomial-time algorithm that either constructs an arborescence rooted at $r$ of cost *exactly* $k$, or reports (correctly) that no such arborescence exists.

# Notes and Further Reading

Due to their conceptual cleanness and intuitive appeal, greedy algorithms have a long history and many applications throughout computer science. In this chapter we focused on cases in which greedy algorithms find the optimal solution. Greedy algorithms are also often used as simple heuristics even when they are not guaranteed to find the optimal solution. In Chapter 11 we will discuss greedy algorithms that find near-optimal approximate solutions.

As discussed in Chapter 1, Interval Scheduling can be viewed as a special case of the Independent Set Problem on a graph that represents the overlaps among a collection of intervals. Graphs arising this way are called *interval graphs*, and they have been extensively studied; see, for example, the book by Golumbic (1980). Not just Independent Set but many hard computational problems become much more tractable when restricted to the special case of interval graphs.

Interval Scheduling and the problem of scheduling to minimize the maximum lateness are two of a range of basic scheduling problems for which a simple greedy algorithm can be shown to produce an optimal solution. A wealth of related problems can be found in the survey by Lawler, Lenstra, Rinnooy Kan, and Shmoys (1993).

The optimal algorithm for caching and its analysis are due to Belady (1966). As we mentioned in the text, under real operating conditions caching algorithms must make eviction decisions in real time without knowledge of future requests. We will discuss such caching strategies in Chapter 13.

The algorithm for shortest paths in a graph with nonnegative edge lengths is due to Dijkstra (1959). Surveys of approaches to the Minimum Spanning Tree Problem, together with historical background, can be found in the reviews by Graham and Hell (1985) and Nesetril (1997).

The single-link algorithm is one of the most widely used approaches to the general problem of clustering; the books by Anderberg (1973), Duda, Hart, and Stork (2001), and Jain and Dubes (1981) survey a variety of clustering techniques.

The algorithm for optimal prefix codes is due to Huffman (1952); the earlier approaches mentioned in the text appear in the books by Fano (1949) and Shannon and Weaver (1949). General overviews of the area of data compression can be found in the book by Bell, Cleary, and Witten (1990) and the survey by Lelewer and Hirschberg (1987). More generally, this topic belongs to the area of *information theory*, which is concerned with the representation and encoding of digital information. One of the founding works in this field is the book by Shannon and Weaver (1949), and the more recent textbook by Cover and Thomas (1991) provides detailed coverage of the subject.

The algorithm for finding minimum-cost arborescences is generally credited to Chu and Liu (1965) and to Edmonds (1967) independently. As discussed in the chapter, this multi-phase approach stretches our notion of what constitutes a greedy algorithm. It is also important from the perspective of linear programming, since in that context it can be viewed as a fundamental application of the *pricing method*, or the *primal-dual* technique, for designing algorithms. The book by Nemhauser and Wolsey (1988) develops these connections to linear programming. We will discuss this method in Chapter 11 in the context of approximation algorithms.

More generally, as we discussed at the outset of the chapter, it is hard to find a precise definition of what constitutes a greedy algorithm. In the search for such a definition, it is not even clear that one can apply the analogue of U.S. Supreme Court Justice Potter Stewart's famous test for obscenity—"I know it when I see it"—since one finds disagreements within the research community on what constitutes the boundary, even intuitively, between greedy and nongreedy algorithms. There has been research aimed at formalizing classes of greedy algorithms: the theory of *matroids* is one very influential example (Edmonds 1971; Lawler 2001); and the paper of Borodin, Nielsen, and Rackoff (2002) formalizes notions of greedy and "greedy-type" algorithms, as well as providing a comparison to other formal work on this question.

***Notes on the Exercises*** Exercise 24 is based on results of M. Edahiro, T. Chao, Y. Hsu, J. Ho, K. Boese, and A. Kahng; Exercise 31 is based on a result of Ingo Althofer, Gautam Das, David Dobkin, and Deborah Joseph.

# Chapter 5

## Divide and Conquer

*Divide and conquer* refers to a class of algorithmic techniques in which one breaks the input into several parts, solves the problem in each part recursively, and then combines the solutions to these subproblems into an overall solution. In many cases, it can be a simple and powerful method.

Analyzing the running time of a divide and conquer algorithm generally involves solving a *recurrence relation* that bounds the running time recursively in terms of the running time on smaller instances. We begin the chapter with a general discussion of recurrence relations, illustrating how they arise in the analysis and describing methods for working out upper bounds from them.

We then illustrate the use of divide and conquer with applications to a number of different domains: computing a distance function on different rankings of a set of objects; finding the closest pair of points in the plane; multiplying two integers; and smoothing a noisy signal. Divide and conquer will also come up in subsequent chapters, since it is a method that often works well when combined with other algorithm design techniques. For example, in Chapter 6 we will see it combined with dynamic programming to produce a space-efficient solution to a fundamental sequence comparison problem, and in Chapter 13 we will see it combined with randomization to yield a simple and efficient algorithm for computing the median of a set of numbers.

One thing to note about many settings in which divide and conquer is applied, including these, is that the natural brute-force algorithm may already be polynomial time, and the divide and conquer strategy is serving to reduce the running time to a lower polynomial. This is in contrast to most of the problems in the previous chapters, for example, where brute force was exponential and the goal in designing a more sophisticated algorithm was to achieve *any* kind of polynomial running time. For example, we discussed in

Chapter 2 that the natural brute-force algorithm for finding the closest pair among $n$ points in the plane would simply measure all $\Theta(n^2)$ distances, for a (polynomial) running time of $\Theta(n^2)$. Using divide and conquer, we will improve the running time to $O(n \log n)$. At a high level, then, the overall theme of this chapter is the same as what we've been seeing earlier: that improving on brute-force search is a fundamental conceptual hurdle in solving a problem efficiently, and the design of sophisticated algorithms can achieve this. The difference is simply that the distinction between brute-force search and an improved solution here will not always be the distinction between exponential and polynomial.

## 5.1 A First Recurrence: The Mergesort Algorithm

To motivate the general approach to analyzing divide-and-conquer algorithms, we begin with the *Mergesort* Algorithm. We discussed the Mergesort Algorithm briefly in Chapter 2, when we surveyed common running times for algorithms. Mergesort sorts a given list of numbers by first dividing them into two equal halves, sorting each half separately by recursion, and then combining the results of these recursive calls—in the form of the two sorted halves—using the linear-time algorithm for merging sorted lists that we saw in Chapter 2.

To analyze the running time of Mergesort, we will abstract its behavior into the following template, which describes many common divide-and-conquer algorithms.

> (†) *Divide the input into two pieces of equal size; solve the two subproblems on these pieces separately by recursion; and then combine the two results into an overall solution, spending only linear time for the initial division and final recombining.*

In Mergesort, as in any algorithm that fits this style, we also need a base case for the recursion, typically having it "bottom out" on inputs of some constant size. In the case of Mergesort, we will assume that once the input has been reduced to size 2, we stop the recursion and sort the two elements by simply comparing them to each other.

Consider any algorithm that fits the pattern in (†), and let $T(n)$ denote its worst-case running time on input instances of size $n$. Supposing that $n$ is even, the algorithm spends $O(n)$ time to divide the input into two pieces of size $n/2$ each; it then spends time $T(n/2)$ to solve each one (since $T(n/2)$ is the worst-case running time for an input of size $n/2$); and finally it spends $O(n)$ time to combine the solutions from the two recursive calls. Thus the running time $T(n)$ satisfies the following *recurrence relation*.

**(5.1)** *For some constant c,*

$$T(n) \leq 2T(n/2) + cn$$

*when n > 2, and*

$$T(2) \leq c.$$

The structure of (5.1) is typical of what recurrences will look like: there's an inequality or equation that bounds $T(n)$ in terms of an expression involving $T(k)$ for smaller values $k$; and there is a base case that generally says that $T(n)$ is equal to a constant when $n$ is a constant. Note that one can also write (5.1) more informally as $T(n) \leq 2T(n/2) + O(n)$, suppressing the constant $c$. However, it is generally useful to make $c$ explicit when analyzing the recurrence.

To keep the exposition simpler, we will generally assume that parameters like $n$ are even when needed. This is somewhat imprecise usage; without this assumption, the two recursive calls would be on problems of size $\lceil n/2 \rceil$ and $\lfloor n/2 \rfloor$, and the recurrence relation would say that

$$T(n) \leq T(\lceil n/2 \rceil) + T(\lfloor n/2 \rfloor) + cn$$

for $n \geq 2$. Nevertheless, for all the recurrences we consider here (and for most that arise in practice), the asymptotic bounds are not affected by the decision to ignore all the floors and ceilings, and it makes the symbolic manipulation much cleaner.

Now (5.1) does not explicitly provide an asymptotic bound on the growth rate of the function $T$; rather, it specifies $T(n)$ implicitly in terms of its values on smaller inputs. To obtain an explicit bound, we need to solve the recurrence relation so that $T$ appears only on the left-hand side of the inequality, not the right-hand side as well.

Recurrence solving is a task that has been incorporated into a number of standard computer algebra systems, and the solution to many standard recurrences can now be found by automated means. It is still useful, however, to understand the process of solving recurrences and to recognize which recurrences lead to good running times, since the design of an efficient divide-and-conquer algorithm is heavily intertwined with an understanding of how a recurrence relation determines a running time.

## Approaches to Solving Recurrences

There are two basic ways one can go about solving a recurrence, each of which we describe in more detail below.

- The most intuitively natural way to search for a solution to a recurrence is to "unroll" the recursion, accounting for the running time across the first few levels, and identify a pattern that can be continued as the recursion expands. One then sums the running times over all levels of the recursion (i.e., until it "bottoms out" on subproblems of constant size) and thereby arrives at a total running time.

- A second way is to start with a guess for the solution, substitute it into the recurrence relation, and check that it works. Formally, one justifies this plugging-in using an argument by induction on $n$. There is a useful variant of this method in which one has a general form for the solution, but does not have exact values for all the parameters. By leaving these parameters unspecified in the substitution, one can often work them out as needed.

We now discuss each of these approaches, using the recurrence in (5.1) as an example.

## Unrolling the Mergesort Recurrence

Let's start with the first approach to solving the recurrence in (5.1). The basic argument is depicted in Figure 5.1.

- *Analyzing the first few levels:* At the first level of recursion, we have a single problem of size $n$, which takes time at most $cn$ plus the time spent in all subsequent recursive calls. At the next level, we have two problems each of size $n/2$. Each of these takes time at most $cn/2$, for a total of at most $cn$, again plus the time in subsequent recursive calls. At the third level, we have four problems each of size $n/4$, each taking time at most $cn/4$, for a total of at most $cn$.

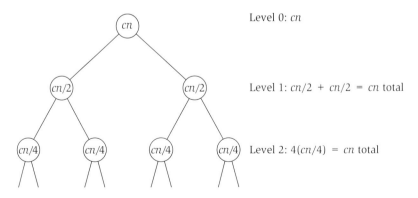

**Figure 5.1**  Unrolling the recurrence $T(n) \leq 2T(n/2) + O(n)$.

- *Identifying a pattern:* What's going on in general? At level $j$ of the recursion, the number of subproblems has doubled $j$ times, so there are now a total of $2^j$. Each has correspondingly shrunk in size by a factor of two $j$ times, and so each has size $n/2^j$, and hence each takes time at most $cn/2^j$. Thus level $j$ contributes a total of at most $2^j(cn/2^j) = cn$ to the total running time.

- *Summing over all levels of recursion:* We've found that the recurrence in (5.1) has the property that the same upper bound of $cn$ applies to total amount of work performed at each level. The number of times the input must be halved in order to reduce its size from $n$ to 2 is $\log_2 n$. So summing the $cn$ work over $\log n$ levels of recursion, we get a total running time of $O(n \log n)$.

We summarize this in the following claim.

**(5.2)**  *Any function $T(\cdot)$ satisfying (5.1) is bounded by $O(n \log n)$, when $n > 1$.*

## Substituting a Solution into the Mergesort Recurrence

The argument establishing (5.2) can be used to determine that the function $T(n)$ is bounded by $O(n \log n)$. If, on the other hand, we have a guess for the running time that we want to verify, we can do so by plugging it into the recurrence as follows.

Suppose we believe that $T(n) \leq cn \log_2 n$ for all $n \geq 2$, and we want to check whether this is indeed true. This clearly holds for $n = 2$, since in this case $cn \log_2 n = 2c$, and (5.1) explicitly tells us that $T(2) \leq c$. Now suppose, by induction, that $T(m) \leq cm \log_2 m$ for all values of $m$ less than $n$, and we want to establish this for $T(n)$. We do this by writing the recurrence for $T(n)$ and plugging in the inequality $T(n/2) \leq c(n/2) \log_2(n/2)$. We then simplify the resulting expression by noticing that $\log_2(n/2) = (\log_2 n) - 1$. Here is the full calculation.

$$
\begin{aligned}
T(n) &\leq 2T(n/2) + cn \\
&\leq 2c(n/2) \log_2(n/2) + cn \\
&= cn[(\log_2 n) - 1] + cn \\
&= (cn \log_2 n) - cn + cn \\
&= cn \log_2 n.
\end{aligned}
$$

This establishes the bound we want for $T(n)$, assuming it holds for smaller values $m < n$, and thus it completes the induction argument.

### An Approach Using Partial Substitution

There is a somewhat weaker kind of substitution one can do, in which one guesses the overall form of the solution without pinning down the exact values of all the constants and other parameters at the outset.

Specifically, suppose we believe that $T(n) = O(n \log n)$, but we're not sure of the constant inside the $O(\cdot)$ notation. We can use the substitution method even without being sure of this constant, as follows. We first write $T(n) \leq kn \log_b n$ for some constant $k$ and base $b$ that we'll determine later. (Actually, the base and the constant we'll end up needing are related to each other, since we saw in Chapter 2 that one can change the base of the logarithm by simply changing the multiplicative constant in front.)

Now we'd like to know whether there is any choice of $k$ and $b$ that will work in an inductive argument. So we try out one level of the induction as follows.

$$T(n) \leq 2T(n/2) + cn \leq 2k(n/2) \log_b(n/2) + cn.$$

It's now very tempting to choose the base $b = 2$ for the logarithm, since we see that this will let us apply the simplification $\log_2(n/2) = (\log_2 n) - 1$. Proceeding with this choice, we have

$$
\begin{aligned}
T(n) &\leq 2k(n/2) \log_2(n/2) + cn \\
&= 2k(n/2)[(\log_2 n) - 1] + cn \\
&= kn[(\log_2 n) - 1] + cn \\
&= (kn \log_2 n) - kn + cn.
\end{aligned}
$$

Finally, we ask: Is there a choice of $k$ that will cause this last expression to be bounded by $kn \log_2 n$? The answer is clearly yes; we just need to choose any $k$ that is at least as large as $c$, and we get

$$T(n) \leq (kn \log_2 n) - kn + cn \leq kn \log_2 n,$$

which completes the induction.

Thus the substitution method can actually be useful in working out the exact constants when one has some guess of the general form of the solution.

## 5.2 Further Recurrence Relations

We've just worked out the solution to a recurrence relation, (5.1), that will come up in the design of several divide-and-conquer algorithms later in this chapter. As a way to explore this issue further, we now consider a class of recurrence relations that generalizes (5.1), and show how to solve the recurrences in this class. Other members of this class will arise in the design of algorithms both in this and in later chapters.

This more general class of algorithms is obtained by considering divide-and-conquer algorithms that create recursive calls on $q$ subproblems of size $n/2$ each and then combine the results in $O(n)$ time. This corresponds to the Mergesort recurrence (5.1) when $q = 2$ recursive calls are used, but other algorithms find it useful to spawn $q > 2$ recursive calls, or just a single ($q = 1$) recursive call. In fact, we will see the case $q > 2$ later in this chapter when we design algorithms for integer multiplication; and we will see a variant on the case $q = 1$ much later in the book, when we design a randomized algorithm for median finding in Chapter 13.

If $T(n)$ denotes the running time of an algorithm designed in this style, then $T(n)$ obeys the following recurrence relation, which directly generalizes (5.1) by replacing 2 with $q$:

**(5.3)** *For some constant $c$,*

$$T(n) \leq qT(n/2) + cn$$

*when $n > 2$, and*

$$T(2) \leq c.$$

We now describe how to solve (5.3) by the methods we've seen above: unrolling, substitution, and partial substitution. We treat the cases $q > 2$ and $q = 1$ separately, since they are qualitatively different from each other—and different from the case $q = 2$ as well.

## The Case of $q > 2$ Subproblems

We begin by unrolling (5.3) in the case $q > 2$, following the style we used earlier for (5.1). We will see that the punch line ends up being quite different.

- *Analyzing the first few levels:* We show an example of this for the case $q = 3$ in Figure 5.2. At the first level of recursion, we have a single problem of size $n$, which takes time at most $cn$ plus the time spent in all subsequent recursive calls. At the next level, we have $q$ problems, each of size $n/2$. Each of these takes time at most $cn/2$, for a total of at most $(q/2)cn$, again plus the time in subsequent recursive calls. The next level yields $q^2$ problems of size $n/4$ each, for a total time of $(q^2/4)cn$. Since $q > 2$, we see that the total work per level is *increasing* as we proceed through the recursion.

- *Identifying a pattern:* At an arbitrary level $j$, we have $q^j$ distinct instances, each of size $n/2^j$. Thus the total work performed at level $j$ is $q^j(cn/2^j) = (q/2)^j cn$.

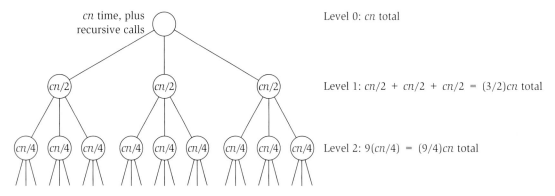

*cn* time, plus recursive calls

Level 0: *cn* total

Level 1: $cn/2 + cn/2 + cn/2 = (3/2)cn$ total

Level 2: $9(cn/4) = (9/4)cn$ total

**Figure 5.2** Unrolling the recurrence $T(n) \le 3T(n/2) + O(n)$.

- *Summing over all levels of recursion:* As before, there are $\log_2 n$ levels of recursion, and the total amount of work performed is the sum over all these:

$$T(n) \le \sum_{j=0}^{\log_2 n - 1} \left(\frac{q}{2}\right)^j cn = cn \sum_{j=0}^{\log_2 n - 1} \left(\frac{q}{2}\right)^j.$$

This is a geometric sum, consisting of powers of $r = q/2$. We can use the formula for a geometric sum when $r > 1$, which gives us the formula

$$T(n) \le cn \left(\frac{r^{\log_2 n} - 1}{r - 1}\right) \le cn \left(\frac{r^{\log_2 n}}{r - 1}\right).$$

Since we're aiming for an asymptotic upper bound, it is useful to figure out what's simply a constant; we can pull out the factor of $r - 1$ from the denominator, and write the last expression as

$$T(n) \le \left(\frac{c}{r - 1}\right) nr^{\log_2 n}.$$

Finally, we need to figure out what $r^{\log_2 n}$ is. Here we use a very handy identity, which says that, for any $a > 1$ and $b > 1$, we have $a^{\log b} = b^{\log a}$. Thus

$$r^{\log_2 n} = n^{\log_2 r} = n^{\log_2(q/2)} = n^{(\log_2 q) - 1}.$$

Thus we have

$$T(n) \le \left(\frac{c}{r - 1}\right) n \cdot n^{(\log_2 q) - 1} \le \left(\frac{c}{r - 1}\right) n^{\log_2 q} = O(n^{\log_2 q}).$$

We sum this up as follows.

**(5.4)**   *Any function $T(\cdot)$ satisfying (5.3) with $q > 2$ is bounded by $O(n^{\log_2 q})$.*

So we find that the running time is more than linear, since $\log_2 q > 1$, but still polynomial in $n$. Plugging in specific values of $q$, the running time is $O(n^{\log_2 3}) = O(n^{1.59})$ when $q = 3$; and the running time is $O(n^{\log_2 4}) = O(n^2)$ when $q = 4$. This increase in running time as $q$ increases makes sense, of course, since the recursive calls generate more work for larger values of $q$.

*Applying Partial Substitution*   The appearance of $\log_2 q$ in the exponent followed naturally from our solution to (5.3), but it's not necessarily an expression one would have guessed at the outset. We now consider how an approach based on partial substitution into the recurrence yields a different way of discovering this exponent.

Suppose we guess that the solution to (5.3), when $q > 2$, has the form $T(n) \le kn^d$ for some constants $k > 0$ and $d > 1$. This is quite a general guess, since we haven't even tried specifying the exponent $d$ of the polynomial. Now let's try starting the inductive argument and seeing what constraints we need on $k$ and $d$. We have

$$T(n) \le qT(n/2) + cn,$$

and applying the inductive hypothesis to $T(n/2)$, this expands to

$$T(n) \le qk\left(\frac{n}{2}\right)^d + cn$$

$$= \frac{q}{2^d}kn^d + cn.$$

This is remarkably close to something that works: if we choose $d$ so that $q/2^d = 1$, then we have $T(n) \le kn^d + cn$, which is almost right except for the extra term $cn$. So let's deal with these two issues: first, how to choose $d$ so we get $q/2^d = 1$; and second, how to get rid of the $cn$ term.

Choosing $d$ is easy: we want $2^d = q$, and so $d = \log_2 q$. Thus we see that the exponent $\log_2 q$ appears very naturally once we decide to discover which value of $d$ works when substituted into the recurrence.

But we still have to get rid of the $cn$ term. To do this, we change the form of our guess for $T(n)$ so as to explicitly subtract it off. Suppose we try the form $T(n) \le kn^d - \ell n$, where we've now decided that $d = \log_2 q$ but we haven't fixed the constants $k$ or $\ell$. Applying the new formula to $T(n/2)$, this expands to

$$T(n) \leq qk\left(\frac{n}{2}\right)^d - q\ell\left(\frac{n}{2}\right) + cn$$

$$= \frac{q}{2^d}kn^d - \frac{q\ell}{2}n + cn$$

$$= kn^d - \frac{q\ell}{2}n + cn$$

$$= kn^d - (\frac{q\ell}{2} - c)n.$$

This now works completely, if we simply choose $\ell$ so that $(\frac{q\ell}{2} - c) = \ell$: in other words, $\ell = 2c/(q-2)$. This completes the inductive step for $n$. We also need to handle the base case $n = 2$, and this we do using the fact that the value of $k$ has not yet been fixed: we choose $k$ large enough so that the formula is a valid upper bound for the case $n = 2$.

## The Case of One Subproblem

We now consider the case of $q = 1$ in (5.3), since this illustrates an outcome of yet another flavor. While we won't see a direct application of the recurrence for $q = 1$ in this chapter, a variation on it comes up in Chapter 13, as we mentioned earlier.

We begin by unrolling the recurrence to try constructing a solution.

- *Analyzing the first few levels:* We show the first few levels of the recursion in Figure 5.3. At the first level of recursion, we have a single problem of size $n$, which takes time at most $cn$ plus the time spent in all subsequent recursive calls. The next level has one problem of size $n/2$, which contributes $cn/2$, and the level after that has one problem of size $n/4$, which contributes $cn/4$. So we see that, unlike the previous case, the total work per level when $q = 1$ is actually *decreasing* as we proceed through the recursion.

- *Identifying a pattern:* At an arbitrary level $j$, we still have just one instance; it has size $n/2^j$ and contributes $cn/2^j$ to the running time.

- *Summing over all levels of recursion:* There are $\log_2 n$ levels of recursion, and the total amount of work performed is the sum over all these:

$$T(n) \leq \sum_{j=0}^{\log_2 n - 1} \frac{cn}{2^j} = cn \sum_{j=0}^{\log_2 n - 1} \left(\frac{1}{2^j}\right).$$

This geometric sum is very easy to work out; even if we continued it to infinity, it would converge to 2. Thus we have

$$T(n) \leq 2cn = O(n).$$

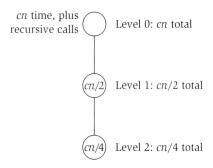

Figure 5.3   Unrolling the recurrence $T(n) \le T(n/2) + O(n)$.

We sum this up as follows.

**(5.5)**   *Any function $T(\cdot)$ satisfying (5.3) with $q = 1$ is bounded by $O(n)$.*

This is counterintuitive when you first see it. The algorithm is performing $\log n$ levels of recursion, but the overall running time is still linear in $n$. The point is that a geometric series with a decaying exponent is a powerful thing: fully half the work performed by the algorithm is being done at the top level of the recursion.

It is also useful to see how partial substitution into the recurrence works very well in this case. Suppose we guess, as before, that the form of the solution is $T(n) \le kn^d$. We now try to establish this by induction using (5.3), assuming that the solution holds for the smaller value $n/2$:

$$T(n) \le T(n/2) + cn$$

$$\le k\left(\frac{n}{2}\right)^d + cn$$

$$= \frac{k}{2^d}n^d + cn.$$

If we now simply choose $d = 1$ and $k = 2c$, we have

$$T(n) \le \frac{k}{2}n + cn = (\frac{k}{2} + c)n = kn,$$

which completes the induction.

***The Effect of the Parameter q.***   It is worth reflecting briefly on the role of the parameter $q$ in the class of recurrences $T(n) \le qT(n/2) + O(n)$ defined by (5.3). When $q = 1$, the resulting running time is linear; when $q = 2$, it's $O(n \log n)$; and when $q > 2$, it's a polynomial bound with an exponent larger than 1 that grows with $q$. The reason for this range of different running times lies in where most of the work is spent in the recursion: when $q = 1$, the total running time is dominated by the top level, whereas when $q > 2$ it's dominated by the work done on constant-size subproblems at the bottom of the recursion. Viewed this way, we can appreciate that the recurrence for $q = 2$ really represents a "knife-edge"—the amount of work done at each level is *exactly the same*, which is what yields the $O(n \log n)$ running time.

## A Related Recurrence: $T(n) \leq 2T(n/2) + O(n^2)$

We conclude our discussion with one final recurrence relation; it is illustrative both as another application of a decaying geometric sum and as an interesting contrast with the recurrence (5.1) that characterized Mergesort. Moreover, we will see a close variant of it in Chapter 6, when we analyze a divide-and-conquer algorithm for solving the Sequence Alignment Problem using a small amount of working memory.

The recurrence is based on the following divide-and-conquer structure.

*Divide the input into two pieces of equal size; solve the two subproblems on these pieces separately by recursion; and then combine the two results into an overall solution, spending quadratic time for the initial division and final recombining.*

For our purposes here, we note that this style of algorithm has a running time $T(n)$ that satisfies the following recurrence.

**(5.6)** *For some constant $c$,*

$$T(n) \leq 2T(n/2) + cn^2$$

*when $n > 2$, and*

$$T(2) \leq c.$$

One's first reaction is to guess that the solution will be $T(n) = O(n^2 \log n)$, since it looks almost identical to (5.1) except that the amount of work per level is larger by a factor equal to the input size. In fact, this upper bound is correct (it would need a more careful argument than what's in the previous sentence), but it will turn out that we can also show a stronger upper bound.

We'll do this by unrolling the recurrence, following the standard template for doing this.

- *Analyzing the first few levels:* At the first level of recursion, we have a single problem of size $n$, which takes time at most $cn^2$ plus the time spent in all subsequent recursive calls. At the next level, we have two problems, each of size $n/2$. Each of these takes time at most $c(n/2)^2 = cn^2/4$, for a total of at most $cn^2/2$, again plus the time in subsequent recursive calls. At the third level, we have four problems each of size $n/4$, each taking time at most $c(n/4)^2 = cn^2/16$, for a total of at most $cn^2/4$. Already we see that something is different from our solution to the analogous recurrence (5.1); whereas the total amount of work per level remained the same in that case, here it's decreasing.

- *Identifying a pattern:* At an arbitrary level $j$ of the recursion, there are $2^j$ subproblems, each of size $n/2^j$, and hence the total work at this level is bounded by $2^j c(\frac{n}{2^j})^2 = cn^2/2^j$.

- *Summing over all levels of recursion:* Having gotten this far in the calculation, we've arrived at almost exactly the same sum that we had for the case $q = 1$ in the previous recurrence. We have

$$T(n) \leq \sum_{j=0}^{\log_2 n - 1} \frac{cn^2}{2^j} = cn^2 \sum_{j=0}^{\log_2 n - 1} \left(\frac{1}{2^j}\right) \leq 2cn^2 = O(n^2),$$

where the second inequality follows from the fact that we have a convergent geometric sum.

In retrospect, our initial guess of $T(n) = O(n^2 \log n)$, based on the analogy to (5.1), was an overestimate because of how quickly $n^2$ decreases as we replace it with $(\frac{n}{2})^2$, $(\frac{n}{4})^2$, $(\frac{n}{8})^2$, and so forth in the unrolling of the recurrence. This means that we get a geometric sum, rather than one that grows by a fixed amount over all $n$ levels (as in the solution to (5.1)).

## 5.3 Counting Inversions

We've spent some time discussing approaches to solving a number of common recurrences. The remainder of the chapter will illustrate the application of divide-and-conquer to problems from a number of different domains; we will use what we've seen in the previous sections to bound the running times of these algorithms. We begin by showing how a variant of the Mergesort technique can be used to solve a problem that is not directly related to sorting numbers.

### The Problem

We will consider a problem that arises in the analysis of *rankings*, which are becoming important to a number of current applications. For example, a number of sites on the Web make use of a technique known as *collaborative filtering*, in which they try to match your preferences (for books, movies, restaurants) with those of other people out on the Internet. Once the Web site has identified people with "similar" tastes to yours—based on a comparison of how you and they rate various things—it can recommend new things that these other people have liked. Another application arises in *meta-search tools* on the Web, which execute the same query on many different search engines and then try to synthesize the results by looking for similarities and differences among the various rankings that the search engines return.

A core issue in applications like this is the problem of comparing two rankings. You rank a set of $n$ movies, and then a collaborative filtering system consults its database to look for other people who had "similar" rankings. But what's a good way to measure, numerically, how similar two people's rankings are? Clearly an identical ranking is very similar, and a completely reversed ranking is very different; we want something that interpolates through the middle region.

Let's consider comparing your ranking and a stranger's ranking of the same set of $n$ movies. A natural method would be to label the movies from 1 to $n$ according to your ranking, then order these labels according to the stranger's ranking, and see how many pairs are "out of order." More concretely, we will consider the following problem. We are given a sequence of $n$ numbers $a_1, \ldots, a_n$; we will assume that all the numbers are distinct. We want to define a measure that tells us how far this list is from being in ascending order; the value of the measure should be 0 if $a_1 < a_2 < \ldots < a_n$, and should increase as the numbers become more scrambled.

A natural way to quantify this notion is by counting the number of *inversions*. We say that two indices $i < j$ form an inversion if $a_i > a_j$, that is, if the two elements $a_i$ and $a_j$ are "out of order." We will seek to determine the number of inversions in the sequence $a_1, \ldots, a_n$.

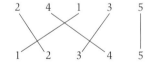

**Figure 5.4** Counting the number of inversions in the sequence $2, 4, 1, 3, 5$. Each crossing pair of line segments corresponds to one pair that is in the opposite order in the input list and the ascending list—in other words, an inversion.

Just to pin down this definition, consider an example in which the sequence is $2, 4, 1, 3, 5$. There are three inversions in this sequence: $(2, 1)$, $(4, 1)$, and $(4, 3)$. There is also an appealing geometric way to visualize the inversions, pictured in Figure 5.4: we draw the sequence of input numbers in the order they're provided, and below that in ascending order. We then draw a line segment between each number in the top list and its copy in the lower list. Each crossing pair of line segments corresponds to one pair that is in the opposite order in the two lists—in other words, an inversion.

Note how the number of inversions is a measure that smoothly interpolates between complete agreement (when the sequence is in ascending order, then there are no inversions) and complete disagreement (if the sequence is in descending order, then every pair forms an inversion, and so there are $\binom{n}{2}$ of them).

## Designing and Analyzing the Algorithm

What is the simplest algorithm to count inversions? Clearly, we could look at every pair of numbers $(a_i, a_j)$ and determine whether they constitute an inversion; this would take $O(n^2)$ time.

We now show how to count the number of inversions much more quickly, in $O(n \log n)$ time. Note that since there can be a quadratic number of inversions, such an algorithm must be able to compute the total number without ever looking at each inversion individually. The basic idea is to follow the strategy (†) defined in Section 5.1. We set $m = \lceil n/2 \rceil$ and divide the list into the two pieces $a_1, \ldots, a_m$ and $a_{m+1}, \ldots, a_n$. We first count the number of inversions in each of these two halves separately. Then we count the number of inversions $(a_i, a_j)$, where the two numbers belong to different halves; the trick is that we must do this part in $O(n)$ time, if we want to apply (5.2). Note that these first-half/second-half inversions have a particularly nice form: they are precisely the pairs $(a_i, a_j)$, where $a_i$ is in the first half, $a_j$ is in the second half, and $a_i > a_j$.

To help with counting the number of inversions between the two halves, we will make the algorithm recursively sort the numbers in the two halves as well. Having the recursive step do a bit more work (sorting as well as counting inversions) will make the "combining" portion of the algorithm easier.

So the crucial routine in this process is `Merge-and-Count`. Suppose we have recursively sorted the first and second halves of the list and counted the inversions in each. We now have two sorted lists $A$ and $B$, containing the first and second halves, respectively. We want to produce a single sorted list $C$ from their union, while also counting the number of pairs $(a, b)$ with $a \in A$, $b \in B$, and $a > b$. By our previous discussion, this is precisely what we will need for the "combining" step that computes the number of first-half/second-half inversions.

This is closely related to the simpler problem we discussed in Chapter 2, which formed the corresponding "combining" step for Mergesort: there we had two sorted lists $A$ and $B$, and we wanted to merge them into a single sorted list in $O(n)$ time. The difference here is that we want to do something extra: not only should we produce a single sorted list from $A$ and $B$, but we should also count the number of "inverted pairs" $(a, b)$ where $a \in A$, $b \in B$, and $a > b$.

It turns out that we will be able to do this in very much the same style that we used for merging. Our `Merge-and-Count` routine will walk through the sorted lists $A$ and $B$, removing elements from the front and appending them to the sorted list $C$. In a given step, we have a *Current* pointer into each list, showing our current position. Suppose that these pointers are currently

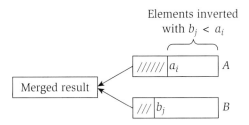

Elements inverted
with $b_j < a_i$

**Figure 5.5** Merging two sorted lists while also counting the number of inversions between them.

at elements $a_i$ and $b_j$. In one step, we compare the elements $a_i$ and $b_j$ being pointed to in each list, remove the smaller one from its list, and append it to the end of list $C$.

This takes care of merging. How do we also count the number of inversions? Because $A$ and $B$ are sorted, it is actually very easy to keep track of the number of inversions we encounter. Every time the element $a_i$ is appended to $C$, no new inversions are encountered, since $a_i$ is smaller than everything left in list $B$, and it comes before all of them. On the other hand, if $b_j$ is appended to list $C$, then it is smaller than all the remaining items in $A$, and it comes after all of them, so we increase our count of the number of inversions by the number of elements remaining in $A$. This is the crucial idea: in constant time, we have accounted for a potentially large number of inversions. See Figure 5.5 for an illustration of this process.

To summarize, we have the following algorithm.

```
Merge-and-Count(A,B)
  Maintain a Current pointer into each list, initialized to
     point to the front elements
  Maintain a variable Count for the number of inversions,
     initialized to 0
  While both lists are nonempty:
     Let aᵢ and bⱼ be the elements pointed to by the Current pointer
     Append the smaller of these two to the output list
     If bⱼ is the smaller element then
        Increment Count by the number of elements remaining in A
     Endif
     Advance the Current pointer in the list from which the
        smaller element was selected.
  EndWhile
```

```
Once one list is empty, append the remainder of the other list
    to the output
Return Count and the merged list
```

The running time of Merge-and-Count can be bounded by the analogue of the argument we used for the original merging algorithm at the heart of Mergesort: each iteration of the While loop takes constant time, and in each iteration we add some element to the output that will never be seen again. Thus the number of iterations can be at most the sum of the initial lengths of $A$ and $B$, and so the total running time is $O(n)$.

We use this Merge-and-Count routine in a recursive procedure that simultaneously sorts and counts the number of inversions in a list $L$.

```
Sort-and-Count(L)
    If the list has one element then
        there are no inversions
    Else
        Divide the list into two halves:
            A contains the first ⌈n/2⌉ elements
            B contains the remaining ⌊n/2⌋ elements
        (r_A, A) = Sort-and-Count(A)
        (r_B, B) = Sort-and-Count(B)
        (r, L) = Merge-and-Count(A, B)
    Endif
    Return r = r_A + r_B + r, and the sorted list L
```

Since our Merge-and-Count procedure takes $O(n)$ time, the running time $T(n)$ of the full Sort-and-Count procedure satisfies the recurrence (5.1). By (5.2), we have

**(5.7)** *The* Sort-and-Count *algorithm correctly sorts the input list and counts the number of inversions; it runs in $O(n \log n)$ time for a list with $n$ elements.*

## 5.4 Finding the Closest Pair of Points

We now describe another problem that can be solved by an algorithm in the style we've been discussing; but finding the right way to "merge" the solutions to the two subproblems it generates requires quite a bit of ingenuity.

## The Problem

The problem we consider is very simple to state: Given $n$ points in the plane, find the pair that is closest together.

The problem was considered by M. I. Shamos and D. Hoey in the early 1970s, as part of their project to work out efficient algorithms for basic computational primitives in geometry. These algorithms formed the foundations of the then-fledgling field of *computational geometry*, and they have found their way into areas such as graphics, computer vision, geographic information systems, and molecular modeling. And although the closest-pair problem is one of the most natural algorithmic problems in geometry, it is surprisingly hard to find an efficient algorithm for it. It is immediately clear that there is an $O(n^2)$ solution—compute the distance between each pair of points and take the minimum—and so Shamos and Hoey asked whether an algorithm asymptotically faster than quadratic could be found. It took quite a long time before they resolved this question, and the $O(n \log n)$ algorithm we give below is essentially the one they discovered. In fact, when we return to this problem in Chapter 13, we will see that it is possible to further improve the running time to $O(n)$ using randomization.

## Designing the Algorithm

We begin with a bit of notation. Let us denote the set of points by $P = \{p_1, \ldots, p_n\}$, where $p_i$ has coordinates $(x_i, y_i)$; and for two points $p_i, p_j \in P$, we use $d(p_i, p_j)$ to denote the standard Euclidean distance between them. Our goal is to find a pair of points $p_i, p_j$ that minimizes $d(p_i, p_j)$.

We will assume that no two points in $P$ have the same $x$-coordinate or the same $y$-coordinate. This makes the discussion cleaner; and it's easy to eliminate this assumption either by initially applying a rotation to the points that makes it true, or by slightly extending the algorithm we develop here.

It's instructive to consider the one-dimensional version of this problem for a minute, since it is much simpler and the contrasts are revealing. How would we find the closest pair of points on a line? We'd first sort them, in $O(n \log n)$ time, and then we'd walk through the sorted list, computing the distance from each point to the one that comes after it. It is easy to see that one of these distances must be the minimum one.

In two dimensions, we could try sorting the points by their $y$-coordinate (or $x$-coordinate) and hoping that the two closest points were near one another in the order of this sorted list. But it is easy to construct examples in which they are very far apart, preventing us from adapting our one-dimensional approach.

Instead, our plan will be to apply the style of divide and conquer used in Mergesort: we find the closest pair among the points in the "left half" of

$P$ and the closest pair among the points in the "right half" of $P$; and then we use this information to get the overall solution in linear time. If we develop an algorithm with this structure, then the solution of our basic recurrence from (5.1) will give us an $O(n \log n)$ running time.

It is the last, "combining" phase of the algorithm that's tricky: the distances that have not been considered by either of our recursive calls are precisely those that occur between a point in the left half and a point in the right half; there are $\Omega(n^2)$ such distances, yet we need to find the smallest one in $O(n)$ time after the recursive calls return. If we can do this, our solution will be complete: it will be the smallest of the values computed in the recursive calls and this minimum "left-to-right" distance.

**Setting Up the Recursion** Let's get a few easy things out of the way first. It will be very useful if every recursive call, on a set $P' \subseteq P$, begins with two lists: a list $P'_x$ in which all the points in $P'$ have been sorted by increasing $x$-coordinate, and a list $P'_y$ in which all the points in $P'$ have been sorted by increasing $y$-coordinate. We can ensure that this remains true throughout the algorithm as follows.

First, before any of the recursion begins, we sort all the points in $P$ by $x$-coordinate and again by $y$-coordinate, producing lists $P_x$ and $P_y$. Attached to each entry in each list is a record of the position of that point in both lists.

The first level of recursion will work as follows, with all further levels working in a completely analogous way. We define $Q$ to be the set of points in the first $\lceil n/2 \rceil$ positions of the list $P_x$ (the "left half") and $R$ to be the set of points in the final $\lfloor n/2 \rfloor$ positions of the list $P_x$ (the "right half"). See Figure 5.6. By a single pass through each of $P_x$ and $P_y$, in $O(n)$ time, we can create the

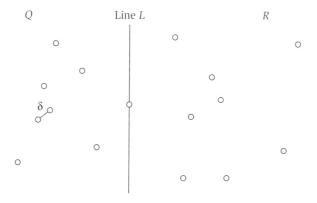

**Figure 5.6** The first level of recursion: The point set $P$ is divided evenly into $Q$ and $R$ by the line $L$, and the closest pair is found on each side recursively.

following four lists: $Q_x$, consisting of the points in $Q$ sorted by increasing $x$-coordinate; $Q_y$, consisting of the points in $Q$ sorted by increasing $y$-coordinate; and analogous lists $R_x$ and $R_y$. For each entry of each of these lists, as before, we record the position of the point in both lists it belongs to.

We now recursively determine a closest pair of points in $Q$ (with access to the lists $Q_x$ and $Q_y$). Suppose that $q_0^*$ and $q_1^*$ are (correctly) returned as a closest pair of points in $Q$. Similarly, we determine a closest pair of points in $R$, obtaining $r_0^*$ and $r_1^*$.

***Combining the Solutions***    The general machinery of divide and conquer has gotten us this far, without our really having delved into the structure of the closest-pair problem. But it still leaves us with the problem that we saw looming originally: How do we use the solutions to the two subproblems as part of a linear-time "combining" operation?

Let $\delta$ be the minimum of $d(q_0^*, q_1^*)$ and $d(r_0^*, r_1^*)$. The real question is: Are there points $q \in Q$ and $r \in R$ for which $d(q, r) < \delta$? If not, then we have already found the closest pair in one of our recursive calls. But if there are, then the closest such $q$ and $r$ form the closest pair in $P$.

Let $x^*$ denote the $x$-coordinate of the rightmost point in $Q$, and let $L$ denote the vertical line described by the equation $x = x^*$. This line $L$ "separates" $Q$ from $R$. Here is a simple fact.

**(5.8)**    *If there exists $q \in Q$ and $r \in R$ for which $d(q, r) < \delta$, then each of $q$ and $r$ lies within a distance $\delta$ of $L$.*

**Proof.**  Suppose such $q$ and $r$ exist; we write $q = (q_x, q_y)$ and $r = (r_x, r_y)$. By the definition of $x^*$, we know that $q_x \le x^* \le r_x$. Then we have

$$x^* - q_x \le r_x - q_x \le d(q, r) < \delta$$

and

$$r_x - x^* \le r_x - q_x \le d(q, r) < \delta,$$

so each of $q$ and $r$ has an $x$-coordinate within $\delta$ of $x^*$ and hence lies within distance $\delta$ of the line $L$.  ∎

So if we want to find a close $q$ and $r$, we can restrict our search to the narrow band consisting only of points in $P$ within $\delta$ of $L$. Let $S \subseteq P$ denote this set, and let $S_y$ denote the list consisting of the points in $S$ sorted by increasing $y$-coordinate. By a single pass through the list $P_y$, we can construct $S_y$ in $O(n)$ time.

We can restate (5.8) as follows, in terms of the set $S$.

**(5.9)** *There exist $q \in Q$ and $r \in R$ for which $d(q, r) < \delta$ if and only if there exist $s, s' \in S$ for which $d(s, s') < \delta$.*

It's worth noticing at this point that $S$ might in fact be the whole set $P$, in which case (5.8) and (5.9) really seem to buy us nothing. But this is actually far from true, as the following amazing fact shows.

**(5.10)** *If $s, s' \in S$ have the property that $d(s, s') < \delta$, then $s$ and $s'$ are within 15 positions of each other in the sorted list $S_y$.*

**Proof.** Consider the subset $Z$ of the plane consisting of all points within distance $\delta$ of $L$. We partition $Z$ into *boxes*: squares with horizontal and vertical sides of length $\delta/2$. One *row* of $Z$ will consist of four boxes whose horizontal sides have the same $y$-coordinates. This collection of boxes is depicted in Figure 5.7.

Suppose two points of $S$ lie in the same box. Since all points in this box lie on the same side of $L$, these two points either both belong to $Q$ or both belong to $R$. But any two points in the same box are within distance $\delta \cdot \sqrt{2}/2 < \delta$, which contradicts our definition of $\delta$ as the minimum distance between any pair of points in $Q$ or in $R$. Thus each box contains at most one point of $S$.

Now suppose that $s, s' \in S$ have the property that $d(s, s') < \delta$, and that they are at least 16 positions apart in $S_y$. Assume without loss of generality that $s$ has the smaller $y$-coordinate. Then, since there can be at most one point per box, there are at least three rows of $Z$ lying between $s$ and $s'$. But any two points in $Z$ separated by at least three rows must be a distance of at least $3\delta/2$ apart—a contradiction.  ■

We note that the value of 15 can be reduced; but for our purposes at the moment, the important thing is that it is an absolute constant.

In view of (5.10), we can conclude the algorithm as follows. We make one pass through $S_y$, and for each $s \in S_y$, we compute its distance to each of the next 15 points in $S_y$. Statement (5.10) implies that in doing so, we will have computed the distance of each pair of points in $S$ (if any) that are at distance less than $\delta$ from each other. So having done this, we can compare the smallest such distance to $\delta$, and we can report one of two things: (i) the closest pair of points in $S$, if their distance is less than $\delta$; or (ii) the (correct) conclusion that no pairs of points in $S$ are within $\delta$ of each other. In case (i), this pair is the closest pair in $P$; in case (ii), the closest pair found by our recursive calls is the closest pair in $P$.

Note the resemblance between this procedure and the algorithm we rejected at the very beginning, which tried to make one pass through $P$ in order

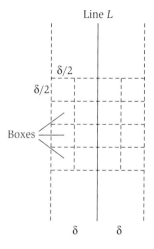

**Figure 5.7** The portion of the plane close to the dividing line $L$, as analyzed in the proof of (5.10).

of $y$-coordinate. The reason such an approach works now is due to the extra knowledge (the value of $\delta$) we've gained from the recursive calls, and the special structure of the set $S$.

This concludes the description of the "combining" part of the algorithm, since by (5.9) we have now determined whether the minimum distance between a point in $Q$ and a point in $R$ is less than $\delta$, and if so, we have found the closest such pair.

A complete description of the algorithm and its proof of correctness are implicitly contained in the discussion so far, but for the sake of concreteness, we now summarize both.

***Summary of the Algorithm***   A high-level description of the algorithm is the following, using the notation we have developed above.

```
Closest-Pair(P)
  Construct Px and Py   (O(n log n) time)
  (p₀*, p₁*) = Closest-Pair-Rec(Px,Py)

Closest-Pair-Rec(Px, Py)
  If |P| ≤ 3 then
    find closest pair by measuring all pairwise distances
  Endif

  Construct Qx, Qy, Rx, Ry (O(n) time)
  (q₀*,q₁*) = Closest-Pair-Rec(Qx, Qy)
  (r₀*,r₁*) = Closest-Pair-Rec(Rx, Ry)

  δ  =  min(d(q₀*,q₁*), d(r₀*,r₁*))
  x* = maximum x-coordinate of a point in set Q
  L  = {(x,y) : x = x*}
  S = points in P within distance δ of L.

  Construct Sy (O(n) time)
  For each point s ∈ Sy, compute distance from s
      to each of next 15 points in Sy
    Let s, s' be pair achieving minimum of these distances
    (O(n) time)

  If d(s,s') < δ then
    Return (s,s')
  Else if d(q₀*,q₁*) < d(r₀*,r₁*) then
    Return (q₀*,q₁*)
```

```
Else
    Return (r_0^*, r_1^*)
Endif
```

## Analyzing the Algorithm

We first prove that the algorithm produces a correct answer, using the facts we've established in the process of designing it.

> **(5.11)**   *The algorithm correctly outputs a closest pair of points in P.*

**Proof.** As we've noted, all the components of the proof have already been worked out, so here we just summarize how they fit together.

We prove the correctness by induction on the size of $P$, the case of $|P| \leq 3$ being clear. For a given $P$, the closest pair in the recursive calls is computed correctly by induction. By (5.10) and (5.9), the remainder of the algorithm correctly determines whether any pair of points in $S$ is at distance less than $\delta$, and if so returns the closest such pair. Now the closest pair in $P$ either has both elements in one of $Q$ or $R$, or it has one element in each. In the former case, the closest pair is correctly found by the recursive call; in the latter case, this pair is at distance less than $\delta$, and it is correctly found by the remainder of the algorithm. ∎

We now bound the running time as well, using (5.2).

> **(5.12)**   *The running time of the algorithm is $O(n \log n)$.*

**Proof.** The initial sorting of $P$ by $x$- and $y$-coordinate takes time $O(n \log n)$. The running time of the remainder of the algorithm satisfies the recurrence (5.1), and hence is $O(n \log n)$ by (5.2). ∎

## 5.5 Integer Multiplication

We now discuss a different application of divide and conquer, in which the "default" quadratic algorithm is improved by means of a different recurrence. The analysis of the faster algorithm will exploit one of the recurrences considered in Section 5.2, in which more than two recursive calls are spawned at each level.

## The Problem

The problem we consider is an extremely basic one: the multiplication of two integers. In a sense, this problem is so basic that one may not initially think of it

$$
\begin{array}{r}
12 \\
\times\ 13 \\
\hline
36 \\
12 \\
\hline
156
\end{array}
\qquad
\begin{array}{r}
1100 \\
\times\ 1101 \\
\hline
1100 \\
0000 \\
1100 \\
1100 \\
\hline
10011100
\end{array}
$$

(a)             (b)

**Figure 5.8** The elementary-school algorithm for multiplying two integers, in (a) decimal and (b) binary representation.

even as an algorithmic question. But, in fact, elementary schoolers are taught a concrete (and quite efficient) algorithm to multiply two $n$-digit numbers $x$ and $y$. You first compute a "partial product" by multiplying each digit of $y$ separately by $x$, and then you add up all the partial products. (Figure 5.8 should help you recall this algorithm. In elementary school we always see this done in base-10, but it works exactly the same way in base-2 as well.) Counting a single operation on a pair of bits as one primitive step in this computation, it takes $O(n)$ time to compute each partial product, and $O(n)$ time to combine it in with the running sum of all partial products so far. Since there are $n$ partial products, this is a total running time of $O(n^2)$.

If you haven't thought about this much since elementary school, there's something initially striking about the prospect of improving on this algorithm. Aren't all those partial products "necessary" in some way? But, in fact, it is possible to improve on $O(n^2)$ time using a different, recursive way of performing the multiplication.

### Designing the Algorithm

The improved algorithm is based on a more clever way to break up the product into partial sums. Let's assume we're in base-2 (it doesn't really matter), and start by writing $x$ as $x_1 \cdot 2^{n/2} + x_0$. In other words, $x_1$ corresponds to the "high-order" $n/2$ bits, and $x_0$ corresponds to the "low-order" $n/2$ bits. Similarly, we write $y = y_1 \cdot 2^{n/2} + y_0$. Thus, we have

$$
\begin{aligned}
xy &= (x_1 \cdot 2^{n/2} + x_0)(y_1 \cdot 2^{n/2} + y_0) \\
&= x_1 y_1 \cdot 2^n + (x_1 y_0 + x_0 y_1) \cdot 2^{n/2} + x_0 y_0. \tag{5.1}
\end{aligned}
$$

Equation (5.1) reduces the problem of solving a single $n$-bit instance (multiplying the two $n$-bit numbers $x$ and $y$) to the problem of solving four $n/2$-bit instances (computing the products $x_1 y_1, x_1 y_0, x_0 y_1,$ and $x_0 y_0$). So we have a first candidate for a divide-and-conquer solution: recursively compute the results for these four $n/2$-bit instances, and then combine them using Equation

(5.1). The combining of the solution requires a constant number of additions of $O(n)$-bit numbers, so it takes time $O(n)$; thus, the running time $T(n)$ is bounded by the recurrence

$$T(n) \leq 4T(n/2) + cn$$

for a constant $c$. Is this good enough to give us a subquadratic running time?

We can work out the answer by observing that this is just the case $q = 4$ of the class of recurrences in (5.3). As we saw earlier in the chapter, the solution to this is $T(n) \leq O(n^{\log_2 q}) = O(n^2)$.

So, in fact, our divide-and-conquer algorithm with four-way branching was just a complicated way to get back to quadratic time! If we want to do better using a strategy that reduces the problem to instances on $n/2$ bits, we should try to get away with only *three* recursive calls. This will lead to the case $q = 3$ of (5.3), which we saw had the solution $T(n) \leq O(n^{\log_2 q}) = O(n^{1.59})$.

Recall that our goal is to compute the expression $x_1 y_1 \cdot 2^n + (x_1 y_0 + x_0 y_1) \cdot 2^{n/2} + x_0 y_0$ in Equation (5.1). It turns out there is a simple trick that lets us determine all of the terms in this expression using just three recursive calls. The trick is to consider the result of the single multiplication $(x_1 + x_0)(y_1 + y_0) = x_1 y_1 + x_1 y_0 + x_0 y_1 + x_0 y_0$. This has the four products above added together, at the cost of a single recursive multiplication. If we now also determine $x_1 y_1$ and $x_0 y_0$ by recursion, then we get the outermost terms explicitly, and we get the middle term by subtracting $x_1 y_1$ and $x_0 y_0$ away from $(x_1 + x_0)(y_1 + y_0)$.

Thus, in full, our algorithm is

```
Recursive-Multiply(x,y):
    Write x = x₁ · 2^{n/2} + x₀
          y = y₁ · 2^{n/2} + y₀
    Compute x₁ + x₀ and y₁ + y₀
    p = Recursive-Multiply(x₁ + x₀, y₁ + y₀)
    x₁y₁ = Recursive-Multiply(x₁, y₁)
    x₀y₀ = Recursive-Multiply(x₀, y₀)
    Return x₁y₁ · 2^n + (p − x₁y₁ − x₀y₀) · 2^{n/2} + x₀y₀
```

## Analyzing the Algorithm

We can determine the running time of this algorithm as follows. Given two $n$-bit numbers, it performs a constant number of additions on $O(n)$-bit numbers, in addition to the three recursive calls. Ignoring for now the issue that $x_1 + x_0$ and $y_1 + y_0$ may have $n/2 + 1$ bits (rather than just $n/2$), which turns out not to affect the asymptotic results, each of these recursive calls is on an instance of size $n/2$. Thus, in place of our four-way branching recursion, we now have a three-way branching one, with a running time that satisfies

$$T(n) \leq 3T(n/2) + cn$$

for a constant $c$.

This is the case $q = 3$ of (5.3) that we were aiming for. Using the solution to that recurrence from earlier in the chapter, we have

**(5.13)**    *The running time of* Recursive-Multiply *on two n-bit factors is* $O(n^{\log_2 3}) = O(n^{1.59})$.

## 5.6 Convolutions and the Fast Fourier Transform

As a final topic in this chapter, we show how our basic recurrence from (5.1) is used in the design of the *Fast Fourier Transform*, an algorithm with a wide range of applications.

### The Problem

Given two vectors $a = (a_0, a_1, \ldots, a_{n-1})$ and $b = (b_0, b_1, \ldots, b_{n-1})$, there are a number of common ways of combining them. For example, one can compute the sum, producing the vector $a + b = (a_0 + b_0, a_1 + b_1, \ldots, a_{n-1} + b_{n-1})$; or one can compute the inner product, producing the real number $a \cdot b = a_0 b_0 + a_1 b_1 + \cdots + a_{n-1} b_{n-1}$. (For reasons that will emerge shortly, it is useful to write vectors in this section with coordinates that are indexed starting from 0 rather than 1.)

A means of combining vectors that is very important in applications, even if it doesn't always show up in introductory linear algebra courses, is the *convolution* $a * b$. The convolution of two vectors of length $n$ (as $a$ and $b$ are) is a vector with $2n - 1$ coordinates, where coordinate $k$ is equal to

$$\sum_{\substack{(i,j):i+j=k \\ i,j<n}} a_i b_j.$$

In other words,

$$a * b = (a_0 b_0, a_0 b_1 + a_1 b_0, a_0 b_2 + a_1 b_1 + a_2 b_0, \ldots,$$
$$a_{n-2} b_{n-1} + a_{n-1} b_{n-2}, a_{n-1} b_{n-1}).$$

This definition is a bit hard to absorb when you first see it. Another way to think about the convolution is to picture an $n \times n$ table whose $(i, j)$ entry is $a_i b_j$, like this,

$$
\begin{array}{ccccc}
a_0 b_0 & a_0 b_1 & \cdots & a_0 b_{n-2} & a_0 b_{n-1} \\
a_1 b_0 & a_1 b_1 & \cdots & a_1 b_{n-2} & a_1 b_{n-1} \\
a_2 b_0 & a_2 b_1 & \cdots & a_2 b_{n-2} & a_2 b_{n-1} \\
\cdots & \cdots & \cdots & \cdots & \cdots \\
a_{n-1} b_0 & a_{n-1} b_1 & \cdots & a_{n-1} b_{n-2} & a_{n-1} b_{n-1}
\end{array}
$$

and then to compute the coordinates in the convolution vector by summing along the diagonals.

It's worth mentioning that, unlike the vector sum and inner product, the convolution can be easily generalized to vectors of different lengths, $a = (a_0, a_1, \ldots, a_{m-1})$ and $b = (b_0, b_1, \ldots, b_{n-1})$. In this more general case, we define $a * b$ to be a vector with $m + n - 1$ coordinates, where coordinate $k$ is equal to

$$
\sum_{\substack{(i,j):i+j=k \\ i<m, j<n}} a_i b_j.
$$

We can picture this using the table of products $a_i b_j$ as before; the table is now rectangular, but we still compute coordinates by summing along the diagonals. (From here on, we'll drop explicit mention of the condition $i < m, j < n$ in the summations for convolutions, since it will be clear from the context that we only compute the sum over terms that are defined.)

It's not just the definition of a convolution that is a bit hard to absorb at first; the motivation for the definition can also initially be a bit elusive. What are the circumstances where you'd want to compute the convolution of two vectors? In fact, the convolution comes up in a surprisingly wide variety of different contexts. To illustrate this, we mention the following examples here.

- A first example (which also proves that the convolution is something that we all saw implicitly in high school) is polynomial multiplication. Any polynomial $A(x) = a_0 + a_1 x + a_2 x^2 + \cdots a_{m-1} x^{m-1}$ can be represented just as naturally using its vector of coefficients, $a = (a_0, a_1, \ldots, a_{m-1})$. Now, given two polynomials $A(x) = a_0 + a_1 x + a_2 x^2 + \cdots a_{m-1} x^{m-1}$ and $B(x) = b_0 + b_1 x + b_2 x^2 + \cdots b_{n-1} x^{n-1}$, consider the polynomial $C(x) = A(x)B(x)$ that is equal to their product. In this polynomial $C(x)$, the coefficient on the $x^k$ term is equal to

$$
c_k = \sum_{(i,j):i+j=k} a_i b_j.
$$

  In other words, the coefficient vector $c$ of $C(x)$ is the convolution of the coefficient vectors of $A(x)$ and $B(x)$.

- Arguably the most important application of convolutions in practice is for *signal processing*. This is a topic that could fill an entire course, so we'll just give a simple example here to suggest one way in which the convolution arises.

Suppose we have a vector $a = (a_0, a_1, \ldots, a_{m-1})$ which represents a sequence of measurements, such as a temperature or a stock price, sampled at $m$ consecutive points in time. Sequences like this are often very noisy due to measurement error or random fluctuations, and so a common operation is to "smooth" the measurements by averaging each value $a_i$ with a weighted sum of its neighbors within $k$ steps to the left and right in the sequence, the weights decaying quickly as one moves away from $a_i$. For example, in *Gaussian smoothing*, one replaces $a_i$ with

$$a_i' = \frac{1}{Z} \sum_{j=i-k}^{i+k} a_j e^{-(j-i)^2},$$

for some "width" parameter $k$, and with $Z$ chosen simply to normalize the weights in the average to add up to 1. (There are some issues with boundary conditions—what do we do when $i - k < 0$ or $i + k > m$?—but we could deal with these, for example, by discarding the first and last $k$ entries from the smoothed signal, or by scaling them differently to make up for the missing terms.)

To see the connection with the convolution operation, we picture this smoothing operation as follows. We first define a "mask"

$$w = (w_{-k}, w_{-(k-1)}, \ldots, w_{-1}, w_0, w_1, \ldots, w_{k-1}, w_k)$$

consisting of the weights we want to use for averaging each point with its neighbors. (For example, $w = \frac{1}{Z}(e^{-k^2}, e^{-(k-1)^2}, \ldots, e^{-1}, 1, e^{-1}, \ldots, e^{-(k-1)^2}, e^{-k^2})$ in the Gaussian case above.) We then iteratively position this mask so it is centered at each possible point in the sequence $a$; and for each positioning, we compute the weighted average. In other words, we replace $a_i$ with $a_i' = \sum_{s=-k}^{k} w_s a_{i+s}$.

This last expression is essentially a convolution; we just have to warp the notation a bit so that this becomes clear. Let's define $b = (b_0, b_1, \ldots, b_{2k})$ by setting $b_\ell = w_{k-\ell}$. Then it's not hard to check that with this definition we have the smoothed value

$$a_i' = \sum_{(j,\ell):j+\ell=i+k} a_j b_\ell.$$

In other words, the smoothed sequence is just the convolution of the original signal and the reverse of the mask (with some meaningless coordinates at the beginning and end).

• We mention one final application: the problem of combining histograms. Suppose we're studying a population of people, and we have the following two histograms: One shows the annual income of all the men in the population, and one shows the annual income of all the women. We'd now like to produce a new histogram, showing for each $k$ the number of *pairs* $(M, W)$ for which man $M$ and woman $W$ have a combined income of $k$.

This is precisely a convolution. We can write the first histogram as a vector $a = (a_0, \ldots, a_{m-1})$, to indicate that there are $a_i$ men with annual income equal to $i$. We can similarly write the second histogram as a vector $b = (b_0, \ldots, b_{n-1})$. Now, let $c_k$ denote the number of pairs $(m, w)$ with combined income $k$; this is the number of ways of choosing a man with income $a_i$ and a woman with income $b_j$, for any pair $(i, j)$ where $i + j = k$. In other words,

$$c_k = \sum_{(i,j):i+j=k} a_i b_j.$$

so the combined histogram $c = (c_0, \ldots, c_{m+n-2})$ is simply the convolution of $a$ and $b$.

(Using terminology from probability that we will develop in Chapter 13, one can view this example as showing how convolution is the underlying means for computing the distribution of the sum of two independent random variables.)

**Computing the Convolution**   Having now motivated the notion of convolution, let's discuss the problem of computing it efficiently. For simplicity, we will consider the case of equal length vectors (i.e., $m = n$), although everything we say carries over directly to the case of vectors of unequal lengths.

Computing the convolution is a more subtle question than it may first appear. The definition of convolution, after all, gives us a perfectly valid way to compute it: for each $k$, we just calculate the sum

$$\sum_{(i,j):i+j=k} a_i b_j$$

and use this as the value of the $k^{\text{th}}$ coordinate. The trouble is that this direct way of computing the convolution involves calculating the product $a_i b_j$ for every pair $(i, j)$ (in the process of distributing over the sums in the different terms) and this is $\Theta(n^2)$ arithmetic operations. Spending $O(n^2)$ time on computing the convolution seems natural, as the definition involves $O(n^2)$ multiplications $a_i b_j$. However, it's not inherently clear that we have to spend quadratic time to compute a convolution, since the input and output both only have size $O(n)$.

Could one design an algorithm that bypasses the quadratic-size definition of convolution and computes it in some smarter way?

In fact, quite surprisingly, this is possible. We now describe a method that computes the convolution of two vectors using only $O(n \log n)$ arithmetic operations. The crux of this method is a powerful technique known as the *Fast Fourier Transform* (FFT). The FFT has a wide range of further applications in analyzing sequences of numerical values; computing convolutions quickly, which we focus on here, is just one of these applications.

### Designing and Analyzing the Algorithm

To break through the quadratic time barrier for convolutions, we are going to exploit the connection between the convolution and the multiplication of two polynomials, as illustrated in the first example discussed previously. But rather than use convolution as a primitive in polynomial multiplication, we are going to exploit this connection in the opposite direction.

Suppose we are given the vectors $a = (a_0, a_1, \ldots, a_{n-1})$ and $b = (b_0, b_1, \ldots, b_{n-1})$. We will view them as the polynomials $A(x) = a_0 + a_1 x + a_2 x^2 + \cdots a_{n-1} x^{n-1}$ and $B(x) = b_0 + b_1 x + b_2 x^2 + \cdots b_{n-1} x^{n-1}$, and we'll seek to compute their product $C(x) = A(x)B(x)$ in $O(n \log n)$ time. If $c = (c_0, c_1, \ldots, c_{2n-2})$ is the vector of coefficients of $C$, then we recall from our earlier discussion that $c$ is exactly the convolution $a * b$, and so we can then read off the desired answer directly from the coefficients of $C(x)$.

Now, rather than multiplying $A$ and $B$ symbolically, we can treat them as functions of the variable $x$ and multiply them as follows.

  (i) First we choose $2n$ values $x_1, x_2, \ldots, x_{2n}$ and evaluate $A(x_j)$ and $B(x_j)$ for each of $j = 1, 2, \ldots, 2n$.

  (ii) We can now compute $C(x_j)$ for each $j$ very easily: $C(x_j)$ is simply the product of the two numbers $A(x_j)$ and $B(x_j)$.

  (iii) Finally, we have to recover $C$ from its values on $x_1, x_2, \ldots, x_{2n}$. Here we take advantage of a fundamental fact about polynomials: any polynomial of degree $d$ can be reconstructed from its values on any set of $d + 1$ or more points. This is known as *polynomial interpolation*, and we'll discuss the mechanics of performing interpolation in more detail later. For the moment, we simply observe that since $A$ and $B$ each have degree at most $n - 1$, their product $C$ has degree at most $2n - 2$, and so it can be reconstructed from the values $C(x_1), C(x_2), \ldots, C(x_{2n})$ that we computed in step (ii).

This approach to multiplying polynomials has some promising aspects and some problematic ones. First, the good news: step (ii) requires only

$O(n)$ arithmetic operations, since it simply involves the multiplication of $O(n)$ numbers. But the situation doesn't look as hopeful with steps (i) and (iii). In particular, evaluating the polynomials $A$ and $B$ on a single value takes $\Omega(n)$ operations, and our plan calls for performing $2n$ such evaluations. This seems to bring us back to quadratic time right away.

The key idea that will make this all work is to find a set of $2n$ values $x_1, x_2, \ldots, x_{2n}$ that are intimately related in some way, such that the work in evaluating $A$ and $B$ on all of them can be shared across different evaluations. A set for which this will turn out to work very well is the *complex roots of unity.*

**The Complex Roots of Unity**   At this point, we're going to need to recall a few facts about complex numbers and their role as solutions to polynomial equations.

Recall that complex numbers can be viewed as lying in the "complex plane," with axes representing their real and imaginary parts. We can write a complex number using polar coordinates with respect to this plane as $re^{\theta i}$, where $e^{\pi i} = -1$ (and $e^{2\pi i} = 1$). Now, for a positive integer $k$, the polynomial equation $x^k = 1$ has $k$ distinct complex roots, and it is easy to identify them. Each of the complex numbers $\omega_{j,k} = e^{2\pi ji/k}$ (for $j = 0, 1, 2, \ldots, k - 1$) satisfies the equation, since

$$(e^{2\pi ji/k})^k = e^{2\pi ji} = (e^{2\pi i})^j = 1^j = 1,$$

and each of these numbers is distinct, so these are all the roots. We refer to these numbers as the $k^{\text{th}}$ *roots of unity.* We can picture these roots as a set of $k$ equally spaced points lying on the unit circle in the complex plane, as shown in Figure 5.9 for the case $k = 8$.

For our numbers $x_1, \ldots, x_{2n}$ on which to evaluate $A$ and $B$, we will choose the $(2n)^{\text{th}}$ roots of unity. It's worth mentioning (although it's not necessary for understanding the algorithm) that the use of the complex roots of unity is the basis for the name *Fast Fourier Transform*: the representation of a degree-$d$

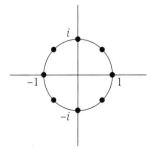

**Figure 5.9** The $8^{\text{th}}$ roots of unity in the complex plane.

polynomial $P$ by its values on the $(d + 1)^{st}$ roots of unity is sometimes referred to as the *discrete Fourier transform* of $P$; and the heart of our procedure is a method for making this computation fast.

*A Recursive Procedure for Polynomial Evaluation*    We want to design an algorithm for evaluating $A$ on each of the $(2n)^{th}$ roots of unity recursively, so as to take advantage of the familiar recurrence from (5.1)—namely, $T(n) \le 2T(n/2) + O(n)$ where $T(n)$ in this case denotes the number of operations required to evaluate a polynomial of degree $n - 1$ on all the $(2n)^{th}$ roots of unity. For simplicity in describing this algorithm, we will assume that $n$ is a power of 2.

How does one break the evaluation of a polynomial into two equal-sized subproblems? A useful trick is to define two polynomials, $A_{even}(x)$ and $A_{odd}(x)$, that consist of the even and odd coefficients of $A$, respectively. That is,

$$A_{even}(x) = a_0 + a_2 x + a_4 x^2 + \cdots + a_{n-2} x^{(n-2)/2},$$

and

$$A_{odd}(x) = a_1 + a_3 x + a_5 x^2 + \cdots + a_{(n-1)} x^{(n-2)/2}.$$

Simple algebra shows us that

$$A(x) = A_{even}(x^2) + x A_{odd}(x^2),$$

and so this gives us a way to compute $A(x)$ in a constant number of operations, given the evaluation of the two constituent polynomials that each have half the degree of $A$.

Now suppose that we evaluate each of $A_{even}$ and $A_{odd}$ on the $n^{th}$ roots of unity. This is exactly a version of the problem we face with $A$ and the $(2n)^{th}$ roots of unity, except that the input is half as large: the degree is $(n - 2)/2$ rather than $n - 1$, and we have $n$ roots of unity rather than $2n$. Thus we can perform these evaluations in time $T(n/2)$ for each of $A_{even}$ and $A_{odd}$, for a total time of $2T(n/2)$.

We're now very close to having a recursive algorithm that obeys (5.1) and gives us the running time we want; we just have to produce the evaluations of $A$ on the $(2n)^{th}$ roots of unity using $O(n)$ additional operations. But this is easy, given the results from the recursive calls on $A_{even}$ and $A_{odd}$. Consider one of these roots of unity $\omega_{j,2n} = e^{2\pi j i/2n}$. The quantity $\omega_{j,2n}^2$ is equal to $(e^{2\pi j i/2n})^2 = e^{2\pi j i/n}$, and hence $\omega_{j,2n}^2$ is an $n^{th}$ root of unity. So when we go to compute

$$A(\omega_{j,2n}) = A_{even}(\omega_{j,2n}^2) + \omega_{j,2n} A_{odd}(\omega_{j,2n}^2),$$

we discover that both of the evaluations on the right-hand side have been performed in the recursive step, and so we can determine $A(\omega_{j,2n})$ using a constant number of operations. Doing this for all $2n$ roots of unity is therefore $O(n)$ additional operations after the two recursive calls, and so the bound $T(n)$ on the number of operations indeed satisfies $T(n) \leq 2T(n/2) + O(n)$. We run the same procedure to evaluate the polynomial $B$ on the $(2n)^{\text{th}}$ roots of unity as well, and this gives us the desired $O(n \log n)$ bound for step (i) of our algorithm outline.

***Polynomial Interpolation*** We've now seen how to evaluate $A$ and $B$ on the set of all $(2n)^{\text{th}}$ roots of unity using $O(n \log n)$ operations and, as noted above, we can clearly compute the products $C(\omega_{j,n}) = A(\omega_{j,2n})B(\omega_{j,2n})$ in $O(n)$ more operations. Thus, to conclude the algorithm for multiplying $A$ and $B$, we need to execute step (iii) in our earlier outline using $O(n \log n)$ operations, reconstructing $C$ from its values on the $(2n)^{\text{th}}$ roots of unity.

In describing this part of the algorithm, it's worth keeping track of the following top-level point: it turns out that the reconstruction of $C$ can be achieved simply by defining an appropriate polynomial (the polynomial $D$ below) and evaluating it at the $(2n)^{\text{th}}$ roots of unity. This is exactly what we've just seen how to do using $O(n \log n)$ operations, so we do it again here, spending an additional $O(n \log n)$ operations and concluding the algorithms.

Consider a polynomial $C(x) = \sum_{s=0}^{2n-1} c_s x^s$ that we want to reconstruct from its values $C(\omega_{s,2n})$ at the $(2n)^{\text{th}}$ roots of unity. Define a new polynomial $D(x) = \sum_{s=0}^{2n-1} d_s x^s$, where $d_s = C(\omega_{s,2n})$. We now consider the values of $D(x)$ at the $(2n)^{\text{th}}$ roots of unity.

$$D(\omega_{j,2n}) = \sum_{s=0}^{2n-1} C(\omega_{s,2n})\omega_{j,2n}^{s}$$

$$= \sum_{s=0}^{2n-1} (\sum_{t=0}^{2n-1} c_t \omega_{s,2n}^{t})\omega_{j,2n}^{s}$$

$$= \sum_{t=0}^{2n-1} c_t (\sum_{s=0}^{2n-1} \omega_{s,2n}^{t}\omega_{j,2n}^{s}),$$

by definition. Now recall that $\omega_{s,2n} = (e^{2\pi i/2n})^s$. Using this fact and extending the notation to $\omega_{s,2n} = (e^{2\pi i/2n})^s$ even when $s \geq 2n$, we get that

$$D(\omega_{j,2n}) = \sum_{t=0}^{2n-1} c_t (\sum_{s=0}^{2n-1} e^{(2\pi i)(st+js)/2n})$$

$$= \sum_{t=0}^{2n-1} c_t (\sum_{s=0}^{2n-1} \omega_{t+j,2n}^{s}).$$

To analyze the last line, we use the fact that for any $(2n)^{\text{th}}$ root of unity $\omega \neq 1$, we have $\sum_{s=0}^{2n-1} \omega^s = 0$. This is simply because $\omega$ is by definition a root of $x^{2n} - 1 = 0$; since $x^{2n} - 1 = (x - 1)(\sum_{t=0}^{2n-1} x^t)$ and $\omega \neq 1$, it follows that $\omega$ is also a root of $(\sum_{t=0}^{2n-1} x^t)$.

Thus the only term of the last line's outer sum that is not equal to 0 is for $c_t$ such that $\omega_{t+j,2n} = 1$; and this happens if $t + j$ is a multiple of $2n$, that is, if $t = 2n - j$. For this value, $\sum_{s=0}^{2n-1} \omega_{t+j,2n}^s = \sum_{s=0}^{2n-1} 1 = 2n$. So we get that $D(\omega_{j,2n}) = 2nc_{2n-j}$. Evaluating the polynomial $D(x)$ at the $(2n)^{\text{th}}$ roots of unity thus gives us the coeffients of the polynomial $C(x)$ in reverse order (multiplied by $2n$ each). We sum this up as follows.

**(5.14)** *For any polynomial $C(x) = \sum_{s=0}^{2n-1} c_s x^s$, and corresponding polynomial $D(x) = \sum_{s=0}^{2n-1} C(\omega_{s,2n})x^s$, we have that $c_s = \frac{1}{2n}D(\omega_{2n-s,2n})$.*

We can do all the evaluations of the values $D(\omega_{2n-s,2n})$ in $O(n \log n)$ operations using the divide-and-conquer approach developed for step (i).

And this wraps everything up: we reconstruct the polynomial $C$ from its values on the $(2n)^{\text{th}}$ roots of unity, and then the coefficients of $C$ are the coordinates in the convolution vector $c = a * b$ that we were originally seeking.

In summary, we have shown the following.

**(5.15)** *Using the Fast Fourier Transform to determine the product polynomial $C(x)$, we can compute the convolution of the original vectors $a$ and $b$ in $O(n \log n)$ time.*

# Solved Exercises

## Solved Exercise 1

Suppose you are given an array $A$ with $n$ entries, with each entry holding a distinct number. You are told that the sequence of values $A[1], A[2], \ldots, A[n]$ is *unimodal*: For some index $p$ between 1 and $n$, the values in the array entries increase up to position $p$ in $A$ and then decrease the remainder of the way until position $n$. (So if you were to draw a plot with the array position $j$ on the $x$-axis and the value of the entry $A[j]$ on the $y$-axis, the plotted points would rise until $x$-value $p$, where they'd achieve their maximum, and then fall from there on.)

You'd like to find the "peak entry" $p$ without having to read the entire array—in fact, by reading as few entries of $A$ as possible. Show how to find the entry $p$ by reading at most $O(\log n)$ entries of $A$.

***Solution***    Let's start with a general discussion on how to achieve a running time of $O(\log n)$ and then come back to the specific problem here. If one needs to compute something using only $O(\log n)$ operations, a useful strategy that we discussed in Chapter 2 is to perform a constant amount of work, throw away half the input, and continue recursively on what's left. This was the idea, for example, behind the $O(\log n)$ running time for binary search.

We can view this as a divide-and-conquer approach: for some constant $c > 0$, we perform at most $c$ operations and then continue recursively on an input of size at most $n/2$. As in the chapter, we will assume that the recursion "bottoms out" when $n = 2$, performing at most $c$ operations to finish the computation. If $T(n)$ denotes the running time on an input of size $n$, then we have the recurrence

**(5.16)**

$$T(n) \leq T(n/2) + c$$

*when $n > 2$, and*

$$T(2) \leq c.$$

It is not hard to solve this recurrence by unrolling it, as follows.

- *Analyzing the first few levels:* At the first level of recursion, we have a single problem of size $n$, which takes time at most $c$ plus the time spent in all subsequent recursive calls. The next level has one problem of size at most $n/2$, which contributes another $c$, and the level after that has one problem of size at most $n/4$, which contributes yet another $c$.

- *Identifying a pattern:* No matter how many levels we continue, each level will have just one problem: level $j$ has a single problem of size at most $n/2^j$, which contributes $c$ to the running time, independent of $j$.

- *Summing over all levels of recursion:* Each level of the recursion is contributing at most $c$ operations, and it takes $\log_2 n$ levels of recursion to reduce $n$ to 2. Thus the total running time is at most $c$ times the number of levels of recursion, which is at most $c \log_2 n = O(\log n)$.

We can also do this by partial substitution. Suppose we guess that $T(n) \leq k \log_b n$, where we don't know $k$ or $b$. Assuming that this holds for smaller values of $n$ in an inductive argument, we would have

$$T(n) \leq T(n/2) + c$$
$$\leq k \log_b(n/2) + c$$
$$= k \log_b n - k \log_b 2 + c.$$

The first term on the right is exactly what we want, so we just need to choose $k$ and $b$ to negate the added $c$ at the end. This we can do by setting $b = 2$ and $k = c$, so that $k \log_b 2 = c \log_2 2 = c$. Hence we end up with the solution $T(n) \leq c \log_2 n$, which is exactly what we got by unrolling the recurrence.

Finally, we should mention that one can get an $O(\log n)$ running time, by essentially the same reasoning, in the more general case when each level of the recursion throws away any constant fraction of the input, transforming an instance of size $n$ to one of size at most $an$, for some constant $a < 1$. It now takes at most $\log_{1/a} n$ levels of recursion to reduce $n$ down to a constant size, and each level of recursion involves at most $c$ operations.

Now let's get back to the problem at hand. If we wanted to set ourselves up to use (5.16), we could probe the midpoint of the array and try to determine whether the "peak entry" $p$ lies before or after this midpoint.

So suppose we look at the value $A[n/2]$. From this value alone, we can't tell whether $p$ lies before or after $n/2$, since we need to know whether entry $n/2$ is sitting on an "up-slope" or on a "down-slope." So we also look at the values $A[n/2 - 1]$ and $A[n/2 + 1]$. There are now three possibilities.

- If $A[n/2 - 1] < A[n/2] < A[n/2 + 1]$, then entry $n/2$ must come strictly before $p$, and so we can continue recursively on entries $n/2 + 1$ through $n$.
- If $A[n/2 - 1] > A[n/2] > A[n/2 + 1]$, then entry $n/2$ must come strictly after $p$, and so we can continue recursively on entries 1 through $n/2 - 1$.
- Finally, if $A[n/2]$ is larger than both $A[n/2 - 1]$ and $A[n/2 + 1]$, we are done: the peak entry is in fact equal to $n/2$ in this case.

In all these cases, we perform at most three probes of the array $A$ and reduce the problem to one of at most half the size. Thus we can apply (5.16) to conclude that the running time is $O(\log n)$.

## Solved Exercise 2

You're consulting for a small computation-intensive investment company, and they have the following type of problem that they want to solve over and over. A typical instance of the problem is the following. They're doing a simulation in which they look at $n$ consecutive days of a given stock, at some point in the past. Let's number the days $i = 1, 2, \ldots, n$; for each day $i$, they have a price $p(i)$ per share for the stock on that day. (We'll assume for simplicity that the price was fixed during each day.) Suppose during this time period, they wanted to buy 1,000 shares on some day and sell all these shares on some (later) day. They want to know: When should they have bought and when should they have sold in order to have made as much money as possible? (If there was no way to make money during the $n$ days, you should report this instead.)

For example, suppose $n = 3$, $p(1) = 9$, $p(2) = 1$, $p(3) = 5$. Then you should return *"buy on 2, sell on 3"* (buying on day 2 and selling on day 3 means they would have made $4 per share, the maximum possible for that period).

Clearly, there's a simple algorithm that takes time $O(n^2)$: try all possible pairs of buy/sell days and see which makes them the most money. Your investment friends were hoping for something a little better.

Show how to find the correct numbers $i$ and $j$ in time $O(n \log n)$.

**Solution**    We've seen a number of instances in this chapter where a brute-force search over pairs of elements can be reduced to $O(n \log n)$ by divide and conquer. Since we're faced with a similar issue here, let's think about how we might apply a divide-and-conquer strategy.

A natural approach would be to consider the first $n/2$ days and the final $n/2$ days separately, solving the problem recursively on each of these two sets, and then figure out how to get an overall solution from this in $O(n)$ time. This would give us the usual recurrence $T(n) \leq 2T\left(\frac{n}{2}\right) + O(n)$, and hence $O(n \log n)$ by (5.1).

Also, to make things easier, we'll make the usual assumption that $n$ is a power of 2. This is no loss of generality: if $n'$ is the next power of 2 greater than $n$, we can set $p(i) = p(n)$ for all $i$ between $n$ and $n'$. In this way, we do not change the answer, and we at most double the size of the input (which will not affect the $O()$ notation).

Now, let $S$ be the set of days $1, \ldots, n/2$, and $S'$ be the set of days $n/2 + 1, \ldots, n$. Our divide-and-conquer algorithm will be based on the following observation: either there is an optimal solution in which the investors are holding the stock at the end of day $n/2$, or there isn't. Now, if there isn't, then the optimal solution is the better of the optimal solutions on the sets $S$ and $S'$. If there is an optimal solution in which they hold the stock at the end of day $n/2$, then the value of this solution is $p(j) - p(i)$ where $i \in S$ and $j \in S'$. But this value is maximized by simply choosing $i \in S$ which minimizes $p(i)$, and choosing $j \in S'$ which maximizes $p(j)$.

Thus our algorithm is to take the best of the following three possible solutions.

- The optimal solution on $S$.
- The optimal solution on $S'$.
- The maximum of $p(j) - p(i)$, over $i \in S$ and $j \in S'$.

The first two alternatives are computed in time $T(n/2)$, each by recursion, and the third alternative is computed by finding the minimum in $S$ and the maximum in $S'$, which takes time $O(n)$. Thus the running time $T(n)$ satisfies

$$T(n) \leq 2T\left(\frac{n}{2}\right) + O(n),$$

as desired.

We note that this is not the best running time achievable for this problem. In fact, one can find the optimal pair of days in $O(n)$ time using dynamic programming, the topic of the next chapter; at the end of that chapter, we will pose this question as Exercise 7.

# Exercises

1. You are interested in analyzing some hard-to-obtain data from two separate databases. Each database contains $n$ numerical values—so there are $2n$ values total—and you may assume that no two values are the same. You'd like to determine the median of this set of $2n$ values, which we will define here to be the $n^{\text{th}}$ smallest value.

   However, the only way you can access these values is through *queries* to the databases. In a single query, you can specify a value $k$ to one of the two databases, and the chosen database will return the $k^{\text{th}}$ smallest value that it contains. Since queries are expensive, you would like to compute the median using as few queries as possible.

   Give an algorithm that finds the median value using at most $O(\log n)$ queries.

2. Recall the problem of finding the number of inversions. As in the text, we are given a sequence of $n$ numbers $a_1, \ldots, a_n$, which we assume are all distinct, and we define an inversion to be a pair $i < j$ such that $a_i > a_j$.

   We motivated the problem of counting inversions as a good measure of how different two orderings are. However, one might feel that this measure is too sensitive. Let's call a pair a *significant inversion* if $i < j$ and $a_i > 2a_j$. Give an $O(n \log n)$ algorithm to count the number of significant inversions between two orderings.

3. Suppose you're consulting for a bank that's concerned about fraud detection, and they come to you with the following problem. They have a collection of $n$ bank cards that they've confiscated, suspecting them of being used in fraud. Each bank card is a small plastic object, containing a magnetic stripe with some encrypted data, and it corresponds to a unique account in the bank. Each account can have many bank cards

corresponding to it, and we'll say that two bank cards are *equivalent* if they correspond to the same account.

It's very difficult to read the account number off a bank card directly, but the bank has a high-tech "equivalence tester" that takes two bank cards and, after performing some computations, determines whether they are equivalent.

Their question is the following: among the collection of $n$ cards, is there a set of more than $n/2$ of them that are all equivalent to one another? Assume that the only feasible operations you can do with the cards are to pick two of them and plug them in to the equivalence tester. Show how to decide the answer to their question with only $O(n \log n)$ invocations of the equivalence tester.

4. You've been working with some physicists who need to study, as part of their experimental design, the interactions among large numbers of very small charged particles. Basically, their setup works as follows. They have an inert lattice structure, and they use this for placing charged particles at regular spacing along a straight line. Thus we can model their structure as consisting of the points $\{1, 2, 3, \ldots, n\}$ on the real line; and at each of these points $j$, they have a particle with charge $q_j$. (Each charge can be either positive or negative.)

They want to study the total force on each particle, by measuring it and then comparing it to a computational prediction. This computational part is where they need your help. The total net force on particle $j$, by Coulomb's Law, is equal to

$$F_j = \sum_{i<j} \frac{Cq_iq_j}{(j-i)^2} - \sum_{i>j} \frac{Cq_iq_j}{(j-i)^2}.$$

They've written the following simple program to compute $F_j$ for all $j$:

```
For j = 1, 2, . . . , n
   Initialize Fⱼ to 0
   For i = 1, 2, . . . , n
      If i < j then
         Add  C qᵢ qⱼ / (j − i)²  to Fⱼ
      Else if i > j then
         Add − C qᵢ qⱼ / (j − i)²  to Fⱼ
      Endif
   Endfor
   Output Fⱼ
Endfor
```

It's not hard to analyze the running time of this program: each invocation of the inner loop, over $i$, takes $O(n)$ time, and this inner loop is invoked $O(n)$ times total, so the overall running time is $O(n^2)$.

The trouble is, for the large values of $n$ they're working with, the program takes several minutes to run. On the other hand, their experimental setup is optimized so that they can throw down $n$ particles, perform the measurements, and be ready to handle $n$ more particles within a few seconds. So they'd really like it if there were a way to compute all the forces $F_j$ much more quickly, so as to keep up with the rate of the experiment.

Help them out by designing an algorithm that computes all the forces $F_j$ in $O(n \log n)$ time.

5. *Hidden surface removal* is a problem in computer graphics that scarcely needs an introduction: when Woody is standing in front of Buzz, you should be able to see Woody but not Buzz; when Buzz is standing in front of Woody, . . . well, you get the idea.

The magic of hidden surface removal is that you can often compute things faster than your intuition suggests. Here's a clean geometric example to illustrate a basic speed-up that can be achieved. You are given $n$ nonvertical lines in the plane, labeled $L_1, \ldots, L_n$, with the $i^{\text{th}}$ line specified by the equation $y = a_i x + b_i$. We will make the assumption that no three of the lines all meet at a single point. We say line $L_i$ is *uppermost* at a given $x$-coordinate $x_0$ if its $y$-coordinate at $x_0$ is greater than the $y$-coordinates of all the other lines at $x_0$: $a_i x_0 + b_i > a_j x_0 + b_j$ for all $j \neq i$. We say line $L_i$ is *visible* if there is some $x$-coordinate at which it is uppermost—intuitively, some portion of it can be seen if you look down from "$y = \infty$."

Give an algorithm that takes $n$ lines as input and in $O(n \log n)$ time returns all of the ones that are visible. Figure 5.10 gives an example.

6. Consider an $n$-node complete binary tree $T$, where $n = 2^d - 1$ for some $d$. Each node $v$ of $T$ is labeled with a real number $x_v$. You may assume that the real numbers labeling the nodes are all distinct. A node $v$ of $T$ is a *local minimum* if the label $x_v$ is less than the label $x_w$ for all nodes $w$ that are joined to $v$ by an edge.

You are given such a complete binary tree $T$, but the labeling is only specified in the following *implicit* way: for each node $v$, you can determine the value $x_v$ by *probing* the node $v$. Show how to find a local minimum of $T$ using only $O(\log n)$ *probes* to the nodes of $T$.

7. Suppose now that you're given an $n \times n$ grid graph $G$. (An $n \times n$ grid graph is just the adjacency graph of an $n \times n$ chessboard. To be completely precise, it is a graph whose node set is the set of all ordered pairs of

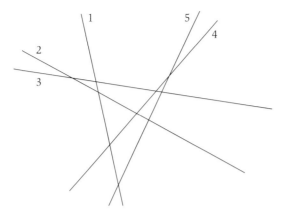

**Figure 5.10** An instance of hidden surface removal with five lines (labeled *1–5* in the figure). All the lines except for *2* are visible.

natural numbers $(i, j)$, where $1 \leq i \leq n$ and $1 \leq j \leq n$; the nodes $(i, j)$ and $(k, \ell)$ are joined by an edge if and only if $|i - k| + |j - \ell| = 1$.)

We use some of the terminology of the previous question. Again, each node $v$ is labeled by a real number $x_v$; you may assume that all these labels are distinct. Show how to find a local minimum of $G$ using only $O(n)$ probes to the nodes of $G$. (Note that $G$ has $n^2$ nodes.)

## Notes and Further Reading

The militaristic coinage "divide and conquer" was introduced somewhat after the technique itself. Knuth (1998) credits John von Neumann with one early explicit application of the approach, the development of the Mergesort Algorithm in 1945. Knuth (1997b) also provides further discussion of techniques for solving recurrences.

The algorithm for computing the closest pair of points in the plane is due to Michael Shamos, and is one of the earliest nontrivial algorithms in the field of computational geometry; the survey paper by Smid (1999) discusses a wide range of results on closest-point problems. A faster randomized algorithm for this problem will be discussed in Chapter 13. (Regarding the nonobviousness of the divide-and-conquer algorithm presented here, Smid also makes the interesting historical observation that researchers originally suspected quadratic time might be the best one could do for finding the closest pair of points in the plane.) More generally, the divide-and-conquer approach has proved very useful in computational geometry, and the books by Preparata and Shamos

(1985) and de Berg et al. (1997) give many further examples of this technique in the design of geometric algorithms.

The algorithm for multiplying two $n$-bit integers in subquadratic time is due to Karatsuba and Ofman (1962). Further background on asymptotically fast multiplication algorithms is given by Knuth (1997b). Of course, the number of bits in the input must be sufficiently large for any of these subquadratic methods to improve over the standard algorithm.

Press et al. (1988) provide further coverage of the Fast Fourier Transform, including background on its applications in signal processing and related areas.

***Notes on the Exercises***   Exercise 7 is based on a result of Donna Llewellyn, Craig Tovey, and Michael Trick.

# Chapter 6

## Dynamic Programming

We began our study of algorithmic techniques with greedy algorithms, which in some sense form the most natural approach to algorithm design. Faced with a new computational problem, we've seen that it's not hard to propose multiple possible greedy algorithms; the challenge is then to determine whether any of these algorithms provides a correct solution to the problem in all cases.

The problems we saw in Chapter 4 were all unified by the fact that, in the end, there really was a greedy algorithm that worked. Unfortunately, this is far from being true in general; for most of the problems that one encounters, the real difficulty is not in determining which of several greedy strategies is the right one, but in the fact that there is *no* natural greedy algorithm that works. For such problems, it is important to have other approaches at hand. Divide and conquer can sometimes serve as an alternative approach, but the versions of divide and conquer that we saw in the previous chapter are often not strong enough to reduce exponential brute-force search down to polynomial time. Rather, as we noted in Chapter 5, the applications there tended to reduce a running time that was unnecessarily large, but already polynomial, down to a faster running time.

We now turn to a more powerful and subtle design technique, *dynamic programming*. It will be easier to say exactly what characterizes dynamic programming after we've seen it in action, but the basic idea is drawn from the intuition behind divide and conquer and is essentially the opposite of the greedy strategy: one implicitly explores the space of all possible solutions, by carefully decomposing things into a series of *subproblems*, and then building up correct solutions to larger and larger subproblems. In a way, we can thus view dynamic programming as operating dangerously close to the edge of brute-force search: although it's systematically working through the exponentially large set of possible solutions to the problem, it does this without ever examining them all explicitly. It is because of this careful balancing act that dynamic programming can be a tricky technique to get used to; it typically takes a reasonable amount of practice before one is fully comfortable with it.

With this in mind, we now turn to a first example of dynamic programming: the Weighted Interval Scheduling Problem that we defined back in Section 1.2. We are going to develop a dynamic programming algorithm for this problem in two stages: first as a recursive procedure that closely resembles brute-force search; and then, by reinterpreting this procedure, as an iterative algorithm that works by building up solutions to larger and larger subproblems.

# 6.1 Weighted Interval Scheduling: A Recursive Procedure

We have seen that a particular greedy algorithm produces an optimal solution to the Interval Scheduling Problem, where the goal is to accept as large a set of nonoverlapping intervals as possible. The Weighted Interval Scheduling Problem is a strictly more general version, in which each interval has a certain *value* (or *weight*), and we want to accept a set of maximum value.

### ✎ Designing a Recursive Algorithm

Since the original Interval Scheduling Problem is simply the special case in which all values are equal to 1, we know already that most greedy algorithms will not solve this problem optimally. But even the algorithm that worked before (repeatedly choosing the interval that ends earliest) is no longer optimal in this more general setting, as the simple example in Figure 6.1 shows.

Indeed, no natural greedy algorithm is known for this problem, which is what motivates our switch to dynamic programming. As discussed above, we will begin our introduction to dynamic programming with a recursive type of algorithm for this problem, and then in the next section we'll move to a more iterative method that is closer to the style we use in the rest of this chapter.

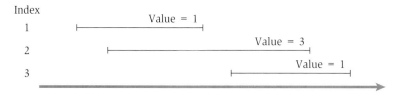

**Figure 6.1** A simple instance of weighted interval scheduling.

We use the notation from our discussion of Interval Scheduling in Section 1.2. We have $n$ requests labeled $1, \ldots, n$, with each request $i$ specifying a start time $s_i$ and a finish time $f_i$. Each interval $i$ now also has a *value*, or *weight* $v_i$. Two intervals are *compatible* if they do not overlap. The goal of our current problem is to select a subset $S \subseteq \{1, \ldots, n\}$ of mutually compatible intervals, so as to maximize the sum of the values of the selected intervals, $\sum_{i \in S} v_i$.

Let's suppose that the requests are sorted in order of nondecreasing finish time: $f_1 \leq f_2 \leq \cdots \leq f_n$. We'll say a request $i$ comes *before* a request $j$ if $i < j$. This will be the natural left-to-right order in which we'll consider intervals. To help in talking about this order, we define $p(j)$, for an interval $j$, to be the largest index $i < j$ such that intervals $i$ and $j$ are disjoint. In other words, $i$ is the leftmost interval that ends before $j$ begins. We define $p(j) = 0$ if no request $i < j$ is disjoint from $j$. An example of the definition of $p(j)$ is shown in Figure 6.2.

Now, given an instance of the Weighted Interval Scheduling Problem, let's consider an optimal solution $\mathcal{O}$, ignoring for now that we have no idea what it is. Here's something completely obvious that we can say about $\mathcal{O}$: either interval $n$ (the last one) belongs to $\mathcal{O}$, or it doesn't. Suppose we explore both sides of this dichotomy a little further. If $n \in \mathcal{O}$, then clearly no interval indexed strictly between $p(n)$ and $n$ can belong to $\mathcal{O}$, because by the definition of $p(n)$, we know that intervals $p(n) + 1, p(n) + 2, \ldots, n - 1$ all overlap interval $n$. Moreover, if $n \in \mathcal{O}$, then $\mathcal{O}$ must include an *optimal* solution to the problem consisting of requests $\{1, \ldots, p(n)\}$—for if it didn't, we could replace $\mathcal{O}$'s choice of requests from $\{1, \ldots, p(n)\}$ with a better one, with no danger of overlapping request $n$.

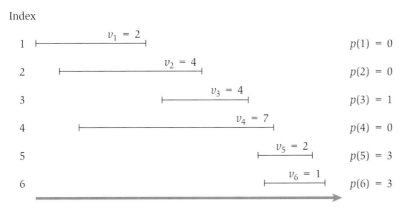

**Figure 6.2** An instance of weighted interval scheduling with the functions $p(j)$ defined for each interval $j$.

On the other hand, if $n \notin \mathcal{O}$, then $\mathcal{O}$ is simply equal to the optimal solution to the problem consisting of requests $\{1, \ldots, n-1\}$. This is by completely analogous reasoning: we're assuming that $\mathcal{O}$ does not include request $n$; so if it does not choose the optimal set of requests from $\{1, \ldots, n-1\}$, we could replace it with a better one.

All this suggests that finding the optimal solution on intervals $\{1, 2, \ldots, n\}$ involves looking at the optimal solutions of smaller problems of the form $\{1, 2, \ldots, j\}$. Thus, for any value of $j$ between 1 and $n$, let $\mathcal{O}_j$ denote the optimal solution to the problem consisting of requests $\{1, \ldots, j\}$, and let $\text{OPT}(j)$ denote the value of this solution. (We define $\text{OPT}(0) = 0$, based on the convention that this is the optimum over an empty set of intervals.) The optimal solution we're seeking is precisely $\mathcal{O}_n$, with value $\text{OPT}(n)$. For the optimal solution $\mathcal{O}_j$ on $\{1, 2, \ldots, j\}$, our reasoning above (generalizing from the case in which $j = n$) says that either $j \in \mathcal{O}_j$, in which case $\text{OPT}(j) = v_j + \text{OPT}(p(j))$, or $j \notin \mathcal{O}_j$, in which case $\text{OPT}(j) = \text{OPT}(j-1)$. Since these are precisely the two possible choices ($j \in \mathcal{O}_j$ or $j \notin \mathcal{O}_j$), we can further say that

**(6.1)**　　$\text{OPT}(j) = \max(v_j + \text{OPT}(p(j)), \text{OPT}(j-1)).$

And how do we decide whether $n$ belongs to the optimal solution $\mathcal{O}_j$? This too is easy: it belongs to the optimal solution if and only if the first of the options above is at least as good as the second; in other words,

**(6.2)**　*Request $j$ belongs to an optimal solution on the set $\{1, 2, \ldots, j\}$ if and only if*

$$v_j + \text{OPT}(p(j)) \geq \text{OPT}(j-1).$$

These facts form the first crucial component on which a dynamic programming solution is based: a recurrence equation that expresses the optimal solution (or its value) in terms of the optimal solutions to smaller subproblems.

Despite the simple reasoning that led to this point, (6.1) is already a significant development. It directly gives us a recursive algorithm to compute $\text{OPT}(n)$, assuming that we have already sorted the requests by finishing time and computed the values of $p(j)$ for each $j$.

```
Compute-Opt(j)
   If j=0 then
      Return 0
   Else
      Return max(v_j+Compute-Opt(p(j)), Compute-Opt(j-1))
   Endif
```

The correctness of the algorithm follows directly by induction on $j$:

**(6.3)** Compute-Opt$(j)$ *correctly computes* OPT$(j)$ *for each* $j = 1, 2, \ldots, n$.

**Proof.** By definition OPT$(0) = 0$. Now, take some $j > 0$, and suppose by way of induction that Compute-Opt$(i)$ correctly computes OPT$(i)$ for all $i < j$. By the induction hypothesis, we know that Compute-Opt$(p(j)) = $ OPT$(p(j))$ and Compute-Opt$(j-1) = $ OPT$(j-1)$; and hence from (6.1) it follows that

$$\text{OPT}(j) = \max(v_j + \texttt{Compute-Opt}(p(j)), \texttt{Compute-Opt}(j-1))$$

$$= \texttt{Compute-Opt}(j). \quad \blacksquare$$

Unfortunately, if we really implemented the algorithm Compute-Opt as just written, it would take exponential time to run in the worst case. For example, see Figure 6.3 for the tree of calls issued for the instance of Figure 6.2: the tree widens very quickly due to the recursive branching. To take a more extreme example, on a nicely layered instance like the one in Figure 6.4, where $p(j) = j - 2$ for each $j = 2, 3, 4, \ldots, n$, we see that Compute-Opt$(j)$ generates separate recursive calls on problems of sizes $j - 1$ and $j - 2$. In other words, the total number of calls made to Compute-Opt on this instance will grow

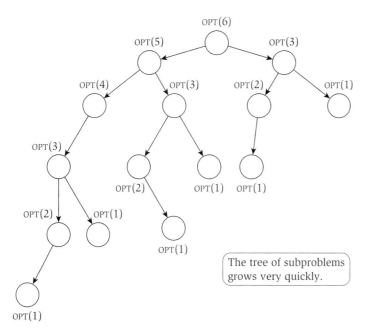

The tree of subproblems grows very quickly.

**Figure 6.3** The tree of subproblems called by Compute-Opt on the problem instance of Figure 6.2.

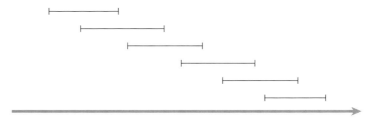

**Figure 6.4** An instance of weighted interval scheduling on which the simple Compute-Opt recursion will take exponential time. The values of all intervals in this instance are 1.

like the Fibonacci numbers, which increase exponentially. Thus we have not achieved a polynomial-time solution.

## Memoizing the Recursion

In fact, though, we're not so far from having a polynomial-time algorithm. A fundamental observation, which forms the second crucial component of a dynamic programming solution, is that our recursive algorithm Compute-Opt is really only solving $n + 1$ different subproblems: Compute-Opt$(0)$, Compute-Opt$(1), \ldots,$ Compute-Opt$(n)$. The fact that it runs in exponential time as written is simply due to the spectacular redundancy in the number of times it issues each of these calls.

How could we eliminate all this redundancy? We could store the value of Compute-Opt in a globally accessible place the first time we compute it and then simply use this precomputed value in place of all future recursive calls. This technique of saving values that have already been computed is referred to as *memoization*.

We implement the above strategy in the more "intelligent" procedure M-Compute-Opt. This procedure will make use of an array $M[0 \ldots n]$; $M[j]$ will start with the value "empty," but will hold the value of Compute-Opt$(j)$ as soon as it is first determined. To determine OPT$(n)$, we invoke M-Compute-Opt$(n)$.

```
M-Compute-Opt(j)
    If j = 0 then
        Return 0
    Else if M[j] is not empty then
        Return M[j]
    Else
```

```
  Define M[j]  =  max(vⱼ+M-Compute-Opt(p(j)), M-Compute-Opt(j − 1))
    Return M[j]
  Endif
```

## Analyzing the Memoized Version

Clearly, this looks very similar to our previous implementation of the algorithm; however, memoization has brought the running time way down.

> **(6.4)** *The running time of* M-Compute-Opt($n$) *is* $O(n)$ *(assuming the input intervals are sorted by their finish times).*

**Proof.** The time spent in a single call to M-Compute-Opt is $O(1)$, excluding the time spent in recursive calls it generates. So the running time is bounded by a constant times the number of calls ever issued to M-Compute-Opt. Since the implementation itself gives no explicit upper bound on this number of calls, we try to find a bound by looking for a good measure of "progress."

The most useful progress measure here is the number of entries in $M$ that are not "empty." Initially this number is 0; but each time the procedure invokes the recurrence, issuing two recursive calls to M-Compute-Opt, it fills in a new entry, and hence increases the number of filled-in entries by 1. Since $M$ has only $n + 1$ entries, it follows that there can be at most $O(n)$ calls to M-Compute-Opt, and hence the running time of M-Compute-Opt($n$) is $O(n)$, as desired. ■

## Computing a Solution in Addition to Its Value

So far we have simply computed the *value* of an optimal solution; presumably we want a full optimal set of intervals as well. It would be easy to extend M-Compute-Opt so as to keep track of an optimal solution in addition to its value: we could maintain an additional array $S$ so that $S[i]$ contains an optimal set of intervals among $\{1, 2, \ldots, i\}$. Naively enhancing the code to maintain the solutions in the array $S$, however, would blow up the running time by an additional factor of $O(n)$: while a position in the $M$ array can be updated in $O(1)$ time, writing down a set in the $S$ array takes $O(n)$ time. We can avoid this $O(n)$ blow-up by not explicitly maintaining $S$, but rather by recovering the optimal solution from values saved in the array $M$ after the optimum value has been computed.

We know from (6.2) that $j$ belongs to an optimal solution for the set of intervals $\{1, \ldots, j\}$ if and only if $v_j + \text{OPT}(p(j)) \geq \text{OPT}(j − 1)$. Using this observation, we get the following simple procedure, which "traces back" through the array $M$ to find the set of intervals in an optimal solution.

```
Find-Solution(j)
  If j = 0 then
    Output nothing
  Else
    If v_j + M[p(j)] ≥ M[j − 1] then
      Output j together with the result of Find-Solution(p(j))
    Else
      Output the result of Find-Solution(j − 1)
    Endif
  Endif
```

Since Find-Solution calls itself recursively only on strictly smaller values, it makes a total of $O(n)$ recursive calls; and since it spends constant time per call, we have

**(6.5)** *Given the array M of the optimal values of the sub-problems,* Find-Solution *returns an optimal solution in $O(n)$ time.*

## 6.2 Principles of Dynamic Programming: Memoization or Iteration over Subproblems

We now use the algorithm for the Weighted Interval Scheduling Problem developed in the previous section to summarize the basic principles of dynamic programming, and also to offer a different perspective that will be fundamental to the rest of the chapter: iterating over subproblems, rather than computing solutions recursively.

In the previous section, we developed a polynomial-time solution to the Weighted Interval Scheduling Problem by first designing an exponential-time recursive algorithm and then converting it (by memoization) to an efficient recursive algorithm that consulted a global array $M$ of optimal solutions to subproblems. To really understand what is going on here, however, it helps to formulate an essentially equivalent version of the algorithm. It is this new formulation that most explicitly captures the essence of the dynamic programming technique, and it will serve as a general template for the algorithms we develop in later sections.

### Designing the Algorithm

The key to the efficient algorithm is really the array $M$. It encodes the notion that we are using the value of optimal solutions to the subproblems on intervals $\{1, 2, \ldots, j\}$ for each $j$, and it uses (6.1) to define the value of $M[j]$ based on values that come earlier in the array. Once we have the array $M$, the problem is solved: $M[n]$ contains the value of the optimal solution on the full instance, and Find-Solution can be used to trace back through $M$ efficiently and return an optimal solution itself.

The point to realize, then, is that we can directly compute the entries in $M$ by an iterative algorithm, rather than using memoized recursion. We just start with $M[0] = 0$ and keep incrementing $j$; each time we need to determine a value $M[j]$, the answer is provided by (6.1). The algorithm looks as follows.

```
Iterative-Compute-Opt
   M[0] = 0
   For  j = 1, 2, . . . , n
      M[j] = max(v_j + M[p(j)], M[j − 1])
   Endfor
```

### Analyzing the Algorithm

By exact analogy with the proof of (6.3), we can prove by induction on $j$ that this algorithm writes OPT($j$) in array entry $M[j]$; (6.1) provides the induction step. Also, as before, we can pass the filled-in array $M$ to Find-Solution to get an optimal solution in addition to the value. Finally, the running time of Iterative-Compute-Opt is clearly $O(n)$, since it explicitly runs for $n$ iterations and spends constant time in each.

An example of the execution of Iterative-Compute-Opt is depicted in Figure 6.5. In each iteration, the algorithm fills in one additional entry of the array $M$, by comparing the value of $v_j + M[p(j)]$ to the value of $M[j − 1]$.

## A Basic Outline of Dynamic Programming

This, then, provides a second efficient algorithm to solve the Weighted Interval Scheduling Problem. The two approaches clearly have a great deal of conceptual overlap, since they both grow from the insight contained in the recurrence (6.1). For the remainder of the chapter, we will develop dynamic programming algorithms using the second type of approach—iterative building up of subproblems—because the algorithms are often simpler to express this way. But in each case that we consider, there is an equivalent way to formulate the algorithm as a memoized recursion.

Most crucially, the bulk of our discussion about the particular problem of selecting intervals can be cast more generally as a rough template for designing dynamic programming algorithms. To set about developing an algorithm based on dynamic programming, one needs a collection of subproblems derived from the original problem that satisfies a few basic properties.

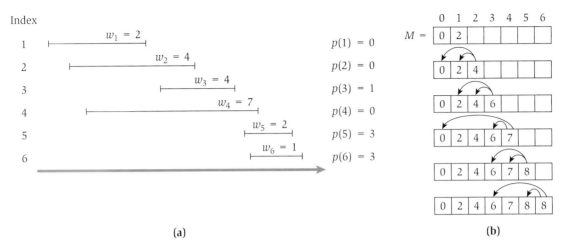

**Figure 6.5** Part (b) shows the iterations of `Iterative-Compute-Opt` on the sample instance of Weighted Interval Scheduling depicted in part (a).

(i) There are only a polynomial number of subproblems.

(ii) The solution to the original problem can be easily computed from the solutions to the subproblems. (For example, the original problem may actually *be* one of the subproblems.)

(iii) There is a natural ordering on subproblems from "smallest" to "largest," together with an easy-to-compute recurrence (as in (6.1) and (6.2)) that allows one to determine the solution to a subproblem from the solutions to some number of smaller subproblems.

Naturally, these are informal guidelines. In particular, the notion of "smaller" in part (iii) will depend on the type of recurrence one has.

We will see that it is sometimes easier to start the process of designing such an algorithm by formulating a set of subproblems that looks natural, and then figuring out a recurrence that links them together; but often (as happened in the case of weighted interval scheduling), it can be useful to first define a recurrence by reasoning about the structure of an optimal solution, and then determine which subproblems will be necessary to unwind the recurrence. This chicken-and-egg relationship between subproblems and recurrences is a subtle issue underlying dynamic programming. It's never clear that a collection of subproblems will be useful until one finds a recurrence linking them together; but it can be difficult to think about recurrences in the absence of the "smaller" subproblems that they build on. In subsequent sections, we will develop further practice in managing this design trade-off.

## 6.3 Segmented Least Squares: Multi-way Choices

We now discuss a different type of problem, which illustrates a slightly more complicated style of dynamic programming. In the previous section, we developed a recurrence based on a fundamentally *binary* choice: either the interval $n$ belonged to an optimal solution or it didn't. In the problem we consider here, the recurrence will involve what might be called "multi-way choices": at each step, we have a polynomial number of possibilities to consider for the structure of the optimal solution. As we'll see, the dynamic programming approach adapts to this more general situation very naturally.

As a separate issue, the problem developed in this section is also a nice illustration of how a clean algorithmic definition can formalize a notion that initially seems too fuzzy and nonintuitive to work with mathematically.

### The Problem

Often when looking at scientific or statistical data, plotted on a two-dimensional set of axes, one tries to pass a "line of best fit" through the data, as in Figure 6.6.

This is a foundational problem in statistics and numerical analysis, formulated as follows. Suppose our data consists of a set $P$ of $n$ points in the plane, denoted $(x_1, y_1), (x_2, y_2), \ldots, (x_n, y_n)$; and suppose $x_1 < x_2 < \cdots < x_n$. Given a line $L$ defined by the equation $y = ax + b$, we say that the *error* of $L$ with respect to $P$ is the sum of its squared "distances" to the points in $P$:

$$\text{Error}(L, P) = \sum_{i=1}^{n} (y_i - ax_i - b)^2.$$

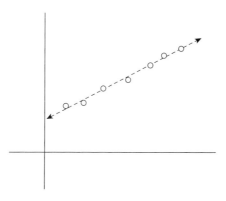

**Figure 6.6** A "line of best fit."

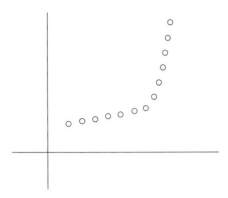

**Figure 6.7** A set of points that lie approximately on two lines.

A natural goal is then to find the line with minimum error; this turns out to have a nice closed-form solution that can be easily derived using calculus. Skipping the derivation here, we simply state the result: The line of minimum error is $y = ax + b$, where

$$a = \frac{n \sum_i x_i y_i - \left(\sum_i x_i\right)\left(\sum_i y_i\right)}{n \sum_i x_i^2 - \left(\sum_i x_i\right)^2} \quad \text{and} \quad b = \frac{\sum_i y_i - a \sum_i x_i}{n}.$$

Now, here's a kind of issue that these formulas weren't designed to cover. Often we have data that looks something like the picture in Figure 6.7. In this case, we'd like to make a statement like: "The points lie roughly on a sequence of two lines." How could we formalize this concept?

Essentially, any single line through the points in the figure would have a terrible error; but if we use two lines, we could achieve quite a small error. So we could try formulating a new problem as follows: Rather than seek a single line of best fit, we are allowed to pass an arbitrary *set* of lines through the points, and we seek a set of lines that minimizes the error. But this fails as a good problem formulation, because it has a trivial solution: if we're allowed to fit the points with an arbitrarily large set of lines, we could fit the points perfectly by having a different line pass through each pair of consecutive points in $P$.

At the other extreme, we could try "hard-coding" the number two into the problem; we could seek the best fit using at most two lines. But this too misses a crucial feature of our intuition: We didn't start out with a preconceived idea that the points lay approximately on two lines; we concluded that from looking at the picture. For example, most people would say that the points in Figure 6.8 lie approximately on three lines.

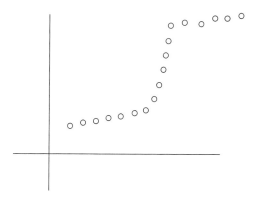

**Figure 6.8** A set of points that lie approximately on three lines.

Thus, intuitively, we need a problem formulation that requires us to fit the points well, using as few lines as possible. We now formulate a problem— the *Segmented Least Squares Problem*—that captures these issues quite cleanly. The problem is a fundamental instance of an issue in data mining and statistics known as *change detection*: Given a sequence of data points, we want to identify a few points in the sequence at which a discrete *change* occurs (in this case, a change from one linear approximation to another).

***Formulating the Problem*** As in the discussion above, we are given a set of points $P = \{(x_1, y_1), (x_2, y_2), \dots, (x_n, y_n)\}$, with $x_1 < x_2 < \dots < x_n$. We will use $p_i$ to denote the point $(x_i, y_i)$. We must first partition $P$ into some number of segments. Each *segment* is a subset of $P$ that represents a contiguous set of $x$-coordinates; that is, it is a subset of the form $\{p_i, p_{i+1}, \dots, p_{j-1}, p_j\}$ for some indices $i \leq j$. Then, for each segment $S$ in our partition of $P$, we compute the line minimizing the error with respect to the points in $S$, according to the formulas above.

The *penalty* of a partition is defined to be a sum of the following terms.

(i) The number of segments into which we partition $P$, times a fixed, given multiplier $C > 0$.

(ii) For each segment, the error value of the optimal line through that segment.

Our goal in the Segmented Least Squares Problem is to find a partition of minimum penalty. This minimization captures the trade-offs we discussed earlier. We are allowed to consider partitions into any number of segments; as we increase the number of segments, we reduce the penalty terms in part (ii) of the definition, but we increase the term in part (i). (The multiplier $C$ is provided with the input, and by tuning $C$, we can penalize the use of additional lines to a greater or lesser extent.)

There are exponentially many possible partitions of $P$, and initially it is not clear that we should be able to find the optimal one efficiently. We now show how to use dynamic programming to find a partition of minimum penalty in time polynomial in $n$.

### Designing the Algorithm

To begin with, we should recall the ingredients we need for a dynamic programming algorithm, as outlined at the end of Section 6.2. We want a polynomial number of subproblems, the solutions of which should yield a solution to the original problem; and we should be able to build up solutions to these subproblems using a recurrence. As with the Weighted Interval Scheduling Problem, it helps to think about some simple properties of the optimal solution. Note, however, that there is not really a direct analogy to weighted interval scheduling: there we were looking for a *subset* of $n$ objects, whereas here we are seeking to *partition* $n$ objects.

For segmented least squares, the following observation is very useful: The last point $p_n$ belongs to a single segment in the optimal partition, and that segment begins at some earlier point $p_i$. This is the type of observation that can suggest the right set of subproblems: if we knew the identity of the *last* segment $p_i, \ldots, p_n$ (see Figure 6.9), then we could remove those points from consideration and recursively solve the problem on the remaining points $p_1, \ldots, p_{i-1}$.

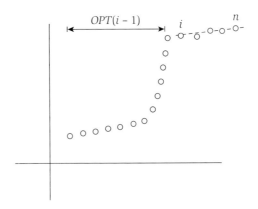

**Figure 6.9** A possible solution: a single line segment fits points $p_i, p_{i+1}, \ldots, p_n$, and then an optimal solution is found for the remaining points $p_1, p_2, \ldots, p_{i-1}$.

Suppose we let OPT($i$) denote the optimum solution for the points $p_1, \ldots, p_i$, and we let $e_{i,j}$ denote the minimum error of any line with respect to $p_i, p_{i+1}, \ldots, p_j$. (We will write OPT($0$) $= 0$ as a boundary case.) Then our observation above says the following.

**(6.6)** *If the last segment of the optimal partition is $p_i, \ldots, p_n$, then the value of the optimal solution is* OPT($n$) $= e_{i,n} + C +$ OPT($i - 1$).

Using the same observation for the subproblem consisting of the points $p_1, \ldots, p_j$, we see that to get OPT($j$) we should find the best way to produce a final segment $p_i, \ldots, p_j$—paying the error plus an additive $C$ for this segment— together with an optimal solution OPT($i - 1$) for the remaining points. In other words, we have justified the following recurrence.

**(6.7)** *For the subproblem on the points $p_1, \ldots, p_j$,*

$$\text{OPT}(j) = \min_{1 \le i \le j} (e_{i,j} + C + \text{OPT}(i - 1)),$$

*and the segment $p_i, \ldots, p_j$ is used in an optimum solution for the subproblem if and only if the minimum is obtained using index $i$.*

The hard part in designing the algorithm is now behind us. From here, we simply build up the solutions OPT($i$) in order of increasing $i$.

```
Segmented-Least-Squares(n)
  Array M[0 . . . n]
  Set M[0] = 0
  For all pairs i ≤ j
    Compute the least squares error e_{i,j} for the segment p_i, . . . , p_j
  Endfor
  For j = 1, 2, . . . , n
    Use the recurrence (6.7) to compute M[j]
  Endfor
  Return M[n]
```

By analogy with the arguments for weighted interval scheduling, the correctness of this algorithm can be proved directly by induction, with (6.7) providing the induction step.

And as in our algorithm for weighted interval scheduling, we can trace back through the array $M$ to compute an optimum partition.

```
Find-Segments(j)
   If j = 0 then
      Output nothing
   Else
      Find an i that minimizes e_{i,j} + C + M[i − 1]
      Output the segment {p_i, . . . , p_j} and the result of
             Find-Segments(i − 1)
   Endif
```

## Analyzing the Algorithm

Finally, we consider the running time of Segmented-Least-Squares. First we need to compute the values of all the least-squares errors $e_{i,j}$. To perform a simple accounting of the running time for this, we note that there are $O(n^2)$ pairs $(i, j)$ for which this computation is needed; and for each pair $(i, j)$, we can use the formula given at the beginning of this section to compute $e_{i,j}$ in $O(n)$ time. Thus the total running time to compute all $e_{i,j}$ values is $O(n^3)$.

Following this, the algorithm has $n$ iterations, for values $j = 1, \ldots, n$. For each value of $j$, we have to determine the minimum in the recurrence (6.7) to fill in the array entry $M[j]$; this takes time $O(n)$ for each $j$, for a total of $O(n^2)$. Thus the running time is $O(n^2)$ once all the $e_{i,j}$ values have been determined.[1]

## 6.4 Subset Sums and Knapsacks: Adding a Variable

We're seeing more and more that issues in scheduling provide a rich source of practically motivated algorithmic problems. So far we've considered problems in which requests are specified by a given interval of time on a resource, as well as problems in which requests have a duration and a deadline but do not mandate a particular interval during which they need to be done.

In this section, we consider a version of the second type of problem, with durations and deadlines, which is difficult to solve directly using the techniques we've seen so far. We will use dynamic programming to solve the problem, but with a twist: the "obvious" set of subproblems will turn out not to be enough, and so we end up creating a richer collection of subproblems. As

---

[1] In this analysis, the running time is dominated by the $O(n^3)$ needed to compute all $e_{i,j}$ values. But, in fact, it is possible to compute all these values in $O(n^2)$ time, which brings the running time of the full algorithm down to $O(n^2)$. The idea, whose details we will leave as an exercise for the reader, is to first compute $e_{i,j}$ for all pairs $(i, j)$ where $j − i = 1$, then for all pairs where $j − i = 2$, then $j − i = 3$, and so forth. This way, when we get to a particular $e_{i,j}$ value, we can use the ingredients of the calculation for $e_{i,j-1}$ to determine $e_{i,j}$ in constant time.

we will see, this is done by adding a new variable to the recurrence underlying the dynamic program.

## The Problem

In the scheduling problem we consider here, we have a single machine that can process jobs, and we have a set of requests $\{1, 2, \ldots, n\}$. We are only able to use this resource for the period between time 0 and time $W$, for some number $W$. Each request corresponds to a job that requires time $w_i$ to process. If our goal is to process jobs so as to keep the machine as busy as possible up to the "cut-off" $W$, which jobs should we choose?

More formally, we are given $n$ items $\{1, \ldots, n\}$, and each has a given nonnegative weight $w_i$ (for $i = 1, \ldots, n$). We are also given a bound $W$. We would like to select a subset $S$ of the items so that $\sum_{i \in S} w_i \leq W$ and, subject to this restriction, $\sum_{i \in S} w_i$ is as large as possible. We will call this the *Subset Sum Problem*.

This problem is a natural special case of a more general problem called the *Knapsack Problem*, where each request $i$ has both a *value* $v_i$ and a *weight* $w_i$. The goal in this more general problem is to select a subset of maximum total value, subject to the restriction that its total weight not exceed $W$. Knapsack problems often show up as subproblems in other, more complex problems. The name *knapsack* refers to the problem of filling a knapsack of capacity $W$ as full as possible (or packing in as much value as possible), using a subset of the items $\{1, \ldots, n\}$. We will use *weight* or *time* when referring to the quantities $w_i$ and $W$.

Since this resembles other scheduling problems we've seen before, it's natural to ask whether a greedy algorithm can find the optimal solution. It appears that the answer is no—at least, no efficient greedy rule is known that always constructs an optimal solution. One natural greedy approach to try would be to sort the items by decreasing weight—or at least to do this for all items of weight at most $W$—and then start selecting items in this order as long as the total weight remains below $W$. But if $W$ is a multiple of 2, and we have three items with weights $\{W/2 + 1, W/2, W/2\}$, then we see that this greedy algorithm will not produce the optimal solution. Alternately, we could sort by *increasing* weight and then do the same thing; but this fails on inputs like $\{1, W/2, W/2\}$.

The goal of this section is to show how to use dynamic programming to solve this problem. Recall the main principles of dynamic programming: We have to come up with a small number of subproblems so that each subproblem can be solved easily from "smaller" subproblems, and the solution to the original problem can be obtained easily once we know the solutions to all the subproblems. The tricky issue here lies in figuring out a good set of subproblems.

## Designing the Algorithm

*A False Start*   One general strategy, which worked for us in the case of Weighted Interval Scheduling, is to consider subproblems involving only the first $i$ requests. We start by trying this strategy here. We use the notation OPT($i$), analogously to the notation used before, to denote the best possible solution using a subset of the requests $\{1, \ldots, i\}$. The key to our method for the Weighted Interval Scheduling Problem was to concentrate on an optimal solution $\mathcal{O}$ to our problem and consider two cases, depending on whether or not the last request $n$ is accepted or rejected by this optimum solution. Just as in that case, we have the first part, which follows immediately from the definition of OPT($i$).

- If $n \notin \mathcal{O}$, then OPT($n$) = OPT($n - 1$).

Next we have to consider the case in which $n \in \mathcal{O}$. What we'd like here is a simple recursion, which tells us the best possible value we can get for solutions that contain the last request $n$. For Weighted Interval Scheduling this was easy, as we could simply delete each request that conflicted with request $n$. In the current problem, this is not so simple. Accepting request $n$ does not immediately imply that we have to reject any other request. Instead, it means that for the subset of requests $S \subseteq \{1, \ldots, n - 1\}$ that we will accept, we have less available weight left: a weight of $w_n$ is used on the accepted request $n$, and we only have $W - w_n$ weight left for the set $S$ of remaining requests that we accept. See Figure 6.10.

*A Better Solution*   This suggests that we need more subproblems: To find out the value for OPT($n$) we not only need the value of OPT($n - 1$), but we also need to know the best solution we can get using a subset of the first $n - 1$ items and total allowed weight $W - w_n$. We are therefore going to use many more subproblems: one for each initial set $\{1, \ldots, i\}$ of the items, and each possible

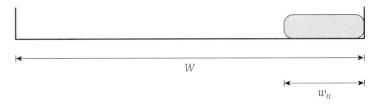

**Figure 6.10** After item $n$ is included in the solution, a weight of $w_n$ is used up and there is $W - w_n$ available weight left.

value for the remaining available weight $w$. Assume that $W$ is an integer, and all requests $i = 1, \ldots, n$ have integer weights $w_i$. We will have a subproblem for each $i = 0, 1, \ldots, n$ and each integer $0 \leq w \leq W$. We will use $\text{OPT}(i, w)$ to denote the value of the optimal solution using a subset of the items $\{1, \ldots, i\}$ with maximum allowed weight $w$, that is,

$$\text{OPT}(i, w) = \max_S \sum_{j \in S} w_j,$$

where the maximum is over subsets $S \subseteq \{1, \ldots, i\}$ that satisfy $\sum_{j \in S} w_j \leq w$. Using this new set of subproblems, we will be able to express the value $\text{OPT}(i, w)$ as a simple expression in terms of values from smaller problems. Moreover, $\text{OPT}(n, W)$ is the quantity we're looking for in the end. As before, let $\mathcal{O}$ denote an optimum solution for the original problem.

- If $n \notin \mathcal{O}$, then $\text{OPT}(n, W) = \text{OPT}(n - 1, W)$, since we can simply ignore item $n$.
- If $n \in \mathcal{O}$, then $\text{OPT}(n, W) = w_n + \text{OPT}(n - 1, W - w_n)$, since we now seek to use the remaining capacity of $W - w_n$ in an optimal way across items $1, 2, \ldots, n - 1$.

When the $n^{\text{th}}$ item is too big, that is, $W < w_n$, then we must have $\text{OPT}(n, W) = \text{OPT}(n - 1, W)$. Otherwise, we get the optimum solution allowing all $n$ requests by taking the better of these two options. Using the same line of argument for the subproblem for items $\{1, \ldots, i\}$, and maximum allowed weight $w$, gives us the following recurrence.

**(6.8)** *If $w < w_i$ then* $\text{OPT}(i, w) = \text{OPT}(i - 1, w)$. *Otherwise*

$$\text{OPT}(i, w) = \max(\text{OPT}(i - 1, w), w_i + \text{OPT}(i - 1, w - w_i)).$$

As before, we want to design an algorithm that builds up a table of all $\text{OPT}(i, w)$ values while computing each of them at most once.

```
Subset-Sum(n, W)
   Array M[0...n, 0...W]
   Initialize M[0, w] = 0 for each w = 0, 1, ..., W
   For i = 1, 2, ..., n
      For w = 0, ..., W
         Use the recurrence (6.8) to compute M[i, w]
      Endfor
   Endfor
   Return M[n, W]
```

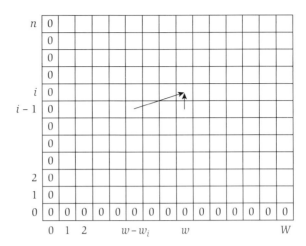

**Figure 6.11** The two-dimensional table of OPT values. The leftmost column and bottom row is always 0. The entry for OPT$(i, w)$ is computed from the two other entries OPT$(i - 1, w)$ and OPT$(i - 1, w - w_i)$, as indicated by the arrows.

Using (6.8) one can immediately prove by induction that the returned value $M[n, W]$ is the optimum solution value for the requests $1, \ldots, n$ and available weight $W$.

## Analyzing the Algorithm

Recall the tabular picture we considered in Figure 6.5, associated with weighted interval scheduling, where we also showed the way in which the array $M$ for that algorithm was iteratively filled in. For the algorithm we've just designed, we can use a similar representation, but we need a two-dimensional table, reflecting the two-dimensional array of subproblems that is being built up. Figure 6.11 shows the building up of subproblems in this case: the value $M[i, w]$ is computed from the two other values $M[i - 1, w]$ and $M[i - 1, w - w_i]$.

As an example of this algorithm executing, consider an instance with weight limit $W = 6$, and $n = 3$ items of sizes $w_1 = w_2 = 2$ and $w_3 = 3$. We find that the optimal value OPT$(3, 6) = 5$ (which we get by using the third item and one of the first two items). Figure 6.12 illustrates the way the algorithm fills in the two-dimensional table of OPT values row by row.

Next we will worry about the running time of this algorithm. As before in the case of weighted interval scheduling, we are building up a table of solutions $M$, and we compute each of the values $M[i, w]$ in $O(1)$ time using the previous values. Thus the running time is proportional to the number of entries in the table.

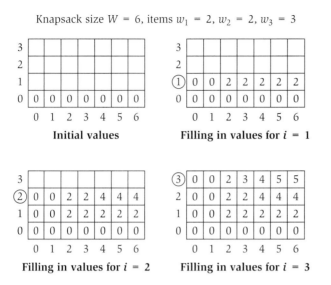

Figure 6.12 The iterations of the algorithm on a sample instance of the Subset Sum Problem.

**(6.9)** *The* Subset-Sum$(n, W)$ *Algorithm correctly computes the optimal value of the problem, and runs in $O(nW)$ time.*

Note that this method is not as efficient as our dynamic program for the Weighted Interval Scheduling Problem. Indeed, its running time is not a polynomial function of $n$; rather, it is a polynomial function of $n$ and $W$, the largest integer involved in defining the problem. We call such algorithms *pseudo-polynomial*. Pseudo-polynomial algorithms can be reasonably efficient when the numbers $\{w_i\}$ involved in the input are reasonably small; however, they become less practical as these numbers grow large.

To recover an optimal set $S$ of items, we can trace back through the array $M$ by a procedure similar to those we developed in the previous sections.

**(6.10)** *Given a table M of the optimal values of the subproblems, the optimal set S can be found in $O(n)$ time.*

## Extension: The Knapsack Problem

The Knapsack Problem is a bit more complex than the scheduling problem we discussed earlier. Consider a situation in which each item $i$ has a nonnegative weight $w_i$ as before, and also a distinct *value* $v_i$. Our goal is now to find a subset $S$ of maximum value $\sum_{i \in S} v_i$, subject to the restriction that the total weight of the set should not exceed $W$: $\sum_{i \in S} w_i \leq W$.

It is not hard to extend our dynamic programming algorithm to this more general problem. We use the analogous set of subproblems, $\text{OPT}(i, w)$, to denote the value of the optimal solution using a subset of the items $\{1, \ldots, i\}$ and maximum available weight $w$. We consider an optimal solution $\mathcal{O}$, and identify two cases depending on whether or not $n \in \mathcal{O}$.

- If $n \notin \mathcal{O}$, then $\text{OPT}(n, W) = \text{OPT}(n - 1, W)$.
- If $n \in \mathcal{O}$, then $\text{OPT}(n, W) = v_n + \text{OPT}(n - 1, W - w_n)$.

Using this line of argument for the subproblems implies the following analogue of (6.8).

**(6.11)**    *If $w < w_i$ then $\text{OPT}(i, w) = \text{OPT}(i - 1, w)$. Otherwise*

$$\text{OPT}(i, w) = \max(\text{OPT}(i - 1, w), v_i + \text{OPT}(i - 1, w - w_i)).$$

Using this recurrence, we can write down a completely analogous dynamic programming algorithm, and this implies the following fact.

**(6.12)**    *The Knapsack Problem can be solved in $O(nW)$ time.*

## 6.5 RNA Secondary Structure: Dynamic Programming over Intervals

In the Knapsack Problem, we were able to formulate a dynamic programming algorithm by adding a new variable. A different but very common way by which one ends up adding a variable to a dynamic program is through the following scenario. We start by thinking about the set of subproblems on $\{1, 2, \ldots, j\}$, for all choices of $j$, and find ourselves unable to come up with a natural recurrence. We then look at the larger set of subproblems on $\{i, i + 1, \ldots, j\}$ for all choices of $i$ and $j$ (where $i \leq j$), and find a natural recurrence relation on these subproblems. In this way, we have added the second variable $i$; the effect is to consider a subproblem for every contiguous *interval* in $\{1, 2, \ldots, n\}$.

There are a few canonical problems that fit this profile; those of you who have studied parsing algorithms for context-free grammars have probably seen at least one dynamic programming algorithm in this style. Here we focus on the problem of RNA secondary structure prediction, a fundamental issue in computational biology.

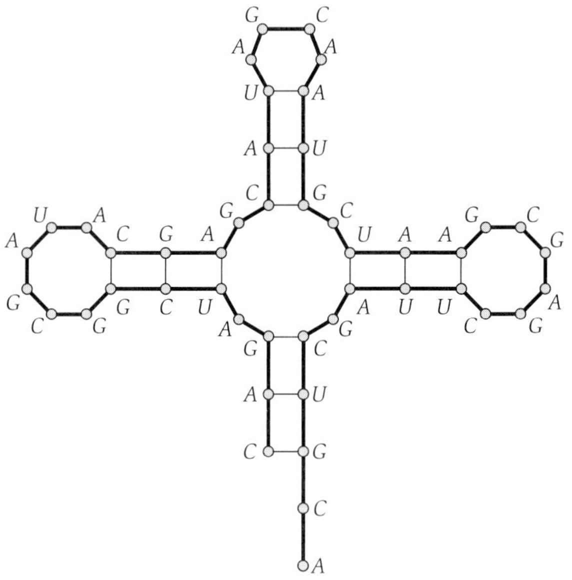

**Figure 6.13** An RNA secondary structure. Thick lines connect adjacent elements of the sequence; thin lines indicate pairs of elements that are matched.

## The Problem

As one learns in introductory biology classes, Watson and Crick posited that double-stranded DNA is "zipped" together by complementary base-pairing. Each strand of DNA can be viewed as a string of *bases*, where each base is drawn from the set $\{A, C, G, T\}$.[2] The bases $A$ and $T$ pair with each other, and the bases $C$ and $G$ pair with each other; it is these $A$-$T$ and $C$-$G$ pairings that hold the two strands together.

Now, single-stranded RNA molecules are key components in many of the processes that go on inside a cell, and they follow more or less the same structural principles. However, unlike double-stranded DNA, there's no "second strand" for the RNA to stick to; so it tends to loop back and form base pairs with itself, resulting in interesting shapes like the one depicted in Figure 6.13. The set of pairs (and resulting shape) formed by the RNA molecule through this process is called the *secondary structure*, and understanding the secondary structure is essential for understanding the behavior of the molecule.

---

[2] Adenine, cytosine, guanine, and thymine, the four basic units of DNA.

For our purposes, a single-stranded RNA molecule can be viewed as a sequence of $n$ symbols (bases) drawn from the alphabet $\{A, C, G, U\}$.[3] Let $B = b_1 b_2 \cdots b_n$ be a single-stranded RNA molecule, where each $b_i \in \{A, C, G, U\}$. To a first approximation, one can model its secondary structure as follows. As usual, we require that $A$ pairs with $U$, and $C$ pairs with $G$; we also require that each base can pair with at most one other base—in other words, the set of base pairs forms a *matching*. It also turns out that secondary structures are (again, to a first approximation) "knot-free," which we will formalize as a kind of *noncrossing* condition below.

Thus, concretely, we say that a *secondary structure on B* is a set of pairs $S = \{(i, j)\}$, where $i, j \in \{1, 2, \ldots, n\}$, that satisfies the following conditions.

   (i)  *(No sharp turns.)* The ends of each pair in $S$ are separated by at least four intervening bases; that is, if $(i, j) \in S$, then $i < j - 4$.

   (ii)  The elements of any pair in $S$ consist of either $\{A, U\}$ or $\{C, G\}$ (in either order).

   (iii)  $S$ is a matching: no base appears in more than one pair.

   (iv)  *(The noncrossing condition.)* If $(i, j)$ and $(k, \ell)$ are two pairs in $S$, then we cannot have $i < k < j < \ell$. (See Figure 6.14 for an illustration.)

Note that the RNA secondary structure in Figure 6.13 satisfies properties (i) through (iv). From a structural point of view, condition (i) arises simply because the RNA molecule cannot bend too sharply; and conditions (ii) and (iii) are the fundamental Watson-Crick rules of base-pairing. Condition (iv) is the striking one, since it's not obvious why it should hold in nature. But while there are sporadic exceptions to it in real molecules (via so-called *pseudoknotting*), it does turn out to be a good approximation to the spatial constraints on real RNA secondary structures.

Now, out of all the secondary structures that are possible for a single RNA molecule, which are the ones that are likely to arise under physiological conditions? The usual hypothesis is that a single-stranded RNA molecule will form the secondary structure with the optimum total free energy. The correct model for the free energy of a secondary structure is a subject of much debate; but a first approximation here is to assume that the free energy of a secondary structure is proportional simply to the *number* of base pairs that it contains.

Thus, having said all this, we can state the basic RNA secondary structure prediction problem very simply: We want an efficient algorithm that takes

---

[3] Note that the symbol $T$ from the alphabet of DNA has been replaced by a $U$, but this is not important for us here.

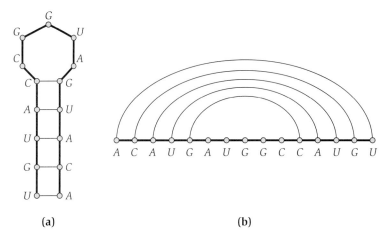

(a)                                        (b)

**Figure 6.14** Two views of an RNA secondary structure. In the second view, (b), the string has been "stretched" lengthwise, and edges connecting matched pairs appear as noncrossing "bubbles" over the string.

a single-stranded RNA molecule $B = b_1 b_2 \cdots b_n$ and determines a secondary structure $S$ with the maximum possible number of base pairs.

## Designing and Analyzing the Algorithm

*A First Attempt at Dynamic Programming* The natural first attempt to apply dynamic programming would presumably be based on the following subproblems: We say that OPT($j$) is the maximum number of base pairs in a secondary structure on $b_1 b_2 \cdots b_j$. By the no-sharp-turns condition above, we know that OPT($j$) = 0 for $j \leq 5$; and we know that OPT($n$) is the solution we're looking for.

The trouble comes when we try writing down a recurrence that expresses OPT($j$) in terms of the solutions to smaller subproblems. We can get partway there: in the optimal secondary structure on $b_1 b_2 \cdots b_j$, it's the case that either

- $j$ is not involved in a pair; or
- $j$ pairs with $t$ for some $t < j - 4$.

In the first case, we just need to consult our solution for OPT($j - 1$). The second case is depicted in Figure 6.15(a); because of the noncrossing condition, we now know that no pair can have one end between 1 and $t - 1$ and the other end between $t + 1$ and $j - 1$. We've therefore effectively isolated two new subproblems: one on the bases $b_1 b_2 \cdots b_{t-1}$, and the other on the bases $b_{t+1} \cdots b_{j-1}$. The first is solved by OPT($t - 1$), but the second is not on our list of subproblems, because it does not begin with $b_1$.

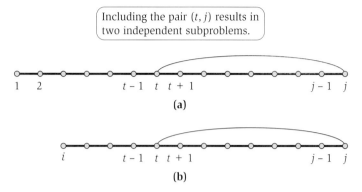

Including the pair $(t, j)$ results in two independent subproblems.

**(a)**

**(b)**

**Figure 6.15** Schematic views of the dynamic programming recurrence using (a) one variable, and (b) two variables.

This is the insight that makes us realize we need to add a variable. We need to be able to work with subproblems that do not begin with $b_1$; in other words, we need to consider subproblems on $b_i b_{i+1} \cdots b_j$ for all choices of $i \leq j$.

***Dynamic Programming over Intervals***    Once we make this decision, our previous reasoning leads straight to a successful recurrence. Let $\text{OPT}(i, j)$ denote the maximum number of base pairs in a secondary structure on $b_i b_{i+1} \cdots b_j$. The no-sharp-turns condition lets us initialize $\text{OPT}(i, j) = 0$ whenever $i \geq j - 4$. (For notational convenience, we will also allow ourselves to refer to $\text{OPT}(i, j)$ even when $i > j$; in this case, its value is 0.)

Now, in the optimal secondary structure on $b_i b_{i+1} \cdots b_j$, we have the same alternatives as before:

- $j$ is not involved in a pair; or
- $j$ pairs with $t$ for some $t < j - 4$.

In the first case, we have $\text{OPT}(i, j) = \text{OPT}(i, j - 1)$. In the second case, depicted in Figure 6.15(b), we recur on the two subproblems $\text{OPT}(i, t - 1)$ and $\text{OPT}(t + 1, j - 1)$; as argued above, the noncrossing condition has isolated these two subproblems from each other.

We have therefore justified the following recurrence.

**(6.13)**    $\text{OPT}(i, j) = \max(\text{OPT}(i, j - 1), \max(1 + \text{OPT}(i, t - 1) + \text{OPT}(t + 1, j - 1)))$, *where the* max *is taken over $t$ such that $b_t$ and $b_j$ are an allowable base pair (under conditions (i) and (ii) from the definition of a secondary structure).*

Now we just have to make sure we understand the proper order in which to build up the solutions to the subproblems. The form of (6.13) reveals that we're always invoking the solution to subproblems on *shorter* intervals: those

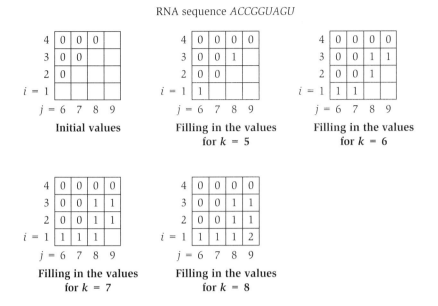

RNA sequence *ACCGGUAGU*

**Figure 6.16** The iterations of the algorithm on a sample instance of the RNA Secondary Structure Prediction Problem.

for which $k = j - i$ is smaller. Thus things will work without any trouble if we build up the solutions in order of increasing interval length.

```
Initialize OPT(i, j) = 0 whenever i ≥ j − 4
For k = 5, 6, . . . , n − 1
   For i = 1, 2, . . . n − k
      Set j = i + k
      Compute OPT(i, j) using the recurrence in (6.13)
   Endfor
Endfor
Return OPT(1, n)
```

As an example of this algorithm executing, we consider the input *ACCGGUAGU*, a subsequence of the sequence in Figure 6.14. As with the Knapsack Problem, we need two dimensions to depict the array $M$: one for the left endpoint of the interval being considered, and one for the right endpoint. In the figure, we only show entries corresponding to $[i, j]$ pairs with $i < j - 4$, since these are the only ones that can possibly be nonzero.

It is easy to bound the running time: there are $O(n^2)$ subproblems to solve, and evaluating the recurrence in (6.13) takes time $O(n)$ for each. Thus the running time is $O(n^3)$.

As always, we can recover the secondary structure itself (not just its value) by recording how the minima in (6.13) are achieved and tracing back through the computation.

## 6.6 Sequence Alignment

For the remainder of this chapter, we consider two further dynamic programming algorithms that each have a wide range of applications. In the next two sections we discuss *sequence alignment*, a fundamental problem that arises in comparing strings. Following this, we turn to the problem of computing shortest paths in graphs when edges have costs that may be negative.

### The Problem

Dictionaries on the Web seem to get more and more useful: often it seems easier to pull up a bookmarked online dictionary than to get a physical dictionary down from the bookshelf. And many online dictionaries offer functions that you can't get from a printed one: if you're looking for a definition and type in a word it doesn't contain—say, *ocurrance*—it will come back and ask, "Perhaps you mean *occurrence*?" How does it do this? Did it truly know what you had in mind?

Let's defer the second question to a different book and think a little about the first one. To decide what you probably meant, it would be natural to search the dictionary for the word most "similar" to the one you typed in. To do this, we have to answer the question: How should we define similarity between two words or strings?

Intuitively, we'd like to say that *ocurrance* and *occurrence* are similar because we can make the two words identical if we add a *c* to the first word and change the *a* to an *e*. Since neither of these changes seems so large, we conclude that the words are quite similar. To put it another way, we can *nearly* line up the two words letter by letter:

```
o-currance
occurrence
```

The hyphen (-) indicates a *gap* where we had to add a letter to the second word to get it to line up with the first. Moreover, our lining up is not perfect in that an *e* is lined up with an *a*.

We want a model in which similarity is determined roughly by the number of gaps and mismatches we incur when we line up the two words. Of course, there are many possible ways to line up the two words; for example, we could have written

```
o-curr-ance
occurre-nce
```

which involves three gaps and no mismatches. Which is better: one gap and one mismatch, or three gaps and no mismatches?

This discussion has been made easier because we know roughly what the correspondence ought to look like. When the two strings don't look like English words—for example, abbbaabbbbaab and ababaaabbbbbab—it may take a little work to decide whether they can be lined up nicely or not:

```
abbbaa--bbbbaab
ababaaabbbbba-b
```

Dictionary interfaces and spell-checkers are not the most computationally intensive application for this type of problem. In fact, determining similarities among strings is one of the central computational problems facing molecular biologists today.

Strings arise very naturally in biology: an organism's *genome*—its full set of genetic material—is divided up into giant linear DNA molecules known as *chromosomes*, each of which serves conceptually as a one-dimensional chemical storage device. Indeed, it does not obscure reality very much to think of it as an enormous linear *tape*, containing a string over the alphabet $\{A, C, G, T\}$. The string of symbols encodes the instructions for building protein molecules; using a chemical mechanism for reading portions of the chromosome, a cell can construct proteins that in turn control its metabolism.

Why is similarity important in this picture? To a first approximation, the sequence of symbols in an organism's genome can be viewed as determining the properties of the organism. So suppose we have two strains of bacteria, $X$ and $Y$, which are closely related evolutionarily. Suppose further that we've determined that a certain substring in the DNA of $X$ codes for a certain kind of toxin. Then, if we discover a very "similar" substring in the DNA of $Y$, we might be able to hypothesize, before performing any experiments at all, that this portion of the DNA in $Y$ codes for a similar kind of toxin. This use of computation to guide decisions about biological experiments is one of the hallmarks of the field of *computational biology*.

All this leaves us with the same question we asked initially, while typing badly spelled words into our online dictionary: How should we define the notion of *similarity* between two strings?

In the early 1970s, the two molecular biologists Needleman and Wunsch proposed a definition of similarity, which, basically unchanged, has become the standard definition in use today. Its position as a standard was reinforced by its simplicity and intuitive appeal, as well as through its independent discovery by several other researchers around the same time. Moreover, this definition of similarity came with an efficient dynamic programming algorithm to compute it. In this way, the paradigm of dynamic programming was independently discovered by biologists some twenty years after mathematicians and computer scientists first articulated it.

The definition is motivated by the considerations we discussed above, and in particular by the notion of "lining up" two strings. Suppose we are given two strings $X$ and $Y$, where $X$ consists of the sequence of symbols $x_1 x_2 \cdots x_m$ and $Y$ consists of the sequence of symbols $y_1 y_2 \cdots y_n$. Consider the sets $\{1, 2, \ldots, m\}$ and $\{1, 2, \ldots, n\}$ as representing the different positions in the strings $X$ and $Y$, and consider a matching of these sets; recall that a *matching* is a set of ordered pairs with the property that each item occurs in at most one pair. We say that a matching $M$ of these two sets is an *alignment* if there are no "crossing" pairs: if $(i, j), (i', j') \in M$ and $i < i'$, then $j < j'$. Intuitively, an alignment gives a way of lining up the two strings, by telling us which pairs of positions will be lined up with one another. Thus, for example,

```
stop-

-tops
```

corresponds to the alignment $\{(2, 1), (3, 2), (4, 3)\}$.

Our definition of similarity will be based on finding the *optimal* alignment between $X$ and $Y$, according to the following criteria. Suppose $M$ is a given alignment between $X$ and $Y$.

- First, there is a parameter $\delta > 0$ that defines a *gap penalty*. For each position of $X$ or $Y$ that is not matched in $M$—it is a *gap*—we incur a cost of $\delta$.

- Second, for each pair of letters $p, q$ in our alphabet, there is a *mismatch cost* of $\alpha_{pq}$ for lining up $p$ with $q$. Thus, for each $(i, j) \in M$, we pay the appropriate mismatch cost $\alpha_{x_i y_j}$ for lining up $x_i$ with $y_j$. One generally assumes that $\alpha_{pp} = 0$ for each letter $p$—there is no mismatch cost to line up a letter with another copy of itself—although this will not be necessary in anything that follows.

- The *cost* of $M$ is the sum of its gap and mismatch costs, and we seek an alignment of minimum cost.

The process of minimizing this cost is often referred to as *sequence alignment* in the biology literature. The quantities $\delta$ and $\{\alpha_{pq}\}$ are external parameters that must be plugged into software for sequence alignment; indeed, a lot of work goes into choosing the settings for these parameters. From our point of view, in designing an algorithm for sequence alignment, we will take them as given. To go back to our first example, notice how these parameters determine which alignment of *ocurrance* and *occurrence* we should prefer: the first is strictly better if and only if $\delta + \alpha_{ae} < 3\delta$.

## Designing the Algorithm

We now have a concrete numerical definition for the similarity between strings $X$ and $Y$: it is the minimum cost of an alignment between $X$ and $Y$. The lower this cost, the more similar we declare the strings to be. We now turn to the problem of computing this minimum cost, and an optimal alignment that yields it, for a given pair of strings $X$ and $Y$.

One of the approaches we could try for this problem is dynamic programming, and we are motivated by the following basic dichotomy.

- In the optimal alignment $M$, either $(m, n) \in M$ or $(m, n) \notin M$. (That is, either the last symbols in the two strings are matched to each other, or they aren't.)

By itself, this fact would be too weak to provide us with a dynamic programming solution. Suppose, however, that we compound it with the following basic fact.

**(6.14)** *Let $M$ be any alignment of $X$ and $Y$. If $(m, n) \notin M$, then either the $m^{th}$ position of $X$ or the $n^{th}$ position of $Y$ is not matched in $M$.*

**Proof.** Suppose by way of contradiction that $(m, n) \notin M$, and there are numbers $i < m$ and $j < n$ so that $(m, j) \in M$ and $(i, n) \in M$. But this contradicts our definition of *alignment*: we have $(i, n), (m, j) \in M$ with $i < m$, but $n > i$ so the pairs $(i, n)$ and $(m, j)$ cross. ∎

There is an equivalent way to write (6.14) that exposes three alternative possibilities, and leads directly to the formulation of a recurrence.

**(6.15)** *In an optimal alignment $M$, at least one of the following is true:*

*(i) $(m, n) \in M$; or*

*(ii) the $m^{th}$ position of $X$ is not matched; or*

*(iii) the $n^{th}$ position of $Y$ is not matched.*

Now, let $\text{OPT}(i, j)$ denote the minimum cost of an alignment between $x_1 x_2 \cdots x_i$ and $y_1 y_2 \cdots y_j$. If case (i) of (6.15) holds, we pay $\alpha_{x_m y_n}$ and then align $x_1 x_2 \cdots x_{m-1}$ as well as possible with $y_1 y_2 \cdots y_{n-1}$; we get $\text{OPT}(m, n) = \alpha_{x_m y_n} + \text{OPT}(m - 1, n - 1)$. If case (ii) holds, we pay a gap cost of $\delta$ since the $m^{th}$ position of $X$ is not matched, and then we align $x_1 x_2 \cdots x_{m-1}$ as well as possible with $y_1 y_2 \cdots y_n$. In this way, we get $\mathrm{OPT}(m, n) = \delta + \mathrm{OPT}(m - 1, n)$. Similarly, if case (iii) holds, we get $\mathrm{OPT}(m, n) = \delta + \mathrm{OPT}(m, n - 1)$.

Using the same argument for the subproblem of finding the minimum-cost alignment between $x_1 x_2 \cdots x_i$ and $y_1 y_2 \cdots y_j$, we get the following fact.

> **(6.16)**   *The minimum alignment costs satisfy the following recurrence for $i \geq 1$ and $j \geq 1$:*
>
> $$\mathrm{OPT}(i, j) = \min[\alpha_{x_i y_j} + \mathrm{OPT}(i - 1, j - 1), \delta + \mathrm{OPT}(i - 1, j), \delta + \mathrm{OPT}(i, j - 1)].$$
>
> *Moreover, $(i, j)$ is in an optimal alignment M for this subproblem if and only if the minimum is achieved by the first of these values.*

We have maneuvered ourselves into a position where the dynamic programming algorithm has become clear: We build up the values of $\mathrm{OPT}(i, j)$ using the recurrence in (6.16). There are only $O(mn)$ subproblems, and $\mathrm{OPT}(m, n)$ is the value we are seeking.

We now specify the algorithm to compute the value of the optimal alignment. For purposes of initialization, we note that $\mathrm{OPT}(i, 0) = \mathrm{OPT}(0, i) = i\delta$ for all $i$, since the only way to line up an $i$-letter word with a 0-letter word is to use $i$ gaps.

```
Alignment(X,Y)
  Array A[0...m, 0...n]
  Initialize A[i, 0] = iδ for each i
  Initialize A[0, j] = jδ for each j
  For j = 1, ..., n
    For i = 1, ..., m
        Use the recurrence (6.16) to compute A[i, j]
    Endfor
  Endfor
  Return A[m, n]
```

As in previous dynamic programming algorithms, we can trace back through the array $A$, using the second part of fact (6.16), to construct the alignment itself.

## Analyzing the Algorithm

The correctness of the algorithm follows directly from (6.16). The running time is $O(mn)$, since the array $A$ has $O(mn)$ entries, and at worst we spend constant time on each.

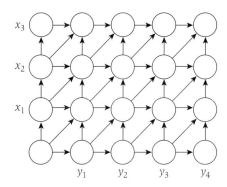

**Figure 6.17** A graph-based picture of sequence alignment.

There is an appealing pictorial way in which people think about this sequence alignment algorithm. Suppose we build a two-dimensional $m \times n$ grid graph $G_{XY}$, with the rows labeled by symbols in the string $X$, the columns labeled by symbols in $Y$, and directed edges as in Figure 6.17.

We number the rows from 0 to $m$ and the columns from 0 to $n$; we denote the node in the $i^{\text{th}}$ row and the $j^{\text{th}}$ column by the label $(i, j)$. We put *costs* on the edges of $G_{XY}$: the cost of each horizontal and vertical edge is $\delta$, and the cost of the diagonal edge from $(i-1, j-1)$ to $(i, j)$ is $\alpha_{x_i y_j}$.

The purpose of this picture now emerges: the recurrence in (6.16) for $\text{OPT}(i, j)$ is precisely the recurrence one gets for the minimum-cost path in $G_{XY}$ from $(0, 0)$ to $(i, j)$. Thus we can show

**(6.17)** *Let $f(i, j)$ denote the minimum cost of a path from $(0, 0)$ to $(i, j)$ in $G_{XY}$. Then for all $i, j$, we have $f(i, j) = \text{OPT}(i, j)$.*

**Proof.** We can easily prove this by induction on $i + j$. When $i + j = 0$, we have $i = j = 0$, and indeed $f(i, j) = \text{OPT}(i, j) = 0$.

Now consider arbitrary values of $i$ and $j$, and suppose the statement is true for all pairs $(i', j')$ with $i' + j' < i + j$. The last edge on the shortest path to $(i, j)$ is either from $(i-1, j-1)$, $(i-1, j)$, or $(i, j-1)$. Thus we have

$$f(i, j) = \min[\alpha_{x_i y_j} + f(i-1, j-1), \delta + f(i-1, j), \delta + f(i, j-1)]$$

$$= \min[\alpha_{x_i y_j} + \text{OPT}(i-1, j-1), \delta + \text{OPT}(i-1, j), \delta + \text{OPT}(i, j-1)]$$

$$= \text{OPT}(i, j),$$

where we pass from the first line to the second using the induction hypothesis, and we pass from the second to the third using (6.16). ∎

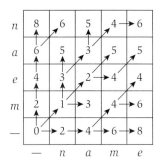

**Figure 6.18** The OPT values for the problem of aligning the words *mean* to *name*.

Thus the value of the optimal alignment is the length of the shortest path in $G_{XY}$ from $(0, 0)$ to $(m, n)$. (We'll call any path in $G_{XY}$ from $(0, 0)$ to $(m, n)$ a *corner-to-corner path*.) Moreover, the diagonal edges used in a shortest path correspond precisely to the pairs used in a minimum-cost alignment. These connections to the Shortest-Path Problem in the graph $G_{XY}$ do not directly yield an improvement in the running time for the sequence alignment problem; however, they do help one's intuition for the problem and have been useful in suggesting algorithms for more complex variations on sequence alignment.

For an example, Figure 6.18 shows the value of the shortest path from $(0, 0)$ to each node $(i, j)$ for the problem of aligning the words *mean* and *name*. For the purpose of this example, we assume that $\delta = 2$; matching a vowel with a different vowel, or a consonant with a different consonant, costs 1; while matching a vowel and a consonant with each other costs 3. For each cell in the table (representing the corresponding node), the arrow indicates the last step of the shortest path leading to that node—in other words, the way that the minimum is achieved in (6.16). Thus, by following arrows backward from node $(4, 4)$, we can trace back to construct the alignment.

## 6.7 Sequence Alignment in Linear Space via Divide and Conquer

In the previous section, we showed how to compute the optimal alignment between two strings $X$ and $Y$ of lengths $m$ and $n$, respectively. Building up the two-dimensional $m$-by-$n$ array of optimal solutions to subproblems, OPT$(\cdot, \cdot)$, turned out to be equivalent to constructing a graph $G_{XY}$ with $mn$ nodes laid out in a grid and looking for the cheapest path between opposite corners. In either of these ways of formulating the dynamic programming algorithm, the running time is $O(mn)$, because it takes constant time to determine the value in each of the $mn$ cells of the array OPT; and the space requirement is $O(mn)$ as well, since it was dominated by the cost of storing the array (or the graph $G_{XY}$).

### The Problem

The question we ask in this section is: Should we be happy with $O(mn)$ as a space bound? If our application is to compare English words, or even English sentences, it is quite reasonable. In biological applications of sequence alignment, however, one often compares very long strings against one another; and in these cases, the $\Theta(mn)$ space requirement can potentially be a more severe problem than the $\Theta(mn)$ time requirement. Suppose, for example, that we are comparing two strings of 100,000 symbols each. Depending on the underlying processor, the prospect of performing roughly 10 billion primitive operations might be less cause for worry than the prospect of working with a single 10-gigabyte array.

Fortunately, this is not the end of the story. In this section we describe a very clever enhancement of the sequence alignment algorithm that makes it work in $O(mn)$ time using only $O(m + n)$ space. In other words, we can bring the space requirement down to linear while blowing up the running time by at most an additional constant factor. For ease of presentation, we'll describe various steps in terms of paths in the graph $G_{XY}$, with the natural equivalence back to the sequence alignment problem. Thus, when we seek the pairs in an optimal alignment, we can equivalently ask for the edges in a shortest corner-to-corner path in $G_{XY}$.

The algorithm itself will be a nice application of divide-and-conquer ideas. The crux of the technique is the observation that, if we divide the problem into several recursive calls, then the space needed for the computation can be reused from one call to the next. The way in which this idea is used, however, is fairly subtle.

## Designing the Algorithm

We first show that if we only care about the *value* of the optimal alignment, and not the alignment itself, it is easy to get away with linear space. The crucial observation is that to fill in an entry of the array $A$, the recurrence in (6.16) only needs information from the current column of $A$ and the previous column of $A$. Thus we will "collapse" the array $A$ to an $m \times 2$ array $B$: as the algorithm iterates through values of $j$, entries of the form $B[i, 0]$ will hold the "previous" column's value $A[i, j - 1]$, while entries of the form $B[i, 1]$ will hold the "current" column's value $A[i, j]$.

```
Space-Efficient-Alignment(X,Y)
   Array B[0...m,0...1]
   Initialize B[i,0]=iδ for each i (just as in column 0 of A)
   For j=1,...,n
      B[0,1]=jδ (since this corresponds to entry A[0,j])
      For i=1,...,m
         B[i,1]= min[α_{x_i y_j} + B[i−1,0],
                     δ + B[i−1,1],  δ + B[i,0]]
      Endfor
      Move column 1 of B to column 0 to make room for next iteration:
         Update B[i,0]=B[i,1] for each i
   Endfor
```

It is easy to verify that when this algorithm completes, the array entry $B[i, 1]$ holds the value of OPT$(i, n)$ for $i = 0, 1, \ldots, m$. Moreover, it uses $O(mn)$ time and $O(m)$ space. The problem is: where is the alignment itself? We haven't left enough information around to be able to run a procedure like Find-Alignment. Since $B$ at the end of the algorithm only contains the last two columns of the original dynamic programming array $A$, if we were to try tracing back to get the path, we'd run out of information after just these two columns. We could imagine getting around this difficulty by trying to "predict" what the alignment is going to be in the process of running our space-efficient procedure. In particular, as we compute the values in the $j^{\text{th}}$ column of the (now implicit) array $A$, we could try hypothesizing that a certain entry has a very small value, and hence that the alignment that passes through this entry is a promising candidate to be the optimal one. But this promising alignment might run into big problems later on, and a different alignment that currently looks much less attractive could turn out to be the optimal one.

There is, in fact, a solution to this problem—we will be able to recover the alignment itself using $O(m + n)$ space—but it requires a genuinely new idea. The insight is based on employing the divide-and-conquer technique that we've seen earlier in the book. We begin with a simple alternative way to implement the basic dynamic programming solution.

***A Backward Formulation of the Dynamic Program***    Recall that we use $f(i, j)$ to denote the length of the shortest path from $(0, 0)$ to $(i, j)$ in the graph $G_{XY}$. (As we showed in the initial sequence alignment algorithm, $f(i, j)$ has the same value as OPT$(i, j)$.) Now let's define $g(i, j)$ to be the length of the shortest path from $(i, j)$ to $(m, n)$ in $G_{XY}$. The function $g$ provides an equally natural dynamic programming approach to sequence alignment, except that we build it up in reverse: we start with $g(m, n) = 0$, and the answer we want is $g(0, 0)$. By strict analogy with (6.16), we have the following recurrence for $g$.

**(6.18)**    *For $i < m$ and $j < n$ we have*

$$g(i, j) = \min[\alpha_{x_{i+1}y_{j+1}} + g(i + 1, j + 1), \delta + g(i, j + 1), \delta + g(i + 1, j)].$$

This is just the recurrence one obtains by taking the graph $G_{XY}$, "rotating" it so that the node $(m, n)$ is in the lower left corner, and using the previous approach. Using this picture, we can also work out the full dynamic programming algorithm to build up the values of $g$, *backward* starting from $(m, n)$. Similarly, there is a space-efficient version of this backward dynamic programming algorithm, analogous to Space-Efficient-Alignment, which computes the value of the optimal alignment using only $O(m + n)$ space. We will refer to this backward version, naturally enough, as `Backward-Space-Efficient-Alignment`.

*Combining the Forward and Backward Formulations*   So now we have symmetric algorithms which build up the values of the functions $f$ and $g$. The idea will be to use these two algorithms in concert to find the optimal alignment. First, here are two basic facts summarizing some relationships between the functions $f$ and $g$.

**(6.19)**   *The length of the shortest corner-to-corner path in $G_{XY}$ that passes through $(i, j)$ is $f(i, j) + g(i, j)$.*

**Proof.**  Let $\ell_{ij}$ denote the length of the shortest corner-to-corner path in $G_{XY}$ that passes through $(i, j)$. Clearly, any such path must get from $(0, 0)$ to $(i, j)$ and then from $(i, j)$ to $(m, n)$. Thus its length is at least $f(i, j) + g(i, j)$, and so we have $\ell_{ij} \geq f(i, j) + g(i, j)$. On the other hand, consider the corner-to-corner path that consists of a minimum-length path from $(0, 0)$ to $(i, j)$, followed by a minimum-length path from $(i, j)$ to $(m, n)$. This path has length $f(i, j) + g(i, j)$, and so we have $\ell_{ij} \leq f(i, j) + g(i, j)$. It follows that $\ell_{ij} = f(i, j) + g(i, j)$. ∎

**(6.20)**   *Let $k$ be any number in $\{0, \ldots, n\}$, and let $q$ be an index that minimizes the quantity $f(q, k) + g(q, k)$. Then there is a corner-to-corner path of minimum length that passes through the node $(q, k)$.*

**Proof.**  Let $\ell^*$ denote the length of the shortest corner-to-corner path in $G_{XY}$. Now fix a value of $k \in \{0, \ldots, n\}$. The shortest corner-to-corner path must use *some* node in the $k^{\text{th}}$ column of $G_{XY}$—let's suppose it is node $(p, k)$—and thus by (6.19)

$$\ell^* = f(p, k) + g(p, k) \geq \min_q f(q, k) + g(q, k).$$

Now consider the index $q$ that achieves the minimum in the right-hand side of this expression; we have

$$\ell^* \geq f(q, k) + g(q, k).$$

By (6.19) again, the shortest corner-to-corner path using the node $(q, k)$ has length $f(q, k) + g(q, k)$, and since $\ell^*$ is the minimum length of *any* corner-to-corner path, we have

$$\ell^* \leq f(q, k) + g(q, k).$$

It follows that $\ell^* = f(q, k) + g(q, k)$. Thus the shortest corner-to-corner path using the node $(q, k)$ has length $\ell^*$, and this proves (6.20). ∎

Using (6.20) and our space-efficient algorithms to compute the *value* of the optimal alignment, we will proceed as follows. We divide $G_{XY}$ along its center column and compute the value of $f(i, n/2)$ and $g(i, n/2)$ for each value of $i$, using our two space-efficient algorithms. We can then determine the minimum value of $f(i, n/2) + g(i, n/2)$, and conclude via (6.20) that there is a shortest corner-to-corner path passing through the node $(i, n/2)$. Given this, we can search for the shortest path recursively in the portion of $G_{XY}$ between $(0, 0)$ and $(i, n/2)$ and in the portion between $(i, n/2)$ and $(m, n)$. The crucial point is that we apply these recursive calls sequentially and reuse the working space from one call to the next. Thus, since we only work on one recursive call at a time, the total space usage is $O(m + n)$. The key question we have to resolve is whether the running time of this algorithm remains $O(mn)$.

In running the algorithm, we maintain a globally accessible list $P$ which will hold nodes on the shortest corner-to-corner path as they are discovered. Initially, $P$ is empty. $P$ need only have $m + n$ entries, since no corner-to-corner path can use more than this many edges. We also use the following notation: $X[i:j]$, for $1 \le i \le j \le m$, denotes the substring of $X$ consisting of $x_i x_{i+1} \cdots x_j$; and we define $Y[i:j]$ analogously. We will assume for simplicity that $n$ is a power of 2; this assumption makes the discussion much cleaner, although it can be easily avoided.

```
Divide-and-Conquer-Alignment(X,Y)
  Let m be the number of symbols in X
  Let n be the number of symbols in Y
  If m ≤ 2 or n ≤ 2 then
     Compute optimal alignment using Alignment(X,Y)
  Call Space-Efficient-Alignment(X,Y[1:n/2])
  Call Backward-Space-Efficient-Alignment(X,Y[n/2+1:n])
  Let q be the index minimizing f(q,n/2)+g(q,n/2)
  Add (q,n/2) to global list P
  Divide-and-Conquer-Alignment(X[1:q],Y[1:n/2])
  Divide-and-Conquer-Alignment(X[q+1:n],Y[n/2+1:n])
  Return P
```

As an example of the first level of recursion, consider Figure 6.19. If the *minimizing index q* turns out to be 1, we get the two subproblems pictured.

## Analyzing the Algorithm

The previous arguments already establish that the algorithm returns the correct answer and that it uses $O(m + n)$ space. Thus, we need only verify the following fact.

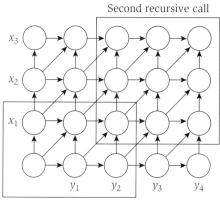

Second recursive call

First recursive call

**Figure 6.19** The first level of recurrence for the space-efficient `Divide-and-Conquer-Alignment`. The two boxed regions indicate the input to the two recursive cells.

**(6.21)** *The running time of* `Divide-and-Conquer-Alignment` *on strings of length m and n is* $O(mn)$.

**Proof.** Let $T(m, n)$ denote the maximum running time of the algorithm on strings of length $m$ and $n$. The algorithm performs $O(mn)$ work to build up the arrays $B$ and $B'$; it then runs recursively on strings of size $q$ and $n/2$, and on strings of size $m - q$ and $n/2$. Thus, for some constant $c$, and some choice of index $q$, we have

$$T(m, n) \leq cmn + T(q, n/2) + T(m - q, n/2)$$
$$T(m, 2) \leq cm$$
$$T(2, n) \leq cn.$$

This recurrence is more complex than the ones we've seen in our earlier applications of divide-and-conquer in Chapter 5. First of all, the running time is a function of two variables ($m$ and $n$) rather than just one; also, the division into subproblems is not necessarily an "even split," but instead depends on the value $q$ that is found through the earlier work done by the algorithm.

So how should we go about solving such a recurrence? One way is to try guessing the form by considering a special case of the recurrence, and then using partial substitution to fill out the details of this guess. Specifically, suppose that we were in a case in which $m = n$, and in which the split point $q$ were exactly in the middle. In this (admittedly restrictive) special case, we could write the function $T(\cdot)$ in terms of the single variable $n$, set $q = n/2$ (since we're assuming a perfect bisection), and have

$$T(n) \leq 2T(n/2) + cn^2.$$

This is a useful expression, since it's something that we solved in our earlier discussion of recurrences at the outset of Chapter 5. Specifically, this recurrence implies $T(n) = O(n^2)$.

So when $m = n$ and we get an even split, the running time grows like the square of $n$. Motivated by this, we move back to the fully general recurrence for the problem at hand and guess that $T(m, n)$ grows like the product of $m$ and $n$. Specifically, we'll guess that $T(m, n) \leq kmn$ for some constant $k$, and see if we can prove this by induction. To start with the base cases $m \leq 2$ and $n \leq 2$, we see that these hold as long as $k \geq c/2$. Now, assuming $T(m', n') \leq km'n'$ holds for pairs $(m', n')$ with a smaller product, we have

$$T(m, n) \leq cmn + T(q, n/2) + T(m - q, n/2)$$
$$\leq cmn + kqn/2 + k(m - q)n/2$$
$$= cmn + kqn/2 + kmn/2 - kqn/2$$
$$= (c + k/2)mn.$$

Thus the inductive step will work if we choose $k = 2c$, and this completes the proof. ∎

## 6.8 Shortest Paths in a Graph

For the final three sections, we focus on the problem of finding shortest paths in a graph, together with some closely related issues.

### 🖋 The Problem

Let $G = (V, E)$ be a directed graph. Assume that each edge $(i, j) \in E$ has an associated *weight* $c_{ij}$. The weights can be used to model a number of different things; we will picture here the interpretation in which the weight $c_{ij}$ represents a *cost* for going directly from node $i$ to node $j$ in the graph.

Earlier we discussed Dijkstra's Algorithm for finding shortest paths in graphs with positive edge costs. Here we consider the more complex problem in which we seek shortest paths when costs may be negative. Among the motivations for studying this problem, here are two that particularly stand out. First, negative costs turn out to be crucial for modeling a number of phenomena with shortest paths. For example, the nodes may represent agents in a financial setting, and $c_{ij}$ represents the cost of a transaction in which we buy from agent $i$ and then immediately sell to agent $j$. In this case, a path would represent a succession of transactions, and edges with negative costs would represent transactions that result in profits. Second, the algorithm that we develop for dealing with edges of negative cost turns out, in certain crucial ways, to be more flexible and *decentralized* than Dijkstra's Algorithm. As a consequence, it has important applications for the design of distributed routing algorithms that determine the most efficient path in a communication network.

In this section and the next two, we will consider the following two related problems.

- Given a graph $G$ with weights, as described above, decide if $G$ has a negative cycle—that is, a directed cycle $C$ such that

$$\sum_{ij \in C} c_{ij} < 0.$$

- If the graph has no negative cycles, find a path $P$ from an origin node $s$ to a destination node $t$ with minimum total cost:

$$\sum_{ij \in P} c_{ij}$$

should be as small as possible for any $s$-$t$ path. This is generally called both the *Minimum-Cost Path Problem* and the *Shortest-Path Problem*.

In terms of our financial motivation above, a negative cycle corresponds to a profitable sequence of transactions that takes us back to our starting point: we buy from $i_1$, sell to $i_2$, buy from $i_2$, sell to $i_3$, and so forth, finally arriving back at $i_1$ with a net profit. Thus negative cycles in such a network can be viewed as good *arbitrage opportunities*.

It makes sense to consider the minimum-cost $s$-$t$ path problem under the assumption that there are no negative cycles. As illustrated by Figure 6.20, if there is a negative cycle $C$, a path $P_s$ from $s$ to the cycle, and another path $P_t$ from the cycle to $t$, then we can build an $s$-$t$ path of arbitrarily negative cost: we first use $P_s$ to get to the negative cycle $C$, then we go around $C$ as many times as we want, and then we use $P_t$ to get from $C$ to the destination $t$.

## Designing and Analyzing the Algorithm

*A Few False Starts*   Let's begin by recalling Dijkstra's Algorithm for the Shortest-Path Problem when there are no negative costs. That method

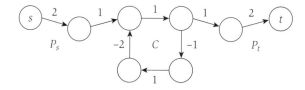

**Figure 6.20**  In this graph, one can find $s$-$t$ paths of arbitrarily negative cost (by going around the cycle $C$ many times).

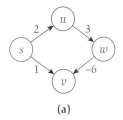

**(a)**

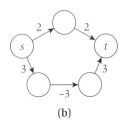

**(b)**

**Figure 6.21** (a) With negative edge costs, Dijkstra's Algorithm can give the wrong answer for the Shortest-Path Problem. (b) Adding 3 to the cost of each edge will make all edges nonnegative, but it will change the identity of the shortest $s$-$t$ path.

computes a shortest path from the origin $s$ to every other node $v$ in the graph, essentially using a greedy algorithm. The basic idea is to maintain a set $S$ with the property that the shortest path from $s$ to each node in $S$ is known. We start with $S = \{s\}$—since we know the shortest path from $s$ to $s$ has cost 0 when there are no negative edges—and we add elements greedily to this set $S$. As our first greedy step, we consider the minimum-cost edge leaving node $s$, that is, $\min_{i \in V} c_{si}$. Let $v$ be a node on which this minimum is obtained. A key observation underlying Dijkstra's Algorithm is that the shortest path from $s$ to $v$ is the single-edge path $\{s, v\}$. Thus we can immediately add the node $v$ to the set $S$. The path $\{s, v\}$ is clearly the shortest to $v$ if there are no negative edge costs: any other path from $s$ to $v$ would have to start on an edge out of $s$ that is at least as expensive as edge $(s, v)$.

The above observation is no longer true if we can have negative edge costs. As suggested by the example in Figure 6.21(a), a path that starts on an expensive edge, but then compensates with subsequent edges of negative cost, can be cheaper than a path that starts on a cheap edge. This suggests that the Dijkstra-style greedy approach will not work here.

Another natural idea is to first modify the costs $c_{ij}$ by adding some large constant $M$ to each; that is, we let $c'_{ij} = c_{ij} + M$ for each edge $(i, j) \in E$. If the constant $M$ is large enough, then all modified costs are nonnegative, and we can use Dijkstra's Algorithm to find the minimum-cost path subject to costs $c'$. However, this approach fails to find the correct minimum-cost paths with respect to the original costs $c$. The problem here is that changing the costs from $c$ to $c'$ changes the minimum-cost path. For example (as in Figure 6.21(b)), if a path $P$ consisting of three edges is only slightly cheaper than another path $P'$ that has two edges, then after the change in costs, $P'$ will be cheaper, since we only add $2M$ to the cost of $P'$ while adding $3M$ to the cost of $P$.

*A Dynamic Programming Approach*   We will try to use dynamic programming to solve the problem of finding a shortest path from $s$ to $t$ when there are negative edge costs but no negative cycles. We could try an idea that has worked for us so far: subproblem $i$ could be to find a shortest path using only the first $i$ nodes. This idea does not immediately work, but it can be made to work with some effort. Here, however, we will discuss a simpler and more efficient solution, the *Bellman-Ford Algorithm*. The development of dynamic programming as a general algorithmic technique is often credited to the work of Bellman in the 1950's; and the Bellman-Ford Shortest-Path Algorithm was one of the first applications.

The dynamic programming solution we develop will be based on the following crucial observation.

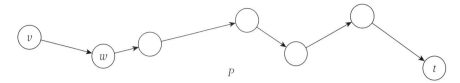

**Figure 6.22** The minimum-cost path $P$ from $v$ to $t$ using at most $i$ edges.

**(6.22)** *If G has no negative cycles, then there is a shortest path from s to t that is simple (i.e., does not repeat nodes), and hence has at most $n - 1$ edges.*

**Proof.** Since every cycle has nonnegative cost, the shortest path $P$ from $s$ to $t$ with the fewest number of edges does not repeat any vertex $v$. For if $P$ did repeat a vertex $v$, we could remove the portion of $P$ between consecutive visits to $v$, resulting in a path of no greater cost and fewer edges. ∎

Let's use $\text{OPT}(i, v)$ to denote the minimum cost of a $v$-$t$ path using at most $i$ edges. By (6.22), our original problem is to compute $\text{OPT}(n - 1, s)$. (We could instead design an algorithm whose subproblems correspond to the minimum cost of an $s$-$v$ path using at most $i$ edges. This would form a more natural parallel with Dijkstra's Algorithm, but it would not be as natural in the context of the routing protocols we discuss later.)

We now need a simple way to express $\text{OPT}(i, v)$ using smaller subproblems. We will see that the most natural approach involves the consideration of many different options; this is another example of the principle of "multi-way choices" that we saw in the algorithm for the Segmented Least Squares Problem.

Let's fix an optimal path $P$ representing $\text{OPT}(i, v)$ as depicted in Figure 6.22.

- If the path $P$ uses at most $i - 1$ edges, then $\text{OPT}(i, v) = \text{OPT}(i - 1, v)$.
- If the path $P$ uses $i$ edges, and the first edge is $(v, w)$, then $\text{OPT}(i, v) = c_{vw} + \text{OPT}(i - 1, w)$.

This leads to the following recursive formula.

**(6.23)** *If $i > 0$ then*

$$\text{OPT}(i, v) = \min(\text{OPT}(i - 1, v), \min_{w \in V}(\text{OPT}(i - 1, w) + c_{vw})).$$

Using this recurrence, we get the following dynamic programming algorithm to compute the value $\text{OPT}(n - 1, s)$.

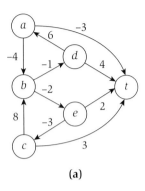

**(a)**

|   | 0 | 1 | 2 | 3 | 4 | 5 |
|---|---|---|---|---|---|---|
| $t$ | 0 | 0 | 0 | 0 | 0 | 0 |
| $a$ | ∞ | −3 | −3 | −4 | −6 | −6 |
| $b$ | ∞ | ∞ | 0 | −2 | −2 | −2 |
| $c$ | ∞ | 3 | 3 | 3 | 3 | 3 |
| $d$ | ∞ | 4 | 3 | 3 | 2 | 0 |
| $e$ | ∞ | 2 | 0 | 0 | 0 | 0 |

**(b)**

**Figure 6.23** For the directed graph in (a), the Shortest-Path Algorithm constructs the dynamic programming table in (b).

```
Shortest-Path(G, s, t)
   n = number of nodes in G
   Array M[0 ... n − 1, V]
   Define M[0, t] = 0 and M[0, v] = ∞ for all other v ∈ V
   For i = 1, ..., n − 1
      For v ∈ V in any order
         Compute M[i, v] using the recurrence (6.23)
      Endfor
   Endfor
   Return M[n − 1, s]
```

The correctness of the method follows directly by induction from (6.23). We can bound the running time as follows. The table $M$ has $n^2$ entries; and each entry can take $O(n)$ time to compute, as there are at most $n$ nodes $w \in V$ we have to consider.

**(6.24)** *The* Shortest-Path *method correctly computes the minimum cost of an s-t path in any graph that has no negative cycles, and runs in $O(n^3)$ time.*

Given the table $M$ containing the optimal values of the subproblems, the shortest path using at most $i$ edges can be obtained in $O(in)$ time, by tracing back through smaller subproblems.

As an example, consider the graph in Figure 6.23(a), where the goal is to find a shortest path from each node to $t$. The table in Figure 6.23(b) shows the array $M$, with entries corresponding to the values $M[i, v]$ from the algorithm. Thus a single row in the table corresponds to the shortest path from a particular node to $t$, as we allow the path to use an increasing number of edges. For example, the shortest path from node $d$ to $t$ is updated four times, as it changes from $d$-$t$, to $d$-$a$-$t$, to $d$-$a$-$b$-$e$-$t$, and finally to $d$-$a$-$b$-$e$-$c$-$t$.

### Extensions: Some Basic Improvements to the Algorithm

*An Improved Running-Time Analysis*   We can actually provide a better running-time analysis for the case in which the graph $G$ does not have too many edges. A directed graph with $n$ nodes can have close to $n^2$ edges, since there could potentially be an edge between each pair of nodes, but many graphs are much sparser than this. When we work with a graph for which the number of edges $m$ is significantly less than $n^2$, we've already seen in a number of cases earlier in the book that it can be useful to write the running-time in terms of both $m$ and $n$; this way, we can quantify our speed-up on graphs with relatively fewer edges.

If we are a little more careful in the analysis of the method above, we can improve the running-time bound to $O(mn)$ without significantly changing the algorithm itself.

**(6.25)** *The* `Shortest-Path` *method can be implemented in* $O(mn)$ *time.*

**Proof.** Consider the computation of the array entry $M[i, v]$ according to the recurrence (6.23); we have

$$M[i, v] = \min(M[i - 1, v], \min_{w \in V}(M[i - 1, w] + c_{vw})).$$

We assumed it could take up to $O(n)$ time to compute this minimum, since there are $n$ possible nodes $w$. But, of course, we need only compute this minimum over all nodes $w$ for which $v$ has an edge to $w$; let us use $n_v$ to denote this number. Then it takes time $O(n_v)$ to compute the array entry $M[i, v]$. We have to compute an entry for every node $v$ and every index $0 \leq i \leq n - 1$, so this gives a running-time bound of

$$O\left(n \sum_{v \in V} n_v\right).$$

In Chapter 3, we performed exactly this kind of analysis for other graph algorithms, and used (3.9) from that chapter to bound the expression $\sum_{v \in V} n_v$ for undirected graphs. Here we are dealing with directed graphs, and $n_v$ denotes the number of edges *leaving* $v$. In a sense, it is even easier to work out the value of $\sum_{v \in V} n_v$ for the directed case: each edge leaves exactly one of the nodes in $V$, and so each edge is counted exactly once by this expression. Thus we have $\sum_{v \in V} n_v = m$. Plugging this into our expression

$$O\left(n \sum_{v \in V} n_v\right)$$

for the running time, we get a running-time bound of $O(mn)$. ∎

***Improving the Memory Requirements*** We can also significantly improve the memory requirements with only a small change to the implementation. A common problem with many dynamic programming algorithms is the large space usage, arising from the $M$ array that needs to be stored. In the Bellman-Ford Algorithm as written, this array has size $n^2$; however, we now show how to reduce this to $O(n)$. Rather than recording $M[i, v]$ for each value $i$, we will use and update a single value $M[v]$ for each node $v$, the length of the shortest path from $v$ to $t$ that we have found so far. We still run the algorithm for iterations $i = 1, 2, \ldots, n - 1$, but the role of $i$ will now simply be as a counter; in each iteration, and for each node $v$, we perform the update

$$M[v] = \min(M[v], \min_{w \in V}(c_{vw} + M[w])).$$

We now observe the following fact.

**(6.26)**  *Throughout the algorithm $M[v]$ is the length of some path from $v$ to $t$, and after $i$ rounds of updates the value $M[v]$ is no larger than the length of the shortest path from $v$ to $t$ using at most $i$ edges.*

Given (6.26), we can then use (6.22) as before to show that we are done after $n - 1$ iterations. Since we are only storing an $M$ array that indexes over the nodes, this requires only $O(n)$ working memory.

**Finding the Shortest Paths**   One issue to be concerned about is whether this space-efficient version of the algorithm saves enough information to recover the shortest paths themselves. In the case of the Sequence Alignment Problem in the previous section, we had to resort to a tricky divide-and-conquer method to recover the solution from a similar space-efficient implementation. Here, however, we will be able to recover the shortest paths much more easily.

To help with recovering the shortest paths, we will enhance the code by having each node $v$ maintain the first node (after itself) on its path to the destination $t$; we will denote this first node by $first[v]$. To maintain $first[v]$, we update its value whenever the distance $M[v]$ is updated. In other words, whenever the value of $M[v]$ is reset to the minimum $\min_{w \in V}(c_{vw} + M[w])$, we set $first[v]$ to the node $w$ that attains this minimum.

Now let $P$ denote the directed "pointer graph" whose nodes are $V$, and whose edges are $\{(v, first[v])\}$. The main observation is the following.

**(6.27)**  *If the pointer graph $P$ contains a cycle $C$, then this cycle must have negative cost.*

**Proof.**  Notice that if $first[v] = w$ at any time, then we must have $M[v] \geq c_{vw} + M[w]$. Indeed, the left- and right-hand sides are equal after the update that sets $first[v]$ equal to $w$; and since $M[w]$ may decrease, this equation may turn into an inequality.

Let $v_1, v_2, \ldots, v_k$ be the nodes along the cycle $C$ in the pointer graph, and assume that $(v_k, v_1)$ is the last edge to have been added. Now, consider the values right before this last update. At this time we have $M[v_i] \geq c_{v_i v_{i+1}} + M[v_{i+1}]$ for all $i = 1, \ldots, k - 1$, and we also have $M[v_k] > c_{v_k v_1} + M[v_1]$ since we are about to update $M[v_k]$ and change $first[v_k]$ to $v_1$. Adding all these inequalities, the $M[v_i]$ values cancel, and we get $0 > \sum_{i=1}^{k-1} c_{v_i v_{i+1}} + c_{v_k v_1}$: a negative cycle, as claimed. ∎

Now note that if $G$ has no negative cycles, then (6.27) implies that the pointer graph $P$ will never have a cycle. For a node $v$, consider the path we get by following the edges in $P$, from $v$ to $first[v] = v_1$, to $first[v_1] = v_2$, and so forth. Since the pointer graph has no cycles, and the sink $t$ is the only node that has no outgoing edge, this path must lead to $t$. We claim that when the algorithm terminates, this is in fact a shortest path in $G$ from $v$ to $t$.

**(6.28)** *Suppose G has no negative cycles, and consider the pointer graph P at the termination of the algorithm. For each node v, the path in P from v to t is a shortest v-t path in G.*

**Proof.** Consider a node $v$ and let $w = first[v]$. Since the algorithm terminated, we must have $M[v] = c_{vw} + M[w]$. The value $M[t] = 0$, and hence the length of the path traced out by the pointer graph is exactly $M[v]$, which we know is the shortest-path distance. ■

Note that in the more space-efficient version of Bellman-Ford, the path whose length is $M[v]$ after $i$ iterations can have substantially more edges than $i$. For example, if the graph is a single path from $s$ to $t$, and we perform updates in the reverse of the order the edges appear on the path, then we get the final shortest-path values in just one iteration. This does not always happen, so we cannot claim a worst-case running-time improvement, but it would be nice to be able to use this fact opportunistically to speed up the algorithm on instances where it does happen. In order to do this, we need a stopping signal in the algorithm—something that tells us it's safe to terminate before iteration $n - 1$ is reached.

Such a stopping signal is a simple consequence of the following observation: If we ever execute a complete iteration $i$ in which *no $M[v]$ value changes*, then no $M[v]$ value will ever change again, since future iterations will begin with exactly the same set of array entries. Thus it is safe to stop the algorithm. Note that it is not enough for a *particular* $M[v]$ value to remain the same; in order to safely terminate, we need for all these values to remain the same for a single iteration.

## 6.9 Shortest Paths and Distance Vector Protocols

One important application of the Shortest-Path Problem is for routers in a communication network to determine the most efficient path to a destination. We represent the network using a graph in which the nodes correspond to routers, and there is an edge between $v$ and $w$ if the two routers are connected by a direct communication link. We define a cost $c_{vw}$ representing the delay on the link $(v, w)$; the Shortest-Path Problem with these costs is to determine the path with minimum delay from a source node $s$ to a destination $t$. Delays are naturally nonnegative, so one could use Dijkstra's Algorithm to compute the shortest path. However, Dijkstra's shortest-path computation requires global knowledge of the network: it needs to maintain a set $S$ of nodes for which shortest paths have been determined, and make a global decision about which node to add next to $S$. While routers can be made to run a protocol in the background that gathers enough global information to implement such an algorithm, it is often cleaner and more flexible to use algorithms that require only local knowledge of neighboring nodes.

If we think about it, the Bellman-Ford Algorithm discussed in the previous section has just such a "local" property. Suppose we let each node $v$ maintain its value $M[v]$; then to update this value, $v$ needs only obtain the value $M[w]$ from each neighbor $w$, and compute

$$\min_{w \in V}(c_{vw} + M[w])$$

based on the information obtained.

We now discuss an improvement to the Bellman-Ford Algorithm that makes it better suited for routers and, at the same time, a faster algorithm in practice. Our current implementation of the Bellman-Ford Algorithm can be thought of as a *pull-based* algorithm. In each iteration $i$, each node $v$ has to contact each neighbor $w$, and "pull" the new value $M[w]$ from it. If a node $w$ has not changed its value, then there is no need for $v$ to get the value again; however, $v$ has no way of knowing this fact, and so it must execute the pull anyway.

This wastefulness suggests a symmetric *push-based* implementation, where values are only transmitted when they change. Specifically, each node $w$ whose distance value $M[w]$ changes in an iteration informs all its neighbors of the new value in the next iteration; this allows them to update their values accordingly. If $M[w]$ has not changed, then the neighbors of $w$ already have the current value, and there is no need to "push" it to them again. This leads to savings in the running time, as not all values need to be pushed in each iteration. We also may terminate the algorithm early, if no value changes during an iteration. Here is a concrete description of the push-based implementation.

```
Push-Based-Shortest-Path(G, s, t)
  n = number of nodes in G
  Array M[V]
  Initialize M[t] = 0 and M[v] = ∞ for all other v ∈ V
  For i = 1, . . . , n − 1
    For w ∈ V in any order
      If M[w] has been updated in the previous iteration then
```

```
          For all edges (v, w) in any order
              M[v] = min(M[v], c_{vw} + M[w])
                  If this changes the value of M[v], then first[v] = w
              Endfor
      Endfor
      If no value changed in this iteration, then end the algorithm
  Endfor
  Return M[s]
```

In this algorithm, nodes are sent updates of their neighbors' distance values in rounds, and each node sends out an update in each iteration in which it has changed. However, if the nodes correspond to routers in a network, then we do not expect everything to run in lockstep like this; some routers may report updates much more quickly than others, and a router with an update to report may sometimes experience a delay before contacting its neighbors. Thus the routers will end up executing an *asynchronous* version of the algorithm: each time a node $w$ experiences an update to its $M[w]$ value, it becomes "active" and eventually notifies its neighbors of the new value. If we were to watch the behavior of all routers interleaved, it would look as follows.

```
Asynchronous-Shortest-Path(G, s, t)
  n = number of nodes in G
  Array M[V]
  Initialize M[t] = 0 and M[v] = ∞ for all other v ∈ V
  Declare t to be active and all other nodes inactive
  While there exists an active node
      Choose an active node w
          For all edges (v, w) in any order
              M[v] = min(M[v], c_{vw} + M[w])
                  If this changes the value of M[v], then
                      first[v] = w
                      v becomes active
              Endfor
          w becomes inactive
  EndWhile
```

One can show that even this version of the algorithm, with essentially no coordination in the ordering of updates, will converge to the correct values of the shortest-path distances to $t$, assuming only that each time a node becomes active, it eventually contacts its neighbors.

The algorithm we have developed here uses a single destination $t$, and all nodes $v \in V$ compute their shortest path to $t$. More generally, we are presumably interested in finding distances and shortest paths between all pairs of nodes in a graph. To obtain such distances, we effectively use $n$ separate computations, one for each destination. Such an algorithm is referred to as a *distance vector protocol*, since each node maintains a vector of distances to every other node in the network.

## Problems with the Distance Vector Protocol

One of the major problems with the distributed implementation of Bellman-Ford on routers (the protocol we have been discussing above) is that it's derived from an initial dynamic programming algorithm that assumes edge costs will remain constant during the execution of the algorithm. Thus far we've been designing algorithms with the tacit understanding that a program executing the algorithm will be running on a single computer (or a centrally managed set of computers), processing some specified input. In this context, it's a rather benign assumption to require that the input not change while the program is actually running. Once we start thinking about routers in a network, however, this assumption becomes troublesome. Edge costs may change for all sorts of reasons: links can become congested and experience slow-downs; or a link $(v, w)$ may even fail, in which case the cost $c_{vw}$ effectively increases to $\infty$.

Here's an indication of what can go wrong with our shortest-path algorithm when this happens. If an edge $(v, w)$ is deleted (say the link goes down), it is natural for node $v$ to react as follows: it should check whether its shortest path to some node $t$ used the edge $(v, w)$, and, if so, it should increase the distance using other neighbors. Notice that this increase in distance from $v$ can now trigger increases at $v$'s neighbors, if they were relying on a path through $v$, and these changes can cascade through the network. Consider the extremely simple example in Figure 6.24, in which the original graph has three edges $(s, v)$, $(v, s)$ and $(v, t)$, each of cost 1.

Now suppose the edge $(v, t)$ in Figure 6.24 is deleted. How does node $v$ react? Unfortunately, it does not have a global map of the network; it only knows the shortest-path distances of each of its neighbors to $t$. Thus it does

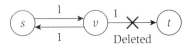

The deleted edge causes an unbounded sequence of updates by $s$ and $v$.

**Figure 6.24** When the edge $(v, t)$ is deleted, the distributed Bellman-Ford Algorithm will begin "counting to infinity."

not know that the deletion of $(v, t)$ has eliminated all paths from $s$ to $t$. Instead, it sees that $M[s] = 2$, and so it updates $M[v] = c_{vs} + M[s] = 3$, assuming that it will use its cost-1 edge to $s$, followed by the supposed cost-2 path from $s$ to $t$. Seeing this change, node $s$ will update $M[s] = c_{sv} + M[v] = 4$, based on its cost-1 edge to $v$, followed by the supposed cost-3 path from $v$ to $t$. Nodes $s$ and $v$ will continue updating their distance to $t$ until one of them finds an alternate route; in the case, as here, that the network is truly disconnected, these updates will continue indefinitely—a behavior known as the problem of *counting to infinity*.

To avoid this problem and related difficulties arising from the limited amount of information available to nodes in the Bellman-Ford Algorithm, the designers of network routing schemes have tended to move from distance vector protocols to more expressive *path vector protocols*, in which each node stores not just the distance and first hop of their path to a destination, but some representation of the entire path. Given knowledge of the paths, nodes can avoid updating their paths to use edges they know to be deleted; at the same time, they require significantly more storage to keep track of the full paths. In the history of the Internet, there has been a shift from distance vector protocols to path vector protocols; currently, the path vector approach is used in the *Border Gateway Protocol* (BGP) in the Internet core.

## * 6.10 Negative Cycles in a Graph

So far in our consideration of the Bellman-Ford Algorithm, we have assumed that the underlying graph has negative edge costs but no negative cycles. We now consider the more general case of a graph that may contain negative cycles.

### The Problem

There are two natural questions we will consider.

- How do we decide if a graph contains a negative cycle?
- How do we actually find a negative cycle in a graph that contains one?

The algorithm developed for finding negative cycles will also lead to an improved practical implementation of the Bellman-Ford Algorithm from the previous sections.

It turns out that the ideas we've seen so far will allow us to find negative cycles that have a path reaching a sink $t$. Before we develop the details of this, let's compare the problem of finding a negative cycle that can reach a given $t$ with the seemingly more natural problem of finding a negative cycle *anywhere* in the graph, regardless of its position related to a sink. It turns out that if we

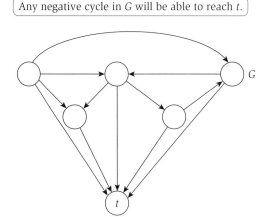

Figure 6.25    The augmented graph.

develop a solution to the first problem, we'll be able to obtain a solution to the second problem as well, in the following way. Suppose we start with a graph $G$, add a new node $t$ to it, and connect each other node $v$ in the graph to node $t$ via an edge of cost 0, as shown in Figure 6.25. Let us call the new "augmented graph" $G'$.

**(6.29)**    *The augmented graph $G'$ has a negative cycle $C$ such that there is a path from $C$ to the sink $t$ if and only if the original graph has a negative cycle.*

**Proof.**    Assume $G$ has a negative cycle. Then this cycle $C$ clearly has an edge to $t$ in $G'$, since all nodes have an edge to $t$.

Now suppose $G'$ has a negative cycle with a path to $t$. Since no edge leaves $t$ in $G'$, this cycle cannot contain $t$. Since $G'$ is the same as $G$ aside from the node $t$, it follows that this cycle is also a negative cycle of $G$.    ■

So it is really enough to solve the problem of deciding whether $G$ has a negative cycle that has a path to a given sink node $t$, and we do this now.

### Designing and Analyzing the Algorithm

To get started thinking about the algorithm, we begin by adopting the original version of the Bellman-Ford Algorithm, which was less efficient in its use of space. We first extend the definitions of $\text{OPT}(i, v)$ from the Bellman-Ford Algorithm, defining them for values $i \geq n$. With the presence of a negative cycle in the graph, (6.22) no longer applies, and indeed the shortest path may get shorter and shorter as we go around a negative cycle. In fact, for any node $v$ on a negative cycle that has a path to $t$, we have the following.

**(6.30)** *If node $v$ can reach node $t$ and is contained in a negative cycle, then*

$$\lim_{i \to \infty} \text{OPT}(i, v) = -\infty.$$

If the graph has no negative cycles, then (6.22) implies following statement.

**(6.31)** *If there are no negative cycles in $G$, then $\text{OPT}(i, v) = \text{OPT}(n - 1, v)$ for all nodes $v$ and all $i \geq n$.*

But for how large an $i$ do we have to compute the values $\text{OPT}(i, v)$ before concluding that the graph has no negative cycles? For example, a node $v$ may satisfy the equation $\text{OPT}(n, v) = \text{OPT}(n - 1, v)$, and yet still lie on a negative cycle. (Do you see why?) However, it turns out that we will be in good shape if this equation holds for all nodes.

**(6.32)** *There is no negative cycle with a path to $t$ if and only if $\text{OPT}(n, v) = \text{OPT}(n - 1, v)$ for all nodes $v$.*

**Proof.** Statement (6.31) has already proved the forward direction. For the other direction, we use an argument employed earlier for reasoning about when it's safe to stop the Bellman-Ford Algorithm early. Specifically, suppose $\text{OPT}(n, v) = \text{OPT}(n - 1, v)$ for all nodes $v$. The values of $\text{OPT}(n + 1, v)$ can be computed from $\text{OPT}(n, v)$; but all these values are the same as the corresponding $\text{OPT}(n - 1, v)$. It follows that we will have $\text{OPT}(n + 1, v) = \text{OPT}(n - 1, v)$. Extending this reasoning to future iterations, we see that none of the values will ever change again, that is, $\text{OPT}(i, v) = \text{OPT}(n - 1, v)$ for all nodes $v$ and all $i \geq n$. Thus there cannot be a negative cycle $C$ that has a path to $t$; for any node $w$ on this cycle $C$, (6.30) implies that the values $\text{OPT}(i, w)$ would have to become arbitrarily negative as $i$ increased. ∎

Statement (6.32) gives an $O(mn)$ method to decide if $G$ has a negative cycle that can reach $t$. We compute values of $\text{OPT}(i, v)$ for nodes of $G$ and for values of $i$ up to $n$. By (6.32), there is no negative cycle if and only if there is some value of $i \leq n$ at which $\text{OPT}(i, v) = \text{OPT}(i - 1, v)$ for all nodes $v$.

So far we have determined whether or not the graph has a negative cycle with a path from the cycle to $t$, but we have not actually found the cycle. To find a negative cycle, we consider a node $v$ such that $\text{OPT}(n, v) \neq \text{OPT}(n - 1, v)$: for this node, a path $P$ from $v$ to $t$ of cost $\text{OPT}(n, v)$ must use *exactly* $n$ edges. We find this minimum-cost path $P$ from $v$ to $t$ by tracing back through the subproblems. As in our proof of (6.22), a simple path can only have $n - 1$

edges, so $P$ must contain a cycle $C$. We claim that this cycle $C$ has negative cost.

**(6.33)** *If $G$ has $n$ nodes and $\text{OPT}(n, v) \neq \text{OPT}(n - 1, v)$, then a path $P$ from $v$ to $t$ of cost $\text{OPT}(n, v)$ contains a cycle $C$, and $C$ has negative cost.*

**Proof.** First observe that the path $P$ must have $n$ edges, as $\text{OPT}(n, v) \neq \text{OPT}(n - 1, v)$, and so every path using $n - 1$ edges has cost greater than that of the path $P$. In a graph with $n$ nodes, a path consisting of $n$ edges must repeat a node somewhere; let $w$ be a node that occurs on $P$ more than once. Let $C$ be the cycle on $P$ between two consecutive occurrences of node $w$. If $C$ were not a negative cycle, then deleting $C$ from $P$ would give us a $v$-$t$ path with fewer than $n$ edges and no greater cost. This contradicts our assumption that $\text{OPT}(n, v) \neq \text{OPT}(n - 1, v)$, and hence $C$ must be a negative cycle. ∎

**(6.34)** *The algorithm above finds a negative cycle in $G$, if such a cycle exists, and runs in $O(mn)$ time.*

### Extensions: Improved Shortest Paths and Negative Cycle Detection Algorithms

At the end of Section 6.8 we discussed a space-efficient implementation of the Bellman-Ford algorithm for graphs with no negative cycles. Here we implement the detection of negative cycles in a comparably space-efficient way. In addition to the savings in space, this will also lead to a considerable speedup in practice even for graphs with no negative cycles. The implementation will be based on the same pointer graph $P$ derived from the "first edges" $(v, first[v])$ that we used for the space-efficient implementation in Section 6.8. By (6.27), we know that if the pointer graph ever has a cycle, then the cycle has negative cost, and we are done. But if $G$ has a negative cycle, does this guarantee that the pointer graph will ever have a cycle? Furthermore, how much extra computation time do we need for periodically checking whether $P$ has a cycle?

Ideally, we would like to determine whether a cycle is created in the pointer graph $P$ every time we add a new edge $(v, w)$ with $first[v] = w$. An additional advantage of such "instant" cycle detection will be that we will not have to wait for $n$ iterations to see that the graph has a negative cycle: We can terminate as soon as a negative cycle is found. Earlier we saw that if a graph $G$ has no negative cycles, the algorithm can be stopped early if in some iteration the shortest path values $M[v]$ remain the same *for all nodes $v$*. Instant negative cycle detection will be an analogous early termination rule for graphs that have negative cycles.

Consider a new edge $(v, w)$, with $first[v] = w$, that is added to the pointer graph $P$. Before we add $(v, w)$ the pointer graph has no cycles, so it consists of paths from each node $v$ to the sink $t$. The most natural way to check whether adding edge $(v, w)$ creates a cycle in $P$ is to follow the current path from $w$ to the terminal $t$ in time proportional to the length of this path. If we encounter $v$ along this path, then a cycle has been formed, and hence, by (6.27), the graph has a negative cycle. Consider Figure 6.26, for example, where in both (a) and (b) the pointer $first[v]$ is being updated from $u$ to $w$; in (a), this does not result in a (negative) cycle, but in (b) it does. However, if we trace out the sequence of pointers from $v$ like this, then we could spend as much as $O(n)$ time following the path to $t$ and still not find a cycle. We now discuss a method that does not require an $O(n)$ blow-up in the running time.

We know that before the new edge $(v, w)$ was added, the pointer graph was a directed tree. Another way to test whether the addition of $(v, w)$ creates a cycle is to consider all nodes in the subtree directed toward $v$. If $w$ is in this subtree, then $(v, w)$ forms a cycle; otherwise it does not. (Again, consider the two sample cases in Figure 6.26.) To be able to find all nodes in the subtree directed toward $v$, we need to have each node $v$ maintain a list of all other nodes whose selected edges point to $v$. Given these pointers, we can find the subtree in time proportional to the size of the subtree pointing to $v$, at most $O(n)$ as before. However, here we will be able to make additional use of the work done. Notice that the current distance value $M[x]$ for all nodes $x$ in the subtree was derived from node $v$'s old value. We have just updated $v$'s distance, and hence we know that the distance values of all these nodes will be updated again. We'll mark each of these nodes $x$ as "dormant," delete the

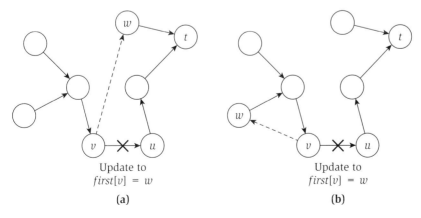

**Figure 6.26** Changing the pointer graph $P$ when $first[v]$ is updated from $u$ to $w$. In (b), this creates a (negative) cycle, whereas in (a) it does not.

edge $(x, first[x])$ from the pointer graph, and not use $x$ for future updates until its distance value changes.

This can save a lot of future work in updates, but what is the effect on the worst-case running time? We can spend as much as $O(n)$ extra time marking nodes dormant after every update in distances. However, a node can be marked dormant only if a pointer had been defined for it at some point in the past, so the time spent on marking nodes dormant is at most as much as the time the algorithm spends updating distances.

Now consider the time the algorithm spends on operations other than marking nodes dormant. Recall that the algorithm is divided into iterations, where iteration $i + 1$ processes nodes whose distance has been updated in iteration $i$. For the original version of the algorithm, we showed in (6.26) that after $i$ iterations, the value $M[v]$ is no larger than the value of the shortest path from $v$ to $t$ using at most $i$ edges. However, with many nodes dormant in each iteration, this may not be true anymore. For example, if the shortest path from $v$ to $t$ using at most $i$ edges starts on edge $e = (v, w)$, and $w$ is dormant in this iteration, then we may not update the distance value $M[v]$, and so it stays at a value higher than the length of the path through the edge $(v, w)$. This seems like a problem—however, in this case, the path through edge $(v, w)$ is not actually the shortest path, so $M[v]$ will have a chance to get updated later to an even smaller value.

So instead of the simpler property that held for $M[v]$ in the original versions of the algorithm, we now have the the following claim.

**(6.35)**    *Throughout the algorithm $M[v]$ is the length of some simple path from $v$ to $t$; the path has at least $i$ edges if the distance value $M[v]$ is updated in iteration $i$; and after $i$ iterations, the value $M[v]$ is the length of the shortest path for all nodes $v$ where there is a shortest $v$-$t$ path using at most $i$ edges.*

**Proof.** The *first* pointers maintain a tree of paths to $t$, which implies that all paths used to update the distance values are simple. The fact that updates in iteration $i$ are caused by paths with at least $i$ edges is easy to show by induction on $i$. Similarly, we use induction to show that after iteration $i$ the value $M[v]$ is the distance on all nodes $v$ where the shortest path from $v$ to $t$ uses at most $i$ edges. Note that nodes $v$ where $M[v]$ is the actual shortest-path distance cannot be dormant, as the value $M[v]$ will be updated in the next iteration for all dormant nodes.  ∎

Using this claim, we can see that the worst-case running time of the algorithm is still bounded by $O(mn)$: Ignoring the time spent on marking nodes dormant, each iteration is implemented in $O(m)$ time, and there can be at most $n - 1$ iterations that update values in the array $M$ without finding a negative cycle, as simple paths can have at most $n - 1$ edges. Finally, the time spent marking nodes dormant is bounded by the time spent on updates. We summarize the discussion with the following claim about the worst-case performance of the algorithm. In fact, as mentioned above, this new version is in practice the fastest implementation of the algorithm even for graphs that do not have negative cycles, or even negative-cost edges.

**(6.36)** *The improved algorithm outlined above finds a negative cycle in G if such a cycle exists. It terminates immediately if the pointer graph P of first[v] pointers contains a cycle C, or if there is an iteration in which no update occurs to any distance value M[v]. The algorithm uses O(n) space, has at most n iterations, and runs in O(mn) time in the worst case.*

# Solved Exercises

### Solved Exercise 1

Suppose you are managing the construction of billboards on the Stephen Daedalus Memorial Highway, a heavily traveled stretch of road that runs west-east for $M$ miles. The possible sites for billboards are given by numbers $x_1, x_2, \ldots, x_n$, each in the interval $[0, M]$ (specifying their position along the highway, measured in miles from its western end). If you place a billboard at location $x_i$, you receive a revenue of $r_i > 0$.

Regulations imposed by the county's Highway Department require that no two of the billboards be within less than or equal to 5 miles of each other. You'd like to place billboards at a subset of the sites so as to maximize your total revenue, subject to this restriction.

**Example.** Suppose $M = 20$, $n = 4$,

$$\{x_1, x_2, x_3, x_4\} = \{6, 7, 12, 14\},$$

and

$$\{r_1, r_2, r_3, r_4\} = \{5, 6, 5, 1\}.$$

Then the optimal solution would be to place billboards at $x_1$ and $x_3$, for a total revenue of 10.

Give an algorithm that takes an instance of this problem as input and returns the maximum total revenue that can be obtained from any valid subset of sites. The running time of the algorithm should be polynomial in $n$.

***Solution*** We can naturally apply dynamic programming to this problem if we reason as follows. Consider an optimal solution for a given input instance; in this solution, we either place a billboard at site $x_n$ or not. If we don't, the optimal solution on sites $x_1, \ldots, x_n$ is really the same as the optimal solution on sites $x_1, \ldots, x_{n-1}$; if we do, then we should eliminate $x_n$ and all other sites that are within 5 miles of it, and find an optimal solution on what's left. The same reasoning applies when we're looking at the problem defined by just the first $j$ sites, $x_1, \ldots, x_j$: we either include $x_j$ in the optimal solution or we don't, with the same consequences.

Let's define some notation to help express this. For a site $x_j$, we let $e(j)$ denote the easternmost site $x_i$ that is more than 5 miles from $x_j$. Since sites are numbered west to east, this means that the sites $x_1, x_2, \ldots, x_{e(j)}$ are still valid options once we've chosen to place a billboard at $x_j$, but the sites $x_{e(j)+1}, \ldots, x_{j-1}$ are not.

Now, our reasoning above justifies the following recurrence. If we let $\text{OPT}(j)$ denote the revenue from the optimal subset of sites among $x_1, \ldots, x_j$, then we have

$$\text{OPT}(j) = \max(r_j + \text{OPT}(e(j)), \text{OPT}(j-1)).$$

We now have most of the ingredients we need for a dynamic programming algorithm. First, we have a set of $n$ subproblems, consisting of the first $j$ sites for $j = 0, 1, 2, \ldots, n$. Second, we have a recurrence that lets us build up the solutions to subproblems, given by $\text{OPT}(j) = \max(r_j + \text{OPT}(e(j)), \text{OPT}(j-1))$.

To turn this into an algorithm, we just need to define an array $M$ that will store the $\text{OPT}$ values and throw a loop around the recurrence that builds up the values $M[j]$ in order of increasing $j$.

```
Initialize M[0]=0 and M[1]=r₁
For j=2,3,...,n:
   Compute M[j] using the recurrence
Endfor
Return M[n]
```

As with all the dynamic programming algorithms we've seen in this chapter, an optimal *set* of billboards can be found by tracing back through the values in array $M$.

Given the values $e(j)$ for all $j$, the running time of the algorithm is $O(n)$, since each iteration of the loop takes constant time. We can also compute all $e(j)$ values in $O(n)$ time as follows. For each site location $x_i$, we define $x_i' = x_i - 5$. We then merge the sorted list $x_1, \ldots, x_n$ with the sorted list $x_1', \ldots, x_n'$ in linear time, as we saw how to do in Chapter 2. We now scan through this merged list; when we get to the entry $x_j'$, we know that anything from this point onward to $x_j$ cannot be chosen together with $x_j$ (since it's within 5 miles), and so we simply define $e(j)$ to be the largest value of $i$ for which we've seen $x_i$ in our scan.

Here's a final observation on this problem. Clearly, the solution looks very much like that of the Weighted Interval Scheduling Problem, and there's a fundamental reason for that. In fact, our billboard placement problem can be directly encoded as an instance of Weighted Interval Scheduling, as follows. Suppose that for each site $x_i$, we define an interval with endpoints $[x_i - 5, x_i]$ and weight $r_i$. Then, given any nonoverlapping set of intervals, the corresponding set of sites has the property that no two lie within 5 miles of each other. Conversely, given any such set of sites (no two within 5 miles), the intervals associated with them will be nonoverlapping. Thus the collections of nonoverlapping intervals correspond precisely to the set of valid billboard placements, and so dropping the set of intervals we've just defined (with their weights) into an algorithm for Weighted Interval Scheduling will yield the desired solution.

## Solved Exercise 2

Through some friends of friends, you end up on a consulting visit to the cutting-edge biotech firm Clones 'R' Us (CRU). At first you're not sure how your algorithmic background will be of any help to them, but you soon find yourself called upon to help two identical-looking software engineers tackle a perplexing problem.

The problem they are currently working on is based on the *concatenation* of sequences of genetic material. If $X$ and $Y$ are each strings over a fixed alphabet $S$, then $XY$ denotes the string obtained by *concatenating* them— writing $X$ followed by $Y$. CRU has identified a *target sequence A* of genetic material, consisting of $m$ symbols, and they want to produce a sequence that is as similar to $A$ as possible. For this purpose, they have a library $\mathcal{L}$ consisting of $k$ (shorter) sequences, each of length at most $n$. They can cheaply produce any sequence consisting of copies of the strings in $\mathcal{L}$ concatenated together (with repetitions allowed).

Thus we say that a *concatenation* over $\mathcal{L}$ is any sequence of the form $B_1 B_2 \cdots B_\ell$, where each $B_i$ belongs the set $\mathcal{L}$. (Again, repetitions are allowed, so $B_i$ and $B_j$ could be the same string in $\mathcal{L}$, for different values of $i$ and $j$.) The problem is to find a concatenation over $\{B_i\}$ for which the sequence alignment cost is as small as possible. (For the purpose of computing the sequence alignment cost, you may assume that you are given a gap cost $\delta$ and a mismatch cost $\alpha_{pq}$ for each pair $p, q \in S$.)

Give a polynomial-time algorithm for this problem.

***Solution***    This problem is vaguely reminiscent of Segmented Least Squares: we have a long sequence of "data" (the string $A$) that we want to "fit" with shorter segments (the strings in $\mathcal{L}$).

If we wanted to pursue this analogy, we could search for a solution as follows. Let $B = B_1 B_2 \cdots B_\ell$ denote a concatenation over $\mathcal{L}$ that aligns as well as possible with the given string $A$. (That is, $B$ is an optimal solution to the input instance.) Consider an optimal alignment $M$ of $A$ with $B$, let $t$ be the first position in $A$ that is matched with some symbol in $B_\ell$, and let $A_\ell$ denote the substring of $A$ from position $t$ to the end. (See Figure 6.27 for an illustration of this with $\ell = 3$.) Now, the point is that in this optimal alignment $M$, the substring $A_\ell$ is optimally aligned with $B_\ell$; indeed, if there were a way to better align $A_\ell$ with $B_\ell$, we could substitute it for the portion of $M$ that aligns $A_\ell$ with $B_\ell$ and obtain a better overall alignment of $A$ with $B$.

This tells us that we can look at the optimal solution as follows. There's some final piece of $A_\ell$ that is aligned with one of the strings in $\mathcal{L}$, and for this piece all we're doing is finding the string in $\mathcal{L}$ that aligns with it as well as possible. Having found this optimal alignment for $A_\ell$, we can break it off and continue to find the optimal solution for the remainder of $A$.

Thinking about the problem this way doesn't tell us exactly how to proceed—we don't know how long $A_\ell$ is supposed to be, or which string in $\mathcal{L}$ it should be aligned with. But this is the kind of thing we can search over in a dynamic programming algorithm. Essentially, we're in about the same spot we were in with the Segmented Least Squares Problem: there we knew that we had to break off some final subsequence of the input points, fit them as well as possible with one line, and then iterate on the remaining input points.

So let's set up things to make the search for $A_\ell$ possible. First, let $A[x:y]$ denote the substring of $A$ consisting of its symbols from position $x$ to position $y$, inclusive. Let $c(x, y)$ denote the cost of the optimal alignment of $A[x:y]$ with any string in $\mathcal{L}$. (That is, we search over each string in $\mathcal{L}$ and find the one that

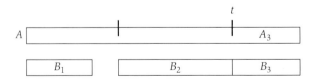

**Figure 6.27** In the optimal concatentation of strings to align with A, there is a final string ($B_3$ in the figure) that aligns with a substring of $A$ ($A_3$ in the figure) that extends from some position $t$ to the end.

aligns best with $A[x:y]$.) Let $\text{OPT}(j)$ denote the alignment cost of the optimal solution on the string $A[1:j]$.

The argument above says that an optimal solution on $A[1:j]$ consists of identifying a final "segment boundary" $t < j$, finding the optimal alignment of $A[t:j]$ with a single string in $\mathcal{L}$, and iterating on $A[1:t-1]$. The cost of this alignment of $A[t:j]$ is just $c(t,j)$, and the cost of aligning with what's left is just $\text{OPT}(t-1)$. This suggests that our subproblems fit together very nicely, and it justifies the following recurrence.

**(6.37)**    $\text{OPT}(j) = \min_{t < j} c(t,j) + \text{OPT}(t-1)$ *for $j \geq 1$, and* $\text{OPT}(0) = 0$.

The full algorithm consists of first computing the quantities $c(t,j)$, for $t < j$, and then building up the values $\text{OPT}(j)$ in order of increasing $j$. We hold these values in an array $M$.

```
Set  M[0] = 0
For all pairs  1 ≤ t ≤ j ≤ m
   Compute the cost  c(t, j) as follows:
   For each string  B ∈ L
      Compute the optimal alignment of  B with  A[t : j]
   Endfor
   Choose the  B that achieves the best alignment, and use
      this alignment cost as  c(t, j)
Endfor
For  j = 1, 2, . . . , n
   Use the recurrence (6.37) to compute  M[j]
Endfor
Return  M[n]
```

As usual, we can get a concatentation that achieves it by tracing back over the array of OPT values.

Let's consider the running time of this algorithm. First, there are $O(m^2)$ values $c(t,j)$ that need to be computed. For each, we try each string of the $k$ strings $B \in \mathcal{L}$, and compute the optimal alignment of $B$ with $A[t:j]$ in time $O(n(j-t)) = O(mn)$. Thus the total time to compute all $c(t,j)$ values is $O(km^3n)$.

This dominates the time to compute all OPT values: Computing $\text{OPT}(j)$ uses the recurrence in (6.37), and this takes $O(m)$ time to compute the minimum. Summing this over all choices of $j = 1, 2, \ldots, m$, we get $O(m^2)$ time for this portion of the algorithm.

# Exercises

1.  Let $G = (V, E)$ be an undirected graph with $n$ nodes. Recall that a subset
    of the nodes is called an *independent set* if no two of them are joined by
    an edge. Finding large independent sets is difficult in general; but here
    we'll see that it can be done efficiently if the graph is "simple" enough.

    Call a graph $G = (V, E)$ a *path* if its nodes can be written as $v_1, v_2, \ldots, v_n$,
    with an edge between $v_i$ and $v_j$ if and only if the numbers $i$ and $j$ differ by
    exactly 1. With each node $v_i$, we associate a positive integer *weight* $w_i$.

    Consider, for example, the five-node path drawn in Figure 6.28. The
    *weights* are the numbers drawn inside the nodes.

    The goal in this question is to solve the following problem:

    *Find an independent set in a path $G$ whose total weight is as large as possible.*

    **(a)**  Give an example to show that the following algorithm *does not* always
    find an independent set of maximum total weight.

    ```
    The "heaviest-first" greedy algorithm
       Start with S equal to the empty set
       While some node remains in G
          Pick a node vi of maximum weight
          Add vi to S
          Delete vi and its neighbors from G
       Endwhile
       Return S
    ```

    **(b)**  Give an example to show that the following algorithm also *does not*
    always find an independent set of maximum total weight.

    ```
    Let S1 be the set of all vi where i is an odd number
    Let S2 be the set of all vi where i is an even number
    (Note that S1 and S2 are both independent sets)
    Determine which of S1 or S2 has greater total weight,
       and return this one
    ```

**Figure 6.28** A paths with weights on the nodes. The maximum weight of an independent
set is 14.

**(c)** Give an algorithm that takes an $n$-node path $G$ with weights and returns an independent set of maximum total weight. The running time should be polynomial in $n$, independent of the values of the weights.

2. Suppose you're managing a consulting team of expert computer hackers, and each week you have to choose a job for them to undertake. Now, as you can well imagine, the set of possible jobs is divided into those that are *low-stress* (e.g., setting up a Web site for a class at the local elementary school) and those that are *high-stress* (e.g., protecting the nation's most valuable secrets, or helping a desperate group of Cornell students finish a project that has something to do with compilers). The basic question, each week, is whether to take on a low-stress job or a high-stress job.

If you select a low-stress job for your team in week $i$, then you get a revenue of $\ell_i > 0$ dollars; if you select a high-stress job, you get a revenue of $h_i > 0$ dollars. The catch, however, is that in order for the team to take on a high-stress job in week $i$, it's required that they do no job (of either type) in week $i - 1$; they need a full week of prep time to get ready for the crushing stress level. On the other hand, it's okay for them to take a low-stress job in week $i$ even if they have done a job (of either type) in week $i - 1$.

So, given a sequence of $n$ weeks, a *plan* is specified by a choice of "low-stress," "high-stress," or "none" for each of the $n$ weeks, with the property that if "high-stress" is chosen for week $i > 1$, then "none" has to be chosen for week $i - 1$. (It's okay to choose a high-stress job in week 1.) The *value* of the plan is determined in the natural way: for each $i$, you add $\ell_i$ to the value if you choose "low-stress" in week $i$, and you add $h_i$ to the value if you choose "high-stress" in week $i$. (You add 0 if you choose "none" in week $i$.)

**The problem.** Given sets of values $\ell_1, \ell_2, \ldots, \ell_n$ and $h_1, h_2, \ldots, h_n$, find a plan of maximum value. (Such a plan will be called *optimal*.)

**Example.** Suppose $n = 4$, and the values of $\ell_i$ and $h_i$ are given by the following table. Then the plan of maximum value would be to choose "none" in week 1, a high-stress job in week 2, and low-stress jobs in weeks 3 and 4. The value of this plan would be $0 + 50 + 10 + 10 = 70$.

|   | Week 1 | Week 2 | Week 3 | Week 4 |
|---|--------|--------|--------|--------|
| $\ell$ | 10 | 1 | 10 | 10 |
| h | 5 | 50 | 5 | 1 |

**(a)** Show that the following algorithm does not correctly solve this problem, by giving an instance on which it does not return the correct answer.

```
For iterations i = 1 to n
    If h_{i+1} > ℓ_i + ℓ_{i+1} then
        Output "Choose no job in week i"
        Output "Choose a high-stress job in week i+1"
        Continue with iteration i+2
    Else
        Output "Choose a low-stress job in week i"
        Continue with iteration i+1
    Endif
End
```

To avoid problems with overflowing array bounds, we define $h_i = \ell_i = 0$ when $i > n$.

In your example, say what the correct answer is and also what the above algorithm finds.

**(b)** Give an efficient algorithm that takes values for $\ell_1, \ell_2, \ldots, \ell_n$ and $h_1, h_2, \ldots, h_n$ and returns the *value* of an optimal plan.

3. Let $G = (V, E)$ be a directed graph with nodes $v_1, \ldots, v_n$. We say that $G$ is an *ordered graph* if it has the following properties.

(i) Each edge goes from a node with a lower index to a node with a higher index. That is, every directed edge has the form $(v_i, v_j)$ with $i < j$.

(ii) Each node except $v_n$ has at least one edge leaving it. That is, for every node $v_i$, $i = 1, 2, \ldots, n-1$, there is at least one edge of the form $(v_i, v_j)$.

The length of a path is the number of edges in it. The goal in this question is to solve the following problem (see Figure 6.29 for an example).

*Given an ordered graph G, find the length of the longest path that begins at $v_1$ and ends at $v_n$.*

**(a)** Show that the following algorithm does not correctly solve this problem, by giving an example of an ordered graph on which it does not return the correct answer.

```
Set w = v_1
Set L = 0
```

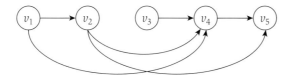

**Figure 6.29** The correct answer for this ordered graph is 3: The longest path from $v_1$ to $v_n$ uses the three edges $(v_1, v_2), (v_2, v_4)$, and $(v_4, v_5)$.

```
While there is an edge out of the node w
  Choose the edge (w, v_j)
      for which j is as small as possible
  Set w = v_j
  Increase L by 1
end while
Return L as the length of the longest path
```

In your example, say what the correct answer is and also what the algorithm above finds.

**(b)** Give an efficient algorithm that takes an ordered graph $G$ and returns the *length* of the longest path that begins at $v_1$ and ends at $v_n$. (Again, the *length* of a path is the number of edges in the path.)

4. Suppose you're running a lightweight consulting business—just you, two associates, and some rented equipment. Your clients are distributed between the East Coast and the West Coast, and this leads to the following question.

Each month, you can either run your business from an office in New York (NY) or from an office in San Francisco (SF). In month $i$, you'll incur an *operating cost* of $N_i$ if you run the business out of NY; you'll incur an operating cost of $S_i$ if you run the business out of SF. (It depends on the distribution of client demands for that month.)

However, if you run the business out of one city in month $i$, and then out of the other city in month $i + 1$, then you incur a fixed *moving cost* of $M$ to switch base offices.

Given a sequence of $n$ months, a *plan* is a sequence of $n$ locations—each one equal to either NY or SF—such that the $i^{\text{th}}$ location indicates the city in which you will be based in the $i^{\text{th}}$ month. The *cost* of a plan is the sum of the operating costs for each of the $n$ months, plus a moving cost of $M$ for each time you switch cities. The plan can begin in either city.

**The problem.** Given a value for the moving cost $M$, and sequences of operating costs $N_1, \ldots, N_n$ and $S_1, \ldots, S_n$, find a plan of minimum cost. (Such a plan will be called *optimal*.)

**Example.** Suppose $n = 4$, $M = 10$, and the operating costs are given by the following table.

|      | Month 1 | Month 2 | Month 3 | Month 4 |
|------|---------|---------|---------|---------|
| NY   | 1       | 3       | 20      | 30      |
| SF   | 50      | 20      | 2       | 4       |

Then the plan of minimum cost would be the sequence of locations

$$[NY, NY, SF, SF],$$

with a total cost of $1 + 3 + 2 + 4 + 10 = 20$, where the final term of 10 arises because you change locations once.

(a) Show that the following algorithm does not correctly solve this problem, by giving an instance on which it does not return the correct answer.

```
For i = 1 to n
   If N_i < S_i then
      Output "NY in Month i"
   Else
      Output "SF in Month i"
End
```

In your example, say what the correct answer is and also what the algorithm above finds.

(b) Give an example of an instance in which every optimal plan must move (i.e., change locations) at least three times.

Provide a brief explanation, saying why your example has this property.

(c) Give an efficient algorithm that takes values for $n$, $M$, and sequences of operating costs $N_1, \ldots, N_n$ and $S_1, \ldots, S_n$, and returns the *cost* of an optimal plan.

5. As some of you know well, and others of you may be interested to learn, a number of languages (including Chinese and Japanese) are written without spaces between the words. Consequently, software that works with text written in these languages must address the *word segmentation problem*—inferring likely boundaries between consecutive words in the

text. If English were written without spaces, the analogous problem would consist of taking a string like "meetateight" and deciding that the best segmentation is "meet at eight" (and not "me et at eight," or "meet ate ight," or any of a huge number of even less plausible alternatives). How could we automate this process?

A simple approach that is at least reasonably effective is to find a segmentation that simply maximizes the cumulative "quality" of its individual constituent words. Thus, suppose you are given a black box that, for any string of letters $x = x_1x_2 \cdots x_k$, will return a number $quality(x)$. This number can be either positive or negative; larger numbers correspond to more plausible English words. (So $quality(\text{"}me\text{"})$ would be positive, while $quality(\text{"}ght\text{"})$ would be negative.)

Given a long string of letters $y = y_1y_2 \cdots y_n$, a segmentation of $y$ is a partition of its letters into contiguous blocks of letters; each block corresponds to a word in the segmentation. The *total quality* of a segmentation is determined by adding up the qualities of each of its blocks. (So we'd get the right answer above provided that $quality(\text{"}meet\text{"}) + quality(\text{"}at\text{"}) + quality(\text{"}eight\text{"})$ was greater than the total quality of any other segmentation of the string.)

Give an efficient algorithm that takes a string $y$ and computes a segmentation of maximum total quality. (You can treat a single call to the black box computing $quality(x)$ as a single computational step.)

(*A final note, not necessary for solving the problem:* To achieve better performance, word segmentation software in practice works with a more complex formulation of the problem—for example, incorporating the notion that solutions should not only be reasonable at the word level, but also form coherent phrases and sentences. If we consider the example "theyouthevent," there are at least three valid ways to segment this into common English words, but one constitutes a much more coherent phrase than the other two. If we think of this in the terminology of formal languages, this broader problem is like searching for a segmentation that also can be parsed well according to a grammar for the underlying language. But even with these additional criteria and constraints, dynamic programming approaches lie at the heart of a number of successful segmentation systems.)

6. In a word processor, the goal of "pretty-printing" is to take text with a ragged right margin, like this,

```
Call me Ishmael.
Some years ago,
never mind how long precisely,
```

```
having little or no money in my purse,
and nothing particular to interest me on shore,
I thought I would sail about a little
and see the watery part of the world.
```

and turn it into text whose right margin is as "even" as possible, like this.

```
Call me Ishmael. Some years ago, never
mind how long precisely, having little
or no money in my purse, and nothing
particular to interest me on shore, I
thought I would sail about a little
and see the watery part of the world.
```

To make this precise enough for us to start thinking about how to write a pretty-printer for text, we need to figure out what it means for the right margins to be "even." So suppose our text consists of a sequence of *words*, $W = \{w_1, w_2, \ldots, w_n\}$, where $w_i$ consists of $c_i$ characters. We have a maximum line length of $L$. We will assume we have a fixed-width font and ignore issues of punctuation or hyphenation.

A *formatting* of $W$ consists of a partition of the words in $W$ into *lines*. In the words assigned to a single line, there should be a space after each word except the last; and so if $w_j, w_{j+1}, \ldots, w_k$ are assigned to one line, then we should have

$$\left\lceil \sum_{i=j}^{k-1}(c_i + 1) \right\rceil + c_k \leq L.$$

We will call an assignment of words to a line *valid* if it satisfies this inequality. The difference between the left-hand side and the right-hand side will be called the *slack* of the line—that is, the number of spaces left at the right margin.

Give an efficient algorithm to find a partition of a set of words $W$ into valid lines, so that the sum of the *squares* of the slacks of all lines (including the last line) is minimized.

7. As a solved exercise in Chapter 5, we gave an algorithm with $O(n \log n)$ running time for the following problem. We're looking at the price of a given stock over $n$ consecutive days, numbered $i = 1, 2, \ldots, n$. For each day $i$, we have a price $p(i)$ per share for the stock on that day. (We'll assume for simplicity that the price was fixed during each day.) We'd like to know: How should we choose a day $i$ on which to buy the stock and a later day $j > i$ on which to sell it, if we want to maximize the profit per

share, $p(j) - p(i)$? (If there is no way to make money during the $n$ days, we should conclude this instead.)

In the solved exercise, we showed how to find the optimal pair of days $i$ and $j$ in time $O(n \log n)$. But, in fact, it's possible to do better than this. Show how to find the optimal numbers $i$ and $j$ in time $O(n)$.

8. The residents of the underground city of Zion defend themselves through a combination of kung fu, heavy artillery, and efficient algorithms. Recently they have become interested in automated methods that can help fend off attacks by swarms of robots.

Here's what one of these robot attacks looks like.

- A swarm of robots arrives over the course of $n$ seconds; in the $i^{th}$ second, $x_i$ robots arrive. Based on remote sensing data, you know this sequence $x_1, x_2, \ldots, x_n$ in advance.

- You have at your disposal an *electromagnetic pulse* (EMP), which can destroy some of the robots as they arrive; the EMP's power depends on how long it's been allowed to charge up. To make this precise, there is a function $f(\cdot)$ so that if $j$ seconds have passed since the EMP was last used, then it is capable of destroying up to $f(j)$ robots.

- So specifically, if it is used in the $k^{th}$ second, and it has been $j$ seconds since it was previously used, then it will destroy $\min(x_k, f(j))$ robots. (After this use, it will be completely drained.)

- We will also assume that the EMP starts off completely drained, so if it is used for the first time in the $j^{th}$ second, then it is capable of destroying up to $f(j)$ robots.

**The problem.** Given the data on robot arrivals $x_1, x_2, \ldots, x_n$, and given the recharging function $f(\cdot)$, choose the points in time at which you're going to activate the EMP so as to destroy as many robots as possible.

**Example.** Suppose $n = 4$, and the values of $x_i$ and $f(i)$ are given by the following table.

| $i$ | 1 | 2 | 3 | 4 |
|-----|---|----|----|---|
| $x_i$ | 1 | 10 | 10 | 1 |
| $f(i)$ | 1 | 2 | 4 | 8 |

The best solution would be to activate the EMP in the $3^{rd}$ and the $4^{th}$ seconds. In the $3^{rd}$ second, the EMP has gotten to charge for 3 seconds, and so it destroys $\min(10, 4) = 4$ robots; In the $4^{th}$ second, the EMP has only gotten to charge for 1 second since its last use, and it destroys $\min(1, 1) = 1$ robot. This is a total of 5.

**(a)** Show that the following algorithm does not correctly solve this problem, by giving an instance on which it does not return the correct answer.

---

```
Schedule-EMP(x₁,  ...,  xₙ)
   Let j be the smallest number for which f(j) ≥ xₙ
      (If no such j exists then set j = n)
   Activate the EMP in the nth second
   If n - j ≥ 1 then
      Continue recursively on the input x₁,...,xₙ₋ⱼ
         (i.e., invoke Schedule-EMP(x₁,...,xₙ₋ⱼ))
```

---

In your example, say what the correct answer is and also what the algorithm above finds.

**(b)** Give an efficient algorithm that takes the data on robot arrivals $x_1, x_2, \ldots, x_n$, and the recharging function $f(\cdot)$, and returns the maximum number of robots that can be destroyed by a sequence of EMP activations.

9. You're helping to run a high-performance computing system capable of processing several terabytes of data per day. For each of $n$ days, you're presented with a quantity of data; on day $i$, you're presented with $x_i$ terabytes. For each terabyte you process, you receive a fixed revenue, but any unprocessed data becomes unavailable at the end of the day (i.e., you can't work on it in any future day).

You can't always process everything each day because you're constrained by the capabilities of your computing system, which can only process a fixed number of terabytes in a given day. In fact, it's running some one-of-a-kind software that, while very sophisticated, is not totally reliable, and so the amount of data you can process goes down with each day that passes since the most recent reboot of the system. On the first day after a reboot, you can process $s_1$ terabytes, on the second day after a reboot, you can process $s_2$ terabytes, and so on, up to $s_n$; we assume $s_1 > s_2 > s_3 > \cdots > s_n > 0$. (Of course, on day $i$ you can only process up to $x_i$ terabytes, regardless of how fast your system is.) To get the system back to peak performance, you can choose to reboot it; but on any day you choose to reboot the system, you can't process any data at all.

**The problem.** Given the amounts of available data $x_1, x_2, \ldots, x_n$ for the next $n$ days, and given the profile of your system as expressed by $s_1, s_2, \ldots, s_n$ (and starting from a freshly rebooted system on day 1), choose the days on which you're going to reboot so as to maximize the total amount of data you process.

**Example.** Suppose $n = 4$, and the values of $x_i$ and $s_i$ are given by the following table.

|   | Day 1 | Day 2 | Day 3 | Day 4 |
|---|-------|-------|-------|-------|
| $x$ | 10 | 1 | 7 | 7 |
| $s$ | 8 | 4 | 2 | 1 |

The best solution would be to reboot on day 2 only; this way, you process 8 terabytes on day 1, then 0 on day 2, then 7 on day 3, then 4 on day 4, for a total of 19. (Note that if you didn't reboot at all, you'd process $8 + 1 + 2 + 1 = 12$; and other rebooting strategies give you less than 19 as well.)

**(a)** Give an example of an instance with the following properties.
- There is a "surplus" of data in the sense that $x_i > s_1$ for every $i$.
- The optimal solution reboots the system at least twice.

In addition to the example, you should say what the optimal solution is. You do not need to provide a proof that it is optimal.

**(b)** Give an efficient algorithm that takes values for $x_1, x_2, \ldots, x_n$ and $s_1, s_2, \ldots, s_n$ and returns the total *number* of terabytes processed by an optimal solution.

**10.** You're trying to run a large computing job in which you need to simulate a physical system for as many discrete *steps* as you can. The lab you're working in has two large supercomputers (which we'll call $A$ and $B$) which are capable of processing this job. However, you're not one of the high-priority users of these supercomputers, so at any given point in time, you're only able to use as many spare cycles as these machines have available.

Here's the problem you face. Your job can only run on one of the machines in any given minute. Over each of the next $n$ minutes, you have a "profile" of how much processing power is available on each machine. In minute $i$, you would be able to run $a_i > 0$ steps of the simulation if your job is on machine $A$, and $b_i > 0$ steps of the simulation if your job is on machine $B$. You also have the ability to move your job from one machine to the other; but doing this costs you a minute of time in which no processing is done on your job.

So, given a sequence of $n$ minutes, a *plan* is specified by a choice of $A$, $B$, or "*move*" for each minute, with the property that choices $A$ and

$B$ cannot appear in consecutive minutes. For example, if your job is on machine $A$ in minute $i$, and you want to switch to machine $B$, then your choice for minute $i + 1$ must be *move*, and then your choice for minute $i + 2$ can be $B$. The *value* of a plan is the total number of steps that you manage to execute over the $n$ minutes: so it's the sum of $a_i$ over all minutes in which the job is on $A$, plus the sum of $b_i$ over all minutes in which the job is on $B$.

**The problem.** Given values $a_1, a_2, \ldots, a_n$ and $b_1, b_2, \ldots, b_n$, find a plan of maximum value. (Such a strategy will be called *optimal.*) Note that your plan can start with either of the machines $A$ or $B$ in minute 1.

**Example.** Suppose $n = 4$, and the values of $a_i$ and $b_i$ are given by the following table.

|   | Minute 1 | Minute 2 | Minute 3 | Minute 4 |
|---|----------|----------|----------|----------|
| A | 10 | 1 | 1 | 10 |
| B | 5 | 1 | 20 | 20 |

Then the plan of maximum value would be to choose $A$ for minute 1, then *move* for minute 2, and then $B$ for minutes 3 and 4. The value of this plan would be $10 + 0 + 20 + 20 = 50$.

**(a)** Show that the following algorithm does not correctly solve this problem, by giving an instance on which it does not return the correct answer.

```
In minute 1, choose the machine achieving the larger of a₁, b₁
Set i = 2
While i ≤ n
    What was the choice in minute i − 1?
    If A:
        If bᵢ₊₁ > aᵢ + aᵢ₊₁ then
            Choose move in minute i and B in minute i + 1
            Proceed to iteration i + 2
        Else
            Choose A in minute i
            Proceed to iteration i + 1
        Endif
    If B: behave as above with roles of A and B reversed
EndWhile
```

In your example, say what the correct answer is and also what the algorithm above finds.

**(b)** Give an efficient algorithm that takes values for $a_1, a_2, \ldots, a_n$ and $b_1, b_2, \ldots, b_n$ and returns the *value* of an optimal plan.

11. Suppose you're consulting for a company that manufactures PC equipment and ships it to distributors all over the country. For each of the next $n$ weeks, they have a projected *supply* $s_i$ of equipment (measured in pounds), which has to be shipped by an air freight carrier.

    Each week's supply can be carried by one of two air freight companies, A or B.

    - Company A charges a fixed rate $r$ per pound (so it costs $r \cdot s_i$ to ship a week's supply $s_i$).

    - Company B makes contracts for a fixed amount $c$ per week, independent of the weight. However, contracts with company B must be made in blocks of four consecutive weeks at a time.

    A *schedule*, for the PC company, is a choice of air freight company (A or B) for each of the $n$ weeks, with the restriction that company B, whenever it is chosen, must be chosen for blocks of four contiguous weeks at a time. The *cost* of the schedule is the total amount paid to company A and B, according to the description above.

    Give a polynomial-time algorithm that takes a sequence of supply values $s_1, s_2, \ldots, s_n$ and returns a *schedule* of minimum cost.

    **Example.** Suppose $r = 1$, $c = 10$, and the sequence of values is

    $$11, 9, 9, 12, 12, 12, 12, 9, 9, 11.$$

    Then the optimal schedule would be to choose company A for the first three weeks, then company B for a block of four consecutive weeks, and then company A for the final three weeks.

12. Suppose we want to replicate a file over a collection of $n$ servers, labeled $S_1, S_2, \ldots, S_n$. To place a copy of the file at server $S_i$ results in a *placement cost* of $c_i$, for an integer $c_i > 0$.

    Now, if a user requests the file from server $S_i$, and no copy of the file is present at $S_i$, then the servers $S_{i+1}, S_{i+2}, S_{i+3} \ldots$ are searched in order until a copy of the file is finally found, say at server $S_j$, where $j > i$. This results in an *access cost* of $j - i$. (Note that the lower-indexed servers $S_{i-1}, S_{i-2}, \ldots$ are not consulted in this search.) The access cost is 0 if $S_i$ holds a copy of the file. We will require that a copy of the file be placed at server $S_n$, so that all such searches will terminate, at the latest, at $S_n$.

We'd like to place copies of the files at the servers so as to minimize the sum of placement and access costs. Formally, we say that a *configuration* is a choice, for each server $S_i$ with $i = 1, 2, \ldots, n - 1$, of whether to place a copy of the file at $S_i$ or not. (Recall that a copy is always placed at $S_n$.) The *total cost* of a configuration is the sum of all placement costs for servers with a copy of the file, plus the sum of all access costs associated with all $n$ servers.

Give a polynomial-time algorithm to find a configuration of minimum total cost.

13. The problem of searching for cycles in graphs arises naturally in financial trading applications. Consider a firm that trades shares in $n$ different companies. For each pair $i \neq j$, they maintain a trade ratio $r_{ij}$, meaning that one share of $i$ trades for $r_{ij}$ shares of $j$. Here we allow the rate $r$ to be fractional; that is, $r_{ij} = \frac{2}{3}$ means that you can trade three shares of $i$ to get two shares of $j$.

A *trading cycle* for a sequence of shares $i_1, i_2, \ldots, i_k$ consists of successively trading shares in company $i_1$ for shares in company $i_2$, then shares in company $i_2$ for shares $i_3$, and so on, finally trading shares in $i_k$ back to shares in company $i_1$. After such a sequence of trades, one ends up with shares in the same company $i_1$ that one starts with. Trading around a cycle is usually a bad idea, as you tend to end up with fewer shares than you started with. But occasionally, for short periods of time, there are opportunities to increase shares. We will call such a cycle an *opportunity cycle*, if trading along the cycle increases the number of shares. This happens exactly if the product of the ratios along the cycle is above 1. In analyzing the state of the market, a firm engaged in trading would like to know if there are any opportunity cycles.

Give a polynomial-time algorithm that finds such an opportunity cycle, if one exists.

14. A large collection of mobile wireless devices can naturally form a network in which the devices are the nodes, and two devices $x$ and $y$ are connected by an edge if they are able to directly communicate with each other (e.g., by a short-range radio link). Such a network of wireless devices is a highly dynamic object, in which edges can appear and disappear over time as the devices move around. For instance, an edge $(x, y)$ might disappear as $x$ and $y$ move far apart from each other and lose the ability to communicate directly.

In a network that changes over time, it is natural to look for efficient ways of *maintaining* a path between certain designated nodes. There are two opposing concerns in maintaining such a path: we want paths that are short, but we also do not want to have to change the path frequently as the network structure changes. (That is, we'd like a single path to continue working, if possible, even as the network gains and loses edges.) Here is a way we might model this problem.

Suppose we have a set of mobile nodes $V$, and at a particular point in time there is a set $E_0$ of edges among these nodes. As the nodes move, the set of edges changes from $E_0$ to $E_1$, then to $E_2$, then to $E_3$, and so on, to an edge set $E_b$. For $i = 0, 1, 2, \ldots, b$, let $G_i$ denote the graph $(V, E_i)$. So if we were to watch the structure of the network on the nodes $V$ as a "time lapse," it would look precisely like the sequence of graphs $G_0, G_1, G_2, \ldots, G_{b-1}, G_b$. We will assume that each of these graphs $G_i$ is connected.

Now consider two particular nodes $s, t \in V$. For an $s$-$t$ path $P$ in one of the graphs $G_i$, we define the *length* of $P$ to be simply the number of edges in $P$, and we denote this $\ell(P)$. Our goal is to produce a sequence of paths $P_0, P_1, \ldots, P_b$ so that for each $i$, $P_i$ is an $s$-$t$ path in $G_i$. We want the paths to be relatively short. We also do not want there to be too many *changes*—points at which the identity of the path switches. Formally, we define $changes(P_0, P_1, \ldots, P_b)$ to be the number of indices $i$ ($0 \le i \le b - 1$) for which $P_i \ne P_{i+1}$.

Fix a constant $K > 0$. We define the *cost* of the sequence of paths $P_0, P_1, \ldots, P_b$ to be

$$cost(P_0, P_1, \ldots, P_b) = \sum_{i=0}^{b} \ell(P_i) + K \cdot changes(P_0, P_1, \ldots, P_b).$$

(a) Suppose it is possible to choose a single path $P$ that is an $s$-$t$ path in each of the graphs $G_0, G_1, \ldots, G_b$. Give a polynomial-time algorithm to find the shortest such path.

(b) Give a polynomial-time algorithm to find a sequence of paths $P_0, P_1, \ldots, P_b$ of minimum cost, where $P_i$ is an $s$-$t$ path in $G_i$ for $i = 0, 1, \ldots, b$.

15. On most clear days, a group of your friends in the Astronomy Department gets together to plan out the astronomical events they're going to try observing that night. We'll make the following assumptions about the events.

- There are $n$ events, which for simplicity we'll assume occur in sequence separated by exactly one minute each. Thus event $j$ occurs at minute $j$; if they don't observe this event at exactly minute $j$, then they miss out on it.

- The sky is mapped according to a one-dimensional coordinate system (measured in degrees from some central baseline); event $j$ will be taking place at coordinate $d_j$, for some integer value $d_j$. The telescope starts at coordinate 0 at minute 0.

- The last event, $n$, is much more important than the others; so it is required that they observe event $n$.

The Astronomy Department operates a large telescope that can be used for viewing these events. Because it is such a complex instrument, it can only move at a rate of one degree per minute. Thus they do not expect to be able to observe all $n$ events; they just want to observe as many as possible, limited by the operation of the telescope and the requirement that event $n$ must be observed.

We say that a subset $S$ of the events is *viewable* if it is possible to observe each event $j \in S$ at its appointed time $j$, and the telescope has adequate time (moving at its maximum of one degree per minute) to move between consecutive events in $S$.

**The problem.** Given the coordinates of each of the $n$ events, find a viewable subset of maximum size, subject to the requirement that it should contain event $n$. Such a solution will be called *optimal*.

**Example.** Suppose the one-dimensional coordinates of the events are as shown here.

| Event | 1 | 2 | 3 | 4 | 5 | 6 | 7 | 8 | 9 |
|---|---|---|---|---|---|---|---|---|---|
| Coordinate | 1 | −4 | −1 | 4 | 5 | −4 | 6 | 7 | −2 |

Then the optimal solution is to observe events 1, 3, 6, 9. Note that the telescope has time to move from one event in this set to the next, even moving at one degree per minute.

(a) Show that the following algorithm does not correctly solve this problem, by giving an instance on which it does not return the correct answer.

```
Mark all events j with |d_n - d_j| > n - j as illegal (as
   observing them would prevent you from observing event n)
Mark all other events as legal
Initialize current position to coordinate 0 at minute 0
While not at end of event sequence
   Find the earliest legal event j that can be reached without
      exceeding the maximum movement rate of the telescope
   Add j to the set S
```

```
    Update current position to be coord.~$d_j$ at minute $j$
Endwhile
Output the set $S$
```

In your example, say what the correct answer is and also what the algorithm above finds.

**(b)** Give an efficient algorithm that takes values for the coordinates $d_1, d_2, \ldots, d_n$ of the events and returns the *size* of an optimal solution.

16. There are many sunny days in Ithaca, New York; but this year, as it happens, the spring ROTC picnic at Cornell has fallen on a rainy day. The ranking officer decides to postpone the picnic and must notify everyone by phone. Here is the mechanism she uses to do this.

Each ROTC person on campus except the ranking officer reports to a unique *superior officer*. Thus the reporting hierarchy can be described by a tree $T$, rooted at the ranking officer, in which each other node $v$ has a parent node $u$ equal to his or her superior officer. Conversely, we will call $v$ a *direct subordinate* of $u$. See Figure 6.30, in which A is the ranking officer, B and D are the direct subordinates of A, and C is the direct subordinate of B.

To notify everyone of the postponement, the ranking officer first calls each of her direct subordinates, one at a time. As soon as each subordinate gets the phone call, he or she must notify each of his or her direct subordinates, one at a time. The process continues this way until everyone has been notified. Note that each person in this process can only call direct subordinates on the phone; for example, in Figure 6.30, A would not be allowed to call C.

We can picture this process as being divided into *rounds*. In one round, each person who has already learned of the postponement can call one of his or her direct subordinates on the phone. The number of rounds it takes for everyone to be notified depends on the sequence in which each person calls their direct subordinates. For example, in Figure 6.30, it will take only two rounds if A starts by calling B, but it will take three rounds if A starts by calling D.

Give an efficient algorithm that determines the minimum number of rounds needed for everyone to be notified, and outputs a sequence of phone calls that achieves this minimum number of rounds.

17. Your friends have been studying the closing prices of tech stocks, looking for interesting patterns. They've defined something called a *rising trend*, as follows.

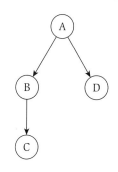

A should call B before D.

**Figure 6.30** A hierarchy with four people. The fastest broadcast scheme is for A to call B in the first round. In the second round, A calls D and B calls C. If A were to call D first, then C could not learn the news until the third round.

They have the closing price for a given stock recorded for $n$ days in succession; let these prices be denoted $P[1], P[2], \ldots, P[n]$. A *rising trend* in these prices is a subsequence of the prices $P[i_1], P[i_2], \ldots, P[i_k]$, for days $i_1 < i_2 < \ldots < i_k$, so that

- $i_1 = 1$, and
- $P[i_j] < P[i_{j+1}]$ for each $j = 1, 2, \ldots, k - 1$.

Thus a rising trend is a subsequence of the days—beginning on the first day and not necessarily contiguous—so that the price strictly increases over the days in this subsequence.

They are interested in finding the longest rising trend in a given sequence of prices.

**Example.** Suppose $n = 7$, and the sequence of prices is

$$10, 1, 2, 11, 3, 4, 12.$$

Then the longest rising trend is given by the prices on days 1, 4, and 7. Note that days 2, 3, 5, and 6 consist of increasing prices; but because this subsequence does not begin on day 1, it does not fit the definition of a rising trend.

(a) Show that the following algorithm does not correctly return the *length* of the longest rising trend, by giving an instance on which it fails to return the correct answer.

```
Define i = 1
       L = 1
For j = 2 to n
  If  P[j] > P[i] then
     Set i = j.
     Add 1 to L
  Endif
Endfor
```

In your example, give the actual length of the longest rising trend, and say what the algorithm above returns.

(b) Give an efficient algorithm that takes a sequence of prices $P[1], P[2], \ldots, P[n]$ and returns the *length* of the longest rising trend.

18. Consider the sequence alignment problem over a four-letter alphabet $\{z_1, z_2, z_3, z_4\}$, with a given gap cost and given mismatch costs. Assume that each of these parameters is a positive integer.

Suppose you are given two strings $A = a_1a_2 \cdots a_m$ and $B = b_1b_2 \cdots b_n$ and a proposed alignment between them. Give an $O(mn)$ algorithm to decide whether this alignment is the *unique* minimum-cost alignment between $A$ and $B$.

19. You're consulting for a group of people (who would prefer not to be mentioned here by name) whose jobs consist of monitoring and analyzing electronic signals coming from ships in coastal Atlantic waters. They want a fast algorithm for a basic primitive that arises frequently: "untangling" a superposition of two known signals. Specifically, they're picturing a situation in which each of two ships is emitting a short sequence of 0s and 1s over and over, and they want to make sure that the signal they're hearing is simply an *interleaving* of these two emissions, with nothing extra added in.

    This describes the whole problem; we can make it a little more explicit as follows. Given a string $x$ consisting of 0s and 1s, we write $x^k$ to denote $k$ copies of $x$ concatenated together. We say that a string $x'$ is a *repetition* of $x$ if it is a prefix of $x^k$ for some number $k$. So $x' = 10110110110$ is a repetition of $x = 101$.

    We say that a string $s$ is an *interleaving* of $x$ and $y$ if its symbols can be partitioned into two (not necessarily contiguous) subsequences $s'$ and $s''$, so that $s'$ is a repetition of $x$ and $s''$ is a repetition of $y$. (So each symbol in $s$ must belong to exactly one of $s'$ or $s''$.) For example, if $x = 101$ and $y = 00$, then $s = 100010101$ is an interleaving of $x$ and $y$, since characters 1,2,5,7,8,9 form 101101—a repetition of $x$—and the remaining characters 3,4,6 form 000—a repetition of $y$.

    In terms of our application, $x$ and $y$ are the repeating sequences from the two ships, and $s$ is the signal we're listening to: We want to make sure $s$ "unravels" into simple repetitions of $x$ and $y$. Give an efficient algorithm that takes strings $s$, $x$, and $y$ and decides if $s$ is an interleaving of $x$ and $y$.

20. Suppose it's nearing the end of the semester and you're taking $n$ courses, each with a final project that still has to be done. Each project will be graded on the following scale: It will be assigned an integer number on a scale of 1 to $g > 1$, higher numbers being better grades. Your goal, of course, is to maximize your average grade on the $n$ projects.

    You have a total of $H > n$ hours in which to work on the $n$ projects cumulatively, and you want to decide how to divide up this time. For simplicity, assume $H$ is a positive integer, and you'll spend an integer number of hours on each project. To figure out how best to divide up your time, you've come up with a set of functions $\{f_i : i = 1, 2, \ldots, n\}$ (rough estimates, of course) for each of your $n$ courses; if you spend $h \leq H$ hours on the project for course $i$, you'll get a grade of $f_i(h)$. (You may assume that the functions $f_i$ are *nondecreasing*: if $h < h'$, then $f_i(h) \leq f_i(h')$.)

So the problem is: Given these functions $\{f_i\}$, decide how many hours to spend on each project (in integer values only) so that your average grade, as computed according to the $f_i$, is as large as possible. In order to be efficient, the running time of your algorithm should be polynomial in $n$, $g$, and $H$; none of these quantities should appear as an exponent in your running time.

21. Some time back, you helped a group of friends who were doing simulations for a computation-intensive investment company, and they've come back to you with a new problem. They're looking at $n$ consecutive days of a given stock, at some point in the past. The days are numbered $i = 1, 2, \ldots, n$; for each day $i$, they have a price $p(i)$ per share for the stock on that day.

For certain (possibly large) values of $k$, they want to study what they call $k$-*shot strategies*. A $k$-shot strategy is a collection of $m$ pairs of days $(b_1, s_1), \ldots, (b_m, s_m)$, where $0 \leq m \leq k$ and

$$1 \leq b_1 < s_1 < b_2 < s_2 \cdots < b_m < s_m \leq n.$$

We view these as a set of up to $k$ nonoverlapping intervals, during each of which the investors buy 1,000 shares of the stock (on day $b_i$) and then sell it (on day $s_i$). The *return* of a given $k$-shot strategy is simply the profit obtained from the $m$ buy-sell transactions, namely,

$$1{,}000 \sum_{i=1}^{m} p(s_i) - p(b_i).$$

The investors want to assess the value of $k$-shot strategies by running simulations on their $n$-day trace of the stock price. Your goal is to design an efficient algorithm that determines, given the sequence of prices, the $k$-shot strategy with the maximum possible return. Since $k$ may be relatively large in these simulations, your running time should be polynomial in both $n$ and $k$; it should not contain $k$ in the exponent.

22. To assess how "well-connected" two nodes in a directed graph are, one can not only look at the length of the shortest path between them, but can also count the *number* of shortest paths.

This turns out to be a problem that can be solved efficiently, subject to some restrictions on the edge costs. Suppose we are given a directed graph $G = (V, E)$, with costs on the edges; the costs may be positive or negative, but every cycle in the graph has strictly positive cost. We are also given two nodes $v, w \in V$. Give an efficient algorithm that computes the number of shortest $v$-$w$ paths in $G$. (The algorithm should not list all the paths; just the number suffices.)

23. Suppose you are given a directed graph $G = (V, E)$ with costs on the edges $c_e$ for $e \in E$ and a sink $t$ (costs may be negative). Assume that you also have finite values $d(v)$ for $v \in V$. Someone claims that, for each node $v \in V$, the quantity $d(v)$ is the cost of the minimum-cost path from node $v$ to the sink $t$.

    (a) Give a linear-time algorithm (time $O(m)$ if the graph has $m$ edges) that verifies whether this claim is correct.

    (b) Assume that the distances are correct, and $d(v)$ is finite for all $v \in V$. Now you need to compute distances to a different sink $t'$. Give an $O(m \log n)$ algorithm for computing distances $d'(v)$ for all nodes $v \in V$ to the sink node $t'$. (*Hint:* It is useful to consider a new cost function defined as follows: for edge $e = (v, w)$, let $c'_e = c_e - d(v) + d(w)$. Is there a relation between costs of paths for the two different costs $c$ and $c'$?)

24. *Gerrymandering* is the practice of carving up electoral districts in very careful ways so as to lead to outcomes that favor a particular political party. Recent court challenges to the practice have argued that through this calculated redistricting, large numbers of voters are being effectively (and intentionally) disenfranchised.

    Computers, it turns out, have been implicated as the source of some of the "villainy" in the news coverage on this topic: Thanks to powerful software, gerrymandering has changed from an activity carried out by a bunch of people with maps, pencil, and paper into the industrial-strength process that it is today. Why is gerrymandering a computational problem? There are database issues involved in tracking voter demographics down to the level of individual streets and houses; and there are algorithmic issues involved in grouping voters into districts. Let's think a bit about what these latter issues look like.

    Suppose we have a set of $n$ *precincts* $P_1, P_2, \ldots, P_n$, each containing $m$ registered voters. We're supposed to divide these precincts into two *districts*, each consisting of $n/2$ of the precincts. Now, for each precinct, we have information on how many voters are registered to each of two political parties. (Suppose, for simplicity, that every voter is registered to one of these two.) We'll say that the set of precincts is *susceptible* to gerrymandering if it is possible to perform the division into two districts in such a way that the same party holds a majority in both districts.

Give an algorithm to determine whether a given set of precincts is susceptible to gerrymandering; the running time of your algorithm should be polynomial in $n$ and $m$.

**Example.** Suppose we have $n = 4$ precincts, and the following information on registered voters.

| Precinct | 1 | 2 | 3 | 4 |
|---|---|---|---|---|
| Number registered for party A | 55 | 43 | 60 | 47 |
| Number registered for party B | 45 | 57 | 40 | 53 |

This set of precincts is susceptible since, if we grouped precincts 1 and 4 into one district, and precincts 2 and 3 into the other, then party A would have a majority in both districts. (Presumably, the "we" who are doing the grouping here are members of party A.) This example is a quick illustration of the basic unfairness in gerrymandering: Although party A holds only a slim majority in the overall population (205 to 195), it ends up with a majority in not one but both districts.

25. Consider the problem faced by a stockbroker trying to sell a large number of shares of stock in a company whose stock price has been steadily falling in value. It is always hard to predict the right moment to sell stock, but owning a lot of shares in a single company adds an extra complication: the mere act of selling many shares in a single day will have an adverse effect on the price.

Since future market prices, and the effect of large sales on these prices, are very hard to predict, brokerage firms use models of the market to help them make such decisions. In this problem, we will consider the following simple model. Suppose we need to sell $x$ shares of stock in a company, and suppose that we have an accurate model of the market: it predicts that the stock price will take the values $p_1, p_2, \ldots, p_n$ over the next $n$ days. Moreover, there is a function $f(\cdot)$ that predicts the effect of large sales: if we sell $y$ shares on a single day, it will permanently decrease the price by $f(y)$ from that day onward. So, if we sell $y_1$ shares on day 1, we obtain a price per share of $p_1 - f(y_1)$, for a total income of $y_1 \cdot (p_1 - f(y_1))$. Having sold $y_1$ shares on day 1, we can then sell $y_2$ shares on day 2 for a price per share of $p_2 - f(y_1) - f(y_2)$; this yields an additional income of $y_2 \cdot (p_2 - f(y_1) - f(y_2))$. This process continues over all $n$ days. (Note, as in our calculation for day 2, that the decreases from earlier days are absorbed into the prices for all later days.)

Design an efficient algorithm that takes the prices $p_1, \ldots, p_n$ and the function $f(\cdot)$ (written as a list of values $f(1), f(2), \ldots, f(x)$) and determines the best way to sell $x$ shares by day $n$. In other words, find natural numbers $y_1, y_2, \ldots, y_n$ so that $x = y_1 + \ldots + y_n$, and selling $y_i$ shares on day $i$ for $i = 1, 2, \ldots, n$ maximizes the total income achievable. You should assume that the share value $p_i$ is monotone decreasing, and $f(\cdot)$ is monotone increasing; that is, selling a larger number of shares causes a larger drop in the price. Your algorithm's running time can have a polynomial dependence on $n$ (the number of days), $x$ (the number of shares), and $p_1$ (the peak price of the stock).

**Example** Consider the case when $n = 3$; the prices for the three days are $90, 80, 40$; and $f(y) = 1$ for $y \leq 40{,}000$ and $f(y) = 20$ for $y > 40{,}000$. Assume you start with $x = 100{,}000$ shares. Selling all of them on day 1 would yield a price of 70 per share, for a total income of 7,000,000. On the other hand, selling 40,000 shares on day 1 yields a price of 89 per share, and selling the remaining 60,000 shares on day 2 results in a price of 59 per share, for a total income of 7,100,000.

26. Consider the following inventory problem. You are running a company that sells some large product (let's assume you sell trucks), and predictions tell you the quantity of sales to expect over the next $n$ months. Let $d_i$ denote the number of sales you expect in month $i$. We'll assume that all sales happen at the beginning of the month, and trucks that are not sold are *stored* until the beginning of the next month. You can store at most $S$ trucks, and it costs $C$ to store a single truck for a month. You receive shipments of trucks by placing orders for them, and there is a fixed ordering fee of $K$ each time you place an order (regardless of the number of trucks you order). You start out with no trucks. The problem is to design an algorithm that decides how to place orders so that you satisfy all the demands $\{d_i\}$, and minimize the costs. In summary:

    - There are two parts to the cost: (1) storage—it costs $C$ for every truck on hand that is not needed that month; (2) ordering fees—it costs $K$ for every order placed.

    - In each month you need enough trucks to satisfy the demand $d_i$, but the number left over after satisfying the demand for the month should not exceed the inventory limit $S$.

    Give an algorithm that solves this problem in time that is polynomial in $n$ and $S$.

27. The owners of an independently operated gas station are faced with the following situation. They have a large underground tank in which they store gas; the tank can hold up to $L$ gallons at one time. Ordering gas is quite expensive, so they want to order relatively rarely. For each order,

they need to pay a fixed price $P$ for delivery in addition to the cost of the gas ordered. However, it costs $c$ to store a gallon of gas for an extra day, so ordering too much ahead increases the storage cost.

They are planning to close for a week in the winter, and they want their tank to be empty by the time they close. Luckily, based on years of experience, they have accurate projections for how much gas they will need each day until this point in time. Assume that there are $n$ days left until they close, and they need $g_i$ gallons of gas for each of the days $i = 1, \ldots, n$. Assume that the tank is empty at the end of day 0. Give an algorithm to decide on which days they should place orders, and how much to order so as to minimize their total cost.

28. Recall the scheduling problem from Section 4.2 in which we sought to minimize the maximum lateness. There are $n$ jobs, each with a deadline $d_i$ and a required processing time $t_i$, and all jobs are available to be scheduled starting at time $s$. For a job $i$ to be done, it needs to be assigned a period from $s_i \geq s$ to $f_i = s_i + t_i$, and different jobs should be assigned nonoverlapping intervals. As usual, such an assignment of times will be called a *schedule*.

In this problem, we consider the same setup, but want to optimize a different objective. In particular, we consider the case in which each job must either be done by its deadline or not at all. We'll say that a subset $J$ of the jobs is *schedulable* if there is a schedule for the jobs in $J$ so that each of them finishes by its deadline. Your problem is to select a schedulable subset of maximum possible size and give a schedule for this subset that allows each job to finish by its deadline.

(a) Prove that there is an optimal solution $J$ (i.e., a schedulable set of maximum size) in which the jobs in $J$ are scheduled in increasing order of their deadlines.

(b) Assume that all deadlines $d_i$ and required times $t_i$ are integers. Give an algorithm to find an optimal solution. Your algorithm should run in time polynomial in the number of jobs $n$, and the maximum deadline $D = \max_i d_i$.

29. Let $G = (V, E)$ be a graph with $n$ nodes in which each pair of nodes is joined by an edge. There is a positive weight $w_{ij}$ on each edge $(i, j)$; and we will assume these weights satisfy the *triangle inequality* $w_{ik} \leq w_{ij} + w_{jk}$. For a subset $V' \subseteq V$, we will use $G[V']$ to denote the subgraph (with edge weights) induced on the nodes in $V'$.

We are given a set $X \subseteq V$ of $k$ *terminals* that must be connected by edges. We say that a *Steiner tree* on $X$ is a set $Z$ so that $X \subseteq Z \subseteq V$, together with a spanning subtree $T$ of $G[Z]$. The *weight* of the Steiner tree is the weight of the tree $T$.

Show that there is function $f(\cdot)$ and a *polynomial function* $p(\cdot)$ so that the problem of finding a minimum-weight Steiner tree on $X$ can be solved in time $O(f(k) \cdot p(n))$.

# Notes and Further Reading

Richard Bellman is credited with pioneering the systematic study of dynamic programming (Bellman 1957); the algorithm in this chapter for segmented least squares is based on Bellman's work from this early period (Bellman 1961). Dynamic programming has since grown into a technique that is widely used across computer science, operations research, control theory, and a number of other areas. Much of the recent work on this topic has been concerned with *stochastic dynamic programming*: Whereas our problem formulations tended to tacitly assume that all input is known at the outset, many problems in scheduling, production and inventory planning, and other domains involve uncertainty, and dynamic programming algorithms for these problems encode this uncertainty using a probabilistic formulation. The book by Ross (1983) provides an introduction to stochastic dynamic programming.

Many extensions and variations of the Knapsack Problem have been studied in the area of combinatorial optimization. As we discussed in the chapter, the pseudo-polynomial bound arising from dynamic programming can become prohibitive when the input numbers get large; in these cases, dynamic programming is often combined with other heuristics to solve large instances of Knapsack Problems in practice. The book by Martello and Toth (1990) is devoted to computational approaches to versions of the Knapsack Problem.

Dynamic programming emerged as a basic technique in computational biology in the early 1970s, in a flurry of activity on the problem of sequence comparison. Sankoff (2000) gives an interesting historical account of the early work in this period. The books by Waterman (1995) and Gusfield (1997) provide extensive coverage of sequence alignment algorithms (as well as many related algorithms in computational biology); Mathews and Zuker (2004) discuss further approaches to the problem of RNA secondary structure prediction. The space-efficient algorithm for sequence alignment is due to Hirschberg (1975).

The algorithm for the Shortest-Path Problem described in this chapter is based originally on the work of Bellman (1958) and Ford (1956). Many optimizations, motivated both by theoretical and experimental considerations, have been added to this basic approach to shortest paths; a Web site maintained by Andrew Goldberg contains state-of-the-art code that he has developed for this problem (among a number of others), based on work by Cherkassky, Goldberg and Radzik (1994). The applications of shortest-path methods to Internet routing, and the trade-offs among the different algorithms for networking applications, are covered in books by Bertsekas and Gallager (1992), Keshav (1997), and Stewart (1998).

***Notes on the Exercises***   Exercise 5 is based on discussions with Lillian Lee; Exercise 6 is based on a result of Donald Knuth; Exercise 25 is based on results of Dimitris Bertsimas and Andrew Lo; and Exercise 29 is based on a result of S. Dreyfus and R. Wagner.

# Chapter 7

## Network Flow

In this chapter, we focus on a rich set of algorithmic problems that grow, in a sense, out of one of the original problems we formulated at the beginning of the course: *Bipartite Matching*.

Recall the set-up of the Bipartite Matching Problem. A *bipartite graph* $G = (V, E)$ is an undirected graph whose node set can be partitioned as $V = X \cup Y$, with the property that every edge $e \in E$ has one end in $X$ and the other end in $Y$. We often draw bipartite graphs as in Figure 7.1, with the nodes in $X$ in a column on the left, the nodes in $Y$ in a column on the right, and each edge crossing from the left column to the right column.

Now, we've already seen the notion of a *matching* at several points in the course: We've used the term to describe collections of pairs over a set, with the property that no element of the set appears in more than one pair. (Think of men ($X$) matched to women ($Y$) in the Stable Matching Problem, or characters in the Sequence Alignment Problem.) In the case of a graph, the edges constitute pairs of nodes, and we consequently say that a *matching* in a graph $G = (V, E)$ is a set of edges $M \subseteq E$ with the property that each node appears in at most one edge of $M$. A set of edges $M$ is a *perfect matching* if every node appears in exactly one edge of $M$.

Matchings in bipartite graphs can model situations in which objects are being *assigned* to other objects. We have seen a number of such situations in our earlier discussions of graphs and bipartite graphs. One natural example arises when the nodes in $X$ represent jobs, the nodes in $Y$ represent machines, and an edge $(x_i, y_j)$ indicates that machine $y_j$ is capable of processing job $x_i$. A perfect matching is, then, a way of assigning each job to a machine that can process it, with the property that each machine is assigned exactly one job. Bipartite graphs can represent many other relations that arise between two

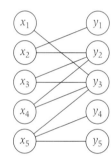

**Figure 7.1** A bipartite graph.

distinct sets of objects, such as the relation between customers and stores; or houses and nearby fire stations; and so forth.

One of the oldest problems in combinatorial algorithms is that of determining the size of the largest matching in a bipartite graph $G$. (As a special case, note that $G$ has a perfect matching if and only if $|X| = |Y|$ and it has a matching of size $|X|$.) This problem turns out to be solvable by an algorithm that runs in polynomial time, but the development of this algorithm needs ideas fundamentally different from the techniques that we've seen so far.

Rather than developing the algorithm directly, we begin by formulating a general class of problems—*network flow* problems—that includes the Bipartite Matching Problem as a special case. We then develop a polynomial-time algorithm for a general problem, the *Maximum-Flow Problem*, and show how this provides an efficient algorithm for Bipartite Matching as well. While the initial motivation for network flow problems comes from the issue of traffic in a network, we will see that they have applications in a surprisingly diverse set of areas and lead to efficient algorithms not just for Bipartite Matching, but for a host of other problems as well.

## 7.1 The Maximum-Flow Problem and the Ford-Fulkerson Algorithm

### The Problem

One often uses graphs to model *transportation networks*—networks whose edges carry some sort of traffic and whose nodes act as "switches" passing traffic between different edges. Consider, for example, a highway system in which the edges are highways and the nodes are interchanges; or a computer network in which the edges are links that can carry packets and the nodes are switches; or a fluid network in which edges are pipes that carry liquid, and the nodes are junctures where pipes are plugged together. Network models of this type have several ingredients: *capacities* on the edges, indicating how much they can carry; *source* nodes in the graph, which generate traffic; *sink* (or destination) nodes in the graph, which can "absorb" traffic as it arrives; and finally, the traffic itself, which is transmitted across the edges.

*Flow Networks* We'll be considering graphs of this form, and we refer to the traffic as *flow*—an abstract entity that is generated at source nodes, transmitted across edges, and absorbed at sink nodes. Formally, we'll say that a *flow network* is a directed graph $G = (V, E)$ with the following features.

- Associated with each edge $e$ is a *capacity*, which is a nonnegative number that we denote $c_e$.

- There is a single *source* node $s \in V$.
- There is a single *sink* node $t \in V$.

Nodes other than $s$ and $t$ will be called *internal* nodes.

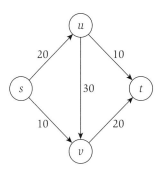

**Figure 7.2** A flow network, with source $s$ and sink $t$. The numbers next to the edges are the capacities.

We will make two assumptions about the flow networks we deal with: first, that no edge enters the source $s$ and no edge leaves the sink $t$; second, that there is at least one edge incident to each node; and third, that all capacities are integers. These assumptions make things cleaner to think about, and while they eliminate a few pathologies, they preserve essentially all the issues we want to think about.

Figure 7.2 illustrates a flow network with four nodes and five edges, and capacity values given next to each edge.

***Defining Flow*** Next we define what it means for our network to carry traffic, or flow. We say that an *s-t flow* is a function $f$ that maps each edge $e$ to a nonnegative real number, $f : E \rightarrow \mathbf{R}^+$; the value $f(e)$ intuitively represents the amount of flow carried by edge $e$. A flow $f$ must satisfy the following two properties.[1]

(i) *(Capacity conditions)* For each $e \in E$, we have $0 \le f(e) \le c_e$.

(ii) *(Conservation conditions)* For each node $v$ other than $s$ and $t$, we have

$$\sum_{e \text{ into } v} f(e) = \sum_{e \text{ out of } v} f(e).$$

Here $\sum_{e \text{ into } v} f(e)$ sums the flow value $f(e)$ over all edges entering node $v$, while $\sum_{e \text{ out of } v} f(e)$ is the sum of flow values over all edges leaving node $v$.

Thus the flow on an edge cannot exceed the capacity of the edge. For every node other than the source and the sink, the amount of flow entering must equal the amount of flow leaving. The source has no entering edges (by our assumption), but it is allowed to have flow going out; in other words, it can generate flow. Symmetrically, the sink is allowed to have flow coming in, even though it has no edges leaving it. The *value* of a flow $f$, denoted $v(f)$, is defined to be the amount of flow generated at the source:

$$v(f) = \sum_{e \text{ out of } s} f(e).$$

To make the notation more compact, we define $f^{\text{out}}(v) = \sum_{e \text{ out of } v} f(e)$ and $f^{\text{in}}(v) = \sum_{e \text{ into } v} f(e)$. We can extend this to sets of vertices; if $S \subseteq V$, we

---

[1] Our notion of flow models traffic as it goes through the network at a steady rate. We have a single variable $f(e)$ to denote the amount of flow on edge $e$. We do not model *bursty* traffic, where the flow fluctuates over time.

define $f^{\text{out}}(S) = \sum_{e \text{ out of } S} f(e)$ and $f^{\text{in}}(S) = \sum_{e \text{ into } S} f(e)$. In this terminology, the conservation condition for nodes $v \neq s, t$ becomes $f^{\text{in}}(v) = f^{\text{out}}(v)$; and we can write $v(f) = f^{\text{out}}(s)$.

**The Maximum-Flow Problem**    Given a flow network, a natural goal is to arrange the traffic so as to make as efficient use as possible of the available capacity. Thus the basic algorithmic problem we will consider is the following: Given a flow network, find a flow of maximum possible value.

As we think about designing algorithms for this problem, it's useful to consider how the structure of the flow network places upper bounds on the maximum value of an *s-t* flow. Here is a basic "obstacle" to the existence of large flows: Suppose we divide the nodes of the graph into two sets, $A$ and $B$, so that $s \in A$ and $t \in B$. Then, intuitively, any flow that goes from $s$ to $t$ must cross from $A$ into $B$ at some point, and thereby use up some of the edge capacity from $A$ to $B$. This suggests that each such "cut" of the graph puts a bound on the maximum possible flow value. The maximum-flow algorithm that we develop here will be intertwined with a proof that the maximum-flow value equals the minimum capacity of any such division, called the *minimum cut*. As a bonus, our algorithm will also compute the minimum cut. We will see that the problem of finding cuts of minimum capacity in a flow network turns out to be as valuable, from the point of view of applications, as that of finding a maximum flow.

### Designing the Algorithm

Suppose we wanted to find a maximum flow in a network. How should we go about doing this? It takes some testing out to decide that an approach such as dynamic programming doesn't seem to work—at least, there is no algorithm known for the Maximum-Flow Problem that could really be viewed as naturally belonging to the dynamic programming paradigm. In the absence of other ideas, we could go back and think about simple greedy approaches, to see where they break down.

Suppose we start with zero flow: $f(e) = 0$ for all $e$. Clearly this respects the capacity and conservation conditions; the problem is that its value is 0. We now try to increase the value of $f$ by "pushing" flow along a path from $s$ to $t$, up to the limits imposed by the edge capacities. Thus, in Figure 7.3, we might choose the path consisting of the edges $\{(s, u), (u, v), (v, t)\}$ and increase the flow on each of these edges to 20, and leave $f(e) = 0$ for the other two. In this way, we still respect the capacity conditions—since we only set the flow as high as the edge capacities would allow—and the conservation conditions—since when we increase flow on an edge entering an internal node, we also increase it on an edge leaving the node. Now, the value of our flow is 20, and we can ask: Is this the maximum possible for the graph in the figure? If we

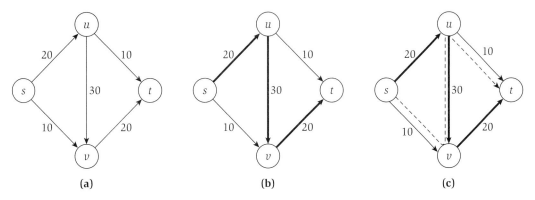

**Figure 7.3** (a) The network of Figure 7.2. (b) Pushing 20 units of flow along the path $s, u, v, t$. (c) The new kind of augmenting path using the edge $(u, v)$ backward.

think about it, we see that the answer is no, since it is possible to construct a flow of value 30. The problem is that we're now stuck—there is no $s$-$t$ path on which we can directly push flow without exceeding some capacity—and yet we do not have a maximum flow. What we need is a more general way of pushing flow from $s$ to $t$, so that in a situation such as this, we have a way to increase the value of the current flow.

Essentially, we'd like to perform the following operation denoted by a dotted line in Figure 7.3(c). We push 10 units of flow along $(s, v)$; this now results in too much flow coming into $v$. So we "undo" 10 units of flow on $(u, v)$; this restores the conservation condition at $v$ but results in too little flow leaving $u$. So, finally, we push 10 units of flow along $(u, t)$, restoring the conservation condition at $u$. We now have a valid flow, and its value is 30. See Figure 7.3, where the dark edges are carrying flow before the operation, and the dashed edges form the new kind of augmentation.

This is a more general way of pushing flow: We can push *forward* on edges with leftover capacity, and we can push *backward* on edges that are already carrying flow, to divert it in a different direction. We now define the *residual graph*, which provides a systematic way to search for forward-backward operations such as this.

**The Residual Graph** Given a flow network $G$, and a flow $f$ on $G$, we define the *residual graph* $G_f$ of $G$ with respect to $f$ as follows. (See Figure 7.4 for the residual graph of the flow on Figure 7.3 after pushing 20 units of flow along the path $s, u, v, t$.)

- The node set of $G_f$ is the same as that of $G$.
- For each edge $e = (u, v)$ of $G$ on which $f(e) < c_e$, there are $c_e - f(e)$ "leftover" units of capacity on which we could try pushing flow forward.

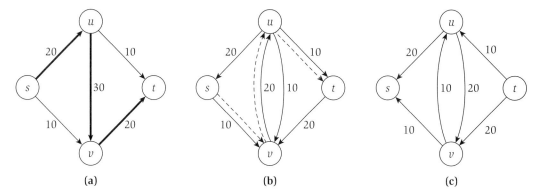

(a)                          (b)                          (c)

**Figure 7.4** (a) The graph $G$ with the path $s, u, v, t$ used to push the first 20 units of flow. (b) The residual graph of the resulting flow $f$, with the residual capacity next to each edge. The dotted line is the new augmenting path. (c) The residual graph after pushing an additional 10 units of flow along the new augmenting path $s, v, u, t$.

So we include the edge $e = (u, v)$ in $G_f$, with a capacity of $c_e - f(e)$. We will call edges included this way *forward edges*.

- For each edge $e = (u, v)$ of $G$ on which $f(e) > 0$, there are $f(e)$ units of flow that we can "undo" if we want to, by pushing flow backward. So we include the edge $e' = (v, u)$ in $G_f$, with a capacity of $f(e)$. Note that $e'$ has the same ends as $e$, but its direction is reversed; we will call edges included this way *backward edges*.

This completes the definition of the residual graph $G_f$. Note that each edge $e$ in $G$ can give rise to one or two edges in $G_f$: If $0 < f(e) < c_e$ it results in both a forward edge and a backward edge being included in $G_f$. Thus $G_f$ has at most twice as many edges as $G$. We will sometimes refer to the capacity of an edge in the residual graph as a *residual capacity*, to help distinguish it from the capacity of the corresponding edge in the original flow network $G$.

***Augmenting Paths in a Residual Graph***    Now we want to make precise the way in which we push flow from $s$ to $t$ in $G_f$. Let $P$ be a simple $s$-$t$ path in $G_f$—that is, $P$ does not visit any node more than once. We define $\texttt{bottleneck}(P, f)$ to be the minimum residual capacity of any edge on $P$, with respect to the flow $f$. We now define the following operation $\texttt{augment}(f, P)$, which yields a new flow $f'$ in $G$.

```
augment(f, P)
  Let b = bottleneck(P, f)
  For each edge (u, v) ∈ P
    If e = (u, v) is a forward edge then
      increase f(e) in G by b
```

```
    Else ((u, v) is a backward edge, and let e = (v, u))
        decrease f(e) in G by b
    Endif
  Endfor
  Return(f)
```

It was purely to be able to perform this operation that we defined the residual graph; to reflect the importance of augment, one often refers to any *s-t* path in the residual graph as an *augmenting path*.

The result of augment($f, P$) is a new flow $f'$ in $G$, obtained by increasing and decreasing the flow values on edges of $P$. Let us first verify that $f'$ is indeed a flow.

**(7.1)**  *$f'$ is a flow in G.*

**Proof.** We must verify the capacity and conservation conditions.

Since $f'$ differs from $f$ only on edges of $P$, we need to check the capacity conditions only on these edges. Thus, let $(u, v)$ be an edge of $P$. Informally, the capacity condition continues to hold because if $e = (u, v)$ is a forward edge, we specifically avoided increasing the flow on $e$ above $c_e$; and if $(u, v)$ is a backward edge arising from edge $e = (v, u) \in E$, we specifically avoided decreasing the flow on $e$ below 0. More concretely, note that bottleneck($P, f$) is no larger than the residual capacity of $(u, v)$. If $e = (u, v)$ is a forward edge, then its residual capacity is $c_e - f(e)$; thus we have

$$0 \le f(e) \le f'(e) = f(e) + \text{bottleneck}(P, f) \le f(e) + (c_e - f(e)) = c_e,$$

so the capacity condition holds. If $(u, v)$ is a backward edge arising from edge $e = (v, u) \in E$, then its residual capacity is $f(e)$, so we have

$$c_e \ge f(e) \ge f'(e) = f(e) - \text{bottleneck}(P, f) \ge f(e) - f(e) = 0,$$

and again the capacity condition holds.

We need to check the conservation condition at each internal node that lies on the path $P$. Let $v$ be such a node; we can verify that the change in the amount of flow entering $v$ is the same as the change in the amount of flow exiting $v$; since $f$ satisfied the conservation condition at $v$, so must $f'$. Technically, there are four cases to check, depending on whether the edge of $P$ that enters $v$ is a forward or backward edge, and whether the edge of $P$ that exits $v$ is a forward or backward edge. However, each of these cases is easily worked out, and we leave them to the reader.  ∎

This augmentation operation captures the type of forward and backward pushing of flow that we discussed earlier. Let's now consider the following algorithm to compute an *s-t* flow in *G*.

```
Max-Flow
    Initially f(e) = 0 for all e in G
    While there is an s-t path in the residual graph Gf
        Let P be a simple s-t path in Gf
        f' = augment(f, P)
        Update f to be f'
        Update the residual graph Gf to be Gf'
    Endwhile
    Return f
```

We'll call this the *Ford-Fulkerson Algorithm*, after the two researchers who developed it in 1956. See Figure 7.4 for a run of the algorithm. The Ford-Fulkerson Algorithm is really quite simple. What is not at all clear is whether its central `While` loop terminates, and whether the flow returned is a maximum flow. The answers to both of these questions turn out to be fairly subtle.

### Analyzing the Algorithm: Termination and Running Time

First we consider some properties that the algorithm maintains by induction on the number of iterations of the `While` loop, relying on our assumption that all capacities are integers.

**(7.2)** *At every intermediate stage of the Ford-Fulkerson Algorithm, the flow values $\{f(e)\}$ and the residual capacities in $G_f$ are integers.*

**Proof.** The statement is clearly true before any iterations of the `While` loop. Now suppose it is true after $j$ iterations. Then, since all residual capacities in $G_f$ are integers, the value `bottleneck`$(P, f)$ for the augmenting path found in iteration $j + 1$ will be an integer. Thus the flow $f'$ will have integer values, and hence so will the capacities of the new residual graph. ■

We can use this property to prove that the Ford-Fulkerson Algorithm terminates. As at previous points in the book we will look for a measure of *progress* that will imply termination.

First we show that the flow value strictly increases when we apply an augmentation.

**(7.3)** *Let $f$ be a flow in $G$, and let $P$ be a simple s-t path in $G_f$. Then $v(f') = v(f) + \text{bottleneck}(P, f)$; and since $\text{bottleneck}(P, f) > 0$, we have $v(f') > v(f)$.*

**Proof.** The first edge $e$ of $P$ must be an edge out of $s$ in the residual graph $G_f$; and since the path is simple, it does not visit $s$ again. Since $G$ has no edges entering $s$, the edge $e$ must be a forward edge. We increase the flow on this edge by `bottleneck`$(P, f)$, and we do not change the flow on any other edge incident to $s$. Therefore the value of $f'$ exceeds the value of $f$ by `bottleneck`$(P, f)$. ∎

We need one more observation to prove termination: We need to be able to bound the maximum possible flow value. Here's one upper bound: If all the edges out of $s$ could be completely saturated with flow, the value of the flow would be $\sum_{e \text{ out of } s} c_e$. Let $C$ denote this sum. Thus we have $v(f) \le C$ for all $s$-$t$ flows $f$. ($C$ may be a huge overestimate of the maximum value of a flow in $G$, but it's handy for us as a finite, simply stated bound.) Using statement (7.3), we can now prove termination.

**(7.4)** *Suppose, as above, that all capacities in the flow network G are integers. Then the Ford-Fulkerson Algorithm terminates in at most C iterations of the* `While` *loop.*

**Proof.** We noted above that no flow in $G$ can have value greater than $C$, due to the capacity condition on the edges leaving $s$. Now, by (7.3), the value of the flow maintained by the Ford-Fulkerson Algorithm increases in each iteration; so by (7.2), it increases by at least 1 in each iteration. Since it starts with the value 0, and cannot go higher than $C$, the `While` loop in the Ford-Fulkerson Algorithm can run for at most $C$ iterations. ∎

Next we consider the running time of the Ford-Fulkerson Algorithm. Let $n$ denote the number of nodes in $G$, and $m$ denote the number of edges in $G$. We have assumed that all nodes have at least one incident edge, hence $m \ge n/2$, and so we can use $O(m + n) = O(m)$ to simplify the bounds.

**(7.5)** *Suppose, as above, that all capacities in the flow network G are integers. Then the Ford-Fulkerson Algorithm can be implemented to run in O(mC) time.*

**Proof.** We know from (7.4) that the algorithm terminates in at most $C$ iterations of the `While` loop. We therefore consider the amount of work involved in one iteration when the current flow is $f$.

The residual graph $G_f$ has at most $2m$ edges, since each edge of $G$ gives rise to at most two edges in the residual graph. We will maintain $G_f$ using an adjacency list representation; we will have two linked lists for each node $v$, one containing the edges entering $v$, and one containing the edges leaving $v$. To find an $s$-$t$ path in $G_f$, we can use breadth-first search or depth-first search, which run in $O(m + n)$ time; by our assumption that $m \geq n/2$, $O(m + n)$ is the same as $O(m)$. The procedure $\texttt{augment}(f, P)$ takes time $O(n)$, as the path $P$ has at most $n - 1$ edges. Given the new flow $f'$, we can build the new residual graph in $O(m)$ time: For each edge $e$ of $G$, we construct the correct forward and backward edges in $G_{f'}$. ∎

A somewhat more efficient version of the algorithm would maintain the linked lists of edges in the residual graph $G_f$ as part of the $\texttt{augment}$ procedure that changes the flow $f$ via augmentation.

## 7.2 Maximum Flows and Minimum Cuts in a Network

We now continue with the analysis of the Ford-Fulkerson Algorithm, an activity that will occupy this whole section. In the process, we will not only learn a lot about the algorithm, but also find that analyzing the algorithm provides us with considerable insight into the Maximum-Flow Problem itself.

### Analyzing the Algorithm: Flows and Cuts

Our next goal is to show that the flow that is returned by the Ford-Fulkerson Algorithm has the maximum possible value of any flow in $G$. To make progress toward this goal, we return to an issue that we raised in Section 7.1: the way in which the structure of the flow network places upper bounds on the maximum value of an $s$-$t$ flow. We have already seen one upper bound: the value $v(f)$ of any $s$-$t$-flow $f$ is at most $C = \sum_{e \text{ out of } s} c_e$. Sometimes this bound is useful, but sometimes it is very weak. We now use the notion of a *cut* to develop a much more general means of placing upper bounds on the maximum-flow value.

Consider dividing the nodes of the graph into two sets, $A$ and $B$, so that $s \in A$ and $t \in B$. As in our discussion in Section 7.1, any such division places an upper bound on the maximum possible flow value, since all the flow must cross from $A$ to $B$ somewhere. Formally, we say that an *$s$-$t$ cut* is a partition $(A, B)$ of the vertex set $V$, so that $s \in A$ and $t \in B$. The *capacity* of a cut $(A, B)$, which we will denote $c(A, B)$, is simply the sum of the capacities of all edges out of $A$: $c(A, B) = \sum_{e \text{ out of } A} c_e$.

Cuts turn out to provide very natural upper bounds on the values of flows, as expressed by our intuition above. We make this precise via a sequence of facts.

**(7.6)** *Let $f$ be any $s$-$t$ flow, and $(A, B)$ any $s$-$t$ cut. Then $v(f) = f^{\text{out}}(A) - f^{\text{in}}(A)$.*

This statement is actually much stronger than a simple upper bound. It says that by watching the amount of flow $f$ sends across a cut, we can exactly *measure* the flow value: It is the total amount that leaves $A$, minus the amount that "swirls back" into $A$. This makes sense intuitively, although the proof requires a little manipulation of sums.

**Proof.** By definition $v(f) = f^{out}(s)$. By assumption we have $f^{in}(s) = 0$, as the source $s$ has no entering edges, so we can write $v(f) = f^{out}(s) - f^{in}(s)$. Since every node $v$ in $A$ other than $s$ is internal, we know that $f^{out}(v) - f^{in}(v) = 0$ for all such nodes. Thus

$$v(f) = \sum_{v \in A} (f^{out}(v) - f^{in}(v)),$$

since the only term in this sum that is nonzero is the one in which $v$ is set to $s$.

Let's try to rewrite the sum on the right as follows. If an edge $e$ has both ends in $A$, then $f(e)$ appears once in the sum with a "+" and once with a "−", and hence these two terms cancel out. If $e$ has only its tail in $A$, then $f(e)$ appears just once in the sum, with a "+". If $e$ has only its head in $A$, then $f(e)$ also appears just once in the sum, with a "−". Finally, if $e$ has neither end in $A$, then $f(e)$ doesn't appear in the sum at all. In view of this, we have

$$\sum_{v \in A} f^{out}(v) - f^{in}(v) = \sum_{e \text{ out of } A} f(e) - \sum_{e \text{ into } A} f(e) = f^{out}(A) - f^{in}(A).$$

Putting together these two equations, we have the statement of (7.6).  ∎

If $A = \{s\}$, then $f^{out}(A) = f^{out}(s)$, and $f^{in}(A) = 0$ as there are no edges entering the source by assumption. So the statement for this set $A = \{s\}$ is exactly the definition of the flow value $v(f)$.

Note that if $(A, B)$ is a cut, then the edges into $B$ are precisely the edges out of $A$. Similarly, the edges out of $B$ are precisely the edges into $A$. Thus we have $f^{out}(A) = f^{in}(B)$ and $f^{in}(A) = f^{out}(B)$, just by comparing the definitions for these two expressions. So we can rephrase (7.6) in the following way.

**(7.7)**    *Let $f$ be any s-t flow, and $(A, B)$ any s-t cut. Then $v(f) = f^{in}(B) - f^{out}(B)$.*

If we set $A = V - \{t\}$ and $B = \{t\}$ in (7.7), we have $v(f) = f^{in}(B) - f^{out}(B) = f^{in}(t) - f^{out}(t)$. By our assumption the sink $t$ has no leaving edges, so we have $f^{out}(t) = 0$. This says that we could have originally defined the *value* of a flow equally well in terms of the sink $t$: It is $f^{in}(t)$, the amount of flow arriving at the sink.

A very useful consequence of (7.6) is the following upper bound.

**(7.8)**    *Let $f$ be any s-t flow, and $(A, B)$ any s-t cut. Then $v(f) \leq c(A, B)$.*

**Proof.**

$$v(f) = f^{\text{out}}(A) - f^{\text{in}}(A)$$

$$\leq f^{\text{out}}(A)$$

$$= \sum_{e \text{ out of } A} f(e)$$

$$\leq \sum_{e \text{ out of } A} c_e$$

$$= c(A, B).$$

Here the first line is simply (7.6); we pass from the first to the second since $f^{\text{in}}(A) \geq 0$, and we pass from the third to the fourth by applying the capacity conditions to each term of the sum. ∎

In a sense, (7.8) looks weaker than (7.6), since it is only an inequality rather than an equality. However, it will be extremely useful for us, since its right-hand side is independent of any particular flow $f$. What (7.8) says is that *the value of every flow is upper-bounded by the capacity of every cut*. In other words, if we exhibit any $s$-$t$ cut in $G$ of some value $c^*$, we know immediately by (7.8) that there cannot be an $s$-$t$ flow in $G$ of value greater than $c^*$. Conversely, if we exhibit any $s$-$t$ flow in $G$ of some value $v^*$, we know immediately by (7.8) that there cannot be an $s$-$t$ cut in $G$ of value less than $v^*$.

## Analyzing the Algorithm: Max-Flow Equals Min-Cut

Let $\bar{f}$ denote the flow that is returned by the Ford-Fulkerson Algorithm. We want to show that $\bar{f}$ has the maximum possible value of any flow in $G$, and we do this by the method discussed above: We exhibit an $s$-$t$ cut $(A^*, B^*)$ for which $v(\bar{f}) = c(A^*, B^*)$. This immediately establishes that $\bar{f}$ has the maximum value of any flow, and that $(A^*, B^*)$ has the minimum capacity of any $s$-$t$ cut.

The Ford-Fulkerson Algorithm terminates when the flow $f$ has no $s$-$t$ path in the residual graph $G_f$. This turns out to be the only property needed for proving its maximality.

**(7.9)** *If $f$ is an s-t-flow such that there is no s-t path in the residual graph $G_f$, then there is an s-t cut $(A^*, B^*)$ in $G$ for which $v(f) = c(A^*, B^*)$. Consequently, $f$ has the maximum value of any flow in $G$, and $(A^*, B^*)$ has the minimum capacity of any s-t cut in $G$.*

**Proof.** The statement claims the existence of a cut satisfying a certain desirable property; thus we must now identify such a cut. To this end, let $A^*$ denote the set of all nodes $v$ in $G$ for which there is an $s$-$v$ path in $G_f$. Let $B^*$ denote the set of all other nodes: $B^* = V - A^*$.

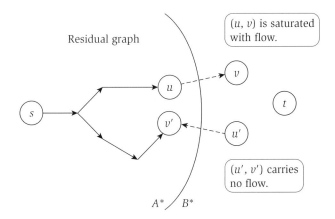

**Figure 7.5** The $(A^*, B^*)$ cut in the proof of (7.9).

First we establish that $(A^*, B^*)$ is indeed an *s-t* cut. It is clearly a partition of $V$. The source $s$ belongs to $A^*$ since there is always a path from $s$ to $s$. Moreover, $t \notin A^*$ by the assumption that there is no *s-t* path in the residual graph; hence $t \in B^*$ as desired.

Next, suppose that $e = (u, v)$ is an edge in $G$ for which $u \in A^*$ and $v \in B^*$, as shown in Figure 7.5. We claim that $f(e) = c_e$. For if not, $e$ would be a forward edge in the residual graph $G_f$, and since $u \in A^*$, there is an *s-u* path in $G_f$; appending $e$ to this path, we would obtain an *s-v* path in $G_f$, contradicting our assumption that $v \in B^*$.

Now suppose that $e' = (u', v')$ is an edge in $G$ for which $u' \in B^*$ and $v' \in A^*$. We claim that $f(e') = 0$. For if not, $e'$ would give rise to a backward edge $e'' = (v', u')$ in the residual graph $G_f$, and since $v' \in A^*$, there is an *s-v'* path in $G_f$; appending $e''$ to this path, we would obtain an *s-u'* path in $G_f$, contradicting our assumption that $u' \in B^*$.

So all edges out of $A^*$ are completely saturated with flow, while all edges into $A^*$ are completely unused. We can now use (7.6) to reach the desired conclusion:

$$v(f) = f^{\text{out}}(A^*) - f^{\text{in}}(A^*)$$

$$= \sum_{e \text{ out of } A^*} f(e) - \sum_{e \text{ into } A^*} f(e)$$

$$= \sum_{e \text{ out of } A^*} c_e - 0$$

$$= c(A^*, B^*). \quad \blacksquare$$

Note how, in retrospect, we can see why the two types of residual edges—forward and backward—are crucial in analyzing the two terms in the expression from (7.6).

Given that the Ford-Fulkerson Algorithm terminates when there is no *s-t* in the residual graph, (7.6) immediately implies its optimality.

**(7.10)**    *The flow $\bar{f}$ returned by the Ford-Fulkerson Algorithm is a maximum flow.*

We also observe that our algorithm can easily be extended to compute a minimum *s-t* cut $(A^*, B^*)$, as follows.

**(7.11)**    *Given a flow $f$ of maximum value, we can compute an s-t cut of minimum capacity in $O(m)$ time.*

**Proof.** We simply follow the construction in the proof of (7.9). We construct the residual graph $G_f$, and perform breadth-first search or depth-first search to determine the set $A^*$ of all nodes that $s$ can reach. We then define $B^* = V - A^*$, and return the cut $(A^*, B^*)$.    ■

Note that there can be many minimum-capacity cuts in a graph $G$; the procedure in the proof of (7.11) is simply finding a particular one of these cuts, starting from a maximum flow $\bar{f}$.

As a bonus, we have obtained the following striking fact through the analysis of the algorithm.

**(7.12)**    *In every flow network, there is a flow $f$ and a cut $(A, B)$ so that $v(f) = c(A, B)$.*

The point is that $f$ in (7.12) must be a maximum *s-t* flow; for if there were a flow $f'$ of greater value, the value of $f'$ would exceed the capacity of $(A, B)$, and this would contradict (7.8). Similarly, it follows that $(A, B)$ in (7.12) is a *minimum cut*—no other cut can have smaller capacity—for if there were a cut $(A', B')$ of smaller capacity, it would be less than the value of $f$, and this again would contradict (7.8). Due to these implications, (7.12) is often called the *Max-Flow Min-Cut Theorem*, and is phrased as follows.

**(7.13)**    *In every flow network, the maximum value of an s-t flow is equal to the minimum capacity of an s-t cut.*

## Further Analysis: Integer-Valued Flows

Among the many corollaries emerging from our analysis of the Ford-Fulkerson Algorithm, here is another extremely important one. By (7.2), we maintain an integer-valued flow at all times, and by (7.9), we conclude with a maximum flow. Thus we have

**(7.14)**   *If all capacities in the flow network are integers, then there is a maximum flow $f$ for which every flow value $f(e)$ is an integer.*

Note that (7.14) does not claim that *every* maximum flow is integer-valued, only that *some* maximum flow has this property. Curiously, although (7.14) makes no reference to the Ford-Fulkerson Algorithm, our algorithmic approach here provides what is probably the easiest way to prove it.

***Real Numbers as Capacities?***   Finally, before moving on, we can ask how crucial our assumption of integer capacities was (ignoring (7.4), (7.5) and (7.14), which clearly needed it). First we notice that allowing capacities to be rational numbers does not make the situation any more general, since we can determine the least common multiple of all capacities, and multiply them all by this value to obtain an equivalent problem with integer capacities.

But what if we have real numbers as capacities? Where in the proof did we rely on the capacities being integers? In fact, we relied on it quite crucially: We used (7.2) to establish, in (7.4), that the value of the flow increased by at least 1 in every step. With real numbers as capacities, we should be concerned that the value of our flow keeps increasing, but in increments that become arbitrarily smaller and smaller; and hence we have no guarantee that the number of iterations of the loop is finite. And this turns out to be an extremely real worry, for the following reason: *With pathological choices for the augmenting path, the Ford-Fulkerson Algorithm with real-valued capacities can run forever.*

However, one can still prove that the Max-Flow Min-Cut Theorem (7.12) is true even if the capacities may be real numbers. Note that (7.9) assumed only that the flow $f$ has no $s$-$t$ path in its residual graph $G_f$, in order to conclude that there is an $s$-$t$ cut of equal value. Clearly, for any flow $f$ of maximum value, the residual graph has no $s$-$t$-path; otherwise there would be a way to increase the value of the flow. So one can prove (7.12) in the case of real-valued capacities by simply establishing that for every flow network, there exists a maximum flow.

Of course, the capacities in any practical application of network flow would be integers or rational numbers. However, the problem of pathological choices for the augmenting paths can manifest itself even with integer capacities: It can make the Ford-Fulkerson Algorithm take a gigantic number of iterations.

In the next section, we discuss how to select augmenting paths so as to avoid the potential bad behavior of the algorithm.

## 7.3 Choosing Good Augmenting Paths

In the previous section, we saw that any way of choosing an augmenting path increases the value of the flow, and this led to a bound of $C$ on the number of augmentations, where $C = \sum_{e \text{ out of } s} c_e$. When $C$ is not very large, this can be a reasonable bound; however, it is very weak when $C$ is large.

To get a sense for how bad this bound can be, consider the example graph in Figure 7.2; but this time assume the capacities are as follows: The edges $(s, v)$, $(s, u)$, $(v, t)$ and $(u, t)$ have capacity 100, and the edge $(u, v)$ has capacity 1, as shown in Figure 7.6. It is easy to see that the maximum flow has value 200, and has $f(e) = 100$ for the edges $(s, v)$, $(s, u)$, $(v, t)$ and $(u, t)$ and value 0 on the edge $(u, v)$. This flow can be obtained by a sequence of two augmentations, using the paths of nodes $s, u, t$ and path $s, v, t$. But consider how bad the Ford-Fulkerson Algorithm can be with pathological choices for the augmenting paths. Suppose we start with augmenting path $P_1$ of nodes $s, u, v, t$ in this order (as shown in Figure 7.6). This path has $\texttt{bottleneck}(P_1, f) = 1$. After this augmentation, we have $f(e) = 1$ on the edge $e = (u, v)$, so the reverse edge is in the residual graph. For the next augmenting path, we choose the path $P_2$ of the nodes $s, v, u, t$ in this order. In this second augmentation, we get $\texttt{bottleneck}(P_2, f) = 1$ as well. After this second augmentation, we have $f(e) = 0$ for the edge $e = (u, v)$, so the edge is again in the residual graph. Suppose we alternate between choosing $P_1$ and $P_2$ for augmentation. In this case, each augmentation will have 1 as the bottleneck capacity, and it will take 200 augmentations to get the desired flow of value 200. This is exactly the bound we proved in (7.4), since $C = 200$ in this example.

### ✎ Designing a Faster Flow Algorithm

The goal of this section is to show that with a better choice of paths, we can improve this bound significantly. A large amount of work has been devoted to finding good ways of choosing augmenting paths in the Maximum-Flow Problem so as to minimize the number of iterations. We focus here on one of the most natural approaches and will mention other approaches at the end of the section. Recall that augmentation increases the value of the maximum flow by the bottleneck capacity of the selected path; so if we choose paths with large bottleneck capacity, we will be making a lot of progress. A natural idea is to select the path that has the largest bottleneck capacity. Having to find such paths can slow down each individual iteration by quite a bit. We will avoid this slowdown by not worrying about selecting the path that has *exactly*

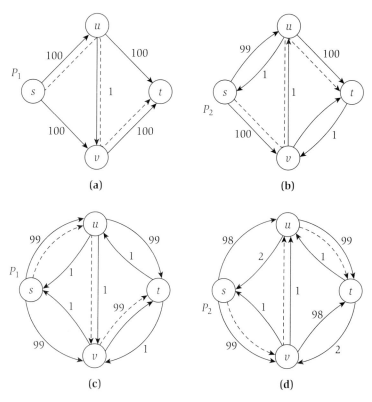

**Figure 7.6** Parts (a) through (d) depict four iterations of the Ford-Fulkerson Algorithm using a bad choice of augmenting paths: The augmentations alternate between the path $P_1$ through the nodes $s$, $u$, $v$, $t$ in order and the path $P_2$ through the nodes $s$, $v$, $u$, $t$ in order.

the largest bottleneck capacity. Instead, we will maintain a so-called *scaling parameter* $\Delta$, and we will look for paths that have bottleneck capacity of at least $\Delta$.

Let $G_f(\Delta)$ be the subset of the residual graph consisting only of edges with residual capacity of at least $\Delta$. We will work with values of $\Delta$ that are powers of 2. The algorithm is as follows.

```
Scaling Max-Flow
  Initially f(e) = 0 for all e in G
  Initially set Δ to be the largest power of 2 that is no larger
        than the maximum capacity out of s: Δ ≤ max_{e out of s} c_e
    While Δ ≥ 1
      While there is an s-t path in the graph G_f(Δ)
        Let P be a simple s-t path in G_f(Δ)
```

$$f' = \text{augment}(f, P)$$

```
        Update f to be f' and update G_f(Δ)
    Endwhile
    Δ = Δ/2
  Endwhile
Return f
```

## Analyzing the Algorithm

First observe that the new Scaling Max-Flow Algorithm is really just an implementation of the original Ford-Fulkerson Algorithm. The new loops, the value $\Delta$, and the restricted residual graph $G_f(\Delta)$ are only used to guide the selection of residual path—with the goal of using edges with large residual capacity for as long as possible. Hence all the properties that we proved about the original Max-Flow Algorithm are also true for this new version: the flow remains integer-valued throughout the algorithm, and hence all residual capacities are integer-valued.

> **(7.15)**   *If the capacities are integer-valued, then throughout the Scaling Max-Flow Algorithm the flow and the residual capacities remain integer-valued. This implies that when $\Delta = 1$, $G_f(\Delta)$ is the same as $G_f$, and hence when the algorithm terminates the flow, f is of maximum value.*

Next we consider the running time. We call an iteration of the outside While loop—with a fixed value of $\Delta$—the $\Delta$-*scaling phase*. It is easy to give an upper bound on the number of different $\Delta$-scaling phases, in terms of the value $C = \sum_{e \text{ out of } s} c_e$ that we also used in the previous section. The initial value of $\Delta$ is at most $C$, it drops by factors of 2, and it never gets below 1. Thus,

> **(7.16)**   *The number of iterations of the outer* While *loop is at most* $1 + \lceil \log_2 C \rceil$.

The harder part is to bound the number of augmentations done in each scaling phase. The idea here is that we are using paths that augment the flow by a lot, and so there should be relatively few augmentations. During the $\Delta$-scaling phase, we only use edges with residual capacity of at least $\Delta$. Using (7.3), we have

> **(7.17)**   *During the $\Delta$-scaling phase, each augmentation increases the flow value by at least $\Delta$.*

The key insight is that at the end of the $\Delta$-scaling phase, the flow $f$ cannot be too far from the maximum possible value.

**(7.18)** *Let $f$ be the flow at the end of the $\Delta$-scaling phase. There is an s-t cut $(A, B)$ in G for which $c(A, B) \leq v(f) + m\Delta$, where m is the number of edges in the graph G. Consequently, the maximum flow in the network has value at most $v(f) + m\Delta$.*

**Proof.** This proof is analogous to our proof of (7.9), which established that the flow returned by the original Max-Flow Algorithm is of maximum value.

As in that proof, we must identify a cut $(A, B)$ with the desired property. Let $A$ denote the set of all nodes $v$ in $G$ for which there is an $s$-$v$ path in $G_f(\Delta)$. Let $B$ denote the set of all other nodes: $B = V - A$. We can see that $(A, B)$ is indeed an $s$-$t$ cut as otherwise the phase would not have ended.

Now consider an edge $e = (u, v)$ in $G$ for which $u \in A$ and $v \in B$. We claim that $c_e < f(e) + \Delta$. For if this were not the case, then $e$ would be a forward edge in the graph $G_f(\Delta)$, and since $u \in A$, there is an $s$-$u$ path in $G_f(\Delta)$; appending $e$ to this path, we would obtain an $s$-$v$ path in $G_f(\Delta)$, contradicting our assumption that $v \in B$. Similarly, we claim that for any edge $e' = (u', v')$ in $G$ for which $u' \in B$ and $v' \in A$, we have $f(e') < \Delta$. Indeed, if $f(e') \geq \Delta$, then $e'$ would give rise to a backward edge $e'' = (v', u')$ in the graph $G_f(\Delta)$, and since $v' \in A$, there is an $s$-$v'$ path in $G_f(\Delta)$; appending $e''$ to this path, we would obtain an $s$-$u'$ path in $G_f(\Delta)$, contradicting our assumption that $u' \in B$.

So all edges $e$ out of $A$ are almost saturated—they satisfy $c_e < f(e) + \Delta$— and all edges into $A$ are almost empty—they satisfy $f(e) < \Delta$. We can now use (7.6) to reach the desired conclusion:

$$v(f) = \sum_{e \text{ out of } A} f(e) - \sum_{e \text{ into } A} f(e)$$

$$\geq \sum_{e \text{ out of } A} (c_e - \Delta) - \sum_{e \text{ into } A} \Delta$$

$$= \sum_{e \text{ out of } A} c_e - \sum_{e \text{ out of } A} \Delta - \sum_{e \text{ into } A} \Delta$$

$$\geq c(A, B) - m\Delta.$$

Here the first inequality follows from our bounds on the flow values of edges across the cut, and the second inequality follows from the simple fact that the graph only contains $m$ edges total.

The maximum-flow value is bounded by the capacity of any cut by (7.8). We use the cut $(A, B)$ to obtain the bound claimed in the second statement. ∎

**(7.19)**    *The number of augmentations in a scaling phase is at most* $2m$.

**Proof.** The statement is clearly true in the first scaling phase: we can use each of the edges out of $s$ only for at most one augmentation in that phase. Now consider a later scaling phase $\Delta$, and let $f_p$ be the flow at the end of the *previous* scaling phase. In that phase, we used $\Delta' = 2\Delta$ as our parameter. By (7.18), the maximum flow $f^*$ is at most $v(f^*) \leq v(f_p) + m\Delta' = v(f_p) + 2m\Delta$. In the $\Delta$-scaling phase, each augmentation increases the flow by at least $\Delta$, and hence there can be at most $2m$ augmentations.    ■

An augmentation takes $O(m)$ time, including the time required to set up the graph and find the appropriate path. We have at most $1 + \lceil \log_2 C \rceil$ scaling phases and at most $2m$ augmentations in each scaling phase. Thus we have the following result.

**(7.20)**    *The Scaling Max-Flow Algorithm in a graph with m edges and integer capacities finds a maximum flow in at most* $2m(1 + \lceil \log_2 C \rceil)$ *augmentations. It can be implemented to run in at most* $O(m^2 \log_2 C)$ *time.*

When $C$ is large, this time bound is much better than the $O(mC)$ bound that applied to an arbitrary implementation of the Ford-Fulkerson Algorithm. In our example at the beginning of this section, we had capacities of size 100, but we could just as well have used capacities of size $2^{100}$; in this case, the generic Ford-Fulkerson Algorithm could take time proportional to $2^{100}$, while the scaling algorithm will take time proportional to $\log_2(2^{100}) = 100$. One way to view this distinction is as follows: The generic Ford-Fulkerson Algorithm requires time proportional to the *magnitude* of the capacities, while the scaling algorithm only requires time proportional to the number of *bits* needed to specify the capacities in the input to the problem. As a result, the scaling algorithm is running in time polynomial in the size of the input (i.e., the number of edges and the numerical representation of the capacities), and so it meets our traditional goal of achieving a polynomial-time algorithm. Bad implementations of the Ford-Fulkerson Algorithm, which can require close to $C$ iterations, do not meet this standard of polynomiality. (Recall that in Section 6.4 we used the term *pseudo-polynomial* to describe such algorithms, which are polynomial in the magnitudes of the input numbers but not in the number of bits needed to represent them.)

## Extensions: Strongly Polynomial Algorithms

Could we ask for something qualitatively better than what the scaling algorithm guarantees? Here is one thing we could hope for: Our example graph (Figure 7.6) had four nodes and five edges; so it would be nice to use a number of iterations that is polynomial in the numbers 4 and 5, completely independently of the values of the capacities. Such an algorithm, which is polynomial in $|V|$ and $|E|$ only, and works with numbers having a polynomial number of bits, is called a *strongly polynomial algorithm*. In fact, there is a simple and natural implementation of the Ford-Fulkerson Algorithm that leads to such a strongly polynomial bound: each iteration chooses the augmenting path with the fewest number of edges. Dinitz, and independently Edmonds and Karp, proved that with this choice the algorithm terminates in at most $O(mn)$ iterations. In fact, these were the first polynomial algorithms for the Maximum-Flow Problem. There has since been a huge amount of work devoted to improving the running times of maximum-flow algorithms. There are currently algorithms that achieve running times of $O(mn \log n)$, $O(n^3)$, and $O(\min(n^{2/3}, m^{1/2})m \log n \log U)$, where the last bound assumes that all capacities are integral and at most $U$. In the next section, we'll discuss a strongly polynomial maximum-flow algorithm based on a different principle.

## * 7.4 The Preflow-Push Maximum-Flow Algorithm

From the very beginning, our discussion of the Maximum-Flow Problem has been centered around the idea of an augmenting path in the residual graph. However, there are some very powerful techniques for maximum flow that are not explicitly based on augmenting paths. In this section we study one such technique, the Preflow-Push Algorithm.

### Designing the Algorithm

Algorithms based on augmenting paths maintain a flow $f$, and use the `augment` procedure to increase the value of the flow. By way of contrast, the Preflow-Push Algorithm will, in essence, increase the flow on an edge-by-edge basis. Changing the flow on a single edge will typically violate the conservation condition, and so the algorithm will have to maintain something less well behaved than a flow—something that does not obey conservation—as it operates.

**Preflows** We say that an *s-t preflow* (*preflow*, for short) is a function $f$ that maps each edge $e$ to a nonnegative real number, $f : E \to \mathbf{R}^+$. A preflow $f$ must satisfy the capacity conditions:

 (i)  For each $e \in E$, we have $0 \le f(e) \le c_e$.

In place of the conservation conditions, we require only inequalities: Each node other than $s$ must have at least as much flow entering as leaving.

 (ii)  For each node $v$ other than the source $s$, we have

$$\sum_{e \text{ into } v} f(e) \ge \sum_{e \text{ out of } v} f(e).$$

We will call the difference

$$e_f(v) = \sum_{e \text{ into } v} f(e) - \sum_{e \text{ out of } v} f(e)$$

the *excess* of the preflow at node $v$. Notice that a preflow where all nodes other than $s$ and $t$ have zero excess is a flow, and the value of the flow is exactly $e_f(t) = -e_f(s)$. We can still define the concept of a residual graph $G_f$ for a preflow $f$, just as we did for a flow. The algorithm will "push" flow along edges of the residual graph (using both forward and backward edges).

**Preflows and Labelings**    The Preflow-Push Algorithm will maintain a preflow and work on converting the preflow into a flow. The algorithm is based on the physical intuition that flow naturally finds its way "downhill." The "heights" for this intuition will be labels $h(v)$ for each node $v$ that the algorithm will define and maintain, as shown in Figure 7.7. We will push flow from nodes with higher labels to those with lower labels, following the intuition that fluid flows downhill. To make this precise, a *labeling* is a function $h : V \to \mathbf{Z}_{\geq 0}$ from the nodes to the nonnegative integers. We will also refer to the labels as *heights* of the nodes. We will say that a labeling $h$ and an *s-t* preflow $f$ are *compatible* if

(i) (*Source and sink conditions*) $h(t) = 0$ and $h(s) = n$,

(ii) (*Steepness conditions*) For all edges $(v, w) \in E_f$ in the residual graph, we have $h(v) \leq h(w) + 1$.

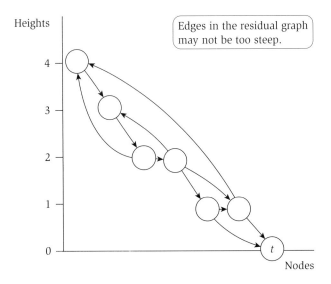

**Figure 7.7** A residual graph and a compatible labeling. No edge in the residual graph can be too "steep"—its tail can be at most one unit above its head in height. The source node $s$ must have $h(s) = n$ and is not drawn in the figure.

Intuitively, the height difference $n$ between the source and the sink is meant to ensure that the flow starts high enough to flow from $s$ toward the sink $t$, while the steepness condition will help by making the descent of the flow gradual enough to make it to the sink.

The key property of a compatible preflow and labeling is that there can be no $s$-$t$ path in the residual graph.

**(7.21)** *If s-t preflow f is compatible with a labeling h, then there is no s-t path in the residual graph $G_f$.*

**Proof.** We prove the statement by contradiction. Let $P$ be a simple $s$-$t$ path in the residual graph $G$. Assume that the nodes along $P$ are $s, v_1, \ldots, v_k = t$. By definition of a labeling compatible with preflow $f$, we have that $h(s) = n$. The edge $(s, v_1)$ is in the residual graph, and hence $h(v_1) \geq h(s) - 1 = n - 1$. Using induction on $i$ and the steepness condition for the edge $(v_{i-1}, v_i)$, we get that for all nodes $v_i$ in path $P$ the height is at least $h(v_i) \geq n - i$. Notice that the last node of the path is $v_k = t$; hence we get that $h(t) \geq n - k$. However, $h(t) = 0$ by definition; and $k < n$ as the path $P$ is simple. This contradiction proves the claim. ∎

Recall from (7.9) that if there is no $s$-$t$ path in the residual graph $G_f$ of a *flow f*, then the flow has maximum value. This implies the following corollary.

**(7.22)** *If s-t flow f is compatible with a labeling h, then f is a flow of maximum value.*

Note that (7.21) applies to preflows, while (7.22) is more restrictive in that it applies only to flows. Thus the Preflow-Push Algorithm will maintain a preflow $f$ and a labeling $h$ compatible with $f$, and it will work on modifying $f$ and $h$ so as to move $f$ toward being a flow. Once $f$ actually becomes a flow, we can invoke (7.22) to conclude that it is a maximum flow. In light of this, we can view the Preflow-Push Algorithm as being in a way orthogonal to the Ford-Fulkerson Algorithm. The Ford-Fulkerson Algorithm maintains a feasible flow while changing it gradually toward optimality. The Preflow-Push Algorithm, on the other hand, maintains a condition that would imply the optimality of a preflow $f$, *if it were to be a feasible flow*, and the algorithm gradually transforms the preflow $f$ into a flow.

To start the algorithm, we will need to define an initial preflow $f$ and labeling $h$ that are compatible. We will use $h(v) = 0$ for all $v \neq s$, and $h(s) = n$, as our initial labeling. To make a preflow $f$ compatible with this labeling, we need to make sure that no edges leaving $s$ are in the residual graph (as these edges do not satisfy the steepness condition). To this end, we define the initial preflow as $f(e) = c_e$ for all edges $e = (s, v)$ leaving the source, and $f(e) = 0$ for all other edges.

**(7.23)**   *The initial preflow f and labeling h are compatible.*

***Pushing and Relabeling***   Next we will discuss the steps the algorithm makes toward turning the preflow $f$ into a feasible flow, while keeping it compatible with some labeling $h$. Consider any node $v$ that has excess—that is, $e_f(v) > 0$. If there is any edge $e$ in the residual graph $G_f$ that leaves $v$ and goes to a node $w$ at a lower height (note that $h(w)$ is at most 1 less than $h(v)$ due to the steepness condition), then we can modify $f$ by pushing some of the excess flow from $v$ to $w$. We will call this a *push* operation.

```
push(f, h, v, w)
   Applicable if  e_f(v) > 0,  h(w) < h(v)  and  (v, w) ∈ E_f
   If  e = (v, w) is a forward edge then
      let  δ = min(e_f(v), c_e − f(e))  and
      increase  f(e) by  δ
   If  (v, w) is a backward edge then
      let  e = (w, v),  δ = min(e_f(v), f(e))  and
      decrease  f(e) by  δ
   Return(f, h)
```

If we cannot push the excess of $v$ along any edge leaving $v$, then we will need to raise $v$'s height. We will call this a *relabel* operation.

```
relabel(f, h, v)
   Applicable if  e_f(v) > 0,  and
        for all edges  (v, w) ∈ E_f  we have  h(w) ≥ h(v)
   Increase  h(v) by 1
   Return(f, h)
```

***The Full Preflow-Push Algorithm***   So, in summary, the Preflow-Push Algorithm is as follows.

```
Preflow-Push
   Initially  h(v) = 0 for all  v ≠ s  and  h(s) = n  and
   f(e) = c_e for all  e = (s, v) and f(e) = 0 for all other edges
   While there is a node  v ≠ t  with excess  e_f(v) > 0
      Let  v be a node with excess
      If there is  w such that push(f, h, v, w) can be applied then
         push(f, h, v, w)
```

```
        Else
            relabel(f, h, v)
    Endwhile
    Return(f)
```

## Analyzing the Algorithm

As usual, this algorithm is somewhat underspecified. For an implementation of the algorithm, we will have to specify which node with excess to choose, and how to efficiently select an edge on which to push. However, it is clear that each iteration of this algorithm can be implemented in polynomial time. (We'll discuss later how to implement it reasonably efficiently.) Further, it is not hard to see that the preflow $f$ and the labeling $h$ are compatible throughout the algorithm. If the algorithm terminates—something that is far from obvious based on its description—then there are no nodes other than $t$ with positive excess, and hence the preflow $f$ is in fact a flow. It then follows from (7.22) that $f$ would be a maximum flow at termination.

We summarize a few simple observations about the algorithm.

> **(7.24)** *Throughout the Preflow-Push Algorithm:*
>
> (i) *the labels are nonnegative integers;*
>
> (ii) *$f$ is a preflow, and if the capacities are integral, then the preflow $f$ is integral; and*
>
> (iii) *the preflow $f$ and labeling $h$ are compatible.*
>
> *If the algorithm returns a preflow $f$, then $f$ is a flow of maximum value.*

**Proof.** By (7.23) the initial preflow $f$ and labeling $h$ are compatible. We will show using induction on the number of push and relabel operations that $f$ and $h$ satisfy the properties of the statement. The push operation modifies the preflow $f$, but the bounds on $\delta$ guarantee that the $f$ returned satisfies the capacity constraints, and that excesses all remain nonnegative, so $f$ is a preflow. To see that the preflow $f$ and the labeling $h$ are compatible, note that $\text{push}(f, h, v, w)$ can add one edge to the residual graph, the reverse edge $(v, w)$, and this edge does satisfy the steepness condition. The relabel operation increases the label of $v$, and hence increases the steepness of all edges leaving $v$. However, it only applies when no edge leaving $v$ in the residual graph is going downward, and hence the preflow $f$ and the labeling $h$ are compatible after relabeling.

The algorithm terminates if no node other than $s$ or $t$ has excess. In this case, $f$ is a flow by definition; and since the preflow $f$ and the labeling $h$

remain compatible throughout the algorithm, (7.22) implies that $f$ is a flow of maximum value.  ■

Next we will consider the number of `push` and `relabel` operations. First we will prove a limit on the `relabel` operations, and this will help prove a limit on the maximum number of `push` operations possible. The algorithm never changes the label of $s$ (as the source never has positive excess). Each other node $v$ starts with $h(v) = 0$, and its label increases by 1 every time it changes. So we simply need to give a limit on how high a label can get. We only consider a node $v$ for `relabel` when $v$ has excess. The only source of flow in the network is the source $s$; hence, intuitively, the excess at $v$ must have originated at $s$. The following consequence of this fact will be key to bounding the labels.

**(7.25)**    *Let $f$ be a preflow. If the node $v$ has excess, then there is a path in $G_f$ from $v$ to the source $s$.*

**Proof.** Let $A$ denote all the nodes $w$ such that there is a path from $w$ to $s$ in the residual graph $G_f$, and let $B = V - A$. We need to show that all nodes with excess are in $A$.

Notice that $s \in A$. Further, no edges $e = (x, y)$ leaving $A$ can have positive flow, as an edge with $f(e) > 0$ would give rise to a reverse edge $(y, x)$ in the residual graph, and then $y$ would have been in $A$. Now consider the sum of excesses in the set $B$, and recall that each node in $B$ has nonnegative excess, as $s \notin B$.

$$0 \leq \sum_{v \in B} e_f(v) = \sum_{v \in B} (f^{\text{in}}(v) - f^{\text{out}}(v))$$

Let's rewrite the sum on the right as follows. If an edge $e$ has both ends in $B$, then $f(e)$ appears once in the sum with a "$+$" and once with a "$-$", and hence these two terms cancel out. If $e$ has only its head in $B$, then $e$ leaves $A$, and we saw above that all edges leaving $A$ have $f(e) = 0$. If $e$ has only its tail in $B$, then $f(e)$ appears just once in the sum, with a "$-$". So we get

$$0 \leq \sum_{v \in B} e_f(v) = -f^{\text{out}}(B).$$

Since flows are nonnegative, we see that the sum of the excesses in $B$ is zero; since each individual excess in $B$ is nonnegative, they must therefore all be 0.

■

Now we are ready to prove that the labels do not change too much. Recall that $n$ denotes the number of nodes in $V$.

**(7.26)** *Throughout the algorithm, all nodes have $h(v) \leq 2n - 1$.*

**Proof.** The initial labels $h(t) = 0$ and $h(s) = n$ do not change during the algorithm. Consider some other node $v \neq s, t$. The algorithm changes $v$'s label only when applying the `relabel` operation, so let $f$ and $h$ be the preflow and labeling returned by a `relabel`$(f, h, v)$ operation. By (7.25) there is a path $P$ in the residual graph $G_f$ from $v$ to $s$. Let $|P|$ denote the number of edges in $P$, and note that $|P| \leq n - 1$. The steepness condition implies that heights of the nodes can decrease by at most 1 along each edge in $P$, and hence $h(v) - h(s) \leq |P|$, which proves the statement. ∎

Labels are monotone increasing throughout the algorithm, so this statement immediately implies a limit on the number of relabeling operations.

**(7.27)** *Throughout the algorithm, each node is relabeled at most $2n - 1$ times, and the total number of relabeling operations is less than $2n^2$.*

Next we will bound the number of `push` operations. We will distinguish two kinds of `push` operations. A `push`$(f, h, v, w)$ operation is *saturating* if either $e = (v, w)$ is a forward edge in $E_f$ and $\delta = c_e - f(e)$, or $(v, w)$ is a backward edge with $e = (w, v)$ and $\delta = f(e)$. In other words, the push is saturating if, after the push, the edge $(v, w)$ is no longer in the residual graph. All other `push` operations will be referred to as *nonsaturating*.

**(7.28)** *Throughout the algorithm, the number of saturating `push` operations is at most $2nm$.*

**Proof.** Consider an edge $(v, w)$ in the residual graph. After a saturating `push`$(f, h, v, w)$ operation, we have $h(v) = h(w) + 1$, and the edge $(v, w)$ is no longer in the residual graph $G_f$, as shown in Figure 7.8. Before we can push again along this edge, first we have to push from $w$ to $v$ to make the edge $(v, w)$ appear in the residual graph. However, in order to push from $w$ to $v$, we first need for $w$'s label to increase by at least 2 (so that $w$ is above $v$). The label of $w$ can increase by 2 at most $n - 1$ times, so a saturating push from $v$ to $w$ can occur at most $n$ times. Each edge $e \in E$ can give rise to two edges in the residual graph, so overall we can have at most $2nm$ saturating pushes. ∎

The hardest part of the analysis is proving a bound on the number of nonsaturating pushes, and this also will be the bottleneck for the theoretical bound on the running time.

**(7.29)** *Throughout the algorithm, the number of nonsaturating `push` operations is at most $2n^2m$.*

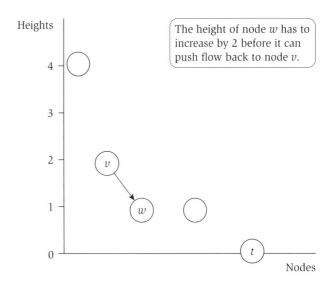

**Figure 7.8** After a saturating push($f, h, v, w$), the height of $v$ exceeds the height of $w$ by 1.

**Proof.** For this proof, we will use a so-called *potential function method*. For a preflow $f$ and a compatible labeling $h$, we define

$$\Phi(f, h) = \sum_{v: e_f(v) > 0} h(v)$$

to be the sum of the heights of all nodes with positive excess. ($\Phi$ is often called a *potential* since it resembles the "potential energy" of all nodes with positive excess.)

In the initial preflow and labeling, all nodes with positive excess are at height 0, so $\Phi(f, h) = 0$. $\Phi(f, h)$ remains nonnegative throughout the algorithm. A nonsaturating $\mathtt{push}(f, h, v, w)$ operation decreases $\Phi(f, h)$ by at least 1, since after the push the node $v$ will have no excess, and $w$, the only node that gets new excess from the operation, is at a height 1 less than $v$. However, each saturating $\mathtt{push}$ and each $\mathtt{relabel}$ operation can increase $\Phi(f, h)$. A $\mathtt{relabel}$ operation increases $\Phi(f, h)$ by exactly 1. There are at most $2n^2$ $\mathtt{relabel}$ operations, so the total increase in $\Phi(f, h)$ due to $\mathtt{relabel}$ operations is $2n^2$. A saturating $\mathtt{push}(f, h, v, w)$ operation does not change labels, but it can increase $\Phi(f, h)$, since the node $w$ may suddenly acquire positive excess after the push. This would increase $\Phi(f, h)$ by the height of $w$, which is at most $2n - 1$. There are at most $2nm$ saturating $\mathtt{push}$ operations, so the total increase in $\Phi(f, h)$ due to $\mathtt{push}$ operations is at most $2mn(2n - 1)$. So, between the two causes, $\Phi(f, h)$ can increase by at most $4mn^2$ during the algorithm.

edge is not in the residual graph. In the first case, we clearly need to relabel $v$ before applying a push on this edge. In the latter case, one needs to apply push to the reverse edge $(w, v)$ to make $(v, w)$ reenter the residual graph. However, when we apply push to edge $(w, v)$, then $w$ is above $v$, and so $v$ needs to be relabeled before one can push flow from $v$ to $w$ again. ∎

Since edges do not have to be considered again for push before relabeling, we get the following.

**(7.32)** *When the* current($v$) *pointer reaches the end of the edge list for $v$, the* relabel *operation can be applied to node $v$.*

After relabeling node $v$, we reset current($v$) to the first edge on the list and start considering edges again in the order they appear on $v$'s list.

**(7.33)** *The running time of the Preflow-Push Algorithm, implemented using the above data structures, is $O(mn)$ plus $O(1)$ for each nonsaturating* push *operation. In particular, the generic Preflow-Push Algorithm runs in $O(n^2m)$ time, while the version where we always select the node at maximum height runs in $O(n^3)$ time.*

**Proof.** The initial flow and relabeling is set up in $O(m)$ time. Both push and relabel operations can be implemented in $O(1)$ time, once the operation has been selected. Consider a node $v$. We know that $v$ can be relabeled at most $2n$ times throughout the algorithm. We will consider the total time the algorithm spends on finding the right edge on which to push flow out of node $v$, between two times that node $v$ gets relabeled. If node $v$ has $d_v$ adjacent edges, then by (7.32) we spend $O(d_v)$ time on advancing the current($v$) pointer between consecutive relabelings of $v$. Thus the total time spent on advancing the current pointers throughout the algorithm is $O(\sum_{v \in V} nd_v) = O(mn)$, as claimed. ∎

## 7.5 A First Application: The Bipartite Matching Problem

Having developed a set of powerful algorithms for the Maximum-Flow Problem, we now turn to the task of developing applications of maximum flows and minimum cuts in graphs. We begin with two very basic applications. First, in this section, we discuss the Bipartite Matching Problem mentioned at the beginning of this chapter. In the next section, we discuss the more general *Disjoint Paths Problem*.

## The Problem

One of our original goals in developing the Maximum-Flow Problem was to be able to solve the Bipartite Matching Problem, and we now show how to do this. Recall that a *bipartite graph* $G = (V, E)$ is an undirected graph whose node set can be partitioned as $V = X \cup Y$, with the property that every edge $e \in E$ has one end in $X$ and the other end in $Y$. A *matching* $M$ in $G$ is a subset of the edges $M \subseteq E$ such that each node appears in at most one edge in $M$. The Bipartite Matching Problem is that of finding a matching in $G$ of largest possible size.

## Designing the Algorithm

The graph defining a matching problem is undirected, while flow networks are directed; but it is actually not difficult to use an algorithm for the Maximum-Flow Problem to find a maximum matching.

Beginning with the graph $G$ in an instance of the Bipartite Matching Problem, we construct a flow network $G'$ as shown in Figure 7.9. First we direct all edges in $G$ from $X$ to $Y$. We then add a node $s$, and an edge $(s, x)$ from $s$ to each node in $X$. We add a node $t$, and an edge $(y, t)$ from each node in $Y$ to $t$. Finally, we give each edge in $G'$ a capacity of 1.

We now compute a maximum $s$-$t$ flow in this network $G'$. We will discover that the value of this maximum is equal to the size of the maximum matching in $G$. Moreover, our analysis will show how one can use the flow itself to recover the matching.

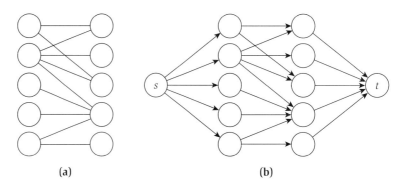

(a)                                (b)

**Figure 7.9** (a) A bipartite graph. (b) The corresponding flow network, with all capacities equal to 1.

## ✐ Analyzing the Algorithm

The analysis is based on showing that integer-valued flows in $G'$ encode matchings in $G$ in a fairly transparent fashion. First, suppose there is a matching in $G$ consisting of $k$ edges $(x_{i_1}, y_{i_1}), \ldots, (x_{i_k}, y_{i_k})$. Then consider the flow $f$ that sends one unit along each path of the form $s, x_{i_j}, y_{i_j}, t$—that is, $f(e) = 1$ for each edge on one of these paths. One can verify easily that the capacity and conservation conditions are indeed met and that $f$ is an $s$-$t$ flow of value $k$.

Conversely, suppose there is a flow $f'$ in $G'$ of value $k$. By the integrality theorem for maximum flows (7.14), we know there is an integer-valued flow $f$ of value $k$; and since all capacities are 1, this means that $f(e)$ is equal to either 0 or 1 for each edge $e$. Now, consider the set $M'$ of edges of the form $(x, y)$ on which the flow value is 1.

Here are three simple facts about the set $M'$.

**(7.34)**  *$M'$ contains $k$ edges.*

**Proof.** To prove this, consider the cut $(A, B)$ in $G'$ with $A = \{s\} \cup X$. The value of the flow is the total flow leaving $A$, minus the total flow entering $A$. The first of these terms is simply the cardinality of $M'$, since these are the edges leaving $A$ that carry flow, and each carries exactly one unit of flow. The second of these terms is 0, since there are no edges entering $A$. Thus, $M'$ contains $k$ edges.  ∎

**(7.35)**  *Each node in $X$ is the tail of at most one edge in $M'$.*

**Proof.** To prove this, suppose $x \in X$ were the tail of at least two edges in $M'$. Since our flow is integer-valued, this means that at least two units of flow leave from $x$. By conservation of flow, at least two units of flow would have to come into $x$—but this is not possible, since only a single edge of capacity 1 enters $x$. Thus $x$ is the tail of at most one edge in $M'$.  ∎

By the same reasoning, we can show

**(7.36)**  *Each node in $Y$ is the head of at most one edge in $M'$.*

Combining these facts, we see that if we view $M'$ as a set of edges in the original bipartite graph $G$, we get a matching of size $k$. In summary, we have proved the following fact.

**(7.37)**  *The size of the maximum matching in $G$ is equal to the value of the maximum flow in $G'$; and the edges in such a matching in $G$ are the edges that carry flow from $X$ to $Y$ in $G'$.*

Note the crucial way in which the integrality theorem (7.14) figured in this construction: we needed to know if there is a maximum flow in $G'$ that takes only the values 0 and 1.

**Bounding the Running Time**  Now let's consider how quickly we can compute a maximum matching in $G$. Let $n = |X| = |Y|$, and let $m$ be the number of edges of $G$. We'll tacitly assume that there is at least one edge incident to each node in the original problem, and hence $m \geq n/2$. The time to compute a maximum matching is dominated by the time to compute an integer-valued maximum flow in $G'$, since converting this to a matching in $G$ is simple. For this flow problem, we have that $C = \sum_{e \text{ out of } s} c_e = |X| = n$, as $s$ has an edge of capacity 1 to each node of $X$. Thus, by using the $O(mC)$ bound in (7.5), we get the following.

> **(7.38)**  *The Ford-Fulkerson Algorithm can be used to find a maximum matching in a bipartite graph in $O(mn)$ time.*

It's interesting that if we were to use the "better" bounds of $O(m^2 \log_2 C)$ or $O(n^3)$ that we developed in the previous sections, we'd get the inferior running times of $O(m^2 \log n)$ or $O(n^3)$ for this problem. There is nothing contradictory in this. These bounds were designed to be good for *all* instances, even when $C$ is very large relative to $m$ and $n$. But $C = n$ for the Bipartite Matching Problem, and so the cost of this extra sophistication is not needed.

It is worthwhile to consider what the augmenting paths mean in the network $G'$. Consider the matching $M$ consisting of edges $(x_2, y_2)$, $(x_3, y_3)$, and $(x_5, y_5)$ in the bipartite graph in Figure 7.1; see also Figure 7.10. Let $f$ be the corresponding flow in $G'$. This matching is not maximum, so $f$ is not a maximum $s$-$t$ flow, and hence there is an augmenting path in the residual graph $G'_f$. One such augmenting path is marked in Figure 7.10(b). Note that the edges $(x_2, y_2)$ and $(x_3, y_3)$ are used backward, and all other edges are used forward. All augmenting paths must alternate between edges used backward and forward, as all edges of the graph $G'$ go from $X$ to $Y$. Augmenting paths are therefore also called *alternating paths* in the context of finding a maximum matching. The effect of this augmentation is to take the edges used backward out of the matching, and replace them with the edges going forward. Because the augmenting path goes from $s$ to $t$, there is one more forward edge than backward edge; thus the size of the matching increases by one.

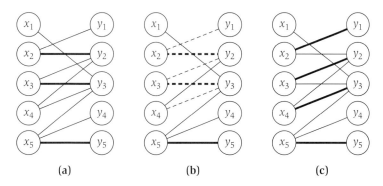

**Figure 7.10** (a) A bipartite graph, with a matching $M$. (b) The augmenting path in the corresponding residual graph. (c) The matching obtained by the augmentation.

## Extensions: The Structure of Bipartite Graphs with No Perfect Matching

Algorithmically, we've seen how to find perfect matchings: We use the algorithm above to find a maximum matching and then check to see if this matching is perfect.

But let's ask a slightly less algorithmic question. Not all bipartite graphs have perfect matchings. What does a bipartite graph without a perfect matching look like? Is there an easy way to see that a bipartite graph does not have a perfect matching—or at least an easy way to convince someone the graph has no perfect matching, after we run the algorithm? More concretely, it would be nice if the algorithm, upon concluding that there is no perfect matching, could produce a short "certificate" of this fact. The certificate could allow someone to be quickly convinced that there is no perfect matching, without having to look over a trace of the entire execution of the algorithm.

One way to understand the idea of such a certificate is as follows. We can decide if the graph $G$ has a perfect matching by checking if the maximum flow in a related graph $G'$ has value at least $n$. By the Max-Flow Min-Cut Theorem, there will be an $s$-$t$ cut of capacity less than $n$ if the maximum-flow value in $G'$ has value less than $n$. So, in a way, a cut with capacity less than $n$ provides such a certificate. However, we want a certificate that has a natural meaning in terms of the original graph $G$.

What might such a certificate look like? For example, if there are nodes $x_1, x_2 \in X$ that have only one incident edge each, and the other end of each edge is the same node $y$, then clearly the graph has no perfect matching: both $x_1$ and $x_2$ would need to get matched to the same node $y$. More generally, consider a subset of nodes $A \subseteq X$, and let $\Gamma(A) \subseteq Y$ denote the set of all nodes that are adjacent to nodes in $A$. If the graph has a perfect matching, then each node in $A$ has to be matched to a different node in $\Gamma(A)$, so $\Gamma(A)$ has to be at least as large as $A$. This gives us the following fact.

**(7.39)**    *If a bipartite graph $G = (V, E)$ with two sides $X$ and $Y$ has a perfect matching, then for all $A \subseteq X$ we must have $|\Gamma(A)| \geq |A|$.*

This statement suggests a type of certificate demonstrating that a graph does not have a perfect matching: a set $A \subseteq X$ such that $|\Gamma(A)| < |A|$. But is the converse of (7.39) also true? Is it the case that whenever there is no perfect matching, there is a set $A$ like this that proves it? The answer turns out to be yes, provided we add the obvious condition that $|X| = |Y|$ (without which there could certainly not be a perfect matching). This statement is known in the literature as *Hall's Theorem*, though versions of it were discovered independently by a number of different people—perhaps first by König—in the early 1900s. The proof of the statement also provides a way to find such a subset $A$ in polynomial time.

**(7.40)**    *Assume that the bipartite graph $G = (V, E)$ has two sides $X$ and $Y$ such that $|X| = |Y|$. Then the graph $G$ either has a perfect matching or there is a subset $A \subseteq X$ such that $|\Gamma(A)| < |A|$. A perfect matching or an appropriate subset $A$ can be found in $O(mn)$ time.*

**Proof.** We will use the same graph $G'$ as in (7.37). Assume that $|X| = |Y| = n$. By (7.37) the graph $G$ has a maximum matching if and only if the value of the maximum flow in $G'$ is $n$.

We need to show that if the value of the maximum flow is less than $n$, then there is a subset $A$ such that $|\Gamma(A)| < |A|$, as claimed in the statement. By the Max-Flow Min-Cut Theorem (7.12), if the maximum-flow value is less than $n$, then there is a cut $(A', B')$ with capacity less than $n$ in $G'$. Now the set $A'$ contains $s$, and may contain nodes from both $X$ and $Y$ as shown in Figure 7.11. We claim that the set $A = X \cap A'$ has the claimed property. This will prove both parts of the statement, as we've seen in (7.11) that a minimum cut $(A', B')$ can also be found by running the Ford-Fulkerson Algorithm.

First we claim that one can modify the minimum cut $(A', B')$ so as to ensure that $\Gamma(A) \subseteq A'$, where $A = X \cap A'$ as before. To do this, consider a node $y \in \Gamma(A)$ that belongs to $B'$ as shown in Figure 7.11 (a). We claim that by moving $y$ from $B'$ to $A'$, we do not increase the capacity of the cut. For what happens when we move $y$ from $B'$ to $A'$? The edge $(y, t)$ now crosses the cut, increasing the capacity by one. But previously there was *at least* one edge $(x, y)$ with $x \in A$, since $y \in \Gamma(A)$; all edges from $A$ and $y$ used to cross the cut, and don't anymore. Thus, overall, the capacity of the cut cannot increase. (Note that we

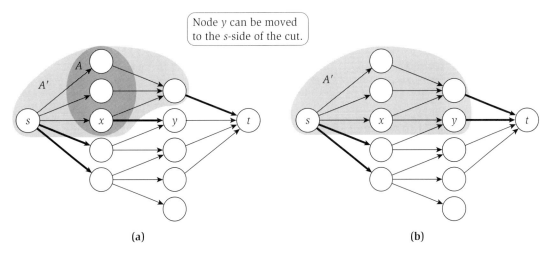

**Figure 7.11** (a) A minimum cut in proof of (7.40). (b) The same cut after moving node $y$ to the $A'$ side. The edges crossing the cut are dark.

don't have to be concerned about nodes $x \in X$ that are not in $A$. The two ends of the edge $(x, y)$ will be on different sides of the cut, but this edge does not add to the capacity of the cut, as it goes from $B'$ to $A'$.)

Next consider the capacity of this minimum cut $(A', B')$ that has $\Gamma(A) \subseteq A'$ as shown in Figure 7.11(b). Since all neighbors of $A$ belong to $A'$, we see that the only edges out of $A'$ are either edges that leave the source $s$ or that enter the sink $t$. Thus the capacity of the cut is exactly

$$c(A', B') = |X \cap B'| + |Y \cap A'|.$$

Notice that $|X \cap B'| = n - |A|$, and $|Y \cap A'| \geq |\Gamma(A)|$. Now the assumption that $c(A', B') < n$ implies that

$$n - |A| + |\Gamma(A)| \leq |X \cap B'| + |Y \cap A'| = c(A', B') < n.$$

Comparing the first and the last terms, we get the claimed inequality $|A| > |\Gamma(A)|$. ∎

## 7.6 Disjoint Paths in Directed and Undirected Graphs

In Section 7.1, we described a flow $f$ as a kind of "traffic" in the network. But our actual definition of a flow has a much more static feel to it: For each edge $e$, we simply specify a number $f(e)$ saying the amount of flow crossing $e$. Let's see if we can revive the more dynamic, traffic-oriented picture a bit, and try formalizing the sense in which units of flow "travel" from the source to the sink. From this more dynamic view of flows, we will arrive at something called the *s-t Disjoint Paths Problem*.

## The Problem

In defining this problem precisely, we will deal with two issues. First, we will make precise this intuitive correspondence between units of flow traveling along paths, and the notion of flow we've studied so far. Second, we will extend the Disjoint Paths Problem to *undirected* graphs. We'll see that, despite the fact that the Maximum-Flow Problem was defined for a directed graph, it can naturally be used also to handle related problems on undirected graphs.

We say that a set of paths is *edge-disjoint* if their edge sets are disjoint, that is, no two paths share an edge, though multiple paths may go through some of the same nodes. Given a directed graph $G = (V, E)$ with two distinguished nodes $s, t \in V$, the *Directed Edge-Disjoint Paths Problem* is to find the maximum number of edge-disjoint *s-t* paths in $G$. The *Undirected Edge-Disjoint Paths Problem* is to find the maximum number of edge-disjoint *s-t* paths in an undirected graph $G$. The related question of finding paths that are not only edge-disjoint, but also node-disjoint (of course, other than at nodes $s$ and $t$) will be considered in the exercises to this chapter.

## Designing the Algorithm

Both the directed and the undirected versions of the problem can be solved very naturally using flows. Let's start with the directed problem. Given the graph $G = (V, E)$, with its two distinguished nodes $s$ and $t$, we define a flow network in which $s$ and $t$ are the source and sink, respectively, and with a capacity of 1 on each edge. Now suppose there are $k$ edge-disjoint *s-t* paths. We can make each of these paths carry one unit of flow: We set the flow to be $f(e) = 1$ for each edge $e$ on any of the paths, and $f(e') = 0$ on all other edges, and this defines a feasible flow of value $k$.

**(7.41)**    *If there are k edge-disjoint paths in a directed graph G from s to t, then the value of the maximum s-t flow in G is at least k.*

Suppose we could show the converse to (7.41) as well: If there is a flow of value $k$, then there exist $k$ edge-disjoint *s-t* paths. Then we could simply compute a maximum *s-t* flow in $G$ and declare (correctly) this to be the maximum number of edge-disjoint *s-t* paths.

We now proceed to prove this converse statement, confirming that this approach using flow indeed gives us the correct answer. Our analysis will also provide a way to extract $k$ edge-disjoint paths from an integer-valued flow sending $k$ units from $s$ to $t$. Thus computing a maximum flow in $G$ will not only give us the maximum *number* of edge-disjoint paths, but the paths as well.

## Analyzing the Algorithm

Proving the converse direction of (7.41) is the heart of the analysis, since it will immediately establish the optimality of the flow-based algorithm to find disjoint paths.

To prove this, we will consider a flow of value at least $k$, and construct $k$ edge-disjoint paths. By (7.14), we know that there is a maximum flow $f$ with integer flow values. Since all edges have a capacity bound of 1, and the flow is integer-valued, each edge that carries flow under $f$ has exactly one unit of flow on it. Thus we just need to show the following.

**(7.42)** *If $f$ is a 0-1 valued flow of value $v$, then the set of edges with flow value $f(e) = 1$ contains a set of $v$ edge-disjoint paths.*

**Proof.** We prove this by induction on the number of edges in $f$ that carry flow. If $v = 0$, there is nothing to prove. Otherwise, there must be an edge $(s, u)$ that carries one unit of flow. We now "trace out" a path of edges that must also carry flow: Since $(s, u)$ carries a unit of flow, it follows by conservation that there is some edge $(u, v)$ that carries one unit of flow, and then there must be an edge $(v, w)$ that carries one unit of flow, and so forth. If we continue in this way, one of two things will eventually happen: Either we will reach $t$, or we will reach a node $v$ for the second time.

If the first case happens—we find a path $P$ from $s$ to $t$—then we'll use this path as one of our $v$ paths. Let $f'$ be the flow obtained by decreasing the flow values on the edges along $P$ to 0. This new flow $f'$ has value $v - 1$, and it has fewer edges that carry flow. Applying the induction hypothesis for $f'$, we get $v - 1$ edge-disjoint paths, which, along with path $P$, form the $v$ paths claimed.

If $P$ reaches a node $v$ for the second time, then we have a situation like the one pictured in Figure 7.12. (The edges in the figure all carry one unit of flow, and the dashed edges indicate the path traversed so far, which has just reached a node $v$ for the second time.) In this case, we can make progress in a different way.

Consider the cycle $C$ of edges visited between the first and second appearances of $v$. We obtain a new flow $f'$ from $f$ by decreasing the flow values on the edges along $C$ to 0. This new flow $f'$ has value $v$, but it has fewer edges that carry flow. Applying the induction hypothesis for $f'$, we get the $v$ edge-disjoint paths as claimed. ∎

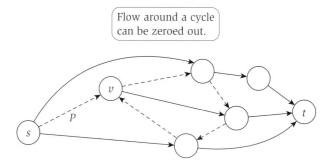

**Figure 7.12** The edges in the figure all carry one unit of flow. The path $P$ of dashed edges is one possible path in the proof of (7.42).

We can summarize (7.41) and (7.42) in the following result.

**(7.43)**   *There are k edge-disjoint paths in a directed graph G from s to t if and only if the value of the maximum value of an s-t flow in G is at least k.*

Notice also how the proof of (7.42) provides an actual procedure for constructing the $k$ paths, given an integer-valued maximum flow in $G$. This procedure is sometimes referred to as a *path decomposition* of the flow, since it "decomposes" the flow into a constituent set of paths. Hence we have shown that our flow-based algorithm finds the maximum number of edge-disjoint $s$-$t$ paths and also gives us a way to construct the actual paths.

***Bounding the Running Time***   For this flow problem, $C = \sum_{e \text{ out of } s} c_e \leq |V| = n$, as there are at most $|V|$ edges out of $s$, each of which has capacity 1. Thus, by using the $O(mC)$ bound in (7.5), we get an integer maximum flow in $O(mn)$ time.

The path decomposition procedure in the proof of (7.42), which produces the paths themselves, can also be made to run in $O(mn)$ time. To see this, note that this procedure, with a little care, can produce a single path from $s$ to $t$ using at most constant work per edge in the graph, and hence in $O(m)$ time. Since there can be at most $n - 1$ edge-disjoint paths from $s$ to $t$ (each must use a different edge out of $s$), it therefore takes time $O(mn)$ to produce all the paths.

In summary, we have shown

**(7.44)**   *The Ford-Fulkerson Algorithm can be used to find a maximum set of edge-disjoint s-t paths in a directed graph G in O(mn) time.*

***A Version of the Max-Flow Min-Cut Theorem for Disjoint Paths***   The Max-Flow Min-Cut Theorem (7.13) can be used to give the following characterization of the maximum number of edge-disjoint $s$-$t$ paths. We say that a set $F \subseteq E$ of edges *separates* $s$ from $t$ if, after removing the edges $F$ from the graph $G$, no $s$-$t$ paths remain in the graph.

**(7.45)** *In every directed graph with nodes s and t, the maximum number of edge-disjoint s-t paths is equal to the minimum number of edges whose removal separates s from t.*

**Proof.** If the removal of a set $F \subseteq E$ of edges separates $s$ from $t$, then each $s$-$t$ path must use at least one edge from $F$, and hence the number of edge-disjoint $s$-$t$ paths is at most $|F|$.

To prove the other direction, we will use the Max-Flow Min-Cut Theorem (7.13). By (7.43) the maximum number of edge-disjoint paths is the value $v$ of the maximum $s$-$t$ flow. Now (7.13) states that there is an $s$-$t$ cut $(A, B)$ with capacity $v$. Let $F$ be the set of edges that go from $A$ to $B$. Each edge has capacity 1, so $|F| = v$ and, by the definition of an $s$-$t$ cut, removing these $v$ edges from $G$ separates $s$ from $t$. ∎

This result, then, can be viewed as the natural special case of the Max-Flow Min-Cut Theorem in which all edge capacities are equal to 1. In fact, this special case was proved by Menger in 1927, much before the full Max-Flow Min-Cut Theorem was formulated and proved; for this reason, (7.45) is often called *Menger's Theorem*. If we think about it, the proof of Hall's Theorem (7.40) for bipartite matchings involves a reduction to a graph with unit-capacity edges, and so it can be proved using Menger's Theorem rather than the general Max-Flow Min-Cut Theorem. In other words, Hall's Theorem is really a special case of Menger's Theorem, which in turn is a special case of the Max-Flow Min-Cut Theorem. And the history follows this progression, since they were discovered in this order, a few decades apart.[2]

## Extensions: Disjoint Paths in Undirected Graphs

Finally, we consider the disjoint paths problem in an undirected graph $G$. Despite the fact that our graph $G$ is now undirected, we can use the maximum-flow algorithm to obtain edge-disjoint paths in $G$. The idea is quite simple: We replace each undirected edge $(u, v)$ in $G$ by two directed edges $(u, v)$ and

---

[2] In fact, in an interesting retrospective written in 1981, Menger relates his version of the story of how he first explained his theorem to König, one of the independent discoverers of Hall's Theorem. You might think that König, having thought a lot about these problems, would have immediately grasped why Menger's generalization of his theorem was true, and perhaps even considered it obvious. But, in fact, the opposite happened; König didn't believe it could be right and stayed up all night searching for a counterexample. The next day, exhausted, he sought out Menger and asked him for the proof.

$(v, u)$, and in this way create a directed version $G'$ of $G$. (We may delete the edges into $s$ and out of $t$, since they are not useful.) Now we want to use the Ford-Fulkerson Algorithm in the resulting directed graph. However, there is an important issue we need to deal with first. Notice that two paths $P_1$ and $P_2$ may be edge-disjoint in the directed graph and yet share an edge in the undirected graph $G$: This happens if $P_1$ uses directed edge $(u, v)$ while $P_2$ uses edge $(v, u)$. However, it is not hard to see that there always exists a maximum flow in any network that uses at most *one* out of each pair of oppositely directed edges.

**(7.46)** *In any flow network, there is a maximum flow $f$ where for all opposite directed edges $e = (u, v)$ and $e' = (v, u)$, either $f(e) = 0$ or $f(e') = 0$. If the capacities of the flow network are integral, then there also is such an integral maximum flow.*

**Proof.** We consider any maximum flow $f$, and we modify it to satisfy the claimed condition. Assume $e = (u, v)$ and $e' = (v, u)$ are opposite directed edges, and $f(e) \neq 0$, $f(e') \neq 0$. Let $\delta$ be the smaller of these values, and modify $f$ by decreasing the flow value on both $e$ and $e'$ by $\delta$. The resulting flow $f'$ is feasible, has the same value as $f$, and its value on one of $e$ and $e'$ is 0. ∎

Now we can use the Ford-Fulkerson Algorithm and the path decomposition procedure from (7.42) to obtain edge-disjoint paths in the undirected graph $G$.

**(7.47)** *There are $k$ edge-disjoint paths in an undirected graph $G$ from $s$ to $t$ if and only if the maximum value of an s-t flow in the directed version $G'$ of $G$ is at least $k$. Furthermore, the Ford-Fulkerson Algorithm can be used to find a maximum set of disjoint s-t paths in an undirected graph $G$ in $O(mn)$ time.*

The undirected analogue of (7.45) is also true, as in any *s-t* cut, at most one of the two oppositely directed edges can cross from the *s*-side to the *t*-side of the cut (for if one crosses, then the other must go from the *t*-side to the *s*-side).

**(7.48)** *In every undirected graph with nodes $s$ and $t$, the maximum number of edge-disjoint s-t paths is equal to the minimum number of edges whose removal separates $s$ from $t$.*

## 7.7 Extensions to the Maximum-Flow Problem

Much of the power of the Maximum-Flow Problem has essentially nothing to do with the fact that it models traffic in a network. Rather, it lies in the fact that many problems with a nontrivial combinatorial search component can be solved in polynomial time because they can be reduced to the problem of finding a maximum flow or a minimum cut in a directed graph.

Bipartite Matching is a natural first application in this vein; in the coming sections, we investigate a range of further applications. To begin with, we stay with the picture of flow as an abstract kind of "traffic," and look for more general conditions we might impose on this traffic. These more general conditions will turn out to be useful for some of our further applications.

In particular, we focus on two generalizations of maximum flow. We will see that both can be reduced to the basic Maximum-Flow Problem.

## The Problem: Circulations with Demands

One simplifying aspect of our initial formulation of the Maximum-Flow Problem is that we had only a single source $s$ and a single sink $t$. Now suppose that there can be a set $S$ of sources generating flow, and a set $T$ of sinks that can absorb flow. As before, there is an integer capacity on each edge.

With multiple sources and sinks, it is a bit unclear how to decide which source or sink to favor in a maximization problem. So instead of maximizing the flow value, we will consider a problem where sources have fixed *supply* values and sinks have fixed *demand* values, and our goal is to ship flow from nodes with available supply to those with given demands. Imagine, for example, that the network represents a system of highways or railway lines in which we want to ship products from factories (which have supply) to retail outlets (which have demand). In this type of problem, we will not be seeking to maximize a particular value; rather, we simply want to satisfy all the demand using the available supply.

Thus we are given a flow network $G = (V, E)$ with capacities on the edges. Now, associated with each node $v \in V$ is a *demand* $d_v$. If $d_v > 0$, this indicates that the node $v$ has a *demand* of $d_v$ for flow; the node is a sink, and it wishes to receive $d_v$ units more flow than it sends out. If $d_v < 0$, this indicates that $v$ has a *supply* of $-d_v$; the node is a source, and it wishes to send out $-d_v$ units more flow than it receives. If $d_v = 0$, then the node $v$ is neither a source nor a sink. We will assume that all capacities and demands are integers.

We use $S$ to denote the set of all nodes with negative demand and $T$ to denote the set of all nodes with positive demand. Although a node $v$ in $S$ wants to send out more flow than it receives, it will be okay for it to have flow that enters on incoming edges; it should just be more than compensated by the flow that leaves $v$ on outgoing edges. The same applies (in the opposite direction) to the set $T$.

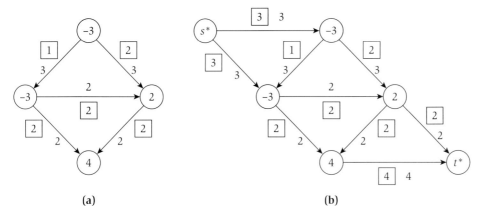

**(a)**                                        **(b)**

**Figure 7.13** (a) An instance of the Circulation Problem together with a solution: Numbers inside the nodes are demands; numbers labeling the edges are capacities and flow values, with the flow values inside boxes. (b) The result of reducing this instance to an equivalent instance of the Maximum-Flow Problem.

In this setting, we say that a *circulation* with demands $\{d_v\}$ is a function $f$ that assigns a nonnegative real number to each edge and satisfies the following two conditions.

  (i)  *(Capacity conditions)* For each $e \in E$, we have $0 \le f(e) \le c_e$.
  (ii) *(Demand conditions)* For each $v \in V$, we have $v, f^{\mathrm{in}}(v) - f^{\mathrm{out}}(v) = d_v$.

Now, instead of considering a maximization problem, we are concerned with a *feasibility problem*: We want to know whether there *exists* a circulation that meets conditions (i) and (ii).

For example, consider the instance in Figure 7.13(a). Two of the nodes are sources, with demands $-3$ and $-3$; and two of the nodes are sinks, with demands 2 and 4. The flow values in the figure constitute a feasible circulation, indicating how all demands can be satisfied while respecting the capacities.

If we consider an arbitrary instance of the Circulation Problem, here is a simple condition that must hold in order for a feasible circulation to exist: The total supply must equal the total demand.

**(7.49)**    *If there exists a feasible circulation with demands $\{d_v\}$, then $\sum_v d_v = 0$.*

**Proof.** Suppose there exists a feasible circulation $f$ in this setting. Then $\sum_v d_v = \sum_v f^{\mathrm{in}}(v) - f^{\mathrm{out}}(v)$. Now, in this latter expression, the value $f(e)$ for each edge $e = (u, v)$ is counted exactly twice: once in $f^{\mathrm{out}}(u)$ and once in $f^{\mathrm{in}}(v)$. These two terms cancel out; and since this holds for all values $f(e)$, the overall sum is 0. ■

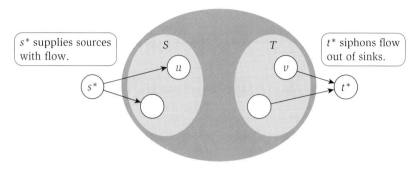

**Figure 7.14** Reducing the Circulation Problem to the Maximum-Flow Problem.

Thanks to (7.49), we know that

$$\sum_{v:d_v>0} d_v = \sum_{v:d_v<0} -d_v.$$

Let $D$ denote this common value.

## ✎ Designing and Analyzing an Algorithm for Circulations

It turns out that we can reduce the problem of finding a feasible circulation with demands $\{d_v\}$ to the problem of finding a maximum $s$-$t$ flow in a different network, as shown in Figure 7.14.

The reduction looks very much like the one we used for Bipartite Matching: we attach a "super-source" $s^*$ to each node in $S$, and a "super-sink" $t^*$ to each node in $T$. More specifically, we create a graph $G'$ from $G$ by adding new nodes $s^*$ and $t^*$ to $G$. For each node $v \in T$—that is, each node $v$ with $d_v > 0$—we add an edge $(v, t^*)$ with capacity $d_v$. For each node $u \in S$—that is, each node with $d_u < 0$—we add an edge $(s^*, u)$ with capacity $-d_u$. We carry the remaining structure of $G$ over to $G'$ unchanged.

In this graph $G'$, we will be seeking a maximum $s^*$-$t^*$ flow. Intuitively, we can think of this reduction as introducing a node $s^*$ that "supplies" all the sources with their extra flow, and a node $t^*$ that "siphons" the extra flow out of the sinks. For example, part (b) of Figure 7.13 shows the result of applying this reduction to the instance in part (a).

Note that there cannot be an $s^*$-$t^*$ flow in $G'$ of value greater than $D$, since the cut $(A, B)$ with $A = \{s^*\}$ only has capacity $D$. Now, if there is a feasible circulation $f$ with demands $\{d_v\}$ in $G$, then by sending a flow value of $-d_v$ on each edge $(s^*, v)$, and a flow value of $d_v$ on each edge $(v, t^*)$, we obtain an $s^*$-$t^*$ flow in $G'$ of value $D$, and so this is a maximum flow. Conversely, suppose there is a (maximum) $s^*$-$t^*$ flow in $G'$ of value $D$. It must be that every edge out of $s^*$, and every edge into $t^*$, is completely saturated with flow. Thus, if we delete these edges, we obtain a circulation $f$ in $G$ with $f^{in}(v) - f^{out}(v) = d_v$ for each node $v$. Further, if there is a flow of value $D$ in $G'$, then there is such a flow that takes integer values.

In summary, we have proved the following.

> **(7.50)** *There is a feasible circulation with demands $\{d_v\}$ in G if and only if the maximum $s^*$-$t^*$ flow in $G'$ has value D. If all capacities and demands in G are integers, and there is a feasible circulation, then there is a feasible circulation that is integer-valued.*

At the end of Section 7.5, we used the Max-Flow Min-Cut Theorem to derive the characterization (7.40) of bipartite graphs that do not have perfect matchings. We can give an analogous characterization for graphs that do not have a feasible circulation. The characterization uses the notion of a *cut*, adapted to the present setting. In the context of circulation problems with demands, a cut $(A, B)$ is any partition of the node set $V$ into two sets, with no restriction on which side of the partition the sources and sinks fall. We include the characterization here without a proof.

**(7.51)** *The graph G has a feasible circulation with demands $\{d_v\}$ if and only if for all cuts $(A, B)$,*

$$\sum_{v \in B} d_v \leq c(A, B).$$

It is important to note that our network has only a single "kind" of flow. Although the flow is supplied from multiple sources, and absorbed at multiple sinks, we cannot place restrictions on which source will supply the flow to which sink; we have to let our algorithm decide this. A harder problem is the *Multicommodity Flow Problem*; here sink $t_i$ must be supplied with flow that originated at source $s_i$, for each $i$. We will discuss this issue further in Chapter 11.

## 🖋 The Problem: Circulations with Demands and Lower Bounds

Finally, let us generalize the previous problem a little. In many applications, we not only want to satisfy demands at various nodes; we also want to force the flow to make use of certain edges. This can be enforced by placing *lower bounds* on edges, as well as the usual upper bounds imposed by edge capacities.

Consider a flow network $G = (V, E)$ with a *capacity* $c_e$ and a *lower bound* $\ell_e$ on each edge $e$. We will assume $0 \leq \ell_e \leq c_e$ for each $e$. As before, each node $v$ will also have a demand $d_v$, which can be either positive or negative. We will assume that all demands, capacities, and lower bounds are integers.

The given quantities have the same meaning as before, and now a lower bound $\ell_e$ means that the flow value on $e$ must be *at least* $\ell_e$. Thus a circulation in our flow network must satisfy the following two conditions.

(i) *(Capacity conditions)* For each $e \in E$, we have $\ell_e \leq f(e) \leq c_e$.

(ii) *(Demand conditions)* For every $v \in V$, we have $f^{in}(v) - f^{out}(v) = d_v$.

As before, we wish to decide whether there exists a *feasible circulation*—one that satisfies these conditions.

## Designing and Analyzing an Algorithm with Lower Bounds

Our strategy will be to reduce this to the problem of finding a circulation with demands but no lower bounds. (We've seen that this latter problem, in turn, can be reduced to the standard Maximum-Flow Problem.) The idea is as follows. We know that on each edge $e$, we need to send at least $\ell_e$ units of flow. So suppose that we define an initial circulation $f_0$ simply by $f_0(e) = \ell_e$. $f_0$ satisfies all the capacity conditions (both lower and upper bounds); but it presumably does not satisfy all the demand conditions. In particular,

$$f_0^{in}(v) - f_0^{out}(v) = \sum_{e \text{ into } v} \ell_e - \sum_{e \text{ out of } v} \ell_e.$$

Let us denote this quantity by $L_v$. If $L_v = d_v$, then we have satisfied the demand condition at $v$; but if not, then we need to superimpose a circulation $f_1$ on top of $f_0$ that will clear the remaining "imbalance" at $v$. So we need $f_1^{in}(v) - f_1^{out}(v) = d_v - L_v$. And how much capacity do we have with which to do this? Having already sent $\ell_e$ units of flow on each edge $e$, we have $c_e - \ell_e$ more units to work with.

These considerations directly motivate the following construction. Let the graph $G'$ have the same nodes and edges, with capacities and demands, but no lower bounds. The capacity of edge $e$ will be $c_e - \ell_e$. The demand of node $v$ will be $d_v - L_v$.

For example, consider the instance in Figure 7.15(a). This is the same as the instance we saw in Figure 7.13, except that we have now given one of the edges a lower bound of 2. In part (b) of the figure, we eliminate this lower bound by sending two units of flow across the edge. This reduces the upper bound on the edge and changes the demands at the two ends of the edge. In the process, it becomes clear that there is no feasible circulation, since after applying the construction there is a node with a demand of $-5$, and a total of only four units of capacity on its outgoing edges.

We now claim that our general construction produces an equivalent instance with demands but no lower bounds; we can therefore use our algorithm for this latter problem.

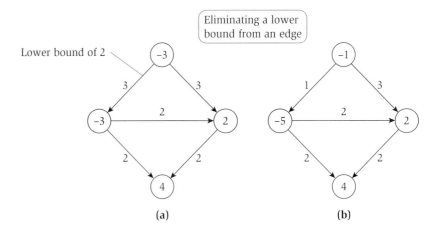

**Figure 7.15** (a) An instance of the Circulation Problem with lower bounds: Numbers inside the nodes are demands, and numbers labeling the edges are capacities. We also assign a lower bound of 2 to one of the edges. (b) The result of reducing this instance to an equivalent instance of the Circulation Problem without lower bounds.

**(7.52)**   *There is a feasible circulation in G if and only if there is a feasible circulation in G'. If all demands, capacities, and lower bounds in G are integers, and there is a feasible circulation, then there is a feasible circulation that is integer-valued.*

**Proof.** First suppose there is a circulation $f'$ in $G'$. Define a circulation $f$ in $G$ by $f(e) = f'(e) + \ell_e$. Then $f$ satisfies the capacity conditions in $G$, and

$$f^{in}(v) - f^{out}(v) = \sum_{e \text{ into } v} (\ell_e + f'(e)) - \sum_{e \text{ out of } v} (\ell_e + f'(e)) = L_v + (d_v - L_v) = d_v,$$

so it satisfies the demand conditions in $G$ as well.

Conversely, suppose there is a circulation $f$ in $G$, and define a circulation $f'$ in $G'$ by $f'(e) = f(e) - \ell_e$. Then $f'$ satisfies the capacity conditions in $G'$, and

$$(f')^{in}(v) - (f')^{out}(v) = \sum_{e \text{ into } v} (f(e) - \ell_e) - \sum_{e \text{ out of } v} (f(e) - \ell_e) = d_v - L_v,$$

so it satisfies the demand conditions in $G'$ as well.   ■

# 7.8 Survey Design

Many problems that arise in applications can, in fact, be solved efficiently by a reduction to Maximum Flow, but it is often difficult to discover when such a reduction is possible. In the next few sections, we give several paradigmatic examples of such problems. The goal is to indicate what such reductions tend to look like and to illustrate some of the most common uses of flows and cuts in the design of efficient combinatorial algorithms. One point that will emerge is the following: Sometimes the solution one wants involves the computation of a maximum flow, and sometimes it involves the computation of a minimum cut; both flows and cuts are very useful algorithmic tools.

We begin with a basic application that we call *survey design*, a simple version of a task faced by many companies wanting to measure customer satisfaction. More generally, the problem illustrates how the construction used to solve the Bipartite Matching Problem arises naturally in any setting where we want to carefully balance decisions across a set of options—in this case, designing questionnaires by balancing relevant questions across a population of consumers.

## The Problem

A major issue in the burgeoning field of *data mining* is the study of consumer preference patterns. Consider a company that sells $k$ products and has a database containing the purchase histories of a large number of customers. (Those of you with "Shopper's Club" cards may be able to guess how this data gets collected.) The company wishes to conduct a survey, sending customized questionnaires to a particular group of $n$ of its customers, to try determining which products people like overall.

Here are the guidelines for designing the survey.

- Each customer will receive questions about a certain subset of the products.
- A customer can only be asked about products that he or she has purchased.
- To make each questionnaire informative, but not too long so as to discourage participation, each customer $i$ should be asked about a number of products between $c_i$ and $c_i'$.
- Finally, to collect sufficient data about each product, there must be between $p_j$ and $p_j'$ distinct customers asked about each product $j$.

More formally, the input to the *Survey Design Problem* consists of a bipartite graph $G$ whose nodes are the customers and the products, and there is an edge between customer $i$ and product $j$ if he or she has ever purchased product $j$. Further, for each customer $i = 1, \ldots, n$, we have limits $c_i \leq c_i'$ on the number of products he or she can be asked about; for each product $j = 1, \ldots, k$, we have limits $p_j \leq p_j'$ on the number of distinct customers that have to be asked about it. The problem is to decide if there is a way to design a questionnaire for each customer so as to satisfy all these conditions.

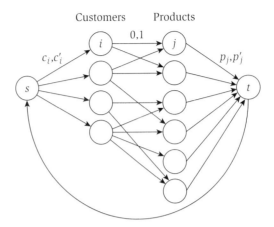

**Figure 7.16** The Survey Design Problem can be reduced to the problem of finding a feasible circulation: Flow passes from customers (with capacity bounds indicating how many questions they can be asked) to products (with capacity bounds indicating how many questions should be asked about each product).

### Designing the Algorithm

We will solve this problem by reducing it to a circulation problem on a flow network $G'$ with demands and lower bounds as shown in Figure 7.16. To obtain the graph $G'$ from $G$, we orient the edges of $G$ from customers to products, add nodes $s$ and $t$ with edges $(s, i)$ for each customer $i = 1, \ldots, n$, edges $(j, t)$ for each product $j = 1, \ldots, k$, and an edge $(t, s)$. The circulation in this network will correspond to the way in which questions are asked. The flow on the edge $(s, i)$ is the number of products included on the questionnaire for customer $i$, so this edge will have a capacity of $c'_i$ and a lower bound of $c_i$. The flow on the edge $(j, t)$ will correspond to the number of customers who were asked about product $j$, so this edge will have a capacity of $p'_j$ and a lower bound of $p_j$. Each edge $(i, j)$ going from a customer to a product he or she bought has capacity 1, and 0 as the lower bound. The flow carried by the edge $(t, s)$ corresponds to the overall number of questions asked. We can give this edge a capacity of $\sum_i c'_i$ and a lower bound of $\sum_i c_i$. All nodes have demand 0.

Our algorithm is simply to construct this network $G'$ and check whether it has a feasible circulation. We now formulate a claim that establishes the correctness of this algorithm.

### Analyzing the Algorithm

**(7.53)** *The graph $G'$ just constructed has a feasible circulation if and only if there is a feasible way to design the survey.*

**Proof.** The construction above immediately suggests a way to turn a survey design into the corresponding flow. The edge $(i, j)$ will carry one unit of flow if customer $i$ is asked about product $j$ in the survey, and will carry no flow otherwise. The flow on the edges $(s, i)$ is the number of questions asked from customer $i$, the flow on the edge $(j, t)$ is the number of customers who were asked about product $j$, and finally, the flow on edge $(t, s)$ is the overall number of questions asked. This flow satisfies the 0 demand, that is, there is flow conservation at every node. If the survey satisfies these rules, then the corresponding flow satisfies the capacities and lower bounds.

Conversely, if the Circulation Problem is feasible, then by (7.52) there is a feasible circulation that is integer-valued, and such an integer-valued circulation naturally corresponds to a feasible survey design. Customer $i$ will be surveyed about product $j$ if and only if the edge $(i, j)$ carries a unit of flow. ∎

# 7.9 Airline Scheduling

The computational problems faced by the nation's large airline carriers are almost too complex to even imagine. They have to produce schedules for thousands of routes each day that are efficient in terms of equipment usage, crew allocation, customer satisfaction, and a host of other factors—all in the face of unpredictable issues like weather and breakdowns. It's not surprising that they're among the largest consumers of high-powered algorithmic techniques.

Covering these computational problems in any realistic level of detail would take us much too far afield. Instead, we'll discuss a "toy" problem that captures, in a very clean way, some of the resource allocation issues that arise in a context such as this. And, as is common in this book, the toy problem will be much more useful for our purposes than the "real" problem, for the solution to the toy problem involves a very general technique that can be applied in a wide range of situations.

## The Problem

Suppose you're in charge of managing a fleet of airplanes and you'd like to create a flight schedule for them. Here's a very simple model for this. Your market research has identified a set of $m$ particular flight segments that would be very lucrative if you could serve them; flight segment $j$ is specified by four parameters: its origin airport, its destination airport, its departure time, and its arrival time. Figure 7.17(a) shows a simple example, consisting of six flight segments you'd like to serve with your planes over the course of a single day:

> (1) Boston (depart 6 A.M.) – Washington DC (arrive 7 A.M.)
> (2) Philadelphia (depart 7 A.M.) – Pittsburgh (arrive 8 A.M.)

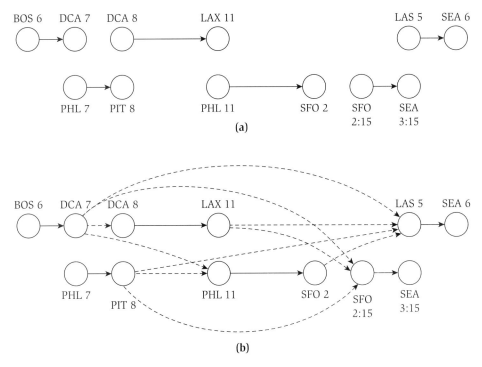

**Figure 7.17** (a) A small instance of our simple Airline Scheduling Problem. (b) An expanded graph showing which flights are reachable from which others.

*(3) Washington DC (depart 8 A.M.) – Los Angeles (arrive 11 A.M.)*
*(4) Philadelphia (depart 11 A.M.) – San Francisco (arrive 2 P.M.)*
*(5) San Francisco (depart 2:15 P.M.) – Seattle (arrive 3:15 P.M.)*
*(6) Las Vegas (depart 5 P.M.) – Seattle (arrive 6 P.M.)*

Note that each segment includes the times you want the flight to serve as well as the airports.

It is possible to use a single plane for a flight segment $i$, and then later for a flight segment $j$, provided that

(a) the destination of $i$ is the same as the origin of $j$, and there's enough time to perform maintenance on the plane in between; or

(b) you can add a flight segment in between that gets the plane from the destination of $i$ to the origin of $j$ with adequate time in between.

For example, assuming an hour for intermediate maintenance time, you could use a single plane for flights (1), (3), and (6) by having the plane sit in Washington, DC, between flights (1) and (3), and then inserting the flight

*Los Angeles (depart 12 noon) – Las Vegas (1 P.M.)*

in between flights (3) and (6).

***Formulating the Problem***    We can model this situation in a very general way as follows, abstracting away from specific rules about maintenance times and intermediate flight segments: We will simply say that flight $j$ is *reachable* from flight $i$ if it is possible to use the same plane for flight $i$, and then later for flight $j$ as well. So under our specific rules (a) and (b) above, we can easily determine for each pair $i, j$ whether flight $j$ is reachable from flight $i$. (Of course, one can easily imagine more complex rules for reachability. For example, the length of maintenance time needed in (a) might depend on the airport; or in (b) we might require that the flight segment you insert be sufficiently profitable on its own.) But the point is that we can handle any set of rules with our definition: The input to the problem will include not just the flight segments, but also a specification of the pairs $(i, j)$ for which a later flight $j$ is reachable from an earlier flight $i$. These pairs can form an arbitrary directed acyclic graph.

The goal in this problem is to determine whether it's possible to serve all $m$ flights on your original list, using at most $k$ planes total. In order to do this, you need to find a way of efficiently reusing planes for multiple flights.

For example, let's go back to the instance in Figure 7.17 and assume we have $k = 2$ planes. If we use one of the planes for flights (1), (3), and (6) as proposed above, we wouldn't be able to serve all of flights (2), (4), and (5) with the other (since there wouldn't be enough maintenance time in San Francisco between flights (4) and (5)). However, there is a way to serve all six flights using two planes, via a different solution: One plane serves flights (1), (3), and (5) (splicing in an LAX–SFO flight), while the other serves (2), (4), and (6) (splicing in PIT–PHL and SFO–LAS).

## Designing the Algorithm

We now discuss an efficient algorithm that can solve arbitrary instances of the Airline Scheduling Problem, based on network flow. We will see that flow techniques adapt very naturally to this problem.

The solution is based on the following idea. Units of flow will correspond to airplanes. We will have an edge for each flight, and upper and lower capacity bounds of 1 on these edges to require that exactly one unit of flow crosses this edge. In other words, each flight must be served by one of the planes. If $(u_i, v_i)$ is the edge representing flight $i$, and $(u_j, v_j)$ is the edge representing flight $j$, and flight $j$ is reachable from flight $i$, then we will have an edge from $v_i$ to $u_j$

with capacity 1; in this way, a unit of flow can traverse $(u_i, v_i)$ and then move directly to $(u_j, v_j)$. Such a construction of edges is shown in Figure 7.17(b).

We extend this to a flow network by including a source and sink; we now give the full construction in detail. The node set of the underlying graph $G$ is defined as follows.

- For each flight $i$, the graph $G$ will have the two nodes $u_i$ and $v_i$.
- $G$ will also have a distinct source node $s$ and sink node $t$.

The edge set of $G$ is defined as follows.

- For each $i$, there is an edge $(u_i, v_i)$ with a lower bound of 1 and a capacity of 1. *(Each flight on the list must be served.)*
- For each $i$ and $j$ so that flight $j$ is reachable from flight $i$, there is an edge $(v_i, u_j)$ with a lower bound of 0 and a capacity of 1. *(The same plane can perform flights i and j.)*
- For each $i$, there is an edge $(s, u_i)$ with a lower bound of 0 and a capacity of 1. *(Any plane can begin the day with flight i.)*
- For each $j$, there is an edge $(v_j, t)$ with a lower bound of 0 and a capacity of 1. *(Any plane can end the day with flight j.)*
- There is an edge $(s, t)$ with lower bound 0 and capacity $k$. *(If we have extra planes, we don't need to use them for any of the flights.)*

Finally, the node $s$ will have a demand of $-k$, and the node $t$ will have a demand of $k$. All other nodes will have a demand of 0.

Our algorithm is to construct the network $G$ and search for a feasible circulation in it. We now prove the correctness of this algorithm.

## Analyzing the Algorithm

**(7.54)** *There is a way to perform all flights using at most $k$ planes if and only if there is a feasible circulation in the network $G$.*

**Proof.** First, suppose there is a way to perform all flights using $k' \le k$ planes. The set of flights performed by each individual plane defines a path $P$ in the network $G$, and we send one unit of flow on each such path $P$. To satisfy the full demands at $s$ and $t$, we send $k - k'$ units of flow on the edge $(s, t)$. The resulting circulation satisfies all demand, capacity, and lower bound conditions.

Conversely, consider a feasible circulation in the network $G$. By (7.52), we know that there is a feasible circulation with integer flow values. Suppose that $k'$ units of flow are sent on edges other than $(s, t)$. Since all other edges have a capacity bound of 1, and the circulation is integer-valued, each such edge that carries flow has exactly one unit of flow on it.

We now convert this to a schedule using the same kind of construction we saw in the proof of (7.42), where we converted a flow to a collection of paths. In fact, the situation is easier here since the graph has no cycles. Consider an edge $(s, u_i)$ that carries one unit of flow. It follows by conservation that $(u_i, v_i)$ carries one unit of flow, and that there is a unique edge out of $v_i$ that carries one unit of flow. If we continue in this way, we construct a path $P$ from $s$ to $t$, so that each edge on this path carries one unit of flow. We can apply this construction to each edge of the form $(s, u_j)$ carrying one unit of flow; in this way, we produce $k'$ paths from $s$ to $t$, each consisting of edges that carry one unit of flow. Now, for each path $P$ we create in this way, we can assign a single plane to perform all the flights contained in this path. ∎

## Extensions: Modeling Other Aspects of the Problem

Airline scheduling consumes countless hours of CPU time in real life. We mentioned at the beginning, however, that our formulation here is really a toy problem; it ignores several obvious factors that would have to be taken into account in these applications. First of all, it ignores the fact that a given plane can only fly a certain number of hours before it needs to be temporarily taken out of service for more significant maintenance. Second, we are making up an optimal schedule for a single day (or at least for a single span of time) as though there were no yesterday or tomorrow; in fact we also need the planes to be optimally positioned for the start of day $N + 1$ at the end of day $N$. Third, all these planes need to be staffed by flight crews, and while crews are also reused across multiple flights, a whole different set of constraints operates here, since human beings and airplanes experience fatigue at different rates. And these issues don't even begin to cover the fact that serving any particular flight segment is not a hard constraint; rather, the real goal is to optimize revenue, and so we can pick and choose among many possible flights to include in our schedule (not to mention designing a good fare structure for passengers) in order to achieve this goal.

Ultimately, the message is probably this: Flow techniques are useful for solving problems of this type, and they are genuinely used in practice. Indeed, our solution above is a general approach to the efficient reuse of a limited set of resources in many settings. At the same time, running an airline efficiently in real life is a very difficult problem.

## 7.10 Image Segmentation

A central problem in image processing is the *segmentation* of an image into various coherent regions. For example, you may have an image representing a picture of three people standing in front of a complex background scene. A natural but difficult goal is to identify each of the three people as coherent objects in the scene.

## The Problem

One of the most basic problems to be considered along these lines is that of foreground/background segmentation: We wish to label each pixel in an image as belonging to either the foreground of the scene or the background. It turns out that a very natural model here leads to a problem that can be solved efficiently by a minimum cut computation.

Let $V$ be the set of *pixels* in the underlying image that we're analyzing. We will declare certain pairs of pixels to be *neighbors*, and use $E$ to denote the set of all pairs of neighboring pixels. In this way, we obtain an *undirected* graph $G = (V, E)$. We will be deliberately vague on what exactly we mean by a "pixel," or what we mean by the "neighbor" relation. In fact, any graph $G$ will yield an efficiently solvable problem, so we are free to define these notions in any way that we want. Of course, it is natural to picture the pixels as constituting a grid of dots, and the neighbors of a pixel to be those that are directly adjacent to it in this grid, as shown in Figure 7.18(a).

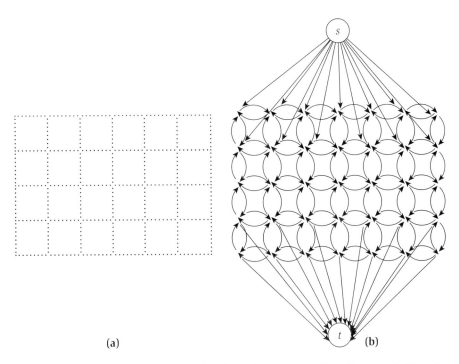

(a)    (b)

**Figure 7.18** (a) A pixel graph. (b) A sketch of the corresponding flow graph. Not all edges from the source or to the sink are drawn.

For each pixel $i$, we have a *likelihood* $a_i$ that it belongs to the foreground, and a *likelihood* $b_i$ that it belongs to the background. For our purposes, we will assume that these likelihood values are arbitrary nonnegative numbers provided as part of the problem, and that they specify how desirable it is to have pixel $i$ in the background or foreground. Beyond this, it is not crucial precisely what physical properties of the image they are measuring, or how they were determined.

In isolation, we would want to label pixel $i$ as belonging to the foreground if $a_i > b_i$, and to the background otherwise. However, decisions that we make about the neighbors of $i$ should affect our decision about $i$. If many of $i$'s neighbors are labeled "background," for example, we should be more inclined to label $i$ as "background" too; this makes the labeling "smoother" by minimizing the amount of foreground/background boundary. Thus, for each pair $(i, j)$ of neighboring pixels, there is a *separation penalty* $p_{ij} \geq 0$ for placing one of $i$ or $j$ in the foreground and the other in the background.

We can now specify our *Segmentation Problem* precisely, in terms of the likelihood and separation parameters: It is to find a partition of the set of pixels into sets $A$ and $B$ (foreground and background, respectively) so as to maximize

$$q(A, B) = \sum_{i \in A} a_i + \sum_{j \in B} b_j - \sum_{\substack{(i,j) \in E \\ |A \cap \{i,j\}| = 1}} p_{ij}.$$

Thus we are rewarded for having high likelihood values and penalized for having neighboring pairs $(i, j)$ with one pixel in $A$ and the other in $B$. The problem, then, is to compute an *optimal labeling*—a partition $(A, B)$ that maximizes $q(A, B)$.

## Designing and Analyzing the Algorithm

We notice right away that there is clearly a resemblance between the minimum-cut problem and the problem of finding an optimal labeling. However, there are a few significant differences. First, we are seeking to maximize an objective function rather than minimizing one. Second, there is no source and sink in the labeling problem; and, moreover, we need to deal with values $a_i$ and $b_i$ on the nodes. Third, we have an undirected graph $G$, whereas for the minimum-cut problem we want to work with a directed graph. Let's address these problems in order.

We deal with the fact that our Segmentation Problem is a maximization problem through the following observation. Let $Q = \sum_i (a_i + b_i)$. The sum $\sum_{i \in A} a_i + \sum_{j \in B} b_j$ is the same as the sum $Q - \sum_{i \in A} b_i - \sum_{j \in B} a_j$, so we can write

$$q(A, B) = Q - \sum_{i \in A} b_i - \sum_{j \in B} a_j - \sum_{\substack{(i,j) \in E \\ |A \cap \{i,j\}|=1}} p_{ij}.$$

Thus we see that the maximization of $q(A, B)$ is the same problem as the minimization of the quantity

$$q'(A, B) = \sum_{i \in A} b_i + \sum_{j \in B} a_j + \sum_{\substack{(i,j) \in E \\ |A \cap \{i,j\}|=1}} p_{ij}.$$

As for the missing source and the sink, we work by analogy with our constructions in previous sections: We create a new "super-source" $s$ to represent the foreground, and a new "super-sink" $t$ to represent the background. This also gives us a way to deal with the values $a_i$ and $b_i$ that reside at the nodes (whereas minimum cuts can only handle numbers associated with edges). Specifically, we will attach each of $s$ and $t$ to every pixel, and use $a_i$ and $b_i$ to define appropriate capacities on the edges between pixel $i$ and the source and sink respectively.

Finally, to take care of the undirected edges, we model each neighboring pair $(i, j)$ with *two* directed edges, $(i, j)$ and $(j, i)$, as we did in the undirected Disjoint Paths Problem. We will see that this works very well here too, since in any $s$-$t$ cut, at most one of these two oppositely directed edges can cross from the $s$-side to the $t$-side of the cut (for if one does, then the other must go from the $t$-side to the $s$-side).

Specifically, we define the following flow network $G' = (V', E')$ shown in Figure 7.18(b). The node set $V'$ consists of the set $V$ of pixels, together with two additional nodes $s$ and $t$. For each neighboring pair of pixels $i$ and $j$, we add directed edges $(i, j)$ and $(j, i)$, each with capacity $p_{ij}$. For each pixel $i$, we add an edge $(s, i)$ with capacity $a_i$ and an edge $(i, t)$ with capacity $b_i$.

Now, an $s$-$t$ cut $(A, B)$ corresponds to a partition of the pixels into sets $A$ and $B$. Let's consider how the capacity of the cut $c(A, B)$ relates to the quantity $q'(A, B)$ that we are trying to minimize. We can group the edges that cross the cut $(A, B)$ into three natural categories.

- Edges $(s, j)$, where $j \in B$; this edge contributes $a_j$ to the capacity of the cut.
- Edges $(i, t)$, where $i \in A$; this edge contributes $b_i$ to the capacity of the cut.
- Edges $(i, j)$ where $i \in A$ and $j \in B$; this edge contributes $p_{ij}$ to the capacity of the cut.

Figure 7.19 illustrates what each of these three kinds of edges looks like relative to a cut, on an example with four pixels.

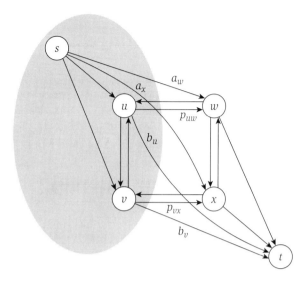

**Figure 7.19** An *s-t* cut on a graph constructed from four pixels. Note how the three types of terms in the expression for $q'(A,B)$ are captured by the cut.

If we add up the contributions of these three kinds of edges, we get

$$c(A,B) = \sum_{i \in A} b_i + \sum_{j \in B} a_j + \sum_{\substack{(i,j) \in E \\ |A \cap \{i,j\}| = 1}} p_{ij}$$

$$= q'(A,B).$$

So everything fits together perfectly. The flow network is set up so that the capacity of the cut $(A,B)$ exactly measures the quantity $q'(A,B)$: The three kinds of edges crossing the cut $(A,B)$, as we have just defined them (edges from the source, edges to the sink, and edges involving neither the source nor the sink), correspond to the three kinds of terms in the expression for $q'(A,B)$.

Thus, if we want to minimize $q'(A,B)$ (since we have argued earlier that this is equivalent to maximizing $q(A,B)$), we just have to find a cut of minimum capacity. And this latter problem, of course, is something that we know how to solve efficiently.

Thus, through solving this minimum-cut problem, we have an optimal algorithm in our model of foreground/background segmentation.

**(7.55)** *The solution to the Segmentation Problem can be obtained by a minimum-cut algorithm in the graph $G'$ constructed above. For a minimum cut $(A', B')$, the partition $(A, B)$ obtained by deleting $s^*$ and $t^*$ maximizes the segmentation value $q(A, B)$.*

## 7.11 Project Selection

Large (and small) companies are constantly faced with a balancing act between projects that can yield revenue, and the expenses needed for activities that can support these projects. Suppose, for example, that the telecommunications giant CluNet is assessing the pros and cons of a project to offer some new type of high-speed access service to residential customers. Marketing research shows that the service will yield a good amount of revenue, but it must be weighed against some costly preliminary projects that would be needed in order to make this service possible: increasing the fiber-optic capacity in the core of their network, and buying a newer generation of high-speed routers.

What makes these types of decisions particularly tricky is that they interact in complex ways: in isolation, the revenue from the high-speed access service might not be enough to justify modernizing the routers; *however*, once the company has modernized the routers, they'll also be in a position to pursue a lucrative additional project with their corporate customers; and maybe this additional project will tip the balance. And these interactions chain together: the corporate project actually would require another expense, but this in turn would enable two other lucrative projects—and so forth. In the end, the question is: Which projects should be pursued, and which should be passed up? It's a basic issue of balancing costs incurred with profitable opportunities that are made possible.

### The Problem

Here's a very general framework for modeling a set of decisions such as this. There is an underlying set $P$ of *projects*, and each project $i \in P$ has an associated *revenue* $p_i$, which can either be positive or negative. (In other words, each of the lucrative opportunities and costly infrastructure-building steps in our example above will be referred to as a separate project.) Certain projects are prerequisites for other projects, and we model this by an underlying directed acyclic graph $G = (P, E)$. The nodes of $G$ are the projects, and there is an edge $(i, j)$ to indicate that project $i$ can only be selected if project $j$ is selected as well. Note that a project $i$ can have many prerequisites, and there can be many projects that have project $j$ as one of their prerequisites. A set of projects $A \subseteq P$ is *feasible* if the prerequisite of every project in $A$ also belongs to $A$: for each $i \in A$, and each edge $(i, j) \in E$, we also have $j \in A$. We will refer to requirements of this form as *precedence constraints*. The profit of a set of projects is defined to be

$$\texttt{profit}(A) = \sum_{i \in A} p_i.$$

The *Project Selection Problem* is to select a feasible set of projects with maximum profit.

This problem also became a hot topic of study in the mining literature, starting in the early 1960s; here it was called the *Open-Pit Mining Problem*.[3] Open-pit mining is a surface mining operation in which blocks of earth are extracted from the surface to retrieve the ore contained in them. Before the mining operation begins, the entire area is divided into a set $P$ of *blocks*, and the net value $p_i$ of each block is estimated: This is the value of the ore minus the processing costs, for this block considered in isolation. Some of these net values will be positive, others negative. The full set of blocks has precedence constraints that essentially prevent blocks from being extracted before others on top of them are extracted. The Open-Pit Mining Problem is to determine the most profitable set of blocks to extract, subject to the precedence constraints. This problem falls into the framework of project selection—each block corresponds to a separate project.

## Designing the Algorithm

Here we will show that the Project Selection Problem can be solved by reducing it to a minimum-cut computation on an extended graph $G'$, defined analogously to the graph we used in Section 7.10 for image segmentation. The idea is to construct $G'$ from $G$ in such a way that the source side of a minimum cut in $G'$ will correspond to an optimal set of projects to select.

To form the graph $G'$, we add a new source $s$ and a new sink $t$ to the graph $G$ as shown in Figure 7.20. For each node $i \in P$ with $p_i > 0$, we add an edge $(s, i)$ with capacity $p_i$. For each node $i \in P$ with $p_i < 0$, we add an edge $(i, t)$ with capacity $-p_i$. We will set the capacities on the edges in $G$ later. However, we can already see that the capacity of the cut $(\{s\}, P \cup \{t\})$ is $C = \sum_{i \in P: p_i > 0} p_i$, so the maximum-flow value in this network is at most $C$.

We want to ensure that if $(A', B')$ is a minimum cut in this graph, then $A = A' - \{s\}$ obeys the precedence constraints; that is, if the node $i \in A$ has an edge $(i, j) \in E$, then we must have $j \in A$. The conceptually cleanest way to ensure this is to give each of the edges in $G$ capacity of $\infty$. We haven't previously formalized what an infinite capacity would mean, but there is no problem in doing this: it is simply an edge for which the capacity condition imposes no upper bound at all. The algorithms of the previous sections, as well as the Max-Flow Min-Cut Theorem, carry over to handle infinite capacities. However, we can also avoid bringing in the notion of infinite capacities by

---

[3] In contrast to the field of data mining, which has motivated several of the problems we considered earlier, we're talking here about actual mining, where you dig things out of the ground.

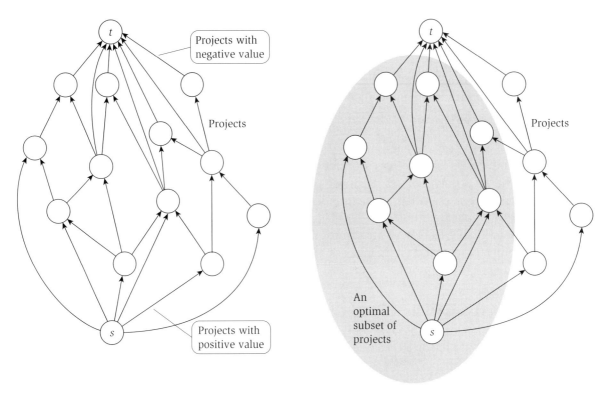

**Figure 7.20** The flow graph used to solve the Project Selection Problem. A possible minimum-capacity cut is shown on the right.

simply assigning each of these edges a capacity that is "effectively infinite." In our context, giving each of these edges a capacity of $C + 1$ would accomplish this: The maximum possible flow value in $G'$ is at most $C$, and so no minimum cut can contain an edge with capacity above $C$. In the description below, it will not matter which of these options we choose.

We can now state the algorithm: We compute a minimum cut $(A', B')$ in $G'$, and we declare $A' - \{s\}$ to be the optimal set of projects. We now turn to proving that this algorithm indeed gives the optimal solution.

### ✎ Analyzing the Algorithm

First consider a set of projects $A$ that satisfies the precedence constraints. Let $A' = A \cup \{s\}$ and $B' = (P - A) \cup \{t\}$, and consider the $s$-$t$ cut $(A', B')$. If the set $A$ satisfies the precedence constraints, then no edge $(i, j) \in E$ crosses this cut, as shown in Figure 7.20. The capacity of the cut can be expressed as follows.

**(7.56)** *The capacity of the cut* $(A', B')$, *as defined from a project set A satisfying the precedence constraints, is* $c(A', B') = C - \sum_{i \in A} p_i$.

**Proof.** Edges of $G'$ can be divided into three categories: those corresponding to the edge set $E$ of $G$, those leaving the source $s$, and those entering the sink $t$. Because $A$ satisfies the precedence constraints, the edges in $E$ do not cross the cut $(A', B')$, and hence do not contribute to its capacity. The edges entering the sink $t$ contribute

$$\sum_{i \in A \text{ and } p_i < 0} -p_i$$

to the capacity of the cut, and the edges leaving the source $s$ contribute

$$\sum_{i \notin A \text{ and } p_i > 0} p_i.$$

Using the definition of $C$, we can rewrite this latter quantity as $C - \sum_{i \in A \text{ and } p_i > 0} p_i$. The capacity of the cut $(A', B')$ is the sum of these two terms, which is

$$\sum_{i \in A \text{ and } p_i < 0} (-p_i) + \left( C - \sum_{i \in A \text{ and } p_i > 0} p_i \right) = C - \sum_{i \in A} p_i,$$

as claimed. ∎

Next, recall that edges of $G$ have capacity more than $C = \sum_{i \in P : p_i > 0} p_i$, and so these edges cannot cross a cut of capacity at most $C$. This implies that such cuts define feasible sets of projects.

**(7.57)** *If* $(A', B')$ *is a cut with capacity at most C, then the set* $A = A' - \{s\}$ *satisfies the precedence constraints.*

Now we can prove the main goal of our construction, that the minimum cut in $G'$ determines the optimum set of projects. Putting the previous two claims together, we see that the cuts $(A', B')$ of capacity at most $C$ are in one-to-one correspondence with feasible sets of project $A = A' - \{s\}$. The capacity of such a cut $(A', B')$ is

$$c(A', B') = C - \texttt{profit}(A).$$

The capacity value $C$ is a constant, independent of the cut $(A', B')$, so the cut with minimum capacity corresponds to the set of projects $A$ with maximum profit. We have therefore proved the following.

**(7.58)** *If* $(A', B')$ *is a minimum cut in* $G'$ *then the set* $A = A' - \{s\}$ *is an optimum solution to the Project Selection Problem.*

## 7.12 Baseball Elimination

*Over on the radio side the producer's saying, "See that thing in the paper last week about Einstein? . . . Some reporter asked him to figure out the mathematics of the pennant race. You know, one team wins so many of their remaining games, the other teams win this number or that number. What are the myriad possibilities? Who's got the edge?"*

*"The hell does he know?"*

*"Apparently not much. He picked the Dodgers to eliminate the Giants last Friday."*

—Don DeLillo, *Underworld*

### 🖋 The Problem

Suppose you're a reporter for the *Algorithmic Sporting News*, and the following situation arises late one September. There are four baseball teams trying to finish in first place in the American League Eastern Division; let's call them New York, Baltimore, Toronto, and Boston. Currently, each team has the following number of wins:

*New York: 92,    Baltimore: 91,    Toronto: 91,    Boston: 90.*

There are five games left in the season: These consist of all possible pairings of the four teams above, except for New York and Boston.

The question is: Can Boston finish with at least as many wins as every other team in the division (that is, finish in first place, possibly in a tie)?

If you think about it, you realize that the answer is no. One argument is the following. Clearly, Boston must win both its remaining games and New York must lose both its remaining games. But this means that Baltimore and Toronto will both beat New York; so then the winner of the Baltimore-Toronto game will end up with the most wins.

Here's an argument that avoids this kind of cases analysis. Boston can finish with at most 92 wins. Cumulatively, the other three teams have 274 wins currently, and their three games against each other will produce exactly three more wins, for a final total of 277. But 277 wins over three teams means that one of them must have ended up with more than 92 wins.

So now you might start wondering: (i) Is there an efficient algorithm to determine whether a team has been eliminated from first place? And (ii) whenever a team has been eliminated from first place, is there an "averaging" argument like this that proves it?

In more concrete notation, suppose we have a set $S$ of teams, and for each $x \in S$, its current number of wins is $w_x$. Also, for two teams $x, y \in S$, they still have to play $g_{xy}$ games against one another. Finally, we are given a specific team $z$.

We will use maximum-flow techniques to achieve the following two things. First, we give an efficient algorithm to decide whether $z$ has been eliminated from first place—or, to put it in positive terms, whether it is possible to choose outcomes for all the remaining games in such a way that the team $z$ ends with at least as many wins as every other team in $S$. Second, we prove the following clean characterization theorem for baseball elimination—essentially, that there is always a short "proof" when a team has been eliminated.

**(7.59)** *Suppose that team $z$ has indeed been eliminated. Then there exists a "proof" of this fact of the following form:*

- *$z$ can finish with at most $m$ wins.*
- *There is a set of teams $T \subseteq S$ so that*

$$\sum_{x \in T} w_x + \sum_{x,y \in T} g_{xy} > m|T|.$$

*(And hence one of the teams in $T$ must end with strictly more than $m$ wins.)*

As a second, more complex illustration of how the averaging argument in (7.59) works, consider the following example. Suppose we have the same four teams as before, but now the current number of wins is

*New York: 90,  Baltimore: 88,  Toronto: 87,  Boston: 79.*

The remaining games are as follows. Boston still has four games against each of the other three teams. Baltimore has one more game against each of New York and Toronto. And finally, New York and Toronto still have six games left to play against each other. Clearly, things don't look good for Boston, but is it actually eliminated?

The answer is yes; Boston has been eliminated. To see this, first note that Boston can end with at most 91 wins; and now consider the set of teams $T = \{$New York, Toronto$\}$. Together New York and Toronto already have 177 wins; their six remaining games will result in a total of 183; and $\frac{183}{2} > 91$. This means that one of them must end up with more than 91 wins, and so Boston can't finish in first. Interestingly, in this instance the set of all three teams ahead of Boston cannot constitute a similar proof: All three teams taken togeher have a total of 265 wins with 8 games left among them; this is a total of 273, and $\frac{273}{3} = 91$ — not enough by itself to prove that Boston couldn't end up in a multi-way tie for first. So it's crucial for the averaging argument that we choose the set $T$ consisting just of New York and Toronto, and omit Baltimore.

### Designing and Analyzing the Algorithm

We begin by constructing a flow network that provides an efficient algorithm for determining whether $z$ has been eliminated. Then, by examining the minimum cut in this network, we will prove (7.59).

Clearly, if there's any way for $z$ to end up in first place, we should have $z$ win all its remaining games. Let's suppose that this leaves it with $m$ wins. We now want to carefully allocate the wins from all remaining games so that no other team ends with more than $m$ wins. Allocating wins in this way can be solved by a maximum-flow computation, via the following basic idea. We have a source $s$ from which all wins emanate. The $i^{\text{th}}$ win can pass through one of the two teams involved in the $i^{\text{th}}$ game. We then impose a capacity constraint saying that at most $m - w_x$ wins can pass through team $x$.

More concretely, we construct the following flow network $G$, as shown in Figure 7.21. First, let $S' = S - \{z\}$, and let $g^* = \sum_{x,y \in S'} g_{xy}$—the total number of games left between all pairs of teams in $S'$. We include nodes $s$ and $t$, a node $v_x$ for each team $x \in S'$, and a node $u_{xy}$ for each pair of teams $x, y \in S'$ with a nonzero number of games left to play against each other. We have the following edges.

- Edges $(s, u_{xy})$ (*wins emanate from s*);
- Edges $(u_{xy}, v_x)$ and $(u_{xy}, v_y)$ (*only x or y can win a game that they play against each other*); and
- Edges $(v_x, t)$ (*wins are absorbed at t*).

Let's consider what capacities we want to place on these edges. We want $g_{xy}$ wins to flow from $s$ to $u_{xy}$ at saturation, so we give $(s, u_{xy})$ a capacity of $g_{xy}$. We want to ensure that team $x$ cannot win more than $m - w_x$ games, so we

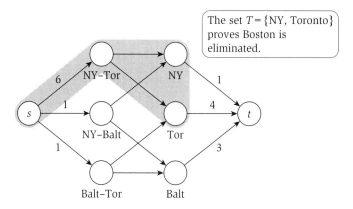

The set $T = \{\text{NY, Toronto}\}$ proves Boston is eliminated.

**Figure 7.21** The flow network for the second example. As the minimum cut indicates, there is no flow of value $g^*$, and so Boston has been eliminated.

give the edge $(v_x, t)$ a capacity of $m - w_x$. Finally, an edge of the form $(u_{xy}, v_y)$ should have *at least* $g_{xy}$ units of capacity, so that it has the ability to transport all the wins from $u_{xy}$ on to $v_x$; in fact, our analysis will be the cleanest if we give it *infinite* capacity. (We note that the construction still works even if this edge is given only $g_{xy}$ units of capacity, but the proof of (7.59) will become a little more complicated.)

Now, if there is a flow of value $g^*$, then it is possible for the outcomes of all remaining games to yield a situation where no team has more than $m$ wins; and hence, if team $z$ wins all its remaining games, it can still achieve at least a tie for first place. Conversely, if there are outcomes for the remaining games in which $z$ achieves at least a tie, we can use these outcomes to define a flow of value $g^*$. For example, in Figure 7.21, which is based on our second example, the indicated cut shows that the maximum flow has value at most 7, whereas $g^* = 6 + 1 + 1 = 8$.

In summary, we have shown

**(7.60)** *Team $z$ has been eliminated if and only if the maximum flow in $G$ has value strictly less than $g^*$. Thus we can test in polynomial time whether $z$ has been eliminated.*

## Characterizing When a Team Has Been Eliminated

Our network flow construction can also be used to prove (7.59). The idea is that the Max-Flow Min-Cut Theorem gives a nice "if and only if" characterization for the existence of flow, and if we interpret this characterization in terms of our application, we get the comparably nice characterization here. This illustrates a general way in which one can generate characterization theorems for problems that are reducible to network flow.

**Proof of (7.59).** Suppose that $z$ has been eliminated from first place. Then the maximum $s$-$t$ flow in $G$ has value $g' < g^*$; so there is an $s$-$t$ cut $(A, B)$ of capacity $g'$, and $(A, B)$ is a minimum cut. Let $T$ be the set of teams $x$ for which $v_x \in A$. We will now prove that $T$ can be used in the "averaging argument" in (7.59).

First, consider the node $u_{xy}$, and suppose one of $x$ or $y$ is not in $T$, but $u_{xy} \in A$. Then the edge $(u_{xy}, v_x)$ would cross from $A$ into $B$, and hence the cut $(A, B)$ would have infinite capacity. This contradicts the assumption that $(A, B)$ is a minimum cut of capacity less than $g^*$. So if one of $x$ or $y$ is not in $T$, then $u_{xy} \in B$. On the other hand, suppose both $x$ and $y$ belong to $T$, but $u_{xy} \in B$. Consider the cut $(A', B')$ that we would obtain by adding $u_{xy}$ to the set $A$ and deleting it from the set $B$. The capacity of $(A', B')$ is simply the capacity of $(A, B)$, minus the capacity $g_{xy}$ of the edge $(s, u_{xy})$—for this edge $(s, u_{xy})$ used to cross from $A$ to $B$, and now it does not cross from $A'$ to $B'$. But since $g_{xy} > 0$, this means that $(A', B')$ has smaller capacity than $(A, B)$, again contradicting our assumption that $(A, B)$ is a minimum cut. So, if both $x$ and $y$ belong to $T$, then $u_{xy} \in A$.

Thus we have established the following conclusion, based on the fact that $(A, B)$ is a minimum cut: $u_{xy} \in A$ if and only if both $x, y \in T$.

Now we just need to work out the minimum-cut capacity $c(A, B)$ in terms of its constituent edge capacities. By the conclusion in the previous paragraph, we know that edges crossing from $A$ to $B$ have one of the following two forms:

- edges of the form $(v_x, t)$, where $x \in T$, and
- edges of the form $(s, u_{xy})$, where at least one of $x$ or $y$ does not belong to $T$ (in other words, $\{x, y\} \not\subset T$).

Thus we have

$$c(A, B) = \sum_{x \in T}(m - w_x) + \sum_{\{x,y\} \not\subset T} g_{xy}$$

$$= m|T| - \sum_{x \in T} w_x + \left(g^* - \sum_{x,y \in T} g_{xy}\right).$$

Since we know that $c(A, B) = g' < g^*$, this last inequality implies

$$m|T| - \sum_{x \in T} w_x - \sum_{x,y \in T} g_{xy} < 0,$$

and hence

$$\sum_{x \in T} w_x + \sum_{x,y \in T} g_{xy} > m|T|. \quad \blacksquare$$

For example, applying the argument in the proof of (7.59) to the instance in Figure 7.21, we see that the nodes for New York and Toronto are on the source side of the minimum cut, and, as we saw earlier, these two teams indeed constitute a proof that Boston has been eliminated.

## * 7.13 A Further Direction: Adding Costs to the Matching Problem

Let's go back to the first problem we discussed in this chapter, Bipartite Matching. Perfect matchings in a bipartite graph formed a way to model the problem of pairing one kind of object with another—jobs with machines, for example. But in many settings, there are a large number of possible perfect matchings on the same set of objects, and we'd like a way to express the idea that some perfect matchings may be "better" than others.

## The Problem

A natural way to formulate a problem based on this notion is to introduce *costs*. It may be that we incur a certain cost to perform a given job on a given machine, and we'd like to match jobs with machines in a way that minimizes the total cost. Or there may be $n$ fire trucks that must be sent to $n$ distinct houses; each house is at a given distance from each fire station, and we'd like a matching that minimizes the average distance each truck drives to its associated house. In short, it is very useful to have an algorithm that finds a perfect matching *of minimum total cost*.

Formally, we consider a bipartite graph $G = (V, E)$ whose node set, as usual, is partitioned as $V = X \cup Y$ so that every edge $e \in E$ has one end in $X$ and the other end in $Y$. Furthermore, each edge $e$ has a nonnegative cost $c_e$. For a matching $M$, we say that the cost of the matching is the total cost of all edges in $M$, that is, $cost(M) = \sum_{e \in M} c_e$. The *Minimum-Cost Perfect Matching Problem* assumes that $|X| = |Y| = n$, and the goal is to find a perfect matching of minimum cost.

## Designing and Analyzing the Algorithm

We now describe an efficient algorithm to solve this problem, based on the idea of augmenting paths but adapted to take the costs into account. Thus, the algorithm will iteratively construct matchings using $i$ edges, for each value of $i$ from 1 to $n$. We will show that when the algorithm concludes with a matching of size $n$, it is a minimum-cost perfect matching. The high-level structure of the algorithm is quite simple. If we have a minimum-cost matching of size $i$, then we seek an augmenting path to produce a matching of size $i + 1$; and rather than looking for any augmenting path (as was sufficient in the case without costs), we use the cheapest augmenting path so that the larger matching will also have minimum cost.

Recall the construction of the residual graph used for finding augmenting paths. Let $M$ be a matching. We add two new nodes $s$ and $t$ to the graph. We add edges $(s, x)$ for all nodes $x \in X$ that are unmatched and edges $(y, t)$ for all nodes $y \in Y$ that are unmatched. An edge $e = (x, y) \in E$ is oriented from $x$ to $y$ if $e$ is not in the matching $M$ and from $y$ to $x$ if $e \in M$. We will use $G_M$ to denote this residual graph. Note that all edges going from $Y$ to $X$ are in the matching $M$, while the edges going from $X$ to $Y$ are not. Any directed $s$-$t$ path $P$ in the graph $G_M$ corresponds to a matching one larger than $M$ by swapping edges along $P$, that is, the edges in $P$ from $X$ to $Y$ are added to $M$ and all edges in $P$ that go from $Y$ to $X$ are deleted from $M$. As before, we will call a path $P$ in $G_M$ an *augmenting path*, and we say that we *augment* the matching $M$ using the path $P$.

Now we would like the resulting matching to have as small a cost as possible. To achieve this, we will search for a cheap augmenting path with respect to the following natural costs. The edges leaving $s$ and entering $t$ will have cost 0; an edge $e$ oriented from $X$ to $Y$ will have cost $c_e$ (as including this edge in the path means that we add the edge to $M$); and an edge $e$ oriented from $Y$ to $X$ will have cost $-c_e$ (as including this edge in the path means that we delete the edge from $M$). We will use $cost(P)$ to denote the cost of a path $P$ in $G_M$. The following statement summarizes this construction.

**(7.61)**    *Let $M$ be a matching and $P$ be a path in $G_M$ from $s$ to $t$. Let $M'$ be the matching obtained from $M$ by augmenting along $P$. Then $|M'| = |M| + 1$ and $cost(M') = cost(M) + cost(P)$.*

Given this statement, it is natural to suggest an algorithm to find a minimum-cost perfect matching: We iteratively find minimum-cost paths in $G_M$, and use the paths to augment the matchings. But how can we be sure that the perfect matching we find is of minimum cost? Or even worse, is this algorithm even meaningful? We can only find minimum-cost paths if we know that the graph $G_M$ has no negative cycles.

*Analyzing Negative Cycles*    In fact, understanding the role of negative cycles in $G_M$ is the key to analyzing the algorithm. First consider the case in which $M$ is a perfect matching. Note that in this case the node $s$ has no leaving edges, and $t$ has no entering edges in $G_M$ (as our matching is perfect), and hence no cycle in $G_M$ contains $s$ or $t$.

**(7.62)**    *Let $M$ be a perfect matching. If there is a negative-cost directed cycle $C$ in $G_M$, then $M$ is not minimum cost.*

**Proof.** To see this, we use the cycle $C$ for augmentation, just the same way we used directed paths to obtain larger matchings. Augmenting $M$ along $C$ involves swapping edges along $C$ in and out of $M$. The resulting new perfect matching $M'$ has cost $cost(M') = cost(M) + cost(C)$; but $cost(C) < 0$, and hence $M$ is not of minimum cost.    ■

More importantly, the converse of this statement is true as well; so in fact a perfect matching $M$ has minimum cost precisely when there is no negative cycle in $G_M$.

**(7.63)**    *Let $M$ be a perfect matching. If there are no negative-cost directed cycles $C$ in $G_M$, then $M$ is a minimum-cost perfect matching.*

**Proof.** Suppose the statement is not true, and let $M'$ be a perfect matching of smaller cost. Consider the set of edges in one of $M$ and $M'$ but not in both.

Observe that this set of edges corresponds to a set of node-disjoint directed cycles in $G_M$. The cost of the set of directed cycles is exactly $cost(M') - cost(M)$. Assuming $M'$ has smaller cost than $M$, it must be that at least one of these cycles has negative cost. ∎

Our plan is thus to iterate through matchings of larger and larger size, maintaining the property that the graph $G_M$ has no negative cycles in any iteration. In this way, our computation of a minimum-cost path will always be well defined; and when we terminate with a perfect matching, we can use (7.63) to conclude that it has minimum cost.

***Maintaining Prices on the Nodes*** It will help to think about a numerical *price* $p(v)$ associated with each node $v$. These prices will help both in understanding how the algorithm runs, and they will also help speed up the implementation. One issue we have to deal with is to maintain the property that the graph $G_M$ has no negative cycles in any iteration. How do we know that after an augmentation, the new residual graph still has no negative cycles? The prices will turn out to serve as a compact proof to show this.

To understand prices, it helps to keep in mind an economic interpretation of them. For this purpose, consider the following scenario. Assume that the set $X$ represents people who need to be assigned to do a set of jobs $Y$. For an edge $e = (x, y)$, the cost $c_e$ is a cost associated with having person $x$ doing job $y$. Now we will think of the price $p(x)$ as an extra bonus we pay for person $x$ to participate in this system, like a "signing bonus." With this in mind, the cost for assigning person $x$ to do job $y$ will become $p(x) + c_e$. On the other hand, we will think of the price $p(y)$ for nodes $y \in Y$ as a reward, or value gained by taking care of job $y$ (no matter which person in $X$ takes care of it). This way the "net cost" of assigning person $x$ to do job $y$ becomes $p(x) + c_e - p(y)$: this is the cost of hiring $x$ for a bonus of $p(x)$, having him do job $y$ for a cost of $c_e$, and then cashing in on the reward $p(y)$. We will call this the *reduced cost* of an edge $e = (x, y)$ and denote it by $c_e^p = p(x) + c_e - p(y)$. However, it is important to keep in mind that only the costs $c_e$ are part of the problem description; the prices (bonuses and rewards) will be a way to think about our solution.

Specifically, we say that a set of numbers $\{p(v) : v \in V\}$ forms a set of *compatible prices* with respect to a matching $M$ if

(i)   for all unmatched nodes $x \in X$ we have $p(x) = 0$ (that is, people not asked to do any job do not need to be paid);

(ii)  for all edges $e = (x, y)$ we have $p(x) + c_e \geq p(y)$ (that is, every edge has a nonnegative reduced cost); and

(iii) for all edges $e = (x, y) \in M$ we have $p(x) + c_e = p(y)$ (every edge used in the assignment has a reduced cost of 0).

Why are such prices useful? Intuitively, compatible prices suggest that the matching is cheap: Along the matched edges reward equals cost, while on all other edges the reward is no bigger than the cost. For a partial matching, this may not imply that the matching has the smallest possible cost for its size (it may be taking care of expensive jobs). However, we claim that if $M$ is any matching for which there exists a set of compatible prices, then $G_M$ has no negative cycles. For a perfect matching $M$, this will imply that $M$ is of minimum cost by (7.63).

To see why $G_M$ can have no negative cycles, we extend the definition of reduced cost to edges in the residual graph by using the same expression $c_e^p = p(v) + c_e - p(w)$ for any edge $e = (v, w)$. Observe that the definition of compatible prices implies that all edges in the residual graph $G_M$ have nonnegative reduced costs. Now, note that for any cycle $C$, we have

$$cost(C) = \sum_{e \in C} c_e = \sum_{e \in C} c_e^p,$$

since all the terms on the right-hand side corresponding to prices cancel out. We know that each term on the right-hand side is nonnegative, and so clearly $cost(C)$ is nonnegative.

There is a second, algorithmic reason why it is useful to have prices on the nodes. When you have a graph with negative-cost edges but no negative cycles, you can compute shortest paths using the Bellman-Ford Algorithm in $O(mn)$ time. But if the graph in fact has no negative-cost edges, then you can use Dijkstra's Algorithm instead, which only requires time $O(m \log n)$—almost a full factor of $n$ faster.

In our case, having the prices around allows us to compute shortest paths with respect to the nonnegative reduced costs $c_e^p$, arriving at an equivalent answer. Indeed, suppose we use Dijkstra's Algorithm to find the minimum cost $d_{p,M}(v)$ of a directed path from $s$ to every node $v \in X \cup Y$ subject to the costs $c_e^p$. Given the minimum costs $d_{p,M}(y)$ for an unmatched node $y \in Y$, the (nonreduced) cost of the path from $s$ to $t$ through $y$ is $d_{p,M}(y) + p(y)$, and so we find the minimum cost in $O(n)$ additional time. In summary, we have the following fact.

**(7.64)** *Let M be a matching, and p be compatible prices. We can use one run of Dijkstra's Algorithm and $O(n)$ extra time to find the minimum-cost path from s to t.*

**Updating the Node Prices**    We took advantage of the prices to improve one iteration of the algorithm. In order to be ready for the next iteration, we need not only the minimum-cost path (to get the next matching), but also a way to produce a set of compatible prices with respect to the new matching.

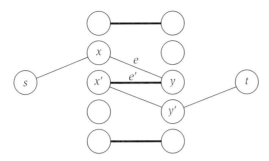

**Figure 7.22** A matching $M$ (the dark edges), and a residual graph used to increase the size of the matching.

To get some intuition on how to do this, consider an unmatched node $x$ with respect to a matching $M$, and an edge $e = (x, y)$, as shown in Figure 7.22. If the new matching $M'$ includes edge $e$ (that is, if $e$ is on the augmenting path we use to update the matching), then we will want to have the reduced cost of this edge to be zero. However, the prices $p$ we used with matching $M$ may result in a reduced cost $c_e^p > 0$ — that is, the assignment of person $x$ to job $y$, in our economic interpretation, may not be viewed as cheap enough. We can arrange the zero reduced cost by either increasing the price $p(y)$ ($y$'s reward) by $c_e^p$, or by decreasing the price $p(x)$ by the same amount. To keep prices nonnegative, we will increase the price $p(y)$. However, node $y$ may be matched in the matching $M$ to some other node $x'$ via an edge $e' = (x', y)$, as shown in Figure 7.22. Increasing the reward $p(y)$ decreases the reduced cost of edge $e'$ to negative, and hence the prices are no longer compatible. To keep things compatible, we can increase $p(x')$ by the same amount. However, this change might cause problems on other edges. Can we update all prices and keep the matching and the prices compatible on all edges? Surprisingly, this can be done quite simply by using the distances from $s$ to all other nodes computed by Dijkstra's Algorithm.

**(7.65)** *Let $M$ be a matching, let $p$ be compatible prices, and let $M'$ be a matching obtained by augmenting along the minimum-cost path from $s$ to $t$. Then $p'(v) = d_{p,M}(v) + p(v)$ is a compatible set of prices for $M'$.*

**Proof.** To prove compatibility, consider first an edge $e = (x', y) \in M$. The only edge entering $x'$ is the directed edge $(y, x')$, and hence $d_{p,M}(x') = d_{p,M}(y) - c_e^p$, where $c_e^p = p(y) + c_e - p(x')$, and thus we get the desired equation on such edges. Next consider edges $(x, y)$ in $M' - M$. These edges are along the minimum-cost path from $s$ to $t$, and hence they satisfy $d_{p,M}(y) = d_{p,M}(x) + c_e^p$ as desired. Finally, we get the required inequality for all other edges since all edges $e = (x, y) \notin M$ must satisfy $d_{p,M}(y) \le d_{p,M}(x) + c_e^p$. ∎

Finally, we have to consider how to initialize the algorithm, so as to get it underway. We initialize $M$ to be the empty set, define $p(x) = 0$ for all $x \in X$, and define $p(y)$, for $y \in Y$, to be the minimum cost of an edge entering $y$. Note that these prices are compatible with respect to $M = \phi$.

We summarize the algorithm below.

---

```
Start with M equal to the empty set
Define p(x) = 0 for x ∈ X, and p(y) = min  c_e  for y ∈ Y
                                     e into y
While M is not a perfect matching
   Find a minimum-cost s-t path P in G_M using (7.64) with prices p
   Augment along P to produce a new matching M'
   Find a set of compatible prices with respect to M' via (7.65)
Endwhile
```

---

The final set of compatible prices yields a proof that $G_M$ has no negative cycles; and by (7.63), this implies that $M$ has minimum cost.

**(7.66)**    *The minimum-cost perfect matching can be found in the time required for n shortest-path computations with nonnegative edge lengths.*

## Extensions: An Economic Interpretation of the Prices

To conclude our discussion of the Minimum-Cost Perfect Matching Problem, we develop the economic interpretation of the prices a bit further. We consider the following scenario. Assume $X$ is a set of $n$ people each looking to buy a house, and $Y$ is a set of $n$ houses that they are all considering. Let $v(x, y)$ denote the value of house $y$ to buyer $x$. Since each buyer wants one of the houses, one could argue that the best arrangement would be to find a perfect matching $M$ that maximizes $\sum_{(x,y) \in M} v(x, y)$. We can find such a perfect matching by using our minimum-cost perfect matching algorithm with costs $c_e = -v(x, y)$ if $e = (x, y)$.

The question we will ask now is this: Can we convince these buyers to buy the house they are allocated? On her own, each buyer $x$ would want to buy the house $y$ that has maximum value $v(x, y)$ to her. How can we convince her to buy instead the house that our matching $M$ allocated? We will use prices to change the incentives of the buyers. Suppose we set a price $P(y)$ for each house $y$, that is, the person buying the house $y$ must pay $P(y)$. With these prices in mind, a buyer will be interested in buying the house with maximum net value, that is, the house $y$ that maximizes $v(x, y) - P(y)$. We say that a perfect matching $M$ and house prices $P$ are in *equilibrium* if, for all edges $(x, y) \in M$ and all other houses $y'$, we have

$$v(x, y) - P(y) \geq v(x, y') - P(y').$$

But can we find a perfect matching and a set of prices so as to achieve this state of affairs, with every buyer ending up happy? In fact, the minimum-cost perfect matching and an associated set of compatible prices provide exactly what we're looking for.

**(7.67)** *Let M be a perfect matching of minimum cost, where $c_e = -v(x, y)$ for each edge $e = (x, y)$, and let p be a compatible set of prices. Then the matching M and the set of prices $\{P(y) = -p(y) : y \in Y\}$ are in equilibrium.*

**Proof.** Consider an edge $e = (x, y) \in M$, and let $e' = (x, y')$. Since $M$ and $p$ are compatible, we have $p(x) + c_e = p(y)$ and $p(x) + c_{e'} \geq p(y')$. Subtracting these two inequalities to cancel $p(x)$, and substituting the values of $p$ and $c$, we get the desired inequality in the definition of equilibrium. ∎

# Solved Exercises

## Solved Exercise 1

Suppose you are given a directed graph $G = (V, E)$, with a positive integer capacity $c_e$ on each edge $e$, a designated source $s \in V$, and a designated sink $t \in V$. You are also given an integer maximum $s$-$t$ flow in $G$, defined by a flow value $f_e$ on each edge $e$.

Now suppose we pick a specific edge $e \in E$ and increase its capacity by one unit. Show how to find a maximum flow in the resulting capacitated graph in time $O(m + n)$, where $m$ is the number of edges in $G$ and $n$ is the number of nodes.

*Solution*    The point here is that $O(m + n)$ is not enough time to compute a new maximum flow from scratch, so we need to figure out how to use the flow $f$ that we are given. Intuitively, even after we add 1 to the capacity of edge $e$, the flow $f$ can't be that far from maximum; after all, we haven't changed the network very much.

In fact, it's not hard to show that the maximum flow value can go up by at most 1.

**(7.68)** *Consider the flow network $G'$ obtained by adding 1 to the capacity of e. The value of the maximum flow in $G'$ is either $v(f)$ or $v(f) + 1$.*

**Proof.** The value of the maximum flow in $G'$ is at least $v(f)$, since $f$ is still a feasible flow in this network. It is also integer-valued. So it is enough to show that the maximum-flow value in $G'$ is at most $v(f) + 1$.

By the Max-Flow Min-Cut Theorem, there is some $s$-$t$ cut $(A, B)$ in the original flow network $G$ of capacity $v(f)$. Now we ask: What is the capacity of $(A, B)$ in the new flow network $G'$? All the edges crossing $(A, B)$ have the same capacity in $G'$ that they did in $G$, with the possible exception of $e$ (in case $e$ crosses $(A, B)$). But $c_e$ only increased by 1, and so the capacity of $(A, B)$ in the new flow network $G'$ is at most $v(f) + 1$. ∎

Statement (7.68) suggests a natural algorithm. Starting with the feasible flow $f$ in $G'$, we try to find a single augmenting path from $s$ to $t$ in the residual graph $G'_f$. This takes time $O(m + n)$. Now one of two things will happen. Either we will fail to find an augmenting path, and in this case we know that $f$ is a maximum flow. Otherwise the augmentation succeeds, producing a flow $f'$ of value at least $v(f) + 1$. In this case, we know by (7.68) that $f'$ must be a maximum flow. So either way, we produce a maximum flow after a single augmenting path computation.

## Solved Exercise 2

You are helping the medical consulting firm Doctors Without Weekends set up the work schedules of doctors in a large hospital. They've got the regular daily schedules mainly worked out. Now, however, they need to deal with all the special cases and, in particular, make sure that they have at least one doctor covering each vacation day.

Here's how this works. There are $k$ vacation periods (e.g., the week of Christmas, the July 4th weekend, the Thanksgiving weekend, . . . ), each spanning several contiguous days. Let $D_j$ be the set of days included in the $j^{\text{th}}$ vacation period; we will refer to the union of all these days, $\cup_j D_j$, as the set of all *vacation days*.

There are $n$ doctors at the hospital, and doctor $i$ has a set of vacation days $S_i$ when he or she is available to work. (This may include certain days from a given vacation period but not others; so, for example, a doctor may be able to work the Friday, Saturday, or Sunday of Thanksgiving weekend, but not the Thursday.)

Give a polynomial-time algorithm that takes this information and determines whether it is possible to select a single doctor to work on each vacation day, subject to the following constraints.

- For a given parameter $c$, each doctor should be assigned to work at most $c$ vacation days total, and only days when he or she is available.

- For each vacation period $j$, each doctor should be assigned to work at most one of the days in the set $D_j$. (In other words, although a particular doctor may work on several vacation days over the course of a year, he or she should not be assigned to work two or more days of the Thanksgiving weekend, or two or more days of the July 4th weekend, etc.)

The algorithm should either return an assignment of doctors satisfying these constraints or report (correctly) that no such assignment exists.

**Solution** This is a very natural setting in which to apply network flow, since at a high level we're trying to match one set (the doctors) with another set (the vacation days). The complication comes from the requirement that each doctor can work at most one day in each vacation period.

So to begin, let's see how we'd solve the problem without that requirement, in the simpler case where each doctor $i$ has a set $S_i$ of days when he or she can work, and each doctor should be scheduled for at most $c$ days total. The construction is pictured in Figure 7.23(a). We have a node $u_i$ representing each doctor attached to a node $v_\ell$ representing each day when he or she can

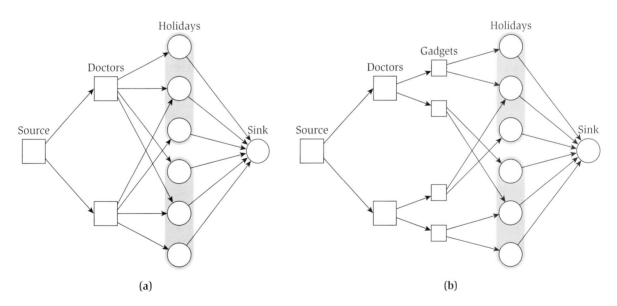

(a)          (b)

**Figure 7.23** (a) Doctors are assigned to holiday days without restricting how many days in one holiday a doctor can work. (b) The flow network is expanded with "gadgets" that prevent a doctor from working more than one day from each vacation period. The shaded sets correspond to the different vacation periods.

work; this edge has a capacity of 1. We attach a super-source $s$ to each doctor node $u_i$ by an edge of capacity $c$, and we attach each day node $v_\ell$ to a super-sink $t$ by an edge with upper and lower bounds of 1. This way, assigned days can "flow" through doctors to days when they can work, and the lower bounds on the edges from the days to the sink guarantee that each day is covered. Finally, suppose there are $d$ vacation days total; we put a demand of $+d$ on the sink and $-d$ on the source, and we look for a feasible circulation. (Recall that once we've introduced lower bounds on some edges, the algorithms in the text are phrased in terms of circulations with demands, not maximum flow.)

But now we have to handle the extra requirement, that each doctor can work at most one day from each vacation period. To do this, we take each pair $(i, j)$ consisting of a doctor $i$ and a vacation period $j$, and we add a "vacation gadget" as follows. We include a new node $w_{ij}$ with an incoming edge of capacity 1 from the doctor node $u_i$, and with outgoing edges of capacity 1 to each day in vacation period $j$ when doctor $i$ is available to work. This gadget serves to "choke off" the flow from $u_i$ into the days associated with vacation period $j$, so that at most one unit of flow can go to them collectively. The construction is pictured in Figure 7.23(b). As before, we put a demand of $+d$ on the sink and $-d$ on the source, and we look for a feasible circulation. The total running time is the time to construct the graph, which is $O(nd)$, plus the time to check for a single feasible circulation in this graph.

The correctness of the algorithm is a consequence of the following claim.

**(7.69)**    *There is a way to assign doctors to vacation days in a way that respects all constraints if and only if there is a feasible circulation in the flow network we have constructed.*

**Proof.** First, if there is a way to assign doctors to vacation days in a way that respects all constraints, then we can construct the following circulation. If doctor $i$ works on day $\ell$ of vacation period $j$, then we send one unit of flow along the path $s, u_i, w_{ij}, v_\ell, t$; we do this for all such $(i, \ell)$ pairs. Since the assignment of doctors satisfied all the constraints, the resulting circulation respects all capacities; and it sends $d$ units of flow out of $s$ and into $t$, so it meets the demands.

Conversely, suppose there is a feasible circulation. For this direction of the proof, we will show how to use the circulation to construct a schedule for all the doctors. First, by (7.52), there is a feasible circulation in which all flow values are integers. We now construct the following schedule: If the edge $(w_{ij}, v_\ell)$ carries a unit of flow, then we have doctor $i$ work on day $\ell$. Because of the capacities, the resulting schedule has each doctor work at most $c$ days, at most one in each vacation period, and each day is covered by one doctor. ∎

# Exercises

1. **(a)** List all the minimum *s-t* cuts in the flow network pictured in Figure 7.24. The capacity of each edge appears as a label next to the edge.

   **(b)** What is the minimum capacity of an *s-t* cut in the flow network in Figure 7.25? Again, the capacity of each edge appears as a label next to the edge.

2. Figure 7.26 shows a flow network on which an *s-t* flow has been computed. The capacity of each edge appears as a label next to the edge, and the numbers in boxes give the amount of flow sent on each edge. (Edges without boxed numbers—specifically, the four edges of capacity 3—have no flow being sent on them.)

   **(a)** What is the value of this flow? Is this a maximum (*s,t*) flow in this graph?

   **(b)** Find a minimum *s-t* cut in the flow network pictured in Figure 7.26, and also say what its capacity is.

3. Figure 7.27 shows a flow network on which an *s-t* flow has been computed. The capacity of each edge appears as a label next to the edge, and the numbers in boxes give the amount of flow sent on each edge. (Edges without boxed numbers have no flow being sent on them.)

   **(a)** What is the value of this flow? Is this a maximum (*s,t*) flow in this graph?

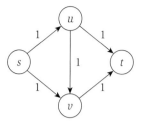

**Figure 7.24** What are the minimum *s-t* cuts in this flow network?

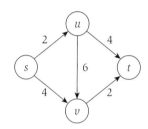

**Figure 7.25** What is the minimum capacity of an *s-t* cut in this flow network?

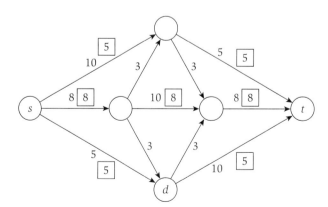

**Figure 7.26** What is the value of the depicted flow? Is it a maximum flow? What is the minimum cut?

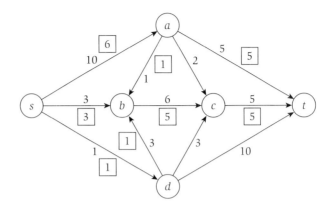

**Figure 7.27** What is the value of the depicted flow? Is it a maximum flow? What is the minimum cut?

    **(b)** Find a minimum *s-t* cut in the flow network pictured in Figure 7.27, and also say what its capacity is.

4. Decide whether you think the following statement is true or false. If it is true, give a short explanation. If it is false, give a counterexample.

> *Let G be an arbitrary flow network, with a source s, a sink t, and a positive integer capacity $c_e$ on every edge e. If f is a maximum s-t flow in G, then f saturates every edge out of s with flow (i.e., for all edges e out of s, we have $f(e) = c_e$).*

5. Decide whether you think the following statement is true or false. If it is true, give a short explanation. If it is false, give a counterexample.

> *Let G be an arbitrary flow network, with a source s, a sink t, and a positive integer capacity $c_e$ on every edge e; and let (A, B) be a mimimum s-t cut with respect to these capacities $\{c_e : e \in E\}$. Now suppose we add 1 to every capacity; then (A, B) is still a minimum s-t cut with respect to these new capacities $\{1 + c_e : e \in E\}$.*

6. Suppose you're a consultant for the Ergonomic Architecture Commission, and they come to you with the following problem.

    They're really concerned about designing houses that are "user-friendly," and they've been having a lot of trouble with the setup of light fixtures and switches in newly designed houses. Consider, for example, a one-floor house with *n* light fixtures and *n* locations for light switches mounted in the wall. You'd like to be able to wire up one switch to control each light fixture, in such a way that a person at the switch can *see* the light fixture being controlled.

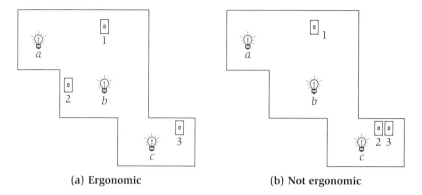

(a) **Ergonomic**          (b) **Not ergonomic**

**Figure 7.28** The floor plan in (a) is ergonomic, because we can wire switches to fixtures in such a way that each fixture is visible from the switch that controls it. (This can be done by wiring switch 1 to $a$, switch 2 to $b$, and switch 3 to $c$.) The floor plan in (b) is not ergonomic, because no such wiring is possible.

Sometimes this is possible and sometimes it isn't. Consider the two simple floor plans for houses in Figure 7.28. There are three light fixtures (labeled $a$, $b$, $c$) and three switches (labeled 1, 2, 3). It is possible to wire switches to fixtures in Figure 7.28(a) so that every switch has a line of sight to the fixture, but this is not possible in Figure 7.28(b).

Let's call a floor plan, together with $n$ light fixture locations and $n$ switch locations, *ergonomic* if it's possible to wire one switch to each fixture so that every fixture is visible from the switch that controls it. A floor plan will be represented by a set of $m$ horizontal or vertical line segments in the plane (the walls), where the $i^{th}$ wall has endpoints $(x_i, y_i), (x_i', y_i')$. Each of the $n$ switches and each of the $n$ fixtures is given by its coordinates in the plane. A fixture is *visible* from a switch if the line segment joining them does not cross any of the walls.

Give an algorithm to decide if a given floor plan is ergonomic. The running time should be polynomial in $m$ and $n$. You may assume that you have a subroutine with $O(1)$ running time that takes two line segments as input and decides whether or not they cross in the plane.

7. Consider a set of mobile computing clients in a certain town who each need to be connected to one of several possible *base stations*. We'll suppose there are $n$ clients, with the position of each client specified by its $(x, y)$ coordinates in the plane. There are also $k$ base stations; the position of each of these is specified by $(x, y)$ coordinates as well.

For each client, we wish to connect it to exactly one of the base stations. Our choice of connections is constrained in the following ways.

There is a *range parameter* $r$—a client can only be connected to a base station that is within distance $r$. There is also a *load parameter* $L$—no more than $L$ clients can be connected to any single base station.

Your goal is to design a polynomial-time algorithm for the following problem. Given the positions of a set of clients and a set of base stations, as well as the range and load parameters, decide whether every client can be connected simultaneously to a base station, subject to the range and load conditions in the previous paragraph.

8. Statistically, the arrival of spring typically results in increased accidents and increased need for emergency medical treatment, which often requires blood transfusions. Consider the problem faced by a hospital that is trying to evaluate whether its blood supply is sufficient.

   The basic rule for blood donation is the following. A person's own blood supply has certain *antigens* present (we can think of antigens as a kind of molecular signature); and a person cannot receive blood with a particular antigen if their own blood does not have this antigen present. Concretely, this principle underpins the division of blood into four *types*: A, B, AB, and O. Blood of type A has the A antigen, blood of type B has the B antigen, blood of type AB has both, and blood of type O has neither. Thus, patients with type A can receive only blood types A or O in a transfusion, patients with type B can receive only B or O, patients with type O can receive only O, and patients with type AB can receive any of the four types.[4]

   (a) Let $s_O$, $s_A$, $s_B$, and $s_{AB}$ denote the supply in whole units of the different blood types on hand. Assume that the hospital knows the projected demand for each blood type $d_O$, $d_A$, $d_B$, and $d_{AB}$ for the coming week. Give a polynomial-time algorithm to evaluate if the blood on hand would suffice for the projected need.

   (b) Consider the following example. Over the next week, they expect to need at most 100 units of blood. The typical distribution of blood types in U.S. patients is roughly 45 percent type O, 42 percent type A, 10 percent type B, and 3 percent type AB. The hospital wants to know if the blood supply it has on hand would be enough if 100 patients arrive with the expected type distribution. There is a total of 105 units of blood on hand. The table below gives these demands, and the supply on hand.

---

[4] The Austrian scientist Karl Landsteiner received the Nobel Prize in 1930 for his discovery of the blood types A, B, O, and AB.

| blood type | supply | demand |
|------------|--------|--------|
| O          | 50     | 45     |
| A          | 36     | 42     |
| B          | 11     | 8      |
| AB         | 8      | 3      |

Is the 105 units of blood on hand enough to satisfy the 100 units of demand? Find an allocation that satisfies the maximum possible number of patients. Use an argument based on a minimum-capacity cut to show why not all patients can receive blood. Also, provide an explanation for this fact that would be understandable to the clinic administrators, who have not taken a course on algorithms. (So, for example, this explanation should not involve the words *flow*, *cut*, or *graph* in the sense we use them in this book.)

9. Network flow issues come up in dealing with natural disasters and other crises, since major unexpected events often require the movement and evacuation of large numbers of people in a short amount of time.

   Consider the following scenario. Due to large-scale flooding in a region, paramedics have identified a set of $n$ injured people distributed across the region who need to be rushed to hospitals. There are $k$ hospitals in the region, and each of the $n$ people needs to be brought to a hospital that is within a half-hour's driving time of their current location (so different people will have different options for hospitals, depending on where they are right now).

   At the same time, one doesn't want to overload any one of the hospitals by sending too many patients its way. The paramedics are in touch by cell phone, and they want to collectively work out whether they can choose a hospital for each of the injured people in such a way that the load on the hospitals is *balanced*: Each hospital receives at most $\lceil n/k \rceil$ people.

   Give a polynomial-time algorithm that takes the given information about the people's locations and determines whether this is possible.

10. Suppose you are given a directed graph $G = (V, E)$, with a positive integer capacity $c_e$ on each edge $e$, a source $s \in V$, and a sink $t \in V$. You are also given a maximum $s$-$t$ flow in $G$, defined by a flow value $f_e$ on each edge $e$. The flow $f$ is *acyclic*: There is no cycle in $G$ on which all edges carry positive flow. The flow $f$ is also integer-valued.

Now suppose we pick a specific edge $e^* \in E$ and reduce its capacity by 1 unit. Show how to find a maximum flow in the resulting capacitated graph in time $O(m + n)$, where $m$ is the number of edges in $G$ and $n$ is the number of nodes.

11. Your friends have written a very fast piece of maximum-flow code based on repeatedly finding augmenting paths as in Section 7.1. However, after you've looked at a bit of output from it, you realize that it's not always finding a flow of *maximum* value. The bug turns out to be pretty easy to find; your friends hadn't really gotten into the whole backward-edge thing when writing the code, and so their implementation builds a variant of the residual graph that *only includes the forward edges*. In other words, it searches for *s-t* paths in a graph $\tilde{G}_f$ consisting only of edges $e$ for which $f(e) < c_e$, and it terminates when there is no augmenting path consisting entirely of such edges. We'll call this the Forward-Edge-Only Algorithm. (Note that we do not try to prescribe how this algorithm chooses its forward-edge paths; it may choose them in any fashion it wants, provided that it terminates only when there are no forward-edge paths.)

It's hard to convince your friends they need to reimplement the code. In addition to its blazing speed, they claim, in fact, that it never returns a flow whose value is less than a fixed fraction of optimal. Do you believe this? The crux of their claim can be made precise in the following statement.

> There is an absolute constant $b > 1$ (independent of the particular input flow network), so that on every instance of the Maximum-Flow Problem, the Forward-Edge-Only Algorithm is guaranteed to find a flow of value at least $1/b$ times the maximum-flow value (regardless of how it chooses its forward-edge paths).

Decide whether you think this statement is true or false, and give a proof of either the statement or its negation.

12. Consider the following problem. You are given a flow network with unit-capacity edges: It consists of a directed graph $G = (V, E)$, a source $s \in V$, and a sink $t \in V$; and $c_e = 1$ for every $e \in E$. You are also given a parameter $k$.

The goal is to delete $k$ edges so as to reduce the maximum *s-t* flow in $G$ by as much as possible. In other words, you should find a set of edges $F \subseteq E$ so that $|F| = k$ and the maximum *s-t* flow in $G' = (V, E - F)$ is as small as possible subject to this.

Give a polynomial-time algorithm to solve this problem.

13. In a standard *s-t* Maximum-Flow Problem, we assume edges have capacities, and there is no limit on how much flow is allowed to pass through a

node. In this problem, we consider the variant of the Maximum-Flow and Minimum-Cut problems with node capacities.

Let $G = (V, E)$ be a directed graph, with source $s \in V$, sink $t \in V$, and nonnegative node capacities $\{c_v \geq 0\}$ for each $v \in V$. Given a flow $f$ in this graph, the flow though a node $v$ is defined as $f^{in}(v)$. We say that a flow is feasible if it satisfies the usual flow-conservation constraints and the node-capacity constraints: $f^{in}(v) \leq c_v$ for all nodes.

Give a polynomial-time algorithm to find an $s$-$t$ maximum flow in such a node-capacitated network. Define an $s$-$t$ cut for node-capacitated networks, and show that the analogue of the Max-Flow Min-Cut Theorem holds true.

14. We define the *Escape Problem* as follows. We are given a directed graph $G = (V, E)$ (picture a network of roads). A certain collection of nodes $X \subset V$ are designated as *populated nodes*, and a certain other collection $S \subset V$ are designated as *safe nodes*. (Assume that $X$ and $S$ are disjoint.) In case of an emergency, we want evacuation routes from the populated nodes to the safe nodes. A set of evacuation routes is defined as a set of paths in $G$ so that (i) each node in $X$ is the tail of one path, (ii) the last node on each path lies in $S$, and (iii) the paths do not share any edges. Such a set of paths gives a way for the occupants of the populated nodes to "escape" to $S$, without overly congesting any edge in $G$.

(a) Given $G$, $X$, and $S$, show how to decide in polynomial time whether such a set of evacuation routes exists.

(b) Suppose we have exactly the same problem as in (a), but we want to enforce an even stronger version of the "no congestion" condition (iii). Thus we change (iii) to say "the paths do not share any *nodes*."

With this new condition, show how to decide in polynomial time whether such a set of evacuation routes exists.

Also, provide an example with the same $G$, $X$, and $S$, in which the answer is yes to the question in (a) but no to the question in (b).

15. Suppose you and your friend Alanis live, together with $n - 2$ other people, at a popular off-campus cooperative apartment, the Upson Collective. Over the next $n$ nights, each of you is supposed to cook dinner for the co-op exactly once, so that someone cooks on each of the nights.

Of course, everyone has scheduling conflicts with some of the nights (e.g., exams, concerts, etc.), so deciding who should cook on which night becomes a tricky task. For concreteness, let's label the people

$$\{p_1, \ldots, p_n\},$$

the nights

$$\{d_1, \ldots, d_n\};$$

and for person $p_i$, there's a set of nights $S_i \subset \{d_1, \ldots, d_n\}$ when they are *not* able to cook.

A *feasible dinner schedule* is an assignment of each person in the co-op to a different night, so that each person cooks on exactly one night, there is someone cooking on each night, and if $p_i$ cooks on night $d_j$, then $d_j \notin S_i$.

**(a)** Describe a bipartite graph $G$ so that $G$ has a perfect matching if and only if there is a feasible dinner schedule for the co-op.

**(b)** Your friend Alanis takes on the task of trying to construct a feasible dinner schedule. After great effort, she constructs what she claims is a feasible schedule and then heads off to class for the day.

Unfortunately, when you look at the schedule she created, you notice a big problem. $n - 2$ of the people at the co-op are assigned to different nights on which they are available: no problem there. But for the other two people, $p_i$ and $p_j$, and the other two days, $d_k$ and $d_\ell$, you discover that she has accidentally assigned both $p_i$ and $p_j$ to cook on night $d_k$, and assigned no one to cook on night $d_\ell$.

You want to fix Alanis's mistake but without having to recompute everything from scratch. Show that it's possible, using her "almost correct" schedule, to decide in only $O(n^2)$ time whether there exists a feasible dinner schedule for the co-op. (If one exists, you should also output it.)

16. Back in the euphoric early days of the Web, people liked to claim that much of the enormous potential in a company like Yahoo! was in the "eyeballs"—the simple fact that millions of people look at its pages every day. Further, by convincing people to register personal data with the site, a site like Yahoo! can show each user an extremely targeted advertisement whenever he or she visits the site, in a way that TV networks or magazines couldn't hope to match. So if a user has told Yahoo! that he or she is a 20-year-old computer science major from Cornell University, the site can present a banner ad for apartments in Ithaca, New York; on the other hand, if he or she is a 50-year-old investment banker from Greenwich, Connecticut, the site can display a banner ad pitching Lincoln Town Cars instead.

But deciding on which ads to show to which people involves some serious computation behind the scenes. Suppose that the managers of a popular Web site have identified $k$ distinct *demographic groups*

$G_1, G_2, \ldots, G_k$. (These groups can overlap; for example, $G_1$ can be equal to all residents of New York State, and $G_2$ can be equal to all people with a degree in computer science.) The site has contracts with $m$ different *advertisers*, to show a certain number of copies of their ads to users of the site. Here's what the contract with the $i^{\text{th}}$ advertiser looks like.

- For a subset $X_i \subseteq \{G_1, \ldots, G_k\}$ of the demographic groups, advertiser $i$ wants its ads shown only to users who belong to at least one of the demographic groups in the set $X_i$.

- For a number $r_i$, advertiser $i$ wants its ads shown to at least $r_i$ users each minute.

Now consider the problem of designing a good *advertising policy*— a way to show a single ad to each user of the site. Suppose at a given minute, there are $n$ users visiting the site. Because we have registration information on each of these users, we know that user $j$ (for $j = 1, 2, \ldots, n$) belongs to a subset $U_j \subseteq \{G_1, \ldots, G_k\}$ of the demographic groups. The problem is: Is there a way to show a single ad to each user so that the site's contracts with each of the $m$ advertisers is satisfied for this minute? (That is, for each $i = 1, 2, \ldots, m$, can at least $r_i$ of the $n$ users, each belonging to at least one demographic group in $X_i$, be shown an ad provided by advertiser $i$?)

Give an efficient algorithm to decide if this is possible, and if so, to actually choose an ad to show each user.

17. You've been called in to help some network administrators diagnose the extent of a failure in their network. The network is designed to carry traffic from a designated source node $s$ to a designated target node $t$, so we will model the network as a directed graph $G = (V, E)$, in which the capacity of each edge is 1 and in which each node lies on at least one path from $s$ to $t$.

Now, when everything is running smoothly in the network, the maximum $s$-$t$ flow in $G$ has value $k$. However, the current situation (and the reason you're here) is that an attacker has destroyed some of the edges in the network, so that there is now no path from $s$ to $t$ using the remaining (surviving) edges. For reasons that we won't go into here, they believe the attacker has destroyed only $k$ edges, the minimum number needed to separate $s$ from $t$ (i.e., the size of a minimum $s$-$t$ cut); and we'll assume they're correct in believing this.

The network administrators are running a monitoring tool on node $s$, which has the following behavior. If you issue the command $ping(v)$, for a given node $v$, it will tell you whether there is currently a path from $s$ to $v$. (So $ping(t)$ reports that no path currently exists; on the other hand, *ping*(s) always reports a path from s to itself.) Since it's not practical to go out and inspect every edge of the network, they'd like to determine the extent of the failure using this monitoring tool, through judicious use of the *ping* command.

So here's the problem you face: Give an algorithm that issues a sequence of *ping* commands to various nodes in the network and then reports the *full* set of nodes that are not currently reachable from s. You could do this by pinging every node in the network, of course, but you'd like to do it using many fewer pings (given the assumption that only k edges have been deleted). In issuing this sequence, your algorithm is allowed to decide which node to ping next based on the outcome of earlier *ping* operations.

Give an algorithm that accomplishes this task using only $O(k \log n)$ pings.

18. We consider the Bipartite Matching Problem on a bipartite graph $G = (V, E)$. As usual, we say that $V$ is partitioned into sets $X$ and $Y$, and each edge has one end in $X$ and the other in $Y$.

If $M$ is a matching in $G$, we say that a node $y \in Y$ is *covered* by $M$ if $y$ is an end of one of the edges in $M$.

(a) Consider the following problem. We are given $G$ and a matching $M$ in $G$. For a given number $k$, we want to decide if there is a matching $M'$ in $G$ so that
   (i)  $M'$ has $k$ more edges than $M$ does, *and*
   (ii) every node $y \in Y$ that is covered by $M$ is also covered by $M'$.
   We call this the *Coverage Expansion Problem*, with input $G$, $M$, and $k$. and we will say that $M'$ is a *solution* to the instance.

   Give a polynomial-time algorithm that takes an instance of Coverage Expansion and either returns a solution $M'$ or reports (correctly) that there is no solution. (You should include an analysis of the running time and a brief proof of why it is correct.)

   **Note:** You may wish to also look at part (b) to help in thinking about this.

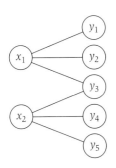

**Figure 7.29** An instance of Coverage Expansion.

**Example.** Consider Figure 7.29, and suppose $M$ is the matching consisting of the edge $(x_1, y_2)$. Suppose we are asked the above question with $k = 1$.

Then the answer to this instance of Coverage Expansion is yes. We can let $M'$ be the matching consisting (for example) of the two edges $(x_1, y_2)$ and $(x_2, y_4)$; $M'$ has one more edge than $M$, and $y_2$ is still covered by $M'$.

(b) Give an example of an instance of Coverage Expansion, specified by $G$, $M$, and $k$, so that the following situation happens.

> *The instance has a solution; but in any solution $M'$, the edges of $M$ do not form a subset of the edges of $M'$.*

(c) Let $G$ be a bipartite graph, and let $M$ be any matching in $G$. Consider the following two quantities.

- $K_1$ is the size of the largest matching $M'$ so that every node $y$ that is covered by $M$ is also covered by $M'$.
- $K_2$ is the size of the largest matching $M''$ in $G$.

Clearly $K_1 \leq K_2$, since $K_2$ is obtained by considering *all possible* matchings in $G$.

> Prove that in fact $K_1 = K_2$; that is, we can obtain a maximum matching even if we're constrained to cover all the nodes covered by our initial matching $M$.

19. You've periodically helped the medical consulting firm Doctors Without Weekends on various hospital scheduling issues, and they've just come to you with a new problem. For each of the next $n$ days, the hospital has determined the number of doctors they want on hand; thus, on day $i$, they have a requirement that *exactly* $p_i$ doctors be present.

There are $k$ doctors, and each is asked to provide a list of days on which he or she is willing to work. Thus doctor $j$ provides a set $L_j$ of days on which he or she is willing to work.

The system produced by the consulting firm should take these lists and try to return to each doctor $j$ a list $L'_j$ with the following properties.

(A) $L'_j$ is a subset of $L_j$, so that doctor $j$ only works on days he or she finds acceptable.

(B) If we consider the whole set of lists $L'_1, \ldots, L'_k$, it causes exactly $p_i$ doctors to be present on day $i$, for $i = 1, 2, \ldots, n$.

(a) Describe a polynomial-time algorithm that implements this system. Specifically, give a polynomial-time algorithm that takes the numbers $p_1, p_2, \ldots, p_n$, and the lists $L_1, \ldots, L_k$, and does one of the following two things.

- Return lists $L'_1, L'_2, \ldots, L'_k$ satisfying properties (A) and (B); or
- Report (correctly) that there is no set of lists $L'_1, L'_2, \ldots, L'_k$ that satisfies both properties (A) and (B).

(b) The hospital finds that the doctors tend to submit lists that are much too restrictive, and so it often happens that the system reports (correctly, but unfortunately) that no acceptable set of lists $L'_1, L'_2, \ldots, L'_k$ exists.

Thus the hospital relaxes the requirements as follows. They add a new parameter $c > 0$, and the system now should try to return to each doctor $j$ a list $L'_j$ with the following properties.

(A*) $L'_j$ contains at most $c$ days that do not appear on the list $L_j$.

(B) *(Same as before)* If we consider the whole set of lists $L'_1, \ldots, L'_k$, it causes exactly $p_i$ doctors to be present on day $i$, for $i = 1, 2, \ldots, n$.

Describe a polynomial-time algorithm that implements this revised system. It should take the numbers $p_1, p_2, \ldots, p_n$, the lists $L_1, \ldots, L_k$, and the parameter $c > 0$, and do one of the following two things.

  - Return lists $L'_1, L'_2, \ldots, L'_k$ satisfying properties (A*) and (B); or
  - Report (correctly) that there is no set of lists $L'_1, L'_2, \ldots, L'_k$ that satisfies both properties (A*) and (B).

20. Your friends are involved in a large-scale atmospheric science experiment. They need to get good measurements on a set $S$ of $n$ different conditions in the atmosphere (such as the ozone level at various places), and they have a set of $m$ balloons that they plan to send up to make these measurements. Each balloon can make at most two measurements.

Unfortunately, not all balloons are capable of measuring all conditions, so for each balloon $i = 1, \ldots, m$, they have a set $S_i$ of conditions that balloon $i$ can measure. Finally, to make the results more reliable, they plan to take each measurement from at least $k$ different balloons. (Note that a single balloon should not measure the same condition twice.) They are having trouble figuring out which conditions to measure on which balloon.

**Example.** Suppose that $k = 2$, there are $n = 4$ conditions labeled $c_1, c_2, c_3, c_4$, and there are $m = 4$ balloons that can measure conditions, subject to the limitation that $S_1 = S_2 = \{c_1, c_2, c_3\}$, and $S_3 = S_4 = \{c_1, c_3, c_4\}$. Then one possible way to make sure that each condition is measured at least $k = 2$ times is to have

  - balloon 1 measure conditions $c_1, c_2$,
  - balloon 2 measure conditions $c_2, c_3$,
  - balloon 3 measure conditions $c_3, c_4$, and
  - balloon 4 measure conditions $c_1, c_4$.

(a) Give a polynomial-time algorithm that takes the input to an instance of this problem (the $n$ conditions, the sets $S_i$ for each of the $m$ balloons, and the parameter $k$) and decides whether there is a way to measure each condition by $k$ different balloons, while each balloon only measures at most two conditions.

**(b)** You show your friends a solution computed by your algorithm from (a), and to your surprise they reply, "This won't do at all—one of the conditions is only being measured by balloons from a single subcontractor." You hadn't heard anything about subcontractors before; it turns out there's an extra wrinkle they forgot to mention. . . .

Each of the balloons is produced by one of three different subcontractors involved in the experiment. A requirement of the experiment is that there be no condition for which all $k$ measurements come from balloons produced by a single subcontractor.

For example, suppose balloon 1 comes from the first subcontractor, balloons 2 and 3 come from the second subcontractor, and balloon 4 comes from the third subcontractor. Then our previous solution no longer works, as both of the measurements for condition $c_3$ were done by balloons from the second subcontractor. However, we could use balloons 1 and 2 to each measure conditions $c_1, c_2$, and use balloons 3 and 4 to each measure conditions $c_3, c_4$.

Explain how to modify your polynomial-time algorithm for part (a) into a new algorithm that decides whether there exists a solution satisfying all the conditions from (a), plus the new requirement about subcontractors.

21. You're helping to organize a class on campus that has decided to give all its students wireless laptops for the semester. Thus there is a collection of $n$ wireless laptops; there is also have a collection of $n$ wireless *access points*, to which a laptop can connect when it is in range.

The laptops are currently scattered across campus; laptop $\ell$ is within range of a *set $S_\ell$* of access points. We will assume that each laptop is within range of at least one access point (so the sets $S_\ell$ are nonempty); we will also assume that every access point $p$ has at least one laptop within range of it.

To make sure that all the wireless connectivity software is working correctly, you need to try having laptops make contact with access points in such a way that each laptop and each access point is involved in at least one connection. Thus we will say that a *test set $T$* is a collection of ordered pairs of the form $(\ell, p)$, for a laptop $\ell$ and access point $p$, with the properties that

(i)   If $(\ell, p) \in T$, then $\ell$ is within range of $p$ (i.e., $p \in S_\ell$).

(ii)  Each laptop appears in at least one ordered pair in $T$.

(iii) Each access point appears in at least one ordered pair in $T$.

This way, by trying out all the connections specified by the pairs in $T$, we can be sure that each laptop and each access point have correctly functioning software.

The problem is: Given the sets $S_\ell$ for each laptop (i.e., which laptops are within range of which access points), and a number $k$, decide whether there is a test set of size at most $k$.

**Example.** Suppose that $n = 3$; laptop 1 is within range of access points 1 and 2; laptop 2 is within range of access point 2; and laptop 3 is within range of access points 2 and 3. Then the set of pairs

> *(laptop 1, access point 1), (laptop 2, access point 2),*
> *(laptop 3, access point 3)*

would form a test set of size 3.

**(a)** Give an example of an instance of this problem for which there is no test set of size $n$. (Recall that we assume each laptop is within range of at least one access point, and each access point $p$ has at least one laptop within range of it.)

**(b)** Give a polynomial-time algorithm that takes the input to an instance of this problem (including the parameter $k$) and decides whether there is a test set of size at most $k$.

22. Let $M$ be an $n \times n$ matrix with each entry equal to either 0 or 1. Let $m_{ij}$ denote the entry in row $i$ and column $j$. A *diagonal entry* is one of the form $m_{ii}$ for some $i$.

*Swapping* rows $i$ and $j$ of the matrix $M$ denotes the following action: we swap the values $m_{ik}$ and $m_{jk}$ for $k = 1, 2, \ldots, n$. Swapping two columns is defined analogously.

We say that $M$ is *rearrangeable* if it is possible to swap some of the pairs of rows and some of the pairs of columns (in any sequence) so that, after all the swapping, all the diagonal entries of $M$ are equal to 1.

**(a)** Give an example of a matrix $M$ that is not rearrangeable, but for which at least one entry in each row and each column is equal to 1.

**(b)** Give a polynomial-time algorithm that determines whether a matrix $M$ with 0-1 entries is rearrangeable.

23. Suppose you're looking at a flow network $G$ with source $s$ and sink $t$, and you want to be able to express something like the following intuitive notion: Some nodes are clearly on the "source side" of the main bottlenecks; some nodes are clearly on the "sink side" of the main bottlenecks; and some nodes are in the middle. However, $G$ can have many minimum cuts, so we have to be careful in how we try making this idea precise.

Here's one way to divide the nodes of $G$ into three categories of this sort.

- We say a node $v$ is *upstream* if, for all minimum $s$-$t$ cuts $(A, B)$, we have $v \in A$—that is, $v$ lies on the source side of every minimum cut.

- We say a node $v$ is *downstream* if, for all minimum $s$-$t$ cuts $(A, B)$, we have $v \in B$—that is, $v$ lies on the sink side of every minimum cut.

- We say a node $v$ is *central* if it is neither upstream nor downstream; there is at least one minimum $s$-$t$ cut $(A, B)$ for which $v \in A$, and at least one minimum $s$-$t$ cut $(A', B')$ for which $v \in B'$.

Give an algorithm that takes a flow network $G$ and classifies each of its nodes as being upstream, downstream, or central. The running time of your algorithm should be within a constant factor of the time required to compute a *single* maximum flow.

24. Let $G = (V, E)$ be a directed graph, with source $s \in V$, sink $t \in V$, and nonnegative edge capacities $\{c_e\}$. Give a polynomial-time algorithm to decide whether $G$ has a *unique* minimum $s$-$t$ cut (i.e., an $s$-$t$ of capacity strictly less than that of all other $s$-$t$ cuts).

25. Suppose you live in a big apartment with a lot of friends. Over the course of a year, there are many occasions when one of you pays for an expense shared by some subset of the apartment, with the expectation that everything will get balanced out fairly at the end of the year. For example, one of you may pay the whole phone bill in a given month, another will occasionally make communal grocery runs to the nearby organic food emporium, and a third might sometimes use a credit card to cover the whole bill at the local Italian-Indian restaurant, Little Idli.

In any case, it's now the end of the year and time to settle up. There are $n$ people in the apartment; and for each ordered pair $(i, j)$ there's an amount $a_{ij} \geq 0$ that $i$ owes $j$, accumulated over the course of the year. We will require that for any two people $i$ and $j$, at least one of the quantities $a_{ij}$ or $a_{ji}$ is equal to $0$. This can be easily made to happen as follows: If it turns out that $i$ owes $j$ a positive amount $x$, and $j$ owes $i$ a positive amount $y < x$, then we will subtract off $y$ from both sides and declare $a_{ij} = x - y$ while $a_{ji} = 0$. In terms of all these quantities, we now define the *imbalance* of a person $i$ to be the sum of the amounts that $i$ is owed by everyone else, minus the sum of the amounts that $i$ owes everyone else. (Note that an imbalance can be positive, negative, or zero.)

In order to restore all imbalances to $0$, so that everyone departs on good terms, certain people will write checks to others; in other words, for certain ordered pairs $(i, j)$, $i$ will write a check to $j$ for an amount $b_{ij} > 0$.

We will say that a set of checks constitutes a *reconciliation* if, for each person $i$, the total value of the checks received by $i$, minus the total value of the checks written by $i$, is equal to the imbalance of $i$. Finally, you and your friends feel it is bad form for $i$ to write $j$ a check if $i$ did not actually owe $j$ money, so we say that a reconciliation is *consistent* if, whenever $i$ writes a check to $j$, it is the case that $a_{ij} > 0$.

Show that, for any set of amounts $a_{ij}$, there is always a consistent reconciliation in which at most $n - 1$ checks get written, by giving a polynomial-time algorithm to compute such a reconciliation.

26. You can tell that cellular phones are at work in rural communities, from the giant microwave towers you sometimes see sprouting out of corn fields and cow pastures. Let's consider a very simplified model of a cellular phone network in a sparsely populated area.

    We are given the locations of $n$ *base stations*, specified as points $b_1, \ldots, b_n$ in the plane. We are also given the locations of $n$ cellular phones, specified as points $p_1, \ldots, p_n$ in the plane. Finally, we are given a *range parameter* $\Delta > 0$. We call the set of cell phones *fully connected* if it is possible to assign each phone to a base station in such a way that

    • Each phone is assigned to a different base station, and

    • If a phone at $p_i$ is assigned to a base station at $b_j$, then the straight-line distance between the points $p_i$ and $b_j$ is at most $\Delta$.

    Suppose that the owner of the cell phone at point $p_1$ decides to go for a drive, traveling continuously for a total of $z$ units of distance due east. As this cell phone moves, we may have to update the assignment of phones to base stations (possibly several times) in order to keep the set of phones fully connected.

    Give a polynomial-time algorithm to decide whether it is possible to keep the set of phones fully connected at all times during the travel of this one cell phone. (You should assume that all other phones remain stationary during this travel.) If it is possible, you should report a sequence of assignments of phones to base stations that will be sufficient in order to maintain full connectivity; if it is not possible, you should report a point on the traveling phone's path at which full connectivity cannot be maintained.

    You should try to make your algorithm run in $O(n^3)$ time if possible.

    **Example.** Suppose we have phones at $p_1 = (0, 0)$ and $p_2 = (2, 1)$; we have base stations at $b_1 = (1, 1)$ and $b_2 = (3, 1)$; and $\Delta = 2$. Now consider the case in which the phone at $p_1$ moves due east a distance of 4 units, ending at $(4, 0)$. Then it is possible to keep the phones fully connected during this motion: We begin by assigning $p_1$ to $b_1$ and $p_2$ to $b_2$, and we reassign $p_1$ to $b_2$ and $p_2$ to $b_1$ during the motion (for example, when $p_1$ passes the point $(2, 0)$).

27. Some of your friends with jobs out West decide they really need some extra time each day to sit in front of their laptops, and the morning commute from Woodside to Palo Alto seems like the only option. So they decide to carpool to work.

    Unfortunately, they all hate to drive, so they want to make sure that any carpool arrangement they agree upon is fair and doesn't overload any individual with too much driving. Some sort of simple round-robin scheme is out, because none of them goes to work every day, and so the subset of them in the car varies from day to day.

    Here's one way to define *fairness*. Let the people be labeled $S = \{p_1, \ldots, p_k\}$. We say that the *total driving obligation* of $p_j$ over a set of days is the expected number of times that $p_j$ would have driven, had a driver been chosen uniformly at random from among the people going to work each day. More concretely, suppose the carpool plan lasts for $d$ days, and on the $i^{\text{th}}$ day a subset $S_i \subseteq S$ of the people go to work. Then the above definition of the total driving obligation $\Delta_j$ for $p_j$ can be written as $\Delta_j = \sum_{i : p_j \in S_i} \frac{1}{|S_i|}$. Ideally, we'd like to require that $p_j$ drives at most $\Delta_j$ times; unfortunately, $\Delta_j$ may not be an integer.

    So let's say that a *driving schedule* is a choice of a driver for each day—that is, a sequence $p_{i_1}, p_{i_2}, \ldots, p_{i_d}$ with $p_{i_t} \in S_t$—and that a *fair driving schedule* is one in which each $p_j$ is chosen as the driver on at most $\lceil \Delta_j \rceil$ days.

    (a) Prove that for any sequence of sets $S_1, \ldots, S_d$, there exists a fair driving schedule.

    (b) Give an algorithm to compute a fair driving schedule with running time polynomial in $k$ and $d$.

28. A group of students has decided to add some features to Cornell's on-line Course Management System (CMS), to handle aspects of course planning that are not currently covered by the software. They're beginning with a module that helps schedule office hours at the start of the semester.

    Their initial prototype works as follows. The office hour schedule will be the same from one week to the next, so it's enough to focus on the scheduling problem for a single week. The course administrator enters a collection of nonoverlapping one-hour time intervals $I_1, I_2, \ldots, I_k$ when it would be possible for teaching assistants (TAs) to hold office hours; the eventual office-hour schedule will consist of a subset of some, but generally not all, of these time slots. Then each of the TAs enters his or her weekly schedule, showing the times when he or she would be available to hold office hours.

Finally, the course administrator specifies, for parameters $a$, $b$, and $c$, that they would like each TA to hold between $a$ and $b$ office hours per week, and they would like a total of exactly $c$ office hours to be held over the course of the week.

The problem, then, is how to assign each TA to some of the office-hour time slots, so that each TA is available for each of his or her office-hour slots, and so that the right number of office hours gets held. (There should be only one TA at each office hour.)

**Example.** Suppose there are five possible time slots for office hours:

$$I_1 = Mon\ 3\text{--}4\ \text{P.M.};\ I_2 = Tue\ 1\text{--}2\ \text{P.M.};\ I_3 = Wed\ 10\text{--}11\ \text{A.M.};\ I_4 = Wed\ 3\text{--}4\ \text{P.M.};\ and\ I_5 = Thu\ 10\text{--}11\ \text{A.M.}.$$

There are two TAs; the first would be able to hold office hours at any time on Monday or Wednesday afternoons, and the second would be able to hold office hours at any time on Tuesday, Wednesday, or Thursday. (In general, TA availability might be more complicated to specify than this, but we're keeping this example simple.) Finally, each TA should hold between $a = 1$ and $b = 2$ office hours, and we want exactly $c = 3$ office hours per week total.

One possible solution would be to have the first TA hold office hours in time slot $I_1$, and the second TA to hold office hours in time slots $I_2$ and $I_5$.

(a) Give a polynomial-time algorithm that takes the input to an instance of this problem (the time slots, the TA schedules, and the parameters $a$, $b$, and $c$) and does one of the following two things:
   - Constructs a valid schedule for office hours, specifying which TA will cover which time slots, or
   - Reports (correctly) that there is no valid way to schedule office hours.

(b) This office-hour scheduling feature becomes very popular, and so course staffs begin to demand more. In particular, they observe that it's good to have a greater density of office hours closer to the due date of a homework assignment.

So what they want to be able to do is to specify an *office-hour density* parameter for each day of the week: The number $d_i$ specifies that they want to have at least $d_i$ office hours on a given day $i$ of the week.

For example, suppose that in our previous example, we add the constraint that we want at least one office hour on Wednesday and at least one office hour on Thursday. Then the previous solution does not work; but there is a possible solution in which we have the first TA hold office hours in time slot $I_1$, and the second TA hold office hours in time slots $I_3$ and $I_5$. (Another solution would be to have the first TA hold office hours in time slots $I_1$ and $I_4$, and the second TA hold office hours in time slot $I_5$.)

Give a polynomial-time algorithm that computes office-hour schedules under this more complex set of constraints. The algorithm should either construct a schedule or report (correctly) that none exists.

29. Some of your friends have recently graduated and started a small company, which they are currently running out of their parents' garages in Santa Clara. They're in the process of porting all their software from an old system to a new, revved-up system; and they're facing the following problem.

    They have a collection of $n$ software applications, $\{1, 2, \ldots, n\}$, running on their old system; and they'd like to port some of these to the new system. If they move application $i$ to the new system, they expect a net (monetary) benefit of $b_i \geq 0$. The different software applications interact with one another; if applications $i$ and $j$ have extensive interaction, then the company will incur an expense if they move one of $i$ or $j$ to the new system but not both; let's denote this expense by $x_{ij} \geq 0$.

    So, if the situation were really this simple, your friends would just port all $n$ applications, achieving a total benefit of $\sum_i b_i$. Unfortunately, there's a problem. . . .

    Due to small but fundamental incompatibilities between the two systems, there's no way to port application 1 to the new system; it will have to remain on the old system. Nevertheless, it might still pay off to port some of the other applications, accruing the associated benefit and incurring the expense of the interaction between applications on different systems.

    So this is the question they pose to you: Which of the remaining applications, if any, should be moved? Give a polynomial-time algorithm to find a set $S \subseteq \{2, 3, \ldots, n\}$ for which the sum of the benefits minus the expenses of moving the applications in $S$ to the new system is maximized.

30. Consider a variation on the previous problem. In the new scenario, any application can potentially be moved, but now some of the benefits $b_i$ for

moving to the new system are in fact *negative*: If $b_i < 0$, then it is preferable (by an amount quantified in $b_i$) to keep $i$ on the old system. Again, give a polynomial-time algorithm to find a set $S \subseteq \{1, 2, \ldots, n\}$ for which the sum of the benefits minus the expenses of moving the applications in $S$ to the new system is maximized.

31. Some of your friends are interning at the small high-tech company Web-Exodus. A running joke among the employees there is that the back room has less space devoted to high-end servers than it does to empty boxes of computer equipment, piled up in case something needs to be shipped back to the supplier for maintainence.

    A few days ago, a large shipment of computer monitors arrived, each in its own large box; and since there are many different kinds of monitors in the shipment, the boxes do not all have the same dimensions. A bunch of people spent some time in the morning trying to figure out how to store all these things, realizing of course that less space would be taken up if some of the boxes could be *nested* inside others.

    Suppose each box $i$ is a rectangular parallelepiped with side lengths equal to $(i_1, i_2, i_3)$; and suppose each side length is strictly between half a meter and one meter. Geometrically, you know what it means for one box to nest inside another: It's possible if you can rotate the smaller so that it fits inside the larger in each dimension. Formally, we can say that box $i$ with dimensions $(i_1, i_2, i_3)$ *nests* inside box $j$ with dimensions $(j_1, j_2, j_3)$ if there is a permutation $a, b, c$ of the dimensions $\{1, 2, 3\}$ so that $i_a < j_1$, and $i_b < j_2$, and $i_c < j_3$. Of course, nesting is recursive: If $i$ nests in $j$, and $j$ nests in $k$, then by putting $i$ inside $j$ inside $k$, only box $k$ is visible. We say that a *nesting arrangement* for a set of $n$ boxes is a sequence of operations in which a box $i$ is put inside another box $j$ in which it nests; and if there were already boxes nested inside $i$, then these end up inside $j$ as well. (Also notice the following: Since the side lengths of $i$ are more than half a meter each, and since the side lengths of $j$ are less than a meter each, box $i$ will take up more than half of each dimension of $j$, and so after $i$ is put inside $j$, nothing else can be put inside $j$.) We say that a box $k$ is *visible* in a nesting arrangement if the sequence of operations does not result in its ever being put inside another box.

    Here is the problem faced by the people at WebExodus: Since only the visible boxes are taking up any space, how should a nesting arrangement be chosen so as to minimize the *number* of visible boxes?

    Give a polynomial-time algorithm to solve this problem.

    **Example.** Suppose there are three boxes with dimensions (.6, .6, .6), (.75, .75, .75), and (.9, .7, .7). The first box can be put into either of the second or third boxes; but in any nesting arrangement, both the second and third boxes will be visible. So the minimum possible number of visible boxes is two, and one solution that achieves this is to nest the first box inside the second.

32. Given a graph $G = (V, E)$, and a natural number $k$, we can define a relation $\xrightarrow{G,k}$ on pairs of vertices of $G$ as follows. If $x, y \in V$, we say that $x \xrightarrow{G,k} y$ if there exist $k$ mutually edge-disjoint paths from $x$ to $y$ in $G$.

    Is it true that for every $G$ and every $k \geq 0$, the relation $\xrightarrow{G,k}$ is transitive? That is, is it always the case that if $x \xrightarrow{G,k} y$ and $y \xrightarrow{G,k} z$, then we have $x \xrightarrow{G,k} z$? Give a proof or a counterexample.

33. Let $G = (V, E)$ be a directed graph, and suppose that for each node $v$, the number of edges into $v$ is equal to the number of edges out of $v$. That is, for all $v$,

$$|\{(u, v) : (u, v) \in E\}| = |\{(v, w) : (v, w) \in E\}|.$$

    Let $x, y$ be two nodes of $G$, and suppose that there exist $k$ mutually edge-disjoint paths from $x$ to $y$. Under these conditions, does it follow that there exist $k$ mutually edge-disjoint paths from $y$ to $x$? Give a proof or a counterexample with explanation.

34. *Ad hoc networks*, made up of low-powered wireless devices, have been proposed for situations like natural disasters in which the coordinators of a rescue effort might want to monitor conditions in a hard-to-reach area. The idea is that a large collection of these wireless devices could be dropped into such an area from an airplane and then configured into a functioning network.

    Note that we're talking about (a) relatively inexpensive devices that are (b) being dropped from an airplane into (c) dangerous territory; and for the combination of reasons (a), (b), and (c), it becomes necessary to include provisions for dealing with the failure of a reasonable number of the nodes.

    We'd like it to be the case that if one of the devices $v$ detects that it is in danger of failing, it should transmit a representation of its current state to some other device in the network. Each device has a limited transmitting range—say it can communicate with other devices that lie within $d$ meters of it. Moreover, since we don't want it to try transmitting its state to a device that has already failed, we should include some redundancy: A device $v$ should have a set of $k$ other devices that it can potentially contact, each within $d$ meters of it. We'll call this a *back-up set* for device $v$.

**(a)** Suppose you're given a set of $n$ wireless devices, with positions represented by an $(x, y)$ coordinate pair for each. Design an algorithm that determines whether it is possible to choose a back-up set for each device (i.e., $k$ other devices, each within $d$ meters), with the further property that, for some parameter $b$, no device appears in the back-up set of more than $b$ other devices. The algorithm should output the back-up sets themselves, provided they can be found.

**(b)** The idea that, for each pair of devices $v$ and $w$, there's a strict dichotomy between being "in range" or "out of range" is a simplified abstraction. More accurately, there's a power decay function $f(\cdot)$ that specifies, for a pair of devices at distance $\delta$, the signal strength $f(\delta)$ that they'll be able to achieve on their wireless connection. (We'll assume that $f(\delta)$ decreases with increasing $\delta$.)

We might want to build this into our notion of back-up sets as follows: among the $k$ devices in the back-up set of $v$, there should be at least one that can be reached with very high signal strength, at least one other that can be reached with moderately high signal strength, and so forth. More concretely, we have values $p_1 \geq p_2 \geq \cdots \geq p_k$, so that if the back-up set for $v$ consists of devices at distances $d_1 \leq d_2 \leq \cdots \leq d_k$, then we should have $f(d_j) \geq p_j$ for each $j$.

Give an algorithm that determines whether it is possible to choose a back-up set for each device subject to this more detailed condition, still requiring that no device should appear in the back-up set of more than $b$ other devices. Again, the algorithm should output the back-up sets themselves, provided they can be found.

**35.** You're designing an interactive image segmentation tool that works as follows. You start with the image segmentation setup described in Section 7.10, with $n$ pixels, a set of neighboring pairs, and parameters $\{a_i\}$, $\{b_i\}$, and $\{p_{ij}\}$. We will make two assumptions about this instance. First, we will suppose that each of the parameters $\{a_i\}$, $\{b_i\}$, and $\{p_{ij}\}$ is a nonnegative integer between 0 and $d$, for some number $d$. Second, we will suppose that the neighbor relation among the pixels has the property that each pixel is a neighbor of at most four other pixels (so in the resulting graph, there are at most four edges out of each node).

You first perform an *initial segmentation* $(A_0, B_0)$ so as to maximize the quantity $q(A_0, B_0)$. Now, this might result in certain pixels being assigned to the background when the user knows that they ought to be in the foreground. So, when presented with the segmentation, the user has the option of mouse-clicking on a particular pixel $v_1$, thereby bringing it to the foreground. But the tool should not simply bring this pixel into the foreground; rather, it should compute a segmentation $(A_1, B_1)$ that maximizes the quantity $q(A_1, B_1)$ *subject to the condition that $v_1$ is in the foreground.* (In practice, this is useful for the following kind of operation: In segmenting a photo of a group of people, perhaps someone is holding a bag that has been accidentally labeled as part of the background. By clicking on a single pixel belonging to the bag, and recomputing an optimal segmentation subject to the new condition, the whole bag will often become part of the foreground.)

In fact, the system should allow the user to perform a sequence of such mouse-clicks $v_1, v_2, \ldots, v_t$; and after mouse-click $v_i$, the system should produce a segmentation $(A_i, B_i)$ that maximizes the quantity $q(A_i, B_i)$ subject to the condition that all of $v_1, v_2, \ldots, v_i$ are in the foreground.

Give an algorithm that performs these operations so that the initial segmentation is computed within a constant factor of the time for a single maximum flow, and then the interaction with the user is handled in $O(dn)$ time per mouse-click.

(*Note:* Solved Exercise 1 from this chapter is a useful primitive for doing this. Also, the symmetric operation of forcing a pixel to belong to the background can be handled by analogous means, but you do not have to work this out here.)

36. We now consider a different variation of the image segmentation problem in Section 7.10. We will develop a solution to an *image labeling* problem, where the goal is to label each pixel with a rough estimate of its distance from the camera (rather than the simple *foreground/background* labeling used in the text). The possible labels for each pixel will be $0, 1, 2, \ldots, M$ for some integer $M$.

Let $G = (V, E)$ denote the graph whose nodes are pixels, and edges indicate neighboring pairs of pixels. A *labeling* of the pixels is a partition of $V$ into sets $A_0, A_1, \ldots, A_M$, where $A_k$ is the set of pixels that is labeled with distance $k$ for $k = 0, \ldots, M$. We will seek a labeling of minimum *cost*; the cost will come from two types of terms. By analogy with the foreground/background segmentation problem, we will have an *assignment cost*: for each pixel $i$ and label $k$, the cost $a_{i,k}$ is the cost of assigning label $k$ to pixel $i$. Next, if two neighboring pixels $(i, j) \in E$ are assigned different labels, there will be a *separation* cost. In Section 7.10, we used a separation penalty $p_{ij}$. In our current problem, the separation cost will also depend on how far the two pixels are separated; specifically, it will be proportional to the difference in value between their two labels.

Thus the overall cost $q'$ of a labeling is defined as follows:

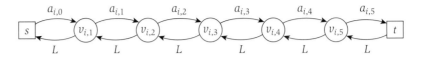

**Figure 7.30** The set of nodes corresponding to a single pixel $i$ in Exercise 36 (shown together with the source $s$ and sink $t$).

$$q'(A_0, \ldots, A_M) = \sum_{k=0}^{M} \sum_{i \in A_i} a_{i,k} + \sum_{k < \ell} \sum_{\substack{(i,j) \in E \\ i \in A_k, j \in A_\ell}} (\ell - k) p_{ij}.$$

The goal of this problem is to develop a polynomial-time algorithm that finds the optimal labeling given the graph $G$ and the penalty parameters $a_{i,k}$ and $p_{ij}$. The algorithm will be based on constructing a flow network, and we will start you off on designing the algorithm by providing a portion of the construction.

The flow network will have a source $s$ and a sink $t$. In addition, for each pixel $i \in V$ we will have nodes $v_{i,k}$ in the flow network for $k = 1, \ldots, M$, as shown in Figure 7.30. ($M = 5$ in the example in the figure.)

For notational convenience, the nodes $v_{i,0}$ and $v_{i,M+1}$ will refer to $s$ and $t$, respectively, for any choice of $i \in V$.

We now add edges $(v_{i,k}, v_{i,k+1})$ with capacity $a_{i,k}$ for $k = 0, \ldots, M$; and edges $(v_{i,k+1}, v_{i,k})$ in the opposite direction with very large capacity $L$. We will refer to this collection of nodes and edges as the *chain* associated with pixel $i$.

Notice that if we make this very large capacity $L$ large enough, then there will be no minimum cut $(A, B)$ so that an edge of capacity $L$ leaves the set $A$. (How large do we have to make it for this to happen?). Hence, for any minimum cut $(A, B)$, and each pixel $i$, there will be exactly one low-capacity edge in the chain associated with $i$ that leaves the set $A$. (You should check that if there were two such edges, then a large-capacity edge would also have to leave the set $A$.)

Finally, here's the question: Use the nodes and edges defined so far to complete the construction of a flow network with the property that a minimum-cost labeling can be efficiently computed from a minimum $s$-$t$ cut. You should prove that your construction has the desired property, and show how to recover the minimum-cost labeling from the cut.

37. In a standard minimum $s$-$t$ cut problem, we assume that all capacities are nonnegative; allowing an arbitrary set of positive and negative capacities results in a problem that is computationally much more difficult. How-

ever, as we'll see here, it is possible to relax the nonnegativity requirement a little and still have a problem that can be solved in polynomial time.

Let $G = (V, E)$ be a directed graph, with source $s \in V$, sink $t \in V$, and edge capacities $\{c_e\}$. Suppose that for every edge $e$ that has neither $s$ nor $t$ as an endpoint, we have $c_e \geq 0$. Thus $c_e$ can be negative for edges $e$ that have at least one end equal to either $s$ or $t$. Give a polynomial-time algorithm to find an $s$-$t$ cut of minimum value in such a graph. (Despite the new nonnegativity requirements, we still define the value of an $s$-$t$ cut $(A, B)$ to be the sum of the capacities of all edges $e$ for which the tail of $e$ is in $A$ and the head of $e$ is in $B$.)

38. You're working with a large database of employee records. For the purposes of this question, we'll picture the database as a two-dimensional table $T$ with a set $R$ of $m$ rows and a set $C$ of $n$ columns; the rows correspond to individual employees, and the columns correspond to different attributes.

To take a simple example, we may have four columns labeled

>        name,   phone number,   start date,   manager's name

and a table with five employees as shown here.

| name | phone number | start date | manager's name |
|---|---|---|---|
| Alanis | 3-4563 | 6/13/95 | Chelsea |
| Chelsea | 3-2341 | 1/20/93 | Lou |
| Elrond | 3-2345 | 12/19/01 | Chelsea |
| Hal | 3-9000 | 1/12/97 | Chelsea |
| Raj | 3-3453 | 7/1/96 | Chelsea |

Given a subset $S$ of the columns, we can obtain a new, smaller table by keeping only the entries that involve columns from $S$. We will call this new table the *projection* of $T$ onto $S$, and denote it by $T[S]$. For example, if $S = \{\text{name}, \text{start date}\}$, then the projection $T[S]$ would be the table consisting of just the first and third columns.

There's a different operation on tables that is also useful, which is to *permute* the columns. Given a permutation $p$ of the columns, we can obtain a new table of the same size as $T$ by simply reordering the columns according to $p$. We will call this new table the *permutation* of $T$ by $p$, and denote it by $T_p$.

All of this comes into play for your particular application, as follows. You have $k$ different subsets of the columns $S_1, S_2, \ldots, S_k$ that you're going to be working with a lot, so you'd like to have them available in a readily accessible format. One choice would be to store the $k$ projections $T[S_1], T[S_2], \ldots, T[S_k]$, but this would take up a lot of space. In considering alternatives to this, you learn that you may not need to explicitly project onto each subset, because the underlying database system can deal with a subset of the columns particularly efficiently if (in some order) the members of the subset constitute a *prefix* of the columns in left-to-right order. So, in our example, the subsets {name, phone number} and {name, start date, phone number,} constitute prefixes (they're the first two and first three columns from the left, respectively); and as such, they can be processed much more efficiently in this table than a subset such as {name, start date}, which does not constitute a prefix. (Again, note that a given subset $S_i$ does not come with a specified order, and so we are interested in whether there is *some* order under which it forms a prefix of the columns.)

So here's the question: Given a parameter $\ell < k$, can you find $\ell$ permutations of the columns $p_1, p_2, \ldots, p_\ell$ so that for every one of the given subsets $S_i$ (for $i = 1, 2, \ldots, k$), it's the case that the columns in $S_i$ constitute a prefix of at least one of the permuted tables $T_{p_1}, T_{p_2}, \ldots, T_{p_\ell}$? We'll say that such a set of permutations constitutes a valid solution to the problem; if a valid solution exists, it means you only need to store the $\ell$ permuted tables rather than all $k$ projections. Give a polynomial-time algorithm to solve this problem; for instances on which there is a valid solution, your algorithm should return an appropriate set of $\ell$ permutations.

**Example.** Suppose the table is as above, the given subsets are

$$S_1 = \{\text{name, phone number}\},$$
$$S_2 = \{\text{name, start date}\},$$
$$S_3 = \{\text{name, manager's name, start date}\},$$

and $\ell = 2$. Then there is a valid solution to the instance, and it could be achieved by the two permutations

$$p_1 = \{\text{name, phone number, start date, manager's name}\},$$
$$p_2 = \{\text{name, start date, manager's name, phone number}\}.$$

This way, $S_1$ constitutes a prefix of the permuted table $T_{p_1}$, and both $S_2$ and $S_3$ constitute prefixes of the permuted table $T_{p_2}$.

39. You are consulting for an environmental statistics firm. They collect statistics and publish the collected data in a book. The statistics are about populations of different regions in the world and are recorded in

multiples of one million. Examples of such statistics would look like the following table.

| Country | A | B | C | Total |
|---|---|---|---|---|
| grown-up men | 11.998 | 9.083 | 2.919 | 24.000 |
| grown-up women | 12.983 | 10.872 | 3.145 | 27.000 |
| children | 1.019 | 2.045 | 0.936 | 4.000 |
| Total | 26.000 | 22.000 | 7.000 | 55.000 |

We will assume here for simplicity that our data is such that all row and column sums are integers. The Census Rounding Problem is to round all data to integers without changing any row or column sum. Each fractional number can be rounded either up or down. For example, a good rounding for our table data would be as follows.

| Country | A | B | C | Total |
|---|---|---|---|---|
| grown-up men | 11.000 | 10.000 | 3.000 | 24.000 |
| grown-up women | 13.000 | 10.000 | 4.000 | 27.000 |
| children | 2.000 | 2.000 | 0.000 | 4.000 |
| Total | 26.000 | 22.000 | 7.000 | 55.000 |

(a) Consider first the special case when all data are between 0 and 1. So you have a matrix of fractional numbers between 0 and 1, and your problem is to round each fraction that is between 0 and 1 to either 0 or 1 without changing the row or column sums. Use a flow computation to check if the desired rounding is possible.

(b) Consider the Census Rounding Problem as defined above, where row and column sums are integers, and you want to round each fractional number $\alpha$ to either $\lfloor \alpha \rfloor$ or $\lceil \alpha \rceil$. Use a flow computation to check if the desired rounding is possible.

(c) Prove that the rounding we are looking for in (a) and (b) always exists.

40. In a lot of numerical computations, we can ask about the "stability" or "robustness" of the answer. This kind of question can be asked for combinatorial problems as well; here's one way of phrasing the question for the Minimum Spanning Tree Problem.

Suppose you are given a graph $G = (V, E)$, with a cost $c_e$ on each edge $e$. We view the costs as quantities that have been measured experimentally, subject to possible errors in measurement. Thus, the minimum spanning tree one computes for $G$ may not in fact be the "real" minimum spanning tree.

Given error parameters $\varepsilon > 0$ and $k > 0$, and a specific edge $e' = (u, v)$, you would like to be able to make a claim of the following form.

> ($*$) *Even if the cost of* each *edge were to be changed by at most $\varepsilon$ (either increased or decreased), and the costs of k of the edges other than $e'$ were further changed to arbitrarily different values, the edge $e'$ would still not belong to any minimum spanning tree of G.*

Such a property provides a type of guarantee that $e'$ is not likely to belong to the minimum spanning tree, even assuming significant measurement error.

Give a polynomial-time algorithm that takes $G$, $e'$, $\varepsilon$, and $k$, and decides whether or not property ($*$) holds for $e'$.

41. Suppose you're managing a collection of processors and must schedule a sequence of jobs over time.

    The jobs have the following characteristics. Each job $j$ has an arrival time $a_j$ when it is first available for processing, a length $\ell_j$ which indicates how much processing time it needs, and a deadline $d_j$ by which it must be finished. (We'll assume $0 < \ell_j \leq d_j - a_j$.) Each job can be run on any of the processors, but only on one at a time; it can also be preempted and resumed from where it left off (possibly after a delay) on another processor.

    Moreover, the collection of processors is not entirely static either: You have an overall pool of $k$ possible processors; but for each processor $i$, there is an interval of time $[t_i, t_i']$ during which it is available; it is unavailable at all other times.

    Given all this data about job requirements and processor availability, you'd like to decide whether the jobs can all be completed or not. Give a polynomial-time algorithm that either produces a schedule completing all jobs by their deadlines or reports (correctly) that no such schedule exists. You may assume that all the parameters associated with the problem are integers.

    **Example.** Suppose we have two jobs $J_1$ and $J_2$. $J_1$ arrives at time 0, is due at time 4, and has length 3. $J_2$ arrives at time 1, is due at time 3, and has length 2. We also have two processors $P_1$ and $P_2$. $P_1$ is available between times 0 and 4; $P_2$ is available between times 2 and 3. In this case, there is a schedule that gets both jobs done.

    • At time 0, we start job $J_1$ on processor $P_1$.

- At time 1, we preempt $J_1$ to start $J_2$ on $P_1$.
- At time 2, we resume $J_1$ on $P_2$. ($J_2$ continues processing on $P_1$.)
- At time 3, $J_2$ completes by its deadline. $P_2$ ceases to be available, so we move $J_1$ back to $P_1$ to finish its remaining one unit of processing there.
- At time 4, $J_1$ completes its processing on $P_1$.

Notice that there is no solution that does not involve preemption and moving of jobs.

42. Give a polynomial-time algorithm for the following minimization analogue of the Maximum-Flow Problem. You are given a directed graph $G = (V, E)$, with a source $s \in V$ and sink $t \in V$, and numbers (capacities) $\ell(v, w)$ for each edge $(v, w) \in E$. We define a flow $f$, and the value of a flow, as usual, requiring that all nodes except $s$ and $t$ satisfy flow conservation. However, the given numbers are lower bounds on edge flow—that is, they require that $f(v, w) \geq \ell(v, w)$ for every edge $(v, w) \in E$, and there is no upper bound on flow values on edges.

    (a) Give a polynomial-time algorithm that finds a feasible flow of minimum possible value.

    (b) Prove an analogue of the Max-Flow Min-Cut Theorem for this problem (i.e., does min-flow = max-cut?).

43. You are trying to solve a circulation problem, but it is not feasible. The problem has demands, but no capacity limits on the edges. More formally, there is a graph $G = (V, E)$, and demands $d_v$ for each node $v$ (satisfying $\sum_{v \in V} d_v = 0$), and the problem is to decide if there is a flow $f$ such that $f(e) \geq 0$ and $f^{in}(v) - f^{out}(v) = d_v$ for all nodes $v \in V$. Note that this problem can be solved via the circulation algorithm from Section 7.7 by setting $c_e = +\infty$ for all edges $e \in E$. (Alternately, it is enough to set $c_e$ to be an extremely large number for each edge—say, larger than the total of all positive demands $d_v$ in the graph.)

    You want to fix up the graph to make the problem feasible, so it would be very useful to know why the problem is not feasible as it stands now. On a closer look, you see that there is a subset $U$ of nodes such that there is no edge into $U$, and yet $\sum_{v \in U} d_v > 0$. You quickly realize that the existence of such a set immediately implies that the flow cannot exist: The set $U$ has a positive total demand, and so needs incoming flow, and yet $U$ has no edges into it. In trying to evaluate how far the problem is from being solvable, you wonder how big the demand of a set with no incoming edges can be.

Give a polynomial-time algorithm to find a subset $S \subset V$ of nodes such that there is no edge into $S$ and for which $\sum_{v \in S} d_v$ is as large as possible subject to this condition.

44. Suppose we are given a directed network $G = (V, E)$ with a root node $r$ and a set of *terminals* $T \subseteq V$. We'd like to disconnect many terminals from $r$, while cutting relatively few edges.

    We make this trade-off precise as follows. For a set of edges $F \subseteq E$, let $q(F)$ denote the number of nodes $v \in T$ such that there is no $r$-$v$ path in the subgraph $(V, E - F)$. Give a polynomial-time algorithm to find a set $F$ of edges that maximizes the quantity $q(F) - |F|$. (Note that setting $F$ equal to the empty set is an option.)

45. Consider the following definition. We are given a set of $n$ countries that are engaged in trade with one another. For each country $i$, we have the value $s_i$ of its budget surplus; this number may be positive or negative, with a negative number indicating a deficit. For each pair of countries $i, j$, we have the total value $e_{ij}$ of all exports from $i$ to $j$; this number is always nonnegative. We say that a subset $S$ of the countries is *free-standing* if the sum of the budget surpluses of the countries in $S$, minus the total value of all exports from countries in $S$ to countries not in $S$, is nonnegative.

    Give a polynomial-time algorithm that takes this data for a set of $n$ countries and decides whether it contains a nonempty free-standing subset that is not equal to the full set.

46. In sociology, one often studies a graph $G$ in which nodes represent people and edges represent those who are friends with each other. Let's assume for purposes of this question that friendship is symmetric, so we can consider an undirected graph.

    Now suppose we want to study this graph $G$, looking for a "close-knit" group of people. One way to formalize this notion would be as follows. For a subset $S$ of nodes, let $e(S)$ denote the number of edges in $S$—that is, the number of edges that have both ends in $S$. We define the *cohesiveness* of $S$ as $e(S)/|S|$. A natural thing to search for would be a set $S$ of people achieving the maximum cohesiveness.

    (a)  Give a polynomial-time algorithm that takes a rational number $\alpha$ and determines whether there exists a set $S$ with cohesiveness at least $\alpha$.

    (b)  Give a polynomial-time algorithm to find a set $S$ of nodes with maximum cohesiveness.

**47.** The goal of this problem is to suggest variants of the Preflow-Push Algorithm that speed up the practical running time without ruining its worst-case complexity. Recall that the algorithm maintains the invariant that $h(v) \le h(w) + 1$ for all edges $(v, w)$ in the residual graph of the current preflow. We proved that if $f$ is a flow (not just a preflow) with this invariant, then it is a maximum flow. Heights were monotone increasing, and the running-time analysis depended on bounding the number of times nodes can increase their heights. Practical experience shows that the algorithm is almost always much faster than suggested by the worst case, and that the practical bottleneck of the algorithm is relabeling nodes (and not the nonsaturating pushes that lead to the worst case in the theoretical analysis). The goal of the problems below is to decrease the number of relabelings by increasing heights faster than one by one. Assume you have a graph $G$ with $n$ nodes, $m$ edges, capacities $c$, source $s$, and sink $t$.

(a) The Preflow-Push Algorithm, as described in Section 7.4, starts by setting the flow equal to the capacity $c_e$ on all edges $e$ leaving the source, setting the flow to 0 on all other edges, setting $h(s) = n$, and setting $h(v) = 0$ for all other nodes $v \in V$. Give an $O(m)$ procedure for initializing node heights that is better than the one we constructed in Section 7.4. Your method should set the height of each node $v$ to be as high as possible given the initial flow.

(b) In this part we will add a new step, called *gap relabeling*, to Preflow-Push, which will increase the labels of lots of nodes by more than one at a time. Consider a preflow $f$ and heights $h$ satisfying the invariant. A *gap* in the heights is an integer $0 < h < n$ so that no node has height exactly $h$. Assume $h$ is a gap value, and let $A$ be the set of nodes $v$ with heights $n > h(v) > h$. Gap relabeling is the process of changing the heights of all nodes in $A$ so they are equal to $n$. Prove that the Preflow-Push Algorithm with gap relabeling is a valid max-flow algorithm. Note that the only new thing that you need to prove is that gap relabeling preserves the invariant above, that $h(v) \le h(w) + 1$ for all edges $(v, w)$ in the residual graph.

(c) In Section 7.4 we proved that $h(v) \le 2n - 1$ throughout the algorithm. Here we will have a variant that has $h(v) \le n$ throughout. The idea is that we "freeze" all nodes when they get to height $n$; that is, nodes at height $n$ are no longer considered active, and hence are not used for `push` and `relabel`. This way, at the end of the algorithm we have a preflow and height function that satisfies the invariant above, and so that all excess is at height $n$. Let $B$ be the set of nodes $v$ so that there is a path from $v$ to $t$ in the residual graph of the current preflow. Let $A = V - B$. Prove that at the end of the algorithm, $(A, B)$ is a minimum-capacity $s$-$t$ cut.

**(d)**  The algorithm in part (c) computes a minimum $s$-$t$ cut but fails to find a maximum flow (as it ends with a preflow that has excesses). Give an algorithm that takes the preflow $f$ at the end of the algorithm of part (c) and converts it into a maximum flow in at most $O(mn)$ time. (*Hint:* Consider nodes with excess, and try to send the excess back to $s$ using only edges that the flow came on.)

48. In Section 7.4 we considered the Preflow-Push Algorithm, and discussed one particular selection rule for considering vertices. Here we will explore a different selection rule. We will also consider variants of the algorithm that terminate early (and find a cut that is close to the minimum possible).

**(a)**  Let $f$ be any preflow. As $f$ is not necessarily a valid flow, it is possible that the value $f^{out}(s)$ is much higher than the maximum-flow value in $G$. Show, however, that $f^{in}(t)$ is a lower bound on the maximum-flow value.

**(b)**  Consider a preflow $f$ and a compatible labeling $h$. Recall that the set $A = \{v : \text{There is an } s\text{-}v \text{ path in the residual graph } G_f\}$, and $B = V - A$ defines an $s$-$t$ cut for any preflow $f$ that has a compatible labeling $h$. Show that the capacity of the cut $(A, B)$ is equal to $c(A, B) = \sum_{v \in B} e_f(v)$.

Combining (a) and (b) allows the algorithm to terminate early and return $(A, B)$ as an approximately minimum-capacity cut, assuming $c(A, B) - f^{in}(t)$ is sufficiently small. Next we consider an implementation that will work on decreasing this value by trying to push flow out of nodes that have a lot of excess.

**(c)**  The scaling version of the Preflow-Push Algorithm maintains a scaling parameter $\Delta$. We set $\Delta$ initially to be a large power of 2. The algorithm at each step selects a node with excess at least $\Delta$ with as small a height as possible. When no nodes (other than $t$) have excess at least $\Delta$, we divide $\Delta$ by 2, and continue. Note that this is a valid implementation of the generic Preflow-Push Algorithm. The algorithm runs in phases. A single phase continues as long as $\Delta$ is unchanged. Note that $\Delta$ starts out at the largest capacity, and the algorithm terminates when $\Delta = 1$. So there are at most $O(\log C)$ scaling phases. Show how to implement this variant of the algorithm so that the running time can be bounded by $O(mn + n \log C + K)$ if the algorithm has $K$ nonsaturating push operations.

**(d)** Show that the number of nonsaturating push operations in the above algorithm is at most $O(n^2 \log C)$. Recall that $O(\log C)$ bounds the number of scaling phases. To bound the number of nonsaturating push operations in a single scaling phase, consider the potential function $\Phi = \sum_{v \in V} h(v) e_f(v)/\Delta$. What is the effect of a nonsaturating push on $\Phi$? Which operation(s) can make $\Phi$ increase?

**49.** Consider an assignment problem where we have a set of $n$ stations that can provide service, and there is a set of $k$ requests for service. Say, for example, that the stations are cell towers and the requests are cell phones. Each request can be served by a given set of stations. The problem so far can be represented by a bipartite graph $G$: one side is the stations, the other the customers, and there is an edge $(x, y)$ between customer $x$ and station $y$ if customer $x$ can be served from station $y$. Assume that each station can serve at most one customer. Using a max-flow computation, we can decide whether or not all customers can be served, or can get an assignment of a subset of customers to stations maximizing the number of served customers.

Here we consider a version of the problem with an additional complication: Each customer offers a different amount of money for the service. Let $U$ be the set of customers, and assume that customer $x \in U$ is willing to pay $v_x \geq 0$ for being served. Now the goal is to find a subset $X \subset U$ maximizing $\sum_{x \in X} v_x$ such that there is an assignment of the customers in $X$ to stations.

Consider the following greedy approach. We process customers in order of decreasing value (breaking ties arbitrarily). When considering customer $x$ the algorithm will either "promise" service to $x$ or reject $x$ in the following greedy fashion. Let $X$ be the set of customers that so far have been promised service. We add $x$ to the set $X$ if and only if there is a way to assign $X \cup \{x\}$ to servers, and we reject $x$ otherwise. Note that rejected customers will not be considered later. (This is viewed as an advantage: If we need to reject a high-paying customer, at least we can tell him/her early.) However, we do not assign accepted customers to servers in a greedy fashion: we only fix the assignment after the set of accepted customers is fixed. Does this greedy approach produce an optimal set of customers? Prove that it does, or provide a counterexample.

**50.** Consider the following scheduling problem. There are $m$ machines, each of which can process jobs, one job at a time. The problem is to assign jobs to machines (each job needs to be assigned to exactly one machine) and order the jobs on machines so as to minimize a cost function.

The machines run at different speeds, but jobs are identical in their processing needs. More formally, each machine $i$ has a parameter $\ell_i$, and each job requires $\ell_i$ time if assigned to machine $i$.

There are $n$ jobs. Jobs have identical processing needs but different levels of urgency. For each job $j$, we are given a cost function $c_j(t)$ that is the cost of completing job $j$ at time $t$. We assume that the costs are nonnegative, and monotone in $t$.

A schedule consists of an assignment of jobs to machines, and on each machine the schedule gives the order in which the jobs are done. The job assigned to machine $i$ as the first job will complete at time $\ell_i$, the second job at time $2\ell_i$ and so on. For a schedule $S$, let $t_S(j)$ denote the completion time of job $j$ in this schedule. The cost of the schedule is $cost(S) = \sum_j c_j(t_S(j))$.

Give a polynomial-time algorithm to find a schedule of minimum cost.

51. Some friends of yours have grown tired of the game "Six Degrees of Kevin Bacon" (after all, they ask, isn't it just breadth-first search?) and decide to invent a game with a little more punch, algorithmically speaking. Here's how it works.

You start with a set $X$ of $n$ actresses and a set $Y$ of $n$ actors, and two players $P_0$ and $P_1$. Player $P_0$ names an actress $x_1 \in X$, player $P_1$ names an actor $y_1$ who has appeared in a movie with $x_1$, player $P_0$ names an actress $x_2$ who has appeared in a movie with $y_1$, and so on. Thus, $P_0$ and $P_1$ collectively generate a sequence $x_1, y_1, x_2, y_2, \ldots$ such that each actor/actress in the sequence has costarred with the actress/actor immediately preceding. A player $P_i$ ($i = 0, 1$) loses when it is $P_i$'s turn to move, and he/she cannot name a member of his/her set who hasn't been named before.

Suppose you are given a specific pair of such sets $X$ and $Y$, with complete information on who has appeared in a movie with whom. A *strategy* for $P_i$, in our setting, is an algorithm that takes a current sequence $x_1, y_1, x_2, y_2, \ldots$ and generates a legal next move for $P_i$ (assuming it's $P_i$'s turn to move). Give a polynomial-time algorithm that decides which of the two players can force a win, in a particular instance of this game.

# Notes and Further Reading

Network flow emerged as a cohesive subject through the work of Ford and Fulkerson (1962). It is now a field of research in itself, and one can easily devote an entire course to the topic; see, for example, the survey by Goldberg, Tardos, and Tarjan (1990) and the book by Ahuja, Magnanti, and Orlin (1993).

Schrijver (2002) provides an interesting historical account of the early work by Ford and Fulkerson on the flow problem. Lending further support to those of us who always felt that the Minimum-Cut Problem had a slightly destructive overtone, this survey cites a recently declassified U.S. Air Force report to show that in the original motivating application for minimum cuts, the network was a map of rail lines in the Soviet Union, and the goal was to disrupt transportation through it.

As we mention in the text, the formulations of the Bipartite Matching and Disjoint Paths Problems predate the Maximum-Flow Problem by several decades; it was through the development of network flows that these were all placed on a common methodological footing. The rich structure of matchings in bipartite graphs has many independent discoverers; P. Hall (1935) and König (1916) are perhaps the most frequently cited. The problem of finding edge-disjoint paths from a source to a sink is equivalent to the Maximum-Flow Problem with all capacities equal to 1; this special case was solved (in essentially equivalent form) by Menger (1927).

The Preflow-Push Maximum-Flow Algorithm is due to Goldberg (1986), and its efficient implementation is due to Goldberg and Tarjan (1986). High-performance code for this and other network flow algorithms can be found at a Web site maintained by Andrew Goldberg.

The algorithm for image segmentation using minimum cuts is due to Greig, Porteous, and Seheult (1989), and the use of minimum cuts has become an active theme in computer vision research (see, e.g., Veksler (1999) and Kolmogorov and Zabih (2004) for overviews); we will discuss some further extensions of this approach in Chapter 12. Wayne (2001) presents further results on baseball elimination and credits Alan Hoffman with initially popularizing this example in the 1960s. Many further applications of network flows and cuts are discussed in the book by Ahuja, Magnanti, and Orlin (1993).

The problem of finding a minimum-cost perfect matching is a special case of the *Minimum-Cost Flow Problem*, which is beyond the scope of our coverage here. There are a number of equivalent ways to state the Minimum-Cost Flow Problem; in one formulation, we are given a flow network with both capacities $c_e$ and costs $C_e$ on the edges; the *cost* of a flow $f$ is equal to the sum of the edge costs weighted by the amount of flow they carry, $\sum_e C_e f(e)$, and the goal is to produce a maximum flow of minimum total cost. The Minimum-Cost Flow Problem can be solved in polynomial time, and it too has many applications;

Cook et al. (1998) and Ahuja, Magnanti, and Orlin (1993) discuss algorithms for this problem.

While network flow models routing problems that can be reduced to the task of constructing a number of paths from a single source to a single sink, there is a more general, and harder, class of routing problems in which paths must be simultaneously constructed between different pairs of senders and receivers. The relationship among these classes of problems is a bit subtle; we discuss this issue, as well as algorithms for some of these harder types of routing problems, in Chapter 11.

*Notes on the Exercises*    Exercise 8 is based on a problem we learned from Bob Bland; Exercise 16 is based on discussions with Udi Manber; Exercise 25 is based on discussions with Jordan Erenrich; Exercise 35 is based on discussions with Yuri Boykov, Olga Veksler, and Ramin Zabih; Exercise 36 is based on results of Hiroshi Ishikawa and Davi Geiger, and of Boykov, Veksler, and Zabih; Exercise 38 is based on a problem we learned from Al Demers; and Exercise 46 is based on a result of J. Picard and H. Ratliff.

# Chapter 8

# NP and Computational Intractability

We now arrive at a major transition point in the book. Up until now, we've developed efficient algorithms for a wide range of problems and have even made some progress on informally categorizing the problems that admit efficient solutions—for example, problems expressible as minimum cuts in a graph, or problems that allow a dynamic programming formulation. But although we've often paused to take note of other problems that we don't see how to solve, we haven't yet made any attempt to actually quantify or characterize the range of problems that *can't be solved efficiently.*

Back when we were first laying out the fundamental definitions, we settled on polynomial time as our working notion of efficiency. One advantage of using a concrete definition like this, as we noted earlier, is that it gives us the opportunity to prove mathematically that certain problems cannot be solved by polynomial-time—and hence "efficient"—algorithms.

When people began investigating computational complexity in earnest, there was some initial progress in proving that certain *extremely hard* problems cannot be solved by efficient algorithms. But for many of the most fundamental discrete computational problems—arising in optimization, artificial intelligence, combinatorics, logic, and elsewhere—the question was too difficult to resolve, and it has remained open since then: We do not know of polynomial-time algorithms for these problems, and we cannot prove that no polynomial-time algorithm exists.

In the face of this formal ambiguity, which becomes increasingly hardened as years pass, people working in the study of complexity have made significant progress. A large class of problems in this "gray area" has been characterized, and it has been proved that they are equivalent in the following sense: a polynomial-time algorithm for any one of them would imply the existence of a polynomial-time algorithm for all of them. These are the *NP-complete problems*, a name that will make more sense as we proceed a little further. There are literally thousands of NP-complete problems, arising in numerous areas, and the class seems to contain a large fraction of the fundamental problems whose complexity we can't resolve. So the formulation of NP-completeness, and the proof that all these problems are equivalent, is a powerful thing: it says that all these open questions are really a *single* open question, a single type of complexity that we don't yet fully understand.

From a pragmatic point of view, NP-completeness essentially means "computationally hard for all practical purposes, though we can't prove it." Discovering that a problem is NP-complete provides a compelling reason to stop searching for an efficient algorithm—you might as well search for an efficient algorithm for any of the famous computational problems already known to be NP-complete, for which many people have tried and failed to find efficient algorithms.

## 8.1 Polynomial-Time Reductions

Our plan is to explore the space of computationally hard problems, eventually arriving at a mathematical characterization of a large class of them. Our basic technique in this exploration is to compare the relative difficulty of different problems; we'd like to formally express statements like, "Problem $X$ is at least as hard as problem $Y$." We will formalize this through the notion of *reduction*: we will show that a particular problem $X$ is at least as hard as some other problem $Y$ by arguing that, if we had a "black box" capable of solving $X$, then we could also solve $Y$. (In other words, $X$ is powerful enough to let us solve $Y$.)

To make this precise, we add the assumption that $X$ can be solved in polynomial time directly to our model of computation. Suppose we had a *black box* that could solve instances of a problem $X$; if we write down the input for an instance of $X$, then in a single step, the black box will return the correct answer. We can now ask the following question:

> (∗) *Can arbitrary instances of problem $Y$ be solved using a polynomial number of standard computational steps, plus a polynomial number of calls to a black box that solves problem $X$?*

If the answer to this question is yes, then we write $Y \leq_P X$; we read this as "$Y$ is polynomial-time reducible to $X$," or "$X$ is at least as hard as $Y$ (with respect to polynomial time)." Note that in this definition, we still pay for the time it takes to write down the input to the black box solving $X$, and to read the answer that the black box provides.

This formulation of reducibility is very natural. When we ask about reductions to a problem $X$, it is as though we've supplemented our computational model with a piece of specialized hardware that solves instances of $X$ in a single step. We can now explore the question: How much extra power does this piece of hardware give us?

An important consequence of our definition of $\leq_P$ is the following. Suppose $Y \leq_P X$ and there actually *exists* a polynomial-time algorithm to solve $X$. Then our specialized black box for $X$ is actually not so valuable; we can replace it with a polynomial-time algorithm for $X$. Consider what happens to our algorithm for problem $Y$ that involved a polynomial number of steps plus a polynomial number of calls to the black box. It now becomes an algorithm that involves a polynomial number of steps, plus a polynomial number of calls to a subroutine that runs in polynomial time; in other words, it has become a polynomial-time algorithm. We have therefore proved the following fact.

**(8.1)** *Suppose $Y \leq_P X$. If $X$ can be solved in polynomial time, then $Y$ can be solved in polynomial time.*

We've made use of precisely this fact, implicitly, at a number of earlier points in the book. Recall that we solved the Bipartite Matching Problem using a polynomial amount of preprocessing plus the solution of a single instance of the Maximum-Flow Problem. Since the Maximum-Flow Problem can be solved in polynomial time, we concluded that Bipartite Matching could as well. Similarly, we solved the foreground/background Image Segmentation Problem using a polynomial amount of preprocessing plus the solution of a single instance of the Minimum-Cut Problem, with the same consequences. Both of these can be viewed as direct applications of (8.1). Indeed, (8.1) summarizes a great way to design polynomial-time algorithms for new problems: by reduction to a problem we already know how to solve in polynomial time.

In this chapter, however, we will be using (8.1) to establish the computational *intractability* of various problems. We will be engaged in the somewhat subtle activity of relating the tractability of problems even when we don't know how to solve *either* of them in polynomial time. For this purpose, we will really be using the contrapositive of (8.1), which is sufficiently valuable that we'll state it as a separate fact.

**(8.2)** *Suppose $Y \leq_P X$. If $Y$ cannot be solved in polynomial time, then $X$ cannot be solved in polynomial time.*

Statement (8.2) is transparently equivalent to (8.1), but it emphasizes our overall plan: If we have a problem $Y$ that is known to be hard, and we show that $Y \leq_P X$, then the hardness has "spread" to $X$; $X$ must be hard or else it could be used to solve $Y$.

In reality, given that we don't actually know whether the problems we're studying can be solved in polynomial time or not, we'll be using $\leq_P$ to establish relative levels of difficulty among problems.

With this in mind, we now establish some reducibilities among an initial collection of fundamental hard problems.

## A First Reduction: Independent Set and Vertex Cover

The Independent Set Problem, which we introduced as one of our five representative problems in Chapter 1, will serve as our first prototypical example of a hard problem. We don't know a polynomial-time algorithm for it, but we also don't know how to prove that none exists.

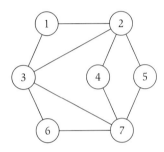

Let's review the formulation of Independent Set, because we're going to add one wrinkle to it. Recall that in a graph $G = (V, E)$, we say a set of nodes $S \subseteq V$ is *independent* if no two nodes in $S$ are joined by an edge. It is easy to find small independent sets in a graph (for example, a single node forms an independent set); the hard part is to find a large independent set, since you need to build up a large collection of nodes without ever including two neighbors. For example, the set of nodes $\{3, 4, 5\}$ is an independent set of size 3 in the graph in Figure 8.1, while the set of nodes $\{1, 4, 5, 6\}$ is a larger independent set.

**Figure 8.1** A graph whose largest independent set has size 4, and whose smallest vertex cover has size 3.

In Chapter 1, we posed the problem of finding the *largest* independent set in a graph $G$. For purposes of our current exploration in terms of reducibility, it will be much more convenient to work with problems that have yes/no answers only, and so we phrase Independent Set as follows.

> *Given a graph $G$ and a number $k$, does $G$ contain an independent set of size at least $k$?*

In fact, from the point of view of polynomial-time solvability, there is not a significant difference between the *optimization version* of the problem (find the maximum size of an independent set) and the *decision version* (decide, yes or no, whether $G$ has an independent set of size at least a given $k$). Given a method to solve the optimization version, we automatically solve the decision version (for any $k$) as well. But there is also a slightly less obvious converse to this: If we can solve the decision version of Independent Set for every $k$, then we can also find a maximum independent set. For given a graph $G$ on $n$ nodes, we simply solve the decision version of Independent Set for each $k$; the largest $k$ for which the answer is "yes" is the size of the largest independent set in $G$. (And using binary search, we need only solve the decision version for $O(\log n)$ different values of $k$.) This simple equivalence between decision and optimization will also hold in the problems we discuss below.

Now, to illustrate our basic strategy for relating hard problems to one another, we consider another fundamental graph problem for which no efficient algorithm is known: *Vertex Cover*. Given a graph $G = (V, E)$, we say that a set of nodes $S \subseteq V$ is a *vertex cover* if every edge $e \in E$ has at least one end in $S$. Note the following fact about this use of terminology: In a vertex cover, the vertices do the "covering," and the edges are the objects being "covered." Now, it is easy to find large vertex covers in a graph (for example, the full vertex set is one); the hard part is to find small ones. We formulate the Vertex Cover Problem as follows.

> *Given a graph G and a number k, does G contain a vertex cover of size at most k?*

For example, in the graph in Figure 8.1, the set of nodes $\{1, 2, 6, 7\}$ is a vertex cover of size 4, while the set $\{2, 3, 7\}$ is a vertex cover of size 3.

We don't know how to solve either Independent Set or Vertex Cover in polynomial time; but what can we say about their relative difficulty? We now show that they are equivalently hard, by establishing that Independent Set $\leq_P$ Vertex Cover and also that Vertex Cover $\leq_P$ Independent Set. This will be a direct consequence of the following fact.

**(8.3)** *Let $G = (V, E)$ be a graph. Then $S$ is an independent set if and only if its complement $V - S$ is a vertex cover.*

**Proof.** First, suppose that $S$ is an independent set. Consider an arbitrary edge $e = (u, v)$. Since $S$ is independent, it cannot be the case that both $u$ and $v$ are in $S$; so one of them must be in $V - S$. It follows that every edge has at least one end in $V - S$, and so $V - S$ is a vertex cover.

Conversely, suppose that $V - S$ is a vertex cover. Consider any two nodes $u$ and $v$ in $S$. If they were joined by edge $e$, then neither end of $e$ would lie in $V - S$, contradicting our assumption that $V - S$ is a vertex cover. It follows that no two nodes in $S$ are joined by an edge, and so $S$ is an independent set. ∎

Reductions in each direction between the two problems follow immediately from (8.3).

**(8.4)**    Independent Set $\leq_P$ Vertex Cover.

**Proof.** If we have a black box to solve Vertex Cover, then we can decide whether $G$ has an independent set of size at least $k$ by asking the black box whether $G$ has a vertex cover of size at most $n - k$.  ∎

---

**(8.5)**    Vertex Cover $\leq_p$ Independent Set.

---

**Proof.** If we have a black box to solve Independent Set, then we can decide whether $G$ has a vertex cover of size at most $k$ by asking the black box whether $G$ has an independent set of size at least $n - k$.  ∎

To sum up, this type of analysis illustrates our plan in general: although we don't know how to solve either Independent Set or Vertex Cover efficiently, (8.4) and (8.5) tell us how we could solve either given an efficient solution to the other, and hence these two facts establish the relative levels of difficulty of these problems.

We now pursue this strategy for a number of other problems.

### Reducing to a More General Case: Vertex Cover to Set Cover

Independent Set and Vertex Cover represent two different genres of problems. Independent Set can be viewed as a *packing problem*: The goal is to "pack in" as many vertices as possible, subject to conflicts (the edges) that try to prevent one from doing this. Vertex Cover, on the other hand, can be viewed as a *covering problem*: The goal is to parsimoniously "cover" all the edges in the graph using as few vertices as possible.

Vertex Cover is a covering problem phrased specifically in the language of graphs; there is a more general covering problem, *Set Cover*, in which you seek to cover an arbitrary set of objects using a collection of smaller sets. We can phrase Set Cover as follows.

> Given a set $U$ of $n$ elements, a collection $S_1, \ldots, S_m$ of subsets of $U$, and a number $k$, does there exist a collection of at most $k$ of these sets whose union is equal to all of $U$?

Imagine, for example, that we have $m$ available pieces of software, and a set $U$ of $n$ *capabilities* that we would like our system to have. The $i^{\text{th}}$ piece of software includes the set $S_i \subseteq U$ of capabilities. In the Set Cover Problem, we seek to include a small number of these pieces of software on our system, with the property that our system will then have all $n$ capabilities.

Figure 8.2 shows a sample instance of the Set Cover Problem: The ten circles represent the elements of the underlying set $U$, and the seven ovals and polygons represent the sets $S_1, S_2, \ldots, S_7$. In this instance, there is a collection

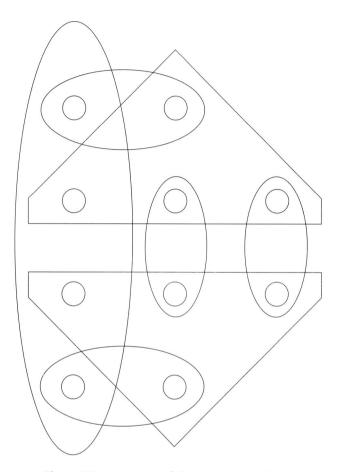

**Figure 8.2** An instance of the Set Cover Problem.

of three of the sets whose union is equal to all of $U$: We can choose the tall thin oval on the left, together with the two polygons.

Intuitively, it feels like Vertex Cover is a special case of Set Cover: in the latter case, we are trying to cover an arbitrary set using arbitrary subsets, while in the former case, we are specifically trying to cover edges of a graph using sets of edges incident to vertices. In fact, we can show the following reduction.

**(8.6)** Vertex Cover $\leq_P$ Set Cover.

**Proof.** Suppose we have access to a black box that can solve Set Cover, and consider an arbitrary instance of Vertex Cover, specified by a graph $G = (V, E)$ and a number $k$. How can we use the black box to help us?

Our goal is to cover the edges in $E$, so we formulate an instance of Set Cover in which the ground set $U$ is equal to $E$. Each time we pick a vertex in the Vertex Cover Problem, we cover all the edges incident to it; thus, for each vertex $i \in V$, we add a set $S_i \subseteq U$ to our Set Cover instance, consisting of all the edges in $G$ incident to $i$.

We now claim that $U$ can be covered with at most $k$ of the sets $S_1, \ldots, S_n$ if and only if $G$ has a vertex cover of size at most $k$. This can be proved very easily. For if $S_{i_1}, \ldots, S_{i_\ell}$ are $\ell \leq k$ sets that cover $U$, then every edge in $G$ is incident to one of the vertices $i_1, \ldots, i_\ell$, and so the set $\{i_1, \ldots, i_\ell\}$ is a vertex cover in $G$ of size $\ell \leq k$. Conversely, if $\{i_1, \ldots, i_\ell\}$ is a vertex cover in $G$ of size $\ell \leq k$, then the sets $S_{i_1}, \ldots, S_{i_\ell}$ cover $U$.

Thus, given our instance of Vertex Cover, we formulate the instance of Set Cover described above, and pass it to our black box. We answer yes if and only if the black box answers yes.

(You can check that the instance of Set Cover pictured in Figure 8.2 is actually the one you'd get by following the reduction in this proof, starting from the graph in Figure 8.1.)  ■

Here is something worth noticing, both about this proof and about the previous reductions in (8.4) and (8.5). Although the definition of $\leq_P$ allows us to issue many calls to our black box for Set Cover, we issued only one. Indeed, our algorithm for Vertex Cover consisted simply of encoding the problem as a single instance of Set Cover and then using the answer to this instance as our overall answer. This will be true of essentially all the reductions that we consider; they will consist of establishing $Y \leq_P X$ by transforming our instance of $Y$ to a single instance of $X$, invoking our black box for $X$ on this instance, and reporting the box's answer as our answer for the instance of $Y$.

Just as Set Cover is a natural generalization of Vertex Cover, there is a natural generalization of Independent Set as a packing problem for arbitrary sets. Specifically, we define the *Set Packing Problem* as follows.

*Given a set $U$ of $n$ elements, a collection $S_1, \ldots, S_m$ of subsets of $U$, and a number $k$, does there exist a collection of at least $k$ of these sets with the property that no two of them intersect?*

In other words, we wish to "pack" a large number of sets together, with the constraint that no two of them are overlapping.

As an example of where this type of issue might arise, imagine that we have a set $U$ of $n$ non-sharable *resources*, and a set of $m$ software processes. The $i^{th}$ process requires the set $S_i \subseteq U$ of resources in order to run. Then the Set Packing Problem seeks a large collection of these processes that can be run simultaneously, with the property that none of their resource requirements overlap (i.e., represent a conflict).

There is a natural analogue to (8.6), and its proof is almost the same as well; we will leave the details as an exercise.

**(8.7)** Independent Set $\leq_P$ Set Packing.

## 8.2 Reductions via "Gadgets": The Satisfiability Problem

We now introduce a somewhat more abstract set of problems, which are formulated in Boolean notation. As such, they model a wide range of problems in which we need to set decision variables so as to satisfy a given set of constraints; such formalisms are common, for example, in artificial intelligence. After introducing these problems, we will relate them via reduction to the graph- and set-based problems that we have been considering thus far.

### The SAT and 3-SAT Problems

Suppose we are given a set $X$ of $n$ *Boolean variables* $x_1, \ldots, x_n$; each can take the value 0 or 1 (equivalently, "false" or "true"). By a *term* over $X$, we mean one of the variables $x_i$ or its negation $\overline{x_i}$. Finally, a *clause* is simply a disjunction of distinct terms

$$t_1 \vee t_2 \vee \cdots \vee t_\ell.$$

(Again, each $t_i \in \{x_1, x_2, \ldots, x_n, \overline{x_1}, \ldots, \overline{x_n}\}$.) We say the clause has length $\ell$ if it contains $\ell$ terms.

We now formalize what it means for an assignment of values to satisfy a collection of clauses. A *truth assignment* for $X$ is an assignment of the value 0 or 1 to each $x_i$; in other words, it is a function $v : X \to \{0, 1\}$. The assignment $v$ implicitly gives $\overline{x_i}$ the opposite truth value from $x_i$. An assignment *satisfies* a clause $C$ if it causes $C$ to evaluate to 1 under the rules of Boolean logic; this is equivalent to requiring that at least one of the terms in $C$ should receive the value 1. An assignment satisfies a collection of clauses $C_1, \ldots, C_k$ if it causes all of the $C_i$ to evaluate to 1; in other words, if it causes the conjunction

$$C_1 \wedge C_2 \wedge \cdots \wedge C_k$$

to evaluate to 1. In this case, we will say that $v$ is a *satisfying assignment* with respect to $C_1, \ldots, C_k$; and that the set of clauses $C_1, \ldots, C_k$ is *satisfiable*.

Here is a simple example. Suppose we have the three clauses

$$(x_1 \vee \overline{x_2}), (\overline{x_1} \vee \overline{x_3}), (x_2 \vee \overline{x_3}).$$

Then the truth assignment $v$ that sets all variables to 1 is not a satisfying assignment, because it does not satisfy the second of these clauses; but the truth assignment $v'$ that sets all variables to 0 is a satisfying assignment.

We can now state the *Satisfiability Problem*, also referred to as *SAT*:

> Given a set of clauses $C_1, \ldots, C_k$ over a set of variables $X = \{x_1, \ldots, x_n\}$, does there exist a satisfying truth assignment?

There is a special case of SAT that will turn out to be equivalently difficult and is somewhat easier to think about; this is the case in which all clauses contain exactly three terms (corresponding to distinct variables). We call this problem *3-Satisfiability*, or *3-SAT*:

> Given a set of clauses $C_1, \ldots, C_k$, each of length 3, over a set of variables $X = \{x_1, \ldots, x_n\}$, does there exist a satisfying truth assignment?

Satisfiability and 3-Satisfiability are really fundamental combinatorial search problems; they contain the basic ingredients of a hard computational problem in very "bare-bones" fashion. We have to make $n$ independent decisions (the assignments for each $x_i$) so as to satisfy a set of constraints. There are several ways to satisfy each constraint in isolation, but we have to arrange our decisions so that all constraints are satisfied simultaneously.

## Reducing 3-SAT to Independent Set

We now relate the type of computational hardness embodied in SAT and 3-SAT to the superficially different sort of hardness represented by the search for independent sets and vertex covers in graphs. Specifically, we will show that 3-SAT $\leq_P$ Independent Set. The difficulty in proving a thing like this is clear; 3-SAT is about setting Boolean variables in the presence of constraints, while Independent Set is about selecting vertices in a graph. To solve an instance of 3-SAT using a black box for Independent Set, we need a way to encode all these Boolean constraints in the nodes and edges of a graph, so that satisfiability corresponds to the existence of a large independent set.

Doing this illustrates a general principle for designing complex reductions $Y \leq_P X$: building "gadgets" out of components in problem $X$ to represent what is going on in problem $Y$.

> **(8.8)**    3-SAT $\leq_P$ Independent Set.

**Proof.** We have a black box for Independent Set and want to solve an instance of 3-SAT consisting of variables $X = \{x_1, \ldots, x_n\}$ and clauses $C_1, \ldots, C_k$.

The key to thinking about the reduction is to realize that there are two conceptually distinct ways of thinking about an instance of 3-SAT.

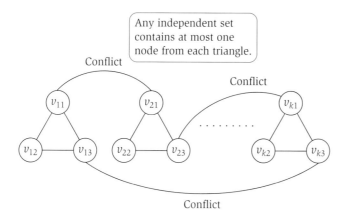

Figure 8.3 The reduction from 3-SAT to Independent Set.

- One way to picture the 3-SAT instance was suggested earlier: You have to make an independent 0/1 decision for each of the $n$ variables, and you succeed if you manage to achieve one of three ways of satisfying each clause.

- A different way to picture the same 3-SAT instance is as follows: You have to choose one term from each clause, and then find a truth assignment that causes all these terms to evaluate to 1, thereby satisfying all clauses. So you succeed if you can select a term from each clause in such a way that no two selected terms "conflict"; we say that two terms *conflict* if one is equal to a variable $x_i$ and the other is equal to its negation $\overline{x_i}$. If we avoid conflicting terms, we can find a truth assignment that makes the selected terms from each clause evaluate to 1.

Our reduction will be based on this second view of the 3-SAT instance; here is how we encode it using independent sets in a graph. First, construct a graph $G = (V, E)$ consisting of $3k$ nodes grouped into $k$ triangles as shown in Figure 8.3. That is, for $i = 1, 2, \ldots, k$, we construct three vertices $v_{i1}, v_{i2}, v_{i3}$ joined to one another by edges. We give each of these vertices a *label*; $v_{ij}$ is labeled with the $j^{\text{th}}$ term from the clause $C_i$ of the 3-SAT instance.

Before proceeding, consider what the independent sets of size $k$ look like in this graph: Since two vertices cannot be selected from the same triangle, they consist of all ways of choosing one vertex from each of the triangles. This is implementing our goal of choosing a term in each clause that will evaluate to 1; but we have so far not prevented ourselves from choosing two terms that conflict.

We encode conflicts by adding some more edges to the graph: For each pair of vertices whose labels correspond to terms that conflict, we add an edge between them. Have we now destroyed all the independent sets of size $k$, or does one still exist? It's not clear; it depends on whether we can still select one node from each triangle so that no conflicting pairs of vertices are chosen. But this is precisely what the 3-SAT instance required.

Let's claim, precisely, that the original 3-SAT instance is satisfiable if and only if the graph $G$ we have constructed has an independent set of size at least $k$. First, if the 3-SAT instance is satisfiable, then each triangle in our graph contains at least one node whose label evaluates to 1. Let $S$ be a set consisting of one such node from each triangle. We claim $S$ is independent; for if there were an edge between two nodes $u, v \in S$, then the labels of $u$ and $v$ would have to conflict; but this is not possible, since they both evaluate to 1.

Conversely, suppose our graph $G$ has an independent set $S$ of size at least $k$. Then, first of all, the size of $S$ is exactly $k$, and it must consist of one node from each triangle. Now, we claim that there is a truth assignment $v$ for the variables in the 3-SAT instance with the property that the labels of all nodes in $S$ evaluate to 1. Here is how we could construct such an assignment $v$. For each variable $x_i$, if neither $x_i$ nor $\overline{x_i}$ appears as a label of a node in $S$, then we arbitrarily set $v(x_i) = 1$. Otherwise, exactly one of $x_i$ or $\overline{x_i}$ appears as a label of a node in $S$; for if one node in $S$ were labeled $x_i$ and another were labeled $\overline{x_i}$, then there would be an edge between these two nodes, contradicting our assumption that $S$ is an independent set. Thus, if $x_i$ appears as a label of a node in $S$, we set $v(x_i) = 1$, and otherwise we set $v(x_i) = 0$. By constructing $v$ in this way, all labels of nodes in $S$ will evaluate to 1.

Since $G$ has an independent set of size at least $k$ if and only if the original 3-SAT instance is satisfiable, the reduction is complete. ∎

## Some Final Observations: Transitivity of Reductions

We've now seen a number of different hard problems, of various flavors, and we've discovered that they are closely related to one another. We can infer a number of additional relationships using the following fact: $\leq_P$ is a *transitive* relation.

**(8.9)**    *If $Z \leq_P Y$, and $Y \leq_P X$, then $Z \leq_P X$.*

**Proof.** Given a black box for $X$, we show how to solve an instance of $Z$; essentially, we just compose the two algorithms implied by $Z \leq_P Y$ and $Y \leq_P X$. We run the algorithm for $Z$ using a black box for $Y$; but each time the black box for $Y$ is called, we *simulate* it in a polynomial number of steps using the algorithm that solves instances of $Y$ using a black box for $X$. ∎

Transitivity can be quite useful. For example, since we have proved

$$\text{3-SAT} \leq_P \text{Independent Set} \leq_P \text{Vertex Cover} \leq_P \text{Set Cover},$$

we can conclude that 3-SAT $\leq_P$ Set Cover.

## 8.3 Efficient Certification and the Definition of NP

Reducibility among problems was the first main ingredient in our study of computational intractability. The second ingredient is a characterization of the class of problems that we are dealing with. Combining these two ingredients, together with a powerful theorem of Cook and Levin, will yield some surprising consequences.

Recall that in Chapter 1, when we first encountered the Independent Set Problem, we asked: Can we say anything *good* about it, from a computational point of view? And, indeed, there was something: If a graph does contain an independent set of size at least $k$, then we could give you an easy proof of this fact by exhibiting such an independent set. Similarly, if a 3-SAT instance is satisfiable, we can prove this to you by revealing the satisfying assignment. It may be an enormously difficult task to actually *find* such an assignment; but if we've done the hard work of finding one, it's easy for you to plug it into the clauses and check that they are all satisfied.

The issue here is the contrast between *finding* a solution and *checking* a proposed solution. For Independent Set or 3-SAT, we do not know a polynomial-time algorithm to find solutions; but *checking* a proposed solution to these problems can be easily done in polynomial time. To see that this is not an entirely trivial issue, consider the problem we'd face if we had to prove that a 3-SAT instance was *not* satisfiable. What "evidence" could we show that would convince you, in polynomial time, that the instance was unsatisfiable?

### Problems and Algorithms

This will be the crux of our characterization; we now proceed to formalize it. The input to a computational problem will be encoded as a finite binary string $s$. We denote the length of a string $s$ by $|s|$. We will identify a decision problem $X$ with the *set* of strings on which the answer is "yes." An algorithm $A$ for a decision problem receives an input string $s$ and returns the value "yes" or "no"—we will denote this returned value by $A(s)$. We say that $A$ *solves* the problem $X$ if for all strings $s$, we have $A(s) = \text{yes}$ if and only if $s \in X$.

As always, we say that $A$ has a *polynomial running time* if there is a polynomial function $p(\cdot)$ so that for every input string $s$, the algorithm $A$ terminates on $s$ in at most $O(p(|s|))$ steps. Thus far in the book, we have been concerned with problems solvable in polynomial time. In the notation above, we can express this as the set $\mathcal{P}$ of all problems $X$ for which there exists an algorithm $A$ with a polynomial running time that solves $X$.

## Efficient Certification

Now, how should we formalize the idea that a solution to a problem can be *checked* efficiently, independently of whether it can be solved efficiently? A "checking algorithm" for a problem $X$ has a different structure from an algorithm that actually seeks to solve the problem; in order to "check" a solution, we need the input string $s$, as well as a separate "certificate" string $t$ that contains the evidence that $s$ is a "yes" instance of $X$.

Thus we say that $B$ is an *efficient certifier* for a problem $X$ if the following properties hold.

- $B$ is a polynomial-time algorithm that takes two input arguments $s$ and $t$.
- There is a polynomial function $p$ so that for every string $s$, we have $s \in X$ if and only if there exists a string $t$ such that $|t| \le p(|s|)$ and $B(s, t) = \text{yes}$.

It takes some time to really think through what this definition is saying. One should view an efficient certifier as approaching a problem $X$ from a "managerial" point of view. It will not actually try to decide whether an input $s$ belongs to $X$ on its own. Rather, it is willing to efficiently evaluate proposed "proofs" $t$ that $s$ belongs to $X$—provided they are not too long—and it is a correct algorithm in the weak sense that $s$ belongs to $X$ if and only if there exists a proof that will convince it.

An efficient certifier $B$ can be used as the core component of a "brute-force" algorithm for a problem $X$: On an input $s$, try all strings $t$ of length $\le p(|s|)$, and see if $B(s, t) = \text{yes}$ for any of these strings. But the existence of $B$ does not provide us with any clear way to design an efficient algorithm that actually solves $X$; after all, it is still up to us to *find* a string $t$ that will cause $B(s, t)$ to say "yes," and there are exponentially many possibilities for $t$.

## NP: A Class of Problems

We define $\mathcal{NP}$ to be the set of all problems for which there exists an efficient certifier.[1] Here is one thing we can observe immediately.

**(8.10)**   $\mathcal{P} \subseteq \mathcal{NP}$.

---

[1] The act of searching for a string $t$ that will cause an efficient certifier to accept the input $s$ is often viewed as a *nondeterministic search* over the space of possible proofs $t$; for this reason, $\mathcal{NP}$ was named as an acronym for "nondeterministic polynomial time."

**Proof.** Consider a problem $X \in \mathcal{P}$; this means that there is a polynomial-time algorithm $A$ that solves $X$. To show that $X \in \mathcal{NP}$, we must show that there is an efficient certifier $B$ for $X$.

This is very easy; we design $B$ as follows. When presented with the input pair $(s, t)$, the certifier $B$ simply returns the value $A(s)$. (Think of $B$ as a very "hands-on" manager that ignores the proposed proof $t$ and simply solves the problem on its own.) Why is $B$ an efficient certifier for $X$? Clearly it has polynomial running time, since $A$ does. If a string $s \in X$, then for every $t$ of length at most $p(|s|)$, we have $B(s, t) = \text{yes}$. On the other hand, if $s \notin X$, then for every $t$ of length at most $p(|s|)$, we have $B(s, t) = \text{no}$. ■

We can easily check that the problems introduced in the first two sections belong to $\mathcal{NP}$: it is a matter of determining how an efficient certifier for each of them will make use of a "certificate" string $t$. For example:

- For the 3-Satisfiability Problem, the certificate $t$ is an assignment of truth values to the variables; the certifier $B$ evaluates the given set of clauses with respect to this assignment.

- For the Independent Set Problem, the certificate $t$ is the identity of a set of at least $k$ vertices; the certifier $B$ checks that, for these vertices, no edge joins any pair of them.

- For the Set Cover Problem, the certificate $t$ is a list of $k$ sets from the given collection; the certifier checks that the union of these sets is equal to the underlying set $U$.

Yet we cannot prove that any of these problems require more than polynomial time to solve. Indeed, we cannot prove that there is any problem in $\mathcal{NP}$ that does not belong to $\mathcal{P}$. So in place of a concrete theorem, we can only ask a question:

**(8.11)**    *Is there a problem in $\mathcal{NP}$ that does not belong to $\mathcal{P}$? Does $\mathcal{P} = \mathcal{NP}$?*

The question of whether $\mathcal{P} = \mathcal{NP}$ is fundamental in the area of algorithms, and it is one of the most famous problems in computer science. The general belief is that $\mathcal{P} \neq \mathcal{NP}$—and this is taken as a working hypothesis throughout the field—but there is not a lot of hard technical evidence for it. It is more based on the sense that $\mathcal{P} = \mathcal{NP}$ would be too amazing to be true. How could there be a general transformation from the task of *checking* a solution to the much harder task of actually *finding* a solution? How could there be a general means for designing efficient algorithms, powerful enough to handle all these hard problems, that we have somehow failed to discover? More generally, a huge amount of effort has gone into failed attempts at designing polynomial-time algorithms for hard problems in $\mathcal{NP}$; perhaps the most natural explanation for this consistent failure is that these problems simply cannot be solved in polynomial time.

## 8.4 NP-Complete Problems

In the absence of progress on the $\mathcal{P} = \mathcal{NP}$ question, people have turned to a related but more approachable question: What are the hardest problems in $\mathcal{NP}$? Polynomial-time reducibility gives us a way of addressing this question and gaining insight into the structure of $\mathcal{NP}$.

Arguably the most natural way to define a "hardest" problem $X$ is via the following two properties: (i) $X \in \mathcal{NP}$; and (ii) for all $Y \in \mathcal{NP}$, $Y \leq_P X$. In other words, we require that every problem in $\mathcal{NP}$ can be reduced to $X$. We will call such an $X$ an *NP-complete* problem.

The following fact helps to further reinforce our use of the term *hardest*.

**(8.12)**  *Suppose X is an NP-complete problem. Then X is solvable in polynomial time if and only if $\mathcal{P} = \mathcal{NP}$.*

**Proof.** Clearly, if $\mathcal{P} = \mathcal{NP}$, then $X$ can be solved in polynomial time since it belongs to $\mathcal{NP}$. Conversely, suppose that $X$ can be solved in polynomial time. If $Y$ is any other problem in $\mathcal{NP}$, then $Y \leq_P X$, and so by (8.1), it follows that $Y$ can be solved in polynomial time. Hence $\mathcal{NP} \subseteq \mathcal{P}$; combined with (8.10), we have the desired conclusion.   ■

A crucial consequence of (8.12) is the following: If there is *any* problem in $\mathcal{NP}$ that cannot be solved in polynomial time, then no NP-complete problem can be solved in polynomial time.

### Circuit Satisfiability: A First NP-Complete Problem

Our definition of NP-completeness has some very nice properties. But before we get too carried away in thinking about this notion, we should stop to notice something: it is not at all obvious that NP-complete problems should even *exist*. Why couldn't there exist two incomparable problems $X'$ and $X''$, so that there is no $X \in \mathcal{NP}$ with the property that $X' \leq_P X$ and $X'' \leq_P X$? Why couldn't there exist an infinite sequence of problems $X_1, X_2, X_3, \ldots$ in $\mathcal{NP}$, each strictly harder than the previous one? To prove a problem is NP-complete, one must show how it could encode *any* problem in $\mathcal{NP}$. This is a much trickier matter than what we encountered in Sections 8.1 and 8.2, where we sought to encode specific, individual problems in terms of others.

In 1971, Cook and Levin independently showed how to do this for very natural problems in $\mathcal{NP}$. Maybe the most natural problem choice for a first NP-complete problem is the following *Circuit Satisfiability Problem.*

To specify this problem, we need to make precise what we mean by a *circuit*. Consider the standard Boolean operators that we used to define the Satisfiability Problem: $\wedge$ (AND), $\vee$ (OR), and $\neg$ (NOT). Our definition of a circuit is designed to represent a physical circuit built out of gates that implement these operators. Thus we define a circuit $K$ to be a labeled, directed acyclic graph such as the one shown in the example of Figure 8.4.

- The *sources* in $K$ (the nodes with no incoming edges) are labeled either with one of the constants 0 or 1, or with the name of a distinct variable. The nodes of the latter type will be referred to as the *inputs* to the circuit.
- Every other node is labeled with one of the Boolean operators $\wedge$, $\vee$, or $\neg$; nodes labeled with $\wedge$ or $\vee$ will have two incoming edges, and nodes labeled with $\neg$ will have one incoming edge.
- There is a single node with no outgoing edges, and it will represent the *output:* the result that is computed by the circuit.

A circuit computes a function of its inputs in the following natural way. We imagine the edges as "wires" that carry the 0/1 value at the node they emanate from. Each node $v$ other than the sources will take the values on its incoming edge(s) and apply the Boolean operator that labels it. The result of this $\wedge$, $\vee$, or $\neg$ operation will be passed along the edge(s) leaving $v$. The overall value computed by the circuit will be the value computed at the output node.

For example, consider the circuit in Figure 8.4. The leftmost two sources are preassigned the values 1 and 0, and the next three sources constitute the

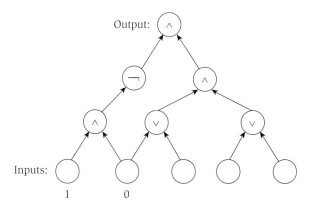

**Figure 8.4** A circuit with three inputs, two additional sources that have assigned truth values, and one output.

inputs. If the inputs are assigned the values $1, 0, 1$ from left to right, then we get values $0, 1, 1$ for the gates in the second row, values $1, 1$ for the gates in the third row, and the value 1 for the output.

Now, the Circuit Satisfiability Problem is the following. We are given a circuit as input, and we need to decide whether there is an assignment of values to the inputs that causes the output to take the value 1. (If so, we will say that the given circuit is *satisfiable*, and a *satisfying assignment* is one that results in an output of 1.) In our example, we have just seen—via the assignment $1, 0, 1$ to the inputs—that the circuit in Figure 8.4 is satisfiable.

We can view the theorem of Cook and Levin as saying the following.

**(8.13)**    Circuit Satisfiability *is NP-complete.*

As discussed above, the proof of (8.13) requires that we consider an arbitrary problem $X$ in $\mathcal{NP}$, and show that $X \leq_P$ Circuit Satisfiability. We won't describe the proof of (8.13) in full detail, but it is actually not so hard to follow the basic idea that underlies it. We use the fact that any algorithm that takes a fixed number $n$ of bits as input and produces a yes/no answer can be represented by a circuit of the type we have just defined: This circuit is equivalent to the algorithm in the sense that its output is 1 on precisely the inputs for which the algorithm outputs yes. Moreover, if the algorithm takes a number of steps that is polynomial in $n$, then the circuit has polynomial size. This transformation from an algorithm to a circuit is the part of the proof of (8.13) that we won't go into here, though it is quite natural given the fact that algorithms implemented on physical computers can be reduced to their operations on an underlying set of $\wedge$, $\vee$, and $\neg$ gates. (Note that fixing the number of input bits is important, since it reflects a basic distinction between algorithms and circuits: an algorithm typically has no trouble dealing with different inputs of varying lengths, but a circuit is structurally hard-coded with the size of the input.)

How should we use this relationship between algorithms and circuits? We are trying to show that $X \leq_P$ Circuit Satisfiability—that is, given an input $s$, we want to decide whether $s \in X$ using a black box that can solve instances of Circuit Satisfiability. Now, all we know about $X$ is that it has an efficient certifier $B(\cdot, \cdot)$. So to determine whether $s \in X$, for some specific input $s$ of length $n$, we need to answer the following question: Is there a $t$ of length $p(n)$ so that $B(s, t) = $ yes?

We will answer this question by appealing to a black box for Circuit Satisfiability as follows. Since we only care about the answer for a specific input $s$, we view $B(\cdot, \cdot)$ as an algorithm on $n + p(n)$ bits (the input $s$ and the certificate $t$), and we convert it to a polynomial-size circuit $K$ with $n + p(n)$ sources. The first $n$ sources will be hard-coded with the values of the bits in $s$, and the remaining $p(n)$ sources will be labeled with variables representing the bits of $t$; these latter sources will be the inputs to $K$.

Now we simply observe that $s \in X$ if and only if there is a way to set the input bits to $K$ so that the circuit produces an output of 1—in other words, if and only if $K$ is satisfiable. This establishes that $X \leq_P$ *Circuit Satisfiability*, and completes the proof of (8.13).

***An Example***    To get a better sense for what's going on in the proof of (8.13), we consider a simple, concrete example. Suppose we have the following problem.

> *Given a graph G, does it contain a two-node independent set?*

Note that this problem belongs to $\mathcal{NP}$. Let's see how an instance of this problem can be solved by constructing an equivalent instance of Circuit Satisfiability.

Following the proof outline above, we first consider an efficient certifier for this problem. The input $s$ is a graph on $n$ nodes, which will be specified by $\binom{n}{2}$ bits: For each pair of nodes, there will be a bit saying whether there is an edge joining this pair. The certificate $t$ can be specified by $n$ bits: For each node, there will be a bit saying whether this node belongs to the proposed independent set. The efficient certifier now needs to check two things: that at least two of the bits in $t$ are set to 1, and that no two bits in $t$ are both set to 1 if they form the two ends of an edge (as determined by the corresponding bit in $s$).

Now, for the specific input length $n$ corresponding to the $s$ that we are interested in, we construct an equivalent circuit $K$. Suppose, for example, that we are interested in deciding the answer to this problem for a graph $G$ on the three nodes $u, v, w$, in which $v$ is joined to both $u$ and $w$. This means that we are concerned with an input of length $n = 3$. Figure 8.5 shows a circuit that is equivalent to an efficient certifier for our problem on arbitrary three-node graphs. (Essentially, the right-hand side of the circuit checks that at least two nodes have been selected, and the left-hand side checks that we haven't selected both ends of any edge.) We encode the edges of $G$ as constants in the first three sources, and we leave the remaining three sources (representing the choice of nodes to put in the independent set) as variables. Now observe that this instance of Circuit Satisfiability is satisfiable, by the assignment $1, 0, 1$ to the inputs. This corresponds to choosing nodes $u$ and $w$, which indeed form a two-node independent set in our three-node graph $G$.

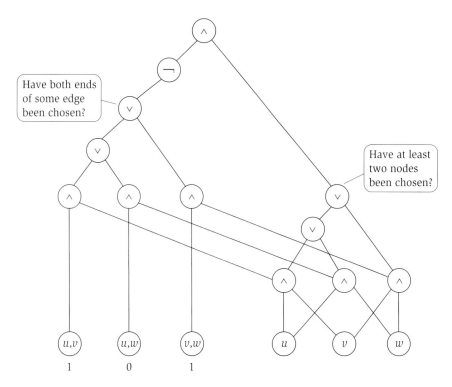

**Figure 8.5** A circuit to verify whether a 3-node graph contains a 2-node independent set.

## Proving Further Problems NP-Complete

Statement (8.13) opens the door to a much fuller understanding of hard problems in $\mathcal{NP}$: Once we have our hands on a first NP-complete problem, we can discover many more via the following simple observation.

**(8.14)**    *If Y is an NP-complete problem, and X is a problem in $\mathcal{NP}$ with the property that $Y \leq_P X$, then X is NP-complete.*

**Proof.** Since $X \in \mathcal{NP}$, we need only verify property (ii) of the definition. So let $Z$ be any problem in $\mathcal{NP}$. We have $Z \leq_P Y$, by the NP-completeness of $Y$, and $Y \leq_P X$ by assumption. By (8.9), it follows that $Z \leq_P X$.  ∎

So while proving (8.13) required the hard work of considering any possible problem in $\mathcal{NP}$, proving further problems NP-complete only requires a reduction from a single problem already known to be NP-complete, thanks to (8.14).

In earlier sections, we have seen a number of reductions among some basic hard problems. To establish their NP-completeness, we need to connect Circuit Satisfiability to this set of problems. The easiest way to do this is by relating it to the problem it most closely resembles, 3-Satisfiability.

**(8.15)**    3-Satisfiability *is NP-complete.*

**Proof.**  Clearly 3-Satisfiability is in $\mathcal{NP}$, since we can verify in polynomial time that a proposed truth assignment satisfies the given set of clauses. We will prove that it is NP-complete via the reduction Circuit Satisfiability $\leq_P$ 3-SAT.

Given an arbitrary instance of Circuit Satisfiability, we will first construct an equivalent instance of SAT in which each clause contains *at most* three variables. Then we will convert this SAT instance to an equivalent one in which each clause has *exactly* three variables. This last collection of clauses will thus be an instance of 3-SAT, and hence will complete the reduction.

So consider an arbitrary circuit $K$. We associate a variable $x_v$ with each node $v$ of the circuit, to encode the truth value that the circuit holds at that node. Now we will define the clauses of the SAT problem. First we need to encode the requirement that the circuit computes values correctly at each gate from the input values. There will be three cases depending on the three types of gates.

- If node $v$ is labeled with $\neg$, and its only entering edge is from node $u$, then we need to have $x_v = \overline{x_u}$. We guarantee this by adding two clauses $(x_v \vee x_u)$, and $(\overline{x_v} \vee \overline{x_u})$.
- If node $v$ is labeled with $\vee$, and its two entering edges are from nodes $u$ and $w$, we need to have $x_v = x_u \vee x_w$. We guarantee this by adding the following clauses: $(x_v \vee \overline{x_u})$, $(x_v \vee \overline{x_w})$, and $(\overline{x_v} \vee x_u \vee x_w)$.
- If node $v$ is labeled with $\wedge$, and its two entering edges are from nodes $u$ and $w$, we need to have $x_v = x_u \wedge x_w$. We guarantee this by adding the following clauses: $(\overline{x_v} \vee x_u)$, $(\overline{x_v} \vee x_w)$, and $(x_v \vee \overline{x_u} \vee \overline{x_w})$.

Finally, we need to guarantee that the constants at the sources have their specified values, and that the output evaluates to 1. Thus, for a source $v$ that has been labeled with a constant value, we add a clause with the single variable $x_v$ or $\overline{x_v}$, which forces $x_v$ to take the designated value. For the output node $o$, we add the single-variable clause $x_o$, which requires that $o$ take the value 1. This concludes the construction.

It is not hard to show that the SAT instance we just constructed is equivalent to the given instance of Circuit Satisfiability. To show the equivalence, we need to argue two things. First suppose that the given circuit $K$ is satisfiable. The satisfying assignment to the circuit inputs can be propagated to create values at all nodes in $K$ (as we did in the example of Figure 8.4). This set of values clearly satisfies the SAT instance we constructed.

To argue the other direction, we suppose that the SAT instance we constructed is satisfiable. Consider a satisfying assignment for this instance, and look at the values of the variables corresponding to the circuit $K$'s inputs. We claim that these values constitute a satisfying assignment for the circuit $K$. To see this, simply note that the SAT clauses ensure that the values assigned to all nodes of $K$ are the same as what the circuit computes for these nodes. In particular, a value of 1 will be assigned to the output, and so the assignment to inputs satisfies $K$.

Thus we have shown how to create a SAT instance that is equivalent to the Circuit Satisfiability Problem. But we are not quite done, since our goal was to create an instance of 3-SAT, which requires that all clauses have length exactly 3—in the instance we constructed, some clauses have lengths of 1 or 2. So to finish the proof, we need to convert this instance of SAT to an equivalent instance in which each clause has exactly three variables.

To do this, we create four new variables: $z_1, z_2, z_3, z_4$. The idea is to ensure that in any satisfying assignment, we have $z_1 = z_2 = 0$, and we do this by adding the clauses $(\overline{z_i} \vee z_3 \vee z_4)$, $(\overline{z_i} \vee \overline{z_3} \vee z_4)$, $(\overline{z_i} \vee z_3 \vee \overline{z_4})$, and $(\overline{z_i} \vee \overline{z_3} \vee \overline{z_4})$ for each of $i = 1$ and $i = 2$. Note that there is no way to satisfy all these clauses unless we set $z_1 = z_2 = 0$.

Now consider a clause in the SAT instance we constructed that has a single term $t$ (where the term $t$ can be either a variable or the negation of a variable). We replace each such term by the clause $(t \vee z_1 \vee z_2)$. Similarly, we replace each clause that has two terms, say, $(t \vee t')$, with the clause $(t \vee t' \vee z_1)$. The resulting 3-SAT formula is clearly equivalent to the SAT formula with at most three variables in each clause, and this finishes the proof. ∎

Using this NP-completeness result, and the sequence of reductions

$$\text{3-SAT} \leq_P \text{Independent Set} \leq_P \text{Vertex Cover} \leq_P \text{Set Cover},$$

summarized earlier, we can use (8.14) to conclude the following.

**(8.16)** *All of the following problems are NP-complete:* Independent Set, Set Packing, Vertex Cover, *and* Set Cover.

**Proof.** Each of these problems has the property that it is in $\mathcal{NP}$ and that 3-SAT (and hence Circuit Satisfiability) can be reduced to it. ∎

## General Strategy for Proving New Problems NP-Complete

For most of the remainder of this chapter, we will take off in search of further NP-complete problems. In particular, we will discuss further genres of hard computational problems and prove that certain examples of these genres are NP-complete. As we suggested initially, there is a very practical motivation in doing this: since it is widely believed that $\mathcal{P} \neq \mathcal{NP}$, the discovery that a problem is NP-complete can be taken as a strong indication that it cannot be solved in polynomial time.

Given a new problem $X$, here is the basic strategy for proving it is NP-complete.

1. Prove that $X \in \mathcal{NP}$.
2. Choose a problem $Y$ that is known to be NP-complete.
3. Prove that $Y \leq_P X$.

We noticed earlier that most of our reductions $Y \leq_P X$ consist of transforming a given instance of $Y$ into a *single* instance of $X$ with the same answer. This is a particular way of using a black box to solve $X$; in particular, it requires only a single invocation of the black box. When we use this style of reduction, we can refine the strategy above to the following outline of an NP-completeness proof.

1. Prove that $X \in \mathcal{NP}$.
2. Choose a problem $Y$ that is known to be NP-complete.
3. Consider an arbitrary instance $s_Y$ of problem $Y$, and show how to construct, in polynomial time, an instance $s_X$ of problem $X$ that satisfies the following properties:
   (a) If $s_Y$ is a "yes" instance of $Y$, then $s_X$ is a "yes" instance of $X$.
   (b) If $s_X$ is a "yes" instance of $X$, then $s_Y$ is a "yes" instance of $Y$.
   In other words, this establishes that $s_Y$ and $s_X$ have the same answer.

There has been research aimed at understanding the distinction between polynomial-time reductions with this special structure—asking the black box a single question and using its answer verbatim—and the more general notion of polynomial-time reduction that can query the black box multiple times. (The more restricted type of reduction is known as a *Karp reduction*, while the more general type is known as a *Cook reduction* and also as a *polynomial-time Turing reduction*.) We will not be pursuing this distinction further here.

## 8.5 Sequencing Problems

Thus far we have seen problems that (like Independent Set and Vertex Cover) have involved searching over subsets of a collection of objects; we have also seen problems that (like 3-SAT) have involved searching over 0/1 settings to a collection of variables. Another type of computationally hard problem involves searching over the set of all *permutations* of a collection of objects.

## The Traveling Salesman Problem

Probably the most famous such sequencing problem is the *Traveling Salesman Problem*. Consider a salesman who must visit $n$ cities labeled $v_1, v_2, \ldots, v_n$. The salesman starts in city $v_1$, his home, and wants to find a *tour*—an order in which to visit all the other cities and return home. His goal is to find a tour that causes him to travel as little total distance as possible.

To formalize this, we will take a very general notion of distance: for each ordered pair of cities $(v_i, v_j)$, we will specify a nonnegative number $d(v_i, v_j)$ as the distance from $v_i$ to $v_j$. We will not require the distance to be symmetric (so it may happen that $d(v_i, v_j) \neq d(v_j, v_i)$), nor will we require it to satisfy the triangle inequality (so it may happen that $d(v_i, v_j)$ plus $d(v_j, v_k)$ is actually less than the "direct" distance $d(v_i, v_k)$). The reason for this is to make our formulation as general as possible. Indeed, Traveling Salesman arises naturally in many applications where the points are not cities and the traveler is not a salesman. For example, people have used Traveling Salesman formulations for problems such as planning the most efficient motion of a robotic arm that drills holes in $n$ points on the surface of a VLSI chip; or for serving I/O requests on a disk; or for sequencing the execution of $n$ software modules to minimize the context-switching time.

Thus, given the set of distances, we ask: Order the cities into a *tour* $v_{i_1}, v_{i_2}, \ldots, v_{i_n}$, with $i_1 = 1$, so as to minimize the total distance $\sum_j d(v_{i_j}, v_{i_{j+1}}) + d(v_{i_n}, v_{i_1})$. The requirement $i_1 = 1$ simply "orients" the tour so that it starts at the home city, and the terms in the sum simply give the distance from each city on the tour to the next one. (The last term in the sum is the distance required for the salesman to return home at the end.)

Here is a decision version of the Traveling Salesman Problem.

*Given a set of distances on n cities, and a bound D, is there a tour of length at most D?*

## The Hamiltonian Cycle Problem

The Traveling Salesman Problem has a natural graph-based analogue, which forms one of the fundamental problems in graph theory. Given a directed graph $G = (V, E)$, we say that a cycle $C$ in $G$ is a *Hamiltonian cycle* if it visits each vertex exactly once. In other words, it constitutes a "tour" of all the vertices, with no repetitions. For example, the directed graph pictured in Figure 8.6 has

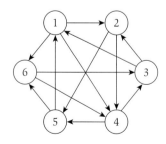

**Figure 8.6** A directed graph containing a Hamiltonian cycle.

several Hamiltonian cycles; one visits the nodes in the order 1, 6, 4, 3, 2, 5, 1, while another visits the nodes in the order 1, 2, 4, 5, 6, 3, 1.

The Hamiltonian Cycle Problem is then simply the following:

*Given a directed graph G, does it contain a Hamiltonian cycle?*

## Proving *Hamiltonian Cycle* is NP-Complete

We now show that both these problems are NP-complete. We do this by first establishing the NP-completeness of Hamiltonian Cycle, and then proceeding to reduce from Hamiltonian Cycle to Traveling Salesman.

**(8.17)** Hamiltonian Cycle *is NP-complete.*

**Proof.** We first show that Hamiltonian Cycle is in $\mathcal{NP}$. Given a directed graph $G = (V, E)$, a certificate that there is a solution would be the ordered list of the vertices on a Hamiltonian cycle. We could then check, in polynomial time, that this list of vertices does contain each vertex exactly once, and that each consecutive pair in the ordering is joined by an edge; this would establish that the ordering defines a Hamiltonian cycle.

We now show that 3-SAT $\leq_P$ Hamiltonian Cycle. Why are we reducing from 3-SAT? Essentially, faced with Hamiltonian Cycle, we really have no idea *what* to reduce from; it's sufficiently different from all the problems we've seen so far that there's no real basis for choosing. In such a situation, one strategy is to go back to 3-SAT, since its combinatorial structure is very basic. Of course, this strategy guarantees at least a certain level of complexity in the reduction, since we need to encode variables and clauses in the language of graphs.

So consider an arbitrary instance of 3-SAT, with variables $x_1, \ldots, x_n$ and clauses $C_1, \ldots, C_k$. We must show how to solve it, given the ability to detect Hamiltonian cycles in directed graphs. As always, it helps to focus on the essential ingredients of 3-SAT: We can set the values of the variables however we want, and we are given three chances to satisfy each clause.

We begin by describing a graph that contains $2^n$ different Hamiltonian cycles that correspond very naturally to the $2^n$ possible truth assignments to the variables. After this, we will add nodes to model the constraints imposed by the clauses.

We construct $n$ paths $P_1, \ldots, P_n$, where $P_i$ consists of nodes $v_{i1}, v_{i2}, \ldots, v_{ib}$ for a quantity $b$ that we take to be somewhat larger than the number of clauses $k$; say, $b = 3k + 3$. There are edges from $v_{ij}$ to $v_{i,j+1}$ and in the other direction from $v_{i,j+1}$ to $v_{ij}$. Thus $P_i$ can be traversed "left to right," from $v_{i1}$ to $v_{ib}$, or "right to left," from $v_{ib}$ to $v_{i1}$.

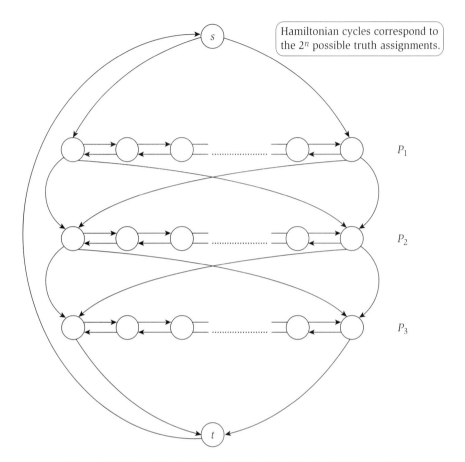

**Figure 8.7** The reduction from 3-SAT to Hamiltonian Cycle: part 1.

We hook these paths together as follows. For each $i = 1, 2, \ldots, n-1$, we define edges from $v_{i1}$ to $v_{i+1,1}$ and to $v_{i+1,b}$. We also define edges from $v_{ib}$ to $v_{i+1,1}$ and to $v_{i+1,b}$. We add two extra nodes $s$ and $t$; we define edges from $s$ to $v_{11}$ and $v_{1b}$; from $v_{n1}$ and $v_{nb}$ to $t$; and from $t$ to $s$.

The construction up to this point is pictured in Figure 8.7. It's important to pause here and consider what the Hamiltonian cycles in our graph look like. Since only one edge leaves $t$, we know that any Hamiltonian cycle $\mathcal{C}$ must use the edge $(t, s)$. After entering $s$, the cycle $\mathcal{C}$ can then traverse $P_1$ either left to right or right to left; regardless of what it does here, it can then traverse $P_2$ either left to right or right to left; and so forth, until it finishes traversing $P_n$ and enters $t$. In other words, there are exactly $2^n$ different Hamiltonian cycles, and they correspond to the $n$ independent choices of how to traverse each $P_i$.

This naturally models the $n$ independent choices of how to set each variables $x_1, \ldots, x_n$ in the 3-SAT instance. Thus we will identify each Hamiltonian cycle uniquely with a truth assignment as follows: If $\mathcal{C}$ traverses $P_i$ left to right, then $x_i$ is set to 1; otherwise, $x_i$ is set to 0.

Now we add nodes to model the clauses; the 3-SAT instance will turn out to be satisfiable if and only if any Hamiltonian cycle survives. Let's consider, as a concrete example, a clause

$$C_1 = x_1 \vee \overline{x_2} \vee x_3.$$

In the language of Hamiltonian cycles, this clause says, "The cycle should traverse $P_1$ left to right; or it should traverse $P_2$ right to left; or it should traverse $P_3$ left to right." So we add a node $c_1$, as in Figure 8.8, that does just this. (Note that certain edges have been eliminated from this drawing, for the sake of clarity.) For some value of $\ell$, node $c_1$ will have edges *from* $v_{1\ell}$, $v_{2,\ell+1}$, and $v_{3\ell}$; it will have edges *to* $v_{1,\ell+1}$, $v_{2,\ell}$, and $v_{3,\ell+1}$. Thus it can be easily spliced into any Hamiltonian cycle that traverses $P_1$ left to right by visiting node $c_1$ between $v_{1\ell}$ and $v_{1,\ell+1}$; similarly, $c_1$ can be spliced into any Hamiltonian cycle that traverses $P_2$ right to left, or $P_3$ left to right. It cannot be spliced into a Hamiltonian cycle that does not do any of these things.

More generally, we will define a node $c_j$ for each clause $C_j$. We will reserve node positions $3j$ and $3j + 1$ in each path $P_i$ for variables that participate in clause $C_j$. Suppose clause $C_j$ contains a term $t$. Then if $t = x_i$, we will add edges $(v_{i,3j}, c_j)$ and $(c_j, v_{i,3j+1})$; if $t = \overline{x_i}$, we will add edges $(v_{i,3j+1}, c_j)$ and $(c_j, v_{i,3j})$.

This completes the construction of the graph $G$. Now, following our generic outline for NP-completeness proofs, we claim that the 3-SAT instance is satisfiable if and only if $G$ has a Hamiltonian cycle.

First suppose there is a satisfying assignment for the 3-SAT instance. Then we define a Hamiltonian cycle following our informal plan above. If $x_i$ is assigned 1 in the satisfying assignment, then we traverse the path $P_i$ left to right; otherwise we traverse $P_i$ right to left. For each clause $C_j$, since it is satisfied by the assignment, there will be at least one path $P_i$ in which we will be going in the "correct" direction relative to the node $c_j$, and we can splice it into the tour there via edges incident on $v_{i,3j}$ and $v_{i,3j+1}$.

Conversely, suppose that there is a Hamiltonian cycle $\mathcal{C}$ in $G$. The crucial thing to observe is the following. If $\mathcal{C}$ enters a node $c_j$ on an edge from $v_{i,3j}$, it must depart on an edge to $v_{i,3j+1}$. For if not, then $v_{i,3j+1}$ will have only one unvisited neighbor left, namely, $v_{i,3j+2}$, and so the tour will not be able to visit this node and still maintain the Hamiltonian property. Symmetrically, if it enters from $v_{i,3j+1}$, it must depart immediately to $v_{i,3j}$. Thus, for each node $c_j$,

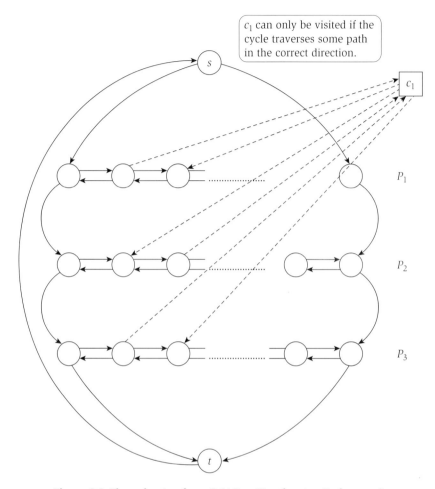

$c_1$ can only be visited if the cycle traverses some path in the correct direction.

**Figure 8.8** The reduction from 3-SAT to Hamiltonian Cycle: part 2.

the nodes immediately before and after $c_j$ in the cycle $\mathcal{C}$ are joined by an edge $e$ in $G$; thus, if we remove $c_j$ from the cycle and insert this edge $e$ for each $j$, then we obtain a Hamiltonian cycle $\mathcal{C}'$ on the subgraph $G - \{c_1, \ldots, c_k\}$. This is our original subgraph, before we added the clause nodes; as we noted above, any Hamiltonian cycle in this subgraph must traverse each $P_i$ fully in one direction or the other. We thus use $\mathcal{C}'$ to define the following truth assignment for the 3-SAT instance. If $\mathcal{C}'$ traverses $P_i$ left to right, then we set $x_i = 1$; otherwise we set $x_i = 0$. Since the larger cycle $\mathcal{C}$ was able to visit each clause node $c_j$, at least one of the paths was traversed in the "correct" direction relative to the node $c_j$, and so the assignment we have defined satisfies all the clauses.

Having established that the 3-SAT instance is satisfiable if and only if $G$ has a Hamiltonian cycle, our proof is complete. ∎

## Proving Traveling Salesman is NP-Complete

Armed with our basic hardness result for Hamiltonian Cycle, we can move on to show the hardness of Traveling Salesman.

**(8.18)**  Traveling Salesman *is NP-complete.*

**Proof.** It is easy to see that Traveling Salesman is in $\mathcal{NP}$: The certificate is a permutation of the cities, and a certifier checks that the length of the corresponding tour is at most the given bound.

We now show that Hamiltonian Cycle $\leq_P$ Traveling Salesman. Given a directed graph $G = (V, E)$, we define the following instance of Traveling Salesman. We have a city $v_i'$ for each node $v_i$ of the graph $G$. We define $d(v_i', v_j')$ to be 1 if there is an edge $(v_i, v_j)$ in $G$, and we define it to be 2 otherwise.

Now we claim that $G$ has a Hamiltonian cycle if and only if there is tour of length at most $n$ in our Traveling Salesman instance. For if $G$ has a Hamiltonian cycle, then this ordering of the corresponding cities defines a tour of length $n$. Conversely, suppose there is a tour of length at most $n$. The expression for the length of this tour is a sum of $n$ terms, each of which is at least 1; thus it must be the case that all the terms are equal to 1. Hence each pair of nodes in $G$ that correspond to consecutive cities on the tour must be connected by an edge; it follows that the ordering of these corresponding nodes must form a Hamiltonian cycle. ∎

Note that allowing *asymmetric* distances in the Traveling Salesman Problem $(d(v_i', v_j') \neq d(v_j', v_i'))$ played a crucial role; since the graph in the Hamiltonian Cycle instance is directed, our reduction yielded a Traveling Salesman instance with asymmetric distances.

In fact, the analogue of the Hamiltonian Cycle Problem for undirected graphs is also NP-complete; although we will not prove this here, it follows via a not-too-difficult reduction from directed Hamiltonian Cycle. Using this undirected Hamiltonian Cycle Problem, an exact analogue of (8.18) can be used to prove that the Traveling Salesman Problem with symmetric distances is also NP-complete.

Of course, the most famous special case of the Traveling Salesman Problem is the one in which the distances are defined by a set of $n$ points in the plane. It is possible to reduce Hamiltonian Cycle to this special case as well, though this is much trickier.

### Extensions: The Hamiltonian Path Problem

It is also sometimes useful to think about a variant of Hamiltonian Cycle in which it is not necessary to return to one's starting point. Thus, given a directed graph $G = (V, E)$, we say that a path $P$ in $G$ is a *Hamiltonian path* if it contains each vertex exactly once. (The path is allowed to start at any node and end at any node, provided it respects this constraint.) Thus such a path consists of distinct nodes $v_{i_1}, v_{i_2}, \ldots, v_{i_n}$ in order, such that they collectively constitute the entire vertex set $V$; by way of contrast with a Hamiltonian cycle, it is not necessary for there to be an edge from $v_{i_n}$ back to $v_{i_1}$. Now, the *Hamiltonian Path Problem* asks:

> *Given a directed graph $G$, does it contain a Hamiltonian path?*

Using the hardness of Hamiltonian Cycle, we show the following.

**(8.19)**    Hamiltonian Path *is NP-complete.*

**Proof.** First of all, Hamiltonian Path is in $\mathcal{NP}$: A certificate could be a path in $G$, and a certifier could then check that it is indeed a path and that it contains each node exactly once.

One way to show that Hamiltonian Path is NP-complete is to use a reduction from 3-SAT that is almost identical to the one we used for Hamiltonian Cycle: We construct the same graph that appears in Figure 8.7, *except* that we do not include an edge from $t$ to $s$. If there is any Hamiltonian path in this modified graph, it must begin at $s$ (since $s$ has no incoming edges) and end at $t$ (since $t$ has no outgoing edges). With this one change, we can adapt the argument used in the Hamiltonian Cycle reduction more or less word for word to argue that there is a satisfying assignment for the instance of 3-SAT if and only if there is a Hamiltonian path.

An alternate way to show that Hamiltonian Path is NP-complete is to prove that Hamiltonian Cycle $\leq_P$ Hamiltonian Path. Given an instance of Hamiltonian Cycle, specified by a directed graph $G$, we construct a graph $G'$ as follows. We choose an arbitrary node $v$ in $G$ and replace it with two new nodes $v'$ and $v''$. All edges out of $v$ in $G$ are now out of $v'$; and all edges into $v$ in $G$ are now into $v''$. More precisely, each edge $(v, w)$ in $G$ is replaced by an edge $(v', w)$; and each edge $(u, v)$ in $G$ is replaced by an edge $(u, v'')$. This completes the construction of $G'$.

We claim that $G'$ contains a Hamiltonian path if and only if $G$ contains a Hamiltonian cycle. Indeed, suppose $C$ is a Hamiltonian cycle in $G$, and consider traversing it beginning and ending at node $v$. It is easy to see that the same ordering of nodes forms a Hamiltonian path in $G'$ that begins at $v'$ and ends at $v''$. Conversely, suppose $P$ is a Hamiltonian path in $G'$. Clearly $P$ must begin at $v'$ (since $v'$ has no incoming edges) and end at $v''$ (since $v''$ has no outgoing edges). If we replace $v'$ and $v''$ with $v$, then this ordering of nodes forms a Hamiltonian cycle in $G$.  ∎

# 8.6 Partitioning Problems

In the next two sections, we consider two fundamental *partitioning* problems, in which we are searching over ways of dividing a collection of objects into subsets. Here we show the NP-completeness of a problem that we call *3-Dimensional Matching*. In the next section we consider *Graph Coloring*, a problem that involves partitioning the nodes of a graph.

## The 3-Dimensional Matching Problem

We begin by discussing the 3-Dimensional Matching Problem, which can be motivated as a harder version of the Bipartite Matching Problem that we considered earlier. We can view the Bipartite Matching Problem in the following way: We are given two sets $X$ and $Y$, each of size $n$, and a set $P$ of pairs drawn from $X \times Y$. The question is: Does there exist a set of $n$ pairs in $P$ so that each element in $X \cup Y$ is contained in exactly one of these pairs? The relation to Bipartite Matching is clear: the set $P$ of pairs is simply the edges of the bipartite graph.

Now Bipartite Matching is a problem we know how to solve in polynomial time. But things get much more complicated when we move from ordered pairs to ordered triples. Consider the following 3-Dimensional Matching Problem:

> *Given disjoint sets $X$, $Y$, and $Z$, each of size $n$, and given a set $T \subseteq X \times Y \times Z$ of ordered triples, does there exist a set of $n$ triples in $T$ so that each element of $X \cup Y \cup Z$ is contained in exactly one of these triples?*

Such a set of triples is called a *perfect three-dimensional matching*.

An interesting thing about 3-Dimensional Matching, beyond its relation to Bipartite Matching, is that it simultaneously forms a special case of both Set Cover and Set Packing: we are seeking to *cover* the ground set $X \cup Y \cup Z$ with a collection of *disjoint* sets. More concretely, *3-Dimensional Matching* is a special case of *Set Cover* since we seek to cover the ground set $U = X \cup Y \cup Z$ using at most $n$ sets from a given collection (the triples). Similarly, 3-Dimensional Matching is a special case of Set Packing, since we are seeking $n$ disjoint subsets of the ground set $U = X \cup Y \cup Z$.

## Proving 3-Dimensional Matching Is NP-Complete

The arguments above can be turned quite easily into proofs that 3-Dimensional Matching $\leq_P$ Set Cover and that 3-Dimensional Matching $\leq_P$ Set Packing.

But this doesn't help us establish the NP-completeness of 3-Dimensional Matching, since these reductions simply show that 3-Dimensional Matching can be reduced to some very hard problems. What we need to show is the other direction: that a known NP-complete problem can be reduced to 3-Dimensional Matching.

**(8.20)**    3-Dimensional Matching *is NP-complete.*

**Proof.** Not surprisingly, it is easy to prove that 3-Dimensional Matching is in $\mathcal{NP}$. Given a collection of triples $T \subset X \times Y \times Z$, a certificate that there is a solution could be a collection of triples $T' \subseteq T$. In polynomial time, one could verify that each element in $X \cup Y \cup Z$ belongs to exactly one of the triples in $T'$.

For the reduction, we again return all the way to 3-SAT. This is perhaps a little more curious than in the case of Hamiltonian Cycle, since 3-Dimensional Matching is so closely related to both Set Packing and Set Cover; but in fact the partitioning requirement is very hard to encode using either of these problems.

Thus, consider an arbitrary instance of 3-SAT, with $n$ variables $x_1, \ldots, x_n$ and $k$ clauses $C_1, \ldots, C_k$. We will show how to solve it, given the ability to detect perfect three-dimensional matchings.

The overall strategy in this reduction will be similar (at a very high level) to the approach we followed in the reduction from 3-SAT to Hamiltonian Cycle. We will first design gadgets that encode the independent choices involved in the truth assignment to each variable; we will then add gadgets that encode the constraints imposed by the clauses. In performing this construction, we will initially describe all the elements in the 3-Dimensional Matching instance simply as "elements," without trying to specify for each one whether it comes from $X$, $Y$, or $Z$. At the end, we will observe that they naturally decompose into these three sets.

Here is the basic gadget associated with variable $x_i$. We define elements $A_i = \{a_{i1}, a_{i2}, \ldots, a_{i,2k}\}$ that constitute the *core* of the gadget; we define elements $B_i = \{b_{i1}, \ldots, b_{i,2k}\}$ at the *tips* of the gadget. For each $j = 1, 2, \ldots, 2k$, we define a triple $t_{ij} = (a_{ij}, a_{i,j+1}, b_{ij})$, where we interpret addition modulo $2k$. Three of these gadgets are pictured in Figure 8.9. In gadget $i$, we will call a triple $t_{ij}$ *even* if $j$ is even, and *odd* if $j$ is odd. In an analogous way, we will refer to a tip $b_{ij}$ as being either *even* or *odd*.

These will be the only triples that contain the elements in $A_i$, so we can already say something about how they must be covered in any perfect matching: we must either use all the even triples in gadget $i$, or all the odd triples in gadget $i$. This will be our basic way of encoding the idea that $x_i$ can

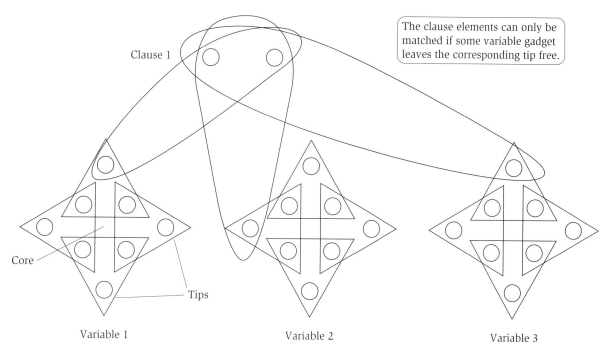

Clause 1

The clause elements can only be matched if some variable gadget leaves the corresponding tip free.

Core

Tips

Variable 1    Variable 2    Variable 3

**Figure 8.9** The reduction from 3-SAT to 3-Dimensional Matching.

be set to either 0 or 1; if we select all the even triples, this will represent setting $x_i = 0$, and if we select all the odd triples, this will represent setting $x_i = 1$.

Here is another way to view the odd/even decision, in terms of the tips of the gadget. If we decide to use the even triples, we cover the even tips of the gadget and leave the odd tips free. If we decide to use the odd triples, we cover the odd tips of the gadget and leave the even tips free. Thus our decision of how to set $x_i$ can be viewed as follows: Leaving the odd tips free corresponds to 0, while leaving the even tips free corresponds to 1. This will actually be the more useful way to think about things in the remainder of the construction.

So far we can make this even/odd choice independently for each of the $n$ variable gadgets. We now add elements to model the clauses and to constrain the assignments we can choose. As in the proof of (8.17), let's consider the example of a clause

$$C_1 = x_1 \vee \overline{x_2} \vee x_3.$$

In the language of three-dimensional matchings, it tells us, "The matching on the cores of the gadgets should leave the even tips of the first gadget free; or it should leave the odd tips of the second gadget free; or it should leave the even tips of the third gadget free." So we add a *clause gadget* that does precisely this. It consists of a set of two *core* elements $P_1 = \{p_1, p'_1\}$, and three triples that contain them. One has the form $(p_1, p'_1, b_{1j})$ for an even tip $b_{1j}$; another includes $p_1$, $p'_1$, and an odd tip $b_{2,j'}$; and a third includes $p_1$, $p'_1$, and an even tip $b_{3,j''}$. These are the only three triples that cover $P_1$, so we know that one of them must be used; this enforces the clause constraint exactly.

In general, for clause $C_j$, we create a gadget with two core elements $P_j = \{p_j, p'_j\}$, and we define three triples containing $P_j$ as follows. Suppose clause $C_j$ contains a term $t$. If $t = x_i$, we define a triple $(p_j, p'_j, b_{i,2j})$; if $t = \overline{x}_i$, we define a triple $(p_j, p'_j, b_{i,2j-1})$. Note that only clause gadget $j$ makes use of tips $b_{im}$ with $m = 2j$ or $m = 2j - 1$; thus, the clause gadgets will never "compete" with each other for free tips.

We are almost done with the construction, but there's still one problem. Suppose the set of clauses has a satisfying assignment. Then we make the corresponding choices of odd/even for each variable gadget; this leaves at least one free tip for each clause gadget, and so all the core elements of the clause gadgets get covered as well. The problem is that *we haven't covered all the tips*. We started with $n \cdot 2k = 2nk$ tips; the triples $\{t_{ij}\}$ covered $nk$ of them; and the clause gadgets covered an additional $k$ of them. This leaves $(n - 1)k$ tips left to be covered.

We handle this problem with a very simple trick: we add $(n - 1)k$ "cleanup gadgets" to the construction. Cleanup gadget $i$ consists of two core elements $Q_i = \{q_i, q'_i\}$, and there is a triple $(q_i, q_i, b)$ for *every* tip $b$ in every variable gadget. This is the final piece of the construction.

Thus, if the set of clauses has a satisfying assignment, then we make the corresponding choices of odd/even for each variable gadget; as before, this leaves at least one free tip for each clause gadget. Using the cleanup gadgets to cover the remaining tips, we see that all core elements in the variable, clause, and cleanup gadgets have been covered, and all tips have been covered as well.

Conversely, suppose there is a perfect three-dimensional matching in the instance we have constructed. Then, as we argued above, in each variable gadget the matching chooses either all the even $\{t_{ij}\}$ or all the odd $\{t_{ij}\}$. In the former case, we set $x_i = 0$ in the 3-SAT instance; and in the latter case, we set $x_i = 1$. Now consider clause $C_j$; has it been satisfied? Because the two core elements in $P_j$ have been covered, at least one of the three variable gadgets corresponding to a term in $C_j$ made the "correct" odd/even decision, and this induces a variable assignment that satisfies $C_j$.

This concludes the proof, except for one last thing to worry about: Have we really constructed an instance of 3-Dimensional Matching? We have a collection of elements, and triples containing certain of them, but can the elements really be partitioned into appropriate sets $X$, $Y$, and $Z$ of equal size?

Fortunately, the answer is yes. We can define $X$ to be set of all $a_{ij}$ with $j$ even, the set of all $p_j$, and the set of all $q_i$. We can define $Y$ to be set of all $a_{ij}$ with $j$ odd, the set of all $p'_j$, and the set of all $q'_i$. Finally, we can define $Z$ to be the set of all tips $b_{ij}$. It is now easy to check that each triple consists of one element from each of $X$, $Y$, and $Z$. ∎

# 8.7 Graph Coloring

When you color a map (say, the states in a U.S. map or the countries on a globe), the goal is to give neighboring regions different colors so that you can see their common borders clearly while minimizing visual distraction by using only a few colors. In the middle of the 19th century, Francis Guthrie noticed that you could color a map of the counties of England this way with only four colors, and he wondered whether the same was true for every map. He asked his brother, who relayed the question to one of his professors, and thus a famous mathematical problem was born: the *Four-Color Conjecture*.

## The Graph Coloring Problem

*Graph coloring* refers to the same process on an undirected graph $G$, with the nodes playing the role of the regions to be colored, and the edges representing pairs that are neighbors. We seek to assign a *color* to each node of $G$ so that if $(u, v)$ is an edge, then $u$ and $v$ are assigned different colors; and the goal is to do this while using a small set of colors. More formally, a $k$-*coloring* of $G$ is a function $f : V \rightarrow \{1, 2, \ldots, k\}$ so that for every edge $(u, v)$, we have $f(u) \neq f(v)$. (So the available colors here are named $1, 2, \ldots, k$, and the function $f$ represents our choice of a color for each node.) If $G$ has a $k$-coloring, then we will say that it is a $k$-*colorable graph*.

In contrast with the case of maps in the plane, it's clear that there's not some fixed constant $k$ so that every graph has a $k$-coloring: For example, if we take a set of $n$ nodes and join each pair of them by an edge, the resulting graph needs $n$ colors. However, the algorithmic version of the problem is very interesting:

> Given a graph $G$ and a bound $k$, does $G$ have a $k$-coloring?

We will refer to this as the *Graph Coloring Problem*, or as $k$-*Coloring* when we wish to emphasize a particular choice of $k$.

Graph Coloring turns out to be a problem with a wide range of applications. While it's not clear there's ever been much genuine demand from cartographers, the problem arises naturally whenever one is trying to allocate resources in the presence of conflicts.

- Suppose, for example, that we have a collection of $n$ processes on a system that can run multiple jobs concurrently, but certain pairs of jobs cannot be scheduled at the same time because they both need a particular resource. Over the next $k$ time steps of the system, we'd like to schedule each process to run in at least one of them. Is this possible? If we construct a graph $G$ on the set of processes, joining two by an edge if they have a conflict, then a $k$-coloring of $G$ represents a conflict-free schedule of the processes: all nodes colored $j$ can be scheduled in step $j$, and there will never be contention for any of the resources.

- Another well-known application arises in the design of compilers. Suppose we are compiling a program and are trying to assign each variable to one of $k$ registers. If two variables are in use at a common point in time, then they cannot be assigned to the same register. (Otherwise one would end up overwriting the other.) Thus we can build a graph $G$ on the set of variables, joining two by an edge if they are both in use at the same time. Now a $k$-coloring of $G$ corresponds to a safe way of allocating variables to registers: All nodes colored $j$ can be assigned to register $j$, since no two of them are in use at the same time.

- A third application arises in wavelength assignment for wireless communication devices: We'd like to assign one of $k$ transmitting wavelengths to each of $n$ devices; but if two devices are sufficiently close to each other, then they need to be assigned different wavelengths to prevent interference. To deal with this, we build a graph $G$ on the set of devices, joining two nodes if they're close enough to interfere with each other; a $k$-coloring of this graph is now an assignment of wavelengths so that any nodes assigned the same wavelength are far enough apart that interference won't be a problem. (Interestingly, this is an application of graph coloring where the "colors" being assigned to nodes are positions on the electromagnetic spectrum—in other words, under a slightly liberal interpretation, they're actually colors.)

## The Computational Complexity of Graph Coloring

What is the complexity of $k$-Coloring? First of all, the case $k = 2$ is a problem we've already seen in Chapter 3. Recall, there, that we considered the problem of determining whether a graph $G$ is bipartite, and we showed that this is equivalent to the following question: Can one color the nodes of $G$ red and blue so that every edge has one red end and one blue end?

But this latter question is precisely the Graph Coloring Problem in the case when there are $k = 2$ colors (i.e., red and blue) available. Thus we have argued that

**(8.21)**   *A graph G is 2-colorable if and only if it is bipartite.*

This means we can use the algorithm from Section 3.4 to decide whether an input graph $G$ is 2-colorable in $O(m + n)$ time, where $n$ is the number of nodes of $G$ and $m$ is the number of edges.

As soon as we move up to $k = 3$ colors, things become much harder. No simple efficient algorithm for the 3-Coloring Problem suggests itself, as it did for 2-Coloring, and it is also a very difficult problem to reason about. For example, one might initially suspect that any graph that is not 3-colorable will contain a "proof" in the form of four nodes that are all mutually adjacent (and hence would need four different colors)—but this is not true. The graph in Figure 8.10, for instance, is not 3-colorable for a somewhat more subtle (though still explainable) reason, and it is possible to draw much more complicated graphs that are not 3-colorable for reasons that seem very hard to state succinctly.

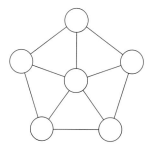

**Figure 8.10** A graph that is not 3-colorable.

In fact, the case of three colors is already a very hard problem, as we show now.

## Proving 3-Coloring Is NP-Complete

**(8.22)**   3-Coloring *is NP-complete.*

**Proof.** It is easy to see why the problem is in $\mathcal{NP}$. Given $G$ and $k$, one certificate that the answer is yes is simply a $k$-coloring: One can verify in polynomial time that at most $k$ colors are used, and that no pair of nodes joined by an edge receive the same color.

Like the other problems in this section, 3-Coloring is a problem that is hard to relate at a superficial level to other NP-complete problems we've seen. So once again, we're going to reach all the way back to 3-SAT. Given an arbitrary instance of 3-SAT, with variables $x_1, \ldots, x_n$ and clauses $C_1, \ldots, C_k$, we will solve it using a black box for 3-Coloring.

The beginning of the reduction is quite intuitive. Perhaps the main power of 3-Coloring for encoding Boolean expressions lies in the fact that we can associate graph nodes with particular terms, and by joining them with edges we ensure that they get different colors; this can be used to set one true and the other false. So with this in mind, we define nodes $v_i$ and $\overline{v_i}$ corresponding to each variable $x_i$ and its negation $\overline{x_i}$. We also define three "special nodes" $T$, $F$, and $B$, which we refer to as *True*, *False*, and *Base*.

To begin, we join each pair of nodes $v_i$, $\overline{v_i}$ to each other by an edge, and we join both these nodes to *Base*. (This forms a triangle on $v_i$, $\overline{v_i}$, and *Base*, for each $i$.) We also join *True*, *False*, and *Base* into a triangle. The simple graph

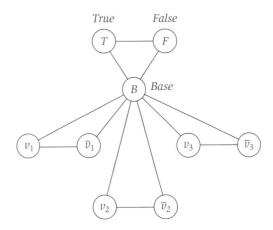

**Figure 8.11** The beginning of the reduction for 3-Coloring.

$G$ we have defined thus far is pictured in Figure 8.11, and it already has some useful properties.

- In any 3-coloring of $G$, the nodes $v_i$ and $\overline{v_i}$ must get different colors, and both must be different from *Base*.

- In any 3-coloring of $G$, the nodes *True*, *False*, and *Base* must get all three colors in some permutation. Thus we can refer to the three colors as the *True* color, the *False* color, and the *Base* color, based on which of these three nodes gets which color. In particular, this means that for each $i$, one of $v_i$ or $\overline{v_i}$ gets the *True* color, and the other gets the *False* color. For the remainder of the construction, we will consider the variable $x_i$ to be set to 1 in the given instance of 3-SAT if and only if the node $v_i$ gets assigned the *True* color.

So in summary, we now have a graph $G$ in which any 3-coloring implicitly determines a truth assignment for the variables in the 3-SAT instance. We now need to grow $G$ so that only satisfying assignments can be extended to 3-colorings of the full graph. How should we do this?

As in other 3-SAT reductions, let's consider a clause like $x_1 \vee \overline{x_2} \vee x_3$. In the language of 3-colorings of $G$, it says, "At least one of the nodes $v_1$, $\overline{v_2}$, or $v_3$ should get the *True* color." So what we need is a little subgraph that we can plug into $G$, so that any 3-coloring that extends into this subgraph must have the property of assigning the *True* color to at least one of $v_1$, $\overline{v_2}$, or $v_3$. It takes some experimentation to find such a subgraph, but one that works is depicted in Figure 8.12.

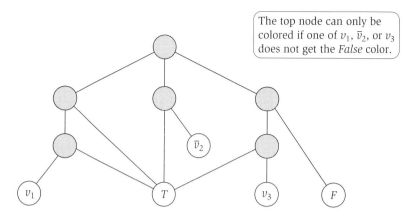

The top node can only be colored if one of $v_1$, $\overline{v}_2$, or $v_3$ does not get the *False* color.

**Figure 8.12** Attaching a subgraph to represent the clause $x_1 \vee \overline{x}_2 \vee x_3$.

This six-node subgraph "attaches" to the rest of $G$ at five existing nodes: *True*, *False*, and those corresponding to the three terms in the clause that we're trying to represent (in this case, $v_1$, $\overline{v}_2$, and $v_3$.) Now suppose that in some 3-coloring of $G$ all three of $v_1$, $\overline{v}_2$, and $v_3$ are assigned the *False* color. Then the lowest two shaded nodes in the subgraph must receive the *Base* color, the three shaded nodes above them must receive, respectively, the *False*, *Base*, and *True* colors, and hence there's no color that can be assigned to the topmost shaded node. In other words, a 3-coloring in which none of $v_1$, $\overline{v}_2$, or $v_3$ is assigned the *True* color cannot be extended to a 3-coloring of this subgraph.[2]

Finally, and conversely, some hand-checking of cases shows that as long as one of $v_1$, $\overline{v}_2$, or $v_3$ is assigned the *True* color, the full subgraph can be 3-colored.

So from this, we can complete the construction: We start with the graph $G$ defined above, and for each clause in the 3-SAT instance, we attach a six-node subgraph as shown in Figure 8.12. Let us call the resulting graph $G'$.

---

[2] This argument actually gives considerable insight into how one comes up with this subgraph in the first place. The goal is to have a node like the topmost one that cannot receive any color. So we start by "plugging in" three nodes corresponding to the terms, all colored *False*, at the bottom. For each one, we then work upward, pairing it off with a node of a known color to force the node above to have the third color. Proceeding in this way, we can arrive at a node that is forced to have any color we want. So we force each of the three different colors, starting from each of the three different terms, and then we plug all three of these differently colored nodes into our topmost node, arriving at the impossibility.

We now claim that the given 3-SAT instance is satisfiable if and only if $G'$ has a 3-coloring. First, suppose that there is a satisfying assignment for the 3-SAT instance. We define a coloring of $G'$ by first coloring *Base*, *True*, and *False* arbitrarily with the three colors, then, for each $i$, assigning $v_i$ the *True* color if $x_i = 1$ and the *False* color if $x_i = 0$. We then assign $\overline{v_i}$ the only available color. Finally, as argued above, it is now possible to extend this 3-coloring into each six-node clause subgraph, resulting in a 3-coloring of all of $G'$.

Conversely, suppose $G'$ has a 3-coloring. In this coloring, each node $v_i$ is assigned either the *True* color or the *False* color; we set the variable $x_i$ correspondingly. Now we claim that in each clause of the 3-SAT instance, at least one of the terms in the clause has the truth value 1. For if not, then all three of the corresponding nodes has the *False* color in the 3-coloring of $G'$ and, as we have seen above, there is no 3-coloring of the corresponding clause subgraph consistent with this—a contradiction.  ∎

When $k > 3$, it is very easy to reduce the 3-Coloring Problem to $k$-Coloring. Essentially, all we do is to take an instance of 3-Coloring, represented by a graph $G$, add $k - 3$ new nodes, and join these new nodes to each other and to every node in $G$. The resulting graph is $k$-colorable if and only if the original graph $G$ is 3-colorable. Thus $k$-Coloring for any $k > 3$ is NP-complete as well.

### Coda: The Resolution of the Four-Color Conjecture

To conclude this section, we should finish off the story of the Four-Color Conjecture for maps in the plane as well. After more than a hundred years, the conjecture was finally proved by Appel and Haken in 1976. The structure of the proof was a simple induction on the number of regions, but the induction step involved nearly two thousand fairly complicated cases, and the verification of these cases had to be carried out by a computer. This was not a satisfying outcome for most mathematicians: Hoping for a proof that would yield some insight into why the result was true, they instead got a case analysis of enormous complexity whose proof could not be checked by hand. The problem of finding a reasonably short, human-readable proof still remains open.

## 8.8 Numerical Problems

We now consider some computationally hard problems that involve arithmetic operations on numbers. We will see that the intractability here comes from the way in which some of the problems we have seen earlier in the chapter can be encoded in the representations of very large integers.

## The Subset Sum Problem

Our basic problem in this genre will be *Subset Sum*, a special case of the Knapsack Problem that we saw before in Section 6.4 when we covered dynamic programming. We can formulate a decision version of this problem as follows.

> Given natural numbers $w_1, \ldots, w_n$, and a target number $W$, is there a subset of $\{w_1, \ldots, w_n\}$ that adds up to precisely $W$?

We have already seen an algorithm to solve this problem; why are we now including it on our list of computationally hard problems? This goes back to an issue that we raised the first time we considered Subset Sum in Section 6.4. The algorithm we developed there has running time $O(nW)$, which is reasonable when $W$ is small, but becomes hopelessly impractical as $W$ (and the numbers $w_i$) grow large. Consider, for example, an instance with 100 numbers, each of which is 100 bits long. Then the input is only $100 \times 100 = 10{,}000$ digits, but $W$ is now roughly $2^{100}$.

To phrase this more generally, since integers will typically be given in bit representation, or base-10 representation, the quantity $W$ is really *exponential* in the size of the input; our algorithm was not a polynomial-time algorithm. (We referred to it as *pseudo-polynomial*, to indicate that it ran in time polynomial in the magnitude of the input numbers, but not polynomial in the size of their representation.)

This is an issue that comes up in many settings; for example, we encountered it in the context of network flow algorithms, where the capacities had integer values. Other settings may be familiar to you as well. For example, the security of a cryptosystem such as RSA is motivated by the sense that factoring a 1,000-bit number is difficult. But if we considered a running time of $2^{1000}$ steps feasible, factoring such a number would not be difficult at all.

It is worth pausing here for a moment and asking: Is this notion of polynomial time for numerical operations too severe a restriction? For example, given two natural numbers $w_1$ and $w_2$ represented in base-$d$ notation for some $d > 1$, how long does it take to add, subtract, or multiply them? This is an issue we touched on in Section 5.5, where we noted that the standard ways that kids in elementary school learn to perform these operations have (low-degree) polynomial running times. Addition and subtraction (with carries) take $O(\log w_1 + \log w_2)$ time, while the standard multiplication algorithm runs in $O(\log w_1 \cdot \log w_2)$ time. (Recall that in Section 5.5 we discussed the design of an asymptotically faster multiplication algorithm that elementary schoolchildren are unlikely to invent on their own.)

So a basic question is: Can Subset Sum be solved by a (genuinely) polynomial-time algorithm? In other words, could there be an algorithm with running time polynomial in $n$ and $\log W$? Or polynomial in $n$ alone?

## Proving Subset Sum Is NP-Complete

The following result suggests that this is not likely to be the case.

> **(8.23)**    Subset Sum *is NP-complete.*

**Proof.** We first show that Subset Sum is in $\mathcal{NP}$. Given natural numbers $w_1, \ldots, w_n$, and a target $W$, a certificate that there is a solution would be the subset $w_{i_1}, \ldots, w_{i_k}$ that is purported to add up to $W$. In polynomial time, we can compute the sum of these numbers and verify that it is equal to $W$.

We now reduce a known NP-complete problem to Subset Sum. Since we are seeking a set that adds up to *exactly* a given quantity (as opposed to being bounded above or below by this quantity), we look for a combinatorial problem that is based on meeting an *exact* bound. The 3-Dimensional Matching Problem is a natural choice; we show that 3-Dimensional Matching $\leq_P$ Subset Sum. The trick will be to encode the manipulation of sets via the addition of integers.

So consider an instance of 3-Dimensional Matching specified by sets $X, Y, Z$, each of size $n$, and a set of $m$ triples $T \subseteq X \times Y \times Z$. A common way to represent sets is via *bit-vectors*: Each entry in the vector corresponds to a different element, and it holds a 1 if and only if the set contains that element. We adopt this type of approach for representing each triple $t = (x_i, y_j, z_k) \in T$: we construct a number $w_t$ with $3n$ digits that has a 1 in positions $i$, $n+j$, and $2n+k$, and a 0 in all other positions. In other words, for some base $d > 1$, $w_t = d^{i-1} + d^{n+j-1} + d^{2n+k-1}$.

Note how taking the union of triples *almost* corresponds to integer addition: The 1s fill in the places where there is an element in any of the sets. But we say *almost* because addition includes *carries*: too many 1s in the same column will "roll over" and produce a nonzero entry in the next column. This has no analogue in the context of the union operation.

In the present situation, we handle this problem by a simple trick. We have only $m$ numbers in all, and each has digits equal to 0 or 1; so if we assume that our numbers are written in base $d = m + 1$, then there will be no carries at all.

Thus we construct the following instance of Subset Sum. For each triple $t = (x_i, y_j, z_k) \in T$, we construct a number $w_t$ in base $m + 1$ as defined above. We define $W$ to be the number in base $m + 1$ with $3n$ digits, each of which is equal to 1, that is, $W = \sum_{i=0}^{3n-1}(m + 1)^i$.

We claim that the set $T$ of triples contains a perfect three-dimensional matching if and only if there is a subset of the numbers $\{w_t\}$ that adds up to $W$. For suppose there is a perfect three-dimensional matching consisting of triples $t_1, \ldots, t_n$. Then in the sum $w_{t_1} + \cdots + w_{t_n}$, there is a single 1 in each of the $3n$ digit positions, and so the result is equal to $W$.

Conversely, suppose there exists a set of numbers $w_{t_1}, \ldots, w_{t_k}$ that adds up to $W$. Then since each $w_{t_i}$ has three 1s in its representation, and there are no carries, we know that $k = n$. It follows that for each of the $3n$ digit positions, exactly one of the $w_{t_i}$ has a 1 in that position. Thus, $t_1, \ldots, t_k$ constitute a perfect three-dimensional matching. ■

## Extensions: The Hardness of Certain Scheduling Problems

The hardness of Subset Sum can be used to establish the hardness of a range of scheduling problems—including some that do not obviously involve the addition of numbers. Here is a nice example, a natural (but much harder) generalization of a scheduling problem we solved in Section 4.2 using a greedy algorithm.

Suppose we are given a set of $n$ jobs that must be run on a single machine. Each job $i$ has a *release time* $r_i$ when it is first available for processing; a *deadline* $d_i$ by which it must be completed; and a *processing duration* $t_i$. We will assume that all of these parameters are natural numbers. In order to be completed, job $i$ must be allocated a contiguous slot of $t_i$ time units somewhere in the interval $[r_i, d_i]$. The machine can run only one job at a time. The question is: Can we schedule all jobs so that each completes by its deadline? We will call this an instance of *Scheduling with Release Times and Deadlines*.

**(8.24)** Scheduling with Release Times and Deadlines *is NP-complete.*

**Proof.** Given an instance of the problem, a certificate that it is solvable would be a specification of the starting time for each job. We could then check that each job runs for a distinct interval of time, between its release time and deadline. Thus the problem is in $\mathcal{NP}$.

We now show that Subset Sum is reducible to this scheduling problem. Thus, consider an instance of Subset Sum with numbers $w_1, \ldots, w_n$ and a target $W$. In constructing an equivalent scheduling instance, one is struck initially by the fact that we have so many parameters to manage: release times, deadlines, and durations. The key is to sacrifice most of this flexibility, producing a "skeletal" instance of the problem that still encodes the Subset Sum Problem.

Let $S = \sum_{i=1}^{n} w_i$. We define jobs $1, 2, \ldots, n$; job $i$ has a release time of 0, a deadline of $S + 1$, and a duration of $w_i$. For this set of jobs, we have the freedom to arrange them in any order, and they will all finish on time.

We now further constrain the instance so that the only way to solve it will be to group together a subset of the jobs whose durations add up precisely to $W$. To do this, we define an $(n + 1)^{st}$ job; it has a release time of $W$, a deadline of $W + 1$, and a duration of 1.

Now consider any feasible solution to this instance of the scheduling problem. The $(n + 1)^{st}$ job must be run in the interval $[W, W + 1]$. This leaves $S$ available time units between the common release time and the common deadline; and there are $S$ time units worth of jobs to run. Thus the machine must not have any idle time, when no jobs are running. In particular, if jobs $i_1, \ldots, i_k$ are the ones that run before time $W$, then the corresponding numbers $w_{i_1}, \ldots, w_{i_k}$ in the Subset Sum instance add up to exactly $W$.

Conversely, if there are numbers $w_{i_1}, \ldots, w_{i_k}$ that add up to exactly $W$, then we can schedule these before job $n + 1$ and the remainder after job $n + 1$; this is a feasible solution to the scheduling instance. ∎

## Caveat: Subset Sum with Polynomially Bounded Numbers

There is a very common source of pitfalls involving the Subset Sum Problem, and while it is closely connected to the issues we have been discussing already, we feel it is worth discussing explicitly. The pitfall is the following.

> *Consider the special case of Subset Sum, with n input numbers, in which W is bounded by a polynomial function of n. Assuming $\mathcal{P} \neq \mathcal{NP}$, this special case is* not *NP-complete.*

It is not NP-complete for the simple reason that it can be solved in time $O(nW)$, by our dynamic programming algorithm from Section 6.4; when $W$ is bounded by a polynomial function of $n$, this is a polynomial-time algorithm.

All this is very clear; so you may ask: Why dwell on it? The reason is that there is a genre of problem that is often wrongly claimed to be NP-complete (even in published papers) via reduction from this special case of Subset Sum. Here is a basic example of such a problem, which we will call *Component Grouping*.

> *Given a graph G that is not connected, and a number k, does there exist a subset of its connected components whose union has size exactly k?*

**Incorrect Claim.** Component Grouping is NP-complete.

**Incorrect Proof.** Component Grouping is in $\mathcal{NP}$, and we'll skip the proof of this. We now attempt to show that Subset Sum $\leq_P$ Component Grouping. Given an instance of Subset Sum with numbers $w_1, \ldots, w_n$ and target $W$, we construct an instance of Component Grouping as follows. For each $i$, we construct a path $P_i$ of length $w_i$. The graph $G$ will be the union of the paths

$P_1, \ldots, P_n$, each of which is a separate connected component. We set $k = W$. It is clear that $G$ has a set of connected components whose union has size $k$ if and only if some subset of the numbers $w_1, \ldots, w_n$ adds up to $W$. ∎

The error here is subtle; in particular, the claim in the last sentence is correct. The problem is that the construction described above does not establish that Subset Sum $\leq_P$ Component Grouping, because it requires more than polynomial time. In constructing the input to our black box that solves Component Grouping, we had to build the encoding of a graph of size $w_1 + \cdots + w_n$, and this takes time exponential in the size of the input to the Subset Sum instance. In effect, Subset Sum works with the numbers $w_1, \ldots, w_n$ in a very compact representation, but Component Grouping does not accept "compact" encodings of graphs.

The problem is more fundamental than the incorrectness of this proof; in fact, Component Grouping is a problem that can be solved in polynomial time. If $n_1, n_2, \ldots, n_c$ denote the sizes of the connected components of $G$, we simply use our dynamic programming algorithm for Subset Sum to decide whether some subset of these numbers $\{n_i\}$ adds up to $k$. The running time required for this is $O(ck)$; and since $c$ and $k$ are both bounded by $n$, this is $O(n^2)$ time.

Thus we have discovered a new polynomial-time algorithm by reducing in the other direction, to a polynomial-time solvable special case of Subset Sum.

## 8.9 Co-NP and the Asymmetry of NP

As a further perspective on this general class of problems, let's return to the definitions underlying the class $\mathcal{NP}$. We've seen that the notion of an efficient certifier doesn't suggest a concrete algorithm for actually solving the problem that's better than brute-force search.

Now here's another observation: The definition of efficient certification, and hence of $\mathcal{NP}$, is fundamentally *asymmetric*. An input string $s$ is a "yes" instance if and only if there exists a short $t$ so that $B(s, t) = \text{yes}$. Negating this statement, we see that an input string $s$ is a "no" instance if and only if *for all* short $t$, it's the case that $B(s, t) = \text{no}$.

This relates closely to our intuition about $\mathcal{NP}$: When we have a "yes" instance, we can provide a short proof of this fact. But when we have a "no" instance, no correspondingly short proof is guaranteed by the definition; the answer is no simply because there is no string that will serve as a proof. In concrete terms, recall our question from Section 8.3: Given an unsatisfiable set of clauses, what evidence could we show to quickly convince you that there is no satisfying assignment?

For every problem $X$, there is a natural *complementary* problem $\overline{X}$: For all input strings $s$, we say $s \in \overline{X}$ if and only if $s \notin X$. Note that if $X \in \mathcal{P}$, then $\overline{X} \in \mathcal{P}$, since from an algorithm $A$ that solves $X$, we can simply produce an algorithm $\overline{A}$ that runs $A$ and then flips its answer.

But it is far from clear that if $X \in \mathcal{NP}$, it should follow that $\overline{X} \in \mathcal{NP}$. The problem $\overline{X}$, rather, has a different property: for all $s$, we have $s \in \overline{X}$ if and only if for all $t$ of length at most $p(|s|)$, $B(s, t) = \text{no}$. This is a fundamentally different definition, and it can't be worked around by simply "inverting" the output of the efficient certifier $B$ to produce $\overline{B}$. The problem is that the "exists $t$" in the definition of $\mathcal{NP}$ has become a "for all $t$," and this is a serious change.

There is a class of problems parallel to $\mathcal{NP}$ that is designed to model this issue; it is called, naturally enough, co-$\mathcal{NP}$. A problem $X$ belongs to co-$\mathcal{NP}$ if and only if the complementary problem $\overline{X}$ belongs to $\mathcal{NP}$. We do not know for sure that $\mathcal{NP}$ and co-$\mathcal{NP}$ are different; we can only ask

**(8.25)**    *Does* $\mathcal{NP} = \text{co-}\mathcal{NP}$?

Again, the widespread belief is that $\mathcal{NP} \neq \text{co-}\mathcal{NP}$: Just because the "yes" instances of a problem have short proofs, it is not clear why we should believe that the "no" instances have short proofs as well.

Proving $\mathcal{NP} \neq \text{co-}\mathcal{NP}$ would be an even bigger step than proving $\mathcal{P} \neq \mathcal{NP}$, for the following reason:

**(8.26)**    *If* $\mathcal{NP} \neq \text{co-}\mathcal{NP}$, *then* $\mathcal{P} \neq \mathcal{NP}$.

**Proof.** We'll actually prove the contrapositive statement: $\mathcal{P} = \mathcal{NP}$ implies $\mathcal{NP} = \text{co-}\mathcal{NP}$. Essentially, the point is that $\mathcal{P}$ is closed under complementation; so if $\mathcal{P} = \mathcal{NP}$, then $\mathcal{NP}$ would be closed under complementation as well. More formally, starting from the assumption $\mathcal{P} = \mathcal{NP}$, we have

$$X \in \mathcal{NP} \implies X \in \mathcal{P} \implies \overline{X} \in \mathcal{P} \implies \overline{X} \in \mathcal{NP} \implies X \in \text{co-}\mathcal{NP}$$

and

$$X \in \text{co-}\mathcal{NP} \implies \overline{X} \in \mathcal{NP} \implies \overline{X} \in \mathcal{P} \implies X \in \mathcal{P} \implies X \in \mathcal{NP}.$$

Hence it would follow that $\mathcal{NP} \subseteq \text{co-}\mathcal{NP}$ and co-$\mathcal{NP} \subseteq \mathcal{NP}$, whence $\mathcal{NP} = \text{co-}\mathcal{NP}$.  ∎

### Good Characterizations: The Class NP ∩ co-NP

If a problem $X$ belongs to both $\mathcal{NP}$ and co-$\mathcal{NP}$, then it has the following nice property: When the answer is yes, there is a short proof; and when the answer is no, there is also a short proof. Thus problems that belong to this intersection

$\mathcal{NP} \cap$ co-$\mathcal{NP}$ are said to have a *good characterization*, since there is always a nice certificate for the solution.

This notion corresponds directly to some of the results we have seen earlier. For example, consider the problem of determining whether a flow network contains a flow of value at least $v$, for some quantity $v$. To prove that the answer is yes, we could simply exhibit a flow that achieves this value; this is consistent with the problem belonging to $\mathcal{NP}$. But we can also prove the answer is no: We can exhibit a cut whose capacity is strictly less than $v$. This duality between "yes" and "no" instances is the crux of the Max-Flow Min-Cut Theorem.

Similarly, Hall's Theorem for matchings from Section 7.5 proved that the Bipartite Perfect Matching Problem is in $\mathcal{NP} \cap$ co-$\mathcal{NP}$: We can exhibit either a perfect matching, or a set of vertices $A \subseteq X$ such that the total number of neighbors of $A$ is strictly less than $|A|$.

Now, if a problem $X$ is in $\mathcal{P}$, then it belongs to both $\mathcal{NP}$ and co-$\mathcal{NP}$; thus, $\mathcal{P} \subseteq \mathcal{NP} \cap$ co-$\mathcal{NP}$. Interestingly, both our proof of the Max-Flow Min-Cut Theorem and our proof of Hall's Theorem came hand in hand with proofs of the stronger results that Maximum Flow and Bipartite Matching are problems in $\mathcal{P}$. Nevertheless, the good characterizations themselves are so clean that formulating them separately still gives us a lot of conceptual leverage in reasoning about these problems.

Naturally, one would like to know whether there's a problem that has a good characterization but no polynomial-time algorithm. But this too is an open question:

**(8.27)**   *Does* $\mathcal{P} = \mathcal{NP} \cap$ co-$\mathcal{NP}$?

Unlike questions (8.11) and (8.25), general opinion seems somewhat mixed on this one. In part, this is because there are many cases in which a problem was found to have a nontrivial good characterization; and then (sometimes many years later) it was also discovered to have a polynomial-time algorithm.

## 8.10 A Partial Taxonomy of Hard Problems

We've now reached the end of the chapter, and we've encountered a fairly rich array of NP-complete problems. In a way, it's useful to know a good number of different NP-complete problems: When you encounter a new problem $X$ and want to try proving it's NP-complete, you want to show $Y \leq_P X$ for some known NP-complete problem $Y$—so the more options you have for $Y$, the better.

At the same time, the more options you have for $Y$, the more bewildering it can be to try choosing the right one to use in a particular reduction. Of course, the whole point of NP-completeness is that one of these problems will work in your reduction if and only if any of them will (since they're all equivalent with respect to polynomial-time reductions); but the reduction to a given problem $X$ can be much, much easier starting from some problems than from others.

With this in mind, we spend this concluding section on a review of the NP-complete problems we've come across in the chapter, grouped into six basic genres. Together with this grouping, we offer some suggestions as to how to choose a starting problem for use in a reduction.

## Packing Problems

Packing problems tend to have the following structure: You're given a collection of objects, and you want to choose at least $k$ of them; making your life difficult is a set of conflicts among the objects, preventing you from choosing certain groups simultaneously.

We've seen two basic packing problems in this chapter.

- *Independent Set*: Given a graph $G$ and a number $k$, does $G$ contain an independent set of size at least $k$?

- *Set Packing*: Given a set $U$ of $n$ elements, a collection $S_1, \ldots, S_m$ of subsets of $U$, and a number $k$, does there exist a collection of at least $k$ of these sets with the property that no two of them intersect?

## Covering Problems

Covering problems form a natural contrast to packing problems, and one typically recognizes them as having the following structure: you're given a collection of objects, and you want to choose a subset that collectively achieves a certain goal; the challenge is to achieve this goal while choosing only $k$ of the objects.

We've seen two basic covering problems in this chapter.

- *Vertex Cover*: Given a graph $G$ and a number $k$, does $G$ contain a vertex cover of size at most $k$?

- *Set Cover*: Given a set $U$ of $n$ elements, a collection $S_1, \ldots, S_m$ of subsets of $U$, and a number $k$, does there exist a collection of at most $k$ of these sets whose union is equal to all of $U$?

## Partitioning Problems

Partitioning problems involve a search over all ways to divide up a collection of objects into subsets so that each object appears in exactly one of the subsets.

One of our two basic partitioning problems, 3-Dimensional Matching, arises naturally whenever you have a collection of sets and you want to solve a covering problem and a packing problem simultaneously: Choose some of the sets in such a way that they are disjoint, yet completely cover the ground set.

- *3-Dimensional Matching*: Given disjoint sets $X$, $Y$, and $Z$, each of size $n$, and given a set $T \subseteq X \times Y \times Z$ of ordered triples, does there exist a set of $n$ triples in $T$ so that each element of $X \cup Y \cup Z$ is contained in exactly one of these triples?

Our other basic partitioning problem, Graph Coloring, is at work whenever you're seeking to partition objects in the presence of conflicts, and conflicting objects aren't allowed to go into the same set.

- *Graph Coloring*: Given a graph $G$ and a bound $k$, does $G$ have a $k$-coloring?

## Sequencing Problems

Our first three types of problems have involved searching over subsets of a collection of objects. Another type of computationally hard problem involves searching over the set of all *permutations* of a collection of objects.

Two of our basic sequencing problems draw their difficulty from the fact that you are required to order $n$ objects, but there are restrictions preventing you from placing certain objects after certain others.

- *Hamiltonian Cycle*: Given a directed graph $G$, does it contain a Hamiltonian cycle?
- *Hamiltonian Path*: Given a directed graph $G$, does it contain a Hamiltonian path?

Our third basic sequencing problem is very similar; it softens these restrictions by simply imposing a cost for placing one object after another.

- *Traveling Salesman*: Given a set of distances on $n$ cities, and a bound $D$, is there a tour of length at most $D$?

## Numerical Problems

The hardness of the numerical problems considered in this chapter flowed principally from Subset Sum, the special case of the Knapsack Problem that we considered in Section 8.8.

- *Subset Sum*: Given natural numbers $w_1, \ldots, w_n$, and a target number $W$, is there a subset of $\{w_1, \ldots, w_n\}$ that adds up to precisely $W$?

It is natural to try reducing from *Subset Sum* whenever one has a problem with weighted objects and the goal is to select objects conditioned on a constraint on the total weight of the objects selected. This, for example, is what happened in the proof of (8.24), showing that Scheduling with Release Times and Deadlines is NP-complete.

At the same time, one must heed the warning that Subset Sum only becomes hard with truly large integers; when the magnitudes of the input numbers are bounded by a polynomial function of $n$, the problem is solvable in polynomial time by dynamic programming.

## Constraint Satisfaction Problems

Finally, we considered basic constraint satisfaction problems, including Circuit Satisfiability, SAT, and 3-SAT. Among these, the most useful for the purpose of designing reductions is 3-SAT.

- *3-SAT*: Given a set of clauses $C_1, \ldots, C_k$, each of length 3, over a set of variables $X = \{x_1, \ldots, x_n\}$, does there exist a satisfying truth assignment?

Because of its expressive flexibility, 3-SAT is often a useful starting point for reductions where none of the previous five categories seem to fit naturally onto the problem being considered. In designing 3-SAT reductions, it helps to recall the advice given in the proof of (8.8), that there are two distinct ways to view an instance of 3-SAT: (a) as a search over assignments to the variables, subject to the constraint that all clauses must be satisfied, and (b) as a search over ways to choose a single term (to be satisfied) from each clause, subject to the constraint that one mustn't choose conflicting terms from different clauses. Each of these perspectives on 3-SAT is useful, and each forms the key idea behind a large number of reductions.

# Solved Exercises

### Solved Exercise 1

You're consulting for a small high-tech company that maintains a high-security computer system for some sensitive work that it's doing. To make sure this system is not being used for any illicit purposes, they've set up some logging software that records the IP addresses that all their users are accessing over time. We'll assume that each user accesses at most one IP address in any given minute; the software writes a log file that records, for each user $u$ and each minute $m$, a value $I(u, m)$ that is equal to the IP address (if any) accessed by user $u$ during minute $m$. It sets $I(u, m)$ to the null symbol $\perp$ if $u$ did not access any IP address during minute $m$.

The company management just learned that yesterday the system was used to launch a complex attack on some remote sites. The attack was carried out by accessing $t$ distinct IP addresses over $t$ consecutive minutes: In minute

1, the attack accessed address $i_1$; in minute 2, it accessed address $i_2$; and so on, up to address $i_t$ in minute $t$.

Who could have been responsible for carrying out this attack? The company checks the logs and finds to its surprise that there's no single user $u$ who accessed each of the IP addresses involved at the appropriate time; in other words, there's no $u$ so that $I(u, m) = i_m$ for each minute $m$ from 1 to $t$.

So the question becomes: What if there were a small *coalition* of $k$ users that collectively might have carried out the attack? We will say a subset $S$ of users is a *suspicious coalition* if, for each minute $m$ from 1 to $t$, there is at least one user $u \in S$ for which $I(u, m) = i_m$. (In other words, each IP address was accessed at the appropriate time by at least one user in the coalition.)

The *Suspicious Coalition Problem* asks: Given the collection of all values $I(u, m)$, and a number $k$, is there a suspicious coalition of size at most $k$?

***Solution***    First of all, Suspicious Coalition is clearly in $\mathcal{NP}$: If we were to be shown a set $S$ of users, we could check that $S$ has size at most $k$, and that for each minute $m$ from 1 to $t$, at least one of the users in $S$ accessed the IP address $i_m$.

Now we want to find a known NP-complete problem and reduce it to Suspicious Coalition. Although Suspicious Coalition has lots of features (users, minutes, IP addresses), it's very clearly a covering problem (following the taxonomy described in the chapter): We need to explain all $t$ suspicious accesses, and we're allowed a limited number of users ($k$) with which to do this. Once we've decided it's a covering problem, it's natural to try reducing Vertex Cover or Set Cover to it. And in order to do this, it's useful to push most of its complicated features into the background, leaving just the bare-bones features that will be used to encode Vertex Cover or Set Cover.

Let's focus on reducing Vertex Cover to it. In Vertex Cover, we need to cover every edge, and we're only allowed $k$ nodes. In Suspicious Coalition, we need to "cover" all the accesses, and we're only allowed $k$ users. This parallelism strongly suggests that, given an instance of Vertex Cover consisting of a graph $G = (V, E)$ and a bound $k$, we should construct an instance of Suspicious Coalition in which the users represent the nodes of $G$ and the suspicious accesses represent the edges.

So suppose the graph $G$ for the Vertex Cover instance has $m$ edges $e_1, \ldots, e_m$, and $e_j = (v_j, w_j)$. We construct an instance of Suspicious Coalition as follows. For each node of $G$ we construct a user, and for each edge $e_t = (v_t, w_t)$ we construct a minute $t$. (So there will be $m$ minutes total.) In minute $t$, the users associated with the two ends of $e_t$ access an IP address $i_t$, and all other users access nothing. Finally, the attack consists of accesses to addresses $i_1, i_2, \ldots, i_m$ in minutes $1, 2, \ldots, m$, respectively.

The following claim will establish that Vertex Cover $\leq_P$ Suspicious Coalition and hence will conclude the proof that Suspicious Coalition is NP-complete. Given how closely our construction of the instance shadows the original Vertex Cover instance, the proof is completely straightforward.

**(8.28)**   *In the instance constructed, there is a suspicious coalition of size at most k if and only if the graph G contains a vertex cover of size at most k.*

**Proof.** First, suppose that $G$ contains a vertex cover $C$ of size at most $k$. Then consider the corresponding set $S$ of users in the instance of Suspicious Coalition. For each $t$ from 1 to $m$, at least one element of $C$ is an end of the edge $e_t$, and the corresponding user in $S$ accessed the IP address $i_t$. Hence the set $S$ is a suspicious coalition.

Conversely, suppose that there is a suspicious coalition $S$ of size at most $k$, and consider the corresponding set of nodes $C$ in $G$. For each $t$ from 1 to $m$, at least one user in $S$ accessed the IP address $i_t$, and the corresponding node in $C$ is an end of the edge $e_t$. Hence the set $C$ is a vertex cover.  ■

## Solved Exercise 2

You've been asked to organize a freshman-level seminar that will meet once a week during the next semester. The plan is to have the first portion of the semester consist of a sequence of $\ell$ guest lectures by outside speakers, and have the second portion of the semester devoted to a sequence of $p$ hands-on projects that the students will do.

There are $n$ options for speakers overall, and in week number $i$ (for $i = 1, 2, \ldots, \ell$) a subset $L_i$ of these speakers is available to give a lecture.

On the other hand, each project requires that the students have seen certain background material in order for them to be able to complete the project successfully. In particular, for each project $j$ (for $j = 1, 2, \ldots, p$), there is a subset $P_j$ of relevant speakers so that the students need to have seen a lecture by *at least one of* the speakers in the set $P_j$ in order to be able to complete the project.

So this is the problem: Given these sets, can you select exactly one speaker for each of the first $\ell$ weeks of the seminar, so that you only choose speakers who are available in their designated week, and so that for each project $j$, the students will have seen at least one of the speakers in the relevant set $P_j$? We'll call this the *Lecture Planning Problem*.

To make this clear, let's consider the following sample instance. Suppose that $\ell = 2$, $p = 3$, and there are $n = 4$ speakers that we denote $A, B, C, D$. The availability of the speakers is given by the sets $L_1 = \{A, B, C\}$ and $L_2 = \{A, D\}$. The relevant speakers for each project are given by the sets $P_1 = \{B, C\}$,

$P_2 = \{A, B, D\}$, and $P_3 = \{C, D\}$. Then the answer to this instance of the problem is yes, since we can choose speaker $B$ in the first week and speaker $D$ in the second week; this way, for each of the three projects, students will have seen at least one of the relevant speakers.

Prove that Lecture Planning is NP-complete.

***Solution***  The problem is in $\mathcal{NP}$ since, given a sequence of speakers, we can check (a) all speakers are available in the weeks when they're scheduled, and (b) that for each project, at least one of the relevant speakers has been scheduled.

Now we need to find a known NP-complete problem that we can reduce to Lecture Planning. This is less clear-cut than in the previous exercise, because the statement of the Lecture Planning Problem doesn't immediately map into the taxonomy from the chapter.

There is a useful intuitive view of Lecture Planning, however, that is characteristic of a wide range of constraint satisfaction problems. This intuition is captured, in a strikingly picturesque way, by a description that appeared in the *New Yorker* of the lawyer David Boies's cross-examination style:

> *During a cross-examination, David takes a friendly walk down the hall with you while he's quietly closing doors. They get to the end of the hall and David turns on you and there's no place to go. He's closed all the doors.*[3]

What does constraint satisfaction have to do with cross-examination? In Lecture Planning, as in many similar problems, there are two conceptual phases. There's a first phase in which you walk through a set of choices, selecting some and thereby closing the door on others; this is followed by a second phase in which you find out whether your choices have left you with a valid solution or not.

In the case of Lecture Planning, the first phase consists of choosing a speaker for each week, and the second phase consists of verifying that you've picked a relevant speaker for each project. But there are many NP-complete problems that fit this description at a high level, and so viewing Lecture Planning this way helps us search for a plausible reduction. We will in fact describe two reductions, first from 3-SAT and then from Vertex Cover. Of course, either one of these by itself is enough to prove NP-completeness, but both make for useful examples.

3-SAT is the canonical example of a problem with the two-phase structure described above: We first walk through the variables, setting each one to true or false; we then look over each clause and see whether our choices

---

[3] Ken Auletta quoting Jeffrey Blattner, *The New Yorker*, 16 August 1999.

have satisfied it. This parallel to Lecture Planning already suggests a natural reduction showing that 3-SAT $\leq_P$ Lecture Planning: We set things up so that the choice of lecturers sets the variables, and then the feasibility of the projects represents the satisfaction of the clauses.

More concretely, suppose we are given an instance of 3-SAT consisting of clauses $C_1, \ldots, C_k$ over the variables $x_1, x_2, \ldots, x_n$. We construct an instance of Lecture Planning as follows. For each variable $x_i$, we create two lecturers $z_i$ and $z_i'$ that will correspond to $x_i$ and its negation. We begin with $n$ weeks of lectures; in week $i$, the only two lecturers available are $z_i$ and $z_i'$. Then there is a sequence of $k$ projects; for project $j$, the set of relevant lecturers $P_j$ consists of the three lecturers corresponding to the terms in clause $C_j$. Now, if there is a satisfying assignment $v$ for the 3-SAT instance, then in week $i$ we choose the lecturer among $z_i, z_i'$ that corresponds to the value assigned to $x_i$ by $v$; in this case, we will select at least one speaker from each relevant set $P_j$. Conversely, if we find a way to choose speakers so that there is at least one from each relevant set, then we can set the variables $x_i$ as follows: $x_i$ is set to 1 if $z_i$ is chosen, and it is set to 0 if $z_i'$ is chosen. In this way, at least one of the three variables in each clause $C_j$ is set in a way that satisfies it, and so this is a satisfying assignment. This concludes the reduction and its proof of correctness.

Our intuitive view of Lecture Planning leads naturally to a reduction from Vertex Cover as well. (What we describe here could be easily modified to work from Set Cover or 3-Dimensional Matching too.) The point is that we can view Vertex Cover as having a similar two-phase structure: We first choose a set of $k$ nodes from the input graph, and we then verify for each edge that these choices have covered all the edges.

Given an input to Vertex Cover, consisting of a graph $G = (V, E)$ and a number $k$, we create a lecturer $z_v$ for each node $v$. We set $\ell = k$, and define $L_1 = L_2 = \cdots = L_k = \{z_v : v \in V\}$. In other words, for the first $k$ weeks, all lecturers are available. After this, we create a project $j$ for each edge $e_j = (v, w)$, with set $P_j = \{z_v, z_w\}$.

Now, if there is a vertex cover $S$ of at most $k$ nodes, then consider the set of lecturers $Z_S = \{z_v : v \in S\}$. For each project $P_j$, at least one of the relevant speakers belongs to $Z_S$, since $S$ covers all edges in $G$. Moreover, we can schedule all the lecturers in $Z_S$ during the first $k$ weeks. Thus it follows that there is a feasible solution to the instance of Lecture Planning.

Conversely, suppose there is a feasible solution to the instance of Lecture Planning, and let $T$ be the set of all lecturers who speak in the first $k$ weeks. Let $X$ be the set of nodes in $G$ that correspond to lecturers in $T$. For each project $P_j$, at least one of the two relevant speakers appears in $T$, and hence at least one end of each edge $e_j$ is in the set $X$. Thus $X$ is a vertex cover with at most $k$ nodes.

This concludes the proof that Vertex Cover $\leq_p$ Lecture Planning.

## Exercises

1. For each of the two questions below, decide whether the answer is (i) "Yes," (ii) "No," or (iii) "Unknown, because it would resolve the question of whether $\mathcal{P} = \mathcal{NP}$." Give a brief explanation of your answer.

   (a) Let's define the decision version of the Interval Scheduling Problem from Chapter 4 as follows: Given a collection of intervals on a time-line, and a bound $k$, does the collection contain a subset of nonoverlapping intervals of size at least $k$?

      Question: Is it the case that Interval Scheduling $\leq_p$ Vertex Cover?

   (b) Question: Is it the case that Independent Set $\leq_p$ Interval Scheduling?

2. A store trying to analyze the behavior of its customers will often maintain a two-dimensional array $A$, where the rows correspond to its customers and the columns correspond to the products it sells. The entry $A[i, j]$ specifies the quantity of product $j$ that has been purchased by customer $i$.

   Here's a tiny example of such an array $A$.

   |         | liquid detergent | beer | diapers | cat litter |
   |---------|------------------|------|---------|------------|
   | Raj     | 0                | 6    | 0       | 3          |
   | Alanis  | 2                | 3    | 0       | 0          |
   | Chelsea | 0                | 0    | 0       | 7          |

   One thing that a store might want to do with this data is the following. Let us say that a subset $S$ of the customers is *diverse* if no two of the of the customers in $S$ have ever bought the same product (i.e., for each product, at most one of the customers in $S$ has ever bought it). A diverse set of customers can be useful, for example, as a target pool for market research.

   We can now define the Diverse Subset Problem as follows: Given an $m \times n$ array $A$ as defined above, and a number $k \leq m$, is there a subset of at least $k$ of customers that is *diverse*?

   Show that Diverse Subset is NP-complete.

3. Suppose you're helping to organize a summer sports camp, and the following problem comes up. The camp is supposed to have at least

one counselor who's skilled at each of the $n$ sports covered by the camp (baseball, volleyball, and so on). They have received job applications from $m$ potential counselors. For each of the $n$ sports, there is some subset of the $m$ applicants qualified in that sport. The question is: For a given number $k < m$, is it possible to hire at most $k$ of the counselors and have at least one counselor qualified in each of the $n$ sports? We'll call this the *Efficient Recruiting Problem*.

Show that Efficient Recruiting is NP-complete.

4. Suppose you're consulting for a group that manages a high-performance real-time system in which asynchronous processes make use of shared resources. Thus the system has a set of $n$ *processes* and a set of $m$ *resources*. At any given point in time, each process specifies a set of resources that it requests to use. Each resource might be requested by many processes at once; but it can only be used by a single process at a time. Your job is to allocate resources to processes that request them. If a process is allocated all the resources it requests, then it is *active*; otherwise it is *blocked*. You want to perform the allocation so that as many processes as possible are active. Thus we phrase the *Resource Reservation Problem* as follows: Given a set of processes and resources, the set of requested resources for each process, and a number $k$, is it possible to allocate resources to processes so that at least $k$ processes will be active?

Consider the following list of problems, and for each problem either give a polynomial-time algorithm or prove that the problem is NP-complete.

(a) The general Resource Reservation Problem defined above.

(b) The special case of the problem when $k = 2$.

(c) The special case of the problem when there are two types of resources—say, people and equipment—and each process requires at most one resource of each type (In other words, each process requires one specific person and one specific piece of equipment.)

(d) The special case of the problem when each resource is requested by at most two processes.

5. Consider a set $A = \{a_1, \ldots, a_n\}$ and a collection $B_1, B_2, \ldots, B_m$ of subsets of $A$ (i.e., $B_i \subseteq A$ for each $i$).

We say that a set $H \subseteq A$ is a *hitting set* for the collection $B_1, B_2, \ldots, B_m$ if $H$ contains at least one element from each $B_i$—that is, if $H \cap B_i$ is not empty for each $i$ (so $H$ "hits" all the sets $B_i$).

We now define the *Hitting Set Problem* as follows. We are given a set $A = \{a_1, \ldots, a_n\}$, a collection $B_1, B_2, \ldots, B_m$ of subsets of $A$, and a number

$k$. We are asked: Is there a hitting set $H \subseteq A$ for $B_1, B_2, \ldots, B_m$ so that the size of $H$ is at most $k$?

   Prove that Hitting Set is NP-complete.

6. Consider an instance of the Satisfiability Problem, specified by clauses $C_1, \ldots, C_k$ over a set of Boolean variables $x_1, \ldots, x_n$. We say that the instance is *monotone* if each term in each clause consists of a nonnegated variable; that is, each term is equal to $x_i$, for some $i$, rather than $\overline{x_i}$. Monotone instances of Satisfiability are very easy to solve: They are always satisfiable, by setting each variable equal to 1.

   For example, suppose we have the three clauses

$$(x_1 \vee x_2), (x_1 \vee x_3), (x_2 \vee x_3).$$

   This is monotone, and indeed the assignment that sets all three variables to 1 satisfies all the clauses. But we can observe that this is not the only satisfying assignment; we could also have set $x_1$ and $x_2$ to 1, and $x_3$ to 0. Indeed, for any monotone instance, it is natural to ask how few variables we need to set to 1 in order to satisfy it.

   Given a monotone instance of Satisfiability, together with a number $k$, the problem of *Monotone Satisfiability with Few True Variables* asks: Is there a satisfying assignment for the instance in which at most $k$ variables are set to 1? Prove this problem is NP-complete.

7. Since the 3-Dimensional Matching Problem is NP-complete, it is natural to expect that the corresponding 4-Dimensional Matching Problem is at least as hard. Let us define *4-Dimensional Matching* as follows. Given sets $W, X, Y$, and $Z$, each of size $n$, and a collection $C$ of ordered 4-tuples of the form $(w_i, x_j, y_k, z_\ell)$, do there exist $n$ 4-tuples from $C$ so that no two have an element in common?

   Prove that 4-Dimensional Matching is NP-complete.

8. Your friends' preschool-age daughter Madison has recently learned to spell some simple words. To help encourage this, her parents got her a colorful set of refrigerator magnets featuring the letters of the alphabet (some number of copies of the letter $A$, some number of copies of the letter $B$, and so on), and the last time you saw her the two of you spent a while arranging the magnets to spell out words that she knows.

   Somehow with you and Madison, things always end up getting more elaborate than originally planned, and soon the two of you were trying to spell out words so as to use up all the magnets in the full set—that is, picking words that she knows how to spell, so that once they were all spelled out, each magnet was participating in the spelling of exactly one of the words. (Multiple copies of words are okay here; so for example, if the set of refrigerator magnets includes two copies each of *C*, *A*, and *T*, it would be okay to spell out *CAT* twice.)

This turned out to be pretty difficult, and it was only later that you realized a plausible reason for this. Suppose we consider a general version of the problem of *Using Up All the Refrigerator Magnets*, where we replace the English alphabet by an arbitrary collection of symbols, and we model Madison's vocabulary as an arbitrary set of strings over this collection of symbols. The goal is the same as in the previous paragraph.

Prove that the problem of Using Up All the Refrigerator Magnets is NP-complete.

9.  Consider the following problem. You are managing a communication network, modeled by a directed graph $G = (V, E)$. There are $c$ *users* who are interested in making use of this network. User $i$ (for each $i = 1, 2, \ldots, c$) issues a *request* to reserve a specific path $P_i$ in $G$ on which to transmit data.

You are interested in accepting as many of these path requests as possible, subject to the following restriction: if you accept both $P_i$ and $P_j$, then $P_i$ and $P_j$ cannot share any nodes.

Thus, the *Path Selection Problem* asks: Given a directed graph $G = (V, E)$, a set of requests $P_1, P_2, \ldots, P_c$—each of which must be a path in $G$—and a number $k$, is it possible to select at least $k$ of the paths so that no two of the selected paths share any nodes?

Prove that Path Selection is NP-complete.

10.  Your friends at WebExodus have recently been doing some consulting work for companies that maintain large, publicly accessible Web sites— contractual issues prevent them from saying which ones—and they've come across the following *Strategic Advertising Problem*.

A company comes to them with the map of a Web site, which we'll model as a directed graph $G = (V, E)$. The company also provides a set of $t$ *trails* typically followed by users of the site; we'll model these trails as directed paths $P_1, P_2, \ldots, P_t$ in the graph $G$ (i.e., each $P_i$ is a path in $G$).

The company wants WebExodus to answer the following question for them: Given $G$, the paths $\{P_i\}$, and a number $k$, is it possible to place advertisements on at most $k$ of the nodes in $G$, so that each path $P_i$ includes at least one node containing an advertisement? We'll call this the Strategic Advertising Problem, with input $G$, $\{P_i : i = 1, \ldots, t\}$, and $k$.

Your friends figure that a good algorithm for this will make them all rich; unfortunately, things are never quite this simple.

**(a)** Prove that Strategic Advertising is NP-complete.

**(b)** Your friends at WebExodus forge ahead and write a pretty fast algorithm $\mathcal{S}$ that produces yes/no answers to arbitrary instances of the Strategic Advertising Problem. You may assume that the algorithm $\mathcal{S}$ is always correct.

   Using the algorithm $\mathcal{S}$ as a black box, design an algorithm that takes input $G$, $\{P_i\}$, and $k$ as in part (a), and does one of the following two things:

   – Outputs a set of at most $k$ nodes in $G$ so that each path $P_i$ includes at least one of these nodes, *or*

   – Outputs (correctly) that no such set of at most $k$ nodes exists.

   Your algorithm should use at most a polynomial number of steps, together with at most a polynomial number of calls to the algorithm $\mathcal{S}$.

11. As some people remember, and many have been told, the idea of hypertext predates the World Wide Web by decades. Even hypertext fiction is a relatively old idea: Rather than being constrained by the linearity of the printed page, you can plot a story that consists of a collection of interlocked virtual "places" joined by virtual "passages."[4] So a piece of hypertext fiction is really riding on an underlying directed graph; to be concrete (though narrowing the full range of what the domain can do), we'll model this as follows.

   Let's view the structure of a piece of hypertext fiction as a directed graph $G = (V, E)$. Each node $u \in V$ contains some text; when the reader is currently at $u$, he or she can choose to follow any edge out of $u$; and if the reader chooses $e = (u, v)$, he or she arrives next at the node $v$. There is a start node $s \in V$ where the reader begins, and an end node $t \in V$; when the reader first reaches $t$, the story ends. Thus any path from $s$ to $t$ is a valid *plot* of the story. Note that, unlike one's experience using a Web browser, there is not necessarily a way to go back; once you've gone from $u$ to $v$, you might not be able to ever return to $u$.

   In this way, the hypertext structure defines a huge number of different plots on the same underlying content; and the relationships among all these possibilities can grow very intricate. Here's a type of problem one encounters when reasoning about a structure like this. Consider a piece of hypertext fiction built on a graph $G = (V, E)$ in which there are certain crucial *thematic elements*: love, death, war, an intense desire to major in computer science, and so forth. Each thematic element $i$ is represented by a set $T_i \subseteq V$ consisting of the nodes in $G$ at which this theme

---

[4] See, e.g., *http://www.eastgate.com*.

appears. Now, given a particular set of thematic elements, we may ask: Is there a valid plot of the story in which each of these elements is encountered? More concretely, given a directed graph $G$, with start node $s$ and end node $t$, and thematic elements represented by sets $T_1, T_2, \ldots, T_k$, the *Plot Fulfillment Problem* asks: Is there a path from $s$ to $t$ that contains at least one node from each of the sets $T_i$?

Prove that Plot Fulfillment is NP-complete.

12. Some friends of yours maintain a popular news and discussion site on the Web, and the traffic has reached a level where they want to begin differentiating their visitors into paying and nonpaying customers. A standard way to do this is to make all the content on the site available to customers who pay a monthly subscription fee; meanwhile, visitors who don't subscribe can still view a subset of the pages (all the while being bombarded with ads asking them to become subscribers).

Here are two simple ways to control access for nonsubscribers: You could (1) designate a fixed subset of pages as viewable by nonsubscribers, or (2) allow any page in principle to be viewable, but specify a maximum number of pages that can be viewed by a nonsubscriber in a single session. (We'll assume the site is able to track the path followed by a visitor through the site.)

Your friends are experimenting with a way of restricting access that is different from and more subtle than either of these two options. They want nonsubscribers to be able to sample different sections of the Web site, so they designate certain subsets of the pages as constituting particular *zones*—for example, there can be a zone for pages on politics, a zone for pages on music, and so forth. It's possible for a page to belong to more than one zone. Now, as a nonsubscribing user passes through the site, the access policy allows him or her to visit one page from each zone, but an attempt by the user to access a second page from the same zone later in the browsing session will be disallowed. (Instead, the user will be directed to an ad suggesting that he or she become a subscriber.)

More formally, we can model the site as a directed graph $G = (V, E)$, in which the nodes represent Web pages and the edges represent directed hyperlinks. There is a distinguished *entry node* $s \in V$, and there are *zones* $Z_1, \ldots, Z_k \subseteq V$. A path $P$ taken by a nonsubscriber is restricted to include at most one node from each zone $Z_i$.

One issue with this more complicated access policy is that it gets difficult to answer even basic questions about reachability, including: Is it possible for a nonsubscriber to visit a given node $t$? More precisely, we define the *Evasive Path Problem* as follows: Given $G, Z_1, \ldots, Z_k, s \in V$, and a *destination node* $t \in V$, is there an *s-t* path in $G$ that includes at most one node from each zone $Z_i$? Prove that Evasive Path is NP-complete.

13. A *combinatorial auction* is a particular mechanism developed by economists for selling a collection of items to a collection of potential buyers. (The Federal Communications Commission has studied this type of auction for assigning stations on the radio spectrum to broadcasting companies.)

    Here's a simple type of combinatorial auction. There are $n$ items for sale, labeled $I_1, \ldots, I_n$. Each item is indivisible and can only be sold to one person. Now, $m$ different people place *bids*: The $i^{\text{th}}$ bid specifies a subset $S_i$ of the items, and an *offering price* $x_i$ that the bidder is willing to pay for the items in the set $S_i$, as a single unit. (We'll represent this bid as the pair $(S_i, x_i)$.)

    An auctioneer now looks at the set of all $m$ bids; she chooses to *accept* some of these bids and to *reject* the others. Each person whose bid $i$ is accepted gets to take all the items in the corresponding set $S_i$. Thus the rule is that no two accepted bids can specify sets that contain a common item, since this would involve giving the same item to two different people.

    The auctioneer collects the sum of the offering prices of all accepted bids. (Note that this is a "one-shot" auction; there is no opportunity to place further bids.) The auctioneer's goal is to collect as much money as possible.

    Thus, the problem of *Winner Determination for Combinatorial Auctions* asks: Given items $I_1, \ldots, I_n$, bids $(S_1, x_1), \ldots, (S_m, x_m)$, and a bound $B$, is there a collection of bids that the auctioneer can accept so as to collect an amount of money that is at least $B$?

    **Example.** Suppose an auctioneer decides to use this method to sell some excess computer equipment. There are four items labeled "PC," "monitor," "printer", and "scanner"; and three people place bids. Define

    $$S_1 = \{\text{PC}, \text{monitor}\}, S_2 = \{\text{PC}, \text{printer}\}, S_3 = \{\text{monitor}, \text{printer}, \text{scanner}\}$$

    and

    $$x_1 = x_2 = x_3 = 1.$$

    The bids are $(S_1, x_1)$, $(S_2, x_2)$, $(S_3, x_3)$, and the bound $B$ is equal to 2.

    Then the answer to this instance is no: The auctioneer can accept at most one of the bids (since any two bids have a desired item in common), and this results in a total monetary value of only 1.

Prove that the problem of Winner Determination in Combinatorial Auctions is NP-complete.

14. We've seen the Interval Scheduling Problem in Chapters 1 and 4. Here we consider a computationally much harder version of it that we'll call *Multiple Interval Scheduling*. As before, you have a processor that is available to run jobs over some period of time (e.g., 9 A.M. to 5 P.M).

    People submit jobs to run on the processor; the processor can only work on one job at any single point in time. Jobs in this model, however, are more complicated than we've seen in the past: each job requires a *set* of intervals of time during which it needs to use the processor. Thus, for example, a single job could require the processor from 10 A.M. to 11 A.M., and again from 2 P.M. to 3 P.M.. If you accept this job, it ties up your processor during those two hours, but you could still accept jobs that need any other time periods (including the hours from 11 A.M. to 2 A.M.).

    Now you're given a set of $n$ jobs, each specified by a set of time intervals, and you want to answer the following question: For a given number $k$, is it possible to accept at least $k$ of the jobs so that no two of the accepted jobs have any overlap in time?

    Show that Multiple Interval Scheduling is NP-complete.

15. You're sitting at your desk one day when a FedEx package arrives for you. Inside is a cell phone that begins to ring, and you're not entirely surprised to discover that it's your friend Neo, whom you haven't heard from in quite a while. Conversations with Neo all seem to go the same way: He starts out with some big melodramatic justification for why he's calling, but in the end it always comes down to him trying to get you to volunteer your time to help with some problem he needs to solve.

    This time, for reasons he can't go into (something having to do with protecting an underground city from killer robot probes), he and a few associates need to monitor radio signals at various points on the electromagnetic spectrum. Specifically, there are $n$ different frequencies that need monitoring, and to do this they have available a collection of *sensors*.

    There are two components to the monitoring problem.

    - A set $L$ of $m$ geographic locations at which sensors can be placed; and
    - A set $S$ of $b$ *interference sources*, each of which blocks certain frequencies at certain locations. Specifically, each interference source $i$ is specified by a pair $(F_i, L_i)$, where $F_i$ is a subset of the frequencies and $L_i$ is a subset of the locations; it signifies that (due to radio inter-

ference) a sensor placed at any location in the set $L_i$ will not be able to receive signals on any frequency in the set $F_i$.

We say that a subset $L' \subseteq L$ of locations is *sufficient* if, for each of the $n$ frequencies $j$, there is some location in $L'$ where frequency $j$ is not blocked by any interference source. Thus, by placing a sensor at each location in a sufficient set, you can successfully monitor each of the $n$ frequencies.

They have $k$ sensors, and hence they want to know whether there is a sufficient set of locations of size at most $k$. We'll call this an instance of the *Nearby Electromagnetic Observation Problem*: Given frequencies, locations, interference sources, and a parameter $k$, is there a sufficient set of size at most $k$?

**Example.** Suppose we have four frequencies $\{f_1, f_2, f_3, f_4\}$ and four locations $\{\ell_1, \ell_2, \ell_3, \ell_4\}$. There are three interference sources, with

$$(F_1, L_1) = (\{f_1, f_2\}, \{\ell_1, \ell_2, \ell_3\})$$
$$(F_2, L_2) = (\{f_3, f_4\}, \{\ell_3, \ell_4\})$$
$$(F_3, L_3) = (\{f_2, f_3\}, \{\ell_1\})$$

Then there is a sufficient set of size 2: We can choose locations $\ell_2$ and $\ell_4$ (since $f_1$ and $f_2$ are not blocked at $\ell_4$, and $f_3$ and $f_4$ are not blocked at $\ell_2$).

Prove that Nearby Electromagnetic Observation is NP-complete.

16. Consider the problem of reasoning about the identity of a set from the size of its intersections with other sets. You are given a finite set $U$ of size $n$, and a collection $A_1, \ldots, A_m$ of subsets of $U$. You are also given numbers $c_1, \ldots, c_m$. The question is: Does there exist a set $X \subset U$ so that for each $i = 1, 2, \ldots, m$, the cardinality of $X \cap A_i$ is equal to $c_i$? We will call this an instance of the *Intersection Inference Problem*, with input $U$, $\{A_i\}$, and $\{c_i\}$.

    Prove that Intersection Inference is NP-complete.

17. You are given a directed graph $G = (V, E)$ with weights $w_e$ on its edges $e \in E$. The weights can be negative or positive. The *Zero-Weight-Cycle Problem* is to decide if there is a simple cycle in $G$ so that the sum of the edge weights on this cycle is exactly 0. Prove that this problem is NP-complete.

18. You've been asked to help some organizational theorists analyze data on group decision-making. In particular, they've been looking at a dataset that consists of decisions made by a particular governmental policy committee, and they're trying to decide whether it's possible to identify a small set of influential members of the committee.

    Here's how the committee works. It has a set $M = \{m_1, \ldots, m_n\}$ of $n$ members, and over the past year it's voted on $t$ different issues. On each issue, each member can vote either "Yes," "No," or "Abstain"; the overall effect is that the committee presents an affirmative decision on the issue if the number of "Yes" votes is strictly greater than the number of "No" votes (the "Abstain" votes don't count for either side), and it delivers a negative decision otherwise.

Now we have a big table consisting of the vote cast by each committee member on each issue, and we'd like to consider the following definition. We say that a subset of the members $M' \subseteq M$ is *decisive* if, had we looked just at the votes cast by the members in $M'$, the committee's decision on *every* issue would have been the same. (In other words, the overall outcome of the voting among the members in $M'$ is the same on every issue as the overall outcome of the voting by the entire committee.) Such a subset can be viewed as a kind of "inner circle" that reflects the behavior of the committee as a whole.

Here's the question: Given the votes cast by each member on each issue, and given a parameter $k$, we want to know whether there is a decisive subset consisting of at most $k$ members. We'll call this an instance of the *Decisive Subset Problem*.

**Example.** Suppose we have four committee members and three issues. We're looking for a decisive set of size at most $k = 2$, and the voting went as follows.

| Issue # | $m_1$ | $m_2$ | $m_3$ | $m_4$ |
|---------|---------|---------|---------|---------|
| Issue 1 | Yes | Yes | Abstain | No |
| Issue 2 | Abstain | No | No | Abstain |
| Issue 3 | Yes | Abstain | Yes | Yes |

Then the answer to this instance is "Yes," since members $m_1$ and $m_3$ constitute a decisive subset.

Prove that Decisive Subset is NP-complete.

19. Suppose you're acting as a consultant for the port authority of a small Pacific Rim nation. They're currently doing a multi-billion-dollar business per year, and their revenue is constrained almost entirely by the rate at which they can unload ships that arrive in the port.

Handling hazardous materials adds additional complexity to what is, for them, an already complicated task. Suppose a convoy of ships arrives in the morning and delivers a total of $n$ cannisters, each containing a different kind of hazardous material. Standing on the dock is a set of $m$ trucks, each of which can hold up to $k$ containers.

Here are two related problems, which arise from different types of constraints that might be placed on the handling of hazardous materials. For each of the two problems, give one of the following two answers:

- A polynomial-time algorithm to solve it; or
- A proof that it is NP-complete.

**(a)** For each cannister, there is a specified subset of the trucks in which it may be safely carried. Is there a way to load all $n$ cannisters into the $m$ trucks so that no truck is overloaded, and each container goes in a truck that is allowed to carry it?

**(b)** In this different version of the problem, any cannister can be placed in any truck; however, there are certain pairs of cannisters that cannot be placed together in the same truck. (The chemicals they contain may react explosively if brought into contact.) Is there a way to load all $n$ cannisters into the $m$ trucks so that no truck is overloaded, and no two cannisters are placed in the same truck when they are not supposed to be?

**20.** There are many different ways to formalize the intuitive problem of *clustering*, where the goal is to divide up a collection of objects into groups that are "similar" to one another.

First, a natural way to express the input to a clustering problem is via a set of objects $p_1, p_2, \ldots, p_n$, with a numerical distance $d(p_i, p_j)$ defined on each pair. (We require only that $d(p_i, p_i) = 0$; that $d(p_i, p_j) > 0$ for distinct $p_i$ and $p_j$; and that distances are symmetric: $d(p_i, p_j) = d(p_j, p_i)$.)

In Section 4.7, earlier in the book, we considered one reasonable formulation of the clustering problem: Divide the objects into $k$ sets so as to *maximize* the minimum distance between any pair of objects in distinct clusters. This turns out to be solvable by a nice application of the Minimum Spanning Tree Problem.

A different but seemingly related way to formalize the clustering problem would be as follows: Divide the objects into $k$ sets so as to *minimize* the maximum distance between any pair of objects in the same cluster. Note the change. Where the formulation in the previous paragraph sought clusters so that no two were "close together," this new formulation seeks clusters so that none of them is too "wide"—that is, no cluster contains two points at a large distance from each other.

Given the similarities, it's perhaps surprising that this new formulation is computationally hard to solve optimally. To be able to think about this in terms of NP-completeness, let's write it first as a yes/no decision problem. Given $n$ objects $p_1, p_2, \ldots, p_n$ with distances on them as above, and a bound $B$, we define the *Low-Diameter Clustering Problem* as follows: Can the objects be partitioned into $k$ sets, so that no two points in the same set are at a distance greater than $B$ from each other?

Prove that Low-Diameter Clustering is NP-complete.

21. After a few too many days immersed in the popular entrepreneurial self-help book *Mine Your Own Business*, you've come to the realization that you need to upgrade your office computing system. This, however, leads to some tricky problems.

In configuring your new system, there are $k$ *components* that must be selected: the operating system, the text editing software, the e-mail program, and so forth; each is a separate component. For the $j^{\text{th}}$ component of the system, you have a set $A_j$ of options; and a *configuration* of the system consists of a selection of one element from each of the sets of options $A_1, A_2, \ldots, A_k$.

Now the trouble arises because certain pairs of options from different sets may not be compatible. We say that option $x_i \in A_i$ and option $x_j \in A_j$ form an *incompatible pair* if a single system cannot contain them both. (For example, Linux (as an option for the operating system) and Microsoft Word (as an option for the text-editing software) form an incompatible pair.) We say that a configuration of the system is *fully compatible* if it consists of elements $x_1 \in A_1, x_2 \in A_2, \ldots x_k \in A_k$ such that none of the pairs $(x_i, x_j)$ is an incompatible pair.

We can now define the *Fully Compatible Configuration (FCC) Problem.* An instance of FCC consists of disjoint sets of options $A_1, A_2, \ldots, A_k$, and a set $P$ of *incompatible pairs* $(x, y)$, where $x$ and $y$ are elements of different sets of options. The problem is to decide whether there exists a fully compatible configuration: a selection of an element from each option set so that no pair of selected elements belongs to the set $P$.

**Example.** Suppose $k = 3$, and the sets $A_1, A_2, A_3$ denote options for the operating system, the text-editing software, and the e-mail program, respectively. We have

$$A_1 = \{\texttt{Linux}, \texttt{Windows NT}\},$$
$$A_2 = \{\texttt{emacs}, \texttt{Word}\},$$
$$A_3 = \{\texttt{Outlook}, \texttt{Eudora}, \texttt{rmail}\},$$

with the set of incompatible pairs equal to

$$P = \{(\texttt{Linux}, \texttt{Word}), (\texttt{Linux}, \texttt{Outlook}), (\texttt{Word}, \texttt{rmail})\}.$$

Then the answer to the decision problem in this instance of FCC is yes—for example, the choices Linux $\in A_1$, emacs $\in A_2$, rmail $\in A_3$ is a fully compatible configuration according to the definitions above.

Prove that Fully Compatible Configuration is NP-complete.

22. Suppose that someone gives you a black-box algorithm $A$ that takes an undirected graph $G = (V, E)$, and a number $k$, and behaves as follows.

    - If $G$ is not connected, it simply returns "$G$ is not connected."

    - If $G$ is connected and has an independent set of size at least $k$, it returns "yes."

    - If $G$ is connected and does not have an independent set of size at least $k$, it returns "no."

    Suppose that the algorithm $A$ runs in time polynomial in the size of $G$ and $k$.

    Show how, using calls to $A$, you could then solve the Independent Set Problem in polynomial time: Given an arbitrary undirected graph $G$, and a number $k$, does $G$ contain an independent set of size at least $k$?

23. Given a set of finite binary strings $S = \{s_1, \ldots, s_k\}$, we say that a string $u$ is a *concatenation* over $S$ if it is equal to $s_{i_1} s_{i_2} \cdots s_{i_t}$ for some indices $i_1, \ldots, i_t \in \{1, \ldots, k\}$.

    A friend of yours is considering the following problem: Given two sets of finite binary strings, $A = \{a_1, \ldots, a_m\}$ and $B = \{b_1, \ldots, b_n\}$, does there exist any string $u$ so that $u$ is both a concatenation over $A$ and a concatenation over $B$?

    Your friend announces, "At least the problem is in $\mathcal{NP}$, since I would just have to exhibit such a string $u$ in order to prove the answer is yes." You point out (politely, of course) that this is a completely inadequate explanation; how do we know that the shortest such string $u$ doesn't have length exponential in the size of the input, in which case it would not be a polynomial-size certificate?

    However, it turns out that this claim can be turned into a proof of membership in $\mathcal{NP}$. Specifically, prove the following statement.

    > *If there is a string $u$ that is a concatenation over both A and B, then there is such a string whose length is bounded by a polynomial in the sum of the lengths of the strings in $A \cup B$.*

24. Let $G = (V, E)$ be a bipartite graph; suppose its nodes are partitioned into sets $X$ and $Y$ so that each edge has one end in $X$ and the other in $Y$. We define an $(a, b)$-*skeleton* of $G$ to be a set of edges $E' \subseteq E$ so that *at most*

$a$ nodes in $X$ are incident to an edge in $E'$, and *at least* $b$ nodes in $Y$ are incident to an edge in $E'$.

Show that, given a bipartite graph $G$ and numbers $a$ and $b$, it is NP-complete to decide whether $G$ has an $(a, b)$-skeleton.

25. For functions $g_1, \ldots, g_\ell$, we define the function $\max(g_1, \ldots, g_\ell)$ via

$$[\max(g_1, \ldots, g_\ell)](x) = \max(g_1(x), \ldots, g_\ell(x)).$$

Consider the following problem. You are given $n$ piecewise linear, continuous functions $f_1, \ldots, f_n$ defined over the interval $[0, t]$ for some integer $t$. You are also given an integer $B$. You want to decide: Do there exist $k$ of the functions $f_{i_1}, \ldots, f_{i_k}$ so that

$$\int_0^t [\max(f_{i_1}, \ldots, f_{i_k})](x)\, dx \geq B?$$

Prove that this problem is NP-complete.

26. You and a friend have been trekking through various far-off parts of the world and have accumulated a big pile of souvenirs. At the time you weren't really thinking about which of these you were planning to keep and which your friend was going to keep, but now the time has come to divide everything up.

Here's a way you could go about doing this. Suppose there are $n$ objects, labeled $1, 2, \ldots, n$, and object $i$ has an agreed-upon *value* $x_i$. (We could think of this, for example, as a monetary resale value; the case in which you and your friend don't agree on the value is something we won't pursue here.) One reasonable way to divide things would be to look for a *partition* of the objects into two sets, so that the total value of the objects in each set is the same.

This suggests solving the following *Number Partitioning Problem*. You are given positive integers $x_1, \ldots, x_n$; you want to decide whether the numbers can be partitioned into two sets $S_1$ and $S_2$ with the same sum:

$$\sum_{x_i \in S_1} x_i = \sum_{x_j \in S_2} x_j.$$

Show that Number Partitioning is NP-complete.

27. Consider the following problem. You are given positive integers $x_1, \ldots, x_n$, and numbers $k$ and $B$. You want to know whether it is possible to *partition*

the numbers $\{x_i\}$ into $k$ sets $S_1, \ldots, S_k$ so that the squared sums of the sets add up to at most $B$:

$$\sum_{i=1}^{k} \left( \sum_{x_j \in S_i} x_j \right)^2 \leq B.$$

Show that this problem is NP-complete.

28. The following is a version of the Independent Set Problem. You are given a graph $G = (V, E)$ and an integer $k$. For this problem, we will call a set $I \subset V$ *strongly independent* if, for any two nodes $v, u \in I$, the edge $(v, u)$ does not belong to $E$, and there is also no path of two edges from $u$ to $v$, that is, there is no node $w$ such that both $(u, w) \in E$ and $(w, v) \in E$. The Strongly Independent Set Problem is to decide whether $G$ has a strongly independent set of size at least $k$.

   Prove that the Strongly Independent Set Problem is NP-complete.

29. You're configuring a large network of workstations, which we'll model as an undirected graph $G$; the nodes of $G$ represent individual workstations and the edges represent direct communication links. The workstations all need access to a common *core database*, which contains data necessary for basic operating system functions.

   You could replicate this database on each workstation; this would make lookups very fast from any workstation, but you'd have to manage a huge number of copies. Alternately, you could keep a single copy of the database on one workstation and have the remaining workstations issue requests for data over the network $G$; but this could result in large delays for a workstation that's many hops away from the site of the database.

   So you decide to look for the following compromise: You want to maintain a small number of copies, but place them so that any workstation either has a copy of the database or is connected by a direct link to a workstation that has a copy of the database. In graph terminology, such a set of locations is called a *dominating set*.

   Thus we phrase the *Dominating Set Problem* as follows. Given the network $G$, and a number $k$, is there a way to place $k$ copies of the database at $k$ different nodes so that every node either has a copy of the database or is connected by a direct link to a node that has a copy of the database?

   Show that Dominating Set is NP-complete.

30. One thing that's not always apparent when thinking about traditional "continuous math" problems is the way discrete, combinatorial issues

of the kind we're studying here can creep into what look like standard calculus questions.

Consider, for example, the traditional problem of minimizing a one-variable function like $f(x) = 3 + x - 3x^2$ over an interval like $x \in [0, 1]$. The derivative has a zero at $x = 1/6$, but this in fact is a maximum of the function, not a minimum; to get the minimum, one has to heed the standard warning to check the values on the boundary of the interval as well. (The minimum is in fact achieved on the boundary, at $x = 1$.)

Checking the boundary isn't such a problem when you have a function in one variable; but suppose we're now dealing with the problem of minimizing a function in $n$ variables $x_1, x_2, \ldots, x_n$ over the unit cube, where each of $x_1, x_2, \ldots, x_n \in [0, 1]$. The minimum may be achieved on the interior of the cube, but it may be achieved on the boundary; and this latter prospect is rather daunting, since the boundary consists of $2^n$ "corners" (where each $x_i$ is equal to either 0 or 1) as well as various pieces of other dimensions. Calculus books tend to get suspiciously vague around here, when trying to describe how to handle multivariable minimization problems in the face of this complexity.

It turns out there's a reason for this: Minimizing an $n$-variable function over the unit cube in $n$ dimensions is as hard as an NP-complete problem. To make this concrete, let's consider the special case of polynomials with integer coefficients over $n$ variables $x_1, x_2, \ldots, x_n$. To review some terminology, we say a *monomial* is a product of a real-number coefficient $c$ and each variable $x_i$ raised to some nonnegative integer power $a_i$; we can write this as $cx_1^{a_1}x_2^{a_2}\cdots x_n^{a_n}$. (For example, $2x_1^2x_2x_3^4$ is a monomial.) A *polynomial* is then a sum of a finite set of monomials. (For example, $2x_1^2x_2x_3^4 + x_1x_3 - 6x_2^2x_3^2$ is a polynomial.)

We define the *Multivariable Polynomial Minimization Problem* as follows: Given a polynomial in $n$ variables with integer coefficients, and given an integer bound $B$, is there a choice of real numbers $x_1, x_2, \ldots, x_n \in [0, 1]$ that causes the polynomial to achieve a value that is $\leq B$?

Choose a problem $Y$ from this chapter that is known to be NP-complete and show that

$$Y \leq_P \text{Multivariable Polynomial Minimization.}$$

31. Given an undirected graph $G = (V, E)$, a *feedback set* is a set $X \subseteq V$ with the property that $G - X$ has no cycles. The *Undirected Feedback Set Problem* asks: Given $G$ and $k$, does $G$ contain a feedback set of size at most $k$? Prove that Undirected Feedback Set is NP-complete.

**32.** The mapping of genomes involves a large array of difficult computational problems. At the most basic level, each of an organism's chromosomes can be viewed as an extremely long string (generally containing millions of symbols) over the four-letter alphabet $\{A, C, G, T\}$. One family of approaches to genome mapping is to generate a large number of short, overlapping snippets from a chromosome, and then to infer the full long string representing the chromosome from this set of overlapping substrings.

While we won't go into these string assembly problems in full detail, here's a simplified problem that suggests some of the computational difficulty one encounters in this area. Suppose we have a set $S = \{s_1, s_2, \ldots, s_n\}$ of short DNA strings over a $q$-letter alphabet; and each string $s_i$ has length $2\ell$, for some number $\ell \geq 1$. We also have a library of additional strings $T = \{t_1, t_2, \ldots, t_m\}$ over the same alphabet; each of these also has length $2\ell$. In trying to assess whether the string $s_b$ might come directly after the string $s_a$ in the chromosome, we will look to see whether the library $T$ contains a string $t_k$ so that the first $\ell$ symbols in $t_k$ are equal to the last $\ell$ symbols in $s_a$, and the last $\ell$ symbols in $t_k$ are equal to the first $\ell$ symbols in $s_b$. If this is possible, we will say that $t_k$ *corroborates* the pair $(s_a, s_b)$. (In other words, $t_k$ could be a snippet of DNA that straddled the region in which $s_b$ directly followed $s_a$.)

Now we'd like to concatenate all the strings in $S$ in some order, one after the other with no overlaps, so that each consecutive pair is corroborated by some string in the library $T$. That is, we'd like to order the strings in $S$ as $s_{i_1}, s_{i_2}, \ldots, s_{i_n}$, where $i_1, i_2, \ldots, i_n$ is a permutation of $\{1, 2, \ldots, n\}$, so that for each $j = 1, 2, \ldots, n-1$, there is a string $t_k$ that corroborates the pair $(s_{i_j}, s_{i_{j+1}})$. (The same string $t_k$ can be used for more than one consecutive pair in the concatenation.) If this is possible, we will say that the set $S$ has a *perfect assembly*.

Given sets $S$ and $T$, the *Perfect Assembly Problem* asks: Does $S$ have a perfect assembly with respect to $T$? Prove that Perfect Assembly is NP-complete.

**Example.** Suppose the alphabet is $\{A, C, G, T\}$, the set $S = \{AG, TC, TA\}$, and the set $T = \{AC, CA, GC, GT\}$ (so each string has length $2\ell = 2$). Then the answer to this instance of Perfect Assembly is yes: We can concatenate the three strings in $S$ in the order $TCAGTA$ (so $s_{i_1} = s_2, s_{i_2} = s_1,$ and $s_{i_3} = s_3$). In this order, the pair $(s_{i_1}, s_{i_2})$ is corroborated by the string $CA$ in the library $T$, and the pair $(s_{i_2}, s_{i_3})$ is corroborated by the string $GT$ in the library $T$.

**33.** In a barter economy, people trade goods and services directly, without money as an intermediate step in the process. Trades happen when each party views the set of goods they're getting as more valuable than the set of goods they're giving in return. Historically, societies tend to move from barter-based to money-based economies; thus various online systems that have been experimenting with barter can be viewed as intentional attempts to regress to this earlier form of economic interaction. In doing this, they've rediscovered some of the inherent difficulties with barter relative to money-based systems. One such difficulty is the complexity of identifying opportunities for trading, even when these opportunities exist.

To model this complexity, we need a notion that each person assigns a *value* to each object in the world, indicating how much this object would be worth to them. Thus we assume there is a set of $n$ people $p_1, \ldots, p_n$, and a set of $m$ distinct objects $a_1, \ldots, a_m$. Each object is owned by one of the people. Now each person $p_i$ has a *valuation function* $v_i$, defined so that $v_i(a_j)$ is a nonnegative number that specifies how much object $a_j$ is worth to $p_i$—the larger the number, the more valuable the object is to the person. Note that everyone assigns a valuation to each object, including the ones they don't currently possess, and different people can assign very different valuations to the same object.

A two-person trade is possible in a system like this when there are people $p_i$ and $p_j$, and subsets of objects $A_i$ and $A_j$ possessed by $p_i$ and $p_j$, respectively, so that each person would prefer the objects in the subset they don't currently have. More precisely,

- $p_i$'s total valuation for the objects in $A_j$ exceeds his or her total valuation for the objects in $A_i$, and

- $p_j$'s total valuation for the objects in $A_i$ exceeds his or her total valuation for the objects in $A_j$.

(Note that $A_i$ doesn't have to be *all* the objects possessed by $p_i$ (and likewise for $A_j$); $A_i$ and $A_j$ can be arbitrary subsets of their possessions that meet these criteria.)

Suppose you are given an instance of a barter economy, specified by the above data on people's valuations for objects. (To prevent problems with representing real numbers, we'll assume that each person's valuation for each object is a natural number.) Prove that the problem of determining whether a two-person trade is possible is NP-complete.

34. In the 1970s, researchers including Mark Granovetter and Thomas Schelling in the mathematical social sciences began trying to develop models of certain kinds of collective human behaviors: Why do particular fads catch on while others die out? Why do particular technological innovations achieve widespread adoption, while others remain focused

on a small group of users? What are the dynamics by which rioting and looting behavior sometimes (but only rarely) emerges from a crowd of angry people? They proposed that these are all examples of *cascade processes*, in which an individual's behavior is highly influenced by the behaviors of his or her friends, and so if a few individuals instigate the process, it can spread to more and more people and eventually have a very wide impact. We can think of this process as being like the spread of an illness, or a rumor, jumping from person to person.

The most basic version of their models is the following. There is some underlying *behavior* (e.g., playing ice hockey, owning a cell phone, taking part in a riot), and at any point in time each person is either an *adopter* of the behavior or a *nonadopter*. We represent the population by a directed graph $G = (V, E)$ in which the nodes correspond to people and there is an edge $(v, w)$ if person $v$ has influence over the behavior of person $w$: If person $v$ adopts the behavior, then this helps induce person $w$ to adopt it as well. Each person $w$ also has a given *threshold* $\theta(w) \in [0, 1]$, and this has the following meaning: At any time when at least a $\theta(w)$ fraction of the nodes with edges to $w$ are adopters of the behavior, the node $w$ will become an adopter as well.

Note that nodes with lower thresholds are more easily convinced to adopt the behavior, while nodes with higher thresholds are more conservative. A node $w$ with threshold $\theta(w) = 0$ will adopt the behavior immediately, with no inducement from friends. Finally, we need a convention about nodes with no incoming edges: We will say that they become adopters if $\theta(w) = 0$, and cannot become adopters if they have any larger threshold.

Given an instance of this model, we can simulate the spread of the behavior as follows.

```
Initially, set all nodes w with θ(w) = 0 to be adopters
    (All other nodes start out as nonadopters)
Until there is no change in the set of adopters:
    For each nonadopter w simultaneously:
        If at least a θ(w) fraction of nodes with edges to w are
            adopters then
                w becomes an adopter
        Endif
    Endfor
End
Output the final set of adopters
```

Note that this process terminates, since there are only $n$ individuals total, and at least one new person becomes an adopter in each iteration.

Now, in the last few years, researchers in marketing and data mining have looked at how a model like this could be used to investigate "word-of-mouth" effects in the success of new products (the so-called *viral marketing* phenomenon). The idea here is that the behavior we're concerned with is the use of a new product; we may be able to convince a few key people in the population to try out this product, and hope to trigger as large a cascade as possible.

Concretely, suppose we choose a set of nodes $S \subseteq V$ and we reset the threshold of each node in $S$ to 0. (By convincing them to try the product, we've ensured that they're adopters.) We then run the process described above, and see how large the final set of adopters is. Let's denote the size of this final set of adopters by $f(S)$ (note that we write it as a function of $S$, since it naturally depends on our choice of $S$). We could think of $f(S)$ as the *influence* of the set $S$, since it captures how widely the behavior spreads when "seeded" at $S$.

The goal, if we're marketing a product, is to find a small set $S$ whose influence $f(S)$ is as large as possible. We thus define the *Influence Maximization Problem* as follows: Given a directed graph $G = (V, E)$, with a threshold value at each node, and parameters $k$ and $b$, is there a set $S$ of at most $k$ nodes for which $f(S) \geq b$?

Prove that Influence Maximization is NP-complete.

**Example.** Suppose our graph $G = (V, E)$ has five nodes $\{a, b, c, d, e\}$, four edges $(a, b), (b, c), (e, d), (d, c)$, and all node thresholds equal to $2/3$. Then the answer to the Influence Maximization instance defined by $G$, with $k = 2$ and $b = 5$, is yes: We can choose $S = \{a, e\}$, and this will cause the other three nodes to become adopters as well. (This is the only choice of $S$ that will work here. For example, if we choose $S = \{a, d\}$, then $b$ and $c$ will become adopters, but $e$ won't; if we choose $S = \{a, b\}$, then none of $c$, $d$, or $e$ will become adopters.)

35. Three of your friends work for a large computer-game company, and they've been working hard for several months now to get their proposal for a new game, *Droid Trader!*, approved by higher management. In the process, they've had to endure all sorts of discouraging comments, ranging from "You're really going to have to work with Marketing on the name" to "Why don't you emphasize the parts where people get to kick each other in the head?"

    At this point, though, it's all but certain that the game is really heading into production, and your friends come to you with one final issue that's been worrying them: What if the overall premise of the game is too simple, so that players get really good at it and become bored too quickly?

It takes you a while, listening to their detailed description of the game, to figure out what's going on; but once you strip away the space battles, kick-boxing interludes, and Stars-Wars-inspired pseudo-mysticism, the basic idea is as follows. A player in the game controls a spaceship and is trying to make money buying and selling droids on different planets. There are $n$ different types of droids and $k$ different planets. Each planet $p$ has the following properties: there are $s(j, p) \geq 0$ droids of type $j$ available for sale, at a fixed price of $x(j, p) \geq 0$ each, for $j = 1, 2, \ldots, n$; and there is a demand for $d(j, p) \geq 0$ droids of type $j$, at a fixed price of $y(j, p) \geq 0$ each. (We will assume that a planet does not simultaneously have both a positive supply and a positive demand for a single type of droid; so for each $j$, at least one of $s(j, p)$ or $d(j, p)$ is equal to 0.)

The player begins on planet $s$ with $z$ units of money and must end at planet $t$; there is a directed acyclic graph $G$ on the set of planets, such that $s$-$t$ paths in $G$ correspond to valid routes by the player. ($G$ is chosen to be acyclic to prevent arbitrarily long games.) For a given $s$-$t$ path $P$ in $G$, the player can engage in transactions as follows. Whenever the player arrives at a planet $p$ on the path $P$, she can buy up to $s(j, p)$ droids of type $j$ for $x(j, p)$ units of money each (provided she has sufficient money on hand) and/or sell up to $d(j, p)$ droids of type $j$ for $y(j, p)$ units of money each (for $j = 1, 2, \ldots, n$). The player's *final score* is the total amount of money she has on hand when she arrives at planet $t$. (There are also bonus points based on space battles and kick-boxing, which we'll ignore for the purposes of formulating this question.)

So basically, the underlying problem is to achieve a high score. In other words, given an instance of this game, with a directed acyclic graph $G$ on a set of planets, all the other parameters described above, and also a target bound $B$, is there a path $P$ in $G$ and a sequence of transactions on $P$ so that the player ends with a final score that is at least $B$? We'll call this an instance of the *High-Score-on-Droid-Trader! Problem*, or HSoDT! for short.

Prove that HSoDT! is NP-complete, thereby guaranteeing (assuming $P \neq NP$) that there isn't a simple strategy for racking up high scores on your friends' game.

36. Sometimes you can know people for years and never really understand them. Take your friends Raj and Alanis, for example. Neither of them is a morning person, but now they're getting up at 6 AM every day to visit

local farmers' markets, gathering fresh fruits and vegetables for the new health-food restaurant they've opened, Chez Alanisse.

In the course of trying to save money on ingredients, they've come across the following thorny problem. There is a large set of $n$ possible raw ingredients they could buy, $I_1, I_2, \ldots, I_n$ (e.g., bundles of dandelion greens, jugs of rice vinegar, and so forth). Ingredient $I_j$ must be purchased in units of size $s(j)$ grams (any purchase must be for a whole number of units), and it costs $c(j)$ dollars per unit. Also, it remains safe to use for $t(j)$ days from the date of purchase.

Now, over the next $k$ days, they want to make a set of $k$ different daily specials, one each day. (The order in which they schedule the specials is up to them.) The $i^{\text{th}}$ daily special uses a subset $S_i \subseteq \{I_1, I_2, \ldots, I_n\}$ of the raw ingredients. Specifically, it requires $a(i, j)$ grams of ingredient $I_j$. And there's a final constraint: The restaurant's rabidly loyal customer base only remains rabidly loyal if they're being served the freshest meals available; so for each daily special, the ingredients $S_i$ are partitioned into two subsets: those that must be purchased on the very day when the daily special is being offered, and those that can be used any day while they're still safe. (For example, the mesclun-basil salad special needs to be made with basil that has been purchased that day; but the arugula-basil pesto with Cornell dairy goat cheese special can use basil that is several days old, as long as it is still safe.)

This is where the opportunity to save money on ingredients comes up. Often, when they buy a unit of a certain ingredient $I_j$, they don't need the whole thing for the special they're making that day. Thus, if they can follow up quickly with another special that uses $I_j$ but doesn't require it to be fresh that day, then they can save money by not having to purchase $I_j$ again. Of course, scheduling the basil recipes close together may make it harder to schedule the goat cheese recipes close together, and so forth—this is where the complexity comes in.

So we define the *Daily Special Scheduling Problem* as follows: Given data on ingredients and recipes as above, and a budget $x$, is there a way to schedule the $k$ daily specials so that the total money spent on ingredients over the course of all $k$ days is at most $x$?

Prove that *Daily Special Scheduling* is NP-complete.

37. There are those who insist that the initial working title for Episode XXVII of the Star Wars series was "$\mathcal{P} = \mathcal{NP}$"—but this is surely apocryphal. In any case, if you're so inclined, it's easy to find NP-complete problems lurking just below the surface of the original *Star Wars* movies.

Consider the problem faced by Luke, Leia, and friends as they tried to make their way from the Death Star back to the hidden Rebel base. We can view the galaxy as an undirected graph $G = (V, E)$, where each node is a star system and an edge $(u, v)$ indicates that one can travel directly from $u$ to $v$. The Death Star is represented by a node $s$, the hidden Rebel base by a node $t$. Certain edges in this graph represent longer distances than others; thus each edge $e$ has an integer *length* $\ell_e \geq 0$. Also, certain edges represent routes that are more heavily patrolled by evil Imperial spacecraft; so each edge $e$ also has an integer *risk* $r_e \geq 0$, indicating the expected amount of damage incurred from special-effects-intensive space battles if one traverses this edge.

It would be safest to travel through the outer rim of the galaxy, from one quiet upstate star system to another; but then one's ship would run out of fuel long before getting to its destination. Alternately, it would be quickest to plunge through the cosmopolitan core of the galaxy; but then there would be far too many Imperial spacecraft to deal with. In general, for any path $P$ from $s$ to $t$, we can define its *total length* to be the sum of the lengths of all its edges; and we can define its *total risk* to be the sum of the risks of all its edges.

So Luke, Leia, and company are looking at a complex type of shortest-path problem in this graph: they need to get from $s$ to $t$ along a path whose total length and total risk are *both* reasonably small. In concrete terms, we can phrase the *Galactic Shortest-Path Problem* as follows: Given a setup as above, and integer bounds $L$ and $R$, is there a path from $s$ to $t$ whose total length is at most $L$, *and* whose total risk is at most $R$?

Prove that Galactic Shortest Path is NP-complete.

38. Consider the following version of the Steiner Tree Problem, which we'll refer to as *Graphical Steiner Tree*. You are given an undirected graph $G = (V, E)$, a set $X \subseteq V$ of vertices, and a number $k$. You want to decide whether there is a set $F \subseteq E$ of at most $k$ edges so that in the graph $(V, F)$, $X$ belongs to a single connected component.

    Show that Graphical Steiner Tree is NP-complete.

39. The *Directed Disjoint Paths Problem* is defined as follows. We are given a directed graph $G$ and $k$ pairs of nodes $(s_1, t_1), (s_2, t_2), \ldots, (s_k, t_k)$. The problem is to decide whether there exist node-disjoint paths $P_1, P_2, \ldots, P_k$ so that $P_i$ goes from $s_i$ to $t_i$.

    Show that Directed Disjoint Paths is NP-complete.

40. Consider the following problem that arises in the design of broadcasting schemes for networks. We are given a directed graph $G = (V, E)$, with a

designated node $r \in V$ and a designated set of "target nodes" $T \subseteq V - \{r\}$. Each node $v$ has a *switching time* $s_v$, which is a positive integer.

At time 0, the node $r$ generates a message that it would like every node in $T$ to receive. To accomplish this, we want to find a scheme whereby $r$ tells some of its neighbors (in sequence), who in turn tell some of their neighbors, and so on, until every node in $T$ has received the message. More formally, a *broadcast scheme* is defined as follows. Node $r$ may send a copy of the message to one of its neighbors at time 0; this neighbor will receive the message at time 1. In general, at time $t \geq 0$, any node $v$ that has already received the message may send a copy of the message to one of its neighbors, provided it has not sent a copy of the message in any of the time steps $t - s_v + 1, t - s_v + 2, \ldots, t - 1$. (This reflects the role of the *switching time*; $v$ needs a pause of $s_v - 1$ steps between successive sendings of the message. Note that if $s_v = 1$, then no restriction is imposed by this.)

The *completion time* of the broadcast scheme is the minimum time $t$ by which all nodes in $T$ have received the message. The *Broadcast Time Problem* is the following: Given the input described above, and a bound $b$, is there a broadcast scheme with completion time at most $b$?

Prove that Broadcast Time is NP-complete.

**Example.** Suppose we have a directed graph $G = (V, E)$, with $V = \{r, a, b, c\}$; edges $(r, a)$, $(a, b)$, $(r, c)$; the set $T = \{b, c\}$; and switching time $s_v = 2$ for each $v \in V$. Then a broadcast scheme with minimum completion time would be as follows: $r$ sends the message to $a$ at time 0; $a$ sends the message to $b$ at time 1; $r$ sends the message to $c$ at time 2; and the scheme completes at time 3 when $c$ receives the message. (Note that $a$ can send the message as soon as it receives it at time 1, since this is its first sending of the message; but $r$ cannot send the message at time 1 since $s_r = 2$ and it sent the message at time 0.)

41. Given a directed graph $G$, a *cycle cover* is a set of node-disjoint cycles so that each node of $G$ belongs to a cycle. The *Cycle Cover Problem* asks whether a given directed graph has a cycle cover.

    (a)   Show that the Cycle Cover Problem can be solved in polynomial time. (*Hint:* Use Bipartite Matching.)

    (b)   Suppose we require each cycle to have at most three edges. Show that determining whether a graph $G$ has such a cycle cover is NP-complete.

42. Suppose you're consulting for a company in northern New Jersey that designs communication networks, and they come to you with the follow-

ing problem. They're studying a specific $n$-node communication network, modeled as a directed graph $G = (V, E)$. For reasons of fault tolerance, they want to divide up $G$ into as many virtual "domains" as possible: A *domain* in $G$ is a set $X$ of nodes, of size at least 2, so that for each pair of nodes $u, v \in X$ there are directed paths from $u$ to $v$ and $v$ to $u$ that are contained entirely in $X$.

Show that the following *Domain Decomposition Problem* is NP-complete. Given a directed graph $G = (V, E)$ and a number $k$, can $V$ be *partitioned* into at least $k$ sets, each of which is a domain?

## Notes and Further Reading

In the notes to Chapter 2, we described some of the early work on formalizing computational efficiency using polynomial time; NP-completeness evolved out of this work and grew into its central role in computer science following the papers of Cook (1971), Levin (1973), and Karp (1972). Edmonds (1965) is credited with drawing particular attention to the class of problems in $\mathcal{NP} \cap$ co-$\mathcal{NP}$—those with "good characterizations." His paper also contains the explicit conjecture that the Traveling Salesman Problem cannot be solved in polynomial time, thereby prefiguring the $P \neq NP$ question. Sipser (1992) is a useful guide to all of this historical context.

The book by Garey and Johnson (1979) provides extensive material on NP-completeness and concludes with a very useful catalog of known NP-complete problems. While this catalog, necessarily, only covers what was known at the time of the book's publication, it is still a very useful reference when one encounters a new problem that looks like it might be NP-complete. In the meantime, the space of known NP-complete problems has continued to expand dramatically; as Christos Papadimitriou said in a lecture, "Roughly 6,000 papers every year contain an NP-completeness result. That means another NP-complete problem has been discovered since lunch." (His lecture was at 2:00 in the afternoon.)

One can interpret NP-completeness as saying that each individual NP-complete problem contains the entire complexity of NP hidden inside it. A concrete reflection of this is the fact that several of the NP-complete problems we discuss here are the subject of entire books: the Traveling Salesman is the subject of Lawler et al. (1985); Graph Coloring is the subject of Jensen and Toft (1995); and the Knapsack Problem is the subject of Martello and Toth (1990). NP-completeness results for scheduling problems are discussed in the survey by Lawler et al. (1993).

***Notes on the Exercises***     A number of the exercises illustrate further problems that emerged as paradigmatic examples early in the development of NP-completeness; these include Exercises 5, 26, 29, 31, 38, 39, 40, and 41. Exercise 33 is based on discussions with Daniel Golovin, and Exercise 34 is based on our work with David Kempe. Exercise 37 is an example of the class of *Bicriteria Shortest-Path problems*; its motivating application here was suggested by Maverick Woo.

# Chapter 9

## PSPACE: A Class of Problems beyond NP

Throughout the book, one of the main issues has been the notion of *time* as a computational resource. It was this notion that formed the basis for adopting *polynomial time* as our working definition of efficiency; and, implicitly, it underlies the distinction between $\mathcal{P}$ and $\mathcal{NP}$. To some extent, we have also been concerned with the *space* (i.e., memory) requirements of algorithms. In this chapter, we investigate a class of problems defined by treating space as the fundamental computational resource. In the process, we develop a natural class of problems that appear to be even harder than $\mathcal{NP}$ and co-$\mathcal{NP}$.

### 9.1 PSPACE

The basic class we study is PSPACE, the set of all problems that can be solved by an algorithm with polynomial space complexity—that is, an algorithm that uses an amount of *space* that is polynomial in the size of the input.

We begin by considering the relationship of PSPACE to classes of problems we have considered earlier. First of all, in polynomial time, an algorithm can consume only a polynomial amount of space; so we can say

**(9.1)** $\mathcal{P} \subseteq PSPACE$.

But PSPACE is much broader than this. Consider, for example, an algorithm that just counts from 0 to $2^n - 1$ in base-2 notation. It simply needs to implement an $n$-bit counter, which it maintains in exactly the same way one increments an odometer in a car. Thus this algorithm runs for an exponential amount of time, and then halts; in the process, it has used only a polynomial amount of space. Although this algorithm is not doing anything particularly interesting, it illustrates an important principle: Space can be reused during a computation in ways that time, by definition, cannot.

Here is a more striking application of this principle.

> **(9.2)** *There is an algorithm that solves 3-SAT using only a polynomial amount of space.*

**Proof.** We simply use a brute-force algorithm that tries all possible truth assignments; each assignment is plugged into the set of clauses to see if it satisfies them. The key is to implement this all in polynomial space.

To do this, we increment an $n$-bit counter from 0 to $2^n - 1$ just as described above. The values in the counter correspond to truth assignments in the following way: When the counter holds a value $q$, we interpret it as a truth assignment $v$ that sets $x_i$ to be the value of the $i^{\text{th}}$ bit of $q$.

Thus we devote a polynomial amount of space to enumerating all possible truth assignments $v$. For each truth assignment, we need only polynomial space to plug it into the set of clauses and see if it satisfies them. If it does satisfy the clauses, we can stop the algorithm immediately. If it doesn't, we delete the intermediate work involved in this "plugging in" operation and *reuse* this space for the next truth assignment. Thus we spend only polynomial space cumulatively in checking all truth assignments; this completes the bound on the algorithm's space requirements. ∎

Since 3-SAT is an NP-complete problem, (9.2) has a significant consequence.

> **(9.3)** $\mathcal{NP} \subseteq PSPACE$.

**Proof.** Consider an arbitrary problem $Y$ in $\mathcal{NP}$. Since $Y \leq_p$ 3-SAT, there is an algorithm that solves $Y$ using a polynomial number of steps plus a polynomial number of calls to a black box for 3-SAT. Using the algorithm in (9.2) to implement this black box, we obtain an algorithm for $Y$ that uses only polynomial space. ∎

Just as with the class $\mathcal{P}$, a problem $X$ is in PSPACE if and only if its complementary problem $\overline{X}$ is in PSPACE as well. Thus we can conclude that co-$\mathcal{NP} \subseteq$ PSPACE. We draw what is known about the relationships among these classes of problems in Figure 9.1.

Given that PSPACE is an enormously large class of problems, containing both $\mathcal{NP}$ and co-$\mathcal{NP}$, it is very likely that it contains problems that cannot be solved in polynomial time. But despite this widespread belief, amazingly

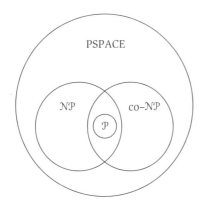

**Figure 9.1** The subset relationships among various classes of problems. Note that we don't know how to prove the conjecture that all of these classes are different from one another.

it has not been proven that $\mathcal{P} \neq$ PSPACE. Nevertheless, the nearly universal conjecture is that PSPACE contains problems that are not even in $\mathcal{NP}$ or co-$\mathcal{NP}$.

## 9.2 Some Hard Problems in PSPACE

We now survey some natural examples of problems in PSPACE that are not known—and not believed—to belong to $\mathcal{NP}$ or co-$\mathcal{NP}$.

As was the case with $\mathcal{NP}$, we can try understanding the structure of PSPACE by looking for *complete problems*—the hardest problems in the class. We will say that a problem $X$ is PSPACE-*complete* if (i) it belongs to PSPACE; and (ii) for all problems $Y$ in PSPACE, we have $Y \leq_P X$.

It turns out, analogously to the case of $\mathcal{NP}$, that a wide range of natural problems are PSPACE-complete. Indeed, a number of the basic problems in artificial intelligence are PSPACE-complete, and we describe three genres of these here.

### Planning

*Planning problems* seek to capture, in a clean way, the task of interacting with a complex environment to achieve a desired set of goals. Canonical applications include large logistical operations that require the movement of people, equipment, and materials. For example, as part of coordinating a disaster-relief effort, we might decide that twenty ambulances are needed at a particular high-altitude location. Before this can be accomplished, we need to get ten snowplows to clear the road; this in turn requires emergency fuel and snowplow crews; but if we use the fuel for the snowplows, then we may not have enough for the ambulances; and . . . you get the idea. Military operations also require such reasoning on an enormous scale, and automated planning techniques from artificial intelligence have been used to great effect in this domain as well.

One can see very similar issues at work in complex solitaire games such as Rubik's Cube or the *fifteen-puzzle*—a $4 \times 4$ grid with fifteen movable tiles labeled $1, 2, \ldots, 15$, and a single *hole*, with the goal of moving the tiles around so that the numbers end up in ascending order. (Rather than ambulances and snowplows, we now are worried about things like getting the tile labeled 6 one position to the left, which involves getting the 11 out of the way; but that involves moving the 9, which was actually in a good position; and so on.) These toy problems can be quite tricky and are often used in artificial intelligence as a test-bed for planning algorithms.

Having said all this, how should we define the problem of planning in a way that's general enough to include each of these examples? Both solitaire puzzles and disaster-relief efforts have a number of abstract features in common: There are a number of *conditions* we are trying to achieve and a set of allowable *operators* that we can apply to achieve these conditions. Thus we model the environment by a set $\mathcal{C} = \{C_1, \ldots, C_n\}$ of *conditions*: A given state of the world is specified by the subset of the conditions that currently hold. We interact with the environment through a set $\{\mathcal{O}_1, \ldots, \mathcal{O}_k\}$ of *operators*. Each operator $\mathcal{O}_i$ is specified by a *prerequisite list*, containing a set of conditions that must hold for $\mathcal{O}_i$ to be invoked; an *add list*, containing a set of conditions that will become true after $\mathcal{O}_i$ is invoked; and a *delete list*, containing a set of conditions that will cease to hold after $\mathcal{O}_i$ is invoked. For example, we could model the fifteen-puzzle by having a condition for each possible location of each tile, and an operator to move each tile between each pair of adjacent locations; the prerequisite for an operator is that its two locations contain the designated tile and the hole.

The problem we face is the following: Given a set $\mathcal{C}_0$ of *initial conditions*, and a set $\mathcal{C}^*$ of *goal conditions*, is it possible to apply a sequence of operators beginning with $\mathcal{C}_0$ so that we reach a situation in which precisely the conditions in $\mathcal{C}^*$ (and no others) hold? We will call this an instance of the *Planning Problem*.

## Quantification

We have seen, in the 3-SAT problem, some of the difficulty in determining whether a set of disjunctive clauses can be simultaneously satisfied. When we add quantifiers, the problem appears to become even more difficult.

Let $\Phi(x_1, \ldots, x_n)$ be a Boolean formula of the form

$$C_1 \wedge C_2 \wedge \cdots \wedge C_k,$$

where each $C_i$ is a disjunction of three terms (in other words, it is an instance of 3-SAT). Assume for simplicity that $n$ is an odd number, and suppose we ask

$$\exists x_1 \forall x_2 \cdots \exists x_{n-2} \forall x_{n-1} \exists x_n \Phi(x_1, \ldots, x_n)?$$

That is, we wish to know whether there is a choice for $x_1$, so that for both choices of $x_2$, there is a choice for $x_3$, and so on, so that $\Phi$ is satisfied. We will refer to this decision problem as *Quantified 3-SAT* (or, briefly, QSAT).

The original 3-SAT problem, by way of comparison, simply asked

$$\exists x_1 \exists x_2 \cdots \exists x_{n-2} \exists x_{n-1} \exists x_n \Phi(x_1, \ldots, x_n)?$$

In other words, in 3-SAT it was sufficient to look for a single setting of the Boolean variables.

Here's an example to illustrate the kind of reasoning that underlies an instance of QSAT. Suppose that we have the formula

$$\Phi(x_1, x_2, x_3) = (x_1 \vee x_2 \vee x_3) \wedge (x_1 \vee x_2 \vee \overline{x_3}) \wedge (\overline{x_1} \vee x_2 \vee x_3) \wedge (\overline{x_1} \vee \overline{x_2} \vee \overline{x_3})$$

and we ask

$$\exists x_1 \forall x_2 \exists x_3 \Phi(x_1, x_2, x_3)?$$

The answer to this question is yes: We can set $x_1$ so that for both choices of $x_2$, there is a way to set $x_3$ so that $\Phi$ is satisfied. Specifically, we can set $x_1 = 1$; then if $x_2$ is set to 1, we can set $x_3$ to 0 (satisfying all clauses); and if $x_2$ is set to 0, we can set $x_3$ to 1 (again satisfying all clauses).

Problems of this type, with a sequence of quantifiers, arise naturally as a form of *contingency planning*—we wish to know whether there is a decision we can make (the choice of $x_1$) so that for all possible responses (the choice of $x_2$) there is a decision we can make (the choice of $x_3$), and so forth.

## Games

In 1996 and 1997, world chess champion Garry Kasparov was billed by the media as the defender of the human race, as he faced IBM's program Deep Blue in two chess matches. We needn't look further than this picture to convince ourselves that computational game-playing is one of the most visible successes of contemporary artificial intelligence.

A large number of two-player games fit naturally into the following framework. Players alternate moves, and the first one to achieve a specific goal wins. (For example, depending on the game, the goal could be capturing the king, removing all the opponent's checkers, placing four pieces in a row, and so on.) Moreover, there is often a natural, polynomial, upper bound on the maximum possible length of a game.

The Competitive Facility Location Problem that we introduced in Chapter 1 fits naturally within this framework. (It also illustrates the way in which games can arise not just as pastimes, but through competitive situations in everyday life.) Recall that in Competitive Facility Location, we are given a graph $G$, with a nonnegative *value* $b_i$ attached to each node $i$. Two players alternately select nodes of $G$, so that the set of selected nodes at all times forms an independent set. Player 2 wins if she ultimately selects a set of nodes of total value at least $B$, for a given bound $B$; Player 1 wins if he prevents this from happening. The question is: Given the graph $G$ and the bound $B$, is there a strategy by which Player 2 can force a win?

## 9.3 Solving Quantified Problems and Games in Polynomial Space

We now discuss how to solve all of these problems in polynomial space. As we will see, this will be trickier—in one case, a lot trickier—than the (simple) task we faced in showing that problems like 3-SAT and Independent Set belong to $\mathcal{NP}$.

We begin here with QSAT and Competitive Facility Location, and then consider Planning in the next section.

### Designing an Algorithm for QSAT

First let's show that QSAT can be solved in polynomial space. As was the case with 3-SAT, the idea will be to run a brute-force algorithm that reuses space carefully as the computation proceeds.

Here is the basic brute-force approach. To deal with the first quantifier $\exists x_1$, we consider both possible values for $x_1$ in sequence. We first set $x_1 = 0$ and see, recursively, whether the remaining portion of the formula evaluates to 1. We then set $x_1 = 1$ and see, recursively, whether the remaining portion of the formula evaluates to 1. The full formula evaluates to 1 if and only if *either* of these recursive calls yields a 1—that's simply the definition of the $\exists$ quantifier.

This is essentially a divide-and-conquer algorithm, which, given an input with $n$ variables, spawns two recursive calls on inputs with $n - 1$ variables each. If we were to save all the work done in both these recursive calls, our space usage $S(n)$ would satisfy the recurrence

$$S(n) \leq 2S(n - 1) + p(n),$$

where $p(n)$ is a polynomial function. This would result in an exponential bound, which is too large.

Fortunately, we can perform a simple optimization that greatly reduces the space usage. When we're done with the case $x_1 = 0$, all we really need to save is the single bit that represents the outcome of the recursive call; we can throw away all the other intermediate work. This is another example of "reuse"—we're reusing the space from the computation for $x_1 = 0$ in order to compute the case $x_1 = 1$.

Here is a compact description of the algorithm.

```
If the first quantifier is ∃ x_i then
    Set x_i = 0 and recursively evaluate the quantified expression
                    over the remaining variables
    Save the result (0 or 1) and delete all other intermediate work
    Set x_i = 1 and recursively evaluate the quantified expression
                    over the remaining variables
    If either outcome yielded an evaluation of 1, then
        return 1
    Else return 0
    Endif
If the first quantifier is ∀ x_i then
    Set x_i = 0 and recursively evaluate the quantified expression
                    over the remaining variables
    Save the result (0 or 1) and delete all other intermediate work
    Set x_i = 1 and recursively evaluate the quantified expression
                    over the remaining variables
    If both outcomes yielded an evaluation of 1, then
        return 1
    Else return 0
    Endif
Endif
```

### Analyzing the Algorithm

Since the recursive calls for the cases $x_1 = 0$ and $x_1 = 1$ overwrite the same space, our space requirement $S(n)$ for an $n$-variable problem is simply a polynomial in $n$ plus the space requirement for one recursive call on an $(n-1)$-variable problem:

$$S(n) \leq S(n-1) + p(n),$$

where again $p(n)$ is a polynomial function. Unrolling this recurrence, we get

$$S(n) \leq p(n) + p(n-1) + p(n-2) + \cdots + p(1) \leq n \cdot p(n).$$

Since $p(n)$ is a polynomial, so is $n \cdot p(n)$, and hence our space usage is polynomial in $n$, as desired.

In summary, we have shown the following.

**(9.4)**   *QSAT can be solved in polynomial space.*

### Extensions: An Algorithm for Competitive Facility Location

We can determine which player has a forced win in a game such as Competitive Facility Location by a very similar type of algorithm.

Suppose Player 1 moves first. We consider all of his possible moves in sequence. For each of these moves, we see who has a forced win in the resulting game, with Player 2 moving first. If Player 1 has a forced win in any of them, then Player 1 has a forced win from the initial position. The crucial point, as in the QSAT algorithm, is that we can reuse the space from one candidate move to the next; we need only store the single bit representing the outcome. In this way, we only consume a polynomial amount of space plus the space requirement for one recursive call on a graph with fewer nodes. As in the case of QSAT, we get the recurrence

$$S(n) \le S(n-1) + p(n)$$

for a polynomial $p(n)$.

In summary, we have shown the following.

**(9.5)**   *Competitive Facility Location can be solved in polynomial space.*

## 9.4 Solving the Planning Problem in Polynomial Space

Now we consider how to solve the basic Planning Problem in polynomial space. The issues here will look quite different, and it will turn out to be a much more difficult task.

### The Problem

Recall that we have a set of *conditions* $\mathcal{C} = \{C_1, \ldots, C_n\}$ and a set of *operators* $\{\mathcal{O}_1, \ldots, \mathcal{O}_k\}$. Each operator $\mathcal{O}_i$ has a *prerequisite list* $P_i$, an *add list* $A_i$, and a *delete list* $D_i$. Note that $\mathcal{O}_i$ can still be applied even if conditions other than those in $P_i$ are present; and it does not affect conditions that are not in $A_i$ or $D_i$.

We define a *configuration* to be a subset $\mathcal{C}' \subseteq \mathcal{C}$; the state of the Planning Problem at any given time can be identified with a unique configuration $\mathcal{C}'$

consisting precisely of the conditions that hold at that time. For an initial configuration $\mathcal{C}_0$ and a goal configuration $\mathcal{C}^*$, we wish to determine whether there is a sequence of operators that will take us from $\mathcal{C}_0$ to $\mathcal{C}^*$.

We can view our Planning instance in terms of a giant, implicitly defined, directed graph $\mathcal{G}$. There is a node of $\mathcal{G}$ for each of the $2^n$ possible configurations (i.e., each possible subset of $\mathcal{C}$); and there is an edge of $\mathcal{G}$ from configuration $\mathcal{C}'$ to configuration $\mathcal{C}''$ if, in one step, one of the operators can convert $\mathcal{C}'$ to $\mathcal{C}''$. In terms of this graph, the Planning Problem has a very natural formulation: Is there a path in $\mathcal{G}$ from $\mathcal{C}_0$ to $\mathcal{C}^*$? Such a path corresponds precisely to a sequence of operators leading from $\mathcal{C}_0$ to $\mathcal{C}^*$.

It's possible for a Planning instance to have a short solution (as in the example of the fifteen-puzzle), but this need not hold in general. That is, there need not always be a short path in $\mathcal{G}$ from $\mathcal{C}_0$ to $\mathcal{C}^*$. This should not be so surprising, since $\mathcal{G}$ has an exponential number of nodes. But we must be careful in applying this intuition, since $\mathcal{G}$ has a special structure: It is defined very compactly in terms of the $n$ conditions and $k$ operators.

**(9.6)** *There are instances of the Planning Problem with $n$ conditions and $k$ operators for which there exists a solution, but the shortest solution has length $2^n - 1$.*

**Proof.** We give a simple example of such an instance; it essentially encodes the task of incrementing an $n$-bit counter from the all-zeros state to the all-ones state.

- We have conditions $C_1, C_2, \ldots, C_n$.
- We have operators $\mathcal{O}_i$ for $i = 1, 2, \ldots, n$.
- $\mathcal{O}_1$ has no prerequisites or delete list; it simply adds $C_1$.
- For $i > 1$, $\mathcal{O}_i$ requires $C_j$ for all $j < i$ as prerequisites. When invoked, it adds $C_i$ and deletes $C_j$ for all $j < i$.

Now we ask: Is there a sequence of operators that will take us from $\mathcal{C}_0 = \phi$ to $\mathcal{C}^* = \{C_1, C_2, \ldots, C_n\}$?

We claim the following, by induction on $i$:

*From any configuration that does not contain $C_j$ for any $j \leq i$, there exists a sequence of operators that reaches a configuration containing $C_j$ for all $j \leq i$; but any such sequence has at least $2^i - 1$ steps.*

This is clearly true for $i = 1$. For larger $i$, here's one solution.

- By induction, achieve conditions $\{C_{i-1}, \ldots, C_1\}$ using operators $\mathcal{O}_1, \ldots, \mathcal{O}_{i-1}$.
- Now invoke operator $\mathcal{O}_i$, adding $C_i$ but deleting everything else.

- Again, by induction, achieve conditions $\{C_{i-1}, \ldots, C_1\}$ using operators $\mathcal{O}_1, \ldots, \mathcal{O}_{i-1}$. Note that condition $C_i$ is preserved throughout this process.

Now we take care of the other part of the inductive step—that *any* such sequence requires at least $2^i - 1$ steps. So consider the first moment when $C_i$ is added. At this step, $C_{i-1}, \ldots, C_1$ must have been present, and by induction, this must have taken at least $2^{i-1} - 1$ steps. $C_i$ can only be added by $\mathcal{O}_i$, which deletes all $C_j$ for $j < i$. Now we have to achieve conditions $\{C_{i-1}, \ldots, C_1\}$ again; this will take another $2^{i-1} - 1$ steps, by induction, for a total of at least $2(2^{i-1} - 1) + 1 = 2^i - 1$ steps.

The overall bound now follows by applying this claim with $i = n$.  ∎

Of course, if every "yes" instance of Planning had a polynomial-length solution, then Planning would be in $\mathcal{NP}$—we could just exhibit the solution. But (9.6) shows that the shortest solution is not necessarily a good certificate for a Planning instance, since it can have a length that is exponential in the input size.

However, (9.6) describes essentially the worst case, for we have the following matching upper bound. The graph $\mathcal{G}$ has $2^n$ nodes, and if there is a path from $\mathcal{C}_0$ to $\mathcal{C}^*$, then the shortest such path does not visit any node more than once. As a result, the shortest path can take at most $2^n - 1$ steps after leaving $\mathcal{C}_0$.

**(9.7)**    *If a Planning instance with n conditions has a solution, then it has one using at most $2^n - 1$ steps.*

## Designing the Algorithm

We've seen that the shortest solution to the Planning Problem may have length exponential in $n$, which is bad news: After all, this means that in polynomial space, we can't even store an explicit representation of the solution. But this fact doesn't necessarily close out our hopes of solving an arbitrary instance of Planning using only polynomial space. It's possible that there could be an algorithm that decides the answer to an instance of Planning without ever being able to survey the entire solution at once.

In fact, we now show that this is the case: we design an algorithm to solve Planning in polynomial space.

***Some Exponential Approaches***    To get some intuition about this problem, we first consider the following brute-force algorithm to solve the Planning instance. We build the graph $\mathcal{G}$ and use any graph connectivity algorithm—depth-first search or breadth-first search—to decide whether there is a path from $\mathcal{C}_0$ to $\mathcal{C}^*$.

Of course, this algorithm is too brute-force for our purposes; it takes exponential space just to construct the graph $\mathcal{G}$. We could try an approach in which we never actually build $\mathcal{G}$, and just simulate the behavior of depth-first search or breadth-first search on it. But this likewise is not feasible. Depth-first search crucially requires us to maintain a list of all the nodes in the current path we are exploring, and this can grow to exponential size. Breadth-first requires a list of all nodes in the current "frontier" of the search, and this too can grow to exponential size.

We seem stuck. Our problem is transparently equivalent to finding a path in $\mathcal{G}$, and all the standard path-finding algorithms we know are too lavish in their use of space. Could there really be a fundamentally different path-finding algorithm out there?

***A More Space-Efficient Way to Construct Paths***    In fact, there is a fundamentally different kind of path-finding algorithm, and it has just the properties we need. The basic idea, proposed by Savitch in 1970, is a clever use of the divide-and-conquer principle. It subsequently inspired the trick for reducing the space requirements in the Sequence Alignment Problem; so the overall approach may remind you of what we discussed there, in Section 6.7. Our plan, as before, is to find a clever way to reuse space, admittedly at the expense of increasing the time spent. Neither depth-first search nor breadth-first search is nearly aggressive enough in its reuse of space; both need to maintain a large history at all times. We need a way to solve half the problem, throw away almost all the intermediate work, and then solve the other half of the problem.

The key is a procedure that we will call $\mathtt{Path}(\mathcal{C}_1, \mathcal{C}_2, L)$. It determines whether there is a sequence of operators, *consisting of at most L steps*, that leads from configuration $\mathcal{C}_1$ to configuration $\mathcal{C}_2$. So our initial problem is to determine the result (yes or no) of $\mathtt{Path}(\mathcal{C}_0, \mathcal{C}^*, 2^n)$. Breadth-first search can be viewed as the following dynamic programming implementation of this procedure: To determine $\mathtt{Path}(\mathcal{C}_1, \mathcal{C}_2, L)$, we first determine all $\mathcal{C}'$ for which $\mathtt{Path}(\mathcal{C}_1, \mathcal{C}', L-1)$ holds; we then see, for each such $\mathcal{C}'$, whether any operator leads directly from $\mathcal{C}'$ to $\mathcal{C}_2$.

This indicates some of the wastefulness, in terms of space, that breadth-first search entails. We are generating a huge number of intermediate configurations just to reduce the parameter $L$ by one. More effective would be to try determining whether there is any configuration $\mathcal{C}'$ that could serve as the *midpoint* of a path from $\mathcal{C}_1$ to $\mathcal{C}_2$. We could first generate all possible midpoints $\mathcal{C}'$. For each $\mathcal{C}'$, we then check recursively whether we can get from $\mathcal{C}_1$ to $\mathcal{C}'$ in at most $L/2$ steps; and also whether we can get from $\mathcal{C}'$ to $\mathcal{C}_2$ in at most $L/2$ steps. This involves two recursive calls, but we care only about the yes/no outcome of each; other than this, we can reuse space from one to the next.

Does this really reduce the space usage to a polynomial amount? We first write down the procedure carefully, and then analyze it. We will think of $L$ as a power of 2, which it is for our purposes.

```
Path(C₁, C₂, L)
  If  L = 1 then
      If there is an operator O converting C₁ to C₂ then
         return ''yes''
      Else
         return ''no''
      Endif
  Else  (L > 1)
      Enumerate all configurations C' using an n-bit counter
      For each C' do the following:
         Compute x  =   Path(C₁, C', ⌈L/2⌉)
         Delete all intermediate work, saving only the return value x
         Compute y  =   Path(C', C₂, ⌈L/2⌉)
         Delete all intermediate work, saving only the return value y
         If both x and y are equal to ''yes'', then return ''yes''
      Endfor
      If ''yes'' was not returned for any C' then
         Return ''no''
      Endif
  Endif
```

Again, note that this procedure solves a generalization of our original question, which simply asked for $\texttt{Path}(C_0, C^*, 2^n)$. This does mean, however, that we should remember to view $L$ as an exponentially large parameter: $\log L = n$.

### 🖊 Analyzing the Algorithm

The following claim therefore implies that Planning can be solved in polynomial space.

> **(9.8)**   $\texttt{Path}(C_1, C_2, L)$ *returns "yes" if and only if there is a sequence of operators of length at most L leading from $C_1$ to $C_2$. Its space usage is polynomial in n, k, and* $\log L$.

**Proof.** The correctness follows by induction on $L$. It clearly holds when $L = 1$, since all operators are considered explicitly. Now consider a larger value of $L$. If there is a sequence of operators from $C_1$ to $C_2$, of length $L' \leq L$, then there is a configuration $C'$ that occurs at position $\lceil L'/2 \rceil$ in this sequence. By induction, $\text{Path}(\mathcal{C}_1, \mathcal{C}', \lceil L/2 \rceil)$ and $\text{Path}(\mathcal{C}', \mathcal{C}_2, \lceil L/2 \rceil)$ will both return "yes," and so $\text{Path}(\mathcal{C}_1, \mathcal{C}_2, L)$ will return "yes." Conversely, if there is a configuration $\mathcal{C}'$ so that $\text{Path}(\mathcal{C}_1, \mathcal{C}', \lceil L/2 \rceil)$ and $\text{Path}(\mathcal{C}', \mathcal{C}_2, \lceil L/2 \rceil)$ both return "yes," then the induction hypothesis implies that there exist corresponding sequences of operators; concatenating these two sequences, we obtain a sequence of operators from $\mathcal{C}_1$ to $\mathcal{C}_2$ of length at most $L$.

Now we consider the space requirements. Aside from the space spent inside recursive calls, each invocation of Path involves an amount of space polynomial in $n$, $k$, and $\log L$. But at any given point in time, only a single recursive call is active, and the intermediate work from all other recursive calls has been deleted. Thus, for a polynomial function $p$, the space requirement $S(n, k, L)$ satisfies the recurrence

$$S(n, k, L) \leq p(n, k, \log L) + S(n, k, \lceil L/2 \rceil).$$
$$S(n, k, 1) \leq p(n, k, 1).$$

Unwinding the recurrence for $O(\log L)$ levels, we obtain the bound $S(n, k, L) = O(\log L \cdot p(n, k, \log L))$, which is a polynomial in $n$, $k$, and $\log L$. ∎

If dynamic programming has an opposite, this is it. Back when we were solving problems by dynamic programming, the fundamental principle was to save all the intermediate work, so you don't have to recompute it. Now that conserving space is our goal, we have just the opposite priorities: throw away all the intermediate work, since it's just taking up space and it can always be recomputed.

As we saw when we designed the space-efficient Sequence Alignment Algorithm, the best strategy often lies somewhere in between, motivated by these two approaches: throw away some of the intermediate work, but not so much that you blow up the running time.

## 9.5 Proving Problems PSPACE-Complete

When we studied $\mathcal{NP}$, we had to prove a *first* problem NP-complete directly from the definition of $\mathcal{NP}$. After Cook and Levin did this for Satisfiability, many other NP-complete problems could follow by reduction.

A similar sequence of events followed for PSPACE, shortly after the results for $\mathcal{NP}$. Recall that we defined PSPACE-completeness, by direct analogy with NP-completeness, in Section 9.1. The natural analogue of Circuit Satisfiability and 3-SAT for PSPACE is played by QSAT, and Stockmeyer and Meyer (1973) proved

**(9.9)** *QSAT is PSPACE-complete.*

This basic PSPACE-complete problem can then serve as a good "root" from which to discover other PSPACE-complete problems. By strict analogy with the case of $\mathcal{NP}$, it's easy to see from the definition that if a problem $Y$ is PSPACE-complete, and a problem $X$ in PSPACE has the property that $Y \leq_P X$, then $X$ is PSPACE-complete as well.

Our goal in this section is to show an example of such a PSPACE-completeness proof, for the case of the Competitive Facility Location Problem; we will do this by reducing QSAT to Competitive Facility Location. In addition to establishing the hardness of Competitive Facility Location, the reduction also gives a sense for how one goes about showing PSPACE-completeness results for games in general, based on their close relationship to quantifiers.

We note that Planning can also be shown to be PSPACE-complete by a reduction from QSAT, but we will not go through that proof here.

### Relating Quantifiers and Games

It is actually not surprising at all that there should be a close relation between quantifiers and games. Indeed, we could have equivalently defined QSAT as the problem of deciding whether the first player has a forced win in the following *Competitive 3-SAT* game. Suppose we fix a formula $\Phi(x_1, \ldots, x_n)$ consisting, as in QSAT, of a conjunction of length-3 clauses. Two players alternate turns picking values for variables: the first player picks the value of $x_1$, then the second player picks the value of $x_2$, then the first player picks the value of $x_3$, and so on. We will say that the first player wins if $\Phi(x_1, \ldots, x_n)$ ends up evaluating to 1, and the second player wins if it ends up evaluating to 0.

When does the first player have a forced win in this game (i.e., when does our instance of Competitive 3-SAT have a yes answer)? Precisely when there is a choice for $x_1$ so that for all choices of $x_2$ there is a choice for $x_3$ so that . . . and so on, resulting in $\Phi(x_1, \ldots, x_n)$ evaluating to 1. That is, the first player has a forced win if and only if (assuming $n$ is an odd number)

$$\exists x_1 \forall x_2 \cdots \exists x_{n-2} \forall x_{n-1} \exists x_n \Phi(x_1, \ldots, x_n).$$

In other words, our Competitive 3-SAT game is directly equivalent to the instance of QSAT defined by the same Boolean formula $\Phi$, and so we have proved the following.

**(9.10)**    *QSAT $\leq_P$ Competitive 3-SAT and Competitive 3-SAT $\leq_P$ QSAT.*

### Proving Competitive Facility Location is PSPACE-Complete

Statement (9.10) moves us into the world of games. We use this connection to establish the PSPACE-completeness of Competitive Facility Location.

**(9.11)**  *Competitive Facility Location is PSPACE-complete.*

**Proof.** We have already shown that Competitive Facility Location is in PSPACE. To prove it is PSPACE-complete, we now show that Competitive 3-SAT $\leq_P$ Competitive Facility Location. Combined with the fact that QSAT $\leq_P$ Competitive 3-SAT, this will show that QSAT $\leq_P$ Competitive Facility Location and hence will establish the PSPACE-completeness result.

We are given an instance of Competitive 3-SAT, defined by a formula $\Phi$. $\Phi$ is the conjunction of clauses

$$C_1 \wedge C_2 \wedge \cdots \wedge C_k;$$

each $C_j$ has length 3 and can be written $C_j = t_{j1} \vee t_{j2} \vee t_{j3}$. As before, we will assume that there is an odd number $n$ of variables. We will also assume, quite naturally, that no clause contains both a term and its negation; after all, such a clause would be automatically satisfied by any truth assignment. We must show how to encode this Boolean structure in the graph that underlies Competitive Facility Location.

We can picture the instance of Competitive 3-SAT as follows. The players alternately select values in a truth assignment, beginning and ending with Player 1; at the end, Player 2 has won if she can select a clause $C_j$ in which none of the terms has been set to 1. Player 1 has won if Player 2 cannot do this.

It is this notion that we would like to encode in an instance of Competitive Facility Location: that the players alternately make a fixed number of moves, in a highly constrained fashion, and then there's a final chance by Player 2 to win the whole thing. But in its general form, Competitive Facility Location looks much more wide-open than this. Whereas the players in Competitive 3-SAT must set one variable at a time, in order, the players in Competitive Facility Location can jump all over the graph, choosing nodes wherever they want.

Our fundamental trick, then, will be to use the values $b_i$ on the nodes to tightly constrain where the players can move, under any "reasonable" strategy. In other words, we will set things up so that if the either of the players deviates from a particular narrow course, he or she will lose instantly.

As with our more complicated NP-completeness reductions in Chapter 8, the construction will have gadgets to represent assignments to the variables, and further gadgets to represent the clauses. Here is how we encode the variables. For each variable $x_i$, we define two nodes $v_i, v_i'$ in the graph $G$, and include an edge $(v_i, v_i')$, as in Figure 9.2. Selecting $v_i$ will represent setting $x_i = 1$; selecting $v_i'$ will represent $x_i = 0$. The constraint that the chosen variables

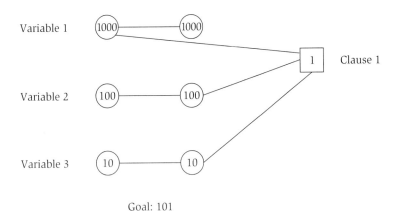

Goal: 101

**Figure 9.2** The reduction from Competitive 3-SAT to Competitive Facility Location.

must form an independent set naturally prevents both $v_i$ and $v_i'$ from being chosen. At this point, we do not define any other edges.

How do we get the players to set the variables in order—first $x_1$, then $x_2$, and so forth? We place values on $v_1$ and $v_1'$ so high that Player 1 will lose instantly if he does not choose them. We place somewhat lower values on $v_2$ and $v_2'$, and continue in this way. Specifically, for a value $c \geq k + 2$, we define the node values $b_{v_i}$ and $b_{v_i'}$ to be $c^{1+n-i}$. We define the bound that Player 2 is trying to achieve to be

$$B = c^{n-1} + c^{n-3} + \cdots + c^2 + 1.$$

Let's pause, before worrying about the clauses, to consider the game played on this graph. In the opening move of the game, Player 1 must select one of $v_1$ or $v_1'$ (thereby obliterating the other one); for if not, then Player 2 will immediately select one of them on her next move, winning instantly. Similarly, in the second move of the game, Player 2 must select one of $v_2$ or $v_2'$. For otherwise, Player 1 will select one on his next move; and then, even if Player 2 acquired all the remaining nodes in the graph, she would not be able to meet the bound $B$. Continuing by induction in this way, we see that to avoid an immediate loss, the player making the $i^{\text{th}}$ move must select one of $v_i$ or $v_i'$. Note that our choice of node values has achieved precisely what we wanted: The players must set the variables in order. And what is the outcome on this graph? Player 2 ends up with a total of value of $c^{n-1} + c^{n-3} + \cdots + c^2 = B - 1$: she has lost by one unit!

We now complete the analogy with Competitive 3-SAT by giving Player 2 one final move on which she can try to win. For each clause $C_j$, we define a node $c_j$ with value $b_{c_j} = 1$ and an edge associated with each of its terms as follows. If $t = x_i$, we add an edge $(c_j, v_i)$; if $t = \overline{x_i}$, we add an edge $(c_j, v_i')$. In other words, we join $c_j$ to the node that represents the term $t$.

This now defines the full graph $G$. We can verify that, because their values are so small, the addition of the clause nodes did not change the property that the players will begin by selecting the variable nodes $\{v_i, v_i'\}$ in the correct order. However, after this is done, Player 2 will win if and only if she can select a clause node $c_j$ that is not adjacent to any selected variable node—in other words, if and only the truth assignment defined alternately by the players failed to satisfy some clause.

Thus Player 2 can win the Competitive Facility Location instance we have defined if and only if she can win the original Competitive 3-SAT instance. The reduction is complete. ■

# Solved Exercises

## Solved Exercise 1

*Self-avoiding walks* are a basic object of study in the area of statistical physics; they can be defined as follows. Let $\mathcal{L}$ denote the set of all points in $\mathbf{R}^2$ with integer coordinates. (We can think of these as the "grid points" of the plane.) A *self-avoiding walk* $W$ of length $n$ is a sequence of points $(p_1, p_2, \ldots, p_n)$ drawn from $\mathcal{L}$ so that

  (i) $p_1 = (0, 0)$. *(The walk starts at the origin.)*
 (ii) No two of the points are equal. *(The walk "avoids" itself.)*
(iii) For each $i = 1, 2, \ldots, n - 1$, the points $p_i$ and $p_{i+1}$ are at distance 1 from each other. *(The walk moves between neighboring points in $\mathcal{L}$.)*

Self-avoiding walks (in both two and three dimensions) are used in physical chemistry as a simple geometric model for the possible conformations of long-chain polymer molecules. Such molecules can be viewed as a flexible chain of beads that flops around, adopting different geometric layouts; self-avoiding walks are a simple combinatorial abstraction for these layouts.

A famous unsolved problem in this area is the following. For a natural number $n \geq 1$, let $A(n)$ denote the number of distinct self-avoiding walks of length $n$. Note that we view walks as *sequences* of points rather than sets; so two walks can be distinct even if they pass through the same set of points, provided that they do so in different orders. (Formally, the walks $(p_1, p_2, \ldots, p_n)$ and $(q_1, q_2, \ldots, q_n)$ are distinct if there is some $i$ ($1 \leq i \leq n$) for which $p_i \neq q_i$.) See Figure 9.3 for an example. In polymer models based on self-avoiding walks, $A(n)$ is directly related to the *entropy* of a chain molecule,

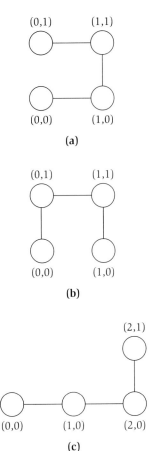

**Figure 9.3** Three distinct self-avoiding walks of length 4. Note that although walks (a) and (b) involve the same set of points, they are considered different walks because they pass through them in a different order.

and so it appears in theories concerning the rates of certain metabolic and organic synthesis reactions.

Despite its importance, no simple formula is known for the value $A(n)$. Indeed, no algorithm is known for computing $A(n)$ that runs in time polynomial in $n$.

(a) Show that $A(n) \geq 2^{n-1}$ for all natural numbers $n \geq 1$.

(b) Give an algorithm that takes a number $n$ as input, and outputs $A(n)$ as a number in binary notation, using space (i.e., memory) that is polynomial in $n$.

(Thus the running time of your algorithm can be exponential, as long as its space usage is polynomial. Note also that *polynomial* here means "polynomial in $n$," not "polynomial in $\log n$." Indeed, by part (a), we see that it will take at least $n - 1$ bits to write the value of $A(n)$, so clearly $n - 1$ is a lower bound on the amount of space you need for producing a correct answer.)

***Solution***    We consider part (b) first. One's first thought is that enumerating all self-avoiding walks sounds like a complicated prospect; it's natural to imagine the search as growing a chain starting from a single bead, exploring possible conformations, and backtracking when there's no way to continue growing and remain self-avoiding. You can picture attention-grabbing screen-savers that do things like this, but it seems a bit messy to write down exactly what the algorithm would be.

So we back up; polynomial space is a very generous bound, and we can afford to take an even more brute-force approach. Suppose that instead of trying just to enumerate all self-avoiding walks of length $n$, we simply enumerate *all* walks of length $n$, and then check which ones turn out to be self-avoiding. The advantage of this is that the space of all walks is much easier to describe than the space of self-avoiding walks.

Indeed, any walk $(p_1, p_2, \ldots, p_n)$ on the set $\mathcal{L}$ of grid points in the plane can be described by the sequence of directions it takes. Each step from $p_i$ to $p_{i+1}$ in the walk can be viewed as moving in one of four directions: north, south, east, or west. Thus any walk of length $n$ can be mapped to a distinct string of length $n - 1$ over the alphabet $\{N, S, E, W\}$. (The three walks in Figure 9.3 would be ENW, NES, and EEN.) Each such string corresponds to a walk of length $n$, but not all such strings correspond to walks that are self-avoiding: for example, the walk NESW revisits the point $(0, 0)$.

We can use this encoding of walks for part (b) of the question as follows. Using a counter in base 4, we enumerate all strings of length $n - 1$ over the alphabet $\{N, S, E, W\}$, by viewing this alphabet equivalently as $\{0, 1, 2, 3\}$. For each such string, we construct the corresponding walk and test, in polynomial space, whether it is self-avoiding. Finally, we increment a second counter $A$ (initialized to 0) if the current walk is self-avoiding. At the end of this algorithm, $A$ will hold the value of $A(n)$.

Now we can bound the space used by this algorithm as follows. The first counter, which enumerates strings, has $n - 1$ positions, each of which requires two bits (since it can take four possible values). Similarly, the second counter holding $A$ can be incremented at most $4^{n-1}$ times, and so it too needs at most $2n$ bits. Finally, we use polynomial space to check whether each generated walk is self-avoiding, but we can reuse the same space for each walk, and so the space needed for this is polynomial as well.

The encoding scheme also provides a way to answer part (a). We observe that all walks that can be encoded using only the letters $\{N, E\}$ are self-avoiding, since they only move up and to the right in the plane. As there are $2^{n-1}$ strings of length $n - 1$ over these two letters, there are at least $2^{n-1}$ self-avoiding walks; in other words, $A(n) \geq 2^{n-1}$.

(Note that we argued earlier that our encoding technique also provides an upper bound, showing immediately that $A(n) \leq 4^{n-1}$.)

# Exercises

1. Let's consider a special case of Quantified 3-SAT in which the underlying Boolean formula has no negated variables. Specifically, let $\Phi(x_1, \ldots, x_n)$ be a Boolean formula of the form

$$C_1 \wedge C_2 \wedge \cdots \wedge C_k,$$

where each $C_i$ is a disjunction of three terms. We say $\Phi$ is *monotone* if each term in each clause consists of a nonnegated variable—that is, each term is equal to $x_i$, for some $i$, rather than $\overline{x_i}$.

We define Monotone QSAT to be the decision problem

$$\exists x_1 \forall x_2 \cdots \exists x_{n-2} \forall x_{n-1} \exists x_n \Phi(x_1, \ldots, x_n)?$$

where the formula $\Phi$ is monotone.

Do one of the following two things: (a) prove that Monotone QSAT is PSPACE-complete; or (b) give an algorithm to solve arbitrary instances of Monotone QSAT that runs in time polynomial in $n$. (Note that in (b), the goal is polynomial *time*, not just polynomial space.)

2. Consider the following word game, which we'll call *Geography*. You have a set of names of places, like the capital cities of all the countries in the world. The first player begins the game by naming the capital city $c$ of the country the players are in; the second player must then choose a city $c'$ that starts with the letter on which $c$ ends; and the game continues in this way, with each player alternately choosing a city that starts with the letter on which the previous one ended. The player who loses is the first one who cannot choose a city that hasn't been named earlier in the game.

For example, a game played in Hungary would start with "Budapest," and then it could continue (for example), "Tokyo, Ottawa, Ankara, Amsterdam, Moscow, Washington, Nairobi."

This game is a good test of geographical knowledge, of course, but even with a list of the world's capitals sitting in front of you, it's also a major strategic challenge. Which word should you pick next, to try forcing your opponent into a situation where they'll be the one who's ultimately stuck without a move?

To highlight the strategic aspect, we define the following abstract version of the game, which we call *Geography on a Graph*. Here, we have a directed graph $G = (V, E)$, and a designated *start node* $s \in V$. Players alternate turns starting from $s$; each player must, if possible, follow an edge out of the current node to a node that hasn't been visited before. The player who loses is the first one who cannot move to a node that hasn't been visited earlier in the game. (There is a direct analogy to *Geography*, with nodes corresponding to words.) In other words, a player loses if the game is currently at node $v$, and for edges of the form $(v, w)$, the node $w$ has already been visited.

Prove that it is PSPACE-complete to decide whether the first player can force a win in *Geography on a Graph*.

3. Give a polynomial-time algorithm to decide whether a player has a forced win in *Geography on a Graph*, in the special case when the underlying graph $G$ has no directed cycles (in other words, when $G$ is a DAG).

## Notes and Further Reading

PSPACE is just one example of a class of intractable problems beyond NP; charting the landscape of computational hardness is the goal of the field of *complexity theory*. There are a number of books that focus on complexity theory; see, for example, Papadimitriou (1995) and Savage (1998).

The PSPACE-completeness of QSAT is due to Stockmeyer and Meyer (1973).

Some basic PSPACE-completeness results for two-player games can be found in Schaefer (1978) and in Stockmeyer and Chandra (1979). The Competitive Facility Location Problem that we consider here is a stylized example of a class of problems studied within the broader area of *facility location*; see, for example, the book edited by Drezner (1995) for surveys of this topic.

Two-player games have provided a steady source of difficult questions for researchers in both mathematics and artificial intelligence. Berlekamp, Conway, and Guy (1982) and Nowakowski (1998) discuss some of the mathematical questions in this area. The design of a world-champion-level chess program was for fifty years the foremost applied challenge problem in the field of computer game-playing. Alan Turing is known to have worked on devising algorithms to play chess, as did many leading figures in artificial intelligence over the years. Newborn (1996) gives a readable account of the history of work on this problem, covering the state of the art up to a year before IBM's Deep Blue finally achieved the goal of defeating the human world champion in a match.

Planning is a fundamental problem in artificial intelligence; it features prominently in the text by Russell and Norvig (2002) and is the subject of a book by Ghallab, Nau, and Traverso (2004). The argument that Planning can be solved in polynomial space is due to Savitch (1970), who was concerned with issues in complexity theory rather than the Planning Problem per se.

***Notes on the Exercises***    Exercise 1 is based on a problem we learned from Maverick Woo and Ryan Williams; Exercise 2 is based on a result of Thomas Schaefer.

# Chapter 10

## Extending the Limits of Tractability

Although we started the book by studying a number of techniques for solving problems efficiently, we've been looking for a while at classes of problems—NP-complete and PSPACE-complete problems—for which no efficient solution is believed to exist. And because of the insights we've gained this way, we've implicitly arrived at a two-pronged approach to dealing with new computational problems we encounter: We try for a while to develop an efficient algorithm; and if this fails, we then try to prove it NP-complete (or even PSPACE-complete). Assuming one of the two approaches works out, you end up either with a solution to the problem (an algorithm), or a potent "reason" for its difficulty: It is as hard as many of the famous problems in computer science.

Unfortunately, this strategy will only get you so far. If there is a problem that people really want your help in solving, they won't be particularly satisfied with the resolution that it's NP-hard[1] and that they should give up on it. They'll still want a solution that's as good as possible, even if it's not the exact, or optimal, answer. For example, in the Independent Set Problem, even if we can't find the largest independent set in a graph, it's still natural to want to compute for as much time as we have available, and output as large an independent set as we can find.

The next few topics in the book will be focused on different aspects of this notion. In Chapters 11 and 12, we'll look at algorithms that provide approximate answers with guaranteed error bounds in polynomial time; we'll also consider *local search heuristics* that are often very effective in practice,

---

even when we are not able to establish any provable guarantees about their behavior.

But to start, we explore some situations in which one can exactly solve instances of NP-complete problems with reasonable efficiency. How do these situations arise? The point is to recall the basic message of NP-completeness: the worst-case instances of these problems are very difficult and not likely to be solvable in polynomial time. On a *particular* instance, however, it's possible that we are not really in the "worst case"—maybe, in fact, the instance we're looking at has some special structure that makes our task easier. Thus the crux of this chapter is to look at situations in which it is possible to quantify some precise senses in which an instance may be easier than the worst case, and to take advantage of these situations when they occur.

We'll look at this principle in several concrete settings. First we'll consider the Vertex Cover Problem, in which there are two natural "size" parameters for a problem instance: the size of the graph, and the size of the vertex cover being sought. The NP-completeness of Vertex Cover suggests that we will have to be exponential in (at least) one of these parameters; but judiciously choosing which one can have an enormous effect on the running time.

Next we'll explore the idea that many NP-complete graph problems become polynomial-time solvable if we require the input to be a tree. This is a concrete illustration of the way in which an input with "special structure" can help us avoid many of the difficulties that can make the worst case intractable. Armed with this insight, one can generalize the notion of a tree to a more general class of graphs—those with small *tree-width*—and show that many NP-complete problems are tractable on this more general class as well.

Having said this, we should stress that our basic point remains the same as it has always been: *Exponential algorithms scale very badly*. The current chapter represents ways of staving off this problem that can be effective in various settings, but there is clearly no way around it in the fully general case. This will motivate our focus on approximation algorithms and local search in subsequent chapters.

## 10.1 Finding Small Vertex Covers

Let us briefly recall the Vertex Cover Problem, which we saw in Chapter 8 when we covered NP-completeness. Given a graph $G = (V, E)$ and an integer $k$, we would like to find a vertex cover of size at most $k$—that is, a set of nodes $S \subseteq V$ of size $|S| \leq k$, such that every edge $e \in E$ has at least one end in $S$.

Like many NP-complete decision problems, Vertex Cover comes with two parameters: $n$, the number of nodes in the graph, and $k$, the allowable size of a vertex cover. This means that the range of possible running-time bounds is much richer, since it involves the interplay between these two parameters.

## The Problem

Let's consider this interaction between the parameters $n$ and $k$ more closely. First of all, we notice that if $k$ is a fixed constant (e.g., $k = 2$ or $k = 3$), then we can solve Vertex Cover in polynomial time: We simply try all subsets of $V$ of size $k$, and see whether any of them constitute a vertex cover. There are $\binom{n}{k}$ subsets, and each takes time $O(kn)$ to check whether it is a vertex cover, for a total time of $O(kn\binom{n}{k}) = O(kn^{k+1})$. So from this we see that the intractability of Vertex Cover only sets in for real once $k$ grows as a function of $n$.

However, even for moderately small values of $k$, a running time of $O(kn^{k+1})$ is quite impractical. For example, if $n = 1,000$ and $k = 10$, then on a computer executing a million high-level instructions per second, it would take at least $10^{24}$ seconds to decide if $G$ has a $k$-node vertex cover—which is several orders of magnitude larger than the age of the universe. And this is for a small value of $k$, where the problem was supposed to be more tractable! It's natural to start asking whether we can do something that is practically viable when $k$ is a small constant.

It turns out that a much better algorithm can be developed, with a running-time bound of $O(2^k \cdot kn)$. There are two things worth noticing about this. First, plugging in $n = 1,000$ and $k = 10$, we see that our computer should be able to execute the algorithm in a few seconds. Second, we see that as $k$ grows, the running time is still increasing very rapidly; it's simply that the exponential dependence on $k$ has been moved out of the exponent on $n$ and into a separate function. From a practical point of view, this is much more appealing.

## Designing the Algorithm

As a first observation, we notice that if a graph has a small vertex cover, then it cannot have very many edges. Recall that the *degree* of a node is the number of edges that are incident to it.

**(10.1)**   *If $G = (V, E)$ has $n$ nodes, the maximum degree of any node is at most $d$, and there is a vertex cover of size at most $k$, then $G$ has at most $kd$ edges.*

**Proof.**  Let $S$ be a vertex cover in $G$ of size $k' \leq k$. Every edge in $G$ has at least one end in $S$; but each node in $S$ can cover at most $d$ edges. Thus there can be at most $k'd \leq kd$ edges in $G$.  ∎

Since the degree of any node in a graph can be at most $n - 1$, we have the following simple consequence of (10.1).

**(10.2)** *If $G = (V, E)$ has n nodes and a vertex cover of size k, then G has at most $k(n - 1) \leq kn$ edges.*

So, as a first step in our algorithm, we can check if $G$ contains more than $kn$ edges; if it does, then we know that the answer to the decision problem—Is there a vertex cover of size at most $k$?—is no. Having done this, we will assume that $G$ contains at most $kn$ edges.

The idea behind the algorithm is conceptually very clean. We begin by considering any edge $e = (u, v)$ in $G$. In any $k$-node vertex cover $S$ of $G$, one of $u$ or $v$ must belong to $S$. Suppose that $u$ belongs to such a vertex cover $S$. Then if we delete $u$ and all its incident edges, it must be possible to cover the remaining edges by at most $k - 1$ nodes. That is, defining $G - \{u\}$ to be the graph obtained by deleting $u$ and all its incident edges, there must be a vertex cover of size at most $k - 1$ in $G - \{u\}$. Similarly, if $v$ belongs to $S$, this would imply there is a vertex cover at most $k - 1$ in $G - \{v\}$.

Here is a concrete way to formulate this idea.

**(10.3)** *Let $e = (u, v)$ be any edge of G. The graph G has a vertex cover of size at most k if and only if at least one of the graphs $G - \{u\}$ and $G - \{v\}$ has a vertex cover of size at most $k - 1$.*

**Proof.** First, suppose $G$ has a vertex cover $S$ of size at most $k$. Then $S$ contains at least one of $u$ or $v$; suppose that it contains $u$. The set $S - \{u\}$ must cover all edges that have neither end equal to $u$. Therefore $S - \{u\}$ is a vertex cover of size at most $k - 1$ for the graph $G - \{u\}$.

Conversely, suppose that one of $G - \{u\}$ and $G - \{v\}$ has a vertex cover of size at most $k - 1$—suppose in particular that $G - \{u\}$ has such a vertex cover $T$. Then the set $T \cup \{u\}$ covers all edges in $G$, so it is a vertex cover for $G$ of size at most $k$. ∎

Statement (10.3) directly establishes the correctness of the following recursive algorithm for deciding whether $G$ has a $k$-node vertex cover.

```
To search for a k-node vertex cover in G:
   If G contains no edges, then the empty set is a vertex cover
   If G contains> k |V| edges, then it has no k-node vertex cover
   Else let e = (u, v) be an edge of G
      Recursively check if either of G-{u} or G-{v}
                   has a vertex cover of size k-1
      If neither of them does, then G has no k-node vertex cover
```

```
    Else, one of them (say, G−{u}) has a (k − 1)-node vertex cover T
        In this case, T ∪ {u} is a k-node vertex cover of G
    Endif
Endif
```

## Analyzing the Algorithm

Now we bound the running time of this algorithm. Intuitively, we are searching a "tree of possibilities"; we can picture the recursive execution of the algorithm as giving rise to a tree, in which each node corresponds to a different recursive call. A node corresponding to a recursive call with parameter $k$ has, as children, two nodes corresponding to recursive calls with parameter $k − 1$. Thus the tree has a total of at most $2^{k+1}$ nodes. In each recursive call, we spend $O(kn)$ time.

Thus, we can prove the following.

**(10.4)** *The running time of the Vertex Cover Algorithm on an n-node graph, with parameter k, is $O(2^k \cdot kn)$.*

We could also prove this by a recurrence as follows. If $T(n, k)$ denotes the running time on an $n$-node graph with parameter $k$, then $T(\cdot, \cdot)$ satisfies the following recurrence, for some absolute constant $c$:

$$T(n, 1) \leq cn,$$
$$T(n, k) \leq 2T(n, k − 1) + ckn.$$

By induction on $k \geq 1$, it is easy to prove that $T(n, k) \leq c \cdot 2^k kn$. Indeed, if this is true for $k − 1$, then

$$T(n, k) \leq 2T(n − 1, k − 1) + ckn$$
$$\leq 2c \cdot 2^{k-1}(k − 1)n + ckn$$
$$= c \cdot 2^k kn − c \cdot 2^k n + ckn$$
$$\leq c \cdot 2^k kn.$$

In summary, this algorithm is a powerful improvement on the simple brute-force approach. However, no exponential algorithm can scale well for very long, and that includes this one. Suppose we want to know whether there is a vertex cover with at most 40 nodes, rather than 10; then, on the same machine as before, our algorithm will take a significant number of years to terminate.

## 10.2 Solving NP-Hard Problems on Trees

In Section 10.1 we designed an algorithm for the Vertex Cover Problem that works well when the size of the desired vertex cover is not too large. We saw that finding a relatively small vertex cover is much easier than the Vertex Cover Problem in its full generality.

Here we consider special cases of NP-complete graph problems with a different flavor—not when the natural "size" parameters are small, but when the input graph is structurally "simple." Perhaps the simplest types of graphs are *trees*. Recall that an undirected graph is a tree if it is connected and has no cycles. Not only are trees structurally easy to understand, but it has been found that many NP-hard graph problems can be solved efficiently when the underlying graph is a tree. At a qualitative level, the reason for this is the following: If we consider a subtree of the input rooted at some node $v$, the solution to the problem restricted to this subtree only "interacts" with the rest of the tree through $v$. Thus, by considering the different ways in which $v$ might figure in the overall solution, we can essentially decouple the problem in $v$'s subtree from the problem in the rest of the tree.

It takes some amount of effort to make this general approach precise and to turn it into an efficient algorithm. Here we will see how to do this for variants of the Independent Set Problem; however, it is important to keep in mind that this principle is quite general, and we could equally well have considered many other NP-complete graph problems on trees.

First we will see that the Independent Set Problem itself can be solved by a greedy algorithm on a tree. Then we will consider the generalization called the *Maximum-Weight Independent Set Problem*, in which nodes have weight, and we seek an independent set of maximum weight. We'll see that the Maximum-Weight Independent Set Problem can be solved on trees via dynamic programming, using a fairly direct implementation of the intuition described above.

### A Greedy Algorithm for Independent Set on Trees

The starting point of our greedy algorithm on a tree is to consider the way a solution looks from the perspective of a single edge; this is a variant on an idea from Section 10.1. Specifically, consider an edge $e = (u, v)$ in $G$. In any independent set $S$ of $G$, at most one of $u$ or $v$ can belong to $S$. We'd like to find an edge $e$ for which we can greedily decide which of the two ends to place in our independent set.

For this we exploit a crucial property of trees: Every tree has at least one *leaf*—a node of degree 1. Consider a leaf $v$, and let $(u, v)$ be the unique edge incident to $v$. How might we "greedily" evaluate the relative benefits of including $u$ or $v$ in our independent set $S$? If we include $v$, the only other node that is directly "blocked" from joining the independent set is $u$. If we include $u$, it blocks not only $v$ but all the other nodes joined to $u$ as well. So if we're trying to maximize the size of the independent set, it seems that including $v$ should be better than, or at least as good as, including $u$.

**(10.5)** *If $T = (V, E)$ is a tree and $v$ is a leaf of the tree, then there exists a maximum-size independent set that contains $v$.*

**Proof.** Consider a maximum-size independent set $S$, and let $e = (u, v)$ be the unique edge incident to node $v$. Clearly, at least one of $u$ or $v$ is in $S$; for if neither is present, then we could add $v$ to $S$, thereby increasing its size. Now, if $v \in S$, then we are done; and if $u \in S$, then we can obtain another independent set $S'$ of the same size by deleting $u$ from $S$ and inserting $v$. ∎

We will use (10.5) repeatedly to identify and delete nodes that can be placed in the independent set. As we do this deletion, the tree $T$ may become disconnected. So, to handle things more cleanly, we actually describe our algorithm for the more general case in which the underlying graph is a *forest* — a graph in which each connected component is a tree. We can view the problem of finding a maximum-size independent set for a forest as really being the same as the problem for trees: an optimal solution for a forest is simply the union of optimal solutions for each tree component, and we can still use (10.5) to think about the problem in any component.

Specifically, suppose we have a forest $F$; then (10.5) allows us to make our first decision in the following greedy way. Consider again an edge $e = (u, v)$, where $v$ is a leaf. We will include node $v$ in our independent set $S$, and not include node $u$. Given this decision, we can delete the node $v$ (since it's already been included) and the node $u$ (since it cannot be included) and obtain a smaller forest. We continue recursively on this smaller forest to get a solution.

```
To find a maximum-size independent set in a forest F:
  Let S be the independent set to be constructed (initially empty)
  While F has at least one edge
    Let e = (u, v) be an edge of F such that v is a leaf
    Add v to S
    Delete from F nodes u and v, and all edges incident to them
  Endwhile
  Return S
```

**(10.6)**  *The above algorithm finds a maximum-size independent set in forests (and hence in trees as well).*

Although (10.5) was a very simple fact, it really represents an application of one of the design principles for greedy algorithms that we saw in Chapter 4: an *exchange argument*. In particular, the crux of our Independent Set Algorithm is the observation that any solution not containing a particular leaf can be "transformed" into a solution that is just as good and contains the leaf.

To implement this algorithm so it runs quickly, we need to maintain the current forest $F$ in a way that allows us to find an edge incident to a leaf efficiently. It is not hard to implement this algorithm in linear time: We need to maintain the forest in a way that allows us to do so on one iteration of the While loop in time proportional to the number of edges deleted when $u$ and $v$ are removed.

**The Greedy Algorithm on More General Graphs**    The greedy algorithm specified above is not guaranteed to work on general graphs, because we cannot be guaranteed to find a leaf in every iteration. However, (10.5) *does* apply to any graph: if we have an arbitrary graph $G$ with an edge $(u, v)$ such that $u$ is the only neighbor of $v$, then it's always safe to put $v$ in the independent set, delete $u$ and $v$, and iterate on the smaller graph.

So if, by repeatedly deleting degree-1 nodes and their neighbors, we're able to eliminate the entire graph, then we're guaranteed to have found an independent set of maximum size—even if the original graph was not a tree. And even if we don't manage to eliminate the whole graph, we may still succeed in running a few iterations of the algorithm in succession, thereby shrinking the size of the graph and making other approaches more tractable. Thus our greedy algorithm is a useful heuristic to try "opportunistically" on arbitrary graphs, in the hope of making progress toward finding a large independent set.

## Maximum-Weight Independent Set on Trees

Next we turn to the more complex problem of finding a maximum-weight independent set. As before, we assume that our graph is a tree $T = (V, E)$. Now we also have a positive *weight* $w_v$ associated with each node $v \in V$. The *Maximum-Weight Independent Set Problem* is to find an independent set $S$ in the graph $T = (V, E)$ so that the total weight $\sum_{v \in S} w_v$ is as large as possible.

First we try the idea we used before to build a greedy solution for the case without weights. Consider an edge $e = (u, v)$, such that $v$ is a leaf. Including $v$ blocks fewer nodes from entering the independent set; so, if the weight of $v$ is at least as large as the weight of $u$, then we can indeed make a greedy decision just as we did in the case without weights. However, if $w_v < w_u$, we face a dilemma: We acquire more weight by including $u$, but we retain more options down the road if we include $v$. There seems to be no easy way to resolve this locally, without considering the rest of the graph. However, there is still something we can say. If node $u$ has many neighbors $v_1, v_2, \ldots$ that are leaves, then we should make the same decision for all of them: Once we decide not to include $u$ in the independent set, we may as well go ahead and include all its adjacent leaves. So for the subtree consisting of $u$ and its adjacent leaves, we really have only two "reasonable" solutions to consider: including $u$, or including all the leaves.

We will use these ideas to design a polynomial-time algorithm using dynamic programming. As we recall, dynamic programming allows us to record a few different solutions, build these up through a sequence of subproblems, and thereby decide only at the end which of these possibilities will be used in the overall solution.

The first issue to decide for a dynamic programming algorithm is what our subproblems will be. For Maximum-Weight Independent Set, we will construct subproblems by *rooting* the tree $T$ at an arbitrary node $r$; recall that this is the operation of "orienting" all the tree's edges away from $r$. Specifically, for any node $u \neq r$, the parent $p(u)$ of $u$ is the node adjacent to $u$ along the path from the root $r$. The other neighbors of $u$ are its children, and we will use *children*$(u)$ to denote the set of children of $u$. The node $u$ and all its descendants form a subtree $T_u$ whose root is $u$.

We will base our subproblems on these subtrees $T_u$. The tree $T_r$ is our original problem. If $u \neq r$ is a leaf, then $T_u$ consists of a single node. For a node $u$ all of whose children are leaves, we observe that $T_u$ is the kind of subtree discussed above.

To solve the problem by dynamic programming, we will start at the leaves and gradually work our way up the tree. For a node $u$, we want to solve the subproblem associated with the tree $T_u$ after we have solved the subproblems for all its children. To get a maximum-weight independent set $S$ for the tree $T_u$, we will consider two cases: Either we include the node $u$ in $S$ or we do not. If we include $u$, then we cannot include any of its children; if we do not include $u$, then we have the freedom to include or omit these children. This suggests that we should define two subproblems for each subtree $T_u$: the subproblem $\text{OPT}_{in}(u)$ will denote the maximum weight of an independent set of $T_u$ that includes $u$, and the subproblem $\text{OPT}_{out}(u)$ will denote the maximum weight of an independent set of $T_u$ that does not include $u$.

Now that we have our subproblems, it is not hard to see how to compute these values recursively. For a leaf $u \neq r$, we have $\text{OPT}_{out}(u) = 0$ and $\text{OPT}_{in}(u) = w_u$. For all other nodes $u$, we get the following recurrence that defines $\text{OPT}_{out}(u)$ and $\text{OPT}_{in}(u)$ using the values for $u$'s children.

**(10.7)** *For a node $u$ that has children, the following recurrence defines the values of the subproblems:*

- $\text{OPT}_{in}(u) = w_u + \displaystyle\sum_{v \in children(u)} \text{OPT}_{out}(v)$

- $\text{OPT}_{out}(u) = \displaystyle\sum_{v \in children(u)} \max(\text{OPT}_{out}(v), \text{OPT}_{in}(v)).$

Using this recurrence, we get a dynamic programming algorithm by building up the optimal solutions over larger and larger subtrees. We define arrays $M_{out}[u]$ and $M_{in}[u]$, which hold the values $\text{OPT}_{out}(u)$ and $\text{OPT}_{in}(u)$, respectively. For building up solutions, we need to process all the children of a node before we process the node itself; in the terminology of tree traversal, we visit the nodes in *post-order*.

```
To find a maximum-weight independent set of a tree T:
    Root the tree at a node r
    For all nodes u of T in post-order
        If u is a leaf then set the values:
            M_out[u] = 0
            M_in[u] = w_u
        Else set the values:
            M_out[u] =   ∑       max(M_out[u], M_in[u])
                      v∈children(u)
            M_in[u] =  w_u  +    ∑      M_out[u].
                            v∈children(u)
        Endif
    Endfor
    Return max(M_out[r], M_in[r])
```

This gives us the value of the maximum-weight independent set. Now, as is standard in the dynamic programming algorithms we've seen before, it's easy to recover an actual independent set of maximum weight by recording the decision we make for each node, and then tracing back through these decisions to determine which nodes should be included. Thus we have

**(10.8)** *The above algorithm finds a maximum-weight independent set in trees in linear time.*

# 10.3 Coloring a Set of Circular Arcs

Some years back, when telecommunications companies began focusing intensively on a technology known as *wavelength-division multiplexing*, researchers at these companies developed a deep interest in a previously obscure algorithmic question: the problem of coloring a set of circular arcs.

After explaining how the connection came about, we'll develop an algorithm for this problem. The algorithm is a more complex variation on the theme of Section 10.2: We approach a computationally hard problem using dynamic programming, building up solutions over a set of subproblems that only "interact" with each other on very small pieces of the input. Having to worry about only this very limited interaction serves to control the complexity of the algorithm.

## The Problem

Let's start with some background on how network routing issues led to the question of circular-arc coloring. Wavelength-division multiplexing (WDM) is a methodology that allows multiple communication streams to share a single portion of fiber-optic cable, provided that the streams are transmitted on this cable using different wavelengths. Let's model the underlying communication network as a graph $G = (V, E)$, with each *communication stream* consisting of a path $P_i$ in $G$; we imagine data flowing along this stream from one endpoint of $P_i$ to the other. If the paths $P_i$ and $P_j$ share some edge in $G$, it is still possible to send data along these two streams simultaneously as long as they are routed using different *wavelengths*. So our goal is the following: Given a set of $k$ available wavelengths (labeled $1, 2, \ldots, k$), we wish to assign a wavelength to each stream $P_i$ in such a way that each pair of streams that share an edge in the graph are assigned different wavelengths. We'll refer to this as an instance of the *Path Coloring Problem*, and we'll call a solution to this instance—a legal assignment of wavelengths to paths—a *k-coloring*.

This is a natural problem that we could consider as it stands; but from the point of view of the fiber-optic routing context, it is useful to make one further simplification. Many applications of WDM take place on networks $G$ that are extremely simple in structure, and so it is natural to restrict the instances of Path Coloring by making some assumptions about this underlying network structure. In fact, one of the most important special cases in practice is also one of the simplest: when the underlying network is simply a ring; that is, it can be modeled using a graph $G$ that is a cycle on $n$ nodes.

This is the case we will focus on here: We are given a graph $G = (V, E)$ that is a cycle on $n$ nodes, and we are given a set of paths $P_1, \ldots, P_m$ on this cycle. The goal, as above, is to assign one of $k$ given wavelengths to each path

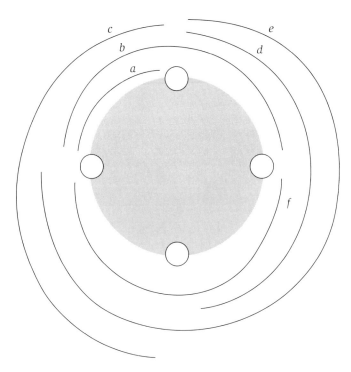

**Figure 10.1** An instance of the Circular-Arc Coloring Problem with six arcs $(a, b, c, d, e, f)$ on a four-node cycle.

$P_i$ so that overlapping paths receive different wavelengths. We will refer to this as a *valid* assignment of wavelengths to the paths. Figure 10.1 shows a sample instance of this problem. In this instance, there is a valid assignment using $k = 3$ wavelengths, by assigning wavelength 1 to the paths $a$ and $e$, wavelength 2 to the paths $b$ and $f$, and wavelength 3 to the paths $c$ and $d$. From the figure, we see that the underlying cycle network can be viewed as a circle, and the paths as arcs on this circle; hence we will refer to this special case of Path Coloring as the *Circular-Arc Coloring Problem*.

***The Complexity of Circular-Arc Coloring***   It's not hard to see that Circular-Arc Coloring can be directly reduced to Graph Coloring. Given an instance of Circular-Arc Coloring, we define a graph $H$ that has a node $z_i$ for each path $P_i$, and we connect nodes $z_i$ and $z_j$ in $H$ if the paths $P_i$ and $P_j$ share an edge in $G$. Now, routing all streams using $k$ wavelengths is simply the problem of coloring $H$ using at most $k$ colors. (In fact, this problem is yet another application of graph coloring in which the abstract "colors," since they encode different wavelengths of light, are actually colors.)

Note that this doesn't imply that Circular-Arc Coloring is NP-complete—all we've done is to reduce it *to* a known NP-complete problem, which doesn't tell us anything about its difficulty. For Path Coloring on general graphs, in fact, it is easy to reduce from Graph Coloring to Path Coloring, thereby establishing that Path Coloring is NP-complete. However, this straightforward reduction does not work when the underlying graph is as simple as a cycle. So what is the complexity of Circular-Arc Coloring?

It turns out that Circular-Arc Coloring can be shown to be NP-complete using a very complicated reduction. This is bad news for people working with optical networks, since it means that optimal wavelength assignment is unlikely to be efficiently solvable. But, in fact, the known reductions that show Circular-Arc Coloring is NP-complete all have the following interesting property: The hard instances of Circular-Arc Coloring that they produce all involve a set of available wavelengths that is quite large. So, in particular, these reductions don't show that the Circular-Arc Coloring is hard in the case when the number of wavelengths is small; they leave open the possibility that for every fixed, *constant* number of wavelengths $k$, it is possible to solve the wavelength assignment problem in time polynomial in $n$ (the size of the cycle) and $m$ (the number of paths). In other words, we could hope for a running time of the form we saw for Vertex Cover in Section 10.1: $O(f(k) \cdot p(n, m))$, where $f(\cdot)$ may be a rapidly growing function but $p(\cdot, \cdot)$ is a polynomial.

Such a running time would be appealing (assuming $f(\cdot)$ does not grow too outrageously), since it would make wavelength assignment potentially feasible when the number of wavelengths is small. One way to appreciate the challenge in obtaining such a running time is to note the following analogy: The general Graph Coloring Problem is already hard for three colors. So if Circular-Arc Coloring were tractable for each fixed number of wavelengths (i.e., colors) $k$, it would show that it's a special case of Graph Coloring with a qualitatively different complexity.

The goal of this section is to design an algorithm with this type of running time, $O(f(k) \cdot p(n, m))$. As suggested at the beginning of the section, the algorithm itself builds on the intuition we developed in Section 10.2 when solving Maximum-Weight Independent Set on trees. There the difficult search inherent in finding a maximum-weight independent set was made tractable by the fact that for each node $v$ in a tree $T$, the problems in the components of $T - \{v\}$ became completely decoupled once we decided whether or not to include $v$ in the independent set. This is a specific example of the general principle of fixing a small set of decisions, and thereby separating the problem into smaller subproblems that can be dealt with independently.

The analogous idea here will be to choose a particular point on the cycle and decide how to color the arcs that cross over this point; fixing these degrees of freedom allows us to define a series of smaller and smaller subproblems on the remaining arcs.

### Designing the Algorithm

Let's pin down some notation we're going to use. We have a graph $G$ that is a cycle on $n$ nodes; we denote the nodes by $v_1, v_2, \ldots, v_n$, and there is an edge $(v_i, v_{i+1})$ for each $i$, and also an edge $(v_n, v_1)$. We have a set of paths $P_1, P_2, \ldots, P_m$ in $G$, we have a set of $k$ available colors; we want to color the paths so that if $P_i$ and $P_j$ share an edge, they receive different colors.

*A Simple Special Case: Interval Coloring*    In order to build up to an algorithm for Circular-Arc Coloring, we first briefly consider an easier coloring problem: the problem of coloring intervals on a line. This can be viewed as a special case of Circular-Arc Coloring in which the arcs lie only in one hemisphere; we will see that once we do not have difficulties from arcs "wrapping around," the problem becomes much simpler. So in this special case, we are given a set of intervals, and we must label each one with a number in such a way that any two overlapping intervals receive different labels.

We have actually seen exactly this problem before: It is the Interval Partitioning (or Interval Coloring) Problem for which we gave an optimal greedy algorithm at the end of Section 4.1. In addition to showing that there is an efficient, optimal algorithm for coloring intervals, our analysis in that earlier section revealed a lot about the structure of the problem. Specifically, if we define the *depth* of a set of intervals to be the maximum number that pass over any single point, then our greedy algorithm from Chapter 4 showed that the minimum number of colors needed is always equal to the depth. Note that the number of colors required is clearly at least the depth, since intervals containing a common point need different colors; the key here is that one never needs a number of colors that is greater than the depth.

It is interesting that this exact relationship between the number of colors and the depth does not hold for collections of arcs on a circle. In Figure 10.2, for example, we see a collection of circular arcs that has depth 2 but needs three colors. This is a basic reflection of the fact that in trying to color a collection of circular arcs, one encounters "long-range" obstacles that render the problem much more complex than the coloring problem for intervals on a line. Despite this, we will see that thinking about the simpler problem of coloring intervals will be useful in designing our algorithm for Circular-Arc Coloring.

*Transforming to an Interval Coloring Problem*    We now return to the Circular-Arc Coloring Problem. For now, we will consider a special case of the problem in which, for each edge $e$ of the cycle, there are exactly $k$ paths that contain $e$. We will call this the *uniform-depth* case. It turns out that al-

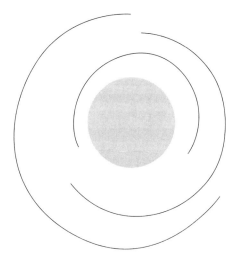

**Figure 10.2** A collection of circular arcs needing three colors, even though at most two arcs pass over any point of the circle.

though this special case may seem fairly restricted, it contains essentially the whole complexity of the problem; once we have an algorithm for the uniform-depth case, it will be easy to translate this to an algorithm for the problem in general.

The first step in designing an algorithm will be to transform the instance into a modified form of Interval Coloring: We "cut" the cycle by slicing through the edge $(v_n, v_1)$, and then "unroll" the cycle into a path $G'$. This process is illustrated in Figure 10.3. The sliced-and-unrolled graph $G'$ has the same nodes as $G$, plus two extra ones where the slicing occurred: a node $v_0$ adjacent to $v_1$ (and no other nodes), and a node $v_{n+1}$ adjacent to $v_n$ (and no other nodes). Also, the set of paths has changed slightly. Suppose that $P_1, P_2, \ldots, P_k$ are the paths that contained the edge $(v_n, v_1)$ in $G$. Each of these paths $P_i$ has now been sliced into two, one that we'll label $P_i'$ (starting at $v_0$) and one that we'll label $P_i''$ (ending at $v_{n+1}$).

Now this is an instance of Interval Coloring, and it has depth $k$. Thus, following our discussion above about the relation between depth and colors, we see that the intervals

$$P_1', P_2', \ldots, P_k', P_{k+1}, \ldots, P_m, P_1'', P_2'', \ldots, P_k''$$

can be colored using $k$ colors. So are we done? Can we just translate this solution into a solution for the paths on $G$?

In fact, this is not so easy; the problem is that our interval coloring may well not have given the paths $P_i'$ and $P_i''$ the same color. Since these are two

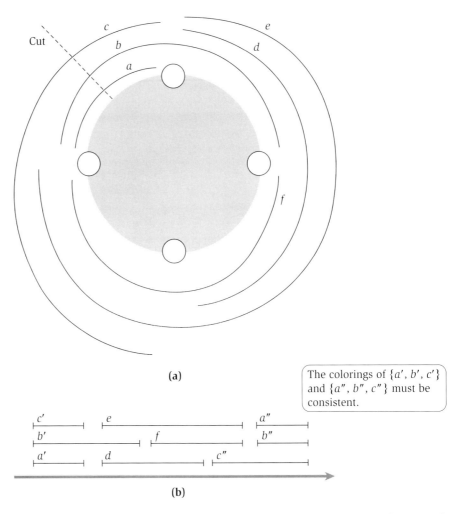

**(a)**

The colorings of $\{a', b', c'\}$ and $\{a'', b'', c''\}$ must be consistent.

$c'$   $e$   $a''$
$b'$   $f$   $b''$
$a'$   $d$   $c''$

**(b)**

**Figure 10.3** (a) Cutting through the cycle in an instance of Circular-Arc Coloring, and then unrolling it so it becomes, in (b), a collection of intervals on a line.

pieces of the same path $P_i$ on $G$, it's not clear how to take the differing colors of $P_i'$ and $P_i''$ and infer from this how to color $P_i$ on $G$. For example, having sliced open the cycle in Figure 10.3(a), we get the set of intervals pictured in Figure 10.3(b). Suppose we compute a coloring so that the intervals in the first row get the color 1, those in the second row get the color 2, and those in the third row get the color 3. Then we don't have an obvious way to figure out a color for $a$ and $c$.

This suggests a way to formalize the relationship between the instance of Circular-Arc Coloring in $G$ and the instance of Interval Coloring in $G'$.

**(10.9)**    *The paths in G can be k-colored if and only if the paths in G' can be k-colored subject to the additional restriction that $P'_i$ and $P''_i$ receive the same color, for each $i = 1, 2, \ldots, k$.*

**Proof.** If the paths in $G$ can be $k$-colored, then we simply use these as the colors in $G'$, assigning each of $P'_i$ and $P''_i$ the color of $P_i$. In the resulting coloring, no two paths with the same color have an edge in common.

Conversely, suppose the paths in $G'$ can be $k$-colored subject to the additional restriction that $P'_i$ and $P''_i$ receive the same color, for each $i = 1, 2, \ldots, k$. Then we assign path $P_i$ (for $i \leq k$) the common color of $P'_i$ and $P''_i$; and we assign path $P_j$ (for $j > k$) the color that $P_j$ gets in $G'$. Again, under this coloring, no two paths with the same color have an edge in common. ∎

We've now transformed our problem into a search for a coloring of the paths in $G'$ subject to the condition in (10.9): The paths $P'_i$ and $P''_i$ (for $1 \leq i \leq k$) should get the same color.

Before proceeding, we introduce some further terminology that makes it easier to talk about algorithms for this problem. First, since the names of the colors are arbitrary, we can assume that path $P'_i$ is assigned the color $i$ for each $i = 1, 2, \ldots, k$. Now, for each edge $e_i = (v_i, v_{i+1})$, we let $S_i$ denote the set of paths that contain this edge. A $k$-coloring of just the paths in $S_i$ has a very simple structure: it is simply a way of assigning exactly one of the colors $\{1, 2, \ldots, k\}$ to each of the $k$ paths in $S_i$. We will think of such a $k$-coloring as a one-to-one function $f : S_i \rightarrow \{1, 2, \ldots, k\}$.

Here's the crucial definition: We say that a $k$-coloring $f$ of $S_i$ and a $k$-coloring $g$ of $S_j$ are *consistent* if there is a single $k$-coloring of all the paths that is equal to $f$ on $S_i$, and also equal to $g$ on $S_j$. In other words, the $k$-colorings $f$ and $g$ on restricted parts of the instance could both arise from a single $k$-coloring of the whole instance. We can state our problem in terms of consistency as follows: If $f'$ denotes the $k$-coloring of $S_0$ that assigns color $i$ to $P'_i$, and $f''$ denotes the $k$-coloring of $S_n$ that assigns color $i$ to $P''_i$, then we need to decide whether $f'$ and $f''$ are consistent.

***Searching for an Acceptable Interval Coloring***    It is not clear how to decide the consistency of $f'$ and $f''$ directly. Instead, we adopt a dynamic programming approach by building up the solution through a series of subproblems.

The subproblems are as follows: For each set $S_i$, working in order over $i = 0, 1, 2, \ldots, n$, we will compute the set $F_i$ of all $k$-colorings on $S_i$ that are consistent with $f'$. Once we have computed $F_n$, we need only check whether it contains $f''$ in order to answer our overall question: whether $f'$ and $f''$ are consistent.

To start the algorithm, we define $F_0 = \{f'\}$: Since $f'$ determines a color for every interval in $S_0$, clearly no other $k$-coloring of $S_0$ can be consistent with it. Now suppose we have computed $F_0, F_1, \ldots, F_i$; we show how to compute $F_{i+1}$ from $F_i$.

Recall that $S_i$ consists of the paths containing the edge $e_i = (v_i, v_{i+1})$, and $S_{i+1}$ consists of the paths containing the next consecutive edge $e_{i+1} = (v_{i+1}, v_{i+2})$. The paths in $S_i$ and $S_{i+1}$ can be divided into three types:

- Those that contain both $e_i$ and $e_{i+1}$. These lie in both $S_i$ and $S_{i+1}$.
- Those that end at node $v_{i+1}$. These lie in $S_i$ but not $S_{i+1}$.
- Those that begin at node $v_{i+1}$. These lie in $S_{i+1}$ but not $S_i$.

Now, for any coloring $f \in F_i$, we say that a coloring $g$ of $S_{i+1}$ is an *extension* of $f$ if all the paths in $S_i \cap S_{i+1}$ have the same colors with respect to $f$ and $g$. It is easy to check that if $g$ is an extension of $f$, and $f$ is consistent with $f'$, then so is $g$. On the other hand, suppose some coloring $g$ of $S_{i+1}$ is consistent with $f'$; in other words, there is a coloring $h$ of all paths that is equal to $f'$ on $S_0$ and is equal to $g$ on $S_{i+1}$. Then, if we consider the colors assigned by $h$ to paths in $S_i$, we get a coloring $f \in F_i$, and $g$ is an extension of $f$.

This proves the following fact.

**(10.10)**    *The set $F_{i+1}$ is equal to the set of all extensions of $k$-colorings in $F_i$.*

So, in order to compute $F_{i+1}$, we simply need to list all extensions of all colorings in $F_i$. For each $f \in F_i$, this means that we want a list of all colorings $g$ of $S_{i+1}$ that agree with $f$ on $S_i \cap S_{i+1}$. To do this, we simply list all possible ways of assigning the colors of $S_i - S_{i+1}$ (with respect to $f$) to the paths in $S_{i+1} - S_i$. Merging these lists for all $f \in F_i$ then gives us $F_{i+1}$.

Thus the overall algorithm is as follows.

```
To determine whether f′ and f″ are consistent:
  Define F₀ = {f′}
  For i = 1, 2,..., n
    For each f ∈ Fᵢ
      Add all extensions of f to Fᵢ₊₁
    Endfor
  Endfor
  Check whether f″ is in Fₙ
```

Figure 10.4 shows the results of executing this algorithm on the example of Figure 10.3. As with all the dynamic programming algorithms we have seen in this book, the actual coloring can be computed by tracing back through the steps that built up the sets $F_1, F_2, \ldots, F_n$.

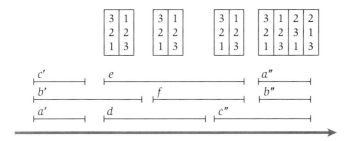

**Figure 10.4** The execution of the coloring algorithm. The initial coloring $f'$ assigns color 1 to $a'$, color 2 to $b'$, and color 3 to $c'$. Above each edge $e_i$ (for $i > 0$) is a table representing the set of all consistent colorings in $F_i$: Each coloring is represented by one of the columns in the table. Since the coloring $f''(a'') = 1$, $f''(b'') = 2$, and $f''(c'') = 3$ appears in the final table, there is a solution to this instance.

We will discuss the running time of this algorithm in a moment. First, however, we show how to remove the assumption that the input instance has uniform depth.

***Removing the Uniform-Depth Assumption***    Recall that the algorithm we just designed assumes that for each edge $e$, exactly $k$ paths contain $e$. In general, each edge may carry a different number of paths, up to a maximum of $k$. (If there were an edge contained in $k + 1$ paths, then all these paths would need a different color, and so we could immediately conclude that the input instance is not colorable with $k$ colors.)

It is not hard to modify the algorithm directly to handle the general case, but it is also easy to reduce the general case to the uniform-depth case. For each edge $e_i$ that carries only $k_i < k$ paths, we add $k - k_i$ paths that consist only of the single edge $e_i$. We now have a uniform-depth instance, and we claim

**(10.11)**    *The original instance can be colored with $k$ colors if and only if the modified instance (obtained by adding single-edge paths) can be colored with $k$ colors.*

**Proof.**  Clearly, if the modified instance has a $k$-coloring, then we can use this same $k$-coloring for the original instance (simply ignoring the colors it assigns to the single-edge paths that we added). Conversely, suppose the original instance has a $k$-coloring $f$. Then we can construct a $k$-coloring of the modified instance by starting with $f$ and considering the extra single-edge paths one at a time, assigning any free color to each of these paths as we consider them. ∎

### Analyzing the Algorithm

Finally, we bound the running time of the algorithm. This is dominated by the time to compute the sets $F_1, F_2, \ldots, F_n$. To build one of these sets $F_{i+1}$, we need to consider each coloring $f \in F_i$, and list all permutations of the colors that $f$ assigns to paths in $S_i - S_{i+1}$. Since $S_i$ has $k$ paths, the number of colorings in $F_i$ is at most $k!$. Listing all permutations of the colors that $f$ assigns to $S_i - S_{i+1}$ also involves enumerating a set of size $\ell!$, where $\ell \leq k$ is the size of $S_i - S_{i+1}$.

Thus the total time to compute $F_{i+1}$ from one $F_i$ has the form $O(f(k))$ for a function $f(\cdot)$ that depends only on $k$. Over the $n$ iterations of the outer loop to compute $F_1, F_2, \ldots, F_n$, this gives a total running time of $O(f(k) \cdot n)$, as desired.

This concludes the description and analysis of the algorithm. We summarize its properties in the following statement.

**(10.12)** *The algorithm described in this section correctly determines whether a collection of paths on an $n$-node cycle can be colored with $k$ colors, and its running time is $O(f(k) \cdot n)$ for a function $f(\cdot)$ that depends only on $k$.*

Looking back on it, then, we see that the running time of the algorithm came from the intuition we described at the beginning of the section: For each $i$, the subproblems based on computing $F_i$ and $F_{i+1}$ fit together along the "narrow" interface consisting of the paths in just $S_i$ and $S_{i+1}$, each of which has size at most $k$. Thus the time needed to go from one to the other could be made to depend only on $k$, and not on the size of the cycle $G$ or on the number of paths.

## * 10.4 Tree Decompositions of Graphs

In the previous two sections, we've seen how particular NP-hard problems (specifically, Maximum-Weight Independent Set and Graph Coloring) can be solved when the input has a restricted structure. When you find yourself in this situation—able to solve an NP-complete problem in a reasonably natural special case—it's worth asking why the approach doesn't work in general. As we discussed in Sections 10.2 and 10.3, our algorithms in both cases were taking advantage of a particular kind of structure: the fact that the input could be broken down into subproblems with very limited interaction.

For example, to solve Maximum-Weight Independent Set on a tree, we took advantage of a special property of (rooted) trees: Once we decide whether or not to include a node $u$ in the independent set, the subproblems in each subtree become completely separated; we can solve each as though the others did not exist. We don't encounter such a nice situation in general graphs, where there might not be a node that "breaks the communication" between subproblems in the rest of the graph. Rather, for the Independent Set Problem in general graphs, decisions we make in one place seem to have complex repercussions all across the graph.

So we can ask a weaker version of our question instead: For how general a class of graphs can we use this notion of "limited interaction"—recursively chopping up the input using small sets of nodes—to design efficient algorithms for a problem like Maximum-Weight Independent Set?

In fact, there is a natural and rich class of graphs that supports this type of algorithm; they are essentially "generalized trees," and for reasons that will become clear shortly, we will refer to them as *graphs of bounded tree-width*. Just as with trees, many NP-complete problems are tractable on graphs of bounded tree-width; and the class of graphs of bounded tree-width turns out to have considerable practical value, since it includes many real-world networks on which NP-complete graph problems arise. So, in a sense, this type of graph serves as a nice example of finding the "right" special case of a problem that simultaneously allows for efficient algorithms and also includes graphs that arise in practice.

In this section, we define tree-width and give the general approach for solving problems on graphs of bounded tree-width. In the next section, we discuss how to tell whether a given graph has bounded tree-width.

## Defining Tree-Width

We now give a precise definition for this class of graphs that is designed to generalize trees. The definition is motivated by two considerations. First, we want to find graphs that we can decompose into disconnected pieces by removing a small number of nodes; this allows us to implement dynamic programming algorithms of the type we discussed earlier. Second, we want to make precise the intuition conveyed by "tree-like" drawings of graphs as in Figure 10.5(b).

We want to claim that the graph $G$ pictured in this figure is decomposable in a tree-like way, along the lines that we've been considering. If we were to encounter $G$ as it is drawn in Figure 10.5(a), it might not be immediately clear why this is so. In the drawing in Figure 10.5(b), however, we see that $G$ is really composed of ten interlocking triangles; and seven of the ten triangles have the property that if we delete them, then the remainder of $G$ falls apart into disconnected pieces that recursively have this interlocking-triangle structure. The other three triangles are attached at the extremities, and deleting them is sort of like deleting the leaves of a tree.

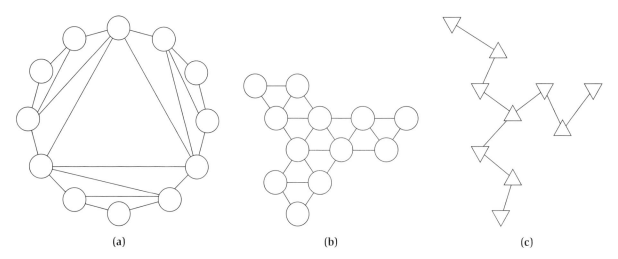

(a)                              (b)                              (c)

**Figure 10.5** Parts (a) and (b) depict the same graph drawn in different ways. The drawing in (b) emphasizes the way in which it is composed of ten interlocking triangles. Part (c) illustrates schematically how these ten triangles "fit together."

So $G$ is tree-like if we view it not as being composed of twelve nodes, as we usually would, but instead as being composed of ten triangles. Although $G$ clearly contains many cycles, it seems, intuitively, to lack cycles when viewed at the level of these ten triangles; and based on this, it inherits many of the nice decomposition properties of a tree.

We will want to represent the tree-like structure of these triangles by having each triangle correspond to a node in a tree, as shown in Figure 10.5(c). Intuitively, the tree in this figure corresponds to this graph, with each node of the tree representing one of the triangles. Notice, however, that the same nodes of the graph occur in multiple triangles, even in triangles that are not adjacent in the tree structure; and there are edges between nodes in triangles very far away in the tree-structure—for example, the central triangle has edges to nodes in every other triangle. How can we make the correspondence between the tree and the graph precise? We do this by introducing the idea of a *tree decomposition* of a graph $G$, so named because we will seek to decompose $G$ according to a tree-like pattern.

Formally, a tree decomposition of $G = (V, E)$ consists of a tree $T$ (on a different node set from $G$), and a subset $V_t \subseteq V$ associated with each node $t$ of $T$. (We will call these subsets $V_t$ the "pieces" of the tree decomposition.) We will sometimes write this as the ordered pair $(T, \{V_t : t \in T\})$. The tree $T$ and the collection of pieces $\{V_t : t \in T\}$ must satisfy the following three properties.

- *(Node Coverage)* Every node of $G$ belongs to at least one piece $V_t$.
- *(Edge Coverage)* For every edge $e$ of $G$, there is some piece $V_t$ containing both ends of $e$.
- *(Coherence)* Let $t_1$, $t_2$, and $t_3$ be three nodes of $T$ such that $t_2$ lies on the path from $t_1$ to $t_3$. Then, if a node $v$ of $G$ belongs to both $V_{t_1}$ and $V_{t_3}$, it also belongs to $V_{t_2}$.

It's worth checking that the tree in Figure 10.5(c) is a tree decomposition of the graph using the ten triangles as the pieces.

Next consider the case when the graph $G$ is a tree. We can build a tree decomposition of it as follows. The decomposition tree $T$ has a node $t_v$ for each node $v$ of $G$, and a node $t_e$ for each edge $e$ of $G$. The tree $T$ has an edge $(t_v, t_e)$ when $v$ is an end of $e$. Finally, if $v$ is a node, then we define the piece $V_{t_v} = \{v\}$; and if $e = (u, v)$ is an edge, then we define the piece $V_{t_e} = \{u, v\}$. One can now check that the three properties in the definition of a tree decomposition are satisfied.

## Properties of a Tree Decomposition

If we consider the definition more closely, we see that the Node Coverage and Edge Coverage Properties simply ensure that the collection of pieces corresponds to the graph $G$ in a minimal way. The crux of the definition is in the Coherence Property. While it is not obvious from its statement that Coherence leads to tree-like separation properties, in fact it does so quite naturally. Trees have two nice separation properties, closely related to each other, that get used all the time. One says that if we delete an edge $e$ from a tree, it falls apart into exactly two connected components. The other says that if we delete a node $t$ from a tree, then this is like deleting all the incident edges, and so the tree falls apart into a number of components equal to the degree of $t$. The Coherence Property is designed to guarantee that separations of $T$, of both these types, correspond naturally to separations of $G$ as well.

If $T'$ is a subgraph of $T$, we use $G_{T'}$ to denote the subgraph of $G$ induced by the nodes in all pieces associated with nodes of $T'$, that is, the set $\cup_{t \in T'} V_t$.

First consider deleting a node $t$ of $T$.

**(10.13)** *Suppose that $T - t$ has components $T_1, \ldots, T_d$. Then the subgraphs*

$$G_{T_1} - V_t, G_{T_2} - V_t, \ldots, G_{T_d} - V_t$$

*have no nodes in common, and there are no edges between them.*

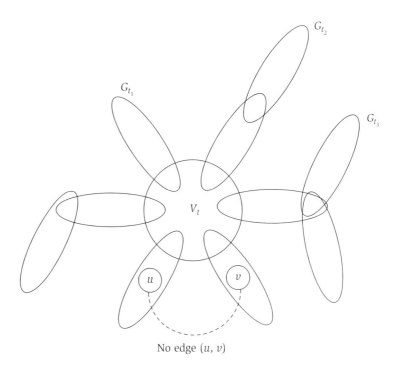

No edge $(u, v)$

**Figure 10.6** Separations of the tree $T$ translate to separations of the graph $G$.

**Proof.** We refer to Figure 10.6 for a general view of what the separation looks like. We first prove that the subgraphs $G_{T_i} - V_t$ do not share any nodes. Indeed, any such node $v$ would need to belong to both $G_{T_i} - V_t$ and $G_{T_j} - V_t$ for some $i \neq j$, and so such a node $v$ belongs to some piece $V_x$ with $x \in T_i$, and to some piece $V_y$ with $y \in T_j$. Since $t$ lies on the $x$-$y$ path in $T$, it follows from the Coherence Property that $v$ lies in $V_t$ and hence belongs to neither $G_{T_i} - V_t$ nor $G_{T_j} - V_t$.

Next we must show that there is no edge $e = (u, v)$ in $G$ with one end $u$ in subgraph $G_{T_i} - V_t$ and the other end $v$ in $G_{T_j} - V_t$ for some $j \neq i$. If there were such an edge, then by the Edge Coverage Property, there would need to be some piece $V_x$ containing both $u$ and $v$. The node $x$ cannot be in both the subgraphs $T_i$ and $T_j$. Suppose by symmetry $x \notin T_i$. Node $u$ is in the subgraph $G_{T_i}$, so $u$ must be in a set $V_y$ for some $y$ in $T_i$. Then the node $u$ belongs to both $V_x$ and $V_y$, and since $t$ lies on the $x$-$y$ path in $T$, it follows that $u$ also belongs to $V_t$, and so it does not lie in $G_{T_i} - V_t$ as required.  ∎

Proving the edge separation property is analogous. If we delete an edge $(x, y)$ from $T$, then $T$ falls apart into two components: $X$, containing $x$, and $Y$,

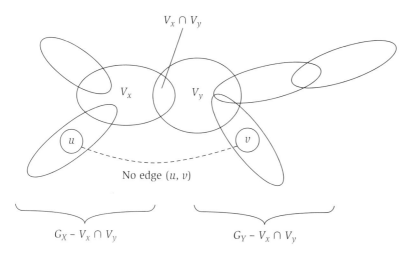

$V_x \cap V_y$

$V_x$

$V_y$

$u$

$v$

No edge $(u, v)$

$G_X - V_x \cap V_y$

$G_Y - V_x \cap V_y$

**Figure 10.7** Deleting an edge of the tree $T$ translates to separation of the graph $G$.

containing $y$. Let's establish the corresponding way in which $G$ is separated by this operation.

**(10.14)** *Let X and Y be the two components of T after the deletion of the edge $(x, y)$. Then deleting the set $V_x \cap V_y$ from V disconnects G into the two subgraphs $G_X - (V_x \cap V_y)$ and $G_Y - (V_x \cap V_y)$ More precisely, these two subgraphs do not share any nodes, and there is no edge with one end in each of them.*

**Proof.** We refer to Figure 10.7 for a general view of what the separation looks like. The proof of this property is analogous to the proof of (10.13). One first proves that the two subgraphs $G_X - (V_x \cap V_y)$ and $G_Y - (V_x \cap V_y)$ do not share any nodes, by showing that a node $v$ that belongs to both $G_X$ and $G_Y$ must belong to both $V_x$ and to $V_y$, and hence it does not lie in either $G_Y - (V_x \cap V_y)$ or $G_X - (V_x \cap V_y)$.

Now we must show that there is no edge $e = (u, v)$ in $G$ with one end $u$ in $G_X - (V_x \cap V_y)$ and the other end $v$ in $G_Y - (V_x \cap V_y)$. If there were such an edge, then by the Edge Coverage Property, there would need to be some piece $V_z$ containing both $u$ and $v$. Suppose by symmetry that $z \in X$. Node $v$ also belongs to some piece $V_w$ for $w \in Y$. Since $x$ and $y$ lie on the $w$-$z$ path in $T$, it follows that $V$ belongs to $V_x$ and $V_y$. Hence $v \in V_x \cap V_y$, and so it does not lie in $G_Y - (V_x \cap V_y)$ as required. ■

So tree decompositions are useful in that the separation properties of $T$ carry over to $G$. At this point, one might think that the key question is: Which graphs have tree decompositions? But this is not the point, for if we think about it, we see that of course every graph has a tree decomposition. Given any $G$, we can let $T$ be a tree consisting of a single node $t$, and let the single piece $V_t$ be equal to the entire node set of $G$. This easily satisfies the three properties required by the definition; and such a tree decomposition is no more useful to us than the original graph.

The crucial point, therefore, is to look for a tree decomposition in which all the pieces are *small*. This is really what we're trying to carry over from trees, by requiring that the deletion of a very small set of nodes breaks apart the graph into disconnected subgraphs. So we define the *width* of a tree decomposition $(T, \{V_t\})$ to be one less than the maximum size of any piece $V_t$:

$$\text{width}(T, \{V_t\}) = \max_t |V_t| - 1.$$

We then define the *tree-width* of $G$ to be the minimum width of any tree decomposition of $G$. Due to the Edge Coverage Property, all tree decompositions must have pieces with at least two nodes, and hence have tree-width at least 1. Recall that our tree decomposition for a tree $G$ has tree-width 1, as the sets $V_t$ each have either one or two nodes. The somewhat puzzling "–1" in this definition is so that trees turn out to have tree-width 1, rather than 2. Also, all graphs with a nontrivial tree decomposition of tree-width $w$ have separators of size $w$, since if $(x, y)$ is an edge of the tree, then, by (10.14), deleting $V_x \cap V_y$ separates $G$ into two components.

Thus we can talk about the set of all graphs of tree-width 1, the set of all graphs of tree-width 2, and so forth. The following fact establishes that trees are the only graphs with tree-width 1, and hence our definitions here indeed generalize the notion of a tree. The proof also provides a good way for us to exercise some of the basic properties of tree decompositions. We also observe that the graph in Figure 10.5 is thus, according to the notion of tree-width, a member of the next "simplest" class of graphs after trees: It is a graph of tree-width 2.

> **(10.15)**    *A connected graph $G$ has tree-width 1 if and only if it is a tree.*

**Proof.** We have already seen that if $G$ is a tree, then we can build a tree decomposition of tree-width 1 for $G$.

To prove the converse, we first establish the following useful fact: If $H$ is a subgraph of $G$, then the tree-width of $H$ is at most the tree-width of $G$. This is simply because, given a tree decomposition $(T, \{V_t\})$ of $G$, we can define a tree decomposition of $H$ by keeping the same underlying tree $T$ and replacing each piece $V_t$ with $V_t \cap H$. It is easy to check that the required three properties still hold. (The fact that certain pieces may now be equal to the empty set does not pose a problem.)

Now suppose by way of contradiction that $G$ is a connected graph of tree-width 1 that is not a tree. Since $G$ is not a tree, it has a subgraph consisting of a simple cycle $C$. By our argument from the previous paragraph, it is now enough for us to argue that the graph $C$ does not have tree-width 1. Indeed, suppose it had a tree decomposition $(T, \{V_t\})$ in which each piece had size at most 2. Choose any two edges $(u, v)$ and $(u', v')$ of $C$; by the Edge Coverage Property, there are pieces $V_t$ and $V_{t'}$ containing them. Now, on the path in $T$ from $t$ to $t'$ there must be an edge $(x, y)$ such that the pieces $V_x$ and $V_y$ are unequal. It follows that $|V_x \cap V_y| \leq 1$. We now invoke (10.14): Defining $X$ and $Y$ to be the components of $T - (x, y)$ containing $x$ and $y$, respectively, we see that deleting $V_x \cap V_y$ separates $C$ into $C_X - (V_x \cap V_y)$ and $C_Y - (V_x \cap V_y)$. Neither of these two subgraphs can be empty, since one contains $\{u, v\} - (V_x \cap V_y)$ and the other contains $\{u', v'\} - (V_x \cap V_y)$. But it is not possible to disconnect a cycle into two nonempty subgraphs by deleting a single node, and so this yields a contradiction. ■

When we use tree decompositions in the context of dynamic programming algorithms, we would like, for the sake of efficiency, that they not have too many pieces. Here is a simple way to do this. If we are given a tree decomposition $(T, \{V_t\})$ of a graph $G$, and we see an edge $(x, y)$ of $T$ such that $V_x \subseteq V_y$, then we can contract the edge $(x, y)$ (folding the piece $V_x$ into the piece $V_y$) and obtain a tree decomposition of $G$ based on a smaller tree. Repeating this process as often as necessary, we end up with a *nonredundant tree decomposition*: There is no edge $(x, y)$ of the underlying tree such that $V_x \subseteq V_y$.

Once we've reached such a tree decomposition, we can be sure that it does not have too many pieces:

**(10.16)** *Any nonredundant tree decomposition of an n-node graph has at most n pieces.*

**Proof.** We prove this by induction on $n$, the case $n = 1$ being clear. Let's consider the case in which $n > 1$. Given a nonredundant tree decomposition $(T, \{V_t\})$ of an $n$-node graph, we first identify a leaf $t$ of $T$. By the nonredundancy condition, there must be at least one node in $V_t$ that does not appear in the neighboring piece, and hence (by the Coherence Property) does not appear in any other piece. Let $U$ be the set of all such nodes in $V_t$. We now observe that by deleting $t$ from $T$, and removing $V_t$ from the collection of pieces, we obtain a nonredundant tree decomposition of $G - U$. By our inductive hypothesis, this tree decomposition has at most $n - |U| \leq n - 1$ pieces, and so $(T, \{V_t\})$ has at most $n$ pieces. ■

While (10.16) is very useful for making sure one has a small tree decomposition, it is often easier in the course of analyzing a graph to start by building a redundant tree decomposition, and only later "condensing" it down to a nonredundant one. For example, our tree decomposition for a graph $G$ that is a tree built a redundant tree decomposition; it would not have been as simple to directly describe a nonredundant one.

Having thus laid the groundwork, we now turn to the algorithmic uses of tree decompositions.

## Dynamic Programming over a Tree Decomposition

We began by claiming that the Maximum-Weight Independent Set could be solved efficiently on any graph for which the tree-width was bounded. Now it's time to deliver on this promise. Specifically, we will develop an algorithm that closely follows the linear-time algorithm for trees. Given an $n$-node graph with an associated tree decomposition of width $w$, it will run in time $O(f(w) \cdot n)$, where $f(\cdot)$ is an exponential function that depends only on the width $w$, not on the number of nodes $n$. And, as in the case of trees, although we are focusing on Maximum-Weight Independent Set, the approach here is useful for many NP-hard problems.

So, in a very concrete sense, the complexity of the problem has been pushed off of the size of the graph and into the tree-width, which may be much smaller. As we mentioned earlier, large networks in the real world often have very small tree-width; and often this is not coincidental, but a consequence of the structured or modular way in which they are designed. So, if we encounter a 1,000-node network with a tree decomposition of width 4, the approach discussed here takes a problem that would have been hopelessly intractable and makes it potentially quite manageable.

Of course, this is all somewhat reminiscent of the Vertex Cover Algorithm from Section 10.1. There we pushed the exponential complexity into the parameter $k$, the size of the vertex cover being sought. Here we did not have an obvious parameter other than $n$ lying around, so we were forced to invent a fairly nonobvious one: the tree-width.

To design the algorithm, we recall what we did for the case of a tree $T$. After rooting $T$, we built the independent set by working our way up from the leaves. At each internal node $u$, we enumerated the possibilities for what to do with $u$—include it or not include it—since once this decision was fixed, the problems for the different subtrees below $u$ became independent.

The generalization for a graph $G$ with a tree decomposition $(T, \{V_t\})$ of width $w$ looks very similar. We root the tree $T$ and build the independent set by considering the pieces $V_t$ from the leaves upward. At an internal node $t$

of $T$, we confront the following basic question: The optimal independent set intersects the piece $V_t$ in some subset $U$, but we don't know which set $U$ it is. So we enumerate all the possibilities for this subset $U$—that is, all possibilities for which nodes to include from $V_t$ and which to leave out. Since $V_t$ may have size up to $w + 1$, this may be $2^{w+1}$ possibilities to consider. But we now can exploit two key facts: first, that the quantity $2^{w+1}$ is a lot more reasonable than $2^n$ when $w$ is much smaller than $n$; and second, that once we fix a particular one of these $2^{w+1}$ possibilities—once we've decided which nodes in the piece $V_t$ to include—the separation properties (10.13) and (10.14) ensure that the problems in the different subtrees of $T$ below $t$ can be solved independently. So, while we settle for doing brute-force search at the level of a *single* piece, we have an algorithm that is quite efficient at the global level when the individual pieces are small.

**Defining the Subproblems**   More precisely, we root the tree $T$ at a node $r$. For any node $t$, let $T_t$ denote the subtree rooted at $t$. Recall that $G_{T_t}$ denotes the subgraph of $G$ induced by the nodes in all pieces associated with nodes of $T_t$; for notational simplicity, we will also write this subgraph as $G_t$. For a subset $U$ of $V$, we use $w(U)$ to denote the total weight of nodes in $U$; that is, $w(U) = \sum_{u \in U} w_u$.

We define a set of subproblems for each subtree $T_t$, one corresponding to each possible subset $U$ of $V_t$ that may represent the intersection of the optimal solution with $V_t$. Thus, for each independent set $U \subseteq V_t$, we write $f_t(U)$ to denote the maximum weight of an independent set $S$ in $G_t$, subject to the requirement that $S \cap V_t = U$. The quantity $f_t(U)$ is undefined if $U$ is not an independent set, since in this case we know that $U$ cannot represent the intersection of the optimal solution with $V_t$.

There are at most $2^{w+1}$ subproblems associated with each node $t$ of $T$, since this is the maximum possible number of independent subsets of $V_t$. By (10.16), we can assume we are working with a tree decomposition that has at most $n$ pieces, and hence there are a total of at most $2^{w+1}n$ subproblems overall. Clearly, if we have the solutions to all these subproblems, we can determine the maximum weight of an independent set in $G$ by looking at the subproblems associated with the root $r$: We simply take the maximum, over all independent sets $U \subseteq V_r$, of $f_r(U)$.

**Building Up Solutions**   Now we must show how to build up the solutions to these sub-problems via a recurrence. It's easy to get started: When $t$ is a leaf, $f_t(U)$ is equal to $w(U)$ for each independent set $U \subseteq V_t$.

Now suppose that $t$ has children $t_1, \ldots, t_d$, and we have already determined the values of $f_{t_i}(W)$ for each child $t_i$ and each independent set $W \subseteq V_{t_i}$. How do we determine the value of $f_t(U)$ for an independent set $U \subseteq V_t$?

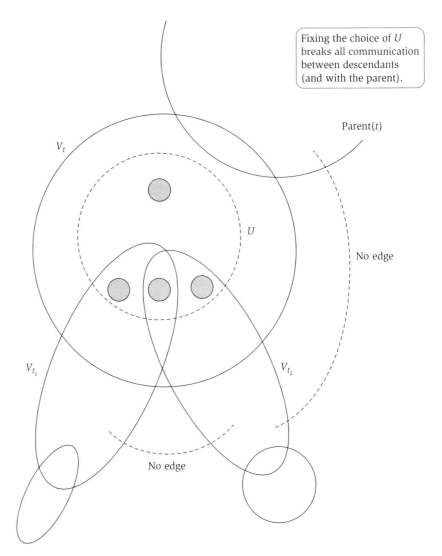

Fixing the choice of $U$ breaks all communication between descendants (and with the parent).

Parent$(t)$

$V_t$

$U$

No edge

$V_{t_1}$

$V_{t_2}$

No edge

**Figure 10.8** The subproblem $f_t(U)$ in the subgraph $G_t$. In the optimal solution to this subproblem, we consider independent sets $S_i$ in the descendant subgraphs $G_{t_i}$, subject to the constraint that $S_i \cap V_t = U \cap V_{t_i}$.

Let $S$ be the maximum-weight independent set in $G_t$ subject to the requirement that $S \cap V_t = U$; that is, $w(S) = f_t(U)$. The key is to understand how this set $S$ looks when intersected with each of the subgraphs $G_{t_i}$, as suggested in Figure 10.8. We let $S_i$ denote the intersection of $S$ with the nodes of $G_{t_i}$.

**(10.17)** $S_i$ *is a maximum-weight independent set of* $G_{t_i}$, *subject to the constraint that* $S_i \cap V_t = U \cap V_{t_i}$.

**Proof.** Suppose there were an independent set $S_i'$ of $G_{t_i}$ with the property that $S_i' \cap V_t = U \cap V_{t_i}$ and $w(S_i') > w(S_i)$. Then consider the set $S' = (S - S_i) \cup S_i'$. Clearly $w(S') > w(S)$. Also, it is easy to check that $S' \cap V_t = U$.

We claim that $S'$ is an independent set in $G$; this will contradict our choice of $S$ as the maximum-weight independent set in $G_t$ subject to $S \cap V_t = U$. For suppose $S'$ is not independent, and let $e = (u, v)$ be an edge with both ends in $S'$. It cannot be that $u$ and $v$ both belong to $S$, or that they both belong to $S_i'$, since these are both independent sets. Thus we must have $u \in S - S_i'$ and $v \in S_i' - S$, from which it follows that $u$ is not a node of $G_{t_i}$ while $v \in G_{t_i} - (V_t \cap V_{t_i})$. But then, by (10.14), there cannot be an edge joining $u$ and $v$. ∎

Statement (10.17) is exactly what we need to design a recurrence relation for our subproblems. It says that the information needed to compute $f_t(U)$ is implicit in the values already computed for the subtrees. Specifically, for each child $t_i$, we need simply determine the value of the maximum-weight independent set $S_i$ of $G_{t_i}$, subject to the constraint that $S_i \cap V_t = U \cap V_{t_i}$. This constraint does not completely determine what $S_i \cap V_{t_i}$ should be; rather, it says that it can be any independent set $U_i \subseteq V_{t_i}$ such that $U_i \cap V_t = U \cap V_{t_i}$. Thus the weight of the optimal $S_i$ is equal to

$$\max\{f_{t_i}(U_i) : U_i \cap V_t = U \cap V_{t_i} \text{ and } U_i \subseteq V_{t_i} \text{ is independent}\}.$$

Finally, the value of $f_t(U)$ is simply $w(U)$ plus these maxima added over the $d$ children of $t$—except that to avoid overcounting the nodes in $U$, we exclude them from the contribution of the children. Thus we have

**(10.18)** *The value of $f_t(U)$ is given by the following recurrence:*

$$f_t(U) = w(U) + \sum_{i=1}^{d} \max\{f_{t_i}(U_i) - w(U_i \cap U) :$$

$$U_i \cap V_t = U \cap V_{t_i} \text{ and } U_i \subseteq V_{t_i} \text{ is independent}\}.$$

The overall algorithm now just builds up the values of all the subproblems from the leaves of $T$ upward.

---

```
To find a maximum-weight independent set of G,
given a tree decomposition (T, {V_t}) of G:
    Modify the tree decomposition if necessary so it is nonredundant
    Root T at a node r
    For each node t of T in post-order
        If t is a leaf then
```

> For each independent set $U$ of $V_t$
> $\quad f_t(U) = w(U)$
> Else
> $\quad$ For each independent set $U$ of $V_t$
> $\quad\quad f_t(U)$ is determined by the recurrence in (10.18)
> Endif
> Endfor
> Return max $\{f_r(U) : U \subseteq V_r$ is independent$\}$.

An actual independent set of maximum weight can be found, as usual, by tracing back through the execution.

We can determine the time required for computing $f_t(U)$ as follows: For each of the $d$ children $t_i$, and for each independent set $U_i$ in $V_{t_i}$, we spend time $O(w)$ checking if $U_i \cap V_t = U \cap V_{t_i}$, to determine whether it should be considered in the computation of (10.18).

This is a total time of $O(2^{w+1}wd)$ for $f_t(U)$; since there are at most $2^{w+1}$ sets $U$ associated with $t$, the total time spent on node $t$ is $O(4^{w+1}wd)$. Finally, we sum this over all nodes $t$ to get the total running time. We observe that the sum, over all nodes $t$, of the number of children of $t$ is $O(n)$, since each node is counted as a child once. Thus the total running time is $O(4^{w+1}wn)$.

## * 10.5 Constructing a Tree Decomposition

In the previous section, we introduced the notion of tree decompositions and tree-width, and we discussed a canonical example of how to solve an NP-hard problem on graphs of bounded tree-width.

### The Problem

There is still a crucial missing piece in our algorithmic use of tree-width, however. Thus far, we have simply provided an algorithm for Maximum-Weight Independent Set on a graph $G$, *provided we have been given a low-width tree decomposition of G*. What if we simply encounter $G$ "in the wild," and no one has been kind enough to hand us a good tree decomposition of it? Can we compute one on our own, and then proceed with the dynamic programming algorithm?

The answer is basically yes, with some caveats. First we must warn that, given a graph $G$, it is NP-hard to determine its tree-width. However, the situation for us is not actually so bad, because we are only interested here in graphs for which the tree-width is a small constant. And, in this case, we will describe an algorithm with the following guarantee: Given a graph $G$ of tree-width less than $w$, it will produce a tree decomposition of $G$ of width less than $4w$ in time $O(f(w) \cdot mn)$, where $m$ and $n$ are the number of edges and nodes of $G$, and $f(\cdot)$ is a function that depends only on $w$. So, essentially, when the tree-width is small, there's a reasonably fast way to produce a tree decomposition whose width is almost as small as possible.

## Designing and Analyzing the Algorithm

*An Obstacle to Low Tree-Width* The first step in designing an algorithm for this problem is to work out a reasonable "obstacle" to a graph $G$ having low tree-width. In other words, as we try to construct a tree decomposition of low width for $G = (V, E)$, might there be some "local" structure we could discover that will tell us the tree-width must in fact be large?

The following idea turns out to provide us with such an obstacle. First, given two sets $Y, Z \subseteq V$ of the same size, we say they are *separable* if some strictly smaller set can completely disconnect them—specifically, if there is a set $S \subseteq V$ such that $|S| < |Y| = |Z|$ and there is no path from $Y - S$ to $Z - S$ in $G - S$. (In this definition, $Y$ and $Z$ need not be disjoint.) Next we say that a set $X$ of nodes in $G$ is *w-linked* if $|X| \geq w$ and $X$ does not contain separable subsets $Y$ and $Z$, such that $|Y| = |Z| \leq w$.

For later algorithmic use of $w$-linked sets, we make note of the following fact.

**(10.19)** *Let $G = (V, E)$ have m edges, let X be a set of k nodes in G, and let $w \leq k$ be a given parameter. Then we can determine whether X is w-linked in time $O(f(k) \cdot m)$, where $f(\cdot)$ depends only on k. Moreover, if X is not w-linked, we can return a proof of this in the form of sets $Y, Z \subseteq X$ and $S \subseteq V$ such that $|S| < |Y| = |Z| \leq w$ and there is no path from $Y - S$ to $Z - S$ in $G - S$.*

**Proof.** We are trying to decide whether $X$ contains separable subsets $Y$ and $Z$ such that $|Y| = |Z| \leq w$. We can first enumerate all pairs of sufficiently small subsets $Y$ and $Z$; since $X$ only has $2^k$ subsets, there are at most $4^k$ such pairs.

Now, for each pair of subsets $Y, Z$, we must determine whether they are separable. Let $\ell = |Y| = |Z| \leq w$. But this is exactly the Max-Flow Min-Cut Theorem when we have an undirected graph with capacities on the nodes: $Y$ and $Z$ are separable if and only there do not exist $\ell$ node-disjoint paths, each with one end in $Y$ and the other in $Z$. (See Exercise 13 in Chapter 7 for the version of maximum flows with capacities on the nodes.) We can determine whether such paths exist using an algorithm for flow with (unit) capacities on the nodes; this takes time $O(\ell m)$. ∎

One should imagine a $w$-linked set as being highly self-entwined—it has no two small parts that can be easily split off from each other. At the same time, a tree decomposition cuts up a graph using very small separators; and so it is intuitively reasonable that these two structures should be in opposition to each other.

**(10.20)**    *If G contains a $(w + 1)$-linked set of size at least $3w$, then G has tree-width at least w.*

**Proof.** Suppose, by way of contradiction, that $G$ has a $(w + 1)$-linked set $X$ of size at least $3w$, and it also has a tree decomposition $(T, \{V_t\})$ of width less than $w$; in other words, each piece $V_t$ has size at most $w$. We may further assume that $(T, \{V_t\})$ is nonredundant.

The idea of the proof is to find a piece $V_t$ that is "centered" with respect to $X$, so that when some part of $V_t$ is deleted from $G$, one small subset of $X$ is separated from another. Since $V_t$ has size at most $w$, this will contradict our assumption that $X$ is $(w + 1)$-linked.

So how do we find this piece $V_t$? We first root the tree $T$ at a node $r$; using the same notation as before, we let $T_t$ denote the subtree rooted at a node $t$, and write $G_t$ for $G_{T_t}$. Now let $t$ be a node that is as far from the root $r$ as possible, subject to the condition that $G_t$ contains more than $2w$ nodes of $X$.

Clearly, $t$ is not a leaf (or else $G_t$ could contain at most $w$ nodes of $X$); so let $t_1, \ldots, t_d$ be the children of $t$. Note that since each $t_i$ is farther than $t$ from the root, each subgraph $G_{t_i}$ contains at most $2w$ nodes of $X$. If there is a child $t_i$ so that $G_{t_i}$ contains at least $w$ nodes of $X$, then we can define $Y$ to be $w$ nodes of $X$ belonging to $G_{t_i}$, and $Z$ to be $w$ nodes of $X$ belonging to $G - G_{t_i}$. Since $(T, \{V_t\})$ is nonredundant, $S = V_{t_i} \cap V_t$ has size at most $w - 1$; but by (10.14), deleting $S$ disconnects $Y - S$ from $Z - S$. This contradicts our assumption that $X$ is $(w + 1)$-linked.

So we consider the case in which there is no child $t_i$ such that $G_{t_i}$ contains at least $w$ nodes of $X$; Figure 10.9 suggests the structure of the argument in this case. We begin with the node set of $G_{t_1}$, combine it with $G_{t_2}$, then $G_{t_3}$, and so forth, until we first obtain a set of nodes containing more than $w$ members of $X$. This will clearly happen by the time we get to $G_{t_d}$, since $G_t$ contains more than $2w$ nodes of $X$, and at most $w$ of them can belong to $V_t$. So suppose our process of combining $G_{t_1}, G_{t_2}, \ldots$ first yields more than $w$ members of $X$ once we reach index $i \leq d$. Let $W$ denote the set of nodes in the subgraphs $G_{t_1}, G_{t_2}, \ldots, G_{t_i}$. By our stopping condition, we have $|W \cap X| > w$. But since $G_{t_i}$ contains fewer than $w$ nodes of $X$, we also have $|W \cap X| < 2w$. Hence we can define $Y$ to be $w + 1$ nodes of $X$ belonging to $W$, and $Z$ to be $w + 1$ nodes of $X$ belonging to $V - W$. By (10.13), the piece $V_t$ is now a set of size at most $w$ whose deletion disconnects $Y - V_t$ from $Z - V_t$. Again this contradicts our assumption that $X$ is $(w + 1)$-linked, completing the proof.  ∎

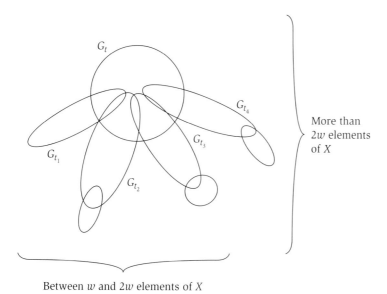

More than $2w$ elements of $X$

Between $w$ and $2w$ elements of $X$

**Figure 10.9** The final step in the proof of (10.20).

***An Algorithm to Search for a Low-Width Tree Decomposition***    Building on these ideas, we now give a greedy algorithm for constructing a tree decomposition of low width. The algorithm will not precisely determine the tree-width of the input graph $G = (V, E)$; rather, given a parameter $w$, either it will produce a tree decomposition of width less than $4w$, or it will discover a $(w + 1)$-linked set of size at least $3w$. In the latter case, this constitutes a proof that the tree-width of $G$ is at least $w$, by (10.20); so our algorithm is essentially capable of narrowing down the true tree-width of $G$ to within a factor of 4. As discussed earlier, the running time will have the form $O(f(w) \cdot mn)$, where $m$ and $n$ are the number of edges and nodes of $G$, and $f(\cdot)$ depends only on $w$.

Having worked with tree decompositions for a little while now, one can start imagining what might be involved in constructing one for an arbitrary input graph $G$. The process is depicted at a high level in Figure 10.10. Our goal is to make $G$ fall apart into tree-like portions; we begin the decomposition by placing the first piece $V_t$ anywhere. Now, hopefully, $G - V_t$ consists of several disconnected components; we recursively move into each of these components, placing a piece in each so that it partially overlaps the piece $V_t$ that we've already defined. We hope that these new pieces cause the graph to break up further, and we thus continue in this way, pushing forward with small sets while the graph breaks apart in front of us. The key to making this algorithm work is to argue the following: If at some point we get stuck, and our

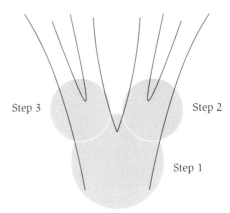

**Figure 10.10** A schematic view of the first three steps in the construction of a tree decomposition. As each step produces a new piece, the goal is to break up the remainder of the graph into disconnected components in which the algorithm can continue iteratively.

small sets don't cause the graph to break up any further, then we can extract a large $(w + 1)$-linked set that proves the tree-width was in fact large.

Given how vague this intuition is, the actual algorithm follows it more closely than you might expect. We start by assuming that there is no $(w + 1)$-linked set of size at least $3w$; our algorithm will produce a tree decomposition provided this holds true, and otherwise we can stop with a proof that the tree-width of $G$ is at least $w$. We grow the underlying tree $T$ of the decomposition, and the pieces $V_t$, in a greedy fashion. At every intermediate stage of the algorithm, we will maintain the property that we have a *partial tree decomposition*: by this we mean that if $U \subseteq V$ denotes the set of nodes of $G$ that belong to at least one of the pieces already constructed, then our current tree $T$ and pieces $V_t$ should form a tree decomposition of the subgraph of $G$ induced on $U$. We define the width of a partial tree decomposition, by analogy with our definition for the width of a tree decomposition, to be one less than the maximum piece size. This means that in order to achieve our goal of having a width of less than $4w$, it is enough to make sure that all pieces have size at most $4w$.

If $C$ is a connected component of $G - U$, we say that $u \in U$ is a *neighbor* of $C$ if there is some node $v \in C$ with an edge to $u$. The key behind the algorithm is not to simply maintain a partial tree decomposition of width less than $4w$, but also to make sure the following invariant is enforced the whole time:

(∗) *At any stage in the execution of the algorithm, each component $C$ of $G - U$ has at most $3w$ neighbors, and there is a single piece $V_t$ that contains all of them.*

Why is this invariant so useful? It's useful because it will let us add a new node $s$ to $T$ and grow a new piece $V_s$ in the component $C$, with the confidence that $s$ can be a leaf hanging off $t$ in the larger partial tree decomposition. Moreover, $(*)$ requires there be at most $3w$ neighbors, while we are trying to produce a tree decomposition of width less than $4w$; this extra $w$ gives our new piece "room" to expand by a little as it moves into $C$.

Specifically, we now describe how to add a new node and a new piece so that we still have a partial tree decomposition, the invariant $(*)$ is still maintained, and the set $U$ has grown strictly larger. In this way, we make at least one node's worth of progress, and so the algorithm will terminate in at most $n$ iterations with a tree decomposition of the whole graph $G$.

Let $C$ be any component of $G-U$, let $X$ be the set of neighbors of $U$, and let $V_t$ be a piece that, as guaranteed by $(*)$, contains all of $X$. We know, again by $(*)$, that $X$ contains at most $3w$ nodes. If $X$ in fact contains strictly fewer than $3w$ nodes, we can make progress right away: For any node $v \in C$ we define a new piece $V_s = X \cup \{v\}$, making $s$ a leaf of $t$. Since all the edges from $v$ into $U$ have their ends in $X$, it is easy to confirm that we still have a partial tree decomposition obeying $(*)$, and $U$ has grown.

Thus, let's suppose that $X$ has exactly $3w$ nodes. In this case, it is less clear how to proceed; for example, if we try to create a new piece by arbitrarily adding a node $v \in C$ to $X$, we may end up with a component of $C-\{v\}$ (which may be all of $C-\{v\}$) whose neighbor set includes all $3w + 1$ nodes of $X \cup \{v\}$, and this would violate $(*)$.

There's no simple way around this; for one thing, $G$ may not actually have a low-width tree decomposition. So this is precisely the place where it makes sense to ask whether $X$ poses a genuine obstacle to the tree decomposition or not: we test whether $X$ is a $(w + 1)$-linked set. By (10.19), we can determine the answer to this in time $O(f(w) \cdot m)$, since $|X| = 3w$. If it turns out that $X$ is $(w + 1)$-linked, then we are all done; we can halt with the conclusion that $G$ has tree-width at least $w$, which was one acceptable outcome of the algorithm. On the other hand, if $X$ is not $(w + 1)$-linked, then we end up with $Y, Z \subseteq X$ and $S \subseteq V$ such that $|S| < |Y| = |Z| \leq w + 1$ and there is no path from $Y-S$ to $Z-S$ in $G-S$. The sets $Y, Z$, and $S$ will now provide us with a means to extend the partial tree decomposition.

Let $S'$ consist of the nodes of $S$ that lie in $Y \cup Z \cup C$. The situation is now as pictured in Figure 10.11. We observe that $S' \cap C$ is not empty: $Y$ and $Z$ each have edges into $C$, and so if $S' \cap C$ were empty, there would be a path from $Y-S$ to $Z-S$ in $G-S$ that started in $Y$, jumped immediately into $C$, traveled through $C$, and finally jumped back into $Z$. Also, $|S'| \leq |S| \leq w$.

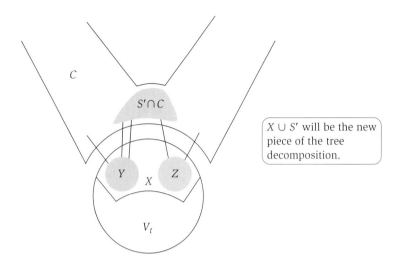

$X \cup S'$ will be the new piece of the tree decomposition.

**Figure 10.11** Adding a new piece to the partial tree decomposition.

We define a new piece $V_s = X \cup S'$, making $s$ a leaf of $t$. All the edges from $S'$ into $U$ have their ends in $X$, and $|X \cup S'| \leq 3w + w = 4w$, so we still have a partial tree decomposition. Moreover, the set of nodes covered by our partial tree decomposition has grown, since $S' \cap C$ is not empty. So we will be done if we can show that the invariant $(*)$ still holds. This brings us exactly the intuition we tried to capture when discussing Figure 10.10: As we add the new piece $X \cup S'$, we are hoping that the component $C$ breaks up into further components in a nice way.

Concretely, our partial tree decomposition now covers $U \cup S'$; and where we previously had a component $C$ of $G - U$, we now may have several components $C' \subseteq C$ of $G - (U \cup S')$. Each of these components $C'$ has all its neighbors in $X \cup S'$; but we must additionally make sure there are at most $3w$ such neighbors, so that the invariant $(*)$ continues to hold. So consider one of these components $C'$. We claim that all its neighbors in $X \cup S'$ actually belong to one of the two subsets $(X - Z) \cup S'$ or $(X - Y) \cup S'$, and each of these sets has size at most $|X| \leq 3w$. For, if this did not hold, then $C'$ would have a neighbor in both $Y - S$ and $Z - S$, and hence there would be a path, through $C'$, from $Y - S$ to $Z - S$ in $G - S$. But we have already argued that there cannot be such a path. This establishes that $(*)$ still holds after the addition of the new piece and completes the argument that the algorithm works correctly.

Finally, what is the running time of the algorithm? The time to add a new piece to the partial tree decomposition is dominated by the time required to check whether $X$ is $(w + 1)$-linked, which is $O(f(w) \cdot m)$. We do this for at most $n$ iterations, since we increase the number of nodes of $G$ that we cover in each iteration. So the total running time is $O(f(w) \cdot mn)$.

We summarize the properties of our tree decomposition algorithm as follows.

**(10.21)** *Given a graph G and a parameter w, the tree decomposition algorithm in this section does one of the following two things:*

- *it produces a tree decomposition of width less than 4w, or*
- *it reports (correctly) that G does not have tree-width less than w.*

*The running time of the algorithm is $O(f(w) \cdot mn)$, for a function $f(\cdot)$ that depends only on w.*

# Solved Exercises

## Solved Exercise 1

As we've seen, 3-SAT is often used to model complex planning and decision-making problems in artificial intelligence: the variables represent binary decisions to be made, and the clauses represent constraints on these decisions. Systems that work with instances of 3-SAT often need to represent situations in which some decisions have been made while others are still undetermined, and for this purpose it is useful to introduce the notion of a *partial assignment* of truth values to variables.

Concretely, given a set of Boolean variables $X = \{x_1, x_2, \ldots, x_n\}$, we say that a *partial assignment* for $X$ is an assignment of the value 0, 1, or ? to each $x_i$; in other words, it is a function $\rho : X \to \{0, 1, ?\}$. We say that a variable $x_i$ is *determined* by the partial assignment if it receives the value 0 or 1, and *undetermined* if it receives the value ?. We can think of a partial assignment as choosing a truth value of 0 or 1 for each of its determined variables, and leaving the truth value of each undetermined variable up in the air.

Now, given a collection of clauses $C_1, \ldots, C_m$, each a disjunction of three distinct terms, we may be interested in whether a partial assignment is sufficient to "force" the collection of clauses to be satisfied, regardless of how we set the undetermined variables. Similarly, we may be interested in whether there exists a partial assignment with only a few determined variables that can force the collection of clauses to be satisfied; this small set of determined variables can be viewed as highly "influential," since their outcomes alone can be enough to force the satisfaction of the clauses.

For example, suppose we are given clauses

$$(x_1 \vee \overline{x_2} \vee \overline{x_4}), (x_2 \vee \overline{x_3} \vee x_4), (\overline{x_2} \vee \overline{x_3} \vee x_5), (x_1 \vee x_3 \vee \overline{x_6}).$$

Then the partial assignment that sets $x_1$ to 1, sets $x_3$ to 0, and sets all other variables to ? has only two determined variables, but it forces the collection of clauses to be satisfied: No matter how we set the remaining four variables, the clauses will be satisfied.

Here's a way to formalize this. Recall that a *truth assignment* for $X$ is an assignment of the value 0 or 1 to each $x_i$; in other words, it must select a truth value for *every* variable and not leave any variables undetermined. We say that a truth assignment $v$ is *consistent* with a partial assignment $\rho$ if each variable that is determined in $\rho$ has the same truth value in both $\rho$ and $v$. (In other words, if $\rho(x_i) \neq ?$, then $\rho(x_i) = v(x_i)$.) Finally, we say that a partial assignment $\rho$ *forces* the collection of clauses $C_1, \ldots, C_m$ if, for every truth assignment $v$ that is consistent with $\rho$, it is the case that $v$ satisfies $C_1, \ldots, C_m$. (We will also call $\rho$ a *forcing partial assignment*.)

Motivated by the issues raised above, here's the question. We are given a collection of Boolean variables $X = \{x_1, x_2, \ldots, x_n\}$, a parameter $b < n$, and a collection of clauses $C_1, \ldots, C_m$ over the variables, where each clause is a disjunction of three distinct terms. We want to decide whether there exists a forcing partial assignment $\rho$ for $X$, such that at most $b$ variables are determined by $\rho$. Give an algorithm that solves this problem with a running time of the form $O(f(b) \cdot p(n, m))$, where $p(\cdot)$ is a polynomial function, and $f(\cdot)$ is an arbitrary function that depends only on $b$, not on $n$ or $m$.

**Solution**    Intuitively, a forcing partial assignment must "hit" each clause in at least one place, since otherwise it wouldn't be able to ensure the truth value. Although this seems natural, it's not actually part of the definition (the definition just talks about truth assignments that are consistent with the partial assignment), so we begin by formalizing and proving this intuition.

**(10.22)**    *A partial assignment $\rho$ forces all clauses if and only if, for each clause $C_i$, at least one of the variables in $C_i$ is determined by $\rho$ in a way that satisfies $C_i$.*

**Proof.** Clearly, if $\rho$ determines at least one variable in each $C_i$ in a way that satisfies it, then no matter how we construct a full truth assignment for the remaining variables, all the clauses are already satisfied. Thus any truth assignment consistent with $\rho$ satisfies all clauses.

Now, for the converse, suppose there is a clause $C_i$ such that $\rho$ does not determine any of the variables in $C_i$ in a way that satisfies $C_i$. We want to show that $\rho$ is not forcing, which, according to the definition, requires us to exhibit a consistent truth assignment that does not satisfy all clauses. So consider the following truth assignment $\nu$: $\nu$ agrees with $\rho$ on all determined variables, it assigns an arbitrary truth value to each undetermined variable not appearing in $C_i$, and it sets each undetermined variable in $C_i$ in a way that fails to satisfy it. We observe that $\nu$ sets each of the variables in $C_i$ so as not to satisfy it, and hence $\nu$ is not a satisfying assignment. But $\nu$ is consistent with $\rho$, and so it follows that $\rho$ is not a forcing partial assignment. ■

In view of (10.22), we have a problem that is very much like the search for small vertex covers at the beginning of the chapter. There we needed to find a set of nodes that covered all edges, and we were limited to choosing at most $k$ nodes. Here we need to find a set of variables that covers all clauses (and with the right true/false values), and we're limited to choosing at most $b$ variables.

So let's try an analogue of the approach we used for finding a small vertex cover. We pick an arbitrary clause $C_\ell$, containing $x_i$, $x_j$, and $x_k$ (each possibly negated). We know from (10.22) that any forcing assignment $\rho$ must set one of these three variables the way it appears in $C_\ell$, and so we can try all three of these possibilities. Suppose we set $x_i$ the way it appears in $C_\ell$; we can then eliminate from the instance all clauses (including $C_\ell$) that are satisfied by this assignment to $x_i$, and consider trying to satisfy what's left. We call this smaller set of clauses the instance *reduced by the assignment to $x_i$*. We can do the same for $x_j$ and $x_k$. Since $\rho$ must determine one of these three variables the way they appear in $C_\ell$, and then still satisfy what's left, we have justified the following analogue of (10.3). (To make the terminology a bit easier to discuss, we say that the *size* of a partial assignment is the number of variables it determines.)

**(10.23)** *There exists a forcing assignment of size at most $b$ if and only if there is a forcing assignment of size at most $b - 1$ on at least one of the instances reduced by the assignment to $x_i$, $x_j$, or $x_k$.*

We therefore have the following algorithm. (It relies on the boundary cases in which there are no clauses (when by definition we can declare success) and in which there are clauses but $b = 0$ (in which case we declare failure).

```
To search for a forcing partial assignment of size at most b:
   If there are no clauses, then by definition we have
      a forcing assignment
   Else if b = 0 then by (10.22) there is no forcing assignment
   Else let Cₗ be an arbitrary clause containing variables xᵢ, xⱼ, xₖ
      For each of xᵢ, xⱼ, xₖ:
         Set xᵢ the way it appears in Cₗ
         Reduce the instance by this assignment
```

```
        Recursively check for a forcing assignment of size at
            most b − 1 on this reduced instance
    Endfor
    If any of these recursive calls (say for xᵢ) returns a
        forcing assignment ρ′ of size most b − 1 then
            Combining ρ′ with the assignment to xᵢ is the desired answer
    Else (none of these recursive calls succeeds)
        There is no forcing assignment of size at most b
    Endif
Endif
```

To bound the running time, we consider the tree of possibilities being searched, just as in the algorithm for finding a vertex cover. Each recursive call gives rise to three children in this tree, and this goes on to a depth of at most $b$. Thus the tree has at most $1 + 3 + 3^2 + \cdots + 3^b \leq 3^{b+1}$ nodes, and at each node we spend at most $O(m + n)$ time to produce the reduced instances. Thus the total running time is $O(3^b(m + n))$.

# Exercises

1. In Exercise 5 of Chapter 8, we claimed that the Hitting Set Problem was NP-complete. To recap the definitions, consider a set $A = \{a_1, \ldots, a_n\}$ and a collection $B_1, B_2, \ldots, B_m$ of subsets of $A$. We say that a set $H \subseteq A$ is a *hitting set* for the collection $B_1, B_2, \ldots, B_m$ if $H$ contains at least one element from each $B_i$—that is, if $H \cap B_i$ is not empty for each $i$. (So $H$ "hits" all the sets $B_i$.)

   Now suppose we are given an instance of this problem, and we'd like to determine whether there is a hitting set for the collection of size at most $k$. Furthermore suppose that each set $B_i$ has at most $c$ elements, for a constant $c$. Give an algorithm that solves this problem with a running time of the form $O(f(c, k) \cdot p(n, m))$, where $p(\cdot)$ is a polynomial function, and $f(\cdot)$ is an arbitrary function that depends only on $c$ and $k$, not on $n$ or $m$.

2. The difficulty in 3-SAT comes from the fact that there are $2^n$ possible assignments to the input variables $x_1, x_2, \ldots, x_n$, and there's no apparent way to search this space in polynomial time. This intuitive picture, however, might create the misleading impression that the fastest algorithms for 3-SAT actually require time $2^n$. In fact, though it's somewhat counterintuitive when you first hear it, there are algorithms for 3-SAT that run in significantly less than $2^n$ time in the worst case; in other words, they

determine whether there's a satisfying assignment in less time than it would take to enumerate all possible settings of the variables.

Here we'll develop one such algorithm, which solves instances of 3-SAT in $O(p(n) \cdot (\sqrt{3})^n)$ time for some polynomial $p(n)$. Note that the main term in this running time is $(\sqrt{3})^n$, which is bounded by $1.74^n$.

(a) For a truth assignment $\Phi$ for the variables $x_1, x_2, \ldots, x_n$, we use $\Phi(x_i)$ to denote the value assigned by $\Phi$ to $x_i$. (This can be either 0 or 1.) If $\Phi$ and $\Phi'$ are each truth assignments, we define the *distance* between $\Phi$ and $\Phi'$ to be the number of variables $x_i$ for which they assign different values, and we denote this distance by $d(\Phi, \Phi')$. In other words, $d(\Phi, \Phi') = |\{i : \Phi(x_i) \neq \Phi'(x_i)\}|$.

A basic building block for our algorithm will be the ability to answer the following kind of question: Given a truth assignment $\Phi$ and a distance $d$, we'd like to know whether there exists a satisfying assignment $\Phi'$ such that the distance from $\Phi$ to $\Phi'$ is at most $d$. Consider the following algorithm, Explore($\Phi, d$), that attempts to answer this question.

```
Explore(Φ,d):
   If Φ is a satisfying assignment then return "yes"
   Else if d = 0 then return "no"
   Else
      Let Cᵢ be a clause that is not satisfied by Φ
         (i.e., all three terms in Cᵢ evaluate to false)
      Let Φ₁ denote the assignment obtained from Φ by
         taking the variable that occurs in the first term of
         clause Cᵢ and inverting its assigned value
      Define Φ₂ and Φ₃ analogously in terms of the
         second and third terms of the clause Cᵢ
      Recursively invoke:
         Explore(Φ₁,d − 1)
         Explore(Φ₂,d − 1)
         Explore(Φ₃,d − 1)
      If any of these three calls returns "yes"
         then return "yes"
      Else return "no"
```

Prove that Explore($\Phi, d$) returns "yes" if and only if there exists a satisfying assignment $\Phi'$ such that the distance from $\Phi$ to $\Phi'$ is at most $d$. Also, give an analysis of the running time of Explore($\Phi, d$) as a function of $n$ and $d$.

(b) Clearly any two assignments $\Phi$ and $\Phi'$ have distance at most $n$ from each other, so one way to solve the given instance of 3-SAT would be to pick an arbitrary starting assignment $\Phi$ and then run `Explore`$(\Phi, n)$. However, this will not give us the running time we want.

Instead, we will need to make several calls to `Explore`, from different starting points $\Phi$, and search each time out to more limited distances. Describe how to do this in such a way that you can solve the instance of 3-SAT in a running time of only $O(p(n) \cdot (\sqrt{3})^n)$.

3. Suppose we are given a directed graph $G = (V, E)$, with $V = \{v_1, v_2, \ldots, v_n\}$, and we want to decide whether $G$ has a Hamiltonian path from $v_1$ to $v_n$. (That is, is there a path in $G$ that goes from $v_1$ to $v_n$, passing through every other vertex exactly once?)

Since the Hamiltonian Path Problem is NP-complete, we do not expect that there is a polynomial-time solution for this problem. However, this does not mean that all nonpolynomial-time algorithms are equally "bad." For example, here's the simplest brute-force approach: For each permutation of the vertices, see if it forms a Hamiltonian path from $v_1$ to $v_n$. This takes time roughly proportional to $n!$, which is about $3 \times 10^{17}$ when $n = 20$.

Show that the Hamiltonian Path Problem can in fact be solved in time $O(2^n \cdot p(n))$, where $p(n)$ is a polynomial function of $n$. This is a much better algorithm for moderate values of $n$; for example, $2^n$ is only about a million when $n = 20$.

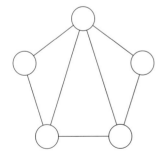

**Figure 10.12** A triangulated cycle graph: The edges form the boundary of a convex polygon together with a set of line segments that divide its interior into triangles.

4. We say that a graph $G = (V, E)$ is a *triangulated cycle graph* if it consists of the vertices and edges of a triangulated convex $n$-gon in the plane—in other words, if it can be drawn in the plane as follows.

The vertices are all placed on the boundary of a convex set in the plane (we may assume on the boundary of a circle), with each pair of consecutive vertices on the circle joined by an edge. The remaining edges are then drawn as straight line segments through the interior of the circle, with no pair of edges crossing in the interior. We require the drawing to have the following property. If we let $S$ denote the set of all points in the plane that lie on vertices or edges of the drawing, then each bounded component of the plane after deleting $S$ is bordered by exactly three edges. (This is the sense in which the graph is a "triangulation.")

A triangulated cycle graph is pictured in Figure 10.12.

Prove that every triangulated cycle graph has a tree decomposition of width at most 2, and describe an efficient algorithm to construct such a decomposition.

5. The *Minimum-Cost Dominating Set Problem* is specified by an undirected graph $G = (V, E)$ and costs $c(v)$ on the nodes $v \in V$. A subset $S \subset V$ is said to be a *dominating set* if all nodes $u \in V - S$ have an edge $(u, v)$ to a node $v$ in $S$. (Note the difference between dominating sets and vertex covers: in a dominating set, it is fine to have an edge $(u, v)$ with neither $u$ nor $v$ in the set $S$ as long as both $u$ and $v$ have neighbors in $S$.)

   (a) Give a polynomial-time algorithm for the Dominating Set Problem for the special case in which $G$ is a tree.

   (b) Give a polynomial-time algorithm for the Dominating Set Problem for the special case in which $G$ has tree-width 2, and we are also given a tree decomposition of $G$ with width 2.

6. The Node-Disjoint Paths Problem is given by an undirected graph $G$ and $k$ pairs of nodes $(s_i, t_i)$ for $i = 1, \ldots, k$. The problem is to decide whether there are node-disjoint paths $P_i$ so that path $P_i$ connects $s_i$ to $t_i$. Give a polynomial-time algorithm for the Node-Disjoint Paths Problem for the special case in which $G$ has tree-width 2, and we are also given a tree decomposition $T$ of $G$ with width 2.

7. The *chromatic number* of a graph $G$ is the minimum $k$ such that it has a $k$-coloring. As we saw in Chapter 8, it is NP-complete for $k \geq 3$ to decide whether a given input graph has chromatic number $\leq k$.

   (a) Show that for every natural number $w \geq 1$, there is a number $k(w)$ so that the following holds. If $G$ is a graph of tree-width at most $w$, then $G$ has chromatic number at most $k(w)$. (The point is that $k(w)$ depends only on $w$, not on the number of nodes in $G$.)

   (b) Given an undirected $n$-node graph $G = (V, E)$ of tree-width at most $w$, show how to compute the chromatic number of $G$ in time $O(f(w) \cdot p(n))$, where $p(\cdot)$ is a polynomial but $f(\cdot)$ can be an arbitrary function.

8. Consider the class of 3-SAT instances in which each of the $n$ variables occurs—counting positive and negated appearances combined—in exactly three clauses. Show that any such instance of 3-SAT is in fact satisfiable, and that a satisfying assignment can be found in polynomial time.

9. Give a polynomial-time algorithm for the following problem. We are given a binary tree $T = (V, E)$ with an even number of nodes, and a nonnegative weight on each edge. We wish to find a partition of the nodes $V$ into two

sets of *equal* size so that the weight of the cut between the two sets is as large as possible (i.e., the total weight of edges with one end in each set is as large as possible). Note that the restriction that the graph is a tree is crucial here, but the assumption that the tree is binary is not. The problem is NP-hard in general graphs.

## Notes and Further Reading

The first topic in this chapter, on how to avoid a running time of $O(kn^{k+1})$ for Vertex Cover, is an example of the general theme of *parameterized complexity*: for problems with two such "size parameters" $n$ and $k$, one generally prefers running times of the form $O(f(k) \cdot p(n))$, where $p(\cdot)$ is a polynomial, rather than running times of the form $O(n^k)$. A body of work has grown up around this issue, including a methodology for identifying NP-complete problems that are unlikely to allow for such improved running times. This area is covered in the book by Downey and Fellows (1999).

The problem of coloring a collection of circular arcs was shown to be NP-complete by Garey, Johnson, Miller, and Papadimitriou (1980). They also described how the algorithm presented in this chapter follows directly from a construction due to Tucker (1975). Both Interval Coloring and Circular-Arc Coloring belong to the following class of problems: Take a collection of geometric objects (such as intervals or arcs), define a graph by joining pairs of objects that intersect, and study the problem of coloring this graph. The book on graph coloring by Jensen and Toft (1995) includes descriptions of a number of other problems in this style.

The importance of tree decompositions and tree-width was brought into prominence largely through the work of Robertson and Seymour (1990). The algorithm for constructing a tree decomposition described in Section 10.5 is due to Diestel et al. (1999). Further discussion of tree-width and its role in both algorithms and graph theory can be found in the survey by Reed (1997) and the book by Diestel (2000). Tree-width has also come to play an important role in inference algorithms for probabilistic models in machine learning (Jordan 1998).

*Notes on the Exercises*    Exercise 2 is based on a result of Uwe Schöning; and Exercise 8 is based on a problem we learned from Amit Kumar.

# Chapter 11

## Approximation Algorithms

Following our encounter with NP-completeness and the idea of computational intractability in general, we've been dealing with a fundamental question: How should we design algorithms for problems where polynomial time is probably an unattainable goal?

In this chapter, we focus on a new theme related to this question: *approximation algorithms*, which run in polynomial time and find solutions that are guaranteed to be close to optimal. There are two key words to notice in this definition: *close* and *guaranteed*. We will not be seeking the optimal solution, and as a result, it becomes feasible to aim for a polynomial running time. At the same time, we will be interested in proving that our algorithms find solutions that are guaranteed to be close to the optimum. There is something inherently tricky in trying to do this: In order to prove an approximation guarantee, we need to compare our solution with—and hence reason about—an optimal solution that is computationally very hard to find. This difficulty will be a recurring issue in the analysis of the algorithms in this chapter.

We will consider four general techniques for designing approximation algorithms. We start with *greedy algorithms*, analogous to the kind of algorithms we developed in Chapter 4. These algorithms will be simple and fast, as in Chapter 4, with the challenge being to find a greedy rule that leads to solutions provably close to optimal. The second general approach we pursue is the *pricing method*. This approach is motivated by an economic perspective; we will consider a price one has to pay to enforce each constraint of the problem. For example, in a graph problem, we can think of the nodes or edges of the graph sharing the cost of the solution in some equitable way. The pricing method is often referred to as the *primal-dual technique*, a term inherited from the study of linear programming, which can also be used to motivate this approach. Our presentation of the pricing method here will not assume familiarity with linear programming. We will introduce linear programming through our third technique in this chapter, *linear programming and rounding*, in which one exploits the relationship between the computational feasibility of linear programming and the expressive power of its more difficult cousin, *integer programming*. Finally, we will describe a technique that can lead to extremely good approximations: using dynamic programming on a rounded version of the input.

## 11.1 Greedy Algorithms and Bounds on the Optimum: A Load Balancing Problem

As our first topic in this chapter, we consider a fundamental *Load Balancing Problem* that arises when multiple servers need to process a set of jobs or requests. We focus on a basic version of the problem in which all servers are identical, and each can be used to serve any of the requests. This simple problem is useful for illustrating some of the basic issues that one needs to deal with in designing and analyzing approximation algorithms, particularly the task of comparing an approximate solution with an optimum solution that we cannot compute efficiently. Moreover, we'll see that the general issue of load balancing is a problem with many facets, and we'll explore some of these in later sections.

### The Problem

We formulate the Load Balancing Problem as follows. We are given a set of $m$ machines $M_1, \ldots, M_m$ and a set of $n$ jobs; each job $j$ has a processing time $t_j$. We seek to assign each job to one of the machines so that the loads placed on all machines are as "balanced" as possible.

More concretely, in any assignment of jobs to machines, we can let $A(i)$ denote the set of jobs assigned to machine $M_i$; under this assignment, machine $M_i$ needs to work for a total time of

$$T_i = \sum_{j \in A(i)} t_j,$$

and we declare this to be the *load* on machine $M_i$. We seek to minimize a quantity known as the *makespan*; it is simply the maximum load on any machine, $T = \max_i T_i$. Although we will not prove this, the scheduling problem of finding an assignment of minimum makespan is NP-hard.

## Designing the Algorithm

We first consider a very simple greedy algorithm for the problem. The algorithm makes one pass through the jobs in any order; when it comes to job $j$, it assigns $j$ to the machine whose load is smallest so far.

```
Greedy-Balance:
Start with no jobs assigned
Set T_i = 0 and A(i) = ∅ for all machines M_i
For j = 1, ..., n
    Let M_i be a machine that achieves the minimum min_k T_k
    Assign job j to machine M_i
    Set A(i) ← A(i) ∪ {j}
    Set T_i ← T_i + t_j
EndFor
```

For example, Figure 11.1 shows the result of running this greedy algorithm on a sequence of six jobs with sizes 2, 3, 4, 6, 2, 2; the resulting makespan is 8, the "height" of the jobs on the first machine. Note that this is not the optimal solution; had the jobs arrived in a different order, so that the algorithm saw the sequence of sizes 6, 4, 3, 2, 2, 2, then it would have produced an allocation with a makespan of 7.

## Analyzing the Algorithm

Let $T$ denote the makespan of the resulting assignment; we want to show that $T$ is not much larger than the minimum possible makespan $T^*$. Of course, in trying to do this, we immediately encounter the basic problem mentioned above: We need to compare our solution to the optimal value $T^*$, even though we don't know what this value is and have no hope of computing it. For the

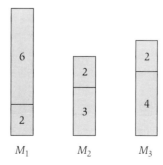

**Figure 11.1** The result of running the greedy load balancing algorithm on three machines with job sizes 2, 3, 4, 6, 2, 2.

analysis, therefore, we will need a *lower bound* on the optimum—a quantity with the guarantee that no matter how good the optimum is, it cannot be less than this bound.

There are many possible lower bounds on the optimum. One idea for a lower bound is based on considering the total processing time $\sum_j t_j$. One of the $m$ machines must do at least a $1/m$ fraction of the total work, and so we have the following.

**(11.1)**    *The optimal makespan is at least*

$$T^* \geq \frac{1}{m} \sum_j t_j.$$

There is a particular kind of case in which this lower bound is much too weak to be useful. Suppose we have one job that is extremely long relative to the sum of all processing times. In a sufficiently extreme version of this, the optimal solution will place this job on a machine by itself, and it will be the last one to finish. In such a case, our greedy algorithm would actually produce the optimal solution; but the lower bound in (11.1) isn't strong enough to establish this.

This suggests the following additional lower bound on $T^*$.

**(11.2)**    *The optimal makespan is at least $T^* \geq \max_j t_j$.*

Now we are ready to evaluate the assignment obtained by our greedy algorithm.

**(11.3)**    *Algorithm* Greedy-Balance *produces an assignment of jobs to machines with makespan $T \leq 2T^*$.*

**Proof.** Here is the overall plan for the proof. In analyzing an approximation algorithm, one compares the solution obtained to what one knows about the optimum—in this case, our lower bounds (11.1) and (11.2). We consider a machine $M_i$ that attains the maximum load $T$ in our assignment, and we ask: What was the last job $j$ to be placed on $M_i$? If $t_j$ is not too large relative to most of the other jobs, then we are not too far above the lower bound (11.1). And, if $t_j$ is a very large job, then we can use (11.2). Figure 11.2 shows the structure of this argument.

Here is how we can make this precise. When we assigned job $j$ to $M_i$, the machine $M_i$ had the smallest load of any machine; this is the key property of our greedy algorithm. Its load just before this assignment was $T_i - t_j$, and since this was the smallest load at that moment, it follows that every machine

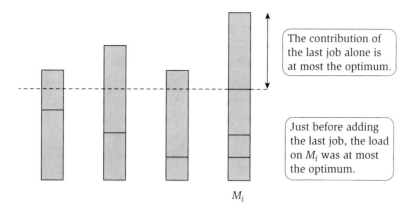

The contribution of the last job alone is at most the optimum.

Just before adding the last job, the load on $M_i$ was at most the optimum.

$M_i$

**Figure 11.2** Accounting for the load on machine $M_i$ in two parts: the last job to be added, and all the others.

had load at least $T_i - t_j$. Thus, adding up the loads of all machines, we have $\sum_k T_k \geq m(T_i - t_j)$, or equivalently,

$$T_i - t_j \leq \frac{1}{m} \sum_k T_k.$$

But the value $\sum_k T_k$ is just the total load of all jobs $\sum_j t_j$ (since every job is assigned to exactly one machine), and so the quantity on the right-hand side of this inequality is exactly our lower bound on the optimal value, from (11.1). Thus

$$T_i - t_j \leq T^*.$$

Now we account for the remaining part of the load on $M_i$, which is just the final job $j$. Here we simply use the other lower bound we have, (11.2), which says that $t_j \leq T^*$. Adding up these two inequalities, we see that

$$T_i = (T_i - t_j) + t_j \leq 2T^*.$$

Since our makespan $T$ is equal to $T_i$, this is the result we want. ∎

It is not hard to give an example in which the solution is indeed close to a factor of 2 away from optimal. Suppose we have $m$ machines and $n = m(m - 1) + 1$ jobs. The first $m(m - 1) = n - 1$ jobs each require time $t_j = 1$. The last job is much larger; it requires time $t_n = m$. What does our greedy algorithm do with this sequence of jobs? It evenly balances the first $n - 1$ jobs, and then has to add the giant job $n$ to one of them; the resulting makespan is $T = 2m - 1$.

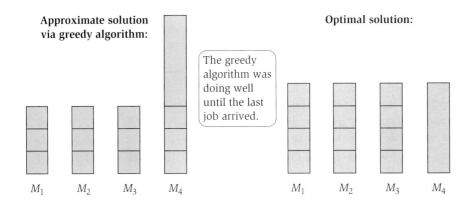

**Figure 11.3** A bad example for the greedy balancing algorithm with $m = 4$.

What does the optimal solution look like in this example? It assigns the large job to one of the machines, say, $M_1$, and evenly spreads the remaining jobs over the other $m - 1$ machines. This results in a makespan of $m$. Thus the ratio between the greedy algorithm's solution and the optimal solution is $(2m - 1)/m = 2 - 1/m$, which is close to a factor of 2 when $m$ is large.

See Figure 11.3 for a picture of this with $m = 4$; one has to admire the perversity of the construction, which misleads the greedy algorithm into perfectly balancing everything, only to mess everything up with the final giant item.

In fact, with a little care, one can improve the analysis in (11.3) to show that the greedy algorithm with $m$ machines is within exactly this factor of $2 - 1/m$ on every instance; the example above is really as bad as possible.

## Extensions: An Improved Approximation Algorithm

Now let's think about how we might develop a better approximation algorithm—in other words, one for which we are always guaranteed to be within a factor strictly smaller than 2 away from the optimum. To do this, it helps to think about the worst cases for our current approximation algorithm. Our earlier bad example had the following flavor: We spread everything out very evenly across the machines, and then one last, giant, unfortunate job arrived. Intuitively, it looks like it would help to get the largest jobs arranged nicely first, with the idea that later, small jobs can only do so much damage. And in fact, this idea does lead to a measurable improvement.

Thus we now analyze the variant of the greedy algorithm that first sorts the jobs in decreasing order of processing time and then proceeds as before.

We will prove that the resulting assignment has a makespan that is at most 1.5 times the optimum.

---

```
Sorted-Balance:
Start with no jobs assigned
Set  T_i = 0 and A(i) = ∅ for all machines M_i
Sort jobs in decreasing order of processing times t_j
Assume that t_1 ≥ t_2 ≥ ... ≥ t_n
For j = 1, ..., n
   Let M_i be the machine that achieves the minimum min_k T_k
   Assign job j to machine M_i
   Set  A(i) ← A(i) ∪ {j}
   Set  T_i ← T_i + t_j
EndFor
```

---

The improvement comes from the following observation. If we have fewer than $m$ jobs, then the greedy solution will clearly be optimal, since it puts each job on its own machine. And if we have more than $m$ jobs, then we can use the following further lower bound on the optimum.

**(11.4)** *If there are more than m jobs, then* $T^* \geq 2t_{m+1}$.

**Proof.** Consider only the first $m + 1$ jobs in the sorted order. They each take at least $t_{m+1}$ time. There are $m + 1$ jobs and only $m$ machines, so there must be a machine that gets assigned two of these jobs. This machine will have processing time at least $2t_{m+1}$. ∎

**(11.5)** *Algorithm* Sorted-Balance *produces an assignment of jobs to machines with makespan* $T \leq \frac{3}{2}T^*$.

**Proof.** The proof will be very similar to the analysis of the previous algorithm. As before, we will consider a machine $M_i$ that has the maximum load. If $M_i$ only holds a single job, then the schedule is optimal.

So let's assume that machine $M_i$ has at least two jobs, and let $t_j$ be the last job assigned to the machine. Note that $j \geq m + 1$, since the algorithm will assign the first $m$ jobs to $m$ distinct machines. Thus $t_j \leq t_{m+1} \leq \frac{1}{2}T^*$, where the second inequality is (11.4).

We now proceed as in the proof of (11.3), with the following single change. At the end of that proof, we had inequalities $T_i - t_j \leq T^*$ and $t_j \leq T^*$, and we added them up to get the factor of 2. But in our case here, the second of these inequalities is, in fact, $t_j \leq \frac{1}{2}T^*$; so adding the two inequalities gives us the bound

$$T_i \leq \frac{3}{2}T^*. \quad \blacksquare$$

## 11.2 The Center Selection Problem

Like the problem in the previous section, the Center Selection Problem, which we consider here, also relates to the general task of allocating work across multiple servers. The issue at the heart of Center Selection is where best to place the servers; in order to keep the formulation clean and simple, we will not incorporate the notion of load balancing into the problem. The Center Selection Problem also provides an example of a case in which the most natural greedy algorithm can result in an arbitrarily bad solution, but a slightly different greedy method is guaranteed to always result in a near-optimal solution.

### The Problem

Consider the following scenario. We have a set $S$ of $n$ *sites*—say, $n$ little towns in upstate New York. We want to select $k$ *centers* for building large shopping malls. We expect that people in each of these $n$ towns will shop at one of the malls, and so we want to select the sites of the $k$ malls to be central.

Let us start by defining the input to our problem more formally. We are given an integer $k$, a set $S$ of $n$ sites (corresponding to the towns), and a distance function. When we consider instances where the sites are points in the plane, the distance function will be the standard Euclidean distance between points, and any point in the plane is an option for placing a center. The algorithm we develop, however, can be applied to more general notions of distance. In applications, distance sometimes means straight-line distance, but can also mean the travel time from point $s$ to point $z$, or the driving distance (i.e., distance along roads), or even the cost of traveling. We will allow any distance function that satisfies the following natural properties.

- $dist(s, s) = 0$ for all $s \in S$
- the distance is symmetric: $dist(s, z) = dist(z, s)$ for all sites $s, z \in S$
- the triangle inequality: $dist(s, z) + dist(z, h) \geq dist(s, h)$

The first and third of these properties tend to be satisfied by essentially all natural notions of distance. Although there are applications with asymmetric distances, most cases of interest also satisfy the second property. Our greedy algorithm will apply to any distance function that satisfies these three properties, and it will depend on all three.

Next we have to clarify what we mean by the goal of wanting the centers to be "central." Let $C$ be a set of centers. We assume that the people in a given town will shop at the closest mall. This suggests we define the distance of a site $s$ to the centers as $dist(s, C) = \min_{c \in C} dist(s, c)$. We say that $C$ forms an $r$-*cover* if each site is within distance at most $r$ from one of the centers—that is, if $dist(s, C) \leq r$ for all sites $s \in S$. The minimum $r$ for which $C$ is an $r$-cover will be called the *covering radius* of $C$ and will be denoted by $r(C)$. In other words, the covering radius of a set of centers $C$ is the farthest that anyone needs to travel to get to his or her nearest center. Our goal will be to select a set $C$ of $k$ centers for which $r(C)$ is as small as possible.

## Designing and Analyzing the Algorithm

***Difficulties with a Simple Greedy Algorithm*** We now discuss greedy algorithms for this problem. As before, the meaning of "greedy" here is necessarily a little fuzzy; essentially, we consider algorithms that select sites one by one in a myopic fashion—that is, choosing each without explicitly considering where the remaining sites will go.

Probably the simplest greedy algorithm would work as follows. It would put the first center at the best possible location for a single center, then keep adding centers so as to reduce the covering radius, each time, by as much as possible. It turns out that this approach is a bit too simplistic to be effective: there are cases where it can lead to very bad solutions.

To see that this simple greedy approach can be really bad, consider an example with only two sites $s$ and $z$, and $k = 2$. Assume that $s$ and $z$ are located in the plane, with distance equal to the standard Euclidean distance in the plane, and that any point in the plane is an option for placing a center. Let $d$ be the distance between $s$ and $z$. Then the best location for a single center $c_1$ is halfway between $s$ and $z$, and the covering radius of this one center is $r(\{c_1\}) = d/2$. The greedy algorithm would start with $c_1$ as the first center. No matter where we add a second center, at least one of $s$ or $z$ will have the center $c_1$ as closest, and so the covering radius of the set of two centers will still be $d/2$. Note that the optimum solution with $k = 2$ is to select $s$ and $z$ themselves as the centers. This will lead to a covering radius of 0. A more complex example illustrating the same problem can be obtained by having two dense "clusters" of sites, one around $s$ and one around $z$. Here our proposed greedy algorithm would start by opening a center halfway between the clusters, while the optimum solution would open a separate center for each cluster.

***Knowing the Optimal Radius Helps*** In searching for an improved algorithm, we begin with a useful thought experiment. Suppose for a minute that someone told us what the optimum radius $r$ is. Would this information help? That is, suppose we *know* that there is a set of $k$ centers $C^*$ with radius $r(C^*) \leq r$, and

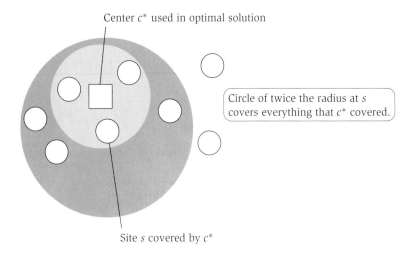

Center $c^*$ used in optimal solution

Circle of twice the radius at $s$ covers everything that $c^*$ covered.

Site $s$ covered by $c^*$

**Figure 11.4** Everything covered at radius $r$ by $c^*$ is also covered at radius $2r$ by $s$.

our job is to find some set of $k$ centers $C$ whose covering radius is not much more than $r$. It turns out that finding a set of $k$ centers with covering radius at most $2r$ can be done relatively easily.

Here is the idea: We can use the existence of this solution $C^*$ in our algorithm even though we do not know what $C^*$ is. Consider any site $s \in S$. There must be a center $c^* \in C^*$ that covers site $s$, and this center $c^*$ is at distance at most $r$ from $s$. Now our idea would be to take this site $s$ as a center in our solution instead of $c^*$, as we have no idea what $c^*$ is. We would like to make $s$ cover all the sites that $c^*$ covers in the unknown solution $C^*$. This is accomplished by expanding the radius from $r$ to $2r$. All the sites that were at distance at most $r$ from center $c^*$ are at distance at most $2r$ from $s$ (by the triangle inequality). See Figure 11.4 for a simple illustration of this argument.

```
S' will represent the sites that still need to be covered
Initialize S' = S
Let C = ∅
While S' ≠ ∅
    Select any site s ∈ S' and add s to C
    Delete all sites from S' that are at distance at most 2r from s
EndWhile
If |C| ≤ k then
    Return C as the selected set of sites
Else
```

```
    Claim (correctly) that there is no set of k centers with
        covering radius at most r
EndIf
```

Clearly, if this algorithm returns a set of at most $k$ centers, then we have what we wanted.

**(11.6)** *Any set of centers C returned by the algorithm has covering radius* $r(C) \leq 2r$.

Next we argue that if the algorithm fails to return a set of centers, then its conclusion that no set can have covering radius at most $r$ is indeed correct.

**(11.7)** *Suppose the algorithm selects more than k centers. Then, for any set* $C^*$ *of size at most k, the covering radius is* $r(C^*) > r$.

**Proof.** Assume the opposite, that there is a set $C^*$ of at most $k$ centers with covering radius $r(C^*) \leq r$. Each center $c \in C$ selected by the greedy algorithm is one of the original sites in $S$, and the set $C^*$ has covering radius at most $r$, so there must be a center $c^* \in C^*$ that is at most a distance of $r$ from $c$—that is, $dist(c, c^*) \leq r$. Let us say that such a center $c^*$ is *close* to $c$. We want to claim that no center $c^*$ in the optimal solution $C^*$ can be close to two different centers in the greedy solution $C$. If we can do this, we are done: each center $c \in C$ has a close optimal center $c^* \in C^*$, and each of these close optimal centers is distinct. This will imply that $|C^*| \geq |C|$, and since $|C| > k$, this will contradict our assumption that $C^*$ contains at most $k$ centers.

So we just need to show that no optimal center $c^* \in C$ can be close to each of two centers $c, c' \in C$. The reason for this is pictured in Figure 11.5. Each pair of centers $c, c' \in C$ is separated by a distance of more than $2r$, so if $c^*$ were within a distance of at most $r$ from each, then this would violate the triangle inequality, since $dist(c, c^*) + dist(c^*, c') \geq dist(c, c') > 2r$. ∎

***Eliminating the Assumption That We Know the Optimal Radius*** Now we return to the original question: How do we select a good set of $k$ centers *without* knowing what the optimal covering radius might be?

It is worth discussing two different answers to this question. First, there are many cases in the design of approximation algorithms where it is conceptually useful to assume that you know the value achieved by an optimal solution. In such situations, you can often start with an algorithm designed under this assumption and convert it into one that achieves a comparable performance guarantee by simply trying out a range of "guesses" as to what the optimal

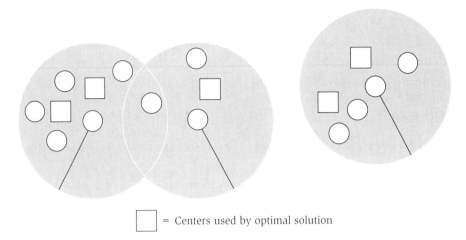

☐ = Centers used by optimal solution

**Figure 11.5** The crucial step in the analysis of the greedy algorithm that knows the optimal radius $r$. No center used by the optimal solution can lie in two different circles, so there must be at least as many optimal centers as there are centers chosen by the greedy algorithm.

value might be. Over the course of the algorithm, this sequence of guesses gets more and more accurate, until an approximate solution is reached.

For the Center Selection Problem, this could work as follows. We can start with some very weak initial guesses about the radius of the optimal solution: We know it is greater than 0, and it is at most the maximum distance $r_{max}$ between any two sites. So we could begin by splitting the difference between these two and running the greedy algorithm we developed above with this value of $r = r_{max}/2$. One of two things will happen, according to the design of the algorithm: Either we find a set of $k$ centers with covering radius at most $2r$, or we conclude that there is no solution with covering radius at most $r$. In the first case, we can afford to lower our guess on the radius of the optimal solution; in the second case, we need to raise it. This gives us the ability to perform a kind of binary search on the radius: in general, we will iteratively maintain values $r_0 < r_1$ so that we know the optimal radius is greater than $r_0$, but we have a solution of radius at most $2r_1$. From these values, we can run the above algorithm with radius $r = (r_0 + r_1)/2$; we will either conclude that the optimal solution has radius greater than $r > r_0$, or obtain a solution with radius at most $2r = (r_0 + r_1) < 2r_1$. Either way, we will have sharpened our estimates on one side or the other, just as binary search is supposed to do. We can stop when we have estimates $r_0$ and $r_1$ that are close to each other; at this point, our solution of radius $2r_1$ is close to being a 2-approximation to the optimal radius, since we know the optimal radius is greater than $r_0$ (and hence close to $r_1$).

*A Greedy Algorithm That Works* For the specific case of the Center Selection Problem, there is a surprising way to get around the assumption of knowing the radius, without resorting to the general technique described earlier. It turns out we can run essentially the same greedy algorithm developed earlier without knowing anything about the value of $r$.

The earlier greedy algorithm, armed with knowledge of $r$, repeatedly selects one of the original sites $s$ as the next center, making sure that it is at least $2r$ away from all previously selected sites. To achieve essentially the same effect without knowing $r$, we can simply select the site $s$ that is farthest away from all previously selected centers: If there is any site at least $2r$ away from all previously chosen centers, then this farthest site $s$ must be one of them. Here is the resulting algorithm.

```
Assume k ≤ |S| (else define C = S)
Select any site s and let C = {s}
While |C| < k
    Select a site s ∈ S that maximizes dist(s, C)
    Add site s to C
EndWhile
Return C as the selected set of sites
```

**(11.8)** *This greedy algorithm returns a set $C$ of $k$ points such that $r(C) \le 2r(C^*)$, where $C^*$ is an optimal set of $k$ points.*

**Proof.** Let $r = r(C^*)$ denote the minimum possible radius of a set of $k$ centers. For the proof, we assume that we obtain a set of $k$ centers $C$ with $r(C) > 2r$, and from this we derive a contradiction.

So let $s$ be a site that is more than $2r$ away from every center in $C$. Consider some intermediate iteration in the execution of the algorithm, where we have thus far selected a set of centers $C'$. Suppose we are adding the center $c'$ in this iteration. We claim that $c'$ is at least $2r$ away from all sites in $C'$. This follows as site $s$ is more than $2r$ away from all sites in the larger set $C$, and we select a site $c$ that is the farthest site from all previously selected centers. More formally, we have the following chain of inequalities:

$$dist(c', C') \ge dist(s, C') \ge dist(s, C) > 2r.$$

It follows that our greedy algorithm is a correct implementation of the first $k$ iterations of the `while` loop of the previous algorithm, which knew the optimal radius $r$: In each iteration, we are adding a center at distance more than $2r$ from all previously selected centers. But the previous algorithm would have $S' \neq \emptyset$ after selecting $k$ centers, as it would have $s \in S'$, and so it would go on and select more than $k$ centers and eventually conclude that $k$ centers cannot have covering radius at most $r$. This contradicts our choice of $r$, and the contradiction proves that $r(C) \leq 2r$. ∎

Note the surprising fact that our final greedy 2-approximation algorithm is a very simple modification of the first greedy algorithm that did not work. Perhaps the most important change is simply that our algorithm always selects sites as centers (i.e., every mall will be built in one of the little towns and not halfway between two of them).

## 11.3 Set Cover: A General Greedy Heuristic

In this section we will consider a very general problem that we also encountered in Chapter 8, the Set Cover Problem. A number of important algorithmic problems can be formulated as special cases of Set Cover, and hence an approximation algorithm for this problem will be widely applicable. We will see that it is possible to design a greedy algorithm here that produces solutions with a guaranteed approximation factor relative to the optimum, although this factor will be weaker than what we saw for the problems in Sections 11.1 and 11.2.

While the greedy algorithm we design for Set Cover will be very simple, the analysis will be more complex than what we encountered in the previous two sections. There we were able to get by with very simple bounds on the (unknown) optimum solution, while here the task of comparing to the optimum is more difficult, and we will need to use more sophisticated bounds. This aspect of the method can be viewed as our first example of the pricing method, which we will explore more fully in the next two sections.

### ✎ The Problem

Recall from our discussion of NP-completeness that the Set Cover Problem is based on a set $U$ of $n$ elements and a list $S_1, \ldots, S_m$ of subsets of $U$; we say that a *set cover* is a collection of these sets whose union is equal to all of $U$.

In the version of the problem we consider here, each set $S_i$ has an associated *weight* $w_i \geq 0$. The goal is to find a set cover $C$ so that the total weight

$$\sum_{S_i \in C} w_i$$

is minimized. Note that this problem is at least as hard as the decision version of Set Cover we encountered earlier; if we set all $w_i = 1$, then the minimum weight of a set cover is at most $k$ if and only if there is a collection of at most $k$ sets that covers $U$.

## Designing the Algorithm

We will develop and analyze a greedy algorithm for this problem. The algorithm will have the property that it builds the cover one set at a time; to choose its next set, it looks for one that seems to make the most progress toward the goal. What is a natural way to define "progress" in this setting? Desirable sets have two properties: They have small weight $w_i$, and they cover lots of elements. Neither of these properties alone, however, would be enough for designing a good approximation algorithm. Instead, it is natural to combine these two criteria into the single measure $w_i/|S_i|$—that is, by selecting $S_i$, we cover $|S_i|$ elements at a cost of $w_i$, and so this ratio gives the "cost per element covered," a very reasonable thing to use as a guide.

Of course, once some sets have already been selected, we are only concerned with how we are doing on the elements still left uncovered. So we will maintain the set $R$ of remaining uncovered elements and choose the set $S_i$ that minimizes $w_i/|S_i \cap R|$.

```
Greedy-Set-Cover:
Start with R = U and no sets selected
While R ≠ ∅
    Select set S_i that minimizes w_i/|S_i ∩ R|
    Delete set S_i from R
EndWhile
Return the selected sets
```

As an example of the behavior of this algorithm, consider what it would do on the instance in Figure 11.6. It would first choose the set containing the four nodes at the bottom (since this has the best weight-to-coverage ratio, 1/4). It then chooses the set containing the two nodes in the second row, and finally it chooses the sets containing the two individual nodes at the top. It thereby chooses a collection of sets of total weight 4. Because it myopically chooses the best option each time, this algorithm misses the fact that there's a way to cover everything using a weight of just $2 + 2\varepsilon$, by selecting the two sets that each cover a full column.

## Analyzing the Algorithm

The sets selected by the algorithm clearly form a set cover. The question we want to address is: How much larger is the weight of this set cover than the weight $w^*$ of an optimal set cover?

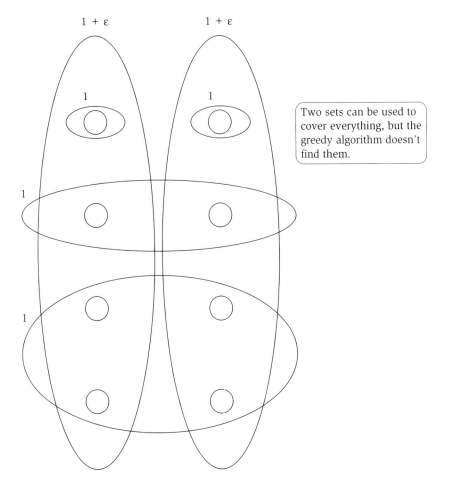

**Figure 11.6** An instance of the Set Cover Problem where the weights of sets are either 1 or $1 + \varepsilon$ for some small $\varepsilon > 0$. The greedy algorithm chooses sets of total weight 4, rather than the optimal solution of weight $2 + 2\varepsilon$.

As in Sections 11.1 and 11.2, our analysis will require a good lower bound on this optimum. In the case of the Load Balancing Problem, we used lower bounds that emerged naturally from the statement of the problem: the average load, and the maximum job size. The Set Cover Problem will turn out to be more subtle; "simple" lower bounds are not very useful, and instead we will use a lower bound that the greedy algorithm implicitly constructs as a by-product.

Recall the intuitive meaning of the ratio $w_i/|S_i \cap R|$ used by the algorithm; it is the "cost paid" for covering each new element. Let's record this cost paid for element $s$ in the quantity $c_s$. We add the following line to the code immediately after selecting the set $S_i$.

---
Define $c_s = w_i/|S_i \cap R|$ for all $s \in S_i \cap R$
---

The values $c_s$ do not affect the behavior of the algorithm at all; we view them as a bookkeeping device to help in our comparison with the optimum $w^*$. As each set $S_i$ is selected, its weight is distributed over the costs $c_s$ of the elements that are newly covered. Thus these costs completely account for the total weight of the set cover, and so we have

**(11.9)** *If $\mathcal{C}$ is the set cover obtained by* Greedy-Set-Cover, *then $\sum_{S_i \in \mathcal{C}} w_i = \sum_{s \in U} c_s$.*

The key to the analysis is to ask how much total cost any single set $S_k$ can account for—in other words, to give a bound on $\sum_{s \in S_k} c_s$ relative to the weight $w_k$ of the set, even for sets not selected by the greedy algorithm. Giving an upper bound on the ratio

$$\frac{\sum_{s \in S_k} c_s}{w_k}$$

that holds for every set says, in effect, "To cover a lot of cost, you must use a lot of weight." We know that the optimum solution must cover the full cost $\sum_{s \in U} c_s$ via the sets it selects; so this type of bound will establish that it needs to use at least a certain amount of weight. This is a lower bound on the optimum, just as we need for the analysis.

Our analysis will use the *harmonic function*

$$H(n) = \sum_{i=1}^{n} \frac{1}{i}.$$

To understand its asymptotic size as a function of $n$, we can interpret it as a sum approximating the area under the curve $y = 1/x$. Figure 11.7 shows how it is naturally bounded above by $1 + \int_1^n \frac{1}{x}\, dx = 1 + \ln n$, and bounded below by $\int_1^{n+1} \frac{1}{x}\, dx = \ln(n + 1)$. Thus we see that $H(n) = \Theta(\ln n)$.

Here is the key to establishing a bound on the performance of the algorithm.

**(11.10)** *For every set $S_k$, the sum $\sum_{s \in S_k} c_s$ is at most $H(|S_k|) \cdot w_k$.*

**Proof.** To simplify the notation, we will assume that the elements of $S_k$ are the first $d = |S_k|$ elements of the set $U$; that is, $S_k = \{s_1, \ldots, s_d\}$. Furthermore, let us assume that these elements are labeled in the order in which they are assigned a cost $c_{s_j}$ by the greedy algorithm (with ties broken arbitrarily). There

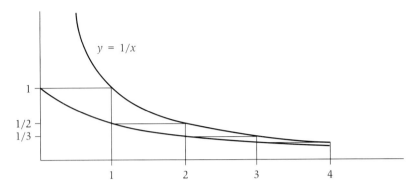

**Figure 11.7** Upper and lower bounds for the Harmonic Function $H(n)$.

is no loss of generality in doing this, since it simply involves a renaming of the elements in $U$.

Now consider the iteration in which element $s_j$ is covered by the greedy algorithm, for some $j \leq d$. At the start of this iteration, $s_j, s_{j+1}, \ldots, s_d \in R$ by our labeling of the elements. This implies that $|S_k \cap R|$ is at least $d - j + 1$, and so the average cost of the set $S_k$ is at most

$$\frac{w_k}{|S_k \cap R|} \leq \frac{w_k}{d - j + 1}.$$

Note that this is not necessarily an equality, since $s_j$ may be covered in the same iteration as some of the other elements $s_{j'}$ for $j' < j$. In this iteration, the greedy algorithm selected a set $S_i$ of minimum average cost; so this set $S_i$ has average cost at most that of $S_k$. It is the average cost of $S_i$ that gets assigned to $s_j$, and so we have

$$c_{s_j} = \frac{w_i}{|S_i \cap R|} \leq \frac{w_k}{|S_k \cap R|} \leq \frac{w_k}{d - j + 1}.$$

We now simply add up these inequalities for all elements $s \in S_k$:

$$\sum_{s \in S_k} c_s = \sum_{j=1}^{d} c_{s_j} \leq \sum_{j=1}^{d} \frac{w_k}{d - j + 1} = \frac{w_k}{d} + \frac{w_k}{d - 1} + \ldots + \frac{w_k}{1} = H(d) \cdot w_k. \quad \blacksquare$$

We now complete our plan to use the bound in (11.10) for comparing the greedy algorithm's set cover to the optimal one. Letting $d^* = \max_i |S_i|$ denote the maximum size of any set, we have the following approximation result.

**(11.11)**  *The set cover $\mathcal{C}$ selected by* `Greedy-Set-Cover` *has weight at most $H(d^*)$ times the optimal weight $w^*$.*

**Proof.** Let $\mathcal{C}^*$ denote the optimum set cover, so that $w^* = \sum_{S_i \in \mathcal{C}^*} w_i$. For each of the sets in $\mathcal{C}^*$, (11.10) implies

$$w_i \geq \frac{1}{H(d^*)} \sum_{s \in S_i} c_s.$$

Because these sets form a set cover, we have

$$\sum_{S_i \in \mathcal{C}^*} \sum_{s \in S_i} c_s \geq \sum_{s \in U} c_s.$$

Combining these with (11.9), we obtain the desired bound:

$$w^* = \sum_{S_i \in \mathcal{C}^*} w_i \geq \sum_{S_i \in \mathcal{C}^*} \frac{1}{H(d^*)} \sum_{s \in S_i} c_s \geq \frac{1}{H(d^*)} \sum_{s \in U} c_s = \frac{1}{H(d^*)} \sum_{S_i \in \mathcal{C}} w_i. \quad \blacksquare$$

Asymptotically, then, the bound in (11.11) says that the greedy algorithm finds a solution within a factor $O(\log d^*)$ of optimal. Since the maximum set size $d^*$ can be a constant fraction of the total number of elements $n$, this is a worst-case upper bound of $O(\log n)$. However, expressing the bound in terms of $d^*$ shows us that we're doing much better if the largest set is small.

It's interesting to note that this bound is essentially the best one possible, since there are instances where the greedy algorithm can do this badly. To see how such instances arise, consider again the example in Figure 11.6. Now suppose we generalize this so that the underlying set of elements $U$ consists of two tall columns with $n/2$ elements each. There are still two sets, each of weight $1 + \varepsilon$, for some small $\varepsilon > 0$, that cover the columns separately. We also create $\Theta(\log n)$ sets that generalize the structure of the other sets in the figure: there is a set that covers the bottommost $n/2$ nodes, another that covers the next $n/4$, another that covers the next $n/8$, and so forth. Each of these sets will have weight 1.

Now the greedy algorithm will choose the sets of size $n/2, n/4, n/8, \ldots$, in the process producing a solution of weight $\Omega(\log n)$. Choosing the two sets that cover the columns separately, on the other hand, yields the optimal solution, with weight $2 + 2\varepsilon$. Through more complicated constructions, one can strengthen this to produce instances where the greedy algorithm incurs a weight that is very close to $H(n)$ times the optimal weight. And in fact, by much more complicated means, it has been shown that no polynomial-time approximation algorithm can achieve an approximation bound much better than $H(n)$ times optimal, unless $P = NP$.

## 11.4 The Pricing Method: Vertex Cover

We now turn to our second general technique for designing approximation algorithms, the *pricing method*. We will introduce this technique by considering a version of the Vertex Cover Problem. As we saw in Chapter 8, Vertex Cover is in fact a special case of Set Cover, and so we will begin this section by considering the extent to which one can use reductions in the design of approximation algorithms. Following this, we will develop an algorithm with a better approximation guarantee than the general bound that we obtained for Set Cover in the previous section.

### ✐ The Problem

Recall that a *vertex cover* in a graph $G = (V, E)$ is a set $S \subseteq V$ so that each edge has at least one end in $S$. In the version of the problem we consider here, each vertex $i \in V$ has a *weight* $w_i \geq 0$, with the weight of a set $S$ of vertices denoted $w(S) = \sum_{i \in S} w_i$. We would like to find a vertex cover $S$ for which $w(S)$ is minimum. When all weights are equal to 1, deciding if there is a vertex cover of weight at most $k$ is the standard decision version of Vertex Cover.

***Approximations via Reductions?***   Before we work on developing an algorithm, we pause to discuss an interesting issue that arises: Vertex Cover is easily reducible to Set Cover, and we have just seen an approximation algorithm for Set Cover. What does this imply about the approximability of Vertex Cover? A discussion of this question brings out some of the subtle ways in which approximation results interact with polynomial-time reductions.

First consider the special case in which all weights are equal to 1—that is, we are looking for a vertex cover of minimum size. We will call this the *unweighted case*. Recall that we showed Set Cover to be NP-complete using a reduction from the decision version of unweighted Vertex Cover. That is,

$$\text{Vertex Cover} \leq_P \text{Set Cover}$$

This reduction says, "If we had a polynomial-time algorithm that solves the Set Cover Problem, then we could use this algorithm to solve the Vertex Cover Problem in polynomial time." We now have a polynomial-time algorithm for the Set Cover Problem that approximates the solution. Does this imply that we can use it to formulate an approximation algorithm for Vertex Cover?

**(11.12)**   *One can use the Set Cover approximation algorithm to give an $H(d)$-approximation algorithm for the weighted Vertex Cover Problem, where $d$ is the maximum degree of the graph.*

**Proof.** The proof is based on the reduction that showed Vertex Cover $\leq_P$ Set Cover, which also extends to the weighted case. Consider an instance of the weighted Vertex Cover Problem, specified by a graph $G = (V, E)$. We define an instance of Set Cover as follows. The underlying set $U$ is equal to $E$. For each node $i$, we define a set $S_i$ consisting of all edges incident to node $i$ and give this set weight $w_i$. Collections of sets that cover $U$ now correspond precisely to vertex covers. Note that the maximum size of any $S_i$ is precisely the maximum degree $d$.

Hence we can use the approximation algorithm for Set Cover to find a vertex cover whose weight is within a factor of $H(d)$ of minimum. ∎

This $H(d)$-approximation is quite good when $d$ is small; but it gets worse as $d$ gets larger, approaching a bound that is logarithmic in the number of vertices. In the following, we will develop a stronger approximation algorithm that comes within a factor of 2 of optimal.

Before turning to the 2-approximation algorithm, we make the following further observation: One has to be very careful when trying to use reductions for designing approximation algorithms. It worked in (11.12), but we made sure to go through an argument for why it worked; it is not the case that every polynomial-time reduction leads to a comparable implication for approximation algorithms.

Here is a cautionary example. We used Independent Set to prove that the Vertex Cover Problem is NP-complete. Specifically, we proved

$$\text{Independent Set} \leq_P \text{Vertex Cover},$$

which states that "if we had a polynomial-time algorithm that solves the Vertex Cover Problem, then we could use this algorithm to solve the Independent Set Problem in polynomial time." Can we use an approximation algorithm for the minimum-size vertex cover to design a comparably good approximation algorithm for the maximum-size independent set?

The answer is no. Recall that a set $I$ of vertices is independent if and only if its complement $S = V - I$ is a vertex cover. Given a minimum-size vertex cover $S^*$, we obtain a maximum-size independent set by taking the complement $I^* = V - S$. Now suppose we use an approximation algorithm for the Vertex Cover Problem to get an approximately minimum vertex cover $S$. The complement $I = V - S$ is indeed an independent set—there's no problem there. The trouble is when we try to determine our approximation factor for the Independent Set Problem; $I$ can be very far from optimal. Suppose, for example, that the optimal vertex cover $S^*$ and the optimal independent set $I^*$ both have size $|V|/2$. If we invoke a 2-approximation algorithm for the Vertex Cover Problem, we may perfectly well get back the set $S = V$. But, in this case, our "approximately maximum independent set" $I = V - S$ has no elements.

### 🖋 Designing the Algorithm: The Pricing Method

Even though (11.12) gave us an approximation algorithm with a provable guarantee, we will be able to do better. Our approach forms a nice illustration of the *pricing method* for designing approximation algorithms.

***The Pricing Method to Minimize Cost***    The pricing method (also known as the *primal-dual method*) is motivated by an economic perspective. For the case of the Vertex Cover Problem, we will think of the weights on the nodes as *costs*, and we will think of each edge as having to pay for its "share" of the cost of the vertex cover we find. We have actually just seen an analysis of this sort, in the greedy algorithm for Set Cover from Section 11.3; it too can be thought of as a pricing algorithm. The greedy algorithm for Set Cover defined values $c_s$, the cost the algorithm paid for covering element $s$. We can think of $c_s$ as the element $s$'s "share" of the cost. Statement (11.9) shows that it is very natural to think of the values $c_s$ as cost-shares, as the sum of the cost-shares $\sum_{s \in U} c_s$ is the cost of the set cover $\mathcal{C}$ returned by the algorithm, $\sum_{S_i \in \mathcal{C}} w_i$. The key to proving that the algorithm is an $H(d^*)$-approximation algorithm was a certain approximate "fairness" property for the cost-shares: (11.10) shows that the elements in a set $S_k$ are charged by at most an $H(|S_k|)$ factor more than the cost of covering them by the set $S_k$.

In this section, we'll develop the pricing technique through another application, Vertex Cover. Again, we will think of the weight $w_i$ of the vertex $i$ as the cost for using $i$ in the cover. We will think of each edge $e$ as a separate "agent" who is willing to "pay" something to the node that covers it. The algorithm will not only find a vertex cover $S$, but also determine prices $p_e \geq 0$ for each edge $e \in E$, so that if each edge $e \in E$ pays the price $p_e$, this will in total approximately cover the cost of $S$. These prices $p_e$ are the analogues of $c_s$ from the Set Cover Algorithm.

Thinking of the edges as agents suggests some natural fairness rules for prices, analogous to the property proved by (11.10). First of all, selecting a vertex $i$ covers all edges incident to $i$, so it would be "unfair" to charge these incident edges in total more than the cost of vertex $i$. We call prices $p_e$ *fair* if, for each vertex $i$, the edges adjacent to $i$ do not have to pay more than the cost of the vertex: $\sum_{e=(i,j)} p_e \leq w_i$. Note that the property proved by (11.10) for Set Cover is an approximate fairness condition, while in the Vertex Cover algorithm we'll actually use the exact fairness defined here. A useful fact about fair prices is that they provide a lower bound on the cost of any solution.

**(11.13)**    *For any vertex cover $S^*$, and any nonnegative and fair prices $p_e$, we have $\sum_{e \in E} p_e \leq w(S^*)$.*

**Proof.** Consider a vertex cover $S^*$. By the definition of fairness, we have $\sum_{e=(i,j)} p_e \le w_i$ for all nodes $i \in S^*$. Adding these inequalities over all nodes in $S^*$, we get

$$\sum_{i \in S^*} \sum_{e=(i,j)} p_e \le \sum_{i \in S^*} w_i = w(S^*).$$

Now the expression on the left-hand side is a sum of terms, each of which is some edge price $p_e$. Since $S^*$ is a vertex cover, each edge $e$ contributes at least one term $p_e$ to the left-hand side. It may contribute more than one copy of $p_e$ to this sum, since it may be covered from both ends by $S^*$; but the prices are nonnegative, and so the sum on the left-hand side is at least as large as the sum of all prices $p_e$. That is,

$$\sum_{e \in E} p_e \le \sum_{i \in S^*} \sum_{e=(i,j)} p_e.$$

Combining this with the previous inequality, we get

$$\sum_{e \in E} p_e \le w(S^*),$$

as desired. ■

*The Algorithm*   The goal of the approximation algorithm will be to find a vertex cover and to set prices at the same time. We can think of the algorithm as being greedy in how it sets the prices. It then uses these prices to drive the way it selects nodes for the vertex cover.

We say that a node $i$ is *tight* (or "paid for") if $\sum_{e=(i,j)} p_e = w_i$.

```
Vertex-Cover-Approx(G, w):
  Set p_e = 0 for all e ∈ E
  While there is an edge e = (i, j) such that neither i nor j is tight
    Select such an edge e
    Increase p_e without violating fairness
  EndWhile
  Let S be the set of all tight nodes
  Return S
```

For example, consider the execution of this algorithm on the instance in Figure 11.8. Initially, no node is tight; the algorithm decides to select the edge $(a, b)$. It can raise the price paid by $(a, b)$ up to 3, at which point the node $b$ becomes tight and it stops. The algorithm then selects the edge $(a, d)$. It can only raise this price up to 1, since at this point the node $a$ becomes tight (due to the fact that the weight of $a$ is 4, and it is already incident to an edge that is

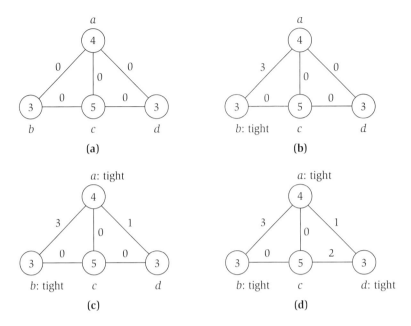

**Figure 11.8** Parts (a)-(d) depict the steps in an execution of the pricing algorithm on an instance of the weighted Vertex Cover Problem. The numbers inside the nodes indicate their weights; the numbers annotating the edges indicate the prices they pay as the algorithm proceeds.

paying 3). Finally, the algorithm selects the edge $(c, d)$. It can raise the price paid by $(c, d)$ up to 2, at which point $d$ becomes tight. We now have a situation where all edges have at least one tight end, so the algorithm terminates. The tight nodes are $a$, $b$, and $d$; so this is the resulting vertex cover. (Note that this is not the minimum-weight vertex cover; that would be obtained by selecting $a$ and $c$.)

## Analyzing the Algorithm

At first sight, one may have the sense that the vertex cover $S$ is fully paid for by the prices: all nodes in $S$ are tight, and hence the edges adjacent to the node $i$ in $S$ can pay for the cost of $i$. But the point is that an edge $e$ can be adjacent to more than one node in the vertex cover (i.e., if both ends of $e$ are in the vertex cover), and hence $e$ may have to pay for more than one node. This is the case, for example, with the edges $(a, b)$ and $(a, d)$ at the end of the execution in Figure 11.8.

However, notice that if we take edges for which both ends happened to show up in the vertex cover, and we charge them their price twice, then we're exactly paying for the vertex cover. (In the example, the cost of the vertex cover is the cost of nodes $a$, $b$, and $d$, which is 10. We can account for this cost exactly by charging $(a, b)$ and $(a, d)$ twice, and $(c, d)$ once.) Now, it's true that this is unfair to some edges, but the amount of unfairness can be bounded: Each edge gets charged its price at most two times (once for each end).

We now make this argument precise, as follows.

> **(11.14)** *The set S and prices p returned by the algorithm satisfy the inequality* $w(S) \leq 2\sum_{e \in E} p_e$.

**Proof.** All nodes in $S$ are tight, so we have $\sum_{e=(i,j)} p_e = w_i$ for all $i \in S$. Adding over all nodes in $S$ we get

$$w(S) = \sum_{i \in S} w_i = \sum_{i \in S} \sum_{e=(i,j)} p_e.$$

An edge $e = (i, j)$ can be included in the sum on the right-hand side at most twice (if both $i$ and $j$ are in $S$), and so we get

$$w(S) = \sum_{i \in S} \sum_{e=(i,j)} p_e \leq 2\sum_{e \in E} p_e,$$

as claimed. ∎

Finally, this factor of 2 carries into an argument that yields the approximation guarantee.

> **(11.15)** *The set S returned by the algorithm is a vertex cover, and its cost is at most twice the minimum cost of any vertex cover.*

**Proof.** First note that $S$ is indeed a vertex cover. Suppose, by contradiction, that $S$ does not cover edge $e = (i, j)$. This implies that neither $i$ nor $j$ is tight, and this contradicts the fact that the While loop of the algorithm terminated.

To get the claimed approximation bound, we simply put together statement (11.14) with (11.13). Let $p$ be the prices set by the algorithm, and let $S^*$ be an optimal vertex cover. By (11.14) we have $2\sum_{e \in E} p_e \geq w(S)$, and by (11.13) we have $\sum_{e \in E} p_e \leq w(S^*)$.

In other words, the sum of the edge prices is a lower bound on the weight of *any* vertex cover, and twice the sum of the edge prices is an upper bound on the weight of our vertex cover:

$$w(S) \leq 2\sum_{e \in E} p_e \leq 2w(S^*). \quad \blacksquare$$

## 11.5 Maximization via the Pricing Method: The Disjoint Paths Problem

We now continue the theme of pricing algorithms with a fundamental problem that arises in network routing: the *Disjoint Paths Problem*. We'll start out by developing a greedy algorithm for this problem and then show an improved algorithm based on pricing.

### The Problem

To set up the problem, it helps to recall one of the first applications we saw for the Maximum-Flow Problem: finding disjoint paths in graphs, which we discussed in Chapter 7. There we were looking for edge-disjoint paths all starting at a node $s$ and ending at a node $t$. How crucial is it to the tractability of this problem that all paths have to start and end at the same node? Using the technique from Section 7.7, one can extend this to find disjoint paths where we are given a set of start nodes $S$ and a set of terminals $T$, and the goal is to find edge-disjoint paths where paths may start at any node in $S$ and end at any node in $T$.

Here, however, we will look at a case where each path to be routed has its own designated starting node and ending node. Specifically, we consider the following *Maximum Disjoint Paths Problem*. We are given a directed graph $G$, together with $k$ pairs of nodes $(s_1, t_1), (s_2, t_2), \ldots, (s_k, t_k)$ and an integer capacity $c$. We think of each pair $(s_i, t_i)$ as a *routing request*, which asks for a path from $s_i$ to $t_i$. A solution to this instance consists of a subset of the requests we will satisfy, $I \subseteq \{1, \ldots, k\}$, together with paths that satisfy them while not overloading any one edge: a path $P_i$ for $i \in I$ so that $P_i$ goes from $s_i$ to $t_i$, and each edge is used by at most $c$ paths. The problem is to find a solution with $|I|$ as large as possible—that is, to satisfy as many requests as possible. Note that the capacity $c$ controls how much "sharing" of edges we allow; when $c = 1$, we are requiring the paths to be fully edge-disjoint, while larger $c$ allows some overlap among the paths.

We have seen in Exercise 39 in Chapter 8 that it is NP-complete to determine whether all $k$ routing requests can be satisfied when the paths are required to be node-disjoint. It is not hard to show that the edge-disjoint version of the problem (corresponding to the case with $c = 1$) is also NP-complete.

Thus it turns out to have been crucial for the application of efficient network flow algorithms that the endpoints of the paths not be explicitly paired up as they are in Maximum Disjoint Paths. To develop this point a little further, suppose we attempted to reduce Maximum Disjoint Paths to a network flow problem by defining the set of sources to be $S = \{s_1, s_2, \ldots, s_k\}$, defining the set of sinks to be $T = \{t_1, t_2, \ldots, t_k\}$, setting each edge capacity to be $c$, and looking for the maximum possible number of disjoint paths starting in $S$ and ending in $T$. Why wouldn't this work? The problem is that there's no way to tell the flow algorithm that a path starting at $s_i \in S$ *must* end at $t_i \in T$; the algorithm guarantees only that this path will end at *some* node in $T$. As a result, the paths that come out of the flow algorithm may well not constitute a solution to the instance of Maximum Disjoint Paths, since they might not link a source $s_i$ to its corresponding endpoint $t_i$.

Disjoint paths problems, where we need to find paths connecting designated pairs of terminal nodes, are very common in networking applications. Just think about paths on the Internet that carry streaming media or Web data, or paths through the phone network carrying voice traffic.[1] Paths sharing edges can interfere with each other, and too many paths sharing a single edge will cause problems in most applications. The maximum allowable amount of sharing will differ from application to application. Requiring the paths to be disjoint is the strongest constraint, eliminating all interference between paths. We'll see, however, that in cases where some sharing is allowed (even just two paths to an edge), better approximation algorithms are possible.

### Designing and Analyzing a Greedy Algorithm

We first consider a very simple algorithm for the case when the capacity $c = 1$: that is, when the paths need to be edge-disjoint. The algorithm is essentially greedy, except that it exhibits a preference for short paths. We will show that this simple algorithm is an $O(\sqrt{m})$-approximation algorithm, where $m = |E|$ is the number of edges in $G$. This may sound like a rather large factor of approximation, and it is, but there is a strong sense in which it is essentially the best we can do. The Maximum Disjoint Paths Problem is not only NP-complete, but it is also hard to approximate: It has been shown that unless $\mathcal{P} = \mathcal{NP}$, it is impossible for any polynomial-time algorithm to achieve an approximation bound significantly better than $O(\sqrt{m})$ in arbitrary directed graphs.

After developing the greedy algorithm, we will consider a slightly more sophisticated pricing algorithm for the capacitated version. It is interesting

---

[1] A researcher from the telecommunications industry once gave the following explanation for the distinction between Maximum Disjoint Paths and network flow, and the broken reduction in the previous paragraph. On Mother's Day, traditionally the busiest day of the year for telephone calls, the phone company must solve an enormous disjoint paths problem: ensuring that each source individual $s_i$ is connected by a path through the voice network to his or her mother $t_i$. Network flow algorithms, finding disjoint paths between a set $S$ and a set $T$, on the other hand, will ensure only that each person gets their call through to *somebody's* mother.

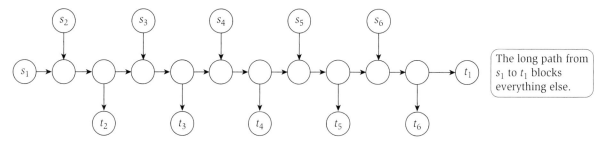

**Figure 11.9** A case in which it's crucial that a greedy algorithm for selecting disjoint paths favors short paths over long ones.

to note that the pricing algorithm does much better than the simple greedy algorithm, even when the capacity $c$ is only slightly more than 1.

```
Greedy-Disjoint-Paths:
Set I = ∅
Until no new path can be found
   Let Pᵢ be the shortest path (if one exists) that is edge-disjoint
       from previously selected paths, and connects some (sᵢ, tᵢ) pair
       that is not yet connected
   Add i to I and select path Pᵢ to connect sᵢ to tᵢ
EndUntil
```

***Analyzing the Algorithm***    The algorithm clearly selects edge-disjoint paths. Assuming the graph $G$ is connected, it must select at least one path. But how does the number of paths selected compare with the maximum possible? A kind of situation we need to worry about is shown in Figure 11.9: One of the paths, from $s_1$ to $t_1$, is very long, so if we select it first, we eliminate up to $\Omega(m)$ other paths.

We now show that the greedy algorithm's preference for short paths not only avoids the problem in this example, but in general it limits the number of other paths that a selected path can interfere with.

**(11.16)**    *The algorithm* Greedy-Disjoint-Paths *is a* $(2\sqrt{m} + 1)$-*approximation algorithm for the Maximum Disjoint Paths Problem.*

**Proof.** Consider an optimal solution: Let $I^*$ be the set of pairs for which a path was selected in this optimum solution, and let $P_i^*$ for $i \in I^*$ be the selected paths. Let $I$ denote the set of pairs returned by the algorithm, and let $P_i$ for $i \in I$ be the corresponding paths. We need to bound $|I^*|$ in terms of $|I|$. The key to the analysis is to make a distinction between short and long paths and to consider them separately. We will call a path *long* if it has at least $\sqrt{m}$ edges, and we will call it *short* otherwise. Let $I_s^*$ denote the set of indices in $I^*$ so that the corresponding path $P_i^*$ is short, and let $I_s$ denote the set of indices in $I$ so that the corresponding path $P_i$ is short.

The graph $G$ has $m$ edges, and each long path uses at least $\sqrt{m}$ edges, so there can be at most $\sqrt{m}$ long paths in $I^*$.

Now consider the short paths in $I^*$. In order for $I^*$ to be much larger than $I$, there would have to be many pairs that are connected in $I^*$ but not in $I$. Thus let us consider pairs that are connected by the optimum using a short path, but are not connected by the greedy algorithm. Since the path $P_i^*$ connecting $s_i$ and $t_i$ in the optimal solution $I^*$ is short, the greedy algorithm would have selected this path, if it had been available, before selecting any long paths. But the greedy algorithm did not connect $s_i$ and $t_i$ at all, and hence one of the edges $e$ along the path $P_i^*$ must occur in a path $P_j$ that was selected earlier by the greedy algorithm. We will say that edge $e$ *blocks* the path $P_i^*$.

Now the lengths of the paths selected by the greedy algorithm are monotone increasing, since each iteration has fewer options for choosing paths. The path $P_j$ was selected before considering $P_i^*$ and hence it must be shorter: $|P_j| \le |P_i^*| \le \sqrt{m}$. So path $P_j$ is short. Since the paths used by the optimum are edge-disjoint, each edge in a path $P_j$ can block at most one path $P_i^*$. It follows that each short path $P_j$ blocks at most $\sqrt{m}$ paths in the optimal solution, and so we get the bound

$$|I_s^* - I| \le \sum_{j \in I_s} |P_j| \le |I_s|\sqrt{m}.$$

We use this to produce a bound on the overall size of the optimal solution. To do this, we view $I^*$ as consisting of three kinds of paths, following the analysis thus far:

- long paths, of which there are at most $\sqrt{m}$;
- paths that are also in $I$; and
- short paths that are not in $I$, which we have just bounded by $|I_s|\sqrt{m}$.

Putting this all together, and using the fact that $|I| \ge 1$ whenever at least one set of terminal pairs can be connected, we get the claimed bound:

$$|I^*| \le \sqrt{m} + |I| + |I_s^* - I| \le \sqrt{m} + |I| + \sqrt{m}|I_s| \le (2\sqrt{m} + 1)|I|. \quad \blacksquare$$

This provides an approximation algorithm for the case when the selected paths have to be disjoint. As we mentioned earlier, the approximation bound of $O(\sqrt{m})$ is rather weak, but unless $\mathcal{P} = \mathcal{NP}$, it is essentially the best possible for the case of disjoint paths in arbitrary directed graphs.

### ✎ Designing and Analyzing a Pricing Algorithm

Not letting any two paths use the same edge is quite extreme; in most applications one can allow a few paths to share an edge. We will now develop an analogous algorithm, based on the pricing method, for the case where $c > 1$ paths may share any edge. In the disjoint case just considered, we viewed all edges as equal and preferred short paths. We can think of this as a simple kind of pricing algorithm: the paths have to pay for using up the edges, and each edge has a unit cost. Here we will consider a pricing scheme in which edges are viewed as more expensive if they have been used already, and hence have less capacity left over. This will encourage the algorithm to "spread out" its paths, rather than piling them up on any single edge. We will refer to the cost of an edge $e$ as its *length* $\ell_e$, and define the *length* of a path to be the sum of the lengths of the edges it contains: $\ell(P) = \sum_{e \in P} \ell_e$. We will use a multiplicative parameter $\beta$ to increase the length of an edge each time an additional path uses it.

```
Greedy-Paths-with-Capacity:
Set I = ∅
Set edge length ℓₑ = 1 for all  e  ∈  E
Until no new path can be found
   Let Pᵢ be the shortest path (if one exists) so that adding Pᵢ to
        the selected set of paths does not use any edge more than c
        times, and Pᵢ connects some (sᵢ, tᵢ) pair not yet connected
   Add i to I and select path Pᵢ to connect sᵢ to tᵢ
   Multiply the length of all edges along Pᵢ by β
EndUntil
```

*Analyzing the Algorithm*    For the analysis we will focus on the simplest case, when at most two paths may use the same edge—that is, when $c = 2$. We'll see that, for this case, setting $\beta = m^{1/3}$ will give the best approximation result for this algorithm. Unlike the disjoint paths case (when $c = 1$), it is not known whether the approximation bounds we obtain here for $c > 1$ are close to the best possible for polynomial-time algorithms in general, assuming $\mathcal{P} \neq \mathcal{NP}$.

The key to the analysis in the disjoint case was to distinguish "short" and "long" paths. For the case when $c = 2$, we will consider a path $P_i$ selected by the algorithm to be *short* if the length is less than $\beta^2$. Let $I_s$ denote the set of short paths selected by the algorithm.

Next we want to compare the number of paths selected with the maximum possible. Let $I^*$ be an optimal solution and $P_i^*$ be the set of paths used in this solution. As before, the key to the analysis is to consider the edges that block the selection of paths in $I^*$. Long paths can block a lot of other paths, so for now we will focus on the short paths in $I_s$. As we try to continue following what we did in the disjoint case, we immediately run into a difficulty, however. In that case, the length of a path in $I^*$ was simply the number of edges it contained; but here, the lengths are changing as the algorithm runs, and so it is not clear how to define the length of a path in $I^*$ for purposes of the analysis. In other words, for the analysis, when should we measure this length? (At the beginning of the execution? At the end?)

It turns out that the crucial moment in the algorithm, for purposes of our analysis, is the first point at which there are no short paths left to choose. Let $\bar{\ell}$ be the length function at this point in the execution of the algorithm; we'll use $\bar{\ell}$ to measure the length of paths in $I^*$. For a path $P$, we use $\bar{\ell}(P)$ to denote its length, $\sum_{e \in P} \bar{\ell}_e$. We consider a path $P_i^*$ in the optimal solution $I^*$ *short* if $\bar{\ell}(P_i^*) < \beta^2$, and *long* otherwise. Let $I_s^*$ denote the set of short paths in $I^*$. The first step is to show that there are no short paths connecting pairs that are not connected by the approximation algorithm.

**(11.17)** *Consider a source-sink pair $i \in I^*$ that is not connected by the approximation algorithm; that is, $i \notin I$. Then $\bar{\ell}(P_i^*) \geq \beta^2$.*

**Proof.** As long as short paths are being selected, we do not have to worry about explicitly enforcing the requirement that each edge be used by at most $c = 2$ paths: any edge $e$ considered for selection by a third path would already have length $\ell_e = \beta^2$, and hence be long.

Consider the state of the algorithm with length $\bar{\ell}$. By the argument in the previous paragraph, we can imagine the algorithm having run up to this point without caring about the limit of $c$; it just selected a short path whenever it could find one. Since the endpoints $s_i, t_i$ of $P_i^*$ are not connected by the greedy algorithm, and since there are no short paths left when the length function reaches $\bar{\ell}$, it must be the case that path $P_i^*$ has length at least $\beta^2$ as measured by $\bar{\ell}$. ∎

The analysis in the disjoint case used the fact that there are only $m$ edges to limit the number of long paths. Here we consider length $\bar{\ell}$, rather than the number of edges, as the quantity that is being consumed by paths. Hence, to be able to reason about this, we will need a bound on the total length in the graph $\sum_e \bar{\ell}_e$. The sum of the lengths over all edges $\sum_e \ell_e$ starts out at $m$ (length 1 for each edge). Adding a short path to the solution $I_s$ can increase the length by at most $\beta^3$, as the selected path has length at most $\beta^2$, and the lengths of the edges are increased by a $\beta$ factor along the path. This gives us a useful comparison between the number of short paths selected and the total length.

**(11.18)**   *The set $I_s$ of short paths selected by the approximation algorithm, and the lengths $\bar{\ell}$, satisfy the relation $\sum_e \bar{\ell}_e \leq \beta^3 |I_s| + m$.*

Finally, we prove an approximation bound for this algorithm. We will find that even though we have simply increased the number of paths allowed on each edge from 1 to 2, the approximation guarantee drops by a significant amount that essentially incorporates this change into the exponent: from $O(m^{1/2})$ down to $O(m^{1/3})$.

**(11.19)**   *The algorithm* Greedy-Paths-with-Capacity, *using $\beta = m^{1/3}$, is a $(4m^{1/3} + 1)$-approximation algorithm in the case when the capacity $c = 2$.*

**Proof.**  We first bound $|I^* - I|$. By (11.17), we have $\bar{\ell}(P_i^*) \geq \beta^2$ for all $i \in I^* - I$. Summing over all paths in $I^* - I$, we get

$$\sum_{i \in I^* - I} \bar{\ell}(P_i^*) \geq \beta^2 |I^* - I|.$$

On the other hand, each edge is used by at most two paths in the solution $I^*$, so we have

$$\sum_{i \in I^* - I} \bar{\ell}(P_i^*) \leq \sum_{e \in E} 2\bar{\ell}_e.$$

Combining these bounds with (11.18) we get

$$\beta^2 |I^*| \leq \beta^2 |I^* - I| + \beta^2 |I| \leq \sum_{i \in I^* - I} \bar{\ell}(P_i^*) + \beta^2 |I|$$

$$\leq \sum_{e \in E} 2\bar{\ell}_e + \beta^2 |I| \leq 2(\beta^3 |I| + m) + \beta^2 |I|.$$

Finally, dividing through by $\beta^2$, using $|I| \geq 1$ and setting $\beta = m^{1/3}$, we get that $|I^*| \leq (4m^{1/3} + 1)|I|$.  ∎

The same algorithm also works for the capacitated Disjoint Path Problem with any capacity $c > 0$. If we choose $\beta = m^{1/(c+1)}$, then the algorithm is a $(2cm^{1/(c+1)} + 1)$-approximation algorithm. To extend the analysis, one has to consider paths to be short if their length is at most $\beta^c$.

**(11.20)**   *The algorithm* Greedy-Paths-with-Capacity, *using $\beta = m^{1/c+1}$, is a $(2cm^{1/(c+1)} + 1)$-approximation algorithm when the the edge capacities are $c$.*

# 11.6 Linear Programming and Rounding: An Application to Vertex Cover

We will start by introducing a powerful technique from operations research: *linear programming*. Linear programming is the subject of entire courses, and we will not attempt to provide any kind of comprehensive overview of it here. In this section, we will introduce some of the basic ideas underlying linear programming and show how these can be used to approximate NP-hard optimization problems.

Recall that in Section 11.4 we developed a 2-approximation algorithm for the weighted Vertex Cover Problem. As a first application for the linear programming technique, we'll give here a different 2-approximation algorithm that is conceptually much simpler (though slower in running time).

## Linear Programming as a General Technique

Our 2-approximation algorithm for the weighted version of Vertex Cover will be based on linear programming. We describe linear programming here not just to give the approximation algorithm, but also to illustrate its power as a very general technique.

So what is linear programming? To answer this, it helps to first recall, from linear algebra, the problem of simultaneous linear equations. Using matrix-vector notation, we have a vector $x$ of unknown real numbers, a given matrix $A$, and a given vector $b$; and we want to solve the equation $Ax = b$. Gaussian elimination is a well-known efficient algorithm for this problem.

The basic Linear Programming Problem can be viewed as a more complex version of this, with inequalities in place of equations. Specifically, consider the problem of determining a vector $x$ that satisfies $Ax \geq b$. By this notation, we mean that each coordinate of the vector $Ax$ should be greater than or equal to the corresponding coordinate of the vector $b$. Such systems of inequalities define regions in space. For example, suppose $x = (x_1, x_2)$ is a two-dimensional vector, and we have the four inequalities

$$x_1 \geq 0, x_2 \geq 0$$
$$x_1 + 2x_2 \geq 6$$
$$2x_1 + x_2 \geq 6$$

Then the set of solutions is the region in the plane shown in Figure 11.10.

Given a region defined by $Ax \geq b$, linear programming seeks to minimize a linear combination of the coordinates of $x$, over all $x$ belonging to the region. Such a linear combination can be written $c^t x$, where $c$ is a vector of coefficients, and $c^t x$ denotes the inner product of two vectors. Thus our standard form for Linear Programming, as an optimization problem, will be the following.

*Given an $m \times n$ matrix $A$, and vectors $b \in R^m$ and $c \in R^n$, find a vector $x \in R^n$ to solve the following optimization problem:*

$$\min(c^t x \text{ such that } x \geq 0; Ax \geq b).$$

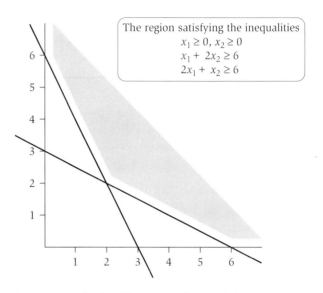

The region satisfying the inequalities
$$x_1 \geq 0,\ x_2 \geq 0$$
$$x_1 + 2x_2 \geq 6$$
$$2x_1 + x_2 \geq 6$$

**Figure 11.10** The feasible region of a simple linear program.

$c^t x$ is often called the *objective function* of the linear program, and $Ax \geq b$ is called the set of *constraints*. For example, suppose we define the vector $c$ to be $(1.5, 1)$ in the example in Figure 11.10; in other words, we are seeking to minimize the quantity $1.5x_1 + x_2$ over the region defined by the inequalities. The solution to this would be to choose the point $x = (2, 2)$, where the two slanting lines cross; this yields a value of $c^t x = 5$, and one can check that there is no way to get a smaller value.

We can phrase Linear Programming as a decision problem in the following way.

> *Given a matrix $A$, vectors $b$ and $c$, and a bound $\gamma$, does there exist $x$ so that $x \geq 0$, $Ax \geq b$, and $c^t x \leq \gamma$?*

To avoid issues related to how we represent real numbers, we will assume that the coordinates of the vectors and matrices involved are integers.

**The Computational Complexity of Linear Programming**   The decision version of Linear Programming is in $\mathcal{NP}$. This is intuitively very believable—we just have to exhibit a vector $x$ satisfying the desired properties. The one concern is that even if all the input numbers are integers, such a vector $x$ may not have integer coordinates, and it may in fact require very large precision to specify: How do we know that we'll be able to read and manipulate it in polynomial time? But, in fact, one can show that if there is a solution, then there is one that is rational and needs only a polynomial number of bits to write down; so this is not a problem.

Linear Programming was also known to be in co-$\mathcal{NP}$ for a long time, though this is not as easy to see. Students who have taken a linear programming course may notice that this fact follows from linear programming duality.[2]

For a long time, indeed, Linear Programming was the most famous example of a problem in both $\mathcal{NP}$ and co-$\mathcal{NP}$ that was not known to have a polynomial-time solution. Then, in 1981, Leonid Khachiyan, who at the time was a young researcher in the Soviet Union, gave a polynomial-time algorithm for the problem. After some initial concern in the U.S. popular press that this discovery might turn out to be a *Sputnik*-like event in the Cold War (it didn't), researchers settled down to understand exactly what Khachiyan had done. His initial algorithm, while polynomial-time, was in fact quite slow and impractical; but since then practical polynomial-time algorithms—so-called *interior point methods*—have also been developed following the work of Narendra Karmarkar in 1984.

Linear programming is an interesting example for another reason as well. The most widely used algorithm for this problem is the *simplex method*. It works very well in practice and is competitive with polynomial-time interior methods on real-world problems. Yet its worst-case running time is known to be exponential; it is simply that this exponential behavior shows up in practice only very rarely. For all these reasons, linear programming has been a very useful and important example for thinking about the limits of polynomial time as a formal definition of efficiency.

For our purposes here, though, the point is that linear programming problems can be solved in polynomial time, and very efficient algorithms exist in practice. You can learn a lot more about all this in courses on linear programming. The question we ask here is this: How can linear programming help us when we want to solve combinatorial problems such as Vertex Cover?

## Vertex Cover as an Integer Program

Recall that a *vertex cover* in a graph $G = (V, E)$ is a set $S \subseteq V$ so that each edge has at least one end in $S$. In the weighted Vertex Cover Problem, each vertex $i \in V$ has a *weight* $w_i \geq 0$, with the weight of a set $S$ of vertices denoted $w(S) = \sum_{i \in S} w_i$. We would like to find a vertex cover $S$ for which $w(S)$ is minimum.

---

[2] Those of you who are familiar with duality may also notice that the *pricing method* of the previous sections is motivated by linear programming duality: the prices are exactly the variables in the dual linear program (which explains why pricing algorithms are often referred to as *primal-dual algorithms*).

We now try to formulate a linear program that is in close correspondence with the Vertex Cover Problem. Thus we consider a graph $G = (V, E)$ with a weight $w_i \geq 0$ on each node $i$. Linear programming is based on the use of vectors of variables. In our case, we will have a *decision variable* $x_i$ for each node $i \in V$ to model the choice of whether to include node $i$ in the vertex cover; $x_i = 0$ will indicate that node $i$ is not in the vertex cover, and $x_i = 1$ will indicate that node $i$ is in the vertex cover. We can create a single $n$-dimensional vector $x$ in which the $i^{\text{th}}$ coordinate corresponds to the $i^{\text{th}}$ decision variable $x_i$.

We use linear inequalities to encode the requirement that the selected nodes form a vertex cover; we use the objective function to encode the goal of minimizing the total weight. For each edge $(i, j) \in E$, it must have one end in the vertex cover, and we write this as the inequality $x_i + x_j \geq 1$. Finally, to express the minimization problem, we write the set of node weights as an $n$-dimensional vector $w$, with the $i^{\text{th}}$ coordinate corresponding to $w_i$; we then seek to minimize $w^t x$. In summary, we have formulated the Vertex Cover Problem as follows.

$$
\text{(VC.IP)} \qquad \text{Min} \quad \sum_{i \in V} w_i x_i
$$

$$
\text{s.t.} \quad x_i + x_j \geq 1 \quad (i, j) \in E
$$

$$
x_i \in \{0, 1\} \quad i \in V.
$$

We claim that the vertex covers of $G$ are in one-to-one correspondence with the solutions $x$ to this system of linear inequalities in which all coordinates are equal to 0 or 1.

**(11.21)**   *S is a vertex cover in G if and only if the vector x, defined as $x_i = 1$ for $i \in S$, and $x_i = 0$ for $i \notin S$, satisfies the constraints in (VC.IP). Further, we have $w(S) = w^t x$.*

We can put this system into the matrix form we used for linear programming, as follows. We define a matrix $A$ whose columns correspond to the nodes in $V$ and whose rows correspond to the edges in $E$; entry $A[e, i] = 1$ if node $i$ is an end of the edge $e$, and 0 otherwise. (Note that each row has exactly two nonzero entries.) If we use $\vec{1}$ to denote the vector with all coordinates equal to 1, and $\vec{0}$ to denote the vector with all coordinates equal to 0, then the system of inequalities above can be written as

$$
Ax \geq \vec{1}
$$

$$
\vec{1} \geq x \geq \vec{0}.
$$

But keep in mind that this is not just an instance of the Linear Programming Problem: We have crucially required that all coordinates in the solution be either 0 or 1. So our formulation suggests that we should solve the problem

$$\min(w^t x \text{ subject to } \vec{1} \geq x \geq \vec{0}, Ax \geq \vec{1}, \ x \text{ has integer coordinates}).$$

This is an instance of the Linear Programming Problem in which we require the coordinates of $x$ to take integer values; without this extra constraint, the coordinates of $x$ could be arbitrary real numbers. We call this problem *Integer Programming*, as we are looking for integer-valued solutions to a linear program.

Integer Programming is considerably harder than Linear Programming; indeed, our discussion really constitutes a reduction from Vertex Cover to the decision version of Integer Programming. In other words, we have proved

**(11.22)** Vertex Cover $\leq_P$ Integer Programming.

To show the NP-completeness of Integer Programming, we would still have to establish that the decision version is in $\mathcal{NP}$. There is a complication here, as with Linear Programming, since we need to establish that there is always a solution $x$ that can be written using a polynomial number of bits. But this can indeed be proven. Of course, for our purposes, the integer program we are dealing with is explicitly constrained to have solutions in which each coordinate is either 0 or 1. Thus it is clearly in $\mathcal{NP}$, and our reduction from Vertex Cover establishes that even this special case is NP-complete.

## Using Linear Programming for Vertex Cover

We have yet to resolve whether our foray into linear and integer programming will turn out to be useful or simply a dead end. Trying to solve the integer programming problem (VC.IP) optimally is clearly not the right way to go, as this is NP-hard.

The way to make progress is to exploit the fact that Linear Programming is not as hard as Integer Programming. Suppose we take (VC.IP) and modify it, dropping the requirement that each $x_i \in \{0, 1\}$ and reverting to the constraint that each $x_i$ is an arbitrary real number between 0 and 1. This gives us an instance of the Linear Programming Problem that we could call (VC.LP), and we can solve it in polynomial time: We can find a set of values $\{x_i^*\}$ between 0 and 1 so that $x_i^* + x_j^* \geq 1$ for each edge $(i, j)$, and $\sum_i w_i x_i^*$ is minimized. Let $x^*$ denote this vector, and $w_{LP} = w^t x^*$ denote the value of the objective function.

We note the following basic fact.

**(11.23)**    *Let $S^*$ denote a vertex cover of minimum weight. Then $w_{LP} \leq w(S^*)$.*

**Proof.** Vertex covers of $G$ correspond to integer solutions of (VC.IP), so the minimum of $\min(w^t x : \vec{1} \geq x \geq 0, Ax \geq 1)$ over all integer $x$ vectors is exactly the minimum-weight vertex cover. To get the minimum of the linear program (VC.LP), we allow $x$ to take arbitrary real-number values—that is, we minimize over many more choices of $x$—and so the minimum of (VC.LP) is no larger than that of (VC.IP). ∎

Note that (11.23) is one of the crucial ingredients we need for an approximation algorithm: a good lower bound on the optimum, in the form of the efficiently computable quantity $w_{LP}$.

However, $w_{LP}$ can definitely be smaller than $w(S^*)$. For example, if the graph $G$ is a triangle and all weights are 1, then the minimum vertex cover has a weight of 2. But, in a linear programming solution, we can set $x_i = \frac{1}{2}$ for all three vertices, and so get a linear programming solution of weight only $\frac{3}{2}$. As a more general example, consider a graph on $n$ nodes in which each pair of nodes is connected by an edge. Again, all weights are 1. Then the minimum vertex cover has weight $n - 1$, but we can find a linear programming solution of value $n/2$ by setting $x_i = \frac{1}{2}$ for all vertices $i$.

So the question is: How can solving this linear program help us actually *find* a near-optimal vertex cover? The idea is to work with the values $x_i^*$ and to infer a vertex cover $S$ from them. It is natural that if $x_i^* = 1$ for some node $i$, then we should put it in the vertex cover $S$; and if $x_i^* = 0$, then we should leave it out of $S$. But what should we do with fractional values in between? What should we do if $x_i^* = .4$ or $x_i^* = .5$? The natural approach here is to *round*. Given a fractional solution $\{x_i^*\}$, we define $S = \{i \in V : x_i^* \geq \frac{1}{2}\}$—that is, we round values at least $\frac{1}{2}$ up, and those below $\frac{1}{2}$ down.

**(11.24)**    *The set $S$ defined in this way is a vertex cover, and $w(S) \leq w_{LP}$.*

**Proof.** First we argue that $S$ is a vertex cover. Consider an edge $e = (i, j)$. We claim that at least one of $i$ and $j$ must be in $S$. Recall that one of our inequalities is $x_i + x_j \geq 1$. So in any solution $x^*$ that satisfies this inequality, either $x_i^* \geq \frac{1}{2}$ or $x_j^* \geq \frac{1}{2}$. Thus at least one of these two will be rounded up, and $i$ or $j$ will be placed in $S$.

Now we consider the weight $w(S)$ of this vertex cover. The set $S$ only has vertices with $x_i^* \geq \frac{1}{2}$; thus the linear program "paid" at least $\frac{1}{2}w_i$ for node $i$, and we only pay $w_i$: at most twice as much. More formally, we have the following chain of inequalities.

$$w_{LP} w^t x^* = \sum_i w_i x_i^* \geq \sum_{i \in S} w_i x_i^* \geq \frac{1}{2} \sum_{i \in S} w_i = \frac{1}{2} w(S). \quad \blacksquare$$

Thus we have a produced a vertex cover $S$ of weight at most $2w_{LP}$. The lower bound in (11.23) showed that the optimal vertex cover has weight at least $w_{LP}$, and so we have the following result.

> **(11.25)** *The algorithm produces a vertex cover S of at most twice the minimum possible weight.*

## * 11.7 Load Balancing Revisited: A More Advanced LP Application

In this section we consider a more general load balancing problem. We will develop an approximation algorithm using the same general outline as the 2-approximation we just designed for Vertex Cover: We solve a corresponding linear program, and then round the solution. However, the algorithm and its analysis here will be significantly more complex than what was needed for Vertex Cover. It turns out that the instance of the Linear Programming Problem we need to solve is, in fact, a flow problem. Using this fact, we will be able to develop a much deeper understanding of what the fractional solutions to the linear program look like, and we will use this understanding in order to round them. For this problem, the only known constant-factor approximation algorithm is based on rounding this linear programming solution.

### The Problem

The problem we consider in this section is a significant, but natural, generalization of the Load Balancing Problem with which we began our study of approximation algorithms. There, as here, we have a set $J$ of $n$ jobs, and a set $M$ of $m$ machines, and the goal is to assign each job to a machine so that the maximum load on any machine will be as small as possible. In the simple Load Balancing Problem we considered earlier, each job $j$ can be assigned to any machine $i$. Here, on the other hand, we will restrict the set of machines that each job may consider; that is, for each job there is just a subset of machines to which it can be assigned. This restriction arises naturally in a number of applications: for example, we may be seeking to balance load while maintaining the property that each job is assigned to a physically nearby machine, or to a machine with an appropriate authorization to process the job.

More formally, each job $j$ has a fixed given size $t_j \geq 0$ and a set of machines $M_j \subseteq M$ that it may be assigned to. The sets $M_j$ can be completely arbitrary. We call an assignment of jobs to machines *feasible* if each job $j$ is assigned to a machine $i \in M_j$. The goal is still to minimize the maximum load on any machine: Using $J_i \subseteq J$ to denote the jobs assigned to a machine $i \in M$ in a feasible assignment, and using $L_i = \sum_{j \in J_i} t_j$ to denote the resulting load, we seek to minimize $\max_i L_i$. This is the definition of the *Generalized Load Balancing Problem*.

In addition to containing our initial Load Balancing Problem as a special case (setting $M_j = M$ for all jobs $j$), Generalized Load Balancing includes the Bipartite Perfect Matching Problem as another special case. Indeed, given a bipartite graph with the same number of nodes on each side, we can view the nodes on the left as jobs and the nodes on the right as machines; we define $t_j = 1$ for all jobs $j$, and define $M_j$ to be the set of machine nodes $i$ such that there is an edge $(i, j) \in E$. There is an assignment of maximum load 1 if and only if there is a perfect matching in the bipartite graph. (Thus, network flow techniques can be used to find the optimum load in this special case.) The fact that Generalized Load Balancing includes both these problems as special cases gives some indication of the challenge in designing an algorithm for it.

## Designing and Analyzing the Algorithm

We now develop an approximation algorithm based on linear programming for the Generalized Load Balancing Problem. The basic plan is the same one we saw in the previous section: we'll first formulate the problem as an equivalent linear program where the variables have to take specific discrete values; we'll then relax this to a linear program by dropping this requirement on the values of the variables; and then we'll use the resulting fractional assignment to obtain an actual assignment that is close to optimal. We'll need to be more careful than in the case of the Vertex Cover Problem in rounding the solution to produce the actual assignment.

***Integer and Linear Programming Formulations***   First we formulate the Generalized Load Balancing Problem as a linear program with restrictions on the variable values. We use variables $x_{ij}$ corresponding to each pair $(i, j)$ of machine $i \in M$ and job $j \in J$. Setting $x_{ij} = 0$ will indicate that job $j$ is not assigned to machine $i$, while setting $x_{ij} = t_j$ will indicate that all the load $t_j$ of job $j$ is assigned to machine $i$. We can think of $x$ as a single vector with $mn$ coordinates.

We use linear inequalities to encode the requirement that each job is assigned to a machine: For each job $j$ we require that $\sum_i x_{ij} = t_j$. The load of a machine $i$ can then be expressed as $L_i = \sum_j x_{ij}$. We require that $x_{ij} = 0$ whenever $i \notin M_j$. We will use the objective function to encode the goal of finding an assignment that minimizes the maximum load. To do this, we will need one more variable, $L$, that will correspond to the load. We use the inequalities $\sum_j x_{ij} \le L$ for all machines $i$. In summary, we have formulated the following problem.

(GL.IP)     $\min L$

$$\sum_i x_{ij} = t_j \quad \text{for all } j \in J$$

$$\sum_j x_{ij} \leq L \quad \text{for all } i \in M$$

$$x_{ij} \in \{0, t_j\} \quad \text{for all } j \in J, i \in M_j.$$

$$x_{ij} = 0 \qquad \text{for all } j \in J, i \notin M_j.$$

First we claim that the feasible assignments are in one-to-one correspondence with the solutions $x$ satisfying the above constraints, and, in an optimal solution to (GL.IP), $L$ is the load of the corresponding assignment.

**(11.26)** *An assignment of jobs to machines has load at most L if and only if the vector x, defined by setting $x_{ij} = t_j$ whenever job j is assigned to machine i, and $x_{ij} = 0$ otherwise, satisfies the constraints in (GL.IP), with L set to the maximum load of the assignment.*

Next we will consider the corresponding linear program obtained by replacing the requirement that each $x_{ij} \in \{0, t_j\}$ by the weaker requirement that $x_{ij} \geq 0$ for all $j \in J$ and $i \in M_j$. Let (GL.LP) denote the resulting linear program. It would also be natural to add $x_{ij} \leq t_j$. We do not add these inequalities explicitly, as they are implied by the nonnegativity and the equation $\sum_i x_{ij} = t_j$ that is required for each job $j$.

We immediately see that if there is an assignment with load at most $L$, then (GL.LP) must have a solution with value at most $L$. Or, in the contrapositive,

**(11.27)** *If the optimum value of (GL.LP) is L, then the optimal load is at least $L^* \geq L$.*

We can use linear programming to obtain such a solution $(x, L)$ in polynomial time. Our goal will then be to use $x$ to create an assignment. Recall that the Generalized Load Balancing Problem is NP-hard, and hence we cannot expect to solve it exactly in polynomial time. Instead, we will find an assignment with load at most two times the minimum possible. To be able to do this, we will also need the simple lower bound (11.2), which we used already in the original Load Balancing Problem.

**(11.28)** *The optimal load is at least $L^* \geq \max_j t_j$.*

***Rounding the Solution When There Are No Cycles*** The basic idea is to round the $x_{ij}$ values to 0 or $t_j$. However, we cannot use the simple idea of just rounding large values up and small values down. The problem is that the linear programming solution may assign small fractions of a job $j$ to each of the $m$ machines, and hence for some jobs there may be no large $x_{ij}$ values. The algorithm we develop will be a rounding of $x$ in the weak sense that each job $j$ will be assigned to a machine $i$ with $x_{ij} > 0$, but we may have to round a few really small values up. This weak rounding already ensures that the assignment is feasible, in the sense that we do not assign any job $j$ to a machine $i$ not in $M_j$ (because if $i \notin M_j$, then we have $x_{ij} = 0$).

The key is to understand what the structure of the fractional solution is like and to show that while a few jobs may be spread out to many machines, this cannot happen to too many jobs. To this end, we'll consider the following bipartite graph $G(x) = (V(x), E(x))$: The nodes are $V(x) = M \cup J$, the set of jobs and the set of machines, and there is an edge $(i, j) \in E(x)$ if and only if $x_{ij} > 0$.

We'll show that, given any solution for (GL.LP), we can obtain a new solution $x$ with the same load $L$, such that $G(x)$ has no cycles. This is the crucial step, as we show that a solution $x$ with no cycles can be used to obtain an assignment with load at most $L + L^*$.

**(11.29)**    *Given a solution $(x, L)$ of (GL.LP) such that the graph $G(x)$ has no cycles, we can use this solution $x$ to obtain a feasible assignment of jobs to machines with load at most $L + L^*$ in $O(mn)$ time.*

**Proof.** Since the graph $G(x)$ has no cycles, each of its connected components is a tree. We can produce the assignment by considering each component separately. Thus, consider one of the components, which is a tree whose nodes correspond to jobs and machines, as shown in Figure 11.11.

First, root the tree at an arbitrary node. Now consider a job $j$. If the node corresponding to job $j$ is a leaf of the tree, let machine node $i$ be its parent. Since $j$ has degree 1 in the tree $G(x)$, machine $i$ is the only machine that has been assigned any part of job $j$, and hence we must have that $x_{ij} = t_j$. Our assignment will assign such a job $j$ to its only neighbor $i$. For a job $j$ whose corresponding node is not a leaf in $G(x)$, we assign $j$ to an arbitrary child of the corresponding node in the rooted tree.

The method can clearly be implemented in $O(mn)$ time (including the time to set up the graph $G(x)$). It defines a feasible assignment, as the linear program (GL.LP) required that $x_{ij} = 0$ whenever $i \notin M_j$. To finish the proof, we need to show that the load is at most $L + L^*$. Let $i$ be any machine, and let $J_i$ be the set of jobs assigned to machine $i$. The jobs assigned to machine $i$ form a subset of the neighbors of $i$ in $G(x)$: the set $J_i$ contains those children of node $i$ that are leaves, plus possibly the parent $p(i)$ of node $i$. To bound the load, we consider the parent $p(i)$ separately. For all other jobs $j \neq p(i)$ assigned to $i$, we have $x_{ij} = t_j$, and hence we can bound the load using the solution $x$, as follows.

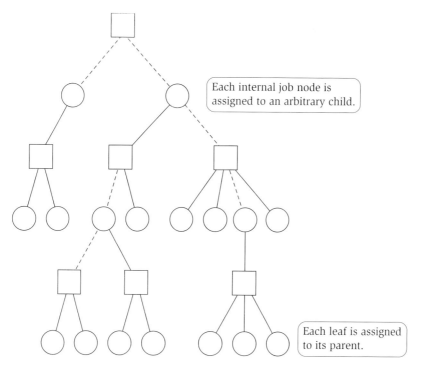

**Figure 11.11** An example of a graph $G(x)$ with no cycles, where the squares are machines and the circles are jobs. The solid lines show the resulting assignment of jobs to machines.

$$\sum_{j \in J_i, j \neq p(i)} t_j \le \sum_{j \in J} x_{ij} \le L,$$

using the inequality bounding the load in (GL.LP). For the parent $j = p(i)$ of node $i$, we use $t_j \le L^*$ by (11.28). Adding the two inequalities, we get that $\sum_{j \in J_i} p_{ij} \le L + L^*$, as claimed. ∎

Now, by (11.27), we know that $L \le L^*$, so a solution whose load is bounded by $L + L^*$ is also bounded by $2L^*$—in other words, twice the optimum. Thus we have the following consequence of (11.29).

**(11.30)** *Given a solution $(x, L)$ of (GL.LP) such that the graph $G(x)$ has no cycles, then we can use this solution $x$ to obtain a feasible assignment of jobs to machines with load at most twice the optimum in $O(mn)$ time.*

***Eliminating Cycles from the Linear Programming Solution*** To wrap up our approximation algorithm, then, we just need to show how to convert

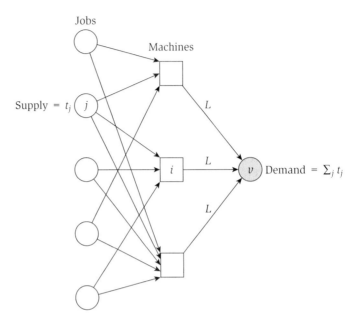

**Figure 11.12** The network flow computation used to find a solution to (GL.LP). Edges between the jobs and machines have infinite capacity.

an arbitrary solution of (GL.LP) into a solution $x$ with no cycles in $G(x)$. In the process, we will also show how to obtain a solution to the linear program (GL.LP) using flow computations. More precisely, given a fixed load value $L$, we show how to use a flow computation to decide if (GL.LP) has a solution with value at most $L$. For this construction, consider the following directed graph $G = (V, E)$ shown in Figure 11.12. The set of vertices of the flow graph $G$ will be $V = M \cup J \cup \{v\}$, where $v$ is a new node. The nodes $j \in J$ will be sources with supply $t_j$, and the only demand node is the new sink $v$, which has demand $\sum_j t_j$. We'll think of the flow in this network as "load" flowing from jobs to the sink $v$ via the machines. We add an edge $(j, i)$ with infinite capacity from job $j$ to machine $i$ if and only if $i \in M_j$. Finally, we add an edge $(i, v)$ for each machine node $i$ with capacity $L$.

**(11.31)**   *The solutions of this flow problem with capacity $L$ are in one-to-one correspondence with solutions of (GL.LP) with value $L$, where $x_{ij}$ is the flow value along edge $(i, j)$, and the flow value on edge $(i, t)$ is the load $\sum_j x_{ij}$ on machine $i$.*

This statement allows us to solve (GL.LP) using flow computations and a binary search for the optimal value $L$: we try successive values of $L$ until we find the smallest one for which there is a feasible flow.

Here we'll use the understanding we gained of (GL.LP) from the equivalent flow formulation to modify a solution $x$ to eliminate all cycles from $G(x)$. In terms of the flow we have just defined, $G(x)$ is the undirected graph obtained from $G$ by ignoring the directions of the edges, deleting the sink $v$ and all adjacent edges, and also deleting all edges from $J$ to $M$ that do not carry flow. We'll eliminate all cycles in $G(x)$ in a sequence of at most $mn$ steps, where the goal of a single step is to eliminate at least one edge from $G(x)$ without increasing the load $L$ or introducing any new edges.

**(11.32)** *Let $(x, L)$ be any solution to (GL.LP) and $C$ be a cycle in $G(x)$. In time linear in the length of the cycle, we can modify the solution $x$ to eliminate at least one edge from $G(x)$ without increasing the load or introducing any new edges.*

**Proof.** Consider the cycle $C$ in $G(x)$. Recall that $G(x)$ corresponds to the set of edges that carry flow in the solution $x$. We will modify the solution by *augmenting* the flow along the cycle $C$, using essentially the procedure `augment` from Section 7.1. The augmentation along a cycle will not change the balance between incoming and outgoing flow at any node; rather, it will eliminate one backward edge from the residual graph, and hence an edge from $G(x)$. Assume that the nodes along the cycle are $i_1, j_1, i_2, j_2, \ldots, i_k, j_k$, where $i_\ell$ is a machine node and $j_\ell$ is a job node. We'll modify the solution by decreasing the flow along all edges $(j_\ell, i_\ell)$ and increasing the flow on the edges $(j_\ell, i_{\ell+1})$ for all $\ell = 1, \ldots, k$ (where $k + 1$ is used to denote 1), by the same amount $\delta$. This change will not affect the flow conservation constraints. By setting $\delta = \min_{\ell=1}^{k} x_{i_\ell j_\ell}$, we ensure that the flow remains feasible and the edge obtaining the minimum is deleted from $G(x)$. ∎

We can use the algorithm contained in the proof of (11.32) repeatedly to eliminate all cycles from $G(x)$. Initially, $G(x)$ may have $mn$ edges, so after at most $O(mn)$ iterations, the resulting solution $(x, L)$ will have no cycles in $G(x)$. At this point, we can use (11.30) to obtain a feasible assignment with at most twice the optimal load. We summarize the result by the following statement.

**(11.33)** *Given an instance of the Generalized Load Balancing Problem, we can find, in polynomial time, a feasible assignment with load at most twice the minimum possible.*

# 11.8 Arbitrarily Good Approximations: The Knapsack Problem

Often, when you talk to someone faced with an NP-hard optimization problem, they're hoping you can give them something that will produce a solution within, say, 1 percent of the optimum, or at least within a small percentage of optimal. Viewed from this perspective, the approximation algorithms we've seen thus far come across as quite weak: solutions within a factor of 2 of the minimum for Center Selection and Vertex Cover (i.e., 100 percent more than optimal). The Set Cover Algorithm in Section 10.3 is even worse: Its cost is not even within a fixed constant factor of the minimum possible!

Here is an important point underlying this state of affairs: NP-complete problems, as you well know, are all equivalent with respect to polynomial-time solvability; but assuming $\mathcal{P} \neq \mathcal{NP}$, they differ considerably in the extent to which their solutions can be efficiently approximated. In some cases, it is actually possible to prove limits on approximability. For example, if $\mathcal{P} \neq \mathcal{NP}$, then the guarantee provided by our Center Selection Algorithm is the best possible for any polynomial-time algorithm. Similarly, the guarantee provided by the Set Cover Algorithm, however bad it may seem, is very close to the best possible, unless $\mathcal{P} = \mathcal{NP}$. For other problems, such as the Vertex Cover Problem, the approximation algorithm we gave is essentially the best known, but it is an open question whether there could be polynomial-time algorithms with better guarantees. We will not discuss the topic of lower bounds on approximability in this book; while some lower bounds of this type are not so difficult to prove (such as for Center Selection), many are extremely technical.

## 🖎 The Problem

In this section, we discuss an NP-complete problem for which it is possible to design a polynomial-time algorithm providing a very strong approximation. We will consider a slightly more general version of the Knapsack (or Subset Sum) Problem. Suppose you have $n$ items that you consider packing in a knapsack. Each item $i = 1, \ldots, n$ has two integer parameters: a weight $w_i$ and a value $v_i$. Given a knapsack capacity $W$, the goal of the Knapsack Problem is to find a subset $S$ of items of maximum value subject to the restriction that the total weight of the set should not exceed $W$. In other words, we wish to maximize $\sum_{i \in S} v_i$ subject to the condition $\sum_{i \in S} w_i \leq W$.

How strong an approximation can we hope for? Our algorithm will take as input the weights and values defining the problem and will also take an extra parameter $\epsilon$, the desired precision. It will find a subset $S$ whose total weight does not exceed $W$, with value $\sum_{i \in S} v_i$ at most a $(1 + \epsilon)$ factor below the maximum possible. The algorithm will run in polynomial time for any *fixed* choice of $\epsilon > 0$; however, the dependence on $\epsilon$ will not be polynomial. We call such an algorithm a *polynomial-time approximation scheme*.

You may ask: How could such a strong kind of approximation algorithm be possible in polynomial time when the Knapsack Problem is NP-hard? With integer values, if we get close enough to the optimum value, we must reach the optimum itself! The catch is in the nonpolynomial dependence on the desired precision: for any fixed choice of $\epsilon$, such as $\epsilon = .5$, $\epsilon = .2$, or even $\epsilon = .01$, the algorithm runs in polynomial time, but as we change $\epsilon$ to smaller and smaller values, the running time gets larger. By the time we make $\epsilon$ small enough to make sure we get the optimum value, it is no longer a polynomial-time algorithm.

## Designing the Algorithm

In Section 6.4 we considered algorithms for the Subset Sum Problem, the special case of the Knapsack Problem when $v_i = w_i$ for all items $i$. We gave a dynamic programming algorithm for this special case that ran in $O(nW)$ time assuming the weights are integers. This algorithm naturally extends to the more general Knapsack Problem (see the end of Section 6.4 for this extension). The algorithm given in Section 6.4 works well when the weights are small (even if the values may be big). It is also possible to extend our dynamic programming algorithm for the case when the values are small, even if the weights may be big. At the end of this section, we give a dynamic programming algorithm for that case running in time $O(n^2 v^*)$, where $v^* = \max_i v_i$. Note that this algorithm does not run in polynomial time: It is only pseudo-polynomial, because of its dependence on the size of the values $v_i$. Indeed, since we proved this problem to be NP-complete in Chapter 8, we don't expect to be able to find a polynomial-time algorithm.

Algorithms that depend on the values in a pseudo-polynomial way can often be used to design polynomial-time approximation schemes, and the algorithm we develop here is a very clean example of the basic strategy. In particular, we will use the dynamic programming algorithm with running time $O(n^2 v^*)$ to design a polynomial-time approximation scheme; the idea is as follows. If the values are small integers, then $v^*$ is small and the problem can be solved in polynomial time already. On the other hand, if the values are large, then we do not have to deal with them exactly, as we only want an approximately optimum solution. We will use a rounding parameter $b$ (whose value we'll set later) and will consider the values rounded to an integer multiple of $b$. We will use our dynamic programming algorithm to solve the problem with the rounded values. More precisely, for each item $i$, let its rounded value be $\tilde{v}_i = \lceil v_i/b \rceil b$. Note that the rounded and the original value are quite close to each other.

**(11.34)**     *For each item $i$ we have $v_i \leq \tilde{v}_i \leq v_i + b$.*

What did we gain by the rounding? If the values were big to start with, we did not make them any smaller. However, the rounded values are all integer multiples of a common value $b$. So, instead of solving the problem with the rounded values $\tilde{v}_i$, we can change the units; we can divide all values by $b$ and get an equivalent problem. Let $\hat{v}_i = \tilde{v}_i / b = \lceil v_i / b \rceil$ for $i = 1, \ldots, n$.

**(11.35)**     *The Knapsack Problem with values $\tilde{v}_i$ and the scaled problem with values $\hat{v}_i$ have the same set of optimum solutions, the optimum values differ exactly by a factor of $b$, and the scaled values are integral.*

Now we are ready to state our approximation algorithm. We will assume that all items have weight at most $W$ (as items with weight $w_i > W$ are not in any solution, and hence can be deleted). We also assume for simplicity that $\epsilon^{-1}$ is an integer.

```
Knapsack-Approx(ε):
    Set  b = (ε/(2n)) max_i v_i
    Solve the Knapsack Problem with values v̂_i (equivalently ṽ_i)
    Return the set S of items found
```

### Analyzing the Algorithm

First note that the solution found is at least feasible; that is, $\sum_{i \in S} w_i \leq W$. This is true as we have rounded only the values and not the weights. This is why we need the new dynamic programming algorithm described at the end of this section.

**(11.36)**     *The set of items $S$ returned by the algorithm has total weight at most $W$, that is $\sum_{i \in S} w_i \leq W$.*

Next we'll prove that this algorithm runs in polynomial time.

**(11.37)**     *The algorithm* `Knapsack-Approx` *runs in polynomial time for any fixed $\epsilon > 0$.*

**Proof.** Setting $b$ and rounding item values can clearly be done in polynomial time. The time-consuming part of this algorithm is the dynamic programming to solve the rounded problem. Recall that for problems with integer values, the dynamic programming algorithm we use runs in time $O(n^2 v^*)$, where $v^* = \max_i v_i$.

Now we are applying this algorithms for an instance in which each item $i$ has weight $w_i$ and value $\hat{v}_i$. To determine the running time, we need to determine $\max_i \hat{v}_i$. The item $j$ with maximum value $v_j = \max_i v_i$ also has maximum value in the rounded problem, so $\max_i \hat{v}_i = \hat{v}_j = \lceil v_j/b \rceil = n\epsilon^{-1}$. Hence the overall running time of the algorithm is $O(n^3 \epsilon^{-1})$. Note that this is polynomial time for any fixed $\epsilon > 0$ as claimed; but the dependence on the desired precision $\epsilon$ is not polynomial, as the running time includes $\epsilon^{-1}$ rather than $\log \epsilon^{-1}$. ∎

Finally, we need to consider the key issue: How good is the solution obtained by this algorithm? Statement (11.34) shows that the values $\tilde{v}_i$ we used are close to the real values $v_i$, and this suggests that the solution obtained may not be far from optimal.

**(11.38)** *If S is the solution found by the* `Knapsack-Approx` *algorithm, and $S^*$ is any other solution satisfying $\sum_{i \in S^*} w_i \leq W$, then we have $(1 + \epsilon) \sum_{i \in S} v_i \geq \sum_{i \in S^*} v_i$.*

**Proof.** Let $S^*$ be any set satisfying $\sum_{i \in S^*} w_i \leq W$. Our algorithm finds the optimal solution with values $\tilde{v}_i$, so we know that

$$\sum_{i \in S} \tilde{v}_i \geq \sum_{i \in S^*} \tilde{v}_i.$$

The rounded values $\tilde{v}_i$ and the real values $v_i$ are quite close by (11.34), so we get the following chain of inequalities.

$$\sum_{i \in S^*} v_i \leq \sum_{i \in S^*} \tilde{v}_i \leq \sum_{i \in S} \tilde{v}_i \leq \sum_{i \in S} (v_i + b) \leq nb + \sum_{i \in S} v_i,$$

showing that the value $\sum_{i \in S} v_i$ of the solution we obtained is at most $nb$ smaller than the maximum value possible. We wanted to obtain a relative error showing that the value obtained, $\sum_{i \in S} v_i$, is at most a $(1 + \epsilon)$ factor less than the maximum possible, so we need to compare $nb$ to the value $\sum_{i \in S} v_i$.

Let $j$ be the item with largest value; by our choice of $b$, we have $v_j = 2\epsilon^{-1} nb$ and $v_j = \tilde{v}_j$. By our assumption that each item alone fits in the knapsack ($w_i \leq W$ for all $i$), we have $\sum_{i \in S} \tilde{v}_i \geq \tilde{v}_j = 2\epsilon^{-1} nb$. Finally, the chain of inequalities above says $\sum_{i \in S} v_i \geq \sum_{i \in S} \tilde{v}_i - nb$, and thus $\sum_{i \in S} v_i \geq (2\epsilon^{-1} - 1)nb$. Hence $nb \leq \epsilon \sum_{i \in S} v_i$ for $\epsilon \leq 1$, and so

$$\sum_{i \in S^*} v_i \leq \sum_{i \in S} v_i + nb \leq (1 + \epsilon) \sum_{i \in S} v_i. ∎$$

## The New Dynamic Programming Algorithm for the Knapsack Problem

To solve a problem by dynamic programming, we have to define a polynomial set of subproblems. The dynamic programming algorithm we defined when we studied the Knapsack Problem earlier uses subproblems of the form $\text{OPT}(i, w)$: the subproblem of finding the maximum value of any solution using a subset of the items $1, \ldots, i$ and a knapsack of weight $w$. When the weights are large, this is a large set of problems. We need a set of subproblems that work well when the values are reasonably small; this suggests that we should use subproblems associated with values, not weights. We define our subproblems as follows. The subproblem is defined by $i$ and a target value $V$, and $\overline{\text{OPT}}(i, V)$ is the smallest knapsack weight $W$ so that one can obtain a solution using a subset of items $\{1, \ldots, i\}$ with value at least $V$. We will have a subproblem for all $i = 0, \ldots, n$ and values $V = 0, \ldots, \sum_{j=1}^{i} v_j$. If $v^*$ denotes $\max_i v_i$, then we see that the largest $V$ can get in a subproblem is $\sum_{j=1}^{n} v_j \leq nv^*$. Thus, assuming the values are integral, there are at most $O(n^2 v^*)$ subproblems. None of these subproblems is precisely the original instance of Knapsack, but if we have the values of all subproblems $\overline{\text{OPT}}(n, V)$ for $V = 0, \ldots, \sum_i v_i$, then the value of the original problem can be obtained easily: it is the largest value $V$ such that $\overline{\text{OPT}}(n, V) \leq W$.

It is not hard to give a recurrence for solving these subproblems. By analogy with the dynamic programming algorithm for Subset Sum, we consider cases depending on whether or not the last item $n$ is included in the optimal solution $\mathcal{O}$.

- If $n \notin \mathcal{O}$, then $\overline{\text{OPT}}(n, V) = \overline{\text{OPT}}(n - 1, V)$.
- If $n \in \mathcal{O}$ is the only item in $\mathcal{O}$, then $\overline{\text{OPT}}(n, V) = w_n$.
- If $n \in \mathcal{O}$ is not the only item in $\mathcal{O}$, then $\overline{\text{OPT}}(n, V) = w_n + \overline{\text{OPT}}(n - 1, V - v_n)$.

These last two options can be summarized more compactly as

- If $n \in \mathcal{O}$, then $\overline{\text{OPT}}(n, V) = w_n + \overline{\text{OPT}}(n - 1, \max(0, V - v_n))$.

This implies the following analogue of the recurrence (6.8) from Chapter 6.

**(11.39)**  *If $V > \sum_{i=1}^{n-1} v_i$, then $\overline{\text{OPT}}(n, V) = w_n + \overline{\text{OPT}}(n - 1, V - v_n)$. Otherwise*

$$\overline{\text{OPT}}(n, V) = \min(\overline{\text{OPT}}(n - 1, V), w_n + \overline{\text{OPT}}(n - 1, \max(0, V - v_n))).$$

We can then write down an analogous dynamic programming algorithm.

```
Knapsack(n):
  Array M[0 ... n,0... V]
```

```
For  i = 0, . . . , n
    M[i, 0]  =  0
Endfor
For  i = 1, 2, . . . , n
    For  V = 1, . . . , ∑_{j=1}^{i} v_j
        If  V > ∑_{j=1}^{i-1} v_j then
            M[i, V] = w_i + M[i − 1, V]
        Else
            M[i, V] = min(M[i − 1, V], w_i + M[i − 1, max(0, V − v_i)])
        Endif
    Endfor
Endfor
Return the maximum value  V  such that  M[n, V] ≤ W
```

**(11.40)** Knapsack($n$) *takes* $O(n^2 v^*)$ *time and correctly computes the optimal values of the subproblems.*

As was done before, we can trace back through the table $M$ containing the optimal values of the subproblems, to find an optimal solution.

## Solved Exercises

### Solved Exercise 1

Recall the Shortest-First greedy algorithm for the Interval Scheduling Problem: Given a set of intervals, we repeatedly pick the shortest interval $I$, delete all the other intervals $I'$ that intersect $I$, and iterate.

In Chapter 4, we saw that this algorithm does *not* always produce a maximum-size set of nonoverlapping intervals. However, it turns out to have the following interesting approximation guarantee. If $s^*$ is the maximum size of a set of nonoverlapping intervals, and $s$ is the size of the set produced by the Shortest-First Algorithm, then $s \geq \frac{1}{2} s^*$ (that is, Shortest-First is a 2-approximation).

Prove this fact.

*Solution* Let's first recall the example in Figure 4.1 from Chapter 4, which showed that Shortest-First does not necessarily find an optimal set of intervals. The difficulty is clear: We may select a short interval $j$ while eliminating two longer flanking intervals $i$ and $i'$. So we have done only half as well as the optimum.

The question is to show that *Shortest-First* could never do worse than this. The issues here are somewhat similar to what came up in the analysis of the greedy algorithm for the Maximum Disjoint Paths Problem in Section 11.5: Each interval we select may "block" some of the intervals in an optimal solution, and we want to argue that by always selecting the shortest possible interval, these blocking effects are not too severe. In the case of disjoint paths, we analyzed the overlaps among paths essentially edge by edge, since the underlying graph there had an arbitrary structure. Here we can benefit from the highly restricted structure of intervals on a line so as to obtain a stronger bound.

In order for Shortest-First to do less than half as well as the optimum, there would have to be a large optimal solution that overlaps with a much smaller solution chosen by Shortest-First. Intuitively, it seems that the only way this could happen would be to have one of the intervals $i$ in the optimal solution nested completely inside one of the intervals $j$ chosen by Shortest-First. This in turn would contradict the behavior of Shortest-First: Why didn't it choose this shorter interval $i$ that's nested inside $j$?

Let's see if we can make this argument precise. Let $A$ denote the set of intervals chosen by Shortest-First, and let $O$ denote an optimal set of intervals. For each interval $j \in A$, consider the set of intervals in $O$ that it conflicts with. We claim

**(11.41)**    *Each interval $j \in A$ conflicts with at most two intervals in $O$.*

**Proof.** Assume by way of contradiction that there is an interval in $j \in A$ that conflicts with at least three intervals in $i_1, i_2, i_3 \in O$. These three intervals do not conflict with one another, as they are part of a single solution $O$, so they are ordered sequentially in time. Suppose they are ordered with $i_1$ first, then $i_2$, and then $i_3$. Since interval $j$ conflicts with both $i_1$ and $i_3$, the interval $i_2$ in between must be shorter than $j$ and fit completely inside it. Moreover, since $i_2$ was never selected by Shortest-First, it must have been available as an option when Shortest-First selected interval $j$. This is a contradiction, since $i_2$ is shorter than $j$.  ∎

The Shortest-First Algorithm only terminates when every unselected interval conflicts with one of the intervals it selected. So, in particular, each interval in $O$ is either included in $A$, or conflicts with an interval in $A$.

Now we use the following accounting scheme to bound the number of intervals in $O$. For each $i \in O$, we have some interval $j \in A$ "pay" for $i$, as follows. If $i$ is also in $A$, then $i$ will pay for itself. Otherwise, we arbitrarily choose an interval $j \in A$ that conflicts with $i$ and have $j$ pay for $i$. As we just argued, every interval in $O$ conflicts with some interval in $A$, so all intervals in $O$ will be paid for under this scheme. But by (11.41), each interval $j \in A$ conflicts with at most two intervals in $O$, and so it will only pay for at most two intervals. Thus, all intervals in $\mathcal{O}$ are paid for by intervals in $A$, and in this process each interval in $A$ pays at most twice. If follows that $A$ must have at least half as many intervals as $\mathcal{O}$.

# Exercises

1. Suppose you're acting as a consultant for the Port Authority of a small Pacific Rim nation. They're currently doing a multi-billion-dollar business per year, and their revenue is constrained almost entirely by the rate at which they can unload ships that arrive in the port.

   Here's a basic sort of problem they face. A ship arrives, with $n$ containers of weight $w_1, w_2, \ldots, w_n$. Standing on the dock is a set of trucks, each of which can hold $K$ units of weight. (You can assume that $K$ and each $w_i$ is an integer.) You can stack multiple containers in each truck, subject to the weight restriction of $K$; the goal is to minimize the number of trucks that are needed in order to carry all the containers. This problem is NP-complete (you don't have to prove this).

   A greedy algorithm you might use for this is the following. Start with an empty truck, and begin piling containers $1, 2, 3, \ldots$ into it until you get to a container that would overflow the weight limit. Now declare this truck "loaded" and send it off; then continue the process with a fresh truck. This algorithm, by considering trucks one at a time, may not achieve the most efficient way to pack the full set of containers into an available collection of trucks.

   (a) Give an example of a set of weights, and a value of $K$, where this algorithm does not use the minimum possible number of trucks.

   (b) Show, however, that the number of trucks used by this algorithm is within a factor of 2 of the minimum possible number, for any set of weights and any value of $K$.

2. At a lecture in a computational biology conference one of us attended a few years ago, a well-known protein chemist talked about the idea of building a "representative set" for a large collection of protein molecules whose properties we don't understand. The idea would be to intensively study the proteins in the representative set and thereby learn (by inference) about all the proteins in the full collection.

   To be useful, the representative set must have two properties.

   • It should be relatively small, so that it will not be too expensive to study it.

- Every protein in the full collection should be "similar" to some protein in the representative set. (In this way, it truly provides some information about all the proteins.)

More concretely, there is a large set $P$ of proteins. We define similarity on proteins by a *distance function* $d$: Given two proteins $p$ and $q$, it returns a number $d(p, q) \geq 0$. In fact, the function $d(\cdot, \cdot)$ most typically used is the *sequence alignment* measure, which we looked at when we studied dynamic programming in Chapter 6. We'll assume this is the distance being used here. There is a predefined distance cut-off $\Delta$ that's specified as part of the input to the problem; two proteins $p$ and $q$ are deemed to be "similar" to one another if and only if $d(p, q) \leq \Delta$.

We say that a subset of $P$ is a *representative set* if, for every protein $p$, there is a protein $q$ in the subset that is similar to it—that is, for which $d(p, q) \leq \Delta$. Our goal is to find a representative set that is as small as possible.

(a) Give a polynomial-time algorithm that approximates the minimum representative set to within a factor of $O(\log n)$. Specifically, your algorithm should have the following property: If the minimum possible size of a representative set is $s^*$, your algorithm should return a representative set of size at most $O(s^* \log n)$.

(b) Note the close similarity between this problem and the Center Selection Problem—a problem for which we considered approximation algorithms in Section 11.2. Why doesn't the algorithm described there solve the current problem?

3. Suppose you are given a set of positive integers $A = \{a_1, a_2, \ldots, a_n\}$ and a positive integer $B$. A subset $S \subseteq A$ is called *feasible* if the sum of the numbers in $S$ does not exceed $B$:

$$\sum_{a_i \in S} a_i \leq B.$$

The sum of the numbers in $S$ will be called the *total sum* of $S$.

You would like to select a feasible subset $S$ of $A$ whose total sum is as large as possible.

**Example.** If $A = \{8, 2, 4\}$ and $B = 11$, then the optimal solution is the subset $S = \{8, 2\}$.

(a) Here is an algorithm for this problem.

---

```
Initially  S = ϕ
Define  T = 0
For  i = 1, 2, . . . , n
```

```
If  T + a_i ≤ B then
    S ← S ∪ {a_i}
    T ← T + a_i
Endif
Endfor
```

Give an instance in which the total sum of the set $S$ returned by this algorithm is less than half the total sum of some other feasible subset of $A$.

(b)  Give a polynomial-time approximation algorithm for this problem with the following guarantee: It returns a feasible set $S \subseteq A$ whose total sum is at least half as large as the maximum total sum of any feasible set $S' \subseteq A$. Your algorithm should have a running time of at most $O(n \log n)$.

4.  Consider an optimization version of the Hitting Set Problem defined as follows. We are given a set $A = \{a_1, \ldots, a_n\}$ and a collection $B_1, B_2, \ldots, B_m$ of subsets of $A$. Also, each element $a_i \in A$ has a *weight* $w_i \geq 0$. The problem is to find a hitting set $H \subseteq A$ such that the total weight of the elements in $H$, that is, $\sum_{a_i \in H} w_i$, is as small as possible. (As in Exercise 5 in Chapter 8, we say that $H$ is a hitting set if $H \cap B_i$ is not empty for each $i$.) Let $b = \max_i |B_i|$ denote the maximum size of any of the sets $B_1, B_2, \ldots, B_m$. Give a polynomial-time approximation algorithm for this problem that finds a hitting set whose total weight is at most $b$ times the minimum possible.

5.  You are asked to consult for a business where clients bring in jobs each day for processing. Each job has a processing time $t_i$ that is known when the job arrives. The company has a set of ten machines, and each job can be processed on any of these ten machines.

At the moment the business is running the simple Greedy-Balance Algorithm we discussed in Section 11.1. They have been told that this may not be the best approximation algorithm possible, and they are wondering if they should be afraid of bad performance. However, they are reluctant to change the scheduling as they really like the simplicity of the current algorithm: jobs can be assigned to machines as soon as they arrive, without having to defer the decision until later jobs arrive.

In particular, they have heard that this algorithm can produce solutions with makespan as much as twice the minimum possible; but their experience with the algorithm has been quite good: They have been running it each day for the last month, and they have not observed it to produce a makespan more than 20 percent above the average load, $\frac{1}{10} \sum_i t_i$.

To try understanding why they don't seem to be encountering this factor-of-two behavior, you ask a bit about the kind of jobs and loads they see. You find out that the sizes of jobs range between 1 and 50, that is, $1 \le t_i \le 50$ for all jobs $i$; and the total load $\sum_i t_i$ is quite high each day: it is always at least 3,000.

Prove that on the type of inputs the company sees, the Greedy-Balance Algorithm will always find a solution whose makespan is at most 20 percent above the average load.

6. Recall that in the basic Load Balancing Problem from Section 11.1, we're interested in placing jobs on machines so as to minimize the *makespan*—the maximum load on any one machine. In a number of applications, it is natural to consider cases in which you have access to machines with different amounts of processing power, so that a given job may complete more quickly on one of your machines than on another. The question then becomes: How should you allocate jobs to machines in these more heterogeneous systems?

Here's a basic model that exposes these issues. Suppose you have a system that consists of $m$ *slow* machines and $k$ *fast* machines. The fast machines can perform twice as much work per unit time as the slow machines. Now you're given a set of $n$ jobs; job $i$ takes time $t_i$ to process on a slow machine and time $\frac{1}{2} t_i$ to process on a fast machine. You want to assign each job to a machine; as before, the goal is to minimize the makespan—that is the maximum, over all machines, of the total processing time of jobs assigned to that machine.

Give a polynomial-time algorithm that produces an assignment of jobs to machines with a makespan that is at most three times the optimum.

7. You're consulting for an e-commerce site that receives a large number of visitors each day. For each visitor $i$, where $i \in \{1, 2, \ldots, n\}$, the site has assigned a value $v_i$, representing the expected revenue that can be obtained from this customer.

Each visitor $i$ is shown one of $m$ possible ads $A_1, A_2, \ldots, A_m$ as they enter the site. The site wants a selection of one ad for each customer so that *each* ad is seen, overall, by a set of customers of reasonably large total weight. Thus, given a selection of one ad for each customer, we will define the *spread* of this selection to be the minimum, over $j = 1, 2, \ldots, m$, of the total weight of all customers who were shown ad $A_j$.

**Example** Suppose there are six customers with values 3, 4, 12, 2, 4, 6, and there are $m = 3$ ads. Then, in this instance, one could achieve a spread of

9 by showing ad $A_1$ to customers $1, 2, 4$, ad $A_2$ to customer 3, and ad $A_3$ to customers 5 and 6.

The ultimate goal is to find a selection of an ad for each customer that maximizes the spread. Unfortunately, this optimization problem is NP-hard (you don't have to prove this). So instead, we will try to approximate it.

**(a)** Give a polynomial-time algorithm that approximates the maximum spread to within a factor of 2. That is, if the maximum spread is $s$, then your algorithm should produce a selection of one ad for each customer that has spread at least $s/2$. In designing your algorithm, you may assume that no single customer has a value that is significantly above the average; specifically, if $\bar{v} = \sum_{i=1}^{n} v_i$ denotes the total value of all customers, then you may assume that no single customer has a value exceeding $\bar{v}/(2m)$.

**(b)** Give an example of an instance on which the algorithm you designed in part (a) does not find an optimal solution (that is, one of maximum spread). Say what the optimal solution is in your sample instance, and what your algorithm finds.

8. Some friends of yours are working with a system that performs real-time scheduling of jobs on multiple servers, and they've come to you for help in getting around an unfortunate piece of legacy code that can't be changed.

Here's the situation. When a batch of jobs arrives, the system allocates them to servers using the simple Greedy-Balance Algorithm from Section 11.1, which provides an approximation to within a factor of 2. In the decade and a half since this part of the system was written, the hardware has gotten faster to the point where, on the instances that the system needs to deal with, your friends find that it's generally possible to compute an optimal solution.

The difficulty is that the people in charge of the system's internals won't let them change the portion of the software that implements the Greedy-Balance Algorithm so as to replace it with one that finds the optimal solution. (Basically, this portion of the code has to interact with so many other parts of the system that it's not worth the risk of something going wrong if it's replaced.)

After grumbling about this for a while, your friends come up with an alternate idea. Suppose they could write a little piece of code that takes the description of the jobs, computes an optimal solution (since they're able to do this on the instances that arise in practice), and then feeds the jobs to the Greedy-Balance Algorithm *in an order that will cause it to allocate them optimally*. In other words, they're hoping to be able to reorder the input in such a way that when Greedy-Balance encounters the input in this order, it produces an optimal solution.

So their question to you is simply the following: Is this always possible? Their conjecture is,

> *For every instance of the load balancing problem from Section 11.1, there exists an order of the jobs so that when Greedy-Balance processes the jobs in this order, it produces an assignment of jobs to machines with the minimum possible makespan.*

Decide whether you think this conjecture is true or false, and give either a proof or a counterexample.

9. Consider the following maximization version of the 3-Dimensional Matching Problem. Given disjoint sets $X$, $Y$, and $Z$, and given a set $T \subseteq X \times Y \times Z$ of ordered triples, a subset $M \subseteq T$ is a *3-dimensional matching* if each element of $X \cup Y \cup Z$ is contained in at most one of these triples. The *Maximum 3-Dimensional Matching Problem* is to find a 3-dimensional matching $M$ of maximum size. (The size of the matching, as usual, is the number of triples it contains. You may assume $|X| = |Y| = |Z|$ if you want.)

   Give a polynomial-time algorithm that finds a 3-dimensional matching of size at least $\frac{1}{3}$ times the maximum possible size.

10. Suppose you are given an $n \times n$ *grid graph* $G$, as in Figure 11.13.

    Associated with each node $v$ is a *weight* $w(v)$, which is a nonnegative integer. You may assume that the weights of all nodes are distinct. Your

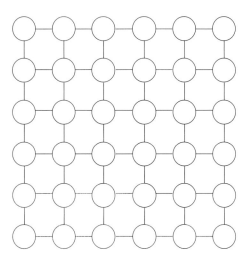

**Figure 11.13** A grid graph.

goal is to choose an independent set $S$ of nodes of the grid, so that the sum of the weights of the nodes in $S$ is as large as possible. (The sum of the weights of the nodes in $S$ will be called its *total weight*.)

Consider the following greedy algorithm for this problem.

```
The "heaviest-first" greedy algorithm:
  Start with S equal to the empty set
  While some node remains in G
    Pick a node v_i of maximum weight
    Add v_i to S
    Delete v_i and its neighbors from G
  Endwhile
  Return S
```

(a) Let $S$ be the independent set returned by the "heaviest-first" greedy algorithm, and let $T$ be any other independent set in $G$. Show that, for each node $v \in T$, either $v \in S$, or there is a node $v' \in S$ so that $w(v) \leq w(v')$ and $(v, v')$ is an edge of $G$.

(b) Show that the "heaviest-first" greedy algorithm returns an independent set of total weight at least $\frac{1}{4}$ times the maximum total weight of any independent set in the grid graph $G$.

11. Recall that in the Knapsack Problem, we have $n$ items, each with a weight $w_i$ and a value $v_i$. We also have a weight bound $W$, and the problem is to select a set of items $S$ of highest possible value subject to the condition that the total weight does not exceed $W$—that is, $\sum_{i \in S} w_i \leq W$. Here's one way to look at the approximation algorithm that we designed in this chapter. If we are told there exists a subset $\mathcal{O}$ whose total weight is $\sum_{i \in \mathcal{O}} w_i \leq W$ and whose total value is $\sum_{i \in \mathcal{O}} v_i = V$ for some $V$, then our approximation algorithm can find a set $A$ with total weight $\sum_{i \in A} w_i \leq W$ and total value at least $\sum_{i \in A} v_i \geq V/(1 + \epsilon)$. Thus the algorithm approximates the best value, while keeping the weights strictly under $W$. (Of course, returning the set $\mathcal{O}$ is always a valid solution, but since the problem is NP-hard, we don't expect to always be able to find $\mathcal{O}$ itself; the approximation bound of $1 + \epsilon$ means that other sets $A$, with slightly less value, can be valid answers as well.)

Now, as is well known, you can always pack a little bit more for a trip just by "sitting on your suitcase"—in other words, by slightly overflowing the allowed weight limit. This too suggests a way of formalizing the approximation question for the Knapsack Problem, but it's the following, different, formalization.

Suppose, as before, that you're given $n$ items with weights and values, as well as parameters $W$ and $V$; and you're told that there is a subset $\mathcal{O}$ whose total weight is $\sum_{i \in \mathcal{O}} w_i \leq W$ and whose total value is $\sum_{i \in \mathcal{O}} v_i = V$ for some $V$. For a given fixed $\epsilon > 0$, design a polynomial-time algorithm that finds a subset of items $A$ such that $\sum_{i \in A} w_i \leq (1 + \epsilon)W$ and $\sum_{i \in A} v_i \geq V$. In other words, you want $A$ to achieve at least as high a total value as the given bound $V$, but you're allowed to exceed the weight limit $W$ by a factor of $1 + \epsilon$.

**Example.** Suppose you're given four items, with weights and values as follows:

$$(w_1, v_1) = (5, 3), (w_2, v_2) = (4, 6)$$

$$(w_3, v_3) = (1, 4), (w_4, v_4) = (6, 11)$$

You're also given $W = 10$ and $V = 13$ (since, indeed, the subset consisting of the first three items has total weight at most 10 and has value 13). Finally, you're given $\epsilon = .1$. This means you need to find (via your approximation algorithm) a subset of weight at most $(1 + .1) * 10 = 11$ and value at least 13. One valid solution would be the subset consisting of the first and fourth items, with value $14 \geq 13$. (Note that this is a case where you're able to achieve a value strictly greater than $V$, since you're allowed to slightly overfill the knapsack.)

12. Consider the following problem. There is a set $U$ of $n$ nodes, which we can think of as users (e.g., these are locations that need to access a service, such as a Web server). You would like to place servers at multiple locations. Suppose you are given a set $S$ possible sites that would be willing to act as locations for the servers. For each site $s \in S$, there is a fee $f_s \geq 0$ for placing a server at that location. Your goal will be to approximately minimize the cost while providing the service to each of the customers. So far this is very much like the Set Cover Problem: The places $s$ are sets, the weight of set $s$ is $f_s$, and we want to select a collection of sets that covers all users. There is one extra complication: Users $u \in U$ can be served from multiple sites, but there is an associated cost $d_{us}$ for serving user $u$ from site $s$. When the value $d_{us}$ is very high, we do not want to serve user $u$ from site $s$; and in general the service cost $d_{us}$ serves as an incentive to serve customers from "nearby" servers whenever possible.

So here is the question, which we call the Facility Location Problem: Given the sets $U$ and $S$, and costs $f$ and $d$, you need to select a subset $A \subseteq S$ at which to place servers (at a cost of $\sum_{s \in A} f_s$), and assign each user $u$ to the active server where it is cheapest to be served, $\min_{s \in A} d_{us}$. The goal is to minimize the overall cost $\sum_{s \in A} f_s + \sum_{u \in U} \min_{s \in A} d_{us}$. Give an $H(n)$-approximation for this problem.

(Note that if all service costs $d_{us}$ are 0 or infinity, then this problem is exactly the Set Cover Problem: $f_s$ is the cost of the set named $s$, and $d_{us}$ is 0 if node $u$ is in set $s$, and infinity otherwise.)

## Notes and Further Reading

The design of approximation algorithms for NP-hard problems is an active area of research, and it is the focus of a book of surveys edited by Hochbaum (1996) and a text by Vazirani (2001).

The greedy algorithm for load balancing and its analysis is due to Graham (1966, 1969); in fact, he proved that when the jobs are first sorted in descending order of size, the greedy algorithm achieves an assignment within a factor $\frac{4}{3}$ of optimal. (In the text, we give a simpler proof for the weaker bound of $\frac{3}{2}$.) Using more complicated algorithms, even stronger approximation guarantees can be proved for this problem (Hochbaum and Shmoys 1987; Hall 1996). The techniques used for these stronger load balancing approximation algorithms are also closely related to the method described in the text for designing arbitrarily good approximations for the Knapsack Problem.

The approximation algorithm for the Center Selection Problem follows the approach of Hochbaum and Shmoys (1985) and Dyer and Frieze (1985). Other geometric location problems of this flavor are discussed by Bern and Eppstein (1996) and in the book of surveys edited by Drezner (1995).

The greedy algorithm for Set Cover and its analysis are due independently to Johnson (1974), Lovász (1975), and Chvatal (1979). Further results for the Set Cover Problem are discussed in the survey by Hochbaum (1996).

As mentioned in the text, the pricing method for designing approximation algorithms is also referred to as the *primal-dual method* and can be motivated using linear programming. This latter perspective is the subject of the survey by Goemans and Williamson (1996). The pricing algorithm to approximate the Weighted Vertex Cover Problem is due to Bar-Yehuda and Even (1981).

The greedy algorithm for the disjoint paths problem is due to Kleinberg and Tardos (1995); the pricing-based approximation algorithm for the case when multiple paths can share an edge is due to Awerbuch, Azar, and Plotkin (1993). Algorithms have been developed for many other variants of the Disjoint Paths Problem; see the book of surveys edited by Korte et al. (1990) for a discussion of cases that can be solved optimally in polynomial time, and Plotkin (1995) and Kleinberg (1996) for surveys of work on approximation.

The linear programming rounding algorithm for the Weighted Vertex Cover Problem is due to Hochbaum (1982). The rounding algorithm for Generalized Load Balancing is due to Lenstra, Shmoys, and Tardos (1990); see the survey by Hall (1996) for other results in this vein. As discussed in the text, these two results illustrate a widely used method for designing approximation algorithms: One sets up an integer programming formulation for the problem, transforms it to a related (but not equivalent) linear programming problem, and then rounds the resulting solution. Vazirani (2001) discusses many further applications of this technique.

Local search and randomization are two other powerful techniques for designing approximation algorithms; we discuss these connections in the next two chapters.

One topic that we do not cover in this book is *inapproximability*. Just as one can prove that a given NP-hard problem can be approximated to within a certain factor in polynomial time, one can also sometimes establish lower bounds, showing that if the problem could be approximated to within better than some factor $c$ in polynomial time, then it could be solved optimally, thereby proving $\mathcal{P} = \mathcal{NP}$. There is a growing body of work that establishes such limits to approximability for many NP-hard problems. In certain cases, these positive and negative results have lined up perfectly to produce an *approximation threshold*, establishing for certain problems that there is a polynomial-time approximation algorithm to within some factor $c$, and it is impossible to do better unless $\mathcal{P} = \mathcal{NP}$. Some of the early results on inapproximability were not very difficult to prove, but more recent work has introduced powerful techniques that become quite intricate. This topic is covered in the survey by Arora and Lund (1996).

***Notes on the Exercises***    Exercises 4 and 12 are based on results of Dorit Hochbaum. Exercise 11 is based on results of Sartaj Sahni, Oscar Ibarra, and Chul Kim, and of Dorit Hochbaum and David Shmoys.

# Chapter 12

## Local Search

In the previous two chapters, we have considered techniques for dealing with computationally intractable problems: in Chapter 10, by identifying structured special cases of NP-hard problems, and in Chapter 11, by designing polynomial-time approximation algorithms. We now develop a third and final topic related to this theme: the design of *local search algorithms*.

Local search is a very general technique; it describes any algorithm that "explores" the space of possible solutions in a sequential fashion, moving in one step from a current solution to a "nearby" one. The generality and flexibility of this notion has the advantage that it is not difficult to design a local search approach to almost any computationally hard problem; the counterbalancing disadvantage is that it is often very difficult to say anything precise or provable about the quality of the solutions that a local search algorithm finds, and consequently very hard to tell whether one is using a good local search algorithm or a poor one.

Our discussion of local search in this chapter will reflect these trade-offs. Local search algorithms are generally heuristics designed to find good, but not necessarily optimal, solutions to computational problems, and we begin by talking about what the search for such solutions looks like at a global level. A useful intuitive basis for this perspective comes from connections with energy minimization principles in physics, and we explore this issue first. Our discussion for this part of the chapter will have a somewhat different flavor from what we've generally seen in the book thus far; here, we'll introduce some algorithms, discuss them qualitatively, but admit quite frankly that we can't prove very much about them.

There are cases, however, in which it is possible to prove properties of local search algorithms, and to bound their performance relative to an optimal solution. This will be the focus of the latter part of the chapter: We begin by considering a case—the dynamics of Hopfield neural networks—in which local search provides the natural way to think about the underlying behavior of a complex process; we then focus on some NP-hard problems for which local search can be used to design efficient algorithms with provable approximation guarantees. We conclude the chapter by discussing a different type of local search: the game-theoretic notions of best-response dynamics and Nash equilibria, which arise naturally in the study of systems that contain many interacting agents.

## 12.1 The Landscape of an Optimization Problem

Much of the core of local search was developed by people thinking in terms of analogies with physics. Looking at the wide range of hard computational problems that require the minimization of some quantity, they reasoned as follows. Physical systems are performing minimization all the time, when they seek to minimize their potential energy. What can we learn from the ways in which nature performs minimization? Does it suggest new kinds of algorithms?

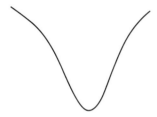

**Figure 12.1** When the potential energy landscape has the structure of a simple funnel, it is easy to find the lowest point.

### Potential Energy

If the world really looked the way a freshman mechanics class suggests, it seems that it would consist entirely of hockey pucks sliding on ice and balls rolling down inclined surfaces. Hockey pucks usually slide because you push them; but why do balls roll downhill? One perspective that we learn from Newtonian mechanics is that the ball is trying to minimize its *potential energy*. In particular, if the ball has mass $m$ and falls a distance of $h$, it loses an amount of potential energy proportional to $mh$. So, if we release a ball from the top of the funnel-shaped landscape in Figure 12.1, its potential energy will be minimized at the lowest point.

If we make the landscape a little more complicated, some extra issues creep in. Consider the "double funnel" in Figure 12.2. Point A is lower than point B, and so is a more desirable place for the ball to come to rest. But if we start the ball rolling from point C, it will not be able to get over the barrier between the two funnels, and it will end up at B. We say that the ball has become trapped in a *local minimum*: It is at the lowest point if one looks in the neighborhood of its current location; but stepping back and looking at the whole landscape, we see that it has missed the *global minimum*.

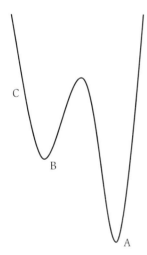

**Figure 12.2** Most landscapes are more complicated than simple funnels; for example, in this "double funnel," there's a deep global minimum and a shallower local minimum.

Of course, enormously large physical systems must also try to minimize their energy. Consider, for example, taking a few grams of some homogeneous substance, heating it up, and studying its behavior over time. To capture the potential energy exactly, we would in principle need to represent the behavior of each atom in the substance, as it interacts with nearby atoms. But it is also useful to speak of the properties of the system as a whole—as an aggregate—and this is the domain of statistical mechanics. We will come back to statistical mechanics in a little while, but for now we simply observe that our notion of an "energy landscape" provides useful visual intuition for the process by which even a large physical system minimizes its energy. Thus, while it would in reality take a huge number of dimensions to draw the true "landscape" that constrains the system, we can use one-dimensional "cartoon" representations to discuss the distinction between local and global energy minima, the "funnels" around them, and the "height" of the energy barriers between them.

Taking a molten material and trying to cool it to a perfect crystalline solid is really the process of trying to guide the underlying collection of atoms to its global potential energy minimum. This can be very difficult, and the large number of local minima in a typical energy landscape represent the pitfalls that can lead the system astray in its search for the global minimum. Thus, rather than the simple example of Figure 12.2, which simply contains a single wrong choice, we should be more worried about landscapes with the schematic cartoon representation depicted in Figure 12.3. This can be viewed as a "jagged funnel," in which there are local minima waiting to trap the system all the way along its journey to the bottom.

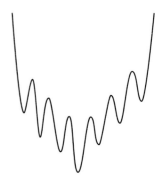

**Figure 12.3** In a general energy landscape, there may be a very large number of local minima that make it hard to find the global minimum, as in the "jagged funnel" drawn here.

## The Connection to Optimization

This perspective on energy minimization has really been based on the following core ingredients: The physical system can be in one of a large number of possible states; its energy is a function of its current state; and from a given state, a small perturbation leads to a "neighboring" state. The way in which these neighboring states are linked together, along with the structure of the energy function on them, defines the underlying energy landscape.

It's from this perspective that we again start to think about computational minimization problems. In a typical such problem, we have a large (typically exponential-size) set $\mathcal{C}$ of possible solutions. We also have a *cost function* $c(\cdot)$ that measures the quality of each solution; for a solution $S \in \mathcal{C}$, we write its cost as $c(S)$. The goal is to find a solution $S^* \in \mathcal{C}$ for which $c(S^*)$ is as small as possible.

So far this is just the way we've thought about such problems all along. We now add to this the notion of a *neighbor relation* on solutions, to capture the idea that one solution $S'$ can be obtained by a small modification of another solution $S$. We write $S \sim S'$ to denote that $S'$ is a neighboring solution of $S$, and we use $N(S)$ to denote the *neighborhood* of $S$, the set $\{S' : S \sim S'\}$. We will primarily be considering symmetric neighbor relations here, though the basic points we discuss will apply to asymmetric neighbor relations as well. A crucial point is that, while the set $\mathcal{C}$ of possible solutions and the cost function $c(\cdot)$ are provided by the specification of the problem, we have the freedom to make up any neighbor relation that we want.

A *local search algorithm* takes this setup, including a neighbor relation, and works according to the following high-level scheme. At all times, it maintains a current solution $S \in \mathcal{C}$. In a given step, it chooses a neighbor $S'$ of $S$, declares $S'$ to be the new current solution, and iterates. Throughout the execution of the algorithm, it remembers the minimum-cost solution that it has seen thus far; so, as it runs, it gradually finds better and better solutions. The crux of a local search algorithm is in the choice of the neighbor relation, and in the design of the rule for choosing a neighboring solution at each step.

Thus one can think of a neighbor relation as defining a (generally undirected) graph on the set of all possible solutions, with edges joining neighboring pairs of solutions. A local search algorithm can then be viewed as performing a walk on this graph, trying to move toward a good solution.

## An Application to the Vertex Cover Problem

This is still all somewhat vague without a concrete problem to think about; so we'll use the Vertex Cover Problem as a running example here. It's important to keep in mind that, while Vertex Cover makes for a good example, there are many other optimization problems that would work just as well for this illustration.

Thus we are given a graph $G = (V, E)$; the set $\mathcal{C}$ of possible solutions consists of all subsets $S$ of $V$ that form vertex covers. Hence, for example, we always have $V \in \mathcal{C}$. The *cost* $c(S)$ of a vertex cover $S$ will simply be its size; in this way, minimizing the cost of a vertex cover is the same as finding one of minimum size. Finally, we will focus our examples on local search algorithms that use a particularly simple neighbor relation: we say that $S \sim S'$ if $S'$ can be obtained from $S$ by adding or deleting a single node. Thus our local search algorithms will be walking through the space of possible vertex covers, adding or deleting a node to their current solution in each step, and trying to find as small a vertex cover as possible.

One useful fact about this neighbor relation is the following.

**(12.1)**   *Each vertex cover $S$ has at most $n$ neighboring solutions.*

The reason is simply that each neighboring solution of $S$ is obtained by adding or deleting a distinct node. A consequence of (12.1) is that we can efficiently examine all possible neighboring solutions of $S$ in the process of choosing which to select.

Let's think first about a very simple local search algorithm, which we'll term *gradient descent*. Gradient descent starts with the full vertex set $V$ and uses the following rule for choosing a neighboring solution.

> Let $S$ denote the current solution. If there is a neighbor $S'$ of $S$ with strictly lower cost, then choose the neighbor whose cost is as small as possible. Otherwise terminate the algorithm.

So gradient descent moves strictly "downhill" as long as it can; once this is no longer possible, it stops.

We can see that gradient descent terminates precisely at solutions that are *local minima*: solutions $S$ such that, for all neighboring $S'$, we have $c(S) \leq c(S')$. This definition corresponds very naturally to our notion of local minima in energy landscapes: They are points from which no one-step perturbation will improve the cost function.

How can we visualize the behavior of a local search algorithm in terms of the kinds of energy landscapes we illustrated earlier? Let's think first about gradient descent. The easiest instance of Vertex Cover is surely an $n$-node graph with no edges. The empty set is the optimal solution (since there are no edges to cover), and gradient descent does exceptionally well at finding this solution: It starts with the full vertex set $V$, and keeps deleting nodes until there are none left. Indeed, the set of vertex covers for this edge-less graph corresponds naturally to the funnel we drew in Figure 12.1: The unique local minimum is the global minimum, and there is a downhill path to it from any point.

When can gradient descent go astray? Consider a "star graph" $G$, consisting of nodes $x_1, y_1, y_2, \ldots, y_{n-1}$, with an edge from $x_1$ to each $y_i$. The minimum vertex cover for $G$ is the singleton set $\{x_1\}$, and gradient descent can reach this solution by successively deleting $y_1, \ldots, y_{n-1}$ in any order. But, if gradient descent deletes the node $x_1$ first, then it is immediately stuck: No node $y_i$ can be deleted without destroying the vertex cover property, so the only neighboring solution is the full node set $V$, which has higher cost. Thus the algorithm has become trapped in the local minimum $\{y_1, y_2, \ldots, y_{n-1}\}$, which has very high cost relative to the global minimum.

Pictorially, we see that we're in a situation corresponding to the double funnel of Figure 12.2. The deeper funnel corresponds to the optimal solution $\{x_1\}$, while the shallower funnel corresponds to the inferior local minimum $\{y_1, y_2, \ldots, y_{n-1}\}$. Sliding down the wrong portion of the slope at the very beginning can send one into the wrong minimum. We can easily generalize this situation to one in which the two minima have any relative depths we want. Consider, for example, a bipartite graph $G$ with nodes $x_1, x_2, \ldots, x_k$ and $y_1, y_2, \ldots, y_\ell$, where $k < \ell$, and there is an edge from every node of the form $x_i$

to every node of the form $y_j$. Then there are two local minima, corresponding to the vertex covers $\{x_1, \ldots, x_k\}$ and $\{y_1, \ldots, y_\ell\}$. Which one is discovered by a run of gradient descent is entirely determined by whether it first deletes an element of the form $x_i$ or $y_j$.

With more complicated graphs, it's often a useful exercise to think about the kind of landscape they induce; and conversely, one sometimes may look at a landscape and consider whether there's a graph that gives rise to something like it.

For example, what kind of graph might yield a Vertex Cover instance with a landscape like the jagged funnel in Figure 12.3? One such graph is simply an $n$-node path, where $n$ is an odd number, with nodes labeled $v_1, v_2, \ldots, v_n$ in order. The unique minimum vertex cover $S^*$ consists of all nodes $v_i$ where $i$ is even. But there are many local optima. For example, consider the vertex cover $\{v_2, v_3, v_5, v_6, v_8, v_9, \ldots\}$ in which every third node is omitted. This is a vertex cover that is significantly larger than $S^*$; but there's no way to delete any node from it while still covering all edges. Indeed, it's very hard for gradient descent to find the minimum vertex cover $S^*$ starting from the full vertex set $V$: Once it's deleted just a single node $v_i$ with an even value of $i$, it's lost the chance to find the global optimum $S^*$. Thus the even/odd parity distinction in the nodes captures a plethora of different wrong turns in the local search, and hence gives the overall funnel its jagged character. Of course, there is not a direct correspondence between the ridges in the drawing and the local optima; as we warned above, Figure 12.3 is ultimately just a cartoon rendition of what's going on.

But we see that even for graphs that are structurally very simple, gradient descent is much too straightforward a local search algorithm. We now look at some more refined local search algorithms that use the same type of neighbor relation, but include a method for "escaping" from local minima.

## 12.2  The Metropolis Algorithm and Simulated Annealing

The first idea for an improved local search algorithm comes from the work of Metropolis, Rosenbluth, Rosenbluth, Teller, and Teller (1953). They considered the problem of simulating the behavior of a physical system according to principles of statistical mechanics. A basic model from this field asserts that the probability of finding a physical system in a state with energy $E$ is proportional to the *Gibbs-Boltzmann function* $e^{-E/(kT)}$, where $T > 0$ is the temperature and $k > 0$ is a constant. Let's look at this function. For any temperature $T$, the function is monotone decreasing in the energy $E$, so this states that a physical system is more likely to be in a lower energy state than in a high energy state. Now let's consider the effect of the temperature $T$. When $T$ is small, the probability for a low-energy state is significantly larger than the probability for a high-energy state. However, if the temperature is large, then the difference between these two probabilities is very small, and the system is almost equally likely to be in any state.

## The Metropolis Algorithm

Metropolis et al. proposed the following method for performing step-by-step simulation of a system at a fixed temperature $T$. At all times, the simulation maintains a current state of the system and tries to produce a new state by applying a perturbation to this state. We'll assume that we're only interested in states of the system that are "reachable" from some fixed initial state by a sequence of small perturbations, and we'll assume that there is only a finite set $\mathcal{C}$ of such states. In a single step, we first generate a small random perturbation to the current state $S$ of the system, resulting in a new state $S'$. Let $E(S)$ and $E(S')$ denote the energies of $S$ and $S'$, respectively. If $E(S') \leq E(S)$, then we update the current state to be $S'$. Otherwise let $\Delta E = E(S') - E(S) > 0$. We update the current state to be $S'$ with probability $e^{-\Delta E/(kT)}$, and otherwise leave the current state at $S$.

Metropolis et al. proved that their simulation algorithm has the following property. To prevent too long a digression, we omit the proof; it is actually a direct consequence of some basic facts about random walks.

**(12.2)**   *Let*

$$Z = \sum_{S \in \mathcal{C}} e^{-E(S)/(kT)}.$$

*For a state $S$, let $f_S(t)$ denote the fraction of the first $t$ steps in which the state of the simulation is in $S$. Then the limit of $f_S(t)$ as $t$ approaches $\infty$ is, with probability approaching 1, equal to $\frac{1}{Z} \cdot e^{-E(S)/(kT)}$.*

This is exactly the sort of fact one wants, since it says that the simulation spends roughly the correct amount of time in each state, according to the Gibbs-Boltzmann equation.

If we want to use this overall scheme to design a local search algorithm for minimization problems, we can use the analogies of Section 12.1 in which states of the system are candidate solutions, with energy corresponding to cost. We then see that the operation of the Metropolis Algorithm has a very desirable pair of features in a local search algorithm: It is biased toward "downhill" moves but will also accept "uphill" moves with smaller probability. In this way, it is able to make progress even when situated in a local minimum. Moreover, as expressed in (12.2), it is globally biased toward lower-cost solutions.

Here is a concrete formulation of the Metropolis Algorithm for a minimization problem.

```
Start with an initial solution S₀, and constants k and T
In one step:
   Let S be the current solution
   Let S' be chosen uniformly at random from the neighbors of S
   If c(S') ≤ c(S) then
      Update S ← S'
   Else
      With probability e^{-(c(S')-c(S))/(kT)}
         Update S ← S'
      Otherwise
         Leave S unchanged
   EndIf
```

Thus, on the Vertex Cover instance consisting of the star graph in Section 12.1, in which $x_1$ is joined to each of $y_1, \ldots, y_{n-1}$, we see that the Metropolis Algorithm will quickly bounce out of the local minimum that arises when $x_1$ is deleted: The neighboring solution in which $x_1$ is put back in will be generated and will be accepted with positive probability. On more complex graphs as well, the Metropolis Algorithm is able, to some extent, to correct the wrong choices it makes as it proceeds.

At the same time, the Metropolis Algorithm does not always behave the way one would want, even in some very simple situations. Let's go back to the very first graph we considered, a graph $G$ with no edges. Gradient descent solves this instance with no trouble, deleting nodes in sequence until none are left. But, while the Metropolis Algorithm will start out this way, it begins to go astray as it nears the global optimum. Consider the situation in which the current solution contains only $c$ nodes, where $c$ is much smaller than the total number of nodes, $n$. With very high probability, the neighboring solution generated by the Metropolis Algorithm will have size $c + 1$, rather than $c - 1$, and with reasonable probability this uphill move will be accepted. Thus it gets harder and harder to shrink the size of the vertex cover as the algorithm proceeds; it is exhibiting a sort of "flinching" reaction near the bottom of the funnel.

This behavior shows up in more complex examples as well, and in more complex ways; but it is certainly striking for it to show up here so simply. In order to figure out how we might fix this behavior, we return to the physical analogy that motivated the Metropolis Algorithm, and ask: What's the meaning of the temperature parameter $T$ in the context of optimization?

We can think of $T$ as a one-dimensional knob that we're able to turn, and it controls the extent to which the algorithm is willing to accept uphill moves. As we make $T$ very large, the probability of accepting an uphill move approaches 1, and the Metropolis Algorithm behaves like a random walk that is basically indifferent to the cost function. As we make $T$ very close to 0, on the other hand, uphill moves are almost never accepted, and the Metropolis Algorithm behaves almost identically to gradient descent.

## Simulated Annealing

Neither of these temperature extremes—very low or very high—is an effective way to solve minimization problems in general, and we can see this in physical settings as well. If we take a solid and heat it to a very high temperature, we do not expect it to maintain a nice crystal structure, even if this is energetically favorable; and this can be explained by the large value of $kT$ in the expression $e^{-E(S)/(kT)}$, which makes the enormous number of less favorable states too probable. This is a way in which we can view the "flinching" behavior of the Metropolis Algorithm on an easy Vertex Cover instance: It's trying to find the lowest energy state at too high a temperature, when all the competing states have too high a probability. On the other hand, if we take a molten solid and freeze it very abruptly, we do not expect to get a perfect crystal either; rather, we get a deformed crystal structure with many imperfections. This is because, with $T$ very small, we've come too close to the realm of gradient descent, and the system has become trapped in one of the numerous ridges of its jagged energy landscape. It is interesting to note that when $T$ is very small, then statement (12.2) shows that in the limit, the random walk spends most of its time in the lowest energy state. The problem is that the random walk will take an enormous amount of time before getting anywhere near this limit.

In the early 1980s, as people were considering the connection between energy minimization and combinatorial optimization, Kirkpatrick, Gelatt, and Vecchi (1983) thought about the issues we've been discussing, and they asked the following question: How do we solve this problem for physical systems, and what sort of algorithm does this suggest? In physical systems, one guides a material to a crystalline state by a process known as *annealing*: The material is cooled very gradually from a high temperature, allowing it enough time to reach equilibrium at a succession of intermediate lower temperatures. In this way, it is able to escape from the energy minima that it encounters all the way through the cooling process, eventually arriving at the global optimum.

We can thus try to mimic this process computationally, arriving at an algorithmic technique known as *simulated annealing*. Simulated annealing works by running the Metropolis Algorithm while gradually decreasing the value of $T$ over the course of the execution. The exact way in which $T$ is updated is called, for natural reasons, a *cooling schedule*, and a number of considerations go into the design of the cooling schedule. Formally, a cooling schedule is a function $\tau$ from $\{1, 2, 3, \ldots\}$ to the positive real numbers; in iteration $i$ of the Metropolis Algorithm, we use the temperature $T = \tau(i)$ in our definition of the probability.

Qualitatively, we can see that simulated annealing allows for large changes in the solution in the early stages of its execution, when the temperature is high. Then, as the search proceeds, the temperature is lowered so that we are less likely to undo progress that has already been made. We can also view simulated annealing as trying to optimize a trade-off that is implicit in (12.2). According to (12.2), values of $T$ arbitrarily close to 0 put the highest probability on minimum-cost solutions; *however*, (12.2) by itself says nothing about the rate of convergence of the functions $f_S(t)$ that it uses. It turns out that these functions converge, in general, much more rapidly for large values of $T$; and so to find minimum-cost solutions quickly, it is useful to speed up convergence by starting the process with $T$ large, and then gradually reducing it so as to raise the probability on the optimal solutions. While we believe that physical systems reach a minimum energy state via annealing, the simulated annealing method has no guarantee of finding an optimal solution. To see why, consider the double funnel of Figure 12.2. If the two funnels take equal area, then at high temperatures the system is essentially equally likely to be in either funnel. Once we cool the temperature, it will become harder and harder to switch between the two funnels. There appears to be no guarantee that at the end of annealing, we will be at the bottom of the lower funnel.

There are many open problems associated with simulated annealing, both in proving properties of its behavior and in determining the range of settings for which it works well in practice. Some of the general questions that come up here involve probabilistic issues that are beyond the scope of this book.

Having spent some time considering local search at a very general level, we now turn, in the next few sections, to some applications in which it is possible to prove fairly strong statements about the behavior of local search algorithms and about the local optima that they find.

# 12.3 An Application of Local Search to Hopfield Neural Networks

Thus far we have been discussing local search as a method for trying to find the global optimum in a computational problem. There are some cases, however, in which, by examining the specification of the problem carefully, we discover that it is really just an arbitrary *local* optimum that is required. We now consider a problem that illustrates this phenomenon.

## The Problem

The problem we consider here is that of finding *stable configurations* in *Hopfield neural networks*. Hopfield networks have been proposed as a simple model of an associative memory, in which a large collection of units are connected by an underlying network, and neighboring units try to correlate their states. Concretely, a Hopfield network can be viewed as an undirected graph $G = (V, E)$, with an integer-valued weight $w_e$ on each edge $e$; each weight may be positive or negative. A *configuration* $S$ of the network is an assignment of the value $-1$ or $+1$ to each node $u$; we will refer to this value as the *state* $s_u$ of the node $u$. The meaning of a configuration is that each node $u$, representing a unit of the neural network, is trying to choose between one of two possible states ("on" or "off"; "yes" or "no"); and its choice is influenced by those of its neighbors as follows. Each edge of the network imposes a *requirement* on its endpoints: If $u$ is joined to $v$ by an edge of negative weight, then $u$ and $v$ want to have the same state, while if $u$ is joined to $v$ by an edge of positive weight, then $u$ and $v$ want to have opposite states. The absolute value $|w_e|$ will indicate the *strength* of this requirement, and we will refer to $|w_e|$ as the *absolute weight* of edge $e$.

Unfortunately, there may be no configuration that respects the requirements imposed by all the edges. For example, consider three nodes $a, b, c$ all mutually connected to one another by edges of weight 1. Then, no matter what configuration we choose, two of these nodes will have the same state and thus will be violating the requirement that they have opposite states.

In view of this, we ask for something weaker. With respect to a given configuration, we say that an edge $e = (u, v)$ is *good* if the requirement it imposes is satisfied by the states of its two endpoints: either $w_e < 0$ and $s_u = s_v$, or $w_e > 0$ and $s_u \neq s_v$. Otherwise we say $e$ is *bad*. Note that we can express the condition that $e$ is good very compactly, as follows: $w_e s_u s_v < 0$. Next we say that a node $u$ is *satisfied* in a given configuration if the total absolute weight of all good edges incident to $u$ is at least as large as the total absolute weight of all bad edges incident to $u$. We can write this as

$$\sum_{v:e=(u,v)\in E} w_e s_u s_v \le 0.$$

Finally, we call a configuration *stable* if all nodes are satisfied.

Why do we use the term *stable* for such configurations? This is based on viewing the network from the perspective of an individual node $u$. On its own, the only choice $u$ has is whether to take the state $-1$ or $+1$; and like all nodes, it wants to respect as many edge requirements as possible (as measured in absolute weight). Suppose $u$ asks: Should I flip my current state? We see that if $u$ does flip its state (while all other nodes keep their states the same), then all the good edges incident to $u$ become bad, and all the bad edges incident to $u$ become good. So, to maximize the amount of good edge weight under its direct control, $u$ should flip its state if and only if it is not satisfied. In other words, a stable configuration is one in which no individual node has an incentive to flip its current state.

A basic question now arises: Does a Hopfield network always have a stable configuration, and if so, how can we find one?

### Designing the Algorithm

We will now design an algorithm that establishes the following result.

> **(12.3)** *Every Hopfield network has a stable configuration, and such a configuration can be found in time polynomial in $n$ and $W = \sum_e |w_e|$.*

We will see that stable configurations in fact arise very naturally as the local optima of a certain local search procedure on the Hopfield network.

To see that the statement of (12.3) is not entirely trivial, we note that it fails to remain true if one changes the model in certain natural ways. For example, suppose we were to define a *directed Hopfield network* exactly as above, except that each edge is directed, and each node determines whether or not it is satisfied by looking only at edges for which it is the tail. Then, in fact, such a network need not have a stable configuration. Consider, for example, a directed version of the three-node network we discussed earlier: There are nodes $a, b, c$, with directed edges $(a, b), (b, c), (c, a)$, all of weight 1. Then, if all nodes have the same state, they will all be unsatisfied; and if one node has a different state from the other two, then the node directly in front of it will be unsatisfied. Thus there is no configuration of this directed network in which all nodes are satisfied.

It is clear that a proof of (12.3) will need to rely somewhere on the undirected nature of the network.

To prove (12.3), we will analyze the following simple iterative procedure, which we call the State-Flipping Algorithm, to search for a stable configuration.

```
While the current configuration is not stable
    There must be an unsatisfied node
    Choose an unsatisfied node u
    Flip the state of u
Endwhile
```

An example of the execution of this algorithm is depicted in Figure 12.4, ending in a stable configuration.

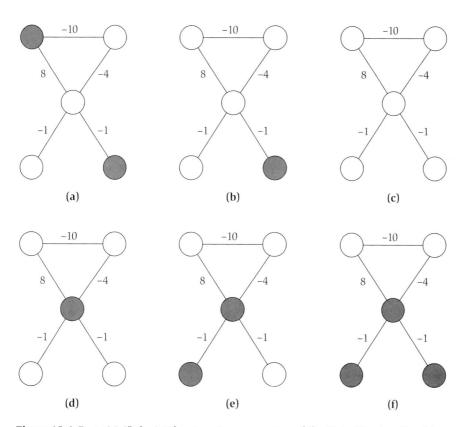

**Figure 12.4** Parts (a)-(f) depict the steps in an execution of the State-Flipping Algorithm for a five-node Hopfield network, ending in a stable configuration. (Nodes are colored black or white to indicate their state.)

## ✒ Analyzing the Algorithm

Clearly, if the *State-Flipping Algorithm* we have just defined terminates, we will have a stable configuration. What is not obvious is whether it must in fact terminate. Indeed, in the earlier directed example, this process will simply cycle through the three nodes, flipping their states sequentially forever.

We now prove that the State-Flipping Algorithm always terminates, and we give a bound on the number of iterations it takes until termination. This will provide a proof of (12.3). The key to proving that this process terminates is an idea we've used in several previous situations: to look for a measure of *progress*—namely, a quantity that strictly increases with every flip and has an absolute upper bound. This can be used to bound the number of iterations.

Probably the most natural progress measure would be the number of satisfied nodes: If this increased every time we flipped an unsatisfied node, the process would run for at most $n$ iterations before terminating with a stable configuration. Unfortunately, this does not turn out to work. When we flip an unsatisfied node $v$, it's true that it has now become satisfied, but several of its previously satisfied neighbors could now become unsatisfied, resulting in a net decrease in the number of satisfied nodes. This actually happens in one of the iterations depicted in Figure 12.4: when the middle node changes state, it renders both of its (formerly satisfied) lower neighbors unsatisfied.

We also can't try to prove termination by arguing that every node changes state at most once during the execution of the algorithm: Again, looking at the example in Figure 12.4, we see that the node in the lower right changes state twice. (And there are more complex examples in which we can get a single node to change state many times.)

However, there is a more subtle progress measure that *does* increase with each flip of an unsatisfied node. Specifically, for a given configuration $S$, we define $\Phi(S)$ to be the total absolute weight of all good edges in the network. That is,

$$\Phi(S) = \sum_{\text{good } e} |w_e|.$$

Clearly, for any configuration $S$, we have $\Phi(S) \geq 0$ (since $\Phi(S)$ is a sum of positive integers), and $\Phi(S) \leq W = \sum_e |w_e|$ (since, at most, every edge is good).

Now suppose that, in a nonstable configuration $S$, we choose a node $u$ that is unsatisfied and flip its state, resulting in a configuration $S'$. What can we say about the relationship of $\Phi(S')$ to $\Phi(S)$? Recall that when $u$ flips its state, all good edges incident to $u$ become bad, all bad edges incident to $u$ become good, and all edges that don't have $u$ as an endpoint remain the same. So, if we let $g_u$ and $b_u$ denote the total absolute weight on good and bad edges incident to $u$, respectively, then we have

$$\Phi(S') = \Phi(S) - g_u + b_u.$$

But, since $u$ was unsatisfied in $S$, we also know that $b_u > g_u$; and since $b_u$ and $g_u$ are both integers, we in fact have $b_u \geq g_u + 1$. Thus

$$\Phi(S') \geq \Phi(S) + 1.$$

Hence the value of $\Phi$ begins at some nonnegative integer, increases by at least 1 on every flip, and cannot exceed $W$. Thus our process runs for at most $W$ iterations, and when it terminates, we must have a stable configuration. Moreover, in each iteration we can identify an unsatisfied node using a number of arithmetic operations that is polynomial in $n$; thus a running-time bound that is polynomial in $n$ and $W$ follows as well.

So we see that, in the end, the existence proof for stable configurations was really about local search. We first set up an objective function $\Phi$ that we sought to maximize. Configurations were the possible solutions to this maximization problem, and we defined what it meant for two configurations $S$ and $S'$ to be neighbors: $S'$ should be obtainable from $S$ by flipping a single state. We then studied the behavior of a simple iterative improvement algorithm for local search (the upside-down form of gradient descent, since we have a maximization problem); and we discovered the following.

**(12.4)** *Any local maximum in the State-Flipping Algorithm to maximize $\Phi$ is a stable configuration.*

It's worth noting that while our algorithm proves the existence of a stable configuration, the running time leaves something to be desired when the absolute weights are large. Specifically, and analogously to what we saw in the Subset Sum Problem and in our first algorithm for maximum flow, the algorithm we obtain here is polynomial only in the actual magnitude of the weights, not in the size of their binary representation. For very large weights, this can lead to running times that are quite infeasible.

However, no simple way around this situation is currently known. It turns out to be an open question to find an algorithm that constructs stable states in time polynomial in $n$ and $\log W$ (rather than $n$ and $W$), or in a number of primitive arithmetic operations that is polynomial in $n$ alone, independent of the value of $W$.

## 12.4 Maximum-Cut Approximation via Local Search

We now discuss a case where a local search algorithm can be used to provide a provable approximation guarantee for an optimization problem. We will do this by analyzing the structure of the local optima, and bounding the quality of these locally optimal solutions relative to the global optimum. The problem we consider is the Maximum-Cut Problem, which is closely related to the problem of finding stable configurations for Hopfield networks that we saw in the previous section.

### The Problem

In the *Maximum-Cut Problem*, we are given an undirected graph $G = (V, E)$, with a positive integer weight $w_e$ on each edge $e$. For a partition $(A, B)$ of the vertex set, we use $w(A, B)$ to denote the total weight of edges with one end in $A$ and the other in $B$:

$$w(A, B) = \sum_{\substack{e=(u,v) \\ u \in A, v \in B}} w_e.$$

The goal is to find a partition $(A, B)$ of the vertex set so that $w(A, B)$ is maximized. Maximum Cut is NP-hard, in the sense that, given a weighted graph $G$ and a bound $\beta$, it is NP-complete to decide whether there is a partition $(A, B)$ of the vertices of $G$ with $w(A, B) \geq \beta$. At the same time, of course, Maximum Cut resembles the polynomially solvable Minimum *s-t* Cut Problem for flow networks; the crux of its intractability comes from the fact that we are seeking to maximize the edge weight across the cut, rather than minimize it.

Although the problem of finding a stable configuration of a Hopfield network was not an optimization problem per se, we can see that Maximum Cut is closely related to it. In the language of Hopfield networks, Maximum Cut is an instance in which all edge weights are positive (rather than negative), and configurations of nodes states $S$ correspond naturally to partitions $(A, B)$: Nodes have state $-1$ if and only if they are in the set $A$, and state $+1$ if and only if they are in the set $B$. The goal is to assign states so that as much weight as possible is on *good edges*—those whose endpoints have opposite states. Phrased this way, Maximum Cut seeks to maximize precisely the quantity $\Phi(S)$ that we used in the proof of (12.3), in the case when all edge weights are positive.

### Designing the Algorithm

The State-Flipping Algorithm used for Hopfield networks provides a local search algorithm to approximate the Maximum Cut objective function $\Phi(S) =$

$w(A, B)$. In terms of partitions, it says the following: If there exists a node $u$ such that the total weight of edges from $u$ to nodes in its own side of the partition exceeds the total weight of edges from $u$ to nodes on the other side of the partition, then $u$ itself should be moved to the other side of the partition.

We'll call this the "single-flip" neighborhood on partitions: Partitions $(A, B)$ and $(A', B')$ are neighboring solutions if $(A', B')$ can be obtained from $(A, B)$ by moving a single node from one side of the partition to the other. Let's ask two basic questions.

- Can we say anything concrete about the quality of the local optima under the single-flip neighborhood?
- Since the single-flip neighborhood is about as simple as one could imagine, what other neighborhoods might yield stronger local search algorithms for Maximum Cut?

We address the first of these questions here, and we take up the second one in the next section.

## Analyzing the Algorithm

The following result addresses the first question, showing that local optima under the single-flip neighborhood provide solutions achieving a guaranteed approximation bound.

**(12.5)** *Let $(A, B)$ be a partition that is a local optimum for Maximum Cut under the single-flip neighborhood. Let $(A^*, B^*)$ be a globally optimal partition. Then $w(A, B) \geq \frac{1}{2} w(A^*, B^*)$.*

**Proof.** Let $W = \sum_e w_e$. We also extend our notation a little: for two nodes $u$ and $v$, we use $w_{uv}$ to denote $w_e$ if there is an edge $e$ joining $u$ and $v$, and $0$ otherwise.

For any node $u \in A$, we must have

$$\sum_{v \in A} w_{uv} \leq \sum_{v \in B} w_{uv},$$

since otherwise $u$ should be moved to the other side of the partition, and $(A, B)$ would not be locally optimal. Suppose we add up these inequalities for all $u \in A$; any edge that has both ends in $A$ will appear on the left-hand side of exactly two of these inequalities, while any edge that has one end in $A$ and one end in $B$ will appear on the right-hand side of exactly one of these inequalities. Thus, we have

$$2 \sum_{\{u,v\} \subseteq A} w_{uv} \leq \sum_{u \in A, v \in B} w_{uv} = w(A, B). \tag{12.1}$$

We can apply the same reasoning to the set $B$, obtaining

$$2 \sum_{\{u,v\}\subseteq B} w_{uv} \leq \sum_{u \in A, v \in B} w_{uv} = w(A,B). \tag{12.2}$$

If we add together inequalities (12.1) and (12.2), and divide by 2, we get

$$\sum_{\{u,v\}\subseteq A} w_{uv} + \sum_{\{u,v\}\subseteq B} w_{uv} \leq w(A,B). \tag{12.3}$$

The left-hand side of inequality (12.3) accounts for all edge weight that does not cross from $A$ to $B$; so if we add $w(A,B)$ to both sides of (12.3), the left-hand side becomes equal to $W$. The right-hand side becomes $2w(A,B)$, so we have $W \leq 2w(A,B)$, or $w(A,B) \geq \frac{1}{2}W$.

Since the globally optimal partition $(A^*,B^*)$ clearly satisfies $w(A^*,B^*) \leq W$, we have $w(A,B) \geq \frac{1}{2}w(A^*,B^*)$. ∎

Notice that we never really thought much about the optimal partition $(A^*,B^*)$ in the proof of (12.5); we really showed the stronger statement that, in any locally optimal solution under the single-flip neighborhood, at least half the total edge weight in the graph crosses the partition.

Statement (12.5) proves that a local optimum is a 2-approximation to the maximum cut. This suggests that the local optimization may be a good algorithm for approximately maximizing the cut value. However, there is one more issue that we need to consider: the running time. As we saw at the end of Section 12.3, the Single-Flip Algorithm is only pseudo-polynomial, and it is an open problem whether a local optimum can be found in polynomial time. However, in this case we can do almost as well, simply by stopping the algorithm when there are no "big enough" improvements.

Let $(A,B)$ be a partition with weight $w(A,B)$. For a fixed $\epsilon > 0$, let us say that a single node flip is a *big-improvement-flip* if it improves the cut value by at least $\frac{2\epsilon}{n}w(A,B)$ where $n = |V|$. Now consider a version of the Single-Flip Algorithm when we only accept big-improvement-flips and terminate once no such flip exists, even if the current partition is not a local optimum. We claim that this will lead to almost as good an approximation and will run in polynomial time. First we can extend the previous proof to show that the resulting cut is almost as good. We simply have to add the term $\frac{2\epsilon}{n}w(A,B)$ to each inequality, as all we know is that there are no big-improvement-flips.

**(12.6)** *Let $(A,B)$ be a partition such that no big-improvement-flip is possible. Let $(A^*,B^*)$ be a globally optimal partition. Then $(2+\epsilon)w(A,B) \geq w(A^*,B^*)$.*

Next we consider the running time.

**(12.7)** *The version of the Single-Flip Algorithm that only accepts big-improvement-flips terminates after at most $O(\epsilon^{-1}n \log W)$ flips, assuming the weights are integral, and $W = \sum_e w_e$.*

**Proof.** Each flip improves the objective function by at least a factor of $(1 + \epsilon/n)$. Since $(1 + 1/x)^x \geq 2$ for any $x \geq 1$, we see that $(1 + \epsilon/n)^{n/\epsilon} \geq 2$, and so the objective function increases by a factor of at least 2 every $n/\epsilon$ flips. The weight cannot exceed $W$, and hence it can only be doubled at most $\log W$ times. ■

## 12.5 Choosing a Neighbor Relation

We began the chapter by saying that a local search algorithm is really based on two fundamental ingredients: the choice of the neighbor relation, and the rule for choosing a neighboring solution at each step. In Section 12.2 we spent time thinking about the second of these: both the Metropolis Algorithm and simulated annealing took the neighbor relation as given and modified the way in which a neighboring solution should be chosen.

What are some of the issues that should go into our choice of the neighbor relation? This can turn out to be quite subtle, though at a high level the trade-off is a basic one.

(i)  The neighborhood of a solution should be rich enough that we do not tend to get stuck in bad local optima; but

(ii)  the neighborhood of a solution should not be too large, since we want to be able to efficiently search the set of neighbors for possible local moves.

If the first of these points were the only concern, then it would seem that we should simply make all solutions neighbors of one another—after all, then there would be no local optima, and the global optimum would always be just one step away! The second point exposes the (obvious) problem with doing this: If the neighborhood of the current solution consists of every possible solution, then the local search paradigm gives us no leverage whatsoever; it reduces simply to brute-force search of this neighborhood.

Actually, we've already encountered one case in which choosing the right neighbor relation had a profound effect on the tractability of a problem, though we did not explicitly take note of this at the time: This was in the Bipartite Matching Problem. Probably the simplest neighbor relation on matchings would be the following: $M'$ is a neighbor of $M$ if $M'$ can be obtained by the insertion or deletion of a single edge in $M$. Under this definition, we get "landscapes" that are quite jagged, quite like the Vertex Cover examples we saw earlier; and we can get locally optimal matchings under this definition that have only half the size of the maximum matching.

But suppose we try defining a more complicated (indeed, asymmetric) neighbor relation: We say that $M'$ is a neighbor of $M$ if, when we set up the corresponding flow network, $M'$ can be obtained from $M$ by a single augmenting path. What can we say about a matching $M$ if it is a local maximum under this neighbor relation? In this case, there is no augmenting path, and so $M$ must in fact be a (globally) maximum matching. In other words, with this neighbor relation, the only local maxima are global maxima, and so direct gradient ascent will produce a maximum matching. If we reflect on what the Ford-Fulkerson algorithm is doing in our reduction from Bipartite Matching to Maximum Flow, this makes sense: the size of the matching strictly increases in each step, and we never need to "back out" of a local maximum. Thus, by choosing the neighbor relation very carefully, we've turned a jagged optimization landscape into a simple, tractable funnel.

Of course, we do not expect that things will always work out this well. For example, since Vertex Cover is NP-complete, it would be surprising if it allowed for a neighbor relation that simultaneously produced "well-behaved" landscapes and neighborhoods that could be searched efficiently. We now look at several possible neighbor relations in the context of the Maximum Cut Problem, which we considered in the previous section. The contrasts among these neighbor relations will be characteristic of issues that arise in the general topic of local search algorithms for computationally hard graph-partitioning problems.

## Local Search Algorithms for Graph Partitioning

In Section 12.4, we considered a state-flipping algorithm for the Maximum-Cut Problem, and we showed that the locally optimal solutions provide a 2-approximation. We now consider neighbor relations that produce larger neighborhoods than the single-flip rule, and consequently attempt to reduce the prevalence of local optima. Perhaps the most natural generalization is the *k-flip neighborhood*, for $k \geq 1$: we say that partitions $(A, B)$ and $(A', B')$ are neighbors under the $k$-flip rule if $(A', B')$ can be obtained from $(A, B)$ by moving at most $k$ nodes from one side of the partition to the other.

Now, clearly if $(A, B)$ and $(A', B')$ are neighbors under the $k$-flip rule, then they are also neighbors under the $k'$-flip rule for every $k' > k$. Thus, if $(A, B)$ is a local optimum under the $k'$-flip rule, it is also a local optimum under the $k$-flip rule for every $k < k'$. But reducing the set of local optima by raising the value of $k$ comes at a steep computational price: to examine the set of neighbors of $(A, B)$ under the $k$-flip rule, we must consider all $\Theta(n^k)$ ways of moving up to

$k$ nodes to the opposite side of the partition. This becomes prohibitive even for small values of $k$.

Kernighan and Lin (1970) proposed an alternate method for generating neighboring solutions; it is computationally much more efficient, but still allows large-scale transformations of solutions in a single step. Their method, which we'll call the K-L heuristic, defines the neighbors of a partition $(A, B)$ according the following $n$-phase procedure.

- In phase 1, we choose a single node to flip, in such a way that the value of the resulting solution is as large as possible. We perform this flip even if the value of the solution decreases relative to $w(A, B)$. We *mark* the node that has been flipped and let $(A_1, B_1)$ denote the resulting solution.

- At the start of phase $k$, for $k > 1$, we have a partition $(A_{k-1}, B_{k-1})$; and $k - 1$ of the nodes are marked. We choose a single unmarked node to flip, in such a way that the value of the resulting solution is as large as possible. (Again, we do this even if the value of the solution decreases as a result.) We mark the node we flip and let $(A_k, B_k)$ denote the resulting solution.

- After $n$ phases, each node is marked, indicating that it has been flipped precisely once. Consequently, the final partition $(A_n, B_n)$ is actually the mirror image of the original partition $(A, B)$: We have $A_n = B$ and $B_n = A$.

- Finally, the K-L heuristic defines the $n - 1$ partitions $(A_1, B_1), \ldots,$ $(A_{n-1}, B_{n-1})$ to be the neighbors of $(A, B)$. Thus $(A, B)$ is a local optimum under the K-L heuristic if and only if $w(A, B) \geq w(A_i, B_i)$ for $1 \leq i \leq n - 1$.

So we see that the K-L heuristic tries a very long sequence of flips, even while it appears to be making things worse, in the hope that some partition $(A_i, B_i)$ generated along the way will turn out better than $(A, B)$. But even though it generates neighbors very different from $(A, B)$, it only performs $n$ flips in total, and each takes only $O(n)$ time to perform. Thus it is computationally much more reasonable than the $k$-flip rule for larger values of $k$. Moreover, the K-L heuristic has turned out to be very powerful in practice, despite the fact that rigorous analysis of its properties has remained largely an open problem.

## * 12.6 Classification via Local Search

We now consider a more complex application of local search to the design of approximation algorithms, related to the Image Segmentation Problem that we considered as an application of network flow in Section 7.10. The more complex version of Image Segmentation that we focus on here will serve as an example where, in order to obtain good performance from a local search algorithm, one needs to use a rather complex neighborhood structure on the set of solutions. We will find that the natural "state-flipping" neighborhood that we saw in earlier sections can result in very bad local optima. To obtain good performance, we will instead use an exponentially large neighborhood. One problem with such a large neighborhood is that we can no longer afford to search though all neighbors of the current solution one by one for an improving solution. Rather, we will need a more sophisticated algorithm to find an improving neighbor whenever one exists.

## The Problem

Recall the basic Image Segmentation Problem that we considered as an application of network flow in Section 7.10. There we formulated the problem of segmenting an image as a *labeling* problem; the goal was to label (i.e., classify) each pixel as belonging to the foreground or the background of the image. At the time, it was clear that this was a very simple formulation of the problem, and it would be nice to handle more complex labeling tasks—for example, to segment the regions of an image based on their distance from the camera. Thus we now consider a labeling problem with more than two labels. In the process, we will end up with a framework for classification that applies more broadly than just to the case of pixels in an image.

In setting up the two-label foreground/background segmentation problem, we ultimately arrived at the following formulation. We were given a graph $G = (V, E)$ where $V$ corresponded to the pixels of the image, and the goal was to classify each node in $V$ as belonging to one of two possible classes: foreground or background. Edges represented pairs of nodes likely to belong to the same class (e.g., because they were next to each other), and for each edge $(i, j)$ we were given a separation penalty $p_{ij} \geq 0$ for placing $i$ and $j$ in different classes. In addition, we had information about the likelihood of whether a node or pixel was more likely to belong to the foreground or the background. These likelihoods translated into penalties for assigning a node to the class where it was less likely to belong. Then the problem was to find a labeling of the nodes that minimized the total separation and assignment penalties. We showed that this minimization problem could be solved via a minimum-cut computation. For the rest of this section, we will refer to the problem we defined there as *Two-Label Image Segmentation*.

Here we will formulate the analogous classification/labeling problem with more than two classes or labels. This problem will turn out to be NP-hard, and we will develop a local search algorithm where the local optima are 2-approximations for the best labeling. The general labeling problem, which we will consider in this section, is formulated as follows. We are given a graph $G = (V, E)$ and a set $L$ of $k$ labels. The goal is to label each node in $V$ with one of the labels in $L$ so as to minimize a certain penalty. There are two competing forces that will guide the choice of the best labeling. For each edge $(i, j) \in E$, we have a *separation penalty* $p_{ij} \geq 0$ for labeling the two nodes $i$ and $j$ with different labels. In addition, nodes are more likely to have certain labels than others. This is expressed through an *assignment penalty*. For each node $i \in V$ and each label $a \in L$, we have a nonnegative penalty $c_i(a) \geq 0$ for assigning label $a$ to node $i$. (These penalties play the role of the likelihoods from the Two-Label Image Segmentation Problem, except that here we view them as costs to be minimized.) The *Labeling Problem* is to find a labeling $f : V \to L$ that minimizes the total penalty:

$$\Phi(f) = \sum_{i \in V} c_i(f(i)) + \sum_{(i,j) \in E: f(i) \neq f(j)} p_{ij}.$$

Observe that the Labeling Problem with only two labels is precisely the Image Segmentation Problem from Section 7.10. For three labels, the Labeling Problem is already NP-hard, though we will not prove this here.

Our goal is to develop a local search algorithm for this problem, in which local optima are good approximations to the optimal solution. This will also serve as an illustration of the importance of choosing good neighborhoods for defining the local search algorithm. There are many possible choices for neighbor relations, and we'll see that some work a lot better than others. In particular, a fairly complex definition of the neighborhoods will be used to obtain the approximation guarantee.

## Designing the Algorithm

*A First Attempt: The Single-Flip Rule*   The simplest and perhaps most natural choice for neighbor relation is the single-flip rule from the State-Flipping Algorithm for the Maximum-Cut Problem: Two labelings are neighbors if we can obtain one from the other by relabeling a single node. Unfortunately, this neighborhood can lead to quite poor local optima for our problem even when there are only two labels.

This may be initially surprising, since the rule worked quite well for the Maximum-Cut Problem. However, our problem is related to the Minimum-Cut Problem. In fact, Minimum $s$-$t$ Cut corresponds to a special case when there are only two labels, and $s$ and $t$ are the only nodes with assignment penalties. It is not hard to see that this State-Flipping Algorithm is not a good approximation algorithm for the Minimum-Cut Problem. See Figure 12.5, which indicates how the edges incident to $s$ may form the global optimum, while the edges incident to $t$ can form a local optimum that is much worse.

*A Closer Attempt: Considering Two Labels at a Time*   Here we will develop a local search algorithm in which the neighborhoods are much more elaborate. One interesting feature of our algorithm is that it allows each solution to have

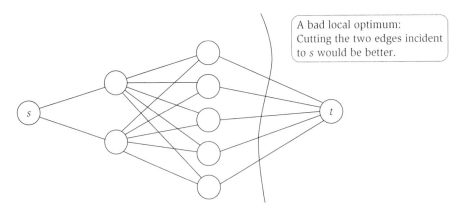

A bad local optimum: Cutting the two edges incident to $s$ would be better.

**Figure 12.5** An instance of the Minimum $s$-$t$ Cut Problem, where all edges have capacity 1.

exponentially many neighbors. This appears to be contrary to the general rule that "the neighborhood of a solution should not be too large," as stated in Section 12.5. However, we will be working with neighborhoods in a more subtle way here. Keeping the size of the neighborhood small is good if the plan is to search for an improving local step by brute force; here, however, we will use a polynomial-time minimum-cut computation to determine whether any of a solution's exponentially many neighbors represent an improvement.

The idea of the local search is to use our polynomial-time algorithm for Two-Label Image Segmentation to find improving local steps. First let's consider a basic implementation of this idea that does not always give a good approximation guarantee. For a labeling $f$, we pick two labels $a, b \in L$ and restrict attention to the nodes that have labels $a$ or $b$ in labeling $f$. In a single local step, we will allow any subset of these nodes to flip labels from $a$ to $b$, or from $b$ to $a$. More formally, two labelings $f$ and $f'$ are neighbors if there are two labels $a, b \in L$ such that for all other labels $c \notin \{a, b\}$ and all nodes $i \in V$, we have $f(i) = c$ if and only if $f'(i) = c$. Note that a state $f$ can have exponentially many neighbors, as an arbitrary subset of the nodes labeled $a$ and $b$ can flip their label. However, we have the following.

**(12.8)** *If a labeling $f$ is not locally optimal for the neighborhood above, then a neighbor with smaller penalty can be found via $k^2$ minimum-cut computations.*

**Proof.** There are fewer than $k^2$ pairs of distinct labels, so we can try each pair separately. Given a pair of labels $a, b \in L$, consider the problem of finding an improved labeling via swapping labels of nodes between labels $a$ and $b$. This is exactly the Segmentation Problem for two labels on the subgraph of nodes that $f$ labels $a$ or $b$. We use the algorithm developed for Two-Label Image Segmentation to find the best such relabeling. ■

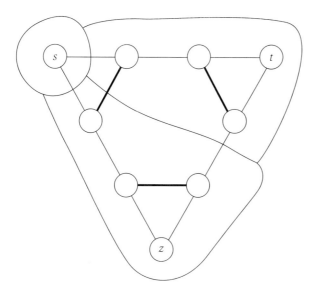

**Figure 12.6** A bad local optimum for the local search algorithm that considers only two labels at a time.

This neighborhood is much better than the single-flip neighborhood we considered first. For example, it solves the case of two labels optimally. However, even with this improved neighborhood, local optima can still be bad, as shown in Figure 12.6. In this example, there are three nodes $s$, $t$, and $z$ that are each required to keep their initial labels. Each other node lies on one of the sides of the triangle; it has to get one of the two labels associated with the nodes at the ends of this side. These requirements can be expressed simply by giving each node a very large assignment penalty for the labels that we are not allowing. We define the edge separation penalties as follows: The light edges in the figure have penalty 1, while the heavy edges have a large separation penalty of $M$. Now observe that the labeling in the figure has penalty $M + 3$ but is locally optimal. The (globally) optimal penalty is only 3 and is obtained from the labeling in the figure by relabeling both nodes next to $s$.

*A Local Search Neighborhood That Works* Next we define a different neighborhood that leads to a good approximation algorithm. The local optimum in Figure 12.6 may be suggestive of what would be a good neighborhood: We need to be able to relabel nodes of different labels in a single step. The key is to find a neighbor relation rich enough to have this property, yet one that still allows us to find an improving local step in polynomial time.

Consider a labeling $f$. As part of a local step in our new algorithm, we will want to do the following. We pick one label $a \in L$ and restrict attention to the nodes that do *not* have label $a$ in labeling $f$. As a single local step, we will allow any subset of these nodes to change their labels to $a$. More formally, for two labelings $f$ and $f'$, we say that $f'$ is a neighbor of $f$ if there is a label $a \in L$ such that, for all nodes $i \in V$, either $f'(i) = f(i)$ or $f'(i) = a$. Note that this neighbor relation is not symmetric; that is, we cannot get $f$ back from $f'$ via a single step. We will now show that for any labeling $f$ we can find its best neighbor via $k$ minimum-cut computations, and further, a local optimum for this neighborhood is a 2-approximation for the minimum penalty labeling.

***Finding a Good Neighbor***    To find the best neighbor, we will try each label $a$ separately. Consider a label $a$. We claim that the best relabeling in which nodes may change their labels to $a$ can be found via a minimum-cut computation. The construction of the minimum-cut graph $G' = (V', E')$ is analogous to the minimum-cut computation developed for Two-Label Image Segmentation. There we introduced a source $s$ and a sink $t$ to represent the two labels. Here we will also introduce a source and a sink, where the source $s$ will represent label $a$, while the sink $t$ will effectively represent the alternate option nodes have—namely, to keep their original labels. The idea will be to find the minimum cut in $G'$ and relabel all nodes on the $s$-side of the cut to label $a$, while letting all nodes on the $t$-side keep their original labels.

For each node of $G$, we will have a corresponding node in the new set $V'$ and will add edges $(i, t)$ and $(s, i)$ to $E'$, as was done in Figure 7.18 from Chapter 7 for the case of two labels. The edge $(i, t)$ will have capacity $c_i(a)$, as cutting the edge $(i, t)$ places node $i$ on the source side and hence corresponds to labeling node $i$ with label $a$. The edge $(i, s)$ will have capacity $c_i(f(i))$, if $f(i) \neq a$, and a very large number $M$ (or $+\infty$) if $f(i) = a$. Cutting edge $(i, t)$ places node $i$ on the sink side and hence corresponds to node $i$ retaining its original label $f(i) \neq a$. The large capacity of $M$ prevents nodes $i$ with $f(i) = a$ from being placed on the sink side.

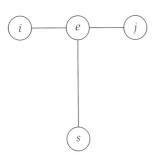

Node $e$ can always be placed so that at most one incident edge is cut.

**Figure 12.7** The construction for edge $e = (i, j)$ with $a \neq f(i) \neq f(j) \neq a$.

In the construction for the two-label problem, we added edges between the nodes of $V$ and used the separation penalties as capacities. This works well for nodes that are separated by the cut, or nodes on the source side that are both labeled $a$. However, if both $i$ and $j$ are on the sink side of the cut, then the edge connecting them is not cut, yet $i$ and $j$ are separated if $f(i) \neq f(j)$. We deal with this difficulty by enhancing the construction of $G'$ as follows. For an edge $(i, j)$, if $f(i) = f(j)$ or one of $i$ or $j$ is labeled $a$, then we add an edge $(i, j)$ to $E'$ with capacity $p_{ij}$. For the edges $e = (i, j)$ where $f(i) \neq f(j)$ and neither has label $a$, we'll have to do something different to correctly encode via the graph $G'$ that $i$ and $j$ remain separated even if they are both on the sink side. For each such edge $e$, we add an extra node $e$ to $V'$ corresponding to edge $e$, and add the edges $(i, e)$, $(e, j)$, and $(e, s)$ all with capacity $p_{ij}$. See Figure 12.7 for these edges.

**(12.9)**   *Given a labeling f and a label a, the minimum cut in the graph $G' = (V', E')$ corresponds to the minimum-penalty neighbor of labeling f obtained by relabeling a subset of nodes to label a. As a result, the minimum-penalty neighbor of f can be found via k minimum-cut computations, one for each label in L.*

**Proof.** Let $(A, B)$ be an $s$-$t$ cut in $G'$. The large value of $M$ ensures that a minimum-capacity cut will not cut any of these high-capacity edges. Now consider a node $e$ in $G'$ corresponding to an edge $e = (i, j) \in E$. The node $e \in V'$ has three adjacent edges, each with capacity $p_{ij}$. Given any partition of the other nodes, we can place $e$ so that at most one of these three edges is cut. We'll call a cut *good* if no edge of capacity $M$ is cut and, for all the nodes corresponding to edges in $E$, at most one of the adjacent edges is cut. So far we have argued that all minimum-capacity cuts are good.

   Good $s$-$t$ cuts in $G'$ are in one-to-one correspondence with relabelings of $f$ obtained by changing the label of a subset of nodes to $a$. Consider the capacity of a good cut. The edges $(s, i)$ and $(i, t)$ contribute exactly the assignment penalty to the capacity of the cut. The edges $(i, j)$ directly connecting nodes in $V$ contribute exactly the separation penalty of the nodes in the corresponding labeling: $p_{ij}$ if they are separated, and 0 otherwise. Finally, consider an edge $e = (i, j)$ with a corresponding node $e \in V'$. If $i$ and $j$ are both on the source side, none of the three edges adjacent to $e$ are cut, and in all other cases exactly one of these edges is cut. So again, the three edges adjacent to $e$ contribute to the cut exactly the separation penalty between $i$ and $j$ in the corresponding labeling. As a result, the capacity of a good cut is exactly the same as the penalty of the corresponding labeling, and so the minimum-capacity cut corresponds to the best relabeling of $f$.   ∎

## Analyzing the Algorithm

Finally, we need to consider the quality of the local optima under this definition of the neighbor relation. Recall that in our previous two attempts at defining neighborhoods, we found that they can both lead to bad local optima. Now, by contrast, we'll show that any local optimum under our new neighbor relation is a 2-approximation to the minimum possible penalty.

   To begin the analysis, consider an optimal labeling $f^*$, and for a label $a \in L$ let $V_a^* = \{i : f^*(i) = a\}$ be the set of nodes labeled by $a$ in $f^*$. Consider a locally optimal labeling $f$. We obtain a neighbor $f_a$ of labeling $f$ by starting with $f$ and relabeling all nodes in $V_a^*$ to $a$. The labeling $f$ is locally optimal, and hence this neighbor $f_a$ has no smaller penalty: $\Phi(f_a) \geq \Phi(f)$. Now consider the difference $\Phi(f_a) - \Phi(f)$, which we know is nonnegative. What quantities contribute to this difference? The only possible change in the assignment penalties could come from nodes in $V_a^*$: for each $i \in V_a^*$, the change is $c_i(f^*(i)) - c_i(f(i))$. The separation penalties differ between the two labelings only in edges $(i, j)$ that have at least one end in $V_a^*$. The following inequality accounts for these differences.

**(12.10)**    *For a labeling $f$ and its neighbor $f_a$, we have*

$$\Phi(f_a) - \Phi(f) \leq \sum_{i \in V_a^*} \left[ c_i(f^*(i)) - c_i(f(i)) \right] + \sum_{\substack{(i,j) \text{ leaving } V_a^*}} p_{ij} - \sum_{\substack{(i,j) \text{ in or leaving } V_a^* \\ f(i) \neq f(j)}} p_{ij}.$$

**Proof.** The change in the assignment penalties is exactly $\sum_{i \in V_a^*} c_i(f^*(i)) - c_i(f(i))$. The separation penalty for an edge $(i, j)$ can differ between the two labelings only if edge $(i, j)$ has at least one end in $V_a^*$. The total separation penalty of labeling $f$ for such edges is exactly

$$\sum_{\substack{(i,j) \text{ in or leaving } V_a^* \\ f(i) \neq f(j)}} p_{ij},$$

while the labeling $f_a$ has a separation penalty of at most

$$\sum_{\substack{(i,j) \text{ leaving } V_a^*}} p_{ij}$$

for these edges. (Note that this latter expression is only an upper bound, since an edge $(i, j)$ leaving $V_a^*$ that has its other end in $a$ does not contribute to the separation penalty of $f_a$.) ∎

Now we are ready to prove our main claim.

**(12.11)**    *For any locally optimal labeling $f$, and any other labeling $f^*$, we have $\Phi(f) \leq 2\Phi(f^*)$.*

**Proof.** Let $f_a$ be the neighbor of $f$ defined previously by relabeling nodes to label $a$. The labeling $f$ is locally optimal, so we have $\Phi(f_a) - \Phi(f) \geq 0$ for all $a \in L$. We use (12.10) to bound $\Phi(f_a) - \Phi(f)$ and then add the resulting inequalities for all labels to obtain the following:

$$0 \leq \sum_{a \in L} (\Phi(f_a) - \Phi(f))$$

$$\leq \sum_{a \in L} \left[ \sum_{i \in V_a^*} c_i(f^*(i)) - c_i(f(i)) + \sum_{\substack{(i,j) \text{ leaving } V_a^*}} p_{ij} - \sum_{\substack{(i,j) \text{ in or leaving } V_a^* \\ f(i) \neq f(j)}} p_{ij} \right].$$

We will rearrange the inequality by grouping the positive terms on the left-hand side and the negative terms on the right-hand side. On the left-hand side, we get $c_i(f^*(i))$ for all nodes $i$, which is exactly the assignment penalty of $f^*$. In addition, we get the term $p_{ij}$ twice for each of the edges separated by $f^*$ (once for each of the two labels $f^*(i)$ and $f^*(j)$).

On the right-hand side, we get $c_i(f(i))$ for each node $i$, which is exactly the assignment penalty of $f$. In addition, we get the terms $p_{ij}$ for edges separated by $f$. We get each such separation penalty at least once, and possibly twice if it is also separated by $f^*$.

In summary, we get the following.

$$2\Phi(f^*) \geq \sum_{a \in L} \left[ \sum_{i \in V_a^*} c_i(f^*(i)) + \sum_{(i,j) \text{ leaving } V_a^*} p_{ij} \right]$$

$$\geq \sum_{a \in L} \left[ \sum_{i \in V_a^*} c_i(f(i)) + \sum_{\substack{(i,j) \text{ in or leaving } V_a^* \\ f(i) \neq f(j)}} p_{ij} \right] \geq \Phi(f),$$

proving the claimed bound. ∎


We proved that all local optima are good approximations to the labeling with minimum penalty. There is one more issue to consider: How fast does the algorithm find a local optimum? Recall that in the case of the Maximum-Cut Problem, we had to resort to a variant of the algorithm that accepts only big improvements, as repeated local improvements may not run in polynomial time. The same is also true here. Let $\epsilon > 0$ be a constant. For a given labeling $f$, we will consider a neighboring labeling $f'$ a *significant improvement* if $\Phi(f') \leq (1 - \epsilon/3k)\Phi(f)$. To make sure the algorithm runs in polynomial time, we should only accept significant improvements, and terminate when no significant improvements are possible. After at most $\epsilon^{-1}k$ significant improvements, the penalty decreases by a constant factor; hence the algorithm will terminate in polynomial time. It is not hard to adapt the proof of (12.11) to establish the following.

**(12.12)** *For any fixed $\epsilon > 0$, the version of the local search algorithm that only accepts significant improvements terminates in polynomial time and results in a labeling $f$ such that $\Phi(f) \leq (2 + \epsilon)\Phi(f^*)$ for any other labeling $f^*$.*

## 12.7 Best-Response Dynamics and Nash Equilibria

Thus far we have been considering local search as a technique for solving optimization problems with a single objective—in other words, applying local operations to a candidate solution so as to minimize its total cost. There are many settings, however, where a potentially large number of agents, each with its own goals and objectives, collectively interact so as to produce a solution to some problem. A solution that is produced under these circumstances often reflects the "tug-of-war" that led to it, with each agent trying to pull the solution in a direction that is favorable to it. We will see that these interactions can be viewed as a kind of local search procedure; analogues of local minima have a natural meaning as well, but having multiple agents and multiple objectives introduces new challenges.

The field of game theory provides a natural framework in which to talk about what happens in such situations, when a collection of agents interacts strategically—in other words, with each trying to optimize an individual objective function. To illustrate these issues, we consider a concrete application, motivated by the problem of routing in networks; along the way, we will introduce some notions that occupy central positions in the area of game theory more generally.

### 🖋 The Problem

In a network like the Internet, one frequently encounters situations in which a number of nodes all want to establish a connection to a single *source node s*. For example, the source $s$ may be generating some kind of data stream that all the given nodes want to receive, as in a style of one-to-many network communication known as *multicast*. We will model this situation by representing the underlying network as a directed graph $G = (V, E)$, with a cost $c_e \geq 0$ on each edge. There is a designated source node $s \in V$ and a collection of $k$ agents located at distinct *terminal nodes* $t_1, t_2, \ldots, t_k \in V$. For simplicity, we will not make a distinction between the agents and the nodes at which they reside; in other words, we will think of the agents as being $t_1, t_2, \ldots, t_k$. Each agent $t_j$ wants to construct a path $P_j$ from $s$ to $t_j$ using as little total cost as possible.

Now, if there were no interaction among the agents, this would consist of $k$ separate shortest-path problems: Each agent $t_j$ would find an $s$-$t_j$ path for which the total cost of all edges is minimized, and use this as its path $P_j$. What makes this problem interesting is the prospect of agents being able to *share* the costs of edges. Suppose that after all the agents have chosen their paths, agent $t_j$ only needs to pay its "fair share" of the cost of each edge $e$ on its path; that is, rather than paying $c_e$ for each $e$ on $P_j$, it pays $c_e$ divided by the number of agents whose paths contain $e$. In this way, there is an incentive for the agents to choose paths that overlap, since they can then benefit by splitting the costs of edges. (This sharing model is appropriate for settings in which the presence of multiple agents on an edge does not significantly degrade the quality of transmission due to congestion or increased latency. If latency effects do come into play, then there is a countervailing penalty for sharing; this too leads to interesting algorithmic questions, but we will stick to our current focus for now, in which sharing comes with benefits only.)

## Best-Response Dynamics and Nash Equilibria: Definitions and Examples

To see how the option of sharing affects the behavior of the agents, let's begin by considering the pair of very simple examples in Figure 12.8. In example (a), each of the two agents has two options for constructing a path: the middle route through $v$, and the outer route using a single edge. Suppose that each agent starts out with an initial path but is continually evaluating the current situation to decide whether it's possible to switch to a better path.

In example (a), suppose the two agents start out using their outer paths. Then $t_1$ sees no advantage in switching paths (since $4 < 5 + 1$), but $t_2$ does (since $8 > 5 + 1$), and so $t_2$ updates its path by moving to the middle. Once this happens, things have changed from the perspective of $t_1$: There is suddenly an advantage for $t_1$ in switching as well, since it now gets to share the cost of the middle path, and hence its cost to use the middle path becomes $2.5 + 1 < 4$. Thus it will switch to the middle path. Once we are in a situation where both

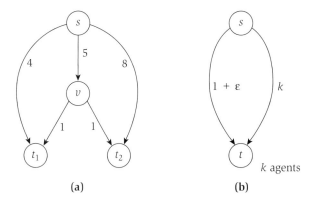

(a)                              (b)

**Figure 12.8** (a) It is in the two agents' interest to share the middle path. (b) It would be better for all the agents to share the edge on the left. But if all $k$ agents start on the right-hand edge, then no one of them will want to unilaterally move from right to left; in other words, the solution in which all agents share the edge on the right is a bad Nash equilibrium.

sides are using the middle path, neither has an incentive to switch, and so this is a stable solution.

Let's discuss two definitions from the area of game theory that capture what's going on in this simple example. While we will continue to focus on our particular multicast routing problem, these definitions are relevant to any setting in which multiple agents, each with an individual objective, interact to produce a collective solution. As such, we will phrase the definitions in these general terms.

- First of all, in the example, each agent was continually prepared to improve its solution in response to changes made by the other agent(s). We will refer to this process as *best-response dynamics*. In other words, we are interested in the dynamic behavior of a process in which each agent updates based on its best response to the current situation.

- Second, we are particularly interested in stable solutions, where the best response of each agent is to stay put. We will refer to such a solution, from which no agent has an incentive to deviate, as a *Nash equilibrium*. (This is named after the mathematician John Nash, who won the Nobel Prize in economics for his pioneering work on this concept.) Hence, in example (a), the solution in which both agents use the middle path is a Nash equilibrium. Note that the Nash equilibria are precisely the solutions at which best-response dynamics terminate.

The example in Figure 12.8(b) illustrates the possibility of multiple Nash equilibria. In this example, there are $k$ agents that all reside at a common node $t$ (that is, $t_1 = t_2 = \cdots = t_k = t$), and there are two parallel edges from $s$ to $t$ with different costs. The solution in which all agents use the left-hand edge is a Nash equilibrium in which all agents pay $(1 + \varepsilon)/k$. The solution in which all agents use the right-hand edge is also a Nash equilibrium, though here the agents each pay $k/k = 1$. The fact that this latter solution is a Nash equilibrium exposes an important point about best-response dynamics. If the agents could somehow synchronously agree to move from the right-hand edge to the left-hand one, they'd all be better off. But under best-response dynamics, each agent is only evaluating the consequences of a unilateral move by itself. In effect, an agent isn't able to make any assumptions about future actions of other agents—in an Internet setting, it may not even know anything about these other agents or their current solutions—and so it is only willing to perform updates that lead to an immediate improvement for itself.

To quantify the sense in which one of the Nash equilibria in Figure 12.8(b) is better than the other, it is useful to introduce one further definition. We say that a solution is a *social optimum* if it minimizes the total cost to all agents. We can think of such a solution as the one that would be imposed by a benevolent central authority that viewed all agents as equally important and hence evaluated the quality of a solution by summing the costs they incurred. Note that in both (a) and (b), there is a social optimum that is also a Nash equilibrium, although in (b) there is also a second Nash equilibrium whose cost is much greater.

## The Relationship to Local Search

Around here, the connections to local search start to come into focus. A set of agents following best-response dynamics are engaged in some kind of gradient descent process, exploring the "landscape" of possible solutions as they try to minimize their individual costs. The Nash equilibria are the natural analogues of local minima in this process: solutions from which no improving move is possible. And the "local" nature of the search is clear as well, since agents are only updating their solutions when it leads to an immediate improvement.

Having said all this, it's important to think a bit further and notice the crucial ways in which this differs from standard local search. In the beginning of this chapter, it was easy to argue that the gradient descent algorithm for a combinatorial problem must terminate at a local minimum: each update decreased the cost of the solution, and since there were only finitely many possible solutions, the sequence of updates could not go on forever. In other words, the cost function itself provided the progress measure we needed to establish termination.

In best-response dynamics, on the other hand, each agent has its own personal objective function to minimize, and so it's not clear what overall "progress" is being made when, for example, agent $t_i$ decides to update its path from $s$. There's progress for $t_i$, of course, since its cost goes down, but this may be offset by an even larger increase in the cost to some other agent. Consider, for example, the network in Figure 12.9. If both agents start on the middle path, then $t_1$ will in fact have an incentive to move to the outer path; its cost drops from 3.5 to 3, but in the process the cost of $t_2$ increases from 3.5 to 6. (Once this happens, $t_2$ will also move to its outer path, and this solution—with both nodes on the outer paths—is the unique Nash equilibrium.)

There are examples, in fact, where the cost-increasing effects of best-response dynamics can be much worse than this. Consider the situation in Figure 12.10, where we have $k$ agents that each have the option to take a common outer path of cost $1 + \varepsilon$ (for some small number $\varepsilon > 0$), or to take their own alternate path. The alternate path for $t_j$ has cost $1/j$. Now suppose we start with a solution in which all agents are sharing the outer path. Each agent pays $(1 + \varepsilon)/k$, and this is the solution that minimizes the total cost to all agents. But running best-response dynamics starting from this solution causes things to unwind rapidly. First $t_k$ switches to its alternate path, since $1/k < (1 + \varepsilon)/k$.

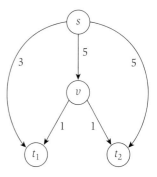

**Figure 12.9** A network in which the unique Nash equilibrium differs from the social optimum.

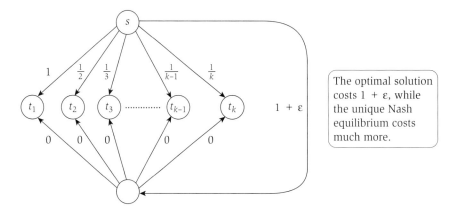

The optimal solution costs $1 + \varepsilon$, while the unique Nash equilibrium costs much more.

**Figure 12.10** A network in which the unique Nash equilibrium costs $H(k) = \Theta(\log k)$ times more than the social optimum.

As a result of this, there are now only $k - 1$ agents sharing the outer path, and so $t_{k-1}$ switches to its alternate path, since $1/(k - 1) < (1 + \varepsilon)/(k - 1)$. After this, $t_{k-2}$ switches, then $t_{k-3}$, and so forth, until all $k$ agents are using the alternate paths directly from $s$. Things come to a halt here, due to the following fact.

**(12.13)**    *The solution in Figure 12.10, in which each agent uses its direct path from s, is a Nash equilibrium, and moreover it is the unique Nash equilibrium for this instance.*

**Proof.** To verify that the given solution is a Nash equilibrium, we simply need to check that no agent has an incentive to switch from its current path. But this is clear, since all agents are paying at most 1, and the only other option—the (currently vacant) outer path—has cost $1 + \varepsilon$.

Now suppose there were some other Nash equilibrium. In order to be different from the solution we have just been considering, it would have to involve at least one of the agents using the outer path. Let $t_{j_1}, t_{j_2}, \ldots, t_{j_\ell}$ be the agents using the outer path, where $j_1 < j_2 < \cdots < j_\ell$. Then all these agents are paying $(1 + \varepsilon)/\ell$. But notice that $j_\ell \geq \ell$, and so agent $t_{j_\ell}$ has the option to pay only $1/j_\ell \leq 1/\ell$ by using its alternate path directly from $s$. Hence $t_{j_\ell}$ has an incentive to deviate from the current solution, and hence this solution cannot be a Nash equilibrium.  ∎

Figure 12.8(b) already illustrated that there can exist a Nash equilibrium whose total cost is much worse than that of the social optimum, but the examples in Figures 12.9 and 12.10 drive home a further point: The total cost to all agents under even the *most favorable* Nash equilibrium solution can be worse than the total cost under the social optimum. How much worse? The total cost of the social optimum in this example is $1 + \varepsilon$, while the cost of the unique Nash equilibrium is $1 + \frac{1}{2} + \frac{1}{3} + \cdots + \frac{1}{k} = \sum_{i=1}^{k} \frac{1}{i}$. We encountered this expression in Chapter 11, where we defined it to be the *harmonic number* $H(k)$ and showed that its asymptotic value is $H(k) = \Theta(\log k)$.

These examples suggest that one can't really view the social optimum as the analogue of the global minimum in a traditional local search procedure. In standard local search, the global minimum is always a stable solution, since no improvement is possible. Here the social optimum can be an unstable solution, since it just requires one agent to have an interest in deviating.

## Two Basic Questions

Best-response dynamics can exhibit a variety of different behaviors, and we've just seen a range of examples that illustrate different phenomena. It's useful at this point to step back, assess our current understanding, and ask some basic questions. We group these questions around the following two issues.

- **The existence of a Nash equilibrium.** At this point, we actually don't have a proof that there even *exists* a Nash equilibrium solution in every instance of our multicast routing problem. The most natural candidate for a progress measure, the total cost to all agents, does not necessarily decrease when a single agent updates its path.

  Given this, it's not immediately clear how to argue that the best-response dynamics must terminate. Why couldn't we get into a cycle where agent $t_1$ improves its solution at the expense of $t_2$, then $t_2$ improves its solution at the expense of $t_1$, and we continue this way forever? Indeed, it's not hard to define other problems in which exactly this can happen and in which Nash equilibria don't exist. So if we want to argue that best-response dynamics leads to a Nash equilibrium in the present case, we need to figure out what's special about our routing problem that causes this to happen.

- **The price of stability.** So far we've mainly considered Nash equilibria in the role of "observers": essentially, we turn the agents loose on the graph from an arbitrary starting point and watch what they do. But if we were viewing this as protocol designers, trying to define a procedure by which agents could construct paths from $s$, we might want to pursue the following approach. Given a set of agents, located at nodes $t_1, t_2, \ldots, t_k$, we could propose a collection of paths, one for each agent, with two properties.

  (i)  The set of paths forms a Nash equilibrium solution; and

  (ii) Subject to (i), the total cost to all agents is as small as possible.

Of course, ideally we'd like just to have the smallest total cost, as this is the social optimum. But if we propose the social optimum and it's not a Nash equilibrium, then it won't be stable: Agents will begin deviating and constructing new paths. Thus properties (i) and (ii) together represent our protocol's attempt to optimize in the face of stability, finding the best solution from which no agent will want to deviate.

We therefore define the *price of stability*, for a given instance of the problem, to be the ratio of the cost of the best Nash equilibrium solution to the cost of the social optimum. This quantity reflects the blow-up in cost that we incur due to the requirement that our solution must be stable in the face of the agents' self-interest.

Note that this pair of questions can be asked for essentially any problem in which self-interested agents produce a collective solution. For our multicast routing problem, we now resolve both these questions. Essentially, we will find that the example in Figure 12.10 captures some of the crucial aspects of the problem in general. We will show that for any instance, best-response dynamics starting from the social optimum leads to a Nash equilibrium whose cost is greater by at most a factor of $H(k) = \Theta(\log k)$.

## Finding a Good Nash Equilibrium

We focus first on showing that best-response dynamics in our problem always terminates with a Nash equilibrium. It will turn out that our approach to this question also provides the necessary technique for bounding the price of stability.

The key idea is that we don't need to use the total cost to all agents as the progress measure against which to bound the number of steps of best-response dynamics. Rather, any quantity that strictly decreases on a path update by any agent, and which can only decrease a finite number of times, will work perfectly well. With this in mind, we try to formulate a measure that has this property. The measure will not necessarily have as strong an intuitive meaning as the total cost, but this is fine as long as it does what we need.

We first consider in more detail why just using the total agent cost doesn't work. Suppose, to take a simple example, that agent $t_j$ is currently sharing, with $x$ other agents, a path consisting of the single edge $e$. (In general, of course, the agents' paths will be longer than this, but single-edge paths are useful to think about for this example.) Now suppose that $t_j$ decides it is in fact cheaper to switch to a path consisting of the single edge $f$, which no agent is currently using. In order for this to be the case, it must be that $c_f < c_e/(x + 1)$. Now, as a result of this switch, the total cost to all agents goes up by $c_f$: Previously,

$x + 1$ agents contributed to the cost $c_e$, and no one was incurring the cost $c_f$; but, after the switch, $x$ agents still collectively have to pay the full cost $c_e$, and $t_j$ is now paying an additional $c_f$.

In order to view this as progress, we need to redefine what "progress" means. In particular, it would be useful to have a measure that could offset the added cost $c_f$ via some notion that the overall "potential energy" in the system has dropped by $c_e/(x + 1)$. This would allow us to view the move by $t_j$ as causing a net decrease, since we have $c_f < c_e/(x + 1)$. In order to do this, we could maintain a "potential" on each edge $e$, with the property that this potential drops by $c_e/(x + 1)$ when the number of agents using $e$ decreases from $x + 1$ to $x$. (Correspondingly, it would need to increase by this much when the number of agents using $e$ increased from $x$ to $x + 1$.)

Thus, our intuition suggests that we should define the potential so that, if there are $x$ agents on an edge $e$, then the potential should decrease by $c_e/x$ when the first one stops using $e$, by $c_e/(x - 1)$ when the next one stops using $e$, by $c_e/(x - 2)$ for the next one, and so forth. Setting the potential to be $c_e(1/x + 1/(x - 1) + \cdots + 1/2 + 1) = c_e \cdot H(x)$ is a simple way to accomplish this. More concretely, we define the *potential* of a set of paths $P_1, P_2, \ldots, P_k$, denoted $\Phi(P_1, P_2, \ldots, P_k)$, as follows. For each edge $e$, let $x_e$ denote the number of agents whose paths use the edge $e$. Then

$$\Phi(P_1, P_2, \ldots, P_k) = \sum_{e \in E} c_e \cdot H(x_e).$$

(We'll define the harmonic number $H(0)$ to be 0, so that the contribution of edges containing no paths is 0.)

The following claim establishes that $\Phi$ really works as a progress measure.

**(12.14)** *Suppose that the current set of paths is $P_1, P_2, \ldots, P_k$, and agent $t_j$ updates its path from $P_j$ to $P_j'$. Then the new potential $\Phi(P_1, \ldots, P_{j-1}, P_j', P_{j+1}, \ldots, P_k)$ is strictly less than the old potential $\Phi(P_1, \ldots, P_{j-1}, P_j, P_{j+1}, \ldots, P_k)$.*

**Proof.** Before $t_j$ switched its path from $P_j$ to $P_j'$, it was paying $\sum_{e \in P_j} c_e/x_e$, since it was sharing the cost of each edge $e$ with $x_e - 1$ other agents. After the switch, it continues to pay this cost on the edges in the intersection $P_j \cap P_j'$, and it also pays $c_f/(x_f + 1)$ on each edge $f \in P_j' - P_j$. Thus the fact that $t_j$ viewed this switch as an improvement means that

$$\sum_{f \in P_j' - P_j} \frac{c_f}{x_f + 1} < \sum_{e \in P_j - P_j'} \frac{c_e}{x_e}.$$

Now let's ask what happens to the potential function $\Phi$. The only edges on which it changes are those in $P'_j - P_j$ and those in $P_j - P'_j$. On the former set, it increases by

$$\sum_{f \in P'_j - P_j} c_f[H(x_f + 1) - H(x_f)] = \sum_{f \in P'_j - P_j} \frac{c_f}{x_f + 1},$$

and on the latter set, it decreases by

$$\sum_{e \in P_j - P'_j} c_e[H(x_e) - H(x_e - 1)] = \sum_{e \in P_j - P'_j} \frac{c_e}{x_e}.$$

So the criterion that $t_j$ used for switching paths is precisely the statement that the total increase is strictly less than the total decrease, and hence the potential $\Phi$ decreases as a result of $t_j$'s switch. ∎

Now there are only finitely many ways to choose a path for each agent $t_j$, and (12.14) says that best-response dynamics can never revisit a set of paths $P_1, \ldots, P_k$ once it leaves it due to an improving move by some agent. Thus we have shown the following.

**(12.15)** *Best-response dynamics always leads to a set of paths that forms a Nash equilibrium solution.*

**Bounding the Price of Stability**   Our potential function $\Phi$ also turns out to be very useful in providing a bound on the price of stability. The point is that, although $\Phi$ is not equal to the total cost incurred by all agents, it tracks it reasonably closely.

To see this, let $C(P_1, \ldots, P_k)$ denote the total cost to all agents when the selected paths are $P_1, \ldots, P_k$. This quantity is simply the sum of $c_e$ over all edges that appear in the union of these paths, since the cost of each such edge is completely covered by the agents whose paths contain it.

Now the relationship between the cost function $C$ and the potential function $\Phi$ is as follows.

**(12.16)** *For any set of paths $P_1, \ldots, P_k$, we have*

$$C(P_1, \ldots, P_k) \leq \Phi(P_1, \ldots, P_k) \leq H(k) \cdot C(P_1, \ldots, P_k).$$

**Proof.**  Recall our notation in which $x_e$ denotes the number of paths containing edge $e$. For the purposes of comparing $C$ and $\Phi$, we also define $E^+$ to be the set of all edges that belong to at least one of the paths $P_1, \ldots, P_k$. Then, by the definition of $C$, we have $C(P_1, \ldots, P_k) = \sum_{e \in E^+} c_e$.

A simple fact to notice is that $x_e \leq k$ for all $e$. Now we simply write

$$C(P_1, \ldots, P_k) = \sum_{e \in E^+} c_e \leq \sum_{e \in E^+} c_e H(x_e) = \Phi(P_1, \ldots, P_k)$$

and

$$\Phi(P_1, \ldots, P_k) = \sum_{e \in E^+} c_e H(x_e) \leq \sum_{e \in E^+} c_e H(k) = H(k) \cdot C(P_1, \ldots, P_k). \quad \blacksquare$$

Using this, we can give a bound on the price of stability.

**(12.17)** *In every instance, there is a Nash equilibrium solution for which the total cost to all agents exceeds that of the social optimum by at most a factor of $H(k)$.*

**Proof.** To produce the desired Nash equilibrium, we start from a social optimum consisting of paths $P_1^*, \ldots, P_k^*$ and run best-response dynamics. By (12.15), this must terminate at a Nash equilibrium $P_1, \ldots, P_k$.

During this run of best-response dynamics, the total cost to all agents may have been going up, but by (12.14) the potential function was decreasing. Thus we have $\Phi(P_1, \ldots, P_k) \leq \Phi(P_1^*, \ldots, P_k^*)$.

This is basically all we need since, for any set of paths, the quantities $C$ and $\Phi$ differ by at most a factor of $H(k)$. Specifically,

$$C(P_1, \ldots, P_k) \leq \Phi(P_1, \ldots, P_k) \leq \Phi(P_1^*, \ldots, P_k^*) \leq H(k) \cdot C(P_1^*, \ldots, P_k^*). \quad \blacksquare$$

Thus we have shown that a Nash equilibrium always exists, and there is always a Nash equilibrium whose total cost is within an $H(k)$ factor of the social optimum. The example in Figure 12.10 shows that it isn't possible to improve on the bound of $H(k)$ in the worst case.

Although this wraps up certain aspects of the problem very neatly, there are a number of questions here for which the answer isn't known. One particularly intriguing question is whether it's possible to construct a Nash equilibrium for this problem in polynomial time. Note that our proof of the existence of a Nash equilibrium argued simply that as best-response dynamics iterated through sets of paths, it could never revisit the same set twice, and hence it could not run forever. But there are exponentially many possible sets of paths, and so this does not give a polynomial-time algorithm. Beyond the question of finding any Nash equilibrium efficiently, there is also the open question of efficiently finding a Nash equilibrium that achieves a bound of $H(k)$ relative to the social optimum, as guaranteed by (12.17).

It's also important to reiterate something that we mentioned earlier: It's not hard to find problems for which best-response dynamics may cycle forever and for which Nash equilibria do not necessarily exist. We were fortunate here that best-response dynamics could be viewed as iteratively improving a *potential function* that guaranteed our progress toward a Nash equilibrium, but the point is that potential functions like this do not exist for all problems in which agents interact.

Finally, it's interesting to compare what we've been doing here to a problem that we considered earlier in this chapter: finding a stable configuration in a Hopfield network. If you recall the discussion of that earlier problem, we analyzed a process in which each node "flips" between two possible states, seeking to increase the total weight of "good" edges incident to it. This can in fact be viewed as an instance of best-response dynamics for a problem in which each node has an objective function that seeks to maximize this measure of good edge weight. However, showing the convergence of best-response dynamics for the Hopfield network problem was much easier than the challenge we faced here: There it turned out that the state-flipping process was in fact a "disguised" form of local search with an objective function obtained simply by adding together the objective functions of all nodes—in effect, the analogue of the total cost to all agents served as a progress measure. In the present case, it was precisely because this total cost function did not work as a progress measure that we were forced to embark on the more complex analysis described here.

## Solved Exercises

### Solved Exercise 1

The Center Selection Problem from Chapter 11 is another case in which one can study the performance of local search algorithms.

Here is a simple local search approach to Center Selection (indeed, it's a common strategy for a variety of problems that involve locating facilities). In this problem, we are given a set of sites $S = \{s_1, s_2, \ldots, s_n\}$ in the plane, and we want to choose a set of $k$ centers $C = \{c_1, c_2, \ldots, c_k\}$ whose *covering radius*—the farthest that people in any one site must travel to their nearest center—is as small as possible.

We start by arbitrarily choosing $k$ points in the plane to be the centers $c_1, c_2, \ldots, c_k$. We now alternate the following two steps.

(i)  Given the set of $k$ centers $c_1, c_2, \ldots, c_k$, we divide $S$ into $k$ sets: For $i = 1, 2, \ldots, k$, we define $S_i$ to be the set of all the sites for which $c_i$ is the closest center.

(ii) Given this division of $S$ into $k$ sets, construct new centers that will be as "central" as possible relative to them. For each set $S_i$, we find the smallest circle in the plane that contains all points in $S_i$, and define center $c_i$ to be the center of this circle.

If steps (i) and (ii) cause the covering radius to strictly decrease, then we perform another iteration; otherwise the algorithm stops.

The alternation of steps (i) and (ii) is based on the following natural interplay between sites and centers. In step (i) we partition the sites as well as possible given the centers; and then in step (ii) we place the centers as well as possible given the partition of the sites. In addition to its role as a heuristic for placing facilities, this type of two-step interplay is also the basis for local search algorithms in statistics, where (for reasons we won't go into here) it is called the *Expectation Maximization* approach.

(a) Prove that this local search algorithm eventually terminates.

(b) Consider the following statement.

*There is an absolute constant $b > 1$ (independent of the particular input instance), so when the local search algorithm terminates, the covering radius of its solution is at most b times the optimal covering radius.*

Decide whether you think this statement is true or false, and give a proof of either the statement or its negation.

**Solution** To prove part (a), one's first thought is the following: The set of covering radii decreases in each iteration; it can't drop below the optimal covering radius; and so the iterations must terminate. But we have to be a bit careful, since we're dealing with real numbers. What if the covering radii decreased in every iteration, but by less and less, so that the algorithm was able to run arbitrarily long as its covering radii converged to some value from above?

It's not hard to take care of this concern, however. Note that the covering radius at the end of step (ii) in each iteration is completely determined by the current partition of the sites into $S_1, S_2, \ldots, S_k$. There are a finite number of ways to partition the sites into $k$ sets, and if the local search algorithm ran for more than this number of iterations, it would have to produce the same partition in two of these iterations. But then it would have the same covering radius at the end of each of these iterations, and this contradicts the assumption that the covering radius strictly decreases from each iteration to the next.

This proves that the algorithm always terminates. (Note that it only gives an exponential bound on the number of iterations, however, since there are exponentially many ways to partition the sites into $k$ sets.)

To disprove part (b), it would be enough to find a run of the algorithm in which the iterations gets "stuck" in a configuration with a very large covering radius. This is not very hard to do. For any constant $b > 1$, consider a set $S$

of four points in the plane that form the corners of a tall, narrow rectangle of width $w$ and height $h = 2bw$. For example, we could have the four points be $(0, 0), (0, h), (w, h), (w, 0)$.

Now suppose $k = 2$, and we start the two centers anywhere to the left and right of the rectangle, respectively (say, at $(-1, h/2)$ and $(w + 1, h/2)$). The first iteration proceeds as follows.

- Step (i) will divide $S$ into the two points $S_1$ on the left side of the rectangle (with $x$-coordinate 0) and the two points $S_2$ on the right side of the rectangle (with $x$-coordinate $w$).
- Step (ii) will place centers at the midpoints of $S_1$ and $S_2$ (i.e., at $(0, h/2)$ and $(w, h/2)$).

We can check that in the next iteration, the partition of $S$ will not change, and so the locations of the centers will not change; the algorithm terminates here at a local minimum.

The covering radius of this solution is $h/2$. But the optimal solution would place centers at the midpoints of the top and bottom sides of the rectangle, for a covering radius of $w/2$. Thus the covering radius of our solution is $h/w = 2b > b$ times that of the optimum.

## Exercises

1. Consider the problem of finding a stable state in a Hopfield neural network, in the special case when all edge weights are positive. This corresponds to the Maximum-Cut Problem that we discussed earlier in the chapter: For every edge $e$ in the graph $G$, the endpoints of $G$ would prefer to have opposite states.

   Now suppose the underlying graph $G$ is connected and bipartite; the nodes can be partitioned into sets $X$ and $Y$ so that each edge has one end in $X$ and the other in $Y$. Then there is a natural "best" configuration for the Hopfield net, in which all nodes in $X$ have the state $+1$ and all nodes in $Y$ have the state $-1$. This way, all edges are *good*, in that their ends have opposite states.

   The question is: In this special case, when the best configuration is so clear, will the State-Flipping Algorithm described in the text (as long as there is an unsatisfied node, choose one and flip its state) always find this configuration? Give a proof that it will, or an example of an input instance, a starting configuration, and an execution of the State-Flipping Algorithm that terminates at a configuration in which not all edges are good.

2. Recall that for a problem in which the goal is to maximize some under-lying quantity, gradient descent has a natural "upside-down" analogue, in which one repeatedly moves from the current solution to a solution of strictly greater value. Naturally, we could call this a *gradient ascent algorithm*. (Often in the literature you'll also see such methods referred to as *hill-climbing* algorithms.)

By straight symmetry, the observations we've made in this chapter about gradient descent carry over to gradient ascent: For many problems you can easily end up with a local optimum that is not very good. But sometimes one encounters problems—as we saw, for example, with the Maximum-Cut and Labeling Problems—for which a local search algorithm comes with a very strong guarantee: Every local optimum is close in value to the global optimum. We now consider the Bipartite Matching Problem and find that the same phenomenon happens here as well.

Thus, consider the following Gradient Ascent Algorithm for finding a matching in a bipartite graph.

> As long as there is an edge whose endpoints are unmatched, add it to the current matching. When there is no longer such an edge, terminate with a locally optimal matching.

(a) Give an example of a bipartite graph $G$ for which this gradient ascent algorithm does not return the maximum matching.

(b) Let $M$ and $M'$ be matchings in a bipartite graph $G$. Suppose that $|M'| > 2|M|$. Show that there is an edge $e' \in M'$ such that $M \cup \{e'\}$ is a matching in $G$.

(c) Use (b) to conclude that any locally optimal matching returned by the gradient ascent algorithm in a bipartite graph $G$ is at least *half* as large as a maximum matching in $G$.

3. Suppose you're consulting for a biotech company that runs experiments on two expensive high-throughput assay machines, each identical, which we'll label $M_1$ and $M_2$. Each day they have a number of jobs that they need to do, and each job has to be assigned to one of the two machines. The problem they need help on is how to assign the jobs to machines to keep the loads balanced each day. The problem is stated as follows. There are $n$ jobs, and each job $j$ has a required processing time $t_j$. They need to partition the jobs into two groups $A$ and $B$, where set $A$ is assigned to $M_1$ and set $B$ to $M_2$. The time needed to process all of the jobs on the two machines is $T_1 = \sum_{j \in A} t_j$ and $T_2 = \sum_{j \in B} t_j$. The problem is to have the two machines work roughly for the same amounts of time—that is, to minimize $|T_1 - T_2|$.

A previous consultant showed that the problem is NP-hard (by a reduction from Subset Sum). Now they are looking for a good local search algorithm. They propose the following. Start by assigning jobs to the two machines arbitrarily (say jobs $1, \ldots, n/2$ to $M_1$, the rest to $M_2$). The local moves are to move a single job from one machine to the other, and we only move jobs if the move decreases the absolute difference in the processing times. You are hired to answer some basic questions about the performance of this algorithm.

(a) The first question is: How good is the solution obtained? Assume that there is no single job that dominates all the processing time—that is, that $t_j \leq \frac{1}{2} \sum_{i=1}^{n} t_i$ for all jobs $j$. Prove that for every locally optimal solution, the times the two machines operate are roughly balanced: $\frac{1}{2} T_1 \leq T_2 \leq 2T_1$.

(b) Next you worry about the running time of the algorithm: How often will jobs be moved back and forth between the two machines? You propose the following small modification in the algorithm. If, in a local move, many different jobs can move from one machine to the other, then the algorithm should always move the job $j$ with maximum $t_j$. Prove that, under this variant, each job will move at most once. (Hence the local search terminates in at most $n$ moves.)

(c) Finally, they wonder if they should work on better algorithms. Give an example in which the local search algorithm above will not lead to an optimal solution.

4. Consider the Load Balancing Problem from Section 11.1. Some friends of yours are running a collection of Web servers, and they've designed a local search heuristic for this problem, different from the algorithms described in Chapter 11.

Recall that we have $m$ machines $M_1, \ldots, M_m$, and we must assign each job to a machine. The load of the $i^{\text{th}}$ job is denoted $t_i$. The makespan of an assignment is the *maximum load* on any machine:

$$\max_{\text{machines } M_i} \sum_{\text{jobs } j \text{ assigned to } M_i} t_j.$$

Your friends' local search heuristic works as follows. They start with an arbitrary assignment of jobs to machines, and they then repeatedly try to apply the following type of "swap move."

Let $A(i)$ and $A(j)$ be the jobs assigned to machines $M_i$ and $M_j$, respectively. To perform a swap move on $M_i$ and $M_j$, choose subsets of jobs $B(i) \subseteq A(j)$ and $B(j) \subseteq A(j)$, and "swap" these jobs between the two machines. That is, update $A(i)$ to be $A(i) \cup B(j) - B(i)$, and update $A(j)$ to be $A(j) \cup B(i) - B(j)$. (One is allowed to have $B(i) = A(i)$, or to have $B(i)$ be the empty set; and analogously for $B(j)$.)

Consider a swap move applied to machines $M_i$ and $M_j$. Suppose the loads on $M_i$ and $M_j$ before the swap are $T_i$ and $T_j$, respectively, and the loads after the swap are $T_i'$ and $T_j'$. We say that the swap move is *improving* if $\max(T_i', T_j') < \max(T_i, T_j)$—in other words, the larger of the two loads involved has strictly decreased. We say that an assignment of jobs to machines is *stable* if there does not exist an improving swap move, beginning with the current assignment.

Thus the local search heuristic simply keeps executing improving swap moves until a stable assignment is reached; at this point, the resulting stable assignment is returned as the solution.

**Example.** Suppose there are two machines: In the current assignment, the machine $M_1$ has jobs of sizes $1, 3, 5, 8$, and machine $M_2$ has jobs of sizes $2, 4$. Then one possible improving swap move would be to define $B(1)$ to consist of the job of size 8, and define $B(2)$ to consist of the job of size 2. After these two sets are swapped, the resulting assignment has jobs of size $1, 2, 3, 5$ on $M_1$, and jobs of size $4, 8$ on $M_2$. This assignment is stable. (It also has an optimal makespan of 12.)

(a) As specified, there is no explicit guarantee that this local search heuristic will always terminate. What if it keeps cycling forever through assignments that are not stable?

Prove that, in fact, the local search heuristic terminates in a finite number of steps, with a stable assignment, on any instance.

(b) Show that any stable assignment has a makespan that is within a factor of 2 of the minimum possible makespan.

# Notes and Further Reading

Kirkpatrick, Gelatt, and Vecchi (1983) introduced simulated annealing, building on an algorithm of Metropolis et al. (1953) for simulating physical systems. In the process, they highlighted the analogy between energy landscapes and the solution spaces of computational problems.

The book of surveys edited by Aarts and Lenstra (1997) covers a wide range of applications of local search techniques for algorithmic problems. Hopfield neural networks were introduced by Hopfield (1982) and are discussed in more detail in the book by Haykin (1999). The heuristic for graph partitioning discussed in Section 12.5 is due to Kernighan and Lin (1970).

The local search algorithm for classification based on the Labeling Problem is due to Boykov, Veksler, and Zabih (1999). Further results and computational experiments are discussed in the thesis by Veksler (1999).

The multi-agent routing problem considered in Section 12.7 raises issues at the intersection of algorithms and game theory, an area concerned with the general issue of strategic interaction among agents. The book by Osborne (2003) provides an introduction to game theory; the algorithmic aspects of the subject are discussed in surveys by Papadimitriou (2001) and Tardos (2004) and the thesis and subsequent book by Roughgarden (2002, 2004). The use of potential functions to prove the existence of Nash equilibria has a long history in game theory (Beckmann, McGuire, and Winsten, 1956; Rosenthal 1973), and potential functions were used to analyze best-response dynamics by Monderer and Shapley (1996). The bound on the price of stability for the routing problem in Section 12.7 is due to Anshelevich et al. (2004).

# Chapter 13

## Randomized Algorithms

The idea that a process can be "random" is not a modern one; we can trace the notion far back into the history of human thought and certainly see its reflections in gambling and the insurance business, each of which reach into ancient times. Yet, while similarly intuitive subjects like geometry and logic have been treated mathematically for several thousand years, the mathematical study of probability is surprisingly young; the first known attempts to seriously formalize it came about in the 1600s. Of course, the history of computer science plays out on a much shorter time scale, and the idea of randomization has been with it since its early days.

Randomization and probabilistic analysis are themes that cut across many areas of computer science, including algorithm design, and when one thinks about random processes in the context of computation, it is usually in one of two distinct ways. One view is to consider the world as behaving randomly: One can consider traditional algorithms that confront randomly generated input. This approach is often termed *average-case analysis*, since we are studying the behavior of an algorithm on an "average" input (subject to some underlying random process), rather than a worst-case input.

A second view is to consider algorithms that behave randomly: The world provides the same worst-case input as always, but we allow our algorithm to make random decisions as it processes the input. Thus the role of randomization in this approach is purely internal to the algorithm and does not require new assumptions about the nature of the input. It is this notion of a *randomized algorithm* that we will be considering in this chapter.

Why might it be useful to design an algorithm that is allowed to make random decisions? A first answer would be to observe that by allowing randomization, we've made our underlying model more powerful. Efficient deterministic algorithms that always yield the correct answer are a special case of efficient randomized algorithms that only need to yield the correct answer with high probability; they are also a special case of randomized algorithms that are always correct, and run efficiently *in expectation*. Even in a worst-case world, an algorithm that does its own "internal" randomization may be able to offset certain worst-case phenomena. So problems that may not have been solvable by efficient deterministic algorithms may still be amenable to randomized algorithms.

But this is not the whole story, and in fact we'll be looking at randomized algorithms for a number of problems where there exist comparably efficient deterministic algorithms. Even in such situations, a randomized approach often exhibits considerable power for further reasons: It may be conceptually much simpler; or it may allow the algorithm to function while maintaining very little internal state or memory of the past. The advantages of randomization seem to increase further as one considers larger computer systems and networks, with many loosely interacting processes—in other words, a *distributed system*. Here random behavior on the part of individual processes can reduce the amount of explicit communication or synchronization that is required; it is often valuable as a tool for *symmetry-breaking* among processes, reducing the danger of contention and "hot spots." A number of our examples will come from settings like this: regulating access to a shared resource, balancing load on multiple processors, or routing packets through a network. Even a small level of comfort with randomized heuristics can give one considerable leverage in thinking about large systems.

A natural worry in approaching the topic of randomized algorithms is that it requires an extensive knowledge of probability. Of course, it's always better to know more rather than less, and some algorithms are indeed based on complex probabilistic ideas. But one further goal of this chapter is to illustrate *how little* underlying probability is really needed in order to understand many of the well-known algorithms in this area. We will see that there is a small set of useful probabilistic tools that recur frequently, and this chapter will try to develop the tools alongside the algorithms. Ultimately, facility with these tools is as valuable as an understanding of the specific algorithms themselves.

## 13.1 A First Application: Contention Resolution

We begin with a first application of randomized algorithms—contention resolution in a distributed system—that illustrates the general style of analysis we will be using for many of the algorithms that follow. In particular, it is a chance to work through some basic manipulations involving *events* and their probabilities, analyzing intersections of events using *independence* as well as unions of events using a simple *Union Bound*. For the sake of completeness, we give a brief summary of these concepts in the final section of this chapter (Section 13.15).

## The Problem

Suppose we have $n$ processes $P_1, P_2, \ldots, P_n$, each competing for access to a single shared database. We imagine time as being divided into discrete *rounds*. The database has the property that it can be accessed by at most one process in a single round; if two or more processes attempt to access it simultaneously, then all processes are "locked out" for the duration of that round. So, while each process wants to access the database as often as possible, it's pointless for all of them to try accessing it in every round; then everyone will be perpetually locked out. What's needed is a way to divide up the rounds among the processes in an equitable fashion, so that all processes get through to the database on a regular basis.

If it is easy for the processes to communicate with one another, then one can imagine all sorts of direct means for resolving the contention. But suppose that the processes can't communicate with one another at all; how then can they work out a protocol under which they manage to "take turns" in accessing the database?

## Designing a Randomized Algorithm

Randomization provides a natural protocol for this problem, which we can specify simply as follows. For some number $p > 0$ that we'll determine shortly, each process will attempt to access the database in each round with probability $p$, independently of the decisions of the other processes. So, if exactly one process decides to make the attempt in a given round, it will succeed; if two or more try, then they will all be locked out; and if none try, then the round is in a sense "wasted." This type of strategy, in which each of a set of identical processes randomizes its behavior, is the core of the *symmetry-breaking* paradigm that we mentioned initially: If all the processes operated in lockstep, repeatedly trying to access the database at the same time, there'd be no progress; but by randomizing, they "smooth out" the contention.

## Analyzing the Algorithm

As with many applications of randomization, the algorithm in this case is extremely simple to state; the interesting issue is to analyze its performance.

***Defining Some Basic Events***    When confronted with a probabilistic system like this, a good first step is to write down some basic events and think about their probabilities. Here's a first event to consider. For a given process $P_i$ and a given round $t$, let $A[i, t]$ denote the event that $P_i$ attempts to access the database in round $t$. We know that each process attempts an access in each round with probability $p$, so the probability of this event, for any $i$ and $t$, is $\Pr[A[i, t]] = p$. For every event, there is also a *complementary event*, indicating that the event did not occur; here we have the complementary event $\overline{A[i, t]}$ that $P_i$ does not attempt to access the database in round $t$, with probability

$$\Pr\left[\overline{A[i, t]}\right] = 1 - \Pr[A[i, t]] = 1 - p.$$

Our real concern is whether a process *succeeds* in accessing the database in a given round. Let $S[i, t]$ denote this event. Clearly, the process $P_i$ must attempt an access in round $t$ in order to succeed. Indeed, succeeding is equivalent to the following: Process $P_i$ attempts to access the database in round $t$, and each other process *does not* attempt to access the database in round $t$. Thus $S[i, t]$ is equal to the intersection of the event $A[i, t]$ with all the complementary events $\overline{A[j, t]}$, for $j \neq i$:

$$S[i, t] = A[i, t] \cap \left( \bigcap_{j \neq i} \overline{A[j, t]} \right).$$

All the events in this intersection are independent, by the definition of the contention-resolution protocol. Thus, to get the probability of $S[i, t]$, we can multiply the probabilities of all the events in the intersection:

$$\Pr[S[i, t]] = \Pr[A[i, t]] \cdot \prod_{j \neq i} \Pr\left[\overline{A[j, t]}\right] = p(1 - p)^{n-1}.$$

We now have a nice, closed-form expression for the probability that $P_i$ succeeds in accessing the database in round $t$; we can now ask how to set $p$ so that this success probability is maximized. Observe first that the success probability is 0 for the extreme cases $p = 0$ and $p = 1$ (these correspond to the extreme case in which processes never bother attempting, and the opposite extreme case in which every process tries accessing the database in every round, so that everyone is locked out). The function $f(p) = p(1 - p)^{n-1}$ is positive for values of $p$ strictly between 0 and 1, and its derivative $f'(p) = (1 - p)^{n-1} - (n - 1)p(1 - p)^{n-2}$ has a single zero at the value $p = 1/n$, where the maximum is achieved. Thus we can maximize the success probability by setting $p = 1/n$. (Notice that $p = 1/n$ is a natural intuitive choice as well, if one wants exactly one process to attempt an access in any round.)

When we set $p = 1/n$, we get $\Pr\left[\mathcal{S}[i,t]\right] = \frac{1}{n}\left(1 - \frac{1}{n}\right)^{n-1}$. It's worth getting a sense for the asymptotic value of this expression, with the help of the following extremely useful fact from basic calculus.

**(13.1)**

(a) *The function* $\left(1 - \frac{1}{n}\right)^{n}$ *converges monotonically from* $\frac{1}{4}$ *up to* $\frac{1}{e}$ *as* $n$ *increases from 2.*

(b) *The function* $\left(1 - \frac{1}{n}\right)^{n-1}$ *converges monotonically from* $\frac{1}{2}$ *down to* $\frac{1}{e}$ *as* $n$ *increases from 2.*

Using (13.1), we see that $1/(en) \leq \Pr\left[\mathcal{S}[i,t]\right] \leq 1/(2n)$, and hence $\Pr\left[\mathcal{S}[i,t]\right]$ is asymptotically equal to $\Theta(1/n)$.

***Waiting for a Particular Process to Succeed*** Let's consider this protocol with the optimal value $p = 1/n$ for the access probability. Suppose we are interested in how long it will take process $P_i$ to succeed in accessing the database at least once. We see from the earlier calculation that the probability of its succeeding in any one round is not very good, if $n$ is reasonably large. How about if we consider multiple rounds?

Let $\mathcal{F}[i,t]$ denote the "failure event" that process $P_i$ does not succeed in *any* of the rounds 1 through $t$. This is clearly just the intersection of the complementary events $\overline{\mathcal{S}[i,r]}$ for $r = 1, 2, \ldots, t$. Moreover, since each of these events is independent, we can compute the probability of $\mathcal{F}[i,t]$ by multiplication:

$$\Pr\left[\mathcal{F}[i,t]\right] = \Pr\left[\bigcap_{r=1}^{t}\overline{\mathcal{S}[i,r]}\right] = \prod_{r=1}^{t}\Pr\left[\overline{\mathcal{S}[i,r]}\right] = \left[1 - \frac{1}{n}\left(1 - \frac{1}{n}\right)^{n-1}\right]^{t}.$$

This calculation does give us the value of the probability; but at this point, we're in danger of ending up with some extremely complicated-looking expressions, and so it's important to start thinking asymptotically. Recall that the probability of success was $\Theta(1/n)$ after one round; specifically, it was bounded between $1/(en)$ and $1/(2n)$. Using the expression above, we have

$$\Pr\left[\mathcal{F}[i,t]\right] = \prod_{r=1}^{t}\Pr\left[\overline{\mathcal{S}[i,r]}\right] \leq \left(1 - \frac{1}{en}\right)^{t}.$$

Now we notice that if we set $t = en$, then we have an expression that can be plugged directly into (13.1). Of course $en$ will not be an integer; so we can take $t = \lceil en \rceil$ and write

$$\Pr\left[\mathcal{F}[i,t]\right] \leq \left(1 - \frac{1}{en}\right)^{\lceil en \rceil} \leq \left(1 - \frac{1}{en}\right)^{en} \leq \frac{1}{e}.$$

This is a very compact and useful asymptotic statement: The probability that process $P_i$ does not succeed in any of rounds 1 through $\lceil en \rceil$ is upper-bounded by the constant $e^{-1}$, independent of $n$. Now, if we increase $t$ by some fairly small factors, the probability that $P_i$ does not succeed in any of rounds 1 through $t$ drops precipitously: If we set $t = \lceil en \rceil \cdot (c \ln n)$, then we have

$$\Pr\left[\mathcal{F}[i, t]\right] \leq \left(1 - \frac{1}{en}\right)^t = \left(\left(1 - \frac{1}{en}\right)^{\lceil en \rceil}\right)^{c \ln n} \leq e^{-c \ln n} = n^{-c}.$$

So, asymptotically, we can view things as follows. After $\Theta(n)$ rounds, the probability that $P_i$ has not yet succeeded is bounded by a constant; and between then and $\Theta(n \ln n)$, this probability drops to a quantity that is quite small, bounded by an inverse polynomial in $n$.

**Waiting for All Processes to Get Through**    Finally, we're in a position to ask the question that was implicit in the overall setup: How many rounds must elapse before there's a high probability that all processes will have succeeded in accessing the database at least once?

To address this, we say that the protocol *fails* after $t$ rounds if some process has not yet succeeded in accessing the database. Let $\mathcal{F}_t$ denote the event that the protocol fails after $t$ rounds; the goal is to find a reasonably small value of $t$ for which $\Pr\left[\mathcal{F}_t\right]$ is small.

The event $\mathcal{F}_t$ occurs if and only if one of the events $\mathcal{F}[i, t]$ occurs; so we can write

$$\mathcal{F}_t = \bigcup_{i=1}^{n} \mathcal{F}[i, t].$$

Previously, we considered intersections of independent events, which were very simple to work with; here, by contrast, we have a union of events that are not independent. Probabilities of unions like this can be very hard to compute exactly, and in many settings it is enough to analyze them using a simple *Union Bound*, which says that the probability of a union of events is upper-bounded by the sum of their individual probabilities:

**(13.2)**    (The Union Bound) *Given events* $\mathcal{E}_1, \mathcal{E}_2, \ldots, \mathcal{E}_n$, *we have*

$$\Pr\left[\bigcup_{i=1}^{n} \mathcal{E}_i\right] \leq \sum_{i=1}^{n} \Pr\left[\mathcal{E}_i\right].$$

Note that this is not an equality; but the upper bound is good enough when, as here, the union on the left-hand side represents a "bad event" that we're trying to avoid, and we want a bound on its probability in terms of constituent "bad events" on the right-hand side.

For the case at hand, recall that $\mathcal{F}_t = \bigcup_{i=1}^{n} \mathcal{F}[i, t]$, and so

$$\Pr\left[\mathcal{F}_t\right] \le \sum_{i=1}^{n} \Pr\left[\mathcal{F}[i, t]\right].$$

The expression on the right-hand side is a sum of $n$ terms, each with the same value; so to make the probability of $\mathcal{F}_t$ small, we need to make each of the terms on the right significantly smaller than $1/n$. From our earlier discussion, we see that choosing $t = \Theta(n)$ will not be good enough, since then each term on the right is only bounded by a constant. If we choose $t = \lceil en \rceil \cdot (c \ln n)$, then we have $\Pr\left[\mathcal{F}[i, t]\right] \le n^{-c}$ for each $i$, which is what we want. Thus, in particular, taking $t = 2\lceil en \rceil \ln n$ gives us

$$\Pr\left[\mathcal{F}_t\right] \le \sum_{i=1}^{n} \Pr\left[\mathcal{F}[i, t]\right] \le n \cdot n^{-2} = n^{-1},$$

and so we have shown the following.

**(13.3)**  *With probability at least $1 - n^{-1}$, all processes succeed in accessing the database at least once within $t = 2\lceil en \rceil \ln n$ rounds.*

An interesting observation here is that if we had chosen a value of $t$ equal to $qn \ln n$ for a very small value of $q$ (rather than the coefficient $2e$ that we actually used), then we would have gotten an upper bound for $\Pr\left[\mathcal{F}[i, t]\right]$ that was larger than $n^{-1}$, and hence a corresponding upper bound for the overall failure probability $\Pr\left[\mathcal{F}_t\right]$ that was larger than 1—in other words, a completely worthless bound. Yet, as we saw, by choosing larger and larger values for the coefficient $q$, we can drive the upper bound on $\Pr\left[\mathcal{F}_t\right]$ down to $n^{-c}$ for any constant $c$ we want; and this is really a very tiny upper bound. So, in a sense, all the "action" in the Union Bound takes place rapidly in the period when $t = \Theta(n \ln n)$; as we vary the hidden constant inside the $\Theta(\cdot)$, the Union Bound goes from providing no information to giving an extremely strong upper bound on the probability.

We can ask whether this is simply an artifact of using the Union Bound for our upper bound, or whether it's intrinsic to the process we're observing. Although we won't do the (somewhat messy) calculations here, one can show that when $t$ is a small constant times $n \ln n$, there really is a sizable probability that some process has not yet succeeded in accessing the database. So a rapid falling-off in the value of $\Pr\left[\mathcal{F}_t\right]$ genuinely does happen over the range $t = \Theta(n \ln n)$. For this problem, as in many problems of this flavor, we're really identifying the asymptotically "correct" value of $t$ despite our use of the seemingly weak Union Bound.

## 13.2 Finding the Global Minimum Cut

Randomization naturally suggested itself in the previous example, since we were assuming a model with many processes that could not directly communicate. We now look at a problem on graphs for which a randomized approach comes as somewhat more of a surprise, since it is a problem for which perfectly reasonable deterministic algorithms exist as well.

### The Problem

Given an undirected graph $G = (V, E)$, we define a *cut* of $G$ to be a partition of $V$ into two non-empty sets $A$ and $B$. Earlier, when we looked at network flows, we worked with the closely related definition of an *s-t cut*: there, given a directed graph $G = (V, E)$ with distinguished source and sink nodes $s$ and $t$, an *s-t cut* was defined to be a partition of $V$ into sets $A$ and $B$ such that $s \in A$ and $t \in B$. Our definition now is slightly different, since the underlying graph is now undirected and there is no source or sink.

For a cut $(A, B)$ in an undirected graph $G$, the *size* of $(A, B)$ is the number of edges with one end in $A$ and the other in $B$. A *global minimum cut* (or "global min-cut" for short) is a cut of minimum size. The term *global* here is meant to connote that any cut of the graph is allowed; there is no source or sink. Thus the global min-cut is a natural "robustness" parameter; it is the smallest number of edges whose deletion disconnects the graph. We first check that network flow techniques are indeed sufficient to find a global min-cut.

**(13.4)**    *There is a polynomial-time algorithm to find a global min-cut in an undirected graph G.*

**Proof.** We start from the similarity between cuts in undirected graphs and *s-t* cuts in directed graphs, and with the fact that we know how to find the latter optimally.

So given an undirected graph $G = (V, E)$, we need to transform it so that there are directed edges and there is a source and sink. We first replace every undirected edge $e = (u, v) \in E$ with two oppositely oriented directed edges, $e' = (u, v)$ and $e'' = (v, u)$, each of capacity 1. Let $G'$ denote the resulting directed graph.

Now suppose we pick two arbitrary nodes $s, t \in V$, and find the minimum *s-t* cut in $G'$. It is easy to check that if $(A, B)$ is this minimum cut in $G'$, then $(A, B)$ is also a cut of minimum size in $G$ *among all those that separate s from t*. But we know that the global min-cut in $G$ must separate $s$ from *something*, since both sides $A$ and $B$ are nonempty, and $s$ belongs to only one of them. So we fix any $s \in V$ and compute the minimum $s$-$t$ cut in $G'$ for every other node $t \in V - \{s\}$. This is $n - 1$ directed minimum-cut computations, and the best among these will be a global min-cut of $G$. ∎

The algorithm in (13.4) gives the strong impression that finding a global min-cut in an undirected graph is in some sense a *harder* problem than finding a minimum $s$-$t$ cut in a flow network, as we had to invoke a subroutine for the latter problem $n - 1$ times in our method for solving the former. But it turns out that this is just an illusion. A sequence of increasingly simple algorithms in the late 1980s and early 1990s showed that global min-cuts in undirected graphs could actually be computed just as efficiently as $s$-$t$ cuts or even more so, and by techniques that didn't require augmenting paths or even a notion of flow. The high point of this line of work came with David Karger's discovery in 1992 of the Contraction Algorithm, a randomized method that is qualitatively simpler than all previous algorithms for global min-cuts. Indeed, it is sufficiently simple that, on a first impression, it is very hard to believe that it actually works.

### Designing the Algorithm

Here we describe the Contraction Algorithm in its simplest form. This version, while it runs in polynomial time, is not among the most efficient algorithms for global min-cuts. However, subsequent optimizations to the algorithm have given it a much better running time.

The Contraction Algorithm works with a connected *multigraph* $G = (V, E)$; this is an undirected graph that is allowed to have multiple "parallel" edges between the same pair of nodes. It begins by choosing an edge $e = (u, v)$ of $G$ uniformly at random and *contracting* it, as shown in Figure 13.1. This means we produce a new graph $G'$ in which $u$ and $v$ have been identified into a single new node $w$; all other nodes keep their identity. Edges that had one end equal to $u$ and the other equal to $v$ are deleted from $G'$. Each other edge $e$ is preserved in $G'$, but if one of its ends was equal to $u$ or $v$, then this end is updated to be equal to the new node $w$. Note that, even if $G$ had at most one edge between any two nodes, $G'$ may end up with parallel edges.

The Contraction Algorithm then continues recursively on $G'$, choosing an edge uniformly at random and contracting it. As these recursive calls proceed, the constituent vertices of $G'$ should be viewed as *supernodes*: Each supernode $w$ corresponds to the subset $S(w) \subseteq V$ that has been "swallowed up" in the contractions that produced $w$. The algorithm terminates when it reaches a graph $G'$ that has only two supernodes $v_1$ and $v_2$ (presumably with a number of parallel edges between them). Each of these super-nodes $v_i$ has a corresponding subset $S(v_i) \subseteq V$ consisting of the nodes that have been

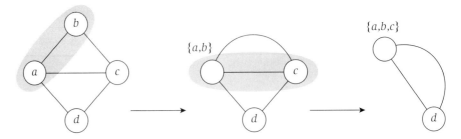

**Figure 13.1** The Contraction Algorithm applied to a four-node input graph.

contracted into it, and these two sets $S(v_1)$ and $S(v_2)$ form a partition of $V$. We output $(S(v_1), S(v_2))$ as the cut found by the algorithm.

```
The Contraction Algorithm applied to a multigraph G = (V, E):
  For each node v, we will record
          the set S(v) of nodes that have been contracted into v
      Initially S(v) = {v} for each v
  If G has two nodes v₁ and v₂, then return the cut (S(v₁), S(v₂))
  Else choose an edge e = (u, v) of G uniformly at random
          Let G′ be the graph resulting from the contraction of e,
              with a new node z_{uv} replacing u and v
          Define S(z_{uv}) = S(u) ∪ S(v)
          Apply the Contraction Algorithm recursively to G′
  Endif
```

## Analyzing the Algorithm

The algorithm is making random choices, so there is some probability that it will succeed in finding a global min-cut and some probability that it won't. One might imagine at first that the probability of success is exponentially small. After all, there are exponentially many possible cuts of $G$; what's favoring the minimum cut in the process? But we'll show first that, in fact, the success probability is only polynomially small. It will then follow that by running the algorithm a polynomial number of times and returning the best cut found in any run, we can actually produce a global min-cut with high probability.

**(13.5)** *The Contraction Algorithm returns a global min-cut of G with probability at least* $1/\binom{n}{2}$.

**Proof.** We focus on a global min-cut $(A, B)$ of $G$ and suppose it has size $k$; in other words, there is a set $F$ of $k$ edges with one end in $A$ and the other in $B$. We want to give a lower bound on the probability that the Contraction Algorithm returns the cut $(A, B)$.

Consider what could go wrong in the first step of the Contraction Algorithm: The problem would be if an edge in $F$ were contracted. For then, a node of $A$ and a node of $B$ would get thrown together in the same supernode, and $(A, B)$ could not be returned as the output of the algorithm. Conversely, if an edge not in $F$ is contracted, then there is still a chance that $(A, B)$ could be returned.

So what we want is an upper bound on the probability that an edge in $F$ is contracted, and for this we need a lower bound on the size of $E$. Notice that if any node $v$ had degree less than $k$, then the cut $(\{v\}, V - \{v\})$ would have size less than $k$, contradicting our assumption that $(A, B)$ is a global min-cut. Thus every node in $G$ has degree at least $k$, and so $|E| \geq \frac{1}{2}kn$. Hence the probability that an edge in $F$ is contracted is at most

$$\frac{k}{\frac{1}{2}kn} = \frac{2}{n}.$$

Now consider the situation after $j$ iterations, when there are $n - j$ supernodes in the current graph $G'$, and suppose that no edge in $F$ has been contracted yet. Every cut of $G'$ is a cut of $G$, and so there are at least $k$ edges incident to every supernode of $G'$. Thus $G'$ has at least $\frac{1}{2}k(n - j)$ edges, and so the probability that an edge of $F$ is contracted in the next iteration $j + 1$ is at most

$$\frac{k}{\frac{1}{2}k(n - j)} = \frac{2}{n - j}.$$

The cut $(A, B)$ will actually be returned by the algorithm if no edge of $F$ is contracted in any of iterations $1, 2, \ldots, n - 2$. If we write $\mathcal{E}_j$ for the event that an edge of $F$ is not contracted in iteration $j$, then we have shown $\Pr\left[\mathcal{E}_1\right] \geq 1 - 2/n$ and $\Pr\left[\mathcal{E}_{j+1} \mid \mathcal{E}_1 \cap \mathcal{E}_2 \cdots \cap \mathcal{E}_j\right] \geq 1 - 2/(n - j)$. We are interested in lower-bounding the quantity $\Pr\left[\mathcal{E}_1 \cap \mathcal{E}_2 \cdots \cap \mathcal{E}_{n-2}\right]$, and we can check by unwinding the formula for conditional probability that this is equal to

$$\Pr\left[\mathcal{E}_1\right] \cdot \Pr\left[\mathcal{E}_2 \mid \mathcal{E}_1\right] \cdots \Pr\left[\mathcal{E}_{j+1} \mid \mathcal{E}_1 \cap \mathcal{E}_2 \cdots \cap \mathcal{E}_j\right] \cdots \Pr\left[\mathcal{E}_{n-2} \mid \mathcal{E}_1 \cap \mathcal{E}_2 \cdots \cap \mathcal{E}_{n-3}\right]$$

$$\geq \left(1 - \frac{2}{n}\right)\left(1 - \frac{2}{n - 1}\right) \cdots \left(1 - \frac{2}{n - j}\right) \cdots \left(1 - \frac{2}{3}\right)$$

$$= \left(\frac{n - 2}{n}\right)\left(\frac{n - 3}{n - 1}\right)\left(\frac{n - 4}{n - 2}\right) \cdots \left(\frac{2}{4}\right)\left(\frac{1}{3}\right)$$

$$= \frac{2}{n(n - 1)} = \binom{n}{2}^{-1}. \quad \blacksquare$$

So we now know that a single run of the Contraction Algorithm fails to find a global min-cut with probability at most $(1 - 1/\binom{n}{2})$. This number is very close to 1, of course, but we can amplify our probability of success simply by repeatedly running the algorithm, with independent random choices, and taking the best cut we find. By fact (13.1), if we run the algorithm $\binom{n}{2}$ times, then the probability that we fail to find a global min-cut in any run is at most

$$\left(1 - 1/\binom{n}{2}\right)^{\binom{n}{2}} \leq \frac{1}{e}.$$

And it's easy to drive the failure probability below $1/e$ with further repetitions: If we run the algorithm $\binom{n}{2} \ln n$ times, then the probability we fail to find a global min-cut is at most $e^{-\ln n} = 1/n$.

The overall running time required to get a high probability of success is polynomial in $n$, since each run of the Contraction Algorithm takes polynomial time, and we run it a polynomial number of times. Its running time will be fairly large compared with the best network flow techniques, since we perform $\Theta(n^2)$ independent runs and each takes at least $\Omega(m)$ time. We have chosen to describe this version of the Contraction Algorithm since it is the simplest and most elegant; it has been shown that some clever optimizations to the way in which multiple runs are performed can improve the running time considerably.

### Further Analysis: The Number of Global Minimum Cuts

The analysis of the Contraction Algorithm provides a surprisingly simple answer to the following question: Given an undirected graph $G = (V, E)$ on $n$ nodes, what is the maximum number of global min-cuts it can have (as a function of $n$)?

For a directed flow network, it's easy to see that the number of minimum $s$-$t$ cuts can be exponential in $n$. For example, consider a directed graph with nodes $s, t, v_1, v_2, \ldots, v_n$, and unit-capacity edges $(s, v_i)$ and $(v_i, t)$ for each $i$. Then $s$ together with any subset of $\{v_1, v_2, \ldots, v_n\}$ will constitute the source side of a minimum cut, and so there are $2^n$ minimum $s$-$t$ cuts.

But for global min-cuts in an undirected graph, the situation looks quite different. If one spends some time trying out examples, one finds that the $n$-node cycle has $\binom{n}{2}$ global min-cuts (obtained by cutting any two edges), and it is not clear how to construct an undirected graph with more.

We now show how the analysis of the Contraction Algorithm settles this question immediately, establishing that the $n$-node cycle is indeed an extreme case.

**(13.6)** *An undirected graph $G = (V, E)$ on $n$ nodes has at most $\binom{n}{2}$ global min-cuts.*

**Proof.** The key is that the proof of (13.5) actually established more than was claimed. Let $G$ be a graph, and let $C_1, \ldots, C_r$ denote all its global min-cuts. Let $\mathcal{E}_i$ denote the event that $C_i$ is returned by the Contraction Algorithm, and let $\mathcal{E} = \cup_{i=1}^{r} \mathcal{E}_i$ denote the event that the algorithm returns any global min-cut.

Then, although (13.5) simply asserts that $\Pr[\mathcal{E}] \geq 1/\binom{n}{2}$, its proof actually shows that for each $i$, we have $\Pr[\mathcal{E}_i] \geq 1/\binom{n}{2}$. Now each pair of events $\mathcal{E}_i$ and $\mathcal{E}_j$ are disjoint—since only one cut is returned by any given run of the algorithm—so by the Union Bound for disjoint events (13.49), we have

$$\Pr[\mathcal{E}] = \Pr\left[\cup_{i=1}^{r}\mathcal{E}_i\right] = \sum_{i=1}^{r} \Pr[\mathcal{E}_i] \geq r/\binom{n}{2}.$$

But clearly $\Pr[\mathcal{E}] \leq 1$, and so we must have $r \leq \binom{n}{2}$. $\blacksquare$

## 13.3 Random Variables and Their Expectations

Thus far our analysis of randomized algorithms and processes has been based on identifying certain "bad events" and bounding their probabilities. This is a qualitative type of analysis, in the sense that the algorithm either succeeds or it doesn't. A more quantitative style of analysis would consider certain parameters associated with the behavior of the algorithm—for example, its running time, or the quality of the solution it produces—and seek to determine the *expected* size of these parameters over the random choices made by the algorithm. In order to make such analysis possible, we need the fundamental notion of a *random variable*.

Given a probability space, a random variable $X$ is a function from the underlying sample space to the natural numbers, such that for each natural number $j$, the set $X^{-1}(j)$ of all sample points taking the value $j$ is an event. Thus we can write $\Pr[X = j]$ as loose shorthand for $\Pr\left[X^{-1}(j)\right]$; it is because we can ask about $X$'s probability of taking a given value that we think of it as a "random variable."

Given a random variable $X$, we are often interested in determining its *expectation*—the "average value" assumed by $X$. We define this as

$$E[X] = \sum_{j=0}^{\infty} j \cdot \Pr[X = j],$$

declaring this to have the value $\infty$ if the sum diverges. Thus, for example, if $X$ takes each of the values in $\{1, 2, \ldots, n\}$ with probability $1/n$, then $E[X] = 1(1/n) + 2(1/n) + \cdots + n(1/n) = \binom{n+1}{2}/n = (n+1)/2$.

## Example: Waiting for a First Success

Here's a more useful example, in which we see how an appropriate random variable lets us talk about something like the "running time" of a simple random process. Suppose we have a coin that comes up heads with probability $p > 0$, and tails with probability $1 - p$. Different flips of the coin have independent outcomes. If we flip the coin until we first get a heads, what's the expected number of flips we will perform? To answer this, we let $X$ denote the random variable equal to the number of flips performed. For $j > 0$, we have $\Pr[X = j] = (1 - p)^{j-1}p$: in order for the process to take exactly $j$ steps, the first $j - 1$ flips must come up tails, and the $j^{\text{th}}$ must come up heads. Now, applying the definition, we have

$$E[X] = \sum_{j=0}^{\infty} j \cdot \Pr[X = j] = \sum_{j=1}^{\infty} j(1-p)^{j-1}p = \frac{p}{1-p} \sum_{j=1}^{\infty} j(1-p)^j$$

$$= \frac{p}{1-p} \cdot \frac{(1-p)}{p^2} = \frac{1}{p}.$$

Thus we get the following intuitively sensible result.

**(13.7)**    *If we repeatedly perform independent trials of an experiment, each of which succeeds with probability $p > 0$, then the expected number of trials we need to perform until the first success is $1/p$.*

## Linearity of Expectation

In Sections 13.1 and 13.2, we broke events down into unions of much simpler events, and worked with the probabilities of these simpler events. This is a powerful technique when working with random variables as well, and it is based on the principle of *linearity of expectation*.

**(13.8)**    Linearity of Expectation. *Given two random variables $X$ and $Y$ defined over the same probability space, we can define $X + Y$ to be the random variable equal to $X(\omega) + Y(\omega)$ on a sample point $\omega$. For any $X$ and $Y$, we have*

$$E[X + Y] = E[X] + E[Y].$$

We omit the proof, which is not difficult. Much of the power of (13.8) comes from the fact that it applies to the sum of *any* random variables; no restrictive assumptions are needed. As a result, if we need to compute the expectation of a complicated random variable $X$, we can first write it as a sum of simpler random variables $X = X_1 + X_2 + \cdots + X_n$, compute each $E[X_i]$, and then determine $E[X] = \sum E[X_i]$. We now look at some examples of this principle in action.

## Example: Guessing Cards

*Memoryless Guessing*   To amaze your friends, you have them shuffle a deck of 52 cards and then turn over one card at a time. Before each card is turned over, you predict its identity. Unfortunately, you don't have any particular psychic abilities—and you're not so good at remembering what's been turned over already—so your strategy is simply to guess a card uniformly at random from the full deck each time. On how many predictions do you expect to be correct?

Let's work this out for the more general setting in which the deck has $n$ distinct cards, using $X$ to denote the random variable equal to the number of correct predictions. A surprisingly effortless way to compute $X$ is to define the random variable $X_i$, for $i = 1, 2, \ldots, n$, to be equal to 1 if the $i^{\text{th}}$ prediction is correct, and 0 otherwise. Notice that $X = X_1 + X_2 + \cdots + X_n$, and

$$E[X_i] = 0 \cdot \Pr[X_i = 0] + 1 \cdot \Pr[X_i = 1] = \Pr[X_i = 1] = \frac{1}{n}.$$

It's worth pausing to note a useful fact that is implicitly demonstrated by the above calculation: If $Z$ is any random variable that only takes the values 0 or 1, then $E[Z] = \Pr[Z = 1]$.

Since $E[X_i] = \frac{1}{n}$ for each $i$, we have

$$E[X] = \sum_{i=1}^{n} E[X_i] = n\left(\frac{1}{n}\right) = 1.$$

Thus we have shown the following.

**(13.9)**   *The expected number of correct predictions under the memoryless guessing strategy is* 1, *independent of n.*

Trying to compute $E[X]$ directly from the definition $\sum_{j=0}^{\infty} j \cdot \Pr[X = j]$ would be much more painful, since it would involve working out a much more elaborate summation. A significant amount of complexity is hidden away in the seemingly innocuous statement of (13.8).

*Guessing with Memory*   Now let's consider a second scenario. Your psychic abilities have not developed any further since last time, but you have become very good at remembering which cards have already been turned over. Thus, when you predict the next card now, you only guess uniformly from among the cards *not yet seen*. How many correct predictions do you expect to make with this strategy?

Again, let the random variable $X_i$ take the value 1 if the $i^{th}$ prediction is correct, and 0 otherwise. In order for the $i^{th}$ prediction to be correct, you need only guess the correct one out of $n - i + 1$ remaining cards; hence

$$E\left[X_i\right] = \Pr\left[X_i = 1\right] = \frac{1}{n - i + 1},$$

and so we have

$$\Pr\left[X\right] = \sum_{i=1}^{n} E\left[X_i\right] = \sum_{i=1}^{n} \frac{1}{n - i + 1} = \sum_{i=1}^{n} \frac{1}{i}.$$

This last expression $\sum_{i=1}^{n} \frac{1}{i} = 1 + \frac{1}{2} + \frac{1}{3} + \cdots + \frac{1}{n}$ is the *harmonic number* $H(n)$, and it is something that has come up in each of the previous two chapters. In particular, we showed in Chapter 11 that $H(n)$, as a function of $n$, closely shadows the value $\int_{1}^{n+1} \frac{1}{x} \, dx = \ln(n + 1)$. For our purposes here, we restate the basic bound on $H(n)$ as follows.

**(13.10)**    $\ln(n + 1) < H(n) < 1 + \ln n$, *and more loosely,* $H(n) = \Theta(\log n)$.

Thus, once you are able to remember the cards you've already seen, the expected number of correct predictions increases significantly above 1.

**(13.11)**    *The expected number of correct predictions under the guessing strategy with memory is* $H(n) = \Theta(\log n)$.

## Example: Collecting Coupons

Before moving on to more sophisticated applications, let's consider one more basic example in which linearity of expectation provides significant leverage.

Suppose that a certain brand of cereal includes a free coupon in each box. There are $n$ different types of coupons. As a regular consumer of this brand, how many boxes do you expect to buy before finally getting a coupon of each type?

Clearly, at least $n$ boxes are needed; but it would be sort of surprising if you actually had all $n$ types of coupons by the time you'd bought $n$ boxes. As you collect more and more different types, it will get less and less likely that a new box has a type of coupon you haven't seen before. Once you have $n - 1$ of the $n$ different types, there's only a probability of $1/n$ that a new box has the missing type you need.

Here's a way to work out the expected time exactly. Let $X$ be the random variable equal to the number of boxes you buy until you first have a coupon of each type. As in our previous examples, this is a reasonably complicated random variable to think about, and we'd like to write it as a sum of simpler random variables. To think about this, let's consider the following natural idea: The coupon-collecting process *makes progress* whenever you buy a box of cereal containing a type of coupon you haven't seen before. Thus the goal of the process is really to make progress $n$ times. Now, at a given point in time, what is the probability that you make progress in the next step? This depends on how many different types of coupons you already have. If you have $j$ types, then the probability of making progress in the next step is $(n - j)/n$: Of the $n$ types of coupons, $n - j$ allow you to make progress. Since the probability varies depending on the number of different types of coupons we have, this suggests a natural way to break down $X$ into simpler random variables, as follows.

Let's say that the coupon-collecting process is in *phase $j$* when you've already collected $j$ different types of coupons and are waiting to get a new type. When you see a new type of coupon, phase $j$ ends and phase $j + 1$ begins. Thus we start in phase 0, and the whole process is done at the end of phase $n - 1$. Let $X_j$ be the random variable equal to the number of steps you spend in phase $j$. Then $X = X_0 + X_1 + \cdots + X_{n-1}$, and so it is enough to work out $E[X_j]$ for each $j$.

**(13.12)**    $E[X_j] = n/(n - j)$.

**Proof.** In each step of phase $j$, the phase ends immediately if and only if the coupon you get next is one of the $n - j$ types you haven't seen before. Thus, in phase $j$, you are really just waiting for an event of probability $(n - j)/n$ to occur, and so, by (13.7), the expected length of phase $j$ is $E[X_j] = n/(n - j)$. ∎

Using this, linearity of expectation gives us the overall expected time.

**(13.13)**    *The expected time before all $n$ types of coupons are collected is* $E[X] = nH(n) = \Theta(n \log n)$.

**Proof.** By linearity of expectation, we have

$$E[X] = \sum_{j=0}^{n-1} E[X_j] = \sum_{j=0}^{n-1} \frac{n}{n - j} = n \sum_{j=0}^{n-1} \frac{1}{n - j} = n \sum_{i=1}^{n} \frac{1}{i} = nH(n).$$

By (13.10), we know this is asymptotically equal to $\Theta(n \log n)$. ∎

It is interesting to compare the dynamics of this process to one's intuitive view of it. Once $n - 1$ of the $n$ types of coupons are collected, you expect to buy $n$ more boxes of cereal before you see the final type. In the meantime, you keep getting coupons you've already seen before, and you might conclude that this final type is "the rare one." But in fact it's just as likely as all the others; it's simply that the final one, whichever it turns out to be, is likely to take a long time to get.

### A Final Definition: Conditional Expectation

We now discuss one final, very useful notion concerning random variables that will come up in some of the subsequent analyses. Just as one can define the conditional probability of one event given another, one can analogously define the expectation of a random variable conditioned on a certain event. Suppose we have a random variable $X$ and an event $\mathcal{E}$ of positive probability. Then we define the *conditional expectation* of $X$, given $\mathcal{E}$, to be the expected value of $X$ computed only over the part of the sample space corresponding to $\mathcal{E}$. We denote this quantity by $E[X \mid \mathcal{E}]$. This simply involves replacing the probabilities $\Pr[X = j]$ in the definition of the expectation with conditional probabilities:

$$E[X \mid \mathcal{E}] = \sum_{j=0}^{\infty} j \cdot \Pr[X = j \mid \mathcal{E}].$$

## 13.4 A Randomized Approximation Algorithm for MAX 3-SAT

In the previous section, we saw a number of ways in which linearity of expectation can be used to analyze a randomized process. We now describe an application of this idea to the design of an approximation algorithm. The problem we consider is a variation of the 3-SAT Problem, and we will see that one consequence of our randomized approximation algorithm is a surprisingly strong general statement about 3-SAT that on its surface seems to have nothing to do with either algorithms or randomization.

### 🖋 The Problem

When we studied NP-completeness, a core problem was 3-SAT: Given a set of clauses $C_1, \ldots, C_k$, each of length 3, over a set of variables $X = \{x_1, \ldots, x_n\}$, does there exist a satisfying truth assignment?

Intuitively, we can imagine such a problem arising in a system that tries to decide the truth or falsehood of statements about the world (the variables $\{x_i\}$), given pieces of information that relate them to one another (the clauses $\{C_j\}$). Now the world is a fairly contradictory place, and if our system gathers enough information, it could well end up with a set of clauses that has no satisfying truth assignment. What then?

A natural approach, if we can't find a truth assignment that satisfies all clauses, is to turn the 3-SAT instance into an optimization problem: Given the set of input clauses $C_1, \ldots, C_k$, find a truth assignment that satisfies *as many as possible*. We'll call this the *Maximum 3-Satisfiability Problem* (or *MAX 3-SAT* for short). Of course, this is an NP-hard optimization problem, since it's NP-complete to decide whether the maximum number of simultaneously satisfiable clauses is equal to $k$. Let's see what can be said about polynomial-time approximation algorithms.

## Designing and Analyzing the Algorithm

A remarkably simple randomized algorithm turns out to give a strong performance guarantee for this problem. Suppose we set each variable $x_1, \ldots, x_n$ independently to 0 or 1 with probability $\frac{1}{2}$ each. What is the expected number of clauses satisfied by such a random assignment?

Let $Z$ denote the random variable equal to the number of satisfied clauses. As in Section 13.3, let's decompose $Z$ into a sum of random variables that each take the value 0 or 1; specifically, let $Z_i = 1$ if the clause $C_i$ is satisfied, and 0 otherwise. Thus $Z = Z_1 + Z_2 + \cdots + Z_k$. Now $E[Z_i]$ is equal to the probability that $C_i$ is satisfied, and this can be computed easily as follows. In order for $C_i$ *not* to be satisfied, each of its three variables must be assigned the value that fails to make it true; since the variables are set independently, the probability of this is $(\frac{1}{2})^3 = \frac{1}{8}$. Thus clause $C_i$ is satisfied with probability $1 - \frac{1}{8} = \frac{7}{8}$, and so $E[Z_i] = \frac{7}{8}$.

Using linearity of expectation, we see that the expected number of satisfied clauses is $E[Z] = E[Z_1] + E[Z_2] + \cdots + E[Z_k] = \frac{7}{8}k$. Since no assignment can satisfy more than $k$ clauses, we have the following guarantee.

**(13.14)** *Consider a 3-SAT formula, where each clause has three different variables. The expected number of clauses satisfied by a random assignment is within an approximation factor $\frac{7}{8}$ of optimal.*

But, if we look at what really happened in the (admittedly simple) analysis of the random assignment, it's clear that something stronger is going on. For any random variable, there must be some point at which it assumes some value at least as large as its expectation. We've shown that for every instance of 3-SAT, a random truth assignment satisfies a $\frac{7}{8}$ fraction of all clauses in expectation; so, in particular, there must *exist* a truth assignment that satisfies a number of clauses that is at least as large as this expectation.

**(13.15)**  *For every instance of 3-SAT, there is a truth assignment that satisfies at least a $\frac{7}{8}$ fraction of all clauses.*

There is something genuinely surprising about the statement of (13.15). We have arrived at a nonobvious fact about 3-SAT—the existence of an assignment satisfying many clauses—whose statement has nothing to do with randomization; but we have done so by a randomized construction. And, in fact, the randomized construction provides what is quite possibly the simplest proof of (13.15). This is a fairly widespread principle in the area of combinatorics—namely, that one can show the existence of some structure by showing that a random construction produces it with positive probability. Constructions of this sort are said to be applications of the *probabilistic method*.

Here's a cute but minor application of (13.15): Every instance of 3-SAT with at most seven clauses is satisfiable. Why? If the instance has $k \leq 7$ clauses, then (13.15) implies that there is an assignment satisfying at least $\frac{7}{8}k$ of them. But when $k \leq 7$, it follows that $\frac{7}{8}k > k - 1$; and since the number of clauses satisfied by this assignment must be an integer, it must be equal to $k$. In other words, all clauses are satisfied.

## Further Analysis: Waiting to Find a Good Assignment

Suppose we aren't satisfied with a "one-shot" algorithm that produces a single assignment with a large number of satisfied clauses in expectation. Rather, we'd like a randomized algorithm whose expected running time is polynomial and that is guaranteed to output a truth assignment satisfying at least a $\frac{7}{8}$ fraction of all clauses.

A simple way to do this is to generate random truth assignments until one of them satisfies at least $\frac{7}{8}k$ clauses. We know that such an assignment exists, by (13.15); but how long will it take until we find one by random trials?

This is a natural place to apply the waiting-time bound we derived in (13.7). If we can show that the probability a random assignment satisfies at least $\frac{7}{8}k$ clauses is at least $p$, then the expected number of trials performed by the algorithm is $1/p$. So, in particular, we'd like to show that this quantity $p$ is at least as large as an inverse polynomial in $n$ and $k$.

For $j = 0, 1, 2, \ldots, k$, let $p_j$ denote the probability that a random assignment satisfies exactly $j$ clauses. So the expected number of clauses satisfied, by the definition of expectation, is equal to $\sum_{j=0}^{k} jp_j$; and by the previous analysis, this is equal to $\frac{7}{8}k$. We are interested in the quantity $p = \sum_{j \geq 7k/8} p_j$. How can we use the lower bound on the expected value to give a lower bound on this quantity?

We start by writing

$$\frac{7}{8}k = \sum_{j=0}^{k} jp_j = \sum_{j<7k/8} jp_j + \sum_{j\geq 7k/8} jp_j.$$

Now let $k'$ denote the largest natural number that is strictly smaller than $\frac{7}{8}k$. The right-hand side of the above equation only increases if we replace the terms in the first sum by $k'p_j$ and the terms in the second sum by $kp_j$. We also observe that $\sum_{j<7k/8} p_j = 1 - p$, and so

$$\frac{7}{8}k \leq \sum_{j<7k/8} k'p_j + \sum_{j\geq 7k/8} kp_j = k'(1-p) + kp \leq k' + kp,$$

and hence $kp \geq \frac{7}{8}k - k'$. But $\frac{7}{8}k - k' \geq \frac{1}{8}$, since $k'$ is a natural number strictly smaller than $\frac{7}{8}$ times another natural number, and so

$$p \geq \frac{\frac{7}{8}k - k'}{k} \geq \frac{1}{8k}.$$

This was our goal—to get a lower bound on $p$—and so by the waiting-time bound (13.7), we see that the expected number of trials needed to find the satisfying assignment we want is at most $8k$.

**(13.16)** *There is a randomized algorithm with polynomial expected running time that is guaranteed to produce a truth assignment satisfying at least a $\frac{7}{8}$ fraction of all clauses.*

# 13.5 Randomized Divide and Conquer: Median-Finding and Quicksort

We've seen the divide-and-conquer paradigm for designing algorithms at various earlier points in the book. Divide and conquer often works well in conjunction with randomization, and we illustrate this by giving divide-and-conquer algorithms for two fundamental problems: computing the median of $n$ numbers, and sorting. In each case, the "divide" step is performed using randomization; consequently, we will use expectations of random variables to analyze the time spent on recursive calls.

## The Problem: Finding the Median

Suppose we are given a set of $n$ numbers $S = \{a_1, a_2, \ldots, a_n\}$. Their *median* is the number that would be in the middle position if we were to sort them. There's an annoying technical difficulty if $n$ is even, since then there is no "middle position"; thus we define things precisely as follows: The median of $S = \{a_1, a_2, \ldots, a_n\}$ is equal to the $k^{\text{th}}$ largest element in $S$, where $k = (n + 1)/2$ if $n$ is odd, and $k = n/2$ if $n$ is even. In what follows, we'll assume for the sake of simplicity that all the numbers are distinct. Without this assumption, the problem becomes notationally more complicated, but no new ideas are brought into play.

It is clearly easy to compute the median in time $O(n \log n)$ if we simply sort the numbers first. But if one begins thinking about the problem, it's far from clear why sorting is *necessary* for computing the median, or even why $\Omega(n \log n)$ time is necessary. In fact, we'll show how a simple randomized approach, based on divide-and-conquer, yields an expected running time of $O(n)$.

### Designing the Algorithm

*A Generic Algorithm Based on Splitters*    The first key step toward getting an expected linear running time is to move from median-finding to the more general problem of *selection*. Given a set of $n$ numbers $S$ and a number $k$ between 1 and $n$, consider the function $\text{Select}(S, k)$ that returns the $k^{\text{th}}$ largest element in $S$. As special cases, $\text{Select}$ includes the problem of finding the median of $S$ via $\text{Select}(S, n/2)$ or $\text{Select}(S, (n + 1)/2)$; it also includes the easier problems of finding the minimum ($\text{Select}(S, 1)$) and the maximum ($\text{Select}(S, n)$). Our goal is to design an algorithm that implements $\text{Select}$ so that it runs in expected time $O(n)$.

The basic structure of the algorithm implementing $\text{Select}$ is as follows. We choose an element $a_i \in S$, the "splitter," and form the sets $S^- = \{a_j : a_j < a_i\}$ and $S^+ = \{a_j : a_j > a_i\}$. We can then determine which of $S^-$ or $S^+$ contains the $k^{\text{th}}$ largest element, and iterate only on this one. Without specifying yet how we plan to choose the splitter, here's a more concrete description of how we form the two sets and iterate.

```
Select(S,k):
   Choose a splitter a_i ∈ S
   For each element a_j of S
      Put a_j in S⁻ if a_j < a_i
      Put a_j in S⁺ if a_j > a_i
   Endfor
   If |S⁻| = k − 1 then
      The splitter a_i was in fact the desired answer
   Else if |S⁻| ≥ k then
      The kth largest element lies in S⁻
      Recursively call Select(S⁻, k)
```

```
    Else suppose |S⁻| = ℓ < k − 1
        The kᵗʰ largest element lies in S⁺
        Recursively call Select(S⁺, k − 1 − ℓ)
    Endif
```

Observe that the algorithm is always called recursively on a strictly smaller set, so it must terminate. Also, observe that if $|S| = 1$, then we must have $k = 1$, and indeed the single element in $S$ will be returned by the algorithm. Finally, from the choice of which recursive call to make, it's clear by induction that the right answer will be returned when $|S| > 1$ as well. Thus we have the following

**(13.17)** *Regardless of how the splitter is chosen, the algorithm above returns the $k^{th}$ largest element of S.*

**Choosing a Good Splitter** Now let's consider how the running time of Select depends on the way we choose the splitter. Assuming we can select a splitter in linear time, the rest of the algorithm takes linear time plus the time for the recursive call. But how is the running time of the recursive call affected by the choice of the splitter? Essentially, it's important that the splitter significantly reduce the size of the set being considered, so that we don't keep making passes through large sets of numbers many times. So a good choice of splitter should produce sets $S^-$ and $S^+$ that are approximately equal in size.

For example, if we could always choose the median as the splitter, then we could show a linear bound on the running time as follows. Let $cn$ be the running time for Select, not counting the time for the recursive call. Then, with medians as splitters, the running time $T(n)$ would be bounded by the recurrence $T(n) \leq T(n/2) + cn$. This is a recurrence that we encountered at the beginning of Chapter 5, where we showed that it has the solution $T(n) = O(n)$.

Of course, hoping to be able to use the median as the splitter is rather circular, since the median is what we want to compute in the first place! But, in fact, one can show that any "well-centered" element can serve as a good splitter: If we had a way to choose splitters $a_i$ such that there were at least $\varepsilon n$ elements both larger and smaller than $a_i$, for any fixed constant $\varepsilon > 0$, then the size of the sets in the recursive call would shrink by a factor of at least $(1 - \varepsilon)$ each time. Thus the running time $T(n)$ would be bounded by the recurrence $T(n) \leq T((1 - \varepsilon)n) + cn$. The same argument that showed the previous recurrence had the solution $T(n) = O(n)$ can be used here: If we unroll this recurrence for any $\varepsilon > 0$, we get

$$T(n) \leq cn + (1 - \varepsilon)cn + (1 - \varepsilon)^2 cn + \cdots = \left[ 1 + (1 - \varepsilon) + (1 - \varepsilon)^2 + \cdots \right]$$

$$cn \leq \frac{1}{\varepsilon} \cdot cn,$$

since we have a convergent geometric series.

Indeed, the only thing to really beware of is a very "off-center" splitter. For example, if we always chose the minimum element as the splitter, then we may end up with a set in the recursive call that's only one element smaller than we had before. In this case, the running time $T(n)$ would be bounded by the recurrence $T(n) \leq T(n-1) + cn$. Unrolling this recurrence, we see that there's a problem:

$$T(n) \leq cn + c(n - 1) + c(n - 2) + \cdots = \frac{cn(n + 1)}{2} = \Theta(n^2).$$

***Random Splitters***   Choosing a "well-centered" splitter, in the sense we have just defined, is certainly similar in flavor to our original problem of choosing the median; but the situation is really not so bad, since *any* well-centered splitter will do.

Thus we will implement the as-yet-unspecified step of selecting a splitter using the following simple rule:

Choose a splitter $a_i \in S$ uniformly at random

The intuition here is very natural: since a fairly large fraction of the elements are reasonably well-centered, we will be likely to end up with a good splitter simply by choosing an element at random.

The analysis of the running time with a random splitter is based on this idea; we expect the size of the set under consideration to go down by a fixed constant fraction every iteration, so we should get a convergent series and hence a linear bound as previously. We now show how to make this precise.

## Analyzing the Algorithm

We'll say that the algorithm is in *phase j* when the size of the set under consideration is at most $n(\frac{3}{4})^j$ but greater than $n(\frac{3}{4})^{j+1}$. Let's try to bound the expected time spent by the algorithm in phase $j$. In a given iteration of the algorithm, we say that an element of the set under consideration is *central* if at least a quarter of the elements are smaller than it and at least a quarter of the elements are larger than it.

Now observe that if a central element is chosen as a splitter, then at least a quarter of the set will be thrown away, the set will shrink by a factor of $\frac{3}{4}$ or better, and the current phase will come to an end. Moreover, half of all the elements in the set are central, and so the probability that our random choice of splitter produces a central element is $\frac{1}{2}$. Hence, by our simple waiting-time bound (13.7), the expected number of iterations before a central element is found is 2; and so the expected number of iterations spent in phase $j$, for any $j$, is at most 2.

This is pretty much all we need for the analysis. Let $X$ be a random variable equal to the number of steps taken by the algorithm. We can write it as the sum $X = X_0 + X_1 + X_2 + \cdots$, where $X_j$ is the expected number of steps spent by the algorithm in phase $j$. When the algorithm is in phase $j$, the set has size at most $n(\frac{3}{4})^j$, and so the number of steps required for one iteration in phase $j$ is at most $cn(\frac{3}{4})^j$ for some constant $c$. We have just argued that the expected number of iterations spent in phase $j$ is at most two, and hence we have $E[X_j] \leq 2cn(\frac{3}{4})^j$. Thus we can bound the total expected running time using linearity of expectation,

$$E[X] = \sum_j E[X_j] \leq \sum_j 2cn \left(\frac{3}{4}\right)^j = 2cn \sum_j \left(\frac{3}{4}\right)^j \leq 8cn,$$

since the sum $\sum_j (\frac{3}{4})^j$ is a geometric series that converges. Thus we have the following desired result.

**(13.18)** *The expected running time of* Select$(n, k)$ *is* $O(n)$.

## A Second Application: Quicksort

The randomized divide-and-conquer technique we used to find the median is also the basis of the sorting algorithm Quicksort. As before, we choose a splitter for the input set $S$, and separate $S$ into the elements below the splitter value and those above it. The difference is that, rather than looking for the median on just one side of the splitter, we sort both sides recursively and glue the two sorted pieces together (with the splitter in between) to produce the overall output. Also, we need to explicitly include a base case for the recursive code: we only use recursion on sets of size at least 4. A complete description of Quicksort is as follows.

```
Quicksort(S):
If |S| ≤ 3 then
    Sort S
    Output the sorted list
Else
    Choose a splitter a_i ∈ S uniformly at random
    For each element a_j of S
```

```
        Put  a_j  in  S^-  if  a_j < a_i
        Put  a_j  in  S^+  if  a_j > a_i
    Endfor
    Recursively call Quicksort(S^-) and Quicksort(S^+)
        Output the sorted set  S^- , then  a_i , then the sorted set  S^+
Endif
```

As with median-finding, the worst-case running time of this method is not so good. If we always select the smallest element as a splitter, then the running time $T(n)$ on $n$-element sets satisfies the same recurrence as before: $T(n) \leq T(n-1) + cn$, and so we end up with a time bound of $T(n) = \Theta(n^2)$. In fact, this is the worst-case running time for Quicksort.

On the positive side, if the splitters selected happened to be the medians of the sets at each iteration, then we get the recurrence $T(n) \leq 2T(n/2) + cn$, which arose frequently in the divide-and-conquer analyses of Chapter 5; the running time in this lucky case is $O(n \log n)$.

Here we are concerned with the *expected running time*; we will show that this can be bounded by $O(n \log n)$, almost as good as in the best case when the splitters are perfectly centered. Our analysis of Quicksort will closely follow the analysis of median-finding. Just as in the Select procedure that we used for median-finding, the crucial definition is that of a *central splitter*—one that divides the set so that each side contains at least a quarter of the elements. (As we discussed earlier, it is enough for the analysis that each side contains at least some fixed constant fraction of the elements; the use of a quarter here is chosen for convenience.) The idea is that a random choice is likely to lead to a central splitter, and central splitters work well. In the case of sorting, a central splitter divides the problem into two considerably smaller subproblems.

To simplify the presentation, we will slightly modify the algorithm so that it only issues its recursive calls when it finds a central splitter. Essentially, this modified algorithm differs from Quicksort in that it prefers to throw away an "off-center" splitter and try again; Quicksort, by contrast, launches the recursive calls even with an off-center splitter, and at least benefits from the work already done in splitting $S$. The point is that the expected running time of this modified algorithm can be analyzed very simply, by direct analogy with our analysis for median-finding. With a bit more work, a very similar but somewhat more involved analysis can also be done for the original Quicksort algorithm as well; however, we will not describe this analysis here.

```
Modified Quicksort(S):
If  |S| ≤ 3  then
    Sort  S
```

```
          Output the sorted list
      Endif
      Else
          While no central splitter has been found
              Choose a splitter a_i ∈ S uniformly at random
              For each element a_j of S
                  Put a_j in S^- if a_j < a_i
                  Put a_j in S^+ if a_j > a_i
              Endfor
              If |S^-| ≥ |S|/4 and |S^+| ≥ |S|/4 then
                  a_i is a central splitter
              Endif
          Endwhile
          Recursively call Quicksort(S^-) and Quicksort(S^+)
          Output the sorted set S^-, then a_i, then the sorted set S^+
      Endif
```

Consider a subproblem for some set $S$. Each iteration of the While loop selects a possible splitter $a_i$ and spends $O(|S|)$ time splitting the set and deciding if $a_i$ is central. Earlier we argued that the number of iterations needed until we find a central splitter is at most 2. This gives us the following statement.

**(13.19)** *The expected running time for the algorithm on a set S, excluding the time spent on recursive calls, is $O(|S|)$.*

The algorithm is called recursively on multiple subproblems. We will group these subproblems by size. We'll say that the subproblem is of *type j* if the size of the set under consideration is at most $n(\frac{3}{4})^j$ but greater than $n(\frac{3}{4})^{j+1}$. By (13.19), the expected time spent on a subproblem of type $j$, excluding recursive calls, is $O(n(\frac{3}{4})^j)$. To bound the overall running time, we need to bound the number of subproblems for each type $j$. Splitting a type $j$ subproblem via a central splitter creates two subproblems of higher type. So the subproblems of a given type $j$ are disjoint. This gives us a bound on the number of subproblems.

**(13.20)** *The number of type j subproblems created by the algorithm is at most $(\frac{4}{3})^{j+1}$.*

There are at most $(\frac{4}{3})^{j+1}$ subproblems of type $j$, and the expected time spent on each is $O(n(\frac{3}{4})^j)$ by (13.19). Thus, by linearity of expectation, the expected time spent on subproblems of type $j$ is $O(n)$. The number of different types is bounded by $\log_{\frac{4}{3}} n = O(\log n)$, which gives the desired bound.

**(13.21)** *The expected running time of* Modified Quicksort *is $O(n \log n)$.*

We considered this modified version of `Quicksort` to simplify the analysis. Coming back to the original `Quicksort`, our intuition suggests that the expected running time is no worse than in the modified algorithm, as accepting the noncentral splitters helps a bit with sorting, even if it does not help as much as when a central splitter is chosen. As mentioned earlier, one can in fact make this intuition precise, leading to an $O(n \log n)$ expected time bound for the original `Quicksort` algorithm; we will not go into the details of this here.

## 13.6 Hashing: A Randomized Implementation of Dictionaries

Randomization has also proved to be a powerful technique in the design of data structures. Here we discuss perhaps the most fundamental use of randomization in this setting, a technique called *hashing* that can be used to maintain a dynamically changing set of elements. In the next section, we will show how an application of this technique yields a very simple algorithm for a problem that we saw in Chapter 5—the problem of finding the closest pair of points in the plane.

### The Problem

One of the most basic applications of data structures is to simply maintain a set of elements that changes over time. For example, such applications could include a large company maintaining the set of its current employees and contractors, a news indexing service recording the first paragraphs of news articles it has seen coming across the newswire, or a search algorithm keeping track of the small part of an exponentially large search space that it has already explored.

In all these examples, there is a *universe $U$* of possible elements that is extremely large: the set of all possible people, all possible paragraphs (say, up to some character length limit), or all possible solutions to a computationally hard problem. The data structure is trying to keep track of a set $S \subseteq U$ whose size is generally a negligible fraction of $U$, and the goal is to be able to insert and delete elements from $S$ and quickly determine whether a given element belongs to $S$.

We will call a data structure that accomplishes this a *dictionary*. More precisely, a dictionary is a data structure that supports the following operations.

- `MakeDictionary`. This operation initializes a fresh dictionary that can maintain a subset $S$ of $U$; the dictionary starts out empty.

- `Insert(u)` adds element $u \in U$ to the set $S$. In many applications, there may be some additional information that we want to associate with $u$

(for example, $u$ may be the name or ID number of an employee, and we want to also store some personal information about this employee), and we will simply imagine this being stored in the dictionary as part of a record together with $u$. (So, in general, when we talk about the element $u$, we really mean $u$ and any additional information stored with $u$.)

- $\texttt{Delete}(u)$ removes element $u$ from the set $S$, if it is currently present.
- $\texttt{Lookup}(u)$ determines whether $u$ currently belongs to $S$; if it does, it also retrieves any additional information stored with $u$.

Many of the implementations we've discussed earlier in the book involve (most of) these operations: For example, in the implementation of the BFS and DFS graph traversal algorithms, we needed to maintain the set $S$ of nodes already visited. But there is a fundamental difference between those problems and the present setting, and that is the size of $U$. The universe $U$ in BFS or DFS is the set of nodes $V$, which is already given explicitly as part of the input. Thus it is completely feasible in those cases to maintain a set $S \subseteq U$ as we did there: defining an array with $|U|$ positions, one for each possible element, and setting the array position for $u$ equal to 1 if $u \in S$, and equal to 0 if $u \notin S$. This allows for insertion, deletion, and lookup of elements in constant time per operation, by simply accessing the desired array entry.

Here, by contrast, we are considering the setting in which the universe $U$ is enormous. So we are not going to be able to use an array whose size is anywhere near that of $U$. The fundamental question is whether, in this case, we can still implement a dictionary to support the basic operations almost as quickly as when $U$ was relatively small.

We now describe a randomized technique called *hashing* that addresses this question. While we will not be able to do quite as well as the case in which it is feasible to define an array over all of $U$, hashing will allow us to come quite close.

## Designing the Data Structure

As a motivating example, let's think a bit more about the problem faced by an automated service that processes breaking news. Suppose you're receiving a steady stream of short articles from various wire services, weblog postings, and so forth, and you're storing the lead paragraph of each article (truncated to at most 1,000 characters). Because you're using many sources for the sake of full coverage, there's a lot of redundancy: the same article can show up many times.

When a new article shows up, you'd like to quickly check whether you've seen the lead paragraph before. So a dictionary is exactly what you want for this problem: The universe $U$ is the set of all strings of length at most 1,000 (or of length exactly 1,000, if we pad them out with blanks), and we're maintaining a set $S \subseteq U$ consisting of strings (i.e., lead paragraphs) that we've seen before.

One solution would be to keep a linked list of all paragraphs, and scan this list each time a new one arrives. But a Lookup operation in this case takes time proportional to $|S|$. How can we get back to something that looks like an array-based solution?

**Hash Functions**    The basic idea of hashing is to work with an array of size $|S|$, rather than one comparable to the (astronomical) size of $U$.

Suppose we want to be able to store a set $S$ of size up to $n$. We will set up an array $H$ of size $n$ to store the information, and use a function $h : U \rightarrow \{0, 1, \dots, n-1\}$ that maps elements of $U$ to array positions. We call such a function $h$ a *hash function*, and the array $H$ a *hash table*. Now, if we want to add an element $u$ to the set $S$, we simply place $u$ in position $h(u)$ of the array $H$. In the case of storing paragraphs of text, we can think of $h(\cdot)$ as computing some kind of numerical signature or "check-sum" of the paragraph $u$, and this tells us the array position at which to store $u$.

This would work extremely well if, for all distinct $u$ and $v$ in our set $S$, it happened to be the case that $h(u) \neq h(v)$. In such a case, we could look up $u$ in constant time: when we check array position $H[h(u)]$, it would either be empty or would contain just $u$.

In general, though, we cannot expect to be this lucky: there can be distinct elements $u, v \in S$ for which $h(u) = h(v)$. We will say that these two elements *collide*, since they are mapped to the same place in $H$. There are a number of ways to deal with collisions. Here we will assume that each position $H[i]$ of the hash table stores a linked list of all elements $u \in S$ with $h(u) = i$. The operation Lookup($u$) would now work as follows.

- Compute the hash function $h(u)$.
- Scan the linked list at position $H[h(u)]$ to see if $u$ is present in this list.

Hence the time required for Lookup($u$) is proportional to the time to compute $h(u)$, plus the length of the linked list at $H[h(u)]$. And this latter quantity, in turn, is just the number of elements in $S$ that collide with $u$. The Insert and Delete operations work similarly: Insert adds $u$ to the linked list at position $H[h(u)]$, and Delete scans this list and removes $u$ if it is present.

So now the goal is clear: We'd like to find a hash function that "spreads out" the elements being added, so that no one entry of the hash table $H$ contains too many elements. This is not a problem for which worst-case analysis is very informative. Indeed, suppose that $|U| \geq n^2$ (we're imagining applications where it's much larger than this). Then, for any hash function $h$ that we choose, there will be some set $S$ of $n$ elements that all map to the same position. In the worst case, we will insert all the elements of this set, and then our Lookup operations will consist of scanning a linked list of length $n$.

Our main goal here is to show that randomization can help significantly for this problem. As usual, we won't make any assumptions about the set of elements $S$ being random; we will simply exploit randomization in the design of the hash function. In doing this, we won't be able to completely avoid collisions, but can make them relatively rare enough, and so the lists will be quite short.

***Choosing a Good Hash Function***   We've seen that the efficiency of the dictionary is based on the choice of the hash function $h$. Typically, we will think of $U$ as a large set of numbers, and then use an easily computable function $h$ that maps each number $u \in U$ to some value in the smaller range of integers $\{0, 1, \ldots, n - 1\}$. There are many simple ways to do this: we could use the first or last few digits of $u$, or simply take $u$ modulo $n$. While these simple choices may work well in many situations, it is also possible to get large numbers of collisions. Indeed, a fixed choice of hash function may run into problems because of the types of elements $u$ encountered in the application: Maybe the particular digits we use to define the hash function encode some property of $u$, and hence maybe only a few options are possible. Taking $u$ modulo $n$ can have the same problem, especially if $n$ is a power of 2. To take a concrete example, suppose we used a hash function that took an English paragraph, used a standard character encoding scheme like ASCII to map it to a sequence of bits, and then kept only the first few bits in this sequence. We'd expect a huge number of collisions at the array entries corresponding to the bit strings that encoded common English words like *The*, while vast portions of the array can be occupied only by paragraphs that begin with strings like *qxf*, and hence will be empty.

A slightly better choice in practice is to take ($u \bmod p$) for a prime number $p$ that is approximately equal to $n$. While in some applications this may yield a good hashing function, it may not work well in all applications, and some primes may work much better than others (for example, primes very close to powers of 2 may not work so well).

Since hashing has been widely used in practice for a long time, there is a lot of experience with what makes for a good hash function, and many hash functions have been proposed that tend to work well empirically. Here we would like to develop a hashing scheme where we can prove that it results in efficient dictionary operations with high probability.

The basic idea, as suggested earlier, is to use randomization in the construction of $h$. First let's consider an extreme version of this: for every element $u \in U$, when we go to insert $u$ into $S$, we select a value $h(u)$ uniformly at random in the set $\{0, 1, \ldots, n - 1\}$, independently of all previous choices. In this case, the probability that two randomly selected values $h(u)$ and $h(v)$ are equal (and hence cause a collision) is quite small.

**(13.22)** *With this uniform random hashing scheme, the probability that two randomly selected values $h(u)$ and $h(v)$ collide—that is, that $h(u) = h(v)$—is exactly $1/n$.*

**Proof.** Of the $n^2$ possible choices for the pair of values $(h(u), h(v))$, all are equally likely, and exactly $n$ of these choices results in a collision.    ■

However, it will not work to use a hash function with independently random chosen values. To see why, suppose we inserted $u$ into $S$, and then later want to perform either Delete($u$) or Lookup($u$). We immediately run into the "Where did I put it?" problem: We will need to know the random value $h(u)$ that we used, so we will need to have stored the value $h(u)$ in some form where we can quickly look it up. But this is exactly the same problem we were trying to solve in the first place.

There are two things that we can learn from (13.22). First, it provides a concrete basis for the intuition from practice that hash functions that spread things around in a "random" way can be effective at reducing collisions. Second, and more crucial for our goals here, we will be able to show how a more controlled use of randomization achieves performance as good as suggested in (13.22), but in a way that leads to an efficient dictionary implementation.

***Universal Classes of Hash Functions***    The key idea is to choose a hash function at random not from the collection of all possible functions into $[0, n - 1]$, but from a carefully selected class of functions. Each function $h$ in our class of functions $\mathcal{H}$ will map the universe $U$ into the set $\{0, 1, \ldots, n - 1\}$, and we will design it so that it has two properties. First, we'd like it to come with the guarantee from (13.22):

- For any pair of elements $u, v \in U$, the probability that a randomly chosen $h \in \mathcal{H}$ satisfies $h(u) = h(v)$ is at most $1/n$.

We say that a class $\mathcal{H}$ of functions is *universal* if it satisfies this first property. Thus (13.22) can be viewed as saying that the class of all possible functions from $U$ into $\{0, 1, \ldots, n - 1\}$ is universal.

However, we also need $\mathcal{H}$ to satisfy a second property. We will state this slightly informally for now and make it more precise later.

- Each $h \in \mathcal{H}$ can be compactly represented and, for a given $h \in \mathcal{H}$ and $u \in U$, we can compute the value $h(u)$ efficiently.

The class of all possible functions failed to have this property: Essentially, the only way to represent an arbitrary function from $U$ into $\{0, 1, \ldots, n-1\}$ is to write down the value it takes on every single element of $U$.

In the remainder of this section, we will show the surprising fact that there exist classes $\mathcal{H}$ that satisfy both of these properties. Before we do this, we first make precise the basic property we need from a universal class of hash functions. We argue that if a function $h$ is selected at random from a universal class of hash functions, then in any set $S \subset U$ of size at most $n$, and any $u \in U$, the expected number of items in $S$ that collide with $u$ is a constant.

---

**(13.23)** *Let $\mathcal{H}$ be a universal class of hash functions mapping a universe $U$ to the set $\{0, 1, \ldots, n-1\}$, let $S$ be an arbitrary subset of $U$ of size at most $n$, and let $u$ be any element in $U$. We define $X$ to be a random variable equal to the number of elements $s \in S$ for which $h(s) = h(u)$, for a random choice of hash function $h \in \mathcal{H}$. (Here $S$ and $u$ are fixed, and the randomness is in the choice of $h \in \mathcal{H}$.) Then $E[X] \leq 1$.*

---

**Proof.** For an element $s \in S$, we define a random variable $X_s$ that is equal to 1 if $h(s) = h(u)$, and equal to 0 otherwise. We have $E[X_s] = \Pr[X_s = 1] \leq 1/n$, since the class of functions is universal.

Now $X = \sum_{s \in S} X_s$, and so, by linearity of expectation, we have

$$E[X] = \sum_{s \in S} E[X_s] \leq |S| \cdot \frac{1}{n} \leq 1. \quad \blacksquare$$

*Designing a Universal Class of Hash Functions* Next we will design a universal class of hash functions. We will use a prime number $p \approx n$ as the size of the hash table $H$. To be able to use integer arithmetic in designing our hash functions, we will identify the universe with vectors of the form $x = (x_1, x_2, \ldots x_r)$ for some integer $r$, where $0 \leq x_i < p$ for each $i$. For example, we can first identify $U$ with integers in the range $[0, N-1]$ for some $N$, and then use consecutive blocks of $\lfloor \log p \rfloor$ bits of $u$ to define the corresponding coordinates $x_i$. If $U \subseteq [0, N-1]$, then we will need a number of coordinates $r \approx \log N / \log n$.

Let $\mathcal{A}$ be the set of all vectors of the form $a = (a_1, \ldots, a_r)$, where $a_i$ is an integer in the range $[0, p-1]$ for each $i = 1, \ldots, r$. For each $a \in \mathcal{A}$, we define the linear function

$$h_a(x) = \left( \sum_{i=1}^{r} a_i x_i \right) \bmod p.$$

This now completes our random implementation of dictionaries. We define the family of hash functions to be $\mathcal{H} = \{h_a : a \in \mathcal{A}\}$. To execute MakeDictionary, we choose a random hash function from $\mathcal{H}$; in other words, we choose a random vector from $\mathcal{A}$ (by choosing each coordinate uniformly at random), and form the function $h_a$. Note that in order to define $\mathcal{A}$, we need to find a prime number $p \geq n$. There are methods for generating prime numbers quickly, which we will not go into here. (In practice, this can also be accomplished using a table of known prime numbers, even for relatively large $n$.)

We then use this as the hash function with which to implement Insert, Delete, and Lookup. The family $\mathcal{H} = \{h_a : a \in \mathcal{A}\}$ satisfies a formal version of the second property we were seeking: It has a compact representation, since by simply choosing and remembering a random $a \in \mathcal{A}$, we can compute $h_a(u)$ for all elements $u \in U$. Thus, to show that $\mathcal{H}$ leads to an efficient, hashing-based implementation of dictionaries, we just need to establish that $\mathcal{H}$ is a universal family of hash functions.

### Analyzing the Data Structure

If we are using a hash function $h_a$ from the class $\mathcal{H}$ that we've defined, then a collision $h_a(x) = h_a(y)$ defines a linear equation modulo the prime number $p$. In order to analyze such equations, it's useful to have the following "cancellation law."

**(13.24)** *For any prime $p$ and any integer $z \neq 0$ mod $p$, and any two integers $\alpha, \beta$, if $\alpha z = \beta z$ mod $p$, then $\alpha = \beta$ mod $p$.*

**Proof.** Suppose $\alpha z = \beta z$ mod $p$. Then, by rearranging terms, we get $z(\alpha - \beta) = 0$ mod $p$, and hence $z(\alpha - \beta)$ is divisible by $p$. But $z \neq 0$ mod $p$, so $z$ is not divisible by $p$. Since $p$ is prime, it follows that $\alpha - \beta$ must be divisible by $p$; that is, $\alpha = \beta$ mod $p$ as claimed. ■

We now use this to prove the main result in our analysis.

**(13.25)** *The class of linear functions $\mathcal{H}$ defined above is universal.*

**Proof.** Let $x = (x_1, x_2, \ldots x_r)$ and $y = (y_1, y_2, \ldots y_r)$ be two distinct elements of $U$. We need to show that the probability of $h_a(x) = h_a(y)$, for a randomly chosen $a \in A$, is at most $1/p$.

Since $x \neq y$, then there must be an index $j$ such that $x_j \neq y_j$. We now consider the following way of choosing the random vector $a \in \mathcal{A}$. We first choose all the coordinates $a_i$ where $i \neq j$. Then, finally, we choose coordinate $a_j$. We will show that regardless of how all the other coordinates $a_i$ were chosen, the probability of $h_a(x) = h_a(y)$, taken over the final choice of $a_j$, is exactly $1/p$. It will follow that the probability of $h_a(x) = h_a(y)$ over the random choice of the full vector $a$ must be $1/p$ as well.

This conclusion is intuitively clear: If the probability is $1/p$ regardless of how we choose all other $a_i$, then it is $1/p$ overall. There is also a direct proof of this using conditional probabilities. Let $\mathcal{E}$ be the event that $h_a(x) = h_a(y)$, and let $\mathcal{F}_b$ be the event that all coordinates $a_i$ (for $i \neq j$) receive a sequence of values $b$. We will show, below, that $\Pr\left[\mathcal{E} \mid \mathcal{F}_b\right] = 1/p$ for all $b$. It then follows that $\Pr\left[\mathcal{E}\right] = \sum_b \Pr\left[\mathcal{E} \mid \mathcal{F}_b\right] \cdot \Pr\left[\mathcal{F}_b\right] = (1/p) \sum_b \Pr\left[\mathcal{F}_b\right] = 1/p$.

So, to conclude the proof, we assume that values have been chosen arbitrarily for all other coordinates $a_i$, and we consider the probability of selecting $a_j$ so that $h_a(x) = h_a(y)$. By rearranging terms, we see that $h_a(x) = h_a(y)$ if and only if

$$a_j(y_j - x_j) = \sum_{i \neq j} a_i(x_i - y_i) \bmod p.$$

Since the choices for all $a_i$ ($i \neq j$) have been fixed, we can view the right-hand side as some fixed quantity $m$. Also, let us define $z = y_j - x_j$.

Now it is enough to show that there is exactly one value $0 \leq a_j < p$ that satisfies $a_j z = m \bmod p$; indeed, if this is the case, then there is a probability of exactly $1/p$ of choosing this value for $a_j$. So suppose there were two such values, $a_j$ and $a_j'$. Then we would have $a_j z = a_j' z \bmod p$, and so by (13.24) we would have $a_j = a_j' \bmod p$. But we assumed that $a_j, a_j' < p$, and so in fact $a_j$ and $a_j'$ would be the same. It follows that there is only one $a_j$ in this range that satisfies $a_j z = m \bmod p$.

Tracing back through the implications, this means that the probability of choosing $a_j$ so that $h_a(x) = h_a(y)$ is $1/p$, however we set the other coordinates $a_i$ in $a$; thus the probability that $x$ and $y$ collide is $1/p$. Thus we have shown that $\mathcal{H}$ is a universal class of hash functions. ∎

## 13.7 Finding the Closest Pair of Points: A Randomized Approach

In Chapter 5, we used the divide-and-conquer technique to develop an $O(n \log n)$ time algorithm for the problem of finding the closest pair of points in the plane. Here we will show how to use randomization to develop a different algorithm for this problem, using an underlying dictionary data structure. We will show that this algorithm runs in $O(n)$ expected time, plus $O(n)$ expected dictionary operations.

There are several related reasons why it is useful to express the running time of our algorithm in this way, accounting for the dictionary operations separately. We have seen in Section 13.6 that dictionaries have a very efficient implementation using hashing, so abstracting out the dictionary operations allows us to treat the hashing as a "black box" and have the algorithm inherit an overall running time from whatever performance guarantee is satisfied by this hashing procedure. A concrete payoff of this is the following. It has been shown that with the right choice of hashing procedure (more powerful, and more complicated, than what we described in Section 13.6), one can make the underlying dictionary operations run in linear expected time as well, yielding an overall expected running time of $O(n)$. Thus the randomized approach we describe here leads to an improvement over the running time of the divide-and-conquer algorithm that we saw earlier. We will talk about the ideas that lead to this $O(n)$ bound at the end of the section.

It is worth remarking at the outset that randomization shows up for two independent reasons in this algorithm: the way in which the algorithm processes the input points will have a random component, regardless of how the dictionary data structure is implemented; and when the dictionary is implemented using hashing, this introduces an additional source of randomness as part of the hash-table operations. Expressing the running time via the number of dictionary operations allows us to cleanly separate the two uses of randomness.

### The Problem

Let us start by recalling the problem's (very simple) statement. We are given $n$ points in the plane, and we wish to find the pair that is closest together. As discussed in Chapter 5, this is one of the most basic geometric *proximity* problems, a topic with a wide range of applications.

We will use the same notation as in our earlier discussion of the closest-pair problem. We will denote the set of points by $P = \{p_1, \ldots, p_n\}$, where $p_i$ has coordinates $(x_i, y_i)$; and for two points $p_i, p_j \in P$, we use $d(p_i, p_j)$ to denote the standard Euclidean distance between them. Our goal is to find the pair of points $p_i, p_j$ that minimizes $d(p_i, p_j)$.

To simplify the discussion, we will assume that the points are all in the unit square: $0 \leq x_i, y_i < 1$ for all $i = 1, \ldots, n$. This is no loss of generality: in linear time, we can rescale all the $x$- and $y$-coordinates of the points so that they lie in a unit square, and then we can translate them so that this unit square has its lower left corner at the origin.

### Designing the Algorithm

The basic idea of the algorithm is very simple. We'll consider the points in random order, and maintain a current value $\delta$ for the closest pair as we process the points in this order. When we get to a new point $p$, we look "in the vicinity" of $p$ to see if any of the previously considered points are at a distance less than $\delta$ from $p$. If not, then the closest pair hasn't changed, and we move on to the next point in the random order. If there is a point within a distance less than $\delta$ from $p$, then the closest pair has changed, and we will need to update it.

The challenge in turning this into an efficient algorithm is to figure out how to implement the task of looking for points in the vicinity of $p$. It is here that the dictionary data structure will come into play.

We now begin making this more concrete. Let us assume for simplicity that the points in our random order are labeled $p_1, \ldots, p_n$. The algorithm proceeds in stages; during each stage, the closest pair remains constant. The first stage starts by setting $\delta = d(p_1, p_2)$, the distance of the first two points. The goal of a stage is to either verify that $\delta$ is indeed the distance of the closest pair of points, or to find a pair of points $p_i, p_j$ with $d(p_i, p_j) < \delta$. During a stage, we'll gradually add points in the order $p_1, p_2, \ldots, p_n$. The stage terminates when we reach a point $p_i$ so that for some $j < i$, we have $d(p_i, p_j) < \delta$. We then let $\delta$ for the next stage be the closest distance found so far: $\delta = \min_{j:j<i} d(p_i, p_j)$.

The number of stages used will depend on the random order. If we get lucky, and $p_1, p_2$ are the closest pair of points, then a single stage will do. It is also possible to have as many as $n - 2$ stages, if adding a new point always decreases the minimum distance. We'll show that the expected running time of the algorithm is within a constant factor of the time needed in the first, lucky case, when the original value of $\delta$ is the smallest distance.

***Testing a Proposed Distance*** The main subroutine of the algorithm is a method to test whether the current pair of points with distance $\delta$ remains the closest pair when a new point is added and, if not, to find the new closest pair.

The idea of the verification is to subdivide the unit square (the area where the points lie) into subsquares whose sides have length $\delta/2$, as shown in Figure 13.2. Formally, there will be $N^2$ subsquares, where $N = \lceil 1/(2\delta) \rceil$: for $0 \leq s \leq N - 1$ and $1 \leq t \leq N - 1$, we define the subsquare $S_{st}$ as

$$S_{st} = \{(x, y) : s\delta/2 \leq x < (s + 1)\delta/2; t\delta/2 \leq y < (t + 1)\delta/2\}.$$

We claim that this collection of subsquares has two nice properties for our purposes. First, any two points that lie in the same subsquare have distance less than $\delta$. Second, and a partial converse to this, any two points that are less than $\delta$ away from each other must fall in either the same subsquare or in very close subsquares.

**(13.26)** *If two points $p$ and $q$ belong to the same subsquare $S_{st}$, then $d(p, q) < \delta$.*

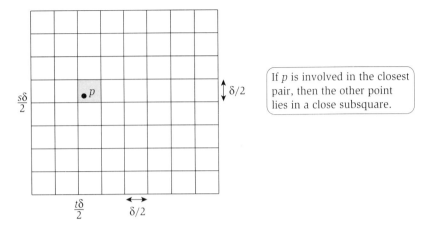

**Figure 13.2** Dividing the square into size $\delta/2$ subsquares. The point $p$ lies in the subsquare $S_{st}$.

**Proof.** If points $p$ and $q$ are in the same subsquare, then both coordinates of the two points differ by at most $\delta/2$, and hence $d(p,q) \leq \sqrt{(\delta/2)^2 + (\delta/2)^2} = \delta/\sqrt{2} < \delta$, as required. ∎

Next we say that subsquares $S_{st}$ and $S_{s't'}$ are *close* if $|s - s'| \leq 2$ and $|t - t'| \leq 2$. (Note that a subsquare is close to itself.)

**(13.27)**  *If for two points $p, q \in P$ we have $d(p,q) < \delta$, then the subsquares containing them are close.*

**Proof.** Consider two points $p, q \in P$ belonging to subsquares that are not close; assume $p \in S_{st}$ and $q \in S_{s't'}$, where one of $s, s'$ or $t, t'$ differs by more than 2. It follows that in one of their respective $x$- or $y$-coordinates, $p$ and $q$ differ by at least $\delta$, and so we cannot have $d(p,q) < \delta$. ∎

Note that for any subsquare $S_{st}$, the set of subsquares close to it form a $5 \times 5$ grid around it. Thus we conclude that there are at most 25 subsquares close to $S_{st}$, counting $S_{st}$ itself. (There will be fewer than 25 if $S_{st}$ is at the edge of the unit square containing the input points.)

Statements (13.26) and (13.27) suggest the basic outline of our algorithm. Suppose that, at some point in the algorithm, we have proceeded partway through the random order of the points and seen $P' \subseteq P$, and suppose that we know the minimum distance among points in $P'$ to be $\delta$. For each of the points in $P'$, we keep track of the subsquare containing it.

Now, when the next point $p$ is considered, we determine which of the subsquares $S_{st}$ it belongs to. If $p$ is going to cause the minimum distance to change, there must be some earlier point $p' \in P'$ at distance less than $\delta$ from it; and hence, by (13.27), the point $p'$ must be in one of the 25 squares around the square $S_{st}$ containing $p$. So we will simply check each of these 25 squares one by one to see if it contains a point in $P'$; for each point in $P'$ that we find this way, we compute its distance to $p$. By (13.26), each of these subsquares contains at most one point of $P'$, so this is at most a constant number of distance computations. (Note that we used a similar idea, via (5.10), at a crucial point in the divide-and-conquer algorithm for this problem in Chapter 5.)

***A Data Structure for Maintaining the Subsquares*** The high-level description of the algorithm relies on being able to name a subsquare $S_{st}$ and quickly determine which points of $P$, if any, are contained in it. A dictionary is a natural data structure for implementing such operations. The *universe U* of possible elements is the set of all subsquares, and the set $S$ maintained by the data structure will be the subsquares that contain points from among the set $P'$ that we've seen so far. Specifically, for each point $p' \in P'$ that we have seen so far, we keep the subsquare containing it in the dictionary, tagged with the index of $p'$. We note that $N^2 = \lceil 1/(2\delta) \rceil^2$ will, in general, be much larger than $n$, the number of points. Thus we are in the type of situation considered in Section 13.6 on hashing, where the universe of possible elements (the set of all subsquares) is much larger than the number of elements being indexed (the subsquares containing an input point seen thus far).

Now, when we consider the next point $p$ in the random order, we determine the subsquare $S_{st}$ containing it and perform a Lookup operation for each of the 25 subsquares close to $S_{st}$. For any points discovered by these Lookup operations, we compute the distance to $p$. If none of these distances are less than $\delta$, then the closest distance hasn't changed; we insert $S_{st}$ (tagged with $p$) into the dictionary and proceed to the next point.

However, if we find a point $p'$ such that $\delta' = d(p, p') < \delta$, then we need to update our closest pair. This updating is a rather dramatic activity: Since the value of the closest pair has dropped from $\delta$ to $\delta'$, our entire collection of subsquares, and the dictionary supporting it, has become useless—it was, after all, designed only to be useful if the minimum distance was $\delta$. We therefore invoke `MakeDictionary` to create a new, empty dictionary that will hold subsquares whose side lengths are $\delta'/2$. For each point seen thus far, we determine the subsquare containing it (in this new collection of subsquares), and we insert this subsquare into the dictionary. Having done all this, we are again ready to handle the next point in the random order.

***Summary of the Algorithm***    We have now actually described the algorithm in full. To recap:

---

Order the points in a random sequence $p_1, p_2, \ldots, p_n$
Let $\delta$ denote the minimum distance found so far
Initialize $\delta = d(p_1, p_2)$
Invoke MakeDictionary for storing subsquares of side length $\delta/2$
For $i = 1, 2, \ldots, n$:
   Determine the subsquare $S_{st}$ containing $p_i$
   Look up the 25 subsquares close to $p_i$
   Compute the distance from $p_i$ to any points found in these subsquares
   If there is a point $p_j$ $(j < i)$ such that $\delta' = d(p_j, p_i) < \delta$ then
     Delete the current dictionary
     Invoke MakeDictionary for storing subsquares of side length $\delta'/2$
     For each of the points $p_1, p_2, \ldots, p_i$:
       Determine the subsquare of side length $\delta'/2$ that contains it
       Insert this subsquare into the new dictionary
     Endfor
   Else
     Insert $p_i$ into the current dictionary
   Endif
Endfor

---

## Analyzing the Algorithm

There are already some things we can say about the overall running time of the algorithm. To consider a new point $p_i$, we need to perform only a constant number of Lookup operations and a constant number of distance computations. Moreover, even if we had to update the closest pair in every iteration, we'd only do $n$ MakeDictionary operations.

The missing ingredient is the total expected cost, over the course of the algorithm's execution, due to reinsertions into new dictionaries when the closest pair is updated. We will consider this next. For now, we can at least summarize the current state of our knowledge as follows.

**(13.28)**    *The algorithm correctly maintains the closest pair at all times, and it performs at most $O(n)$ distance computations, $O(n)$ Lookup operations, and $O(n)$ MakeDictionary operations.*

We now conclude the analysis by bounding the expected number of Insert operations. Trying to find a good bound on the total expected number of Insert operations seems a bit problematic at first: An update to the closest pair in iteration $i$ will result in $i$ insertions, and so each update comes at a high cost once $i$ gets large. Despite this, we will show the surprising fact that the expected number of insertions is only $O(n)$. The intuition here is that, even as the cost of updates becomes steeper as the iterations proceed, these updates become correspondingly less likely.

Let $X$ be a random variable specifying the number of Insert operations performed; the value of this random variable is determined by the random order chosen at the outset. We are interested in bounding $E[X]$, and as usual in this type of situation, it is helpful to break $X$ down into a sum of simpler random variables. Thus let $X_i$ be a random variable equal to 1 if the $i^{th}$ point in the random order causes the minimum distance to change, and equal to 0 otherwise.

Using these random variables $X_i$, we can write a simple formula for the total number of Insert operations. Each point is inserted once when it is first encountered; and $i$ points need to be reinserted if the minimum distance changes in iteration $i$. Thus we have the following claim.

**(13.29)** *The total number of* Insert *operations performed by the algorithm is* $n + \sum_i iX_i$.

Now we bound the probability $\Pr[X_i = 1]$ that considering the $i^{th}$ point causes the minimum distance to change.

**(13.30)** $\Pr[X_i = 1] \leq 2/i$.

**Proof.** Consider the first $i$ points $p_1, p_2, \ldots, p_i$ in the random order. Assume that the minimum distance among these points is achieved by $p$ and $q$. Now the point $p_i$ can only cause the minimum distance to decrease if $p_i = p$ or $p_i = q$. Since the first $i$ points are in a random order, any of them is equally likely to be last, so the probability that $p$ or $q$ is last is $2/i$. ∎

Note that $2/i$ is only an upper bound in (13.30) because there could be multiple pairs among the first $i$ points that define the same smallest distance.

By (13.29) and (13.30), we can bound the total number of Insert operations as

$$E[X] = n + \sum_i i \cdot E[X_i] \leq n + 2n = 3n.$$

Combining this with (13.28), we obtain the following bound on the running time of the algorithm.

**(13.31)** *In expectation, the randomized closest-pair algorithm requires* $O(n)$ *time plus* $O(n)$ *dictionary operations.*

## Achieving Linear Expected Running Time

Up to this point, we have treated the dictionary data structure as a black box, and in (13.31) we bounded the running time of the algorithm in terms of computational time plus dictionary operations. We now want to give a bound on the actual expected running time, and so we need to analyze the work involved in performing these dictionary operations.

To implement the dictionary, we'll use a universal hashing scheme, like the one discussed in Section 13.6. Once the algorithm employs a hashing scheme, it is making use of randomness in two distinct ways: First, we randomly order the points to be added; and second, for each new minimum distance $\delta$, we apply randomization to set up a new hash table using a universal hashing scheme.

When inserting a new point $p_i$, the algorithm uses the hash-table Lookup operation to find all nodes in the 25 subsquares close to $p_i$. However, if the hash table has collisions, then these 25 Lookup operations can involve inspecting many more than 25 nodes. Statement (13.23) from Section 13.6 shows that each such Lookup operation involves considering $O(1)$ previously inserted points, in expectation. It seems intuitively clear that performing $O(n)$ hash-table operations in expectation, each of which involves considering $O(1)$ elements in expectation, will result in an expected running time of $O(n)$ overall. To make this intuition precise, we need to be careful with how these two sources of randomness interact.

**(13.32)** *Assume we implement the randomized closest-pair algorithm using a universal hashing scheme. In expectation, the total number of points considered during the* Lookup *operations is bounded by* $O(n)$.

**Proof.** From (13.31) we know that the expected number of Lookup operations is $O(n)$, and from (13.23) we know that each of these Lookup operations involves considering only $O(1)$ points in expectation. In order to conclude that this implies the expected number of points considered is $O(n)$, we now consider the relationship between these two sources of randomness.

Let $X$ be a random variable denoting the number of Lookup operations performed by the algorithm. Now the random order $\sigma$ that the algorithm chooses for the points completely determines the sequence of minimum-distance values the algorithm will consider and the sequence of dictionary operations it will perform. As a result, the choice of $\sigma$ determines the value of $X$; we let $X(\sigma)$ denote this value, and we let $\mathcal{E}_\sigma$ denote the event the algorithm chooses the random order $\sigma$. Note that the conditional expectation $E\left[X \mid \mathcal{E}_\sigma\right]$ is equal to $X(\sigma)$. Also, by (13.31), we know that $E\left[X\right] \le c_0 n$, for some constant $c_0$.

Now consider this sequence of Lookup operations for a fixed order $\sigma$. For $i = 1, \ldots, X(\sigma)$, let $Y_i$ be the number of points that need to be inspected during the $i^{\text{th}}$ Lookup operations—namely, the number of previously inserted points that collide with the dictionary entry involved in this Lookup operation. We would like to bound the expected value of $\sum_{i=1}^{X(\sigma)} Y_i$, where expectation is over both the random choice of $\sigma$ and the random choice of hash function.

By (13.23), we know that $E\left[Y_i \mid \mathcal{E}_\sigma\right] = O(1)$ for all $\sigma$ and all values of $i$. It is useful to be able to refer to the constant in the expression $O(1)$ here, so we will say that $E\left[Y_i \mid \mathcal{E}_\sigma\right] \leq c_1$ for all $\sigma$ and all values of $i$. Summing over all $i$, and using linearity of expectation, we get $E\left[\sum_i Y_i \mid \mathcal{E}_\sigma\right] \leq c_1 X(\sigma)$. Now we have

$$E\left[\sum_{i=1}^{X(\sigma)} Y_i\right] = \sum_\sigma \Pr\left[\mathcal{E}_\sigma\right] E\left[\sum_i Y_i \mid \mathcal{E}_\sigma\right]$$

$$\leq \sum_\sigma \Pr\left[\mathcal{E}_\sigma\right] \cdot c_1 X(\sigma)$$

$$= c_1 \sum_\sigma E\left[X \mid \mathcal{E}_\sigma\right] \cdot \Pr\left[\mathcal{E}_\sigma\right] = c_1 E\left[X\right].$$

Since we know that $E[X]$ is at most $c_0 n$, the total expected number of points considered is at most $c_0 c_1 n = O(n)$, which proves the claim. ∎

Armed with this claim, we can use the universal hash functions from Section 13.6 in our closest-pair algorithm. In expectation, the algorithm will consider $O(n)$ points during the Lookup operations. We have to set up multiple hash tables—a new one each time the minimum distance changes—and we have to compute $O(n)$ hash-function values. All hash tables are set up for the same size, a prime $p \geq n$. We can select one prime and use the same table throughout the algorithm. Using this, we get the following bound on the running time.

**(13.33)** *In expectation, the algorithm uses $O(n)$ hash-function computations and $O(n)$ additional time for finding the closest pair of points.*

Note the distinction between this statement and (13.31). There we counted each dictionary operation as a single, atomic step; here, on the other hand, we've conceptually opened up the dictionary operations so as to account for the time incurred due to hash-table collisions and hash-function computations.

Finally, consider the time needed for the $O(n)$ hash-function computations. How fast is it to compute the value of a universal hash function $h$? The class of universal hash functions developed in Section 13.6 breaks numbers in our universe $U$ into $r \approx \log N / \log n$ smaller numbers of size $O(\log n)$ each, and then uses $O(r)$ arithmetic operations on these smaller numbers to compute the hash-function value. So computing the hash value of a single point involves $O(\log N/\log n)$ multiplications, on numbers of size $\log n$. This is a total of $O(n \log N/\log n)$ arithmetic operations over the course of the algorithm, more than the $O(n)$ we were hoping for.

In fact, it is possible to decrease the number of arithmetic operations to $O(n)$ by using a more sophisticated class of hash functions. There are other classes of universal hash functions where computing the hash-function value can be done by only $O(1)$ arithmetic operations (though these operations will have to be done on larger numbers, integers of size roughly $\log N$). This class of improved hash functions also comes with one extra difficulty for this application: the hashing scheme needs a prime that is bigger than the size of the universe (rather than just the size of the set of points). Now the universe in this application grows inversely with the minimum distance $\delta$, and so, in particular, it increases every time we discover a new, smaller minimum distance. At such points, we will have to find a new prime and set up a new hash table. Although we will not go into the details of this here, it is possible to deal with these difficulties and make the algorithm achieve an expected running time of $O(n)$.

## 13.8 Randomized Caching

We now discuss the use of randomization for the caching problem, which we first encountered in Chapter 4. We begin by developing a class of algorithms, the *marking algorithms*, that include both deterministic and randomized approaches. After deriving a general performance guarantee that applies to all marking algorithms, we show how a stronger guarantee can be obtained for a particular marking algorithm that exploits randomization.

### 🖋 The Problem

We begin by recalling the *Cache Maintenance Problem* from Chapter 4. In the most basic setup, we consider a processor whose full memory has $n$ addresses; it is also equipped with a *cache* containing $k$ slots of memory that can be accessed very quickly. We can keep copies of $k$ items from the full memory in the cache slots, and when a memory location is accessed, the processor will first check the cache to see if it can be quickly retrieved. We say the request is a *cache hit* if the cache contains the requested item; in this case, the access is very quick. We say the request is a *cache miss* if the requested item is not in the cache; in this case, the access takes much longer, and moreover, one of the items currently in the cache must be *evicted* to make room for the new item. (We will assume that the cache is kept full at all times.)

The goal of a Cache Maintenance Algorithm is to minimize the number of cache misses, which are the truly expensive part of the process. The sequence of memory references is not under the control of the algorithm—this is simply dictated by the application that is running—and so the job of the algorithms we consider is simply to decide on an *eviction policy*: Which item currently in the cache should be evicted on each cache miss?

In Chapter 4, we saw a greedy algorithm that is optimal for the problem: Always evict the item that will be needed the *farthest in the future*. While this algorithm is useful to have as an absolute benchmark on caching performance, it clearly cannot be implemented under real operating conditions, since we don't know ahead of time when each item will be needed next. Rather, we need to think about eviction policies that operate *online*, using only information about past requests without knowledge of the future.

The eviction policy that is typically used in practice is to evict the item that was used the least recently (i.e., whose most recent access was the longest ago in the past); this is referred to as the Least-Recently-Used, or LRU, policy. The empirical justification for LRU is that algorithms tend to have a certain locality in accessing data, generally using the same set of data frequently for a while. If a data item has not been accessed for a long time, this is a sign that it may not be accessed again for a long time.

Here we will evaluate the performance of different eviction policies without making any assumptions (such as locality) on the sequence of requests. To do this, we will compare the number of misses made by an eviction policy on a sequence $\sigma$ with the minimum number of misses it is possible to make on $\sigma$. We will use $f(\sigma)$ to denote this latter quantity; it is the number of misses achieved by the optimal Farthest-in-Future policy. Comparing eviction policies to the optimum is very much in the spirit of providing performance guarantees for approximation algorithms, as we did in Chapter 11. Note, however, the following interesting difference: the reason the optimum was not attainable in our approximation analyses from that chapter (assuming $\mathcal{P} \neq \mathcal{NP}$) is that the algorithms were constrained to run in polynomial time; here, on the other hand, the eviction policies are constrained in their pursuit of the optimum by the fact that they do not know the requests that are coming in the future.

For eviction policies operating under this online constraint, it initially seems hopeless to say something interesting about their performance: Why couldn't we just design a request sequence that completely confounds any online eviction policy? The surprising point here is that it is in fact possible to give absolute guarantees on the performance of various online policies relative to the optimum.

We first show that the number of misses incurred by LRU, on any request sequence, can be bounded by roughly $k$ times the optimum. We then use randomization to develop a variation on LRU that has an exponentially stronger bound on its performance: Its number of misses is never more than $O(\log k)$ times the optimum.

### Designing the Class of Marking Algorithms

The bounds for both LRU and its randomized variant will follow from a general template for designing online eviction policies—a class of policies called *marking algorithms*. They are motivated by the following intuition. To do well against the benchmark of $f(\sigma)$, we need an eviction policy that is sensitive to the difference between the following two possibilities: (a) in the recent past, the request sequence has contained more than $k$ distinct items; or (b) in the recent past, the request sequence has come exclusively from a set of at most $k$ items. In the first case, we know that $f(\sigma)$ must be increasing, since no algorithm can handle more than $k$ distinct items without incurring a cache miss. But, in the second case, it's possible that $\sigma$ is passing through a long stretch in which an optimal algorithm need not incur any misses at all. It is here that our policy must make sure that it incurs very few misses.

Guided by these considerations, we now describe the basic outline of a marking algorithm, which prefers evicting items that don't seem to have been used in a long time. Such an algorithm operates in *phases*; the description of one phase is as follows.

```
Each memory item can be either marked or unmarked
At the beginning of the phase, all items are unmarked
On a request to item s:
   Mark s
   If s is in the cache, then evict nothing
   Else s is not in the cache:
      If all items currently in the cache are marked then
         Declare the phase over
         Processing of s is deferred to start of next phase
      Else evict an unmarked item from the cache
      Endif
   Endif
```

Note that this describes a class of algorithms, rather than a single specific algorithm, because the key step—evict an unmarked item from the cache—does not specify which unmarked item should be selected. We will see that eviction policies with different properties and performance guarantees arise depending on how we resolve this ambiguity.

We first observe that, since a phase starts with all items unmarked, and items become marked only when accessed, the unmarked items have all been accessed less recently than the marked items. This is the sense in which a marking algorithm is trying to evict items that have not been requested recently. Also, at any point in a phase, if there are any unmarked items in the cache, then the least recently used item must be unmarked. It follows that the LRU policy evicts an unmarked item whenever one is available, and so we have the following fact.

**(13.34)**    *The LRU policy is a marking algorithm.*

### ✎ Analyzing Marking Algorithms

We now describe a method for analyzing marking algorithms, ending with a bound on performance that applies to all marking algorithms. After this, when we add randomization, we will need to strengthen this analysis.

Consider an arbitrary marking algorithm operating on a request sequence $\sigma$. For the analysis, we picture an optimal caching algorithm operating on $\sigma$ alongside this marking algorithm, incurring an overall cost of $f(\sigma)$. Suppose that there are $r$ phases in this sequence $\sigma$, as defined by the marking algorithm.

To make the analysis easier to discuss, we are going to "pad" the sequence $\sigma$ both at the beginning and the end with some extra requests; these will not add any extra misses to the optimal algorithm—that is, they will not cause $f(\sigma)$ to increase—and so any bound we show on the performance of the marking algorithm relative to the optimum for this padded sequence will also apply to $\sigma$. Specifically, we imagine a "phase 0" that takes place before the first phase, in which all the items initially in the cache are requested once. This does not affect the cost of either the marking algorithm or the optimal algorithm. We also imagine that the final phase $r$ ends with an epilogue in which every item currently in the cache of the optimal algorithm is requested twice in round-robin fashion. This does not increase $f(\sigma)$; and by the end of the second pass through these items, the marking algorithm will contain each of them in its cache, and each will be marked.

For the performance bound, we need two things: an upper bound on the number of misses incurred by the marking algorithm, and a lower bound saying that the optimum must incur at least a certain number of misses.

The division of the request sequence $\sigma$ into phases turns out to be the key to doing this. First of all, here is how we can picture the history of a phase, from the marking algorithm's point of view. At the beginning of the phase, all items are unmarked. Any item that is accessed during the phase is marked, and it then remains in the cache for the remainder of the phase. Over the course of the phase, the number of marked items grows from 0 to $k$, and the next phase begins with a request to a $(k+1)^{\text{st}}$ item, different from all of these marked items. We summarize some conclusions from this picture in the following claim.

**(13.35)** *In each phase, $\sigma$ contains accesses to exactly $k$ distinct items. The subsequent phase begins with an access to a different $(k+1)^{\text{st}}$ item.*

Since an item, once marked, remains in the cache until the end of the phase, the marking algorithm cannot incur a miss for an item more than once in a phase. Combined with (13.35), this gives us an upper bound on the number of misses incurred by the marking algorithm.

**(13.36)** *The marking algorithm incurs at most $k$ misses per phase, for a total of at most $kr$ misses over all $r$ phases.*

As a lower bound on the optimum, we have the following fact.

**(13.37)** *The optimum incurs at least $r - 1$ misses. In other words, $f(\sigma) \geq r - 1$.*

**Proof.** Consider any phase but the last one, and look at the situation just after the first access (to an item $s$) in this phase. Currently $s$ is in the cache maintained by the optimal algorithm, and (13.35) tells us that the remainder of the phase will involve accesses to $k - 1$ other distinct items, and the first access of the next phase will involve a $k^{\text{th}}$ other item as well. Let $S$ be this set of $k$ items other than $s$. We note that at least one of the members of $S$ is not currently in the cache maintained by the optimal algorithm (since, with $s$ there, it only has room for $k - 1$ other items), and the optimal algorithm will incur a miss the first time this item is accessed.

What we've shown, therefore, is that for every phase $j < r$, the sequence from the second access in phase $j$ through the first access in phase $j + 1$ involves at least one miss by the optimum. This makes for a total of at least $r - 1$ misses.
■

Combining (13.36) and (13.37), we have the following performance guarantee.

**(13.38)** *For any marking algorithm, the number of misses it incurs on any sequence $\sigma$ is at most $k \cdot f(\sigma) + k$.*

**Proof.** The number of misses incurred by the marking algorithm is at most

$$kr = k(r-1) + k \leq k \cdot f(\sigma) + k,$$

where the final inequality is just (13.37). ∎

Note that the "$+k$" in the bound of (13.38) is just an additive constant, independent of the length of the request sequence $\sigma$, and so the key aspect of the bound is the factor of $k$ relative to the optimum. To see that this factor of $k$ is the best bound possible for some marking algorithms, and for LRU in particular, consider the behavior of LRU on a request sequence in which $k+1$ items are repeatedly requested in a round-robin fashion. LRU will each time evict the item that will be needed just in the next step, and hence it will incur a cache miss on each access. (It's possible to get this kind of terrible caching performance in practice for precisely such a reason: the program is executing a loop that is just slightly too big for the cache.) On the other hand, the optimal policy, evicting the page that will be requested farthest in the future, incurs a miss only every $k$ steps, so LRU incurs a factor of $k$ more misses than the optimal policy.

### Designing a Randomized Marking Algorithm

The bad example for LRU that we just saw implies that, if we want to obtain a better bound for an online caching algorithm, we will not be able to reason about fully general marking algorithms. Rather, we will define a simple *Randomized Marking Algorithm* and show that it never incurs more than $O(\log k)$ times the number of misses of the optimal algorithm—an exponentially better bound.

Randomization is a natural choice in trying to avoid the unfortunate sequence of "wrong" choices in the bad example for LRU. To get this bad sequence, we needed to define a sequence that always evicted precisely the wrong item. By randomizing, a policy can make sure that, "on average," it is throwing out an unmarked item that will at least not be needed right away.

Specifically, where the general description of a marking contained the line

```
Else evict an unmarked item from the cache
```

without specifying how this unmarked item is to be chosen, our Randomized Marking Algorithm uses the following rule:

```
Else evict an unmarked item chosen uniformly at random
      from the cache
```

This is arguably the simplest way to incorporate randomization into the marking framework.[1]

## Analyzing the Randomized Marking Algorithm

Now we'd like to get a bound for the Randomized Marking Algorithm that is stronger than (13.38); but in order to do this, we need to extend the analysis in (13.36) and (13.37) to something more subtle. This is because there are sequences $\sigma$, with $r$ phases, where the Randomized Marking Algorithm can really be made to incur $kr$ misses—just consider a sequence that never repeats an item. But the point is that, on such sequences, the optimum will incur many more than $r - 1$ misses. We need a way to bring the upper and lower bounds closer together, based on the structure of the sequence.

This picture of a "runaway sequence" that never repeats an item is an extreme instance of the distinction we'd like to draw: It is useful to classify the unmarked items in the middle of a phase into two further categories. We call an unmarked item *fresh* if it was not marked in the previous phase either, and we call it *stale* if it was marked in the previous phase.

Recall the picture of a single phase that led to (13.35): The phase begins with all items unmarked, and it contains accesses to $k$ distinct items, each of which goes from unmarked to marked the first time it is accessed. Among these $k$ accesses to unmarked items in phase $j$, let $c_j$ denote the number of these that are to fresh items.

To strengthen the result from (13.37), which essentially said that the optimum incurs at least one miss per phase, we provide a bound in terms of the number of fresh items in a phase.

**(13.39)**    $f(\sigma) \geq \frac{1}{2} \sum_{j=1}^{r} c_j.$

**Proof.** Let $f_j(\sigma)$ denote the number of misses incurred by the optimal algorithm in phase $j$, so that $f(\sigma) = \sum_{j=1}^{r} f_j(\sigma)$. From (13.35), we know that in any phase $j$, there are requests to $k$ distinct items. Moreover, by our definition of *fresh*, there are requests to $c_{j+1}$ further items in phase $j + 1$; so between phases $j$ and $j + 1$, there are at least $k + c_{j+1}$ distinct items requested. It follows that the optimal algorithm must incur at least $c_{j+1}$ misses over the course of phases $j$

---

[1] It is not, however, the simplest way to incorporate randomization into a caching algorithm. We could have considered the *Purely Random Algorithm* that dispenses with the whole notion of marking, and on each cache miss selects one of its $k$ current items for eviction uniformly at random. (Note the difference: The Randomized Marking Algorithm randomizes only over the unmarked items.) Although we won't prove this here, the Purely Random Algorithm can incur at least $c$ times more misses than the optimum, for any constant $c < k$, and so it does not lead to an improvement over LRU.

and $j + 1$, so $f_j(\sigma) + f_{j+1}(\sigma) \geq c_{j+1}$. This holds even for $j = 0$, since the optimal algorithm incurs $c_1$ misses in phase 1. Thus we have

$$\sum_{j=0}^{r-1} (f_j(\sigma) + f_{j+1}(\sigma)) \geq \sum_{j=0}^{r-1} c_{j+1}.$$

But the left-hand side is at most $2\sum_{j=1}^{r} f_j(\sigma) = 2f(\sigma)$, and the right-hand side is $\sum_{j=1}^{r} c_j$. ∎

We now give an upper bound on the expected number of misses incurred by the Randomized Marking Algorithm, also quantified in terms of the number of fresh items in each phase. Combining these upper and lower bounds will yield the performance guarantee we're seeking. In the following statement, let $M_\sigma$ denote the random variable equal to the number of cache misses incurred by the Randomized Marking Algorithm on the request sequence $\sigma$.

**(13.40)** *For every request sequence $\sigma$, we have $E\left[M_\sigma\right] \leq H(k) \sum_{j=1}^{r} c_j$.*

**Proof.** Recall that we used $c_j$ to denote the number of requests in phase $j$ to fresh items. There are $k$ requests to unmarked items in a phase, and each unmarked item is either fresh or stale, so there must be $k - c_j$ requests in phase $j$ to unmarked stale items.

Let $X_j$ denote the number of misses incurred by the Randomized Marking Algorithm in phase $j$. Each request to a fresh item results in a guaranteed miss for the Randomized Marking Algorithm; since the fresh item was not marked in the previous phase, it cannot possibly be in the cache when it is requested in phase $j$. Thus the Randomized Marking Algorithm incurs at least $c_j$ misses in phase $j$ because of requests to fresh items.

Stale items, by contrast, are a more subtle matter. The phase starts with $k$ stale items in the cache; these are the items that were unmarked *en masse* at the beginning of the phase. On a request to a stale item $s$, the concern is whether the Randomized Marking Algorithm evicted it earlier in the phase and now incurs a miss as it has to bring it back in. What is the probability that the $i^{\text{th}}$ request to a stale item, say $s$, results in a miss? Suppose that there have been $c \leq c_j$ requests to fresh items thus far in the phase. Then the cache contains the $c$ formerly fresh items that are now marked, $i - 1$ formerly stale items that are now marked, and $k - c - i + 1$ items that are stale and not yet marked in this phase. But there are $k - i + 1$ items overall that are still stale; and since exactly $k - c - i + 1$ of them are in the cache, the remaining $c$ of them are not. Each of the $k - i + 1$ stale items is equally likely to be no longer in the cache, and so $s$ is not in the cache at this moment with probability $\frac{c}{k-i+1} \leq \frac{c_j}{k-i+1}$.

This is the probability of a miss on the request to $s$. Summing over all requests to unmarked items, we have

$$E\left[X_j\right] \le c_j + \sum_{i=1}^{k-c_j} \frac{c_j}{k-i+1} \le c_j \left[1 + \sum_{\ell=c_j+1}^{k} \frac{1}{\ell}\right] = c_j(1 + H(k) - H(c_j)) \le c_j H(k).$$

Thus the total expected number of misses incurred by the Randomized Marking Algorithm is

$$E\left[M_\sigma\right] = \sum_{j=1}^{r} E\left[X_j\right] \le H(k) \sum_{j=1}^{r} c_j. \quad \blacksquare$$

Combining (13.39) and (13.40), we immediately get the following performance guarantee.

**(13.41)**   *The expected number of misses incurred by the Randomized Marking Algorithm is at most* $2H(k) \cdot f(\sigma) = O(\log k) \cdot f(\sigma)$.

## 13.9 Chernoff Bounds

In Section 13.3, we defined the expectation of a random variable formally and have worked with this definition and its consequences ever since. Intuitively, we have a sense that the value of a random variable ought to be "near" its expectation with reasonably high probability, but we have not yet explored the extent to which this is true. We now turn to some results that allow us to reach conclusions like this, and see a sampling of the applications that follow.

We say that two random variables $X$ and $Y$ are *independent* if, for any values $i$ and $j$, the events $\Pr[X = i]$ and $\Pr[Y = j]$ are independent. This definition extends naturally to larger sets of random variables. Now consider a random variable $X$ that is a sum of several independent 0-1-valued random variables: $X = X_1 + X_2 + \cdots + X_n$, where $X_i$ takes the value 1 with probability $p_i$, and the value 0 otherwise. By linearity of expectation, we have $E[X] = \sum_{i=1}^{n} p_i$. Intuitively, the independence of the random variables $X_1, X_2, \ldots, X_n$ suggests that their fluctuations are likely to "cancel out," and so their sum $X$ will have a value close to its expectation with high probability. This is in fact true, and we state two concrete versions of this result: one bounding the probability that $X$ deviates above $E[X]$, the other bounding the probability that $X$ deviates below $E[X]$. We call these results *Chernoff bounds*, after one of the probabilists who first established bounds of this form.

**(13.42)** *Let* $X, X_1, X_2, \ldots, X_n$ *be defined as above, and assume that* $\mu \geq E[X]$. *Then, for any* $\delta > 0$, *we have*

$$\Pr[X > (1+\delta)\mu] < \left[\frac{e^{\delta}}{(1+\delta)^{(1+\delta)}}\right]^{\mu}.$$

**Proof.** To bound the probability that $X$ exceeds $(1+\delta)\mu$, we go through a sequence of simple transformations. First note that, for any $t > 0$, we have $\Pr[X > (1+\delta)\mu] = \Pr\left[e^{tX} > e^{t(1+\delta)\mu}\right]$, as the function $f(x) = e^{tx}$ is monotone in $x$. We will use this observation with a $t$ that we'll select later.

Next we use some simple properties of the expectation. For a random variable $Y$, we have $\gamma \Pr[Y > \gamma] \leq E[Y]$, by the definition of the expectation. This allows us to bound the probability that $Y$ exceeds $\gamma$ in terms of $E[Y]$. Combining these two ideas, we get the following inequalities.

$$\Pr[X > (1+\delta)\mu] = \Pr\left[e^{tX} > e^{t(1+\delta)\mu}\right] \leq e^{-t(1+\delta)\mu}E\left[e^{tX}\right].$$

Next we need to bound the expectation $E\left[e^{tX}\right]$. Writing $X$ as $X = \sum_i X_i$, the expectation is $E\left[e^{tX}\right] = E\left[e^{t\sum_i X_i}\right] = E\left[\prod_i e^{tX_i}\right]$. For independent variables $Y$ and $Z$, the expectation of the product $YZ$ is $E[YZ] = E[Y]E[Z]$. The variables $X_i$ are independent, so we get $E\left[\prod_i e^{tX_i}\right] = \prod_i E\left[e^{tX_i}\right]$.

Now, $e^{tX_i}$ is $e^t$ with probability $p_i$ and $e^0 = 1$ otherwise, so its expectation can be bounded as

$$E\left[e^{tX_i}\right] = p_i e^t + (1 - p_i) = 1 + p_i(e^t - 1) \leq e^{p_i(e^t - 1)},$$

where the last inequality follows from the fact that $1 + \alpha \leq e^{\alpha}$ for any $\alpha \geq 0$. Combining the inequalities, we get the following bound.

$$\Pr[X > (1+\delta)\mu] \leq e^{-t(1+\delta)\mu}E\left[e^{tX}\right] = e^{-t(1+\delta)\mu}\prod_i E\left[e^{tX_i}\right]$$

$$\leq e^{-t(1+\delta)\mu}\prod_i e^{p_i(e^t - 1)} \leq e^{-t(1+\delta)\mu}e^{\mu(e^t - 1)}.$$

To obtained the bound claimed by the statement, we substitute $t = \ln(1+\delta)$. ∎

Where (13.42) provided an upper bound, showing that $X$ is not likely to deviate far above its expectation, the next statement, (13.43), provides a lower bound, showing that $X$ is not likely to deviate far below its expectation. Note that the statements of the results are not symmetric, and this makes sense: For the upper bound, it is interesting to consider values of $\delta$ much larger than 1, while this would not make sense for the lower bound.

**(13.43)**   *Let $X, X_1, X_2, \ldots, X_n$ and $\mu$ be as defined above, and assume that $\mu \leq E[X]$. Then for any $1 > \delta > 0$, we have*

$$\Pr\left[X < (1 - \delta)\mu\right] < e^{-\frac{1}{2}\mu\delta^2}.$$

The proof of (13.43) is similar to the proof of (13.42), and we do not give it here. For the applications that follow, the statements of (13.42) and (13.43), rather than the internals of their proofs, are the key things to keep in mind.

## 13.10 Load Balancing

In Section 13.1, we considered a distributed system in which communication among processes was difficult, and randomization to some extent replaced explicit coordination and synchronization. We now revisit this theme through another stylized example of randomization in a distributed setting.

### The Problem

Suppose we have a system in which $m$ jobs arrive in a stream and need to be processed immediately. We have a collection of $n$ identical processors that are capable of performing the jobs; so the goal is to assign each job to a processor in a way that balances the workload evenly across the processors. If we had a central controller for the system that could receive each job and hand it off to the processors in round-robin fashion, it would be trivial to make sure that each processor received at most $\lceil m/n \rceil$ jobs—the most even balancing possible.

But suppose the system lacks the coordination or centralization to implement this. A much more lightweight approach would be to simply assign each job to one of the processors uniformly at random. Intuitively, this should also balance the jobs evenly, since each processor is equally likely to get each job. At the same time, since the assignment is completely random, one doesn't expect everything to end up perfectly balanced. So we ask: How well does this simple randomized approach work?

Although we will stick to the motivation in terms of jobs and processors here, it is worth noting that comparable issues come up in the analysis of hash functions, as we saw in Section 13.6. There, instead of assigning jobs to processors, we're assigning elements to entries in a hash table. The concern about producing an even balancing in the case of hash tables is based on wanting to keep the number of collisions at any particular entry relatively small. As a result, the analysis in this section is also relevant to the study of hashing schemes.

## Analyzing a Random Allocation

We will see that the analysis of our random load balancing process depends on the relative sizes of $m$, the number of jobs, and $n$, the number of processors. We start with a particularly clean case: when $m = n$. Here it is possible for each processor to end up with exactly one job, though this is not very likely. Rather, we expect that some processors will receive no jobs and others will receive more than one. As a way of assessing the quality of this randomized load balancing heuristic, we study how heavily loaded with jobs a processor can become.

Let $X_i$ be the random variable equal to the number of jobs assigned to processor $i$, for $i = 1, 2, \ldots, n$. It is easy to determine the expected value of $X_i$: We let $Y_{ij}$ be the random variable equal to 1 if job $j$ is assigned to processor $i$, and 0 otherwise; then $X_i = \sum_{i=1}^{n} Y_{ij}$ and $E\left[Y_{ij}\right] = 1/n$, so $E\left[X_i\right] = \sum_{j=1}^{n} E\left[Y_{ij}\right] = 1$. But our concern is with how far $X_i$ can deviate above its expectation: What is the probability that $X_i > c$? To give an upper bound on this, we can directly apply (13.42): $X_i$ is a sum of independent 0-1-valued random variables $\{Y_{ij}\}$; we have $\mu = 1$ and $1 + \delta = c$. Thus the following statement holds.

**(13.44)**

$$\Pr\left[X_i > c\right] < \left(\frac{e^{c-1}}{c^c}\right).$$

In order for there to be a small probability of *any* $X_i$ exceeding $c$, we will take the Union Bound over $i = 1, 2, \ldots, n$; and so we need to choose $c$ large enough to drive $\Pr\left[X_i > c\right]$ down well below $1/n$ for each $i$. This requires looking at the denominator $c^c$ in (13.44). To make this denominator large enough, we need to understand how this quantity grows with $c$, and we explore this by first asking the question: What is the $x$ such that $x^x = n$?

Suppose we write $\gamma(n)$ to denote this number $x$. There is no closed-form expression for $\gamma(n)$, but we can determine its asymptotic value as follows. If $x^x = n$, then taking logarithms gives $x \log x = \log n$; and taking logarithms again gives $\log x + \log \log x = \log \log n$. Thus we have

$$2 \log x > \log x + \log \log x = \log \log n > \tfrac{1}{2} \log x,$$

and, using this to divide through the equation $x \log x = \log n$, we get

$$\frac{1}{2}x \leq \frac{\log n}{\log \log n} \leq x = \gamma(n).$$

Thus $\gamma(n) = \Theta\left(\dfrac{\log n}{\log \log n}\right).$

Now, if we set $c = e\gamma(n)$, then by (13.44) we have

$$\Pr\left[X_i > c\right] < \left(\frac{e^{c-1}}{c^c}\right) < \left(\frac{e}{c}\right)^c = \left(\frac{1}{\gamma(n)}\right)^{e\gamma(n)} < \left(\frac{1}{\gamma(n)}\right)^{2\gamma(n)} = \frac{1}{n^2}.$$

Thus, applying the Union Bound over this upper bound for $X_1, X_2, \ldots, X_n$, we have the following.

**(13.45)** *With probability at least $1 - n^{-1}$, no processor receives more than $e\gamma(n) = \Theta\left(\frac{\log n}{\log\log n}\right)$ jobs.*

With a more involved analysis, one can also show that this bound is asymptotically tight: with high probability, some processor actually receives $\Omega\left(\frac{\log n}{\log\log n}\right)$ jobs.

So, although the load on some processors will likely exceed the expectation, this deviation is only logarithmic in the number of processors.

***Increasing the Number of Jobs*** We now use Chernoff bounds to argue that, as more jobs are introduced into the system, the loads "smooth out" rapidly, so that the number of jobs on each processor quickly become the same to within constant factors.

Specifically, if we have $m = 16n \ln n$ jobs, then the expected load per processor is $\mu = 16 \ln n$. Using (13.42), we see that the probability of any processor's load exceeding $32 \ln n$ is at most

$$\Pr\left[X_i > 2\mu\right] < \left(\frac{e}{4}\right)^{16 \ln n} < \left(\frac{1}{e^2}\right)^{\ln n} = \frac{1}{n^2}.$$

Also, the probability that any processor's load is below $8 \ln n$ is at most

$$\Pr\left[X_i < \frac{1}{2}\mu\right] < e^{-\frac{1}{2}\left(\frac{1}{2}\right)^2(16 \ln n)} = e^{-2 \ln n} = \frac{1}{n^2}.$$

Thus, applying the Union Bound, we have the following.

**(13.46)** *When there are $n$ processors and $\Omega(n \log n)$ jobs, then with high probability, every processor will have a load between half and twice the average.*

## 13.11 Packet Routing

We now consider a more complex example of how randomization can alleviate contention in a distributed system—namely, in the context of *packet routing*.

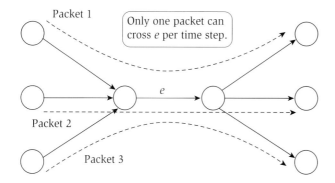

**Figure 13.3** Three packets whose paths involve a shared edge $e$.

## The Problem

*Packet routing* is a mechanism to support communication among nodes of a large network, which we can model as a directed graph $G = (V, E)$. If a node $s$ wants to send data to a node $t$, this data is discretized into one or more *packets*, each of which is then sent over an *s-t* path $P$ in the network. At any point in time, there may be many packets in the network, associated with different sources and destinations and following different paths. However, the key constraint is that a single edge $e$ can only transmit a single packet per time step. Thus, when a packet $p$ arrives at an edge $e$ on its path, it may find there are several other packets already waiting to traverse $e$; in this case, $p$ joins a *queue* associated with $e$ to wait until $e$ is ready to transmit it. In Figure 13.3, for example, three packets with different sources and destinations all want to traverse edge $e$; so, if they all arrive at $e$ at the same time, some of them will be forced to wait in a queue for this edge.

Suppose we are given a network $G$ with a set of packets that need to be sent across specified paths. We'd like to understand how many steps are necessary in order for all packets to reach their destinations. Although the paths for the packets are all specified, we face the algorithmic question of timing the movements of the packets across the edges. In particular, we must decide when to release each packet from its source, as well as a *queue management policy* for each edge $e$—that is, how to select the next packet for transmission from $e$'s queue in each time step.

It's important to realize that these *packet scheduling* decisions can have a significant effect on the amount of time it takes for all the packets to reach their destinations. For example, let's consider the tree network in Figure 13.4, where there are nine packets that want to traverse the respective dotted paths up the tree. Suppose all packets are released from their sources immediately, and each edge $e$ manages its queue by always transmitting the packet that is

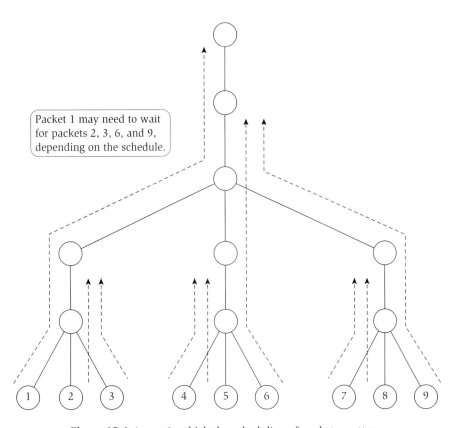

**Figure 13.4** A case in which the scheduling of packets matters.

closest to its destination. In this case, packet 1 will have to wait for packets 2 and 3 at the second level of the tree; and then later it will have to wait for packets 6 and 9 at the fourth level of the tree. Thus it will take nine steps for this packet to reach its destination. On the other hand, suppose that each edge $e$ manages its queue by always transmitting the packet that is farthest from its destination. Then packet 1 will never have to wait, and it will reach its destination in five steps; moreover, one can check that every packet will reach its destination within six steps.

There is a natural generalization of the tree network in Figure 13.4, in which the tree has height $h$ and the nodes at every other level have $k$ children. In this case, the queue management policy that always transmits the packet nearest its destination results in some packet requiring $\Omega(hk)$ steps to reach its destination (since the packet traveling farthest is delayed by $\Omega(k)$ steps at each of $\Omega(h)$ levels), while the policy that always transmits the packet farthest from its destination results in all packets reaching their destinations within $O(h + k)$ steps. This can become quite a large difference as $h$ and $k$ grow large.

***Schedules and Their Durations***   Let's now move from these examples to the question of scheduling packets and managing queues in an arbitrary network $G$. Given packets labeled $1, 2, \ldots, N$ and associated paths $P_1, P_2, \ldots, P_N$, a *packet schedule* specifies, for each edge $e$ and each time step $t$, which packet will cross edge $e$ in step $t$. Of course, the schedule must satisfy some basic consistency properties: at most one packet can cross any edge $e$ in any one step; and if packet $i$ is scheduled to cross $e$ at step $t$, then $e$ should be on the path $P_i$, and the earlier portions of the schedule should cause $i$ to have already reached $e$. We will say that the *duration* of the schedule is the number of steps that elapse until every packet reaches its destination; the goal is to find a schedule of minimum duration.

What are the obstacles to having a schedule of low duration? One obstacle would be a very long path that some packet must traverse; clearly, the duration will be at least the length of this path. Another obstacle would be a single edge $e$ that many packets must cross; since each of these packets must cross $e$ in a distinct step, this also gives a lower bound on the duration. So, if we define the *dilation* $d$ of the set of paths $\{P_1, P_2, \ldots, P_N\}$ to be the maximum length of any $P_i$, and the *congestion* $c$ of the set of paths to be the maximum number that have any single edge in common, then the duration is at least $\max(c, d) = \Omega(c + d)$.

In 1988, Leighton, Maggs, and Rao proved the following striking result: Congestion and dilation are the only obstacles to finding fast schedules, in the sense that there is always a schedule of duration $O(c + d)$. While the statement of this result is very simple, it turns out to be extremely difficult to prove; and it yields only a very complicated method to actually *construct* such a schedule. So, instead of trying to prove this result, we'll analyze a simple algorithm (also proposed by Leighton, Maggs, and Rao) that can be easily implemented in a distributed setting and yields a duration that is only worse by a logarithmic factor: $O(c + d \log(mN))$, where $m$ is the number of edges and $N$ is the number of packets.

## Designing the Algorithm

***A Simple Randomized Schedule***   If each edge simply transmits an arbitrary waiting packet in each step, it is easy to see that the resulting schedule has duration $O(cd)$: at worst, a packet can be blocked by $c - 1$ other packets on each of the $d$ edges in its path. To reduce this bound, we need to set things up so that each packet only waits for a much smaller number of steps over the whole trip to its destination.

The reason a bound as large as $O(cd)$ can arise is that the packets are very badly timed with respect to one another: Blocks of $c$ of them all meet at an edge at the same time, and once this congestion has cleared, the same thing happens at the next edge. This sounds pathological, but one should remember that a very natural queue management policy caused it to happen in Figure 13.4. However, it is the case that such bad behavior relies on very unfortunate synchronization in the motion of the packets; so it is believable that, if we introduce some randomization in the timing of the packets, then this kind of behavior is unlikely to happen. The simplest idea would be just to randomly shift the times at which the packets are released from their sources. Then if there are many packets all aimed at the same edge, they are unlikely to hit it all at the same time, as the contention for edges has been "smoothed out." We now show that this kind of randomization, properly implemented, in fact works quite well.

Consider first the following algorithm, which will not quite work. It involves a parameter $r$ whose value will be determined later.

```
Each packet i behaves as follows:
  i chooses a random delay s between 1 and r
  i waits at its source for s time steps
  i then moves full speed ahead, one edge per time step
     until it reaches its destination
```

If the set of random delays were really chosen so that no two packets ever "collided"—reaching the same edge at the same time—then this schedule would work just as advertised; its duration would be at most $r$ (the maximum initial delay) plus $d$ (the maximum number of edges on any path). However, unless $r$ is chosen to be very large, it is likely that a collision will occur somewhere in the network, and so the algorithm will probably fail: Two packets will show up at the same edge $e$ in the same time step $t$, and both will be required to cross $e$ in the next step.

***Grouping Time into Blocks***     To get around this problem, we consider the following generalization of this strategy: rather than implementing the "full speed ahead" plan at the level of individual time steps, we implement it at the level of contiguous *blocks* of time steps.

```
For a parameter b, group intervals of b consecutive time steps
     into single blocks of time
Each packet i behaves as follows:
  i chooses a random delay s between 1 and r
  i waits at its source for s blocks
```

```
i then moves forward one edge per block,
    until it reaches its destination
```

This schedule will work provided that we avoid a more extreme type of collision: It should not be the case that more than $b$ packets are supposed to show up at the same edge $e$ at the start of the same block. If this happens, then at least one of them will not be able to cross $e$ in the next block. However, if the initial delays smooth things out enough so that no more than $b$ packets arrive at any edge in the same block, then the schedule will work just as intended. In this case, the duration will be at most $b(r + d)$—the maximum number of blocks, $r + d$, times the length of each block, $b$.

**(13.47)** *Let $\mathcal{E}$ denote the event that more than $b$ packets are required to be at the same edge $e$ at the start of the same block. If $\mathcal{E}$ does not occur, then the duration of the schedule is at most $b(r + d)$.*

Our goal is now to choose values of $r$ and $b$ so that both the probability $\Pr[\mathcal{E}]$ and the duration $b(r + d)$ are small quantities. This is the crux of the analysis since, if we can show this, then (13.47) gives a bound on the duration.

### Analyzing the Algorithm

To give a bound on $\Pr[\mathcal{E}]$, it's useful to decompose it into a union of simpler bad events, so that we can apply the Union Bound. A natural set of bad events arises from considering each edge and each time block separately; if $e$ is an edge, and $t$ is a block between 1 and $r + d$, we let $\mathcal{F}_{et}$ denote the event that more than $b$ packets are required to be at $e$ at the start of block $t$. Clearly, $\mathcal{E} = \cup_{e,t}\mathcal{F}_{et}$. Moreover, if $N_{et}$ is a random variable equal to the number of packets scheduled to be at $e$ at the start of block $t$, then $\mathcal{F}_{et}$ is equivalent to the event $[N_{et} > b]$.

The next step in the analysis is to decompose the random variable $N_{et}$ into a sum of independent 0-1-valued random variables so that we can apply a Chernoff bound. This is naturally done by defining $X_{eti}$ to be equal to 1 if packet $i$ is required to be at edge $e$ at the start of block $t$, and equal to 0 otherwise. Then $N_{et} = \sum_i X_{eti}$; and for different values of $i$, the random variables $X_{eti}$ are independent, since the packets are choosing independent delays. (Note that $X_{eti}$ and $X_{e't'i}$, where the value of $i$ is the same, would certainly not be independent; but our analysis does not require us to add random variables of this form together.) Notice that, of the $r$ possible delays that packet $i$ can choose, at most one will require it to be at $e$ at block $t$; thus $E\left[X_{eti}\right] \leq 1/r$. Moreover, at most $c$ packets have paths that include $e$; and if $i$ is not one of these packets, then clearly $E\left[X_{eti}\right] = 0$. Thus we have

$$E\left[N_{et}\right] = \sum_i E\left[X_{eti}\right] \leq \frac{c}{r}.$$

We now have the setup for applying the Chernoff bound (13.42), since $N_{et}$ is a sum of the independent 0-1-valued random variables $X_{eti}$. Indeed, the quantities are sort of like what they were when we analyzed the problem of throwing $m$ jobs at random onto $n$ processors: in that case, each constituent random variable had expectation $1/n$, the total expectation was $m/n$, and we needed $m$ to be $\Omega(n \log n)$ in order for each processor load to be close to its expectation with high probability. The appropriate analogy in the case at hand is for $r$ to play the role of $n$, and $c$ to play the role of $m$: This makes sense symbolically, in terms of the parameters; it also accords with the picture that the packets are like the jobs, and the different time blocks of a single edge are like the different processors that can receive the jobs. This suggests that if we want the number of packets destined for a particular edge in a particular block to be close to its expectation, we should have $c = \Omega(r \log r)$.

This will work, except that we have to increase the logarithmic term a little to make sure that the Union Bound over all $e$ and all $t$ works out in the end. So let's set

$$r = \frac{c}{q \log(mN)},$$

where $q$ is a constant that will be determined later.

Let's fix a choice of $e$ and $t$ and try to bound the probability that $N_{et}$ exceeds a constant times $\frac{c}{r}$. We define $\mu = \frac{c}{r}$, and observe that $E\left[N_{et}\right] \le \mu$, so we are in a position to apply the Chernoff bound (13.42). We choose $\delta = 2$, so that $(1 + \delta)\mu = \frac{3c}{r} = 3q \log(mN)$, and we use this as the upper bound in the expression $\Pr\left[N_{et} > \frac{3c}{r}\right] = \Pr\left[N_{et} > (1 + \delta)\mu\right]$. Now, applying (13.42), we have

$$\Pr\left[N_{et} > \frac{3c}{r}\right] < \left[\frac{e^{\delta}}{(1 + \delta)^{(1+\delta)}}\right]^{\mu} < \left[\frac{e^{1+\delta}}{(1 + \delta)^{(1+\delta)}}\right]^{\mu} = \left(\frac{e}{1 + \delta}\right)^{(1+\delta)\mu}$$

$$= \left(\frac{e}{3}\right)^{(1+\delta)\mu} = \left(\frac{e}{3}\right)^{3c/r} = \left(\frac{e}{3}\right)^{3q \log(mN)} = \frac{1}{(mN)^{z}},$$

where $z$ is a constant that can be made as large as we want by choosing the constant $q$ appropriately.

We can see from this calculation that it's safe to set $b = 3c/r$; for, in this case, the event $\mathcal{F}_{et}$ that $N_{et} > b$ will have very small probability for each choice of $e$ and $t$. There are $m$ different choices for $e$, and $d + r$ different choice for $t$, where we observe that $d + r \le d + c - 1 \le N$. Thus we have

$$\Pr\left[\mathcal{E}\right] = \Pr\left[\bigcup_{e,t} \mathcal{F}_{et}\right] \le \sum_{e,t} \Pr\left[\mathcal{F}_{et}\right] \le mN \cdot \frac{1}{(mN)^{z}} = \frac{1}{(mN)^{z-1}},$$

which can be made as small as we want by choosing $z$ large enough.

Our choice of the parameters $b$ and $r$, combined with (13.44), now implies the following.

**(13.48)** *With high probability, the duration of the schedule for the packets is $O(c + d \log (mN))$.*

**Proof.** We have just argued that the probability of the bad event $\mathcal{E}$ is very small, at most $(mN)^{-(z-1)}$ for an arbitrarily large constant $z$. And provided that $\mathcal{E}$ does not happen, (13.47) tells us that the duration of the schedule is bounded by

$$b(r + d) = \frac{3c}{r}(r + d) = 3c + d \cdot \frac{3c}{r} = 3c + d(3q \log(mN)) = O(c + d \log(mN)).$$

∎

## 13.12 Background: Some Basic Probability Definitions

For many, though certainly not all, applications of randomized algorithms, it is enough to work with probabilities defined over finite sets only; and this turns out to be much easier to think about than probabilities over arbitrary sets. So we begin by considering just this special case. We'll then end the section by revisiting all these notions in greater generality.

### Finite Probability Spaces

We have an intuitive understanding of sentences like, "If a fair coin is flipped, the probability of 'heads' is 1/2." Or, "If a fair die is rolled, the probability of a '6' is 1/6." What we want to do first is to describe a mathematical framework in which we can discuss such statements precisely. The framework will work well for carefully circumscribed systems such as coin flips and rolls of dice; at the same time, we will avoid the lengthy and substantial philosophical issues raised in trying to model statements like, "The probability of rain tomorrow is 20 percent." Fortunately, most algorithmic settings are as carefully circumscribed as those of coins and dice, if perhaps somewhat larger and more complex.

To be able to compute probabilities, we introduce the notion of a *finite probability space*. (Recall that we're dealing with just the case of finite sets for now.) A finite probability space is defined by an underlying *sample space* $\Omega$, which consists of the possible *outcomes* of the process under consideration. Each point $i$ in the sample space also has a nonnegative *probability mass* $p(i) \geq 0$; these probability masses need only satisfy the constraint that their total sum is 1; that is, $\sum_{i \in \Omega} p(i) = 1$. We define an *event* $\mathcal{E}$ to be any subset of

$\Omega$—an event is defined simply by the set of outcomes that constitute it—and we define the *probability* of the event to be the sum of the probability masses of all the points in $\mathcal{E}$. That is,

$$\Pr[\mathcal{E}] = \sum_{i \in \mathcal{E}} p(i).$$

In many situations that we'll consider, all points in the sample space have the same probability mass, and then the probability of an event $\mathcal{E}$ is simply its size relative to the size of $\Omega$; that is, in this special case, $\Pr[\mathcal{E}] = |\mathcal{E}|/|\Omega|$. We use $\overline{\mathcal{E}}$ to denote the complementary event $\Omega - \mathcal{E}$; note that $\Pr\left[\overline{\mathcal{E}}\right] = 1 - \Pr[\mathcal{E}]$.

Thus the points in the sample space and their respective probability masses form a complete description of the system under consideration; it is the events—the subsets of the sample space—whose probabilities we are interested in computing. So to represent a single flip of a "fair" coin, we can define the sample space to be $\Omega = \{\texttt{heads}, \texttt{tails}\}$ and set $p(\texttt{heads}) = p(\texttt{tails}) = 1/2$. If we want to consider a biased coin in which "heads" is twice as likely as "tails," we can define the probability masses to be $p(\texttt{heads}) = 2/3$ and $p(\texttt{tails}) = 1/3$. A key thing to notice even in this simple example is that defining the probability masses is a part of defining the underlying problem; in setting up the problem, we are specifying whether the coin is fair or biased, not deriving this from some more basic data.

Here's a slightly more complex example, which we could call the *Process Naming*, or *Identifier Selection Problem*. Suppose we have $n$ processes in a distributed system, denoted $p_1, p_2, \ldots, p_n$, and each of them chooses an identifier for itself uniformly at random from the space of all $k$-bit strings. Moreover, each process's choice happens concurrently with those of all the other processes, and so the outcomes of these choices are unaffected by one another. If we view each identifier as being chosen from the set $\{0, 1, 2, \ldots, 2^k - 1\}$ (by considering the numerical value of the identifier as a number in binary notation), then the sample space $\Omega$ could be represented by the set of all $n$-tuples of integers, with each integer between 0 and $2^k - 1$. The sample space would thus have $(2^k)^n = 2^{kn}$ points, each with probability mass $2^{-kn}$.

Now suppose we are interested in the probability that processes $p_1$ and $p_2$ each choose the same name. This is an event $\mathcal{E}$, represented by the subset consisting of all $n$-tuples from $\Omega$ whose first two coordinates are the same. There are $2^{k(n-1)}$ such $n$-tuples: we can choose any value for coordinates 3 through $n$, then any value for coordinate 2, and then we have no freedom of choice in coordinate 1. Thus we have

$$\Pr[\mathcal{E}] = \sum_{i \in \mathcal{E}} p(i) = 2^{k(n-1)} \cdot 2^{-kn} = 2^{-k}.$$

This, of course, corresponds to the intuitive way one might work out the probability, which is to say that we can choose any identifier we want for process $p_2$, after which there is only 1 choice out of $2^k$ for process $p_1$ that will cause the names to agree. It's worth checking that this intuition is really just a compact description of the calculation above.

## Conditional Probability and Independence

If we view the probability of an event $\mathcal{E}$, roughly, as the likelihood that $\mathcal{E}$ is going to occur, then we may also want to ask about its probability given additional information. Thus, given another event $\mathcal{F}$ of positive probability, we define the *conditional probability of $\mathcal{E}$ given $\mathcal{F}$* as

$$\Pr[\mathcal{E} \mid \mathcal{F}] = \frac{\Pr[\mathcal{E} \cap \mathcal{F}]}{\Pr[\mathcal{F}]}.$$

This is the "right" definition intuitively, since it's performing the following calculation: Of the portion of the sample space that consists of $\mathcal{F}$ (the event we "know" to have occurred), what fraction is occupied by $\mathcal{E}$?

One often uses conditional probabilities to analyze $\Pr[\mathcal{E}]$ for some complicated event $\mathcal{E}$, as follows. Suppose that the events $\mathcal{F}_1, \mathcal{F}_2, \ldots, \mathcal{F}_k$ each have positive probability, and they partition the sample space; in other words, each outcome in the sample space belongs to exactly one of them, so $\sum_{j=1}^{k} \Pr[\mathcal{F}_j] = 1$. Now suppose we know these values $\Pr[\mathcal{F}_j]$, and we are also able to determine $\Pr[\mathcal{E} \mid \mathcal{F}_j]$ for each $j = 1, 2, \ldots, k$. That is, we know what the probability of $\mathcal{E}$ is if we assume that any one of the events $\mathcal{F}_j$ has occurred. Then we can compute $\Pr[\mathcal{E}]$ by the following simple formula:

$$\Pr[\mathcal{E}] = \sum_{j=1}^{k} \Pr[\mathcal{E} \mid \mathcal{F}_j] \cdot \Pr[\mathcal{F}_j].$$

To justify this formula, we can unwind the right-hand side as follows:

$$\sum_{j=1}^{k} \Pr[\mathcal{E} \mid \mathcal{F}_j] \cdot \Pr[\mathcal{F}_j] = \sum_{j=1}^{k} \frac{\Pr[\mathcal{E} \cap \mathcal{F}_j]}{\Pr[\mathcal{F}_j]} \cdot \Pr[\mathcal{F}_j] = \sum_{j=1}^{k} \Pr[\mathcal{E} \cap \mathcal{F}_j] = \Pr[\mathcal{E}].$$

**Independent Events** Intuitively, we say that two events are *independent* if information about the outcome of one does not affect our estimate of the likelihood of the other. One way to make this concrete would be to declare events $\mathcal{E}$ and $\mathcal{F}$ independent if $\Pr[\mathcal{E} \mid \mathcal{F}] = \Pr[\mathcal{E}]$, and $\Pr[\mathcal{F} \mid \mathcal{E}] = \Pr[\mathcal{F}]$. (We'll assume here that both have positive probability; otherwise the notion of independence is not very interesting in any case.) Actually, if one of these two equalities holds, then the other must hold, for the following reason: If $\Pr[\mathcal{E} \mid \mathcal{F}] = \Pr[\mathcal{E}]$, then

$$\frac{\Pr\left[\mathcal{E} \cap \mathcal{F}\right]}{\Pr\left[\mathcal{F}\right]} = \Pr\left[\mathcal{E}\right],$$

and hence $\Pr\left[\mathcal{E} \cap \mathcal{F}\right] = \Pr\left[\mathcal{E}\right] \cdot \Pr\left[\mathcal{F}\right]$, from which the other equality holds as well.

It turns out to be a little cleaner to adopt this equivalent formulation as our working definition of independence. Formally, we'll say that events $\mathcal{E}$ and $\mathcal{F}$ are *independent* if $\Pr\left[\mathcal{E} \cap \mathcal{F}\right] = \Pr\left[\mathcal{E}\right] \cdot \Pr\left[\mathcal{F}\right]$.

This product formulation leads to the following natural generalization. We say that a collection of events $\mathcal{E}_1, \mathcal{E}_2, \ldots, \mathcal{E}_n$ is *independent* if, for every set of indices $I \subseteq \{1, 2, \ldots, n\}$, we have

$$\Pr\left[\bigcap_{i \in I} \mathcal{E}_i\right] = \prod_{i \in I} \Pr\left[\mathcal{E}_i\right].$$

It's important to notice the following: To check if a large set of events is independent, it's not enough to check whether every pair of them is independent. For example, suppose we flip three independent fair coins: If $\mathcal{E}_i$ denotes the event that the $i^{\text{th}}$ coin comes up heads, then the events $\mathcal{E}_1, \mathcal{E}_2, \mathcal{E}_3$ are independent and each has probability $1/2$. Now let $A$ denote the event that coins 1 and 2 have the same value; let $B$ denote the event that coins 2 and 3 have the same value; and let $C$ denote the event that coins 1 and 3 have different values. It's easy to check that each of these events has probability $1/2$, and the intersection of any two has probability $1/4$. Thus every pair drawn from $A, B, C$ is independent. But the set of all three events $A, B, C$ is not independent, since $\Pr\left[A \cap B \cap C\right] = 0$.

## The Union Bound

Suppose we are given a set of events $\mathcal{E}_1, \mathcal{E}_2, \ldots, \mathcal{E}_n$, and we are interested in the probability that *any* of them happens; that is, we are interested in the probability $\Pr\left[\cup_{i=1}^{n} \mathcal{E}_i\right]$. If the events are all pairwise disjoint from one another, then the probability mass of their union is comprised simply of the separate contributions from each event. In other words, we have the following fact.

**(13.49)**    *Suppose we have events $\mathcal{E}_1, \mathcal{E}_2, \ldots, \mathcal{E}_n$ such that $\mathcal{E}_i \cap \mathcal{E}_j = \phi$ for each pair. Then*

$$\Pr\left[\bigcup_{i=1}^{n} \mathcal{E}_i\right] = \sum_{i=1}^{n} \Pr\left[\mathcal{E}_i\right].$$

In general, a set of events $\mathcal{E}_1, \mathcal{E}_2, \ldots, \mathcal{E}_n$ may overlap in complex ways. In this case, the equality in (13.49) no longer holds; due to the overlaps among

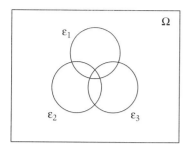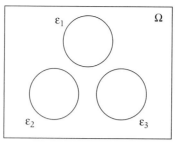

**Figure 13.5** The Union Bound: The probability of a union is maximized when the events have no overlap.

events, the probability mass of a point that is counted once on the left-hand side will be counted one *or more* times on the right-hand side. (See Figure 13.5.) This means that for a general set of events, the equality in (13.49) is relaxed to an inequality; and this is the content of the Union Bound. We have stated the Union Bound as (13.2), but we state it here again for comparison with (13.49).

**(13.50)**    (The Union Bound) *Given events* $\mathcal{E}_1, \mathcal{E}_2, \ldots, \mathcal{E}_n$, *we have*

$$\Pr\left[\bigcup_{i=1}^{n} \mathcal{E}_i\right] \leq \sum_{i=1}^{n} \Pr\left[\mathcal{E}_i\right].$$

Given its innocuous appearance, the Union Bound is a surprisingly powerful tool in the analysis of randomized algorithms. It draws its power mainly from the following ubiquitous style of analyzing randomized algorithms. Given a randomized algorithm designed to produce a correct result with high probability, we first tabulate a set of "bad events" $\mathcal{E}_1, \mathcal{E}_2, \ldots, \mathcal{E}_n$ with the following property: if none of these bad events occurs, then the algorithm will indeed produce the correct answer. In other words, if $\mathcal{F}$ denotes the event that the algorithm fails, then we have

$$\Pr\left[\mathcal{F}\right] \leq \Pr\left[\bigcup_{i=1}^{n} \mathcal{E}_i\right].$$

But it's hard to compute the probability of this union, so we apply the Union Bound to conclude that

$$\Pr\left[\mathcal{F}\right] \leq \Pr\left[\bigcup_{i=1}^{n} \mathcal{E}_i\right] \leq \sum_{i=1}^{n} \Pr\left[\mathcal{E}_i\right].$$

Now, if in fact we have an algorithm that succeeds with very high probability, and if we've chosen our bad events carefully, then each of the probabilities $\Pr[\mathcal{E}_i]$ will be so small that even their sum—and hence our overestimate of the failure probability—will be small. This is the key: decomposing a highly complicated event, the failure of the algorithm, into a horde of simple events whose probabilities can be easily computed.

Here is a simple example to make the strategy discussed above more concrete. Recall the Process Naming Problem we discussed earlier in this section, in which each of a set of processes chooses a random identifier. Suppose that we have 1,000 processes, each choosing a 32-bit identifier, and we are concerned that two of them will end up choosing the same identifier. Can we argue that it is unlikely this will happen? To begin with, let's denote this event by $\mathcal{F}$. While it would not be overwhelmingly difficult to compute $\Pr[\mathcal{F}]$ exactly, it is much simpler to bound it as follows. The event $\mathcal{F}$ is really a union of $\binom{1000}{2}$ "atomic" events; these are the events $\mathcal{E}_{ij}$ that processes $p_i$ and $p_j$ choose the same identifier. It is easy to verify that indeed, $\mathcal{F} = \cup_{i<j} \mathcal{E}_{ij}$. Now, for any $i \neq j$, we have $\Pr[\mathcal{E}_{ij}] = 2^{-32}$, by the argument in one of our earlier examples. Applying the Union Bound, we have

$$\Pr[\mathcal{F}] \leq \sum_{i,j} \Pr[\mathcal{E}_{ij}] = \binom{1000}{2} \cdot 2^{-32}.$$

Now, $\binom{1000}{2}$ is at most half a million, and $2^{32}$ is (a little bit) more than 4 billion, so this probability is at most $\frac{.5}{4000} = .000125$.

## Infinite Sample Spaces

So far we've gotten by with finite probability spaces only. Several of the sections in this chapter, however, consider situations in which a random process can run for arbitrarily long, and so cannot be well described by a sample space of finite size. As a result, we pause here to develop the notion of a probability space more generally. This will be somewhat technical, and in part we are providing it simply for the sake of completeness: Although some of our applications require infinite sample spaces, none of them really exercises the full power of the formalism we describe here.

Once we move to infinite sample spaces, more care is needed in defining a probability function. We cannot simply give each point in the sample space $\Omega$ a probability mass and then compute the probability of every set by summing. Indeed, for reasons that we will not go into here, it is easy to get into trouble if one even allows every subset of $\Omega$ to be an event whose probability can be computed. Thus a general probability space has three components:

(i) The sample space $\Omega$.

(ii) A collection $S$ of subsets of $\Omega$; these are the only events on which we are allowed to compute probabilities.

(iii) A probability function Pr, which maps events in $S$ to real numbers in $[0, 1]$.

The collection $S$ of allowable events can be any family of sets that satisfies the following basic closure properties: the empty set and the full sample space $\Omega$ both belong to $S$; if $\mathcal{E} \in S$, then $\overline{\mathcal{E}} \in S$ (closure under complement); and if $\mathcal{E}_1, \mathcal{E}_2, \mathcal{E}_3, \ldots \in S$, then $\cup_{i=1}^{\infty} \mathcal{E}_i \in S$ (closure under countable union). The probability function Pr can be any function from $S$ to $[0, 1]$ that satisfies the following basic consistency properties: $\Pr[\phi] = 0$, $\Pr[\Omega] = 1$, $\Pr[\mathcal{E}] = 1 - \Pr[\overline{\mathcal{E}}]$, and the Union Bound for disjoint events (13.49) should hold even for countable unions—if $\mathcal{E}_1, \mathcal{E}_2, \mathcal{E}_3, \ldots \in S$ are all pairwise disjoint, then

$$\Pr\left[\bigcup_{i=1}^{\infty} \mathcal{E}_i\right] = \sum_{i=1}^{\infty} \Pr[\mathcal{E}_i].$$

Notice how, since we are not building up Pr from the more basic notion of a probability mass anymore, (13.49) moves from being a theorem to simply a required property of Pr.

When an infinite sample space arises in our context, it's typically for the following reason: we have an algorithm that makes a sequence of random decisions, each one from a fixed finite set of possibilities; and since it may run for arbitrarily long, it may make an arbitrarily large number of decisions. Thus we consider sample spaces $\Omega$ constructed as follows. We start with a finite set of symbols $X = \{1, 2, \ldots, n\}$, and assign a *weight* $w(i)$ to each symbol $i \in X$. We then define $\Omega$ to be the set of all infinite sequences of symbols from $X$ (with repetitions allowed). So a typical element of $\Omega$ will look like $\langle x_1, x_2, x_3, \ldots \rangle$ with each entry $x_i \in X$.

The simplest type of event we will be concerned with is as follows: it is the event that a point $\omega \in \Omega$ begins with a particular finite sequence of symbols. Thus, for a finite sequence $\sigma = x_1 x_2 \ldots x_s$ of length $s$, we define the *prefix event associated with $\sigma$* to be the set of all sample points of $\Omega$ whose first $s$ entries form the sequence $\sigma$. We denote this event by $\mathcal{E}_\sigma$, and we define its probability to be $\Pr[\mathcal{E}_\sigma] = w(x_1)w(x_2)\cdots w(x_s)$.

The following fact is in no sense easy to prove.

> **(13.51)** *There is a probability space* $(\Omega, \mathcal{S}, \mathrm{Pr})$, *satisfying the required closure and consistency properties, such that* $\Omega$ *is the sample space defined above,* $\mathcal{E}_\sigma \in \mathcal{S}$ *for each finite sequence* $\sigma$, *and* $\mathrm{Pr}\left[\mathcal{E}_\sigma\right] = w(x_1)w(x_2) \cdots w(x_s)$.

Once we have this fact, the closure of $\mathcal{S}$ under complement and countable union, and the consistency of $\mathrm{Pr}$ with respect to these operations, allow us to compute probabilities of essentially any "reasonable" subset of $\Omega$.

In our infinite sample space $\Omega$, with events and probabilities defined as above, we encounter a phenomenon that does not naturally arise with finite sample spaces. Suppose the set $X$ used to generate $\Omega$ is equal to $\{0, 1\}$, and $w(0) = w(1) = 1/2$. Let $\mathcal{E}$ denote the set consisting of all sequences that contain at least one entry equal to 1. (Note that $\mathcal{E}$ omits the "all-0" sequence.) We observe that $\mathcal{E}$ is an event in $\mathcal{S}$, since we can define $\sigma_i$ to be the sequence of $i - 1$ 0s followed by a 1, and observe that $\mathcal{E} = \cup_{i=1}^{\infty} \mathcal{E}_{\sigma_i}$. Moreover, all the events $\mathcal{E}_{\sigma_i}$ are pairwise disjoint, and so

$$\mathrm{Pr}\left[\mathcal{E}\right] = \sum_{i=1}^{\infty} \mathrm{Pr}\left[\mathcal{E}_{\sigma_i}\right] = \sum_{i=1}^{\infty} 2^{-i} = 1.$$

Here, then, is the phenomenon: It's possible for an event to have probability 1 even when it's not equal to the whole sample space $\Omega$. Similarly, $\mathrm{Pr}\left[\overline{\mathcal{E}}\right] = 1 - \mathrm{Pr}\left[\mathcal{E}\right] = 0$, and so we see that it's possible for an event to have probability 0 even when it's not the empty set. There is nothing wrong with any of these results; in a sense, it's a necessary step if we want probabilities defined over infinite sets to make sense. It's simply that in such cases, we should be careful to distinguish between the notion that an event has probability 0 and the intuitive idea that the event "can't happen."

## Solved Exercises

### Solved Exercise 1

Suppose we have a collection of small, low-powered devices scattered around a building. The devices can exchange data over short distances by wireless communication, and we suppose for simplicity that each device has enough range to communicate with $d$ other devices. Thus we can model the wireless connections among these devices as an undirected graph $G = (V, E)$ in which each node is incident to exactly $d$ edges.

Now we'd like to give some of the nodes a stronger *uplink transmitter* that they can use to send data back to a base station. Giving such a transmitter to every node would ensure that they can all send data like this, but we can achieve this while handing out fewer transmitters. Suppose that we find a subset $S$ of the nodes with the property that every node in $V - S$ is adjacent to a node in $S$. We call such a set $S$ a *dominating set*, since it "dominates" all other nodes in the graph. If we give uplink transmitters only to the nodes in a dominating set $S$, we can still extract data from all nodes: Any node $u \notin S$ can choose a neighbor $v \in S$, send its data to $v$, and have $v$ relay the data back to the base station.

The issue is now to find a dominating set $S$ of minimum possible size, since this will minimize the number of uplink transmitters we need. This is an NP-hard problem; in fact, proving this is the crux of Exercise 29 in Chapter 8. (It's also worth noting here the difference between dominating sets and vertex covers: in a dominating set, it is fine to have an edge $(u, v)$ with neither $u$ nor $v$ in the set $S$ as long as both $u$ and $v$ have neighbors in $S$. So, for example, a graph consisting of three nodes all connected by edges has a dominating set of size 1, but no vertex cover of size 1.)

Despite the NP-hardness, it's important in applications like this to find as small a dominating set as one can, even if it is not optimal. We will see here that a simple randomized strategy can be quite effective. Recall that in our graph $G$, each node is incident to exactly $d$ edges. So clearly any dominating set will need to have size at least $\frac{n}{d+1}$, since each node we place in a dominating set can take care only of itself and its $d$ neighbors. We want to show that a random selection of nodes will, in fact, get us quite close to this simple lower bound.

Specifically, show that for some constant $c$, a set of $\frac{cn \log n}{d+1}$ nodes chosen uniformly at random from $G$ will be a dominating set with high probability. (In other words, this completely random set is likely to form a dominating set that is only $O(\log n)$ times larger than our simple lower bound of $\frac{n}{d+1}$.)

**Solution**    Let $k = \frac{cn \log n}{d}$, where we will choose the constant $c$ later, once we have a better idea of what's going on. Let $\mathcal{E}$ be the event that a random choice of $k$ nodes is a dominating set for $G$. To make the analysis simpler, we will consider a model in which the nodes are selected one at a time, and the same node may be selected twice (if it happens to be picked twice by our sequence of random choices).

Now we want to show that if $c$ (and hence $k$) is large enough, then $\Pr[\mathcal{E}]$ is close to 1. But $\mathcal{E}$ is a very complicated-looking event, so we begin by breaking it down into much simpler events whose probabilities we can analyze more easily.

To start with, we say that a node $w$ *dominates* a node $v$ if $w$ is a neighbor of $v$, or $w = v$. We say that a set $S$ dominates a node $v$ if some element of $S$ dominates $v$. (These definitions let us say that a dominating set is simply a set of nodes that dominates every node in the graph.) Let $\mathcal{D}[v, t]$ denote the event that the $t^{\text{th}}$ random node we choose dominates node $v$. The probability of this event can be determined quite easily: of the $n$ nodes in the graph, we must choose $v$ or one of its $d$ neighbors, and so

$$\Pr\left[\mathcal{D}[v,t]\right] = \frac{d+1}{n}.$$

Let $\mathcal{D}_v$ denote the event that the random set consisting of all $k$ selected nodes dominates $v$. Thus

$$\mathcal{D}_v = \bigcup_{t=1}^{k} \mathcal{D}[v,t].$$

For independent events, we've seen in the text that it's easier to work with intersections—where we can simply multiply out the probabilities—than with unions. So rather than thinking about $\mathcal{D}_v$, we'll consider the complementary "failure event" $\overline{\mathcal{D}_v}$, that no node in the random set dominates $v$. In order for no node to dominate $v$, each of our choices has to fail to do so, and hence we have

$$\overline{\mathcal{D}_v} = \bigcap_{t=1}^{k} \overline{\mathcal{D}[v,t]}.$$

Since the events $\overline{\mathcal{D}[v,t]}$ are independent, we can compute the probability on the right-hand side by multiplying all the individual probabilities; thus

$$\Pr\left[\overline{\mathcal{D}_v}\right] = \prod_{t=1}^{k} \Pr\left[\overline{\mathcal{D}[v,t]}\right] = \left(1 - \frac{d+1}{n}\right)^{k}.$$

Now, $k = \frac{cn\log n}{d+1}$, so we can write this last expression as

$$\left(1 - \frac{d+1}{n}\right)^{k} = \left[\left(1 - \frac{d+1}{n}\right)^{n/(d+1)}\right]^{c\log n} \leq \left(\frac{1}{e}\right)^{c\log n},$$

where the inequality follows from (13.1) that we stated earlier in the chapter.

We have not yet specified the base of the logarithm we use to define $k$, but it's starting to look like base $e$ is a good choice. Using this, we can further simplify the last expression to

$$\Pr\left[\overline{\mathcal{D}_v}\right] \leq \left(\frac{1}{e}\right)^{c\ln n} = \frac{1}{n^c}.$$

We are now very close to done. We have shown that for each node $v$, the probability that our random set fails to dominate it is at most $n^{-c}$, which we can drive down to a very small quantity by making $c$ moderately large. Now recall the original event $\mathcal{E}$, that our random set is a dominating set. This fails to occur if and only if one of the events $\mathcal{D}_v$ fails to occur, so $\overline{\mathcal{E}} = \cup_v \overline{\mathcal{D}_v}$. Thus, by the Union Bound (13.2), we have

$$\Pr\left[\overline{\mathcal{E}}\right] \leq \sum_{v \in V} \Pr\left[\overline{\mathcal{D}_v}\right] \leq n \cdot \frac{1}{n^c} = \frac{1}{n^{c-1}}.$$

Simply choosing $c = 2$ makes this probability $\frac{1}{n}$, which is much less than 1. Thus, with high probability, the event $\mathcal{E}$ holds and our random choice of nodes is indeed a dominating set.

It's interesting to note that the probability of success, as a function of $k$, exhibits behavior very similar to what we saw in the contention-resolution example in Section 13.1. Setting $k = \Theta(n/d)$ is enough to guarantee that each individual node is dominated with constant probability. This, however, is not enough to get anything useful out of the Union Bound. Then, raising $k$ by another logarithmic factor is enough to drive up the probability of dominating each node to something very close to 1, at which point the Union Bound can come into play.

## Solved Exercise 2

Suppose we are given a set of $n$ variables $x_1, x_2, \ldots, x_n$, each of which can take one of the values in the set $\{0, 1\}$. We are also given a set of $k$ equations; the $r^{\text{th}}$ equation has the form

$$(x_i + x_j) \bmod 2 = b_r$$

for some choice of two distinct variables $x_i, x_j$, and for some value $b_r$ that is either 0 or 1. Thus each equation specifies whether the sum of two variables is even or odd.

Consider the problem of finding an assignment of values to variables that maximizes the number of equations that are satisfied (i.e., in which equality actually holds). This problem is NP-hard, though you don't have to prove this.

For example, suppose we are given the equations

$$(x_1 + x_2) \bmod 2 = 0$$

$$(x_1 + x_3) \bmod 2 = 0$$

$$(x_2 + x_4) \bmod 2 = 1$$

$$(x_3 + x_4) \bmod 2 = 0$$

over the four variables $x_1, \ldots, x_4$. Then it's possible to show that no assignment of values to variables will satisfy all equations simultaneously, but setting all variables equal to 0 satisfies three of the four equations.

(a) Let $c^*$ denote the maximum possible number of equations that can be satisfied by an assignment of values to variables. Give a polynomial-time algorithm that produces an assignment satisfying at least $\frac{1}{2}c^*$ equations. If you want, your algorithm can be randomized; in this case, the *expected* number of equations it satisfies should be at least $\frac{1}{2}c^*$. In either case, you should prove that your algorithm has the desired performance guarantee.

(b) Suppose we drop the condition that each equation must have exactly two variables; in other words, now each equation simply specifies that the sum of an arbitrary subset of the variables, mod 2, is equal to a particular value $b_r$.

Again let $c^*$ denote the maximum possible number of equations that can be satisfied by an assignment of values to variables, and give a polynomial-time algorithm that produces an assignment satisfying at least $\frac{1}{2}c^*$ equations. (As before, your algorithm can be randomized.) If you believe that your algorithm from part (a) achieves this guarantee here as well, you can state this and justify it with a proof of the performance guarantee for this more general case.

**Solution**    Let's recall the punch line of the simple randomized algorithm for MAX 3-SAT that we saw earlier in the chapter: If you're given a constraint satisfaction problem, assigning variables at random can be a surprisingly effective way to satisfy a constant fraction of all constraints.

We now try applying this principle to the problem here, beginning with part (a). Consider the algorithm that sets each variable independently and uniformly at random. How well does this random assignment do, in expectation? As usual, we will approach this question using linearity of expectation: If $X$ is a random variable denoting the number of satisfied equations, we'll break $X$ up into a sum of simpler random variables.

For some $r$ between 1 and $k$, let the $r^{\text{th}}$ equation be

$$(x_i + x_j) \bmod 2 = b_r.$$

Let $X_r$ be a random variable equal to 1 if this equation is satisfied, and 0 otherwise. $E\left[X_r\right]$ is the probability that equation $r$ is satisfied. Of the four possible assignments to equation $i$, there are two that cause it to evaluate to 0 mod 2 ($x_i = x_j = 0$ and $x_i = x_j = 1$) and two that cause it to evaluate to 1 mod 2 ($x_i = 0; x_j = 1$ and $x_i = i; x_j = 0$). Thus $E\left[X_r\right] = 2/4 = 1/2$.

Now, by linearity of expectation, we have $E[X] = \sum_r E\left[X_r\right] = k/2$. Since the maximum number of satisfiable equations $c^*$ must be at most $k$, we satisfy at least $c^*/2$ in expectation. Thus, as in the case of MAX 3-SAT, a simple random assignment to the variables satisfies a constant fraction of all constraints.

For part (b), let's press our luck by trying the same algorithm. Again let $X_r$ be a random variable equal to 1 if the $r^{th}$ equation is satisfied, and 0 otherwise; let $X$ be the total number of satisfied equations; and let $c^*$ be the optimum.

We want to claim that $E[X_r] = 1/2$ as before, even when there can be an arbitrary number of variables in the $r^{th}$ equation; in other words, the probability that the equation takes the correct value mod 2 is exactly $1/2$. We can't just write down all the cases the way we did for two variables per equation, so we will use an alternate argument.

In fact, there are two natural ways to prove that $E[X_r] = 1/2$. The first uses a trick that appeared in the proof of (13.25) in Section 13.6 on hashing: We consider assigning values arbitrarily to all variables but the last one in the equation, and then we randomly assign a value to the last variable $x$. Now, regardless of how we assign values to all other variables, there are two ways to assign a value to $x$, and it is easy to check that one of these ways will satisfy the equation and the other will not. Thus, regardless of the assignments to all variables other than $x$, the probability of setting $x$ so as to satisfy the equation is exactly $1/2$. Thus the probability the equation is satisfied by a random assignment is $1/2$.

(As in the proof of (13.25), we can write this argument in terms of conditional probabilities. If $\mathcal{E}$ is the event that the equation is satisfied, and $\mathcal{F}_b$ is the event that the variables other than $x$ receive a sequence of values $b$, then we have argued that $\Pr[\mathcal{E} \mid \mathcal{F}_b] = 1/2$ for all $b$, and so $\Pr[\mathcal{E}] = \sum_b \Pr[\mathcal{E} \mid \mathcal{F}_b] \cdot \Pr[\mathcal{F}_b] = (1/2) \sum_b \Pr[\mathcal{F}_b] = 1/2$.)

An alternate proof simply counts the number of ways for the $r^{th}$ equation to have an even sum, and the number of ways for it to have an odd sum. If we can show that these two numbers are equal, then the probability that a random assignment satisfies the $r^{th}$ equation is the probability it gives it a sum with the right even/odd parity, which is $1/2$.

In fact, at a high level, this proof is essentially the same as the previous one, with the difference that we make the underlying counting problem explicit. Suppose that the $r^{th}$ equation has $t$ terms; then there are $2^t$ possible assignments to the variables in this equation. We want to claim that $2^{t-1}$ assignments produce an even sum, and $2^{t-1}$ produce an odd sum, which will show that $E[X_r] = 1/2$. We prove this by induction on $t$. For $t = 1$, there are just two assignments, one of each parity; and for $t = 2$, we already proved this earlier by considering all $2^2 = 4$ possible assignments. Now suppose the claim holds for an arbitrary value of $t - 1$. Then there are exactly $2^{t-1}$ ways to get an even sum with $t$ variables, as follows:

- $2^{t-2}$ ways to get an even sum on the first $t - 1$ variables (by induction), followed by an assignment of 0 to the $t^{th}$, plus

- $2^{t-2}$ ways to get an odd sum on the first $t-1$ variables (by induction), followed by an assignment of 1 to the $t^{\text{th}}$.

The remaining $2^{t-1}$ assignments give an odd sum, and this completes the induction step.

Once we have $E\left[X_r\right] = 1/2$, we conclude as in part (a): Linearity of expectation gives us $E\left[X\right] = \sum_r E\left[X_r\right] = k/2 \geq c^*/2$.

## Exercises

1. *3-Coloring* is a yes/no question, but we can phrase it as an optimization problem as follows.

   Suppose we are given a graph $G = (V, E)$, and we want to color each node with one of three colors, even if we aren't necessarily able to give different colors to every pair of adjacent nodes. Rather, we say that an edge $(u, v)$ is *satisfied* if the colors assigned to $u$ and $v$ are different.

   Consider a 3-coloring that maximizes the number of satisfied edges, and let $c^*$ denote this number. Give a polynomial-time algorithm that produces a 3-coloring that satisfies at least $\frac{2}{3}c^*$ edges. If you want, your algorithm can be randomized; in this case, the *expected* number of edges it satisfies should be at least $\frac{2}{3}c^*$.

2. Consider a county in which 100,000 people vote in an election. There are only two candidates on the ballot: a Democratic candidate (denoted $D$) and a Republican candidate (denoted $R$). As it happens, this county is heavily Democratic, so 80,000 people go to the polls with the intention of voting for $D$, and 20,000 go to the polls with the intention of voting for $R$.

   However, the layout of the ballot is a little confusing, so each voter, independently and with probability $\frac{1}{100}$, votes for the wrong candidate— that is, the one that he or she *didn't* intend to vote for. (Remember that in this election, there are only two candidates on the ballot.)

   Let $X$ denote the random variable equal to the number of votes received by the Democratic candidate $D$, when the voting is conducted with this process of error. Determine the expected value of $X$, and give an explanation of your derivation of this value.

3. In Section 13.1, we saw a simple distributed protocol to solve a particular contention-resolution problem. Here is another setting in which randomization can help with contention resolution, through the distributed construction of an independent set.

Suppose we have a system with $n$ processes. Certain pairs of processes are in *conflict*, meaning that they both require access to a shared resource. In a given time interval, the goal is to schedule a large subset $S$ of the processes to run—the rest will remain idle—so that no two conflicting processes are both in the scheduled set $S$. We'll call such a set $S$ *conflict-free*.

One can picture this process in terms of a graph $G = (V, E)$ with a node representing each process and an edge joining pairs of processes that are in conflict. It is easy to check that a set of processes $S$ is conflict-free if and only if it forms an independent set in $G$. This suggests that finding a maximum-size conflict-free set $S$, for an arbitrary conflict $G$, will be difficult (since the general Independent Set Problem is reducible to this problem). Nevertheless, we can still look for heuristics that find a reasonably large conflict-free set. Moreover, we'd like a simple method for achieving this without centralized control: Each process should communicate with only a small number of other processes and then decide whether or not it should belong to the set $S$.

We will suppose for purposes of this question that each node has exactly $d$ neighbors in the graph $G$. (That is, each process is in conflict with exactly $d$ other processes.)

(a) Consider the following simple protocol.

> Each process $P_i$ independently picks a random value $x_i$; it sets $x_i$ to 1 with probability $\frac{1}{2}$ and sets $x_i$ to 0 with probability $\frac{1}{2}$. It then decides to enter the set $S$ if and only if it chooses the value 1, and each of the processes with which it is in conflict chooses the value 0.

Prove that the set $S$ resulting from the execution of this protocol is conflict-free. Also, give a formula for the expected size of $S$ in terms of $n$ (the number of processes) and $d$ (the number of conflicts per process).

(b) The choice of the probability $\frac{1}{2}$ in the protocol above was fairly arbitrary, and it's not clear that it should give the best system performance. A more general specification of the protocol would replace the probability $\frac{1}{2}$ by a parameter $p$ between 0 and 1, as follows.

> Each process $P_i$ independently picks a random value $x_i$; it sets $x_i$ to 1 with probability $p$ and sets $x_i$ to 0 with probability $1 - p$. It then decides to enter the set $S$ if and only if it chooses the value 1, and each of the processes with which it is in conflict chooses the value 0.

In terms of the parameters of the graph $G$, give a value of $p$ so that the expected size of the resulting set $S$ is as large as possible. Give a formula for the expected size of $S$ when $p$ is set to this optimal value.

4. A number of *peer-to-peer systems* on the Internet are based on *overlay networks*. Rather than using the physical Internet topology as the network on which to perform computation, these systems run protocols by which nodes choose collections of virtual "neighbors" so as to define a higher-level graph whose structure may bear little or no relation to the underlying physical network. Such an overlay network is then used for sharing data and services, and it can be extremely flexible compared with a physical network, which is hard to modify in real time to adapt to changing conditions.

Peer-to-peer networks tend to grow through the arrival of new participants, who join by linking into the existing structure. This growth process has an intrinsic effect on the characteristics of the overall network. Recently, people have investigated simple abstract models for network growth that might provide insight into the way such processes behave, at a qualitative level, in real networks.

Here's a simple example of such a model. The system begins with a single node $v_1$. Nodes then join one at a time; as each node joins, it executes a protocol whereby it forms a directed link to a single other node chosen uniformly at random from those already in the system. More concretely, if the system already contains nodes $v_1, v_2, \ldots, v_{k-1}$ and node $v_k$ wishes to join, it randomly selects one of $v_1, v_2, \ldots, v_{k-1}$ and links to this node.

Suppose we run this process until we have a system consisting of nodes $v_1, v_2, \ldots, v_n$; the random process described above will produce a directed network in which each node other than $v_1$ has exactly one outgoing edge. On the other hand, a node may have multiple incoming links, or none at all. The incoming links to a node $v_j$ reflect all the other nodes whose access into the system is via $v_j$; so if $v_j$ has many incoming links, this can place a large load on it. To keep the system load-balanced, then, we'd like all nodes to have a roughly comparable number of incoming links. That's unlikely to happen here, however, since nodes that join earlier in the process are likely to have more incoming links than nodes that join later. Let's try to quantify this imbalance as follows.

(a) Given the random process described above, what is the expected number of incoming links to node $v_j$ in the resulting network? Give an exact formula in terms of $n$ and $j$, and also try to express this quantity

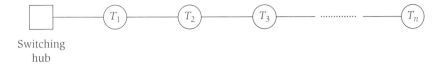

Switching
hub

**Figure 13.6** Towns $T_1, T_2 \ldots, T_n$ need to decide how to share the cost of the cable.

asymptotically (via an expression without large summations) using $\Theta(\cdot)$ notation.

(b) Part (a) makes precise a sense in which the nodes that arrive early carry an "unfair" share of the connections in the network. Another way to quantify the imbalance is to observe that, in a run of this random process, we expect many nodes to end up with no incoming links.

Give a formula for the expected number of nodes with no incoming links in a network grown randomly according to this model.

5. Out in a rural part of the county somewhere, $n$ small towns have decided to get connected to a large Internet switching hub via a high-volume fiber-optic cable. The towns are labeled $T_1, T_2, \ldots, T_n$, and they are all arranged on a single long highway, so that town $T_i$ is $i$ miles from the switching hub (See Figure 13.6).

Now this cable is quite expensive; it costs $k$ dollars per mile, resulting in an overall cost of $kn$ dollars for the whole cable. The towns get together and discuss how to divide up the cost of the cable.

First, one of the towns way out at the far end of the highway makes the following proposal.

**Proposal A.** *Divide the cost evenly among all towns, so each pays $k$ dollars.*

There's some sense in which Proposal A is fair, since it's as if each town is paying for the mile of cable directly leading up to it.

But one of the towns very close to the switching hub objects, pointing out that the faraway towns are actually benefiting from a large section of the cable, whereas the close-in towns only benefit from a short section of it. So they make the following counterproposal.

**Proposal B.** *Divide the cost so that the contribution of town $T_i$ is proportional to $i$, its distance from the switching hub.*

One of the other towns very close to the switching hub points out that there's another way to do a nonproportional division that is also natural. This is based on conceptually dividing the cable into $n$ equal-length "edges" $e_1, \ldots, e_n$, where the first edge $e_1$ runs from the switching hub to $T_1$, and the $i^{\text{th}}$ edge $e_i$ ($i > 1$) runs from $T_{i-1}$ to $T_i$. Now we observe that, while all the towns benefit from $e_1$, only the last town benefits from $e_n$. So they suggest

> **Proposal C.** *Divide the cost separately for each edge $e_i$. The cost of $e_i$ should be shared equally by the towns $T_i, T_{i+1}, \ldots, T_n$, since these are the towns "downstream" of $e_i$.*

So now the towns have many different options; which is the fairest? To resolve this, they turn to the work of Lloyd Shapley, one of the most famous mathematical economists of the 20th century. He proposed what is now called the *Shapley value* as a general mechanism for sharing costs or benefits among several parties. It can be viewed as determining the "marginal contribution" of each party, *assuming the parties arrive in a random order.*

Here's how it would work concretely in our setting. Consider an ordering $\mathcal{O}$ of the towns, and suppose that the towns "arrive" in this order. The *marginal cost of town $T_i$ in order* $\mathcal{O}$ is determined as follows. If $T_i$ is first in the order $\mathcal{O}$, then $T_i$ pays $ki$, the cost of running the cable all the way from the switching hub to $T_i$. Otherwise, look at the set of towns that come before $T_i$ in the order $\mathcal{O}$, and let $T_j$ be the farthest among these towns from the switching hub. When $T_i$ arrives, we assume the cable already reaches out to $T_j$ but no farther. So if $j > i$ ($T_j$ is farther out than $T_i$), then the marginal cost of $T_i$ is 0, since the cable already runs past $T_i$ on its way out to $T_j$. On the other hand, if $j < i$, then the marginal cost of $T_i$ is $k(i - j)$: the cost of extending the cable from $T_j$ out to $T_i$.

(For example, suppose $n = 3$ and the towns arrive in the order $T_1, T_3, T_2$. First $T_1$ pays $k$ when it arrives. Then, when $T_3$ arrives, it only has to pay $2k$ to extend the cable from $T_1$. Finally, when $T_2$ arrives, it doesn't have to pay anything since the cable already runs past it out to $T_3$.)

Now, let $X_i$ be the random variable equal to the marginal cost of town $T_i$ when the order $\mathcal{O}$ is selected uniformly at random from all permutations of the towns. Under the rules of the Shapley value, the amount that $T_i$ should contribute to the overall cost of the cable is the expected value of $X_i$.

The question is: Which of the three proposals above, if any, gives the same division of costs as the Shapley value cost-sharing mechanism? Give a proof for your answer.

6. One of the (many) hard problems that arises in genome mapping can be formulated in the following abstract way. We are given a set of $n$ *markers* $\{\mu_1, \ldots, \mu_n\}$—these are positions on a chromosome that we are trying to map—and our goal is to output a linear ordering of these markers. The output should be consistent with a set of $k$ *constraints*, each specified by a triple $(\mu_i, \mu_j, \mu_k)$, requiring that $\mu_j$ lie *between* $\mu_i$ and $\mu_k$ in the total ordering that we produce. (Note that this constraint does not specify which of $\mu_i$ or $\mu_k$ should come first in the ordering, only that $\mu_j$ should come between them.)

Now it is not always possible to satisfy all constraints simultaneously, so we wish to produce an ordering that satisfies as many as possible. Unfortunately, deciding whether there is an ordering that satisfies at least $k'$ of the $k$ constraints is an NP-complete problem (you don't have to prove this.)

Give a constant $\alpha > 0$ (independent of $n$) and an algorithm with the following property. If it is possible to satisfy $k^*$ of the constraints, then the algorithm produces an ordering of markers satisfying at least $\alpha k^*$ of the constraints. Your algorithm may be randomized; in this case it should produce an ordering for which the *expected* number of satisfied constraints is at least $\alpha k^*$.

7. In Section 13.4, we designed an approximation algorithm to within a factor of 7/8 for the MAX 3-SAT Problem, where we assumed that each clause has terms associated with three different variables. In this problem, we will consider the analogous MAX SAT Problem: Given a set of clauses $C_1, \ldots, C_k$ over a set of variables $X = \{x_1, \ldots, x_n\}$, find a truth assignment satisfying as many of the clauses as possible. Each clause has at least one term in it, and all the variables in a single clause are distinct, but otherwise we do not make any assumptions on the length of the clauses: There may be clauses that have a lot of variables, and others may have just a single variable.

(a) First consider the randomized approximation algorithm we used for MAX 3-SAT, setting each variable independently to *true* or *false* with probability 1/2 each. Show that the expected number of clauses satisfied by this random assignment is at least $k/2$, that is, at least half of the clauses are satisfied in expectation. Give an example to show that there are MAX SAT instances such that no assignment satisfies more than half of the clauses.

(b) If we have a clause that consists only of a single term (e.g., a clause consisting just of $x_1$, or just of $\overline{x_2}$), then there is only a single way to satisfy it: We need to set the corresponding variable in the appropriate way. If we have two clauses such that one consists of just the term $x_i$, and the other consists of just the negated term $\overline{x_i}$, then this is a pretty direct contradiction.

Assume that our instance has no such pair of "conflicting clauses"; that is, for no variable $x_i$ do we have both a clause $C = \{x_i\}$ and a clause $C' = \{\overline{x_i}\}$. Modify the randomized procedure above to improve the approximation factor from $1/2$ to at least .6. That is, change the algorithm so that the expected number of clauses satisfied by the process is at least .6$k$.

(c) Give a randomized polynomial-time algorithm for the general MAX SAT Problem, so that the expected number of clauses satisfied by the algorithm is at least a .6 fraction of the maximum possible.

(Note that, by the example in part (a), there are instances where one cannot satisfy more than $k/2$ clauses; the point here is that we'd still like an efficient algorithm that, in expectation, can satisfy a .6 fraction *of the maximum that can be satisfied by an optimal assignment*.)

8. Let $G = (V, E)$ be an undirected graph with $n$ nodes and $m$ edges. For a subset $X \subseteq V$, we use $G[X]$ to denote the subgraph *induced* on $X$—that is, the graph whose node set is $X$ and whose edge set consists of all edges of $G$ for which both ends lie in $X$.

We are given a natural number $k \le n$ and are interested in finding a set of $k$ nodes that induces a "dense" subgraph of $G$; we'll phrase this concretely as follows. Give a polynomial-time algorithm that produces, for a given natural number $k \le n$, a set $X \subseteq V$ of $k$ nodes with the property that the induced subgraph $G[X]$ has at least $\frac{mk(k-1)}{n(n-1)}$ edges.

You may give either (a) a deterministic algorithm, or (b) a randomized algorithm that has an expected running time that is polynomial, and that only outputs correct answers.

9. Suppose you're designing strategies for selling items on a popular auction Web site. Unlike other auction sites, this one uses a *one-pass auction*, in which each bid must be immediately (and irrevocably) accepted or refused. Specifically, the site works as follows.

   • First a seller puts up an item for sale.

   • Then buyers appear in sequence.

   • When buyer $i$ appears, he or she makes a bid $b_i > 0$.

   • The seller must decide immediately whether to accept the bid or not. If the seller accepts the bid, the item is sold and all future buyers are turned away. If the seller rejects the bid, buyer $i$ departs and the bid is withdrawn; and only then does the seller see any future buyers.

Suppose an item is offered for sale, and there are $n$ buyers, each with a distinct bid. Suppose further that the buyers appear in a random order, and that the seller knows the number $n$ of buyers. We'd like to design a strategy whereby the seller has a reasonable chance of accepting the highest of the $n$ bids. By a *strategy*, we mean a rule by which the seller decides whether to accept each presented bid, based only on the value of $n$ and the sequence of bids seen so far.

For example, the seller could always accept the first bid presented. This results in the seller accepting the highest of the $n$ bids with probability only $1/n$, since it requires the highest bid to be the first one presented.

Give a strategy under which the seller accepts the highest of the $n$ bids with probability at least $1/4$, regardless of the value of $n$. (For simplicity, you may assume that $n$ is an even number.) Prove that your strategy achieves this probabilistic guarantee.

10. Consider a very simple online auction system that works as follows. There are $n$ *bidding agents*; agent $i$ has a bid $b_i$, which is a positive natural number. We will assume that all bids $b_i$ are distinct from one another. The bidding agents appear in an order chosen uniformly at random, each proposes its bid $b_i$ in turn, and at all times the system maintains a variable $b^*$ equal to the highest bid seen so far. (Initially $b^*$ is set to 0.)

What is the expected number of times that $b^*$ is updated when this process is executed, as a function of the parameters in the problem?

**Example.** Suppose $b_1 = 20$, $b_2 = 25$, and $b_3 = 10$, and the bidders arrive in the order $1, 3, 2$. Then $b^*$ is updated for $1$ and $2$, but not for $3$.

11. *Load balancing algorithms* for parallel or distributed systems seek to spread out collections of computing jobs over multiple machines. In this way, no one machine becomes a "hot spot." If some kind of central coordination is possible, then the load can potentially be spread out almost perfectly. But what if the jobs are coming from diverse sources that can't coordinate? As we saw in Section 13.10, one option is to assign them to machines at random and hope that this randomization will work to prevent imbalances. Clearly, this won't generally work as well as a perfectly centralized solution, but it can be quite effective. Here we try analyzing some variations and extensions on the simple load balancing heuristic we considered in Section 13.10.

Suppose you have $k$ machines, and $k$ jobs show up for processing. Each job is assigned to one of the $k$ machines independently at random (with each machine equally likely).

(a) Let $N(k)$ be the expected number of machines that do not receive any jobs, so that $N(k)/k$ is the expected fraction of machines with nothing to do. What is the value of the limit $\lim_{k\to\infty} N(k)/k$? Give a proof of your answer.

(b) Suppose that machines are not able to queue up excess jobs, so if the random assignment of jobs to machines sends more than one job to a machine $M$, then $M$ will do the first of the jobs it receives and reject the rest. Let $R(k)$ be the expected number of rejected jobs; so $R(k)/k$ is the expected fraction of rejected jobs. What is $\lim_{k\to\infty} R(k)/k$? Give a proof of your answer.

(c) Now assume that machines have slightly larger buffers; each machine $M$ will do the first two jobs it receives, and reject any additional jobs. Let $R_2(k)$ denote the expected number of rejected jobs under this rule. What is $\lim_{k\to\infty} R_2(k)/k$? Give a proof of your answer.

12. Consider the following analogue of Karger's algorithm for finding minimum $s$-$t$ cuts. We will contract edges iteratively using the following randomized procedure. In a given iteration, let $s$ and $t$ denote the possibly contracted nodes that contain the original nodes $s$ and $t$, respectively. To make sure that $s$ and $t$ do not get contracted, at each iteration we delete any edges connecting $s$ and $t$ and select a random edge to contract among the remaining edges. Give an example to show that the probability that this method finds a minimum $s$-$t$ cut can be exponentially small.

13. Consider a balls-and-bins experiment with $2n$ balls but only two bins. As usual, each ball independently selects one of the two bins, both bins equally likely. The expected number of balls in each bin is $n$. In this problem, we explore the question of how big their difference is likely to be. Let $X_1$ and $X_2$ denote the number of balls in the two bins, respectively. ($X_1$ and $X_2$ are random variables.) Prove that for any $\varepsilon > 0$ there is a constant $c > 0$ such that the probability $\Pr\left[X_1 - X_2 > c\sqrt{n}\right] \le \varepsilon$.

14. Some people designing parallel physical simulations come to you with the following problem. They have a set $P$ of $k$ *basic processes* and want to assign each process to run on one of two machines, $M_1$ and $M_2$. They are then going to run a sequence of $n$ jobs, $J_1, \ldots, J_n$. Each job $J_i$ is represented by a set $P_i \subseteq P$ of exactly $2n$ basic processes which must be running (each on its assigned machine) while the job is processed. An assignment of basic processes to machines will be called *perfectly balanced* if, for

each job $J_i$, exactly $n$ of the basic processes associated with $J_i$ have been assigned to each of the two machines. An assignment of basic processes to machines will be called *nearly balanced* if, for each job $J_i$, no more than $\frac{4}{3}n$ of the basic processes associated with $J_i$ have been assigned to the same machine.

(a) Show that for arbitrarily large values of $n$, there exist sequences of jobs $J_1, \ldots, J_n$ for which no perfectly balanced assignment exists.

(b) Suppose that $n \geq 200$. Give an algorithm that takes an arbitrary sequence of jobs $J_1, \ldots, J_n$ and produces a nearly balanced assignment of basic processes to machines. Your algorithm may be randomized, in which case its expected running time should be polynomial, and it should always produce the correct answer.

15. Suppose you are presented with a very large set $S$ of real numbers, and you'd like to approximate the median of these numbers by sampling. You may assume all the numbers in $S$ are distinct. Let $n = |S|$; we will say that a number $x$ is an $\varepsilon$-*approximate median* of $S$ if at least $(\frac{1}{2} - \varepsilon)n$ numbers in $S$ are less than $x$, and at least $(\frac{1}{2} - \varepsilon)n$ numbers in $S$ are greater than $x$.

Consider an algorithm that works as follows. You select a subset $S' \subseteq S$ uniformly at random, compute the median of $S'$, and return this as an approximate median of $S$. Show that there is an absolute constant $c$, independent of $n$, so that if you apply this algorithm with a sample $S'$ of size $c$, then with probability at least $.99$, the number returned will be a $(.05)$-approximate median of $S$. (You may consider either the version of the algorithm that constructs $S'$ by sampling with replacement, so that an element of $S$ can be selected multiple times, or one without replacement.)

16. Consider the following (partially specified) method for transmitting a message securely between a sender and a receiver. The message will be represented as a string of bits. Let $\Sigma = \{0, 1\}$, and let $\Sigma^*$ denote the set of all strings of 0 or more bits (e.g., $0, 00, 1110001 \in \Sigma^*$). The "empty string," with no bits, will be denoted $\lambda \in \Sigma^*$.

The sender and receiver share a secret function $f : \Sigma^* \times \Sigma \to \Sigma$. That is, $f$ takes a word and a bit, and returns a bit. When the receiver gets a sequence of bits $\alpha \in \Sigma^*$, he or she runs the following method to decipher it.

---

```
Let α = α₁α₂···αₙ, where n is the number of bits in α,
The goal is to produce an n-bit deciphered message,
β = β₁β₂···βₙ
Set β₁ = f(λ, α₁)
```

```
For i = 2, 3, 4, ..., n
    Set β_i = f(β_1 β_2 ··· β_{i-1}, α_i)
    Endfor
Output β
```

One could view this is as a type of "stream cipher with feedback." One problem with this approach is that, if any bit $\alpha_i$ gets corrupted in transmission, it will corrupt the computed value of $\beta_j$ for all $j \geq i$.

We consider the following problem. A sender $S$ wants to transmit the same (plain-text) message $\beta$ to each of $k$ receivers $R_1, \ldots, R_k$. With each one, he shares a different secret function $f^{(i)}$. Thus he sends a different encrypted message $\alpha^{(i)}$ to each receiver, so that $\alpha^{(i)}$ decrypts to $\beta$ when the above algorithm is run with the function $f^{(i)}$.

Unfortunately, the communication channels are very noisy, so each of the $n$ bits in each of the $k$ transmissions is *independently* corrupted (i.e., flipped to its complement) with probability $1/4$. Thus no single receiver on his or her own is likely to be able to decrypt the message correctly. Show, however, that if $k$ is large enough as a function of $n$, then the $k$ receivers can jointly reconstruct the plain-text message in the following way. They get together, and without revealing any of the $\alpha^{(i)}$ or the $f^{(i)}$, they interactively run an algorithm that will produce the correct $\beta$ with probability at least $9/10$. (How large do you need $k$ to be in your algorithm?)

17. Consider the following simple model of gambling in the presence of bad odds. At the beginning, your net profit is 0. You play for a sequence of $n$ rounds; and in each round, your net profit increases by 1 with probability $1/3$, and decreases by 1 with probability $2/3$.

Show that the expected number of steps in which your net profit is positive can be upper-bounded by an absolute constant, independent of the value of $n$.

18. In this problem, we will consider the following simple randomized algorithm for the Vertex Cover Algorithm.

```
Start with S = ∅
While S is not a vertex cover,
    Select an edge e not covered by S
    Select one end of e at random (each end equally likely)
    Add the selected node to S
Endwhile
```

We will be interested in the expected cost of a vertex cover selected by this algorithm.

(a) Is this algorithm a $c$-approximation algorithm for the Minimum Weight Vertex Cover Problem for some constant $c$? Prove your answer.

(b) Is this algorithm a $c$-approximation algorithm for the Minimum Cardinality Vertex Cover Problem for some constant $c$? Prove your answer.

   *(Hint:* For an edge, let $p_e$ denote the probability that edge $e$ is selected as an uncovered edge in this algorithm. Can you express the expected value of the solution in terms of these probabilities? To bound the value of an optimal solution in terms of the $p_e$ probabilities, try to bound the sum of the probabilities for the edges incident to a given vertex $v$, namely, $\sum_{e \text{ incident to } v} p_e$.)

# Notes and Further Reading

The use of randomization in algorithms is an active research area; the books by Motwani and Raghavan (1995) and Mitzenmacher and Upfal (2005) are devoted to this topic. As the contents of this chapter make clear, the types of probabilistic arguments used in the study of basic randomized algorithms often have a discrete, combinatorial flavor; one can get background in this style of probabilistic analysis from the book by Feller (1957).

The use of randomization for contention resolution is common in many systems and networking applications. Ethernet-style shared communication media, for example, use randomized *backoff* protocols to reduce the number of collisions among different senders; see the book by Bertsekas and Gallager (1992) for a discussion of this topic.

The randomized algorithm for the Minimum-Cut Problem described in the text is due to Karger, and after further optimizations due to Karger and Stein (1996), it has become one of the most efficient approaches to the minimum cut problem. A number of further extensions and applications of the algorithm appear in Karger's (1995) Ph.D. thesis.

The approximation algorithm for MAX 3-SAT is due to Johnson (1974), in a paper that contains a number of early approximation algorithms for NP-hard problems. The surprising punch line to that section—that every instance of 3-SAT has an assignment satisfying at least 7/8 of the clauses—is an example of the *probabilistic method*, whereby a combinatorial structure with a desired property is shown to exist simply by arguing that a random structure has the property with positive probability. This has grown into a highly refined technique in the area of combinatorics; the book by Alon and Spencer (2000) covers a wide range of its applications.

Hashing is a topic that remains the subject of extensive study, in both theoretical and applied settings, and there are many variants of the basic method. The approach we focus on in Section 13.6 is due to Carter and Wegman (1979). The use of randomization for finding the closest pair of points in the plane was originally proposed by Rabin (1976), in an influential early paper that exposed the power of randomization in many algorithmic settings. The algorithm we describe in this chapter was developed by Golin et al. (1995). The technique used there to bound the number of dictionary operations, in which one sums the expected work over all stages of the random order, is sometimes referred to as *backwards analysis*; this was originally proposed by Chew (1985) for a related geometric problem, and a number of further applications of backwards analysis are described in the survey by Seidel (1993).

The performance guarantee for the LRU caching algorithm is due to Sleator and Tarjan (1985), and the bound for the Randomized Marking algorithm is due to Fiat, Karp, Luby, McGeoch, Sleator, and Young (1991). More generally, the paper by Sleator and Tarjan highlighted the notion of *online algorithms*, which must process input without knowledge of the future; caching is one of the fundamental applications that call for such algorithms. The book by Borodin and El-Yaniv (1998) is devoted to the topic of online algorithms and includes many further results on caching in particular.

There are many ways to formulate bounds of the type in Section 13.9, showing that a sum of 0-1-valued independent random variables is unlikely to deviate far from its mean. Results of this flavor are generally called *Chernoff bounds*, or *Chernoff-Hoeffding* bounds, after the work of Chernoff (1952) and Hoeffding (1963). The books by Alon and Spencer (1992), Motwani and Raghavan (1995), and Mitzenmacher and Upfal (2005) discuss these kinds of bounds in more detail and provide further applications.

The results for packet routing in terms of congestion and dilation are due to Leighton, Maggs, and Rao (1994). Routing is another area in which randomization can be effective at reducing contention and hot spots; the book by Leighton (1992) covers many further applications of this principle.

***Notes on the Exercises***    Exercise 6 is based on a result of Benny Chor and Madhu Sudan; Exercise 9 is a version of the *Secretary Problem*, whose popularization is often credited to Martin Gardner.

# *Epilogue: Algorithms That Run Forever*

Every decade has its addictive puzzles; and if Rubik's Cube stands out as the preeminent solitaire recreation of the early 1980s, then Tetris evokes a similar nostalgia for the late eighties and early nineties. Rubik's Cube and Tetris have a number of things in common—they share a highly mathematical flavor, based on stylized geometric forms—but the differences between them are perhaps more interesting.

Rubik's Cube is a game whose complexity is based on an enormous search space; given a scrambled configuration of the Cube, you have to apply an intricate sequence of operations to reach the ultimate goal. By contrast, Tetris—in its pure form—has a much fuzzier definition of success; rather than aiming for a particular endpoint, you're faced with a basically infinite stream of events to be dealt with, and you have to react continuously so as to keep your head above water.

These novel features of Tetris parallel an analogous set of themes that has emerged in recent thinking about algorithms. Increasingly, we face settings in which the standard view of algorithms—in which one begins with an input, runs for a finite number of steps, and produces an output—does not really apply. Rather, if we think about Internet routers that move packets while avoiding congestion, or decentralized file-sharing mechanisms that replicate and distribute content to meet user demand, or machine learning routines that form predictive models of concepts that change over time, then we are dealing with algorithms that effectively are designed *to run forever*. Instead of producing an eventual output, they succeed if they can keep up with an environment that is in constant flux and continuously throws new tasks at them. For such applications, we have shifted from the world of Rubik's Cube to the world of Tetris.

There are many settings in which we could explore this theme, and as our final topic for the book we consider one of the most compelling: the design of algorithms for high-speed packet switching on the Internet.

## The Problem

A packet traveling from a source to a destination on the Internet can be thought of as traversing a path in a large graph whose nodes are switches and whose edges are the cables that link switches together. Each packet $p$ has a header from which a switch can determine, when $p$ arrives on an input link, the output link on which $p$ needs to depart. The goal of a switch is thus to take streams of packets arriving on its input links and move each packet, as quickly as possible, to the particular output link on which it needs to depart. How quickly? In high-volume settings, it is possible for a packet to arrive on each input link once every few tens of nanoseconds; if they aren't offloaded to their respective output links at a comparable rate, then traffic will back up and packets will be dropped.

In order to think about the algorithms operating inside a switch, we model the switch itself as follows. It has $n$ *input links* $I_1, \ldots, I_n$ and $n$ *output links* $O_1, \ldots, O_n$. Packets arrive on the input links; a given packet $p$ has an associated input/output *type* $(I[p], O[p])$ indicating that it has arrived at input link $I[p]$ and needs to depart on output link $O[p]$. Time moves in discrete *steps*; in each step, at most one new packet arrives on each input link, and at most one packet can depart on each output link.

Consider the example in Figure E.1. In a single time step, the three packets $p$, $q$, and $r$ have arrived at an empty switch on input links $I_1$, $I_3$, and $I_4$, respectively. Packet $p$ is destined for $O_1$, packet $q$ is destined for $O_3$, and packet $r$ is also destined for $O_3$. Now there's no problem sending packet $p$ out on link $O_1$; but only one packet can depart on link $O_3$, and so the switch has to resolve the contention between $q$ and $r$. How can it do this?

The simplest model of switch behavior is known as *pure output queueing*, and it's essentially an idealized picture of how we wished a switch behaved. In this model, all nodes that arrive in a given time step are placed in an *output buffer* associated with their output link, and one of the packets in each output buffer actually gets to depart. More concretely, here's the model of a single time step.

```
One step under pure output queueing:
  Packets arrive on input links
  Each packet p of type (I[p], O[p]) is moved to output buffer O[p]
  At most one packet departs from each output buffer
```

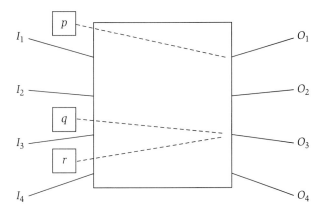

**Figure E.1** A switch with $n = 4$ inputs and outputs. In one time step, packets $p$, $q$, and $r$ have arrived.

So, in Figure E.1, the given time step could end with packets $p$ and $q$ having departed on their output links, and with packet $r$ sitting in the output buffer $O_3$. (In discussing this example here and below, we'll assume that $q$ is favored over $r$ when decisions are made.) Under this model, the switch is basically a "frictionless" object through which packets pass unimpeded to their output buffer.

In reality, however, a packet that arrives on an input link must be copied over to its appropriate output link, and this operation requires some processing that ties up both the input and output links for a few nanoseconds. So, really, constraints within the switch do pose some obstacles to the movement of packets from inputs to outputs.

The most restrictive model of these constraints, *input/output queueing*, works as follows. We now have an *input buffer* for each input link $I$, as well as an output buffer for each output link $O$. When each packet arrives, it immediately lands in its associated input buffer. In a single time step, a switch can read at most one packet from each input buffer and write at most one packet to each output buffer. So under input/output queueing, the example of Figure E.1 would work as follows. Each of $p$, $q$, and $r$ would arrive in different input buffers; the switch could then move $p$ and $q$ to their output buffers, but it could not move all three, since moving all three would involve writing two packets into the output buffer $O_3$. Thus the first step would end with $p$ and $q$ having departed on their output links, and $r$ sitting in the input buffer $I_4$ (rather than in the output buffer $O_3$).

More generally, the restriction of limited reading and writing amounts to the following: If packets $p_1, \ldots, p_\ell$ are moved in a single time step from input buffers to output buffers, then all their input buffers and all their output buffers must be distinct. In other words, their types $\{(I[p_i], O[p_i]) : i = 1, 2, \ldots, \ell\}$ must form a bipartite matching. Thus we can model a single time step as follows.

---

One step under input/output queueing:
  Packets arrive on input links and are placed in input buffers
  A set of packets whose types form a matching are moved to their
    associated output buffers
  At most one packet departs from each output buffer

---

The choice of which matching to move is left unspecified for now; this is a point that will become crucial later.

So under input/output queueing, the switch introduces some "friction" on the movement of packets, and this is an observable phenomenon: if we view the switch as a black box, and simply watch the sequence of departures on the output links, then we can see the difference between pure output queueing and input/output queueing. Consider an example whose first step is just like Figure E.1, and in whose second step a single packet $s$ of type $(I_4, O_4)$ arrives. Under pure output queueing, $p$ and $q$ would depart in the first step, and $r$ and $s$ would depart in the second step. Under input/output queueing, however, the sequence of events depicted in Figure E.2 occurs: At the end of the first step, $r$ is still sitting in the input buffer $I_4$, and so, at the end of the second step, one of $r$ or $s$ is still in the input buffer $I_4$ and has not yet departed. This conflict between $r$ and $s$ is called *head-of-line blocking*, and it causes a switch with input/output queueing to exhibit inferior delay characteristics compared with pure output queueing.

***Simulating a Switch with Pure Output Queueing***   While pure output queueing would be nice to have, the arguments above indicate why it's not feasible to design a switch with this behavior: In a single time step (lasting only tens of nanoseconds), it would not generally be possible to move packets from each of $n$ input links to a common output buffer.

But what if we were to take a switch that used input/output queueing and ran it somewhat faster, moving several matchings in a single time step instead of just one? Would it be possible to simulate a switch that used pure output queueing? By this we mean that the sequence of departures on the output links (viewing the switch as a black box) should be the same under the behavior of pure output queueing and the behavior of our sped-up input/output queueing algorithm.

It is not hard to see that a speed-up of $n$ would suffice: If we could move $n$ matchings in each time step, then even if every arriving packet needed to reach the same output buffer, we could move them all in the course of one

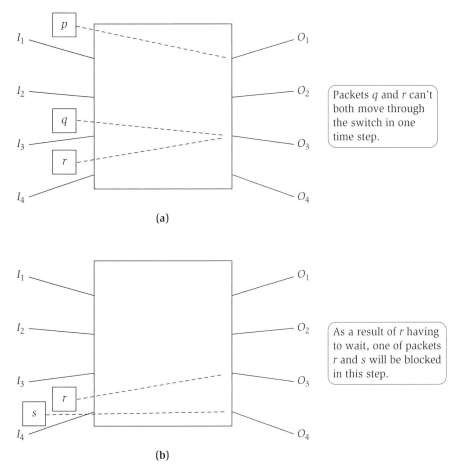

Packets $q$ and $r$ can't both move through the switch in one time step.

**(a)**

As a result of $r$ having to wait, one of packets $r$ and $s$ will be blocked in this step.

**(b)**

**Figure E.2** Parts (a) and (b) depict a two-step example in which head-of-line blocking occurs.

step. But a speed-up of $n$ is completely infeasible; and if we think about this worst-case example, we begin to worry that we might need a speed-up of $n$ to make this work—after all, what if all the arriving packets really did need to go to the same output buffer?

The crux of this section is to show that a much more modest speed-up is sufficient. We'll describe a striking result of Chuang, Goel, McKeown, and Prabhakar (1999), showing that a switch using input/output queueing with a speed-up of 2 can simulate a switch that uses pure output queueing. Intuitively, the result exploits the fact that the behavior of the switch at an internal level need not resemble the behavior under pure output queueing, provided that the sequence of output link departures is the same. (Hence, to continue the example in the previous paragraph, it's okay that we don't move all $n$ arriving packets to a common output buffer in one time step; we can afford more time for this, since their departures on this common output link will be spread out over a long period of time anyway.)

## ✐ Designing the Algorithm

Just to be precise, here's our model for a speed-up of 2.

---

```
One step under sped-up input/output queueing:
  Packets arrive on input links and are placed in input buffers
  A set of packets whose types form a matching are moved to their
    associated output buffers
  At most one packet departs from each output buffer
  A set of packets whose types form a matching are moved to their
    associated output buffers
```

---

In order to prove that this model can simulate pure output queueing, we need to resolve the crucial underspecified point in the model above: *Which matchings should be moved in each step?* The answer to this question will form the core of the result, and we build up to it through a sequence of intermediate steps. To begin with, we make one simple observation right away: If a packet of type $(I, O)$ is part of a matching selected by the switch, then the switch will move the packet of this type that has the *earliest* time to leave.

***Maintaining Input and Output Buffers***     To decide which two matchings the switch should move in a given time step, we define some quantities that track the current state of the switch relative to pure output queueing. To begin with, for a packet $p$, we define its *time to leave*, $TL(p)$, to be the time step in which it would depart on its output link from a switch that was running pure output queueing. The goal is to make sure that each packet $p$ departs from our switch (running sped-up input/output queueing) in precisely the time step $TL(p)$.

Conceptually, each input buffer is maintained as an ordered list; however, we retain the freedom to insert an arriving packet into the middle of this order, and to move a packet to its output buffer even when it is not yet at the front of the line. Despite this, the linear ordering of the buffer will form a useful progress measure. Each output buffer, by contrast, does not need to be ordered; when a packet's time to leave comes up, we simply let it depart. We can think of the whole setup as resembling a busy airport terminal, with the input buffers corresponding to check-in counters, the output buffers to the departure lounge, and the internals of the switch to a congested security checkpoint. The input buffers are stressful places: If you don't make it to the head of the line by the time your departure is announced, you could miss your time to leave; to mitigate this, there are airport personnel who are allowed to helpfully extract you from the middle of the line and hustle you through security. The output buffers, by way of contrast, are relaxing places: You sit around until your time to leave is announced, and then you just go. The goal is to get everyone through the congestion in the middle so that they depart on time.

One consequence of these observations is that we don't need to worry about packets that are already in output buffers; they'll just depart at the right time. Hence we refer to a packet $p$ as *unprocessed* if it is still in its input buffer, and we define some further useful quantities for such packets. The *input cushion* $IC(p)$ is the number of packets ordered in front of $p$ in its input buffer. The *output cushion* $OC(p)$ is the number of packets already in $p$'s output buffer that have an earlier time to leave. Things are going well for an unprocessed packet $p$ if $OC(p)$ is significantly greater than $IC(p)$; in this case, $p$ is near the front of the line in its input buffer, and there are still a lot of packets before it in the output buffer. To capture this relationship, we define $Slack(p) = OC(p) - IC(p)$, observing that large values of $Slack(p)$ are good.

Here is our plan: We will move matchings through the switch so as to maintain the following two properties at all times.

(i)  $Slack(p) \geq 0$ for all unprocessed packets $p$.

(ii) In any step that begins with $IC(p) = OC(p) = 0$, packet $p$ will be moved to its output buffer in the first matching.

We first claim that it is sufficient to maintain these two properties.

**(E.1)**    *If properties (i) and (ii) are maintained for all unprocessed packets at all times, then every packet $p$ will depart at its time to leave $TL(p)$.*

**Proof.** If $p$ is in its output buffer at the start of step $TL(p)$, then it can clearly depart. Otherwise it must be in its input buffer. In this case, we have $OC(p) = 0$ at the start of the step. By property (i), we have $Slack(p) = OC(p) - IC(p) \geq 0$, and hence $IC(p) = 0$. It then follows from property (ii) that $p$ will be moved to the output buffer in the first matching of this step, and hence will depart in this step as well.  ∎

It turns out that property (ii) is easy to guarantee (and it will arise naturally from the solution below), so we focus on the tricky task of choosing matchings so as to maintain property (i).

***Moving a Matching through a Switch***    When a packet $p$ first arrives on an input link, we insert it as far back in the input buffer as possible (potentially somewhere in the middle) consistent with the requirement $Slack(p) \geq 0$. This makes sure property (i) is satisfied initially for $p$.

Now, if we want to maintain nonnegative slacks over time, then we need to worry about counterbalancing events that cause $Slack(p)$ to decrease. Let's return to the description of a single time step and think about how such decreases can occur.

---

```
One step under sped-up input/output queueing:
  Packets arrive on input links and are placed in input buffers
  The switch moves a matching
  At most one packet departs from each output buffer
  The switch moves a matching
```

---

Consider a given packet $p$ that is unprocessed at the beginning of a time step. In the arrival phase of the step, $IC(p)$ could increase by 1 if the arriving packet is placed in the input buffer ahead of $p$. This would cause $Slack(p)$ to decrease by 1. In the departure phase of the step, $OC(p)$ could decrease by 1, since a packet with an earlier time to leave will no longer be in the output buffer. This too would cause $Slack(p)$ to decrease by 1. So, in summary, $Slack(p)$ can potentially decrease by 1 in each of the arrival and departure phases. Consequently, we will be able to maintain property (i) if we can guarantee that $Slack(p)$ increases by at least 1 each time the switch moves a matching. How can we do this?

If the matching to be moved includes a packet in $I[p]$ that is *ahead* of $p$, then $IC(p)$ will decrease and hence $Slack(p)$ will increase. If the matching includes a packet destined for $O[p]$ with an earlier time to leave than $p$, then $OC(p)$ and $Slack(p)$ will increase. So the only problem is if neither of these things happens. Figure E.3 gives a schematic picture of such a situation. Suppose that packet $x$ is moved out of $I[p]$ even though it is farther back in order, and packet $y$ is moved to $O[p]$ even though it has a later time to leave. In this situation, it seems that buffers $I[p]$ and $O[p]$ have both been treated "unfairly": It would have been better for $I[p]$ to send a packet like $p$ that was farther forward, and it would have been better for $O[p]$ to receive a packet like $p$ that had an earlier time to leave. Taken together, the two buffers form something reminiscent of an *instability* from the Stable Matching Problem.

In fact, we can make this precise, and it provides the key to finishing the algorithm. Suppose we say that output buffer $O$ *prefers* input buffer $I$ to $I'$ if the earliest time to leave among packets of type $(I, O)$ is smaller than the earliest time to leave among packets of type $(I', O)$. (In other words, buffer $I$ is more in need of sending something to buffer $O$.) Further, we say that input buffer $I$ *prefers* output buffer $O$ to output buffer $O'$ if the forwardmost packet of type $(I, O)$ comes ahead of the forwardmost packet of type $(I, O')$ in the ordering of $I$. We construct a preference list for each buffer from these rules;

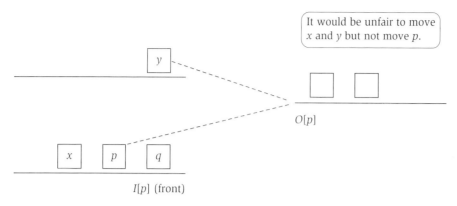

**Figure E.3** Choosing a matching to move.

and if there are no packets at all of type $(I, O)$, then $I$ and $O$ are placed at the end of each other's preference lists, with ties broken arbitrarily. Finally, we determine a stable matching $M$ with respect to these preference lists, and the switch moves this matching $M$.

## Analyzing the Algorithm

The following fact establishes that choosing a stable matching will indeed yield an algorithm with the performance guarantee that we want.

**(E.2)** *Suppose the switch always moves a stable matching $M$ with respect to the preference lists defined above. (And for each type $(I, O)$ contained in $M$, we select the packet of this type with the earliest time to leave). Then, for all unprocessed packets $p$, the value Slack$(p)$ increases by at least 1 when the matching $M$ is moved.*

**Proof.** Consider any unprocessed packet $p$. Following the discussion above, suppose that no packet ahead of $p$ in $I[p]$ is moved as part of the matching $M$, and no packet destined for $O[p]$ with an earlier time to leave is moved as part of $M$. So, in particular, the pair $(I[p], O[p])$ is not in $M$; suppose that pairs $(I', O[p])$ and $(I[p], O')$ belong to $M$.

Now $p$ has an earlier time to leave than any packet of type $(I', O[p])$, and it comes ahead of every packet of type $(I[p], O')$ in the ordering of $I[p]$. It follows that $I[p]$ prefers $O[p]$ to $O'$, and $O[p]$ prefers $I[p]$ to $I'$. Hence the pair $(I[p], O[p])$ forms an instability, which contradicts our assumption that $M$ is stable. ∎

Thus, by moving a stable matching in every step, the switch maintains the property Slack$(p) \geq 0$ for all packets $p$; hence, by (E.1), we have shown the following.

**(E.3)**   *By moving two stable matchings in each time step, according to the preferences just defined, the switch is able to simulate the behavior of pure output queueing.*

Overall, the algorithm makes for a surprising last-minute appearance by the topic with which we began the book—and rather than matching men with women or applicants with employers, we find ourselves matching input links to output links in a high-speed Internet router.

This has been one glimpse into the issue of algorithms that run forever, keeping up with an infinite stream of new events. It is an intriguing topic, full of open directions and unresolved issues. But that is for another time, and another book; and, as for us, we are done.

# References

E. Aarts and J. K. Lenstra (eds.). *Local Search in Combinatorial Optimization*. Wiley, 1997.

R. K. Ahuja, T. L. Magnanti, and J. B. Orlin. *Network Flows: Theory, Algorithms, and Applications*. Prentice Hall, 1993.

N. Alon and J. Spencer. *The Probabilistic Method* (2nd edition). Wiley, 2000.

M. Anderberg. *Cluster Analysis for Applications*. Academic Press, 1973.

E. Anshelevich, A. Dasgupta, J. Kleinberg, É. Tardos, T. Wexler, and T. Roughgarden. The price of stability for network design with fair cost allocation. *Proc. 45th IEEE Symposium on Foundations of Computer Science*, pp. 295–304, 2004.

K. Appel and W. Haken. The solution of the four-color-map problem. *Scientific American*, 237:4(1977), 108–121.

S. Arora and C. Lund. Hardness of approximations. In *Approximation Algorithms for NP-Hard Problems*, edited by D. S. Hochbaum. PWS Publishing, 1996.

B. Awerbuch, Y. Azar, and S. Plotkin. Throughput-competitive online routing, *Proc. 34th IEEE Symposium on Foundations of Computer Science*, pp. 32–40, 1993.

R. Bar-Yehuda and S. Even. A linear-time approximation algorithm for the weighted vertex cover problem. *J. Algorithms* 2 (1981), 198–203.

A.-L. Barabasi. *Linked: The New Science of Networks*. Perseus, 2002.

M. Beckmann, C. B. McGuire, and C. B. Winsten. *Studies in the Economics of Transportation*. Yale University Press, 1956.

L. Belady. A study of replacement algorithms for virtual storage computers. *IBM Systems Journal* 5 (1966), 78–101.

T. C. Bell, J. G. Cleary, and I. H. Witten. *Text Compression*. Prentice Hall, 1990.

R. E. Bellman. *Dynamic Programming*. Princeton University Press, 1957.

R. Bellman. On a routing problem. *Quarterly of Applied Mathematics* 16 (1958), 87–90.

R. Bellman. On the approximation of curves by line segments using dynamic programming. *Communications of the ACM*, 4:6 (June 1961), 284.

M. de Berg, M. van Kreveld, M. Overmars, and O. Schwarzkopf. *Computational Geometry: Algorithms and Applications*. Springer-Verlag, 1997.

C. Berge. *Graphs and Hypergraphs*. North-Holland Mathematical Library, 1976.

E. R. Berlekamp, J. H. Conway, and R. K. Guy. *Winning Ways for Your Mathematical Plays*. Academic Press, 1982.

M. Bern and D. Eppstein. Approximation algorithms for geometric problems. In *Approximation Algorithms for NP-Hard Problems*, edited by D. S. Hochbaum. PWS Publishing, 1996.

D. Bertsekas and R. Gallager. *Data Networks*. Prentice Hall, 1992.

B. Bollobas. *Modern Graph Theory*. Springer-Verlag, 1998.

A. Borodin and R. El-Yaniv. *Online Computation and Competitive Analysis*. Cambridge University Press, 1998.

A. Borodin, M. N. Nielsen, and C. Rackoff. (Incremental) priority algorithms. *Proc. 13th Annual ACM-SIAM Symposium on Discrete Algorithms*, pp. 752–761, 2002.

Y. Boykov, O. Veksler, and R. Zabih. Fast approximate energy minimization via graph cuts. *International Conference on Computer Vision*, pp. 377–384, 1999.

L. J. Carter and M. L. Wegman. Universal classes of hash functions. *J. Computer and System Sciences* 18:2 (1979), 143–154.

B. V. Cherkassky, A. V. Goldberg, and T. Radzik. Shortest paths algorithms: Theory and experimental evaluation. *Proc. 5th ACM-SIAM Symposium on Discrete Algorithms*, pp. 516–525, 1994.

H. Chernoff. A measure of asymptotic efficiency for tests of a hypothesis based on the sum of observations. *Annals of Mathematical Statistics*, 23 (1952), 493–509.

L. P. Chew. Building Voronoi diagrams for convex polygons in linear expected time. Technical Report, Dept. of Math and Computer Science, Dartmouth College, Hanover, NH, 1985.

Y. J. Chu and T. H. Liu. On the shortest arborescence of a directed graph. *Sci. Sinica 14* (1965), 1396–1400.

S.-T. Chuang, A. Goel, N. McKeown, and B. Prabhakar. Matching output queueing with a combined input output queued switch. *IEEE J. on Selected Areas in Communications*, 17:6 (1999), 1030–1039.

V. Chvatal. A greedy heuristic for the set covering problem. *Mathematics of Operations Research*, 4 (1979), 233–235.

S. A. Cook. The complexity of theorem proving procedures. *Proc. 3rd ACM Symp. on Theory of Computing*, pp. 151–158. 1971.

W. J. Cook, W. H. Cunningham, W. R. Pulleyblank, and A. Schrijver. *Combinatorial Optimization*. Wiley, 1998.

T. Cover and J. Thomas. *Elements of Information Theory*. Wiley, 1991.

R. Diestel, K. Yu. Gorbunov, T.R. Jensen, and C. Thomassen. Highly connected sets and the excluded grid theorem. *J. Combinatorial Theory, Series B* 75(1999), 61–73.

R. Diestel. *Graph Theory* (2nd edition). Springer-Verlag, 2000.

E. W. Dijkstra. A note on two problems in connexion with graphs. *Numerische Matematik*, 1 (1959), 269–271.

E. A. Dinitz. Algorithm for solution of a problem of maximum flow in networks with power estimation. *Soviet Mathematics Doklady*, 11(1970), 1277–1280.

R. Downey and M. Fellows. *Parametrized Complexity*. Springer-Verlag, 1999.

Z. Drezner (ed.). Facility location. Springer-Verlag, 1995.

R. Duda, P. Hart, and D. Stork. *Pattern Classification* (2nd edition). Wiley, 2001.

M. E. Dyer and A. M. Frieze. A simple heuristic for the $p$-centre problem. *Operations Research Letters*, 3 (1985), 285–288.

J. Edmonds. Minimum partition of a matroid into independent subsets. *J. Research of the National Bureau of Standards B*, 69 (1965), 67–72.

J. Edmonds. Optimum branchings. *J. Research of the National Bureau of Standards*, 71B (1967), 233–240.

J. Edmonds. Matroids and the Greedy Algorithm. *Math. Programming* 1 (1971), 127–136.

J. Edmonds and R. M. Karp. Theoretical improvements in algorithmic efficiency for network flow problems. *Journal of the ACM* 19:2(1972), 248–264.

L. Euler. Solutio problematis ad geometriam situs pertinentis. *Commetarii Academiae Scientiarum Imperialis Petropolitanae* 8 (1736), 128–140.

R. M. Fano. *Transmission of Information*. M.I.T. Press, 1949.

W. Feller. *An Introduction to Probability Theory and Its Applications*, Vol. 1. Wiley, 1957.

A. Fiat, R. M. Karp, M. Luby, L. A. McGeoch, D. D. Sleator, and N. E. Young. Competitive paging algorithms. *J. Algorithms* 12 (1991), 685–699.

R. W. Floyd. Algorithm 245 (TreeSort). *Communications of the ACM*, 7 (1964), 701.

L. R. Ford. Network Flow Theory. RAND Corporation Technical Report P-923, 1956.

L. R. Ford and D. R. Fulkerson. *Flows in Networks*. Princeton University Press, 1962.

D. Gale. The two-sided matching problem: Origin, development and current issues. *International Game Theory Review*, 3:2/3 (2001), 237–252.

D. Gale and L. Shapley. College admissions and the stability of marriage. *American Mathematical Monthly* 69 (1962), 9–15.

M. R. Garey and D. S. Johnson. *Computers and Intractability. A Guide to the Theory of NP-Completeness*. Freeman, 1979.

M. Garey, D. Johnson, G. Miller, and C. Papadimitriou. The complexity of coloring circular arcs and chords. *SIAM J. Algebraic and Discrete Methods*, 1:2 (June 1980), 216–227.

M. Ghallab, D. Nau, and P. Traverso. *Automated Planning: Theory and Practice*. Morgan Kaufmann, 2004.

M. X. Goemans and D. P. Williamson. The primal-dual method for approximation algorithms and its application to network design problems. In *Approximation Algorithms for NP-Hard Problems*, edited by D. S. Hochbaum. PWS Publishing, 1996.

A. Goldberg. Efficient Graph Algorithms for Sequential and Parallel Computers. Ph.D. thesis, MIT, 1986.

A. Goldberg. Network Optimization Library. *http://www.avglab.com/andrew /soft.html*.

A. Goldberg, É. Tardos, and R. E. Tarjan. Network flow algorithms. In *Paths, Flows, and VLSI-Layout*, edited by B. Korte et al. Springer-Verlag, 1990.

A. Goldberg and R. Tarjan. A new approach to the maximum flow problem. *Proc. 18th ACM Symposium on Theory of Computing*, pp. 136–146, 1986.

M. Golin, R. Raman, C. Schwarz, and M. Smid. Simple randomized algorithms for closest pair problems. *Nordic J. Comput.*, 2 (1995), 3–27.

M. C. Golumbic. *Algorithmic Graph Theory and Perfect Graphs*. Academic Press, 1980.

R. L. Graham. Bounds for certain multiprocessing anomalies. *Bell System Technical Journal* 45 (1966), 1563–1581.

R. L. Graham. Bounds for multiprocessing timing anomalies. *SIAM J. Applied Mathematics* 17 (1969), 263–269.

R. L. Graham and P. Hell. On the history of the minimum spanning tree problem. *Annals of the History of Computing*, 7 (1985), 43–57.

M. Granovetter. Threshold models of collective behavior. *American Journal of Sociology* 83:6(1978), 1420–1443.

D. Greig, B. Porteous, and A. Seheult. Exact maximum *a posteriori* estimation for binary images. *J. Royal Statistical Society B*, 51:2(1989), pp. 271–278.

D. Gusfield. *Algorithms on Strings, Trees, and Sequences: Computer Science and Computational Biology.* Cambridge University Press, 1997.

D. R. Gusfield and R. W. Irving. *The Stable Marriage Problem: Structure and Algorithms.* MIT Press, 1989.

L. A. Hall. Approximation algorithms for scheduling. In *Approximation Algorithms for NP-Hard Problems*, edited by D. S. Hochbaum. PWS Publishing, 1996.

P. Hall. On representation of subsets. *J. London Mathematical Society* 10 (1935), 26–30.

S. Haykin. *Neural Networks: A Comprehensive Foundation* (2nd ed.). Macmillan, 1999.

D. S. Hirschberg. A linear space algorithm for computing maximal common subsequences. *Communications of the ACM* 18 (1975) 341–343.

D. S. Hochbaum. Approximation algorithms for the set covering and vertex cover problems. *SIAM J. on Computing*, 11:3 (1982), 555–556.

D. S. Hochbaum (ed.). *Approximation Algorithms for NP-Hard Problems.* PWS Publishing, 1996.

D. S. Hochbaum. Approximating covering and packing problems: set cover, vertex cover, independent set and related problems. In *Approximation Algorithms for NP-Hard Problems*, edited by D. S. Hochbaum. PWS Publishing, 1996.

D. S. Hochbaum and D. B. Shmoys. A best possible heuristic for the $k$-center problem. *Mathematics of Operations Research* 10:2 (1985), 180–184.

D. S. Hochbaum and D. B. Shmoys. Using dual approximation algorithms for scheduling problems: Theoretical and practical results. *Journal of the ACM* 34 (1987), 144–162.

W. Hoeffding. Probability inequalities for sums of bounded random variables. *J. American Statistical Association*, 58 (1963), 13–30.

J. Hopfield. Neural networks and physical systems with emergent collective computational properties. *Proc. National Academy of Sciences of the USA*, 79 (1982), 2554–2588.

D. A. Huffman. A method for the construction of minimum-redundancy codes. *Proc. IRE* 40: 9 (Sept. 1952), 1098–1101.

A. Jain and R. Dubes. *Algorithms for Clustering Data.* Prentice Hall, 1981.

T. R. Jensen and B. Toft. *Graph Coloring Problems.* Wiley Interscience, 1995.

D. S. Johnson. Approximation algorithms for combinatorial problems. *J. of Computer and System Sciences*, 9 (1974), 256–278.

M. Jordan (ed.). *Learning in Graphical Models*. MIT Press, 1998.

A. Karatsuba and Y. Ofman. Multiplication of multidigit numbers on automata. *Soviet Physics Doklady*, 7 (1962), 595–596.

D. Karger. Random Sampling in Graph Optimization Problems. Ph.D. Thesis, Stanford University, 1995.

D. R. Karger, C. Stein. A new approach to the minimum cut problem. *Journal of the ACM* 43:4(1996), 601–640.

N. Karmarkar. A new polynomial-time algorithm for linear programming. *Combinatorica*, 4:4(1984), 373–396.

R. M. Karp. Reducibility among combinatorial problems. In *Complexity of Computer Computations*, edited by R. Miller and J. Thatcher, pp. 85–103. Plenum Press, 1972.

B. Kernighan and S. Lin. An efficient heuristic procedure for partitioning graphs. *The Bell System Technical Journal*, 49:2 (1970), 291–307.

S. Keshav. *An Engineering Approach to Computer Networking*. Addison-Wesley, 1997.

L. Khachiyan. A polynomial algorithm in linear programming. *Soviet Mathematics Doklady*, 20:1(1979), 191–194.

S. Kirkpatrick, C. D. Gelatt, Jr., and M. P. Vecchi. Optimization by simulated annealing. *Science*, 220:4598 (1983), 671–680.

J. Kleinberg. Approximation Algorithms for Disjoint Paths Problems. Ph.D Thesis, MIT, 1996.

J. Kleinberg and É. Tardos. Disjoint paths in densely embedded graphs. *Proc. 36th IEEE Symposium on Foundations of Computer Science*, pp. 52–61, 1995.

D. E. Knuth, *The Art of Computer Programming*, Vol. 1: *Fundamental Algorithms* (3rd edition). Addison-Wesley, 1997a.

D. E. Knuth. *The Art of Computer Programming*, Vol. 2: *Seminumerical Algorithms* (3rd edition). Addison-Wesley, 1997b.

D. E. Knuth. Stable marriage and its relation to other combinatorial problems. *CRM Proceedings and Lecture Notes*, vol. 10. American Mathematical Society, 1997c.

D. E. Knuth. *The Art of Computer Programming*, Vol. 3: *Sorting and Searching* (3rd edition). Addison-Wesley, 1998.

V. Kolmogorov and R. Zabih. What energy functions can be minimized via graph cuts? *IEEE Transactions on Pattern Analysis and Machine Intelligence (PAMI)*, 26:2 (2004), 147–159.

D. Konig. Uber Graphen und ihre Anwendung auf Determinantentheorie und Mengenlehre. *Mathematische Annalen*, 77 (1916), 453–465.

B. Korte, L. Lovász, H. J. Prömel, A. Schrijver (eds.). *Paths, Flows, and VLSI-Layout* Springer-Verlag, 1990.

E. Lawler. *Combinatorial Optimization: Networks and Matroids*. Dover, 2001.

E. L. Lawler, J. K. Lenstra, A. H. G. Rinnooy Kan, and D. B. Shmoys. *The Traveling Salesman Problem: A Guided Tour of Combinatorial Optimization*. Wiley, 1985.

E. L. Lawler, J. K. Lenstra, A. H. G. Rinnooy Kan, and D. B. Shmoys. Sequencing and scheduling: Algorithms and complexity. In *Handbooks in Operations Research and Management Science* 4, edited by S. C. Graves, A. H. G. Rinnooy Kan, and P. H. Zipkin. Elsevier, 1993.

F. T. Leighton, *Introduction to Parallel Algorithms and Architectures*. Morgan Kaufmann, 1992.

F. T. Leighton, B. M. Maggs, and S. Rao. Packet routing and job-shop scheduling in O(congestion + dilation) steps. *Combinatorica*, 14:2 (1994), 167–186.

D. Lelewer and D. S. Hirshberg. Data Compression. *Computing Surveys* 19:3 (1987), 261–297.

J. K. Lenstra, D. Shmoys, and É. Tardos. Approximation algorithms for scheduling unrelated parallel machines. *Mathematical Programming*, 46 (1990), 259–271.

L. Levin. Universal Search Problems (in Russian). *Problemy Peredachi Informatsii*, 9:3 (1973), pp. 265–266. For a partial English translation, see B. A. Trakhtenbrot, A survey of Russian approaches to Perebor (brute-force search) algorithms. *Annals of the History of Computing* 6:4 (1984), 384–400.

L. Lovász. On the ratio of the optimal integral and fractional covers. *Discrete Mathematics* 13 (1975), 383–390.

S. Martello and P. Toth. *Knapsack Problems: Algorithms and Computer Implementations*. Wiley, 1990.

D. H. Mathews and M. Zuker. RNA secondary structure prediction. In *Encyclopedia of Genetics, Genomics, Proteomics and Bioinformatics*, edited by P. Clote. Wiley, 2004.

K. Mehlhorn and St. Näher. *The LEDA Platform of Combinatorial and Geometric Computing*. Cambridge University Press, 1999.

K. Menger. Zur allgemeinen Kurventheorie. *Fundam. Math.* 19 (1927), 96–115.

K. Menger. On the origin of the *n*-Arc Theorem. *J. Graph Theory* 5 (1981), 341–350.

N. Metropolis, A. W. Rosenbluth, M. N. Rosenbluth. A. H. Teller, and E. Teller. Equation of state calculations by fast computing machines. *J. Chemical Physics* 21 (1953), 1087–1092.

M. Mitzenmacher and E. Upfal. *Probability and Computing: Randomized Algorithms and Probabilistic Analysis*. Cambridge University Press, 2005.

D. Monderer and L. Shapley. Potential Games. *Games and Economic Behavior* 14 (1996), 124–143.

R. Motwani and P. Raghavan. *Randomized Algorithms*. Cambridge University Press, 1995.

John F. Nash, Jr. Equilibrium points in $n$-person games. *Proc. National Academy of Sciences of the USA*, 36 (1950), 48–49.

S. B. Needleman and C. D. Wunsch. *J. Molecular Biology*. 48 (1970), 443–453.

G. L. Nemhauser and L. A. Wolsey. *Integer and Combinatorial Optimization*. Wiley, 1988.

J. Nesetril. A few remarks on the history of MST-problem. *Archivum Mathematicum Brno*, 33 (1997), 15–22.

M. Newborn. *Kasparov versus Deep Blue: Computer Chess Comes of Age*. Springer-Verlag, 1996.

R. Nowakowski (ed.). *Games of No Chance*. Cambridge University Press, 1998.

M. Osborne. *An Introduction to Game Theory.* Oxford University Press, 2003.

C. H. Papadimitriou. *Computational Complexity*. Addison-Wesley, 1995.

C. H. Papadimitriou. Algorithms, games, and the Internet. *Proc. 33rd ACM Symposium on Theory of Computing*, pp. 749–753, 2001.

S. Plotkin. Competitive routing in ATM networks. *IEEE J. Selected Areas in Communications*, 1995, pp. 1128–1136.

F. P. Preparata and M. I. Shamos. *Computational Geometry: An Introduction*. Springer-Verlag, 1985.

W. H. Press, B. P. Flannery, S. A. Teukolsky, and W. T. Vetterling. *Numerical Recipes in C*. Cambridge University Press, 1988.

M. O. Rabin. Probabilistic algorithms. In *Algorithms and Complexity: New Directions and Recent Results*, edited by J. Traub, 21–39. Academic Press, 1976.

B. Reed. Tree width and tangles, a new measure of connectivity and some applications. *Surveys in Combinatorics*, edited by R. Bailey. Cambridge University Press, 1997.

N. Robertson and P. D. Seymour. An outline of a disjoint paths algorithm. In *Paths, Flows, and VLSI-Layout*, edited by B. Korte et al. Springer-Verlag, 1990.

R. W. Rosenthal. The network equilibrium problem in integers. *Networks* 3 (1973), 53–59.

S. Ross. *Introduction to Stochastic Dynamic Programming*, Academic Press, 1983.

T. Roughgarden. Selfish Routing. Ph.D. thesis, Cornell University, 2002.

T. Roughgarden. *Selfish Routing and the Price of Anarchy*. MIT Press, 2004.

S. Russell and P. Norvig. *Artificial Intelligence: A Modern Approach* (2nd edition). Prentice Hall, 2002.

D. Sankoff. The early introduction of dynamic programming into computational biology. *Bioinformatics* 16:1 (2000), 41–47.

J. E. Savage. *Models of Computation*. Addison-Wesley, 1998.

W. Savitch. Relationships between nondeterministic and deterministic tape complexities. *J. Computer and System Sciences* 4 (1970), 177–192.

T. Schaefer. On the complexity of some two-person perfect-information games. *J. Computer and System Sciences* 16:2 (April 1978), 185–225.

T. Schelling. *Micromotives and Macrobehavior*. Norton, 1978.

A. Schrijver. On the history of the transportation and maximum flow problems. *Math. Programming* 91 (2002), 437–445.

R. Seidel. Backwards analysis of randomized geometric algorithms. In *New Trends in Discrete and Computational Geometry*, edited by J. Pach, pp. 37–68. Springer-Verlag, 1993.

M. I. Shamos and D. Hoey. Closest-point problems. *Proc. 16th IEEE Symposium on Foundations of Computer Science*, pp. 151–162, 1975.

C. E. Shannon and W. Weaver. *The Mathematical Theory of Communication*. University of Illinois Press, 1949.

M. Sipser. The history and status of the *P* versus *NP* question. *Proc. 24th ACM Symposium on the Theory of Computing*, pp. 603–618, 1992.

D. D. Sleator and R. E. Tarjan. Amortized efficiency of list update and paging rules. *Communications of the ACM*, 28:2 (1985), 202–208.

M. Smid. Closest-point problems in computational geometry. In *Handbook of Computational Geometry*, edited by J. Rudiger Sack and J. Urrutia, pp. 877–935. Elsevier Science Publishers, B.V. North-Holland, 1999.

J. W. Stewart. *BGP4: Inter-Domain Routing in the Internet*. Addison-Wesley, 1998.

L. Stockmeyer and A. K. Chandra. Provably difficult combinatorial games. *SIAM J. on Computing* 8 (1979), 151–174.

L. Stockmeyer and A. Meyer. Word problems requiring exponential time. *Proc. 5th Annual ACM Symposium on Theory of Computing*, pp. 1–9, 1973.

É. Tardos. Network Games. *Proc. 36th ACM Symposium on Theory of Computing*, pp. 341–342, 2004.

R. E. Tarjan. Data structures and network algorithms. CBMS-NSF *Regional Conference Series in Applied Mathematics* 44. Society for Industrial and Applied Mathematics, 1983.

R. E. Tarjan. Algorithmic design. *Communications of the ACM*, 30:3 (1987), 204–212.

A. Tucker. Coloring a family of circular arcs. *SIAM J. Applied Mathematics*, 29:3 (November 1975), 493–502.

V. Vazirani. *Approximation Algorithms*. Springer-Verlag, 2001.

O. Veksler. Efficient Graph-Based Energy Minimization Methods in Computer Vision. Ph.D. thesis, Cornell University, 1999.

M. Waterman. *Introduction to Computational Biology: Sequences, Maps and Genomes*. Chapman Hall, 1995.

D. J. Watts. *Six Degrees: The Science of a Connected Age*. Norton, 2002.

K. Wayne. A new property and faster algorithm for baseball elimination. *SIAM J. Discrete Mathematics*, 14:2 (2001), 223–229.

J. W. J. Williams. Algorithm 232 (Heapsort). *Communications of the ACM*, 7 (1964), 347–348.

# Index

A page number ending in *ex* refers to a topic that is discussed in an exercise.